UNIVERSITY CASEBOOK SERIES®

FEDERAL ADMINISTRATIVE LAW

CASES AND MATERIALS

SECOND EDITION

by

KRISTIN E. HICKMAN
Harlan Albert Rogers Professor of Law
University of Minnesota Law School

RICHARD J. PIERCE, JR.
Lyle T. Alverson Professor of Law
George Washington University Law School

FOUNDATION PRESS

University Casebook Series is a trademark registered in the U.S. Patent and Trademark Office.

© 2010 By THOMSON REUTERS/FOUNDATION PRESS
© 2014 LEG, Inc. d/b/a West Academic
    444 Cedar Street, Suite 700
    St. Paul, MN 55101
    1-877-888-1330

Printed in the United States of America

ISBN: 978-1-60930-337-2

Mat #41431993

For Trey, Charles, and Jack

PREFACE

Several years ago, Justice Antonin Scalia began a lecture on administrative law with the following comment: "Administrative law is not for sissies—so you should lean back, clutch the sides of your chairs, and steel yourselves for a pretty dull lecture." Antonin Scalia, *Judicial Deference to Administrative Interpretations of Law*, 1989 DUKE L.J. 511. Administrative law is a notoriously difficult course to study and to teach because the doctrines at its heart are often very abstract and nuanced while the key administrative law cases frequently concern seemingly obscure and arcane questions scattered across a wide array of statutes and areas of legal practice. To the lay reader, the academic literature on administrative law issues, and perhaps some of the jurisprudence as well, may resemble a competition to see who can cram more angels on the head of a pin. The danger is that students will finish a course on administrative law perhaps knowing a little more than when they started, but hopelessly confused about what they know.

Yet, for all of the challenges that studying and teaching the course present, administrative law is an exciting and dynamic subject with enormous implications for legal practice and society at large. It is virtually impossible to live or work in the United States without realizing the benefits and/or consequences of federal administrative action. Practicing lawyers in a plethora of practice areas routinely assist their clients in engaging with federal agencies and challenging the actions of those agencies in court. Furthermore, administrative law as a field of study is blessed with a rich evolutionary history and with an ever-present theoretical subtext concerning the nature, use, and abuse of governmental power. Can you imagine a more interesting topic to contemplate as a law student than governmental power?

Our principal goal in writing this casebook was to provide a resource that addresses the key issues and doctrines of which any lawyer who routinely deals with federal administrative agencies ought to be aware as clearly, accessibly, and practically as we could explain them. Our goal remains unchanged with this Second Edition. Toward that end, we continue to provide practical questions, examples, and discussion problems throughout to help ground the material in the real world. We have continue, however, to expose readers of this casebook to some of the history and theory that, to us, makes administrative law such a fascinating topic of study. We offer this Second Edition of the casebook partly to update the materials to reflect changes in the courts' jurisprudence regarding several issues. In this Second Edition, we also expand the casebook's coverage to incorporate a few new topics that seem more significant in light of recent cases.

Finally, recognizing that there is no clear "right" or "wrong" way to approach the study of administrative law, we have organized this casebook to be pedagogically flexible. We ourselves cover the materials in a different order based on differing pedagogic beliefs. Professor Hickman assigns the chapters in the order in which they appear. She discusses the relationship between agencies, the President and the Congress before she discusses the decisionmaking procedures agencies use and the relationship between agencies and courts. She believes that students should have a good understanding of the place of agencies in relation to the politically accountable branches of government before they begin to study the ways in which agencies make decisions and the ways in which courts review those decisions. Professor Pierce, by contrast, assigns Chapters 2 and 3 last. He believes that students will gain a better understanding of the implications of alternative relationships between agencies, the President and the Congress if they already have a basic grasp of the ways in which agencies make decisions and the ways in which courts review those decisions. No matter where you begin your study of administrative law, we recommend you keep in mind that the various topics and doctrines discussed in this casebook will circle back to material that you have already covered and forward to material that you have yet to address. We hope that you find these materials useful and that you come to appreciate and enjoy the study of administrative law as much as we do.

KRISTIN E. HICKMAN

RICHARD J. PIERCE, JR.

July 1, 2014

ACKNOWLEDGMENTS

We would be remiss if we did not thank the law students who contributed to the writing of this book. We thank the many, many students who have contributed through their classroom participation to our thinking about how best to teach the material contained in this textbook. For excellent research assistance, we also thank particularly Jessica Edwards, Hans Grong, and Lindsey Hopper in connection with the First Edition and Caitlinrose Fisher in connection with this Second Edition.

We also wish to acknowledge and express our appreciation to those authors and publishers who graciously granted us permission to reprint excerpts from the following publications.

Lisa Schultz Bressman, Chevron's Mistake, 58 DUKE L.J. 549, 559–66 (2009).

JOHN HART ELY, DEMOCRACY AND DISTRUST: A THEORY OF JUDICIAL REVIEW 132–34 (1980), pp. 131–133 reprinted by permission of the publisher, Harvard University Press, Cambridge, Mass., Copyright © 1980 by the President and Fellows of Harvard College.

William N. Eskridge, Jr., Relationships Between Formalism and Functionalism in Separation of Powers Cases, 22 HARV. J. L. & PUB. POL'Y 21, 21–22 (1998).

Henry J. Friendly, Some Kind of Hearing, 123 U. PA. L. REV. 1267 (1975), copyright 1975 by University of Pennsylvania Law Review, reproduced with permission of University of Pennsylvania Law Review.

Owen Fiss, The War Against Terrorism and the Rule of Law, 26 OXFORD J. LEGAL STUD. 235, 244–45 (2006).

Gary Lawson, Territorial Governments and the Limits of Formalism, 78 CAL. L. REV. 853, 857–60 (1990), © 1990 by California Law Review, Inc., reprinted by permission of the author and California Law Review, Inc.

RICHARD J. PIERCE, JR., ADMINISTRATIVE LAW TREATISE § 6.8 (5th ed. 2010).

Richard J. Pierce, Jr., Waiting for Vermont Yankee II, III, and IV, 75 GEO. WASH. L. REV. 902 (2007).

Richard J. Pierce, Jr., Chevron and its Aftermath, 41 VAND. L. REV. 301, 304–08 (1988).

Antonin Scalia, Judicial Deference to Administrative Interpretations of Law, 1989 DUKE L.J. 511, 513–17, 520–21 (1989).

Peter L. Strauss, Overseer, or "The Decider"? The President in Administrative Law, 75 GEO. WASH. L. REV. 696 (2007).

SUMMARY OF CONTENTS

PREFACE...V

ACKNOWLEDGMENTS.. VII

TABLE OF CASES.. XXI

Chapter 1. Introduction..1
A.   The Study of Administrative Law...1
B.   What Is an Agency? 5
C.   The History of Administrative Law 15

Chapter 2. Congress and Agencies......................................**23**
A.   The Constitutionality of Delegating Policymaking Authority 23
B.   The Constitutionality of Delegating Adjudicatory Power 91
C.   Other Means Through Which Congress Influences Agencies............121
D.   Limits on Congressional Power..129

Chapter 3. Presidential Control of Agencies.....................**155**
A.   The Power to Appoint 157
B.   The Power to Remove 217
C.   Other Presidential Attempts to Control Agencies 247

Chapter 4. Adjudication **277**
A.   The Role of the Due Process Clause...277
B.   Statutes as a Source of Procedural Requirements............................343
C.   Permissible Decisionmaking Structures and Impermissible
     Bias 357
D.   Judicial Review of Agency Adjudications 385

Chapter 5. Rules and Rulemaking **417**
A.   Why Rulemaking?..418
B.   APA Rulemaking Procedures..458
C.   Arbitrary and Capricious ("Hard Look") Review 560
D.   Ossification and Responses 590

Chapter 6. Statutory Interpretation in Administrative Law **597**
A.   The Pre-*Chevron* Approach 598
B.   The *Chevron* "Revolution" 613
C.   *Chevron*'s Scope and the *Mead* Counter-Revolution............................711
D.   *Chevron* and Stare Decisis 737
E.   *Chevron* and Jurisdictional Questions 758
F.   Agency Interpretations of Agency Regulations..................................774

Chapter 7. Prerequisites to Judicial Review **795**
A.   Reviewability...795
B.   The Timing of Judicial Review..855
C.   Standing to Obtain Judicial Review 919

Appendix A. The Constitution of the United States 989

Appendix B. Administrative Procedure Act 1005

INDEX 1017

TABLE OF CONTENTS

PREFACE...V

ACKNOWLEDGMENTS.. VII

TABLE OF CASES... XXI

Chapter 1. Introduction...1
A. The Study of Administrative Law 1
    1. What Is Administrative Law? 1
    2. Why Study Administrative Law? 3
B. What Is an Agency? 5
    1. Statutory Definitions 5
        Citizens for Responsibility and Ethics in Washington v. Office
           of Administration 7
        Notes and Questions 10
    2. Executive Branch and Independent Agencies................................10
    3. Agencies and the Three Branches...12
    4. Quasi-judicial and Quasi-legislative Versus Bureaucratic
        Actions 14
C. The History of Administrative Law 15
    1. The Early Republic..15
    2. The Progressive Era and the New Deal...17
    3. The Administrative Procedure Act 18
    4. The 1960s and 1970s..20
    5. The Modern Era 21

Chapter 2. Congress and Agencies...23
A. The Constitutionality of Delegating Policymaking Authority 23
    1. The Nondelegation Doctrine...23
        Panama Refining Co. v. Ryan...26
        A.L.A. Schechter Poultry Corp. v. United States 30
        Notes and Questions 34
        a. The Decline of the Nondelegation Doctrine...........................35
        b. Renewed Interest in the Nondelegation Doctrine in the
            1970s 37
            Industrial Union Dept., AFL-CIO v. American Petroleum
               Institute (The Benzene Case) 38
            Notes and Questions 43
        c. Apparent Rejection of the Attempt to Reinvigorate the
            Nondelegation Doctrine 45
            Mistretta v. United States 45
            Notes and Questions 52
            Discussion Problem 53
        d. A "New" Nondelegation Doctrine?..53
            American Trucking Ass'ns, Inc. v. EPA 55
            American Trucking Ass'ns, Inc. v. EPA 59
            Whitman v. American Trucking Ass'ns, Inc. 60
            Notes and Questions 65

                e.   Subdelegation 66
                     United States Telecom Association v. Federal
                         Communications Commission 67
                     Notes and Questions 73
                f.   Privatization 73
                     Association of American Railroads v. United States
                         Department of Transportation 75
                     Notes and Questions 84
           2.   If Broad Delegations Are a Problem, Are Detailed Instructions
                the Answer? 84
                a.   The Food Stamp Program 85
                     U.S. Department of Agriculture v. Murry 85
                     Notes and Questions 87
                b.   The Delaney Clause 88
                     Les v. Reilly 89
                     Notes and Questions 90
      B.   The Constitutionality of Delegating Adjudicatory Power 91
           Crowell v. Benson 93
           Notes and Questions 97
           Northern Pipeline Const. Co. v. Marathon Pipe Line Co. 98
           Notes and Questions 105
           Commodity Futures Trading Commission v. Schor 106
           Notes and Questions 114
           Granfinanciera v. Nordberg 115
           Notes and Questions 120
           Discussion Problem 121
      C.   Other Means Through Which Congress Influences Agencies 121
           1.   Other Statutes 121
                a.   Administrative Procedure Act 122
                b.   Freedom of Information Act 122
                c.   National Environmental Policy Act 124
                d.   Civil Service Act 125
                e.   Information Quality Act 126
           2.   Allocation of Litigating Authority 126
           3.   The Confirmation Process 127
           4.   The Appropriations Process 127
           5.   The Oversight Process 128
           6.   Casework 128
      D.   Limits on Congressional Power 129
           1.   Due Process 129
                Pillsbury Co. v. Federal Trade Commission 129
                Notes and Questions 134
           2.   The Procedures Required to Legislate 135
                a.   The Legislative Veto 135
                     Immigration & Naturalization Service v. Chadha 135
                     Notes and Questions 142
                     Discussion Problem 144
                b.   Gramm-Rudman-Hollings and the Comptroller General 145
                     Bowsher v. Synar 146

Notes and Questions 153
Discussion Problem 154

Chapter 3. Presidential Control of Agencies.......................................155
Formalism versus Functionalism 155
Gary Lawson, Territorial Governments and the Limits of Formalism 156
Harold H. Bruff, The Incompatibility Principle.............................157
William N. Eskridge, Jr., Relationships Between Formalism and
    Functionalism in Separation of Powers Cases 157
A.   The Power to Appoint 157
    1.   Who Is an Officer of the United States? 158
        Buckley v. Valeo 158
        Notes and Questions 162
        Federal Election Commission v. NRA Political Victory Fund.......164
        Notes and Questions 167
        Landry v. FDIC 168
        Notes and Questions 170
        Discussion Problem 171
    2.   What Kind of Officer: Principal or Inferior?.................................171
        Morrison v. Olson 172
        Notes and Questions 178
        Edmond v. United States...179
        Notes and Questions 183
        Discussion Problem 183
    3.   Who Is Head of a Department? 183
        Freytag v. Commissioner of Internal Revenue 184
        Notes and Questions 191
    4.   The Recess Appointments Clause 193
        National Labor Relations Board v. Noel Canning 196
        Notes and Questions 216
        Discussion Problem 216
B.   The Power to Remove 217
    Myers v. United States 217
    Notes and Questions 221
    Humphrey's Executor v. United States 222
    Notes and Questions 225
    Wiener v. United States 226
    Notes and Questions 227
    Morrison v. Olson 228
    Notes and Questions 231
    Free Enterprise Fund v. Public Company Accounting Oversight
        Board...232
    Notes and Questions 246
C.   Other Presidential Attempts to Control Agencies 247
    1.   The Nature and Scope of Presidential Authority.........................247
        Youngstown Sheet & Tube Co. v. Sawyer 248
        Notes and Questions 253
        Discussion Problem 255

    2.   Tools Presidents Use to Control Agencies 255
        Presidential Signing Statements 257
        Executive Orders..258
        OMB and OIRA 259
        Executive Order 12291 of February 17, 1981............................260
        Notes and Questions 264
        Major Changes to Executive Order 12291 265
        Peter L. Strauss, Overseer, or "The Decider"? The President
            in Administrative Law 267
        Other Presidential Efforts to Influence Rulemaking...................272
        Ad Hoc Jawboning 274

Chapter 4. Adjudication 277
A.   The Role of the Due Process Clause 277
    1.   When Due Process Applies...278
        a.   Adjudication Versus Rulemaking 278
            Londoner v. Denver..279
            Bi-Metallic Investment Co. v. State Board of
                Equalization..280
            Notes and Questions 281
            Explaining the *Londoner/Bi-Metallic* Distinction................283
            Discussion Problem 285
        b.   Life, Liberty, or Property...286
            Goldberg v. Kelly...287
            Notes and Questions 294
            Discussion Problems 296
            Wisconsin v. Constantineau 297
            Notes and Questions 298
            Board of Regents of State Colleges v. Roth 298
            Perry v. Sindermann...303
            Notes and Questions 306
            Paul v. Davis..308
            Notes and Questions 310
            Discussion Problems 312
    2.   Procedures Required by Due Process 312
        Mathews v. Eldridge 316
        Notes and Questions 323
        Discussion Problem..326
        The Bitter with the Sweet Model 326
        Cleveland Board of Education v. Loudermill 327
    3.   The Limits of Procedural Balancing 332
        Hamdi v. Rumsfeld 333
        Notes and Questions 341
B.   Statutes as a Source of Procedural Requirements 343
    1.   Formal Adjudication 343
        Dominion Energy Brayton Point, LLC v. Johnson 345
        Notes and Questions 349
    2.   Informal Adjudication...350
        Citizens to Preserve Overton Park, Inc. v. Volpe........................350

Pension Benefit Guaranty Corp. v. LTV Corp. 354
Notes and Questions 357
C. Permissible Decisionmaking Structures and Impermissible Bias 357
   1. Judicial Models: Separation of Functions and Split-
      Enforcement 358
      Withrow v. Larkin 359
      Notes and Questions 363
      The Split-Enforcement Model 365
   2. The Judicial Model versus the Bureaucratic Model 366
      Nash v. Bowen...368
      Notes and Questions 370
      Ongoing Issues with ALJs in the Social Security Disability
        System..372
      Notes and Questions 373
      The Bureaucratic Model 374
   3. Public versus Private Adjudicators.................................374
      Gibson v. Berryhill 375
      Notes and Questions 378
      Schweiker v. McClure 378
      Notes and Questions 384
D. Judicial Review of Agency Adjudications 385
   1. Judicial Review of Agency Fact Finding.............................386
      Universal Camera Corp. v. NLRB 386
      Notes and Questions 389
      Allentown Mack Sales & Serv., Inc. v. National Labor
        Relations Board 390
      Notes and Questions 399
      Richardson v. Perales 400
      Notes and Questions 407
      Fact-Finding in Informal Adjudication..............................408
      Ass'n of Data Processing Serv. Organizations, Inc. v. Board
        of Governors of the Federal Reserve System.........................408
      Notes and Questions 413
   2. Judicial Review of Issues of Law and of the Agency
      Reasoning Process..413

Chapter 5. Rules and Rulemaking **417**
A. Why Rulemaking? 418
   1. Agency Power to Issue Rules..418
      National Petroleum Refiners Ass'n v. FTC 419
      Notes and Questions 422
      Richard J. Pierce, Jr., The Many Advantages of Rules and
        Rulemaking...424
      Discussion Problem 425
   2. The Functional Relationship Between Rules and
      Adjudications..426
      Heckler v. Campbell..427
      Notes and Questions 429
      Bowen v. Yuckert 430

Notes and Questions 435
Yetman v. Garvey 435
Notes and Questions 440
Discussion Problem 441
3. Making "Rules" Through Adjudication 441
SEC v. Chenery Corp. ("Chenery II") 442
Notes and Questions 447
The Ongoing Vitality of *Chenery II* 447
Bowen v. Georgetown University Hospital 452
Notes and Questions 457
B. APA Rulemaking Procedures 458
1. The Decline of Formal Rulemaking 459
United States v. Florida East Coast Ry. Co. 460
Notes and Questions 464
2. The Evolution of Informal Rulemaking 465
a. Oral Hearings in Informal Rulemaking 467
Vermont Yankee Nuclear Power Corp. v. NRDC 468
Notes and Questions 472
Discussion Problem 473
b. The Notice Requirement 473
Shell Oil Co. v. EPA 474
Notes and Questions 477
Discussion Problems 479
Portland Cement Ass'n v. Ruckelshaus 479
Notes and Questions 482
American Radio Relay League, Inc. v. FCC 484
Notes and Questions 489
c. The "Concise" Statement of Basis and Purpose 489
United States v. Nova Scotia Food Products Corp. 490
Notes and Questions 494
Discussion Problem 494
d. Ex Parte Communications in Rulemakings 495
Home Box Office, Inc. v. FCC 495
Notes and Questions 499
Action for Children's Television v. FCC 500
Notes and Questions 504
Sierra Club v. Costle 505
Notes and Questions 511
e. Impermissible Bias in Rulemakings 513
Association of National Advertisers v. FTC 513
Notes and Questions 522
Discussion Problem 523
3. Exemptions from APA Rulemaking Procedures 523
a. Subject Matter Exemptions 524
b. The Good Cause Exemption 524
Mack Trucks, Inc. v. Environmental Protection Agency 526
Discussion Problem 530
United States v. Johnson 532
Notes and Questions 539

       c.   The Procedural Rule Exemption 539

             Discussion Problem 541

       d.   The Interpretative Rule Exemption...................................542

             American Mining Congress v. Mine Safety & Health

                 Administration..543

             Notes and Questions 548

       e.   The Policy Statement Exemption.....................................549

             Pacific Gas & Electric Co. v. Federal Power Commission 550

             Notes and Questions 554

             Community Nutrition Institute v. Young...........................555

             Notes and Questions 557

             Discussion Problems 557

             The Practically Binding Standard....................................558

C.   Arbitrary and Capricious ("Hard Look") Review 560

    National Tire Dealers & Retreaders Ass'n, Inc. v. Brinegar..............562

    Notes and Questions 567

    Motor Vehicle Manufacturers Ass'n of U.S., Inc. v. State Farm

       Mutual Auto. Insurance Co. 568

    Notes and Questions 577

    FCC v. Fox Television Stations, Inc...578

    Notes and Questions 589

D.   Ossification and Responses 590

    Negotiated Rulemaking...593

    Direct Final Rulemaking...594

    Remand Without Vacatur..595

Chapter 6. Statutory Interpretation in Administrative Law 597

A.   The Pre-*Chevron* Approach 598

    NLRB v. Hearst Publications..599

    Notes and Questions 604

    Skidmore v. Swift & Co. 605

    Notes and Questions 608

    Discussion Problem: *Benzene* Revisited....................................609

B.   The *Chevron* "Revolution" 613

    Chevron U.S.A. Inc. v. Natural Resources Defense Council, Inc........613

    Notes and Questions 620

    Debating the Theory of *Chevron* 621

    Antonin Scalia, Judicial Deference to Administrative

       Interpretations of Law 621

    Richard J. Pierce, Jr., *Chevron* and Its Aftermath 624

    Lisa Schultz Bressman, *Chevron*'s Mistake 627

    1.   How Clear Is Clear? 629

       Yellow Transportation, Inc. v. Michigan 630

       American Bar Association v. Federal Trade Commission 635

       Notes and Questions 643

    2.   The "Tools" of Step One Analysis.....................................643

       Department of Housing & Urban Development v. Rucker..........647

       General Dynamics Land Systems, Inc. v. Cline 651

       Notes and Questions 661

3. *Chevron* and Substantive Canons 661
Solid Waste Agency of Northern Cook County v. United
    States Army Corps of Engineers 662
Notes and Questions 666
Babbitt v. Sweet Home Chapter of Communities for a Greater
    Oregon 667
Notes and Questions 676
Carter v. Welles-Bowen Realty, Inc. 677
Notes and Questions 683
4. *Chevron* Step Two: What's Left? 684
AT&T Corp. v. Iowa Utilities Board 685
Notes and Questions 692
Rapanos v. United States 693
Notes and Questions 706
Hard Look Review and *Chevron* Step Two 708
5. *Chevron* Applied 709
C. *Chevron*'s Scope and the *Mead* Counter-Revolution 711
Christensen v. Harris County 712
Notes and Questions 717
United States v. Mead Corp. 718
Notes and Questions 728
Barnhart v. Walton 730
Notes and Questions 735
The Modern *Skidmore* Doctrine 736
D. *Chevron* and Stare Decisis 737
National Cable & Telecomm. Ass'n v. Brand X Internet Services 738
Notes and Questions 746
United States v. Home Concrete & Supply, LLC 747
Notes and Questions 758
E. *Chevron* and Jurisdictional Questions 758
City of Arlington, Tex. v. FCC 759
Notes and Questions 773
F. Agency Interpretations of Agency Regulations 774
Talk America, Inc. v. Michigan Bell Telephone Co. 777
Christopher v. SmithKline Beecham Corp. 779
Decker v. Northwest Environmental Defense Center 784
Notes and Questions 793

Chapter 7. Prerequisites to Judicial Review 795
A. Reviewability 795
1. Preclusion 796
    a. Express Preclusion 796
        Johnson v. Robison 797
        Notes and Questions 798
        Discussion Problem 799
    b. Implied Preclusion 799
        Block v. Community Nutrition Institute 800
        Bowen v. Michigan Academy of Family Physicians 804
        Notes and Questions 809

	2.	Committed to Agency Discretion	810
		Citizens to Preserve Overton Park, Inc. v. Volpe	811
		Notes and Questions	815
		Webster v. Doe	820
		Notes and Questions	831
		Lincoln v. Vigil	832
		Notes and Questions	836
	3.	Agency Inaction	836
		Dunlop v. Bachowski	837
		Notes and Questions	840
		Heckler v. Chaney	842
		Notes and Questions	848
		American Horse Protection Ass'n, Inc. v. Lyng	850
		Notes and Questions	852
		Discussion Problem	854
B.	The Timing of Judicial Review		855
	1.	Final Agency Action	856
		Franklin v. Massachusetts	857
		Dalton v. Specter	860
		Notes and Questions	863
		Bennett v. Spear	865
		Notes and Questions	867
		Discussion Problem	868
	2.	Ripeness for Judicial Review	868
		Abbott Laboratories v. Gardner	870
		Toilet Goods Ass'n, Inc. v. Gardner	874
		Notes and Questions	876
		Reno v. Catholic Social Services, Inc.	879
		Notes and Questions	889
	3.	Duty to Exhaust Administrative Remedies	889
		McKart v. United States	890
		McGee v. United States	893
		Notes and Questions	897
		McCarthy v. Madigan	898
		Notes and Questions	904
		Discussion Problem	906
		Statutory Exhaustion	906
		Darby v. Cisneros	907
		Notes and Questions	911
		Issue Exhaustion	912
	4.	Agency Delay	913
		Discussion Problem	917
	5.	Primary Jurisdiction	917
C.	Standing to Obtain Judicial Review		919
	Association of Data Processing Service Organizations, Inc. v. Camp		919
	1.	Constitutional Standing	922
		Allen v. Wright	922
		Notes and Questions	924

FEC v. Akins 925
Notes and Questions 930
Lujan v. National Wildlife Federation..........................932
Notes and Questions 934
Lujan v. Defenders of Wildlife......................................936
Notes and Questions 944
Steel Co. v. Citizens for a Better Environment...........946
Notes and Questions 949
Friends of the Earth, Inc. v. Laidlaw Environmental
         Services 950
Notes and Questions 955
Massachusetts v. EPA 956
Notes and Questions 965
2.   Statutory Standing and the "Zone of Interests".........968
National Credit Union Administration v. First National Bank
         & Trust Co. 973
Notes and Questions 984
Match-E-Be-Nash-She-Wish Band of Pottawatomi Indians v.
         Patchak 985
Notes and Questions 987

Appendix A. The Constitution of the United States **989**

Appendix B. Administrative Procedure Act.....................**1005**

INDEX 1017

TABLE OF CASES

The principal cases are in bold type.

37712, Inc. v. Ohio Department of Liquor Control 282

75 Acres, LLC v. Miami-Dade County, Fla. 282

A.L.A. Schechter Poultry Corp. v. United States................30, 40, 47, 62, 73, 74, 77

Abbott Laboratories v. Gardner....................352, 796, **870**

Abilene, City of v. FCC 642

Accardi, United States ex rel. v. Shaughnessy 349

Ace Telephone Ass'n v. Koppendrayer..........................413

Action for Children's Television v. FCC.......................................**500**

Adamo Wrecking Co. v. United States 878

Adams v. Richardson 846

Addington v. Texas 342

Air Courier Conf. of Amer. v. Amer. Postal Workers Union, AFL-CIO 973, 978, 979, 980

Aircraft Owners & Pilots Ass'n v. FAA 411

Alaska Department of Environmental Conservation v. EPA 737

Albertini, United States v.............650

Alden v. Maine 768

Alexander Sprunt & Son, Inc. v. United States............................970

Allen v. Wright...................**922**, 937, 941, 961, 962, 968, 969

Allentown Mack Sales & Serv., Inc. v. National Labor Relations Board......................**390**

Allocco, United States v. 195, 196

Amalgamated Meat Cutters v. Connally.......................................36

American Bar Association v. Federal Trade Commission **635**

American Fed'n of Gov't Employees, AFL-CIO 798, 832

American Horse Protection Ass'n, Inc. v. Lyng......................**850**, 853

American Hospital Assn. v. NLRB 767

American Insurance Co. v. Canter 186, 188

American Liberty Oil Co. v. Commissioner 752

American Mining Congress v. Mine Safety & Health Administration....................**543**, 717

American Power & Light Co. v. SEC 47, 59, 62

American Pub. Gas Ass'n v. FPC 411

American Radio Relay League, Inc. v. FCC................**484**, 591, 592

American Trucking Ass'ns v. United States...353

American Trucking Ass'ns, Inc. v. EPA......................................**55, 59**

Anderson, United States v. 245

Appalachian Elec. Power Co., United States v..............................694, 699

Aptheker v. Sec'y of State 339

Arent v. Shalala............................708

Arlington, Tex., City of v. FCC.................................683, **759**

Armour & Co. v. Wantock et al.........................605, 606, 607

Armstrong v. Executive Office of the President 8, 9

Armstrong v. Manzo.............290, 318

Arnett v. Kennedy 326, 328, 329, 331, 332

Arnold Tours, Inc. v. Camp..........921, 975

Arver v. United States 92

ASARCO Inc. v. Kadish 937, 965

Assiniboine & Sioux Tribes v. Bd. of Oil and Gas 71, 72

Association of Am. R.R. v. Costle..915

Association of American Railroads v. United States Department of Transportation...........................**75**

Association of Battery Recyclers, Inc. v. EPA...969

Association of Data Processing Serv. Organizations, Inc. v. Board of Governors of the Federal Reserve System **408**

Association of Data Processing Service Organizations, Inc. v. Camp **919**

Association of Flight Attendants-CWA v. Chao 897

Association of National Advertisers v. FTC **513**

AT&T Corp. v. Iowa Utilities Board....................67, 68, **685**, 740

AT&T Corp. v. Portland 740, 742, 743, 746, 747

AT&T v. United States..................598

Atascadero State Hosp. v. Scanlon.......................................642

Atchison, Topeka & Santa Fe Railway v. Scarlett....................598

Atchison, Topeka & Santa Fe Railway Co., United States v. 3

Atlantic Cleaners & Dyers, Inc. v. United States 6

Atlantic Mut. Ins. Co. v. Comm'r.

Auer v. Robbins 714, 716, 731

Ayuda, Inc. v. Thornburgh....887, 888
Babbitt v. Sweet Home Chapter of Communities for a Greater Oregon **667**, 682
Baccarat Fremont Developers, LLC v. Army Corps of Engineers 697
Bachowski v. Brennan 846
Bailey v. Richardson 286
Bakelite Corp., Ex parte 94, 101, 117, 118
Baker v. Carr..........................827, 962
Baldwin v. Hale 337
Ballard v. Commissioner..............349
Baltimore Gas & Elec. Co. v. Natural Res. Def. Council........................124
Bangura v. Hansen 905
Barlow v. Collins 801
Barnhart v. Thomas......................657
Barnhart v. Walton 640, 680, **730**, 766
Barrentine v. Arkansas-Best Freight System, Inc.............................779
Barrows v. Jackson 920
Barry v. Barchi......................325, 901
Bass, United States v...........664, 670, 678, 679
Batterton v. Francis......608, 609, 620
Beecham v. United States..............674
Bell v. Burson 297, 329
Bennett v. Spear..............**865**, 926, 945, 978, 980, 981, 983
Beth Israel Hospital v. NLRB......394, 399
BFP v. Resolution Trust Corp.......700
Bi-Metallic Investment Co. v. State Board of Equalization **280**, 282
Bishop v. Wood 327, 329
Bivens v. Six Unknown Federal Narcotics Agents..........84, 898, 904
Black & Decker Disability Plan v. Nord...407
Blakely v. Washington 757
Block v. Community Nutrition Institute............................**800**, 806
Board of Governors of the Fed. Reserve Sys. v. Inv. Co. Inst. (ICI) 410
Board of Regents of State Colleges v. Roth **298**, 305, 306, 328
Bob Jones University v. United States 922
Boddie v. Connecticut 297, 329
Bonanno Linen Service v. NLRB..............................608, 646
Bonhometre v. Gonzales 905
Booth v. Churner...........................904
Boumediene v. Bush......................342
Bowen v. City of New York 900
Bowen v. Georgetown University Hospital **452**, 716, 782
Bowen v. Massachusetts 911

Bowen v. Michigan Academy of Family Physicians **804**
Bowen v. Yuckert **430**, 435
Bowles v. Seminole Rock & Sand Co. 774, 778, 789, 790
Bowman Transportation, Inc. v. Arkansas-Best Freight System, Inc..355, 356
Bowsher v. Synar 64, **146**, 154, 166
Bragdon v. Abbott..........................720
Briggs Plumbingware, Inc. v. NLRB...396
Brock v. Roadway Express............324
Brown v. Board of Education 284, 818
Brown v. Secretary of Health & Human Servs...............................905
Buckley v. Valeo 99, 109, 138, 152, **158**, 881
Burgin v. Nix 311
Buttfield v. Stranahan 25
Cabiya San Miguel v. United States Veterans Admin. 798
Cafeteria Workers v. McElroy..... 288, 298, 318
Calhoon v. Harvey.........................838
Califano v. Sanders 799, 880
Califano v. Yamasaki 330, 384
California Coastal Comm'n v. Granite Rock Co. 665
Camp v. Pitts 408, 412
Carey v. Piphus 330
Carmel-By-The-Sea, City of v. Department of Transp. 124
Carter v. Carter Coal.....35, 74, 77, 82
Carter v. Welles-Bowen Realty, Inc. **677**, 684
CC&F Western Operations L.P. v. Commissioner.............................758
Chambless, United States v............50
Chapman v. United States............742
Chase Bank USA, N.A. v. McCoy...............776, 777, 781, 788
Chemical Foundation, United States v..................................66, 352
Chemical Waste Management, Inc. v. EPA...344
Chen v. Mukasey...........................390
Chevron U.S.A. Inc. v. Natural Resources Defense Council, Inc. 21, 54, 255, 344, 345, 597, **613**, 701, 704, 706, 709, 714, 731, 759, 854
Chicago & Southern Air Lines, Inc. v. Waterman S.S. Corp. 745, 866
Chicago v. Atchison, T. & S.F.R. Co..921
Christensen v. Harris County............. 656, **712**, 729, 776
Christopher v. SmithKline Beecham Corp. 763, **779**, 789

Citizens for Responsibility and
    Ethics in Washington v. Office
    of Administration......................7
Citizens to Preserve Overton
    Park, Inc. v. Volpe.........350, 356,
    811
Clackamas Gastroenterology
    Associates v. Wells....................736
Clapper v. Amnesty
    International..............................967
Clark v. Martinez.........................678
Clarke v. Securities Industry
    Assn..................969, 973, 976, 977,
    981, 983, 986
Cleveland Board of Education v.
    Loudermill.......................327, 337
Clinton v. Jones.....................211, 236
Coeur Alaska, Inc. v. Southeast
    Alaska Conservation Council.....776
Cohen v. United States.................877
Cohens v. Virginia........................900
Coit Independence Joint Venture v.
    FSLIC......................................904
Coleman v. Miller..................926, 927
Colony, Inc. v. Commissioner......747,
    748, 749, 750, 751, 752, 753, 755,
    756
Colorado River Water Conservation
    Dist. v. United States...............900
Commodity Futures Trading
    Commission v. Schor....105, 106,
    239, 733, 830
Community Ass'n for Restoration of
    Env't v. Henry Bosma Dairy.....696
Community for Creative Non-
    Violence v. Reid..........................658
Community Nutrition Institute v.
    Young.......................................555
Concentrated Export Ass'n, Inc.,
    United States v...........................954
Concerned Area Residents for Env't
    v. Southview Farm....................702
Connecticut Nat'l Bank v.
    Germain....................................658
Connell v. Higginbotham......301, 307
Consolidated Edison Co. v.
    NLRB..................................387, 392
Constance v. Sec'y of Health &
    Human Servs. 623
Cowart, Estate of v. Nicklos Drilling
    Co. 781, 782
Crandon v. United States............662,
    678, 679, 747
Crowell v. Benson.................92, 93,
    101, 105, 109, 117, 120, 240
Currin v. Wallace............................78
Curtis v. Loether..................115, 118
Curtiss-Wright Export Corp., United
    States v. 823, 827
Dague v. Burlington....................702
DaimlerChrysler Corp. v. Cuno.....970
Dalton v. Specter..............860, 866
Dames & Moore v. Regan.............208
Dandridge v. Williams...................87
Darby v. Cisneros.....................907

Data Processing Serv. v. Camp.....803,
    926, 974, 975, 977, 978, 986
Davies Warehouse Co. v.
    Bowles......................................609
Davis v. Hightower......................752
Deaton, United States v...............696
Decatur Liquors, Inc. v. District of
    Columbia.................................282
Decker v. Northwest
    Environmental Defense
    Center 784
Dehainaut v. Pena.......................283
Department of Air Force v. Rose......8
Department of Commerce v. U.S.
    House of Representatives.........864
Department of Housing & Urban
    Development v. Rucker........647
Department of Navy v.
    Egan 341, 824
Department of Revenue of Ore. v.
    ACF Industries, Inc. 734
Department of Transp. v. Public
    Citizen.....................................912
Department of Transportation v.
    Ass'n of Amer. Railroads.............84
DeVito v. Schultz (DeVito I).........839
DeVito v. Schultz (DeVito II)........840
Dia v. Ashcroft............................414
Dickinson v. Zurko......................413
Dierckman, United States v..........661
Dirks v. SEC...............................609
Dixon v. Love..............................330
Dixson v. United States...............683
Dobson v. Comm'r......................189
Dominion Energy Brayton
    Point, LLC v. Johnson..........345
Dong v. Smithsonian Inst. 10
Duke Power Co. v. Carolina Env'tl
    Study Group, Inc........................959
Dunlop v. Bachowski...............806,
    809, 837, 843, 846
Eaton, United States v..........180, 681
Edelman v. Lynchburg College.....656
Edmond v. United States.........179
Edward J. DeBartolo Corp. v. Florida
    Gulf Coast Building & Constr.
    Trades Council...................664, 667
EEOC v. Arabian American Oil
    Co..679
Eidson, United States v................695
Elk Grove Unified School Dist. v.
    Newdow...............................969, 982
Entergy Corp. v. Riverkeeper,
    Inc....................................643, 753
Environmental Defense Center v.
    Babbitt.....................................127
EPA v. National Crushed Stone
    Assn. 885
Erika, Inc., United States
    v. 379, 807
Ervine's Appeal...........................284
Esso Standard Oil Co. v. Lopez-
    Freytes.....................................385
Ethnic Employees of the Library of
    Cong. v. Boorstin..........................6
Evans v. Stephens.................195, 196

Ewing v. Mytinger & Casselberry, Inc........871, 872
Fahey v. Mallonee 59
Fall River Dyeing & Finishing Corp. v. NLRB............395, 398
FCC v. Fox Television Stations, Inc........414, **578**
FCC v. Sanders Bros. Radio Station........920, 926, 971
FDA v. Brown & Williamson Tobacco Corp.........758, 759
Federal Deposit Ins. Corp. v. Mallen 325
Federal Election Comm'n v. Akins **925**, 959
Federal Election Comm'n v. Legi-Tech, Inc............167
Federal Election Comm'n v. NRA Political Victory Fund..........127, **164**
Federal Express Corp. v. Holowecki............775
Federal Maritime Comm'n v. South Carolina Ports Authority...........768
Federal Power Commission v. Hope Natural Gas Co. 35
Federal Radio Comm'n v. Nelson Bros. Bond & Mortgage Co.........51, 59
Federal Trade Comm'n v. Cement Institute 360, 361
Federal Trade Comm'n v. Gibson 67
Federal Trade Comm'n v. Keppel & Bro. 32
Federal Trade Comm'n v. Raladam Co............32
Fidelity Mortgage Investors, In re 6
Fiduccia v. Department of Justice 123
Field v. Clark............24, 25
First Jersey Sec., Inc. v. Bergen 78
First Nat'l Bank & Trust Co. v. National Credit Union Administration..................982, 983
Flast v. Cohen............957
Fleming v. Mohawk Wrecking & Lumber Co............70
Florida East Coast Railway, United States v.........281, 344, **460**
Ford Motor Co. v. NLRB 608
Ford Motor Credit Co. v. Milhollin............764
Foucha v. Louisiana 335
Frame, United States v............78
Franklin v. Massachusetts..........6, 834, **857**
Free Enterprise Fund v. Public Co. Accounting Oversight Bd............79, 80, 192, 202, 207, **232**, 374, 768
French, United States ex rel. v. Weeks............66

Freytag v. Commissioner of Internal Revenue.............13, 169, **184**, 209
Friedman v. Rogers 363, 378
Friends of the Earth, Inc. v. Laidlaw Environmental Services............ **950**, 967
Fuentes v. Shevin 337
Fund for Animals v. Kempthorne 73
Fusari v. Steinberg............321, 329
Gagnon v. Scarpelli 330
Garcia v. San Antonio Metropolitan Transit Authority............712
Gardner v. Toilet Goods Assn., Inc............881
Gates & Fox Co. v. Occupational Safety and Health Review Comm'n............782
Geer v. Connecticut 672
General Atomics v. U.S. Nuclear Regulatory Comm'n 905
General Dynamics Land Systems, Inc. v. Cline **651**
Georgia v. Tennessee Copper Co............958, 962
Germaine, United States v.......... 160, 174, 175, 177, 185
Gibson v. Berryhill............360, 363, **375**, 382, 900
Gideon v. Wainwright 293
Gilbert v. Homar............325
Gilmore v. City of Montgomery.....923
Giordano, United States v............70
Glickman v. Wileman Bros. & Elliott, Inc............78
Go-Bart Importing Co. v. United States............180
Goldberg v. Kelly...... **287**, 297, 301, 317, 384
Golden State Bottling Co. v. NLRB............394
Gonzales v. Oregon........678, 766, 776
Gonzales, United States v. 649
Goodenow v. Commisioner............752
Goodyear's Rubber Manufacturing Co. v. Goodyear Rubber Co..........31
Goss v. Lopez 324, 329, 330, 331
Grand River Enterprises Six Nations v. Pryor 282
Granfinanciera v. Nordberg **115**
Grannis v. Ordean 290
Gray v. Powell............603
Greater Los Angeles Council on Deafness v. Baldrige 848
Greene v. McElroy............291
Greene v. Meese............906
Gregory v. Ashcroft............642, 681
Grimaud, United States v. 25, 681
Group Life & Health Ins. Co. v. Royal Drug Co. 638
GTE South, Inc. v. Morrison 413
Hagans v. Commissioner of Social Security 735
Hahn v. Gottlieb 816

Haig v. Agee 339, 341
Halverson v. Slater 70
Hamdan v. Rumsfeld 253
Hamdi v. Rumsfeld **333**
Hamilton v. Caterpillar Inc. 651
Hannah v. Larche 162
Hanousek v. United States 693
Hanover Star Milling Co. v.
    Metcalf 31
Hardin v. Kentucky Utilities
    Co. 921
Hartwell, United States v. 177
Hazen Paper Co. v. Biggins 654
Headwaters, Inc. v. Talent Irrigation
    Dist. 696
Heckler v. Campbell **427**, 429,
    430, 432, 433
Heckler v. Chaney 782, 819, **842**
Hennen, Ex parte 160, 180, 235
Hess v. Port Authority Trans-Hudson
    Corporation 665
High Country Citizens Alliance v.
    Clarke 810
Hodel v. Virginia Surface Mining &
    Reclamation Assn., Inc. 665
**Home Box Office, Inc. v.
    FCC** **495**, 503, 504, 508
**Home Concrete & Supply, LLC,
    United States v.** **747**
Howe Scale Co. v. Wyckoff, Seamans
    & Benedict 31
Hudson v. United States 953
**Humphrey's Executor v. United
    States** 52, 79, 147, 162, **222**
Hunt v. Washington Apple
    Advertising Comm'n 935
ICC v. Locomotive Engineers 834
Illinois Cent. R.R. Co. v. Interstate
    Commerce Comm'n 223
Illinois Cent. R.R. v. Norfolk &
    W. Ry. 411
Implementation of the Local
    Competition Provisions in the
    Telecomm. Act of 1996, In re 687
**Industrial Union Dept., AFL-CIO
    v. American Petroleum
    Institute (The Benzene
    Case)** **38**, 47, 58, 59, 62, 609
Ingraham v. Wright 324
Inland Empire Pub. Lands Council v.
    Glickman 70
Inquiry Concerning High-Speed
    Access to the Internet Over Cable
    & Other Facilities, In re 738
INS v. Aguirre-Aguirre 715
INS v. Cardoza-Fonseca 751, 765
INS v. Chadha 64, **135**, 144, 148,
    149, 150, 207, 222
INS v. St. Cyr 679, 683
INS v. Wang 608
INS v. Yang 414
International News Service v.
    Associated Press 31
International Union, United Auto.,
    Aerospace & Agricultural

Implement Workers of Amer. v.
    Brock 935
Interport Pilots Agency v.
    Sammis 283
Investment Company Institute v.
    Camp 976, 981
Irwin Mem'l Blood Bank of San
    Francisco Med. Soc. v. American
    Nat'l Red Cross 10
J.W. Hampton, Jr. & Co. v. United
    States 25, 28, 46, 47,
    56, 61, 63, 77
Jerome v. United States 602
Jewell Ridge Coal Corp. v. Mine
    Workers 618
John R. Sand & Gravel Co. v. United
    States 749
Johnson v. Eisentrager 341
Johnson v. Robison **797**, 822,
    830
Johnson, United States v. **532**,
    707
Joint Anti-Fascist Committee v.
    McGrath 288, 298, 300, 310
Jones v. United States 335, 655
Jones, United States v. 166
Judulang v. Holder 709
K Mart Corp. v. Cartier, Inc. 661
Karlen v. City Colls. of Chi. 651
Kasten v. Saint-Gobain Performance
    Plastics Corp. 678
Keene Corp. v. United States 675
Kentucky Div., Horsemen's
    Benevolent and Protective Ass'n v.
    Turfway Park Racing Ass'n 78
Kirschbaum v. Walling 606
Kissinger v. Reporters Comm. for
    Freedom of the Press 8
Kyle v. Morton High School 296
L. Singer & Sons v. Union Pac. R.R.
    Co. 927
Laird v. Tatum 364, 365, 941
Lance v. Coffman 970
Landry v. FDIC **168**, 373
Langevin v. Chenango Court,
    Inc. 817
Lead Industries Ass'n v. EPA 57,
    60, 65
Lebron v. National Railroad
    Passenger Corp. 82, 83, 234
Lechmere, Inc. v. NLRB 745
Lefkowitz v. Turley 330
Lehigh Valley Coal Co. v.
    Yensavage 603
Leocal v. Ashcroft 678
Les v. Reilly **89**
Lewis v. Continental Bank
    Corp. 949
Lexmark Int'l, Inc. v. Static Control
    Components, Inc. 969
Lincoln v. Vigil **832**
Linda R.S. v. Richard D. 924
Londoner v. Denver **279**, 281
Long Island Care at Home, Ltd. v.
    Coke 782
Lopez, United States v. 83, 664

Los Angeles v. Lyons.....937, 938, 963
Los Angeles, City of v. David........325
Louisiana Pub. Serv. Comm'n v.
    FCC 770
Loving v. United States 45, 54
Lujan v. Defenders of
    Wildlife 929, 930, **936**, 948,
    957, 959, 961, 962, 963, 965, 970
Lujan v. National Wildlife
    Federation 886, 887, **932**,
    939, 978, 979, 980, 981
Mack Trucks, Inc. v.
    Environmental Protection
    Agency **526**
Mackey v. Lanier Collection Agency
    & Service, Inc.............................669
Maislin Indus., U.S., Inc. v. Primary
    Steel, Inc. 742, 745
Mallette v. Arlington County........296
Mango, United States v...................70
Manhattan Gen. Equipment Co. v.
    Commissioner 758
Maracich v. Spears.......................678
Marathon Oil Co. v. EPA 344, 346
Marbury v. Madison.............292, 621,
    770, 805
Marshall v. Jerrico, Inc. 382
Massachusetts v. EPA.............852,
    853, 854, **956**, 965, 966, 967
Massachusetts v. Mellon.......941, 968
Match-E-Be-Nash-She-Wish Band
    of Pottawatomi Indians v.
    Patchak...................................**985**
Matherson, United States v............71
Mathews v. Eldridge **316**, 323,
    324, 326, 329, 331, 332, 333, 335,
    336, 338, 339, 341, 342, 367, 381
Mayo Foundation for Medical Ed.
    and Research v. United
    States 750, 753, 757
Mazurie, United States v................71
McAuliffe v. City of New
    Bedford.............................286, 307
McBoyle v. United States.............680
McCarthy v. Madigan.......**898**, 910,
    911, 912
McClure v. Harris..........379, 380, 383
McCulloch v. Maryland..........81, 198,
    239
McGee v. United States.....**893**, 899
MCI Telecommunications v.
    AT&T..707
McKart v. United States **890**,
    894, 895, 900
McKinley v. United States.............34
McMurtray v. Holladay.................283
Meachum v. Fano.........................330
Mead Corp., United States
    v.........................598, 632, 634, 656,
    680, 683, **718**, 732, 764
Medellin v. Texas 208, 253, 681
Mescalero Apache Tribe v.
    Jones...986

Mesquite, City of v. Aladdin's Castle,
    Inc. 954
Metropolitan Washington Airports
    Authority v. Citizens for
    Abatement of Aircraft Noise,
    Inc. 166, 185, 237
Meyer v. Bush................................8, 9
Meyer v. Nebraska 300
Michigan Gambling Opposition v.
    Kempthorne..................................81
Michigan v. EPA...........................640
Miller v. French 239
Minnesota Board for Community
    Colleges v. Knight 281, 283
Mississippi Power & Light Co. v.
    Mississippi ex rel. Moore 762
Missouri v. Holland 664
Mistretta v. United States **45**,
    58, 62, 63, 77, 166, 371, 757
Monongahela Bridge Co. v. United
    States..92
Morgan v. Comm'r 602
Morgan, United States v. 353,
    382, 815
Morrison v. Olson........ 79, **172**, **228**
Morrison, United States v.............664
Morrissey v. Brewer 318, 384
Morton v. Ruiz 615, 734
Morton, United States v...............734
Moskal v. United States........674, 683
Motor Vehicle Manufacturers
    Ass'n of U.S., Inc. v. State
    Farm Mutual Auto. Insurance
    Co. 21, **568**, 641, 708, 741
Mullane v. Cent. Hanover Bank &
    Trust Co.....................................329
Murchison, In re 360
Murray's Lessee v. Hoboken Land &
    Improvement Company 94,
    100, 101, 112
Myers v. Bethlehem Shipbuilding
    Corp. 890
Myers v. United States 139, 147,
    160, 197, **217**
Nash v. Bowen........................... **368**
National Ass'n of Home Builders v.
    Defenders of Wildlife 776
National Ass'n of Reg. Util. Comm'rs
    ("NARUC") v. FCC 70, 77, 81, 82
National Association of Psychiatric
    Treatment v. Mendez..................72
National Broadcasting Co. v. United
    States...............................35, 49, 50
National Cable & Telecomm.
    Ass'n v. Brand X Internet
    Services............ 347, 348, 676, **738**
National Cable & Telecomm. Ass'n,
    Inc. v. Gulf Power Co. 743, 763
National Cable Television Assn. v.
    United States 47
National Credit Union
    Administration v. First
    National Bank & Trust
    Co. 926, **973**, 987

National Customs Brokers & Forwarders Ass'n of Am., Inc. v. United States 853
National Ins. Co. v. Tidewater Co. 109
National Organization of Veterans' Advocates, Inc. v. Secretary of Veterans' Affairs 709
National Park and Conservation Ass'n v. Stanton 70, 72
National Petroleum Refiners Ass'n v. FTC **419**
National Tire Dealers & Retreaders Ass'n, Inc. v. Brinegar **562**
NationsBank of N.C., N.A. v. Variable Annuity Life Ins. Co. 715, 721, 734
Natural Res. Def. Council, Inc. v. Train 915
Neagle, In re 247
Neal v. United States............ 742, 744
New State Ice Co. v. Liebmann 286
New York Cent. Secs. Corp. v. United States 50
New York v. United States 81, 208
NLRB v. Bell Aerospace Co. 609, 782
NLRB v. Columbian Enameling & Stamping Co. 387, 392, 411
NLRB v. Curtin Matheson Scientific, Inc. 395
NLRB v. Donnelly Garment Co. 361
NLRB v. Enterprise Leasing Co. Se., LLC 195
NLRB v. Hearst Publications **599**
NLRB v. New Vista Nursing & Rehab. 195
NLRB v. Noel Canning **196**, 221, 224, 232, 235, 239
NLRB v. Std. Oil Co. 387
Noel Canning v. NLRB 195
North Haven Bd. of Ed. v. Bell 733
Northeast Marine Terminal v. Caputo.......................609
Northeastern Fla. Chapter, Associated Gen. Contractors of America v. Jacksonville............888, 889
Northern Pipeline Const. Co. v. Marathon Pipe Line Co.........**98**, 107, 110, 111, 112, 117, 118, 119, 207, 239
Norton v. Southern Utah Wilderness Alliance 916
Norwood v. Harrison....................923
Nourse, United States v...............805
Nova Scotia Food Products Corp., United States v. **490**
O'Connor v. Consol. Coin Caterers Corp.............................651
O'Connor v. Donaldson 335
O'Hagan, United States v. 681

O'Rourke v. Smithsonian Inst. Press 10
O'Shea v. Littleton.......................938
Oakland Cannabis Buyers' Cooperative, United States v.....650
Office Employees v. NLRB...........609
Old Colony Trust Co. v. Comm'r 189
Olenhouse v. Commodity Credit Corp. 413
Oncale v. Sundowner Offshore Servs., Inc......................660
Open America v. Watergate Special Prosecution Force.....................123
Ortiz, United States v. 702
Pacific Gas & Elec. Co. v. State Energy Resources Conservation and Development Comm'n........886
Pacific Gas & Electric Co. v. Federal Power Commission **550**
Pacific Legal Found. v. Dep't of Transp. 411
Pacific States Box & Basket Co. v. White.............................352
Page v. Celebrezze......................406
Page, United States v......................66
Panama Refining Co. v. Ryan **26**, 33, 34, 40, 47, 62, 78, 860
Parham v. J.R......................342, 384
Parker v. Summerfield....................67
Parson's v. Bedford........................115
Patsy v. Bd. of Regents of Fla. 899
Patterson v. McLean Credit Union...........................749
Paul v. Davis **308**
PBGC v. LTV Corp. 818
Pension Benefit Guar. Corp. v. LTV Corp. **354**, 715
Pension Benefit Guar. Corp. v. R.A. Gray & Co.................................354
Perkins, United States v. 232
Perry v. Sindermann.........**303**, 329
Pickus v. United States Bd. of Parole 6
Pierce v. Sisters 286
Pillsbury Co. v. Federal Trade Commission **129**
Plaut v. Spendthrift Farm, Inc. 207
Port of Boston Marine Terminal Ass'n v. Rederiaktiebolaget Transatl. 866
Porter v. Nussle...........................904
Portland Cement Ass'n v. Ruckelshaus 412, **479**
Powell v. Alabama.........................291
Pozo v. McCaughtry 905
Process Gas Consumers Group v. United States Dep't of Agric......623
Providence Journal Co., United States v......................167
Public Citizen v. Department of Justice 208
Quivira Mining Co. v. EPA 695
R.H. Johnson & Co. v. SEC.............78

R.L.C., United States v. 683
Raddatz, United States v. 102, 112
Radio Officers v. NLRB.................396
Railway Labor Exec. Ass'n v. Nat'l
    Mediation Bd.....................639, 640
Rancho Palos Verdes v.
    Abrams.................................759
Rapanos v. United States 667,
    693
Ratzlaf v. United States................675
Raymond B. Yates, M.D., P.C. Profit
    Sharing Plan v. Hendon 736
Rea v. Matteuchi 282
Reno v. Catholic Social Services,
    Inc....**879**
Reno v. Flores..............................650
Richardson v. Perales......322, 361,
    383, **400**
Richardson, United States v. 927,
    929, 930
Riverside Bayview Homes, Inc.,
    United States v. 665, 695, 763
Rogers v. Bennett 905
Ross v. Bernhard 116
Ross v. County of Bernalillo..........905
Rueth Dev. Co., United States
    v. 697
Runkle v. United States.................66
Rushforth v. Council of Econ.
    Advisers...9
Rusk v. Cort...........................806, 883
Rust v. Sullivan 735
S & D Maint. Co. v. Goldin 307
Sackett v. EPA..............769, 788, 867
Salt Institute v. Leavitt 126
Sandin v. Conner..........................311
Santos, United States v. 683
Save Our Sonoran, Inc. v.
    Flowers.....................................696
Scenic Hudson Preservation
    Conference v. FPC 920
Scheidler v. Nat'l Org. for
    Women..678
Schilling v. Rogers........................352
Schlesinger v. Reservists Committee
    to Stop the War.................930, 962
Schoenthal v. Irving Trust Co. 116
Schware v. Board of Bar
    Examiners..................................301
Schweiker v. McClure......**378**, 384,
    385
Seacoast Anti-Pollution League v.
    Costle..............................344, 345
Sea-Land Serv., Inc. v. Dep't of
    Transp. 640
Sealed Case, In re..........................182
Sebelius v. Auburn Regional Medical
    Center...763
SEC v. Chenery Corp. ("Chenery
    II")..................................**442**, 608
SEC v. Sloan.................................609
Securities Indus. Ass'n v. Bd. of
    Governors of the Fed. Reserve Sys.
    (SIA) 410

Sequoia Orange Co. v. Yeutter........78
Service v. Dulles 349
Sevoian v. Ashcroft.......................413
Shalala v. Illinois Council on Long
    Term Care 878
Shapiro v. Thompson.....................288
Sheldon v. Sill..............................825
Shell Oil Co. v. EPA.................. **474**
Shelley v. Brock 841
Shields v. Utah Idaho Cent. R.R.
    Co...92
Shimer, United States v. 615, 620
Shook v. District of Columbia Fin.
    Responsibility & Mgmt. Assistance
    Auth. 70, 72
Sibbach v. Wilson & Co. 51
Siebold, Ex parte 180
Sierra Club v. Andrus 8
Sierra Club v. Costle......... 275, **505**
Sierra Club v. EPA 935
Sierra Club v. Morton..........938, 942,
    952
Sierra Club v. Sigler.......................82
Simon v. Eastern Ky. Welfare Rights
    Org..................................924, 937
Sims v. Apfel................................912
Singleton v. Wulff.........................968
Skidmore v. Swift & Co........... **605**,
    609, 656, 714, 766
Skinner v. Mid-America Pipeline
    Co...45
Slaff v. Commisioner 752
Smiley v. Citibank 620, 724,
    734, 761
Snepp v. United States..........822, 827
Sniadach v. Family Finance
    Corp. 329
Socialist Labor Party v.
    Gilligan.....................................881
Solid Waste Agency of Northern
    Cook County v. United States
    Army Corps of Engineers.... **662**,
    676, 682, 695
Sorenson v. Secretary of
    Treasury....................................734
Sorrell v. IMS Health Inc. 780
Sorrell v. SEC 78
SoundExchange, Inc. v. Librarian of
    Congress 183
South Fla. Water Mgmt. Dist. v.
    Miccosukee Tribe 702
South Texas Lumber Co.,
    Commissioner v............................598
Southern Pacific Transp. Co. v.
    Watt...71
Southern R.R. Co. v. Seabord Allied
    Milling Corp. 824
Specter v. Garrett.................861, 862
Speiser v. Randall.........................304
Standard Oil Co. of California v.
    United States 130
Standard Oil Co. of New Jersey v.
    United States 51

Standard Oil Co. v. United
States 223
Stanley, United States v. 827
Staples v. United States 674
Stark v. Wickard 881
State Farm Mut. Auto. Ins. Co. v.
Dep't of Transp. 852
**Steel Co. v. Citizens for a Better
Environment** **946**, 954, 955,
969
Stone v. INS 670
Storer Broadcasting Co., United
States v. 885
Strickland v. Comm'r, Me. Dep't of
Human Servs. 348
Students Challenging Regulatory
Agency Procedures (SCRAP),
United States v. 931, 939
Succar v. Ashcroft 661
Sunshine Anthracite Coal Co. v.
Adkins 78, 80, 92, 140, 945
Swan v. Clinton 196
Sweetland v. Walters 8, 9
Sykes v. United States 683
Tabor v. Joint Board for Enrollment
of Actuaries 72
**Talk America, Inc. v. Michigan
Bell Telephone Co.** 769,
777, 783, 790, 792
Telecommunications Research &
Action Center v. FCC 914, 915
The Brig Aurora 24
The Daniel Ball 694, 699
Thirty-Seven Photographs, United
States v. 797
Thomas Jefferson Univ. v.
Shalala 782, 791, 792
Thomas v. Union Carbide
Agricultural Products Co. 105,
107, 109, 110, 111, 117
Thomas v. Woolum 905
Thompson v. Gleason 798
Thompson/Center Arms Co., United
States v. 676, 677, 678, 682, 747
Thunder Basin Coal Co. v.
Reich 878
Ticor Title Insurance Co. v.
FTC 856
Tigner v. Texas 953
Todd & Co. v. SEC 78
**Toilet Goods Ass'n, Inc. v.
Gardner** **874**, 881, 887, 888
Totten, United States ex rel. v.
Bombardier Corp. 81, 83
Touby v. United States 45, 62,
63, 681
Tracy v. Gleason 798
Traynor v. Turnage 798
Trbovich v. Mine Workers 839
Treacy v. Newdunn Ass'n 696
Truax v. Raich 303
Tucker Truck Lines, Inc., United
States v. 314
Tull v. United States 115, 116, 953
Tumey v. Ohio 363, 377
Turner v. Safley 902

Turner v. Williams 92
TVA v. Hill 620, 669
**U.S. Department of Agriculture v.
Murry** **85**
U.S. Steel Corp. v. Train 346
Udall v. Tallman 731
Union Pacific R. Co. v. Locomotive
Engineers 769
United Public Workers v.
Mitchell 869
United States Health Club v.
Major 67
**United States Telecom
Association v. Federal
Communications
Commission** **67**
**Universal Camera Corp. v.
NLRB** **386**, 392, 394
Valley Forge Christian Coll. v. Ams.
United for Separation of Church &
State, Inc. 943, 970
**Vermont Yankee Nuclear Power
Corp. v. NRDC** 281, 356,
468, 755
Vigil v. Rhoades 832
Vitek v. Jones 384
Vlandis v. Kline 86
W.T. Grant Co., United States
v. 954
Ward v. Village of Monroeville 363,
377, 382
Warth v. Seldin 922, 927, 962, 983
Washington Legal Found. v. United
States Sentencing Comm'n 6
Washington, Virginia & Maryland
Coach Co. v. NLRB 387
Watt v. Alaska 735
Wayman v. Southard 51
Webster v. Doe **820**, 834,
835, 836
Weiman v. Updegraff 298
Weinberger v. Salfi 905
West Chicago, Illinois, City of v.
NRC 344
West v. Bergland 900
Western Pacific R.R. Co., United
States v. 918, 919
**Whitman v. American Trucking
Ass'ns, Inc.** 45, 55, **60**,
79, 80, 126, 264, 638
Whitmore v. Arkansas 937, 963
Widdowson, United States v. 70
Wieman v. Updegraff 310
Wiener v. United States **226**
Wilkins v. United States 905
Will v. Mich. Dep't of State
Police 642
Will, United States v. 109
Williams v. United States 186
Williamson County Regional
Planning Comm'n v. Hamilton
Bank of Johnson City 910
Wilson & Co. v. NLRB 387
Wilson v. MVM, Inc. 897
Wiltberger, United States
v. 678, 683

Winston, United States v. 167
Wirtz v. Bottle Blowers
    Ass'n 838, 839
Wirtz v. Laborers' Union.............. 839
Wisconsin Gas Co. v. F.E.R.C. 282
Wisconsin v. Constantineau **297**,
    300, 309
Withrow v. Larkin.............**359**, 382
Wolff v. McDonnell................ 297, 314
Woodford v. Ngo 905, 913
Woodley, United States v...... 195, 196
WWHT, Inc. v. FCC...................... 852
Yakus v. United States 35, 47,
    49, 50, 681
Yellow Transportation, Inc. v.
    Michigan................................**630**
Yetman v. Garvey......................**435**
Yi v. Sterling Collision Centers,
    Inc... 783
Yick Wo v. Hopkins 902
Yonkers, City of v. United
    States 353
Young v. Cmty. Nutrition Inst...... 715
Youngstown Sheet & Tube Co. v.
    Sawyer 80, 166, **248**, 860
Zakonaite v. Wolf 92
Zemel v. Rusk 35
Zivotofsky v. Clinton 207, 773

UNIVERSITY CASEBOOK SERIES®

FEDERAL ADMINISTRATIVE LAW

CASES AND MATERIALS

SECOND EDITION

CHAPTER 1

INTRODUCTION

A. THE STUDY OF ADMINISTRATIVE LAW

Many students of administrative law enroll in the course with no real conception of what it is about. They hear that it is a good course to take, but they may not know why. In fact, it is difficult to avoid administrative law in modern legal practice. Why is this so?

1. WHAT IS ADMINISTRATIVE LAW?

The high school civics model of American government recognizes three branches as outlined in the United States Constitution: the legislative, *i.e.*, Congress; the executive, *i.e.*, the President; and the judicial, *i.e.*, the Supreme Court and lower federal courts. Many students do not really appreciate that, in fact, this model only barely scratches the surface of contemporary American government.

In addition to Congress, the President, and the courts, the federal government encompasses fifteen Cabinet-level departments and dozens of other agencies, boards, commissions, bureaus, and departmental divisions that commonly fall under the heading of administrative agencies and that often seem to operate both in conjunction with and independently of Congress, the President, and the courts. Administrative agencies are responsible for administering thousands of pages of federal statutes, including promulgating and implementing regulations and adjudicating individual cases as well as prosecuting enforcement actions. In fact, administrative agencies create many more legally-binding rules than Congress and adjudicate far more individual disputes than the courts. It seems fair, then, to assume that the field of administrative law relates to administrative agencies; but how?

Indeed, a precise definition of administrative law has proven elusive for many decades. Twenty-five years ago, Henry Friendly provided the following sweeping description:

> Administrative law includes the entire range of action by government with respect to the citizen or by the citizen with respect to the government, except for those matters dealt with by the criminal law and those left to private civil litigation where the government's participation is in furnishing an impartial tribunal with the power of enforcement.[1]

A quarter century earlier, Frank Cooper offered a similarly broad conception, that

> administrative law may be defined as including all those branches of public law which relate to the organization of government administration ... cover[ing] many of the principles and doctrines comprising the fields usually described as constitutional law, legislation, public

---

[1]   Henry Friendly, *New Trends in Administrative Law*, 6 MD. BAR J., No. 3, at 9 (1974).

corporations, public officers, civil service, and taxation, and includes, in fact, all branches of the law affecting the executive activities of the government.[2]

These descriptions certainly capture the scope of the administrative law enterprise, which along with the size of the federal government has only grown larger and more complicated since.

Given the breadth of these definitions, however, it is perhaps not too surprising that other scholars have wondered whether there really is or can be a coherent definition of administrative law as a subject for legal study. In 1936, J.F. Davison observed,

> [t]o many lawyers and laymen, however, the phrase "administrative law" suggests the rules and principles by which administrative agencies formulate their decisions. In so far as such rules and principles exist, they should and could be included in a complete study of administrative law. However, the decisions by these various administrative bodies are, as Mr. Justice Holmes expressed it, based on, "an intuition of experience which outruns analysis." Hence, it must be seriously questioned as to whether it is possible to find rules and principles comparable to those said to exist in the common law and statute law as it is studied at the present time. * * * When courts or legislatures approve of administrative action based upon intuitive judgments, it may be considered that they have enunciated a principle of law to the effect that an intuitive judgment is the proper one. It is such principles and the field for their use that constitute the principles of administrative law as we know them at the present time.[3]

Forty years later, Ernest Gellhorn and Glen Robinson picked up on Davison's point and also asked whether a definition of administrative law was possible, noting the "changing conception of administrative law . . . which in turn reflects developments in the nature and scope of administrative government." Nevertheless, Gellhorn and Robinson also conceded that, "for all this evolution, perhaps the more noteworthy thing is not how much but how little has actually changed in the basic conception of administrative law."[4] In other words, plus ça change, plus c'est la même chose; the more things change, the more they stay the same?

Whatever the merits of this debate in the abstract, such conceptions offer little guidance for discerning what a student of administrative law should, in fact, study. Scholarly approaches to the study of administrative law resolve this question with different, though of course related and overlapping, emphases. Some scholars focus their inquiry on the constitutional relationships between administrative agencies and the other three traditional branches of government: what are the sources of and limitations upon agency authority in our system

---

[2]   FRANK E. COOPER, ADMINISTRATIVE AGENCIES AND THE COURTS 4 (1951).

[3]   J.F. Davison, *Administrative and Judicial Self–Limitation*, 4 GEO. WASH. L. REV. 291, 296–99 (1936).

[4]   Ernest Gellhorn & Glen O. Robinson, *Perspectives on Administrative Law,* 75 COLUM. L. REV. 771 (1975).

of separated and shared powers? Chapters 2 and 3 of this casebook are particularly dedicated to these issues.

Other scholars consider more closely the actions of the agencies themselves: what they do and how they do it. More specifically, agencies adopt rules and adjudicate claims, and some scholars fairly describe administrative law as the study of the processes and procedures by which agencies pursue those activities. Perhaps it is this perspective that prompted Adrian Vermeule to observe that "[o]ne of the main functions of administrative law is to regulate the powers and duties of administrative agencies and the processes by which they act."[5] Consistent with the observations of Gellhorn and Byse, what agencies do and how they do it often varies tremendously. This is perhaps not surprising, as individual agencies are responsible for administering federal statutes covering everything from immigration, environment, workplace safety, and employment discrimination to patents, securities, taxes, and pension benefits. Nevertheless, agency processes and procedures are also governed by a set of common statutes and legal requirements, including but by no means limited to the Administrative Procedure Act. Chapters 4 and 5 focus especially on these commonalities of agency practice and procedure.

Finally, whatever agencies may do, they are all subject to judicial oversight. Thus, some scholarly conceptions of administrative law place greater emphasis upon judicial oversight of agency action and the standards and doctrines that courts apply in such cases. As Kenneth Culp Davis once offered, "Administrative law is the law concerning the powers and procedures of administrative agencies, including especially the law governing judicial review of administrative action."[6] Chapters 6 and 7 address primarily topics fitting this description.

In sum, administrative law is a field of great breadth, encompassing the efforts of dozens of administrative agencies and impacting virtually everyone. Every agency and substantive area of government regulation possesses its own unique statutes, practices, customs, and understandings, such that generalization is often difficult. Yet, these myriad areas of law and regulation do share in common statutes, principles, standards, and doctrines that influence both agency behavior and judicial evaluation thereof. Those statutes, principles, standards, and doctrines have evolved over time and continue to do so, yet remain a source of commonality among administrative agencies. The purpose of this casebook is to explore those sources of commonality.

2. WHY STUDY ADMINISTRATIVE LAW?

It is virtually impossible to practice law in the United States today without encountering federal government agencies and administrative law issues. To highlight merely a few of the agencies with which different types of lawyers work routinely:

- Environmental lawyers must work with the Environmental Protection Agency and the Department of the Interior;

---

[5]   Adrian Vermeule, *Our Schmittian Administrative Law*, 122 HARV. L. REV. 1095, 1107 (2009).

[6]   1 KENNETH CULP DAVIS, ADMINISTRATIVE LAW TREATISE § 1.01 (1958).

- Energy lawyers with the Department of Energy and the Federal Energy Regulatory Commission;

- Immigration lawyers with the Department of Homeland Security and its subsidiary agencies, U.S. Citizenship and Immigration Services and U.S. Immigration and Customs Enforcement;

- Tax lawyers with the Treasury Department and the Internal Revenue Service;

- Labor and employment lawyers with the Department of Labor, the National Labor Relations Board, the Occupational Safety and Health Administration, and the Equal Employment Opportunity Commission;

- Patent lawyers with the U.S. Patent Office;

- Securities lawyers with the Treasury Department and the Securities and Exchange Commission; and

- Banking lawyers with the Treasury Department's Office of the Comptroller of the Currency and Office of Thrift Supervision, the Federal Deposit Insurance Corporation, and the Federal Reserve Board.

Federal regulatory regimes, and the agencies that administer them, intrude into virtually every sphere of American life. Agencies like the Environmental Protection Agency, the Food and Drug Administration, the Consumer Product Safety Commission, and the National Highway Traffic Safety Administration administer regulatory programs that protect public health, safety, and the environment, imposing private costs that exceed the total annual expenditures of the federal government. Agencies like the Social Security Administration and the Center for Medicare and Medicaid Services implement benefit systems that account for a substantial and growing percentage of federal government expenditures. The Internal Revenue Service collects taxes from a few hundred million individuals and entities every year.

Other courses address the particular statutes, regulations, and practices of individual agencies and areas of legal practice. By contrast, the materials in this casebook are designed to introduce you to the procedures that many if not most federal agencies use to issue rules and to adjudicate disputes, the standards that judges apply in reviewing those rules and adjudications, and the doctrines that generally govern the relationships between federal government agencies and the three branches of government recognized in the Constitution. Although this casebook is dedicated to federal administrative law practices and doctrines, because state and local agencies, legislatures, and courts borrow liberally from their federal analogues, this introduction to federal administrative law will also help you to understand state and local administrative law systems as well.[7]

---

[7]   State and local administrative law systems are too vast and variable to be susceptible to easy generalization. Each state and local administrative law system differs from the federal system in important respects. With the exception of materials concerning due process in Section A of Chapter Four, the materials in this textbook are not directly applicable to the administrative law systems of any state or locality unless explicitly adopted by state or local governments and courts.

B. WHAT IS AN AGENCY?

As noted, administrative agencies are central to the study of administrative law. Yet, just as scholars have struggled to define administrative law, bright lines for characterizing government offices or entities as agencies and for explaining their role in American government have proven similarly elusive. Kenneth Culp Davis offered that "[a]n administrative agency is a governmental authority, other than a court and other than a legislative body, which affects the rights of private parties through either adjudication or rulemaking."[8] James Freedman, meanwhile, suggested that agencies represent "centers of gravity of the exercise of administrative power . . . where substantial 'powers to act' . . . are vested."[9] Do these explanations help you understand what an agency is and does?

1. STATUTORY DEFINITIONS

Distinguishing agencies from other government offices and entities is often essential for establishing the applicability of various statutes that govern federal agency action. Hence, some of these statutes explicitly define agency for their purposes, although not necessarily in the same way. Why do you think different statutes might define agency differently?

The Administrative Procedure Act, 5 U.S.C. § 551 *et seq.*, which imposes procedural rules for agency actions and standards for judicial review thereof, offers a broad definition that serves for most, though not all, administrative law purposes:

[A]gency means each authority of the Government of the United States, whether or not it is within or subject to review by another agency, but does not include—

(A) the Congress;

(B) the courts of the United States;

(C) the governments of the territories or possessions of the United States;

(D) the government of the District of Columbia;

or except as to the requirements of section 552 of this title—

(E) agencies composed of representatives of the parties or of representatives of organizations of the parties to the disputes determined by them;

(F) courts martial and military commissions;

(G) military authority exercised in the field in time of war or in occupied territory; or

(H) functions conferred by [various provisions of the U.S. Code]. . . .[10]

---

[8]   1 KENNETH CULP DAVIS, ADMINISTRATIVE LAW TREATISE § 1.01 (1958).

[9]   James Freedman, *Administrative Procedure and the Control of Foreign Direct Investment*, 119 U. PA. L. REV. 1, 419 (1970).

[10]   5 U.S.C. § 551(1).

As you can see, rather than offering a particular description of what constitutes an agency, the APA definition is most clear in its identification of particular government entities that are not agencies. Notably, while the APA expressly excludes Congress and the courts from its definition of agency, the APA does not address the status of the President and members of his Executive Office. Despite this omission, the Supreme Court in *Franklin v. Massachusetts*, 505 U.S. 788, 800–01 (1992), declared that the President of the United States is most definitely not an agency for purposes of the APA:

> The President is not explicitly excluded from the APA's purview, but he is not explicitly included, either. Out of respect for the separation of powers and the unique constitutional position of the President, we find that textual silence is not enough to subject the President to the provisions of the APA. We would require an express statement by Congress before assuming it intended the President's performance of his statutory duties to be reviewed for abuse of discretion. As the APA does not expressly allow review of the President's actions, we must presume that his actions are not subject to its requirements.

Further, the courts have interpreted the APA's exclusion of Congress and the courts from its definition of agency broadly to encompass other government offices in the legislative and judicial branches, respectively. Thus, the United States Judicial Conference,[11] the United States Probation Service,[12] and the United States Sentencing Commission[13] are not agencies for purposes of the APA because they are part of the judicial branch; likewise, the Library of Congress is not an agency subject to APA requirements because it is part of the legislative branch.[14]

Another notable feature of the APA definition of agency is its division of listed non-agency entities into two groups: those authorities listed in (A)–(D) that are exempt from APA governance entirely, including § 552; and those authorities listed in (E)–(H) that are not exempt from § 552. Section 552 of Title 5 of the U.S. Code, more commonly called the Freedom of Information Act, or FOIA, requires agencies to make various government documents and information available to the public. FOIA § 552(e) offers its own definition of agency that is based upon but deviates from APA § 551(1):

> [F]or purposes of this section, the term "agency" as defined in section 551(1) of this title includes any executive department, Government corporation, Government controlled corporation, or other establishment in the executive branch of the Government (including the Executive Office of the President), or any independent regulatory agency.

---

[11] In re Fidelity Mortgage Investors, 690 F.2d 35, 38–39 (2d Cir. 1982), *cert. denied sub nom.* Lifetime Communities, Inc. v. Administrative Office of U.S. Courts, 462 U.S. 1106 (1983).

[12] Pickus v. United States Bd. of Parole, 507 F.2d 1107, 1112 (D.C. Cir. 1974).

[13] Washington Legal Found. v. United States Sentencing Comm'n, 17 F.3d 1446, 1449 (D.C. Cir. 1994).

[14] Ethnic Employees of the Library of Cong. v. Boorstin, 751 F.2d 1405, 1416 n. 15 (D.C. Cir. 1985).

Legislative history reflects that Congress intended the definition of agency in FOIA to be broader than the APA definition. Why do you think this might be so?

Other statutes that regulate agency conduct both track and deviate from the APA and FOIA definitions of agency. The Privacy Act, 5 U.S.C. § 552a, which limits the types of information agencies may disclose, uses the same definition of agency as FOIA. The Government in the Sunshine Act, 5 U.S.C. § 552b, which requires that covered agencies hold many of their meetings open to the public, limits its scope to those agencies as defined by FOIA that are "headed by a collegial body composed of two or more individual members, a majority of whom are appointed to such position by the President with the advice and consent of the Senate, and any subdivision thereof authorized to act on behalf of the agency." Only a narrow subset of agencies subject to either the APA or FOIA satisfies the Sunshine Act definition. Meanwhile, the Federal Advisory Committee Act (FACA), 5 U.S.C. App.1, which similarly requires government advisory committees to open many of their meetings and records to the public, simply utilizes the APA definition of agency.

In summary, for all of these statutes, whether or not a particular government office or entity is an agency begins with the definition of § 551(1), with or without modification. For a government office or entity that is not explicitly excluded by the APA definition, the question may arise whether that office or entity represents an "authority" of the United States Government and, thus, an agency. The following case offers a nice summary of the courts' reasoning in cases concerning this issue.

Citizens for Responsibility and Ethics in Washington v. Office of Administration

566 F.3d 219 (D.C. Cir. 2009).

■ GRIFFITH, CIRCUIT JUDGE:

Citizens for Responsibility and Ethics in Washington (CREW) alleges that the Office of Administration (OA) discovered in October 2005 that entities in the Executive Office of the President (EOP) had lost millions of White House e-mails. In April 2007, CREW made a FOIA request of OA asking for information about the missing e-mails. CREW sought records about the EOP's e-mail management system, reports analyzing potential problems with the system, records of retained e-mails and possibly missing ones, documents discussing plans to find the missing e-mails, and proposals to institute a new e-mail record system. * * *

In June 2007, the parties agreed to a timeline for producing the records, but within weeks OA changed course and told CREW, for the first time in this dispute, that it is not covered by FOIA because it provides administrative support and services directly to the President and the staff in the EOP, putting it outside FOIA's definition of "agency." * * * OA refused to turn over the bulk of the potentially responsive records-more than 3000 pages.

* * *

Congress enacted the Freedom of Information Act in 1966 to provide public access to certain categories of government records. The Act strives "to pierce the veil of administrative secrecy and to open agency action to the light of public scrutiny." *Dep't of Air Force v. Rose,* 425 U.S. 352, 361 (1976). Described in its most general terms, FOIA requires covered federal entities to disclose information to the public upon reasonable request, *see* 5 U.S.C. § 552(a), unless the information falls within the statute's exemptions, *see id.* § 552(b).

By its terms, FOIA applies only to an "agency," and the key inquiry of this appeal is whether the Office of Administration is an agency under the Act. In the original statute, "agency" was defined broadly as any "authority of the Government of the United States. . . ." Administrative Procedure Act, Pub.L. No. 89–554, § 551(1), 80 Stat. 378, 381 (1966) (codified as amended at 5 U.S.C. § 551(1)). In 1974, Congress amended the definition of "agency" to include, more specifically, "any executive department, military department, Government corporation, Government controlled corporation, or other establishment in the executive branch of the Government (including the Executive Office of the President), or any independent regulatory agency." 5 U.S.C. § 552(f)(1). Although the 1974 amendments expressly include the EOP within the definition of "agency," the Supreme Court relied upon their legislative history to hold that FOIA does not extend to "the President's immediate personal staff or units in the Executive Office [of the President] whose sole function is to advise and assist the President," *Kissinger v. Reporters Comm. for Freedom of the Press,* 445 U.S. 136, 156 (1980). The Supreme Court's use of FOIA's legislative history as an interpretive tool has given rise to several tests for determining whether an EOP unit is subject to FOIA. These tests have asked, variously, "whether the entity exercises substantial independent authority," *Armstrong v. Executive Office of the President,* 90 F.3d 553, 558 (D.C.Cir.1996), "whether . . . the entity's sole function is to advise and assist the President," *id.,* and in an effort to harmonize these tests, "how close operationally the group is to the President," "whether it has a self-contained structure," and "the nature of its delegat[ed]" authority, *Meyer v. Bush,* 981 F.2d 1288, 1293 (D.C.Cir.1993).

However the test has been stated, common to every case in which we have held that an EOP unit is subject to FOIA has been a finding that the entity in question "wielded substantial authority independently of the President." *Sweetland v. Walters,* 60 F.3d 852, 854 (D.C.Cir.1995) (per curiam). In *Soucie v. David,* we concluded that the Office of Science and Technology (OST) is an agency covered by FOIA because it has independent authority to evaluate federal scientific research programs, initiate and fund research projects, and award scholarships. 448 F.2d 1067, 1073–75 (D.C.Cir.1971). Similarly, we determined that the Office of Management and Budget (OMB) exercises substantial independent authority because it has a statutory duty to prepare the annual federal budget, which aids both Congress and the President. *See Sierra Club v. Andrus,* 581 F.2d 895, 902 (D.C.Cir.1978). We noted that "Congress signified the importance of OMB's power and function, over and above its role as presidential advisor, when it provided . . . for Senate confirmation of the Director and Deputy Director of OMB." *Id.* * * *

By the same token, we have consistently refused to extend FOIA to an EOP unit that lacks substantial independent authority. We held that the Council of Economic Advisors (CEA) was not covered by FOIA because it "has no independent authority such as that enjoyed either by CEQ or OST." *Rushforth v. Council of Econ. Advisers,* 762 F.2d 1038, 1042 (D.C.Cir.1985). Specifically, we noted that CEA "has no regulatory power under [its] statute. It cannot fund projects based on [its] appraisal, as OST might, nor can it issue regulations for procedures based on the appraisals, as CEQ might." *Id.* at 1043. And although President Ronald Reagan's Task Force on Regulatory Relief comprised senior White House staffers and cabinet officers whose agencies fall under FOIA, we concluded that the Task Force was not a FOIA agency because it lacked substantial authority independent of the President "to direct executive branch officials." *Meyer,* 981 F.2d at 1297. The Task Force reviewed agency rules and proposed regulatory revisions to the President, but it could not issue guidelines or other types of directives. Nor is the National Security Council (NSC) covered by FOIA because it plays no "substantive role apart from that of the President, as opposed to a coordinating role on behalf of the President." *Armstrong,* 90 F.3d at 565.

And in *Sweetland,* we held that members of the Executive Residence staff do not exercise substantial authority independent of the President because they only "assist[ ] the President in maintaining his home and carrying out his various ceremonial duties." 60 F.3d at 854. Specifically, they "provide[ ] for the operation of the [residence]" by preparing meals, greeting visitors, making repairs, improving the rooms' mechanical systems, and providing needed services for official functions. *Id. Sweetland*'s analysis and disposition have special force in this matter because it involved an EOP unit that, like OA, provided to the President only operational and administrative support. Where that is the purpose and function of the unit, it lacks the substantial independent authority we have required to find an agency covered by FOIA.

OA's charter documents created an office within the EOP to perform tasks that are entirely operational and administrative in nature. President Jimmy Carter proposed OA as the "base for an effective EOP budget/planning system through which the President can manage an integrated EOP rather than a collection of disparate units." OA "shall provide components of the [EOP] with such administrative services as the President shall from time to time direct." President Carter ordered OA to "provide common administrative support and services to all units within [the EOP], except for such services provided [by the White House] primarily in direct support of the President." However, OA "shall, upon request, assist the White House Office in performing its role of providing those administrative services which are primarily in direct support of the President." OA continues to exercise these same functions and duties today. Significantly, OA's director is "not accountable for the program and management responsibilities of units within the [EOP]"; instead, "the head of each unit . . . remain[s] responsible for those functions."

As its name suggests, everything the Office of Administration does is directly related to the operational and administrative support of the work of the President and his EOP staff. OA's services include personnel management; financial management; data processing; library, records, and information services; and "office services and operations, including: mail, messenger, printing and duplication, graphics, word processing, procurement, and supply services." CREW contends that OA's support of non-EOP entities—including the Navy, the Secret Service, and the General Services Administration— undermines the government's argument. But those units only receive OA support if they work at the White House complex in support of the President and his staff. Assisting these entities in these activities is consistent with OA's mission. Because nothing in the record indicates that OA performs or is authorized to perform tasks other than operational and administrative support for the President and his staff, we conclude that OA lacks substantial independent authority and is therefore not an agency under FOIA.

NOTES AND QUESTIONS

1. In *Citizens for Responsibility and Ethics*, the D.C. Circuit applied what is known as the substantial independent authority standard for assessing whether the Office of Administration was an "authority of the Government of the United States" under the APA's definition of agency, 5 U.S.C. § 551(1), for purposes of FOIA. The D.C. Circuit has applied the same standard in interpreting 5 U.S.C. § 551(1) for Privacy Act purposes as well. *See, e.g., Dong v. Smithsonian Inst.*, 125 F.3d 877, 881 (D.C. Cir. 1997). Other circuits have concurred in this interpretation of the APA's definition of agency. *See, e.g., O'Rourke v. Smithsonian Inst. Press*, 399 F.3d 113, 120 (2d Cir. 2005); *Irwin Mem'l Blood Bank of San Francisco Med. Soc. v. American Nat'l Red Cross*, 640 F.2d 1051, 1053 (9th Cir. 1981). In other words, even if statutes like FOIA and the Privacy Act, for their own purposes, add or subtract from the APA's definition of agency, in all such contexts, the courts have consistently applied the substantial independent authority standard in identifying whether a particular entity is an authority of the Government of the United States under 5 U.S.C. § 551(1). Given that these statutes serve different purposes and define agency somewhat differently, does the courts' use of the substantial independent authority standard to interpret 5 U.S.C. § 551(1) seem sensible to you? Why or why not?

2. If, as the D.C. Circuit maintains, the goal of FOIA is "to pierce the veil of administrative secrecy and to open agency action to the light of public scrutiny," and FOIA explicitly recognizes the Executive Office of the President as an agency, why do you think the courts have excluded the President and his immediate staff from FOIA's document disclosure requirements?

2. EXECUTIVE BRANCH AND INDEPENDENT AGENCIES

Government entities that do qualify as agencies under one or more of the above definitions come in many sizes and configurations. Two categories of agencies are particularly relevant for some of the materials in this text: traditional or executive branch agencies, and independent agencies. Again, no single definition captures either category completely, but certain characteristics are more typical than not.

Traditional agencies include and/or are sited in one of the Cabinet-level departments. Presently, the President's Cabinet includes representatives from fifteen executive branch departments; they are the Departments of State, Treasury, Defense, Justice, Interior, Agriculture, Commerce, Labor, Health and Human Services, Housing and Urban Development, Transportation, Energy, Education, Veterans' Affairs, and Homeland Security.[15] Although each of these Departments employs many, many officers and employees, each is also headed by an individual Secretary or, in the case of the Justice Department, the Attorney General. As we will discuss further in Chapter 3, these individual Department heads are appointed by the President with the advice and consent of the Senate, and they are removable at will by the President as well within certain political constraints.

Somewhat confusingly, the organizational structures of these Departments also contain other agencies—i.e., agencies within agencies. For example,

- the Occupational Safety and Health Administration and the Mine Safety and Health Administration are agencies that are part of the Department of Labor;

- the Food and Drug Administration, the National Institutes of Health, and the Indian Health Service are all part of the Department of Health and Human Services; and

- the Bureau of Indian Affairs, National Park Service, and Bureau of Land Management are part of the Department of the Interior.

Like the Departments themselves, each of these agencies within agencies typically is headed by a single person, although these individuals carry various titles—e.g., Commissioner, Administrator, or Director. These individual agency heads are also appointed by the President with the advice and consent of the Senate. That said, it is not always easy to distinguish an agency within an agency from a subgroup within a single agency.

Independent agencies, by contrast, exist and function outside the control of the traditional executive branch departments. They also tend to be structured differently from traditional executive agencies, with the goal of insulating them from political pressure and direct control by either Congress or the President. Although there is no precise set of features that designates an agency as independent, these agencies tend to be headed by multi-member commissions, boards, or councils rather than by single individuals. The President appoints the heads of independent agencies with the advice and consent of the Senate, but the statutes that create these agencies often establish staggered, fixed-year terms of office for their members, provide that the President may only remove those members from office for cause, and/or specify that only a certain number of the members may belong to the same political party. In the Paperwork Reduction Act of 1980, Congress provided a nonexclusive list of agencies it considered to be independent, including

---

[15] The Administrator of the Environmental Protection Agency and the United States Trade Representative are accorded cabinet-level status, but the Environmental Protection Agency and the Office of the United States Trade Representative are not themselves cabinet departments.

the Federal Communications Commission, the National Labor Relations Board, the Consumer Products Safety Commission, and the Securities and Exchange Commission, all of which resemble the above description.

Federal government agencies reflect a wide variety of institutional arrangements that do not fit either of these two categories precisely. For example:

- The Federal Energy Regulatory Commission (FERC) possesses all of the typical characteristics of an independent agency; it is headed by a collegial body, the members of which serve staggered terms of years and cannot be removed except for cause, with the qualification that no more than a bare majority may be from the same political party. Yet, unlike many independent agencies, according to its organic statute, FERC is an agency "within the Department" of Energy. 42 U.S.C. § 7134. Thus, for example, the Inspector General for the Department of Energy also has investigatory powers with respect to FERC.

- The Social Security Administration (SSA) is headed by an individual Administrator rather than a multi-member body. Yet, the head of the Social Security Administration serves for a fixed term of years and cannot be removed from office except for cause. The statute creating the SSA describes it as "an independent agency in the executive branch of the Government." 42 U.S.C. § 901.

- The Internal Revenue Service (IRS) is also headed by a single Commissioner who is removable at will by the President. The IRS is an agency within the Treasury Department. As of 1997, however, the Commissioner is appointed for a fixed, five-year term. 26 U.S.C. § 7803(a).

3. AGENCIES AND THE THREE BRANCHES

The standard categorization of agencies as between executive branch agencies and independent agencies belies the broader relationships between agencies and all three traditional branches of government. In fact, in important respects, the relationship between agencies, whether traditional or independent, and the other parts of government can be depicted most accurately by the following organization chart.

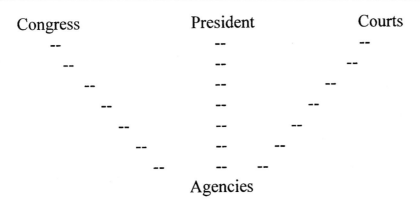

Congress   President   Courts

Agencies

The dotted lines we have drawn between each of the three branches of government reflect the jurisprudential uncertainty with respect to the details of the relationships between the agencies and each of the three branches. To some extent, this uncertainty derives from the Constitution's relative silence regarding the role of agencies in its otherwise tripartite scheme. The Constitution clearly contemplates the existence of agencies, but it offers no vision of what they might do or how they might do it.

It is clear that agencies are accountable to Congress, the President, and the courts in many important contexts and respects. It is also clear that the constitutionally-permissible relationships between and among the four institutions varies with context. Remarkably, however, some of the most important characteristics of the relationships remain uncertain even in the third century of our constitutional republic. Thus, for instance, as recently as 1991, the Justices engaged in a lively and inconclusive debate about the characteristics of an institution that cause it to be a court of law or an executive department.[16] For that matter, the Justices still have not resolved definitively the controversy that led to the impeachment of President Andrew Johnson in 1868—to what extent and in what circumstances can Congress insulate an agency official from the otherwise plenary power of the President to remove an officer or inferior officer of the United States?

Some things, however, are known and accepted. Whether traditional or independent, agency power begins with Congress, with a presidential assist. With the President's signature (and thus acquiescence), Congress enacts legislation that assigns an agency the responsibility, and thus the authority and a fair amount of discretion, to administer a statute by enforcing its requirements and/or pursuing its goals. Congress may endeavor to control how an agency exercises that authority and discretion. Congress may narrow the parameters of the delegation substantively, for example by explicitly removing particular questions from the agency's jurisdiction or requiring judicial approval before an agency's orders are enforceable as a matter of law. Congress can, and often does, enact other legislation imposing procedural hurdles that agencies must surmount before they can act. Yet, that initial

---

[16] *See* Freytag v. Commissioner, 501 U.S. 868 (1991). The *Freytag* case is discussed at some length in Chapter 3.

delegation of authority to administer, regulate, and adjudicate gives an agency the power to act in the first instance.

Furthermore, there is little doubt that a congressional delegation of authority to an agency serves to shift power not only to the agency but also to the President and the courts. Presidents have the power to appoint top agency officials, albeit with the advice and consent of the Senate. Presidents often seek appointees who share their policy goals and preferences. Presidents may also enjoy the power to remove from office many top agency officials should they decline to pursue the President's agenda. Presidents commonly utilize a variety of less formal mechanisms to influence agency action. In sum, Presidents enjoy a fair amount of control or at least influence over agency actions, so legislation that grants power to agency officials ultimately empowers the President as well. The courts meanwhile exercise the power of judicial review over the substance, procedure, and process of agency action. While standards of judicial review often counsel deference to agencies, courts ultimately have tremendous power to derail agency actions of which they disapprove. The materials in this casebook examine all of these issues at some length.

4.   QUASI-JUDICIAL AND QUASI-LEGISLATIVE VERSUS BUREAUCRATIC ACTIONS

Because neither the Constitution nor statutes provide definitive answers to most important administrative law questions, courts have long attempted to draw analogies to two institutions whose characteristics and functions are better known and more settled than those of agencies—legislatures and courts. In other words, when a court is called upon to decide whether a decision-making procedure used by an agency is lawful or whether a relationship between an agency and another institution of government is permissible, that reviewing court may attempt to analogize to some legislative or judicial function. Thus, many judicial opinions addressing administrative law disputes have passages reasoning that a particular decision-making procedure or relationship with another institution is or is not permissible because the agency is performing a function that is "quasi-legislative" or "quasi-judicial."

It is important to recognize that, while this analogical reasoning process may be quite useful for some purposes, in other cases it may be of limited utility and may produce bad reasoning and bad results. In some contexts, agencies behave similarly to legislatures, and in other contexts they bear some resemblance to courts, but of course they are neither. Legal scholars have recognized that, as institutions, agencies possess their own unique characteristics and norms. Arguably, therefore, assessments of agency actions should recognize and take into account agencies' institutional uniqueness.

For example, Jerry Mashaw has recognized that agencies follow their own particular bureaucratic norms that are not law per se but that nevertheless operate to direct and constrain agency behavior toward desirable ends; Mashaw also contends that, in many contexts, bureaucratic justice is superior—*i.e.*, provides more accurate results—

when compared to the justice that courts provide.[17] Perhaps, therefore, administrative disputes are better resolved by considering agencies' institutional context rather than by evaluating agency actions through the prism of legislative or judicial conventions. In fact, in the last few decades, courts have shown increased awareness of and consideration for agencies' institutional distinctiveness in adjudicating some administrative law cases.

C. THE HISTORY OF ADMINISTRATIVE LAW

It is difficult to appreciate many administrative law doctrines fully without knowing at least some of their history. Agencies have grown dramatically over the nation's history in number, size, and scope. Scholarly and popular perceptions of agencies' essential nature have changed quite a bit as well.

Many legal scholars think of administrative law as largely a twentieth century development. A typical summary of the history of federal administrative law begins with the creation of the Interstate Commerce Commission in 1887, followed by the proliferation of agencies regulating economic activity and administering government benefits during the New Deal, and subsequently the addition of numerous health, safety, and environmental regulatory agencies in the 1960s and 1970s. Indeed, lawyers really only began to think of administrative law as a separate legal field in the late nineteenth century. Yet, federal administrative activity in the United States extends back at least to the founding, and debates and decisions of that era remain part of the administrative law discussion today.

Unsurprisingly, as the administrative state has expanded, and as administrative law doctrine has evolved, different theories of the administrative state have emerged. Although certain theoretical models are often associated with particular time periods, none of the various theories has ever been completely dropped or discredited. Rather, each continues to exist alongside others that have developed subsequently.

1. THE EARLY REPUBLIC

The principal architect of the United States Constitution, James Madison, cautioned that "[t]he accumulation of all powers, legislative, executive, and judiciary, in the same hands, whether of one, a few, or many, and whether hereditary, self-appointed, or elective, may justly be pronounced the very definition of tyranny."[18] The United States Constitution provides for a federal government of limited authority that is both divided and shared among three co-equal branches. In theory, consistent with the Constitution's structure, the primary function of the President and other executive branch officers is to execute the laws that Congress enacts, although of course the President, with his veto power, often enjoys tremendous influence in shaping legislation.

Nevertheless, legal scholars have long recognized that the Constitution contemplates the creation of executive branch departments for the purpose of implementing congressionally-enacted

---

[17] JERRY MASHAW, BUREAUCRATIC JUSTICE, 213–27 (1983).

[18] THE FEDERALIST NO. 47, at 266 (James Madison) (Scott, ed. 1898).

statutes. The First Congress and President George Washington established Departments of War, Treasury, and Foreign Affairs to assist the President in performing the executive function. The First Congress also authorized the President to create regulations to implement the provision of military pensions for Revolutionary War veterans[19]; and delegated administrative power over statutorily-created programs to other executive branch officials, for example by assigning responsibility for "estimat[ing] the duties payable" on imported goods to appointed district tax collectors.[20] Subsequent Congresses followed suit, creating agencies and delegating administrative authority to address problems as diverse as implementing embargos against hostile countries, allocating and regulating most of the nation's land, and establishing and regulating a national banking system. Congress placed most of these agencies directly within cabinet departments like the Treasury Department. Others were more "independent"; for example, the Patent Office, created in 1790, was headed collectively by the Secretaries of State and War and the Attorney General, rather than falling solely within the sphere of any one department.[21]

Moreover, while federal regulation of economic activity did not at all approximate contemporary norms, it did exist. Even beyond the discretion granted to tax collectors to administer the revenue laws, consider Jerry Mashaw's account of the Steamship Safety Act of 1852.[22] In the mid-nineteenth century, steamship explosions were commonplace, with large resulting losses of lives. Congress responded by creating a Board of Supervising Inspectors and empowering it to issue licenses to operate steamships, to issue legally-binding rules, and to adjudicate disputes involving steamship safety. Congress did not impose any procedural safeguards upon the agency for when it issued rules or adjudicated disputes, except for the requirement that the agency state its reasons for issuing a rule or for resolving a dispute in a particular manner. Within three years, the Commission was able to reduce the incidence of steamship explosions by roughly eighty per cent.

While performing important functions and exercising substantial power, nineteenth century agencies operated largely unchecked by the courts. A court could not review an agency action that was considered discretionary, and discretion was defined to include any agency action in which an agency had some degree of choice—a broad definition that arguably served to eliminate judicial review of all but a handful of federal agency actions. In that early era, the sole means by which any court could exercise power over an agency was through a suit at common law against an agency employee. Individuals who were injured by conduct that they believed to be ultra vires could file a common law action for trespass or conversion in state court against the federal official who took the action. The federal official would defend on the basis of his claim that he was performing a lawful function on behalf of

---

[19]   Ch. 24, § 1, 1 Stat. 95 (1789).

[20]   Ch. 5, § 5, 1 Stat. 29, 36 (1789).

[21]   *See, e.g.,* Jerry Mashaw, *Recovering American Administrative Law: Federalist Foundations, 1787–1801,* 115 YALE L. J. 1256 (2006).

[22]   *See* Jerry Mashaw, *Administration and "The Democracy": Administrative Law from Jackson to Lincoln, 1829–1861,* 117 YALE L. J. 1568 (2008).

the federal government, and his fate would depend on whether a state judge and/or jury agreed with that claim.

Still, although agencies were perhaps more prevalent in these early years than typically realized, and notwithstanding the discretion those agencies exercised, common assumptions regarding administration during this era resemble what Richard Stewart has described as the "transmission belt" theory of agency action.[23] Agencies merely apply legislative commands to individual facts and circumstances. The courts, meanwhile, ensure that agencies follow congressional orders. Stewart rightly associates the transmission belt model of administration with the first half of the twentieth century rather than the nineteenth. While judicial opinions during the latter time period continued to reflect this theory, many theorists had already moved on.

2. THE PROGRESSIVE ERA AND THE NEW DEAL

Any account of federal administrative law recognizes 1887 as a pivotal moment. In that year, responding to complaints by Western farmers and others about the economic power and discriminatory rate practices of the railroads, Congress established the Interstate Commerce Commission (ICC). Congress empowered the ICC to determine "reasonable and just" rates for railroad services and to enforce various anti-discriminatory provisions it adopted simultaneously. Legal scholars herald the creation of the ICC as the beginning of a new era of federal regulation for a few reasons. Scholars sometimes describe the statute creating the ICC as the first time that Congress enacted a broad legislative scheme to regulate a single industry considered vitally important to the national economy. Also, the ICC is often thought to be the first independent agency and an initial effort toward a more technocratic form of governance.

New era: ICC

A hallmark of both the Progressive and New Deal eras was a broadly-shared faith in administrative agencies as neutral bodies of experts, untainted by political considerations, dedicated to the essentially technocratic business of regulating key economic sectors, acting in the public interest. Hence, both of the "firsts" attributed to the ICC and its organic statute were repeated numerous times throughout this extended time period. Among the avalanche of economic and social legislation:

- Congress expanded the size, power, and jurisdiction of the ICC with the Hepburn Act in 1906;

- Congress enacted the Sherman Act in 1890, followed by the Clayton Act in 1914 and the Robinson-Patman Act in 1936, and created the Federal Trade Commission as an independent agency in 1914, all for the purposes of preventing monopolization and preserving competition in the marketplace;

- Congress adopted the Pure Food and Drug Act in 1906 to protect the public from adulterated and misbranded food and drugs, assigned responsibility for its administration first to the Bureau of Chemistry in the U.S. Department of Agriculture and

---

[23] Richard Stewart, *The Reformation of American Administrative Law*, 88 HARV. L. REV. 1667, 1675 (1975).

subsequently to a new Food and Drug Administration in 1927, and then expanded the FDA's authority with the Federal Food, Drug and Cosmetics Act in 1938;

- After the Sixteenth Amendment was ratified in 1913, Congress adopted an initial series of revenue acts that established corporate and individual income taxes and formed the statutory basis for the modern Internal Revenue Code;

- Congress established the Federal Power Commission in 1920, restructured it as an independent agency in 1930, and tasked it with regulating electricity, natural gas and oil pipelines, and hydroelectric projects;

- Congress enacted the Securities Act of 1933, the Securities and Exchange Act of 1934, and created the Securities and Exchange Commission in 1934 to administer both these and related future statutes and to oversee the securities markets;

- Congress passed the Social Security Act in 1935, dramatically expanding the provision of government benefits to the poor, the unemployed, and the elderly, and created the Social Security Board to administer its programs.

Other prominent Progressive and New Deal era agencies, both executive branch and other independent, include the Federal Communications Commission, the National Labor Relations Board, the Federal Deposit Insurance Corporation, the Federal Reserve System, and the Civil Aeronautics Administration (now the Federal Aviation Administration).

According to one account, by 1941, the United States Government Manual listed more than 200 agencies, boards, commissions, bureaus, and departmental divisions, 111 of which had published rules and regulations in the Code of Federal Regulations, and at least 51 of which conducted rulemakings or adjudications that substantially affected persons outside the government.[24] Of those 51 particularly significant agencies, Congress created 6 agencies, including the ICC, between 1865 and 1900; 9 agencies between 1900 and 1918; another 9 agencies between 1918 and 1929; and 17 agencies between 1930 and 1940. Fully 22 of those agencies fell outside the traditional executive branch departments.

3. THE ADMINISTRATIVE PROCEDURE ACT

It is perhaps not surprising that dramatic proliferation of federal government agencies during the Progressive and New Deal eras prompted calls for some coordinated effort to study and improve upon agency practices and procedures. The result, after several years, was the Administrative Procedure Act.

First enacted in 1946, the Administrative Procedure Act (APA), which is contained in Appendix A to this book, is to administrative law what the Constitution is to constitutional law. Agencies, courts, and practitioners invariably refer to it as an authoritative source for purposes of resolving all major federal administrative law disputes.

---

[24] *See* FINAL REPORT OF ATTORNEY GENERAL'S COMMITTEE ON ADMINISTRATIVE PROCEDURE, S. DOC. NO. 8, 77th Cong. (1st Sess. 1941).

George Shepherd's account of the decade-long congressional debate that preceded enactment of the APA helps to gain an understanding of both the function of the APA and its limitations.[25] The APA was originally proposed in the early days of the New Deal as a means of obtaining greater uniformity with respect to the procedures used by the plethora of new agencies Congress was creating to make various types of decisions and with respect to the relationships between those agencies and the courts. For several years prior to World War II, Congress engaged in bitter debates about the basic contours of the APA. Some members saw agencies as the answer to all of the nation's problems. They urged enactment of a statute that would create powerful agencies that were largely unconstrained by either mandatory procedures or potentially intrusive judicial review. Other members were skeptical that the new agencies would engage in socially-beneficial actions and were concerned that they would overreach, abuse their vast powers, and interfere with the smooth-functioning of the economy. They urged passage of a statute that would limit agency power, require agencies to use elaborate procedures to make all decisions, and subject agency actions to de novo judicial review. By the time that World War II interrupted that debate, Congress had made no discernable progress in resolving the differences between those two groups.

After the War, Congress returned to the APA debate with an increased emphasis on compromise. After considerable painstaking work, committees of Congress produced a proposed statute that bridged the gap among the members so successfully that it was enacted in 1946 by unanimous votes in both the House and the Senate. Not surprisingly, however, the drafters of the APA were able to please all members of Congress only by using language that is susceptible to many meanings. Agencies and courts have struggled in their efforts to give the flexible words of the statute sensible meanings for over half a century, with mixed and highly incomplete results.

The APA alone resolves few administrative law disputes. In many cases, the APA describes dramatically different procedures for issuing rules or for adjudicating disputes and refers to the provisions of other statutes to indicate which procedure an agency must follow. Thus, the APA must be read in conjunction with the organic acts that authorize each agency to take particular types of actions. In addition, the APA is drafted in much the same manner as a constitution—its language is sufficiently malleable to support many different interpretations. As a result, the APA must be read along with the many judicial decisions in which courts have given meaning to its protean provisions.

Although the story of the APA as legislative compromise demonstrates that not everyone agreed, in the years that followed, most legal scholars generally continued to view administrative agencies as working diligently to resolve complex social and economic problems in the public interest. Nevertheless, some scholars in the 1950s began to question the public interest theory of administrative agencies. One scholar, Samuel Huntington, set off a small uproar when he asserted that the quality of the ICC's personnel had deteriorated and that political support for its activities had shifted from the farm groups that

---

[25] George Shepherd, *Fierce Compromise: The Administrative Procedure Act Emerges from New Deal Politics*, 90 NW. L. REV. 1557 (1996).

prompted its creation to the railroads that it was supposed to regulate.[26] Huntington did not altogether repudiate the public interest theory of agencies. Rather, Huntington merely suggested reorganizing and combining the ICC with other agencies responsible for various transportation issues to broaden their collective base of political support and better enable them to act in the public interest.

4.   THE 1960S AND 1970S

While one might consider the 1940s and 1950s as a period of consolidation and reflection regarding the administrative expansion that had gone before, the 1960s and 1970s were a time of substantial upheaval in administrative law. Beginning with the Great Society program under President Lyndon Baines Johnson and continuing through the administrations of Presidents Richard Nixon and Gerald Ford,

- Congress adopted the Social Security Act of 1965, establishing the Medicare and Medicaid programs to fund medical care for the elderly and the poor;

- Congress enacted statutes like the Federal Coal Mine Safety and Health Act in 1969 and the Occupational Safety and Health Act in 1970 to promote workplace safety, and established agencies like the Mine Safety and Health Administration, the Occupational Safety and Health Administration, and the Occupational Safety and Health Commission to administer those statutes;

- Congress established the Environmental Agency and adopted dozens of environmental statutes, including the National Environmental Policy Act of 1969, the Clean Air Act of 1970, and the Clean Water Act of 1972;

- Congress enacted the Consumer Product Safety Act of 1972 and established the Consumer Product Safety Commission to protect consumers from unsafe products;

- Congress passed the Endangered Species Act of 1973 and several related statutes to protect wildlife; and

- Congress passed the Employee Retirement Income Security Act of 1974 to protect workers' pensions and created the Pension Benefit Guarantee Corporation as an independent agency to facilitate the continuation and maintenance of private pension plans.

These are just a few examples of the regulatory and administrative expansion that characterized this time period.

This explosive growth of administrative laws and agencies was accompanied by significant developments in agency practices and administrative law doctrine. Interestingly, at the same time that

[handwritten note in margin: more laws & agencies]

---

[26] Samuel P. Huntington, *The Marasmus of the ICC: the Commission, the Railroads, and the Public Interest*, 61 YALE L.J. 467 (1952); *see also* Samuel P. Huntington, C. Dickerman Williams, & Charles S. Morgan, *The ICC Re-examined: A Colloquy*, 63 YALE L.J. 44 (1953); C. Dickerman Williams, *Transportation Regulation and the Department of Commerce*, 62 YALE L.J. 563 (1953); Charles S. Morgan, *A Critique of "The Marasmus of the ICC: The Commission, the Railroads, and the Public Interest,"* 62 YALE L.J. 171 (1953).

[handwritten margin notes: more skepticism / broader P standing]

Congress was again dramatically expanding the administrative state, skepticism of agency action was growing. Building off the observations of Samuel Huntington and others, scholars and courts routinely saw agencies as aligned with and captured by the very agencies they were supposed to regulate. Hence, administrative law doctrine shifted substantially to allow for broader plaintiff standing, a presumption in favor of judicial review, and expanded due process requirements for agency adjudications. Also, new statutes and revised interpretations of old ones prompted many agencies to begin pursuing their policy agendas by promulgating extensive regulations rather than case-by-case enforcement actions. Finally, Congress enacted statutes like the Freedom of Information Act (1966), the Privacy Act (1974), and the Government in the Sunshine Act (1976), which prompted agencies to alter many of their practices to accommodate new process and procedure requirements.

5. THE MODERN ERA

Characterizing more recent years in the context of history is often a difficult and dicey proposition. Nevertheless, it seems at least fair to say that the past thirty years have been an exciting period of change in administrative law.

The Supreme Court has considered a number of key structural issues that this casebook addresses: Does Congress have the power to delegate to agencies the authority to resolve policy through legally-binding regulations? Can Congress establish agencies that are independent of the President? Can agencies perform adjudicatory functions that are traditionally reserved for the Article III courts? These questions are all addressed in Chapters 2 and 3 of this casebook.

The Supreme Court has also developed new standards for judicial review that have had profound effects on agency actions and interactions with the courts. For example, in *Motor Vehicle Manufacturers Ass'n v. State Farm Automobile Insurance Co.*, 463 U.S. 29 (1983), the Court held that agencies must engage in reasoned decisionmaking and consider obvious alternatives to their policies in order to avoid judicial reversal of their policy choices as arbitrary and capricious. The following year, in *Chevron, U.S.A., Inc. v. NRDC*, 467 U.S. 837 (1984), the Court established a new two-step standard for judicial review of agency legal interpretations that requires courts to defer to agencies' reasonable interpretations of the statutes that they administer. These doctrines are addressed by Chapters 5 and 6, respectively.

Meanwhile, the courts have adopted new interpretations of the Administrative Procedure Act that have significantly altered agency behavior, for good and for ill, leading to complaints that the APA no longer works and that reform is needed. Scholarly and judicial debates have raged over the merits and significance of all of these developments. As Thomas Merrill has observed, "law schools have become a veritable cornucopia—or perhaps cacophony is a better word—of 'theory,' "[27] complicating assessments of administrative law

---

[27] Thomas W. Merrill, *Capture Theory and the Courts: 1967–1983*, 72 CHI.-KENT L. REV. 1039, 1067 (1997).

doctrine and making it difficult to identify a dominant theory of administration, but enriching the discussion.

Finally, as globalization, modern telecommunication and transportation systems, and other technological developments have made life more complex, and as the federal government has sought to address ever more problems and issues, government agencies (and sometimes Congress directly) have turned increasingly to private actors to perform a variety of government functions. As a result, modern governance is a complex web of public and private relationships, with an array of command and cooperative structures, wielding hard rules and soft guidance with real legal consequences. The academic literature assigns different labels to this approach: privatization, public/private partnerships, and new governance, to name just a few. The cooperation of the public and private sectors to achieve public goals is not new. At the height of the New Deal, Louis Jaffe lauded the longstanding and substantial involvement of private groups in the regulatory sphere.[28] But as the scope, range, and legal significance of public/private relationships have expanded, at least some legal scholars have begun to question the legitimacy of the results. Old arguments are new again, clear answers are often elusive, and the administrative law doctrines covered by this case book continue to evolve.

---

[28] Louis Jaffe, *Law Making By Private Groups*, 51 HARV. L. REV. 201 (1937).

CHAPTER 2

CONGRESS AND AGENCIES

Agencies exercise a wide variety of powers. The most important are rulemaking and adjudication. Both have long existed under a constitutional cloud.

A high proportion of agency rulemaking seems to consist of the exercise of legislative power delegated to agencies by Congress. Congress authorizes or even mandates that agencies promulgate rules and regulations to accomplish various statutory purposes and impose penalties upon regulated parties who fail to comply with those rules and regulations. Such delegations of power arguably violate Article I of the Constitution, which provides in relevant part that "all legislative Powers herein granted shall be vested in a Congress of the United States."

Similarly, a substantial number of agency adjudications seem to entail exercise of the judicial power. Congress authorizes agencies to adjudicate the rights and obligations of regulated parties under various statutory provisions. Such delegations of power arguably violate Article III of the Constitution, which provides that "the judicial Power of the United States, shall be vested in one supreme Court, and in such inferior Courts as the Congress may from time to time ordain and establish." They also arguably deny the right to jury trial guaranteed in the Seventh Amendment.

While agencies enjoy tremendous authority as a result of congressional delegations of policymaking and adjudicative responsibilities, Congress has also imposed numerous procedural and other burdens to curtail the discretion of agencies in exercising those powers. In this Chapter, we explore constitutional and other legal implications of congressional delegations of power to administrative agencies and also some of the alternative means by which Congress has acted to curtail agency discretion.

A. THE CONSTITUTIONALITY OF DELEGATING POLICYMAKING AUTHORITY

Article I, § 1 vests "all legislative powers" in Congress. From the earliest days of the Republic, the Supreme Court equated the legislative power with the authority to issue legally binding general rules of conduct and held that Congress could not delegate the legislative power. Thus was born the nondelegation doctrine. Yet, as the following materials demonstrate, the doctrine has never fit comfortably with reality on the ground.

1. THE NONDELEGATION DOCTRINE

Article I of the Constitution grants Congress the power to enact the laws that govern primary behavior, and Article II vests in the President the power to execute those laws. The line between making the law and executing the law has always been a murky one. Statutory meaning is often ambiguous. Executing a congressional statute thus often requires selecting one interpretation from among two or more reasonable alternatives. Such decisions are often fraught with policy implications, and the choices that the executive makes do not always correspond with legislative preferences.

Further, as regards the executive function, the Constitution authorizes the President to obtain written advice from "the principal Officer in each of the executive Departments" and, with advice and consent of the Senate, to appoint "Officers of the United States." The Constitution also gives Congress the power to "vest the appointment of . . . inferior Officers . . . in the Heads of Departments." It is difficult to conceive how an executive department differs from an administrative agency, or how any number of officers of the United States, inferior officers, and heads of departments could be organized except as administrative agencies. Thus, it seems the Constitution clearly anticipated the inclusion of administrative agencies as part of the federal government.

Finally, notwithstanding the nondelegation doctrine, Congress has been quite explicit in creating agencies with the power to issue legally binding rules since 1789. The First Congress and President George Washington established Departments of War, Treasury, and Foreign Affairs to assist the President in serving the executive function. The First Congress also adopted one statute designating particular officials to "estimate the duties payable" on imports and perform related duties, and another statute providing for military pensions for "invalids who were wounded and disabled during the late war," to be paid "under such regulations as the President of the United States may direct." The number of agencies with powers similar to these has only increased over the ensuing centuries, to the point at which rules issued by federal agencies now outnumber by far rules enacted in statutes.

The Court has attempted to reconcile its conclusion that Congress cannot delegate the legislative power with these realities in several ways. The Court's initial effort to legitimize broad delegations of power came in the case of *The Brig Aurora*, 11 U.S. 382 (1813). Congress had authorized the President to lift trade embargoes against France and England when those countries "ceased to violate the neutral commerce of the United States." The Court rejected the argument that Congress had unconstitutionally delegated legislative power to the President by characterizing the President's role as that of a mere finder of facts, ascertaining when events had occurred to trigger congressionally defined legal consequences. Similarly, in *Field v. Clark*, 143 U.S. 649, 693 (1892), the Court upheld legislation giving the President the power to impose tariffs upon finding, as a factual matter, that tariff-free trade with a country would be "reciprocally unequal and unreasonable." The Court approved the legislation because the President's authority was limited to taking the specific action prescribed by Congress when the "named contingency" occurred.

The fiction that Congress makes all policy decisions, leaving agencies only the job of determining the factual predicates for application of congressional policies, proved insufficient to legitimize many congressional delegations. The Court abandoned the named contingency test as soon as cases arose in which its application would have required the Court to hold a statute unconstitutional. In *Buttfield v. Stranahan*, 192 U.S. 470 (1904), the Court upheld a statute that authorized the Secretary of the Treasury to "fix and establish uniform standards of purity, quality, and fitness" for imported tea. Because the named contingency test could not be stretched to authorize such broad rulemaking authority, the Court substituted a "legislative standards" test: Congress could delegate legislative power if it set standards sufficient to limit the scope of the agency's discretion. In *United States v. Grimaud*, 220 U.S. 506, 517 (1911), the Court rationalized a similarly broad delegation of rulemaking power as authorizing an agency only to "fill up the details." In other words, as long as Congress made the major policy decisions, it could delegate interstitial policymaking to an agency.

Like the named contingency test applied in *Brig Aurora* and *Field v. Clark*, the legislative standards test survived only until its application would have required the Court to hold a statute unconstitutional. In *J.W. Hampton, Jr. & Co. v. United States*, 276 U.S. 394 (1928), the Court considered yet another tariff statute. In this case, however, the statute did not only authorize a designated tariff increase upon a particular finding by the President, but granted the President the power to increase tariffs by the amount he deemed necessary to "equalize . . . differences in costs of production" between producers of goods in the United States and competing countries. Since the statutory specifications were was too open-ended to permit the Court to uphold the statute as authorizing only interstitial policymaking, the Court announced a new standard: A statute delegating power to an agency could be upheld if it established an "intelligible principle" to guide the exercise of that power. *J. W. Hampton*, 276 U.S. at 409.

In sum, the Supreme Court has gone to great lengths to avoid declaring statutes unconstitutional on nondelegation grounds. The Court has held delegations of power to agencies unconstitutional in only two cases. Both were decided the same year, 1935, and both involved delegations under the same statute. The decisions are best understood in their unique historical context. First, the challenged statute, the National Industrial Recovery Act (NIRA), was the most radical component of President Franklin D. Roosevelt's revolutionary program to bring the nation out of a deep economic depression. Viewed as a whole, the NIRA delegated enormous power to agencies; in effect, it authorized cartelization of virtually all sectors of the economy. Second, many of the powers created by the NIRA were delegated to groups of private citizens who had financial interests in the markets they were assigned to regulate. Third, Justices on the Supreme Court in 1935 were extremely skeptical of President Roosevelt's plan for economic recovery through massive government intervention. That year was the peak of this period of great judicial hostility toward the politically accountable branches of government.

Panama Refining Co. v. Ryan

293 U.S. 388 (1935).

■ MR. CHIEF JUSTICE HUGHES delivered the opinion of the Court.

On July 11, 1933, the President, by Executive Order No. 6199 prohibited "the transportation in interstate and foreign commerce of petroleum and the products thereof produced or withdrawn from storage in excess of the amount permitted to be produced or withdrawn from storage by any State law or valid regulation or order prescribed thereunder, by any board, commission, officer, or other duly authorized agency of a State." This action was based on section 9(c) of Title I of the National Industrial Recovery Act of 1933, 15 U.S.C. § 709(c). That section provides:

"Sec. 9. . . .

"(c) The President is authorized to prohibit the transportation in interstate and foreign commerce of petroleum and the products thereof produced or withdrawn from storage in excess of the amount permitted to be produced or withdrawn from storage by any State law or valid regulation or order prescribed thereunder, by any board, commission, officer, or other duly authorized agency of a State. Any violation of any order of the President issued under the provisions of this subsection shall be punishable by fine of not to exceed $1,000, or imprisonment for not to exceed six months, or both."

* * *

Section 9(c) is assailed upon the ground that it is an unconstitutional delegation of legislative power. The section purports to authorize the President to pass a prohibitory law. The subject to which this authority relates is defined. It is the transportation in interstate and foreign commerce of petroleum and petroleum products which are produced or withdrawn from storage in excess of the amount permitted by state authority. Assuming for the present purpose, without deciding, that the Congress has the power to interdict the transportation of that excess in interstate and foreign commerce, the question whether that transportation shall be prohibited by law is obviously one of legislative policy. Accordingly, we look to the statute to see whether Congress has declared a policy with respect to that subject; whether the Congress has set up a standard for the President's action; whether the Congress has required any finding by the President in the exercise of the authority to enact the prohibition.

Section 9(c) is brief and unambiguous. It does not attempt to control the production of petroleum and petroleum products within a state. It does not seek to lay down rules for the guidance of state legislatures or state officers. It leaves to the states and to their constituted authorities the determination of what production shall be permitted. It does not qualify the President's authority by reference to the basis or extent of the state's limitation of production. Section 9(c) does not state whether, or in what circumstances or under what conditions, the President is to prohibit the transportation of the amount of petroleum or petroleum products produced in excess of the State's permission. It establishes no criterion to govern the President's course.

It does not require any finding by the President as a condition of his action. The Congress in § 9(c) thus declares no policy as to the transportation of the excess production. So far as this section is concerned, it gives to the President an unlimited authority to determine the policy and to lay down the prohibition, or not to lay it down, as he may see fit. And disobedience to his order is made a crime punishable by fine and imprisonment.

We examine the context to ascertain if it furnishes a declaration of policy or a standard of action, which can be deemed to relate to the subject of § 9(c) and thus to imply what is not there expressed. * * *

We turn to the other provisions of Title I of the Act. The first section is a "declaration of policy."[6] It declares that a national emergency exists which is "productive of widespread unemployment and disorganization of industry, which burdens interstate and foreign commerce, affects the public welfare, and undermines the standards of living of the American people." 15 U.S.C. § 701. It is declared to be the policy of Congress "to remove obstructions to the free flow of interstate and foreign commerce which tend to diminish the amount thereof"; "to provide for the general welfare by promoting the organization of industry for the purpose of cooperative action among trade groups"; "to induce and maintain united action of labor and management under adequate governmental sanctions and supervision"; "to eliminate unfair competitive practices, to promote the fullest possible utilization of the present productive capacity of industries, to avoid undue restriction of production (except as may be temporarily required), to increase the consumption of industrial and agricultural products by increasing purchasing power, to reduce and relieve unemployment, to improve standards of labor, and otherwise to rehabilitate industry and to conserve natural resources." *Id.*

This general outline of policy contains nothing as to the circumstances or conditions in which transportation of petroleum or petroleum products should be prohibited,—nothing as to the policy of prohibiting, or not prohibiting, the transportation of production exceeding what the States allow. The general policy declared is "to remove obstructions to the free flow of interstate and foreign commerce." *Id.* As to production, the section lays down no policy of limitation. It favors the fullest possible utilization of the present productive capacity of industries. It speaks, parenthetically, of a

---

[6]   The text of § 1 is as follows:

"Section 1.   A national emergency productive of widespread unemployment and disorganization of industry, which burdens interstate and foreign commerce, affects the public welfare, and undermines the standards of living of the American people, is hereby declared to exist. It is hereby declared to be the policy of Congress to remove obstructions to the free flow of interstate and foreign commerce which tend to diminish the amount thereof; and to provide for the general welfare by promoting the organization of industry for the purpose of cooperative action among trade groups, to induce and maintain united action of labor and management under adequate governmental sanctions and supervision, to eliminate unfair competitive practices, to promote the fullest possible utilization of the present productive capacity of industries, to avoid undue restriction of production (except as may be temporarily required), to increase the consumption of industrial and agricultural products by increasing purchasing power, to reduce and relieve unemployment, to improve standards of labor, and otherwise to rehabilitate industry and to conserve natural resources." 15 U.S.C. § 701.

possible temporary restriction of production, but of what, or in what circumstances, it gives no suggestion. The section also speaks in general terms of the conservation of natural resources, but it prescribes no policy for the achievement of that end. It is manifest that this broad outline is simply an introduction of the Act, leaving the legislative policy as to particular subjects to be declared and defined, if at all, by the subsequent sections.

* * *

The question whether such a delegation of legislative power is permitted by the Constitution is not answered by the argument that it should be assumed that the President has acted, and will act, for what he believes to be the public good. The point is not one of motives, but of constitutional authority, for which the best of motives is not a substitute. While the present controversy relates to a delegation to the President, the basic question has a much wider application. If the Congress can make a grant of legislative authority of the sort attempted by § 9(c), we find nothing in the Constitution which restricts the Congress to the selection of the President as grantee. The Congress may vest the power in the officer of its choice or in a board or commission such as it may select or create for the purpose. * * *

The Constitution provides that "All legislative Powers herein granted shall be vested in a Congress of the United States, which shall consist of a Senate and House of Representatives." Art. I, § 1. And the Congress is empowered "To make all Laws which shall be necessary and proper for carrying into execution" its general powers. Art. I, § 8, cl. 18. The Congress manifestly is not permitted to abdicate or to transfer to others the essential legislative functions with which it is thus vested. Undoubtedly legislation must often be adapted to complex conditions involving a host of details with which the national legislature cannot deal directly. The Constitution has never been regarded as denying to the Congress the necessary resources of flexibility and practicality, which will enable it to perform its function in laying down policies and establishing standards, while leaving to selected instrumentalities the making of subordinate rules within prescribed limits and the determination of facts to which the policy as declared by the legislature is to apply. Without capacity to give authorizations of that sort we should have the anomaly of a legislative power which in many circumstances calling for its exertion would be but a futility. But the constant recognition of the necessity and validity of such provisions and the wide range of administrative authority which has been developed by means of them cannot be allowed to obscure the limitations of the authority to delegate, if our constitutional system is to be maintained.

The Court has had frequent occasion to refer to these limitations and to review the course of congressional action.

* * *

The applicable considerations were reviewed in *[J.W.] Hampton & Co. v. United States*, 276 U.S. 394, where the Court dealt with the so-called "flexible tariff provision" of the Act of September 21, 1922, and with the authority it conferred upon the President. The Court applied the same principle that permitted the Congress to exercise its ratemaking power in interstate commerce, and found that a similar provision was justified for the fixing of customs duties; that is, as the Court said, "If Congress shall lay down by legislative act an intelligible principle to which the person or body authorized to fix such rates is directed to conform, such legislative action is not a forbidden delegation of legislative power.* * *" * * *

[I]n every case in which the question has been raised, the Court has recognized that there are limits of delegation which there is no constitutional authority to transcend. We think that § 9(c) goes beyond those limits. As to the transportation of oil production in excess of state permission, the Congress has declared no policy, has established no standard, has laid down no rule. There is no requirement, no definition of circumstances and conditions in which the transportation is to be allowed or prohibited.

If § 9(c) were held valid, it would be idle to pretend that anything would be left of limitations upon the power of the Congress to delegate its law-making function. The reasoning of the many decisions we have reviewed would be made vacuous and their distinctions nugatory. Instead of performing its law-making function, the Congress could at will and as to such subjects as it chooses transfer that function to the President or other officer or to an administrative body. The question is not of the intrinsic importance of the particular statute before us, but of the constitutional processes of legislation which are an essential part of our system of government.

■ MR. JUSTICE CARDOZO, dissenting.

* * *

I am unable to assent to the conclusion that § 9(c) of the National Recovery Act, a section delegating to the President a very different power from any that is involved in the regulation of production or in the promulgation of a code, is to be nullified upon the ground that his discretion is too broad or for any other reason. My point of difference with the majority of the court is narrow. I concede that to uphold the delegation there is need to discover in the terms of the act a standard reasonably clear whereby discretion must be governed. I deny that such a standard is lacking in respect of the prohibitions permitted by this section when the act with all its reasonable implications is considered as a whole. What the standard is becomes the pivotal inquiry.

As to the nature of the *act* which the President is authorized to perform there is no need for implication. That at least is definite beyond the possibility of challenge. He may prohibit the transportation in interstate and foreign commerce of petroleum and the products thereof produced or withdrawn from storage in excess of the amount permitted by any state law or valid regulation or order prescribed thereunder. He is not left to roam at will among all the possible subjects of interstate transportation, picking and choosing as he pleases. I am far from asserting now that delegation would be valid if accompanied by all that latitude of choice. In the laying of his interdict he is to confine himself to a particular commodity, and to that commodity when produced or withdrawn from storage in contravention of the policy and statutes of the states. He has choice, though within limits, as to the occasion, but none whatever as to the means. The means have been prescribed by

Congress. There has been no grant to the Executive of any roving commission to inquire into evils and then, upon discovering them, do anything he pleases. His act being thus defined, what else must he ascertain in order to regulate his discretion and bring the power into play? The answer is not given if we look to § 9(c) only, but it comes to us by implication from a view of other sections where the standards are defined. The prevailing opinion concedes that a standard will be as effective if imported into § 9(c) by reasonable implication as if put there in so many words. If we look to the whole structure of the statute, the test is plainly this, that the President is to forbid the transportation of the oil when he believes, in the light of the conditions of the industry as disclosed from time to time, that the prohibition will tend to effectuate the declared policies of the act,—not merely his own conception of its policies, undirected by any extrinsic guide, but the policies announced by § 1 in the forefront of the statute as an index to the meaning of everything that follows.

* * *

I am persuaded that a reference, express or implied, to the policy of Congress as declared in § 1, is a sufficient definition of a standard to make the statute valid. Discretion is not unconfined and vagrant. It is canalized within banks that keep it from overflowing.

A.L.A. Schechter Poultry Corp. v. United States
295 U.S. 495 (1935).

■ MR. CHIEF JUSTICE HUGHES delivered the opinion of the Court.

Petitioners . . . were convicted in the District Court of the United States for the Eastern District of New York on eighteen counts of an indictment charging violations of what is known as the "Live Poultry Code," and on an additional count for conspiracy to commit such violations. By demurrer to the indictment and appropriate motions on the trial, the defendants contended (1) that the code had been adopted pursuant to an unconstitutional delegation by Congress of legislative power; . . .

* * *

The "Live Poultry Code" was promulgated under § 3 of the National Industrial Recovery Act. That section—the pertinent provisions of which are set forth in the margin,[4]—authorizes the President to

---

[4]   CODES OF FAIR COMPETITION.

"Sec. 3. (a) Upon the application to the President by one or more trade or industrial associations or groups, the President may approve a code or codes of fair competition for the trade or industry or subdivision thereof, represented by the applicant or applicants, if the President finds (1) that such associations or groups impose no inequitable restrictions on admission to membership therein and are truly representative of such trades or industries or subdivisions thereof, and (2) that such code or codes are not designed to promote monopolies or to eliminate or oppress small enterprises and will not operate to discriminate against them, and will tend to effectuate the policy of this title: Provided, That such code or codes shall not permit monopolies or monopolistic practices: Provided further, That where such code or codes affect the services and welfare of persons engaged in other steps of the economic process,

approve "codes of fair competition." * * * Violation of any provision of a code (so approved or prescribed) "in any transaction in or affecting interstate or foreign commerce" is made a misdemeanor punishable by a fine of not more than $500 for each offense, and each day the violation continues is to be deemed a separate offense.

* * *

[W]e look to the statute to see whether Congress has overstepped these limitations—whether Congress in authorizing "codes of fair competition" has itself established the standards of legal obligation, thus performing its essential legislative function, or, by the failure to enact such standards, has attempted to transfer that function to others.

* * *

What is meant by "fair competition" as the term is used in the act? Does it refer to a category established in the law, and is the authority to make codes limited accordingly? Or is it used as a convenient designation for whatever set of laws the formulators of a code for a particular trade or industry may propose and the President may approve (subject to certain restrictions), or the President may himself prescribe, as being wise and beneficent provisions for the government of the trade or industry in order to accomplish the broad purposes of rehabilitation, correction, and expansion which are stated in the first section of Title I?

The act does not define "fair competition." "Unfair competition," as known to the common law, is a limited concept. Primarily, and strictly, it relates to the palming off of one's goods as those of a rival trader. *Goodyear's Rubber Manufacturing Co. v. Goodyear Rubber Co.*, 128 U.S. 598, 604; *Howe Scale Co. v. Wyckoff, Seamans & Benedict*, 198 U.S. 118, 140; *Hanover Star Milling Co. v. Metcalf*, 240 U.S. 403, 413. In recent years, its scope has been extended. It has been held to apply to misappropriation as well as misrepresentation, to the selling of another's goods as one's own—to misappropriation of what equitably belongs to a competitor. *International News Service v. Associated Press*, 248 U.S. 215, 241, 242. Unairness in competition has been predicated of acts which lie outside the ordinary course of business and are tainted by fraud or coercion or conduct otherwise prohibited by law. *Id.*, p. 258. But it is evident that in its widest range, "unfair competition," as it has been understood in the law, does not reach the objectives of the codes which are authorized by the National Industrial Recovery Act. The codes may, indeed, cover conduct which existing law condemns, but they are not limited to conduct of that sort. The government does not contend that the act contemplates such a limitation. It would be opposed both to the declared purposes of the act and to its administrative construction.

---

nothing in this section shall deprive such persons of the right to be heard prior to approval by the President of such code or codes. The President may, as a condition of his approval of any such code, impose such conditions (including requirements for the making of reports and the keeping of accounts) for the protection of consumers, competitors, employees, and others, and in furtherance of the public interest, and may provide such exceptions to and exemptions from the provisions of such code. as the President in his discretion deems necessary to effectuate the policy herein declared." 5 U.S.C. § 703(a).

The Federal Trade Commission Act (§ 5) introduced the expression "unfair methods of competition," which were declared to be unlawful. That was an expression new in the law. Debate apparently convinced the sponsors of the legislation that the words "unfair competition," in light of their meaning at common law, were too narrow. We have said that the substituted phrase has a broader meaning, that it does not admit of precise definition, its scope being left to judicial determination as controversies arise. *Federal Trade Comm'n v. Raladam Co.*, 283 U.S. 643, 648, 649; *Federal Trade Comm'n v. Keppel & Bro.*, 291 U.S. 304, 310–12. * * * To make this possible, Congress set up a special procedure. A Commission, a quasi-judicial body, was created. Provision was made for formal complaint, for notice and hearing, for appropriate findings of fact supported by adequate evidence, and for judicial review to give assurance that the action of the Commission is taken with in its statutory authority. *Federal Trade Comm'n v. Raladam Co., supra; Federal Trade Comm'n v. Klesner, supra.*

In providing for codes, the National Industrial Recovery Act dispenses with this administrative procedure and with any administrative procedure of an analogous character. But the difference between the code plan of the Recovery Act and the scheme of the Federal Trade Commission Act lies not only in procedure but in subject matter. We cannot regard the "fair competition" of the codes as antithetical to the "unfair methods of competition" of the Federal Trade Commission Act. The "fair competition" of the codes has a much broader range and a new significance.

* * *

We think the conclusion is inescapable that the authority sought to be conferred by § 3 was not merely to deal with "unfair competitive practices" which offend against existing law, and could be the subject of judicial condemnation without further legislation, or to create administrative machinery for the application of established principles of law to particular instances of violation. Rather, the purpose is clearly disclosed to authorize new and controlling prohibitions through codes of laws which would embrace what the formulators would propose, and what the President would approve or prescribe, as wise and beneficent measures for the government of trades and industries in order to bring about their rehabilitation, correction, and development, according to the general declaration of policy in section one. Codes of laws of this sort are styled "codes of fair competition."

* * *

The government urges that the codes will "consist of rules of competition deemed fair for each industry by representative members of that industry—by the persons most vitally concerned and most familiar with its problems." * * * But would it be seriously contended that Congress could delegate its legislative authority to trade or industrial associations or groups so as to empower them to enact the laws they deem to be wise and beneficent for the rehabilitation and expansion of their trade or industries? Could trade or industrial associations or groups be constituted legislative bodies for that purpose because such associations or groups are familiar with the problems of their enterprises? And could an effort of that sort be made valid by such a preface of generalities as to permissible aims as we find in section 1 of title 1? The answer is obvious. Such a delegation of legislative power is unknown to our law, and is utterly inconsistent with the constitutional prerogatives and duties of Congress.

one thing perhaps whether the Pres. has the power to decide the meaning?

The question, then, turns upon the authority which § 3 of the Recovery Act vests in the President to approve or prescribe. If the codes have standing as penal statutes, this must be due to the effect of the executive action. But Congress cannot delegate legislative power to the President to exercise an unfettered discretion to make whatever laws he thinks may be needed or advisable for the rehabilitation and expansion of trade or industry. *See Panama Refining Company v. Ryan*, 293 U.S. 388 (1935).

Accordingly we turn to the Recovery Act to ascertain what limits have been set to the exercise of the President's discretion: First, the President, as a condition of approval, is required to find that the trade or industrial associations or groups which propose a code "impose no inequitable restrictions on admission to membership" and are "truly representative." That condition, however, relates only to the status of the initiators of the new laws and not to the permissible scope of such laws. Second, the President is required to find that the code is not "designed to promote monopolies or to eliminate or oppress small enterprises and will not operate to discriminate against them." And to this is added a proviso that the code "shall not permit monopolies or monopolistic practices." But these restrictions leave virtually untouched the field of policy envisaged by one, and, in that wide field of legislative possibilities, the proponents of a code, refraining from monopolistic designs, may roam at will, and the President may approve or disapprove their proposals as he may see fit. That is the precise effect of the further finding that the President is to make—that the code "will tend to effectuate the policy of this title." While this is called a finding, it is really but a statement of an opinion as to the general effect upon the promotion of trade or industry of a scheme of laws. These are the only findings which Congress has made essential in order to put into operation a legislative code having the aims described in the "Declaration of Policy."

Nor is the breadth of the President's discretion left to the necessary implications of this limited requirement as to his findings. As already noted, the President in approving a code may impose his own conditions, adding to or taking from what is proposed, as "in his discretion" he thinks necessary "to effectuate the policy" declared by the Act. Of course, he has no less liberty when he prescribes a code on his own motion or on complaint, and he is free to prescribe one if a code has not been approved. The Act provides for the creation by the President of administrative agencies to assist him, but the action or reports of such agencies, or of his other assistants—their recommendations and findings in relation to the making of codes—have no sanction beyond the will of the President, who may accept, modify, or reject them as he pleases. Such recommendations or findings in no way limit the authority which § 3 undertakes to vest in the President with no other conditions than those there specified. And this authority relates to a host of different trades and industries, thus extending the President's discretion to all the varieties of laws which he may deem to be beneficial in dealing with the vast array of commercial and industrial activities throughout the country.

* * *

To summarize and conclude upon this point: Section 3 of the Recovery Act is without precedent. It supplies no standards for any trade, industry or activity. It does not undertake to prescribe rules of conduct to be applied to particular states of fact determined by appropriate administrative procedure. Instead of prescribing rules of conduct, it authorizes the making of codes to prescribe them. For that legislative undertaking, § 3 sets up no standards, aside from the statement of the general aims of rehabilitation, correction and expansion described in section one. In view of the scope of that broad delegation, and of the nature of the few restrictions that are imposed, the discretion of the President in approving or prescribing codes, and thus enacting laws for the government of trade and industry throughout the country, is virtually unfettered. We think that the code-making authority thus conferred is an unconstitutional delegation of legislative power.

* * *

■ MR. JUSTICE CARDOZO, concurring.

The delegated power of legislation which has found expression in this code is not canalized within banks that keep it from overflowing. It is unconfined and vagrant, if I may borrow my own words in an earlier opinion. *Panama Refining Co. v. Ryan*, 293 U.S. 388, 440 (1935) (Cardozo, J., dissenting).

NOTES AND QUESTIONS

1.   Many statutes upheld by the Supreme Court, both before and after *J.W. Hampton*, *Panama Refining*, and *Schechter Poultry*, seem to fall short of even the intelligible principle standard. Consider the following examples:

- In *McKinley v. United States*, 249 U.S. 397 (1919), the Court upheld as constitutional a statute authorizing the Secretary of War for the duration of the First World War "to do everything by him deemed necessary to suppress and prevent the keeping or setting up of houses of ill fame, brothels, or bawdy houses, within such distance as he may deem needful of any military camp, station, fort, post, cantonment, training or mobilization place."

- In *United States v. Atchison, Topeka, & Santa Fe Railway Co.*, 234 U.S. 476 (1914) (also known as the Intermountain Rate Cases), the Court considered a statute that precluded common carriers (*e.g.*, railroads) from charging different rates for transporting passengers for shorter than for longer distances, and upheld language granting the Interstate Commerce Commission the power, "upon application" and "after investigation," to authorize a railroad "to charge less for longer than for shorter distances" and also the authority to "from time to time prescribe the extent to which such designated common carrier may be relieved from" the general nondiscrimination requirement.

- In *Federal Power Commission v. Hope Natural Gas Co.*, 320 U.S. 591 (1944), the Supreme Court upheld a grant of authority to the Federal Power Commission to set the "just and reasonable rate" to be charged for the transportation or sale of natural gas and to "order a decrease where existing rates are unjust, unduly discriminatory, preferential, otherwise unlawful, or are not the lowest reasonable rates," even though Congress did not provide any formula, rule, or fixed principle by which the Commission was to make such assessments.

2. Compare the National Industrial Relations Act language at issue in *Panama Refining* and *Schechter Poultry* with the statutory language quoted in the above examples from cases in which the Supreme Court has upheld broad delegations of authority to agencies. How is the National Industrial Recovery Act distinguishable from the delegations in those cases?

3. Is the lack of an intelligible principle to guide executive branch action under the National Industrial Recovery Act the Court's only objection to that statute's delegation of legislative authority? Did it also matter to the Court who possessed delegated power?

4. In *Carter v. Carter Coal*, 298 U.S. 238 (1936), the Supreme Court considered the constitutionality of the Bituminous Coal Conservation Act, which said that when the producers of more than two-thirds of the annual national tonnage of coal production for the preceding calendar year and the representatives of more than one-half of the mine workers employed by such producers agreed upon maximum daily and weekly hours of labor and minimum wages, then all coal producers and miners would have to abide by that agreement. In other words, the statute required a dissenting minority of producers, miners, or both to follow the wage and hour agreements of the majority. The Court declared this statutory requirement "an intolerable and unconstitutional interference of liberty and private property" in violation of the Due Process Clause, which is discussed at length in Chapter 4. But the Court also suggested that the statute might be unconstitutional as well under the reasoning of *Schechter Poultry*. In what way might the Court have applied *Schechter Poultry* to invalidate this statute?

a. THE DECLINE OF THE NONDELEGATION DOCTRINE

Notwithstanding its decisions in *Schechter Poultry* and *Panama Refining*, the Supreme Court upheld broad delegations of power in many subsequent cases.

In *Zemel v. Rusk*, 381 U.S. 1 (1965), the Court considered the constitutionality of the Passport Act of 1926, which granted the Secretary of State the authority to "grant and issue passports . . . under such rules as the President shall designate and prescribe. . . ." The Court upheld the upheld that delegation because Congress "must of necessity paint with a broad brush" when it legislates on foreign affairs. In *Yakus v. United States*, 321 U.S. 414 (1944), the Court said that, as a "war emergency measure," Congress could constitutionally delegate authority to the Administrator of the Office of Price Administration to establish price controls for commodities that "in his judgment" would be "fair and equitable." In *National Broadcasting Co. v. United States*, 319 U.S. 190 (1943), the Court upheld a delegation of authority to the

Federal Communications Commission to regulate broadcasting to further "public interest, convenience or necessity." The Court has not held a delegation unconstitutional since 1935.

The three-judge district court opinion in *Amalgamated Meat Cutters v. Connally*, 337 F.Supp. 737 (D.D.C. 1971), provides a particularly good illustration of the extraordinarily broad delegations that have been upheld and of the many techniques courts use to uphold broad delegations. In the Economic Stabilization Act of 1970, 84 Stat. 799, Congress authorized the President to stabilize prices, rents, wages, and salaries, "with such adjustments as might be necessary to prevent gross inequities." It is hard to imagine a broader delegation of power less channeled by statutory standards. Yet, the court upheld the statute.

The court relied on some uncertain combination of features and history to avoid holding the statute unconstitutional. At least some of the court's reasoning can be fairly characterized as imaginative.

- The statute applied for only a limited time. (Congress later extended it.)

- Individuals could protect themselves from arbitrary action through use of the procedural safeguards the agency was required to use. (The statute provided virtually no procedural safeguards.)

- Actions under the statute were subject to potential judicial review. (The courts affirmed virtually all of the thousands of actions taken under the statute.)

- The statutory reference to avoidance of "gross inequity" reflected a congressional decision to adopt a "fair and equitable" standard. ("Fair and equitable" is not much of a standard, and Congress did not include that phrase in the statute in any event.)

- Although the statute itself lacked explicit standards to guide its application, the agency and reviewing courts could use the standards employed to administer war emergency price controls to channel the application of the new peacetime controls. (Neither the agency nor a reviewing court ever referred to the standards adopted to administer war emergency controls.)

- Congress must have broad leeway when it legislates in areas affecting national security and foreign relations. (If peacetime price controls affect these areas, it is hard to imagine a government program that does not.)

Notwithstanding the breadth of delegations that the Court was willing to recognize as passing constitutional muster, one common type of delegation continued for some time after *Panama Refining* and *Schechter Poultry* to implicate nondelegation doctrine concerns. Many regulatory statutes, including but not limited to the Internal Revenue Code, the Communications Act of 1934, and the Food, Drug and Cosmetic Act of 1938, granted government agencies broad, general authority to promulgate "all necessary rules and regulations" to effectuate or enforce those statutes. While the Court concluded repeatedly that the nondelegation doctrine did not preclude agencies from adopting legally binding substantive regulations under more specific statutory authority grants, government officials and legal commentators agreed that a general, "all necessary rules and regulations" grant that permitted binding regulations carrying the force and effect of law would be inconsistent with the nondelegation doctrine and thus constitutionally invalid. Instead, such general authority grants merely recognized by statute already-existing executive power to execute, and thus interpret and enforce, congressionally enacted laws. *See, e.g.*, 1 KENNETH CULP DAVIS, ADMINISTRATIVE LAW TREATISE § 5.04 (1958); 1 F. TROWBRIDGE VOM BAUR, FEDERAL ADMINISTRATIVE LAW § 489 (1942); Stanley S. Surrey, *The Scope and Effect of Treasury Regulations under the Income, Estate, and Gift Taxes*, 88 U. PA. L. REV. 556, 557–58 (1940). Hence, the courts routinely treated agency rules and regulations promulgated pursuant to such authority as mere litigation positions, and thus avoided altogether the perceived nondelegation issue such rules and regulations raised. Eventually, however, this last bastion of nondelegation faded as agencies in the 1970s asserted the legal force of regulations issued in the exercise of general rulemaking grants and the courts acquiesced to those assertions.

b. RENEWED INTEREST IN THE NONDELEGATION DOCTRINE IN THE 1970S

For four decades following *Schechter* and *Panama Refining*, courts consistently declined to apply the nondelegation doctrine, and commentators pronounced it moribund. The 1970s brought renewed interest in the doctrine. Many distinguished scholars and judges became so concerned about the enormous discretionary power of agencies that they urged reinvigoration of the doctrine. *See, e.g.*, Peter H. Aranson, Ernest Gellhorn & Glen O. Robinson, *A Theory of Legislative Delegation*, 68 CORNELL L. REV. 1, 7–17 (1982); JOHN HART ELY, DEMOCRACY AND DISTRUST: A THEORY OF JUDICIAL REVIEW 132–34 (1980); JAMES O. FREEDMAN, CRISIS AND LEGITIMACY: THE ADMINISTRATIVE PROCESS AND AMERICAN GOVERNMENT 93–94 (1978); Carl McGowan, *Congress, Court, and Control of Delegated Power*, 77 COLUM. L. REV. 1119 (1977); THEODORE J. LOWI, THE END OF LIBERALISM: THE SECOND REPUBLIC OF THE UNITED STATES 93 (1969). These critics saw Congress's increasing tendency to delegate most policy decisions to agencies as a major flaw in our attempt to construct a system of government based on democratic principles. By declining to make most policy decisions, Congress was abdicating its responsibility as the most politically accountable branch of government. Moreover, by conferring vast discretionary power on agencies, Congress was placing citizens in an increasingly subservient relationship to the agencies that control their fates. The only solution to this serious problem, according to the critics, was judicial enforcement of a meaningful prohibition on congressional delegation of standardless power.

John Hart Ely, then-Dean of Stanford Law School, made the case for reinvigoration of the nondelegation doctrine in his award-winning book, Democracy and Distrust:

In theory, it is the legislature that makes the laws and the administrators who apply them. Anyone who has seen

Congress in action, however, . . . will know that the actual situation is very nearly upside down. Much of the typical representative's time is consumed . . . with running errands . . . for . . . constituents—"making calls to public agencies on behalf of businessmen and interested parties back home. . . ." This is not to say that our representatives are unconcerned with substantive questions. But often that concern is expressed not in the form of legislation but rather by second-guessing the decisions of executive and administrative officials—questioning them at hearings and in various less formal ways. Much of the law is made by the legions of unelected administrators whose duty it becomes to give operative meaning to the broad delegations the statutes contain. . . .

The reasons things got switched around are not hard to discern. One is that it is simply easier, and it pays more visible political dividends, to play errand-boy-cum-ombudsman than to play one's part in a genuinely legislative process. . . . [O]n most hard issues our representatives quite shrewdly prefer not to have to stand up and be counted but rather to let some executive-branch bureaucrat . . . "take the inevitable political heat." . . . [W]hat comes later is a virtually no loss situation: "[T]hen we stand back and say when our constituents are aggrieved or oppressed by various rules and regulations, 'Hey, it's not me. We didn't mean that. . . .' "

Now this is wrong . . . because it is undemocratic, in the quite obvious sense that by refusing to legislate, our legislators are escaping the sort of accountability that is crucial to the intelligible functioning of a democratic republic. . . .

There can be little point in worrying about the distribution of the franchise and other personal political rights unless the important policy choices are made by elected officials. Courts thus should ensure not only that administrators follow those legislative policy directions that do exist . . . but also that such directions are given.

JOHN HART ELY, DEMOCRACY AND DISTRUST: A THEORY OF JUDICIAL REVIEW 131–33 (1980)

In 1980, the Court decided a case in which a majority of Justices strongly suggested that they were receptive to the arguments of Dean Ely and the other distinguished scholars who were urging the Court to reinvigorate the nondelegation doctrine.

Industrial Union Dept., AFL-CIO v. American Petroleum Institute (The Benzene Case)

448 U.S. 607 (1980).

■ MR. JUSTICE STEVENS announced the judgment of the Court and delivered an opinion, in which THE CHIEF JUSTICE and MR. JUSTICE STEWART joined and in Parts I, II, III–A, III–B, III–C and III–E of which MR. JUSTICE POWELL joined.

The Occupational Safety and Health Act of 1970 (Act), 84 Stat. 1590, 29 U.S.C. § 651 *et seq.*, was enacted for the purpose of ensuring safe and healthful working conditions for every working man and woman in the Nation. This litigation concerns a standard promulgated by the Secretary of Labor to regulate occupational exposure to benzene, a substance which has been shown to cause cancer at high exposure levels. The principal question is whether such a showing is a sufficient basis for a standard that places the most stringent limitation on exposure to benzene that is technologically and economically possible.

The Act delegates broad authority to the Secretary to promulgate different kinds of standards. The basic definition of an "occupational safety and health standard" is found in § 3(8), which provides:

> "The term 'occupational safety and health standard' means a standard which requires conditions, or the adoption or use of one or more practices, means, methods, operations, or processes, reasonably necessary or appropriate to provide safe or healthful employment and places of employment." 84 Stat. 1591, 29 U.S.C. § 652(8).

Where toxic materials or harmful physical agents are concerned, a standard must also comply with § 6(b)(5), which provides:

> "The Secretary, in promulgating standards dealing with toxic materials or harmful physical agents under this subsection, shall set the standard which most adequately assures, to the extent feasible, on the basis of the best available evidence, that no employee will suffer material impairment of health or functional capacity even if such employee has regular exposure to the hazard dealt with by such standard for the period of his working life. Development of standards under this subsection shall be based upon research, demonstrations, experiments, and such other information as may be appropriate. In addition to the attainment of the highest degree of health and safety protection for the employee, other considerations shall be the latest available scientific data in the field, the feasibility of the standards, and experience gained under this and other health and safety laws." 84 Stat. 1594, 29 U.S.C. § 655(b)(5).

Wherever the toxic material to be regulated is a carcinogen, the Secretary has taken the position that no safe exposure level can be determined and that § 6(b)(5) requires him to set an exposure limit at the lowest technologically feasible level that will not impair the viability of the industries regulated. In this case, after having determined that there is a causal connection between benzene and leukemia (a cancer of the white blood cells), the Secretary set an exposure limit on airborne concentrations of benzene of one part benzene per million parts of air (1 ppm), regulated dermal and eye contact with solutions containing benzene, and imposed complex monitoring and medical testing requirements on employers whose workplaces contain 0.5 ppm or more of benzene. 29 CFR §§ 1910.1028(c), (e) (1979).

* * *

We [hold] that § 3(8) requires the Secretary to find, as a threshold matter, that the toxic substance in question poses a significant health risk in the workplace and that a new, lower standard is therefore "reasonably necessary or appropriate to provide safe or healthful employment and places of employment."

* * *

Any discussion of the 1 ppm exposure limit must, of course, begin with the Agency's rationale for imposing that limit. The written explanation of the standard fills 184 pages of the printed appendix. Much of it is devoted to a discussion of the voluminous evidence of the adverse effects of exposure to benzene at levels of concentration well above 10 ppm. This discussion demonstrates that there is ample justification for regulating occupational exposure to benzene and that the prior limit of 10 ppm, with a ceiling of 25 ppm (or a peak of 50 ppm) was reasonable. It does not, however, provide direct support for the Agency's conclusion that the limit should be reduced from 10 ppm to 1 ppm.

The evidence in the administrative record of adverse effects of benzene exposure at 10 ppm is sketchy at best. OSHA noted that there was "no dispute" that certain nonmalignant blood disorders, evidenced by a reduction in the level of red or white cells or platelets in the blood, could result from exposures of 25–40 ppm. It then stated that several studies had indicated that relatively slight changes in normal blood values could result from exposures below 25 ppm and perhaps below 10 ppm. OSHA did not attempt to make any estimate based on these studies of how significant the risk of nonmalignant disease would be at exposures of 10 ppm or less. Rather, it stated that because of the lack of data concerning the linkage between low-level exposures and blood abnormalities, it was impossible to construct a dose-response curve at this time.

* * *

Under the Government's view, § 3(8), if it has any substantive content at all, merely requires OSHA to issue standards that are reasonably calculated to produce a safer or more healthy work environment.

* * *

If the Government was correct in arguing that neither § 3(8) nor § 6(b)(5) requires that the risk from a toxic substance be quantified sufficiently to enable the Secretary to characterize it as significant in an understandable way, the statute would make such a "sweeping delegation of legislative power" that it might be unconstitutional under the Court's reasoning in *A.L.A. Schechter Poultry Corp. v. United States*, 295 U.S. 495, 539 (1935), and *Panama Refining Co. v. Ryan*, 293 U.S. 388 (1935). A construction of the statute that avoids this kind of open-ended grant should certainly be favored.

■ MR. JUSTICE REHNQUIST, concurring in the judgment.

According to the Secretary, who is one of the petitioners herein, § 6(b)(5) imposes upon him an absolute duty, in regulating harmful substances like benzene for which no safe level is known, to set the standard for permissible exposure at the lowest level that "can be achieved at bearable cost with available technology." While the

Secretary does not attempt to refine the concept of "bearable cost," he apparently believes that a proposed standard is economically feasible so long as its impact "will not be such as to threaten the financial welfare of the affected firms or the general economy." 43 Fed. Reg. 5939 (1978).

Respondents reply, and the lower court agreed, that § 6(b)(5) must be read in light of another provision in the same Act, § 3(8), which defines an "occupational health and safety standard" as

". . . a standard which requires conditions, or the adoption or use of one or more practices, means, methods, operations, or processes, reasonably necessary or appropriate to provide safe or healthful employment and places of employment." 84 Stat. 1591, 29 U.S.C. § 652(8).

According to respondents, § 6(b)(5), as tempered by § 3(8), requires the Secretary to demonstrate that any particular health standard is justifiable on the basis of a rough balancing of costs and benefits.

In considering these alternative interpretations, my colleagues manifest a good deal of uncertainty, and ultimately divide over whether the Secretary produced sufficient evidence that the proposed standard for benzene will result in any appreciable benefits at all. This uncertainty, I would suggest, is eminently justified, since I believe that this litigation presents the Court with what has to be one of the most difficult issues that could confront a decisionmaker: whether the statistical possibility of future deaths should ever be disregarded in light of the economic costs of preventing those deaths. I would also suggest that the widely varying positions advanced in the briefs of the parties and in the opinions of Mr. Justice STEVENS, THE CHIEF JUSTICE, Mr. Justice POWELL, and Mr. Justice MARSHALL demonstrate, perhaps better than any other fact, that Congress, the governmental body best suited and most obligated to make the choice confronting us in this litigation, has improperly delegated that choice to the Secretary of Labor and, derivatively, to this Court.

* * *

[D]elegations of legislative authority must be judged "according to common sense and the inherent necessities of the governmental co-ordination."

Viewing the legislation at issue here in light of these principles, I believe that it fails to pass muster. Read literally, the relevant portion of § 6(b)(5) is completely precatory, admonishing the Secretary to adopt the most protective standard if he can, but excusing him from that duty if he cannot. In the case of a hazardous substance for which a "safe" level is either unknown or impractical, the language of § 6(b)(5) gives the Secretary absolutely no indication where on the continuum of relative safety he should draw his line. Especially in light of the importance of the interests at stake, I have no doubt that the provision at issue, standing alone, would violate the doctrine against uncanalized delegations of legislative power. For me the remaining question, then, is whether additional standards are ascertainable from the legislative history or statutory context of § 6(b)(5) or, if not, whether such a standardless delegation was justifiable in light of the "inherent necessities" of the situation.

* * *

I believe that the legislative history demonstrates that the feasibility requirement, as employed in § 6(b)(5), is a legislative mirage, appearing to some Members but not to others, and assuming any form desired by the beholder.

* * *

As formulated and enforced by this Court, the nondelegation doctrine serves three important functions. First, and most abstractly, it ensures to the extent consistent with orderly governmental administration that important choices of social policy are made by Congress, the branch of our Government most responsive to the popular will. Second, the doctrine guarantees that, to the extent Congress finds it necessary to delegate authority, it provides the recipient of that authority with an "intelligible principle" to guide the exercise of the delegated discretion. Third, and derivative of the second, the doctrine ensures that courts charged with reviewing the exercise of delegated legislative discretion will be able to test that exercise against ascertainable standards.

I believe the legislation at issue here fails on all three counts. The decision whether the law of diminishing returns should have any place in the regulation of toxic substances is quintessentially one of legislative policy. For Congress to pass that decision on to the Secretary in the manner it did violates, in my mind, John Locke's caveat—reflected in the cases cited earlier in this opinion—that legislatures are to make laws, not legislators. Nor, as I think the prior discussion amply demonstrates, do the provisions at issue or their legislative history provide the Secretary with any guidance that might lead him to his somewhat tentative conclusion that he must eliminate exposure to benzene as far as technologically and economically possible. Finally, I would suggest that the standard of "feasibility" renders meaningful judicial review impossible.

We ought not to shy away from our judicial duty to invalidate unconstitutional delegations of legislative authority solely out of concern that we should thereby reinvigorate discredited constitutional doctrines of the pre-New Deal era. If the nondelegation doctrine has fallen into the same desuetude as have substantive due process and restrictive interpretations of the Commerce Clause, it is, as one writer has phrased it, "a case of death by association." J. Ely, Democracy and Distrust, A Theory of Judicial Review 133 (1980). Indeed, a number of observers have suggested that this Court should once more take up its burden of ensuring that Congress does not unnecessarily delegate important choices of social policy to politically unresponsive administrators. * * *

If we are ever to reshoulder the burden of ensuring that Congress itself make the critical policy decisions, these are surely the cases in which to do it. It is difficult to imagine a more obvious example of Congress simply avoiding a choice which was both fundamental for purposes of the statute and yet politically so divisive that the necessary decision or compromise was difficult, if not impossible, to hammer out in the legislative forge. Far from detracting from the substantive authority of Congress, a declaration that the first sentence of § 6(b)(5) of the Occupational Safety and Health Act constitutes an invalid delegation to the Secretary of Labor would preserve the authority of Congress. If Congress wishes to legislate in an area which it has not previously sought to enter, it will in today's political world undoubtedly run into opposition no matter how the legislation is formulated. But that is the very essence of legislative authority under our system. It is the hard choices, and not the filling in of the blanks, which must be made by the elected representatives of the people. When fundamental policy decisions underlying important legislation about to be enacted are to be made, the buck stops with Congress and the President insofar as he exercises his constitutional role in the legislative process.

■ MR. JUSTICE MARSHALL, with whom MR. JUSTICE BRENNAN, MR. JUSTICE WHITE, and MR. JUSTICE BLACKMUN join, dissenting.

In cases of statutory construction, this Court's authority is limited. If the statutory language and legislative intent are plain, the judicial inquiry is at an end. Under our jurisprudence, it is presumed that ill-considered or unwise legislation will be corrected through the democratic process; a court is not permitted to distort a statute's meaning in order to make it conform with the Justices' own views of sound social policy.

Today's decision flagrantly disregards these restrictions on judicial authority. The plurality ignores the plain meaning of the Occupational Safety and Health Act of 1970 in order to bring the authority of the Secretary of Labor in line with the plurality's own views of proper regulatory policy. The unfortunate consequence is that the Federal Government's efforts to protect American workers from cancer and other crippling diseases may be substantially impaired.

NOTES AND QUESTIONS

1. Compare the statutory language quoted by the Court in the *Benzene* case with its holding that the statute requires the Secretary to make a threshold finding that a toxic substance poses "a significant health risk in the workplace." Can you trace the significant health risk standard to the statutory language? On what basis might the Justices who joined the plurality opinion justify attributing that standard to Congress?

2. Do the Justices in the *Benzene* case differ with respect to the meaning of the statute, or is their disagreement more about what a court should do when Congress declines to incorporate a decisional standard in a statute?

3. In his concurrence, Justice Rehnquist contends that, where statutory text fails to offer guiding standards, agencies and courts may ascertain such standards from legislative history or statutory context. Justice Rehnquist further suggests that a delegation of fundamental policymaking authority might pass constitutional muster if "inherent necessities" justify a broad grant. Justice Rehnquist clearly does not feel the statute at bar reflects such inherent necessities. What circumstances do you think might demonstrate inherent necessities?

4. Notwithstanding the Court's opinion in *Benzene*, arguments persist that the Occupational Safety and Health Act contains an unconstitutional delegation of legislative power. Professor Cass Sunstein recently contended that OSHA's "reasonably necessary or appropriate" standard is unconstitutionally lacking both textually and contextually. *See* Cass R. Sunstein, *Is OSHA Unconstitutional?*, 94 VA. L. REV. 1407 (2008). According to Sunstein, OSHA's standard fails on two grounds: first, "reasonably necessary" and "appropriate" are both too permissive and open-ended on their own to constrain agency action; and second, the statute does not connect the reasonably necessary or appropriate language with a substantive provision that would instruct (and thus limit) the Secretary of Labor regarding what to consider in deciding what actions to take. Can you reconcile Professor Sunstein's analysis with the various opinions in *Benzene*?

5. It seems apparent that Justice Rehnquist accepts Dean Ely's explanation for the failure of Congress to include a justiciable standard in the statute, but the political science literature also provides alternative explanations. Any legislative decision to delegate broad policymaking power to an agency can be explained by reference to some combination of three theories of legislative behavior.

First, legislators may be motivated by the selfish and cynical reasoning Dean Ely attributes to them.

Second, legislators may be motivated by the public interest. Members of Congress are neither omniscient nor prescient. They lack the expertise necessary to understand the implications of the thousands of policy decisions government must make annually. Even if they were capable of obtaining complete mastery of a field at the time they enact a statute governing a field, their correct decisions at the time of enactment of a statute can turn into terrible mistakes within a short period of time. The world and our understanding of it changes rapidly. Given its cognitive limitations, Congress wisely chooses to delegate most policy decisions to expert bodies that can react rapidly to new developments and to new understandings in their areas of expertise. The public interest theory of delegation has deep historical roots. Its proponents include Professor (later President) Woodrow Wilson. *See* Woodrow Wilson, *The Study of Administration*, 2 POL. SCI. Q. 197 (1897).

The third theory of legislative behavior is often called the "social choice" theory. It too has deep roots. In 1785, the Marquis de Condorcet demonstrated that majority rule cannot yield a stable choice among three alternative decisions when there are sharp differences of opinion with respect to the three options. CONDORCET, ESSAI SUR L'APPLICATION DE L'ANALYSE A LA PROBILITE DES DECISION RESIDUES A LA PLURALITE DES VOIX (1785). Modern scholars have extended Condorcet's work. In an important class of cases, a multimember body cannot make a choice among policy options without violating principles of fairness and majority rule. AMARTYA K. SEN, COLLECTIVE CHOICE AND SOCIAL WELFARE (1970); DUNCAN BLACK, THE THEORY OF COMMITTEES AND ELECTIONS (1958); KENNETH J. ARROW, SOCIAL CHOICE AND INDIVIDUAL VALUES (1951). In such circumstances, Congress' only choice is between an indeterminate outcome (delegation of broad authority to an agency) and a determinate outcome that is dictated by a minority with the power to determine the sequence of votes on the competing alternatives.

Which of these theories do you think best explains the extraordinarily broad and arguably standardless delegation of power to OSHA? Is it possible that the legislative process conforms to some uncertain extent with each of these theories? Should it matter to a court which theory explains the outcome of the legislative process? How could a court determine which of the three theories of legislative behavior best explains a particular broad delegation of power to an agency?

c. APPARENT REJECTION OF THE ATTEMPT TO REINVIGORATE THE NONDELEGATION DOCTRINE

Benzene seemed to foreshadow increased Supreme Court reliance on some version of the nondelegation doctrine. The Court's subsequent jurisprudence failed, however, to follow through on that suggestion. The Court has applied the intelligible principles standard to uphold broad delegations of power in five cases by votes of nine to zero or eight to one:

- In *Mistretta v. United States*, 488 U.S. 361 (1989), the Court upheld a delegation of power to a special commission established to issue sentencing guidelines that bind the courts. This case is discussed in greater detail below.

- In *Skinner v. Mid-America Pipeline Co.*, 490 U.S. 212 (1989), the Court upheld a statute delegating to the Secretary of Transportation the authority to "establish a schedule of fees based on the usage, in reasonable relationship to volume-miles, miles, revenues, or an appropriate combination thereof, of natural gas and hazardous liquid pipelines,"—*i.e.* to determine both the incidence and level of a tax.

- In *Touby v. United States*, 500 U.S. 160 (1991), the Court upheld a grant of power to the Attorney General to designate a substance as a "controlled substance," and thereby determine an element of various drug crimes.

- In *Loving v. United States*, 517 U.S. 748 (1996), the Court upheld a statute allowing the President to determine when a court martial should impose the death penalty.

- In *Whitman v. American Trucking Assns.*, 531 U.S. 457 (2001), the Court upheld a broad grant of power to the EPA to set air quality standards. This case is discussed in greater detail later in this Chapter.

In the three decades since the Court decided the *Benzene* case, Justice Scalia in his dissenting opinion in *Mistretta* is the only Justice to have relied on the nondelegation doctrine as justification for invalidating a statute. Even Justice Scalia's dissenting opinion emphasized primarily his disquiet with respect to the legitimacy of independent agencies, rather than the scope of the particular delegation in question.

Mistretta v. United States

488 U.S. 361 (1989).

■ BLACKMUN delivered the opinion of the Court.

In this litigation, we granted certiorari before judgment in the United States Court of Appeals for the Eighth Circuit in order to consider the constitutionality of the Sentencing Guidelines promulgated by the United States Sentencing Commission. The Commission is a body created under the Sentencing Reform Act of 1984 (Act), as amended, 18 U.S.C. § 3551 *et seq.* (1982 ed., Supp. IV), and 28 U.S.C. §§ 991–98 (1982 ed., Supp. IV).

* * *

The Commission is established "as an independent commission in the judicial branch of the United States." § 991(a). It has seven voting members (one of whom is the Chairman) appointed by the President "by and with the advice and consent of the Senate." "At least three of the members shall be Federal judges selected after considering a list of six judges recommended to the President by the Judicial Conference of the United States." *Id.* No more than four members of the Commission shall be members of the same political party. The Attorney General, or his designee, is an ex officio non-voting member. The Chairman and other members of the Commission are subject to removal by the President "only for neglect of duty or malfeasance in office or for other good cause shown." *Id.* Except for initial staggering of terms, a voting member serves for six years and may not serve more than two full terms. §§ 992(a), (b).

* * *

In addition to the duty the Commission has to promulgate determinative-sentence guidelines, it is under an obligation periodically to "review and revise" the guidelines. § 994(*o*). It is to "consult with authorities on, and individual and institutional representatives of, various aspects of the Federal criminal justice system." *Id.* It must report to Congress "any amendments of the guidelines." § 994(p). It is to make recommendations to Congress whether the grades or maximum penalties should be modified. § 994(r). It must submit to Congress at least annually an analysis of the operation of the guidelines. § 994(w). It is to issue "general policy statements" regarding their application. § 994(a)(2). And it has the power to "establish general policies . . . as are necessary to carry out the purposes" of the legislation, § 995(a)(1); to "monitor the performance of probation officers" with respect to the guidelines, § 995(a)(9); to "devise and conduct periodic training programs of instruction in sentencing techniques for judicial and probation personnel" and others, § 995(a)(18); and to "perform such other functions as are required to permit Federal courts to meet their responsibilities" as to sentencing, § 995(a)(22).

* * *

Petitioner argues that in delegating the power to promulgate sentencing guidelines for every federal criminal offense to an independent Sentencing Commission, Congress has granted the Commission excessive legislative discretion in violation of the constitutionally based nondelegation doctrine. We do not agree.

* * * In a passage now enshrined in our jurisprudence, Chief Justice Taft, writing for the Court, explained our approach to such cooperative ventures: "In determining what [Congress] may do in seeking assistance from another branch, the extent and character of that assistance must be fixed according to common sense and the inherent necessities of the government co-ordination." *J.W. Hampton,*

Jr., & Co. v. United States, 276 U.S. 394, 406 (1928). So long as Congress "shall lay down by legislative act an intelligible principle to which the person or body authorized to [exercise the delegated authority] is directed to conform, such legislative action is not a forbidden delegation of legislative power." *Id.*, at 409.

Applying this "intelligible principle" test to congressional delegations, our jurisprudence has been driven by a practical understanding that in our increasingly complex society, replete with ever changing and more technical problems, Congress simply cannot do its job absent an ability to delegate power under broad general directives. "The Constitution has never been regarded as denying to the Congress the necessary resources of flexibility and practicality, which will enable it to perform its function." *Panama Refining Co. v. Ryan*, 293 U.S. 388, 421 (1935). Accordingly, this Court has deemed it "constitutionally sufficient if Congress clearly delineates the general policy, the public agency which is to apply it, and the boundaries of this delegated authority." *American Power & Light Co. v. SEC*, 329 U.S. 90, 105 (1946).

Until 1935, this Court never struck down a challenged statute on delegation grounds. After invalidating in 1935 two statutes as excessive delegations, *see A.L.A. Schechter Poultry Corp. v. United States*, 295 U.S. 495 and *Panama Refining Co. v. Ryan*, 293 U.S. 388, we have upheld, again without deviation, Congress' ability to delegate power under broad standards.[7]

In light of our approval of these broad delegations, we harbor no doubt that Congress' delegation of authority to the Sentencing Commission is sufficiently specific and detailed to meet constitutional requirements. Congress charged the Commission with three goals: to "assure the meeting of the purposes of sentencing as set forth" in the Act; to "provide certainty and fairness in meeting the purposes of sentencing, avoiding unwarranted sentencing disparities among defendants with similar records . . . while maintaining sufficient flexibility to permit individualized sentences," where appropriate; and to "reflect, to the extent practicable, advancement in knowledge of human behavior as it relates to the criminal justice process." 28 U.S.C. § 991(b)(1). Congress further specified four "purposes" of sentencing that the Commission must pursue in carrying out its mandate: "to reflect the seriousness of the offense, to promote respect for the law, and to provide just punishment for the offense"; "to afford adequate deterrence to criminal conduct"; "to protect the public from further crimes of the defendant"; and "to provide the defendant with needed . . . correctional treatment." 18 U.S.C. § 3553(a)(2).

---

[7] In *Schechter Poultry* and *Panama Refining* the Court concluded that Congress had failed to articulate any policy or standard that would serve to confine the discretion of the authorities to whom Congress had delegated power. No delegation of the kind at issue in those cases is present here. The Act does not make crimes of acts never before criminalized, *see Fahey v. Mallonee*, 332 U.S. 245, 249 (1947) (analyzing *Panama Refining*), or delegate regulatory power to private individuals, *see Yakus v. United States*, 321 U.S. 414, 424 (1944) (analyzing *Schechter*). In recent years, our application of the nondelegation doctrine principally has been limited to the interpretation of statutory texts, and, more particularly, to giving narrow constructions to statutory delegations that might otherwise be thought to be unconstitutional. *See, e.g., Indus. Union Dept. v. Am. Petroleum Inst.*, 448 U.S. 607, 646 (1980); *Nat'l Cable Television Assn. v. United States,* 415 U.S. 336, 342 (1974).

In addition, Congress prescribed the specific tool—the guidelines system—for the Commission to use in regulating sentencing. More particularly, Congress directed the Commission to develop a system of "sentencing ranges" applicable "for each category of offense involving each category of defendant." 28 U.S.C. § 994(b).[8] Congress instructed the Commission that these sentencing ranges must be consistent with pertinent provisions of Title 18 of the United States Code and could not include sentences in excess of the statutory maxima. Congress also required that for sentences of imprisonment, "the maximum of the range established for such a term shall not exceed the minimum of that range by more than the greater of 25 percent or 6 months, except that, if the minimum term of the range is 30 years or more, the maximum may be life imprisonment." § 994(b)(2). Moreover, Congress directed the Commission to use current average sentences "as a starting point" for its structuring of the sentencing ranges. § 994(m).

To guide the Commission in its formulation of offense categories, Congress directed it to consider seven factors: the grade of the offense; the aggravating and mitigating circumstances of the crime; the nature and degree of the harm caused by the crime; the community view of the gravity of the offense; the public concern generated by the crime; the deterrent effect that a particular sentence may have on others; and the current incidence of the offense. §§ 994(c)(1)–(7).[9] Congress set forth 11 factors for the Commission to consider in establishing categories of defendants. These include the offender's age, education, vocational skills, mental and emotional condition, physical condition (including drug dependence), previous employment record, family ties and responsibilities, community ties, role in the offense, criminal history, and degree of dependence upon crime for a livelihood. § 994(d)(1)–(11).[10] Congress also prohibited the Commission from considering the "race, sex, national origin, creed, and socioeconomic status of offenders," § 994(d), and instructed that the guidelines should reflect the "general inappropriateness" of considering certain other factors, such as current unemployment, that might serve as proxies for forbidden factors, § 994(e).

In addition to these overarching constraints, Congress provided even more detailed guidance to the Commission about categories of offenses and offender characteristics. Congress directed that guidelines require a term of confinement at or near the statutory maximum for

---

[8]   Congress mandated that the guidelines include:

"(A) a determination whether to impose a sentence to probation, a fine, or a term of imprisonment;

"(B) a determination as to the appropriate amount of a fine or the appropriate length of a term of probation or a term of imprisonment;

"(C) a determination whether a sentence to a term of imprisonment should include a requirement that the defendant be placed on a term of supervised release after imprisonment, and, if so, the appropriate length of such a term; and

"(D) a determination whether multiple sentences to terms of imprisonment should be ordered to run concurrently or consecutively." 28 U.S.C. § 994(a)(1).

[9]   The Senate Report on the legislation elaborated on the purpose to be served by each factor. * * * The Report, moreover, gave specific examples of areas in which prevailing sentences might be too lenient, including the treatment of major white-collar criminals.

[10]   Again, the legislative history provides additional guidance for the Commission's consideration of the statutory factors. * * *

certain crimes of violence and for drug offenses, particularly when committed by recidivists. § 994(h). Congress further directed that the Commission assure a substantial term of imprisonment for an offense constituting a third felony conviction, for a career felon, for one convicted of a managerial role in a racketeering enterprise, for a crime of violence by an offender on release from a prior felony conviction, and for an offense involving a substantial quantity of narcotics. § 994(i). Congress also instructed "that the guidelines reflect . . . the general appropriateness of imposing a term of imprisonment" for a crime of violence that resulted in serious bodily injury. On the other hand, Congress directed that guidelines reflect the general inappropriateness of imposing a sentence of imprisonment "in cases in which the defendant is a first offender who has not been convicted of a crime of violence or an otherwise serious offense." § 994(j). Congress also enumerated various aggravating and mitigating circumstances, such as, respectively, multiple offenses or substantial assistance to the Government, to be reflected in the guidelines. §§ 994(*l*), (n). In other words, although Congress granted the Commission substantial discretion in formulating guidelines, in actuality it legislated a full hierarchy of punishment—from near maximum imprisonment, to substantial imprisonment, to some imprisonment, to alternatives—and stipulated the most important offense and offender characteristics to place defendants within these categories.

We cannot dispute petitioner's contention that the Commission enjoys significant discretion in formulating guidelines. The Commission does have discretionary authority to determine the relative severity of federal crimes and to assess the relative weight of the offender characteristics that Congress listed for the Commission to consider. *See* §§ 994(c), (d) (Commission instructed to consider enumerated factors as it deems them to be relevant). The Commission also has significant discretion to determine which crimes have been punished too leniently, and which too severely. § 994(m). Congress has called upon the Commission to exercise its judgment about which types of crimes and which types of criminals are to be considered similar for the purposes of sentencing.

But our cases do not at all suggest that delegations of this type may not carry with them the need to exercise judgment on matters of policy. In *Yakus v. United States*, 321 U.S. 414 (1944), the Court upheld a delegation to the Price Administrator to fix commodity prices that "in his judgment will be generally fair and equitable and will effectuate the purposes of this Act" to stabilize prices and avert speculation. *See id.*, at 420. In *National Broadcasting Co. v. United States*, 319 U.S. 190 (1943), we upheld a delegation to the Federal Communications Commission granting it the authority to promulgate regulations in accordance with its view of the "public interest." In *Yakus*, the Court laid down the applicable principle:

> "It is no objection that the determination of facts and the inferences to be drawn from them in the light of the statutory standards and declaration of policy call for the exercise of judgment, and for the formulation of subsidiary administrative policy within the prescribed statutory framework. . . .

"... Only if we could say that that there is an absence of standards for the guidance of the Administrator's action, so that it would be impossible in a proper proceeding to ascertain whether the will of Congress has been obeyed, would we be justified in overriding its choice of means for effecting its declared purpose...." 321 U.S. at 425–26.

Congress has met that standard here. The Act sets forth more than merely an "intelligible principle" or minimal standards. One court has aptly put it: "The statute outlines the policies which prompted establishment of the Commission, explains what the Commission should do and how it should do it, and sets out specific directives to govern particular situations." *United States v. Chambless*, 680 F.Supp. 793, 796 (E.D. La. 1988).

■ JUSTICE SCALIA, dissenting.

While the products of the Sentencing Commission's labors have been given the modest name "Guidelines," *see* 28 U.S.C. § 994(a)(1) (1982 ed., Supp. IV); United States Sentencing Commission Guidelines Manual (June 15, 1988), they have the force and effect of laws, prescribing the sentences criminal defendants are to receive. A judge who disregards them will be reversed, 18 U.S.C. § 3742 (1982 ed., Supp. IV). I dissent from today's decision because I can find no place within our constitutional system for an agency created by Congress to exercise no governmental power other than the making of laws.

* * *

Petitioner's most fundamental and far-reaching challenge to the Commission is that Congress' commitment of such broad policy responsibility to any institution is an unconstitutional delegation of legislative power. It is difficult to imagine a principle more essential to democratic government than that upon which the doctrine of unconstitutional delegation is founded: Except in a few areas constitutionally committed to the Executive Branch, the basic policy decisions governing society are to be made by the Legislature. Our Members of Congress could not, even if they wished, vote all power to the President and adjourn *sine die*.

But while the doctrine of unconstitutional delegation is unquestionably a fundamental element of our constitutional system, it is not an element readily enforceable by the courts. Once it is conceded, as it must be, that no statute can be entirely precise, and that some judgments, even some judgments involving policy considerations, must be left to the officers executing the law and to the judges applying it, the debate over unconstitutional delegation becomes a debate not over a point of principle but over a question of degree. * * * What legislated standard, one must wonder, can possibly be too vague to survive judicial scrutiny, when we have repeatedly upheld, in various contexts, a "public interest" standard? *See, e.g., Nat'l Broad. Co. v. United States*, 319 U.S. 190, 216–17 (1943); *N.Y. Cent. Secs. Corp. v. United States*, 287 U.S. 12, 24–25 (1932).

In short, I fully agree with the Court's rejection of petitioner's contention that the doctrine of unconstitutional delegation of legislative authority has been violated because of the lack of intelligible, congressionally prescribed standards to guide the Commission.

Precisely because the scope of delegation is largely uncontrollable by the courts, we must be particularly rigorous in preserving the Constitution's structural restrictions that deter excessive delegation. The major one, it seems to me, is that the power to make law cannot be exercised by anyone other than Congress, except in conjunction with the lawful exercise of executive or judicial power.

The whole theory of *lawful* congressional "delegation" is not that Congress is sometimes too busy or too divided and can therefore assign its responsibility of making law to someone else; but rather that a certain degree of discretion, and thus of lawmaking, *inheres* in most executive or judicial action, and it is up to Congress, by the relative specificity or generality of its statutory commands, to determine—up to a point—how small or how large that degree shall be. Thus, the courts could be given the power to say precisely what constitutes a "restraint of trade," *see Standard Oil Co. of New Jersey v. United States*, 221 U.S. 1 (1911), or to adopt rules of procedure, *see Sibbach v. Wilson & Co.*, 312 U.S. 1, 22 (1941), or to prescribe by rule the manner in which their officers shall execute their judgments, *Wayman v. Southard*, 23 U.S. (10 Wheat.) 1, 45 (1825), because that "lawmaking" was ancillary to their exercise of judicial powers. And the Executive could be given the power to adopt policies and rules specifying in detail what radio and television licenses will be in the "public interest, convenience or necessity," because that was ancillary to the exercise of its executive powers in granting and policing licenses and making a "fair and equitable allocation" of the electromagnetic spectrum. *Fed. Radio Comm'n v. Nelson Bros. Bond & Mortgage Co.*, 289 U.S. 266, 285 (1933). Or to take examples closer to the case before us: Trial judges could be given the power to determine what factors justify a greater or lesser sentence within the statutorily prescribed limits because that was ancillary to their exercise of the judicial power of pronouncing sentence upon individual defendants. And the President, through the Parole Commission subject to his appointment and removal, could be given the power to issue Guidelines specifying when parole would be available, because that was ancillary to the President's exercise of the executive power to hold and release federal prisoners. *See* 18 U.S.C. §§ 4203(a)(1), (b); 28 CFR § 2.20 (1988).

* * * In the present case, however, a pure delegation of legislative power is precisely what we have before us. It is irrelevant whether the standards are adequate, because they are not standards related to the exercise of executive or judicial powers; they are, plainly and simply, standards for further legislation.

The lawmaking function of the Sentencing Commission is completely divorced from any responsibility for execution of the law or adjudication of private rights under the law. It is divorced from responsibility for execution of the law not only because the Commission is not said to be "located in the Executive Branch" (as I shall discuss presently, I doubt whether Congress can "locate" an entity within one Branch or another for constitutional purposes by merely saying so); but, more importantly, because the Commission neither exercises any executive power on its own, nor is subject to the control of the President who does. The only functions it performs, apart from prescribing the law, conducting the investigations useful and necessary for prescribing the law, and clarifying the intended application of the law that it prescribes, are data collection and intragovernmental advice giving and education. These latter activities—similar to functions performed by congressional agencies and even congressional staff—neither determine nor affect private rights, and do not constitute an exercise of governmental power. *See Humphrey's Executor v. United States*, 295 U.S. 602, 628 (1935). And the Commission's lawmaking is completely divorced from the exercise of judicial powers since, not being a court, it has no judicial powers itself, nor is it subject to the control of any other body with judicial powers. The power to make law at issue here, in other words, is not ancillary but quite naked. The situation is no different in principle from what would exist if Congress gave the same power of writing sentencing laws to a congressional agency such as the General Accounting Office, or to members of its staff.

The delegation of lawmaking authority to the Commission is, in short, unsupported by any legitimating theory to explain why it is not a delegation of legislative power. * * *

By reason of today's decision, I anticipate that Congress will find delegation of its lawmaking powers much more attractive in the future. If rulemaking can be entirely unrelated to the exercise of judicial or executive powers, I foresee all manner of "expert" bodies, insulated from the political process, to which Congress will delegate various portions of its lawmaking responsibility. How tempting to create an expert Medical Commission (mostly M.D.'s, with perhaps a few Ph.D.'s in moral philosophy) to dispose of such thorny, "no-win" political issues as the withholding of life-support systems in federally funded hospitals, or the use of fetal tissue for research. This is an undemocratic precedent that we set—not because of the scope of the delegated power, but because its recipient is not one of the three Branches of Government. The only governmental power the Commission possesses is the power to make law; and it is not the Congress.

* * *

I think the Court errs, in other words, not so much because it mistakes the degree of commingling, but because it fails to recognize that this case is not about commingling, but about the creation of a new Branch altogether, a sort of junior varsity Congress. It may well be that in some circumstances such a Branch would be desirable; perhaps the agency before us here will prove to be so. But there are many desirable dispositions that do not accord with the constitutional structure we live under. And in the long run the improvisation of a constitutional structure on the basis of currently perceived utility will be disastrous.

NOTES AND QUESTIONS

1.   Consider the relevant statutory language in the *Benzene* and *Mistretta* cases and compare it with the language of the National Industrial Recovery Act that the Supreme Court rejected in *Panama Refining* and *Schechter Poultry*. How is the delegation contained in the National Industrial Recovery Act distinguishable from those in the Occupational Safety & Health Act and the Sentencing Reform Act? Could you parse the National

Industrial Recovery Act language to find standards, goals, purposes, and factors that might constrain agency action?

2.   Justice Scalia's dissent in *Mistretta* addresses not only the scope of delegated power but also the makeup of the body exercising such authority. What was the nature of the body to which the Sentencing Reform Act of 1984 delegated authority? How is that body similar or different from the recipients of delegated power in *Panama Refining*? *Schechter Poultry*? *Benzene*?

DISCUSSION PROBLEM

Section 5 of the Indian Reorganization Act, 25 U.S.C. § 465, authorizes the Secretary of the Interior,

> in his discretion, to acquire, through purchase, relinquishment, gift, exchange, or assignment, any interest in lands, water rights, or surface rights to lands, within or without existing reservations, . . . for the purpose of providing lands for Indians.

> For the acquisition of such lands, interests in lands, water rights, and surface rights, and for expenses incident to such acquisition, there is authorized to be appropriated, out of any funds in the Treasury not otherwise appropriated, a sum not to exceed $2,000,000 in any one year. . . .

> Title to any lands or rights acquired pursuant to this Act . . . shall be taken in the name of the United States in trust for the Indian tribe . . . for which the land is acquired, and such lands or rights shall be exempt from State and local taxation.

The Match-E-Be-Nash-She-Wish Band of Pottawotami Indians (the "Tribe") has been working with the Bureau of Indian Affairs (BIA) to acquire land for a reservation for the Tribe using the Secretary of the Interior's authority under § 5. The Tribe identified a tract of land in a largely rural area that they would like to acquire for such use and on which they would also like to build a facility that would include a gambling casino, restaurants, stores, and offices. The BIA has recommended that the Secretary move forward with the land purchase. A not-for-profit membership organization representing citizens who reside in the area of the proposed reservation and who are opposed to gambling sued to stop the acquisition, claiming that § 5 represents an impermissible delegation of legislative power to the Secretary of the Interior because that provision lacks standards to guide or limit the Secretary's discretion in acquiring land for Indians.

Does the quoted statutory language satisfy the intelligible principles standard? Why or why not?

d.   A "NEW" NONDELEGATION DOCTRINE?

It is not possible to know why the Justices abandoned so quickly the interest in a reinvigorated nondelegation doctrine that they expressed in the opinions in *Benzene*. They have not stated any reasons for their change in direction. It is possible, however, to draw inferences from the language they used in those opinions and in their opinions in subsequent cases.

For example, in *Benzene*, Justice Rehnquist expressed the view that Congress cannot "delegate important choices of social policy to politically unresponsive administrators." Yet, only a few years later, in *Chevron, U.S.A., Inc. v. Natural Resources Defense Council, Inc.*, 467 U.S. 837 (1984), a unanimous Supreme Court expressed a different view. In *Chevron*, the Court announced a new two-step test that courts must apply to agency interpretations of agency-administered statutes. *Chevron* instructs courts to assess first whether the meaning of an agency-administered statute is clear, and if not, then to uphold any reasonable agency interpretation of that statutory ambiguity. We discuss *Chevron* at length in Chapter 6. For present purposes, *Chevron*'s significance lies in the Court's reasons for instructing courts to defer to agency statutory constructions:

> Judges are not experts in the field, and are not part of either political branch of the Government. Courts must, in some cases, reconcile competing political interests, but not on the basis of the judges' personal policy preferences. In contrast, an agency to which Congress has delegated policy-making responsibilities may, within the limits of that delegation, properly rely upon the incumbent administration's views of wise policy to inform its judgments. While agencies are not directly accountable to the people, the Chief Executive is, and it is entirely appropriate for this political branch of the Government to make such policy choices—resolving the competing interests which Congress itself either inadvertently did not resolve, or intentionally left to be resolved by the agency charged with the administration of the statute in light of everyday realities.

Chevron, 467 U.S. at 865–66.

Other Justices have attempted to explain and/or defend the Court's refusal to invoke the nondelegation doctrine on other grounds. Justice O'Conner joined Justice Scalia in such an effort in their concurring opinion in *Loving v. United States*, 517 U.S. 748, 777 (1996) (Scalia, J., concurring):

> Legislative power is nondelegable. . . . What Congress does is to assign responsibility to the Executive; and when the Executive undertakes those assigned responsibilities it acts, not as the "delegate" of Congress, but as the agent of the People. At some point the responsibilities assigned can be so extensive and so unconstrained that Congress has in effect delegated its legislative power; but until that point of excess is reached, there exists not a "lawful" delegation, but no delegation at all.

Regardless of the reason, it seems fair to say that the nondelegation doctrine, particularly as reflected in the intelligible principles standard, is an unworkable and meaningless limitation on congressional delegations of policymaking authority to agencies. Nevertheless, a majority of the Supreme Court thus far has refused to abandon the nondelegation doctrine altogether, and continues to express platitudinous statements in its favor. The concerns that motivate the nondelegation doctrine continue to inspire litigants, courts, and scholars to pursue new arguments under the nondelegation label.

One approach, dubbed the "new nondelegation doctrine" by some scholars, derived from a 1969 essay by Professor Kenneth Culp Davis. *See* Kenneth Culp Davis, *A New Approach to Delegation*, 36 U. CHI. L. REV. 713 (1969). In contemplating the nondelegation doctrine, Professor Davis contended reviewing courts should require agencies to adopt their own standards, principles, and rules to limit their policymaking discretion.

> The crucial consideration is not what the statute says but what administrators do. The safeguards that count are the ones the administrators use, not the ones mentioned in the statute. The standards that matter are the ones that guide the administrative determination, not merely the ones stated by the legislative body.

In other words, argued Davis, courts should require agencies to interpret the scope of their authority narrowly to avoid the constitutional concerns raised by nondelegation doctrine theory. In a similar vein, other scholars have suggested that courts employ certain canons of statutory construction to interpret statutes narrowly to require Congress to be explicit in delegating authority of a scope that implicates important constitutional concerns. Indeed, some scholars contend that the *Chevron* test itself represents an incarnation of the new nondelegation doctrine, allowing courts the opportunity to use an array of statutory construction tools to impose standards limiting agency discretion with the imprimatur of congressional intent, while simultaneously allowing courts to approve agency-developed standards where statutory text offers none.

Arguably, the Supreme Court in *Benzene* followed a version of the new nondelegation doctrine when it relied on the avoidance canon—adopting an interpretation of the Occupational Safety and Health Act that avoids raising the nondelegation question—to justify its attribution to Congress of a requirement that OSHA find a "significant risk of material health impairment" before imposing more demanding workplace safety standards. More recently, in *Whitman v. American Trucking Ass'ns, Inc.*, 531 U.S. 457 (2001), the Supreme Court addressed at least one strand of new nondelegation doctrine theory. The Supreme Court opinions in the case are easier to understand against the backdrop of the circuit court opinion that the Court reversed.

American Trucking Ass'ns, Inc. v. EPA

175 F.3d 1027 (D.C. Cir. 1999).

■ WILLIAMS, GINSBURG and TATEL, CIRCUIT JUDGES (PER CURIAM):

The Clean Air Act requires EPA to promulgate and periodically revise national ambient air quality standards ("NAAQS") for each air pollutant identified by the agency as meeting certain statutory criteria. *See* Clean Air Act §§ 108–09, 42 U.S.C. §§ 7408–09. For each pollutant, EPA sets a "primary standard"—a concentration level "requisite to protect the public health" with an "adequate margin of safety"—and a "secondary standard"—a level "requisite to protect the public welfare." *Id.* § 7409(b).

In July 1997 EPA issued final rules revising the primary and secondary NAAQS for particulate matter ("PM") and ozone. *See* National Ambient Air Quality Standards for Particulate Matter, 62 Fed. Reg. 38,652 (1997) ("PM Final Rule"); National Ambient Air Quality Standards for Ozone, 62 Fed. Reg. 38,856 (1997) ("Ozone Final Rule"). Numerous petitions for review have been filed for each rule.

* * *

Certain "Small Business Petitioners" argue in each case that EPA has construed §§ 108 & 109 of the Clean Air Act so loosely as to render them unconstitutional delegations of legislative power. We agree. Although the factors EPA uses in determining the degree of public health concern associated with different levels of ozone and PM are reasonable, EPA appears to have articulated no "intelligible principle" to channel its application of these factors; nor is one apparent from the statute. The nondelegation doctrine requires such a principle. *See J.W. Hampton, Jr. & Co. v. United States,* 276 U.S. 394, 409 (1928). Here it is as though Congress commanded EPA to select "big guys," and EPA announced that it would evaluate candidates based on height and weight, but revealed no cut-off point. The announcement, though sensible in what it does say, is fatally incomplete. The reasonable person responds, "How tall? How heavy?"

EPA regards ozone definitely, and PM likely, as non-threshold pollutants, i.e., ones that have some possibility of some adverse health impact (however slight) at any exposure level above zero. *See* Ozone Final Rule, 62 Fed. Reg. at 38,863/3 ("Nor does it seem possible, in the Administrator's judgment, to identify [an ozone concentration] level at which it can be concluded with confidence that no 'adverse' effects are likely to occur."); National Ambient Air Quality Standards for Ozone and Particulate Matter, 61 Fed. Reg. 65,637, 65,651/3 (1996) (proposed rule) ("[T]he single most important factor influencing the uncertainty associated with the risk estimates is whether or not a threshold concentration exists below which PM-associated health risks are not likely to occur."). For convenience, we refer to both as non-threshold pollutants; the indeterminacy of PM's status does not affect EPA's analysis, or ours.

Thus the only concentration for ozone and PM that is utterly risk-free, in the sense of direct health impacts, is zero. Section 109(b)(1) says that EPA must set each standard at the level "requisite to protect the public health" with an "adequate margin of safety." 42 U.S.C. § 7409(b)(1). These are also the criteria by which EPA must determine whether a revision to existing NAAQS is appropriate. *See* 42 U.S.C. § 7409(d)(1) (EPA shall "promulgate such new standards as may be appropriate in accordance with . . . [§ 7409(b)]"). For EPA to pick any non-zero level it must explain the degree of imperfection permitted. The factors that EPA has elected to examine for this purpose in themselves pose no inherent nondelegation problem. But what EPA lacks is any determinate criterion for drawing lines. It has failed to state intelligibly how much is too much.

We begin with the criteria EPA has announced for assessing health effects in setting the NAAQS for non-threshold pollutants. They are "the nature and severity of the health effects involved, the size of the sensitive population(s) at risk, the types of health information available, and the kind and degree of uncertainties that must be addressed." Ozone Final Rule, 62 Fed. Reg. at 38,883/2; EPA, Review of the National Ambient Air Quality Standards for Particulate Matter: Policy Assessment of Scientific and Technical Information: OAQPS Staff Paper, at II–2 (July 1996) ("PM Staff paper") (listing the same factors). Although these criteria, so stated, are a bit vague, they do focus the inquiry on pollution's effects on public health. And most of the vagueness in the abstract formulation melts away as EPA applies the criteria: EPA basically considers severity of effect, certainty of effect, and size of population affected. These criteria, long ago approved by the judiciary, *see Lead Industries Ass'n v. EPA*, 647 F.2d 1130, 1161 (D.C. Cir. 1980), do not themselves speak to the issue of degree.

Read in light of these factors, EPA's explanations for its decisions amount to assertions that a less stringent standard would allow the relevant pollutant to inflict a greater quantum of harm on public health, and that a more stringent standard would result in less harm. Such arguments only support the intuitive proposition that more pollution will not benefit public health, not that keeping pollution at or below any particular level is "requisite" or not requisite to "protect the public health" with an "adequate margin of safety," the formula set out by § 109(b)(1).

Consider EPA's defense of the 0.08 ppm level of the ozone NAAQS. EPA explains that its choice is superior to retaining the existing level, 0.09 ppm, because more people are exposed to more serious effects at 0.09 than at 0.08. *See* Ozone Final Rule, 62 Fed. Reg. at 38,868/1. In defending the decision not to go down to 0.07, EPA never contradicts the intuitive proposition, confirmed by data in its Staff Paper, that reducing the standard to that level would bring about comparable changes.

* * *

In addition to the assertion quoted above, EPA cited the consensus of the Clean Air Scientific Advisory Committee ("CASAC") that the standard should not be set below 0.08. That body gave no specific reasons for its recommendations, so the appeal to its authority, also made in defense of other standards in the PM Final Rule, adds no enlightenment. The dissent stresses the undisputed eminence of CASAC's members, but the question whether EPA acted pursuant to lawfully delegated authority is not a scientific one. Nothing in what CASAC says helps us discern an intelligible principle derived by EPA from the Clean Air Act.

Finally, EPA argued that a 0.07 standard would be "closer to peak background levels that infrequently occur in some areas due to nonanthropogenic sources of O_3 precursors, and thus more likely to be inappropriately targeted in some areas on such sources." Ozone Final Rule, 62 Fed. Reg. at 38,868/3. But a 0.08 level, of course, is also *closer* to these peak levels than 0.09. The dissent notes that a single background observation fell between 0.07 and 0.08, and says that

EPA's decision "ensured that if a region surpasses the ozone standard, it will do so because of controllable human activity, not uncontrollable natural levels of ozone." EPA's language, coupled with the data on background ozone levels, may add up to a backhanded way of saying that, given the national character of the NAAQS, it is inappropriate to set a standard below a level that can be achieved throughout the country without action affirmatively *extracting* chemicals from nature. That may well be a sound reading of the statute, but EPA has not explicitly adopted it.

* * *

The arguments EPA offers here show only that EPA is applying the stated factors and that larger public health harms (including increased probability of such harms) are, as expected, associated with higher pollutant concentrations. The principle EPA invokes for each increment in stringency (such as for adopting the annual coarse particulate matter standard that it chose here)—that it is "possible but not certain" that health effects exist at that level, *see* PM Final Rule, 62 Fed. Reg. at 38,678/3—could as easily, for any nonthreshold pollutant, justify a standard of zero. The same indeterminacy prevails in EPA's decisions *not* to pick a still more stringent level. * * * Thus, the agency rightly recognizes that the question is one of degree, but offers no intelligible principle by which to identify a stopping point.

* * *

Where (as here) statutory language and an existing agency interpretation involve an unconstitutional delegation of power, but an interpretation without the constitutional weakness is or may be available, our response is not to strike down the statute but to give the agency an opportunity to extract a determinate standard on its own. Doing so serves at least two of three basic rationales for the nondelegation doctrine. If the agency develops determinate, binding standards for itself, it is less likely to exercise the delegated authority arbitrarily. And such standards enhance the likelihood that meaningful judicial review will prove feasible. A remand of this sort of course does not serve the third key function of nondelegation doctrine, to "ensure[ ] to the extent consistent with orderly governmental administration that important choices of social policy are made by Congress, the branch of our Government most responsive to the popular will," *Industrial Union Dep't, AFL-CIO v. American Petroleum Inst. ("Benzene")*, 448 U.S. 607, 685 (1980) (Rehnquist, J., concurring). The agency will make the fundamental policy choices. But the remand does ensure that the courts not hold unconstitutional a statute that an agency, with the application of its special expertise, could salvage. In any event, we do not read current Supreme Court cases as applying the strong form of the nondelegation doctrine voiced in Justice Rehnquist's concurrence. *See Mistretta v. United States*, 488 U.S. 361, 377–79 (1989).

American Trucking Ass'ns, Inc. v. EPA

195 F.3d 4 (D.C. Cir. 1999).

■ WILLIAMS, GINSBURG, and TATEL, CIRCUIT JUDGES (PER CURIAM) on petitions for rehearing.

* * *

As we noted in our first opinion in this case, when "statutory language and an existing agency interpretation involve an unconstitutional delegation of power, but an interpretation without the constitutional weakness is or may be available, our response is not to strike down the statute but to give the agency an opportunity to extract a determinate standard on its own." 175 F.3d at 1038. Counsel for the EPA have now extracted from the statute what they contend is an intelligible principle limiting the EPA's discretion. We express no opinion upon the sufficiency of that principle; only after the EPA itself has applied it in setting a NAAQS can we say whether the principle, in practice, fulfills the purposes of the nondelegation doctrine.

A final word about our nondelegation holding: The Supreme Court has long held that an ambiguous principle in a statute delegating power to an agency can gain "meaningful content from the purpose of the Act, its factual background and the statutory context in which [it] appear[s]." *Am. Power & Light Co. v. SEC*, 329 U.S. 90, 104 (1946); *see also Fed. Radio Comm'n v. Nelson Bros. Bond & Mortgage Co.*, 289 U.S. 266, 285 (1933) (upholding delegation to Federal Radio Commission to grant licenses "as public convenience, interest or necessity requires" in light of "its context [and] the nature of radio transmission and reception"); *Fahey v. Mallonee,* 332 U.S. 245, 250 (1947) (upholding delegation to the Federal Home Loan Bank Board to promulgate regulations for the appointment of a conservator for savings and loan associations in view of the banking industry's "well-defined practices for the appointment of conservators"). This court has done the same. To choose among permissible interpretations of an ambiguous principle, of course, is to make a policy decision, and since *Chevron* it has been clear that "[t]he responsibilities for assessing the wisdom of such policy choices . . . are not judicial ones." *Chevron U.S.A. Inc. v. NRDC*, 467 U.S. 837, 866 (1984). Accordingly, just as we must defer to an agency's reasonable interpretation of an ambiguous statutory term, we must defer to an agency's reasonable interpretation of a statute containing only an ambiguous principle by which to guide its exercise of delegated authority. In sum, the approach of the *Benzene* case, in which the Supreme Court itself identified an intelligible principle in an ambiguous statute, has given way to the approach of *Chevron. See Indus. Union Dep't v. Am. Petroleum Inst. ("Benzene")*, 448 U.S. 607, 642, 646 (1980) (Stevens, J., plurality) (interpreting § 3(8) of the Occupational Health and Safety Act to require "a threshold finding . . . that significant risks are present," thereby finding in the statute an intelligible principle).

Whitman v. American Trucking Ass'ns, Inc.

531 U.S. 457 (2001).

■ JUSTICE SCALIA delivered the opinion of the Court.

These cases present the following questions: (1) Whether § 109(b)(1) of the Clean Air Act (CAA) delegates legislative power to the Administrator of the Environmental Protection Agency (EPA). (2) Whether the Administrator may consider the costs of implementation in setting national ambient air quality standards (NAAQS) under § 109(b)(1).

I

Section 109(a) of the CAA, as added, 84 Stat. 1679, and amended, 42 U.S.C. § 7409(a), requires the Administrator of the EPA to promulgate NAAQS for each air pollutant for which "air quality criteria" have been issued under § 108, 42 U.S.C. § 7408. Once a NAAQS has been promulgated, the Administrator must review the standard (and the criteria on which it is based) "at five-year intervals" and make "such revisions . . . as may be appropriate." CAA § 109(d)(1), 42 U.S.C. § 7409(d)(1). These cases arose when, on July 18, 1997, the Administrator revised the NAAQS for particulate matter and ozone. American Trucking Associations, Inc. * * * challenged the new standards in the Court of Appeals for the District of Columbia Circuit.

The District of Columbia Circuit accepted some of the challenges and rejected others. It agreed with the No. 99–1257 respondents (hereinafter respondents) that § 109(b)(1) delegated legislative power to the Administrator in contravention of the United States Constitution, art. I, § 1, because it found that the EPA had interpreted the statute to provide no "intelligible principle" to guide the agency's exercise of authority. The court thought, however, that the EPA could perhaps avoid the unconstitutional delegation by adopting a restrictive construction of § 109(b)(1), so instead of declaring the section unconstitutional the court remanded the NAAQS to the agency.

* * *

II

In *Lead Industries Ass'n, Inc. v. EPA*, 647 F.2d 1130, 1148 (D.C. Cir. 1980), the District of Columbia Circuit held that "economic considerations [may] play no part in the promulgation of ambient air quality standards under Section 109" of the CAA. In the present cases, the court adhered to that holding, as it had done on many other occasions. Respondents argue that these decisions are incorrect. We disagree; and since the first step in assessing whether a statute delegates legislative power is to determine what authority the statute confers, we address that issue of interpretation first and reach respondents' constitutional arguments in Part III, *infra*.

Section 109(b)(1) instructs the EPA to set primary ambient air quality standards "the attainment and maintenance of which . . . are requisite to protect the public health" with "an adequate margin of safety." 42 U.S.C. § 7409(b)(1). Were it not for the hundreds of pages of briefing respondents have submitted on the issue, one would have thought it fairly clear that this text does not permit the EPA to consider costs in setting the standards. The language, as one scholar has noted, "is absolute." D. Currie, Air Pollution: Federal Law and Analysis 4–15 (1981). The EPA, "based on" the information about health effects contained in the technical "criteria" documents compiled under § 108(a)(2), 42 U.S.C. § 7408(a)(2), is to identify the maximum airborne concentration of a pollutant that the public health can tolerate, decrease the concentration to provide an "adequate" margin of safety, and set the standard at that level. Nowhere are the costs of achieving such a standard made part of that initial calculation.

* * *

It should be clear from what we have said that the canon requiring texts to be so construed as to avoid serious constitutional problems has no application here. No matter how severe the constitutional doubt, courts may choose only between reasonably available interpretations of a text. The text of § 109(b), interpreted in its statutory and historical context and with appreciation for its importance to the CAA as a whole, unambiguously bars cost considerations from the NAAQS-setting process, and thus ends the matter for us as well as the EPA.[4] We therefore affirm the judgment of the Court of Appeals on this point.

III

Section 109(b)(1) of the CAA instructs the EPA to set "ambient air quality standards the attainment and maintenance of which in the judgment of the Administrator, based on [the] criteria [documents of § 108] and allowing an adequate margin of safety, are requisite to protect the public health." 42 U.S.C. § 7409(b)(1). The Court of Appeals held that this section as interpreted by the Administrator did not provide an "intelligible principle" to guide the EPA's exercise of authority in setting NAAQS. "[The] EPA," it said, "lack[ed] any determinate criteria for drawing lines. It has failed to state intelligibly how much is too much." The court hence found that the EPA's interpretation (but not the statute itself) violated the nondelegation doctrine. We disagree.

In a delegation challenge, the constitutional question is whether the statute has delegated legislative power to the agency. Article I, § 1, of the Constitution vests "[a]ll legislative Powers herein granted . . . in a Congress of the United States." This text permits no delegation of those powers, and so we repeatedly have said that when Congress confers decisionmaking authority upon agencies *Congress* must "lay down by legislative act an intelligible principle to which the person or body authorized to [act] is directed to conform." *J.W. Hampton, Jr., & Co. v. United States*, 267 U.S. 394, 409 (1928). We have never suggested that an agency can cure an unlawful delegation of legislative power by adopting in its discretion a limiting construction of the statute. * * * The idea that an agency can cure an unconstitutionally standardless delegation of power by declining to exercise some of that power seems to

---

[4]   Respondents' speculation that the EPA is secretly considering the costs of attainment without telling anyone is irrelevant to our interpretive inquiry. If such an allegation could be proved, it would be grounds for vacating the NAAQS, because the Administrator had not followed the law. *See, e.g., Chevron U.S.A. Inc. v. NRDC*, 467 U.S. 837, 842–43 (1984); *Atl. Mut. Ins. Co. v. Comm'r*, 523 U.S. 382, 387 (1998). It would not, however, be grounds for this Court's changing the law.

us internally contradictory. The very choice of which portion of the power to exercise—that is to say, the prescription of the standard that Congress had omitted—would *itself* be an exercise of the forbidden legislative authority. Whether the statute delegates legislative power is a question for the courts, and an agency's voluntary self-denial has no bearing upon the answer.

We agree with the Solicitor General that the text of § 109(b)(1) of the CAA at a minimum requires that "[f]or a discrete set of pollutants and based on published air quality criteria that reflect the latest scientific knowledge, [the] EPA must establish uniform national standards at a level that is requisite to protect public health from the adverse effects of the pollutant in the ambient air." Requisite, in turn, "mean[s] sufficient, but not more than necessary." These limits on the EPA's discretion are strikingly similar to the ones we approved in *Touby v. United States,* 500 U.S. 160 (1991), which permitted the Attorney General to designate a drug as a controlled substance for purposes of criminal drug enforcement if doing so was " 'necessary to avoid an imminent hazard to the public safety.' " *Id.* at 163. They also resemble the Occupational Safety and Health Act of 1970 provision requiring the agency to " 'set the standard which most adequately assures, to the extent feasible, on the basis of the best available evidence, that no employee will suffer any impairment of health' "— which the Court upheld in *Industrial Union Dept., AFL-CIO v. American Petroleum Institute* ("*Benzene*"), 448 U.S. 607, 646 (1980). * * *

The scope of discretion § 109(b)(1) allows is in fact well within the outer limits of our nondelegation precedents. In the history of the Court we have found the requisite "intelligible principle" lacking in only two statutes, one of which provided literally no guidance for the exercise of discretion, and the other of which conferred authority to regulate the entire economy on the basis of no more precise a standard than stimulating the economy by assuring "fair competition." *See Panama Refining Co. v. Ryan,* 293 U.S. 388 (1935); *A.L.A. Schechter Poultry Corp. v. United States,* 295 U.S. 495 (1935). We have, on the other hand, upheld the validity of § 11(b)(2) of the Public Utility Holding Company Act of 1935, 49 Stat. 821, which gave the Securities and Exchange Commission authority to modify the structure of holding company systems so as to ensure that they are not "unduly or unnecessarily complicate[d]" and do not "unfairly or inequitably distribute voting power among security holders." *Am. Power & Light Co. v. SEC,* 329 U.S. 90, 104 (1946). We have approved the wartime conferral of agency power to fix the prices of commodities at a level that " 'will be generally fair and equitable and will effectuate the [in some respects conflicting] purposes of th[e] Act.' " And we have found an "intelligible principle" in various statutes authorizing regulation in the "public interest." In short, we have "almost never felt qualified to second-guess Congress regarding the permissible degree of policy judgment that can be left to those executing or applying the law." *Mistretta v. United States,* 488 U.S. 361, 416 (1989) (Scalia, J., dissenting); *id.* at 373 (majority opinion).

It is true enough that the degree of agency discretion that is acceptable varies according to the scope of the power congressionally conferred. While Congress need not provide any direction to the EPA regarding the manner in which it is to define "country elevators," which are to be exempt from new-stationary-source regulations governing grain elevators, it must provide substantial guidance on setting air standards that affect the entire national economy. But even in sweeping regulatory schemes we have never demanded, as the Court of Appeals did here, that statutes provide a "determinate criterion" for saying "how much [of the regulated harm] is too much." In *Touby,* for example, we did not require the statute to decree how "imminent" was too imminent, or how "necessary" was necessary enough, or even—most relevant here—how "hazardous" was too hazardous. 500 U.S. at 165–67. Similarly, the statute at issue in *Lichter* authorized agencies to recoup "excess profits" paid under wartime Government contracts, yet we did not insist that Congress specify how much profit was too much. 344 U.S. at 783–86. It is therefore not conclusive for delegation purposes that, as respondents argue, ozone and particulate matter are "nonthreshold" pollutants that inflict a continuum of adverse health effects at any airborne concentration greater than zero, and hence require the EPA to make judgments of degree.

"[A] certain degree of discretion, and thus of lawmaking, inheres in most executive or judicial action." *Mistretta*, 488 U.S. at 417 (Scalia, J., dissenting) (emphasis deleted); *id.* at 378–79 (majority opinion). Section 109(b)(1) of the CAA, which to repeat we interpret as requiring the EPA to set air quality standards at the level that is "requisite"—that is, not lower or higher than is necessary—to protect the public health with an adequate margin of safety, fits comfortably within the scope of discretion permitted by our precedent.

We therefore reverse the judgment of the Court of Appeals remanding for reinterpretation that would avoid a supposed delegation of legislative power.

■ JUSTICE THOMAS, concurring.

I agree with the majority that § 109's directive to the agency is no less an "intelligible principle" than a host of other directives that we have approved. I also agree that the Court of Appeals' remand to the agency to make its own corrective interpretation does not accord with our understanding of the delegation issue. I write separately, however, to express my concern that there may nevertheless be a genuine constitutional problem with § 109, a problem which the parties did not address.

The parties to these cases who briefed the constitutional issue wrangled over constitutional doctrine with barely a nod to the text of the Constitution. Although this Court since 1928 has treated the "intelligible principle" requirement as the only constitutional limit on congressional grants of power to administrative agencies, *see J.W. Hampton, Jr., & Co. v. United States*, 276 U.S. 394, 409 (1928), the Constitution does not speak of "intelligible principles." Rather, it speaks in much simpler terms: "*All* legislative Powers herein granted shall be vested in a Congress." U.S. CONST., art. I, § 1 (emphasis added). I am not convinced that the intelligible principle doctrine serves to prevent all cessions of legislative power. I believe that there are cases in which the principle is intelligible and yet the significance of the delegated decision is simply too great for the decision to be called anything other than "legislative."

As it is, none of the parties to these cases has examined the text of the Constitution or asked us to reconsider our precedents on cessions of legislative power. On a future day, however, I would be willing to address the question whether our delegation jurisprudence has strayed too far from our Founders' understanding of separation of powers.

■ JUSTICE STEVENS, with whom JUSTICE SOUTER joins, concurring in part and concurring in the judgment.

* * *

The Court has two choices. We could choose to articulate our ultimate disposition of this issue by frankly acknowledging that the power delegated to the EPA is "legislative" but nevertheless conclude that the delegation is constitutional because adequately limited by the terms of the authorizing statute. Alternatively, we could pretend, as the Court does, that the authority delegated to the EPA is somehow not "legislative power." Despite the fact that there is language in our opinions that supports the Court's articulation of our holding, I am persuaded that it would be both wiser and more faithful to what we have actually done in delegation cases to admit that agency rulemaking authority is "legislative power."

The proper characterization of governmental power should generally depend on the nature of the power, not on the identity of the person exercising it. *See* BLACK'S LAW DICTIONARY 899 (6th ed.1990) (defining "legislation" as, *inter alia,* "[f]ormulation of rule[s] for the future"); 1 K. DAVIS & R. PIERCE, ADMINISTRATIVE LAW TREATISE § 2.3 (3d ed. 1994) ("If legislative power means the power to make rules of conduct that bind everyone based on resolution of major policy issues, scores of agencies exercise legislative power routinely by promulgating what are candidly called 'legislative rules' "). If the NAAQS that the EPA promulgated had been prescribed by Congress, everyone would agree that those rules would be the product of an exercise of "legislative power." The same characterization is appropriate when an agency exercises rulemaking authority pursuant to a permissible delegation from Congress.

My view is not only more faithful to normal English usage, but is also fully consistent with the text of the Constitution. In Article I, the Framers vested "All legislative Powers" in the Congress, art. I, § 1, just as in Article II they vested the "executive Power" in the President, art. II, § 1. Those provisions do not purport to limit the authority of either recipient of power to delegate authority to others. *See Bowsher v. Synar*, 478 U.S. 714, 752 (1986) (Stevens, J., concurring in judgment) ("Despite the statement in Article I of the Constitution that 'All legislative powers herein granted shall be vested in a Congress of the United States,' it is far from novel to acknowledge that independent agencies do indeed exercise legislative powers"); *INS v. Chadha*, 462 U.S. 919, 985–86 (1983) (White, J., dissenting) ("[L]egislative power can be exercised by independent agencies and Executive departments . . ."); 1 K. DAVIS & R. PIERCE, ADMINISTRATIVE LAW TREATISE § 2.6 ("The Court was probably mistaken from the outset in interpreting Article I's grant of power to Congress as an implicit limit on Congress' authority to delegate legislative power"). Surely the authority granted to members of the Cabinet and federal law enforcement agents is properly characterized as "Executive" even though not exercised by the President.

It seems clear that an executive agency's exercise of rulemaking authority pursuant to a valid delegation from Congress is "legislative." As long as the delegation provides a sufficiently intelligible principle, there is nothing inherently unconstitutional about it.

NOTES AND QUESTIONS

1. The various opinions from both the Court and the D.C. Circuit reflect different conceptions of the nondelegation doctrine. Can you isolate the different suggested approaches? In particular, in both its original per curiam opinion and its opinion per curiam on petitions for rehearing, the D.C. Circuit panel takes the position that agencies are responsible for adopting interpretations of statutes that are sufficiently narrow to avoid nondelegation concerns. On what basis does the D.C. Circuit adopt this position? On what basis does the Supreme Court reject this approach to the nondelegation doctrine?

2. Compared to some delegations, the congressional command to the Environmental Protection Agency in Clean Air Act § 109 seems rather clear. The EPA is to set national primary ambient air quality standards at the level "requisite to protect the public health," "allowing adequate margin of safety." 42 U.S.C. § 7409(b)(1). The problem the Court addresses arises because there is no such level applicable to a non-threshhold pollutant. The best available evidence suggests that the adverse health effects of exposure to ozone and particulate matter, including fatal asthma attacks, increase at every level of concentration down to zero. To make the situation worse, non-anthropogenic sources of particulate matter sometimes account for ambient concentrations as high as 0.7 ppm. For instance, a high proportion of the particulate matter in the air in Florida comes across the Atlantic Ocean from sandstorms in the Kalahari Desert. Congress has been apprised of this situation many times and refuses to amend the statute to reflect an attainable standard. Why do you think Congress has declined to amend the statute to address these conditions? What should an agency do in this situation? What should reviewing courts do?

3. As the Supreme Court in *American Trucking* recognized, in an earlier case, *Lead Industries Ass'n, Inc. v. EPA*, 647 F.2d 1130 (D.C. Cir. 1980), the D.C. Circuit had held that the EPA is not permitted to consider costs in setting primary air standards. The Supreme Court affirmed that decision in *American Trucking*.

Interestingly, the EPA is permitted to calculate the costs and benefits of proposed primary air standards but is not allowed to consider them in its decision-making process. In fact, each of the last four Presidents has ordered the EPA to calculate the costs and benefits of all proposed major rules, and the EPA did so in this case. The EPA's cost/benefit analysis of the rules at issue in *American Trucking* was available to anyone on the EPA's website; the cost/benefit analysis found that the benefits of the standards EPA adopted exceeded the costs of the standards. The EPA stated that it did not consider its cost/benefit analysis in its decision-making process. Do you believe that none of the officials at the EPA who participated in the decision-making process and none of the Advisory

Committee members on whom the EPA relied in making its decision considered the cost/benefit analysis in their decision-making process? If you were an EPA decisionmaker or a member of the Advisory Committee, would you sneak a quick look at the cost/benefit analysis? If you did, do you think that the cost/benefit analysis might influence you, whether or not you were legally authorized to consider it in your decision-making process?

e.   SUBDELEGATION

The Court has repeatedly demonstrated its inclination to glean intelligible principles from even the most vague, subjective, and open-ended statutory language. In *American Trucking*, the Court also clearly rejected the nondelegation doctrine as a canon of statutory construction requiring agencies to adopt narrow interpretations of the statutes that they administer in order to avoid the doctrine's implications. Yet a majority of the Justices still maintain that Congress's power to delegate legislative authority is not limitless. What limitations, then, might the Court impose on Congress in the name of nondelegation?

One possible limitation focuses instead on *who* is eligible to exercise delegated power. Sometimes the head of an agency will transfer powers and responsibilities to subordinates—a practice known as subdelegation. For many years, Supreme Court precedent disapproved of subdelegation. In 1887, the Court held that a statute that called for the President to approve the dismissal of an officer from the army after court martial thus required the President to exercise his own personal judgment. *Runkle v. United States*, 122 U.S. 543 (1887). The Court never overruled *Runkle*, but it did find various ways around *Runkle*'s holding. Instead, for example, the Court presumed the exercise of personal judgment in *United States v. Page*, 137 U.S. 673 (1891); the Court liberally interpreted statutes calling for presidential action as not actually requiring personal action in *United States ex rel. French v. Weeks*, 259 U.S. 326 (1922); and in *United States v. Chemical Foundation*, 272 U.S. 1 (1926), the Court in dictum stated that "[o]bviously all the functions of his great office cannot be exercised by the President in person."

In 1951, Congress expressly authorized subdelegation of presidential authority with the Subdelegation Act, codified at 3 U.S.C. §§ 301–303. In pertinent part, that statute authorizes the President

> to designate and empower the head of any department or agency in the executive branch, or any official thereof who is required to be appointed by and with the advice and consent of the Senate, to perform without approval, ratification, or other action by the President (1) any function which is vested in the President by law, or (2) any function which such officer is required or authorized by law to perform only with or subject to the approval, ratification, or other action of the President.

3 U.S.C. § 301. Elsewhere, Congress has separately adopted statutory language approving subdelegation by particular agency heads charged with administering particular statutes. For example, the Federal Communications Commission may "delegate any of its functions . . . to a panel of commissioners, an individual commissioner, an employee board, or an individual employee," with only a few narrow limitations. 47 U.S.C. § 155(c)(1). Similarly, the Securities and Exchange

Commission enjoys the power to delegate "any of its functions to a division of the Commission, an individual Commissioner, an administrative law judge, or an employee or employee board." 15 U.S.C. § 78d–1(a). Subsequent court decisions have upheld delegations such as these. *See, e.g., United States Health Club v. Major,* 292 F.2d 665 (3d Cir.), *cert. denied,* 368 U.S. 896 (1961); *Parker v. Summerfield,* 265 F.2d 359 (D.C. Cir. 1959).

Today, subdelegation is a mainstay of government operation. Parties no longer challenge normal subdelegations within agencies. Perhaps the most significant modern case concerning an ordinary instance of subdelegation is *FTC v. Gibson,* 460 F.2d 605 (5th Cir. 1972), in which the court easily held that the Federal Trade Commission could delegate to the Assistant Attorney in the New Orleans Field Office the power to sign and issue a subpoena. Courts generally permit subdelegations when Congress has authorized them or when the statute is silent on the matter. Nevertheless, the courts' acceptance of subdelegations is not completely unequivocal. The following case explores at some length the limitations of the courts' willingness to uphold subdelegations.

United States Telecom Association v. Federal Communications Commission

359 F.3d 554 (D.C. Cir. 2004).

■ WILLIAMS, SENIOR CIRCUIT JUDGE:

The Telecommunications Act of 1996 (the "Act") sought to foster a competitive market in telecommunications. To enable new firms to enter the field despite the advantages of the incumbent local exchange carriers ("ILECs"), the Act gave the Federal Communications Commission broad powers to require ILECs to make "network elements" available to other telecommunications carriers, most importantly the competitive local exchange carriers ("CLECs"). The most obvious candidates for such obligatory provision were the copper wire loops historically used to carry telephone service over the "last mile" into users' homes. But Congress left to the Commission the choice of elements to be "unbundled," specifying that in doing so it was to

> consider, at a minimum, whether . . . the failure to provide access to such network elements would *impair* the ability of the telecommunications carrier seeking access to provide the services that it seeks to offer.

Id. § 251(d)(2) (emphasis added).

The Act became effective on February 8, 1996, a little more than eight years ago. Twice since then the courts have faulted the Commission's efforts to identify the elements to be unbundled. The Supreme Court invalidated the first effort in *AT&T Corp. v. Iowa Utilities Board,* 525 U.S. 366, 389–90 (1999) ("*AT&T*"). We invalidated much of the second effort (including separately adopted "line-sharing" rules) in *United States Telecom Association v. FCC,* 290 F.3d 415 (D.C.Cir. 2002) ("*USTA I*"). The Commission consolidated our remand in that case with its "triennial review" of the scope of obligatory unbundling and issued the Order on review here. Again, regrettably, much of the resulting work is unlawful.

* * *

In its first effort to interpret the "impairment" standard of § 251(d)(2), the Commission held that lack of unbundled access to an element would "impair" a CLEC's ability to provide telecommunications service "if the quality of the service the entrant can offer, absent access to the requested element, declines and/or the cost of providing the service rises." *Implementation of the Local Competition Provisions in the Telecommunications Act of 1996,* First Report and Order, 11 FCC Rcd 15499, 15643 (1996) ("First Report and Order").

The Supreme Court found this reading of "impair" unreasonable in two respects. First, the Commission had irrationally refused to consider whether a CLEC could self-provision or acquire the requested element from a third party. *AT&T,* 525 U.S. at 389. Second, the Commission had considered *any* increase in cost or decrease in quality, no matter how small, sufficient to establish impairment—a result the Court concluded could not be squared with the "ordinary and fair meaning" of the word "impair." *Id.* at 389–90 & n. 11. The Court admonished the FCC that in assessing which cost differentials would "impair" a new entrant's competition within the meaning of the statute, it must "apply *some* limiting standard, rationally related to the goals of the Act." *Id.* at 388.

Responding to the *AT&T* decision, the Commission adopted a new interpretation under which a would-be entrant is "impaired" if, "taking into consideration the availability of alternative elements outside the incumbent's network, including self-provisioning by a requesting carrier or acquiring an alternative from a third-party supplier, lack of access to that element *materially diminishes* a requesting carrier's ability to provide the services it seeks to offer." *Implementation of the Local Competition Provisions of the Telecommunications Act of 1996,* Third Report and Order and Fourth Further Notice of Proposed Rulemaking, 15 FCC Rcd 3696, 3725 (1999) (emphasis added). But in *USTA I* we held that this new interpretation of "impairment," while an improvement, was still unreasonable in light of the Act's underlying purposes.

The fundamental problem, we held, was that the Commission did not differentiate between those cost disparities that a new entrant in *any* market would be likely to face and those that arise from market characteristics "linked (in some degree) to natural monopoly . . . that would make genuinely competitive provision of an element's function wasteful." *USTA I,* 290 F.3d at 427. This distinction between different kinds of incumbent/entrant cost differentials is qualitative, not merely quantitative, which is why the Commission's addition of a requirement that the cost disparity be "material" was inadequate.

* * *

We also objected to the Commission's decision to issue, with respect to most elements, broad unbundling requirements that would apply "in every geographic market and customer class, without regard to the state of competitive impairment in any particular market." *USTA I,* 290 F.3d at 422. Though the Act does not necessarily require the

Commission to determine "on a localized state-by-state or market-by-market basis which unbundled elements are to be made available," it does require "a more nuanced concept of impairment than is reflected in findings . . . detached from any specific markets or market categories." *Id.* at 425–26. Thus, the Commission is obligated to establish unbundling criteria that are at least aimed at tracking relevant market characteristics and capturing significant variation.

* * *

In response to *USTA I* the Commission again revised its definition of impairment.

* * *

The Commission responded to our demand for a more "nuanced" application of the impairment standard by purporting to adopt a "granular" approach that would consider "such factors as specific services, specific geographic locations, the different types and capacities of facilities, and customer and business considerations." Where the Commission believed that the record could not support an absolute national impairment finding but at the same time contained too little information to make "granular" determinations, it adopted a provisional nationwide rule, subject to the possibility of specific exclusions, to be created by state regulatory commissions under a purported delegation of the Commission's own authority.

* * *

The Commission made a nationwide finding that CLECs are impaired without unbundled access to ILEC switches for the "mass market," consisting of residential and relatively small business users. This finding was based primarily on the costs associated with "hot cuts" * * *, which must be performed when a CLEC provides its own switch. But the Commission, apparently concerned that a blanket nationwide impairment determination might be unlawfully overbroad in light of the record evidence of substantial market-by-market variation in hot cut costs, delegated authority to state commissions to make more "nuanced" and "granular" impairment determinations.

First, the Commission directed the state commissions to eliminate unbundling if a market contained at least three competitors in addition to the ILEC, or at least two non-ILEC third parties that offered access to their own switches on a wholesale basis. For purposes of this exercise the Commission gave the states virtually unlimited discretion over the definition of the relevant market. Second, where these "competitive triggers" are not met, the Commission instructed the states to consider whether, despite the many economic and operational entry barriers deemed relevant by the Commission, competitive supply of mass market switching was nevertheless feasible. The Commission also instructed the states to explore specific mechanisms to ameliorate or eliminate the costs of the "hot cut" process. The Commission mentioned, for example, the possible use of "rolling" hot cuts, a process in which CLECs could use ILEC switches for some time after a customer selected the CLEC as its provider, and after an accumulation of such customer changes, the ILEC would make all the necessary hot cuts in one fell swoop. If a state failed to perform the requisite analysis within nine months, the Commission would step into the position of the state commission and do the analysis itself. Finally, the Order provided that a party "aggrieved" by a state commission decision could seek a declaratory ruling from the Commission, though with no assurance when, or even whether, the Commission might respond.

We consider first whether the Commission's subdelegation of authority to the state commissions is lawful. We conclude that it is not. * * *

The FCC acknowledges that § 251(d)(2) instructs "the Commission" to "determine[ ]" which network elements shall be made available to CLECs on an unbundled basis. But it claims that agencies have the presumptive power to subdelegate to state commissions, so long as the statute authorizing agency action refrains from foreclosing such a power. * * *

The Commission's position is based on a fundamental misreading of the relevant case law. When a statute delegates authority to a federal officer or agency, subdelegation to a subordinate federal officer or agency is presumptively permissible absent affirmative evidence of a contrary congressional intent. See *United States v. Giordano,* 416 U.S. 505, 512–13 (1974); *Fleming v. Mohawk Wrecking & Lumber Co.,* 331 U.S. 111, 121–22 (1947); *Halverson v. Slater,* 129 F.3d 180, 185–86 (D.C.Cir. 1997); *United States v. Mango,* 199 F.3d 85, 90–91 (2d Cir. 1999); *Inland Empire Pub. Lands Council v. Glickman,* 88 F.3d 697, 702 (9th Cir. 1996); *United States v. Widdowson,* 916 F.2d 587, 592 (10th Cir. 1990), vacated on other grounds, 502 U.S. 801 (1991). But the cases recognize an important distinction between subdelegation to a *subordinate* and subdelegation to an *outside party*. The presumption that subdelegations are valid absent a showing of contrary congressional intent applies only to the former. There is no such presumption covering subdelegations to outside parties. Indeed, if anything, the case law strongly suggests that subdelegations to outside parties are assumed to be improper absent an affirmative showing of congressional authorization. See *Shook v. District of Columbia Fin. Responsibility & Mgmt. Assistance Auth.,* 132 F.3d 775, 783–84 & n. 6 (D.C.Cir. 1998). See also *Nat'l Ass'n of Reg. Util. Comm'rs ("NARUC") v. FCC,* 737 F.2d 1095, 1143–44 & n.41 (D.C. Cir. 1984); *Nat'l Park and Conservation Ass'n v. Stanton,* 54 F.Supp.2d 7, 18–20 (D.D.C. 1999). * * *

This distinction is entirely sensible. When an agency delegates authority to its subordinate, responsibility—and thus accountability—clearly remain with the federal agency. But when an agency delegates power to outside parties, lines of accountability may blur, undermining an important democratic check on government decision-making. See *NARUC,* 737 F.2d at 1143 n.41. Also, delegation to outside entities increases the risk that these parties will not share the agency's "national vision and perspective," *Stanton,* 54 F.Supp.2d at 20, and thus may pursue goals inconsistent with those of the agency and the underlying statutory scheme. In short, subdelegation to outside entities aggravates the risk of policy drift inherent in any principal-agent relationship.

The fact that the subdelegation in this case is to state commissions rather than private organizations does not alter the analysis. Although *United States v. Mazurie,* 419 U.S. 544 (1975), noted that "limits on the authority of *Congress* to delegate its legislative power . . . are [ ] less stringent in cases where the entity exercising the delegated authority itself possesses independent authority over the subject matter," *id.* at 556–57 (emphasis added), that decision has no application here: it involved a constitutional challenge to an express *congressional* delegation, rather than an administrative subdelegation, and the point of the discussion was to distinguish the still somewhat suspect case of congressional delegation to purely private organizations.

* * *

We therefore hold that, while federal agency officials may subdelegate their decision-making authority to subordinates absent evidence of contrary congressional intent, they may not subdelegate to outside entities—private or sovereign—absent affirmative evidence of authority to do so.

* * *

The FCC invokes a number of other cases in support of its idea of a presumptive authority to subdelegate to entities other than subordinates. These are inapposite because they do not involve subdelegation of decision-making authority. They merely recognize three specific types of legitimate outside party input into agency decision-making processes: (1) establishing a reasonable condition for granting federal approval; (2) fact gathering; and (3) advice giving. The scheme established in the Order fits none of these models.

First, a federal agency entrusted with broad discretion to permit or forbid certain activities may condition its grant of permission on the decision of another entity, such as a state, local, or tribal government, so long as there is a reasonable connection between the outside entity's decision and the federal agency's determination. Thus in *United States v. Matherson,* 367 F.Supp. 779, 782–83 (E.D.N.Y.1973), aff'd 493 F.2d 1339 (2d Cir.1974), the court upheld the decision of the Fire Island National Seashore Superintendent to condition issuance of federal seashore motor vehicle permits on the applicant's acquisition of an analogous permit from an adjacent town. And [*Southern Pacific Transp. Co. v. Watt,* 700 F.2d 550, 556 (9th Cir. 1983)], citing *Matherson,* sustained the Secretary of Interior's conditioning of right-of-way permits across tribal lands on the tribal government's approval. In contrast to these cases, where an agency with broad permitting authority had adopted an obviously relevant local concern as an element of its decision process, the Commission here has delegated to another actor almost the entire determination of whether a specific statutory requirement—impairment—has been satisfied.

Second, there is some authority for the view that a federal agency may use an outside entity, such as a state agency or a private contractor, to provide the agency with factual information. While *Assiniboine & Sioux Tribes* [*v. Bd. Of Oil and Gas,* 792 F.2d 782 (9th Cir. 1986),] found that a delegation of decision-making power to a state board would be unlawful, it left open whether reliance by the federal agency on the state board for "nondiscretionary activities such as compiling, hearing, and transmitting technical information might not be permissible and desirable." 792 F.2d at 795. And *National Association of Psychiatric Treatment v. Mendez,* 857 F.Supp. 85, 91 (D.D.C.1994), upheld a federal certifying agency's decision to hire a private contractor to conduct surveys of residential treatment centers and pass its results on to the agency, which retained final certification authority. While the FCC has sought to characterize the state commissions' role here as fact finding, in fact the Order lets the states make crucial decisions regarding market definition and application of the FCC's general impairment standard to the specific circumstances of those markets, with FCC oversight neither timely nor assured. The Commission's attempted punt does not remotely resemble nondiscretionary information gathering.

Our own decision in *Tabor v. Joint Board for Enrollment of Actuaries,* 566 F.2d 705, 708 n. 5 (D.C.Cir.1977), seems to straddle the two above variants of permissible relationships. There the federal Joint Board for Enrollment of Actuaries, exercising its broad discretion to set conditions for certifying actuaries to administer ERISA pension plans, required applicants *either* to pass a Board exam *or* to pass an exam administered by one of the recognized private national actuarial societies. 566 F.2d at 708 n. 5. The court found that the process was "superintended by the Board in every respect," and that the Board had not abdicated its decision-making authority but merely created a reasonable "short-cut," contingent on the approval of certain private organizations, to satisfy one of the Board's own regulatory requirements. *Id.* The opinions in both *Southern Pacific* (from our first category) and *Mendez* (from our second) invoke *Tabor.*

* * *

Third, a federal agency may turn to an outside entity for advice and policy recommendations, provided the agency makes the final decisions itself. Thus in *Shook,* 132 F.3d at 784, we disapproved the D.C. Control Board's delegation of governance powers over D.C. schools to a private Board of Trustees, but we suggested that the Control Board could use an entity of that sort "as an advisory board charged with recommending certain actions and policies to the Control Board." See also *Stanton,* 54 F.Supp.2d at 19–20 & n. 6; *Mendez,* 857 F.Supp. at 91. An agency may not, however, merely "rubber-stamp" decisions made by others under the guise of seeking their "advice," see *Assiniboine & Sioux Tribes,* 792 F.2d at 795, nor will vague or inadequate assertions of final reviewing authority save an unlawful subdelegation, see *Stanton,* 54 F.Supp.2d at 19, 20–21.

* * *

We therefore vacate, as an unlawful subdelegation of the Commission's § 251(d)(2) responsibilities, those portions of the Order that delegate to state commissions the authority to determine whether CLECs are impaired without access to network elements, and in particular we vacate the Commission's scheme for subdelegating mass market switching determinations. * * *

NOTES AND QUESTIONS

1. In *U.S. Telecom Assoc. v. FCC*, the D.C. Circuit distinguished subdelegation of discretionary decisionmaking authority from subdelegation of nondiscretionary functions such as "(1) establishing a reasonable condition for granting federal approval; (2) fact gathering; and (3) advice giving," which the court described as "legitimate outside party input into agency decision-making processes." Do you see the difference?

2. Since the D.C. Circuit decided *U.S. Telecom Assoc. v. FCC*, other courts have drawn the line between permissible and impermissible subdelegations somewhat differently, focusing instead on the degree or scope of discretionary power subdelegated. For example, the Migratory Bird Treaty Act authorizes the U.S. Fish and Wildlife Service (FWS) "to determine when, to what extent, if at all, and by what means" to permit the killing of migratory birds. 16 U.S.C. § 704(a). In *Fund for Animals v. Kempthorne*, 538 F.3d 124 (2d Cir. 2007), the Second Circuit upheld a FWS Depredation Order authorizing state fish and wildlife agencies, Indian Tribes, and the U.S. Department of Agriculture to kill an unspecified number of federally-protected double-crested cormorants in 25 states, without advance notice to the FWS, as they deem necessary "to prevent depredations on the public resources of fish . . . , wildlife, plants, and their habitats." 50 C.F.R. § 21.48(c). While endorsing the D.C. Circuit's decision in *U.S. Telecom Ass'n v. FCC* regarding the impermissibility of subdelegation absent statutory authorization, the Second Circuit court nevertheless concluded that the discretionary powers extended by the FWS Depredation Order to state fish and wildlife agencies and others was a sufficiently narrow subset of the authority given to the FWS by the restricted as not to constitute a subdelegation of authority at all. "[T]he authority delegated by Congress to the FWS under the MBTA bears little resemblance to the far narrower band of discretion afforded to those acting under the Depredation Order." Can you anticipate any difficulties in applying this approach to evaluating subdelegations? Would you expect such a standard to be easier or more difficult to apply than that of the D.C. Circuit in *U.S. Telecom Assoc. v. FCC*?

3. Why do you think an agency might choose to subdelegate decisionmaking authority to other federal agencies, to state government agencies, or to private parties? In *U.S. Telecom Assoc. v. FCC*, the D.C. Circuit dwelled on the negative implications of subdelegation for agency accountability and democratic legitimacy. Can you think of what benefits subdelegation might offer? How would you weigh the benefits versus the costs of subdelegation?

f. PRIVATIZATION

Cases evaluating subdelegations represent only one strain of those that consider the "who" aspect of congressional delegations of legislative power. Another line of contemporary jurisprudence considers delegations of government responsibilities to private actors.

Recall that, in *A.L.A. Schechter Poultry v. United States*, 295 U.S. 495 (1935), the Supreme Court rejected the constitutionality of the National Industrial Recovery Act on the ground that it lacked intelligible principles to limit the President's actions. That case concerned persons convicted of violating the Live Poultry Code, which had been developed by industry participants and approved by the President. In further explaining its decision, the Court additionally objected that the delegation of legislative power had been to private parties.

> But would it be seriously contended that Congress could delegate its legislative authority to trade or industrial associations or groups so as to empower them to enact the laws they deem to be wise and beneficent for the rehabilitation and expansion of their trade or industries? Could trade or industrial associations or groups be constituted legislative bodies for that purpose because such associations or groups are familiar with the problems of their enterprises? And could an effort of that sort be made valid by such a preface of generalities as to permissible aims as we find in section 1 of title 1? The answer is obvious. Such a delegation of legislative power is unknown to our law, and is utterly inconsistent with the constitutional prerogatives and duties of Congress.

Id. at 537. Subsequently, in *Carter v. Carter Coal*, 298 U.S. 238 (1936), the Supreme Court considered the constitutionality of the Bituminous Coal Conservation Act, which said that when the producers of more than two-thirds of the annual national tonnage of coal production for the preceding calendar year and the representatives of more than one-half of the mine workers employed by such producers agreed upon maximum daily and weekly hours of labor and minimum wages, then all coal producers and miners would have to abide by that agreement. In other words, the statute required a dissenting minority of producers, miners, or both to follow the wage and hour agreements of the majority. The Court declared this statutory requirement "an intolerable and unconstitutional interference of liberty and private property" under the Due Process Clause, discussed at length in Chapter 4. But the Court also recognized that the statute might be unconstitutional as well under the reasoning of *Schechter Poultry*, presumably for delegating legislative power to private parties.

Notwithstanding the Court's objection to the delegation of lawmaking power to industry groups, the federal government routinely relies quite heavily on private actors both to perform a variety of regulatory and other government functions. To some extent, such has always been the case. At the height of the New Deal, Louis Jaffe lauded the longstanding and substantial involvement of private groups in the regulatory sphere. *See* Louis Jaffe, *Law Making By Private Groups*, 51 HARV. L. REV. 201 (1937). Nevertheless, the blending of the public and private spheres has grown substantially in recent decades. In the 1990s, President Bill Clinton and Vice President Al Gore worked to "reinvent" government by downsizing government bureaucracies and outsourcing government functions to private actors thought to be more efficient as a result of their participation in a competitive marketplace. President George W. Bush followed suit, seeking new ways to contract with private vendors to perform functions previously handled by government employees.

Today, private companies run federal prisons, subject to regulations adopted by the Federal Bureau of Prisons, but with tremendous latitude in applying those regulations in managing the day-to-day circumstances of federal prisoners. Private companies also own and operate Medicare- and Medicaid-funded nursing homes and managed care organizations, also subject to extensive regulation and oversight by federal agencies, but with tremendous discretion in managing individual patient care case by case. Federal financial regulators rely heavily on self-regulated organizations like the New York Stock Exchange to establish and enforce standards of conduct for their members. Professional and trade groups develop health, safety, and product standards for their members that Congress and federal agencies, in turn, incorporate by reference into federal statutes and regulations. Although the courts generally have been quite permissive of these arrangements, they do not always approve of them.

Association of American Railroads v. United States Department of Transportation

721 F.3d 666 (D.C. Cir. 2013).

■ BROWN, CIRCUIT JUDGE:

Imagine a scenario in which Congress has given to General Motors the power to coauthor, alongside the Department of Transportation, regulations that will govern all automobile manufacturers. And, if the two should happen to disagree on what form those regulations will take, then neither will have the ultimate say. Instead, an unspecified arbitrator will make the call. Constitutional? The Department of Transportation seems to think so.

Next consider a parallel statutory scheme—the one at issue in this case. This time, instead of General Motors, it is Amtrak (officially, the "National Railroad Passenger Corporation") wielding joint regulatory power with a government agency. This new stipulation further complicates the issue. Unlike General Motors, Amtrak is a curious entity that occupies the twilight between the public and private sectors. And the regulations it codevelops govern not the automotive industry, but the priority freight railroads must give Amtrak's trains over their own. Whether the Constitution permits Congress to delegate such joint regulatory authority to Amtrak is the question that confronts us now.

Section 207 of the Passenger Rail Investment and Improvement Act of 2008 empowers Amtrak and the Federal Railroad Administration (FRA) to jointly develop performance measures to enhance enforcement of the statutory priority Amtrak's passenger rail service has over other trains. * * * We conclude § 207 constitutes an unlawful delegation of regulatory power to a private entity.

I

A

To reinvigorate a national passenger rail system that had, by mid-century, grown moribund and unprofitable, Congress passed the Rail Passenger Service Act of 1970. Most prominently, the legislation created the passenger rail corporation now known as Amtrak, which would "employ[ ] innovative operating and marketing concepts so as to fully develop the potential of modern rail service in meeting the Nation's intercity passenger transportation requirements." Rail Passenger Service Act, § 301. The act also made railroad companies languishing under the prior regime an offer they could not refuse: if these companies consented to certain conditions, such as permitting Amtrak to use their tracks and other facilities, they could shed their cumbersome common carrier obligation to offer intercity passenger service. Pursuant to statute, Amtrak negotiates these arrangements with individual railroads, the terms of which are enshrined in Operating Agreements. *See* 49 U.S.C. § 24308(a). Today, freight railroads own roughly 97% of the track over which Amtrak runs its passenger service.

Naturally, sharing tracks can cause coordination problems, which is why Congress has prescribed that, absent an emergency, Amtrak's passenger rail "has preference over freight transportation in using a rail line, junction, or crossing." *Id.* at § 24308(c). More recently, this same concern prompted enactment of the Passenger Rail Investment and Improvement Act of 2008 ("PRIIA"). At issue in this case is the PRIIA's § 207, which directs the FRA and Amtrak to "jointly . . . develop new or improve existing metrics and minimum standards for measuring the performance and service quality of intercity passenger train operations, including cost recovery, on-time performance and minutes of delay, ridership, on-board services, stations, facilities, equipment, and other services." PRIIA § 207(a), 49 U.S.C. § 24101 (note). If Amtrak and the FRA disagree about the composition of these "metrics and standards," either "may petition the Surface Transportation Board to appoint an arbitrator to assist the parties in resolving their disputes through binding arbitration." *Id.* § 207(d), 49 U.S.C. § 24101 (note). "To the extent practicable," Amtrak and its host rail carriers must incorporate the metrics and standards into their Operating Agreements. *Id.* § 207(c), 49 U.S.C. § 24101 (note).

Though § 207 provides the means for devising the metrics and standards, § 213 is the enforcement mechanism. If the "on-time performance" or "service quality" of any intercity passenger train proves inadequate under the metrics and standards for two consecutive quarters, the STB may launch an investigation "to determine whether and to what extent delays or failure to achieve minimum standards are due to causes that could reasonably be addressed by a rail carrier over whose tracks the intercity passenger train operates or reasonably addressed by Amtrak or other intercity passenger rail operators." PRIIA § 213(a), 49 U.S.C. § 24308(f)(1). Similarly, if "Amtrak, an intercity passenger rail operator, a host freight railroad over which Amtrak operates, or an entity for which Amtrak operates intercity passenger rail service" files a complaint, the STB "*shall*" initiate such an investigation. *Id.* (emphasis added). Should the STB determine the failure to satisfy the metrics and standards is "attributable to a rail carrier's failure to provide preference to Amtrak over freight transportation as required," it may award damages or other relief against the offending host rail carrier. *Id.* § 24308(f)(2).

B

Following § 207's mandate, the FRA and Amtrak jointly drafted proposed metrics and standards, which they submitted to public comment on March 13, 2009. *See Metrics and Standards for Intercity Passenger Rail Service Under Section 207 of Public Law 110–432*, 74 Fed. Reg. 10,983 (Mar. 13, 2009). The proposal attracted criticism, with much vitriol directed at three metrics formulated to measure on-time performance: "effective speed" (the ratio of route's distance to the average time required to travel it), "endpoint on-time performance" (the portion of a route's trains that arrive on schedule), and "all-stations on-time performance" (the degree to which trains arrive on time at each station along the route). [The Association of American Railroads (AAR)], among others, derided these metrics as "unrealistic" and worried that certain aspects would create "an excessive administrative and financial burden." The FRA responded to the comments, and a final version of the metrics and standards took effect in May 2010. *See Metrics and Standards for Intercity Passenger Rail Service Under Section 207 of the Passenger Rail Investment and Improvement Act of 2008,* 75 Fed. Reg. 26,839 (May 11, 2010).

* * *

II

AAR's argument takes the following form: Delegating regulatory authority to a private entity is unconstitutional. Amtrak is a private entity. Ergo, § 207 is unconstitutional. This proposed syllogism is susceptible, however, to attacks on both its validity and soundness. In other words, does the conclusion actually follow from the premises? And, if it does, are both premises true? Our discussion follows the same path.

A

We open our discussion with a principle upon which both sides agree: Federal lawmakers cannot delegate regulatory authority to a private entity. To do so would be "legislative delegation in its most obnoxious form." *Carter v. Carter Coal Co.,* 298 U.S. 238, 311 (1936). This constitutional prohibition is the lesser-known cousin of the doctrine that Congress cannot delegate its legislative function to an agency of the Executive Branch. *See* U.S. CONST. art. I, § 1 ("All legislative Powers herein granted shall be vested in a Congress of the United States. . . ."); *see A.L.A. Schechter Poultry Corp. v. United States,* 295 U.S. 495, 529 (1935). This latter proposition finds scarce practical application, however, because "no statute can be entirely precise," meaning "some judgments, even some judgments involving policy considerations, must be left to the officers executing the law and to the judges applying it." *Mistretta v. United States,* 488 U.S. 361, 415 (1989) (Scalia, J., dissenting). All that is required then to legitimate a delegation to a government agency is for Congress to prescribe an intelligible principle governing the statute's enforcement. *See J.W. Hampton, Jr., & Co. v. United States,* 276 U.S. 394, 409 (1928).

Not so, however, in the case of private entities to whom the Constitution commits no executive power. Although objections to delegations are "typically presented in the context of a transfer of legislative authority from the Congress to agencies," we have reaffirmed that "the difficulties sparked by such allocations are even more prevalent in the context of agency delegations to private individuals." *Nat'l Ass'n of Regulatory Util. Comm'rs v. FCC ("NARUC"),* 737 F.2d 1095, 1143 (D.C.Cir.1984) (per curiam). Even an intelligible principle cannot rescue a statute empowering private parties to wield regulatory authority. Such entities may, however, help a government agency make its regulatory decisions, for "[t]he Constitution has never been regarded as denying to the Congress the necessary resources of flexibility and practicality" that such schemes facilitate. *Pan. Ref. Co. v. Ryan,* 293 U.S. 388, 421 (1935). Yet precisely how much involvement may a private entity have in the administrative process before its advisory role trespasses into an unconstitutional delegation? Discerning that line is the task at hand.

Preliminarily, we note the Supreme Court has never approved a regulatory scheme that so drastically empowers a private entity in the way § 207 empowers Amtrak. True, § 207 has a passing resemblance to the humbler statutory frameworks in *Currin v. Wallace,* 306 U.S. 1 (1939), and *Sunshine Anthracite Coal Co. v. Adkins,* 310 U.S. 381 (1940). In *Currin* Congress circumscribed its delegations of administrative authority—in that case, by requiring two thirds of regulated industry members to approve an agency's new regulations before they took effect. *Adkins,* meanwhile, affirmed a modest principle: Congress may formalize the role of private parties in proposing regulations so long as that role is merely "as an aid" to a government agency that retains the discretion to "approve[ ], disapprove[ ], or modif[y]" them. 310 U.S. at 388. Like the private parties in *Currin,* Amtrak has an effective veto over regulations developed by the FRA. And like those in *Adkins,* Amtrak has a role in filling the content of regulations. But the similarities end there. The industries in *Currin* did not craft the regulations, while *Adkins* involved no private check on an agency's regulatory authority.[4] Even more damningly, the agency in *Adkins* could unilaterally change regulations proposed to it by private parties, whereas Amtrak enjoys authority equal the FRA. Should the FRA prefer an alternative to Amtrak's proposed metrics and standards, § 207 leaves it impotent to choose its version without Amtrak's permission. No case prefigures the unprecedented regulatory powers delegated to Amtrak.[5]

The government also points out that the metrics and standards themselves impose no liability. Rather, they define the circumstances in which the STB will investigate whether infractions are attributable to a freight railroad's failure to meet its preexisting statutory obligation to accord preference to Amtrak's trains. *See* PRIIA § 213(a), 49 U.S.C. § 24308(f). We are not entirely certain what to make of this argument. Taken to its logical extreme, it would preclude all preenforcement

---

[4] For what it is worth, *Currin* also involved the collective participation of two thirds of industry members, and the regulations in *Adkins* arose from district boards comprising multiple members of the regulated industry. Neither upheld a statute that favored a single firm over all its market rivals.

[5] The government also cites various decisions from other circuits that purportedly support its position. All are distinguishable. Several upheld schemes like that in *Currin* in which the effect of regulations was contingent upon the assent of a certain portion of the regulated industry. *See Ky. Div., Horsemen's Benevolent and Protective Ass'n v. Turfway Park Racing Ass'n,* 20 F.3d 1406, 1416 (6th Cir.1994); *Sequoia Orange Co. v. Yeutter,* 973 F.2d 752, 759 (9th Cir.1992). The others resemble *Adkins* insofar as they approve structures in which private industry members serve in purely advisory or ministerial functions. *See Pittston Co. v. United States,* 368 F.3d 385, 394–97 (4th Cir.2004); *United States v. Frame,* 885 F.2d 1119, 1128–29 (3d Cir.1989), *abrogated on other grounds by Glickman v. Wileman Bros. & Elliott, Inc.,* 521 U.S. 457 (1997); *Sorrell v. SEC,* 679 F.2d 1323, 1325–26 (9th Cir.1982); *First Jersey Sec., Inc. v. Bergen,* 605 F.2d 690, 697 (3d Cir.1979); *Todd & Co. v. SEC,* 557 F.2d 1008, 1012–13 (3d Cir.1977); *R.H. Johnson & Co. v. SEC,* 198 F.2d 690, 695 (2d Cir.1952). In none of these cases did a private party stand on equal footing with a government agency.

review of agency rulemaking, so it is probably unlikely the government is pressing so immodest a claim. If the point is merely that the STB adds another layer of government "oversight" to Amtrak's exercise of regulatory power, this precaution does not alter the analysis. Government enforcement power did not save the rulemaking authority of the private coal companies in *Carter Coal* * * *. As is often the case in administrative law, the metrics and standards lend definite regulatory force to an otherwise broad statutory mandate. *See, e.g., Whitman v. Am. Trucking Ass'ns*, 531 U.S. 457, 465 (2001). The preference for Amtrak's traffic may predate the PRIIA, but the metrics and standards are what channel its enforcement. Certainly the FRA and Amtrak saw things that way, responding to one public comment by noting the STB "is the primary enforcement body *of the standards.*" Not only that, § 207 directs "Amtrak and its host carriers" to include the metrics and standards in their Operating Agreements "[t]o the extent practicable." PRIIA § 207(c), 49 U.S.C. § 24101 (note). The STB's involvement is no safe harbor from AAR's constitutional challenge to § 207.

As far as we know, no court has invalidated a scheme like § 207's, but perhaps that is because no parallel exists. Unprecedented constitutional questions, after all, lack clear and controlling precedent. We nevertheless believe *Free Enterprise Fund v. Public Co. Accounting Oversight Board,* 130 S.Ct. 3138 (2010), offers guidance. There the Supreme Court deemed it a violation of separation of powers to endow inferior officers with two layers of good-cause tenure insulating them from removal by the President. Two principles from that case are particularly resonant. To begin with, just because two structural features raise no constitutional concerns independently does not mean Congress may combine them in a single statute. *Free Enterprise Fund* deemed invalid a regime blending two limitations on the President's removal power that, taken separately, were unproblematic: the establishment of independent agencies headed by principal officers shielded from dismissal without cause, *see Humphrey's Ex'r v. United States,* 295 U.S. 602, 629–31 (1935), and the protection of certain inferior officers from removal by principal officers directly accountable to the President, *see Morrison v. Olson,* 487 U.S. 654, 691–93 (1988). *See* 130 S.Ct. at 3146–47. So even if the government is right that § 207 merely synthesizes elements approved by *Currin* and *Adkins*, that would be no proof of constitutionality.

As for the second principle, *Free Enterprise Fund* also clarifies that novelty may, in certain circumstances, signal unconstitutionality. That double good-cause tenure, for example, lacked an antecedent in the history of the administrative state was one reason to suspect its legality:

> Perhaps the most telling indication of the severe constitutional problem with the PCAOB is the lack of historical precedent for this entity. Neither the majority opinion nor the PCAOB nor the United States as intervenor has located any historical analogues for this novel structure. They have not identified any independent agency other than the PCAOB that is appointed by and removable only for cause by another independent agency.

Id. at 3159. In defending § 207, the government revealingly cites no case—nor have we found any—embracing the position that a private entity may jointly exercise regulatory power on equal footing with an administrative agency. This fact is not trivial. Section 207 is as close to the blatantly unconstitutional scheme in *Carter Coal* as we have seen. The government would essentially limit *Carter Coal* to its facts, arguing that "[n]o more is constitutionally required" than the government's "active oversight, participation, and assent" in its private partner's rulemaking decisions. This proposition—one we find nowhere in the case law—vitiates the principle that private parties must be limited to an advisory or subordinate role in the regulatory process.

To make matters worse, § 207 fails to meet even the government's ad hoc standard. Consider what would have happened if Amtrak and the FRA could not have reached an agreement on the content of the metrics and standards within 180 days of the PRIIA's enactment. Amtrak could have "petition[ed] the Surface Transportation Board to appoint an arbitrator to assist the parties in resolving their disputes through binding arbitration." PRIIA 207(d), 49 U.S.C. § 24101 (note). And nothing in the statute precludes the appointment of a private party as arbitrator.[7] That means it would have been entirely possible for metrics and standards to go into effect that had not been assented to by a single representative of the government. Though that did not in fact occur here, § 207's arbitration provision still polluted the rulemaking process over and above the other defects besetting the statute. As a formal matter, that the recipients of illicitly delegated authority opted not to make use of it is no antidote. It is *Congress's* decision to delegate that is unconstitutional. *See Whitman,* 531 U.S. at 473. As a practical matter, the FRA's failure to reach an agreement with Amtrak would have meant forfeiting regulatory power to an arbitrator the agency would have had no hand in picking. Rather than ensuring Amtrak would "function subordinately" to the FRA, *Adkins,* 310 U.S. at 399, this backdrop stacked the deck in favor of compromise. Even for government agencies, half an apple is better than none at all.

We remain mindful that the Constitution "contemplates that practice will integrate the dispersed powers into a workable government." *Youngstown Sheet & Tube Co. v. Sawyer,* 343 U.S. 579, 635 (1952) (Jackson, J., concurring). But a flexible Constitution must not be so yielding as to become twisted. Unless it can be established that Amtrak is an organ of the government, therefore, § 207 is an unconstitutional delegation of regulatory power to a private party.

B

Now the crucial question: is Amtrak indeed a private corporation? If not—if it is just one more government agency—then the regulatory power it wields under § 207 is of no constitutional moment.

---

[7]   The government notes § 207's arbitration provision does not *require* the arbitrator be a private party. This is irrelevant. "[A]n agency can[not] cure an unlawful delegation of legislative power by adopting in its discretion a limiting construction of the statute." *Whitman,* 531 U.S. at 472. Nor does the canon of constitutional avoidance offer a solution. The statute's text precludes the government's suggestion that we construe the open-ended language "an arbitrator" to include only federal entities. The constitutional avoidance canon is an interpretive aid, not an invitation to rewrite statutes to satisfy constitutional strictures.

Many of the details of Amtrak's makeup support the government's position that it is not a private entity of the sort described in *Carter Coal*. Amtrak's Board of Directors includes the Secretary of Transportation (or his designee), seven other presidential appointees, and the President of Amtrak. *See* 49 U.S.C. § 24302(a). The President of Amtrak—the one Board member not appointed by the President of the United States—is in turn selected by the eight other members of the Board. *See id.* § 24303(a). Amtrak is also subject to the Freedom of Information Act. *See id.* § 24301(e). Amtrak's equity structure is similarly suggestive. As of September 30, 2011, four common stockholders owned 9,385,694 outstanding shares, which they acquired from the four railroads whose intercity passenger service Amtrak assumed in 1971. At the same time, however, the federal government owned all 109,396,994 shares of Amtrak's preferred stock, each share of which is convertible into 10 shares of common stock. And, all that stands between Amtrak and financial ruin is congressional largesse.

That being said, Amtrak's legislative origins are not determinative of its constitutional status. Congress's power to charter private corporations was recognized early in our nation's history. *See McCulloch v. Maryland,* 17 U.S. (4 Wheat.) 316, 409 (1819). And, as far as Congress was concerned, that is exactly what it was doing when it created Amtrak. As Congress explained it, Amtrak "shall be operated and managed as a for-profit corporation" and "is not a department, agency, or instrumentality of the United States Government." 49 U.S.C. § 24301(a). We have previously taken Congress at its word and relied on this declaration in deciding whether the False Claims Act applies to Amtrak. *See United States ex rel. Totten v. Bombardier Corp.,* 380 F.3d 488, 490 (D.C.Cir.2004) ("Amtrak is not the Government."); *id.* at 491 ("Amtrak is not the Government."); *id.* at 502 ("Amtrak is not the Government."). Amtrak agrees: "The National Railroad Passenger Corporation, also known as Amtrak, is not a government agency or establishment [but] a private corporation operated for profit." NAT'L R.R. PASSENGER CORP., FREEDOM OF INFORMATION ACT HANDBOOK 1 (2008). And, somewhat tellingly, Amtrak's website is www.amtrak.com—not www.amtrak.gov.

How to decide? Since, in support of its claim that Amtrak is a public entity, the government looks past labels to how the corporation functions, it is worth examining what functional purposes the public-private distinction serves when it comes to delegating regulatory power. We identify two of particular importance. First, delegating the government's powers to private parties saps our political system of democratic accountability. *See Mich. Gambling Opposition v. Kempthorne,* 525 F.3d 23, 34 (D.C. Cir. 2008) (Brown, J., dissenting in part). This threat is particularly dangerous where both Congress and the Executive can deflect blame for unpopular policies by attributing them to the choices of a private entity. *See NARUC,* 737 F.2d at 1143 n. 41; *cf. New York v. United States,* 505 U.S. 144, 169 (1992) ("[W]here the Federal Government directs the States to regulate, it may be state officials who will bear the brunt of public disapproval, while the federal officials who devised the regulatory program may remain insulated from the electoral ramifications of their decision."). This worry is certainly present in the case of § 207, since Congress has expressly forsworn Amtrak's status as a "department, agency, or instrumentality of the United States Government." 49 U.S.C. § 24301(a)(3). Dislike the metrics and standards Amtrak has concocted? It's not the federal government's fault—Amtrak is a "for-profit corporation." *Id.* § 24301(a)(2).

Second, fundamental to the public-private distinction in the delegation of regulatory authority is the belief that disinterested government agencies ostensibly look to the public good, not private gain. For this reason, delegations to private entities are particularly perilous. *Carter Coal* specifically condemned delegations made not "to an official or an official body, presumptively disinterested, but to private persons whose interests may be and often are adverse to the interests of others in the same business." 298 U.S. at 311. Partly echoing the Constitution's guarantee of due process, this principle ensures that regulations are not dictated by those who "are not bound by any official duty," but may instead act "for selfish reasons or arbitrarily." *Roberge,* 278 U.S. at 122. More recent decisions are also consistent with this view. *See Pittston Co.,* 368 F.3d at 398; *NARUC,* 737 F.2d at 1143–44; *Sierra Club v. Sigler,* 695 F.2d 957, 962 n. 3 (5th Cir.1983). Amtrak may not compete with the freight railroads for customers, but it does compete with them for use of their scarce track. Like the "power conferred upon the majority . . . to regulate the affairs of an unwilling minority" in *Carter Coal,* § 207 grants Amtrak a distinct competitive advantage: a hand in limiting the freight railroads' exercise of their property rights over an essential resource. 298 U.S. at 311.

Because Amtrak must "be operated and managed as a for-profit corporation," 49 U.S.C. § 24301(a)(2), the fact that the President has appointed the bulk of its Board does nothing to exonerate its management from its fiduciary duty to maximize company profits. Also consistent with this purpose, "Amtrak is encouraged to make agreements with the private sector and undertake initiatives that are consistent with good business judgment and designed to maximize its revenues and minimize Government subsidies." *Id.* § 24101(d). Yet § 207 directs Amtrak and its host carriers to incorporate the metrics and standards in their Operating Agreements. *See id.* § 24101(c) note. So to summarize: Amtrak must negotiate contracts that will maximize its profits; those contracts generally must, by law, include certain terms; and Amtrak has the power to define those terms. Perverse incentives abound. Nothing about the government's involvement in Amtrak's operations restrains the corporation from devising metrics and standards that inure to its own financial benefit rather than the common good. And that is the very essence of the public-private distinction when a claim of unconstitutional delegation arises.

No discussion of Amtrak's status as a private or public institution would be complete, however, without an examination of the Supreme Court's decision in *Lebron v. National Railroad Passenger Corp.,* 513 U.S. 374 (1995). There the Court held that Amtrak "is part of the Government for purposes of the First Amendment." *Id.* at 400. Otherwise, the majority cautioned, the government could "evade the most solemn obligations imposed in the Constitution by simply resorting to the corporate form." *Id.* at 397. What the Court did not do in *Lebron* was conclude that Amtrak counted as part of the government for all purposes. On some questions—Does the Administrative

Procedure Act apply to Amtrak? Does Amtrak enjoy sovereign immunity from suit?—Congress's disclaimer of Amtrak's governmental status is dispositive. *See id.* at 392; *Totten,* 380 F.3d at 491–92. This makes sense: Congress has the power to waive certain governmental privileges, like sovereign immunity, that are within its legislative control; but it cannot circumvent the Bill of Rights by simply dubbing something private.

Whether § 207 effects an unconstitutional delegation is a constitutional question, not a statutory one. But just because *Lebron* treated Amtrak as a government agency for purposes of the First Amendment does not dictate the same result with respect to all other constitutional provisions. To view *Lebron* in this way entirely misses the point. In *Lebron,* viewing Amtrak as a strictly private entity would have permitted the government to avoid a constitutional prohibition; in this case, deeming Amtrak to be just another governmental entity would allow the government to ignore a constitutional obligation. Just as it is impermissible for Congress to employ the corporate form to sidestep the First Amendment, neither may it reap the benefits of delegating regulatory authority while absolving the federal government of all responsibility for its exercise. The federal government cannot have its cake and eat it too. In any event, *Lebron*'s holding was comparatively narrow, deciding only that Amtrak is an agency of the United States for the purpose of the First Amendment. 513 U.S. at 394. It did not opine on Amtrak's status with respect to the federal government's structural powers under the Constitution—the issue here.

This distinction is more than academic. When *Lebron* contrasted "the constitutional obligations of Government" from "the 'privileges of the government,'" it was not drawing a distinction between questions that are constitutional from those that are not. Any "privilege" of the federal government must also be anchored in the Constitution. *Id.* at 399. As our federal government is one of enumerated powers, the Constitution's structural provisions are the source of Congress's power to act in the first place. *See United States v. Lopez,* 514 U.S. 549, 552 (1995); THE FEDERALIST NO. 45 (James Madison). And, generally speaking, these provisions authorize action without mandating it. Congress's power to regulate interstate commerce, for example, does not dictate the enactment of this or that bill within its proper scope. By contrast, individual rights are "affirmative prohibitions" on government action that become relevant "only where the Government possesses authority to act in the first place." *Nat'l Fed'n of Ind. Bus.,* 132 S.Ct. at 2577. While often phrased in terms of an affirmative prohibition, Congress's inability to delegate government power to private entities is really just a function of its constitutional authority not extending that far in the first place. In other words, rather than proscribing what Congress *cannot* do, the doctrine defines the limits of what Congress *can* do. And, by designing Amtrak to operate as a private corporation— to seek profit on behalf of private interests—Congress has elected to deny itself the power to delegate it regulatory authority under § 207. *Cf.* Religious Freedom Restoration Act of 1993, 42 U.S.C. §§ 2000bb to bb–4 (requiring, beyond what the Constitution mandates, that the federal government "not substantially burden a person's exercise of religion even if the burden results from a rule of general applicability" unless the restriction satisfies strict scrutiny).

We therefore hold that Amtrak is a private corporation with respect to Congress's power to delegate regulatory authority. Though the federal government's involvement in Amtrak is considerable, Congress has both designated it a private corporation and instructed that it be managed so as to maximize profit. In deciding Amtrak's status for purposes of congressional delegations, these declarations are dispositive. Skewed incentives are precisely the danger forestalled by restricting delegations to government instrumentalities. And as a private entity, Amtrak cannot be granted the regulatory power prescribed in § 207.

III

We conclude § 207 of the PRIIA impermissibly delegates regulatory authority to Amtrak. * * *

NOTES AND QUESTIONS

1. Why do you think that Congress might choose to delegate decisionmaking authority to private parties? Can you think of public benefits such delegations might offer?

2. In supporting the government's petition for certiorari in the *Association of American Railroads* case, Alexander Volokh has offered an alternative approach to that taken by the D.C. Circuit. *See* Brief of Professor Alexander Volokh as Amicus Curiae in Support of Petitioners, *Department of Transportation v. Ass'n of Amer. Railroads*, No. 13–1080 (Sup. Ct. Apr. 10, 2014), 2014 WL 1430811. Instead of invalidating the statutory scheme, Volokh suggests instead designating Amtrak a state actor subject to constitutional due process limitations, meaning that Amtrak could not develop performance standards for passenger trains without complying with procedural requirements of the Due Process Clause. Volokh contends that this approach better protects regulated parties from bias and unfairness while also enabling them to pursue damages through *Bivens* actions under 42 U.S.C. § 1983 and *Bivens v. Six Unknown Named Agents of Federal Bureau of Narcotics*, 403 U.S. 388 (1971). Which approach do you think best protects the interests of regulated parties: precluding delegations of discretionary power to private parties in the first instance, or permitting regulated parties to sue for damages in the event they are aggrieved by the actions of otherwise-private parties exercising delegated power?

2. IF BROAD DELEGATIONS ARE A PROBLEM, ARE DETAILED INSTRUCTIONS THE ANSWER?

Turning back to broad delegations to federal agencies, despite many attempts, proponents of reinvigorating the nondelegation doctrine seem not to have persuaded the Court to take up the daunting challenge of giving life to that constitutional law doctrine. They have persuaded almost everyone that broad delegations of vast power to agencies have many undesirable effects, however. It would seem to follow logically that Congress is at its best when it addresses policy issues with clarity and particularity and gives agencies detailed instructions. That is not always the case. Congress often creates serious problems when it acts in this manner. The following cases illustrate this phenomenon.

a.   THE FOOD STAMP PROGRAM

The first case arose in the context of an agency-administered welfare program. Welfare programs are politically fragile. Beneficiaries constitute a small percentage of the population, and they have little political power. Support from the broader population, based on feelings of empathy and compassion, waxes and wanes over time. Moreover, welfare programs are highly vulnerable to demagogic rhetoric that portrays welfare recipients as lazy, immoral frauds. One of the few welfare programs that has continued in effect in a relatively generous form for decades is the Food Stamp program. The political durability of that program undoubtedly is attributable in part to the fact that it has a second group of beneficiaries with considerable political clout—farmers and other agricultural interests.

During the late 1960s and early 1970s, however, the continued political viability of the Food Stamp program was jeopardized by a highly-publicized scandal. Some college students who were children of rich parents "abused" the program by collecting Food Stamps. Many were technically eligible because they had no assets and no income, but the image of the indulged offspring of multi-millionaires driving up to Food Stamp offices in their Porsches each month and driving off with a few hundred dollars in taxpayer-funded benefits created tremendous political pressure to "do something" about this alleged abuse of Food Stamps. Congress responded by enacting the amendment to the Food Stamp statute that is the subject of the following case.

U.S. Department of Agriculture v. Murry

413 U.S. 508 (1973).

■ MR. JUSTICE DOUGLAS:

The Food Stamp Act of 1964, 7 U.S.C. § 2011 *et seq.*, as amended in 1971, 84 Stat. 2048, has been applied to these appellees so as to lead the three-judge District Court to hold one provision of it unconstitutional. We noted probable jurisdiction.

Appellee Murry has two sons and ten grandchildren in her household. Her monthly income is $57.50, which comes from her ex-husband as support for her sons. Her expenses far exceed her monthly income. By payment, however, of $11 she received $128 in food stamps. But she has now been denied food stamps because her ex-husband (who has remarried) had claimed her two sons and one grandchild as tax dependents in his 1971 income tax return. That claim, plus the fact that her eldest son is 19 years old, disqualified her household for food stamps under § 5(b) of the Act.

* * *

Appellees are members of households that have been denied food stamp eligibility solely because the households contain persons 18 years or older who have been claimed as "dependents" for federal income tax purposes by taxpayers who are themselves ineligible for food stamp relief. Section 5(b) makes the entire household of which a "tax dependent" was a member ineligible for food stamps for two years: (1) during the tax year for which the dependency was claimed and (2) during the next 12 months. During these two periods of time § 5(b) creates a conclusive presumption that the "tax dependent's" household is not needy and has access to nutritional adequacy.

* * *

The tax dependency provision was generated by congressional concern about nonneedy households participating in the food stamp program. The legislative history reflects a concern about abuses of the program by "college students, children of wealthy parents." But, as the District Court said, the Act goes far beyond that goal and its operation is inflexible. "Households containing no college student, that had established clear eligibility for Food Stamps and which still remain in dire need and otherwise eligible are now denied stamps if it appears that a household member 18 years or older is claimed by someone as a tax dependent."

* * *

We have difficulty in concluding that it is rational to assume that a child is not indigent this year because the parent declared the child as a dependent in his tax return for the prior year. But even on that assumption our problem is not at an end. Under the Act the issue is not the indigency of the child but the indigency of a different household with which the child happens to be living. Members of that different household are denied food stamps if one of its present members was used as a tax deduction in the past year by his parents even though the remaining members have no relation to the parent who used the tax deduction, even though they are completely destitute, and even though they are one, or 10 or 20 in number. We conclude that the deduction taken for the benefit of the parent in the prior year is not a rational measure of the need of a different household with which the child of the tax-deducting parent lives and rests on an irrebuttable presumption often contrary to fact. It therefore lacks critical ingredients of due process found wanting in *Vlandis v. Kline*, 412 U.S. 441, 452 (1973) [holding that an irrebuttable presumption is unconstitutional unless it is "necessarily or universally true"—Ed.]

■ MR. JUSTICE MARSHALL, concurring.

* * *

It is, of course, quite simple for Congress to provide an administrative mechanism to guarantee that abusers of the program were eliminated from it. All that is needed is some way for a person whose household would otherwise be ineligible for food stamps because of this statute to show that the support presently available from the person claiming a member of the household as a tax dependent does not in fact offset the loss of benefits. Reasonable rules stating what a claimant must show before receiving a hearing on the question could easily be devised. We deal here with a general rule that may seriously affect the ability of persons genuinely in need to provide an adequate diet for their households. In the face of readily available alternatives that might prevent abuse of the program, Congress did not choose a method of reducing abuses that was "fairly related to the object of the regulation," by enacting the statute challenged in this case.

■ MR. JUSTICE REHNQUIST, with whom THE CHIEF JUSTICE and MR. JUSTICE POWELL concur, dissenting.

Appellees challenge on constitutional grounds a section of the most recent congressional revision of the Food Stamp Act whereby households containing persons 18 years or older who have been claimed as "dependents" for income tax purposes are made ineligible to receive food stamps. The Court's opinion sustains this challenge. Referring to what it conceives to be the legislative aim in enacting such a limitation, "a concern about abuses of the program by 'college students, children of wealthy parents,'" the opinion states that "the Act goes far beyond that goal and its operation is inflexible."

Notions that in dispensing public funds to the needy Congress may not impose limitations which "go beyond the goal" of Congress, or may not be "inflexible," have not heretofore been thought to be embodied in the Constitution. In *Dandridge v. Williams*, 397 U.S. 471, 484–85 (1970), the Court rejected this approach in an area of welfare legislation that is indistinguishable from the food stamp program here involved. * * * [T]he Court [in *Danbridge*] * * * held:

> * * * "For this Court to approve the invalidation of state economic or social regulation as 'overreaching' would be far too reminiscent of an era when the Court thought the Fourteenth Amendment gave it power to strike down state laws 'because they may be unwise, improvident or out of harmony with a particular school of thought'. . . .

> "In the area of economics and social welfare, a State does not violate the Equal Protection Clause merely because the classifications made by its laws are imperfect. If the classification has some 'reasonable basis,' it does not offend the Constitution simply because the classification 'is not made with mathematical nicety or because in practice it results in some inequality.'"

NOTES AND QUESTIONS

1.   Do you agree with Justice Marshall's claim that it would be "quite simple" to solve this problem by conducting a hearing in each case to determine whether a college student actually has financial need sufficient to justify his or her eligibility for welfare?

2.   The *Murry* case represents just one example of the Supreme Court's application of the irrebuttable presumption doctrine. That doctrine holds that, where statutory requirements rely upon presumptions that are not always true and also affect important individual rights, as for example by limiting government benefits to people who satisfy certain criteria that are not sufficiently tailored to correspond to legislative goals, due process requires that affected individuals be allowed to rebut the presumptions. In a few cases in the 1970s, the Court applied the irrebuttable presumption doctrine as the basis to hold statues unconstitutional. It then seemed to abandon the doctrine with no explanation. Why might the Court have abandoned the irrebuttable presumption doctrine? What difficulties might

the Court have encountered in applying the doctrine? Consider, for instance, all statutes that use age as a conclusive proxy for maturity, *e.g.,* statutes that limit eligibility to purchase alcohol and cigarettes, statutes that limit eligibility to vote, and statutes that limit eligibility for a driver's license. Would any of those statutes survive application of the test the Court applied in cases like *Murry*? Is any age "necessarily and universally" an accurate measure of maturity?

3. Do the nondelegation doctrine and the irrebuttable presumption doctrine share similarities in their application? Is it possible that the Court's silent abandonment of both the nondelegation doctrine and irrebuttable presumption doctrine reflect a more realistic and empathetic perspective on the difficulty of the task of drafting statutes that are not too broad and not too detailed? If you were a member of Congress, how might you go about drafting legislation to address the problem that Congress confronted?

b.   THE DELANEY CLAUSE

The second illustration of the potential adverse effects of statutes that give agencies detailed instructions is drawn from the context of government regulation. The Food, Drug, and Cosmetics Act (FDCA) contains a provision called the Delaney Clause. The Delaney Clause provides that: "no (food) additive shall be deemed to be safe if it is found to induce cancer when ingested by man or animal. . . ." The same statutory prohibition applies to veterinary drugs and to pesticides if any amount of the drug or pesticide remains on or in any food. The pesticide provision is implemented by Environmental Protection Agency (EPA), while the food additive and veterinary drug provisions are implemented by Food and Drug Administration (FDA). *See* Richard Merrill, *Regulating Carcinogens in Food: A Legislator's Guide to the Food Safety Provisions of the Federal Food, Drug and Cosmetic Act,* 77 MICH. L. REV. 171 (1978).

The Delaney Clause was added to the FDCA in 1958. At that time, it had little effect, and the effect it had may have been beneficial. In 1958, only four substances had been shown to induce cancer in man or animals. Scientists' limited understanding of cancer made it reasonable to assume that any substance that induced cancer in animals also was likely to induce cancer in humans. Moreover, the available methods of testing a food to determine whether it contained a particular substance, *e.g.,* a veterinary drug or a pesticide, permitted detection of only relatively large quantities that were likely to pose a health risk. The Delaney Clause is now, however, having significant unintended effects on agencies' ability to do their jobs.

Scientists have made great progress in their understanding of cancer since 1958. There is now scientific consensus with respect to several issues relevant to this debate. Hundreds of substances induce cancer in animals if they are ingested in massive doses. About 50 percent of all substances tested are carcinogenic in this sense, including many substances that occur naturally in most fruits and vegetables. Only a small fraction of those substances induce cancer in humans when they are ingested in quantities relevant to the human diet. Substances vary considerably in their potential to induce cancer in humans. Moreover, available methods of detecting the existence of a substance in food have improved to such an extent since 1958 that we now can detect the presence of substances in infinitesimally small quantities. As a result of these scientific changes, the Delaney Clause now requires the FDA and the EPA to ban the use of some food additives, veterinary drugs, and pesticides that pose no risk to human health.

The literature documenting these changes in our understanding of cancer and their relationships with the Delaney Clause is voluminous. *See, e.g.*, Bruce N. Ames & Lois Swirsky Gold, *Too Many Rodent Carcinogens: Mitogenesis Increases Mutagenesis*, 249 SCIENCE 970 (1990); Cass R. Sunstein, *Interpreting Statutes in the Regulatory State*, 103 HARV. L. REV. 405, 496–497 (1989); NATIONAL RESEARCH COUNCIL, REGULATING PESTICIDES IN FOOD: THE DELANEY PARADOX (1987); Margaret Gilhooley, *Plain Meaning, Absurd Results and the Legislative Purpose: The Interpretation of the Delaney Clause*, 40 ADMIN. L. REV. 267 (1988); Lester B. Lave, THE STRATEGY OF SOCIAL REGULATION 9–26 (1981); Charles H. Blank, *The Delaney Clause: Technical Naivete and Scientific Advocacy in the Formulation of Public Health Policies*, 62 CAL. L. REV. 1084 (1974).

Imagine that you represented the sugar industry in the 1970s. Public concern about obesity, diabetes, and other adverse health effects of ingestion of large quantities of sugar have combined with the availability of a sugar substitute, saccharin, to reduce sales of sugar and the your client's profits. By this time, it is well known that about half of all substances that are subjected to animal studies are shown to induce cancer in rats when, as typically is the case, the rats are injected with massive quantities of the substance. What might you do to help your client?

The American Sugar Institute commissioned a study of saccharin in which rats were injected with quantities of saccharin equivalent to the amount a human would ingest if he or she drank 800 cans of diet soda each day. Some of the rats died of cancer. The FDA then banned saccharin. Congress responded to the resulting public furor by enacting an indefinite moratorium on the saccharin ban, but it did not amend or repeal the Delaney Clause.

Many judges are aware of the unintended effects of the Delaney Clause, but they are powerless to avoid those effects, as the following opinion illustrates.

Les v. Reilly

968 F.2d 985 (9th Cir. 1992).

■ SCHROEDER, CIRCUIT JUDGE:

Petitioners seek review of a final order of the Environmental Protection Agency permitting the use of four pesticides as food additives although they have been found to induce cancer. Petitioners challenge the final order on the ground that it violates the provisions of the Delaney clause, which prohibits the use of any food additive that is found to induce cancer.

Prior to 1988, EPA regulations promulgated in the absence of evidence of carcinogenicity permitted use of the four pesticides at issue here as food additives. In 1988, however, the EPA found these pesticides to be carcinogens. Notwithstanding the Delaney clause, the EPA refused to revoke the earlier regulations, reasoning that, although the chemicals posed a measurable risk of causing cancer, that risk was "de minimis."

We set aside the EPA's order because we agree with the petitioners that the language of the Delaney clause, its history and purpose all reflect that Congress intended the EPA to prohibit all additives that are carcinogens, regardless of the degree of risk involved.

* * *

[T]he EPA argues that a de minimis exception to the Delaney clause is necessary in order to bring about a more sensible application of the regulatory scheme. It relies particularly on a recent study suggesting that the criterion of concentration level in processed foods may bear little or no relation to actual risk of cancer, and that some pesticides might be barred by rigid enforcement of the Delaney clause while others, with greater cancer-causing risk, may be permitted through the flow-through provisions because they do not concentrate in processed foods. The EPA in effect asks us to approve what it deems to be a more enlightened system than that which Congress established. The EPA is not alone in criticizing the scheme established by the Delaney clause. *See, e.g.*, Richard A. Merrill, *FDA's Implementation of the Delaney Clause: Repudiation of Congressional Choice or Reasoned Adaptation to Scientific Progress*, 5 YALE J. ON REG. 1, 87 (1988) (concluding that the Delaney clause is both unambiguous and unwise: "at once an explicit and imprudent expression of legislative will"). Revising the existing statutory scheme, however, is neither our function nor the function of the EPA. There are currently bills pending before the House and the Senate which would amend the food additive provision to allow the Secretary to establish tolerance levels for carcinogens, including pesticide residues in processed foods, which impose a negligible risk. If there is to be a change, it is for Congress to direct.

NOTES AND QUESTIONS

1. During the Clinton Administration, the Ninth Circuit's opinion in *Les* gave rise to widespread concern among regulators, academics, and most public health officials that the Delaney Clause might be applied in the near future in ways that would increase significantly the incidence of cancer. There was reason to believe that the vast majority of pesticides would soon be the subject of animal studies finding that they induce cancer in rats when they are ingested in the massive quantities typically employed in animal tests. Those findings would, in turn, force EPA to ban use of most pesticides. What effect would such bans have on the cost and availability of fruits and vegetables? What effect would an increase in the price of fruits and vegetables have on the quantity of fruits and vegetables consumed? What effect would a reduction in consumption of fruits and vegetables have on the incidence of cancer?

2. Carol Browner, EPA Administrator under President Bill Clinton, convinced Congress to enact an amendment to the pesticide regulatory statute that has the effect of creating a situation in which the Delaney

Clause can never require EPA to ban a pesticide. In Administrator Browner's opinion, Congress would have been unlikely to repeal the Delaney Clause but would be willing to amend the statute in ways that make it ineffective through means the general public will never detect. Do you think she was correct in that judgment? If you were a member of Congress, why might you be reluctant to vote to repeal the Delaney Clause?

B. THE CONSTITUTIONALITY OF DELEGATING ADJUDICATORY POWER

Article III, § 1 vests "the judicial Power" in "one supreme Court, and in such inferior Courts as the Congress may from time to time ordain and establish." Yet, while the Constitution thus seems to assign responsibility for the adjudicative functions of government to the courts, reading this assignment literally is impractical if not impossible. As Professor Paul Bator recognized, "[e]very time an official of the executive branch, in determining how faithfully to execute the laws, goes through the process of finding facts and determining the meaning and application of the relevant law, he is doing something which functionally is akin to the exercise of judicial power." Paul M. Bator, *The Constitution as Architecture: Legislative and Administrative Courts Under Article III*, 65 IND. L.J. 233, 264 (1990). Professor Gary Lawson similarly observed, "[m]uch adjudicative activity by executive officials— such as granting or denying benefits under entitlement statutes—is execution of the laws by any rational standard, though it also fits comfortably within the concept of the judicial power if conducted by judicial officers." Gary Lawson, *The Rise and Rise of the Administrative State*, 107 HARV. L. REV. 1231, 1246 (1994).

Viewed in this light, it is hardly surprising that Congress first began authorizing adjudication by agencies as early as 1789, when it empowered the Comptroller within the Treasury Department to resolve all disputes concerning claims against the Treasury. Madison characterized this function as "of a judiciary quality," 12 THE PAPERS OF JAMES MADISON 265 (C. Hobson & R. Rutland eds. 1989). Today, federal agencies adjudicate far more disputes involving individual rights than do the federal courts. Scores of agencies exercise a wide variety of adjudicatory functions and collectively adjudicate millions of cases each year. For example, in its 2012 fiscal year, the Social Security Administration alone received about 3.2 million initial disability claims and conducted more than 672,352 disability hearings. By contrast, the federal district courts received roughly 372,600 combined civil and criminal filings and concluded 369,300 civil and criminal cases in 2012.

Some scholars contend that agency adjudication offers enormous advantages over court adjudication. They maintain that agency adjudication is less expensive and yields superior results in terms of accuracy and consistency. Others suggest that, at least in some administrative contexts, relaxed evidentiary rules may increase both the cost and duration of agency adjudications. At a minimum, agency adjudication relieves federal courts of a burden they could not possibly assume. Indeed, the federal courts already experience grave problems attempting to manage their existing caseload without adding to their dockets the millions of adjudications that agencies currently conduct annually. Yet, agencies also sometimes have a hard time clearing their dockets.

Whatever the potential advantages of agency adjudication and its widespread use for two centuries, some doubt remains concerning the constitutionality of agency adjudication of many important types of disputes. Because agency power to adjudicate is susceptible to challenge particularly under Article III and the Seventh Amendments, the Court has attempted to answer two general questions. In what circumstances does Article III compel adjudication by a life-tenured federal judge? In what circumstances does the Seventh Amendment require trial by jury? The Court has had a hard time establishing stable, sensible tests to govern disputes in these areas.

The Supreme Court has upheld numerous statutory delegations of adjudicatory power to agencies. Congress can authorize agencies to adjudicate cases involving aliens, *Zakonaite v. Wolf*, 226 U.S. 272 (1912), *Turner v. Williams*, 194 U.S. 279 (1904); unreasonable obstructions to navigation, *Monongahela Bridge Co. v. United States*, 216 U.S. 177 (1910); and the draft law of the First World War, *Arver v. United States*, 245 U.S. 366 (1918). The Court upheld administrative adjudication in railroad regulation, *Shields v. Utah Idaho Cent. R.R. Co.*, 305 U.S. 177 (1938), and in fixing prices of coal, *Sunshine Anthracite Coal Co. v. Adkins*, 310 U.S. 381 (1940). In *Sunshine*, the Court emphatically asserted: "Nor is there an invalid delegation of judicial power. To hold that there was would turn back the clock on at least a half century of administrative law." 310 U.S. at 400.

Nevertheless, in *Crowell v. Benson*, 285 U.S. 22 (1932), a six-Justice majority rejected the argument that the Longshoremen's and Harbor Workers Act was an unconstitutional delegation of adjudicatory power to an agency. A bit of background with respect to the history of the statute will help to place in context the dispute animating that case.

During the nineteenth century, workers injured on the job could sue their employers in tort for damages. They tended to fare poorly in such actions, however, because they had to prove negligence and they had to overcome both the fellow servant rule (an employer was not liable for negligence of a fellow servant) and a strong version of the assumption of risk defense. In the early twentieth century, states changed from the traditional court-administered, negligence-based system of workers compensation to the agency-administered, no-fault system of workers compensation that exists in all states today. States lacked jurisdiction over some types of employees, however, including longshoremen and harbor workers. Congress enacted statutes that had approximately the same transformative effects with respect to those categories of employees as the state statutes had with respect to other categories of employees. The categories of employees that were subject to exclusive federal jurisdiction no longer could bring tort actions against their employers in federal court. They were given instead the right to seek no-fault based compensation from their employers in actions they brought against their employers in a federal agency.

Benson was a broad-based attack on the constitutionality of the statutory transfer of jurisdiction from the federal courts to an agency. The majority opinion in *Benson* stated the applicable law until the

1980s, and it still provides the legal framework within which modern disputes are resolved.

Crowell v. Benson

285 U.S. 22 (1932).

■ MR. CHIEF JUSTICE HUGHES delivered the opinion of the Court.

This suit was brought in the District Court to enjoin the enforcement of an award made by petitioner Crowell, as Deputy Commissioner of the United States Employees' Compensation Commission, in favor of the petitioner Knudsen and against the respondent Benson. The award was made under the Longshoremen's and Harbor Workers' Compensation Act, and rested upon the finding of the deputy commissioner that Knudsen was injured while in the employ of Benson and performing service upon the navigable waters of the United States. . . . An amended complaint charged that the act was unconstitutional upon the grounds that it violated the due process clause of the Fifth Amendment, the provision of the Seventh Amendment as to trial by jury, that of the Fourth Amendment as to unreasonable search and seizure, and the provisions of Article III with respect to the judicial power of the United States.

* * *

The act has two limitations that are fundamental. It deals exclusively with compensation in respect of disability or death resulting "from an injury occurring upon the navigable waters of the United States" if recovery "through workmen's compensation proceedings may not validly be provided by State law," and it applies only when the relation of master and servant exists. "Injury," within the statute, "means accidental injury or death arising out of and in the course of employment," and the term "employer" means one "any of whose employees are employed in maritime employment, in whole or in part," upon such navigable waters.

* * *

The contention under the due process clause of the Fifth Amendment relates to the determination of questions of fact. Rulings of the deputy commissioner upon questions of law are without finality. So far as the latter are concerned, full opportunity is afforded for their determination by the Federal courts through proceedings to suspend or to set aside a compensation order, by the requirement that judgment is to be entered on a supplementary order declaring default only in case the order follows the law, and by the provision that the issue of injunction or other process in a proceeding by a beneficiary to compel obedience to a compensation order is dependent upon a determination by the court that the order was lawfully made and served. Moreover, the statute contains no express limitation attempting to preclude the court, in proceedings to set aside an order as not in accordance with law, from making its own examination and determination of facts whenever that is deemed to be necessary to enforce a constitutional right properly asserted. * * *

Apart from cases involving constitutional rights to be appropriately enforced by proceedings in court, there can be no doubt that the act contemplates that as to questions of fact, arising with respect to injuries to employees within the purview of the act, the findings of the deputy commissioner, supported by evidence and within the scope of his authority, shall be final. To hold otherwise would be to defeat the obvious purpose of the legislation to furnish a prompt, continuous, expert, and inexpensive method for dealing with a class of questions of fact which are peculiarly suited to examination and determination by an administrative agency specially assigned to that task.

* * *

As to determinations of fact, the distinction is at once apparent between cases of private right and those which arise between the government and persons subject to its authority in connection with the performance of the constitutional functions of the executive or legislative departments. The Court referred to this distinction in *Murray's Lessee v. Hoboken Land & Improvement Company*, 59 U.S. (18 How.) 272, 284 (1855), pointing out that "there are matters, involving public rights, which may be presented in such form that the judicial power is capable of acting on them, and which are susceptible of judicial determination, but which Congress may or may not bring within the cognizance of the courts of the United States, as it may deem proper." Thus the Congress, in exercising the powers confided to it, may establish 'legislative' courts (as distinguished from 'constitutional courts in which the judicial power conferred by the Constitution can be deposited') which are to form part of the government of territories or of the District of Columbia, or to serve as special tribunals "to examine and determine various matters, arising between the government and others, which from their nature do not require judicial determination and yet are susceptible of it." But "the mode of determining matters of this class is completely within congressional control. Congress may reserve to itself the power to decide, may delegate that power to executive officers, or may commit it to judicial tribunals." *Ex parte Bakelite Corp.*, 279 U.S. 438, 451 (1929). Familiar illustrations of administrative agencies created for the determination of such matters are found in connection with the exercise of the congressional power as to interstate and foreign commerce, taxation, immigration, the public lands, public health, the facilities of the post office, pensions, and payments to veterans.

The present case does not fall within the categories just described, but is one of private right, that is, of the liability of one individual to another under the law as defined. But, in cases of that sort, there is no requirement that, in order to maintain the essential attributes of the judicial power, all determinations of fact in constitutional courts shall be made by judges. On the common law side of the Federal courts, the aid of juries is not only deemed appropriate but is required by the Constitution itself. In cases of equity and admiralty, it is historic practice to call to the assistance of the courts, without the consent of the parties, masters, and commissioners or assessors, to pass upon certain classes of questions, as, for example, to take and state an account or to find the amount of damages. While the reports of masters and commissioners in such cases are essentially of an advisory nature, it has not been the practice to disturb their findings when they are properly based upon evidence, in the absence of errors of law, and the parties have no right to demand that the court shall redetermine the facts thus found.

* * *

In deciding whether the Congress, in enacting the statute under review, has exceeded the limits of its authority to prescribe procedure in cases of injury upon navigable waters, regard must be had, as in other cases where constitutional limits are invoked, not to mere matters of form, but to the substance of what is required. The statute has a limited application, being confined to the relation of master and servant, and the method of determining the questions of fact, which arise in the routine of making compensation awards to employees under the Act, is necessary to its effective enforcement. The Act itself, where it applies, establishes the measure of the employer's liability, thus leaving open for determination the questions of fact as to the circumstances, nature, extent, and consequences of the injuries sustained by the employee for which compensation is to be made in accordance with the prescribed standards. Findings of fact by the deputy commissioner upon such questions are closely analogous to the findings of the amount of damages that are made according to familiar practice by commissioners or assessors; and the reservation of full authority to the court to deal with matters of law provides for the appropriate exercise of the judicial function in this class of cases. For the purposes stated, we are unable to find any constitutional obstacle to the action of the Congress in availing itself of a method shown by experience to be essential in order to apply its standards to the thousands of cases involved, thus relieving the courts of a most serious burden while preserving their complete authority to insure the proper application of the law.

What has been said thus far relates to the determination of claims of employees within the purview of the Act. A different question is presented where the determinations of fact are fundamental or 'jurisdictional,' in the sense that their existence is a condition precedent to the operation of the statutory scheme. These fundamental requirements are that the injury occur upon the navigable waters of the United States, and that the relation of master and servant exists. These conditions are indispensable to the application of the statute, not only because the Congress has so provided explicitly, but also because the power of the Congress to enact the legislation turns upon the existence of these conditions.

* * * In the present instance, the Congress has imposed liability without fault only where the relation of master and servant exists in maritime employment, and, while we hold that the Congress could do this, the fact of that relation is the pivot of the statute, and, in the absence of any other justification, underlies the constitutionality of this enactment. If the person injured was not an employee of the person sought to be held, or if the injury did not occur upon the navigable waters of the United States, there is no ground for an assertion that the person against whom the proceeding was directed could constitutionally be subjected, in the absence of fault upon his part, to the liability which the statute creates.

In relation to these basic facts, the question is not the ordinary one as to the propriety of provision for administrative determinations. Nor have we simply the question of due process in relation to notice and hearing. It is rather a question of the appropriate maintenance of the Federal judicial power in requiring the observance of constitutional restrictions. It is the question whether the Congress may substitute for constitutional courts, in which the judicial power of the United States is vested, an administrative agency—in this instance a single deputy commissioner—for the final determination of the existence of the facts upon which the enforcement of the constitutional rights of the citizen depend. The recognition of the utility and convenience of administrative agencies for the investigation and finding of facts within their proper province, and the support of their authorized action, does not require the conclusion that there is no limitation of their use, and that the Congress could completely oust the courts of all determinations of fact by vesting the authority to make them with finality in its own instrumentalities or in the Executive Department. That would be to sap the judicial power as it exists under the Federal Constitution, and to establish a government of a bureaucratic character alien to our system, wherever fundamental rights depend, as not infrequently they do depend, upon the facts, and finality as to facts becomes in effect finality in law.

* * * [W]here administrative bodies have been appropriately created to meet the exigencies of certain classes of cases and their action is of a judicial character, the question of the conclusiveness of their administrative findings of fact generally arises where the facts are clearly not jurisdictional and the scope of review as to such facts has been determined by the applicable legislation. None of the decisions of this sort touch the question which is presented where the facts involved are jurisdictional or where the question concerns the proper exercise of the judicial power of the United States in enforcing constitutional limitations.

Even where the subject lies within the general authority of the Congress, the propriety of a challenge by judicial proceedings of the determinations of fact deemed to be jurisdictional, as underlying the authority of executive officers, has been recognized.

* * *

In the present instance, the argument that the Congress has constituted the deputy commissioner a fact-finding tribunal is unavailing, as the contention makes the untenable assumption that the constitutional courts may be deprived in all cases of the determination of facts upon evidence even though a constitutional right may be involved.

* * *

As the question is one of the constitutional authority of the deputy commissioner as an administrative agency, the court is under no obligation to give weight to his proceedings pending the determination of that question. If the court finds that the facts existed which gave the deputy commissioner jurisdiction to pass upon the claim for compensation, the injunction will be denied in so far as these fundamental questions are concerned; if, on the contrary, the court is satisfied that the deputy commissioner had no jurisdiction of the proceedings before him, that determination will deprive them of their effectiveness for any purpose. We think that the essential independence of the exercise of the judicial power of the United States, in the enforcement of constitutional rights requires that the federal court should determine such an issue upon its own record and the facts elicited before it.

NOTES AND QUESTIONS

1. The Court in *Crowell v. Benson* emphasizes that the agency's jurisdiction is narrow and that the class of cases Congress transferred from courts to the agency is limited. How important is that factor to the court's decision? Should the breadth of a delegation's scope be important?

2. The *Benson* Court distinguishes between public rights disputes and private rights disputes. Although the Court downplays its significance for resolving the case at bar, the public/private rights distinction remains an important component of Article III jurisprudence today. Some adjudicatory disputes are easy to characterize. Thus, for instance, workers compensation cases are private rights cases because they have a clear common law antecedent and they pit private parties against each other; social security disability cases, by contrast, are public rights cases because they involve only the applicant and the government, and they have no common law antecedent. Other classes of adjudications, however, are more difficult to characterize. During the nineteenth century, courts resolved economic regulatory disputes. In the early twentieth century, state and federal legislatures reallocated all such disputes to newly created agencies, usually with no change in applicable substantive standards. *See* Edward A. Adler, *Business Jurisprudence*, 28 HARV. L. REV. 135 (1914). Do cases involving government regulation of economic activity—*e.g.*, setting the rates that common carriers or utilities can charge their customers—concern private rights or public rights?

3. The Court in *Benson* seems to place great emphasis on the jurisdictional and constitutional fact doctrines. The doctrine of jurisdictional fact holds that the presence or absence of a fact on which an agency's statutory authority depends must be decided independently by an Article III court, including allowing the court to consider different or additional evidence from that considered by the agency. Similarly, the constitutional fact doctrine requires de novo review by an Article III court of factual findings that dictate constitutionality. Accordingly, as the *Benson* Court notes, courts did not defer to any extent to an agency's finding with respect to any fact that had constitutional or jurisdictional implications, but rather engaged de novo review, including a whole new evidentiary hearing. The Court has never explicitly overruled the old cases in which it announced and applied these doctrines, but they have long been moribund. As we discuss in greater detail in Chapter 4, with the narrow exception of facts that are relevant to First Amendment disputes, modern courts apply extremely deferential tests to agency findings of fact, including those that have jurisdictional or constitutional implications. *See* Henry P. Monaghan, *Constitutional Fact Review*, 85 COLUM. L. REV. 229 (1985). Why do you think the Court eventually abandoned the constitutional and jurisdictional fact doctrines? Given the demise of those doctrines, can you think of a basis on which *Benson* remains a reliable precedent?

————————

The Court said nothing new or important about the constitutionality of Congressional delegations of adjudicatory power to agencies between 1932 and 1982. The Court then decided a case that created grave doubt about the continuing viability of the reasoning and holding in *Benson*. The case involved congressional reallocation of bankruptcy cases from Article III courts to a newly created class of Article I courts, rather than a delegation of adjudicatory power to an agency. Nevertheless, is there an obvious reason why the law should distinguish between an agency and an Article I court?

Northern Pipeline Const. Co. v. Marathon Pipe Line Co.

458 U.S. 50 (1982).

■ JUSTICE BRENNAN announced the judgment of the Court and delivered an opinion in which JUSTICE MARSHALL, JUSTICE BLACKMUN, and JUSTICE STEVENS joined.

The question presented is whether the assignment by Congress to bankruptcy judges of the jurisdiction granted by § 241(a) of the Bankruptcy Act of 1978 violates Art. III of the Constitution.

* * *

In 1978, after almost 10 years of study and investigation, Congress enacted a comprehensive revision of the bankruptcy laws. The Bankruptcy Act of 1978 (Act) made significant changes in both the substantive and procedural law of bankruptcy. It is the changes in the latter that are at issue in this case.

Before the Act, federal district courts served as bankruptcy courts and employed a "referee" system. Bankruptcy proceedings were generally conducted before referees, except in those instances in which the district court elected to withdraw a case from a referee. The referee's final order was appealable to the district court. The bankruptcy courts were vested with "summary jurisdiction"—that is, with jurisdiction over controversies involving property in the actual or constructive possession of the court. And, with consent, the bankruptcy court also had jurisdiction over some "plenary" matters—such as disputes involving property in the possession of a third person.

The Act eliminates the referee system and establishes "in each judicial district, as an adjunct to the district court for such district, a bankruptcy court which shall be a court of record known as the United States Bankruptcy Court for the district." 28 U.S.C. § 151(a) (1976 ed., Supp. IV). The judges of these courts are appointed to office for 14-year terms by the President, with the advice and consent of the Senate. They are subject to removal by the "judicial council of the circuit" on account of "incompetency, misconduct, neglect of duty or physical or mental disability." § 153(b). In addition, the salaries of the bankruptcy judges are set by statute and are subject to adjustment under the Federal Salary Act.

The jurisdiction of the bankruptcy courts created by the Act is much broader than that exercised under the former referee system. Eliminating the distinction between "summary" and "plenary" jurisdiction, the Act grants the new courts jurisdiction over all "civil proceedings arising under title 11 [the Bankruptcy title] or arising in or *related to* cases under title 11." 28 U.S.C. § 1471(b) (1976 ed., Supp. IV) (emphasis added). This jurisdictional grant empowers bankruptcy courts to entertain a wide variety of cases involving claims that may affect the property of the estate once a petition has been filed under Title 11. Included within the bankruptcy courts' jurisdiction are suits to recover accounts, controversies involving exempt property, actions to avoid transfers and payments as preferences or fraudulent conveyances, and causes of action owned by the debtor at the time of the petition for bankruptcy. The bankruptcy courts can hear claims based on state law as well as those based on federal law.

The judges of the bankruptcy courts are vested with all of the "powers of a court of equity, law, and admiralty," except that they "may not enjoin another court or punish a criminal contempt not committed in the presence of the judge of the court or warranting a punishment of imprisonment." 28 U.S.C. § 1481 (1976 ed., Supp.IV). In addition to this broad grant of power, Congress has allowed bankruptcy judges the power to hold jury trials, to issue declaratory judgments, to issue writs of habeas corpus under certain circumstances, to issue all writs necessary in aid of the bankruptcy court's expanded jurisdiction, and to issue any order, process or judgment that is necessary or appropriate to carry out the provisions of Title 11.

* * *

Basic to the constitutional structure established by the Framers was their recognition that "[t]he accumulation of all powers, legislative, executive, and judiciary, in the same hands, whether of one, a few, or many, and whether hereditary, self-appointed, or elective, may justly be pronounced the very definition of tyranny." THE FEDERALIST NO. 47, 300 (James Madison). To ensure against such tyranny, the Framers provided that the Federal Government would consist of three distinct Branches, each to exercise one of the governmental powers recognized by the Framers as inherently distinct. "The Framers regarded the checks and balances that they had built into the tripartite Federal Government as a self-executing safeguard against the encroachment or aggrandizement of one branch at the expense of the other." *Buckley v. Valeo*, 424 U.S. 1, 122 (1976).

The Federal Judiciary was therefore designed by the Framers to stand independent of the Executive and Legislature—to maintain the checks and balances of the constitutional structure, and also to guarantee that the process of adjudication itself remained impartial.

* * *

As an inseparable element of the constitutional system of checks and balances, and as a guarantee of judicial impartiality, Art. III both defines the power and protects the independence of the Judicial Branch.

It provides that "The judicial Power of the United States, shall be vested in one supreme Court, and in such inferior Courts as the Congress may from time to time ordain and establish." U.S. CONST. art. III, § 1. The inexorable command of this provision is clear and definite. The judicial power of the United States must be exercised by courts having the attributes prescribed in Art. III. Those attributes are also clearly set forth:

> "The Judges, both of the supreme and inferior Courts, shall hold their Offices during good Behaviour, and shall, at stated Times, receive for their Services, a Compensation, which shall not be diminished during their Continuance in Office." *Id.*

* * *

In sum, our Constitution unambiguously enunciates a fundamental principle—that the "judicial Power of the United States" must be reposed in an independent Judiciary. It commands that the independence of the Judiciary be jealously guarded, and it provides clear institutional protections for that independence.

B

It is undisputed that the bankruptcy judges whose offices were created by the Bankruptcy Act of 1978 do not enjoy the protections constitutionally afforded to Art. III judges. The bankruptcy judges do not serve for life subject to their continued "good Behaviour." Rather, they are appointed for 14-year terms, and can be removed by the judicial council of the circuit in which they serve on grounds of "incompetency, misconduct, neglect of duty, or physical or mental disability." Second, the salaries of the bankruptcy judges are not immune from diminution by Congress. In short, there is no doubt that the bankruptcy judges created by the Act are not Art. III judges.

[We have omitted here a long discussion of cases involving the constitutionality of territorial courts and military courts. Ed.]

* * *

Finally, appellants rely on a third group of cases, in which this Court has upheld the constitutionality of legislative courts and administrative agencies created by Congress to adjudicate cases involving "public rights."[18] The "public rights" doctrine was first set forth in *Murray's Lessee v. Hoboken Land & Improvement Co.*, 59 U.S. (18 How.) 272 (1855):

> "[W]e do not consider congress can either withdraw from judicial cognizance any matter which, from its nature, is the subject of a suit at the common law, or in equity, or admiralty; nor, on the other hand, can it bring under the judicial power a matter which, from its nature, is not a subject for judicial determination. At the same time there are matters, *involving public rights*, which may be presented in such form that the judicial power is capable of acting on them, and which are

---

[18] Congress' power to create legislative courts to adjudicate public rights carries with it the lesser power to create administrative agencies for the same purpose, and to provide for review of those agency decisions in Art. III courts. *See, e.g., Atlas Roofing Co. v. Occupational Safety & Health Review Comm'n*, 430 U.S. 442, 452 (1977).

susceptible of judicial determination, but which congress may or may not bring within the cognizance of the courts of the United States, as it may deem proper." *Id.* at 284 (emphasis added).

This doctrine may be explained in part by reference to the traditional principle of sovereign immunity, which recognizes that the Government may attach conditions to its consent to be sued. But the public-rights doctrine also draws upon the principle of separation of powers, and a historical understanding that certain prerogatives were reserved to the political Branches of Government. The doctrine extends only to matters arising "between the Government and persons subject to its authority in connection with the performance of the constitutional functions of the executive or legislative departments," *Crowell v. Benson*, 285 U.S. 22, 50 (1932), and only to matters that historically could have been determined exclusively by those departments. The understanding of these cases is that the Framers expected that Congress would be free to commit such matters completely to nonjudicial executive determination, and that as a result there can be no constitutional objection to Congress' employing the less drastic expedient of committing their determination to a legislative court or an administrative agency. *Benson*, 285 U.S. at 50.

* * *

The distinction between public rights and private rights has not been definitively explained in our precedents. Nor is it necessary to do so in the present cases, for it suffices to observe that a matter of public rights must at a minimum arise "between the government and others." *Ex parte Bakelite Corp.*, 279 U.S. 438, 451 (1929). In contrast, "the liability of one individual to another under the law as defined," *Crowell*, 285 U.S. at 51, is a matter of private rights. Our precedents clearly establish that *only* controversies in the former category may be removed from Art. III courts and delegated to legislative courts or administrative agencies for their determination. *See Crowell v. Benson*, 285 U.S. at 50–51. Private-rights disputes, on the other hand, lie at the core of the historically recognized judicial power.

* * *

[T]he substantive legal rights at issue in the present action cannot be deemed "public rights." Appellants argue that a discharge in bankruptcy is indeed a "public right," similar to such congressionally created benefits as "radio station licenses, pilot licenses, or certificates for common carriers" granted by administrative agencies. But the restructuring of debtor-creditor relations, which is at the core of the federal bankruptcy power, must be distinguished from the adjudication of state-created private rights, such as the right to recover contract damages that is at issue in this case. The former may well be a "public right," but the latter obviously is not.

* * *

Crowell involved the adjudication of congressionally created rights. But this Court has sustained the use of adjunct factfinders even in the adjudication of constitutional rights—so long as those adjuncts were subject to sufficient control by an Art. III district court. In *United States v. Raddatz*, 447 U.S. 667 (1980), the Court upheld the 1978 Federal Magistrates Act, which permitted district court judges to refer certain pretrial motions, including suppression motions based on alleged violations of constitutional rights, to a magistrate for initial determination. The Court observed that the magistrate's proposed findings and recommendations were subject to *de novo* review by the district court, which was free to rehear the evidence or to call for additional evidence. Moreover, it was noted that the magistrate considered motions only upon reference from the district court, and that the magistrates were appointed, and subject to removal, by the district court. In short, the ultimate decisionmaking authority respecting all pretrial motions clearly remained with the district court. Under these circumstances, the Court held that the Act did not violate the constraints of Art. III.

* * *

We hold that the Bankruptcy Act of 1978 carries the possibility of * * * an unwarranted encroachment [on the jurisdiction of Article III courts]. Many of the rights subject to adjudication by the Act's bankruptcy courts, like the rights implicated in *Raddatz*, are not of Congress' creation. Indeed, the cases before us, which center upon appellant Northern's claim for damages for breach of contract and misrepresentation, involve a right created by *state* law, a right independent of and antecedent to the reorganization petition that conferred jurisdiction upon the Bankruptcy Court. Accordingly, Congress' authority to control the manner in which that right is adjudicated, through assignment of historically judicial functions to a non-Art. III "adjunct," plainly must be deemed at a minimum. Yet it is equally plain that Congress has vested the "adjunct" bankruptcy judges with powers over Northern's state-created right that far exceed the powers that it has vested in administrative agencies that adjudicate only rights of Congress' own creation.

Unlike the administrative scheme that we reviewed in *Crowell*, the Act vests all "essential attributes" of the judicial power of the United States in the "adjunct" bankruptcy court. First, the agency in *Crowell* made only specialized, narrowly confined factual determinations regarding a particularized area of law. In contrast, the subject-matter jurisdiction of the bankruptcy courts encompasses not only traditional matters of bankruptcy, but also "all civil proceedings arising under title 11 or arising in or *related to* cases under title 11." 28 U.S.C. § 1471(b) (emphasis added). Second, while the agency in *Crowell* engaged in statutorily channeled factfinding functions, the bankruptcy courts exercise "*all* of the jurisdiction" conferred by the Act on the district courts. § 1471(c) (emphasis added). Third, the agency in *Crowell* possessed only a limited power to issue compensation orders pursuant to specialized procedures, and its orders could be enforced only by order of the district court. By contrast, the bankruptcy courts exercise all ordinary powers of district courts, including the power to preside over jury trials, the power to issue declaratory judgments, the power to issue writs of habeas corpus, and the power to issue any order, process, or judgment appropriate for the enforcement of the provisions of Title 11, Fourth, while orders issued by the agency in *Crowell* were to be set aside if "not supported by the evidence," the judgments of the bankruptcy courts are apparently subject to review only under the more deferential "clearly erroneous" standard. Finally, the agency in *Crowell* was required by law to seek enforcement of its compensation orders in the district court. In contrast, the bankruptcy courts issue final judgments, which are binding and enforceable even in the absence of an appeal. In short, the "adjunct" bankruptcy courts created by the Act exercise jurisdiction behind the facade of a grant to the district courts, and are exercising powers far greater than those lodged in the adjuncts approved in either *Crowell* or *Raddatz*.

■ JUSTICE REHNQUIST, with whom JUSTICE O'CONNOR joins, concurring in the judgment.

Were I to agree with the plurality that the question presented by these cases is "whether the assignment by Congress to bankruptcy judges of the jurisdiction granted by § 241(a) of the Bankruptcy Act of 1978 violates Art. III of the Constitution," I would with considerable reluctance embark on the duty of deciding this broad question. But appellee Marathon Pipe Line Co. has not been subjected to the full range of authority granted bankruptcy courts by § 1471.

* * *

From the record before us, the lawsuit in which Marathon was named defendant seeks damages for breach of contract, misrepresentation, and other counts which are the stuff of the traditional actions at common law tried by the courts at Westminster in 1789. There is apparently no federal rule of decision provided for any of the issues in the lawsuit; the claims of Northern arise entirely under state law. No method of adjudication is hinted, other than the traditional common-law mode of judge and jury. The lawsuit is before the Bankruptcy Court only because the plaintiff has previously filed a petition for reorganization in that court.

The cases dealing with the authority of Congress to create courts other than by use of its power under Art. III do not admit of easy synthesis.

* * *

I would, therefore, hold so much of the Bankruptcy Act of 1978 as enables a Bankruptcy Court to entertain and decide Northern's lawsuit over Marathon's objection to be violative of Art. III of the United States Constitution. Because I agree with the plurality that this grant of authority is not readily severable from the remaining grant of authority to bankruptcy courts under § 1471, I concur in the judgment.

■ CHIEF JUSTICE BURGER, dissenting.

I join Justice WHITE's dissenting opinion, but I write separately to emphasize that, notwithstanding the plurality opinion, the Court does *not* hold today that Congress' broad grant of jurisdiction to the new bankruptcy courts is generally inconsistent with Art. III of the Constitution. Rather, the Court's holding is limited to the proposition stated by Justice REHNQUIST in his concurrence in the judgment— that a "traditional" state common-law action, not made subject to a federal rule of decision, and related only peripherally to an adjudication of bankruptcy under federal law, must, absent the consent of the litigants, be heard by an "Art. III court" if it is to be heard by any court or agency of the United States. This limited holding, of course, does not suggest that there is something inherently unconstitutional about the new bankruptcy courts; nor does it preclude such courts from adjudicating all but a relatively narrow category of claims "arising under" or "arising in or related to cases under" the Bankruptcy Act.

■ JUSTICE WHITE, with whom THE CHIEF JUSTICE and JUSTICE POWELL join, dissenting.

Article III, § 1, of the Constitution is straightforward and uncomplicated on its face:

> "The judicial Power of the United States, shall be vested in one supreme Court, and in such inferior Courts as the Congress may from time to time ordain and establish. The Judges, both of the supreme and inferior Courts, shall hold their Offices during good Behaviour, and shall at stated Times, receive for their Services, a Compensation, which shall not be diminished during their Continuance in Office."

Any reader could easily take this provision to mean that although Congress was free to establish such lower courts as it saw fit, any court that it did establish would be an "inferior" court exercising "judicial Power of the United States" and so must be manned by judges possessing both life tenure and a guaranteed minimal income. This would be an eminently sensible reading and one that, as the plurality shows, is well founded in both the documentary sources and the political doctrine of separation of powers that stands behind much of our constitutional structure.

If this simple reading were correct and we were free to disregard 150 years of history, these would be easy cases and the plurality opinion could end with its observation that "[i]t is undisputed that the bankruptcy judges whose offices were created by the Bankruptcy Act of 1978 do not enjoy the protections constitutionally afforded to Art. III judges." The fact that the plurality must go on to deal with what has been characterized as one of the most confusing and controversial areas of constitutional law itself indicates the gross oversimplification implicit in the plurality's claim that "our Constitution unambiguously enunciates a fundamental principle-that the 'judicial Power of the United States' must be reposed in an independent Judiciary [and] provides clear institutional protections for that independence." While this is fine rhetoric, analytically it serves only to put a distracting and superficial gloss on a difficult question.

That question is what limits Art. III places on Congress' ability to create adjudicative institutions designed to carry out federal policy established pursuant to the substantive authority given Congress elsewhere in the Constitution. Whether fortunate or unfortunate, at this point in the history of constitutional law that question can no longer be answered by looking only to the constitutional text. This Court's cases construing that text must also be considered. In its attempt to pigeonhole these cases, the plurality does violence to their meaning and creates an artificial structure that itself lacks coherence.

* * *

The distinction between public and private rights as the principle delineating the proper domains of legislative and constitutional courts respectively received its death blow, I had believed, in *Crowell v. Benson*, 285 U.S. 22 (1932).

NOTES AND QUESTIONS

1.   There are several plausible ways of distinguishing *Crowell v. Benson* and *Northern Pipeline*. For example, bankruptcy courts have broad jurisdiction over a large class of disputes, while the agency in *Benson* has narrow jurisdiction over a small class of disputes. Bankruptcy judges also have a range of ancillary powers that is similar to the powers of Article III judges, while agency decisionmakers lack many of those powers. Do you find either of these distinctions between bankruptcy courts and agencies persuasive in explaining the outcomes of *Benson* and *Northern Pipeline*?

2.   The *Northern Pipeline* plurality refers to other potential bases for distinguishing between bankruptcy courts and administrative agencies. At least some of these bases are implausible because they do not exist. For example, the plurality stated that the Bankruptcy Act instructed reviewing courts to accord greater deference to the factual findings of bankruptcy courts than to those of administrative agencies. In fact, agency decisionmakers receive roughly the same deference from reviewing courts as bankruptcy judges did in the legal regime the Court struck down. The plurality also emphasized that the Bankruptcy Act of 1978 granted bankruptcy court judges fewer job protections than those enjoyed by Article III judges—*e.g.,* 14-year terms instead of life tenure. Yet, agency decisionmakers, particularly those without fixed terms of office, tend to have even less job security than bankruptcy judges. Why do you suppose the plurality referred to these theoretical but practically non-existent bases for distinguishing between bankruptcy courts and administrative agencies?

3.   The Court in *Northern Pipeline* cites *Crowell v. Benson* for the proposition that "only controversies in the [public rights] category may be removed from Art. III courts and delegated to legislative courts or administrative agencies for their determination," while "[p]rivate-rights disputes, on the other hand, lie at the core of the historically recognized judicial power" and thus must be adjudicated by Art. III courts. Consider again what the *Benson* court had to say about the public/private rights distinction as a limit on Congress's ability to delegate evidentiary factfinding to administrative agencies. Do you read *Benson* as supporting the proposition the Court in *Northern Pipeline* attributes to it? Why or why not?

————————

The outcome of *Northern Pipeline* encouraged parties to challenge the constitutionality of several agency adjudicatory regimes. The Court rejected the only two challenges that reached it, in *Thomas v. Union Carbide Agricultural Products Co.*, 473 U.S. 568 (1985), and *Commodity Futures Trading Commission v. Schor*, 478 U.S. 833 (1986). In *Union Carbide*, the Court unanimously upheld a provision of the Federal Insecticide, Fungicide & Rodenticide Act (FIFRA) that authorized applicants for approval of pesticides that were similar to pesticides that had been previously approved at the behest of another applicant to use some of the data submitted by that earlier applicant. This authorization was subject to a constitutionally imposed duty to compensate the earlier applicant for the use of its property. The statute instructed the EPA to subject all disputes with respect to the proper compensation to binding arbitration. The Court upheld that feature of the compensation system over an Article III challenge.

The six-Justice majority rejected the public/private rights dichotomy: "In essence, the public rights doctrine reflects simply the pragmatic understanding that when Congress selects a quasi-judicial method of resolving matters that could be conclusively determined by the Executive and Legislative Branches, the danger of encroaching on judicial powers is reduced." How persuasive is this reasoning? Does it leave any class of adjudications that Congress could not assign to an agency?

Three concurring Justices applied the public/private rights distinction but concluded that the FIFRA disputes concerned public rights: "Although a compensation dispute under FIFRA involves a determination of the duty owed one party by another, at its heart the dispute involves the exercise of authority by a Federal Government arbitrator in the course of administration of FIFRA's comprehensive regulatory scheme." How persuasive is this reasoning? Does it leave any class of adjudications that Congress could not assign to an agency?

In one important sense, *Union Carbide* goes further than any Article III case, since the binding agency arbitration regime the Court upheld left virtually no role for reviewing courts: an arbitrator's decision under FIFRA can be overturned only for fraud, misconduct, or misrepresentation. A year after it decided *Union Carbide*, the Court divided in resolving another Article III dispute.

Commodity Futures Trading Commission v. Schor
478 U.S. 833 (1986).

■ JUSTICE O'CONNOR delivered the opinion of the Court.

The question presented is whether the Commodity Exchange Act (CEA or Act), 7 U.S.C. § 1 *et seq.*, empowers the Commodity Futures Trading Commission (CFTC or Commission) to entertain state law counterclaims in reparation proceedings and, if so, whether that grant of authority violates Article III of the Constitution.

I

The CEA broadly prohibits fraudulent and manipulative conduct in connection with commodity futures transactions. In 1974, Congress "overhaul[ed]" the Act in order to institute a more "comprehensive regulatory structure to oversee the volatile and esoteric futures trading complex." H.R.Rep. No. 93–975, p. 1 (1974). * * *

Among the duties assigned to the CFTC was the administration of a reparations procedure through which disgruntled customers of professional commodity brokers could seek redress for the brokers' violations of the Act or CFTC regulations. * * *

In conformance with the congressional goal of promoting efficient dispute resolution, the CFTC promulgated a regulation in 1976 which allows it to adjudicate counterclaims "aris[ing] out of the transaction or occurrence or series of transactions or occurrences set forth in the complaint." 41 Fed. Reg. 3994, 3995, 4002 (1976) (codified at 17 CFR § 12.23(b)(2) (1983)). This permissive counterclaim rule leaves the respondent in a reparations proceeding free to seek relief against the reparations complainant in other fora.

The instant dispute arose in February 1980, when respondents Schor and Mortgage Services of America, Inc., invoked the CFTC's reparations jurisdiction by filing complaints against petitioner ContiCommodity Services, Inc. (Conti), a commodity futures broker, and Richard L. Sandor, a Conti employee. Schor had an account with Conti which contained a debit balance because Schor's net futures trading losses and expenses, such as commissions, exceeded the funds deposited in the account. Schor alleged that this debit balance was the result of Conti's numerous violations of the CEA.

Before receiving notice that Schor had commenced the reparations proceeding, Conti had filed a diversity action in Federal District Court to recover the debit balance. * * *

Although the District Court declined to stay or dismiss the suit, Conti voluntarily dismissed the federal court action and presented its debit balance claim by way of a counterclaim in the CFTC reparations proceeding. Conti denied violating the CEA and instead insisted that the debit balance resulted from Schor's trading, and was therefore a simple debt owed by Schor.

After discovery, briefing, and a hearing, the Administrative Law Judge (ALJ) in Schor's reparations proceeding ruled in Conti's favor on both Schor's claims and Conti's counterclaims. After this ruling, Schor for the first time challenged the CFTC's statutory authority to adjudicate Conti's counterclaim. The ALJ rejected Schor's challenge, stating himself "bound by agency regulations and published agency policies." The Commission declined to review the decision and allowed it to become final, at which point Schor filed a petition for review with the Court of Appeals for the District of Columbia Circuit. Prior to oral argument, the Court of Appeals, *sua sponte,* raised the question whether CFTC could constitutionally adjudicate Conti's counterclaims in light of *Northern Pipeline Construction Co. v. Marathon Pipe Line Co.,* 458 U.S. 50 (1982), in which this Court held that "Congress may not vest in a non-Article III court the power to adjudicate, render final judgment, and issue binding orders in a traditional contract action arising under state law, without consent of the litigants, and subject only to ordinary appellate review." *Thomas v. Union Carbide Agric. Prods. Co.,* 473 U.S. 568, 584 (1985).

After briefing and argument, the Court of Appeals upheld the CFTC's decision on Schor's claim in most respects, but ordered the dismissal of Conti's counterclaims on the ground that "the CFTC lacks authority (subject matter competence) to adjudicate" common law counterclaims.

* * *

II

* * *

Congress' assumption that the CFTC would have the authority to adjudicate counterclaims is evident on the face of the statute.

* * *

Moreover, quite apart from congressional statements of intent, the broad grant of power in § 12a(5) clearly authorizes the promulgation of regulations providing for adjudication of common law counterclaims arising out of the same transaction as a reparations complaint because such jurisdiction is necessary, if not critical, to accomplish the purposes behind the reparations program.

Reference to the instant controversy illustrates the crippling effect that the Court of Appeals' restrictive reading of the CFTC's counterclaim jurisdiction would have on the efficacy of the reparations remedy. The dispute between Schor and Conti is typical of the disputes adjudicated in reparations proceedings: a customer and a professional commodities broker agree that there is a debit balance in the customer's account, but the customer attributes the deficit to the broker's alleged CEA violations and the broker attributes it to the customer's lack of success in the market. The customer brings a reparations claim; the broker counterclaims for the amount of the debit balance. In the usual case, then, the counterclaim "arises out of precisely the same course of events" as the principal claim and requires resolution of many of the same disputed factual issues.

Under the Court of Appeals' approach, the entire dispute may not be resolved in the administrative forum. Consequently, the entire dispute will typically end up in court, for when the broker files suit to recover the debit balance, the customer will normally be compelled either by compulsory counterclaim rules or by the expense and inconvenience of litigating the same issues in two fora to forgo his reparations remedy and to litigate his claim in court. * * *

As our discussion makes manifest, the CFTC's long-held position that it has the power to take jurisdiction over counterclaims such as Conti's is eminently reasonable and well within the scope of its delegated authority.

* * *

III

Article III, § 1, directs that the "judicial Power of the United States shall be vested in one supreme Court and in such inferior Courts as the Congress may from time to time ordain and establish," and provides that these federal courts shall be staffed by judges who hold office during good behavior, and whose compensation shall not be diminished during tenure in office. Schor claims that these provisions prohibit Congress from authorizing the initial adjudication of common law counterclaims by the CFTC, an administrative agency whose adjudicatory officers do not enjoy the tenure and salary protections embodied in Article III.

Although our precedents in this area do not admit of easy synthesis, they do establish that the resolution of claims such as Schor's cannot turn on conclusory reference to the language of Article III. Rather, the constitutionality of a given congressional delegation of adjudicative functions to a non-Article III body must be assessed by reference to the purposes underlying the requirements of Article III. This inquiry, in turn, is guided by the principle that "practical attention to substance rather than doctrinaire reliance on formal categories should inform application of Article III." *Thomas*, 473 U.S. at 587; *see also Crowell v. Benson*, 285 U.S. 22, 53 (1932).

A

Article III, § 1, serves both to protect "the role of the independent judiciary within the constitutional scheme of tripartite government," *Thomas*, 473 U.S. at 583, and to safeguard litigants' "right to have claims decided before judges who are free from potential domination by other branches of government." *United States v. Will*, 449 U.S. 200, 218 (1980). * * *

Our precedents also demonstrate, however, that Article III does not confer on litigants an absolute right to the plenary consideration of every nature of claim by an Article III court. Moreover, as a personal right, Article III's guarantee of an impartial and independent federal adjudication is subject to waiver, just as are other personal constitutional rights that dictate the procedures by which civil and criminal matters must be tried. * * *

In the instant cases, Schor indisputably waived any right he may have possessed to the full trial of Conti's counterclaim before an Article III court. Schor expressly demanded that Conti proceed on its counterclaim in the reparations proceeding rather than before the District Court and was content to have the entire dispute settled in the forum he had selected until the ALJ ruled against him on all counts; it was only after the ALJ rendered a decision to which he objected that Schor raised any challenge to the CFTC's consideration of Conti's counterclaim.

* * *

B

As noted above, our precedents establish that Article III, § 1, not only preserves to litigants their interest in an impartial and independent federal adjudication of claims within the judicial power of the United States, but also serves as "an inseparable element of the constitutional system of checks and balances." Article III, § 1, safeguards the role of the Judicial Branch in our tripartite system by barring congressional attempts "to transfer jurisdiction [to non-Article III tribunals] for the purpose of emasculating" constitutional courts, *Nat'l Ins. Co. v. Tidewater Co.*, 337 U.S. 582, 644 (1949), and thereby preventing "the encroachment or aggrandizement of one branch at the expense of the other." *Buckley v. Valeo*, 424 U.S. 1, 122 (1976) (*per curiam*). To the extent that this structural principle is implicated in a given case, the parties cannot by consent cure the constitutional difficulty for the same reason that the parties by consent cannot confer on federal courts subject-matter jurisdiction beyond the limitations imposed by Article III, § 2. When these Article III limitations are at issue, notions of consent and waiver cannot be dispositive because the limitations serve institutional interests that the parties cannot be expected to protect.

In determining the extent to which a given congressional decision to authorize the adjudication of Article III business in a non-Article III tribunal impermissibly threatens the institutional integrity of the Judicial Branch, the Court has declined to adopt formalistic and unbending rules. Although such rules might lend a greater degree of coherence to this area of the law, they might also unduly constrict Congress' ability to take needed and innovative action pursuant to its Article I powers. Thus, in reviewing Article III challenges, we have weighed a number of factors, none of which has been deemed determinative, with an eye to the practical effect that the congressional action will have on the constitutionally assigned role of the federal judiciary. Among the factors upon which we have focused are the extent to which the "essential attributes of judicial power" are reserved to Article III courts, and, conversely, the extent to which the non-Article III forum exercises the range of jurisdiction and powers normally vested only in Article III courts, the origins and importance of the right to be adjudicated, and the concerns that drove Congress to depart from the requirements of Article III. *See, e.g., Thomas,* 473 U.S. at 587, 588–89; *Northern Pipeline,* 458 U.S. at 84–86.

An examination of the relative allocation of powers between the CFTC and Article III courts in light of the considerations given prominence in our precedents demonstrates that the congressional scheme does not impermissibly intrude on the province of the judiciary. The CFTC's adjudicatory powers depart from the traditional agency model in just one respect: the CFTC's jurisdiction over common law counterclaims. While wholesale importation of concepts of pendent or ancillary jurisdiction into the agency context may create greater constitutional difficulties, we decline to endorse an absolute prohibition on such jurisdiction out of fear of where some hypothetical "slippery slope" may deposit us.

* * *

The CFTC, like the agency in *Crowell,* deals only with a "particularized area of law," whereas the jurisdiction of the bankruptcy courts found unconstitutional in *Northern Pipeline* extended to broadly "all civil proceedings arising under title 11 or arising in or *related to* cases under title 11." *Northern Pipeline,* 458 U.S. at 85 (quoting 28 U.S.C. § 1471(b)) (emphasis added). CFTC orders, like those of the agency in *Crowell,* but unlike those of the bankruptcy courts under the 1978 Act, are enforceable only by order of the district court. CFTC orders are also reviewed under the same "weight of the evidence" standard sustained in *Crowell,* rather than the more deferential standard found lacking in *Northern Pipeline.* The legal rulings of the CFTC, like the legal determinations of the agency in *Crowell,* are subject to *de novo* review. Finally, the CFTC, unlike the bankruptcy courts under the 1978 Act, does not exercise "all ordinary powers of district courts," and thus may not, for instance, preside over jury trials or issue writs of habeas corpus. *Northern Pipeline,* 458 U.S. at 85.

Of course, the nature of the claim has significance in our Article III analysis quite apart from the method prescribed for its adjudication. The counterclaim asserted in this litigation is a "private" right for which state law provides the rule of decision. It is therefore a claim of the kind assumed to be at the "core" of matters normally reserved to Article III courts. Yet this conclusion does not end our inquiry; just as this Court has rejected any attempt to make determinative for Article III purposes the distinction between public rights and private rights, there is no reason inherent in separation of powers principles to accord the state law character of a claim talismanic power in Article III inquiries.

We have explained that "the public rights doctrine reflects simply a pragmatic understanding that when Congress selects a quasi-judicial method of resolving matters that 'could be conclusively determined by the Executive and Legislative Branches,' the danger of encroaching on the judicial powers" is less than when private rights, which are normally within the purview of the judiciary, are relegated as an initial matter to administrative adjudication. *Thomas*, 473 U.S. at 589 (quoting *Northern Pipeline*, 458 U.S. at 68).

* * *

In so doing, we have also been faithful to our Article III precedents, which counsel that bright-line rules cannot effectively be employed to yield broad principles applicable in all Article III inquiries. Rather, due regard must be given in each case to the unique aspects of the congressional plan at issue and its practical consequences in light of the larger concerns that underlie Article III. We conclude that the limited jurisdiction that the CFTC asserts over state law claims as a necessary incident to the adjudication of federal claims willingly submitted by the parties for initial agency adjudication does not contravene separation of powers principles or Article III.

■ JUSTICE BRENNAN, with whom JUSTICE MARSHALL joins, dissenting.

On its face, Article III, § 1, seems to prohibit the vesting of *any* judicial functions in either the Legislative or the Executive Branch. The Court has, however, recognized three narrow exceptions to the otherwise absolute mandate of Article III: territorial courts, courts-martial, and courts that adjudicate certain disputes concerning public rights. Unlike the Court, I would limit the judicial authority of non-Article III federal tribunals to these few, long-established exceptions and would countenance no further erosion of Article III's mandate.

I

The Framers knew that "[t]he accumulation of all powers, Legislative, Executive, and Judiciary, in the same hands, whether of one, a few, or many, and whether hereditary, self-appointed, or elective, may justly be pronounced the very definition of tyranny." THE FEDERALIST NO. 46, at 334 (James Madison). * * *

The Framers also understood that a principal benefit of the separation of the judicial power from the legislative and executive powers would be the protection of individual litigants from decisionmakers susceptible to majoritarian pressures. Article III's salary and tenure provisions promote impartial adjudication by placing the judicial power of the United States "in a body of judges insulated from majoritarian pressures and thus able to enforce [federal law] without fear of reprisal or public rebuke." *United States v. Raddatz*, 447 U.S. 667, 704 (1980) (Marshall, J., dissenting). * * *

These important functions of Article III are too central to our constitutional scheme to risk their incremental erosion. The exceptions we have recognized for territorial courts, courts-martial, and administrative courts were each based on "certain exceptional powers bestowed upon Congress by the Constitution or by historical consensus." *Northern Pipeline*, 458 U.S. at 70 (opinion of Brennan, J.). Here, however, there is no equally forceful reason to extend further these exceptions to situations that are distinguishable from existing precedents. The Court, however, engages in just such an extension. By sanctioning the adjudication of state-law counterclaims by a federal administrative agency, the Court far exceeds the analytic framework of our precedents.

More than a century ago, we recognized that Congress may not "withdraw from [Article III] judicial cognizance any matter *which, from its nature, is the subject of a suit at the common law,* or in equity, or admiralty." *Murray's Lessee v. Hoboken Land & Improvement Company*, 59 U.S. (18 How.) 272, 284 (1855) (emphasis added). More recently, in *Northern Pipeline*, 458 U.S. at 70, the view of a majority of the Court that the breach-of-contract and misrepresentation claims at issue in that case lay "at the core of the historically recognized judicial power," and were "the stuff of the traditional actions at common law tried by the courts at Westminster in 1789," *id.* at 90 (Rehnquist, J., concurring in judgment), contributed significantly to the Court's conclusion that the bankruptcy courts could not constitutionally adjudicate Northern Pipeline's common-law claims. In the instant litigation, the Court lightly discards both history and our precedents. The Court attempts to support the substantial alteration it works today in our Article III jurisprudence by pointing, *inter alia,* to legislative convenience; to the fact that Congress does not altogether eliminate federal-court jurisdiction over ancillary state-law counterclaims; and to Schor's "consent" to CFTC adjudication of Conti Commodity's counterclaims. In my view, the Court's effort fails.

The Court states that in reviewing Article III challenges, one of several factors we have taken into account is "the concerns that drove Congress to depart from the requirements of Article III." The Court identifies the desire of Congress "to create an inexpensive and expeditious alternative forum through which customers could enforce the provisions of the CEA against professional brokers" as the motivating congressional concern here. The Court further states that "[i]t was only to ensure the effectiveness of this scheme that Congress authorized the CFTC to assert jurisdiction over common-law counterclaims[;] . . . absent the CFTC's exercise of that authority, the purposes of the reparations procedure would have been confounded." Were we to hold that the CFTC's authority to decide common-law counterclaims offends Article III, the Court declares, "it is clear that we would 'defeat the obvious purpose of the legislation.'" Article III, the Court concludes, does not "compe[l] this degree of prophylaxis."

I disagree—Article III's prophylactic protections were intended to prevent just this sort of abdication to claims of legislative convenience. The Court requires that the legislative interest in convenience and efficiency be weighed against the competing interest in judicial independence. In doing so, the Court pits an interest the benefits of which are immediate, concrete, and easily understood against one, the benefits of which are almost entirely prophylactic, and thus often seem remote and not worth the cost in any single case. Thus, while this balancing creates the illusion of objectivity and ineluctability, in fact the result was foreordained, because the balance is weighted against judicial independence. The danger of the Court's balancing approach is, of course, that as individual cases accumulate in which the Court finds that the short-term benefits of efficiency outweigh the long-term benefits of judicial independence, the protections of Article III will be eviscerated.

Perhaps the resolution of reparations claims such as respondents' may be accomplished more conveniently under the Court's decision than under my approach, but the Framers foreswore this sort of convenience in order to preserve freedom.

* * *

According to the Court, the intrusion into the province of the Federal Judiciary caused by the CFTC's authority to adjudicate state-law counterclaims is insignificant, both because the CFTC *shares* in, rather than displaces, federal district court jurisdiction over these claims and because only a very narrow class of state-law issues are involved. The "sharing" justification fails under the reasoning used by the Court to support the CFTC's authority. If the administrative reparations proceeding is so much more convenient and efficient than litigation in federal district court that abrogation of Article III's commands is warranted, it seems to me that complainants would rarely, if ever, choose to go to district court in the first instance. Thus, any "sharing" of jurisdiction is more illusory than real.

More importantly, the Court, in emphasizing that *this litigation* will permit solely a narrow class of state-law claims to be decided by a non-Article III court, ignores the fact that it establishes a broad principle. The decision today may authorize the administrative adjudication only of state-law claims that stem from the same transaction or set of facts that allow the customer of a professional commodity broker to initiate reparations proceedings before the CFTC, but the *reasoning* of this decision strongly suggests that, given "legislative necessity" and party consent, any federal agency may decide state-law issues that are ancillary to federal issues within the agency's jurisdiction. Thus, while in this litigation "the magnitude of any intrusion on the Judicial Branch" may conceivably be characterized as "de minimis," the potential impact of the Court's decision on federal-court jurisdiction is substantial. The Court dismisses warnings about the dangers of its approach, asserting simply that it does not fear the slippery slope and that this litigation does not involve the creation by Congress of a "phalanx of non-Article III tribunals equipped to handle the entire business of the Article III courts." A healthy respect for the precipice on which we stand is warranted, however, for this reason:

Congress can seriously impair Article III's structural and individual protections without assigning away "the *entire* business of the Article III courts." It can do so by *diluting* the judicial power of the federal courts. And, contrary to the Court's intimations, dilution of judicial power operates to impair the protections of Article III regardless of whether Congress acted with the "good intention" of providing a more efficient dispute resolution system or with the "bad intention" of strengthening the Legislative Branch at the expense of the Judiciary.

* * *

Our Constitution unambiguously enunciates a fundamental principle—that the "judicial Power of the United States" be reposed in an independent Judiciary. It is our obligation zealously to guard that independence so that our tripartite system of government remains strong and that individuals continue to be protected against decisionmakers subject to majoritarian pressures. Unfortunately, today the Court forsakes that obligation for expediency. I dissent.

NOTES AND QUESTIONS

1. Much like *Union Carbide* respecting binding arbitration, *Schor* is unprecedented among Article III cases for the following reason: Congress did not expressly delegate the power to adjudicate common law counterclaims to the CFTC; instead, the CFTC asserted that power in a rule as its interpretation of the Commodity Exchange Act. Should that make a difference in the Court's Article III analysis?

2. The Court in *Schor* rejects the public/private rights distinction as an absolute basis for resolving when Congress can delegate adjudicatory authority to non-Article III tribunals. Instead, the *Schor* majority finds two limits on the power of Congress to delegate power to adjudicate private rights disputes to agencies.

The first is the individual right of the litigant. The majority concludes that Schor waived his right to adjudicate in an Article III court by filing his counterclaim with the CFTC and withdrawing his district court complaint after the district court refused to dismiss or stay that complaint. As the majority notes, as a practical matter, the reparations proceeding and the common law counterclaim must be adjudicated in the same forum at the same time. Do you find the majority's waiver theory convincing? Can you imagine a district court refusing to dismiss or to stay proceedings to consider a common law counterclaim once the Supreme Court holds that the CFTC can hear both reparations cases and common law counterclaims? In Chapter 6, we discuss the doctrine of primary jurisdiction. Does that discussion influence your answer to these questions?

The other limit on Congress's power to delegate adjudicatory authority is the right of the judiciary to protect its jurisdiction from potential encroachment by Congress. How does the majority interpret and apply that limit? Does the majority opinion impose any real limit as long as Congress gives some plausible reason for the decision to reallocate a class of disputes from Article III courts to an agency and engages in only piecemeal reallocation of discrete categories of disputes?

3. The dissenting justices in *Schor* were concerned that Congress would reallocate large numbers of disputes over time and that any such reallocation would jeopardize individual rights or the core functions of the judicial branch. How valid are these concerns?

———————

Notably, the plurality that prevailed in *Northern Pipeline* became a two-Justice dissent in *Schor*. Of course, those two Justices—Brennan and Marshall—are no longer on the Court, and none of the present Justices seems to share their judicial philosophy in this area of law. It would seem to follow that any cloud over the power of Congress to reallocate adjudication of a class of disputes from Article III courts to agencies has been lifted. At least, most scholars believed that to be the case until the Court decided the following case.

Granfinanciera v. Nordberg

492 U.S. 33 (1989).

■ BRENNAN, J., delivered the opinion of the Court, in which REHNQUIST, C.J., and MARSHALL, STEVENS, and KENNEDY, JJ., joined, and in Parts I, II, III, and V, of which SCALIA, J., joined. SCALIA, J., filed an opinion concurring in part and concurring in the judgment. WHITE, J., filed a dissenting opinion. BLACKMUN, J., filed a dissenting opinion, in which O'CONNOR, J., joined.

The question presented is whether a person who has not submitted a claim against a bankruptcy estate has a right to a jury trial when sued by the trustee in bankruptcy to recover an allegedly fraudulent monetary transfer. We hold that the Seventh Amendment entitles such a person to a trial by jury, notwithstanding Congress' designation of fraudulent conveyance actions as "core proceedings."

* * *

III

Petitioners rest their claim to a jury trial on the Seventh Amendment alone. The Seventh Amendment provides: "In Suits at common law, where the value in controversy shall exceed twenty dollars, the right of trial by jury shall be preserved. . . ." We have consistently interpreted the phrase "Suits at common law" to refer to "suits in which *legal* rights were to be ascertained and determined, in contradistinction to those where equitable rights alone were recognized, and equitable remedies were administered." *Parson's v. Bedford*, 28 U.S. (3 Pet.) 433, 447 (1830). Although "the thrust of the Amendment was to preserve the right to jury trial as it existed in 1791," the Seventh Amendment also applies to actions brought to enforce statutory rights that are analogous to common-law causes of action ordinarily decided in English law courts in the late 18th century, as opposed to those customarily heard by courts of equity or admiralty. *Curtis v. Loether*, 415 U.S. 189, 193 (1974).

The form of our analysis is familiar. "First, we compare the statutory action to 18th-century actions brought in the courts of England prior to the merger of the courts of law and equity. Second, we examine the remedy sought and determine whether it is legal or equitable in nature." *Tull v. United States*, 481 U.S. 412, 417–18 (1987) (citations omitted). The second stage of this analysis is more important than the first. If, on balance, these two factors indicate that a party is entitled to a jury trial under the Seventh Amendment, we must decide whether Congress may assign and has assigned resolution of the relevant claim to a non-Article III adjudicative body that does not use a jury as factfinder.[4]

A

There is no dispute that actions to recover preferential or fraudulent transfers were often brought at law in late 18th-century England.

* * *

IV

Prior to passage of the Bankruptcy Reform Act of 1978, "[s]uits to recover preferences constitute[d] no part of the proceedings in bankruptcy." *Schoenthal v. Irving Trust Co.*, 287 U.S. 92, 94–95 (1932). Although related to bankruptcy proceedings, fraudulent conveyance and preference actions brought by a trustee in bankruptcy were deemed separate, plenary suits to which the Seventh Amendment applied. While the 1978 Act brought those actions within the jurisdiction of the bankruptcy courts, it preserved parties' rights to trial by jury as they existed prior to the effective date of the 1978 Act. The 1984 Amendments, however, designated fraudulent conveyance actions "core proceedings," which bankruptcy judges may adjudicate and in which they may issue final judgments if a district court has referred the matter to them. * * *

A

In *Atlas Roofing*, we noted that "when Congress creates new statutory 'public rights,' it may assign their adjudication to an administrative agency with which a jury trial would be incompatible, without violating the Seventh Amendment's injunction that jury trial is to be 'preserved' in 'suits at common law.' " 430 U.S. at 455. We emphasized, however, that Congress' power to block application of the Seventh Amendment to a cause of action has limits. Congress may only deny trials by jury in actions at law, we said, in cases where "public rights" are litigated. * * *

We adhere to that general teaching. As we said in *Atlas Roofing*: " 'On the common law side of the federal courts, the aid of juries is not

---

[4] This quite distinct inquiry into whether Congress has permissibly entrusted the resolution of certain disputes to an administrative agency or specialized court of equity, and whether jury trials would impair the functioning of the legislative scheme, appears to be what the Court contemplated when, in *Ross v. Bernhard*, 396 U.S. 531, 538 n.10 (1970), it identified "the practical abilities and limitations of juries" as an additional factor to be consulted in determining whether the Seventh Amendment confers a jury trial right. *Tull v. United States*, 481 U.S. at 418 n.4; *Atlas Roofing Co. v. Occupational Safety & Health Rev. Comm'n*, 430 U.S. 442, 454–455 (1977). We consider this issue in Part IV, *infra*. Contrary to Justice WHITE's contention, we do not declare that the Seventh Amendment provides a right to a jury trial on all legal rather than equitable claims. If a claim that is legal in nature asserts a "public right," as we define that term in Part IV, then the Seventh Amendment does not entitle the parties to a jury trial if Congress assigns its adjudication to an administrative agency or specialized court of equity. The Seventh Amendment protects a litigant's right to a jury trial only if a cause of action is legal in nature and it involves a matter of "private right."

only deemed appropriate but is required by the Constitution itself.' " *Id.* at 450 n.7 (quoting *Crowell v. Benson*, 285 U.S. 22, 51 (1932)). Congress may devise novel causes of action involving public rights free from the strictures of the Seventh Amendment if it assigns their adjudication to tribunals without statutory authority to employ juries as factfinders. But it lacks the power to strip parties contesting matters of private right of their constitutional right to a trial by jury. As we recognized in *Atlas Roofing*, to hold otherwise would be to permit Congress to eviscerate the Seventh Amendment's guarantee by assigning to administrative agencies or courts of equity all causes of action not grounded in state law, whether they originate in a newly fashioned regulatory scheme or possess a long line of common-law forebears. * * *

In certain situations, of course, Congress may fashion causes of action that are closely *analogous* to common-law claims and place them beyond the ambit of the Seventh Amendment by assigning their resolution to a forum in which jury trials are unavailable.

* * *

[O]ur decisions point to the conclusion that, if a statutory cause of action is legal in nature, the question whether the Seventh Amendment permits Congress to assign its adjudication to a tribunal that does not employ juries as factfinders requires the same answer as the question whether Article III allows Congress to assign adjudication of that cause of action to a non-Article III tribunal. For if a statutory cause of action, such as respondent's right to recover a fraudulent conveyance under 11 U.S.C. § 548(a)(2), is not a "public right" for Article III purposes, then Congress may not assign its adjudication to a specialized non-Article III court lacking "the essential attributes of the judicial power." *Crowell v. Benson*, 285 U.S. at 51. And if the action must be tried under the auspices of an Article III court, then the Seventh Amendment affords the parties a right to a jury trial whenever the cause of action is legal in nature. Conversely, if Congress may assign the adjudication of a statutory cause of action to a non-Article III tribunal, then the Seventh Amendment poses no independent bar to the adjudication of that action by a nonjury factfinder. * * *

In our most recent discussion of the "public rights" doctrine as it bears on Congress' power to commit adjudication of a statutory cause of action to a non-Article III tribunal, we rejected the view that "a matter of public rights must at a minimum arise 'between the government and others.' " *Northern Pipeline*, 458 U.S. at 69 (opinion of Brennan, J.) (quoting *Ex parte Bakelite Corp.*, 279 U.S. at 451). We held, instead, that the Federal Government need not be a party for a case to revolve around "public rights." *Thomas v. Union Carbide Agric. Prods. Co.*, 473 U.S. 568, 586 (1985). The crucial question, in cases not involving the Federal Government, is whether "Congress, acting for a valid legislative purpose pursuant to its constitutional powers under Article I, [has] create[d] a seemingly 'private' right that is so closely integrated into a public regulatory scheme as to be a matter appropriate for agency resolution with limited involvement by the Article III judiciary." *Id.* at 600 (Brennan, J., concurring). If a statutory right is not closely intertwined with a federal regulatory program Congress has power to enact, and if that right neither belongs to nor exists against the Federal

Government, then it must be adjudicated by an Article III court. If the right is legal in nature, then it carries with it the Seventh Amendment's guarantee of a jury trial.

B

Although the issue admits of some debate, a bankruptcy trustee's right to recover a fraudulent conveyance under 11 U.S.C. § 548(a)(2) seems to us more accurately characterized as a private rather than a public right as we have used those terms in our Article III decisions.

* * *

It may be that providing jury trials in some fraudulent conveyance actions—if not in this particular case, because respondent's suit was commenced after the Bankruptcy Court approved the debtor's plan of reorganization—would impede swift resolution of bankruptcy proceedings and increase the expense of Chapter 11 reorganizations. But "these considerations are insufficient to overcome the clear command of the Seventh Amendment." *Curtis v. Loether*, 415 U.S. 189, 198 (1974).

■ JUSTICE SCALIA, concurring in part and concurring in the judgment.

I join all but Part IV of the Court's opinion. I make that exception because I do not agree with the premise of its discussion: that "the Federal Government need not be a party for a case to revolve around 'public rights.'" In my view a matter of "public rights," whose adjudication Congress may assign to tribunals lacking the essential characteristics of Article III courts, "must at a minimum arise 'between the government and others.'" *Northern Pipeline*, 458 U.S. at 69 (1982) (quoting *Ex parte Bakelite*, 279 U.S. at 451). * * *

The notion that the power to adjudicate a legal controversy between two private parties may be assigned to a non-Article III, yet federal, tribunal is entirely inconsistent with the origins of the public rights doctrine.

* * *

It is clear that what we meant by public rights were not rights important to the public, or rights created by the public, but rights *of the public*—that is, rights pertaining to claims brought by or against the United States.

* * *

We thus held in *Thomas*, for the first time, that a purely private federally created action did not require Article III courts.

There was in my view no constitutional basis for that decision. * * *

I do not think one can preserve a system of separation of powers on the basis of such intuitive judgments regarding "practical effects," * * *.

■ JUSTICE WHITE, dissenting.

The Court's decision today calls into question several of our previous decisions, strikes down at least one federal statute, and potentially concludes for the first time that the Seventh Amendment guarantees litigants in a specialized non-Article III forum the right to a jury trial. Because I cannot accept these departures from established law, I respectfully dissent.

* * *

The Court's decision today ignores our statement in *Atlas Roofing* that "even if the Seventh Amendment would have required a jury where the adjudication of [some types of] rights is assigned to a federal court of law instead of an administrative agency," this constitutional provision does not apply when Congress assigns the adjudication of these rights to specialized tribunals where juries have no place. 430 U.S. at 455.

* * *

The Court's decision also substantially cuts back on Congress' power to assign selected causes of action to specialized forums and tribunals (such as bankruptcy courts), by holding that these forums will have to employ juries when hearing claims like the one before us today—a requirement that subverts in large part Congress' decision to create such forums in the first place. Past decisions have accorded Congress far more discretion in making these assignments.

■ JUSTICE BLACKMUN, with whom JUSTICE O'CONNOR joins, dissenting.

I agree generally with what Justice WHITE has said, but write separately to clarify, particularly in my own mind, the nature of the relevant inquiry.

* * *

[T]he question remains whether the assignment is one Congress may constitutionally make. Under *Atlas Roofing*, that question turns on whether the claim involves a "public right." When Congress was faced with the task of divining the import of our fragmented decision in *Northern Pipeline Construction Co. v. Marathon Pipe Line Co.*, it gambled and predicted that a statutory right which is an integral part of a pervasive regulatory scheme may qualify as a "public right." Doing its best to observe the constraints of *Northern Pipeline* while at the same time preserving as much as it could of the policy goals of the major program of bankruptcy reform the decision in *Northern Pipeline* dismantled, Congress struck a compromise. It identified those proceedings which it viewed as integral to the bankruptcy scheme as "core" and assigned them to a specialized equitable tribunal.

I agree with Justice WHITE, that it would be improper for this Court to employ, in its Seventh Amendment analysis, a century-old conception of what is and is not central to the bankruptcy process, a conception that Congress has expressly rejected. To do so would, among other vices, trivialize the efforts Congress has engaged in for more than a decade to bring the bankruptcy system into the modern era.

There are, nonetheless, some limits to what Congress constitutionally may designate as a "core proceeding," if the designation has an impact on constitutional rights. Congress, for example, could not designate as "core bankruptcy proceedings" state-law contract actions brought by debtors against third parties. Otherwise, *Northern Pipeline* would be rendered a nullity. In this case, however, Congress has not exceeded these limits.

* * *

[I]t must be acknowledged that Congress has legislated treacherously close to the constitutional line by denying a jury trial in a fraudulent conveyance action in which the defendant has no claim against the estate. Nonetheless, given the significant federal interests involved, and the importance of permitting Congress at long last to fashion a modern bankruptcy system which places the basic rudiments of the bankruptcy process in the hands of an expert equitable tribunal, I cannot say that Congress has crossed the constitutional line on the facts of this case.

NOTES AND QUESTIONS

1.   If you think the reasoning in the majority opinion in *Granfinanciera* resembles the reasoning in the plurality opinion in *Northern Pipeline* and the dissenting opinion in *Schor*, you are in good company. That should come as no surprise, since all three opinions were written by Justice Brennan. It is notable, however, that in addition to Justice Marshall, who had joined him in the prior opinions, Justice Brennan was able to recruit Justices Rehnquist, Scalia, Stevens, and Kennedy, to create a new majority of six Justices. The Court has not decided a major Article III or Seventh Amendment case since 1989, and has experienced significant turnover since then. We cannot yet know the views of Chief Justice Roberts or Justices Breyer, Ginsburg, Alito, or Sotomayor.

2.   The public/private rights dichotomy that a majority seemed to abandon in *Schor* seems to have returned with renewed strength in *Granfinanciera*. In fact, Justice Scalia would go further than the Court has ever previously gone by defining public rights to exclude any adjudication between two private individuals. Would the workers compensation regime the Court upheld in *Crowell v. Benson* survive application of Justice Scalia's test, given the present administrative law environment in which courts apply highly deferential methods of review to all agency findings of fact including issues of jurisdictional and constitutional fact?

3.   Deriving clear, coherent, and consistent principles of law from the foregoing Article III and Seventh Amendment cases is a challenge. Leading scholars on this question have struggled to reconcile the Court's decisions in this area. *See, e.g.*, Caleb Nelson, *Adjudication in the Political Branches*, 107 COLUM. L. REV. 559 (2007); Richard H. Fallon, Jr., *Of Legislative Courts, Administrative Agencies, and Article III*, 101 HARV. L. REV. 915 (1988). Nevertheless, these cases reflect at least one discernible pattern: in cases that do not involve agencies, the Court has issued opinions that create grave doubt with respect to the constitutionality of many agency adjudicatory regimes; yet, in cases that do involve agencies, the Court has declined to hold any agency adjudicatory regime unconstitutional as a violation of either Article III or the Seventh Amendment. What, if any, inference do you draw from that peculiar pattern of decisions?

4.   The decision in *Granfinanciera* turned on the Court's interpretation of the Seventh Amendment jury trial right as applied in a common law cause of action in the civil context. Consider the text of the Fifth and Sixth

Amendments, located in Appendix [A]. Would the majority's reasoning in *Granfianciera* also apply to the application of Fifth and Sixth Amendment rights in criminal cases? Why or why not?

DISCUSSION PROBLEM

Medical malpractice cases traditionally have been resolved through case-by-case litigation in state courts. In an effort to gain control of perceived costs and inequities of existing medical malpractice litigation, and in conjunction with other efforts to reform the health care delivery system, proposed legislation would replace this traditional system of litigating individual medical malpractice cases with a new system of specialized federal administrative health courts with administrative law judges with medical expertise and neutral expert witnesses instead of juries to resolve medical malpractice claims. The proposed legislation would empower the new federal health courts with the ability to award compensatory damages in full, but damages for pain and suffering only as consistent with a predetermined schedule. Would these proposed federal health courts satisfy the requirements of Article III and the Seventh Amendment? Why or why not? Does it matter to your analysis whether the health courts are established in conjunction with broader reforms that provide benefits to patients by lowering health care costs and improving patient access and safety?

C. OTHER MEANS THROUGH WHICH CONGRESS INFLUENCES AGENCIES

We discussed in section A the most obvious and direct way in which Congress exercises control over agencies—through enactment of statutes that simultaneously delegate power to agencies and limit the scope of those powers. Statutes of that type are frequently referred to as agency organic acts. We will return to that topic in detail in Chapters 4 and 5, where we discuss judicial application of statutory limits on agency actions. Statutes of that type are only one important means through which Congress influences agency actions, however. The other mechanisms of influence and control that Congress uses with considerable effect include other statutes that shape agency actions, allocation of litigating authority between agencies and the Department of Justice, the process of confirming nominees to agency decision-making positions, the appropriations process, oversight hearings, and casework. We will discuss each in turn.

1. OTHER STATUTES

Congress has enacted scores of statutes, in addition to agency organic acts, that apply to agencies. We discuss just a few of those statutes that we believe to have particularly significant effects on agencies. All of these statutes have both intended socially beneficial effects and unintended detrimental effects. There is a lively debate with respect to the net effects of each. The debates often generate more heat than light, however, because of the near impossibility of measuring either the benefits or the adverse effects of each statute. It is easy to collect anecdotes that illustrate both the beneficial and the detrimental effects of any agency-influencing statute. Each such statute has pervasive but subtle and indirect effects that render them poor candidates for systematic empirical study, however.

a.   ADMINISTRATIVE PROCEDURE ACT

As we discussed in Chapter 1, Congress enacted the Administrative Procedure Act (APA) in 1946 to create greater uniformity with respect to the procedures agencies use to make decisions and the standards courts apply in reviewing those decisions. The APA is to administrative law what the Constitution is to constitutional law. It specifies the procedures agencies must use to make various categories of decisions and the relationship between agencies and reviewing courts. It is so important to an understanding of administrative law that we have included it as Appendix A. Most of the cases in this book include discussions, interpretations, and applications of the APA.

b.   FREEDOM OF INFORMATION ACT

Congress enacted the Freedom of Information Act (FOIA) in 1966 and has amended it many times since. It is codified at 5 U.S.C. § 552. FOIA was intended to make the functions of government agencies more transparent to the public so that the public could identify problems in the functioning of government and bring pressure to bear on agency officials, the President, and the Congress to address those problems. FOIA requires each agency to publish its rules in the Federal Register, to make its final decisions in adjudications available at a publicly accessible location, and to disclose information contained in its records to any person who requests that information, subject to nine exemptions. FOIA has achieved its goals in many important respects. Agencies respond to tens of thousands of FOIA requests each year. Members of the general public, the press, agency regulatees, and beneficiaries of agency-administered programs obtain vital information about agency functions through this route.

Like all statutes, however, FOIA also has unintended adverse effects. FOIA has been used by organized crime to identify and kill informants and to learn how law enforcement agencies function, so that they can engage in criminal activities with less risk of detection and prosecution. It has also been used by foreign intelligence services to obtain information they can analyze to draw inferences with respect to matters important to U.S. national security. Because of these well-known potential abuses of FOIA, Congress has amended some of the exemptions several times to provide agencies greater discretion to refrain from disclosing information that could harm the nation if revealed, and agencies have established elaborate and expensive procedures to screen FOIA requests with reference to the exemptions for the duty to disclose.

Agencies are required by statute to respond to FOIA requests within 20 days, but many agencies cannot come close to complying with that deadline. The task of screening requests is extremely difficult, particularly at agencies like FBI and CIA, and the staffing and funding Congress provides many agencies for this purpose falls far short of what is required for prompt compliance with FOIA requests. This systemic problem is a source of great frustration for parties that request information, agencies that must respond to large numbers of such requests with woefully inadequate resources, and courts that are called upon to enforce FOIA against agencies.

The problem of delay in complying with FOIA requests first came to court in *Open America v. Watergate Special Prosecution Force*, 547 F.2d 605 (D.C. Cir. 1976). The plaintiffs asked the Attorney General and FBI Director for all documents relating to the role of Patrick Gray in any aspect of the "Watergate affair." The FBI on the day of the request had 5,137 FOIA requests on hand, the FBI so responded more than 20 days later, an appeal was denied for the same reason, and the district court then issued an order to compel the FBI to comply with or deny immediately plaintiffs' request. The government then sought an immediate temporary stay of the district court's order in the court of appeals.

Part of the problem for the court was miscalculation by Congress of the burden on the agencies. The House Committee in 1974 estimated additional cost of FOIA amendments for all agencies at $50,000 for that year and $100,000 for each of the succeeding five years. An FBI officer subsequently filed an affidavit stating that FBI costs of implementing the FOIA were as follows: 1974, $160,000; 1975, $462,000; 1976, an estimated $2,675,000; and the same amount estimated for 1977. The cost of implementation of FOIA has increased steadily every year since, but Congress has not appropriated funds that remotely approach the amount needed to comply with all requests promptly.

The *Open America* court found that the FBI was using "due diligence." It divided requests into difficult and simple ones. The *Open America* request was a difficult one, because the name of L. Patrick Gray had not been included in the index of 58 million index cards of subjects and individuals, and 38,000 pages had been located that required review. The team working on the request had 33 projects pending, all started earlier. At FBI headquarters, 191 employees worked solely on FOIA requests.

Because the plaintiffs alleged no reason for urgency, the court dealt only with the question whether an applicant for records may go to the head of the line simply by going to court. It held that Congress intended a court to give priority to a request only "if some exceptional need or urgency attached to the request justified putting it ahead of all other requests received by the same agency prior thereto."

The problem of delay in responding to FOIA requests persists at most agencies and has become worse at many. All circuits have adopted the D.C. Circuit's reasoning and holding in *Open America,* but courts often express frustration with the extreme delays in responses to FOIA requests at many agencies. The Ninth Circuit's opinion in *Fiduccia v. Department of Justice*, 185 F.3d 1035 (9th Cir. 1999), illustrates the problem. The plaintiffs requested information from the FBI in 1986. The FBI had not complied by 1999, and stated that the queue of FOIA requests at the FBI was so long that it could not comply until 2001. The court expressed its agreement with the reasoning and holding of *Open America* and stated that it was unwilling to allow the plaintiffs to jump the queue by filing a lawsuit. The court went on to complain: "But the queue is too long. . . . Congress gave agencies 20 *days*, not years, to [comply with an FOIA request.]" The court recognized that the root of the problem is the refusal of Congress to provide the FBI and other agencies resources sufficient to comply with FOIA requests in a timely manner. It urged the FBI to "educate Congress" with respect to its need for increased resources to comply with FOIA or for a statutory amendment that allows agencies more time to comply. That is a good suggestion in theory, but it has no chance of success. Congress has demonstrated its unwillingness to provide agencies the resources required to comply with FOIA or to amend the FOIA deadlines for decades. The problem is not lack of education on this issue but lack of political will to address the issue.

The problem of systemic delay in responding to FOIA requests is part of a much broader problem. Congress routinely assigns agencies a host of difficult tasks, couples those assignments with demanding decision-making procedures, declines to provide agencies the resources required to perform all of those tasks, and imposes on the agencies unrealistic statutory compliance deadlines. The result is systemic delay that neither agencies nor courts are capable of addressing in an effective manner. We discuss that broader problem in Chapter 6.

c.   NATIONAL ENVIRONMENTAL POLICY ACT

Congress enacted the National Environmental Policy Act (NEPA) in 1969. It is codified at 42 U.S.C. § 4331 *et seq.* NEPA requires every agency to prepare an environmental impact statement before it takes any major federal action that has a significant effect on the environment. The Supreme Court has held repeatedly that NEPA has no substantive standard. *See, e.g., Baltimore Gas & Elec. Co. v. Natural Res. Def. Council*, 462 U.S. 87 (1983).

Thus, in theory, an agency could prepare an environmental impact statement in which it finds that the action it is contemplating would have a devastating impact on the environment and still take the action without violating NEPA. Does it follow that NEPA does not affect agency decisionmaking? Consider two potential indirect effects. First, every agency action is subject to judicial review through application of the arbitrary and capricious standard, as we discuss in detail in Chapters 4 and 5. How would you expect a reviewing court to apply that test to an agency decision to take an action that the agency finds would have a devastating effect on the environment? Second, in order to comply with NEPA, every agency had to create and staff a unit that engages in preparation of environmental impact statements. A representative of that unit is now routinely included as a member of the team that makes major decisions at most agencies. How, if at all, would you expect that change in the composition of the decision-making team to affect agency decisionmaking?

Of course, like all statutes, NEPA also has unintended adverse effects. NEPA increases the cost of engaging in many socially beneficial actions and delays implementation of such actions. Thus, in one extreme case, a court held that a much-needed highway that was first proposed in 1947 could not go forward without extensive additional study of its effects on the environment even though the agency responsible for the project had already prepared a 10,000 page environmental impact statement. *See City of Carmel-By-The-Sea v. Department of Transp.*, 123 F.3d 1142 (9th Cir. 1997).

d.   CIVIL SERVICE ACT

Congress enacted the Civil Service Act (CSA) in 1883. It is codified in scattered sections of Title 5. CSA eliminated the prior practice of hiring and firing based on patronage and required the government to create a meritocratic system of hiring, evaluating, and promoting employees. There is no doubt that the CSA has improved the quality of the federal workforce. It too has had unintended adverse effects, however. The CSA makes it difficult for managers to fire or otherwise discipline inefficient workers. The CSA also makes it difficult for the President to implement his agenda when key civil servants do not share the President's values and preferences. Since we elect Presidents to make good on the promises they make to us during their campaigns for election, the CSA sacrifices to some extent the democratic values on which our form of government is based.

Over the past several decades, the number of government employees who are political appointees rather than civil servants has increased substantially, from 451 in 1960 to 2,393 in 1992 to 2,786 in 2005. *See* PAUL C. LIGHT, THICKENING GOVERNMENT: FEDERAL HIERARCHY AND THE DIFFUSION OF ACCOUNTABILITY 7 (1995); UNITED STATES HOUSE OF REPRESENTATIVES COMMITTEE ON GOVERNMENT REFORM—MINORITY STAFF, SPECIAL INVESTIGATIONS DIVISION, GROWTH OF POLITICAL APPOINTEES IN THE BUSH ADMINISTRATION 5 (2006). By contrast, the federal government employed roughly 2.5 million civilian, executive branch employees in the mid-1960s, increasing to over 3 million in the early 1990s, and declining back to around 2.7 million in 2012 largely as a result of increased outsourcing of various government functions to private contracts. *See* PAUL C. LIGHT, THE TRUE SIZE OF GOVERNMENT 42–43 (1999); OFFICE OF PERSONNEL MANAGEMENT, FEDERAL EMPLOYMENT REPORTS, HISTORICAL FEDERAL WORKFORCE TABLES, TOTAL GOVERNMENT EMPLOYMENT SINCE 1962, *at* http://www. opm.gov/policy-data-oversight/data-analysis-documentation/federal-employment-reports/historical-tables/total-government-employment-since-1962/ (last visited July 2, 2014). Though political appointees remain only a tiny percentage of the total federal workforce, the sizeable increase in their numbers has had major effects—both good and bad. Political appointees tend to fill leadership roles, and their expanded presence probably has increased the responsiveness of the bureaucracy to the preferences of the President and, derivatively, to the preferences of the people expressed through the electoral process. Yet, the larger number of political appointees leading government agencies arguably has politicized agencies in less benign ways. Commentators regularly accuse the President and other White House personnel acting in his name of subverting scientific and economic analysis performed by professionals to the whims of political advisors who are more concerned about obtaining and retaining political support from important constituencies. Not surprisingly, therefore, scholars and others have criticized the increased number of political appointees in federal government agencies. *See, e.g.*, REPORT OF THE NATIONAL COMMISSION ON PUBLIC SERVICE, URGENT BUSINESS FOR AMERICA: REVITALIZING THE FEDERAL GOVERNMENT FOR THE TWENTY-FIRST CENTURY 34–37 (2005).

e.   INFORMATION QUALITY ACT

Congress enacted the Information Quality Act (IQA) in 2000 as a rider to a large 2001 appropriations bill. Also known as the Data Quality Act, the IQA is codified at 44 U.S.C. § 3516, note. The IQA requires agencies to act only on the basis of high quality information. Passage of the IQA was inspired in part by an incident that occurred during the rulemaking in which the EPA issued the controversial rules that the Supreme Court upheld in *Whitman v. American Trucking Ass'ns, Inc.*, 531 U.S. 457 (2001), reproduced and discussed in Part A of this Chapter. One of the most important sources of data the EPA relied on was a study done by researchers from Harvard. When participants in the rulemaking asked the EPA for the working papers for that study, the EPA responded that the authors were unwilling to provide the working papers. Many participants were angry when the EPA relied on the study even though the authors were not willing to make the working papers public. Congress responded to the anger produced by that and other similar incidents by enacting the IQA. Of course, as that incident illustrates, information quality is a slippery and controversial concept. There was no reason to believe that the Harvard study was a source of low quality data.

In *Salt Institute v. Leavitt*, 440 F.3d 156 (4th Cir. 2006), the Fourth Circuit observed that the IQA "does not create any legal right to information or its correctness." Instead, the IQA merely instructs the Office of Management and Budget to publish implementing guidelines and enforce the IQA against agencies. We know from the experience with NEPA, however, that a statute can have major effects even though it is not enforceable by courts. It may be too soon to fully evaluate the good or bad effects of the IQA. Nevertheless, legal scholars have criticized the IQA and OMB's implementing guidelines, linking them to a parade of problems including allowing special interests to harass agency officials by raising frivolous challenges against scientific studies that support particular policy preferences; ossifying agency rulemaking; and reducing agency disclosures of information to the public. *See, e.g.,* THOMAS O. MCGARITY & WENDY E. WAGNER, BENDING SCIENCE: HOW SPECIAL INTERESTS CORRUPT PUBLIC HEALTH RESEARCH 147, 150–54, 282–83 (2008); *see also* Sidney A. Shapiro, *The Information Quality Act and Environmental Protection: The Perils of Reform By Appropriations Rider*, 28 WM. & MARY ENVTL. L. & POL'Y REV. 339, 349–63 (2004) (summarizing potential benefits as well as possible costs).

2.   ALLOCATION OF LITIGATING AUTHORITY

Some agencies have the statutory authority to go to court to enforce their statutes and rules, while other agencies do not. Those agencies that lack such authority must rely on the Department of Justice (DOJ) to enforce the statutes for which they are responsible. The efficacy of an agency that lacks the authority to go to court depends critically on the attitudes of the DOJ and local U.S. Attorneys toward the importance of the agency's mission. If the DOJ and/or the U.S. Attorneys do not attach a great deal of significance to an agency's mission, they will allocate their scarce enforcement and litigation resources elsewhere, and the agency will be largely powerless to perform its mission.

Of the agencies that possess the statutory authority to go to court, few have the power to litigate before the Supreme Court. The Supreme Court has held that an agency must have explicit statutory authority to represent the government before it. *See Federal Election Comm'n v. NRA Political Victory Fund*, 513 U.S. 88 (1994). Congress rarely grants that authority. Agencies lacking the power to litigate before the Supreme Court must rely upon the Solicitor General to do it for them. As a result, the Solicitor General often has de facto power to veto a position taken by an agency by refusing to argue in support of that position before the Supreme Court.

3. THE CONFIRMATION PROCESS

Article II, section 2 of the Constitution gives the President the power "to nominate, and by and with the Advice and Consent of the Senate, . . . appoint . . . Officers of the United States." Article II, section 2 also grants Congress the authority to vest the President with the power to appoint "inferior Officers," which Congress has often done. We discuss the appointments process and the definition of an "Officer" in detail in Chapter 3. For now, it is sufficient to know that any agency official who has the power to make any final, legally binding decision must be an Officer. It follows that the President cannot appoint anyone to a position in which he or she can make final, legally binding decisions without confirmation by the Senate.

The Senate can and often does use the confirmation process for at least four purposes. First and most directly, the Senate can use the confirmation process as a means of vetoing the President's choice of an individual for a decision-making position in an agency. Second, the Senate can use the confirmation process as a source of leverage to extract commitments from a nominee. Thus, for instance, a member of the Senate committee that conducts a confirmation hearing might inform a nominee that the member will not vote to confirm unless the nominee agrees to take specified actions once in office. If the nominee believes that the Senator has enough votes to back up that demand, he or she has little choice but to agree to take the actions demanded by the Senator. Third, members of the Senate committee that has jurisdiction to hold the confirmation hearing can influence the agency by embarrassing it, or threatening to embarrass it, at the confirmation hearings. Fourth, the Senate can deter the President from removing from office an individual the President wants to remove, even if the individual serves at the pleasure of the President, by threatening not to confirm the individual's successor or by threatening to use that successor's confirmation hearing to embarrass the President.

4. THE APPROPRIATIONS PROCESS

All funds spent by the government must be appropriated by Congress. Congress sometimes adds to appropriations bills provisions that prohibit an agency from using any appropriated funds to take an action the agency otherwise would have the power or even the duty to take. The effects of such provisions are illustrated by *Environmental Defense Center v. Babbitt*, 73 F.3d 867 (9th Cir. 1995) (*EDF*). The Endangered Species Act (ESA) requires the Department of Interior (DOI) to act on a petition to list a species as endangered within a specified period of time after it receives a petition. In *EDF*, the DOI attempted to defend its failure to act on petitions within the statutory deadline by referring to a provision of each of the past several annual appropriations bills that prohibited the DOI from using any appropriated funds for purposes of deciding whether to list a species as endangered. The court resolved the obvious conflict between the ESA and the appropriations bills by holding that the statutory deadline continued to apply notwithstanding the provision of the appropriations bills, but that the DOI's statutory duty to act on the petition was suspended during the periods in which it was prohibited from using appropriated funds for that purpose.

Congress also uses the appropriations process in other ways. A member of an appropriations committee can inform an agency head that the amount of money Congress appropriates for the agency will depend to some extent on whether the agency takes an action that is favored by the member. If the agency head believes that the member has the votes needed to make good on that threat, the agency will experience great budgetary pressure to act in accordance with the wishes of the member. Members of congressional appropriations committees also often use appropriations hearings as an opportunity to influence an agency's behavior by embarrassing or threatening to embarrass the agency unless it acts in ways the member prefers.

5.   THE OVERSIGHT PROCESS

There is at least one, and sometimes more than one, committee of each House of Congress with jurisdiction to conduct hearings to evaluate an agency's performance. Members often use oversight hearings to influence agency actions by embarrassing an agency, or threatening to embarrass an agency, unless it acts in ways preferred by the member.

6.   CASEWORK

All members of Congress engage in extensive "casework"—communications with agencies to assist constituents in obtaining the results they desire from agencies in a timely manner. Such casework spans a long spectrum, from helping individual constituents obtain benefits from the Social Security Administration, to ensuring businesses gain prompt action on a license application from a regulatory agency. In fact, empirical studies of the behavior of members of Congress find that members spend far more time engaged in casework than engaged in the process of legislating. *See, e.g.*, MICHAEL J. MALBIN, UNELECTED REPRESENTATIVES: CONGRESSIONAL STAFF AND THE FUTURE OF REPRESENTATIVE GOVERNMENT 243–44 (1980). Those studies played a role in the efforts of some scholars to reinvigorate the nondelegation doctrine, discussed in Part A of this Chapter. Those scholars have suggested that members of Congress increasingly prefer to create agencies with vast discretionary powers so that the members could then curry favor with constituents by engaging in influence peddling with the agencies.

D. LIMITS ON CONGRESSIONAL POWER

Two key sources limit the power of Congress to control or to influence agency actions: the Due Process Clause of the Fifth Amendment and provisions of Article I of the Constitution that prescribe the manner in which Congress can take legislative action.

1. DUE PROCESS

As we discuss at great length in Chapter 4, the Due Process Clause imposes substantial procedural requirements on federal government agencies when they seek to deprive persons of life, liberty, or property. The Due Process Clause also limits the ability of Congress to act in certain ways that are designed to influence agency action in some contexts, as the next case illustrates.

Pillsbury Co. v. Federal Trade Commission

354 F.2d 952 (5th Cir. 1966).

■ TUTTLE, Chief Judge.

This is a petition by the Pillsbury Company to review and set aside an order of the Federal Trade Commission requiring Pillsbury to divest itself of the assets of Ballard & Ballard Company and of Duff's Baking Mix Division of American Home Products Corporation which the Federal Trade Commission found it had acquired in violation of § 7 of the Clayton Act * * *.

* * *

Since a resolution of one of the attacks made under the procedural due process heading, if decided favorably to Pillsbury, would make unnecessary our consideration of any of the other matters, we shall deal with that first. It is the alleged improper interference by committees of Congress with the decisional process of the Federal Trade Commission while the Pillsbury case was pending before it. The alleged interference, we hasten to add, was not alleged improper influence behind closed doors but was rather interference in the nature of questions and statements made by members of two Senate and House subcommittees having responsibility for legislation dealing with antitrust matters, all clearly spread upon the record.

Briefly stated, the criticism of the conduct of the members of the House and Senate arises in this manner: following the filing of the complaint against Pillsbury on June 16, 1952, the Government undertook to make out its case in chief. On April 22, 1953, the hearing examiner granted Pillsbury's motion to dismiss, taking the position that the record lacked figures showing the sales volume of the various Pillsbury products after the challenged acquisitions had taken place and that there were no "authentic or reliable" figures showing the sales and production of competing companies in the industry. On appeal, the Commission reversed by an order dated December 21, 1953. Thereafter, the Pillsbury Company undertook to introduce its evidence, and evidence for both parties continued to be received for the next several years.

During the months of May and June, 1955, hearings were held before the subcommittee on antitrust and monopoly of the Committee of the Judiciary of the United States Senate, and before the antitrust subcommittee of the Committee on Judiciary of the House of Representatives. At these hearings, Mr. Howrey, the then Chairman of the Commission, and several of the members of his staff, appeared including Mr. Kintner, the then General Counsel and later Chairman of the Commission, who wrote the final opinion from which this appeal is prosecuted.

It is to be noted that these hearings were held after the Commission had issued its interlocutory order, but long before the examiner made his Initial Decision on the merits, and, of course, before the Commission made its final Decision in 1960.

In this interlocutory opinion of the Commission, reversing the dismissal of the Pillsbury case by the examiner, the Commission rejected an argument made by the Government (counsel supporting the complaint) to the effect that where a showing that a company in the field having a substantial share of the business of the industry acquires the assets of competitors so that the resulting merged entity would meet the "substantiality" test of *Standard Oil Co. of California v. United States*, 337 U.S. 293 (1949), no further proof need be introduced in support of the complaint. This is what will be hereafter spoken of as the "per se" doctrine. The Commission in its order reversing the order of dismissal rejected this contention and expressly held that the per se doctrine did not apply under § 7, as amended.

The posture of the case at the time of Mr. Howrey's appearance before the Senate Committee, therefore, was that the Commission had found sufficient evidence to make a prima facie case of acquisition of competitors by a company having a substantial share of the business in the specified fields of industry, and a prima facie case of other conditions in the industry to make out an affirmative case of a "substantial lessening of competition." The Commission had, thus, given Pillsbury an opportunity to introduce countervailing evidence. Some had already been introduced and the prospects were that this would continue for a considerable period of time.

When Chairman Howrey appeared before the Senate subcommittee on June 1, 1955, he met a barrage of questioning by the members of the committee challenging his view of the requirements of § 7 and the application of the per se doctrine announced by the Supreme Court in the Standard Stations case, *Standard Oil Co. of California v. United States*, 337 U.S. 293 (1949), in a Clayton Act § 3 case, to § 7 proceedings. A number of the members of the committee challenged the correctness of his and the Commission's position in holding that a mere showing of a substantial increase in the share of the market after merger would not be sufficient to satisfy the requirement of § 7 of a showing that "the effect of such acquisition may be substantially to lessen competition."

Much of the questioning criticized by the petitioner here is in the nature of questions and comments by members of the committee in which they forcefully expressed their own opinions that the per se doctrine should apply and that it was the intent of Congress that it should apply.

The thrust of the comments and questions was that there was no need to carry on the long and complicated inquiry into all of the surrounding matters reflecting on the conditions in the industry if the Commission should determine that there was a substantial acquisition by a substantial number of the industry; that monopolies ought to be stopped quickly, and that Congress did not intend the Commission to apply the "rule of reason" in § 7 proceedings.

The questions were so probing that Mr. Howrey, the chairman of the Commission, announced to chairman Kefauver of the subcommittee that he would have to disqualify himself from further participation in the Pillsbury case (see quotations below).

Unfortunately, substantial portions of the questions and answers must be quoted in order that our opinion can be understood. The persons present and the positions they occupied at the time of the hearing, and their participation in the Commission's final Order are here outlined:

* * *

[Chairman Kilgore]: "On the problem of mergers Congress enacted the Celler-Kefauver Antimerger Act of 1950 primarily for the purpose of plugging a loop-hole in section 7 of the Clayton Act in order to slow down the merger movement and stop those which might substantially lessen competition. We wish to learn why mergers have continued at a great pace. Is it because section 7 is still not adequate to prohibit undesirable mergers? Is it because the law has not been vigorously enforced? Or can it be said that most of the mergers do not substantially lessen competition and should not be prohibited? This subcommittee hopes to throw light on this perplexing problem through testimony at these and succeeding days' hearings." * * *

[Chairman Kilgore]: "In the legislative history of the Act and in the Attorney General's Committee report, it is emphasized that the tendency to monopoly provision would reach even a relatively minor acquisition in the light of a historical pattern of acquisition. What has the Commission done to combat this type of acquisition since the enactment of the law?

[Mr. Howrey]: "Well, I think I agree with that wholeheartedly, that is, where there has been a pattern of minor acquisitions, and that is exactly what occurred in our Pillsbury case, where they had acquired a couple of small mills in Iowa and other mills in various parts of the country and there was a historical pattern of acquisitions of small companies.

And so, we agree, we follow that policy and work on it in our examination." * * *

[Mr. Howrey]: "That is, if it [Standard Stations case] held, just as International Salt did under section 3, that just dollar volume was enough why, clearly, we did not—we rejected that in Pillsbury.

Now, if that held that quantitative substantiality meant share of the market, why, we rejected that in the Pillsbury case, standing alone. I mean, we rejected that theory as being applicable to all cases." * * *

[Chairman Kilgore]: "Now, under the Pillsbury case, I think you pointed out that this company by acquiring two competitors, the second largest miller in the country, increased its share of the mix market in the Southeast from approximately 20 to 23 percent to 45 percent, which also put it in first place nationally in the mix field, its share increasing from 16 percent to 23 percent.

Shouldn't those figures have been practically sufficient to determine the issue of substantial lessening of competition or tendency to monopoly in the Southeast markets?

[Mr. Howrey]: "That is something that is a hard question for me to answer. The other facts are in the record.

I think that the share of the market, where it is of sufficient size, may in many cases be enough, standing by itself.

On the other hand, I can think in some instances where the share of the market might be insufficient, where there is plenty of remaining competition, and where there may have been other reasons for the merger, such as bad financial condition or something, which might involve a substantial share but still might not affect competition.

I think the goal in each case to determine whether the competitive pattern in the market has been involved and the percentage share of the market may in some cases be enough to show that and in other cases may not.

I hate to fix on any one percentage, because Judge Hand did that in the ALCOA case and has never been able to live it down.

[The Chairman]: "Yes.

Now, has the Commission found that the Department of Justice does not deem it necessary to consider all the factors relied upon by the Commission in its Pillsbury decision in deciding the legality of certain horizontal acquisions.

[Mr. Howrey]: "I don't know, of course, what the Department of Justice thinks." * * *

[Senator Kefauver]: "Then, Mr. Howrey, on the statement you made this morning, and as set forth in your opinion here, generally, insofar as dough mix or whatever it may be, in the southeastern part of the United States, Pillsbury had approximately 22 or 23 percent, and Duff and Ballard had 22 or 23 percent, and so somewhere they were winding up with between 45 and 48 percent of the dough-mix business in the southeastern part of the country. Those are rough figures, but that is substantially correct, is it not?

[Mr. Howrey]: "Yes, that is substantially correct.

I can give you the precise figures.

[Senator Kefauver]: "Well, they are in your opinion here. But that would be quite an obvious lessening of competition, particularly in view of the fact that there have been so many acquisitions prior to that time in the flour business. Wouldn't you have thought so?

[Mr. Howrey]: "Yes, and I so said and so held."

[At this point, it should be noted that members of the Committee spoke as if the basic facts as to substantiality of shares in the market had already been determined. Actually, these facts were still being litigated before the Commission. The Commission's order which Howrey was being questioned about held merely that a prima facie case as to substantiality had been made out by the Government. Pillsbury had not yet had its turn at bat]. * * *

[Senator Kefauver]: "It would seem to me that in a case where it is quite obvious and plain that there is a lessening of competition and, therefore, a violation of section 7 of the law, that perhaps the companies themselves would be relieved of future headaches if, upon their refusal to hold off until after the litigation can be settled, the Department of Justice were asked to institute injunction proceedings.

[Mr. Howrey]: "I want to say, if I may, that the opinion we rendered was after the close of the Government's case, and we said in the opinion, and I should say in my testimony, because I am a quasi-judicial officer, and if anybody reads it, they will see that I made up my mind, and will ask that I disqualify myself and, I think, rightly so—I should qualify what I said before, that we so held that the history of acquisitions and the relative share, and so forth, when I characterized that, I meant to characterize that solely what they made was what we think is a prima facie case and, of course, Pillsbury has an opportunity to come back and is putting in its case right now so that the case has not been decided and I should not indicate that it has.

[Senator Kefauver]: "Mr. Howrey, that is another thing that worries me about this decision. I do not see how you can hardly ever get to an end of litigation if the decision of the Federal Trade Commission is merely that [a] prima facie case violation has been found, and then it goes eventually to the courts, where there is still more argument.

Did not Pillsbury already submit information at the time this decision was rendered?

[Mr. Howrey]: "Yes; but under long established procedures and more particularly under the Administrative Procedure Act, every person, every corporation, has his right to his day in court, and we have to decide these things on sworn testimony made upon the public record and under the procedures established by Congress.

So whatever delay occurs in that respect, I think is due to the type of jurisprudence under which this country lives.

But I should, if I may, just add to that, the record in the Pillsbury case at the close of the Government's case was not a big record. It was 3,500 pages.

Now, in an antimonopoly or antitrust case, unfortunately or fortunately that is considered a small record.

[Senator Kefauver]: "Well, I appreciate the fact that there must be some consideration given to size and the effect upon competition, and you must have some standards to go by. But is not this Pillsbury case a pretty good example of what your rule of reason is going to get you into?

[Mr. Howrey]: "Yes; I think it is a very good example of it, and, of course, I conclude differently from you. I think it proves 100 percent that you can apply the rule of reason approach and have a relatively small record and relatively quick trial because, as I say, the case in chief was put in in 3,500 pages.

Now, the old Cement case went to 30,000 pages.

[Senator Kefauver]: "But, Mr. Howrey, it has just started. The thing has been going on ever since December 1953, and the hearing examiner is still hearing all this, that, and the other, under your rule of reason. When does this terminate?

[The court continued with similar quotes from the congressional hearing for several more pages. Ed.]

* * *

The foregoing quotations are not nearly all the references to the Pillsbury case in the course of the Committee hearings. This case or the Pillsbury name was referred to more than 100 times during the several hearings. We have here quoted only from a morning and afternoon session before the Senate subcommittee.

We think it is not necessary to consider the contention of petitioner here that the House hearings, conducted a little earlier, were also damaging to Pillsbury and were of such a nature as to deprive it of procedural due process. We conclude that the proceedings just outlined constituted an improper intrusion into the adjudicatory processes of the Commission and were of such a damaging character as to have required at least some of the members in addition to the chairman to disqualify themselves. We think it illuminating to quote Chairman Howrey's statement relative to his decision to disqualify himself, which he read into the record at the House subcommittee hearing. He said:

"* * * I wrote the opinion [in the Pillsbury case]. It is still a pending adjudication; and because of some of the penetrating questions over on the Senate side, I felt compelled to withdraw from the case because I did not think I could be judicial any more when I had been such an advocate of its views in answering questions."

* * * [C]ommon justice to a litigant requires that we invalidate the order entered by a quasi-judicial tribunal that was importuned by members of the United States Senate, however innocent they intended their conduct to be, to arrive at the ultimate conclusion which they did reach.

NOTES AND QUESTIONS

Not all agency proceedings are subject to the Due Process Clause and, hence, to the limits on permissible congressional exercises of influence that the Court applied in *Pillsbury*. The Due Process Clause prohibits a government official from attempting to influence an agency to decide an adjudicatory proceeding against a private party. The Due Process Clause does not apply to agency rulemaking or to an attempt to persuade an agency to act in favor of a private party when there is no private party on the other side of the case. What might be some non-legal reasons why members of Congress must be cautious in intervening on behalf of a private party when there is no private party on the other side? How might a political opponent of the member use that type of intervention on behalf of a private party?

2. THE PROCEDURES REQUIRED TO LEGISLATE

The Due Process Clause is not the only limit on the power of Congress to influence agency actions through informal means. No provision of the Constitution explicitly authorizes Congress to use informal means to persuade agencies to act in ways that are preferred by members of Congress, but the ability of Congress to do so is an inherent by-product of the formal powers conferred on Congress by the Constitution. Those formal powers are described in detail in Article I. Congress has long attempted to circumvent the limits on those powers, as the following materials illustrate.

a. THE LEGISLATIVE VETO

Beginning in the 1930s and continuing up until *Immigration & Naturalization Service v. Chadha*, below, Congress enacted more than 200 statutes with provisions allowing Congress to approve or disapprove agency actions through measures that fell short of full-blown legislation, such as a simple resolution passed by one or both Houses of Congress, or perhaps even by a single congressional committee. At the time the Court decided *Chadha*, Congress was poised to enact an amendment to the Administrative Procedure Act that would have conferred on either House acting alone the power to veto any action taken by any agency.

Immigration & Naturalization Service v. Chadha
462 U.S. 919 (1983).

■ CHIEF JUSTICE BURGER delivered the opinion of the Court.

[This case] presents a challenge to the constitutionality of the provision in § 244(c)(2) of the Immigration and Nationality Act authorizing one House of Congress, by resolution, to invalidate the decision of the Executive Branch, pursuant to authority delegated by Congress to the Attorney General of the United States, to allow a particular deportable alien to remain in the United States.

I

Chadha is an East Indian who was born in Kenya and holds a British passport. He was lawfully admitted to the United States in 1966 on a nonimmigrant student visa. His visa expired on June 30, 1972. On October 11, 1973, the District Director of the Immigration and Naturalization Service ordered Chadha to show cause why he should not be deported for having "remained in the United States for a longer time than permitted." Pursuant to § 242(b) of the Immigration and Nationality Act (Act), a deportation hearing was held before an immigration judge on January 11, 1974. Chadha conceded that he was deportable for overstaying his visa and the hearing was adjourned to enable him to file an application for suspension of deportation under § 244(a)(1) of the Act. Section 244(a)(1), 8 U.S.C. § 1254(a)(1), at the time in question, provided:

> "As hereinafter prescribed in this section, the Attorney General may, in his discretion, suspend deportation and adjust the status to that of an alien lawfully admitted for permanent residence, in the case of an alien who applies to the Attorney General for suspension of deportation and—

> "(1) is deportable under any law of the United States except the provisions specified in paragraph (2) of this subsection; has been physically present in the United States for a continuous period of not less than seven years immediately preceding the date of such application, and proves that during all of such period he was and is a person of good moral character; and is a person whose deportation would, in the opinion of the Attorney General, result in extreme hardship to the alien or to his spouse, parent, or child, who is a citizen of the United States or an alien lawfully admitted for permanent residence."

After Chadha submitted his application for suspension of deportation, the deportation hearing was resumed on February 7, 1974. On the basis of evidence adduced at the hearing, affidavits submitted with the application, and the results of a character investigation conducted by the INS, the Immigration Judge, on June 25, 1974, ordered that Chadha's deportation be suspended. The Immigration Judge found that Chadha met the requirements of § 244(a)(1): he had resided continuously in the United States for over seven years, was of good moral character, and would suffer "extreme hardship" if deported.

Pursuant to § 244(c)(1) of the Act, the Immigration Judge suspended Chadha's deportation and a report of the suspension was transmitted to Congress. Section 244(c)(1) provides:

> "Upon application by any alien who is found by the Attorney General to meet the requirements of subsection (a) of this section the Attorney General may in his discretion suspend deportation of such alien. If the deportation of any alien is suspended under the provisions of this subsection, a complete and detailed statement of the facts and pertinent provisions of law in the case shall be reported to the Congress with the reasons for such suspension. Such reports shall be submitted on the first day of each calendar month in which Congress is in session."

Once the Attorney General's recommendation for suspension of Chadha's deportation was conveyed to Congress, Congress had the power under § 244(c)(2) of the Act, to veto the Attorney General's determination that Chadha should not be deported. Section 244(c)(2) provides:

"(2) In the case of an alien specified in paragraph (1) of subsection (a) of this subsection—

"if during the session of the Congress at which a case is reported, or prior to the close of the session of the Congress next following the session at which a case is reported, either the Senate or the House of Representatives passes a resolution stating in substance that it does not favor the suspension of such deportation, the Attorney General shall thereupon deport such alien or authorize the alien's voluntary departure at his own expense under the order of deportation in the manner provided by law. If, within the time above specified, neither the Senate nor the House of Representatives shall pass such a resolution, the Attorney General shall cancel deportation proceedings."

* * *

On December 12, 1975, Representative Eilberg, Chairman of the Judiciary Subcommittee on Immigration, Citizenship, and International Law, introduced a resolution opposing "the granting of permanent residence in the United States to [six] aliens," including Chadha. * * * So far as the record before us shows, the House consideration of the resolution was based on Representative Eilberg's statement from the floor that

"[i]t was the feeling of the committee, after reviewing 340 cases, that the aliens contained in the resolution [Chadha and five others] did not meet these statutory requirements, particularly as it relates to hardship; and it is the opinion of the committee that their deportation should not be suspended."

The resolution was passed without debate or recorded vote. Since the House action was pursuant to § 244(c)(2), the resolution was not treated as an Article I legislative act; it was not submitted to the Senate or presented to the President for his action.

* * *

III

A

We turn now to the question whether action of one House of Congress under § 244(c)(2) violates strictures of the Constitution. * * *

[O]ur inquiry is sharpened rather than blunted by the fact that Congressional veto provisions are appearing with increasing frequency in statutes which delegate authority to executive and independent agencies:

"Since 1932, when the first veto provision was enacted into law, 295 congressional veto-type procedures have been inserted in 196 different statutes as follows: from 1932 to 1939, five statutes were affected; from 1940–49, nineteen statutes; between 1950–59, thirty-four statutes; and from 1960–69, forty-nine. From the year 1970 through 1975, at least one hundred sixty-three such provisions were included in eighty-nine laws." Abourezk, *The Congressional Veto: A Contemporary*

Response to Executive Encroachment on Legislative Prerogatives, 52 IND. L. REV. 323, 324 (1977).

Justice WHITE undertakes to make a case for the proposition that the one-House veto is a useful "political invention," and we need not challenge that assertion. We can even concede this utilitarian argument although the long-range political wisdom of this "invention" is arguable. It has been vigorously debated and it is instructive to compare the views of the protagonists. But policy arguments supporting even useful "political inventions" are subject to the demands of the Constitution which defines powers and, with respect to this subject, sets out just how those powers are to be exercised.

Explicit and unambiguous provisions of the Constitution prescribe and define the respective functions of the Congress and of the Executive in the legislative process. Since the precise terms of those familiar provisions are critical to the resolution of this case, we set them out verbatim. Article I provides:

> "All legislative Powers herein granted shall be vested in a Congress of the United States, which shall consist of a Senate *and* a House of Representatives." U.S. CONST. art. I, § 1. (emphasis added).

> "Every Bill which shall have passed the House of Representatives *and* the Senate, *shall*, before it becomes a Law, be presented to the President of the United States. . . ." U.S. CONST. art. I, § 7, cl. 2. (emphasis added).

> "*Every* Order, Resolution, or Vote to which the Concurrence of the Senate and House of Representatives may be necessary (except on a question of Adjournment) *shall be* presented to the President of the United States; and before the Same shall take Effect, *shall be* approved by him, or being disapproved by him, *shall be* repassed by two thirds of the Senate and House of Representatives, according to the Rules and Limitations prescribed in the Case of a Bill." U.S. CONST. art. I, § 7, cl. 3. (emphasis added).

These provisions of Art. I are integral parts of the constitutional design for the separation of powers. We have recently noted that "[t]he principle of separation of powers was not simply an abstract generalization in the minds of the Framers: it was woven into the documents that they drafted in Philadelphia in the summer of 1787." *Buckley v. Valeo*, 424 U.S. 1, 124 (1976). * * * [W]e see that the purposes underlying the Presentment Clauses and the bicameral requirement of Art. I guide our resolution of the important question presented in this case. The very structure of the Articles delegating and separating powers under Arts. I, II, and III exemplify the concept of separation of powers and we now turn to Art. I.

B

The Presentment Clauses

The records of the Constitutional Convention reveal that the requirement that all legislation be presented to the President before becoming law was uniformly accepted by the Framers. Presentment to the President and the Presidential veto were considered so imperative that the draftsmen took special pains to assure that these requirements could not be circumvented. During the final debate on Art. I, § 7, cl. 2, James Madison expressed concern that it might easily be evaded by the simple expedient of calling a proposed law a "resolution" or "vote" rather than a "bill." As a consequence, Art. I, § 7, cl. 3, was added.

The decision to provide the President with a limited and qualified power to nullify proposed legislation by veto was based on the profound conviction of the Framers that the powers conferred on Congress were the powers to be most carefully circumscribed. It is beyond doubt that lawmaking was a power to be shared by both Houses and the President. In The Federalist No. 73, Hamilton focused on the President's role in making laws:

> "If even no propensity had ever discovered itself in the legislative body to invade the rights of the Executive, the rules of just reasoning and theoretic propriety would of themselves teach us that the one ought not to be left to the mercy of the other, but ought to possess a constitutional and effectual power of self-defense."

THE FEDERALIST NO. 73, at 458 (Alexander Hamilton). In his Commentaries on the Constitution, Joseph Story makes the same point. 1 JOSEPH STORY, COMMENTARIES ON THE CONSTITUTION OF THE UNITED STATES 614–15 (1858).

The President's role in the lawmaking process also reflects the Framers' careful efforts to check whatever propensity a particular Congress might have to enact oppressive, improvident, or ill-considered measures. The President's veto role in the legislative process was described later during public debate on ratification:

> "It establishes a salutary check upon the legislative body, calculated to guard the community against the effects of faction, precipitancy, or of any impulse unfriendly to the public good which may happen to influence a majority of that body.
>
> ". . . The primary inducement to conferring the power in question upon the Executive is to enable him to defend himself; the secondary one is to increase the chances in favor of the community against the passing of bad laws through haste, inadvertence, or design." THE FEDERALIST NO. 73, at 458 (Alexander Hamilton).

The Court also has observed that the Presentment Clauses serve the important purpose of assuring that a "national" perspective is grafted on the legislative process:

> "The President is a representative of the people just as the members of the Senate and of the House are, and it may be, at some times, on some subjects, that the President elected by all the people is rather more representative of them all than are the members of either body of the Legislature whose constituencies are local and not countrywide. . . ." *Myers v. United States*, 272 U.S. 52, 123 (1926).

C

Bicameralism

The bicameral requirement of Art. I, §§ 1, 7 was of scarcely less concern to the Framers than was the Presidential veto and indeed the two concepts are interdependent. By providing that no law could take effect without the concurrence of the prescribed majority of the Members of both Houses, the Framers reemphasized their belief, already remarked upon in connection with the Presentment Clauses, that legislation should not be enacted unless it has been carefully and fully considered by the Nation's elected officials. In the Constitutional Convention debates on the need for a bicameral legislature, James Wilson, later to become a Justice of this Court, commented:

> "Despotism comes on mankind in different shapes. sometimes [sic] in an Executive, sometimes in a military, one. Is there danger of a Legislative despotism? Theory & practice both proclaim it. If the Legislative authority be not restrained, there can be neither liberty nor stability; and it can only be restrained by dividing it within itself, into distinct and independent branches. In a single house there is no check, but the inadequate one, of the virtue & good sense of those who compose it." 1 Farrand 254.

Hamilton argued that a Congress comprised of a single House was antithetical to the very purposes of the Constitution. Were the Nation to adopt a Constitution providing for only one legislative organ, he warned:

> "[W]e shall finally accumulate, in a single body, all the most important prerogatives of sovereignty, and thus entail upon our posterity one of the most execrable forms of government that human infatuation ever contrived. Thus we should create in reality that very tyranny which the adversaries of the new Constitution either are, or affect to be, solicitous to avert." THE FEDERALIST NO. 22, at 135 (Alexander Hamilton).

This view was rooted in a general skepticism regarding the fallibility of human nature later commented on by Joseph Story:

> "Public bodies, like private persons, are occasionally under the dominion of strong passions and excitements; impatient, irritable, and impetuous. . . . If [a legislature] feels no check but its own will, it rarely has the firmness to insist upon holding a question long enough under its own view, to see and mark it in all its bearings and relations to society." 1 STORY, *supra* at 383–84.

These observations are consistent with what many of the Framers expressed, none more cogently than Hamilton in pointing up the need to divide and disperse power in order to protect liberty:

> "In republican government, the legislative authority necessarily predominates. The remedy for this inconveniency is to divide the legislature into different branches; and to render them, by different modes of election and different principles of action, as little connected with each other as the nature of their common functions and their common dependence on the

society will admit." THE FEDERALIST NO. 51, at 324 (James Madison).

However familiar, it is useful to recall that apart from their fear that special interests could be favored at the expense of public needs, the Framers were also concerned, although not of one mind, over the apprehensions of the smaller states. Those states feared a commonality of interest among the larger states would work to their disadvantage; representatives of the larger states, on the other hand, were skeptical of a legislature that could pass laws favoring a minority of the people. It need hardly be repeated here that the Great Compromise, under which one House was viewed as representing the people and the other the states, allayed the fears of both the large and small states.

We see therefore that the Framers were acutely conscious that the bicameral requirement and the Presentment Clauses would serve essential constitutional functions. The President's participation in the legislative process was to protect the Executive Branch from Congress and to protect the whole people from improvident laws. The division of the Congress into two distinctive bodies assures that the legislative power would be exercised only after opportunity for full study and debate in separate settings. The President's unilateral veto power, in turn, was limited by the power of two thirds of both Houses of Congress to overrule a veto thereby precluding final arbitrary action of one person. It emerges clearly that the prescription for legislative action in Art. I, §§ 1, 7 represents the Framers' decision that the legislative power of the Federal government be exercised in accord with a single, finely wrought and exhaustively considered, procedure.

IV

* * *

Finally, we see that when the Framers intended to authorize either House of Congress to act alone and outside of its prescribed bicameral legislative role, they narrowly and precisely defined the procedure for such action. There are but four provisions in the Constitution, explicit and unambiguous, by which one House may act alone with the unreviewable force of law, not subject to the President's veto:

(a) The House of Representatives alone was given the power to initiate impeachments. U.S. CONST. art. I, § 2, cl. 6;

(b) The Senate alone was given the power to conduct trials following impeachment on charges initiated by the House and to convict following trial. U.S. CONST. art. I, § 3, cl. 5;

(c) The Senate alone was given final unreviewable power to approve or to disapprove presidential appointments. U.S. CONST. art. II, § 2, cl. 2;

(d) The Senate alone was given unreviewable power to ratify treaties negotiated by the President. U.S. CONST. art. II, § 2, cl. 2.

Clearly, when the Draftsmen sought to confer special powers on one House, independent of the other House, or of the President, they did so in explicit, unambiguous terms. * * *

Since it is clear that the action by the House under § 244(c)(2) was not within any of the express constitutional exceptions authorizing one

House to act alone, and equally clear that it was an exercise of legislative power, that action was subject to the standards prescribed in Art. I. The bicameral requirement, the Presentment Clauses, the President's veto, and Congress' power to override a veto were intended to erect enduring checks on each Branch and to protect the people from the improvident exercise of power by mandating certain prescribed steps. To preserve those checks, and maintain the separation of powers, the carefully defined limits on the power of each Branch must not be eroded. To accomplish what has been attempted by one House of Congress in this case requires action in conformity with the express procedures of the Constitution's prescription for legislative action: passage by a majority of both Houses and presentment to the President.

■ [An opinion by JUSTICE POWELL, concurring in the judgment, is omitted. Ed.]

■ JUSTICE WHITE, dissenting.

Today the Court not only invalidates § 244(c)(2) of the Immigration and Nationality Act, but also sounds the death knell for nearly 200 other statutory provisions in which Congress has reserved a "legislative veto." For this reason, the Court's decision is of surpassing importance. And it is for this reason that the Court would have been well advised to decide the case, if possible, on the narrower grounds of separation of powers, leaving for full consideration the constitutionality of other congressional review statutes operating on such varied matters as war powers and agency rulemaking, some of which concern the independent regulatory agencies.

The prominence of the legislative veto mechanism in our contemporary political system and its importance to Congress can hardly be overstated. It has become a central means by which Congress secures the accountability of executive and independent agencies. Without the legislative veto, Congress is faced with a Hobson's choice: either to refrain from delegating the necessary authority, leaving itself with a hopeless task of writing laws with the requisite specificity to cover endless special circumstances across the entire policy landscape, or in the alternative, to abdicate its lawmaking function to the Executive Branch and independent agencies. To choose the former leaves major national problems unresolved; to opt for the latter risks unaccountable policymaking by those not elected to fill that role. Accordingly, over the past five decades, the legislative veto has been placed in nearly 200 statutes. The device is known in every field of governmental concern: reorganization, budgets, foreign affairs, war powers, and regulation of trade, safety, energy, the environment and the economy.

NOTES AND QUESTIONS

1.   *Chadha* was an unusual case in one respect. It involved the exercise of a legislative veto in the context of an action an agency had taken in an adjudication. That unusual characteristic of the case was the basis for Justice Powell's concurring opinion, in which he relied on the Bill of Attainder Clause as a narrower basis for holding that the congressional action was unconstitutional. We have omitted that opinion because the issue Justice Powell addressed arises only in the context of an adjudication,

and the legislative veto was rarely exercised in that context. Congress more frequently used the legislative veto to reject agency rules. Of course, the majority opinion in *Chadha* is broad enough to apply to all exercise of one-House or two-House legislative vetoes.

2. As Justice White's dissenting opinion notes, Congress had come to view the legislative veto as a critical means of exercising control over agencies. Proponents of the legislative veto related it to the nondelegation doctrine in an interesting way. The argument could be summarized as follows: "We lack the omniscience and prescience needed to include clear substantive standards in the statutes in which we delegate power to agencies, but we have the capability and the responsibility to review agency actions after an agency has created a record that we can use to understand the underlying facts, identify the reasons for and against the agency action, and decide whether the agency action is consistent with our original intent and the preferences of the public we represent." How persuasive is that argument? Do the legislative veto and the nondelegation doctrine interact in other ways? If you were a member of Congress, how if at all would the availability of the legislative veto affect your incentives to delegate broad powers to agencies?

3. Justice White expressed particular concern that the lack of availability of the legislative veto would render it difficult or impossible for any politically-accountable institution to exercise control over the so-called "independent agencies." The existence and status of agencies that are independent of the Executive Branch in some way has long been the subject of great controversy. We discuss that controversy in detail in Chapter 3. Why might Justice White have been particularly concerned about the lack of political accountability of independent agencies in the absence of the legislative veto power? Is that a justifiable concern? If so, are there other ways of satisfying that concern?

4. The legislative veto power was used infrequently when it existed. Does it follow that its existence had little effect on agency actions? Consider the following hypothetical.

You are Administrator of the EPA. You issue a Notice of Proposed Rulemaking in which you propose to issue a major new rule that will improve air quality and reduce the incidences of mortality and morbidity attributable to asthma and heart disease at considerable cost to some corporations. You have discussed the proposal with the President, and he has expressed his strong support. You receive a call from the Congressman Jones, who chairs the House committee with jurisdiction over your agency. He orders you to come to his office for a meeting. (As an aside, what do you think about the option of refusing to come to his office to meet with him?) At the meeting, he orders you not to issue the proposed rule. He tells you that it will have an unacceptable adverse effect on his most important constituent, Acme Industries. You know enough about the power structure of the House to be able to predict that Chairman Jones can convince a majority of the members of his committee and a majority of the members of the House to vote for a resolution of disapproval of the rule you have proposed if you issue it. (As an aside, is that a realistic belief in some cases?)

What are your options with and without a legislative veto provision? Consider that question in three contexts. In the first, the chair of the Senate committee with jurisdiction over your agency supports your proposed rule, but there is a one-House veto provision in effect. In the second, both Houses are controlled by the opposition party, and you believe that a majority of members of the Senate also will vote for a resolution of disapproval if you issue the proposed rule, but there is a two-House veto provision in effect. In the third situation, there is no legislative veto provision in effect. Predict the outcome of this dispute in each situation.

5.   Notwithstanding the Supreme Court's decision in *Chadha*, Congress continues to utilize variations of the legislative veto. Some of the mechanisms used are informal. For example, agency officials and members of congressional appropriations committees might reach an informal agreement, documented in congressional committee and conference reports, that the agency would seek committee approval before pursuing particular actions in exchange for receiving certain funding. More formally, notwithstanding *Chadha*, Congress still includes legislative vetoes in bills; between 1983 and 2005, Congress adopted more than 400 such legislative vetoes. Although Presidents often reject the constitutionality of such provisions even while signing the accompanying legislation, agency documents often acknowledge the need to seek preclearance of certain actions in compliance with legislative veto requirements. *See* LOUIS FISHER, CONGRESSIONAL RESEARCH SERVICE REPORT FOR CONGRESS: LEGISLATIVE VETOES AFTER CHADHA (2005).

6.   In 1996, Congress created yet another new version of the legislative veto by enacting subtitle E of Public Law 104–121, entitled the Congressional Review Act, and codified as a new chapter eight of the Administrative Procedure Act, 5 U.S.C. §§ 801–808. In the new version of the legislative veto, Congress can veto a major rule only by enacting a joint resolution of disapproval subject to presentment to, and potential veto by, the President. Is this version of the legislative veto vulnerable to constitutional attack? *See* Stephen Breyer, *The Legislative Veto after* Chadha, 72 GEO. L.J. 785 (1984). Would you expect the new version of the legislative veto to be effective? The new version of the legislative veto has been used only once—when a newly inaugurated President signed a joint resolution to veto a rule that an agency had issued just days before the then-incumbent President left office. Why might it be possible for Congress to exercise the legislative veto power in that situation? Can you think of any other situation in which Congress could successfully exercise the new legislative veto power?

DISCUSSION PROBLEM

Proposed legislation requires agencies to submit all regulations that they adopt for consideration by Congress. Most agency regulations would fall under the definition of a "nonmajor rule" and would go into effect unless Congress adopts a joint resolution disapproving the regulation. By contrast, a regulation that qualifies as a "major rule," which is defined by reference to various potential features including but not limited to having an annual effect on the economy of $100,000,000 or more, will not go into effect unless Congress adopts a joint resolution approving the regulation. Critics of the proposed regulation contend that it violates the Supreme Court's decision in *INS v. Chadha* by allowing one house of Congress effectively to veto agency action. Supporters of the legislation counter that it merely converts major regulations into proposed legislation, and that it satisfies bicameralism and presentment by requiring both houses of

Congress to act before such regulations take effect. Is the proposed legislation constitutional? Assuming it is constitutional, what would the legislation accomplish, and what drawbacks might the legislation present?

b.   GRAMM-RUDMAN-HOLLINGS AND THE COMPTROLLER GENERAL

Congress has attempted other ways of shortcutting the legislative process, as the following case illustrates. A little bit of background about the history of the exercise of the spending power may help to put the case in perspective. Originally, Presidents enjoyed a great deal of discretion with respect to expenditures of funds that Congress appropriated. That discretion had two sources.

First, the early budgets of the United States consisted of only four broad accounts. As a result, the President enjoyed considerable discretion with respect to the types of expenditures he made within each broad category. That source of Presidential discretion disappeared gradually over the years as Congress broke the budget into thousands of accounts and sub-accounts.

Second, Congress traditionally worded appropriations statutes in the following form: "Congress hereby appropriates and authorizes the expenditure of. . . ." That traditional way of wording appropriations statutes gave the President discretion not to spend some appropriated funds. Presidents used that discretion with considerable frequency for a variety of reasons. Thus, for instance, President Jefferson declined to spend money Congress had appropriated to build a fleet of gunboats because of his conclusion that the foreign policy emergency that motivated Congress to authorize construction of the fleet had passed, and several Presidents used the discretion to implement across-the-board reductions in spending to avoid running unacceptably high budget deficits. For a detailed account of the history of the spending power, see Louis Fisher, Presidential Spending Power (1975).

Congress eliminated that second source of Presidential discretion in 1974 in response to many perceived abuses of the power by then-President Nixon. When Congress appropriated funds for any purpose with which President Nixon disagreed, he ordered the agency charged with responsibility for the funds appropriated for that purpose not to spend the funds. Congress was so angry at this circumvention of its power that it enacted a statute that instructs courts to interpret every appropriations statute as providing that: "Congress hereby appropriates and orders the expenditure of. . . ." That, of course, eliminated all Presidential discretion to decline to spend any funds appropriated by Congress for any purpose. It also left the Congress with the sole power and responsibility to avoid running unsustainably high budget deficits. Congress has had great difficulty fulfilling that responsibility. Can you identify the motives of individual legislators and the collective action problems that combine to render it difficult for Congress to keep the budget tolerably near balance?

Bowsher v. Synar

478 U.S. 714 (1986).

■ CHIEF JUSTICE BURGER delivered the opinion of the Court.

The question presented by these appeals is whether the assignment by Congress to the Comptroller General of the United States of certain functions under the Balanced Budget and Emergency Deficit Control Act of 1985 violates the doctrine of separation of powers.

On December 12, 1985, the President signed into law the Balanced Budget and Emergency Deficit Control Act of 1985, popularly known as the "Gramm-Rudman-Hollings Act." The purpose of the Act is to eliminate the federal budget deficit. To that end, the Act sets a "maximum deficit amount" for federal spending for each of fiscal years 1986 through 1991. The size of that maximum deficit amount progressively reduces to zero in fiscal year 1991. If in any fiscal year the federal budget deficit exceeds the maximum deficit amount by more than a specified sum, the Act requires across-the-board cuts in federal spending to reach the targeted deficit level, with half of the cuts made to defense programs and the other half made to nondefense programs. The Act exempts certain priority programs from these cuts.

These "automatic" reductions are accomplished through a rather complicated procedure, spelled out in § 251, the so-called "reporting provisions" of the Act. Each year, the Directors of the Office of Management and Budget (OMB) and the Congressional Budget Office (CBO) independently estimate the amount of the federal budget deficit for the upcoming fiscal year. If that deficit exceeds the maximum targeted deficit amount for that fiscal year by more than a specified amount, the Directors of OMB and CBO independently calculate, on a program-by-program basis, the budget reductions necessary to ensure that the deficit does not exceed the maximum deficit amount. The Act then requires the Directors to report jointly their deficit estimates and budget reduction calculations to the Comptroller General.

The Comptroller General, after reviewing the Directors' reports, then reports his conclusions to the President. § 251(b). The President in turn must issue a "sequestration" order mandating the spending reductions specified by the Comptroller General. § 252. There follows a period during which Congress may by legislation reduce spending to obviate, in whole or in part, the need for the sequestration order. If such reductions are not enacted, the sequestration order becomes effective and the spending reductions included in that order are made.

* * *

A three-judge District Court, appointed pursuant to 2 U.S.C. § 922(a)(5), invalidated the reporting provisions. [Then-Circuit Judge Scalia was appointed a member of the three-judge District Court. He is widely believed to have been the author of that court's decision even though it was characterized as a per curiam opinion. Ed.]

* * *

Although the District Court concluded that the Act survived a delegation doctrine challenge, it held that the role of the Comptroller

General in the deficit reduction process violated the constitutionally imposed separation of powers. The court first explained that the Comptroller General exercises executive functions under the Act. However, the Comptroller General, while appointed by the President with the advice and consent of the Senate, is removable not by the President but only by a joint resolution of Congress or by impeachment. The District Court reasoned that this arrangement could not be sustained under this Court's decisions in *Myers v. United States*, and *Humphrey's Executor v. United States*. Under the separation of powers established by the Framers of the Constitution, the court concluded, Congress may not retain the power of removal over an officer performing executive functions. The congressional removal power created a "here-and-now subservience" of the Comptroller General to Congress. The District Court therefore held that:

> "since the powers conferred upon the Comptroller General as part of the automatic deficit reduction process are executive powers, which cannot constitutionally be exercised by an officer removable by Congress, those powers cannot be exercised and therefore the automatic deficit reduction process to which they are central cannot be implemented."

Appeals were taken directly to this Court pursuant to § 274(b) of the Act. We noted probable jurisdiction and expedited consideration of the appeals. We affirm.

* * *

The Constitution does not contemplate an active role for Congress in the supervision of officers charged with the execution of the laws it enacts. The President appoints "Officers of the United States" with the "Advice and Consent of the Senate. . . ." U.S. CONST. art. II, § 2. Once the appointment has been made and confirmed, however, the Constitution explicitly provides for removal of Officers of the United States by Congress only upon impeachment by the House of Representatives and conviction by the Senate. An impeachment by the House and trial by the Senate can rest only on "Treason, Bribery or other high Crimes and Misdemeanors." U.S. CONST. art. II, § 4. A direct congressional role in the removal of officers charged with the execution of the laws beyond this limited one is inconsistent with separation of powers.

* * *

[W]e conclude that Congress cannot reserve for itself the power of removal of an officer charged with the execution of the laws except by impeachment. To permit the execution of the laws to be vested in an officer answerable only to Congress would, in practical terms, reserve in Congress control over the execution of the laws. As the District Court observed: "Once an officer is appointed, it is only the authority that can remove him, and not the authority that appointed him, that he must fear and, in the performance of his functions, obey." The structure of the Constitution does not permit Congress to execute the laws; it follows that Congress cannot grant to an officer under its control what it does not possess.

Our decision in *INS v. Chadha*, 462 U.S. 919 (1983), supports this conclusion. * * *

To permit an officer controlled by Congress to execute the laws would be, in essence, to permit a congressional veto. Congress could simply remove, or threaten to remove, an officer for executing the laws in any fashion found to be unsatisfactory to Congress. This kind of congressional control over the execution of the laws, *Chadha* makes clear, is constitutionally impermissible.

* * *

Appellants urge that the Comptroller General performs his duties independently and is not subservient to Congress. We agree with the District Court that this contention does not bear close scrutiny.

The critical factor lies in the provisions of the statute defining the Comptroller General's office relating to removability. Although the Comptroller General is nominated by the President from a list of three individuals recommended by the Speaker of the House of Representatives and the President *pro tempore* of the Senate, and confirmed by the Senate, he is removable only at the initiative of Congress.

* * *

Appellants suggest that the duties assigned to the Comptroller General in the Act are essentially ministerial and mechanical so that their performance does not constitute "execution of the law" in a meaningful sense. On the contrary, we view these functions as plainly entailing execution of the law in constitutional terms. Interpreting a law enacted by Congress to implement the legislative mandate is the very essence of "execution" of the law. Under § 251, the Comptroller General must exercise judgment concerning facts that affect the application of the Act. He must also interpret the provisions of the Act to determine precisely what budgetary calculations are required. Decisions of that kind are typically made by officers charged with executing a statute.

The executive nature of the Comptroller General's functions under the Act is revealed in § 252(a)(3) which gives the Comptroller General the ultimate authority to determine the budget cuts to be made. Indeed, the Comptroller General commands the President himself to carry out, without the slightest variation (with exceptions not relevant to the constitutional issues presented), the directive of the Comptroller General as to the budget reductions . .

■ JUSTICE STEVENS, with whom JUSTICE MARSHALL joins, concurring in the judgment.

* * *

Everyone agrees that the powers assigned to the Comptroller General by § 251(b) and § 251(c)(2) of the Gramm-Rudman-Hollings Act are extremely important. They require him to exercise sophisticated economic judgment concerning anticipated trends in the Nation's economy, projected levels of unemployment, interest rates, and the special problems that may be confronted by the many components of a vast federal bureaucracy. His duties are anything but ministerial—he is not merely a clerk wearing a "green eye-shade" as he undertakes these tasks. Rather, he is vested with the kind of responsibilities that Congress has elected to discharge itself under the fallback provision that will become effective if and when § 251(b) and § 251(c)(2) are held invalid. Unless we make the naive assumption that the economic destiny of the Nation could be safely entrusted to a mindless bank of computers, the powers that this Act vests in the Comptroller General must be recognized as having transcendent importance.

The Court concludes that the Gramm-Rudman-Hollings Act impermissibly assigns the Comptroller General "executive powers." Justice WHITE's dissent agrees that "the powers exercised by the Comptroller under the Act may be characterized as 'executive' in that they involve the interpretation and carrying out of the Act's mandate." This conclusion is not only far from obvious but also rests on the unstated and unsound premise that there is a definite line that distinguishes executive power from legislative power.

* * *

One reason that the exercise of legislative, executive, and judicial powers cannot be categorically distributed among three mutually exclusive branches of Government is that governmental power cannot always be readily characterized with only one of those three labels. On the contrary, as our cases demonstrate, a particular function, like a chameleon, will often take on the aspect of the office to which it is assigned. For this reason, "[w]hen any Branch acts, it is presumptively exercising the power the Constitution has delegated to it." *INS v. Chadha*, 462 U.S. 919, 951 (1983).

The *Chadha* case itself illustrates this basic point. The governmental decision that was being made was whether a resident alien who had overstayed his student visa should be deported. From the point of view of the Administrative Law Judge who conducted a hearing on the issue—or as Justice POWELL saw the issue in his concurrence— the decision took on a judicial coloring. From the point of view of the Attorney General of the United States to whom Congress had delegated the authority to suspend deportation of certain aliens, the decision appeared to have an executive character. But, as the Court held, when the House of Representatives finally decided that Chadha must be deported, its action "was essentially legislative in purpose and effect." *Id.* at 952.

The powers delegated to the Comptroller General by § 251 of the Act before us today have a similar chameleon-like quality. The District Court persuasively explained why they may be appropriately characterized as executive powers. But, when that delegation is held invalid, the "fallback provision" provides that the report that would otherwise be issued by the Comptroller General shall be issued by Congress itself. In the event that the resolution is enacted, the congressional report will have the same legal consequences as if it had been issued by the Comptroller General. In that event, moreover, surely no one would suggest that Congress had acted in any capacity other than "legislative."

* * *

Thus, I do not agree that the Comptroller General's responsibilities under the Gramm-Rudman-Hollings Act must be termed "executive powers," or even that our inquiry is much advanced by using that term. For, whatever the label given the functions to be performed by the Comptroller General under § 251—or by the Congress under § 274—the District Court had no difficulty in concluding that Congress could delegate the performance of those functions to another branch of the Government. If the delegation to a stranger is permissible, why may not Congress delegate the same responsibilities to one of its own agents? That is the central question before us today.

Congress regularly delegates responsibility to a number of agents who provide important support for its legislative activities. * * *

The Gramm-Rudman-Hollings Act assigns to the Comptroller General the duty to make policy decisions that have the force of law. The Comptroller General's report is, in the current statute, the engine that gives life to the ambitious budget reduction process. It is the Comptroller General's report that "provide[s] for the determination of reductions" and that "contain[s] estimates, determinations, and specifications for all of the items contained in the report" submitted by the Office of Management and Budget and the Congressional Budget Office. § 251(b). It is the Comptroller General's report that the President must follow and that will have conclusive effect. § 252. It is, in short, the Comptroller General's report that will have a profound, dramatic, and immediate impact on the Government and on the Nation at large.

Article I of the Constitution specifies the procedures that Congress must follow when it makes policy that binds the Nation: its legislation must be approved by both of its Houses and presented to the President. In holding that an attempt to legislate by means of a "one-House veto" violated the procedural mandate in Article I, we explained:

> "We see therefore that the Framers were acutely conscious that the bicameral requirement and the Presentment Clauses would serve essential constitutional functions. The President's participation in the legislative process was to protect the Executive Branch from Congress and to protect the whole people from improvident laws. The division of the Congress into two distinctive bodies assures that the legislative power would be exercised only after opportunity for full study and debate in separate settings. The President's unilateral veto power, in turn, was limited by the power of two-thirds of both Houses of Congress to overrule a veto thereby precluding final arbitrary action of one person. . . . It emerges clearly that the prescription for legislative action in Art. I, §§ 1, 7, represents the Framers' decision that the legislative power of the Federal Government be exercised in accord with a single, finely wrought and exhaustively considered, procedure." *INS v. Chadha*, 462 U.S. at 951.

If Congress were free to delegate its policymaking authority to one of its components, or to one of its agents, it would be able to evade "the carefully crafted restraints spelled out in the Constitution." *Id.* at 959.

That danger—congressional action that evades constitutional restraints—is not present when Congress delegates lawmaking power to the executive or to an independent agency.

* * *

As a result, to decide this case there is no need to consider the Decision of 1789, the President's removal power, or the abstract nature of "executive powers." Once it is clear that the Comptroller General, whose statutory duties define him as an agent of Congress, has been assigned the task of making policy determinations that will bind the Nation, the question is simply one of congressional process. There can be no doubt that the Comptroller General's statutory duties under Gramm-Rudman-Hollings do not follow the constitutionally prescribed procedures for congressional lawmaking.

In short, even though it is well settled that Congress may delegate legislative power to independent agencies or to the Executive, and thereby divest itself of a portion of its lawmaking power, when it elects to exercise such power itself, it may not authorize a lesser representative of the Legislative Branch to act on its behalf. It is for this reason that I believe § 251(b) and § 251(c)(2) of the Act are unconstitutional.

■ JUSTICE WHITE, dissenting.

The Court, acting in the name of separation of powers, takes upon itself to strike down the Gramm-Rudman-Hollings Act, one of the most novel and far-reaching legislative responses to a national crisis since the New Deal.

* * *

To be sure, if the budget-cutting mechanism required the responsible officer to exercise a great deal of policymaking discretion, one might argue that having created such broad discretion Congress had some obligation based upon Art. II to vest it in the Chief Executive or his agents. In Gramm-Rudman-Hollings, however, Congress has done no such thing; instead, it has created a precise and articulated set of criteria designed to minimize the degree of policy choice exercised by the officer executing the statute and to ensure that the relative spending priorities established by Congress in the appropriations it passes into law remain unaltered. Given that the exercise of policy choice by the officer executing the statute would be inimical to Congress' goal in enacting "automatic" budget-cutting measures, it is eminently reasonable and proper for Congress to vest the budget-cutting authority in an officer who is to the greatest degree possible nonpartisan and independent of the President and his political agenda and who therefore may be relied upon not to allow his calculations to be colored by political considerations.

* * *

The question to be answered is whether the threat of removal of the Comptroller General for cause through joint resolution as authorized by the Budget and Accounting Act renders the Comptroller sufficiently subservient to Congress that investing him with "executive" power can be realistically equated with the unlawful retention of such power by Congress itself; more generally, the question is whether there is a genuine threat of "encroachment or aggrandizement of one branch at the expense of the other," *Buckley v. Valeo*, 424 U.S. 1, 122 (1976). Common sense indicates that the existence of the removal provision poses no such threat to the principle of separation of powers.

The statute does not permit anyone to remove the Comptroller at will; removal is permitted only for specified cause, with the existence of cause to be determined by Congress following a hearing. Any removal under the statute would presumably be subject to post-termination judicial review to ensure that a hearing had in fact been held and that the finding of cause for removal was not arbitrary. These procedural and substantive limitations on the removal power militate strongly against the characterization of the Comptroller as a mere agent of Congress by virtue of the removal authority. Indeed, similarly qualified grants of removal power are generally deemed to protect the officers to whom they apply and to establish their independence from the domination of the possessor of the removal power. Removal authority limited in such a manner is more properly viewed as motivating adherence to a substantive standard established by law than as inducing subservience to the particular institution that enforces that standard. That the agent enforcing the standard is Congress may be of some significance to the Comptroller, but Congress' substantively limited removal power will undoubtedly be less of a spur to subservience than Congress' unquestionable and unqualified power to enact legislation reducing the Comptroller's salary, cutting the funds available to his department, reducing his personnel, limiting or expanding his duties, or even abolishing his position altogether.

More importantly, the substantial role played by the President in the process of removal through joint resolution reduces to utter insignificance the possibility that the threat of removal will induce subservience to the Congress. As I have pointed out above, a joint resolution must be presented to the President and is ineffective if it is vetoed by him, unless the veto is overridden by the constitutionally prescribed two-thirds majority of both Houses of Congress. The requirement of Presidential approval obviates the possibility that the Comptroller will perceive himself as so completely at the mercy of Congress that he will function as its tool. If the Comptroller's conduct in office is not so unsatisfactory to the President as to convince the latter that removal is required under the statutory standard, Congress will have no independent power to coerce the Comptroller unless it can muster a two-thirds majority in both Houses—a feat of bipartisanship more difficult than that required to impeach and convict. The incremental *in terrorem* effect of the possibility of congressional removal in the face of a Presidential veto is therefore exceedingly unlikely to have any discernible impact on the extent of congressional influence over the Comptroller.

The practical result of the removal provision is not to render the Comptroller unduly dependent upon or subservient to Congress, but to render him one of the most independent officers in the entire federal establishment.

NOTES AND QUESTIONS

1. Justice White disagreed with the other Justices on two issues. The first is the nature and significance of the task assigned to the Comptroller General. The concurring Justices characterized the task as "extremely important," and the Justices who join the majority opinion seemed to agree with that characterization. Yet, the appellants characterized the task as "essentially ministerial and mechanical," and Justice White seemed to agree with that characterization. Indeed, he conceded that "if the budget-cutting mechanism required the responsible official to exercise a great deal of policymaking discretion, one might argue that . . . Congress had some obligation based upon Art. II to vest it in the Chief Executive or his agents." Which characterization of the Comptroller General's task do you find more persuasive, and why?

2. The second issue on which Justice White differed with the other Justices was with respect to the question of what individual or institution, if any, can exercise control over the Comptroller General. The other Justices agreed with then-Judge Scalia that, since Congress is the only institution that can initiate the process of removing the Comptroller General, the Comptroller General has a "here-and-now subservience" to Congress that will cause him to follow instructions from congressional leaders. Justice White, by contrast, believed that the process of removing the Comptroller General is so difficult to complete that the Comptroller General is independent of both Congress and the Executive. Which characterization of the Comptroller General's position do you find more persuasive, and why?

3. Unless the Comptroller General is removed from office, he serves a statutory term of fifteen years. If Justice White is correct with respect to his conclusion that the Comptroller General is so independent of both Congress and the Executive, would the budget-cutting mechanism adopted in Gramm-Rudman-Hollings create even larger constitutional problems? Why might we find it problematic if budgetary decisions are made by someone who cannot be removed from office and who was appointed by a President whose term ended over a dozen years ago?

4. Both the majority and Justice White characterized the spending function as an Executive function. The concurring Justices disagreed. They argued that it defies characterization on any basis except the identity of the institution and the procedures used to perform it. Which of these positions do you find more persuasive, and why?

5. Both the majority and the concurrence concluded that the unconstitutionality of the budget-cutting mechanism adopted in Gramm-Rudman-Hollings followed logically from *Chadha*. If Congress could delegate discretionary power to agencies so wholly within its control, would Congress then have an incentive to delegate power even more broadly to agencies? Why or why not? If Congress could delegate power to agencies within its control, what incentive would Congress have to impose any substantive limits on the power of such agencies?

6. Once again you see lurking in the background the long-standing dispute with respect to the constitutionality of so-called "independent agencies." We will discuss that dispute in detail in the next Chapter. It may help you to understand the differences of opinion among the Justices on this issue that are apparent in the opinions in *Chadha* and *Bowsher* if we tell you about two basic characteristics of independent agencies now. The heads of "independent agencies" *can* be removed from office by the President, albeit only "for cause" and Congress *can play no role* in the process of removing such an agency official. Compare that with removal provision at issue in *Bowsher v. Synar*: the President cannot remove the Comptroller General for any reason, and only Congress can begin the process of removing the Comptroller General. As a practical matter, would you expect these two removal mechanisms to achieve different results in influencing agency action? If so, in what way?

DISCUSSION PROBLEM

The Secretary of State wants Congress to authorize $50 million in humanitarian aid for use in Pakistan. Several members of Congress have expressed concern that some of the funds will find their way into the hands of groups actively engaged in attacking United States soldiers serving in Afghanistan. In return for receiving the $50 million, the Secretary of State agrees that a portion of the funds will only be released with the approval of certain congressional committees. The agreement is documented in a letter from the Secretary of State to congressional leaders. Is this informal agreement constitutional? Why or why not?

CHAPTER 3

PRESIDENTIAL CONTROL OF AGENCIES

As you no doubt discerned from the Chapter 2, Congress devoted much of the twentieth century (and some of the nineteenth and twenty-first) to establishing and delegating power to executive branch and independent agencies. Just as these acts highlighted existing questions regarding the power of Congress to make such delegations, they also brought to the fore debates over the nature and scope of presidential authority.

Presidents have long complained about their inability to control the sprawling federal government bureaucracy, and every President has attempted to exercise control in a wide variety of ways. The Constitution says little that is helpful in identifying the tools available to a President to control agencies or the limits on those tools. Article 2, Section 1, Clause 1 provides that: "The executive power shall be vested in the President. . . ." Section 2, Clause 1 empowers the President to "require the opinion, in writing, of the principal officer in each of the executive departments, upon any subject relating to their respective offices, . . ." Section 3 provides that the President "shall take care that the laws be faithfully executed, . . ."

Each of these provisions is difficult to interpret. What is the executive power? What does it mean to vest it in the President? Does the Opinions in Writing Clause imply that all principal officers in each of the executive departments must follow the orders of the President? What is an executive department? Does the Take Care Clause confer power on the President? If so, what powers does it confer? Does the Take Care Clause implicitly preclude individuals or institutions other than those that are accountable to the President from executing the laws? Is that clause also a limit on presidential power? If so, how does it limit presidential power? The Court has wrestled with some of these and other questions concerning presidential power and administrative agencies, but the Court has not yet provided definitive answers to most of them.

Formalism versus Functionalism

Supreme Court and other judicial opinions construing Article II are often difficult to square with one another. One way of thinking meaningfully about these cases and reconciling the seemingly irreconcilable opinions requires some understanding of two competing theories of constitutional interpretation: formalism and functionalism. Legal scholars have debated the merits, flaws, and implications of these theories ad nauseum, offering several interesting perspectives that you might find illuminating in considering the cases in this Chapter.

Gary Lawson, Territorial Governments and the
Limits of Formalism

78 Cal. L. Rev. 853, 857–60 (1990).

Formalists treat the Constitution's three "vesting" clauses as effecting a complete division of otherwise unallocated federal governmental authority among the constitutionally specified legislative, executive, and judicial institutions. Any exercise of governmental power, and any governmental institution exercising that power, must either fit within one of the three formal categories thus established or find explicit constitutional authorization for such deviation. The separation of powers principle is violated whenever the categorizations of the exercised power and the exercising institution do not match and the Constitution does not specifically permit such blending.

The formalist method is concededly easier to describe than to apply, because not all governmental activities are associated with only one particular institution. For example, Congress can resolve disputes concerning government contracts by passing private bills or by entrusting the dispute resolution to courts. The activity can thus be either legislative or judicial, depending upon which institution performs it. Similarly, certain political bodies can be simultaneously part of more than one governmental institution. One can imagine—and Congress has on occasion created—bodies that perform both judicial and executive functions, enjoying independence in the exercise of the former but answering to the President for the performance of the latter. The formalist, however, views these areas of overlap among the three constitutional functions and institutions as limited. Outside of these areas, and absent constitutional authorization to the contrary, formalism maintains that each institution must exercise its correlative power and no others, without regard to the pragmatic usefulness or harmlessness of having the "wrong" institution exercise a power.

* * *

Formalism can usefully be contrasted with functionalism, its principal methodological competitor in the separation of powers arena. In its simplest formulation, functionalism asks "whether the exercise of the contested function by one branch impermissibly intrudes into the *core* function or domain of another branch." In other words, the question of blending is treated as one of degree rather than, as with formalism, one of kind. A different strand of functionalism begins with the (correct) observation that "the constitutional text addresses the powers *only* of the elected members of Congress, of the President as an individual, and of the federal courts." The Constitution does not speak of "branches" as such, nor does it discuss the institutions of government subordinate to the three named heads of authority. The functionalist thus infers that Congress is free to allocate authority as it pleases among subordinate institutions (however formalists would characterize them), as long as the "overall character or quality" of the relationships between those institutions and the named heads of government is consistent with the latters' performance of their core functions.

Harold H. Bruff, The Incompatibility Principle
59 Admin. L. Rev. 225, 226 (2007).

Formalism is very fierce; it consumes statutes that may serve real needs of government. Functionalism is quite permissive; it blesses statutes that may contain serious flaws.

William N. Eskridge, Jr., Relationships Between Formalism and Functionalism in Separation of Powers Cases
22 Harv. J. L. & Pub. Pol'y 21, 21–22 (1998).

Formalism might be understood as deduction from authoritative constitutional text, structure, original intent, or all three working together. Functionalism might be understood as induction from constitutional policy and practice, with practice typically being examined over time. Formalist reasoning promises stability and continuity of analysis over time; functionalist reasoning promises adaptability and evolution.

Finally and relatedly, formalism and functionalism could be contrasted as emphasizing different goals for law. Formalism might be understood as giving priority to rule of law values such as transparency, predictability, and continuity in law. Functionalism, in turn, might be understood as emphasizing pragmatic values like adaptability, efficacy, and justice in law.

Professor Lawson, for one, has opined that the Supreme Court is "solidly, consistently, unshakably functionalist." Gary Lawson, *Prolegomenon to Any Future Administrative Law Course: Separation of Powers and the Transcendental Deduction*, 49 ST. LOUIS U. L.J. 885, 891 (2005). Formalist versus functionalist reasoning is by no means limited to the materials in this Chapter; nevertheless, in evaluating the judicial opinions contained herein, you might consider whether or not you think Lawson's assessment of the Supreme Court's preferred interpretive methodology is correct.

A. THE POWER TO APPOINT

The provision of the Constitution that most clearly confers power over agencies on the President is the Appointments Clause. Article 2, Section 2, Clause 2 provides that "he shall nominate and, by and with the advice and consent of the Senate, shall appoint . . . all . . . officers of the United States, . . . but the Congress may by law vest the appointment of such inferior officers, as they think proper, in the President alone, in the courts of law, or in the heads of departments." Under any plausible interpretation, the Appointments Clause gives the President a great deal of power to choose agency decision makers. Moreover, the Court has issued several important opinions in which it has interpreted the Appointments Clause in ways that give the President the dominant role in choosing the individuals who are the ultimate decisionmakers in agencies. Nevertheless, like the other clauses in Article II, the Appointments Clause raises difficult interpretive issues.

1.   WHO IS AN OFFICER OF THE UNITED STATES?

Officers of the United States must be appointed in accordance with the Appointments Clause. Other federal government employees do not. The Appointments Clause provides explicitly that ambassadors and Supreme Court Justices are Officers of the United States, but also makes clear that the category stretches more broadly to include "other public Ministers and Consuls" and "all other Officers" without offering further guidance as to who is included. By what criteria do the courts evaluate which employees of the federal government are Officers? The Federal Election Commission has provided fertile ground for exploring this question, as the following cases demonstrate.

Buckley v. Valeo
424 U.S. 1 (1976).

■ PER CURIAM.

These appeals present constitutional challenges to the key provisions of the Federal Election Campaign Act of 1971 (Act), and related provisions of the Internal Revenue Code of 1954, all as amended in 1974.

The Court of Appeals, in sustaining the legislation in large part against various constitutional challenges, viewed it as "by far the most comprehensive reform legislation (ever) passed by Congress concerning the election of the President, Vice-President, and members of Congress." The statutes at issue summarized in broad terms, contain the following provisions: (a) individual political contributions are limited to $1,000 to any single candidate per election, with an overall annual limitation of $25,000 by any contributor; independent expenditures by individuals and groups "relative to a clearly identified candidate" are limited to $1,000 a year; campaign spending by candidates for various federal offices and spending for national conventions by political parties are subject to prescribed limits; (b) contributions and expenditures above certain threshold levels must be reported and publicly disclosed; (c) a system for public funding of presidential campaign activities is established by Subtitle H of the Internal Revenue Code; and (d) a Federal Election Commission is established to administer and enforce the legislation.

* * *

[The Justices divided in complicated ways in their views with respect to many of the issues raised, but they were unanimous with respect to the views expressed in section IV of the opinion. Ed.]

IV. THE FEDERAL ELECTION COMMISSION

The 1974 amendments to the Act create an eight-member Federal Election Commission (Commission) and vest in it primary and substantial responsibility for administering and enforcing the Act. The question that we address in this portion of the opinion is whether, in view of the manner in which a majority of its members are appointed, the Commission may under the Constitution exercise the powers conferred upon it. * * *

Chapter 14 of Title 2 makes the Commission the principal repository of the numerous reports and statements which are required by that chapter to be filed by those engaging in the regulated political activities. Its duties . . . with respect to these reports and statements include filing and indexing, making them available for public inspection, preservation, and auditing and field investigations. It is directed to "serve as a national clearinghouse for information in respect to the administration of elections." Federal Election Campaign Act of 1971, 2 U.S.C. § 438(b).

Beyond these recordkeeping, disclosure, and investigative functions, however, the Commission is given extensive rulemaking and adjudicative powers. * * *

The Commission's enforcement power is both direct and wide ranging. * * *

The body in which this authority is reposed consists of eight members. The Secretary of the Senate and the Clerk of the House of Representatives are *ex officio* members of the Commission without the right to vote. Two members are appointed by the President *pro tempore* of the Senate "upon the recommendations of the majority leader of the Senate and the minority leader of the Senate." Two more are to be appointed by the Speaker of the House of Representatives, likewise upon the recommendations of its respective majority and minority leaders. The remaining two members are appointed by the President. Each of the six voting members of the Commission must be confirmed by the majority of both Houses of Congress, and each of the three appointing authorities is forbidden to choose both of their appointees from the same political party.

Appellants argue that given the Commission's extensive powers the method of choosing its members * * * runs afoul of the separation of powers embedded in the Constitution, and urge that as presently constituted the Commission's "existence be held unconstitutional by this Court."

* * *

Appellants urge that since Congress has given the Commission wide-ranging rulemaking and enforcement powers with respect to the substantive provisions of the Act, Congress is precluded under the principle of separation of powers from vesting in itself the authority to appoint those who will exercise such authority. Their argument is based on the language of Art. II, § 2, cl. 2, of the Constitution, which provides in pertinent part as follows:

"[The President] shall nominate, and by and with the Advice and Consent of the Senate, shall appoint . . . all other Officers of the United States, whose Appointments are not herein otherwise provided for, and which shall be established by Law: but the Congress may by Law vest the Appointment of such inferior Officers, as they think proper, in the President alone, in the Courts of Law, or in the Heads of Departments."

Appellants' argument is that this provision is the exclusive method by which those charged with executing the laws of the United States may be chosen. Congress, they assert, cannot have it both ways. If the Legislature wishes the Commission to exercise all of the conferred powers, then its members are in fact "Officers of the United States" and must be appointed under the Appointments Clause. But if Congress insists upon retaining the power to appoint, then the members of the Commission may not discharge those many functions of the Commission which can be performed only by "Officers of the United States," as that term must be construed within the doctrine of separation of powers.

Appellee Commission and *amici* in support of the Commission urge that the Framers of the Constitution, while mindful of the need for checks and balances among the three branches of the National Government, had no intention of denying to the Legislative Branch authority to appoint its own officers. Congress, either under the Appointments Clause or under its grants of substantive legislative authority and the Necessary and Proper Clause in Art. I, is in their view empowered to provide for the appointment to the Commission in the manner which it did because the Commission is performing "appropriate legislative functions."

* * *

We think that the term "Officers of the United States" as used in Art. II, defined to include "all persons who can be said to hold an office under the government" in *United States v. Germaine*, 99 U.S. 508 (1879), is a term intended to have substantive meaning. We think its fair import is that any appointee exercising significant authority pursuant to the laws of the United States is an "Officer of the United States," and must, therefore, be appointed in the manner prescribed by § 2, cl. 2, of that Article.

If "all persons who can be said to hold an office under the government about to be established under the Constitution were intended to be included within one or the other of these modes of appointment," *United States v. Germaine*, 99 U.S. 508, it is difficult to see how the members of the Commission may escape inclusion. If a postmaster first class, *Myers v. United States*, 272 U.S. 52 (1926), and the clerk of a district court, *Ex parte Hennen*, 38 U.S. (13 Pet.) 225 (1839), are inferior officers of the United States within the meaning of the Appointments Clause, as they are, surely the Commissioners before us are at the very least such "inferior Officers" within the meaning of that Clause.[162]

---

[162] "Officers of the United States" does not include all employees of the United States, but there is no claim made that the Commissioners are employees of the United States rather than officers. Employees are lesser functionaries subordinate to officers of the United States, whereas the Commissioners, appointed for a statutory term, are not subject to the control or direction of any other executive, judicial, or legislative authority.

Although two members of the Commission are initially selected by the President, his nominations are subject to confirmation not merely by the Senate, but by the House of Representatives as well. The remaining four voting members of the Commission are appointed by the President *pro tempore* of the Senate and by the Speaker of the House. While the second part of the Clause authorizes Congress to vest the appointment of the officers described in that part in "the Courts of Law, or in the Heads of Departments," neither the Speaker of the House nor the President *pro tempore* of the Senate comes within this language.

The phrase "Heads of Departments," used as it is in conjunction with the phrase "Courts of Law," suggests that the Departments referred to are themselves in the Executive Branch or at least have some connection with that branch. While the Clause expressly authorizes Congress to vest the appointment of certain officers in the "Courts of Law," the absence of similar language to include Congress must mean that neither Congress nor its officers were included within the language "Heads of Departments" in this part of cl. 2.

Thus with respect to four of the six voting members of the Commission, neither the President, the head of any department, nor the Judiciary has any voice in their selection.

The Appointments Clause specifies the method of appointment only for "Officers of the United States" whose appointment is not "otherwise provided for" in the Constitution. But there is no provision of the Constitution remotely providing any alternative means for the selection of the members of the Commission or for anybody like them.

* * *

Thus, on the assumption that all of the powers granted in the statute may be exercised by an agency whose members *have been* appointed in accordance with the Appointments Clause, the ultimate question is which, if any, of those powers may be exercised by the present voting Commissioners, none of whom was appointed as provided by that Clause. * * * [T]he Commission's powers fall generally into three categories: functions relating to the flow of necessary information—receipt, dissemination, and investigation; functions with respect to the Commission's task of fleshing out the statute—rulemaking and advisory opinions; and functions necessary to ensure compliance with the statute and rules—informal procedures, administrative determinations and hearings, and civil suits.

Insofar as the powers confided in the Commission are essentially of an investigative and informative nature, falling in the same general category as those powers which Congress might delegate to one of its own committees, there can be no question that the Commission as presently constituted may exercise them. * * *

But when we go beyond this type of authority to the more substantial powers exercised by the Commission, we reach a different result. The Commission's enforcement power, exemplified by its discretionary power to seek judicial relief, is authority that cannot possibly be regarded as merely in aid of the legislative function of Congress. A lawsuit is the ultimate remedy for a breach of the law, and it is to the President, and not to the Congress, that the Constitution entrusts the responsibility to "take Care that the Laws be faithfully executed." U.S. CONST. art. II, § 3.

* * *

We hold that these provisions of the Act, vesting in the Commission primary responsibility for conducting civil litigation in the courts of the United States for vindicating public rights, violate Art. II, § 2, cl. 2, of the Constitution. Such functions may be discharged only by persons who are "Officers of the United States" within the language of that section.

All aspects of the Act are brought within the Commission's broad administrative powers: rulemaking, advisory opinions, and determinations of eligibility for funds and even for federal elective office itself. These functions, exercised free from day-to-day supervision of either Congress or the Executive Branch, are more legislative and judicial in nature than are the Commission's enforcement powers, and are of kinds usually performed by independent regulatory agencies or by some department in the Executive Branch under the direction of an Act of Congress. Congress viewed these broad powers as essential to effective and impartial administration of the entire substantive framework of the Act. Yet each of these functions also represents the performance of a significant governmental duty exercised pursuant to a public law. While the President may not insist that such functions be delegated to an appointee of his removable at will, *Humphrey's Executor v. United States*, 295 U.S. 602 (1935), none of them operates merely in aid of congressional authority to legislate or is sufficiently removed from the administration and enforcement of public law to allow it to be performed by the present Commission. These administrative functions may therefore be exercised only by persons who are "Officers of the United States."

NOTES AND QUESTIONS

1.   During the 1960s, the Civil Rights Commission was one of the most powerful agencies. It conducted investigations of alleged deprivations of civil rights, with particular emphasis on racism in the south. Its investigations and reports identified horrible conditions and led to enactment of the many federal statutes that gradually transformed the legal and social environment of the southern states. The Civil Rights Commission had (and still has) the same composition that the Court held to be unconstitutional in *Buckley*—its members are appointed by the President, the leaders of the Senate, and the leaders of the House. Yet, in rejecting a due process challenge to investigative hearing procedures employed by the Civil Rights Commission in *Hannah v. Larche*, 363 U.S. 420 (1960), the Court was clearly untroubled by that agency's composition, notwithstanding a dissent that was clearly disturbed by the scope and practical impact of the agency's powers. Why do you think the Civil Rights Commission's composition was permissible but the original composition of the FEC was not?

2.   Most federal agencies are headed by a single individual who is appointed by the President subject to confirmation by the Senate; many if not most such individuals serve at the pleasure of the President and can be removed at will by him. Alternatively, some federal agencies, referred to as

"independent agencies," share a different structure: decision making by majority vote of an odd number of commissioners, each of whom serves a specified term of years and cannot be removed from office except for cause, and no more than a majority of whom can be members of the same political party. Some people believe that the "for cause" restriction on the power of the President to remove a Commissioner insulates the independent agencies from presidential control to some extent. We will explore the debate about the removal power and its effects in detail in Part B of this Chapter. Regardless, both agencies headed by single individuals and independent agencies are subject to the holding in *Buckley* if they have powers similar to those of the FEC. Thus, commissioners can only be appointed through the process of nomination by the President subject to confirmation by the Senate. Why do you think the supporters of the FEC originally rejected the above-described traditional models and adopted instead a structure that consisted of six voting Commissioners—two appointed by the President, two by the Senate, and two by the House? What goals might they have been attempting to further with this structure? Do you think the structure they chose would have been effective in furthering that goal if the Court had held it constitutional? Given the mission of the FEC, what structure would be effective and fair?

3. After the Court's decision in *Buckley*, Congress reenacted the statute with one change in the FEC's composition: all six voting Commissioners must be nominated by the President subject to confirmation by the Senate. Still, no more than three Commissioners may belong to a single political party. Would you expect this structure to be effective? During significant periods of time, the FEC has not been able to take any action because the President and the Senate leadership have not been able to agree on appointees and the FEC consequently lacked a quorum. In what conditions would you expect the lack of quorum problem to exist? Under what circumstances would you expect the President and the leaders of the Senate to agree on appointees? How would you rate the likelihood of a filibuster over appointments to the FEC? If the same party has control of the White House and a filibuster-proof majority of the Senate, would you anticipate the confirmed nominees to be politically neutral individuals?

———————————

Although Congress amended the Federal Election Campaign Act to provide for presidential appointment of all six voting Commissioners, the Secretary of the Senate and the Clerk of the House of Representatives continue to serve as non-voting, *ex officio* members of the Commission. The Secretary of the Senate and the Clerk of the House of Representatives are appointed by Congress, not by the President. What are the ramifications of these non-voting, *ex officio* members for the constitutionality of the FEC?

Additionally, under current law, consistent with original statutory requirements, no more than three FEC Commissioners can be members of the same political party. How important is this statutory requirement? Is that requirement consistent with the Appointments Clause? At least one commentator suggests not. *See* Hanah Metchis Volokh, *The Two Appointments Clauses: Statutory Qualifications for Federal Officers*, 10 U. PA. J. CONST. L. 745 (2008).

The D.C. Circuit addressed both of these issues in the following opinion.

Federal Election Commission v. NRA Political Victory Fund

6 F.3d 821 (D.C. Cir. 1993), cert. dismissed, 513 U.S. 88 (1994).

■ SILBERMAN, CIRCUIT JUDGE:

This enforcement action by the Federal Election Commission concerns a transfer of $415,744.72 from the National Rifle Association Institute for Legislative Action (NRA-ILA) to its political action committee, the NRA Political Victory Fund (PVF). The district court held that the transfer was a "contribution" prohibited by the Federal Election Campaign Act (FECA), 2 U.S.C. §§ 431 *et seq.* (1988), and rejected appellants' various constitutional arguments based on the First Amendment and separation of powers.

We believe that the Commission lacks authority to bring this enforcement action because its composition violates the Constitution's separation of powers. Congress exceeded its legislative authority when it placed its agents, the Secretary of the Senate and the Clerk of the House of Representatives, on the independent Commission as non-voting *ex officio* members. We therefore reverse.

* * *

Appellants claim that the composition of the Commission, particularly its two *ex officio* members, violates the Constitution's separation of powers. In 1974, Congress amended FECA to create the Commission and charged it with administering the Act. The Commission then, as now, had eight members: the Secretary of the Senate and the Clerk of the House of Representatives (non-voting and *ex officio*), and six voting members whom Congress played varying roles in appointing. In *Buckley v. Valeo*, 424 U.S. 1 (1976), the Supreme Court held, *inter alia*, that the limitations Congress placed on the President's power to nominate voting members of the Commission violated the Appointments Clause. Although the Court mentioned the *ex officio* members, *see id.* at 113, it never discussed the constitutionality of their status.

After *Buckley*, Congress reconstituted the Commission as follows:

> The Commission is composed of the Secretary of the Senate and the Clerk of the House of Representatives or their designees, ex officio and without the right to vote, and 6 members appointed by the President, by and with the advice and consent of the Senate. No more than 3 members of the Commission appointed under this paragraph may be affiliated with the same political party.

2 U.S.C. § 437c(a)(1) (1988).

It is argued that the reconstituted Commission still violates separation of powers principles in several respects. First, appellants urge that FECA's requirement that "[n]o more than 3 members of the Commission . . . may be affiliated with the same political party," impermissibly limits the President's nomination power under the Appointments Clause. * * * And finally, they assert that Congress exceeded its Article I authority by placing the Secretary and the Clerk on the Commission as *ex officio* members.

* * *

We agree with the district court * * * that appellants' challenge to the alleged restriction on the President's appointment power to select more than three commissioners from one party is not justiciable. Congressional limitations—even the placement of burdens—on the President's appointment power may raise serious constitutional questions. But it is impossible to determine in this case whether the *statute* actually limited the President's appointment power. Appellants do not argue, nor can we assume, that the President wished to appoint more than three members of one party and was restrained by FECA from doing so. Presidents have often viewed restrictions on their appointment power not to be legally binding. Of course, such legislation may impose political restraints. Particularly with respect to the Commission—for which, because of the sensitive political nature of its work, an equal number of members from each party was contemplated—it is hard to imagine that the President would wish to alter that balance, even if the understanding had not been reflected in the statutory language. More important, as appellants recognize, under its Advice and Consent authority the Senate may reject or approve the President's nominees for whatever reason it deems proper. Since all commissioners must be confirmed by the Senate, it would seem that a Senate resolution or even an informal communication to the President would have the same effect as the statute. It is not the law, therefore, which arguably restrains the President, but his perception of the present Senate's view as it may be assumed to be reflected in the statute.

* * *

We turn now to appellants' more substantial claim. It is undisputed that both *ex officio* members are appointed by and are agents of Congress, and it is also settled that Congress may not appoint the voting members of this Commission or, indeed, any agency with executive powers. There remains only the question whether *ex officio* non-voting members enjoy a different status for purposes of constitutional analysis.

The Commission would have us conclude that the *ex officio* members are constitutionally harmless. Non-voting members cannot serve as chairman, cannot call or adjourn a meeting, and are not counted in determining a quorum. In short, we are told that the *ex officio* members have no actual influence on agency decisionmaking. If that were so, congressional intent as reflected in the legislative history would seem frustrated. At least certain members of Congress clearly intended that the appointed officers serve its interests while serving as commissioners.

Legislative history aside, we cannot conceive why Congress would wish or expect its officials to serve as *ex officio* members if not to exercise some influence. Even if the *ex officio* members were to remain completely silent during all deliberations (a rather unlikely scenario), their mere presence as agents of Congress conveys a tacit message to the other commissioners. The message may well be an entirely appropriate one—but it nevertheless has the potential to influence the other commissioners. Federal law recognizes in other contexts that non-voting participation can influence a decisionmaking process. For example, FED.R.CRIM.P. 24(c) states: "An alternate juror who does not replace a regular juror shall be discharged after the jury retires to consider its verdict." An alternate juror, of course, does not have a right to vote. The rationale animating this rule is that "[w]hen alternate jurors are present during the deliberations, the possible prejudice is that defendants are being tried not by a jury of 12, as is their right, but by a larger group." *United States v. Jones*, 763 F.2d 518, 523 (2d Cir. 1985) (citations omitted).

In *Metropolitan Washington Airports Authority v. Citizens for Abatement of Aircraft Noise, Inc.*, 501 U.S. 252 (1991) ("*MWAA*"), the Supreme Court held unconstitutional a board of review composed entirely of members of Congress that had veto power over the decisions of regional airports authority. In so doing, the Court recognized that the "unique" arrangement "might prove innocuous." *Id.* at 254. The Court invalidated the law, however, because "the statutory scheme challenged today provides a blueprint for extensive expansion of the legislative power beyond its constitutionally-confined role." *Id.* The Court recalled that the Framers recognized that "power is of an encroaching nature," THE FEDERALIST NO. 48, at 332 (James Madison), and therefore the Constitution imposes a structural ban on legislative intrusions into other governmental functions. It is true that the Court has not considered the circumstances of this case; the members of Congress in *MWAA* and the Comptroller General in *Bowsher v. Synar*, 478 U.S. 714 (1986), possessed explicit voting or decisionmaking power that is not present here. However, since "the legislature 'can with the greater facility, mask under complicated and indirect measures, the encroachments which it makes on the co-ordinate departments,'" *MWAA*, 501 U.S at 274 (quoting THE FEDERALIST NO. 48, at 334), the mere presence of agents of Congress on an entity with executive powers offends the Constitution.

To be sure, as the Court has said often, the Constitution does not require a "hermetic sealing off of the three branches of Government." *Buckley*, 424 U.S. at 121. The Constitution "enjoins upon its branches separateness but interdependence, autonomy but reciprocity," *Youngstown Sheet & Tube Co. v. Sawyer*, 343 U.S. 579, 635 (1952) (Jackson, J., concurring), and it "anticipates that the coordinate Branches will converse with each other on matters of vital common interest." *Mistretta v. United States*, 488 U.S. 361, 408 (1989). The Commission argues that Congress intended *ex officio* membership to fulfill this coordinating function by having the Secretary and the Clerk play a mere "informational or advisory role" in agency decisionmaking. Advice, however, surely implies influence, and Congress must limit the exercise of its influence, whether in the form of advice or not, to its legislative role. In that capacity, Congress enjoys ample channels to advise, coordinate, and even directly influence an executive agency. It can do so through oversight hearings, appropriation and authorization legislation, or direct communication with the Commission. What the

Constitution prohibits Congress from doing, and what Congress does in this case, is to place its agents "beyond the legislative sphere" by naming them to membership on an entity with executive powers.

NOTES AND QUESTIONS

1. Though it declined to resolve the constitutionality of the statutory requirement that no more than three FEC Commissioners be members of the same political party, the D.C. Circuit expressed skepticism that, as a practical matter, the President would want to alter that balance. Do you think the court is accurate in its assessment? Can you think of circumstances in which the President might pursue a different policy in appointing FEC Commissioners?

2. The Supreme Court initially granted certiorari in the *NRA* case, but it dismissed the case after it held that the FEC lacks power to litigate in the Supreme Court. The Court had held previously that the general power to litigate in other courts does not automatically give an agency the power to litigate before the Supreme Court; rather, an agency can litigate before the Supreme Court only if Congress has explicitly granted it that power. *See, e.g., United States v. Providence Journal Co.*, 485 U.S. 693 (1988); *cf. United States v. Winston*, 170 U.S. 522 (1898). Congress rarely gives an agency the power to litigate before the Supreme Court, so the Solicitor General is the only entity with the power to file a petition for writ of certiorari. This is another means through which the President exercises some degree of control over agencies. The Solicitor General frequently refuses to file a petition for a writ that an agency requests it to file, either because he does not consider the issue worth pursuing in the Supreme Court or because he (and presumably the President) disagrees with the agency's position on the issue. Occasionally, the Solicitor General takes a position before the Supreme Court that differs from the position the agency takes on the issue.

3. Four days after the D.C. Circuit decided the *NRA* case, the FEC voted to reconstitute itself, excluding the ex officio members from all of its proceedings. The reconstituted FEC subsequently considered recommendations concerning whether or not to proceed with enforcement actions pending at the time of the *NRA* decision, and in particular decided to continue civil enforcement litigation against one Legi-Tech, Inc., which stood accused of violating the Federal Election Campaign Act. When the D.C. Circuit had occasion to consider the FEC's actions in the *Legi-Tech* case, it upheld both the FEC's self-reconstitution and its ratification of prior FEC decisions as an appropriate remedy for the constitutional violation recognized in the *NRA* case. *See Federal Election Comm'n v. Legi-Tech, Inc.*, 75 F.3d 704 (D.C. Cir. 1996). Are you persuaded that the FEC's remedial efforts suffice to resolve the *NRA* court's concerns regarding the influence of the FEC's ex officio members? Should the FEC be able to reconstitute itself, or should the court have required congressional action? Why or why not?

4. Even when the FEC has a quorum, it is often unable to make decisions because it often divides three-to-three on an issue. When the FEC is able to agree on a decision, it is often criticized for reaching a decision that renders the regulatory regime largely ineffective. The main proponents of effective regulation of federal elections, Senators McCain and Feingold, are understandably frustrated by the relative impotence of the FEC. They are constantly searching for ways of making FEC more effective and more "independent." At one point they proposed to give the Administrative Law Judges (ALJs) who work for the FEC greater power in two ways: ALJs would have the power to issue rules as well as to adjudicate cases, and they would have the power to issue final decisions in adjudications.

As we discuss in detail in Chapter 4, ALJs play important roles in adjudicating many disputes that come before agencies. ALJs are considered to be highly independent decisionmakers. ALJs are chosen primarily through a meritocratic process. The Office of Personnel Management (OPM) decides who is eligible to be an ALJ and compiles a list of such persons. Each agency then decides which ALJs to hire from the OPM's list of eligible ALJs. Would the proposal to increase the powers of FEC ALJs pass constitutional muster? Some people have urged enactment of a statute that would increase the independence of many agencies by increasing the powers of all ALJs. Would those proposals survive a challenge under the Appointments Clause? In your efforts to answer those questions, consider the following D.C. Circuit opinion.

Landry v. FDIC

204 F.3d 1125 (D.C. Cir. 2000).

■ STEPHEN F. WILLIAMS, CIRCUIT JUDGE:

Congress has given the Federal Deposit Insurance Corporation ("FDIC") a variety of weapons to use against individuals whose actions threaten the integrity of federally insured banks or savings associations. Among these is the power to remove a bank officer from his position and to bar him from further participation in the operations of a federally insured depository institution. On April 30, 1996 the FDIC notified Michael D. Landry that it intended to seek such an order against him because of his conduct as Senior Vice President, Chief Financial Officer, and Cashier of First Guaranty Bank, Hammond, Louisiana.

As required by statute, the FDIC assigned the matter to an administrative law judge for a formal, on-the-record, administrative hearing. The ALJ held a two-week hearing and then issued a decision recommending that the FDIC issue the proposed prohibition order. Landry filed exceptions to the ALJ's recommendation, and the case was forwarded to the FDIC's Board of Directors for a final decision. The Board agreed with the recommendation and issued an order of removal and prohibition. Landry filed a timely petition for review. The principal issue for review is Landry's argument that the FDIC's method of appointing ALJs violates the Appointments Clause of the Constitution, art. II, § 2, cl. 2.

* * *

Landry would classify ALJs who conduct administrative proceedings for the various federal banking agencies as "inferior officers" of the United States. If so, Congress's instruction to the banking agencies to "establish their own pool of administrative law judges" to conduct such hearings, *see* Federal Institutions Reform, Recovery, and Enforcement Act ("FIRREA"), § 916, 103 Stat. 486

(codified at 12 U.S.C. § 1818 note), would be unconstitutional because it vests appointment authority in a set of agencies that are not (according to Landry) "departments" under the Appointments Clause. The FDIC counters that the ALJs in question need not be appointed by heads of departments because they are employees rather than inferior officers.

* * *

The line between "mere" employees and inferior officers is anything but bright. In fact, the earliest Appointments Clause cases often employed circular logic, granting officer status to an official based in part upon his appointment by the head of a department. In an attempt to clarify the inquiry, the Court has often said that "any appointee exercising significant authority pursuant to the laws of the United States is an 'Officer of the United States,'" *Buckley v. Valeo*, 424 U.S. 1, 126 n.162 (1976), but ascertaining the test's real meaning requires a look at the roles of the employees whose status was at issue in other cases.

In the most analogous case, *Freytag*, the Court decided that STJs [special trial judges of the Tax Court] were inferior officers. *Freytag v. Commissioner*, 501 U.S. 868, 881–82 (1991). In so finding, the Court relied on authority of the STJs not matched by the ALJs here. In particular, the Court noted that STJs have the authority to render the *final* decision of the Tax Court in declaratory judgment proceedings and in certain small-amount tax cases. *See id.* at 882. But the ALJs here can never render the decision of the FDIC. Final decisions are issued only by the FDIC Board of Directors. Moreover, even for the non-final decisions of the type made by the STJ in *Freytag*, the Tax Court was required to defer to the STJ's factual and credibility findings unless they were clearly erroneous, whereas here the FDIC Board makes its own factual findings. Landry argues that the FDIC Board did not undertake a de novo review of his case, but his characterization of the FDIC's work goes only to its carefulness, not its authority.

It is, to be sure, uncertain just what role the STJs' power to make final decisions played in *Freytag*. Many of the features of the STJ job that the Court found to contribute to its being covered by the Appointments Clause have analogues here. The office of STJ was "established by Law" (the threshold trigger for the Appointments Clause) and the "duties, salary, and means of appointment" for the office were specified by statute, a factor that has proved relevant in the Court's Appointments Clause jurisprudence. *Freytag*, 501 U.S. at 881. The ALJ position here is also "established by Law," as are its specific duties, salary, and means of appointment. *See* 5 U.S.C. § 5372 (pay scales for ALJs); 5 U.S.C. § 3105 (hiring practices); 5 U.S.C. §§ 556–557 (functions); 12 CFR pt. 308 (same). Similarly, both the ALJs here and the STJs in *Freytag* "take testimony, conduct trials, rule on the admissibility of evidence, and have the power to enforce compliance with discovery orders." *Freytag*, 501 U.S. at 881–82. And, the Court observed, "In the course of carrying out these important functions, the special trial judges exercise significant discretion," *id.* at 882, rather a magic phrase under the *Buckley* test. Further, the Court introduced mention of the STJs' power to render final decisions with something of a shrug: "Even if the duties" of STJs involving conduct of nonfinal proceedings "were not as significant as we and the two courts [Tax Court and Fifth Circuit] have found them to be, our conclusion would be unchanged." *Id.* Only then did it go on to discuss the STJs' power to make final decisions.

Nonetheless, in another way the Court laid exceptional stress on the STJs' final decisionmaking power. After noting those powers, the Court went on to explain why Freytag could raise the claim even though in his case the STJ had not been exercising them:

> Special trial judges are not inferior officers for purposes of some of their duties under [the enabling statute], but mere employees with respect to other responsibilities. The fact that an inferior officer on occasion performs duties that may be performed by an employee not subject to the Appointments Clause does not transform his status under the Constitution.

Id. All this explanation would have been quite unnecessary if the purely recommendatory powers were fatal in themselves. Accordingly, we believe that the STJs' power of final decision in certain classes of cases was critical to the Court's decision. As the ALJs hired pursuant to § 916 of FIRREA have no such powers, we conclude that they are not inferior officers.

■ RANDOLPH, CIRCUIT JUDGE, concurring in part and concurring in the judgment:

I join the court's opinion except for its disposition of Landry's claim under the Appointments Clause of the Constitution. In my view, *Freytag v. Commissioner*, 501 U.S. 868 (1991), cannot be distinguished. The Administrative Law Judge who presided over Landry's case was as much an "inferior Officer" under Article II, § 2, cl. 2 of the Constitution as the special trial judge in *Freytag*. I nevertheless would sustain the FDIC's decision and order because Landry suffered no prejudicial error.

NOTES AND QUESTIONS

1. Both the majority and dissenting opinions in Landry compare the circumstances of that case to those of *Freytag v. Commissioner*, 501 U.S. 868 (1991). The primary issue in that case was whether of the Tax Reform Act of 1969, in granting the Chief Judge of the United States Tax Court the power to appoint special trial judges, violated the Appointments Clause. According to the statute, the special trial judges were authorized to preside over certain statutorily-specified proceedings and "any other proceeding which the chief judge may designate." 26 U.S.C. §§ 7443A(a), (b). Consistent with this authority, in the complex litigation at issue in *Freytag*, the Chief Judge authorized a special trial judge to preside over evidentiary hearings and prepare proposed findings and an opinion, but the final decision was rendered by a regular judge of the Tax Court. The Chief Judge and other regular Tax Court judges are appointed to 15-year terms by the President, with advice and consent of the Senate.

In a relatively brief passage in *Freytag*, the Supreme Court held that Tax Court special trial judges are inferior officers who must be appointed in a manner consistent with the Appointments Clause, rather than mere employees. Applying *Buckley v. Valeo*, the Court offered the following reasons for characterizing special trial judges as inferior Officers rather than mere employees:

The office of special trial judge is "established by Law," Art. II, § 2, cl. 2, and the duties, salary, and means of appointment for that office are specified by statute. * * * Furthermore, special trial judges perform more than ministerial tasks. They take testimony, conduct trials, rule on the admissibility of evidence, and have the power to enforce compliance with discovery orders. In the course of carrying out these important functions, the special trial judges exercise significant discretion.

* * * Under §§ 7443A(b)(1)–(3), (c), the Chief Judge may assign special trial judges to render the decisions of the Tax Court in declaratory judgment proceedings and limited-amount tax cases. * * *

Freytag, 501 U.S. at 881–82. Why do you think the *Landry* majority held that ALJs are employees even though the Supreme Court held that STJs are inferior officers? Who has the better of the argument between the majority and Judge Randolph?

2.   If Judge Randolph's view had prevailed in *Landry*, Congress would have to change the method of appointing ALJs to comply with the appointments clause. The nature and magnitude of the required changes would depend in part on whether the FDIC and the many other agencies that employ ALJS are "departments" within the meaning of the appointments clause. The meaning of "department" was a subject of disagreement among the Justices in *Freytag*. We discuss this issue further in Part A.3 of this Chapter below.

DISCUSSION PROBLEM

In the False Claims Act, 31 U.S.C. § 3730(b)(1), Congress authorized private citizens to bring civil enforcement actions against persons whom they allege to be guilty of submitting fraudulent claims for payment to the federal government. In several environmental statutes such as the Clean Air Act, 42 U.S.C. § 7604, the Clean Water Act, 33 U.S.C. § 1365, and the Endangered Species Act, 16 U.S.C. § 1540(g), Congress adopted similar citizen provisions authorizing lawsuits by persons who are adversely affected or aggrieved by a defendant's violations of statutory requirements. Do these provisions violate the Appointments Clause by delegating such power to individuals who have not been appointed according to the Appointments Clause? In other words, are private citizens who pursue enforcement actions under these provisions Officers of the United States, or does the Constitution permit non-officers to pursue government enforcement actions against private parties?

2.   WHAT KIND OF OFFICER: PRINCIPAL OR INFERIOR?

Establishing that a particular person is an Officer of the United States is often only the beginning of the Appointments Clause inquiry. The Appointments Clause provides two different avenues of appointment for Officers of the United States. It expressly requires that some officers, commonly referred to as principal officers, be appointed by the President and approved by the Senate. The Appointments Clause also recognizes a separate class of inferior officers who may be appointed, as Congress sees fit, by the President, the Courts of Law, or the Heads of Departments. Observe that the Appointments Clause does not authorize Congress to appoint even inferior officers. Why do you think that is?

Whether an officer is a principal officer or an inferior officer obviously matters for purposes of determining whether or not Congress may vest the power of appointment in someone other than the President. Yet, the Constitution offers little guidance for distinguishing principal from inferior officers. The following cases explore this issue.

Morrison v. Olson

487 U.S. 654 (1988).

■ CHIEF JUSTICE REHNQUIST delivered the opinion of the Court.

This case presents us with a challenge to the independent counsel provisions of the Ethics in Government Act of 1978, 28 U.S.C. §§ 49, 591 *et seq.* (1982, Supp. V). We hold today that these provisions of the Act do not violate the Appointments Clause of the Constitution, Art. II, § 2, cl. 2 * * *.

Briefly stated, Title VI of the Ethics in Government Act (Title VI or the Act), allows for the appointment of an "independent counsel" to investigate and, if appropriate, prosecute certain high-ranking Government officials for violations of federal criminal laws. The Act requires the Attorney General, upon receipt of information that he determines is "sufficient to constitute grounds to investigate whether any person [covered by the Act] may have violated any Federal criminal law," to conduct a preliminary investigation of the matter. When the Attorney General has completed this investigation, or 90 days has elapsed, he is required to report to a special court (the Special Division) created by the Act "for the purpose of appointing independent counsels." 28 U.S.C. § 49 (1982 ed., Supp. V).[3] If the Attorney General determines that "there are no reasonable grounds to believe that further investigation is warranted," then he must notify the Special Division of this result. In such a case, "the division of the court shall have no power to appoint an independent counsel." § 592(b)(1). If, however, the Attorney General has determined that there are "reasonable grounds to believe that further investigation or prosecution is warranted," then he "shall apply to the division of the court for the appointment of an independent counsel." The Attorney General's application to the court "shall contain sufficient information to assist the [court] in selecting an independent counsel and in defining that independent counsel's prosecutorial jurisdiction." § 592(d). Upon receiving this application, the Special Division "shall appoint an appropriate independent counsel and shall define that independent counsel's prosecutorial jurisdiction." § 593(b).

---

[3]   The Special Division is a division of the United States Court of Appeals for the District of Columbia Circuit. 28 U.S.C. § 49 (1982, Supp. V). The court consists of three circuit court judges or justices appointed by the Chief Justice of the United States. One of the judges must be a judge of the United States Court of Appeals for the District of Columbia Circuit, and no two of the judges may be named to the Special Division from a particular court. The judges are appointed for 2–year terms, with any vacancy being filled only for the remainder of the 2–year period. *Id.*

With respect to all matters within the independent counsel's jurisdiction, the Act grants the counsel "full power and independent authority to exercise all investigative and prosecutorial functions and powers of the Department of Justice, the Attorney General, and any other officer or employee of the Department of Justice." § 594(a). The functions of the independent counsel include conducting grand jury proceedings and other investigations, participating in civil and criminal court proceedings and litigation, and appealing any decision in any case in which the counsel participates in an official capacity. §§ 594(a)(1)–(3). Under § 594(a)(9), the counsel's powers include "initiating and conducting prosecutions in any court of competent jurisdiction, framing and signing indictments, filing informations, and handling all aspects of any case, in the name of the United States." The counsel may appoint employees, § 594(c), may request and obtain assistance from the Department of Justice, § 594(d), and may accept referral of matters from the Attorney General if the matter falls within the counsel's jurisdiction as defined by the Special Division, § 594(e). The Act also states that an independent counsel "shall, except where not possible, comply with the written or other established policies of the Department of Justice respecting enforcement of the criminal laws." § 594(f). In addition, whenever a matter has been referred to an independent counsel under the Act, the Attorney General and the Justice Department are required to suspend all investigations and proceedings regarding the matter. § 597(a). An independent counsel has "full authority to dismiss matters within [his or her] prosecutorial jurisdiction without conducting an investigation or at any subsequent time before prosecution, if to do so would be consistent" with Department of Justice policy. § 594(g).

Two statutory provisions govern the length of an independent counsel's tenure in office. The first defines the procedure for removing an independent counsel. Section 596(a)(1) provides:

> "An independent counsel appointed under this chapter may be removed from office, other than by impeachment and conviction, only by the personal action of the Attorney General and only for good cause, physical disability, mental incapacity, or any other condition that substantially impairs the performance of such independent counsel's duties."

* * *

The other provision governing the tenure of the independent counsel defines the procedures for "terminating" the counsel's office. Under § 596(b)(1), the office of an independent counsel terminates when he or she notifies the Attorney General that he or she has completed or substantially completed any investigations or prosecutions undertaken pursuant to the Act. In addition, the Special Division, acting either on its own or on the suggestion of the Attorney General, may terminate the office of an independent counsel at any time if it finds that "the investigation of all matters within the prosecutorial jurisdiction of such independent counsel . . . have been completed or so substantially completed that it would be appropriate for the Department of Justice to complete such investigations and prosecutions." § 596(b)(2).

Finally, the Act provides for congressional oversight of the activities of independent counsel. An independent counsel may from time to time send Congress statements or reports on his or her activities. § 595(a)(2). The "appropriate committees of the Congress" are given oversight jurisdiction in regard to the official conduct of an independent counsel, and the counsel is required by the Act to cooperate with Congress in the exercise of this jurisdiction. § 595(a)(1). The counsel is required to inform the House of Representatives of "substantial and credible information which [the counsel] receives . . . that may constitute grounds for an impeachment." § 595(c). In addition, the Act gives certain congressional committee members the power to "request in writing that the Attorney General apply for the appointment of an independent counsel." § 592(g)(1). The Attorney General is required to respond to this request within a specified time but is not required to accede to the request. § 592(g)(2).

[The Court then described the manner in which the case reached the Court. Briefly, an independent counsel subpoenaed individuals to testify before a grand jury. The individuals claimed that they were not required to comply because the underlying statute was unconstitutional. A district court rejected that claim and held the individuals in contempt. A divided panel of the D.C. Circuit held the statute unconstitutional, and the independent counsel filed a petition for writ of certiorari. Ed.]

* * *

The parties do not dispute that "[t]he Constitution for purposes of appointment . . . divides all its officers into two classes." *United States v. Germaine*, 99 U.S. 508, 509 (1879). As we stated in *Buckley v. Valeo*, 424 U.S. 1, 132 (1976): "[P]rincipal officers are selected by the President with the advice and consent of the Senate. Inferior officers Congress may allow to be appointed by the President alone, by the heads of departments, or by the Judiciary." The initial question is, accordingly, whether appellant is an "inferior" or a "principal" officer. If she is the latter, as the Court of Appeals concluded, then the Act is in violation of the Appointments Clause.

The line between "inferior" and "principal" officers is one that is far from clear, and the Framers provided little guidance into where it should be drawn. We need not attempt here to decide exactly where the line falls between the two types of officers, because in our view appellant clearly falls on the "inferior officer" side of that line. Several factors lead to this conclusion.

First, appellant is subject to removal by a higher Executive Branch official. Although appellant may not be "subordinate" to the Attorney General (and the President) insofar as she possesses a degree of independent discretion to exercise the powers delegated to her under the Act, the fact that she can be removed by the Attorney General indicates that she is to some degree "inferior" in rank and authority. Second, appellant is empowered by the Act to perform only certain, limited duties. An independent counsel's role is restricted primarily to investigation and, if appropriate, prosecution for certain federal crimes. Admittedly, the Act delegates to appellant "full power and independent authority to exercise all investigative and prosecutorial functions and powers of the Department of Justice," § 594(a), but this grant of authority does not include any authority to formulate policy for the Government or the Executive Branch, nor does it give appellant any administrative duties outside of those necessary to operate her office. The Act specifically provides that in policy matters appellant is to comply to the extent possible with the policies of the Department. § 594(f).

Third, appellant's office is limited in jurisdiction. Not only is the Act itself restricted in applicability to certain federal officials suspected of certain serious federal crimes, but an independent counsel can only act within the scope of the jurisdiction that has been granted by the Special Division pursuant to a request by the Attorney General. Finally, appellant's office is limited in tenure. There is concededly no time limit on the appointment of a particular counsel. Nonetheless, the office of independent counsel is "temporary" in the sense that an independent counsel is appointed essentially to accomplish a single task, and when that task is over the office is terminated, either by the counsel herself or by action of the Special Division. Unlike other prosecutors, appellant has no ongoing responsibilities that extend beyond the accomplishment of the mission that she was appointed for and authorized by the Special Division to undertake. In our view, these factors relating to the "ideas of tenure, duration . . . and duties" of the independent counsel, *Germaine*, 99 U.S. at 511, are sufficient to establish that appellant is an "inferior" officer in the constitutional sense.

■ JUSTICE KENNEDY took no part in the consideration or decision of this case.

■ JUSTICE SCALIA, dissenting.

Article II, § 2, cl. 2, of the Constitution provides as follows:

"[The President] shall nominate, and by and with the Advice and Consent of the Senate, shall appoint Ambassadors, other public Ministers and Consuls, Judges of the supreme Court, and all other Officers of the United States, whose Appointments are not herein otherwise provided for, and which shall be established by Law: but the Congress may by Law vest the Appointment of such inferior Officers, as they think proper, in the President alone, in the Courts of Law, or in the Heads of Departments."

Because appellant (who all parties and the Court agree is an officer of the United States) was not appointed by the President with the advice and consent of the Senate, but rather by the Special Division of the United States Court of Appeals, her appointment is constitutional only if (1) she is an "inferior" officer within the meaning of the above Clause, and (2) Congress may vest her appointment in a court of law.

As to the first of these inquiries, the Court does not attempt to "decide exactly" what establishes the line between principal and "inferior" officers, but is confident that, whatever the line may be, appellant "clearly falls on the 'inferior officer' side" of it. The Court gives three reasons: *First,* she "is subject to removal by a higher Executive Branch official," namely, the Attorney General. *Second,* she is "empowered by the Act to perform only certain, limited duties." *Third,* her office is "limited in jurisdiction" and "limited in tenure."

The first of these lends no support to the view that appellant is an inferior officer. Appellant is removable only for "good cause" or physical or mental incapacity. 28 U.S.C. § 596(a)(1) (1982, Supp. V). By contrast, most (if not all) *principal* officers in the Executive Branch may be removed by the President *at will*. I fail to see how the fact that appellant is more difficult to remove than most principal officers helps to establish that she is an inferior officer. And I do not see how it could possibly make any difference to her superior or inferior status that the President's limited power to remove her must be exercised through the Attorney General. If she were removable at will by the Attorney General, then she would be subordinate to him and thus properly designated as inferior; but the Court essentially admits that she is not subordinate. If it were common usage to refer to someone as "inferior" who is subject to removal for cause by another, then one would say that the President is "inferior" to Congress.

The second reason offered by the Court—that appellant performs only certain, limited duties—may be relevant to whether she is an inferior officer, but it mischaracterizes the extent of her powers. As the Court states: "Admittedly, the Act delegates to appellant [the] *'full power and independent authority to exercise all investigative and prosecutorial functions and powers of the Department of Justice.'*" Moreover, in addition to this general grant of power she is given a broad range of specifically enumerated powers, including a power not even the Attorney General possesses: to "contes[t] in court . . . any claim of privilege or attempt to withhold evidence on grounds of national security." § 594(a)(6). Once all of this is "admitted," it seems to me impossible to maintain that appellant's authority is so "limited" as to render her an inferior officer. The Court seeks to brush this away by asserting that the independent counsel's power does not include any authority to "formulate policy for the Government or the Executive Branch." But the same could be said for all officers of the Government, with the single exception of the President. All of them only formulate policy within their respective spheres of responsibility—as does the independent counsel, who must comply with the policies of the Department of Justice only to the extent possible. § 594(f).

The final set of reasons given by the Court for why the independent counsel clearly is an inferior officer emphasizes the limited nature of her jurisdiction and tenure. Taking the latter first, I find nothing unusually limited about the independent counsel's tenure. To the contrary, unlike most high-ranking Executive Branch officials, she continues to serve until she (or the Special Division) decides that her work is substantially completed. This particular independent prosecutor has already served more than two years, which is at least as long as many Cabinet officials. As to the scope of her jurisdiction, there can be no doubt that is small (though far from unimportant). But within it she exercises more than the full power of the Attorney General. The Ambassador to Luxembourg is not anything less than a principal officer, simply because Luxembourg is small. And the federal judge who sits in a small district is not for that reason "inferior in rank and authority." If the mere fragmentation of executive responsibilities into small compartments suffices to render the heads of each of those compartments inferior officers, then Congress could deprive the President of the right to appoint his chief law enforcement officer by dividing up the Attorney General's responsibilities among a number of "lesser" functionaries.

More fundamentally, however, it is not clear from the Court's opinion why the factors it discusses—even if applied correctly to the facts of this case—are determinative of the question of inferior officer status. The apparent source of these factors is a statement in *United States v. Germaine,* 99 U.S. 508, 511 (1879) (discussing *United States v. Hartwell,* 6 Wall. 385, 393 (1868)), that "the term [officer] embraces the ideas of tenure, duration, emolument, and duties." Besides the fact that this was dictum, it was dictum in a case where the distinguishing characteristics of inferior officers versus superior officers were in no way relevant, but rather only the distinguishing characteristics of an "officer of the United States" (to which the criminal statute at issue applied) as opposed to a mere *employee.* Rather than erect a theory of who is an inferior officer on the foundation of such an irrelevancy, I think it preferable to look to the text of the Constitution and the division of power that it establishes. These demonstrate, I think, that the independent counsel is not an inferior officer because she is not *subordinate* to any officer in the Executive Branch (indeed, not even to the President).

* * *

To be sure, it is not a *sufficient* condition for "inferior" officer status that one be subordinate to a principal officer. Even an officer who is subordinate to a department head can be a principal officer. That is clear from the brief exchange following Gouverneur Morris' suggestion of the addition of the exceptions clause for inferior officers. Madison responded:

> "It does not go far enough if it be necessary at all—*Superior Officers below Heads of Departments* ought in some cases to have the appointment of the lesser offices." 2 M. FARRAND, RECORDS OF THE FEDERAL CONVENTION, OF 1787, at 627 (rev. ed. 1966) (emphasis added).

But it is surely a *necessary* condition for inferior officer status that the officer be subordinate to another officer.

The independent counsel is not even subordinate to the President. The Court essentially admits as much, noting that "appellant may not be 'subordinate' to the Attorney General (and the President) insofar as she possesses a degree of independent discretion to exercise the powers delegated to her under the Act." In fact, there is no doubt about it. As noted earlier, the Act specifically grants her the "*full* power and *independent* authority to exercise *all* investigative and prosecutorial functions of the Department of Justice," 28 U.S.C. § 594(a) (1982, Supp. V) (emphasis added), and makes her removable only for "good cause," a limitation specifically intended to ensure that she be *independent* of, not *subordinate* to, the President and the Attorney General. *See* H.R. REP. No. 100–452, at 37 (1987) (Conf. Rep.).

Because appellant is not subordinate to another officer, she is not an "inferior" officer and her appointment other than by the President with the advice and consent of the Senate is unconstitutional.

NOTES AND QUESTIONS

1.   Congress adopted the independent counsel provisions in 1978 as a response to the controversy known as the "Saturday Night Massacre." Under pressure from Congress and the press, Attorney General Elliot Richardson appointed a special counsel, Archibald Cox, to investigate the facts surrounding an alleged burglary of the Democratic Party headquarters in the Watergate apartment building. When it appeared that Cox was about to find the "smoking gun" that would link the White House to the burglary and its cover-up, President Nixon attempted to derail the investigation by ordering first Attorney General Richardson and then Deputy Attorney General William Rucklehaus to fire Cox, and he fired Richardson and Rucklehaus when they refused. Solicitor General Robert Bork, in his new capacity as Acting Attorney General, complied with Nixon's demand and fired Cox.

The theory behind the Act was that removing the power to prosecute high-level executive branch officials from the exclusive jurisdiction of the executive branch would eliminate conflicts of interest. In his dissent in *Morrison v. Olson*, Justice Scalia protested both the breadth of an independent counsel's powers and her lack of meaningful supervision under the Act, and predicted much mischief as a result. In the decades to follow, independent counsel investigations of both Republican and Democratic officeholders were sharply criticized for being too broad, too long, too expensive, and too political. The investigations of Reagan Administration officials who sold arms to Iran and sent the profits to Nicaragua's Contra rebels and of President Bill Clinton for various indiscretions culminating in his impeachment were particularly controversial. Although the independent counsel provisions were renewed several times, in 1999, Congress allowed them to expire. In the view of many, therefore, the predictions of Justice Scalia's dissent in *Morrison* proved prophetic.

2.   Justice Scalia's dissenting opinion is powerful but contains some key inaccuracies and omissions. For example, in a portion of the opinion not included in the excerpt, Justice Scalia asserts that "prosecution has always and everywhere" been conducted by the Executive. As a student Note documented, however, the history of prosecution in the United States is highly variable, and it includes many contexts in which prosecutors were appointed by courts and legislatures. *See* Note, *Is Prosecution a Core Executive Function?*, 99 YALE L.J. 1069 (1990). Also, Justice Scalia begins his opinion by quoting the separation of powers provision in the Massachusetts Constitution, but neglects to mention that the Framers of the U.S. Constitution rejected a similar provision that was proposed for the U.S. Constitution. Indeed, there is no separation of powers provision in the U.S. Constitution. *See* Gerhard Casper, *An Essay on Separation of Powers: Some Early Versions and Practices*, 30 WM. & MARY L. REV. 211, 216–221 (1989). Justice Scalia's opinion relies heavily on excerpts from the Federalist Papers that are, of course, legislative history—a source that Justice Scalia is unwilling to consider in any context except constitutional interpretation.

3.   One of the factors that the Supreme Court considered relevant in deciding that independent counsels are inferior officers was that they are "subject to removal by a higher Executive Branch official," namely the Attorney General. The Court did not acknowledge, however, that the statute only authorized the Attorney General to remove an independent

counsel "for good cause, physical disability, mental incapacity, or any other condition that substantially impairs the performance of such independent counsel's duties." 28 U.S.C. § 596(a)(1) (1982, Supp. V). Should for cause limitations on a principal officer's removal authority matter in assessing whether a particular government official is a principal or inferior officer? Why or why not?

In his dissent in *Morrison v. Olson*, Justice Scalia maintained that being subordinate to another government official is a necessary but not sufficient condition for characterization as an inferior officer. He did not, however, offer guidance concerning what conditions other than subordination might also be necessary to classify an Officer of the United States as inferior. What factors do you think might be relevant? In answering these questions, consider Justice Scalia's opinion in the following case.

Edmond v. United States

520 U.S. 651 (1997).

■ JUSTICE SCALIA delivered the opinion of the Court.

We must determine in this case whether Congress has authorized the Secretary of Transportation to appoint civilian members of the Coast Guard Court of Criminal Appeals, and if so, whether this authorization is constitutional under the Appointments Clause of Article II.

The Coast Guard Court of Criminal Appeals (formerly known as the Coast Guard Court of Military Review) is an intermediate court within the military justice system. It is one of four military Courts of Criminal Appeals; others exist for the Army, the Air Force, and the Navy-Marine Corps. The Coast Guard Court of Criminal Appeals hears appeals from the decisions of courts-martial, and its decisions are subject to review by the United States Court of Appeals for the Armed Forces (formerly known as the United States Court of Military Appeals).

Appellate military judges who are assigned to a Court of Criminal Appeals must be members of the bar, but may be commissioned officers or civilians. Uniform Code of Military Justice (UCMJ) art. 66(a), 10 U.S.C. § 866(a). During the times relevant to this case, the Coast Guard Court of Criminal Appeals has had two civilian members, Chief Judge Joseph H. Baum and Associate Judge Alfred F. Bridgman, Jr. These judges were originally assigned to serve on the court by the General Counsel of the Department of Transportation, who is, ex officio, the Judge Advocate General of the Coast Guard, UCMJ art. 1(a), 10 U.S.C. § 801(1).

* * *

On January 15, 1993, the Secretary of Transportation issued a memorandum "adopting" the General Counsel's assignments to the Coast Guard Court of Military Review "as judicial appointments of my own." The memorandum then listed the names of "[t]hose judges presently assigned and appointed by me," including Chief Judge Baum and Judge Bridgman.

* * *

The prescribed manner of appointment for principal officers is also the default manner of appointment for inferior officers. * * * Section 323(a), which confers appointment power upon the Secretary of Transportation, can constitutionally be applied to the appointment of Court of Criminal Appeals judges only if those judges are "inferior Officers."

Our cases have not set forth an exclusive criterion for distinguishing between principal and inferior officers for Appointments Clause purposes. Among the offices that we have found to be inferior are that of a district court clerk, *Ex parte Hennen,* 38 U.S. (13 Pet.) 225, 229 (1839), an election supervisor, *Ex parte Siebold,* 100 U.S. 371, 397–98 (1880), a vice consul charged temporarily with the duties of the consul, *United States v. Eaton,* 169 U.S. 331, 343 (1898), and a "United States commissioner" in district court proceedings, *Go-Bart Importing Co. v. United States,* 282 U.S. 344, 352–54 (1931). Most recently, in *Morrison v. Olson,* 487 U.S. 654 (1988), we held that the independent counsel created by provisions of the Ethics in Government Act of 1978, 28 U.S.C. §§ 591–99, was an inferior officer. In reaching that conclusion, we relied on several factors: that the independent counsel was subject to removal by a higher officer (the Attorney General), that she performed only limited duties, that her jurisdiction was narrow, and that her tenure was limited. 487 U.S. at 671–72.

Petitioners are quite correct that the last two of these conclusions do not hold with regard to the office of military judge at issue here. It is not "limited in tenure," as that phrase was used in *Morrison* to describe "appoint[ment] essentially to accomplish a single task [at the end of which] the office is terminated." *Id.* at 672. Nor are military judges "limited in jurisdiction," as used in *Morrison* to refer to the fact that an independent counsel may investigate and prosecute only those individuals, and for only those crimes, that are within the scope of jurisdiction granted by the special three judge appointing panel. However, *Morrison* did not purport to set forth a definitive test for whether an office is "inferior" under the Appointments Clause. To the contrary, it explicitly stated: "We need not attempt here to decide exactly where the line falls between the two types of officers, because in our view [the independent counsel] clearly falls on the 'inferior officer' side of that line." 487 U.S. at 671.

To support principal-officer status, petitioners emphasize the importance of the responsibilities that Court of Criminal Appeals judges bear. They review those court-martial proceedings that result in the most serious sentences, including those "in which the sentence, as approved, extends to death, dismissal . . . , dishonorable or bad-conduct discharge, or confinement for one year or more." UCMJ art. 66(b)(1), 10 U.S.C. § 866(b)(1). They must ensure that the court-martial's finding of guilt and its sentence are "correct in law and fact," *id.* art. 66(c), § 866(c), which includes resolution of constitutional challenges. And finally, unlike most appellate judges, Court of Criminal Appeals judges are not required to defer to the trial court's factual findings, but may independently "weigh the evidence, judge the credibility of witnesses, and determine controverted questions of fact, recognizing that the trial court saw and heard the witnesses." *Id.* We do not dispute that military appellate judges are charged with exercising significant authority on behalf of the United States. This, however, is also true of offices that we have held were "inferior" within the meaning of the Appointments Clause. *See, e.g., Freytag v. Comm'r*, 501 U.S. at 881–82 (special trial judges having "significan[t] . . . duties and discretion" are inferior officers). The exercise of "significant authority pursuant to the laws of the United States" marks, not the line between principal and inferior officer for Appointments Clause purposes, but rather, as we said in *Buckley*, the line between officer and nonofficer. 424 U.S. at 126.

Generally speaking, the term "inferior officer" connotes a relationship with some higher ranking officer or officers below the President: Whether one is an "inferior" officer depends on whether he has a superior. It is not enough that other officers may be identified who formally maintain a higher rank, or possess responsibilities of a greater magnitude. If that were the intention, the Constitution might have used the phrase "lesser officer." Rather, in the context of a Clause designed to preserve political accountability relative to important Government assignments, we think it evident that "inferior officers" are officers whose work is directed and supervised at some level by others who were appointed by presidential nomination with the advice and consent of the Senate.

* * *

Supervision of the work of Court of Criminal Appeals judges is divided between the Judge Advocate General (who in the Coast Guard is subordinate to the Secretary of Transportation) and the Court of Appeals for the Armed Forces. The Judge Advocate General exercises administrative oversight over the Court of Criminal Appeals. He is charged with the responsibility to "prescribe uniform rules of procedure" for the court, and must "meet periodically [with other Judge Advocates General] to formulate policies and procedure in regard to review of court-martial cases." UCMJ art. 66(f), 10 U.S.C. § 866(f). It is conceded by the parties that the Judge Advocate General may also remove a Court of Criminal Appeals judge from his judicial assignment without cause. The power to remove officers, we have recognized, is a powerful tool for control. *Bowsher v. Synar*, 478 U.S. 714, 727 (1986).

The Judge Advocate General's control over Court of Criminal Appeals judges is, to be sure, not complete. He may not attempt to influence (by threat of removal or otherwise) the outcome of individual proceedings and has no power to reverse decisions of the court. This latter power does reside, however, in another Executive Branch entity, the Court of Appeals for the Armed Forces. That court reviews every decision of the Courts of Criminal Appeals in which: (a) the sentence extends to death; (b) the Judge Advocate General orders such review; or (c) the court itself grants review upon petition of the accused. UCMJ art. 67(a), 10 U.S.C. § 867(a). The scope of review is narrower than that exercised by the Court of Criminal Appeals: so long as there is some competent evidence in the record to establish each element of the offense beyond a reasonable doubt, the Court of Appeals for the Armed

Forces will not reevaluate the facts. *Id.* art. 67(c), § 867(c). This limitation upon review does not in our opinion render the judges of the Court of Criminal Appeals principal officers. What is significant is that the judges of the Court of Criminal Appeals have no power to render a final decision on behalf of the United States unless permitted to do so by other Executive officers.

Finally, petitioners argue that *Freytag v. Commissioner,* 501 U.S. 868 (1991), which held that special trial judges charged with assisting Tax Court judges were inferior officers and could be appointed by the Chief Judge of the Tax Court, suggests that Court of Criminal Appeals judges are principal officers. Petitioners contend that Court of Criminal Appeals judges more closely resemble Tax Court judges—who we implied (according to petitioners) were principal officers—than they do special trial judges. We note initially that *Freytag* does not hold that Tax Court judges are principal officers; only the appointment of special trial judges was at issue in that case. Moreover, there are two significant distinctions between Tax Court judges and Court of Criminal Appeals judges. First, there is no Executive Branch tribunal comparable to the Court of Appeals for the Armed Forces that reviews the work of the Tax Court; its decisions are appealable only to courts of the Third Branch. And second, there is no officer comparable to a Judge Advocate General who supervises the work of the Tax Court, with power to determine its procedural rules, to remove any judge without cause, and to order any decision submitted for review. *Freytag* does not control our decision here.

■ JUSTICE SOUTER, concurring in part and concurring in the judgment.

Because the term "inferior officer" implies an official superior, one who has no superior is not an inferior officer. This unexceptionable maxim will in some instances be dispositive of status; it might, for example, lead to the conclusion that United States district judges cannot be inferior officers, since the power of appellate review does not extend to them personally, but is limited to their judgments. *See In re Sealed Case,* 838 F.2d 476, 483 (D.C. Cir.) (suggesting that "lower federal judges . . . are principal officers" because they are "not subject to personal supervision"), *rev'd sub nom. Morrison v. Olson,* 487 U.S. 654 (1988).

It does not follow, however, that if one is subject to some supervision and control, one is an inferior officer. Having a superior officer is necessary for inferior officer status, but not sufficient to establish it. *See, e.g., Morrison v. Olson,* 487 U.S. at 654, 722 (Scalia, J., dissenting) ("To be sure, it is not a *sufficient* condition for 'inferior' officer status that one be subordinate to a principal officer. Even an officer who is subordinate to a department head can be a principal officer."). Accordingly, in *Morrison,* the Court's determination that the independent counsel was "to some degree 'inferior' "to the Attorney General, *see id.* at 671, did not end the enquiry. The Court went on to weigh the duties, jurisdiction, and tenure associated with the office before concluding that the independent counsel was an inferior officer. Thus, under *Morrison,* the Solicitor General of the United States, for example, may well be a principal officer, despite his statutory "inferiority" to the Attorney General. The mere existence of a "superior" officer is not dispositive.

* * *

In having to go beyond the Court's opinion to decide that the criminal appeals judges are inferior officers, I do not claim the convenience of a single sufficient condition, and, indeed, at this stage of the Court's thinking on the matter, I would not try to derive a single rule of sufficiency. What is needed, instead, is a detailed look at the powers and duties of these judges to see whether reasons favoring their inferior officer status within the constitutional scheme weigh more heavily than those to the contrary.

NOTES AND QUESTIONS

In light of the Court's opinion in *Edmond*, is the test established in *Morrison v. Olson* for distinguishing principal from inferior officers still good law? How would you reconcile the opinions of the Court in *Morrison* and *Edmond*? What is the standard for determining whether an Officer of the United States is an inferior officer?

DISCUSSION PROBLEM

A copyright grants the owner of a musical work an exclusive right to perform that work in public, enabling copyright holders to charge royalties for performances by others. In 1995, Congress expanded copyrights to encompass performances of copyrighted work "by means of a digital audio transmission," *i.e.* on a satellite radio service. 17 U.S.C. §§ 106(6), 114(d). Under the Copyright Royalty and Distribution Reform Act of 2004, if the satellite radio service and the copyright holder cannot agree upon an appropriate license fee, then three Copyright Royalty Judges (CRJs), who collectively form the Copyright Royalty Board (CRB), may set "reasonable rates and terms of royalty payments." *Id.* § 114(f)(1)(A). The CRJs together as the CRB conduct hearings, which may include discovery, live testimony, and other trial-like elements, after which the CRB by majority determination sets royalty rates. The CRJs are appointed by the Librarian of Congress. In a concurring opinion in *SoundExchange, Inc. v. Librarian of Congress*, 571 F.3d 1220 (D.C. Cir. 2009), Judge Kavanaugh suggested that the CRB violates the Appointments Clause on the ground that CRB members "plainly are officers of the United States" and that they appear to be principal rather than inferior officers "because they are not removable at will and their decisions regarding royalty rates are not reversible by the Librarian of Congress or any other Executive Branch official." Do you agree with Judge Kavanaugh's assertion? Why or why not?

3.   WHO IS HEAD OF A DEPARTMENT?

In 1924, Congress created the Board of Tax Appeals as an independent agency within the Executive Branch. In 1942, Congress changed its name to "Tax Court of the United States" in 1942, but retained its status as an independent agency in the Executive Branch. In 1969, Congress designated the United States Tax Court as an "Article I Court," but did not materially change its composition or function and left it in the Executive Branch. The United States Tax Court performs the single function of adjudicating disputes concerning federal tax liability. Its judges are appointed to 15-year terms by the

President with the advice and consent of the Senate; its judges do not have life tenure, and they are subject to presidential removal for cause. Also in 1969, Congress granted the Chief Judge of the United States Tax Court the authority to appoint special trial judges to preside over certain matters.

In *Freytag v. Commissioner of Internal Revenue*, below, the Supreme Court held unanimously that special trial judges of the United States Tax Court are inferior officers who can be appointed by the Chief Judge of the Tax Court. The Justices disagreed, however, in every step of the reasoning process that produced this holding. Under the Appointments Clause, an inferior officer can be appointed only by the President, the courts of law, or the heads of departments. Obviously, the Chief Judge of the Tax Court is not the President; so is he the head of a department, or is the Tax Court a court of law? The Court devoted a substantial portion of its analysis in *Freytag* to that precisely that question.

Freytag v. Commissioner of Internal Revenue

501 U.S. 868 (1991).

■ JUSTICE BLACKMUN delivered the opinion of the Court.

* * * In this litigation, we must decide whether the authority that Congress has granted the Chief Judge of the United States Tax Court to appoint special trial judges transgresses our structure of separated powers. We answer that inquiry in the negative.

* * *

Can the Chief Judge of the Tax Court constitutionally be vested by Congress with the power to appoint? The Appointments Clause names the possible repositories for the appointment power. It is beyond question in this litigation that Congress did not intend to grant to the President the power to appoint special trial judges. We therefore are left with three other possibilities. First, as the Commissioner urges, the Tax Court could be treated as a department with the Chief Judge as its head. Second, as the *amicus* suggests, the Tax Court could be considered one of "the Courts of Law." Third, we could agree with petitioners that the Tax Court is neither a "Departmen[t]" nor a "Cour[t] of Law." Should we agree with petitioners, it would follow that the appointment power could not be vested in the Chief Judge of the Tax Court.

* * *

We cannot accept the Commissioner's assumption that every part of the Executive Branch is a department, the head of which is eligible to receive the appointment power. The Appointments Clause prevents Congress from distributing power too widely by limiting the actors in whom Congress may vest the power to appoint. The Clause reflects our Framers' conclusion that widely distributed appointment power subverts democratic government. Given the inexorable presence of the administrative state, a holding that every organ in the Executive Branch is a department would multiply indefinitely the number of actors eligible to appoint. The Framers recognized the dangers posed by an excessively diffuse appointment power and rejected efforts to expand that power. So do we. For the Chief Judge of the Tax Court to qualify as a "Hea[d] of [a] Departmen[t]," the Commissioner must demonstrate not only that the Tax Court is a part of the Executive Branch but also that it is a department.

We are not so persuaded. This Court for more than a century has held that the term "Departmen[t]" refers only to " 'a part or division of the executive government, as the Department of State, or of the Treasury,' " expressly "creat[ed]" and "giv[en] . . . the name of a department" by Congress. *United States v. Germaine*, 99 U.S. 508, 510–11 (1879). Accordingly, the term "Heads of Departments" does not embrace "inferior commissioners and bureau officers." *Id.* at 511.

Confining the term "Heads of Departments" in the Appointments Clause to executive divisions like the Cabinet-level departments constrains the distribution of the appointment power just as the Commissioner's interpretation, in contrast, would diffuse it. The Cabinet-level departments are limited in number and easily identified. Their heads are subject to the exercise of political oversight and share the President's accountability to the people.

* * *

Even if we were not persuaded that the Commissioner's view threatened to diffuse the appointment power and was contrary to the meaning of "Departmen[t]" in the Constitution, we still could not accept his treatment of the intent of Congress, which enacted legislation in 1969 with the express purpose of "making the Tax Court an Article I court rather than an executive agency." S. REP. NO. 91–552, at 303 (1969), 1969 U.S.C.C.A.N. 1645, 2027. Congress deemed it "anomalous to continue to classify" the Tax Court with executive agencies, *id.* at 302, and questioned whether it was "appropriate for one executive agency [the pre-1969 tribunal] to be sitting in judgment on the determinations of another executive agency [the IRS]." *Id.*

Treating the Tax Court as a "Department" and its Chief Judge as its "Hea[d]" would defy the purpose of the Appointments Clause, the meaning of the Constitution's text, and the clear intent of Congress to transform the Tax Court into an Article I legislative court. The Tax Court is not a "Departmen[t]."

Having so concluded, we now must determine whether it is one of the "Courts of Law," as *amicus* suggests. Petitioners and the Commissioner both take the position that the Tax Court cannot be a "Cour[t] of Law" within the meaning of the Appointments Clause because, they say, that term is limited to Article III courts.

The text of the Clause does not limit the "Courts of Law" to those courts established under Article III of the Constitution. The Appointments Clause does not provide that Congress can vest appointment power only in "one Supreme Court" and other courts established under Article III, or only in tribunals that exercise broad common-law jurisdiction. * * *

Our cases involving non-Article III tribunals have held that these courts exercise the judicial power of the United States. In both

American Insurance Co. v. Canter, 26 U.S. (1 Pet.) 511, 546 (1828) and *Williams v. United States*, 289 U.S. 553, 565–67 (1933), this Court rejected arguments similar to the literalistic one now advanced by petitioners, that only Article III courts could exercise the judicial power because the term "judicial Power" appears only in Article III. * * * We cannot hold that an Article I court, such as the Court of Claims in *Williams* or the Territorial Court of Florida in *Canter*, can exercise the judicial power of the United States and yet cannot be one of the "Courts of Law."

* * *

The Tax Court exercises judicial power to the exclusion of any other function. It is neither advocate nor rulemaker. As an adjudicative body, it construes statutes passed by Congress and regulations promulgated by the Internal Revenue Service. It does not make political decisions.

The Tax Court's function and role in the federal judicial scheme closely resemble those of the federal district courts, which indisputably are "Courts of Law." Furthermore, the Tax Court exercises its judicial power in much the same way as the federal district courts exercise theirs. It has authority to punish contempts by fine or imprisonment, 26 U.S.C. § 7456(c); to grant certain injunctive relief, § 6213(a); to order the Secretary of the Treasury to refund an overpayment determined by the court, § 6512(b)(2); and to subpoena and examine witnesses, order production of documents, and administer oaths, § 7456(a). All these powers are quintessentially judicial in nature.

The Tax Court remains independent of the Executive and Legislative Branches. Its decisions are not subject to review by either the Congress or the President. Nor has Congress made Tax Court decisions subject to review in the federal district courts. Rather, like the judgments of the district courts, the decisions of the Tax Court are appealable only to the regional United States courts of appeals, with ultimate review in this Court. The courts of appeals, moreover, review those decisions "in the same manner and to the same extent as decisions of the district courts in civil actions tried without a jury." § 7482(a). This standard of review contrasts with the standard applied to agency rulemaking by the courts of appeals under § 10(e) of the Administrative Procedure Act, 5 U.S.C. § 706(2)(A).

The Tax Court's exclusively judicial role distinguishes it from other non-Article III tribunals that perform multiple functions and provides the limit on the diffusion of appointment power that the Constitution demands. * * * Including Article I courts, such as the Tax Court, that exercise judicial power and perform exclusively judicial functions among the "Courts of Law" does not significantly expand the universe of actors eligible to receive the appointment power.

■ JUSTICE SCALIA, with whom JUSTICE O'CONNOR, JUSTICE KENNEDY, and JUSTICE SOUTER join, concurring in part and concurring in the judgment.

The Appointments Clause provides:

"[T]he Congress may by Law vest the Appointment of such inferior Officers, as they think proper, in the President alone, in the Courts of Law, or in the Heads of Departments." U.S. CONST. art. II, § 2, cl. 2.

I agree with the Court that a special trial judge is an "inferior Office[r]" within the meaning of this Clause, with the result that, absent Presidential appointment, he must be appointed by a court of law or the head of a department. I do not agree, however, with the Court's conclusion that the Tax Court is a "Cour[t] of Law" within the meaning of this provision. I would find the appointment valid because the Tax Court is a "Departmen[t]" and the Chief Judge is its head.

A careful reading of the Constitution and attention to the apparent purpose of the Appointments Clause make it clear that the Tax Court cannot be one of those "Courts of Law" referred to there. The Clause does not refer generally to "Bodies exercising judicial Functions," or even to "Courts" generally, or even to "Courts of Law" generally. It refers to "*the* Courts of Law." Certainly this does not mean *any* "Cour[t] of Law" (the Supreme Court of Rhode Island would not do). The definite article "the" obviously narrows the class of eligible "Courts of Law" to those courts of law envisioned by the Constitution. Those are Article III courts, and the Tax Court is not one of them.

* * * The Framers contemplated no other national judicial tribunals. * * *

We recognized this in *Buckley*, and it was indeed an essential part of our reasoning. Responding to the argument that a select group of Congressmen was a "Department," we said:

"The phrase 'Heads of Departments,' used as it is in conjunction with the phrase 'Courts of Law,' suggests that the Departments referred to are themselves in the Executive Branch or at least have some connection with that branch. While the Clause expressly authorizes Congress to vest the appointment of certain officers in the 'Courts of Law,' the absence of similar language to include Congress must mean that neither Congress nor its officers were included within the language 'Heads of Departments' in this part of cl. 2.

"Thus, with respect to four of the six voting members of the Commission, neither the President, the head of any department, *nor the Judiciary* has any voice in their selection." *Buckley*, 424 U.S. at 127 (emphasis added).

The whole point of this passage is that "the Heads of Departments" must reasonably be understood to refer exclusively to the Executive Branch (thereby excluding officers of Congress) because "the Courts of Law" obviously refers exclusively to the Judicial Branch. We were right in *Buckley*, and the Court is wrong today.

* * *

Having concluded, against all odds, that "the Courts of Law" referred to in Article II, § 2, are not the courts of law established by Article III, the Court is confronted with the difficult problem of determining what courts of law they *are*. It acknowledges that they must be courts which exercise "the judicial power of the United States" and concludes that the Tax Court is such a court-even though it is not an Article III court. This is quite a feat, considering that Article III begins "*The* judicial Power of the United States"—not "*Some of* the judicial Power of the United States," or even "*Most of* the judicial Power of the United States"—"shall be vested in one supreme Court, and in such inferior Courts as the Congress may from time to time ordain and establish." Despite this unequivocal text, the Court sets forth the startling proposition that "the judicial power of the United States is not limited to the judicial power defined under Article III." It turns out, however—to our relief, I suppose it must be said—that this is really only a pun. "The judicial power," as the Court uses it, bears no resemblance to the constitutional term of art we are all familiar with, but means only "the power to adjudicate in the manner of courts." So used, as I shall proceed to explain, the phrase covers an infinite variety of individuals exercising *executive* rather than *judicial* power (in the constitutional sense), and has nothing to do with the separation of powers or with any other characteristic that might cause one to believe *that* is what was meant by "the Courts of Law." As far as I can tell, the only thing to be said for this approach is that it makes the Tax Court a "Cour[t] of Law"—which is perhaps the object of the exercise.

I agree with the unremarkable proposition that "Congress [has] wide discretion to assign the task of adjudication in cases arising under federal law to legislative tribunals." Congress may also assign that task to subdivisions of traditional executive departments, as it did in 1924 when it created the Tax Court's predecessor, the Tax Board of Appeals—or to take a more venerable example, as it did in 1791 when it created within the Treasury Department the Comptroller of the United States, who "decide[d] on appeal, without further review by the Secretary, all claims concerning the settlement of accounts." Casper, *An Essay in Separation of Powers: Some Early Versions and Practices*, 30 WM. & MARY L. REV. 211, 238 (1989). Such tribunals, like any other administrative board, exercise the executive power, not the judicial power of the United States. They are, in the words of the great Chief Justice, "incapable of receiving [the judicial power]"—unless their members serve for life during good behavior and receive permanent salary. *Am. Ins. Co. v. Canter*, 26 U.S. (1 Pet.) 511, 546 (1828) (Marshall, C.J.).

It is no doubt true that all such bodies "adjudicate," *i.e.*, they determine facts, apply a rule of law to those facts, and thus arrive at a decision. But there is nothing "inherently judicial" about "adjudication." To be a federal officer and to adjudicate are necessary but not sufficient conditions for the exercise of federal judicial power, as we recognized almost a century and a half ago. * * * Today, the Federal Government has a corps of administrative law judges numbering more than 1,000, whose principal statutory function is the conduct of adjudication under the Administrative Procedure Act. They are all *executive* officers. "Adjudication," in other words, is no more an "inherently" judicial function than the promulgation of rules governing primary conduct is an "inherently" legislative one.

* * *

The Tax Court * * * reviews determinations by Executive Branch officials (the Internal Revenue Service) that this much or that much tax is owed—a classic executive function. For 18 years its predecessor, the

Board of Tax Appeals, did the very same thing, and no one suggested that body exercised "the judicial power." We held just the opposite:

> "The Board of Tax Appeals is not a court. It is an executive or administrative board, upon the decision of which the parties are given an opportunity to base a petition for review to the courts after the administrative inquiry of the Board has been had and decided." *Old Colony Trust Co. v. Comm'r*, 279 U.S. 716, 725 (1929).

Though renamed "the Tax Court of the United States" in 1942, it remained "an independent agency in the Executive Branch," 26 U.S.C. § 1100 (1952), and continued to perform the same function. As an *executive* agency, it possessed many of the accoutrements the Court considers "quintessentially judicial." It administered oaths, for example, and subpoenaed and examined witnesses; its findings were reviewed "in the same manner and to the same extent as decisions of the district courts in civil actions tried without a jury," § 1141(a). This Court continued to treat it as an administrative agency, akin to the Federal Communications Commission (FCC) or the National Labor Relations Board (NLRB). *See Dobson v. Comm'r*, 320 U.S. 489, 495–501 (1943).

When the Tax Court was statutorily denominated an "Article I Court" in 1969, its judges did not magically acquire the judicial power. They still lack life tenure; their salaries may still be diminished; they are still removable by the President for "inefficiency, neglect of duty, or malfeasance in office." 26 U.S.C. § 7443(f). (In *Bowsher v. Synar*, 478 U.S. at 729, we held that these latter terms are "very broad" and "could sustain removal . . . for any number of actual or perceived transgressions.") How anyone with these characteristics can exercise *judicial* power "independent . . . [of] the Executive Branch" is a complete mystery. It seems to me entirely obvious that the Tax Court, like the Internal Revenue Service, the FCC, and the NLRB, exercises executive power.

* * *

Since the Tax Court is not a court of law, unless the Chief Judge is the head of a department, the appointment of the Special Trial Judge was void. Unlike the Court, I think he is.

I have already explained that the Tax Court, like its predecessors, exercises the executive power of the United States. This does not, of course, suffice to make it a "Departmen[t]" for purposes of the Appointments Clause. If, for instance, the Tax Court were a subdivision of the Department of the Treasury—as the Board of Tax Appeals used to be—it would not qualify. In fact, however, the Tax Court is a free-standing, self-contained entity in the Executive Branch, whose Chief Judge is removable by the President (and, save impeachment, no one else).

* * *

The Court reserves the right to consider as "Cabinet-like" and hence as "Departments" those agencies which, above all others, are at the farthest remove from Cabinet status, and whose heads are specifically designed *not* to have the quality that the Court earlier thinks important, of being "subject to the exercise of political oversight and shar[ing] the President's accountability to the people,"—namely, independent regulatory agencies such as the Federal Trade Commission and the Securities and Exchange Commission. Indeed, lest any conceivable improbability be excluded, the Court even reserves the right to consider as a "Departmen[t]" an entity that is not headed by an officer of the United States—the Federal Reserve Bank of St. Louis, whose president is appointed in none of the manners constitutionally permitted for federal officers, but rather by a Board of Directors, two-thirds of whom are elected by regional banks. It is as impossible to respond to this random argumentation as it is to derive a comprehensible theory of the appointments power from it. I shall address, therefore, what was petitioners' point, what I originally took to be the point of the Court's opinion, and what is the only trace of a flesh-and-blood point that subsists: the proposition that "Departmen[t]" means "Cabinet-level agency."

There is no basis in text or precedent for this position. The term "Cabinet" does not appear in the Constitution, the Founders having rejected proposals to create a Cabinet-like entity. The existence of a Cabinet, its membership, and its prerogatives (except to the extent the Twenty-fifth Amendment speaks to them), are entirely matters of Presidential discretion. Nor does any of our cases hold that "the Heads of Departments" are Cabinet members.

* * *

[T]here is no reason, in text, judicial decision, history, or policy, to limit the phrase "the Heads of Departments" in the Appointments Clause to those officials who are members of the President's Cabinet. I would give the term its ordinary meaning, something which Congress has apparently been doing for decades without complaint. As an American dictionary roughly contemporaneous with adoption of the Appointments Clause provided, and as remains the case, a department is "[a] separate allotment or part of business; a distinct province, in which a class of duties are allotted to a particular person. ..." 1 WEBSTER'S AMERICAN DICTIONARY 58 (1828). I readily acknowledge that applying this word to an entity such as the Tax Court would have seemed strange to the Founders, as it continues to seem strange to modern ears. But that is only because the Founders did not envision that an independent establishment of such small size and specialized function would be created. They chose the word "Departmen[t]," however, not to connote size or function (much less Cabinet status), but separate organization—a connotation that still endures even in colloquial usage today ("that is not my department"). The Constitution is clear, I think, about the chain of appointment and supervision that it envisions: Principal officers could be permitted by law to appoint their subordinates. That should subsist, however much the nature of federal business or of federal organizational structure may alter.

I must confess that in the case of the Tax Court, as with some other independent establishments (notably, the so-called "independent regulatory agencies" such as the FCC and the Federal Trade Commission) permitting appointment of inferior officers by the agency head may not ensure the high degree of insulation from congressional control that was the purpose of the appointments scheme elaborated in the Constitution. That is a consequence of our decision in *Humphrey's Executor v. United States*, 295 U.S. 602 (1935), which approved congressional restriction upon arbitrary dismissal of the heads of such agencies by the President, a scheme avowedly designed to made such agencies less accountable to him, and hence he less responsible for them. Depending upon how broadly one reads the President's power to dismiss "for cause," it may be that he has no control over the appointment of inferior officers in such agencies; and if those agencies are publicly regarded as beyond his control—a "headless Fourth Branch"—he may have less incentive to care about such appointments. It could be argued, then, that much of the *raison d'être* for permitting appointive power to be lodged in "Heads of Departments," does not exist with respect to the heads of *these* agencies, because they, in fact, will not be shored up by the President and are thus not resistant to congressional pressures. That is a reasonable position—though I tend to the view that adjusting the remainder of the Constitution to compensate for *Humphrey's Executor* is a fruitless endeavor. But in any event it is not a reasonable position that supports the Court's decision today—both because a "Cour[t] of Law" artificially defined as the Court defines it is even *less* resistant to those pressures, and because the distinction between those agencies that are subject to full Presidential control and those that are not is entirely unrelated to the distinction between Cabinet agencies and non-Cabinet agencies, and to all the other distinctions that the Court successively embraces. (The Central Intelligence Agency and the Environmental Protection Agency, for example, though not Cabinet agencies or components of Cabinet agencies, are not "independent" agencies in the sense of independence from Presidential control.) In sum, whatever may be the distorting effects of later innovations that this Court has approved, considering the Chief Judge of the Tax Court to be the head of a department seems to me the only reasonable construction of Article II, § 2.

NOTES AND QUESTIONS

1.   The majority in *Freytag* expressed its view that the Appointments Clause was intended to limit strictly the potential diffusion of the appointment power. For that reason, the majority suggested strongly that no agency can be a department for purposes of the Appointments Clause unless it is a cabinet-level agency. Yet, the federal government includes an enormous number of non-cabinet agencies, including but by no means limited to the Federal Trade Commission, the Securities and Exchange Commission, the Federal Energy Regulatory Commission, and the Federal Reserve Bank of St. Louis, the heads of which are currently considered principal officers to be appointed by the President with the advice and consent of the Senate. In footnote 4 of the majority opinion, which is not included in your excerpt, the majority specifically disavowed any opinion with respect to the status of the five non-cabinet agencies listed in the preceding sentence. Should we read the majority's reasoning as requiring either expansion of the President's cabinet to encompass hundreds of additional agencies or direct presidential appointment (without advice and consent of the Senate) of the thousands of inferior officers who serve in non-cabinet agencies? If not, then how should we apply the Appointments Clause to non-cabinet agency officials?

2. Recall the discussion in Chapter 1 of traditional versus independent agencies, and observe that the Federal Trade Commission, the Securities and Exchange Commission, the Federal Energy Regulatory Commission, and the Federal Reserve Bank of St. Louis are all independent agencies. Should we distinguish between traditional and independent status in evaluating whether or not an agency is a department for purposes of the Appointments Clause?

3. In *Free Enterprise Fund v. Public Company Accounting Oversight Board*, 561 U.S. 477 (2010), the Supreme Court held that, as a "freestanding component of the Executive Branch, not subordinate to or contained within any other such component, . . . constitutes a 'Departmen[t]' for the purposes of the Appointments Clause," with its several Commissioners acting collectively (rather than merely the Commission's Chairman) as its "Head." Although the Court acknowledged that the Constitution's framers "vested the nomination of principal officers in the President to avoid the perceived evils of collective appointments," the Court saw no such difficulty in having multimember agencies appoint inferior officers such as those at issue in *Free Enterprise Fund*. Justices dissenting from the Court's opinion in *Free Enterprise Fund* did not address this issue. The *Free Enterprise Fund* decision is excerpted and discussed at greater length in the part of this Chapter addressing the President's power to remove officers of the United States.

4. One could argue that the majority's conclusion that the Tax Court is not a department was based primarily on its observation that the Tax Court performs only adjudicative powers, and that it has no power to advocate, administer, or issue substantive rules. The Occupational Safety and Health Regulatory Commission (OSHRC), the Mine Safety and Health Regulatory Commission (MSHRC) exercise only adjudicatory powers. Should we read the majority's opinion to mean that the OSHRC and the MSHRC are also courts of law? What about other executive-branch agencies that only engage in adjudication?

5. The concurring opinion is based on reasoning that is entirely consistent with the present structure of government—with the critical exception of the last paragraph of the excerpt questioning the legitimacy of independent agencies. The concurring Justices expressed the view that the Framers were attempting to limit congressional involvement in the appointments process by centralizing the appointments power in the President and his direct appointees. According to the concurrence, independent agencies, whose heads are insulated from plenary presidential control by limits on the President's removal power, provide an opportunity for Congress to exert control over the appointment of inferior officers that is inconsistent with the intent of the Framers. For example, Congress could increase the power of ALJs by giving them the power to make final decisions, at which point ALJs would be inferior officers, rather than employees, even under the reasoning of the majority in *Landry*. At present, ALJs at many agencies are hired through use of a largely meritocratic, apolitical process. If ALJs were given the power to make final decisions and were classified as inferior officers under the Appointments Clause, would you expect Congress to change the process of hiring ALJs?

6. Think back to *Buckley v. Valeo* and the NRA case, both excerpted earlier in this Chapter, and the structure of the Federal Election Commission (FEC). As a member of Congress, would you be comfortable with an FEC structure in which ALJs have the power to issue final decisions and in which either the President or the President's appointee as Chair of the FEC has unilateral power to appoint ALJs? If ALJs have the power to make final decisions in the intensely political adjudications that come before the FEC, would you rather that their appointments require confirmation by the Senate? If so, would you feel the same way about ALJs with the power to make final decisions at other agencies like the FCC, FTC, etc.? Does the Constitution require the ALJs with the power to make final decisions be appointed by the President and confirmed by the Senate? Remember that Congress can only authorize the President, a court of law, or a head of department to appoint an inferior officer. If ALJs had the power to make final decisions, would they be inferior officers? To whom would they be inferior?

4.   THE RECESS APPOINTMENTS CLAUSE

Article II, Section 2, Clause 3 of the United States Constitution provides, "The President shall have Power to fill up all Vacancies that may happen during the Recess of the Senate, by granting Commissions which shall expire at the End of their next Session." Particularly in times when travel was difficult and the Senate might be adjourned for months, the Recess Appointments Clause served as a pragmatic exception from the Senate consent requirement of the Appointments Clause. President George Washington utilized the Recess Appointments Clause numerous times, as did most if not all of his successors; recess appointments have been a frequent source of friction between Presidents and Senators. In the past few decades, however, controversial recess appointments to executive branch positions in recent decades have prompted new interest in the meaning and scope of the Recess Appointments Clause.

Historically, much of the controversy surrounding the Recess Appointments Clause related to recess appointments of federal judges. From 1789 through 1960, Presidents made more than 300 judicial recess appointments, including several Supreme Court Justices. *See* Henry B. Hogue, *The Law: Recess Appointments to Article III Courts*, 34 PRESIDENTIAL STUDIES Q. 656, 659–60 (2004). In 1960, however, the Senate adopted a resolution discouraging recess appointments to the Supreme Court, at least, as not "wholly consistent with the best interests of the Supreme Court, the nominee who may be involved, the litigants before the Court, nor indeed the people of the United States." S. Res. 334, 86th Cong., 106 CONG. REC. 12761 (1960). Since 1960, only four judges have received recess appointments: President Jimmy Carter appointed Judge Walter Heen to the United States District Court for the District of Hawaii on December 31, 1981, just before President Ronald Reagan took office; President Bill Clinton appointed Roger Gregory to the Fourth Circuit on December 27, 2000, just before President George W. Bush took office; and in 2004, President George W. Bush appointed Judges Charles Pickering and William Pryor to the United States Courts of Appeals for the Fifth, and Eleventh Circuits, respectively.

Nevertheless, Presidents have continued making recess appointments to fill executive branch positions. President Reagan exercised the recess appointment power 240 times over eight years.

President George H.W. Bush made 77 recess appointments during his single, four-year term. President Clinton made 139 during his two terms of office. President George W. Bush made 171 over the eight years of his presidency. President Barack Obama had made 32 recess appointments as of June 4, 2013. *See* HENRY B. HOGUE, CONGRESSIONAL RESEARCH SERVICE, RECESS APPOINTMENTS: FREQUENTLY ASKED QUESTIONS, CRS REPORT RS21308 at 2 (updated June 7, 2013); Patrick Hein, *In Defense of Broad Recess Appointment Power: The Effectiveness of Political Counterweights*, 96 CAL. L. REV. 235, 236 (2008). Although the Recess Appointments Clause clearly serves as a limited, pragmatic exception from the mechanism for appointments provided by the Appointments Clause, many of these recess appointments were quite controversial, as Presidents used the recess appointment power to appoint individuals whose nominations have garnered significant opposition in the Senate. In 2004, President George W. Bush used the recess appointment power to appoint William Pryor to a judgeship on the United States Court of Appeals for the Eleventh Circuit over Senate opposition, although the Senate later confirmed Judge Pryor. In 2012, President Obama gave Richard Cordray a recess appointment to serve as head of the new Consumer Financial Protection Board after Senate Republicans blocked his appointment to register their dissatisfaction with the CFPB's organizational structure.

Since November 2013, a change in the rules governing the Senate has substantially decreased the need for Presidents to rely upon the recess appointment power to appoint controversial nominees to judicial or executive branch positions. Although the votes of only a simple majority of 51 senators are needed to confirm a judicial or executive branch nomination, before November 2013, a longstanding Senate rule required 60 senators to agree to end debate, known as cloture, before the Senate could hold a confirmation vote. The cloture rule thus allowed a minority of senators to block the presidential nominations they found objectionable—a common occurrence during the administrations of Presidents Obama and George W. Bush. On November 21, 2013, a majority of senators voted to change the cloture rule to allow a simple majority of 51 votes to end debate with respect to most judicial and all executive branch nominations; only nominations to the Supreme Court were excluded from the rule change. At the time of the rule change, both the President and the majority of senators were Democrats. Immediately after the change, Senate Democrats acted to advance several nominations previously blocked by Republicans. Critics of the rule change (as well as some supporters) have observed that the more relaxed cloture requirement will permit the appointment of more ideologically extreme nominees whenever the same party controls both the Presidency and the Senate. Supporters of the rule change contend that it will make the Senate more responsive to the wishes of the electorate. Who do you think is right?

The circumstances surrounding various recess appointments have raised a number of questions regarding the proper interpretation of the Recess Appointments Clause. For example, what constitutes "the Recess of the Senate" for purposes of the Recess Appointments Clause? In addition to the annual *sine die* adjournment, also known as an "intersession" recess, which represents the end of one congressional session and the beginning of the next and which often runs several weeks, the Senate also adjourns "intrasession" for a few days most every weekend and for longer periods throughout the year.

In 1901, Attorney General P.C. Knox concluded that Presidents could only make recess appointments during the *sine die* adjournment between sessions. *See* 23 Op. Att'y Gen. 599, 601 (1901). On December 7, 1903, when the 57th Congress commenced its second session immediately after adjourning the first, President Theodore Roosevelt declared the divide between the sessions a "constructive recess" and made 160 recess appointments. *See* Hogue, *supra*, at 671. In 1921, Attorney General Harry Daugherty expressed a different view, concluding that Presidents could make recess appointments during intrasession adjournments of substantial duration. *See* 33 Op. Att'y Gen. 20, 21–25 (1921). Daugherty further opined that an intrasession adjournment from August 24 through September 21 was long enough, but that intrasession adjournments of two, five, or even ten days would be inadequate to support a recess appointment. *See id.* at 24–25. Later interpretations by Department of Justice attorneys were consistent with Daugherty's view. *See, e.g.*, 3 Op. Off. Legal Counsel 314 (1979) (supporting recess appointments during an intrasession recess from August 2 through September 4); 41 Op. Att'y Gen. 463 (1960) (supporting recess appointments during an intrasession recess from July 3 through August 8).

The federal circuit courts divided over the meaning of "the Recess of the Senate." For example, in considering a challenge to the intrasession recess appointment of Judge William Pryor, the Eleventh Circuit held that the Recess includes intrasession recesses. *Evans v. Stephens*, 387 F.3d 1220 (11th Cir. 2004) (en banc), *cert. denied*, 544 U.S. 942 (2005). Although the *Evans* court did not set a specific duration for a Senate break to qualify as a recess for this purpose, Judge Pryor's appointment occurred during a ten-or eleven-day intrasession break of the Senate, and the court recognized favorably previous recess appointments during intrasession breaks of nine, eleven, and thirteen days. The *Evans* court's conclusion was consistent with previous decisions by the Second and Ninth Circuits upholding intrasession recess appointments. *See United States v. Woodley*, 751 F.2d 1008 (9th Cir. 1985) (en banc); *United States v. Allocco*, 305 F.2d 704 (2d Cir. 1962), cert. denied, 371 U.S. 964 (1963). By contrast, in evaluating a challenge to the recess appointments of three members of the National Labor Relations Board, the D.C. Circuit rejected intrasession recess appointments altogether, reasoning that the Constitution's use of "the Recess" (rather than "a Recess") was a clear reference to the annual *sine die* adjournment. *Noel Canning v. NLRB*, 705 F.3d 490 (D.C. Cir. 2013), *cert. granted*, 133 S. Ct. 2861. Subsequently, two other circuits similarly held that the Constitution does not permit the President to make recess appointments during intrasession adjournments of the Senate. *See NLRB v. Enterprise Leasing Co. Se., LLC*, 722 F.3d 609 (4th Cir. 2013); *NLRB v. New Vista Nursing & Rehab.*, 719 F.3d 203 (3d Cir. 2013).

Another common question regarding the Recess Appointments Clause is whether the requirement that vacancies "happen" during a Senate recess means that they must initially arise or merely exist at that time. In several cases involving recess appointments of federal judges, the courts have upheld the "exist" interpretation, on the theory that the "arise" interpretation would merely "create Executive paralysis and do violence to the orderly functioning of our complex government." *United States v. Allocco*, 305 F.2d 704, 712 (2d Cir. 1962); *see also Evans v. Stephens*, 387 F.3d 1220, 1224 (11th Cir. 2004) (en banc) (following similar rationale); *United States v. Woodley*, 751 F.2d 1008, 1013 (9th Cir. 1985) (en banc) (same). By contrast, in considering recess appointments to the NLRB in the *Noel Canning* case, the D.C. Circuit concluded that the President may only make recess appointments to fill vacancies that arise during a recess of the Senate. 705 F.3d at 508. Relying primarily on the Constitution's text and structure as supporting its interpretation of "happen," the D.C. Circuit noted further that a contrary interpretation would effectively gut the Appointments Clause of Article II, Section 2, Clause 2. "A President at odds with the Senate over nominations would never have to submit his nominees for confirmation. He could simply wait for a 'recess' (however defined) and then fill up all vacancies." *Id.*

Finally, many statutes establishing multi-member commissions whose members serve limited terms—including the Federal Trade Commission, the Federal Elections Commission, the Security and Exchange Commission, and the International Trade Commission— contain "holdover clauses" calling for any member whose term has expired to continue to serve until his or her successor takes office. Where a statute contains a holdover clause, can the President use a recess appointment to replace a member serving an expired term, or must the Senate confirm the successor to remove the holdover? Does the Constitution allow Congress to constrain presidential exercise of the recess appointment power with a holdover clause? In *Swan v. Clinton*, 100 F.3d 973, 988 (D.C. Cir. 1996), the D.C. Circuit decided to avoid the latter, constitutional question by declining, absent clear congressional intent, to read a holdover clause governing membership on the National Credit Union Administration as limiting the President's authority to exercise his recess appointment authority to replace a holdover officer.

The following opinion of the Supreme Court resolves some but not all of these issues, while potentially creating new questions for the future regarding proper interpretation of the Recess Appointments Clause.

National Labor Relations Board v. Noel Canning

134 S. Ct. 2550 (2014).

■ JUSTICE BREYER delivered the opinion of the Court.

Ordinarily the President must obtain "the Advice and Consent of the Senate" before appointing an "Office[r] of the United States." U.S. Const., Art. II, § 2, cl. 2. But the Recess Appointments Clause creates an exception. It gives the President alone the power "to fill up all Vacancies that may happen during the Recess of the Senate, by granting Commissions which shall expire at the End of their next Session." Art. II, § 2, cl. 3. We here consider three questions about the application of this Clause.

* * *

I

The case before us arises out of a labor dispute. The National Labor Relations Board (NLRB) found that a Pepsi-Cola distributor, Noel Canning, had unlawfully refused to reduce to writing and execute a collective-bargaining agreement with a labor union. The Board ordered the distributor to execute the agreement and to make employees whole for any losses.

The Pepsi-Cola distributor * * * claimed that three of the five Board members had been invalidly appointed, leaving the Board without the three lawfully appointed members necessary for it to act.

The three members in question were Sharon Block, Richard Griffin, and Terence Flynn. In 2011 the President had nominated each of them to the Board. As of January 2012, Flynn's nomination had been pending in the Senate awaiting confirmation for approximately a year. The nominations of each of the other two had been pending for a few weeks. On January 4, 2012, the President, invoking the Recess Appointments Clause, appointed all three to the Board.

* * *

II

Before turning to the specific questions presented, we shall mention two background considerations that we find relevant to all three. First, *the Recess Appointments Clause sets forth a subsidiary, not a primary, method for appointing officers of the United States.* The immediately preceding Clause—Article II, Section 2, Clause 2— provides the primary method of appointment. It says that the President "shall nominate, *and by and with the Advice and Consent of the Senate,* shall appoint Ambassadors, other public Ministers and Consuls, Judges of the supreme Court, and all other Officers of the United States" (emphasis added).

* * *

Thus the Recess Appointments Clause reflects the tension between, on the one hand, the President's continuous need for "the assistance of subordinates," *Myers v. United States*, 272 U.S. 52, 117 (1926), and, on the other, the Senate's practice, particularly during the Republic's early years, of meeting for a single brief session each year. We seek to interpret the Clause as granting the President the power to make appointments during a recess but not offering the President the authority routinely to avoid the need for Senate confirmation.

Second, *in interpreting the Clause, we put significant weight upon historical practice.* For one thing, the interpretive questions before us concern the allocation of power between two elected branches of Government. Long ago Chief Justice Marshall wrote that

> a doubtful question, one on which human reason may pause, and the human judgment be suspended, in the decision of which the great principles of liberty are not concerned, but the respective powers of those who are equally the representatives of the people, are to be adjusted; if not put at rest by the practice of the government, ought to receive a considerable

impression from that practice. *McCulloch v. Maryland,* 4 Wheat. 316, 401 (1819).

And we later confirmed that "[l]ong settled and established practice is a consideration of great weight in a proper interpretation of constitutional provisions" regulating the relationship between Congress and the President. *The Pocket Veto Case,* 279 U.S. 655, 689 (1929).

* * *

There is a great deal of history to consider here. Presidents have made recess appointments since the beginning of the Republic. Their frequency suggests that the Senate and President have recognized that recess appointments can be both necessary and appropriate in certain circumstances. We have not previously interpreted the Clause, and, when doing so for the first time in more than 200 years, we must hesitate to upset the compromises and working arrangements that the elected branches of Government themselves have reached.

III

The first question concerns the scope of the phrase "*the recess* of the Senate." Art. II, § 2, cl. 3 (emphasis added). The Constitution provides for congressional elections every two years. And the 2-year life of each elected Congress typically consists of two formal 1-year sessions, each separated from the next by an "inter-session recess." Congressional Research Service, H. Hogue, Recess Appointments: Frequently Asked Questions 2 (2013). The Senate or the House of Representatives announces an inter-session recess by approving a resolution stating that it will "adjourn *sine die,*" *i.e.,* without specifying a date to return (in which case Congress will reconvene when the next formal session is scheduled to begin).

The Senate and the House also take breaks in the midst of a session. The Senate or the House announces any such "intra-session recess" by adopting a resolution stating that it will "adjourn" to a fixed date, a few days or weeks or even months later. All agree that the phrase "the recess of the Senate" covers inter-session recesses. The question is whether it includes intra-session recesses as well.

In our view, the phrase "the recess" includes an intra-session recess of substantial length. Its words taken literally can refer to both types of recess. Founding-era dictionaries define the word "recess," much as we do today, simply as "a period of cessation from usual work." 13 The Oxford English Dictionary 322–323 (2d ed.1989) (hereinafter OED) (citing 18th- and 19th-century sources for that definition of "recess"); 2 N. Webster, An American Dictionary of the English Language (1828) ("[r]emission or suspension of business or procedure"); 2 S. Johnson, A Dictionary of the English Language 1602–1603 (4th ed. 1773) (hereinafter Johnson) (same). The Founders themselves used the word to refer to intra-session, as well as to inter-session, breaks. See, *e.g.,* 3 Records of the Federal Convention of 1787, p. 76 (M. Farrand rev.1966) (hereinafter Farrand) (letter from George Washington to John Jay using "the recess" to refer to an intra-session break of the Constitutional Convention); *id.,* at 191 (speech of Luther Martin with a similar usage); 1 T. Jefferson, A Manual of Parliamentary Practice § LI, p. 165 (2d ed. 1812) (describing a "recess by adjournment" which did *not* end a session).

We recognize that the word "the" in "*the* recess" might suggest that the phrase refers to the single break separating formal sessions of Congress. That is because the word "the" frequently (but not always) indicates "a particular thing." 2 Johnson 2003. But the word can also refer "to a term used generically or universally." 17 OED 879. The Constitution, for example, directs the Senate to choose a President *pro tempore* "in *the* Absence of the Vice-President." Art. I, § 3, cl. 5 (emphasis added). And the Federalist Papers refer to the chief magistrate of an ancient Achaean league who "administered the government in *the* recess of the Senate." The Federalist No. 18, at 113 (J. Madison) (emphasis added). Reading "the" generically in this way, there is no linguistic problem applying the Clause's phrase to both kinds of recess. * * *

The constitutional text is thus ambiguous. And we believe the Clause's purpose demands the broader interpretation. The Clause gives the President authority to make appointments during "the recess of the Senate" so that the President can ensure the continued functioning of the Federal Government when the Senate is away. The Senate is equally away during both an inter-session and an intra-session recess, and its capacity to participate in the appointments process has nothing to do with the words it uses to signal its departure.

History also offers strong support for the broad interpretation. We concede that pre-Civil War history is not helpful. But it shows only that Congress generally took long breaks between sessions, while taking no significant intra-session breaks at all (five times it took a break of a week or so at Christmas). Obviously, if there are no significant intra-session recesses, there will be no intra-session recess appointments. In 1867 and 1868, Congress for the first time took substantial, nonholiday intra-session breaks, and President Andrew Johnson made dozens of recess appointments. * * *

In all, between the founding and the Great Depression, Congress took substantial intra-session breaks (other than holiday breaks) in four years: 1867, 1868, 1921, and 1929. And in each of those years the President made intra-session recess appointments.

Since 1929, and particularly since the end of World War II, Congress has shortened its inter-session breaks as it has taken longer and more frequent intra-session breaks; Presidents have correspondingly made more intra-session recess appointments. * * *

Not surprisingly, the publicly available opinions of Presidential legal advisers that we have found are nearly unanimous in determining that the Clause authorizes these appointments.

* * *

What about the Senate? Since Presidents began making intra-session recess appointments, individual Senators have taken differing views about the proper definition of "the recess." But neither the Senate considered as a body nor its committees, despite opportunities to express opposition to the practice of intra-session recess appointments, has done so. Rather, to the extent that the Senate or a Senate committee has expressed a view, that view has favored a functional definition of "recess," and a functional definition encompasses intra-session recesses.

Most notably, in 1905 the Senate Committee on the Judiciary objected strongly to President Theodore Roosevelt's use of the Clause to make more than 160 recess appointments during a "fictitious" inter-session recess. S. Rep. No. 4389, 58th Cong., 3d Sess., p. 2 (hereinafter 1905 Senate Report). At noon on December 7, 1903, the Senate President *pro tempore* had "declare[d]" a formal, "extraordinary session" of the Senate "adjourned without day," and the next formal Senate session began immediately afterwards. 37 Cong. Rec. 544 (1903). President Roosevelt made over 160 recess appointments during the instantaneous inter-session interval. The Judiciary Committee, when stating its strong objection, defined "recess" in functional terms as

> the period of time when the Senate is not sitting in regular or extraordinary session as a branch of the Congress . . . ; when its members owe no duty of attendance; when its Chamber is empty; when, because of its absence, it can not receive communications from the President or participate as a body in making appointments. 1905 Senate Report, at 2 (emphasis deleted).

That functional definition encompasses intra-session, as well as inter-session, recesses.

* * *

The upshot is that restricting the Clause to inter-session recesses would frustrate its purpose. It would make the President's recess-appointment power dependent on a formalistic distinction of Senate procedure. Moreover, the President has consistently and frequently interpreted the word "recess" to apply to intra-session recesses, and has acted on that interpretation. The Senate as a body has done nothing to deny the validity of this practice for at least three-quarters of a century. And three-quarters of a century of settled practice is long enough to entitle a practice to "great weight in a proper interpretation" of the constitutional provision. *The Pocket Veto Case,* 279 U.S., at 689.

* * *

The greater interpretive problem is determining how long a recess must be in order to fall within the Clause. Is a break of a week, or a day, or an hour too short to count as a "recess"? The Clause itself does not say.

* * *

[T]he most likely reason the Framers did not place a textual floor underneath the word "recess" is that they did not foresee the *need* for one. They might have expected that the Senate would meet for a single session lasting at most half a year. The Federalist No. 84, at 596 (A. Hamilton). And they might not have anticipated that intra-session recesses would become lengthier and more significant than inter-session ones. The Framers' lack of clairvoyance on that point is not dispositive. * * *

Moreover, the lack of a textual floor raises a problem that plagues *both* interpretations—Justice SCALIA's and ours. Today a brief inter-session recess is just as possible as a brief intra-session recess. And though Justice SCALIA says that the "notion that the Constitution empowers the President to make unilateral appointments every time the Senate takes a half-hour lunch break is *so absurd as to be self-refuting*," he must immediately concede (in a footnote) that the President "can make recess appointments during any break *between* sessions, *no matter how short*." (emphasis added).

Even the Solicitor General, arguing for a broader interpretation, acknowledges that there is a lower limit applicable to both kinds of recess. He argues that the lower limit should be three days by analogy to the Adjournments Clause of the Constitution. That Clause says: "Neither House, during the Session of Congress, shall, without the Consent of the other, adjourn for more than three days." Art. I, § 5, cl. 4.

We agree with the Solicitor General that a 3-day recess would be too short. * * * The Adjournments Clause reflects the fact that a 3-day break is not a significant interruption of legislative business. As the Solicitor General says, it is constitutionally *de minimis*. A Senate recess that is so short that it does not require the consent of the House is not long enough to trigger the President's recess-appointment power.

That is not to say that the President may make recess appointments during any recess that is "more than three days." Art. I, § 5, cl. 4. The Recess Appointments Clause seeks to permit the Executive Branch to function smoothly when Congress is unavailable. And though Congress has taken short breaks for almost 200 years, and there have been many thousands of recess appointments in that time, we have not found a single example of a recess appointment made during an intra-session recess that was shorter than 10 days.

* * *

We therefore conclude, in light of historical practice, that a recess of more than 3 days but less than 10 days is presumptively too short to fall within the Clause. We add the word "presumptively" to leave open the possibility that some very unusual circumstance—a national catastrophe, for instance, that renders the Senate unavailable but calls for an urgent response—could demand the exercise of the recess-appointment power during a shorter break. (It should go without saying—except that Justice SCALIA compels us to say it—that political opposition in the Senate would not qualify as an unusual circumstance.)

In sum, we conclude that the phrase "the recess" applies to both intra-session and inter-session recesses. If a Senate recess is so short that it does not require the consent of the House, it is too short to trigger the Recess Appointments Clause. See Art. I, § 5, cl. 4. And a recess lasting less than 10 days is presumptively too short as well.

IV

The second question concerns the scope of the phrase "vacancies *that may happen* during the recess of the Senate." Art. II, § 2, cl. 3 (emphasis added). All agree that the phrase applies to vacancies that initially occur during a recess. But does it also apply to vacancies that initially occur before a recess and continue to exist during the recess? In our view the phrase applies to both kinds of vacancy.

We believe that the Clause's language, read literally, permits, though it does not naturally favor, our broader interpretation. We concede that the most natural meaning of "happens" as applied to a "vacancy" (at least to a modern ear) is that the vacancy "happens" when it initially occurs. See 1 Johnson 913 (defining "happen" in relevant part as meaning "[t]o fall out; to chance; to come to pass"). But that is not the only possible way to use the word.

* * *

In any event, the linguistic question here is not whether the phrase can be, but whether it must be, read more narrowly. The question is whether the Clause is ambiguous. *The Pocket Veto Case,* 279 U.S., at 690. And the broader reading, we believe, is at least a permissible reading of a " 'doubtful' " phrase. *Ibid.* We consequently go on to consider the Clause's purpose and historical practice.

The Clause's purpose strongly supports the broader interpretation. That purpose is to permit the President to obtain the assistance of subordinate officers when the Senate, due to its recess, cannot confirm them. Attorney General [William] Wirt clearly described how the narrower interpretation would undermine this purpose:

> "Put the case of a vacancy occurring in an office, held in a distant part of the country, on the last day of the Senate's session. Before the vacancy is made known to the President, the Senate rises. The office may be an important one; the vacancy may paralyze a whole line of action in some essential branch of our internal police; the public interests may imperiously demand that it shall be immediately filled. But the vacancy happened to occur during the session of the Senate; and if the President's power is to be limited to such vacancies only as happen to occur during the recess of the Senate, the vacancy in the case put must continue, however ruinous the consequences may be to the public." 1 Op. Atty. Gen., at 632.

* * *

We do not agree with Justice SCALIA's suggestion that the Framers would have accepted the catastrophe envisioned by Wirt because Congress can always provide for acting officers, see 5 U.S.C. § 3345, and the President can always convene a special session of Congress, see U.S. Const., Art. II, § 3. Acting officers may have less authority than Presidential appointments. 6 Op. OLC 119, 121 (1982). Moreover, to rely on acting officers would lessen the President's ability to staff the Executive Branch with people of his own choosing, and thereby limit the President's control and political accountability. Cf. *Free Enterprise Fund v. Public Company Accounting Oversight Bd.,* 561 U.S. 477, 497–498 (2010). Special sessions are burdensome (and would have been especially so at the time of the founding). The point of the Recess Appointments Clause was to *avoid* reliance on these inadequate expedients.

At the same time, we recognize one important purpose-related consideration that argues in the opposite direction. A broad interpretation might permit a President to avoid Senate confirmations as a matter of course. If the Clause gives the President the power to "fill up all vacancies" that occur before, and continue to exist during, the Senate's recess, a President might not submit any nominations to the Senate. He might simply wait for a recess and then provide all potential nominees with recess appointments. He might thereby routinely avoid the constitutional need to obtain the Senate's "advice and consent."

Wirt thought considerations of character and politics would prevent Presidents from abusing the Clause in this way. 1 Op. Atty. Gen., at 634. He might have added that such temptations should not often arise. It is often less desirable for a President to make a recess appointment. A recess appointee only serves a limited term. That, combined with the lack of Senate approval, may diminish the recess appointee's ability, as a practical matter, to get a controversial job done. And even where the President and Senate are at odds over politically sensitive appointments, compromise is normally possible. * * * In any event, the Executive Branch has adhered to the broader interpretation for two centuries, and Senate confirmation has always remained the norm for officers that require it.

While we concede that both interpretations carry with them some risk of undesirable consequences, we believe the narrower interpretation risks undermining constitutionally conferred powers more seriously and more often. It would prevent the President from making any recess appointment that arose before a recess, no matter who the official, no matter how dire the need, no matter how uncontroversial the appointment, and no matter how late in the session the office fell vacant. Overall, like Attorney General Wirt, we believe the broader interpretation more consistent with the Constitution's "reason and spirit." 1 Op. Atty. Gen., at 632.

Historical practice over the past 200 years strongly favors the broader interpretation.

[The Court then proceeded to document numerous presidential uses of the recess appointment power and Senate reactions thereto. Ed.]

* * *

The upshot is that the President has consistently and frequently interpreted the Recess Appointments Clause to apply to vacancies that initially occur before, but continue to exist during, a recess of the Senate. The Senate as a body has not countered this practice for nearly three-quarters of a century, perhaps longer. * * * The tradition is long enough to entitle the practice "to great regard in determining the true construction" of the constitutional provision. *The Pocket Veto Case,* 279 U.S., at 690. And we are reluctant to upset this traditional practice where doing so would seriously shrink the authority that Presidents have believed existed and have exercised for so long.

In light of some linguistic ambiguity, the basic purpose of the Clause, and the historical practice we have described, we conclude that the phrase "all vacancies" includes vacancies that come into existence while the Senate is in session.

V

The third question concerns the calculation of the length of the Senate's "recess." On December 17, 2011, the Senate by unanimous consent adopted a resolution to convene " *pro forma* session[s]" only, with "no business . . . transacted," on every Tuesday and Friday from December 20, 2011, through January 20, 2012. At the end of each *pro forma* session, the Senate would "adjourn until" the following *pro forma* session. During that period, the Senate convened and adjourned as agreed. It held *pro forma* sessions on December 20, 23, 27, and 30, and on January 3, 6, 10, 13, 17, and 20; and at the end of each *pro forma* session, it adjourned until the time and date of the next.

The President made the recess appointments before us on January 4, 2012, in between the January 3 and the January 6 *pro forma* sessions. We must determine the significance of these sessions—that is, whether, for purposes of the Clause, we should treat them as periods when the Senate was in session or as periods when it was in recess. If the former, the period between January 3 and January 6 was a 3-day recess, which is too short to trigger the President's recess-appointment power. If the latter, however, then the 3-day period was part of a much longer recess during which the President did have the power to make recess appointments.

* * *

In our view, however, the *pro forma* sessions count as sessions, not as periods of recess. We hold that, for purposes of the Recess Appointments Clause, the Senate is in session when it says it is, provided that, under its own rules, it retains the capacity to transact Senate business. The Senate met that standard here.

The standard we apply is consistent with the Constitution's broad delegation of authority to the Senate to determine how and when to conduct its business. The Constitution explicitly empowers the Senate to "determine the Rules of its Proceedings." Art. 1, § 5, cl. 2. And we have held that "all matters of method are open to the determination" of the Senate, as long as there is "a reasonable relation between the mode or method of proceeding established by the rule and the result which is sought to be attained" and the rule does not "ignore constitutional restraints or violate fundamental rights." *United States v. Ballin*, 144 U.S. 1, 5 (1892).

In addition, the Constitution provides the Senate with extensive control over its schedule. There are only limited exceptions. See Amdt. 20, § 2 (Congress must meet once a year on January 3, unless it specifies another day by law); Art. II, § 3 (Senate must meet if the President calls it into special session); Art. I, § 5, cl. 4 (neither House may adjourn for more than three days without consent of the other). See also Art. II, § 3 ("[I]n Case of Disagreement between [the Houses], with Respect to the Time of Adjournment, [the President] may adjourn them to such Time as he shall think proper"). The Constitution thus gives the Senate wide latitude to determine whether and when to have a session, as well as how to conduct the session. This suggests that the Senate's determination about what constitutes a session should merit great respect.

Furthermore, this Court's precedents reflect the breadth of the power constitutionally delegated to the Senate. We generally take at face value the Senate's own report of its actions. * * *

For these reasons, we conclude that we must give great weight to the Senate's own determination of when it is and when it is not in session. But our deference to the Senate cannot be absolute. When the Senate is without the *capacity* to act, under its own rules, it is not in session even if it so declares. In that circumstance, the Senate is not simply unlikely or unwilling to act upon nominations of the President. It is *unable* to do so. The purpose of the Clause is to ensure the continued functioning of the Federal Government while the Senate is unavailable. This purpose would count for little were we to treat the Senate as though it were in session even when it lacks the ability to provide its "advice and consent." Art. II, § 2, cl. 2. Accordingly, we conclude that when the Senate declares that it is in session and possesses the capacity, under its own rules, to conduct business, it is in session for purposes of the Clause.

Applying this standard, we find that the *pro forma* sessions were sessions for purposes of the Clause. First, the Senate said it was in session. The Journal of the Senate and the Congressional Record indicate that the Senate convened for a series of twice-weekly "sessions" from December 20 through January 20. And these reports of the Senate "must be assumed to speak the truth." *Ballin, supra,* at 4.

Second, the Senate's rules make clear that during its *pro forma* sessions, despite its resolution that it would conduct no business, the Senate retained the power to conduct business. During any *pro forma* session, the Senate could have conducted business simply by passing a unanimous consent agreement. The Senate in fact conducts much of its business through unanimous consent. Senate rules presume that a quorum is present unless a present Senator questions it. And when the Senate has a quorum, an agreement is unanimously passed if, upon its proposal, no present Senator objects. It is consequently unsurprising that the Senate *has* enacted legislation during *pro forma* sessions even when it has said that no business will be transacted. Indeed, the Senate passed a bill by unanimous consent during the second *pro forma* session after its December 17 adjournment. And that bill quickly became law. Pub.L. 112–78, 125 Stat. 1280.

By way of contrast, we do not see how the Senate could conduct business during a recess. It could terminate the recess and then, when in session, pass a bill. But in that case, of course, the Senate would no longer be in recess. It would be in session. And that is the crucial point. Senate rules make clear that, once in session, the Senate can act even if it has earlier said that it would not.

* * *

The Solicitor General asks us to engage in a more realistic appraisal of what the Senate actually did. He argues that, during the relevant *pro forma* sessions, business was not in fact conducted; messages from the President could not be received in any meaningful way because they could not be placed before the Senate; the Senate Chamber was, according to C-SPAN coverage, almost empty; and in practice attendance was not required.

We do not believe, however, that engaging in the kind of factual appraisal that the Solicitor General suggests is either legally or practically appropriate. From a legal perspective, this approach would run contrary to precedent instructing us to "respect . . . coequal and independent departments" by, for example, taking the Senate's report of its official action at its word. [*Marshall Field & Co. v. Clark*, 143 U.S. 649, 672 (1892)]; see *Ballin,* 144 U.S., at 4. From a practical perspective, judges cannot easily determine such matters as who is, and who is not, in fact present on the floor during a particular Senate session. Judicial efforts to engage in these kinds of inquiries would risk undue judicial interference with the functioning of the Legislative Branch.

VI

The Recess Appointments Clause responds to a structural difference between the Executive and Legislative Branches: The Executive Branch is perpetually in operation, while the Legislature only acts in intervals separated by recesses. The purpose of the Clause is to allow the Executive to continue operating while the Senate is unavailable. We believe that the Clause's text, standing alone, is ambiguous. It does not resolve whether the President may make appointments during intra-session recesses, or whether he may fill pre-recess vacancies. But the broader reading better serves the Clause's structural function. Moreover, that broader reading is reinforced by centuries of history, which we are hesitant to disturb. We thus hold that the Constitution empowers the President to fill any existing vacancy during any recess—intra-session or inter-session—of sufficient length.

Justice SCALIA would render illegitimate thousands of recess appointments reaching all the way back to the founding era. More than that: Calling the Clause an "anachronism," he would basically read it out of the Constitution. He performs this act of judicial excision in the name of liberty. We fail to see how excising the Recess Appointments Clause preserves freedom. In fact, Alexander Hamilton observed in the very first Federalist Paper that "the vigour of government is essential to the security of liberty." The Federalist No. 1, at 5. And the Framers included the Recess Appointments Clause to preserve the "vigour of government" at times when an important organ of Government, the United States Senate, is in recess. Justice SCALIA's interpretation of the Clause would defeat the power of the Clause to achieve that objective.

* * *

Given our answer to the last question before us, we conclude that the Recess Appointments Clause does not give the President the constitutional authority to make the appointments here at issue. * * *

[Appendices A and B to the Court's opinion, documenting "the dates of all the intra-session and inter-session recesses that Congress has taken since the founding" and "the proportion of recent appointments that have filled pre-recess vacancies," respectively, are omitted. Ed.]

■ JUSTICE SCALIA, with whom THE CHIEF JUSTICE, JUSTICE THOMAS, and JUSTICE ALITO join, concurring in the judgment.

* * * This case requires us to decide whether the Recess Appointments Clause authorized three appointments made by President Obama to the National Labor Relations Board in January 2012 without the Senate's consent.

* * *

Today's Court agrees that the appointments were invalid, but for the far narrower reason that they were made during a 3-day break in the Senate's session. On its way to that result, the majority sweeps away the key textual limitations on the recess-appointment power. It holds, first, that the President can make appointments without the

Senate's participation even during short breaks in the middle of the Senate's session, and second, that those appointments can fill offices that became vacant long before the break in which they were filled. The majority justifies those atextual results on an adverse-possession theory of executive authority: Presidents have long claimed the powers in question, and the Senate has not disputed those claims with sufficient vigor, so the Court should not "upset the compromises and working arrangements that the elected branches of Government themselves have reached."

The Court's decision transforms the recess-appointment power from a tool carefully designed to fill a narrow and specific need into a weapon to be wielded by future Presidents against future Senates. To reach that result, the majority casts aside the plain, original meaning of the constitutional text in deference to late-arising historical practices that are ambiguous at best. The majority's insistence on deferring to the Executive's untenably broad interpretation of the power is in clear conflict with our precedent and forebodes a diminution of this Court's role in controversies involving the separation of powers and the structure of government. I concur in the judgment only.

I. Our Responsibility

Today's majority disregards two overarching principles that ought to guide our consideration of the questions presented here.

First, the Constitution's core, government-structuring provisions are no less critical to preserving liberty than are the later adopted provisions of the Bill of Rights. Indeed, "[s]o convinced were the Framers that liberty of the person inheres in structure that at first they did not consider a Bill of Rights necessary." *Clinton v. City of New York,* 524 U.S. 417, 450 (1998) (KENNEDY, J., concurring). Those structural provisions reflect the founding generation's deep conviction that "checks and balances were the foundation of a structure of government that would protect liberty." *Bowsher v. Synar,* 478 U.S. 714, 722 (1986). It is for that reason that "the claims of individuals—not of Government departments—have been the principal source of judicial decisions concerning separation of powers and checks and balances." *Bond v. United States,* 564 U.S. ___, ___ (2011) (slip op., at 10); see, *e.g., Free Enterprise Fund v. Public Company Accounting Oversight Bd.,* 561 U.S. 477 (2010); *Clinton, supra*; *Plaut v. Spendthrift Farm, Inc.,* 514 U.S. 211 (1995); *Bowsher, supra*; *INS v. Chadha,* 462 U.S. 919 (1983); *Northern Pipeline Constr. Co. v. Marathon Pipe Line Co.,* 458 U.S. 50 (1982). Those decisions all rest on the bedrock principle that "the constitutional structure of our Government" is designed first and foremost not to look after the interests of the respective branches, but to "protec[t] individual liberty." *Bond, supra,* at ___ (slip op., at 11).

Second and relatedly, when questions involving the Constitution's government-structuring provisions are presented in a justiciable case, it is the solemn responsibility of the Judicial Branch " 'to say what the law is.' " *Zivotofsky v. Clinton,* 566 U.S. ___, ___ (2012) (slip op., at 7) (quoting *Marbury v. Madison,* 1 Cranch 137, 177 (1803)). This Court does not defer to the other branches' resolution of such controversies; as Justice KENNEDY has previously written, our role is in no way "lessened" because it might be said that "the two political branches are adjusting their own powers between themselves." *Clinton, supra,* at 449 (concurring opinion). Since the separation of powers exists for the protection of individual liberty, its vitality "does not depend" on "whether 'the encroached-upon branch approves the encroachment.'" *Free Enterprise Fund, supra,* at 497 (quoting *New York v. United States,* 505 U.S. 144, 182 (1992)). Rather, policing the "enduring structure" of constitutional government when the political branches fail to do so is "one of the most vital functions of this Court." *Public Citizen v. Department of Justice,* 491 U.S. 440, 468 (1989) (KENNEDY, J., concurring in judgment).

* * *

Of course, where a governmental practice has been open, widespread, and unchallenged since the early days of the Republic, the practice should guide our interpretation of an ambiguous constitutional provision. But "'[p]ast practice does not, by itself, create power.'" *Medellín v. Texas,* 552 U.S. 491, 532 (2008) (quoting *Dames & Moore v. Regan,* 453 U.S. 654, 686 (1981)). That is a necessary corollary of the principle that the political branches cannot by agreement alter the constitutional structure. Plainly, then, a self-aggrandizing practice adopted by one branch well after the founding, often challenged, and never before blessed by this Court—in other words, the sort of practice on which the majority relies in this case—does not relieve us of our duty to interpret the Constitution in light of its text, structure, and original understanding.

* * *

II. Intra-Session Breaks
* * *

A. Plain Meaning

A sensible interpretation of the Recess Appointments Clause should start by recognizing that the Clause uses the term "Recess" in contradistinction to the term "Session." As Alexander Hamilton wrote: "The time within which the power is to operate 'during the recess of the Senate' and the duration of the appointments 'to the end of the next session' of that body, conspire to elucidate the sense of the provision." The Federalist No. 67, p. 455 (J. Cooke ed.1961).

In the founding era, the terms "recess" and "session" had well-understood meanings in the marking-out of legislative time. The life of each elected Congress typically consisted (as it still does) of two or more formal sessions separated by adjournments *sine die,* that is, without a specified return date. The period *between* two sessions was known as "the recess." See 26 Annals of Cong. 748 (1814) (Sen. Gore) ("The time of the Senate consists of two periods, viz: their session and their recess"). * * * By contrast, other provisions of the Constitution use the verb "adjourn" rather than "recess" to refer to the commencement of breaks *during* a formal legislative session. See, *e.g.,* Art. I, § 5, cl. 1; *id.,* § 5, cl. 4.

* * *

More importantly, neither the Solicitor General nor the majority argues that the Clause uses "session" in its loose, colloquial sense. And if "the next Session" denotes a *formal* session, then "the Recess" must mean the break *between* formal sessions. * * * It is linguistically implausible to suppose—as the majority does—that the Clause uses one of those terms ("Recess") informally and the other ("Session") formally in a single sentence, with the result that an event can occur during *both* the "Recess" *and* the "Session."

Besides being linguistically unsound, the majority's reading yields the strange result that an appointment made during a short break near the beginning of one official session will not terminate until the end of the *following* official session, enabling the appointment to last for up to two years. * * * The Clause's self-evident design is to have the President's unilateral appointment last only until the Senate has "had an *opportunity* to act on the subject." 3 J. Story, Commentaries on the Constitution of the United States § 1551, p. 410 (1833) (emphasis added).

* * *

The boundlessness of the colloquial reading of "the Recess" thus refutes the majority's assertion that the Clause's "purpose" of "ensur[ing] the continued functioning of the Federal Government" demands that it apply to intra-session breaks as well as inter-session recesses. The majority disregards another self-evident purpose of the Clause: to preserve the Senate's role in the appointment process—which the founding generation regarded as a critical protection against " 'despotism,' " [*Freytag v. Commissioner,* 501 U.S. 868, 883 (1992)]—by clearly delineating the times when the President can appoint officers without the Senate's consent. Today's decision seriously undercuts *that* purpose. In doing so, it demonstrates the folly of interpreting constitutional provisions designed to establish "a structure of government that would protect liberty," *Bowsher,* 478 U.S., at 722, on the narrow-minded assumption that their only purpose is to make the government run as efficiently as possible. "Convenience and efficiency," we have repeatedly recognized, "are not the primary objectives" of our constitutional framework. *Free Enterprise Fund,* 561 U.S., at 499 (internal quotation marks omitted).

Relatedly, the majority contends that the Clause's supposed purpose of keeping the wheels of government turning demands that we interpret the Clause to maintain its relevance in light of the "new circumstance" of the Senate's taking an increasing number of intra-session breaks that exceed three days. Even if I accepted the canard that courts can alter the Constitution's meaning to accommodate changed circumstances, I would be hard pressed to see the relevance of that notion here. The rise of intra-session adjournments has occurred in tandem with the development of modern forms of communication and transportation that mean the Senate "is always available" to consider nominations, even when its Members are temporarily dispersed for an intra-session break. Tr. of Oral Arg. 21 (GINSBURG, J.). The Recess Appointments Clause therefore is, or rather, should be, an anachronism—"essentially an historic relic, something whose original purpose has disappeared." *Id.,* at 19 (KAGAN, J.). The need it was designed to fill no longer exists, and its only remaining use is the ignoble one of enabling the President to circumvent the Senate's role in the appointment process. That does not justify "read[ing] it out of the Constitution" and, contra the majority, I would not do so; but neither would I distort the Clause's original meaning, as the majority does, to ensure a prominent role for the recess-appointment power in an era when its influence is far more pernicious than beneficial.

To avoid the absurd results that follow from its colloquial reading of "the Recess," the majority is forced to declare that some intra-session breaks—though undisputedly within the phrase's colloquial meaning—are simply "too short to trigger the Recess Appointments Clause." But it identifies no textual basis whatsoever for limiting the length of "the Recess," nor does it point to any clear standard for determining how short is too short. * * *

Fumbling for some textually grounded standard, the majority seizes on the Adjournments Clause, which bars either House from adjourning for more than three days without the other's consent. *Id.,* § 5, cl. 4. According to the majority, that clause establishes that a 3-day break is *always* "too short" to trigger the Recess Appointments Clause. It goes without saying that nothing in the constitutional text supports that disposition. If (as the majority concludes) "the Recess" means a recess in the colloquial sense, then it necessarily includes breaks shorter than three days. And the fact that the Constitution includes a 3-day limit in one clause but omits it from the other weighs strongly against finding such a limit to be implicit in the clause in which it does not appear. * * *

And what about breaks longer than three days? The majority says that a break of four to nine days is "presumptively too short" but that the presumption may be rebutted in an "unusual circumstance," such as a "national catastrophe . . . that renders the Senate unavailable but calls for an urgent response." The majority must hope that the *in terrorem* effect of its "presumptively too short" pronouncement will deter future Presidents from making any recess appointments during 4-to-9-day breaks and thus save us from the absurd spectacle of unelected judges evaluating (after an evidentiary hearing?) whether an alleged "catastrophe" was sufficiently "urgent" to trigger the recess-appointment power. The majority also says that "political opposition in the Senate would not qualify as an unusual circumstance." So if the Senate should refuse to confirm a nominee whom the President considers highly qualified; or even if it should refuse to confirm any nominee for an office, thinking the office better left vacant for the time being; the President's power would not be triggered during a 4-to-9-day break, no matter how "urgent" the President's perceived need for the officer's assistance. (The majority protests that this "should go without saying—except that Justice SCALIA compels us to say it," seemingly forgetting that the appointments at issue in this very case were justified on those grounds and that the Solicitor General has asked us to view the recess-appointment power as a "safety valve" against Senatorial "intransigence.")

As for breaks of 10 or more days: We are presumably to infer that such breaks do not trigger any "presumpt[ion]" against recess appointments, but does that mean the President has an utterly free hand? Or can litigants seek invalidation of an appointment made during a 10-day break by pointing to an absence of "unusual" or "urgent" circumstances necessitating an immediate appointment, albeit without the aid of a "presumpt[ion]" in their favor? Or, to put the question as it will present itself to lawyers in the Executive Branch:

Can the President make an appointment during a 10-day break simply to overcome "political opposition in the Senate" despite the absence of any "national catastrophe," even though it "go[es] without saying" that he cannot do so during a 9-day break? Who knows? The majority does not say, and neither does the Constitution.

Even if the many questions raised by the majority's failure to articulate a standard could be answered, a larger question would remain: If the Constitution's text empowers the President to make appointments during any break in the Senate's proceedings, by what right does the majority subject the President's exercise of that power to vague, court-crafted limitations with no textual basis? The majority claims its temporal guideposts are informed by executive practice, but a President's self-restraint cannot "bind his successors by diminishing their powers." *Free Enterprise Fund,* 561 U.S., at 497; cf. *Clinton v. Jones,* 520 U.S. 681, 718 (1997) (BREYER, J., concurring in judgment) ("voluntary actions" by past Presidents "tel[l] us little about what the Constitution commands").

An interpretation that calls for this kind of judicial adventurism cannot be correct. * * *

B. Historical Practice

For the foregoing reasons, the Constitution's text and structure unambiguously refute the majority's freewheeling interpretation of "the Recess." It is not plausible that the Constitution uses that term in a sense that authorizes the President to make unilateral appointments during *any* break in Senate proceedings, subject only to hazy, atextual limits crafted by this Court centuries after ratification. The majority, however, insists that history "offers strong support" for its interpretation. The historical practice of the political branches is, of course, irrelevant when the Constitution is clear. But even if the Constitution were thought ambiguous on this point, history does not support the majority's interpretation.

[Justice Scalia then proceeded to offer his own extensive survey of the history of the Recess Appointments Clause and objections to presidential exercises thereof. Ed.]

* * *

What does all this amount to? In short: Intra-session recess appointments were virtually unheard of for the first 130 years of the Republic, were deemed unconstitutional by the first Attorney General to address them, were not openly defended by the Executive until 1921, were not made in significant numbers until after World War II, and have been repeatedly criticized as unconstitutional by Senators of both parties. It is astonishing for the majority to assert that this history lends "strong support," to its interpretation of the Recess Appointments Clause. And the majority's contention that recent executive practice in this area merits deference because the Senate has not done more to oppose it is utterly divorced from our precedent. * * *

Moreover, the majority's insistence that the Senate gainsay an executive practice "as a body" in order to prevent the Executive from acquiring power by adverse possession will systematically favor the expansion of executive power at the expense of Congress. In any controversy between the political branches over a separation-of-powers question, staking out a position and defending it over time is far easier for the Executive Branch than for the Legislative Branch. All Presidents have a high interest in expanding the powers of their office, since the more power the President can wield, the more effectively he can implement his political agenda; whereas individual Senators may have little interest in opposing Presidential encroachment on legislative prerogatives, especially when the encroacher is a President who is the leader of their own party. (The majority would not be able to point to a lack of "formal action" by the Senate "as a body" challenging intra-session recess appointments had the appointing President's party in the Senate not blocked such action on multiple occasions.) And when the President wants to assert a power and establish a precedent, he faces neither the collective-action problems nor the procedural inertia inherent in the legislative process. The majority's methodology thus all but guarantees the continuing aggrandizement of the Executive Branch.

III. Pre-Recess Vacancies

* * *

A. Plain Meaning

As the majority concedes, "the most natural meaning of 'happens' as applied to a 'vacancy' . . . is that the vacancy 'happens' when it initially occurs." The majority adds that this meaning is most natural "to a modern ear," but it fails to show that founding-era ears heard it differently. "Happen" meant then, as it does now, "[t]o fall out; to chance; to come to pass." 1 Johnson, Dictionary of the English Language 913. Thus, a vacancy that *happened* during the Recess was most reasonably understood as one that *arose* during the recess. It was, of course, possible in certain contexts for the word "happen" to mean "happen to be" rather than "happen to occur," as in the idiom "it so happens." But that meaning is not at all natural when the subject is a vacancy, a state of affairs that comes into existence at a particular moment in time.

In any event, no reasonable reader would have understood the Recess Appointments Clause to use the word "happen" in the majority's "happen to be" sense, and thus to empower the President to fill all vacancies that might *exist* during a recess, regardless of when they arose. For one thing, the Clause's language would have been a surpassingly odd way of giving the President that power. The Clause easily could have been written to convey that meaning clearly: It could have referred to "all Vacancies that may exist during the Recess," or it could have omitted the qualifying phrase entirely and simply authorized the President to "fill up all Vacancies during the Recess." Given those readily available alternative phrasings, the reasonable reader might have wondered, why would any intelligent drafter intending the majority's reading have inserted the words "that may happen"—words that, as the majority admits, make the majority's desired reading awkward and unnatural, and that must be effectively read out of the Clause to achieve that reading?

For another thing, the majority's reading not only strains the Clause's language but distorts its constitutional role, which was meant to be subordinate. As Hamilton explained, appointment with the advice and consent of the Senate was to be "the general mode of appointing officers of the United States." The Federalist No. 67, at 455. The Senate's check on the President's appointment power was seen as vital because " 'manipulation of official appointments' had long been one of the American revolutionary generation's greatest grievances against executive power." *Freytag,* 501 U.S., at 883. The unilateral power conferred on the President by the Recess Appointments Clause was therefore understood to be "nothing more than a supplement" to the "general method" of advice and consent. The Federalist No. 67, at 455.

If, however, the Clause had allowed the President to fill *all* pre-existing vacancies during the recess by granting commissions that would last throughout the following session, it would have been impossible to regard it—as the Framers plainly did—as a mere codicil to the Constitution's principal, power-sharing scheme for filling federal offices. On the majority's reading, the President would have had no need *ever* to seek the Senate's advice and consent for his appointments: Whenever there was a fair prospect of the Senate's rejecting his preferred nominee, the President could have appointed that individual unilaterally during the recess, allowed the appointment to expire at the end of the next session, renewed the appointment the following day, and so on *ad infinitum.* (Circumvention would have been especially easy if, as the majority also concludes, the President was authorized to make such appointments during any intra-session break of more than a few days.) It is unthinkable that such an obvious means for the Executive to expand its power would have been overlooked during the ratification debates.

* * *

The majority, however, relies heavily on a contrary account of the Clause given by Attorney General William Wirt in 1823. See 1 Op. Atty. Gen 631. Wirt notably began—as does the majority—by acknowledging that his predecessors' reading was "most accordant with the letter of the constitution." *Id.,* at 632. But he thought the "most natural" reading had to be rejected because it would interfere with the "substantial purpose of the constitution," namely, "keep[ing] . . . offices filled." *Id.,* at 631–632. He was chiefly concerned that giving the Clause its plain meaning would produce "embarrassing inconveniences" if a distant office were to become vacant during the Senate's session, but news of the vacancy were not to reach the President until the recess. *Id.,* at 632, 634. The majority fully embraces Wirt's reasoning.

Wirt's argument is doubly flawed. To begin, the Constitution provides ample means, short of rewriting its text, for dealing with the hypothetical dilemma Wirt posed. Congress can authorize "acting" officers to perform the duties associated with a temporarily vacant office—and has done that, in one form or another, since 1792. See 5 U.S.C. § 3345; Act of May 8, 1792, ch. 37, § 8, 1 Stat. 281. And on "extraordinary Occasions" the President can call the Senate back into session to consider a nomination. Art. II, § 3. If the Framers had thought those options insufficient and preferred to authorize the President to make recess appointments to fill vacancies arising late in the session, they would have known how to do so. Massachusetts, for example, had authorized its Governor to make certain recess appointments "in case a vacancy shall happen . . . in the recess of the

General Court [*i.e.,* the state legislature], *or at so late a period in any session of the same Court, that the vacancy . . . shall not be supplied in the same session thereof.*" 1783 Mass. Acts ch. 12, in Acts and Laws of the Commonwealth of Massachusetts 523 (1890) (emphasis added).

The majority protests that acting appointments, unlike recess appointments, are an "inadequate" solution to Wirt's hypothetical dilemma because acting officers "may have less authority than Presidential appointments." * * * But just a few lines later, the majority says that "the lack of Senate approval . . . may diminish the recess appointee's ability, as a practical matter, to get a controversial job done." The majority does not explain why an acting officer would have less authority "as a practical matter" than a recess appointee. The majority also objects that requiring the President to rely on acting officers would "lessen the President's ability to staff the Executive Branch with people of his own choosing,"—a surprising charge, since that is the very purpose of the Constitution's advice-and-consent requirement. As for special sessions, the majority thinks it a sufficient answer to say that they are "burdensome," an observation that fails to distinguish them from many procedures required by our structural Constitution.

More fundamentally, Wirt and the majority are mistaken to say that the Constitution's "'substantial purpose' " is to " 'keep . . . offices filled.' " The Constitution is not a road map for maximally efficient government, but a system of "carefully crafted restraints" designed to "protect the people from the improvident exercise of power." *Chadha,* 462 U.S., at 957, 959. Wirt's and the majority's *argumentum ab inconvenienti* thus proves far too much. There are many circumstances other than a vacancy that can produce similar inconveniences if they arise late in the session: For example, a natural disaster might occur to which the Executive cannot respond effectively without a supplemental appropriation. But in those circumstances, the Constitution would not permit the President to appropriate funds himself. See Art. I, § 9, cl. 7. Congress must either anticipate such eventualities or be prepared to be haled back into session. The troublesome need to do so is not a bug to be fixed by this Court, but a calculated feature of the constitutional framework. As we have recognized, while the Constitution's government-structuring provisions can seem "clumsy" and "inefficient," they reflect "hard choices . . . consciously made by men who had lived under a form of government that permitted arbitrary governmental acts to go unchecked." *Chadha, supra,* at 959.

B. Historical Practice

For the reasons just given, it is clear that the Constitution authorizes the President to fill unilaterally only those vacancies that arise during a recess, not every vacancy that happens to exist during a recess. Again, however, the majority says "[h]istorical practice" requires the broader interpretation. And again the majority is mistaken. Even if the Constitution were wrongly thought to be ambiguous on this point, a fair recounting of the relevant history does not support the majority's interpretation.

[Justice Scalia then proceeded to offer further history of the Recess Appointments Clause and interpretations thereof. Ed.]

* * *

In sum: Washington's and Adams' Attorneys General read the Constitution to restrict recess appointments to vacancies arising during the recess, and there is no evidence that any of the first four Presidents consciously departed from that reading. The contrary reading was first defended by an executive official in 1823, was vehemently rejected by the Senate in 1863, was vigorously resisted by legislation in place from 1863 until 1940, and is arguably inconsistent with legislation in place from 1940 to the present. The Solicitor General has identified only about 100 appointments that have ever been made under the broader reading, and while it seems likely that a good deal more have been made in the last few decades, there is good reason to doubt that many were made before 1940 (since the appointees could not have been compensated). I can conceive of no sane constitutional theory under which this evidence of "historical practice"—which is actually evidence of a long-simmering inter-branch conflict—would require us to defer to the views of the Executive Branch.

IV. Conclusion

What the majority needs to sustain its judgment is an ambiguous text and a clear historical practice. What it has is a clear text and an at-best-ambiguous historical practice. Even if the Executive could accumulate power through adverse possession by engaging in a *consistent* and *unchallenged* practice over a long period of time, the oft-disputed practices at issue here would not meet that standard. Nor have those practices created any justifiable expectations that could be disappointed by enforcing the Constitution's original meaning. There is thus no ground for the majority's deference to the unconstitutional recess-appointment practices of the Executive Branch.

The majority replaces the Constitution's text with a new set of judge-made rules to govern recess appointments. Henceforth, the Senate can avoid triggering the President's now-vast recess-appointment power by the odd contrivance of never adjourning for more than three days without holding a *pro forma* session at which it is understood that no business will be conducted. How this new regime will work in practice remains to be seen. Perhaps it will reduce the prevalence of recess appointments. But perhaps not: Members of the President's party in Congress may be able to prevent the Senate from holding *pro forma* sessions with the necessary frequency, and if the House and Senate disagree, the President may be able to adjourn both "to such Time as he shall think proper." U.S. Const., Art. II, § 3. In any event, the limitation upon the President's appointment power is there not for the benefit of the Senate, but for the protection of the people; it should not be dependent on Senate action for its existence.

The real tragedy of today's decision is not simply the abolition of the Constitution's limits on the recess-appointment power and the substitution of a novel framework invented by this Court. It is the damage done to our separation-of-powers jurisprudence more generally. It is not every day that we encounter a proper case or controversy requiring interpretation of the Constitution's structural provisions. Most of the time, the interpretation of those provisions is left to the political branches—which, in deciding how much respect to afford the constitutional text, often take their cues from this Court. We should therefore take every opportunity to affirm the primacy of the Constitution's enduring principles over the politics of the moment. Our failure to do so today will resonate well beyond the particular dispute at hand. Sad, but true: The Court's embrace of the adverse-possession theory of executive power (a characterization the majority resists but does not refute) will be cited in diverse contexts, including those presently unimagined, and will have the effect of aggrandizing the Presidency beyond its constitutional bounds and undermining respect for the separation of powers.

NOTES AND QUESTIONS

1. In *Noel Canning*, the Supreme Court relied heavily on past presidential practice as a reason to uphold a broad recess appointment power, claiming that a narrower interpretation "would render illegitimate thousands of recess appointments reaching all the way back to the founding era." Yet, as Justice Scalia noted in his concurrence, the Supreme Court only infrequently has the opportunity to address the constitutionality under separation-of-powers principles of practices engaged in by Congress and the President. In other words, by the time that cases such as *Noel Canning* find their way to the Supreme Court, the practices that they question almost invariably have been around for some time. Indeed, notwithstanding numerous past recess appointments, *Noel Canning* represented the first time the Supreme Court had the opportunity to address the meaning of the Recess Appointments Clause. Under such circumstances, how much weight should the Supreme Court give to past practice in evaluating the constitutionality thereof? Should the Court be wary of declaring a longstanding government practice unconstitutional?

2. Writing for the majority in *Noel Canning*, Justice Breyer placed great emphasis on the Senate's availability (or lack thereof) to act on presidential appointments in the event of a vacancy, describing an out-of-session Senate as "not simply unlikely or unwilling to act" on presidential nominations but "*unable* to do so." Yet, all of the Justices in *Noel Canning* recognize that the circumstances of Senate availability to act on presidential nominations have changed substantially since the Constitution was ratified. Instead of letters and horses or telegraphs and trains, we now have Skype and airplanes. Rather than meeting for a single, unbroken session followed by a lengthy recess each year, the Senate meets more or less continually, with many short intra-session breaks and, sometimes, virtually nonexistent inter-session ones. Meanwhile, for a variety of reasons, the appointment process often extends for weeks or months, not because the Senate is out of session but because the Senate confirmation process entails many steps and, often, some controversy. Given the contemporary reality, is the Senate ever really unavailable to act on presidential nominations, or is the Senate's availability or unavailability a matter of form over substance?

DISCUSSION PROBLEM

In *Noel Canning*, the Supreme Court said that a Senate adjournment of three days or less will always be too short to support a recess appointment, and a Senate adjournment of four to nine days duration is presumptively too short to support a recess appointment, but a Senate adjournment of ten days or longer generally will support a recess appointment. The Adjournments Clause of U.S. Constitution Article I, § 5 says that neither the Senate nor the House of Representatives "shall, without the Consent of the other, adjourn for more than three days." The Prorogation Clause of U.S. Constitution Article II, § 3 provides that "in Case of Disagreement between" the Senate and the House "with Respect to the Time of Adjournment, [the President] may adjourn them to such Time as he shall think proper." Imagine that a majority of Senators belong to the Democratic Party, but the President and a majority of the House of Representatives belong to the Republican Party (or vice versa). Imagine, too, that the Senate objects to a particular presidential nominee and wants to hold pro forma sessions every three days—*i.e.*, not adjourn—to preclude the President from making a recess appointment. Can the House, in coordination with the President, claim a desire to adjourn for a longer period, and thereby allow the President to forcibly adjourn the House and the Senate for more than ten days, thereby giving the President the opportunity to make the recess appointment that the Senate prefers to forestall?

B. THE POWER TO REMOVE

Unlike the power to appoint officers, the Constitution does not mention the power to remove officers at all. Nevertheless, Presidents from George Washington to George W. Bush have asserted the power to remove subordinate executive officials from office. *See* STEVEN G. CALABRESI & CHRISOPHER S. YOO, THE UNITARY EXECUTIVE (2008) (documenting removal power claims of each President). As a result, the Court has been required to draw inferences with respect to the removal power based on other characteristics of the Constitution. It has done so in four famous opinions, each of which appears below in edited form. Before you begin to read the opinions, however, we should caution that, although each still has considerable significance today, the first three no longer mean what they were widely believed to mean when they were issued. Thus, one task that anyone assessing the removal power must undertake is to determine what each opinion means today in light of the subsequent opinions the Court has issued.

Myers v. United States

272 U.S. 52 (1926).

■ MR. CHIEF JUSTICE TAFT delivered the opinion of the Court.

This case presents the question whether under the Constitution the President has the exclusive power of removing executive officers of the United States whom he has appointed by and with the advice and consent of the Senate.

Myers, appellant's intestate, was on July 21, 1917, appointed by the President, by and with the advice and consent of the Senate, to be a postmaster of the first class at Portland, Oregon, for a term of four years. On January 20, 1920, Myers' resignation was demanded. He refused the demand. On February 2, 1920, he was removed from office by order of the Postmaster General, acting by direction of the President. February 10th, Myers sent a petition to the President and another to the Senate Committee on Post Offices, asking to be heard, if any charges were filed. He protested to the Department against his removal, and continued to do so until the end of his term. He pursued no other occupation and drew compensation for no other service during the interval. On April 21, 1921, he brought this suit in the Court of Claims for his salary from the date of his removal, which, as claimed by supplemental petition filed after July 21, 1921, the end of his term, amounted to $8,838.71. In August, 1920, the President made a recess appointment of one Jones, who took office September 19, 1920.

* * *

By the 6th section of the Act of Congress of July 12, 1876, 19 Stat. 80, 81, c. 179 (Comp. Stat. § 7190), under which Myers was appointed with the advice and consent of the Senate as a first-class postmaster, it is provided that:

> 'Postmasters of the first, second and third classes shall be appointed and may be removed by the President by and with the advice and consent of the Senate, and shall hold their offices for four years unless sooner removed or suspended according to law.'

The Senate did not consent to the President's removal of Myers during his term. If this statute, in its requirement that his term should be four years unless sooner removed by the President by and with the consent of the Senate, is valid, the appellant, Myers' administratrix, is entitled to recover his unpaid salary for his full term and the judgment of the Court of Claims must be reversed. The Government maintains that the requirement is invalid, for the reason that under Article II of the Constitution the President's power of removal of executive officers appointed by him with the advice and consent of the Senate is full and complete without consent of the Senate. If this view is sound, the removal of Myers by the President without the Senate's consent was legal, and the judgment of the Court of Claims against the appellant was correct, and must be affirmed, though for a different reason from the given by that court. We are therefore confronted by the constitutional question and cannot avoid it.

* * *

The question where the power of removal of executive officers appointed by the President by and with the advice and consent of the Senate was vested, was presented early in the first session of the First Congress. There is no express provision respecting removals in the Constitution, except as Section 4 of Article II provides for removal from office by impeachment. The subject was not discussed in the Constitutional Convention. Under the Articles of Confederation, Congress was given the power of appointing certain executive officers of the Confederation, and during the Revolution and while the articles were given effect, Congress exercised the power of removal.

* * *

The vesting of the executive power in the President was essentially a grant of the power to execute the laws. But the President alone and unaided could not execute the laws. He must execute them by the assistance of subordinates. This view has since been repeatedly affirmed by this Court. As he is charged specifically to take care that they be faithfully executed, the reasonable implication, even in the absence of express words, was that as part of his executive power he should select those who were to act for him under his direction in the execution of the laws. The further implication must be, in the absence of any express limitation respecting removals, that as his selection of administrative officers is essential to the execution of the laws by him, so must be his power of removing those for whom he cannot continue to be responsible. It was urged that the natural meaning of the term "executive power" granted the President included the appointment and removal of executive subordinates. If such appointments and removals were not an exercise of the executive power, what were they? They certainly were not the exercise of legislative or judicial power in government as usually understood.

* * *

[T]he power of removal, though equally essential to the executive power, is different in its nature from that of appointment. A veto by the Senate—a part of the legislative branch of the Government—upon removals is a much greater limitation upon the executive branch, and a much more serious blending of the legislative with the executive, than a rejection of a proposed appointment. It is not to be implied. The rejection of a nominee of the President for a particular office does not greatly embarrass him in the conscientious discharge of his high duties in the selection of those who are to aid him, because the President usually has an ample field from which to select for office, according to his preference, competent and capable men. The Senate has full power to reject newly proposed appointees whenever the President shall remove the incumbents. Such a check enables the Senate to prevent the filling of offices with bad or incompetent men, or with those against whom there is tenable objection.

The power to prevent the removal of an officer who has served under the President is different from the authority to consent to or reject his appointment. When a nomination is made, it may be presumed that the Senate is, or may become, as well advised as to the fitness of the nominee as the President, but in the nature of things the defects in ability or intelligence or loyalty in the administration of the laws of one who has served as an officer under the President are facts as to which the President, or his trusted subordinates, must be better informed than the Senate, and the power to remove him may, therefore, be regarded as confined for very sound and practical reasons, to the governmental authority which has administrative control. The power of removal is incident to the power of appointment, not to the power of advising and consenting to appointment, and when the grant of the executive power is enforced by the express mandate to take care that the laws be faithfully executed, it emphasizes the necessity for including within the executive power as conferred the exclusive power of removal.

* * *

It is reasonable to suppose also that, had it been intended to give to Congress power to regulate or control removals in the manner suggested, it would have been included among the specifically enumerated legislative powers in Article I, or in the specified limitations on the executive power in Article II. The difference between the grant of legislative power under Article I to Congress which is limited to powers therein enumerated, and the more general grant of the executive power to the President under Article II is significant. The fact that the executive power is given in general terms strengthened by specific terms where emphasis is appropriate, and limited by direct expressions where limitation is needed, and that no express limit is placed on the power of removal by the executive, is a convincing indication that none was intended.

* * *

Made responsible under the Constitution for the effective enforcement of the law, the President needs as an indispensable aid to meet it the disciplinary influence upon those who act under him of a reserve power of removal. But it is contended that executive officers appointed by the President with the consent of the Senate are bound by the statutory law and are not his servants to do his will, and that his obligation to care for the faithful execution of the laws does not authorize him to treat them as such. The degree of guidance in the discharge of their duties that the President may exercise over executive officers varies with the character of their service as prescribed in the law under which they act. The highest and most important duties which his subordinates perform are those in which they act for him. In such cases they are exercising not their own but his discretion. This field is a very large one. It is sometimes described as political. Each head of a department is and must be the President's *alter ego* in the matters of that department where the President is required by law to exercise authority.

* * *

In all such cases, the discretion to be exercised is that of the President in determining the national public interest and in directing the action to be taken by his executive subordinates to protect it. In this field his cabinet officers must do his will. He must place in each member of his official family, and his chief executive subordinates, implicit faith. The moment that he loses confidence in the intelligence, ability, judgment, or loyalty of any one of them, he must have the power to remove him without delay. To require him to file charges and submit them to the consideration of the Senate might make impossible that unity and co-ordination in executive administration essential to effective action.

The duties of the heads of departments and bureaus in which the discretion of the President is exercised and which we have described are the most important in the whole field of executive action of the Government. There is nothing in the Constitution which permits a distinction between the removal of the head of a department or a bureau, when he discharges a political duty of the President or exercises his discretion, and the removal of executive officers engaged in the discharge of their other normal duties. The imperative reasons requiring an unrestricted power to remove the most important of his subordinates in their most important duties must, therefore, control the interpretation of the Constitution as to all appointed by him.

But this is not to say that there are not strong reasons why the President should have a like power to remove his appointees charged with other duties than those above described. The ordinary duties of officers prescribed by statute come under the general administrative control of the President by virtue of the general grant to him of the executive power, and he may properly supervise and guide their construction of the statutes under which they act in order to secure that unitary and uniform execution of the laws which Article II of the Constitution evidently contemplated in vesting general executive power in the President alone. Laws are often passed with specific provision for adoption of regulations by a department or bureau head to make the law workable and effective. The ability and judgment manifested by the official thus empowered, as well as his energy and stimulation of his subordinates, are subjects which the President must consider and supervise in his administrative control. Finding such officers to be negligent and inefficient, the President should have the power to remove them. Of course there may be duties so peculiarly and specifically committed to the discretion of a particular officer as to raise a question whether the President may overrule or revise the officer's interpretation of his statutory duty in a particular instance. Then there may be duties of a quasi-judicial character imposed on executive officers and members of executive tribunals whose decisions after hearing affect interests of individuals, the discharge of which the President cannot in a particular case properly influence or control. But even in such a case he may consider the decision after its rendition as a reason for removing the officer, on the ground that the discretion regularly entrusted to that officer by statute has not been on the whole intelligently or wisely exercised. Otherwise he does not discharge his own constitutional duty of seeing that the laws be faithfully executed.

■ [We have omitted the dissenting opinions of JUSTICES MCREYNOLDS, BRANDEIS, and HOLMES. Ed.]

NOTES AND QUESTIONS

1.   The author of the majority opinion in *Myers*, Chief Justice William Howard Taft, served as President from 1909 to 1913, before assuming the position of Chief Justice in 1921. As President, Taft had exercised the removal power to remove Forestry Bureau Chief Gifford Pinchot from office after Pinchot disagreed publicly with Taft and his Interior Secretary, Richard Ballinger, over management of the national forest system. *See* CALABRESI & YOO, *supra*, at 248–49. What impact might Chief Justice Taft's experiences as President have had on his strong support for presidential removal power in *Myers*?

2.   The statute the Court held unconstitutional in *Myers* was called the Tenure in Office Act. It had a rich history. The sole count of the Bill of Particulars that was the basis for the successful impeachment of President Andrew Johnson in 1868 alleged his refusal to comply with the Tenure in Office Act. The vote in the Senate was only one short of the number required to remove a President from office. Thus, a President was impeached and nearly removed for refusing to comply with a statute the Court held to be unconstitutional fifty years later.

3. At the time the Court decided *Myers*, its opinion was widely interpreted to stand for the broad proposition that Congress cannot limit in any way the power of the President to remove any officer of the United States. As the next three opinions demonstrate, *Myers* can no longer carry that meaning. Yet, it clearly stands for one or more propositions that remain important today. For example, recall *INS v. Chadha*, 462 U.S. 919 (1983), and *Bowsher v. Synar*, 478 U.S. 714 (1986), discussed in Chapter 2. In *Chadha*, the Court rejected legislative vetoes of agency action by one or both Houses or a committee of Congress without presentment to the President as an unconstitutional violation of the executive power. In *Bowsher*, the Court held that Congress could not retain removal power over an executive officer. Comparing the reasoning of the Court in those cases with the precise requirement of the Tenure in Office Act, requiring Senate consent before the President could remove a Postmaster, for what proposition might you conclude that *Myers* remains good law?

Humphrey's Executor v. United States

295 U.S. 602 (1935).

■ MR. JUSTICE SUTHERLAND delivered the opinion of the Court.

Plaintiff brought suit in the Court of Claims against the United States to recover a sum of money alleged to be due the deceased for salary as a Federal Trade Commissioner from October 8, 1933, when the President undertook to remove him from office, to the time of his death on February 14, 1934. The court below has certified to this court two questions in respect of the power of the President to make the removal. The material facts which give rise to the questions are as follows:

William E. Humphrey, the decedent, on December 10, 1931, was nominated by President Hoover to succeed himself as a member of the Federal Trade Commission, and was confirmed by the United States Senate. He was duly commissioned for a term of seven years, expiring September 25, 1938; and, after taking the required oath of office, entered upon his duties. On July 25, 1933, President Roosevelt addressed a letter to the commissioner asking for his resignation, on the ground "that the aims and purposes of the Administration with respect to the work of the Commission can be carried out most effectively with personnel of my own selection," but disclaiming any reflection upon the commissioner personally or upon his services. The commissioner replied, asking time to consult his friends. After some further correspondence upon the subject, the President on August 31, 1933, wrote the commissioner expressing the hope that the resignation would be forthcoming, and saying: "You will, I know, realize that I do not feel that your mind and my mind go along together on either the policies or the administering of the Federal Trade Commission, and, frankly, I think it is best for the people of this country that I should have a full confidence."

The commissioner declined to resign; and on October 7, 1933, the President wrote him: "Effective as of this date you are hereby removed from the office of Commissioner of the Federal Trade Commission."

Humphrey never acquiesced in this action, but continued thereafter to insist that he was still a member of the commission, entitled to perform its duties and receive the compensation provided by law at the rate of $10,000 per annum.

* * *

The Federal Trade Commission Act creates a commission of five members to be appointed by the President by and with the advice and consent of the Senate, and § 1 provides:

"Not more than three of the commissioners shall be members of the same political party. The first commissioners appointed shall continue in office for terms of three, four, five, six, and seven years, respectively, from the date of the taking effect of this Act, the term of each to be designated by the President, but their successors shall be appointed for terms of seven years, except that any person chosen to fill a vacancy shall be appointed only for the unexpired term of the commissioner whom he shall succeed. The commission shall choose a chairman from its own membership. No commissioner shall engage in any other business, vocation, or employment. Any commissioner may be removed by the President for inefficiency, neglect of duty, or malfeasance in office. . . ."

* * *

The question first to be considered is whether, by the provisions of § 1 of the Federal Trade Commission Act already quoted, the President's power is limited to removal for the specific causes enumerated therein.

* * *

[T]he fixing of a definite term subject to removal for cause, unless there be some countervailing provision or circumstance indicating the contrary, which here we are unable to find, is enough to establish the legislative intent that the term is not to be curtailed in the absence of such cause. But if the intention of Congress that no removal should be made during the specified term except for one or more of the enumerated causes were not clear upon the face of the statute, as we think it is, it would be made clear by a consideration of the character of the commission and the legislative history which accompanied and preceded the passage of the act.

The commission is to be nonpartisan; and it must, from the very nature of its duties, act with entire impartiality. It is charged with the enforcement of no policy except the policy of the law. Its duties are neither political nor executive, but predominantly quasi-judicial and quasi-legislative. Like the Interstate Commerce Commission, its members are called upon to exercise the trained judgment of a body of experts "appointed by law and informed by experience." *Ill. Cent. R.R. Co. v. Interstate Commerce Comm'n*, 206 U.S. 441, 454 (1907); *Std. Oil Co. v. United States*, 283 U.S. 235, 238–39 (1931).

The legislative reports in both houses of Congress clearly reflect the view that a fixed term was necessary to the effective and fair administration of the law.

* * *

The debates in both houses demonstrate that the prevailing view was that the Commission was not to be "subject to anybody in the government but . . . only to the people of the United States"; free from "political domination or control" or the "probability or possibility of such a thing"; to be "separate and apart from any existing department of the government-not subject to the orders of the President."

* * *

We conclude that the intent of the act is to limit the executive power of removal to the causes enumerated, the existence of none of which is claimed here; and we pass to the second question.

Second. To support its contention that the removal provision of § 1, as we have just construed it, is an unconstitutional interference with the executive power of the President, the government's chief reliance is *Myers v. United States*, 272 U.S. 52 (1926). * * * In the course of the opinion of the court, expressions occur which tend to sustain the government's contention, but these are beyond the point involved and, therefore, do not come within the rule of stare decisis. In so far as they are out of harmony with the views here set forth, these expressions are disapproved.

* * *

The office of a postmaster is so essentially unlike the office now involved that the decision in the *Myers* case cannot be accepted as controlling our decision here. A postmaster is an executive officer restricted to the performance of executive functions. He is charged with no duty at all related to either the legislative or judicial power. The actual decision in the *Myers* case finds support in the theory that such an officer is merely one of the units in the executive department and, hence, inherently subject to the exclusive and illimitable power of removal by the Chief Executive, whose subordinate and aid he is. Putting aside dicta, which may be followed if sufficiently persuasive but which are not controlling, the necessary reach of the decision goes far enough to include all purely executive officers. It goes no farther;— much less does it include an officer who occupies no place in the executive department and who exercises no part of the executive power vested by the Constitution in the President.

The Federal Trade Commission is an administrative body created by Congress to carry into effect legislative policies embodied in the statute in accordance with the legislative standard therein prescribed, and to perform other specified duties as a legislative or as a judicial aid. Such a body cannot in any proper sense be characterized as an arm or an eye of the executive. Its duties are performed without executive leave and, in the contemplation of the statute, must be free from executive control. In administering the provisions of the statute in respect of "unfair methods of competition"—that is to say, in filling in and administering the details embodied by that general standard—the commission acts in part quasi-legislatively and in part quasi-judicially. In making investigations and reports thereon for the information of Congress under § 6, in aid of the legislative power, it acts as a legislative agency. Under § 7, which authorizes the commission to act as a master in chancery under rules prescribed by the court, it acts as an agency of the judiciary. To the extent that it exercises any executive function, as distinguished from executive power in the constitutional sense, it does so in the discharge and effectuation of its quasi-legislative or quasi-judicial powers, or as an agency of the legislative or judicial departments of the government.

NOTES AND QUESTIONS

1. The case of *Humphrey's Executor* was decided at a time of unprecedented disagreement between the Supreme Court and the politically-accountable branches of government. At the time, the Court was extremely suspicious of the "New Deal" agenda that President Franklin D. Roosevelt was attempting to implement in response to the Great Depression: imposing widespread economic regulation to counter widespread unemployment and drive economic recovery. Justices James Clark McReynolds, George Sutherland, Willis van Devanter, and Pierce Butler—nicknamed the "Four Horsemen"—were particularly noted for the opposition to New Deal economic policies and, along with either or both of Justices Charles Evans Hughes and Owen J. Roberts, repeatedly voided legislation promoted by the Roosevelt Administration to regulate economic activity. Although the case of *Humphrey's Executor* involved a presidential exercise of the removal power rather than legislation, the FTC's responsibility for investigating anti-competitive behavior was certainly relevant to the Roosevelt Administration's economic agenda. Recognizing nevertheless that the Court's decision in *Humphrey's Executor* was unanimous, what role if any do you suppose that the Four Horsemen's attitude toward President Roosevelt and the New Deal played in the decision-making process of the Justices?

2. The Court's decision in *Humphrey's Executor*, coupled with the other statutes that provide for a term of years and a limit on the President's removal power, are cited as the reason why some agencies are labeled as independent. Indeed, the Court in *Humphrey's Executor* emphasizes that the FTC and its Commissioners are "not to be 'subject to anybody in the government but . . . only to the people of the United States'. . . ." FTC Commissioners are appointed by the President with the advice and consent of the Senate, not elected. How independent of the President can an agency be when its members are nominated by the President and can be removed by the President, albeit only for cause? To the extent that agencies like FTC are independent of the President, how important is the limit on the President's removal power in explaining that independence? Yet, what does it mean for a government official to be subject to the people of the United States without being either elected or subject to removal by, and thus directly accountable to, the President or other elected official?

3. The Court seems to place considerable emphasis on the functions of the FTC, characterizing its duties as not political or executive but rather as solely quasi judicial and quasi legislative. What do you think the Court means when it refers to the FTC's duties by these terms?

In considering the characterization of the FTC's responsibilities as quasi legislative, it may be important to know that Congress did not have access to a large staff or to any other institution that could evaluate the need for legislation at the time *Humphrey's Executor* was decided. As a result, Congress routinely asked the FTC to evaluate the need for proposed legislation. Thus, for instance, the FTC issued multi-volume reports in which it analyzed the performance of the natural gas and electricity markets and recommended that Congress enact legislation that became the Federal Power Act and the Natural Gas Act. Is there a justification for insulating an agency that serves functions of that type from what otherwise would be the President's plenary power to control the agency?

Nevertheless, despite the FTC's role in helping Congress shape legislation, at the time the Court decided *Humphrey's Executor*, the common understanding was that the FTC did not have the power to issue rules. Recalling the materials from Chapter 2 concerning congressional delegations of rulemaking power to agencies, do you think the Court could characterize the FTC's duties as quasi legislative rather than "executive" if the FTC had the power to issue rules? Is it possible for an agency to issue rules that are apolitical?

4. Note that President Roosevelt did not specify any cause for removing Humphrey. What would the Court have done if Roosevelt had stated that he was removing Humphrey for neglect of duty or malfeasance? Would the Court require the President to provide a detailed description and/or proof of Humphrey's alleged neglect of duty? If FTC had the power to issue rules, and Humphrey refused to issue a rule that the President considered essential, would that qualify as neglect of duty or malfeasance?

Wiener v. United States

357 U.S. 349 (1958).

■ MR. JUSTICE FRANKFURTER delivered the opinion of the Court.

This is a suit for back pay, based on petitioner's alleged illegal removal as a member of the War Claims Commission. The facts are not in dispute. By the War Claims Act of 1948, Congress established that Commission with "jurisdiction to receive and adjudicate according to law," claims for compensating internees, prisoners of war, and religious organizations, who suffered personal injury or property damage at the hands of the enemy in connection with World War II. The Commission was to be composed of three persons, at least two of whom were to be members of the bar, to be appointed by the President, by and with the advice and consent of the Senate. The Commission was to wind up its affairs not later than three years after the expiration of the time for filing claims, originally limited to two years but extended by successive legislation first to March 1, 1951, and later to March 31, 1952. This limit on the Commission's life was the mode by which the tenure of the Commissioners was defined, and Congress made no provision for removal of a Commissioner.

Having been duly nominated by President Truman, the petitioner was confirmed on June 2, 1950, and took office on June 8, following. On his refusal to heed a request for his resignation, he was, on December 10, 1953, removed by President Eisenhower in the following terms: "I regard it as in the national interest to complete the administration of the War Claims Act of 1948, as amended, with personnel of my own selection." * * * [P]etitioner brought this proceeding in the Court of Claims for recovery of his salary as a War Claims Commissioner from December 10, 1953, the day of his removal by the President, to June 30, 1954, the last day of the Commission's existence.

* * *

Humphrey's case was a *cause célèbre*—and not least in the halls of Congress. And what is the essence of the decision in Humphrey's case? It drew a sharp line of cleavage between officials who were part of the Executive establishment and were thus removable by virtue of the President's constitutional powers, and those who are members of a body "to exercise its judgment without the leave or hindrance of any other official or any department of the government," *Humphrey's Executor v. United States*, 295 U.S. 602, 625–626 (1935), as to whom a power of removal exists only if Congress may fairly be said to have conferred it. This sharp differentiation derives from the difference in functions between those who are part of the Executive establishment and those whose tasks require absolute freedom from Executive interference. "For it is quite evident," again to quote *Humphrey's Executor*, "that one who holds his office only during the pleasure of another, cannot be depended upon to maintain an attitude of independence against the latter's will." *Id.* at 629.

Thus, the most reliable factor for drawing an inference regarding the President's power of removal in our case is the nature of the function that Congress vested in the War Claims Commission. What were the duties that Congress confided to this Commission? And can the inference fairly be drawn from the failure of Congress to provide for removal that these Commissioners were to remain in office at the will of the President? For such is the assertion of power on which petitioner's removal must rest. The ground of President Eisenhower's removal of petitioner was precisely the same as President Roosevelt's removal of Humphrey. Both Presidents desired to have Commissioners, one on the Federal Trade Commission, the other on the War Claims Commission, "of my own selection." They wanted these Commissioners to be their men. The terms of removal in the two cases are identic and express the assumption that the agencies of which the two Commissioners were members were subject in the discharge of their duties to the control of the Executive. An analysis of the Federal Trade Commission Act left this Court in no doubt that such was not the conception of Congress in creating the Federal Trade Commission. The terms of the War Claims Act of 1948 leave no doubt that such was not the conception of Congress regarding the War Claims Commission.

NOTES AND QUESTIONS

Given the President's role as Commander in Chief, the functional case for limiting the President's removal power in the context of the War Claims Commission is apparent. Nevertheless, the War Claims Act contained no statutory limit on the power of the President to remove members of the War Claims Commission. Instead, the Court relied on a combination of congressional silence and the agency's functions to support an inference that Congress intended to limit the President's removal power. Thus, *Wiener* seems to support a canon of construction that congressional silence combined with assignment of quasi-judicial functions to an agency should be interpreted as an indication of congressional intent to limit the President's removal power.

Yet, recall that in *Federal Election Commission v. NRA Political Victory Fund*, 6 F.3d 821, 826 (D.C. Cir. 1993), the D.C. Circuit said the following of the statute that created the FEC, which also serves quasi-judicial functions:

> Here the statute is silent as to the President's removal authority, and therefore appellants argue that he has none. However, statutory silence could imply that the President actually enjoys an unrestricted power of removal. The Commission suggests that the President can remove the commissioners only for good cause, which limitation is implied by the Commission's structure and mission as well as the commissioners' terms. We think the Commission is likely correct, but, in any event, we can safely assume that the President would at minimum have authority to discharge a commissioner for good cause—if for no other.

Putting these opinions together, can you discern a single, consistent rule regarding congressional silence, quasi-judicial functions, and the President's removal power? If not, how might you distinguish and reconcile these two cases?

Morrison v. Olson

487 U.S. 654 (1988).

■ CHIEF JUSTICE REHNQUIST delivered the opinion of the Court.

[An excerpt of the background section of this opinion is provided in the materials in this Chapter discussing the appointment power. Ed.]

We now turn to consider whether the Act is invalid under the constitutional principle of separation of powers. * * * The first [issue that must be addressed] is whether the provision of the Act restricting the Attorney General's power to remove the independent counsel to only those instances in which he can show "good cause," taken by itself, impermissibly interferes with the President's exercise of his constitutionally appointed functions.

* * *

Unlike both *Bowsher* and *Myers*, this case does not involve an attempt by Congress itself to gain a role in the removal of executive officials other than its established powers of impeachment and conviction. The Act instead puts the removal power squarely in the hands of the Executive Branch; an independent counsel may be removed from office, "only by the personal action of the Attorney General, and only for good cause." 28 U.S.C. § 596(a)(1). There is no requirement of congressional approval of the Attorney General's removal decision, though the decision is subject to judicial review. In our view, the removal provisions of the Act make this case more analogous to *Humphrey's Executor* and *Wiener*, than to *Myers* or *Bowsher*.

* * *

Appellees contend that *Humphrey's Executor* and *Wiener* are distinguishable from this case because they did not involve officials who performed a "core executive function." They argue that our decision in *Humphrey's Executor* rests on a distinction between "purely executive" officials and officials who exercise "quasi-legislative" and "quasi-judicial" powers. In their view, when a "purely executive" official is involved, the governing precedent is *Myers*, not *Humphrey's Executor*. And, under *Myers*, the President must have absolute discretion to discharge "purely" executive officials at will.

We undoubtedly did rely on the terms "quasi-legislative" and "quasi-judicial" to distinguish the officials involved in *Humphrey's Executor* and *Wiener* from those in *Myers*, but our present considered view is that the determination of whether the Constitution allows Congress to impose a "good cause"-type restriction on the President's power to remove an official cannot be made to turn on whether or not that official is classified as "purely executive." The analysis contained in our removal cases is designed not to define rigid categories of those officials who may or may not be removed at will by the President, but to ensure that Congress does not interfere with the President's exercise of the "executive power" and his constitutionally appointed duty to "take care that the laws be faithfully executed" under Article II. *Myers* was undoubtedly correct in its holding, and in its broader suggestion that there are some "purely executive" officials who must be removable by the President at will if he is to be able to accomplish his constitutional role. * * * At the other end of the spectrum from *Myers*, the characterization of the agencies in *Humphrey's Executor* and *Wiener* as "quasi-legislative" or "quasi-judicial" in large part reflected our judgment that it was not essential to the President's proper execution of his Article II powers that these agencies be headed up by individuals who were removable at will. We do not mean to suggest that an analysis of the functions served by the officials at issue is irrelevant. But the real question is whether the removal restrictions are of such a nature that they impede the President's ability to perform his constitutional duty, and the functions of the officials in question must be analyzed in that light.

Considering for the moment the "good cause" removal provision in isolation from the other parts of the Act at issue in this case, we cannot say that the imposition of a "good cause" standard for removal by itself unduly trammels on executive authority. There is no real dispute that the functions performed by the independent counsel are "executive" in the sense that they are law enforcement functions that typically have been undertaken by officials within the Executive Branch. As we noted above, however, the independent counsel is an inferior officer under the Appointments Clause, with limited jurisdiction and tenure and lacking policymaking or significant administrative authority. Although the counsel exercises no small amount of discretion and judgment in deciding how to carry out his or her duties under the Act, we simply do not see how the President's need to control the exercise of that discretion is so central to the functioning of the Executive Branch as to require as a matter of constitutional law that the counsel be terminable at will by the President.

Nor do we think that the "good cause" removal provision at issue here impermissibly burdens the President's power to control or supervise the independent counsel, as an executive official, in the execution of his or her duties under the Act. This is not a case in which the power to remove an executive official has been completely stripped from the President, thus providing no means for the President to ensure the "faithful execution" of the laws. Rather, because the independent counsel may be terminated for "good cause," the Executive, through the Attorney General, retains ample authority to assure that the counsel is competently performing his or her statutory responsibilities in a manner that comports with the provisions of the Act. Although we need not decide in this case exactly what is encompassed within the term "good cause" under the Act, the legislative history of the removal provision also makes clear that the Attorney General may remove an independent counsel for "misconduct." Here, as with the provision of the Act conferring the appointment authority of the independent counsel on the special court, the congressional determination to limit the removal power of the Attorney General was essential, in the view of Congress, to establish the necessary independence of the office. We do not think that this limitation as it presently stands sufficiently deprives the President of control over the independent counsel to interfere impermissibly with his constitutional obligation to ensure the faithful execution of the laws.

■ JUSTICE SCALIA, dissenting.

There is, of course, no provision in the Constitution stating who may remove executive officers, except the provisions for removal by impeachment. Before the present decision it was established, however, (1) that the President's power to remove principal officers who exercise purely executive powers could not be restricted, and (2) that his power to remove inferior officers who exercise purely executive powers, and whose appointment Congress had removed from the usual procedure of Presidential appointment with Senate consent, could be restricted, at least where the appointment had been made by an officer of the Executive Branch.

The Court could have resolved the removal power issue in this case by simply relying upon its erroneous conclusion that the independent counsel was an inferior officer, and then extending our holding that the removal of inferior officers appointed by the Executive can be restricted, to a new holding that even the removal of inferior officers appointed by the courts can be restricted. That would in my view be a considerable and unjustified extension, giving the Executive full discretion in *neither* the selection *nor* the removal of a purely executive officer. The course the Court has chosen, however, is even worse.

Since our 1935 decision in *Humphrey's Executor*, 295 U.S. 602 (1935)—which was considered by many at the time the product of an activist, anti-New Deal Court bent on reducing the power of President Franklin Roosevelt—it has been established that the line of permissible restriction upon removal of principal officers lies at the point at which the powers exercised by those officers are no longer purely executive. Thus, removal restrictions have been generally regarded as lawful for so-called "independent regulatory agencies," such as the Federal Trade Commission, the Interstate Commerce Commission, and the Consumer Product Safety Commission, which engage substantially in what has been called the "quasi-legislative activity" of rulemaking, and for members of Article I courts, such as the Court of Military Appeals who engage in the "quasi-judicial" function of adjudication. It has often been observed, correctly in my view, that the line between "purely executive" functions and "quasi-legislative" or "quasi-judicial" functions is not a clear one or even a rational one. But at least it permitted the identification of certain officers, and certain agencies, whose functions were entirely within the control of the President. Congress had to be aware of that restriction in its legislation. Today, however, *Humphrey's Executor* is swept into the dustbin of repudiated constitutional principles. "[O]ur present considered view," the Court says, "is that the determination of whether the Constitution allows Congress to impose a 'good cause'-type restriction on the President's power to remove an official cannot be made to turn on whether or not that official is classified as 'purely executive.' "What *Humphrey's Executor* (and presumably *Myers*) really means, we are now told, is not that there are any "rigid categories of those officials who may or may not be removed at will by the President," but simply that Congress cannot "interfere with the President's exercise of the 'executive power' and his constitutionally appointed duty to 'take care that the laws be faithfully executed.' "

* * * There are now no lines. If the removal of a prosecutor, the virtual embodiment of the power to "take care that the laws be faithfully executed," can be restricted, what officer's removal cannot? This is an open invitation for Congress to experiment. What about a special Assistant Secretary of State, with responsibility for one very narrow area of foreign policy, who would not only have to be confirmed by the Senate but could also be removed only pursuant to certain carefully designed restrictions? Could this possibly render the President "[un]able to accomplish his constitutional role"? Or a special Assistant Secretary of Defense for Procurement? The possibilities are endless, and the Court does not understand what the separation of powers, what "[a]mbition ... counteract[ing] ambition," THE FEDERALIST NO. 51 (James Madison), is all about, if it does not expect Congress to try them. As far as I can discern from the Court's opinion, it is now open season upon the President's removal power for all executive officers, with not even the superficially principled restriction of *Humphrey's Executor* as cover. The Court essentially says to the President: "Trust us. We will make sure that you are able to accomplish your constitutional role." I think the Constitution gives the President—and the people—more protection than that.

NOTES AND QUESTIONS

1. Justice Scalia complains that the majority has "swept into the dustbin" the unsatisfactory test with respect to the limits of the power of Congress to limit the President's removal power that the Court had announced particularly in *Humphrey's Executor*, and replaced that test with nothing. Is that a fair criticism of the majority opinion? Can you find in the majority opinion a new test for drawing that line? If not, can you use the majority opinion in *Morrison*, combined with some of the Court's modern opinions in related contexts, to draw inferences with respect to the line the Court might draw in future cases?

2. In evaluating Appointments Clause claims in *Morrison*, and also in other cases such as *Freytag v. Commissioner*, the Court has relied in part upon whether or not the government officials in question possess the power to make policy decisions. Could the power to make policy decisions form a potential basis for drawing a new line around the removal power? *See* Richard J. Pierce, Jr., Morrison v. Olson: *Separation of Powers and the Structure of Government*, 1988 SUP. CT. REV..

3.   In discussing the removal power, Justice Scalia references three hypothetical statutes to illustrate the absence of a clear standard in the majority opinion. He hypothesizes statutes in which Congress limits the President's power to remove an Assistant Secretary of State with a specific narrow area of responsibility, an Assistant Secretary of Defense for Procurement, and an Assistant Attorney General with a specific narrow area of responsibility. Do you believe the Court would uphold any of those hypothetical statutes? If not, what reasoning would you expect the Court to use to distinguish *Morrison*, *Weiner*, and *Humphrey's Executor*? Might the Court extract some quotes from its opinion in *Myers*? What passages in *Myers* might resonate with a majority of the Justices today?

Free Enterprise Fund v.
Public Company Accounting Oversight Board
561 U.S. 477 (2010).

■ CHIEF JUSTICE ROBERTS delivered the opinion of the Court.

Our Constitution divided the "powers of the new Federal Government into three defined categories, Legislative, Executive, and Judicial." *INS v. Chadha,* 462 U.S. 919, 951 (1983). Article II vests "[t]he executive Power . . . in a President of the United States of America," who must "take Care that the Laws be faithfully executed." Art. II, § 1, cl. 1; *id.,* § 3. In light of "[t]he impossibility that one man should be able to perform all the great business of the State," the Constitution provides for executive officers to "assist the supreme Magistrate in discharging the duties of his trust." 30 Writings of George Washington 334 (J. Fitzpatrick ed.1939).

Since 1789, the Constitution has been understood to empower the President to keep these officers accountable—by removing them from office, if necessary. See generally *Myers v. United States,* 272 U.S. 52 (1926). This Court has determined, however, that this authority is not without limit. In *Humphrey's Executor v. United States,* 295 U.S. 602 (1935), we held that Congress can, under certain circumstances, create independent agencies run by principal officers appointed by the President, whom the President may not remove at will but only for good cause. Likewise, in *United States v. Perkins,* 116 U.S. 483 (1886), and *Morrison v. Olson,* 487 U.S. 654 (1988), the Court sustained similar restrictions on the power of principal executive officers—themselves responsible to the President—to remove their own inferiors. The parties do not ask us to reexamine any of these precedents, and we do not do so.

We are asked, however, to consider a new situation not yet encountered by the Court. The question is whether these separate layers of protection may be combined. May the President be restricted in his ability to remove a principal officer, who is in turn restricted in his ability to remove an inferior officer, even though that inferior officer determines the policy and enforces the laws of the United States?

We hold that such multilevel protection from removal is contrary to Article II's vesting of the executive power in the President. The President cannot "take Care that the Laws be faithfully executed" if he cannot oversee the faithfulness of the officers who execute them. Here the President cannot remove an officer who enjoys more than one level of good-cause protection, even if the President determines that the officer is neglecting his duties or discharging them improperly. That judgment is instead committed to another officer, who may or may not agree with the President's determination, and whom the President cannot remove simply because that officer disagrees with him. This contravenes the President's "constitutional obligation to ensure the faithful execution of the laws." *Id.,* at 693.

I

A

After a series of celebrated accounting debacles, Congress enacted the Sarbanes-Oxley Act of 2002 (or Act), 116 Stat. 745. Among other measures, the Act introduced tighter regulation of the accounting industry under a new Public Company Accounting Oversight Board. The Board is composed of five members, appointed to staggered 5-year terms by the Securities and Exchange Commission. It was modeled on private self-regulatory organizations in the securities industry—such as the New York Stock Exchange—that investigate and discipline their own members subject to Commission oversight. Congress created the Board as a private "nonprofit corporation," and Board members and employees are not considered Government "officer[s] or employee[s]" for statutory purposes. 15 U.S.C. §§ 7211(a), (b). The Board can thus recruit its members and employees from the private sector by paying salaries far above the standard Government pay scale. See §§ 7211(f)(4), 7219.

Unlike the self-regulatory organizations, however, the Board is a Government-created, Government-appointed entity, with expansive powers to govern an entire industry. Every accounting firm—both foreign and domestic—that participates in auditing public companies under the securities laws must register with the Board, pay it an annual fee, and comply with its rules and oversight. §§ 7211(a), 7212(a), (f), 7213, 7216(a)(1). The Board is charged with enforcing the Sarbanes-Oxley Act, the securities laws, the Commission's rules, its own rules, and professional accounting standards. §§ 7215(b)(1), (c)(4). To this end, the Board may regulate every detail of an accounting firm's practice, including hiring and professional development, promotion, supervision of audit work, the acceptance of new business and the continuation of old, internal inspection procedures, professional ethics rules, and "such other requirements as the Board may prescribe." § 7213(a)(2)(B).

The Board promulgates auditing and ethics standards, performs routine inspections of all accounting firms, demands documents and testimony, and initiates formal investigations and disciplinary proceedings. §§ 7213–7215 (2006 ed. and Supp. II). The willful violation of any Board rule is treated as a willful violation of the Securities Exchange Act of 1934, 48 Stat. 881, 15 U.S.C. § 78a *et seq.*—a federal crime punishable by up to 20 years' imprisonment or $25 million in fines ($5 million for a natural person). §§ 78ff(a), 7202(b)(1) (2006 ed.). And the Board itself can issue severe sanctions in its disciplinary proceedings, up to and including the permanent revocation of a firm's registration, a permanent ban on a person's associating with any registered firm, and money penalties of $15 million ($750,000 for a natural person). § 7215(c)(4). Despite the provisions specifying that Board members are not Government officials for statutory purposes, the parties agree that the Board is "part of the Government" for constitutional purposes, *Lebron v. National Railroad Passenger Corporation,* 513 U.S. 374, 397 (1995), and that its members are " 'Officers of the United States' " who "exercis[e] significant authority pursuant to the laws of the United States," *Buckley v. Valeo,* 424 U.S. 1, 125–126 (1976) (*per curiam*) (quoting Art. II, § 2, cl. 2).

The Act places the Board under the SEC's oversight, particularly with respect to the issuance of rules or the imposition of sanctions (both of which are subject to Commission approval and alteration). §§ 7217(b)–(c). But the individual members of the Board—like the officers and directors of the self-regulatory organizations—are substantially insulated from the Commission's control. The Commission cannot remove Board members at will, but only "for good cause shown," "in accordance with" certain procedures. § 7211(e)(6).

* * *

The parties agree that the Commissioners [of the SEC] cannot themselves be removed by the President except under the *Humphrey's Executor* standard of "inefficiency, neglect of duty, or malfeasance in office," 295 U.S., at 620 (internal quotation marks omitted), and we decide the case with that understanding.

* * *

III

We hold that the dual for-cause limitations on the removal of Board members contravene the Constitution's separation of powers.

A

The Constitution provides that "[t]he executive Power shall be vested in a President of the United States of America." Art. II, § 1, cl. 1. As Madison stated on the floor of the First Congress, "if any power whatsoever is in its nature Executive, it is the power of appointing, overseeing, and controlling those who execute the laws." 1 Annals of Cong. 463 (1789).

The removal of executive officers was discussed extensively in Congress when the first executive departments were created. The view that "prevailed, as most consonant to the text of the Constitution" and "to the requisite responsibility and harmony in the Executive Department," was that the executive power included a power to oversee executive officers through removal; because that traditional executive power was not "expressly taken away, it remained with the President." Letter from James Madison to Thomas Jefferson (June 30, 1789), 16 Documentary History of the First Federal Congress 893 (2004). "This Decision of 1789 provides contemporaneous and weighty evidence of the Constitution's meaning since many of the Members of the First Congress had taken part in framing that instrument." *Bowsher v. Synar,* 478 U.S. 714, 723–724 (1986) (internal quotation marks omitted). And it soon became the "settled and well understood construction of the Constitution." *Ex parte Hennen,* 38 U.S. 230 (1839).

The landmark case of *Myers v. United States* reaffirmed the principle that Article II confers on the President "the general administrative control of those executing the laws." 272 U.S., at 164. It is *his* responsibility to take care that the laws be faithfully executed. The buck stops with the President, in Harry Truman's famous phrase. As we explained in *Myers,* the President therefore must have some "power of removing those for whom he can not continue to be responsible." *Id.,* at 117.

Nearly a decade later in *Humphrey's Executor,* this Court held that *Myers* did not prevent Congress from conferring good-cause tenure on the principal officers of certain independent agencies. That case concerned the members of the Federal Trade Commission, who held 7-year terms and could not be removed by the President except for " 'inefficiency, neglect of duty, or malfeasance in office.' " 295 U.S., at 620 (quoting 15 U.S.C. § 41). The Court distinguished *Myers* on the ground that *Myers* concerned "an officer [who] is merely one of the units in the executive department and, hence, inherently subject to the exclusive and illimitable power of removal by the Chief Executive, whose subordinate and aid he is." 295 U.S., at 627. By contrast, the Court characterized the FTC as "quasi-legislative and quasi-judicial" rather than "purely executive," and held that Congress could require it "to act . . . independently of executive control." *Id.,* at 627–629. Because "one who holds his office only during the pleasure of another, cannot be depended upon to maintain an attitude of independence against the latter's will," the Court held that Congress had power to "fix the period during which [the Commissioners] shall continue in office, and to forbid their removal except for cause in the meantime." *Id.,* at 629.

Humphrey's Executor did not address the removal of inferior officers, whose appointment Congress may vest in heads of departments. If Congress does so, it is ordinarily the department head, rather than the President, who enjoys the power of removal. See *Myers, supra,* at 119, 127; *Hennen, supra,* at 259–260. This Court has upheld for-cause limitations on that power as well.

* * *

B

As explained, we have previously upheld limited restrictions on the President's removal power. In those cases, however, only one level of protected tenure separated the President from an officer exercising executive power. It was the President—or a subordinate he could remove at will—who decided whether the officer's conduct merited removal under the good-cause standard.

The Act before us does something quite different. It not only protects Board members from removal except for good cause, but withdraws from the President any decision on whether that good cause exists. That decision is vested instead in other tenured officers—the Commissioners—none of whom is subject to the President's direct control. The result is a Board that is not accountable to the President, and a President who is not responsible for the Board.

The added layer of tenure protection makes a difference. Without a layer of insulation between the Commission and the Board, the Commission could remove a Board member at any time, and therefore would be fully responsible for what the Board does. The President could then hold the Commission to account for its supervision of the Board, to the same extent that he may hold the Commission to account for everything else it does.

A second level of tenure protection changes the nature of the President's review. Now the Commission cannot remove a Board member at will. The President therefore cannot hold the Commission fully accountable for the Board's conduct, to the same extent that he may hold the Commission accountable for everything else that it does. The Commissioners are not responsible for the Board's actions. They are only responsible for their own determination of whether the Act's rigorous good-cause standard is met. And even if the President disagrees with their determination, he is powerless to intervene—unless that determination is so unreasonable as to constitute "inefficiency, neglect of duty, or malfeasance in office." *Humphrey's Executor,* 295 U.S., at 620 (internal quotation marks omitted).

This novel structure does not merely add to the Board's independence, but transforms it. Neither the President, nor anyone directly responsible to him, nor even an officer whose conduct he may review only for good cause, has full control over the Board. The President is stripped of the power our precedents have preserved, and his ability to execute the laws—by holding his subordinates accountable for their conduct—is impaired.

That arrangement is contrary to Article II's vesting of the executive power in the President. Without the ability to oversee the Board, or to attribute the Board's failings to those whom he *can* oversee, the President is no longer the judge of the Board's conduct. He is not the one who decides whether Board members are abusing their offices or neglecting their duties. He can neither ensure that the laws are faithfully executed, nor be held responsible for a Board member's breach of faith. This violates the basic principle that the President "cannot delegate ultimate responsibility or the active obligation to supervise that goes with it," because Article II "makes a single President responsible for the actions of the Executive Branch." *Clinton v. Jones,* 520 U.S. 681, 712–713 (1997) (Breyer, J., concurring in judgment).[4]

Indeed, if allowed to stand, this dispersion of responsibility could be multiplied. If Congress can shelter the bureaucracy behind two layers of good-cause tenure, why not a third? At oral argument, the Government was unwilling to concede that even *five* layers between the President and the Board would be too many. The officers of such an agency—

---

[4] Contrary to the dissent's suggestion, the second layer of tenure protection does compromise the President's ability to remove a Board member the Commission wants to retain. Without a second layer of protection, the Commission has no excuse for retaining an officer who is not faithfully executing the law. With the second layer in place, the Commission can shield its decision from Presidential review by finding that good cause is absent—a finding that, given the Commission's own protected tenure, the President cannot easily overturn. The dissent describes this conflict merely as one of four possible "scenarios," but it is the central issue in this case: The second layer matters precisely when the President finds it necessary to have a subordinate officer removed, and a statute prevents him from doing so.

safely encased within a Matryoshka doll of tenure protections—would be immune from Presidential oversight, even as they exercised power in the people's name.

* * *

The diffusion of power carries with it a diffusion of accountability. The people do not vote for the "Officers of the United States." Art. II, § 2, cl. 2. They instead look to the President to guide the "assistants or deputies . . . subject to his superintendence." The Federalist No. 72, p. 487 (J. Cooke ed.1961) (A. Hamilton). Without a clear and effective chain of command, the public cannot "determine on whom the blame or the punishment of a pernicious measure, or series of pernicious measures ought really to fall." *Id.*, No. 70, at 476 (same). That is why the Framers sought to ensure that "those who are employed in the execution of the law will be in their proper situation, and the chain of dependence be preserved; the lowest officers, the middle grade, and the highest, will depend, as they ought, on the President, and the President on the community." 1 Annals of Cong., at 499 (J. Madison).

By granting the Board executive power without the Executive's oversight, this Act subverts the President's ability to ensure that the laws are faithfully executed—as well as the public's ability to pass judgment on his efforts. The Act's restrictions are incompatible with the Constitution's separation of powers.

C

Respondents and the dissent resist this conclusion, portraying the Board as "the kind of practical accommodation between the Legislature and the Executive that should be permitted in a 'workable government.'" *Metropolitan Washington Airports Authority v. Citizens for Abatement of Aircraft Noise, Inc.,* 501 U.S. 252, 276 (1991) (*MWAA*) (quoting *Youngstown Sheet & Tube Co. v. Sawyer,* 343 U.S. 579, 635 (1952) (Jackson, J., concurring)). According to the dissent, Congress may impose multiple levels of for-cause tenure between the President and his subordinates when it "rests agency independence upon the need for technical expertise." The Board's mission is said to demand both "technical competence" and "apolitical expertise," and its powers may only be exercised by "technical professional experts." * * *

No one doubts Congress's power to create a vast and varied federal bureaucracy. But where, in all this, is the role for oversight by an elected President? The Constitution requires that a President chosen by the entire Nation oversee the execution of the laws. And the "'fact that a given law or procedure is efficient, convenient, and useful in facilitating functions of government, standing alone, will not save it if it is contrary to the Constitution,'" for "'[c]onvenience and efficiency are not the primary objectives—or the hallmarks—of democratic government.'" *Bowsher,* 478 U.S., at 736 (quoting *Chadha,* 462 U.S., at 944).

One can have a government that functions without being ruled by functionaries, and a government that benefits from expertise without being ruled by experts. Our Constitution was adopted to enable the people to govern themselves, through their elected leaders. The growth of the Executive Branch, which now wields vast power and touches almost every aspect of daily life, heightens the concern that it may slip from the Executive's control, and thus from that of the people. This concern is largely absent from the dissent's paean to the administrative state.

* * *

The Framers created a structure in which "[a] dependence on the people" would be the "primary control on the government." The Federalist No. 51, at 349 (J. Madison). That dependence is maintained, not just by "parchment barriers," *id.,* No. 48, at 333 (same), but by letting "[a]mbition . . . counteract ambition," giving each branch "the necessary constitutional means, and personal motives, to resist encroachments of the others," *id.,* No. 51, at 349. A key "constitutional means" vested in the President—perhaps *the* key means—was "the power of appointing, overseeing, and controlling those who execute the laws." 1 Annals of Cong., at 463. And while a government of "opposite and rival interests" may sometimes inhibit the smooth functioning of administration, The Federalist No. 51, at 349, "[t]he Framers recognized that, in the long term, structural protections against abuse of power were critical to preserving liberty." *Bowsher, supra,* at 730.

Calls to abandon those protections in light of "the era's perceived necessity," *New York,* 505 U.S., at 187, are not unusual. Nor is the argument from bureaucratic expertise limited only to the field of accounting. The failures of accounting regulation may be a "pressing national problem," but "a judiciary that licensed extraconstitutional government with each issue of comparable gravity would, in the long run, be far worse." *Id.,* at 187–188. Neither respondents nor the dissent explains why the Board's task, unlike so many others, requires *more* than one layer of insulation from the President * * *.

* * *

The President has been given the power to oversee executive officers; he is not limited, as in Harry Truman's lament, to "persuad[ing]" his unelected subordinates "to do what they ought to do without persuasion." In its pursuit of a "workable government," Congress cannot reduce the Chief Magistrate to a cajoler-in-chief.

* * *

The Constitution that makes the President accountable to the people for executing the laws also gives him the power to do so. That power includes, as a general matter, the authority to remove those who assist him in carrying out his duties. Without such power, the President could not be held fully accountable for discharging his own responsibilities; the buck would stop somewhere else. Such diffusion of authority "would greatly diminish the intended and necessary responsibility of the chief magistrate himself." The Federalist No. 70, at 478.

While we have sustained in certain cases limits on the President's removal power, the Act before us imposes a new type of restriction—two levels of protection from removal for those who nonetheless exercise significant executive power. Congress cannot limit the President's authority in this way.

■ JUSTICE BREYER, with whom JUSTICE STEVENS, JUSTICE GINSBURG, and JUSTICE SOTOMAYOR join, dissenting.

[I]n my view the statute does not significantly interfere with the President's "executive Power." Art. II, § 1. It violates no separation-of-powers principle. And the Court's contrary holding threatens to disrupt severely the fair and efficient administration of the laws. I consequently dissent.

I

A

The legal question before us arises at the intersection of two general constitutional principles. On the one hand, Congress has broad power to enact statutes "necessary and proper" to the exercise of its specifically enumerated constitutional authority. Art. I, § 8, cl. 18. As Chief Justice Marshall wrote for the Court nearly 200 years ago, the Necessary and Proper Clause reflects the Framers' efforts to create a Constitution that would "endure for ages to come." *McCulloch v. Maryland,* 17 U.S. 316 (1819). It embodies their recognition that it would be "unwise" to prescribe "the means by which government should, in all future time, execute its powers." *Ibid.* Such "immutable rules" would deprive the Government of the needed flexibility to respond to future "exigencies which, if foreseen at all, must have been seen dimly." *Ibid.* Thus the Necessary and Proper Clause affords Congress broad authority to "create" governmental "offices" and to structure those offices "as it chooses." *Buckley v. Valeo,* 424 U.S. 1, 138 (1976) *(per curiam).* And Congress has drawn on that power over the past century to create numerous federal agencies in response to "various crises of human affairs" as they have arisen. *McCulloch, supra,* at 415 (emphasis deleted).

On the other hand, the opening sections of Articles I, II, and III of the Constitution separately and respectively vest "all legislative Powers" in Congress, the "executive Power" in the President, and the "judicial Power" in the Supreme Court (and such "inferior Courts as Congress may from time to time ordain and establish"). In doing so, these provisions imply a structural separation-of-powers principle. *See, e.g., Miller v. French,* 530 U.S. 327, 341–342 (2000). And that principle, along with the instruction in Article II, § 3 that the President "shall take Care that the Laws be faithfully executed," limits Congress' power to structure the Federal Government. *See, e.g., INS v. Chadha,* 462 U.S. 919, 946 (1983); *Freytag v. Commissioner,* 501 U.S. 868, 878 (1991); *Northern Pipeline Constr. Co. v. Marathon Pipe Line Co.,* 458 U.S. 50, 64 (1982); *Commodity Futures Trading Comm'n v. Schor,* 478 U.S. 833, 859–860 (1986). Indeed, this Court has held that the separation-of-powers principle guarantees the President the authority to dismiss certain Executive Branch officials at will. *Myers v. United States,* 272 U.S. 52 (1926).

But neither of these two principles is absolute in its application to removal cases. The Necessary and Proper Clause does not grant Congress power to free *all* Executive Branch officials from dismissal at the will of the President. *Ibid.* Nor does the separation-of-powers principle grant the President an absolute authority to remove *any and all* Executive Branch officials at will. Rather, depending on, say, the nature of the office, its function, or its subject matter, Congress sometimes may, consistent with the Constitution, limit the President's authority to remove an officer from his post. See *Humphrey's Executor v. United States,* 295 U.S. 602 (1935), overruling in part *Myers, supra; Morrison v. Olson,* 487 U.S. 654 (1988). And we must here decide whether the circumstances surrounding the statute at issue justify such a limitation.

* * *

In short, the question presented lies at the intersection of two sets of conflicting, broadly framed constitutional principles. And no text, no history, perhaps no precedent provides any clear answer.

B

When previously deciding this kind of nontextual question, the Court has emphasized the importance of examining how a particular provision, taken in context, is likely to function. Thus, in *Crowell v. Benson,* 285 U.S. 22, 53 (1932), a foundational separation-of-powers case, the Court said that "regard must be had, as in other cases where constitutional limits are invoked, not to mere matters of form, but to the substance of what is required." * * * The Court has thereby written into law Justice Jackson's wise perception that "the Constitution . . . contemplates that practice will integrate the dispersed powers into *a workable government." Youngstown Sheet & Tube Co. v. Sawyer,* 343 U.S. 579, 635 (1952) (opinion concurring in judgment) (emphasis added).

It is not surprising that the Court in these circumstances has looked to function and context, and not to bright-line rules. For one thing, that approach embodies the intent of the Framers. As Chief Justice Marshall long ago observed, our Constitution is fashioned so as to allow the three coordinate branches, including this Court, to exercise practical judgment in response to changing conditions and "exigencies," which at the time of the founding could be seen only "dimly," and perhaps not at all. *McCulloch,* 4 Wheat., at 415.

For another, a functional approach permits Congress and the President the flexibility needed to adapt statutory law to changing circumstances. That is why the "powers conferred upon the Federal Government by the Constitution were phrased in language broad enough to allow for the expansion of the Federal Government's role" over time. *New York v. United States,* 505 U.S. 144, 157 (1992). Indeed, the Federal Government at the time of the founding consisted of about 2,000 employees and served a population of about 4 million. Today, however, the Federal Government employs about *4.4 million workers* who serve a Nation of more than 310 million people living in a society characterized by rapid technological, economic, and social change.

Federal statutes now require or permit Government officials to provide, regulate, or otherwise administer, not only foreign affairs and defense, but also a wide variety of such subjects as taxes, welfare, social security, medicine, pharmaceutical drugs, education, highways, railroads, electricity, natural gas, nuclear power, financial instruments, banking, medical care, public health and safety, the environment, fair employment practices, consumer protection and much else besides.

Those statutes create a host of different organizational structures. Sometimes they delegate administrative authority to the President directly; sometimes they place authority in a long-established Cabinet department; sometimes they delegate authority to an independent commission or board; sometimes they place authority directly in the hands of a single senior administrator; sometimes they place it in a sub-cabinet bureau, office, division or other agency; sometimes they vest it in multimember or multiagency task groups; sometimes they vest it in commissions or advisory committees made up of members of more than one branch; sometimes they divide it among groups of departments, commissions, bureaus, divisions, and administrators; and sometimes they permit state or local governments to participate as well. Statutes similarly grant administrators a wide variety of powers—for example, the power to make rules, develop informal practices, investigate, adjudicate, impose sanctions, grant licenses, and provide goods, services, advice, and so forth.

The upshot is that today vast numbers of statutes governing vast numbers of subjects, concerned with vast numbers of different problems, provide for, or foresee, their execution or administration through the work of administrators organized within many different kinds of administrative structures, exercising different kinds of administrative authority, to achieve their legislatively mandated objectives. And, given the nature of the Government's work, it is not surprising that administrative units come in many different shapes and sizes.

The functional approach required by our precedents recognizes this administrative complexity and, more importantly, recognizes the various ways presidential power operates within this context—and the various ways in which a removal provision might affect that power. As human beings have known ever since Ulysses tied himself to the mast so as safely to hear the Sirens' song, sometimes it is necessary to disable oneself in order to achieve a broader objective. Thus, legally enforceable commitments—such as contracts, statutes that cannot instantly be changed, and, as in the case before us, the establishment of independent administrative institutions—hold the potential to empower precisely because of their ability to constrain. If the President seeks to regulate through impartial adjudication, then insulation of the adjudicator from removal at will can help him achieve that goal. And to free a technical decisionmaker from the fear of removal without cause can similarly help create legitimacy with respect to that official's regulatory actions by helping to insulate his technical decisions from nontechnical political pressure.

Neither is power always susceptible to the equations of elementary arithmetic. A rule that takes power from a President's friends and allies may weaken him. But a rule that takes power from the President's opponents may strengthen him. And what if the rule takes power from a functionally *neutral* independent authority? In that case, it is difficult to predict how the President's power is affected in the abstract.

These practical reasons not only support our precedents' determination that cases such as this should examine the specific functions and context at issue; they also indicate that judges should hesitate before second-guessing a "for cause" decision made by the other branches. *See, e.g., Chadha,* 462 U.S., at 944 (applying a "presumption that the challenged statute is valid"). Compared to Congress and the President, the Judiciary possesses an inferior understanding of the realities of administration, and the manner in which power, including and most especially political power, operates in context.

There is no indication that the two comparatively more expert branches were divided in their support for the "for cause" provision at issue here. In this case, the Act embodying the provision was passed by a vote of 423 to 3 in the House of Representatives and a by vote of 99 to 0 in the Senate. The creation of the Accounting Board was discussed at great length in both bodies without anyone finding in its structure any constitutional problem. The President signed the Act. And, when he did so, he issued a signing statement that critiqued multiple provisions of the Act but did not express any separation-of-powers concerns.

Thus, here, as in similar cases, we should decide the constitutional question in light of the provision's practical functioning in context. And our decision should take account of the Judiciary's comparative lack of institutional expertise.

II

A

To what extent then is the Act's "for cause" provision likely, as a practical matter, to limit the President's exercise of executive authority? In practical terms no "for cause" provision can, in isolation, define the full measure of executive power. This is because a legislative decision to place ultimate administrative authority in, say, the Secretary of Agriculture rather than the President, the way in which the statute defines the scope of the power the relevant administrator can exercise, the decision as to who controls the agency's budget requests and funding, the relationships between one agency or department and another, as well as more purely political factors (including Congress' ability to assert influence) are more likely to affect the President's power to get something done. That is why President Truman complained that " 'the powers of the President amount to' " bringing " 'people in and try[ing] to persuade them to do what they ought to do without persuasion.' " C. Rossiter, The American Presidency 154 (2d rev. ed.1960). And that is why scholars have written that the President "is neither dominant nor powerless" in his relationships with many Government entities, "whether denominated executive or independent." Strauss, The Place of Agencies in Government: Separation of Powers and the Fourth Branch, 84 Colum. L.Rev. 573, 583 (1984) (hereinafter Strauss). Those entities "are *all* subject to presidential direction in significant aspects of their functioning, and [are each] able to resist presidential direction in others." *Ibid.* (emphasis added).

Indeed, notwithstanding the majority's assertion that the removal authority is "*the* key" mechanism by which the President oversees inferior officers in the independent agencies, it appears that no President has ever actually sought to exercise that power by testing the scope of a "for cause" provision.

But even if we put all these other matters to the side, we should still conclude that the "for cause" restriction before us will not restrict presidential power significantly. For one thing, the restriction directly limits, not the President's power, but the power of an already independent agency. The Court seems to have forgotten that fact when it identifies its central constitutional problem: According to the Court, the President "is powerless to intervene" if he has determined that the Board members' "conduct merit[s] removal" because "[t]hat decision is vested instead in other tenured officers—the Commissioners—none of whom is subject to the President's direct control." But so long as the President is *legitimately* foreclosed from removing the *Commissioners* except for cause (as the majority assumes), nullifying the Commission's power to remove Board members only for cause will not resolve the problem the Court has identified: The President will *still* be "powerless to intervene" by removing the Board members if the Commission reasonably decides not to do so.

In other words, the Court fails to show why *two* layers of "for cause" protection-Layer One insulating the Commissioners from the President, and Layer Two insulating the Board from the Commissioners—impose any more serious limitation upon the *President's* powers than *one* layer. Consider the four scenarios that might arise:

1. The President and the Commission both want to keep a Board member in office. Neither layer is relevant.

2. The President and the Commission both want to dismiss a Board member. Layer Two stops them both from doing so without cause. The President's ability to remove the Commission (Layer One) is irrelevant, for he and the Commission are in agreement.

3. The President wants to dismiss a Board member, but the Commission wants to keep the member. Layer One allows the Commission to make that determination notwithstanding the President's contrary view. Layer Two is irrelevant because the Commission does not seek to remove the Board member.

4. The President wants to keep a Board member, but the Commission wants to dismiss the Board member. Here, Layer Two *helps the President,* for it hinders the Commission's ability to dismiss a Board member whom the President wants to keep in place.

Thus, the majority's decision to eliminate only *Layer Two* accomplishes virtually nothing. And that is because a removal restriction's effect upon presidential power depends not on the presence of a "double-layer" of for-cause removal, as the majority pretends, but rather on the real-world nature of the President's relationship with the Commission. If the President confronts a Commission that seeks to *resist* his policy preferences—a distinct possibility when, as here, a Commission's membership must reflect both political parties—the restriction on the *Commission's* ability to remove a Board member is either irrelevant (as in scenario 3) or may actually help the President (as in scenario 4). And if the President faces a Commission that seeks to *implement* his policy preferences, Layer One is irrelevant, for the President and Commission see eye to eye.

In order to avoid this elementary logic, the Court creates two alternative scenarios. In the first, the Commission and the President *both* want to remove a Board member, but have varying judgments as to whether they have good "cause" to do so—*i.e.*, the President and the Commission both conclude that a Board member should be removed, but disagree as to whether that conclusion (which they have both reached) is *reasonable*. In the second, the President wants to remove a Board member and the Commission disagrees; but, notwithstanding its freedom to make reasonable decisions independent of the President (afforded by Layer One), the Commission (while apparently telling the President that it agrees with him and would like to remove the Board member) uses Layer Two as an "excuse" to pursue its actual aims-an excuse which, given Layer One, it does not need.

Both of these circumstances seem unusual. I do not know if they have ever occurred. But I do not deny their logical possibility. I simply doubt their importance. And the fact that, with respect to the President's power, the double layer of for-cause removal sometimes might help, sometimes might hurt, leads me to conclude that its overall effect is at most indeterminate.

But once we leave the realm of hypothetical logic and view the removal provision at issue in the context of the entire Act, its lack of practical effect becomes readily apparent. That is because the statute provides the Commission with full authority and virtually comprehensive control over all of the Board's functions.

* * *

[T]he statute here gives the Accounting Board the power to adopt rules and standards "relating to the preparation of audit reports"; to adjudicate disciplinary proceedings involving accounting firms that fail to follow these rules; to impose sanctions; and to engage in other related activities, such as conducting inspections of accounting firms registered as the law requires and investigations to monitor compliance with the rules and related legal obligations. But, at the same time,

- No Accounting Board rule takes effect unless and until the Commission approves it, § 7217(b)(2);

- The Commission may "abrogat[e], delet[e] or ad[d] to" any rule or any portion of a rule promulgated by the Accounting Board whenever, in the Commission's view, doing so "further[s] the purposes" of the securities and accounting-oversight laws, § 7217(b)(5);

- The Commission may review any sanction the Board imposes and "enhance, modify, cancel, reduce, or require the remission of" that sanction if it finds the Board's action not "appropriate," §§ 7215(e), 7217(c)(3);

- *The Commission may promulgate rules restricting or directing the Accounting Board's conduct of all inspections and investigations,* §§ 7211(c)(3), 7214(h), 7215(b)(1)–(4);

- *The Commission may itself initiate any investigation or promulgate any rule within the Accounting Board's purview,* § 7202, and may also *remove any Accounting Board member who has unreasonably "failed to enforce compliance with" the relevant "rule[s], or any professional standard,"* § 7217(d)(3)(C) (emphasis added);

- *The Commission may at any time "relieve the Board of any responsibility to enforce compliance with any provision" of the Act, the rules, or professional standards if, in the Commission's view, doing so is in "the public interest," § 7217(d)(1) (emphasis added).*

As these statutory provisions make clear, the Court is simply wrong when it says that "the Act nowhere gives the Commission effective power to start, stop, or alter" Board investigations. On the contrary, the Commission's control over the Board's investigatory and legal functions is virtually absolute. Moreover, the Commission has general supervisory powers over the Accounting Board itself: It controls the Board's budget, §§ 7219(b), (d)(1); it can assign to the Board any "duties or functions" that it "determines are necessary or appropriate," § 7211(c)(5); it has full "oversight and enforcement authority over the Board," § 7217(a), *including the authority to inspect the Board's activities whenever it believes it "appropriate" to do so,* § 7217(d)(2) (emphasis added). And it can censure the Board or its members, as well as remove the members from office, if the members, for example, fail to enforce the Act, violate any provisions of the Act, or abuse the authority granted to them under the Act, § 7217(d)(3).

What is left? The Commission's inability to remove a Board member whose perfectly *reasonable* actions cause the Commission to overrule him with great frequency? What is the practical likelihood of that occurring, or, if it does, of the President's serious concern about such a matter? Everyone concedes that the President's control over the Commission is constitutionally sufficient. And if the President's control over the Commission is sufficient, and the Commission's control over the Board is virtually absolute, then, as a practical matter, the President's control over the Board should prove sufficient as well.

B

At the same time, Congress and the President had good reason for enacting the challenged "for cause" provision. First and foremost, the Board adjudicates cases. This Court has long recognized the appropriateness of using "for cause" provisions to protect the personal independence of those who even only sometimes engage in adjudicatory functions. *Humphrey's Executor, supra,* at 623–628. * * *

Moreover, in addition to their adjudicative functions, the Accounting Board members supervise, and are themselves, technical professional experts. This Court has recognized that the "difficulties involved in the preparation of" sound auditing reports require the application of "scientific accounting principles." *United States v. Anderson,* 269 U.S. 422, 440 (1926). And this Court has recognized the constitutional legitimacy of a justification that rests agency independence upon the need for technical expertise. See *Humphrey's Executor, supra,* at 624–626.

Here, the justification for insulating the "technical experts" on the Board from fear of losing their jobs due to political influence is particularly strong. Congress deliberately sought to provide that kind of protection. And historically, this regulatory subject matter—financial regulation—has been thought to exhibit a particular need for independence. And Congress, by, for example, providing the Board with a revenue stream independent of the congressional appropriations process, helped insulate the Board from congressional, as well as other, political influences.

In sum, Congress and the President could reasonably have thought it prudent to insulate the adjudicative Board members from fear of purely politically based removal. And in a world in which we count on the Federal Government to regulate matters as complex as, say, nuclear-power production, the Court's assertion that we should simply learn to get by "without being" regulated "by experts" is, at best, unrealistic—at worst, dangerously so.

NOTES AND QUESTIONS

1.   The Sarbanes-Oxley Act of 2002 and the Public Accounting Oversight Board (PCAOB) created by that legislation, were both enormously controversial. In a bid effectively to undermine Sarbanes-Oxley and the PCAOB, the petitioners in *Free Enterprise Foundation* had asked the Supreme Court to invalidate the actions of the PCAOB as a remedy for finding its insulation from the presidential removal power unconstitutional. The Court declined to do so, however, leaving undisturbed the Board's prior acts and concluding instead that merely allowing the SEC to remove members of the Board without cause henceforth was a more appropriate remedy. Imagine that you are a member of Congress and that you disagree with the Court's conclusion regarding the constitutionality of two levels of "for cause" removal restrictions. Faced with the possibility of such a consequence for violating the President's removal power, would you be inclined to adopt similar removal restrictions in future legislation establishing other governmental bodies?

2.   Elsewhere in his dissenting opinion and in an accompanying appendix, Justice Breyer identified 573 government officials who he claimed resemble members of the Public Company Accounting Oversight Board in that they can only be removed from office "for cause" by superiors who themselves are only removable from office by the President "for cause." Indeed, given the uncertainty surrounding the identification of particular government officials as inferior officers, Justice Breyer suggested there could be thousands of government officers currently protected by two levels of for cause removal restrictions and who now might be potentially subject to removal by their superiors at will as a result of *Free Enterprise Foundation*. In light of the remedy offered by the Court in this case, would you expect regulated parties to challenge the constitutionality of the for cause restrictions protecting these government officers from removal?

3.   Now imagine that you are an inferior officer working in a government agency, and that the Court's decision in *Free Enterprise Foundation* raises a question regarding the constitutionality of a "for cause" removal restriction for your position. In other words, while the President may or may not know your name today, the head of your agency (who herself is only removable "for cause") may now have the power to fire you without first establishing good cause for doing so. Would you be inclined under such circumstances to do your job differently? How so? Would you expect the ability to fire inferior officers at will to have good or bad consequences for the operation of government?

C. OTHER PRESIDENTIAL ATTEMPTS TO CONTROL AGENCIES

Every President over the past century has complained of his inability to control the sprawling bureaucracy. Presidents have all attempted to impose control, but in a variety of different ways.

1. THE NATURE AND SCOPE OF PRESIDENTIAL AUTHORITY

The legal framework by which Presidents may exercise power is surprisingly underdeveloped. The Supreme Court has decided only a handful of cases that focus on the scope of Presidential power, and most of the opinions tell us little of real value. In an excellent scholarly analysis of the few relevant cases, Henry Monaghan concluded that, absent a delegation of power from Congress, the President may behave in a way that adversely affects private rights only when he is acting to "preserve, protect, and defend the personnel, property, and instrumentalities of the national government." Henry P. Monaghan, *The Protective Power of the Presidency*, 93 COLUM. LAW REV. 1, 61–62 (1993).

One of the most interesting of the opinions on the subject comes from *In re Neagle*, 135 U.S. 1 (1890). Like all Justices at that time, Justice Field was assigned to "ride circuit," *i.e.* travel, to California to decide some cases. He told the Attorney General that he feared that an individual who had a grudge against him might attack him in California. Without any statutory authority, the Attorney General hired a body guard to protect Justice Field. When the individual appeared in the vicinity of the Justice and engaged in conduct that was ambiguous at best but that the bodyguard interpreted as threatening, the bodyguard shot him dead. The State of California then arrested the bodyguard and charged him with murder. The bodyguard defended his actions on the bases that he had lawful authority to kill the individual and that, under the Supremacy Clause, his authorization from the Attorney General trumped the State's power to try him. The State argued that the bodyguard's defense was invalid and that he had no authority to shoot the alleged assailant because the Attorney General lacked the power to hire a bodyguard to protect a Supreme Court Justice. The Supreme Court upheld both the defense put forth by the bodyguard and the Attorney General's inherent power to hire bodyguards to protect Supreme Court Justices. Does that result surprise you?

Perhaps the most important case addressing the scope of presidential power is *Youngstown Sheet & Tube Co. v. Sawyer*, 343 U.S. 579 (1952). The case arose when the steelworkers' union and the owners of the steel mills were unable or unwilling to resolve a labor dispute, and the union called a nationwide strike. President Truman became incensed because of his belief that a shutdown of the steel mills would adversely affect the nation's ability to fight the Korean War. After inappropriately conferring with two Justices and receiving their private assurances that the Court would uphold his action, President Truman seized the steel mills so they could be operated by the government. The secret assurances of two Justices proved to be unfounded. A majority of the Court held that the seizure was illegal. Except for the concurring opinion of Justice Jackson, the opinions issued in the case are generally regarded as poor in the quality of their reasoning; later court opinions have largely ignored them. Justice Jackson's concurring opinion, by contrast, has elicited considerable praise.

Youngstown Sheet & Tube Co. v. Sawyer
343 U.S. 579 (1952).

■ MR. JUSTICE JACKSON, concurring in the judgment and opinion of the Court.

That comprehensive and undefined presidential powers hold both practical advantages and grave dangers for the country will impress anyone who has served as legal adviser to a President in time of transition and public anxiety. While an interval of detached reflection may temper teachings of that experience, they probably are a more realistic influence on my views than the conventional materials of judicial decision which seem unduly to accentuate doctrine and legal fiction. But as we approach the question of presidential power, we half overcome mental hazards by recognizing them. The opinions of judges, no less than executives and publicists, often suffer the infirmity of confusing the issue of a power's validity with the cause it is invoked to promote, of confounding the permanent executive office with its temporary occupant. The tendency is strong to emphasize transient results upon policies-such as wages or stabilization-and lose sight of enduring consequences upon the balanced power structure of our Republic.

A judge, like an executive adviser, may be surprised at the poverty of really useful and unambiguous authority applicable to concrete problems of executive power as they actually present themselves. Just what our forefathers did envision, or would have envisioned had they foreseen modern conditions, must be divined from materials almost as enigmatic as the dreams Joseph was called upon to interpret for Pharaoh. A century and a half of partisan debate and scholarly speculation yields no net result but only supplies more or less apt quotations from respected sources on each side of any question. They largely cancel each other. And court decisions are indecisive because of the judicial practice of dealing with the largest questions in the most narrow way.

The actual art of governing under our Constitution does not and cannot conform to judicial definitions of the power of any of its branches based on isolated clauses or even single Articles torn from context. While the Constitution diffuses power the better to secure liberty, it also contemplates that practice will integrate the dispersed powers into a workable government. It enjoins upon its branches separateness but interdependence, autonomy but reciprocity. Presidential powers are not fixed but fluctuate, depending upon their disjunction or conjunction with those of Congress. We may well begin by a somewhat over-simplified grouping of practical situations in which a President may doubt, or others may challenge, his powers, and by distinguishing roughly the legal consequences of this factor of relativity.

1.   When the President acts pursuant to an express or implied authorization of Congress, his authority is at its maximum, for it

includes all that he possesses in his own right plus all that Congress can delegate. In these circumstances, and in these only, may he be said (for what it may be worth), to personify the federal sovereignty. If his act is held unconstitutional under these circumstances, it usually means that the Federal Government as an undivided whole lacks power. A seizure executed by the President pursuant to an Act of Congress would be supported by the strongest of presumptions and the widest latitude of judicial interpretation, and the burden of persuasion would rest heavily upon any who might attack it.

2.   When the President acts in absence of either a congressional grant or denial of authority, he can only rely upon his own independent powers, but there is a zone of twilight in which he and Congress may have concurrent authority, or in which its distribution is uncertain. Therefore, congressional inertia, indifference or quiescence may sometimes, at least as a practical matter, enable, if not invite, measures on independent presidential responsibility. In this area, any actual test of power is likely to depend on the imperatives of events and contemporary imponderables rather than on abstract theories of law.

3.   When the President takes measures incompatible with the expressed or implied will of Congress, his power is at its lowest ebb, for then he can rely only upon his own constitutional powers minus any constitutional powers of Congress over the matter. Courts can sustain exclusive Presidential control in such a case only by disabling the Congress from acting upon the subject. Presidential claim to a power at once so conclusive and preclusive must be scrutinized with caution, for what is at stake is the equilibrium established by our constitutional system.

Into which of these classifications does this executive seizure of the steel industry fit? It is eliminated from the first by admission, for it is conceded that no congressional authorization exists for this seizure. That takes away also the support of the many precedents and declarations which were made in relation, and must be confined, to this category.

Can it then be defended under flexible tests available to the second category? It seems clearly eliminated from that class because Congress has not left seizure of private property an open field but has covered it by three statutory policies inconsistent with this seizure. In cases where the purpose is to supply needs of the Government itself, two courses are provided: one, seizure of a plant which fails to comply with obligatory orders placed by the Government, another, condemnation of facilities, including temporary use under the power of eminent domain. The third is applicable where it is the general economy of the country that is to be protected rather than exclusive governmental interests. None of these were invoked. In choosing a different and inconsistent way of his own, the President cannot claim that it is necessitated or invited by failure of Congress to legislate upon the occasions, grounds and methods for seizure of industrial properties.

This leaves the current seizure to be justified only by the severe tests under the third grouping, where it can be supported only by any remainder of executive power after subtraction of such powers as Congress may have over the subject. In short, we can sustain the President only by holding that seizure of such strike-bound industries is within his domain and beyond control by Congress. Thus, this Court's first review of such seizures occurs under circumstances which leave Presidential power most vulnerable to attack and in the least favorable of possible constitutional postures.

This leaves the current seizure to be justified only by the severe tests under the third grouping, where it can be supported only by any remainder of executive power after subtraction of such powers as Congress may have over the subject. In short, we can sustain the President only by holding that seizure of such strike-bound industries is within his domain and beyond control by Congress. Thus, this Court's first review of such seizures occurs under circumstances which leave Presidential power most vulnerable to attack and in the least favorable of possible constitutional postures.

I did not suppose, and I am not persuaded, that history leaves it open to question, at least in the courts, that the executive branch, like the Federal Government as a whole, possesses only delegated powers. The purpose of the Constitution was not only to grant power, but to keep it from getting out of hand. However, because the President does not enjoy unmentioned powers does not mean that the mentioned ones should be narrowed by a niggardly construction. Some clauses could be made almost unworkable, as well as immutable, by refusal to indulge some latitude of interpretation for changing times. I have heretofore, and do now, give to the enumerated powers the scope and elasticity afforded by what seem to be reasonable practical implications instead of the rigidity dictated by a doctrinaire textualism.

The Solicitor General seeks the power of seizure in three clauses of the Executive Article, the first reading, "The executive Power shall be vested in a President of the United States of America." Lest I be thought to exaggerate, I quote the interpretation which his brief puts upon it: "In our view, this clause constitutes a grant of all the executive powers of which the Government is capable." If that be true, it is difficult to see why the forefathers bothered to add several specific items, including some trifling ones.

* * * I cannot accept the view that this clause is a grant in bulk of all conceivable executive power but regard it as an allocation to the presidential office of the generic powers thereafter stated.

The clause on which the Government next relies is that "The President shall be Commander in Chief of the Army and Navy of the United States. . . ." These cryptic words have given rise to some of the most persistent controversies in our constitutional history. Of course, they imply something more than an empty title. But just what authority goes with the name has plagued Presidential advisers who would not waive or narrow it by nonassertion yet cannot say where it begins or ends. It undoubtedly puts the Nation's armed forces under Presidential command. Hence, this loose appellation is sometimes advanced as support for any Presidential action, internal or external, involving use of force, the idea being that it vests power to do anything, anywhere, that can be done with an army or navy.

That seems to be the logic of an argument tendered at our bar—that the President having, on his own responsibility, sent American troops abroad derives from that act "affirmative power" to seize the means of producing a supply of steel for them. To quote, "Perhaps the most forceful illustrations of the scope of Presidential power in this connection is the fact that American troops in Korea, whose safety and effectiveness are so directly involved here, were sent to the field by an exercise of the President's constitutional powers." Thus, it is said he has invested himself with "war powers."

I cannot foresee all that it might entail if the Court should indorse this argument. Nothing in our Constitution is plainer than that declaration of a war is entrusted only to Congress. Of course, a state of war may in fact exist without a formal declaration. But no doctrine that the Court could promulgate would seem to me more sinister and alarming than that a President whose conduct of foreign affairs is so largely uncontrolled, and often even is unknown, can vastly enlarge his mastery over the internal affairs of the country by his own commitment of the Nation's armed forces to some foreign venture. I do not, however, find it necessary or appropriate to consider the legal status of the Korean enterprise to discountenance argument based on it.

* * *

We should not use this occasion to circumscribe, much less to contract, the lawful role of the President as Commander-in-Chief. I should indulge the widest latitude of interpretation to sustain his exclusive function to command the instruments of national force, at least when turned against the outside world for the security of our society. But, when it is turned inward, not because of rebellion but because of a lawful economic struggle between industry and labor, it should have no such indulgence. His command power is not such an absolute as might be implied from that office in a militaristic system but is subject to limitations consistent with a constitutional Republic whose law and policy-making branch is a representative Congress. The purpose of lodging dual titles in one man was to insure that the civilian would control the military, not to enable the military to subordinate the presidential office. No penance would ever expiate the sin against free government of holding that a President can escape control of executive powers by law through assuming his military role. What the power of command may include I do not try to envision, but I think it is not a military prerogative, without support of law, to seize persons or property because they are important or even essential for the military and naval establishment.

The third clause in which the Solicitor General finds seizure powers is that "he shall take Care that the Laws be faithfully executed. . . ." That authority must be matched against words of the Fifth Amendment that "No person shall be deprived of life, liberty, or property, without due process of law." One gives a governmental authority that reaches so far as there is law, the other gives a private right that authority shall go no farther. These signify about all there is of the principle that ours is a government of laws, not of men, and that we submit ourselves to rulers only if under rules.

The Solicitor General lastly grounds support of the seizure upon nebulous, inherent powers never expressly granted but said to have accrued to the office from the customs and claims of preceding administrations. The plea is for a resulting power to deal with a crisis or an emergency according to the necessities of the case, the unarticulated assumption being that necessity knows no law.

Loose and irresponsible use of adjectives colors all non-legal and much legal discussion of presidential powers. "Inherent" powers, "implied" powers, "incidental" powers, "plenary" powers, "war" powers, and "emergency" powers are used, often interchangeably and without fixed or ascertainable meanings.

The vagueness and generality of the clauses that set forth presidential powers afford a plausible basis for pressures within and without an administration for presidential action beyond that supported by those whose responsibility it is to defend his actions in court. The claim of inherent and unrestricted presidential powers has long been a persuasive dialectical weapon in political controversy. While it is not surprising that counsel should grasp support from such unadjudicated claims of power, a judge cannot accept self-serving press statements of the attorney for one of the interested parties as authority in answering a constitutional question, even if the advocate was himself. But prudence has counseled that actual reliance on such nebulous claims stop short of provoking a judicial test.

The appeal, however, that we declare the existence of inherent powers ex necessitate to meet an emergency asks us to do what many think would be wise, although it is something the forefathers omitted. They knew what emergencies were, knew the pressures they engender for authoritative action, knew, too, how they afford a ready pretext for usurpation. We may also suspect that they suspected that emergency powers would tend to kindle emergencies. Aside from suspension of the privilege of the writ of habeas corpus in time of rebellion or invasion, when the public safety may require it, they made no express provision for exercise of extraordinary authority because of a crisis. I do not think we rightfully may so amend their work, and, if we could, I am not convinced it would be wise to do so, although many modern nations have forthrightly recognized that war and economic crises may upset the normal balance between liberty and authority. Their experience with emergency powers may not be irrelevant to the argument here that we should say that the Executive, of his own volition, can invest himself with undefined emergency powers.

* * *

In view of the ease, expedition and safety with which Congress can grant and has granted large emergency powers, certainly ample to embrace this crisis, I am quite unimpressed with the argument that we should affirm possession of them without statute. Such power either has no beginning or it has no end. If it exists, it need submit to no legal restraint. I am not alarmed that it would plunge us straightway into dictatorship, but it is at least a step in that wrong direction.

As to whether there is imperative necessity for such powers, it is relevant to note the gap that exists between the President's paper powers and his real powers. The Constitution does not disclose the measure of the actual controls wielded by the modern presidential office. That instrument must be understood as an Eighteenth-Century sketch of a government hoped for, not as a blueprint of the Government that is. Vast accretions of federal power, eroded from that reserved by the States, have magnified the scope of presidential activity. Subtle shifts take place in the centers of real power that do not show on the face of the Constitution.

Executive power has the advantage of concentration in a single head in those choices the whole Nation has a part, making him the focus of public hopes and expectations. In drama, magnitude and finality his decisions so far overshadow any others that almost alone he fills the public eye and ear. No other personality in public life can begin to compete with him in access to the public mind through modern methods of communications. By his prestige as head of state and his influence upon public opinion he exerts a leverage upon those who are supposed to check and balance his power which often cancels their effectiveness.

Moreover, rise of the party system has made a significant extraconstitutional supplement to real executive power. No appraisal of his necessities is realistic which overlooks that he heads a political system as well as a legal system. Party loyalties and interests, sometimes more binding than law, extend his effective control into branches of government other than his own and he often may win, as a political leader, what he cannot command under the Constitution. Indeed, Woodrow Wilson, commenting on the President as leader both of his party and of the Nation, observed, "If he rightly interpret the national thought and boldly insist upon it, he is irresistible. . . . His office is anything he has the sagacity and force to make it." I cannot be brought to believe that this country will suffer if the Court refuses further to aggrandize the presidential office, already so potent and so relatively immune from judicial review, at the expense of Congress.

NOTES AND QUESTIONS

1. Although Justice Jackson wrote alone in concurrence and not for a majority of the Court, his words continue to resonate with the Supreme Court. The Court frequently treats his opinion in *Youngstown* as authoritative. In *Medellin v. Texas*, 552 U.S. 491, 128 S.Ct. 1346, 1350 (2008), for example, the Court recognized Justice Jackson's tripartite analysis in *Youngstown* as "the accepted framework for evaluating executive action." In *Hamdan v. Rumsfeld*, 548 U.S. 557, 638 (2006), Justice Kennedy writing in concurrence identified Justice Jackson's *Youngstown* opinion as providing "[t]he proper framework for assessing whether executive actions are authorized."

2. There are no cases in Justice Jackson's third category in which the Supreme Court has upheld a presidential action that the Court determined to be forbidden by a statute—*i.e.*, contrary to "the expressed or implied will of Congress." There are several cases, including *Youngstown*, in which the Court has held such a presidential action unlawful. Note, however, that Jackson does not completely rule out the possibility that a President might someday take an action that is forbidden by a statute but that the Court determines to be lawful. Instead, he characterizes that situation as one in which the President's power is "at its lowest ebb." Can you think of any circumstances in which the President could lawfully act contrary to statute?

3. The Constitution's Article II provides that "[t]he executive Power shall be vested in a President of the United States of America." Justice Jackson rejected the argument that this vesting clause "is a grant in bulk of all conceivable executive power," and maintained instead that this language merely "allocat[ed] to the presidential office" the various specific powers listed in Article II. While many legal scholars agree with Jackson's assessment, in the past few decades, others have advanced an alternative vision of executive power, known as the unitary executive theory, that attributes more substance to the Article II vesting clause. Saikrishna Prakash, *Fragmented Features of the Constitution's Unitary Executive*, 45 WILLAMETTE L. REV. 701, 701 (2009), describes the unitary executive theory as follows:

> The assertion that the original Constitution creates a "unitary executive" can be understood as a claim that the Constitution empowers the President to control the execution of federal law. This generic assertion has as many as three sub-claims: that the President, as the "constitutional executor" of the laws, personally may execute any federal law himself; that the President, as Chief Executive, may direct all executive officers in their execution of federal law; and that the President, as the Supreme Executive Magistrate charged with ensuring faithful law execution, may remove executive officers.

4. Most of the cases discussed in the other chapters of this casebook would seem to involve a President or one of his agents exercising power that falls within Justice Jackson's first category—where presidential power is "at its maximum." As you saw in Chapter 2, Congress routinely delegates authority to the President or executive branch or independent agencies that are, to one or another degree, subordinated to him. Agency actions taken pursuant to such delegated authority would seem to reflect a combination of presidential power plus the power that Congress has and can delegate to the President or his agent.

Yet, as you have also seen, the same statutes that grant agencies such substantial authority also contain extensive gaps and ambiguities that the agency must resolve. In fact, the President and members of Congress routinely disagree over the proper interpretation of statutes, *e.g.*, with individual members of Congress asserting that a particular statute requires a given agency to act in a certain way, and the President disagreeing. When the President and members of Congress disagree over the meaning of a statute, are agency officials bound to follow the President's interpretation? The materials in the next section of this Chapter 3 discuss presidential signing statements, executive orders, and other presidential actions undertaken in an effort to control or at least influence the interpretive policy choices of executive branch and independent agency officials. Do these actions fall in Justice Jackson's second category—where presidential power is uncertain because Congress has neither authorized nor forbidden the action at issue? Or, at least on occasion, might these actions fall into Justice Jackson's third category?

There are few decided cases that address issues of this type directly because it is nearly impossible to devise a way of getting such disputes before a court in a form a court can, or will, decide. Such disputes typically come before the courts only after the agency has chosen its course of action.

As a result, these cases tend not to be framed as questions of presidential exercises of power in contradiction to clear congressional mandates, but rather as disagreements over statutory meaning that the courts must mediate. Implicitly and through dicta, however, the Supreme Court has approved of the powers that Presidents have claimed in this context. For example, in justifying judicial deference to agency interpretations of the statutes that they administer, the Supreme Court observed that,

> [w]hile agencies are not directly accountable to the people, the Chief Executive is, and it is entirely appropriate for this political branch of the Government to make such policy choices—resolving the competing interests which Congress itself either inadvertently did not resolve, or intentionally left to be resolved by the agency charged with the administration of the statute in light of everyday realities.

Chevron U.S.A. Inc. v. Natural Resources Defense Council, Inc., 467 U.S. 837, 865–66 (1984). Do you think Justice Jackson would concur with this assessment? Would a proponent of the unitary executive theory?

DISCUSSION PROBLEM

Assume that the U.S. is involved in a war in which U.S. military personnel are fighting on foreign soil, and assume that Congress has adopted a statute that withdraws funding for the war on a timetable that is not consistent with safe withdrawal of the troops. A retreat under fire is a very dangerous military action. A Department of Defense study concluded that safe withdrawal of U.S. forces from Iraq would require one year, and that a more precipitous withdrawal would produce a high risk of unnecessary loss of life. The Department of Defense conducted similar studies reaching similar conclusions in the contexts of the Vietnam War and the Korean War. Assume in the present case, however, that Congress enacted a statute requiring withdrawal of all forces from the field of battle within three months of the date of enactment, and the Department of Defense estimated that such a withdrawal would increase U.S. casualties by 5000 in comparison with withdrawal on a one-year timetable. Would the President be acting within his power as Commander-in-Chief if he withdrew the forces on the fastest timetable consistent with safe withdrawal even if that timetable is slower than the statutorily mandated timetable?

2.   TOOLS PRESIDENTS USE TO CONTROL AGENCIES

Independent of the legal limits on the scope of presidential power, the President confronts practical limits on the means through which he can control the bureaucracy. The primary tools by which the President controls agency decisions were discussed at length in Parts A and B of this Chapter—the power to appoint and the power to remove executive branch and independent agency officers. By appointing officers who are likely to share his policy preferences and who are likely to defer to his views in circumstances in which they do not, the President minimizes the potential for conflict with the officers to whom Congress has delegated the power to make decisions. By threatening explicitly, or more often implicitly, to remove an officer who disagrees with him on some important matter, the President further reduces the risk that an agency will make a decision that displeases him. The powers of appointment and removal are not always sufficient, however, to create a situation in which an agency head acts in accordance with the President's preferences.

The Senate is not always willing to confirm the President's first choice for a given office. The President may not wish to expend political capital and antagonize members of the Senate to secure the appointment of his first choice. Thus, the President may be forced to nominate a compromise candidate whose views are less closely aligned to his own.

Also, notwithstanding the jurisprudence in Part B of this Chapter, Presidents have the power to remove most officers without giving any reason for doing so. Yet, Presidents are extremely reluctant to use their removal power. Imagine that you are a political advisor to the President when it appears that some agency head is about to make a decision that the President dislikes or when an agency head refuses to take an action the President wants him to take. Suppose that the President has done everything he can to persuade the agency head not to take the action the President does not want him to take or to take the action he refuses to take, but has been unsuccessful. What factors would you consider in advising the President whether to remove the agency head?

- Would it matter whether the agency head has an independent constituency? A Secretary of Agriculture might be popular with farmers and agribusiness. A Secretary of the Treasury could be highly regarded and trusted by Wall Street and the Chamber of Commerce.

- Would it matter whether the agency head has an excellent reputation? At various times during the tenure of President George W. Bush, Secretaries of State Colin Powell and Condoleeza Rice had much higher public approval ratings than the President.

- Would it matter whether you fear that the public may side with the agency head on the issue on which he disagrees with the President? Also under President George W. Bush, Attorney General John Ashcroft refused to say that certain aggressive interrogation techniques that many consider to be torture are legal even though the President urged him to make such a determination.

- Would it matter whether the agency head is popular with Congress, and prominent members of Congress happen to agree with the agency head's position? Would you consider the difficulty and/or embarrassment the President is likely to suffer in Senate confirmation hearings when he nominates a potential replacement for that agency head?

Because of these practical limitations on his appointment and removal powers, Presidents have endeavored to develop other mechanisms to control or at least influence agencies. Some of these efforts have been more successful than others.

Presidential Signing Statements

Article I, Section 7 of the United States Constitution calls for bills that have passed both houses of Congress to be presented to the President who, "if he approve . . . shall sign it." Since at least President James Monroe, who served as President from 1817 to 1825, Presidents have taken the opportunity when signing bills to issue formal statements offering their views regarding the legislation's constitutionality or meaning. These presidential signing statements have been controversial at various times. President Andrew Jackson in 1830 used a signing statement to raise objections to a particular provision in an appropriations bill, and members of the House of Representatives criticized that action as an attempted line item veto. President John Tyler in 1842 issued a signing statement expressing doubts as to whether a bill regarding the apportionment of congressional districts was constitutional and was rebuked by Congress for defacing public records. *See* T.J. HALSTED, CONGRESSIONAL RESEARCH SERVICE REPORT FOR CONGRESS: PRESIDENTIAL SIGNING STATEMENTS: CONSTITUTIONAL AND INSTITUTIONAL IMPLICATIONS 2 (Sept. 17, 2007).

President Ronald Reagan significantly expanded both the use and significance of presidential signing statements; he issued 250 of them, one third of which raised objections regarding one or more provisions of the laws that he was signing. Subsequent Presidents followed his lead. Presidents George H.W. Bush and Bill Clinton both issued a few hundred signing statements, a significant number of which also documented constitutional or legal objections to the laws in question. President George W. Bush in turn issued fewer signing statements, but his contained more constitutional and statutory complaints. Moreover, a few of the latter President Bush's signing statements—those accompanying statutes addressing aspects of his administration's actions against terrorism—made particularly controversial assertions of unitary executive authority and other presidential powers. For an interesting empirical analysis of the signing statements of Presidents Jimmy Carter through George W. Bush, see Curtis A. Bradley and Eric A. Posner, *Presidential Signing Statements and Executive Power*, 23 CONST. COMMENT. 321–34 (2006).

Presidents use signing statements for a variety of purposes. Some are merely rhetorical or political, for example praising the legislation or thanking those who have been instrumental in its passage, or perhaps expressing disappointment that the legislation did not contain additional provisions that the President wanted. Presidents have been particularly criticized for using signing statements to express doubts regarding the constitutionality of a statute or some of its provisions, and also to advocate particular interpretations of arguably ambiguous statutory language that may not comport with the views of some members of Congress.

Setting aside the question whether Presidents have a duty to enforce statutes that they believe are unconstitutional, critics of signing statements that raise constitutional questions argue that a President should not sign a bill that he believes is unconstitutional. They also contend that these signing statements serve as a form of line item veto, enabling the President as a practical matter to accept or reject provisions of a bill according to his preference. Defenders of signing statements observe that they are not legally binding, that the statutes remain validly on the books, and that the concerns about constitutionality typically relate to potential applications of the provisions in question. At worst, defenders maintain signing statements represent a determination not to enforce a statute that may or may not actually lead to nonenforcement. Even when raising constitutional concerns, Presidents rarely use signing statements to declare outright an intent not to enforce a statutory provision.

For signing statements that advocate particular interpretations of ambiguous statutes, the principal question is the extent to which reviewing courts might be willing to defer to them. Critics express concern that, if courts give weight to signing statements in evaluating statutory meaning, the President will be able essentially to veto legislation without facing the possibility of a congressional override, or at least possess an effective line item veto. It is not at all clear that courts give signing statements as such any more weight than they give congressional legislative history. Nevertheless, courts routinely defer to interpretations of ambiguous statutes advanced by administrative agencies. We discuss judicial deference to agency interpretations of statutes at length in Chapter 6. The real question, therefore, may be the extent to which presidential signing statements lead to agency interpretations to which courts ultimately defer.

Executive Orders

Executive orders are presidential directives that govern the actions of government officials and agencies. Unlike presidential signing statements, they often carry the force of law. Except for William Henry Harrison, every President from George Washington to Barack Obama has issued at least one executive order; collectively, they have produced thousands. *See, e.g.*, JOHN CONTRUBIS, CONGRESSIONAL RESEARCH SERVICE REPORT FOR CONGRESS: EXECUTIVE ORDERS AND PROCLAMATIONS 25–26 (Mar. 9, 1999).

Many executive orders deal with minor administrative matters, for example, ordering federal government employees not to engage in text messaging while driving on official government business or in government vehicles. See E.O. 13513, 74 Fed. Reg. 51225 (2009). Others have been quite controversial. President Franklin D. Roosevelt used executive orders to order the internment of Americans of Japanese ancestry during World War II, *see* E.O, 9066, 7 Fed. Reg. 1407 (1942), and to forbid racial discrimination in employment of workers in government and the defense industry. *See* E.O, 8022, 6 Fed. Reg. 3109 (1941). President Truman's steel mill seizure, at issue in *Youngstown Sheet & Tube Co. v. Sawyer*, 343 U.S. 579 (1952), was undertaken by executive order. *See* E.O. 10340, 17 Fed. Reg. 3139 (1952).

The Constitution does not explicitly authorize the President to issue executive orders. Even when they carry legal force, executive orders are not automatically subject to a congressional vote. Sometimes legislation explicitly authorizes the President to act by executive order, or Congress decides to ratify an executive order after the President issues it. Nevertheless, even in the face of congressional opposition, Presidents have often claimed that provisions in Article II of the

Constitution or more ambiguous statutory language authorize particular executive orders. Further, in many instances, Presidents have based their executive orders on rather nonspecific assertions of authority. In fact, Presidents have occasionally issued executive orders claiming simply authority under "the Constitution and statutes of the United States of America, and as President of the United States of America." *See, e.g.*, E.O. 12052, 43 Fed. Reg. 15133 (1978).

The ambiguity surrounding the President's authority to issue executive orders naturally leads to difficult questions, particularly when an order is controversial. If a President claims statutory authority for an executive order, then presumably Congress has at least some power to alter the statute. What power does Congress have to challenge an order, however, if a President claims constitutional authority as supporting a controversial executive order? If a controversial executive order becomes the subject of a legal challenge, what standard of review should a court apply in evaluating the order? Consider these questions in connection with the following materials, which discuss a series of controversial executive orders asserting presidential control over the regulatory process.

OMB and OIRA

Practically since the expansion of the administrative state began over 100 years ago, Presidents have attempted to implement systematic methods of controlling agencies. One way in which they do so is through the Office of Management and Budget (OMB) and its subsidiary agency, the Office of Information and Regulatory Affairs (OIRA).[1]

The OMB evolved from the Bureau of the Budget, which Congress created in 1921 within the Treasury Department "to assemble, correlate, revise, reduce, or increase the [budget] estimates of the several departments or establishments." 42 Stat. 22 (1921). With this power, the Bureau quickly became instrumental as a sort of information clearinghouse, helping the President discern what various government agencies were doing and influence their actions. Under President Franklin D. Roosevelt, the Bureau moved from the Treasury Department to the Executive Office of the President. President Richard Nixon transformed the Bureau into the OMB and gave it certain nonbudgetary powers over federal government agencies as part of a larger executive reorganization plan. President Gerald Ford expanded OMB review of agency actions for their inflationary impact (a big concern in the 1970s). President Jimmy Carter issued Executive Order (E.O.) 12044, which replaced the Nixon and Ford agency oversight programs with a requirement that agencies analyze and consider the costs of proposed rules as well as possible alternatives to regulation, and select from the "least burdensome of the acceptable alternatives."

---

[1] OIRA is a subsidiary agency within the OMB. See 44 U.S.C. § 3503. Congress established OIRA in the Paperwork Reduction Act of 1980. Under that statute, OIRA is responsible for monitoring and reducing the burden of paperwork across the federal government and also with respect to private entities. See 44 U.S.C. § 3504. Over time, OIRA has acquired additional administrative responsibilities over various statutes that govern agency behavior, including but by no means limited to the Information Quality Act discussed in Chapter 2. OIRA has also assumed responsibility for the OMB's duties under the executive orders discussed in the following pages of this text.

As Frank Cross observes in documenting the history of the OMB, these Presidents all "recognized a need for some centralized supervision of agency activities," with Presidents Nixon, Ford, and Carter, that need encompassed "alleviating the economic burdens of regulation." Frank B. Cross, *Executive Orders 12,291 and 12,498: A Test Case in Presidential Control of Executive Agencies*, 4 J.L. & POL. 483 (1988).

President Reagan, however, took the single most important step toward systematic presidential control of administrative agencies in 1981 when he issued E.O. 12291, superseding President Carter's E.O. 12044 and providing for the OMB to play an expanded supervisory role in directing agency rulemaking efforts.

Executive Order 12291 of February 17, 1981
FEDERAL REGULATION
46 Fed. Reg. 13,193 (1981).

By the authority vested in me as President by the Constitution and laws of the United States of America, and in order to reduce the burdens of existing and future regulations, increase agency accountability for regulatory actions, provide for presidential oversight of the regulatory process, minimize duplication and conflict of regulations, and insure well-reasoned regulations, it is hereby ordered as follows:

Section 1. *Definitions.* For the purposes of this Order:

* * *

(b) "Major rule" means any regulation that is likely to result in:

(1) An annual effect on the economy of $100 million or more;

(2) A major increase in costs or prices for consumers, individual industries, Federal, State, or local government agencies, or geographic regions; or

(3) Significant adverse effects on competition, employment, investment, productivity, innovation, or on the ability of United States-based enterprises to compete with foreign-based enterprises in domestic or export markets.

(c) "Director" means the Director of the Office of Management and Budget.

* * *

(e) "Task Force" means the Presidential Task Force on Regulatory Relief.

Sec. 2. *General Requirements.* In promulgating new regulations, reviewing existing regulations, and developing legislative proposals concerning regulation, all agencies, to the extent permitted by law, shall adhere to the following requirements:

(a) Administrative decisions shall be based on adequate information concerning the need for and consequences of proposed government action;

(b) Regulatory action shall not be undertaken unless the potential benefits to society for the regulation outweigh the potential costs to society;

(c) Regulatory objectives shall be chosen to maximize the net benefits to society;

(d) Among alternative approaches to any given regulatory objective, the alternative involving the least net cost to society shall be chosen; and

(e) Agencies shall set regulatory priorities with the aim of maximizing the aggregate net benefits to society, taking into account the condition of the particular industries affected by regulations, the condition of the national economy, and other regulatory actions contemplated for the future.

Sec. 3. *Regulatory Impact Analysis and Review.*

(a) In order to implement Section 2 of this Order, each agency shall, in connection with every major rule, prepare, and to the extent permitted by law consider, a Regulatory Impact Analysis.

* * *

(c) Except as provided in Section 8 of this Order, agencies shall prepare Regulatory Impact Analyses of major rules and transmit them, along with all notices of proposed rulemaking and all final rules, to the Director as follows:

* * *

(2) With respect to all other major rules, the agency shall prepare a preliminary Regulatory Impact Analysis, which shall be transmitted, along with a notice of proposed rulemaking, to the Director at least 60 days prior to the publication of a notice of proposed rulemaking, and a final Regulatory Impact Analysis, which shall be transmitted along with the final rule at least 30 days prior to the publication of the major rule as a final rule;

* * *

(d) To permit each proposed major rule to be analyzed in light of the requirements stated in Section 2 of this Order, each preliminary and final Regulatory Impact Analysis shall contain the following information:

(1) A description of the potential benefits of the rule, including any beneficial effects that cannot be quantified in monetary terms, and the identification of those likely to receive the benefits;

(2) A description of the potential costs of the rule, including any adverse effects that cannot be quantified in

monetary terms, and the identification of those likely to bear the costs;

(3) A determination of the potential net benefits of the rule, including an evaluation of effects that cannot be quantified in monetary terms;

(4) A description of alternative approaches that could substantially achieve the same regulatory goal at lower cost, together with an analysis of this potential benefit and costs and a brief explanation of the legal reasons why such alternatives, if proposed, could not be adopted; and

(5) Unless covered by the description required under paragraph (4) of this subsection, an explanation of any legal reasons why the rule cannot be based on the requirements set forth in Section 2 of this Order.

(e) (1) The Director, subject to the direction of the Task Force, which shall resolve any issues raised under this Order or ensure that they are presented to the President, is authorized to review any preliminary or final Regulatory Impact Analysis, notice of proposed rulemaking, or final rule based on the requirements of this Order.

(2) The Director shall be deemed to have concluded review unless the Director advises an agency to the contrary under subsection (f) of this Section:

* * *

(B) Within 30 days of the submission of a final Regulatory Impact Analysis and a final rule under subsection (c)(2);

* * *

(f) (1) Upon the request of the Director, an agency shall consult with the Director concerning the review of a preliminary Regulatory Impact Analysis or notice of proposed rulemaking under this Order, and shall, subject to Section 8(a)(2) of this Order, refrain from publishing its preliminary Regulatory Impact Analysis or notice of proposed rulemaking until such review is concluded.

* * *

(g) For every rule for which an agency publishes a notice of proposed rulemaking, the agency shall include in its notice:

(1) A brief statement setting forth the agency's initial determination whether the proposed rule is a major rule, together with the reasons underlying that determination; and

(2) For each proposed major rule, a brief summary of the agency's preliminary Regulatory Impact Analysis.

* * *

(h) Agencies shall make their preliminary and final Regulatory Impact Analyses available to the public.

(i) Agencies shall initiate reviews of currently effective rules in accordance with the purposes of this Order, and perform Regulatory Impact Analyses of currently effective major rules. The Director, subject to the direction of the Task Force, may designate currently effective rules for review in accordance with this Order, and establish schedules for reviews and Analyses under this Order.

* * *

Sec. 5. *Regulatory Agendas.*

(a) Each agency shall publish, in October and April of each year, an agenda of proposed regulations that the agency has issued or expects to issue, and currently effective rules that are under agency review pursuant to this Order. These agendas may be incorporated with the agendas published under 5 U.S.C. 602, and must contain at the minimum:

(1) A summary of the nature of each major rule being considered, the objectives and legal basis for the issuance of the rule, and an approximate schedule for completing action on any major rule for which the agency has issued a notice of proposed rulemaking;

(2) The name and telephone number of a knowledgeable agency official for each item on the agenda; and

(3) A list of existing regulations to be reviewed under the terms of this Order, and a brief discussion of each such regulation.

(b) The Director, subject to the direction of the Task Force, may, to the extent permitted by law:

(1) Require agencies to provide additional information in an agenda; and

(2) Require publication of the agenda in any form.

Sec. 6. *The Task Force and Office of Management and Budget.*

(a) To the extent permitted by law, the Director shall have authority, subject to the direction of the Task Force, to:

* * *

(3) Require an agency to obtain and evaluate, in connection with a regulation, any additional relevant data from any appropriate source;

* * *

Sec. 9. *Judicial Review.* This Order is intended only to improve the internal management of the Federal government, and is not intended to create any right or benefit, substantive or procedural, enforceable at law by a party against the United

States, its agencies, its officers or any person. The determinations made by agencies under Section 4 of this Order, and any Regulatory Impact Analyses for any rule, shall be made part of the whole record of agency action in connection with the rule.

NOTES AND QUESTIONS

1. Why do you suppose E.O. 12291 is limited to rules and does not apply to adjudications? Might the potential relationship between attempts by the White House to influence agency actions and the application of due process to agency decision making discussed in Chapter 4 play a role?

Why do you suppose E.O. 12291 is limited to "major" rules? Hint: No one knows exactly how many rules agencies collectively issue each year, but the number is somewhere in the thousands. Between one hundred and two hundred of the rules issued in any given year may be characterized as major.

2. If you are head of an agency that wants to avoid White House review of your decisions, you can make all major policy decisions in the process of adjudicating individual disputes. NLRB is famous for avoiding political scrutiny of its policy decisions by announcing all major changes in its policies in the lengthy opinions it writes to resolve adjudicatory disputes. Is that appropriate? What, if anything, can the President or Congress do about the practice? Do you think that the President or Congress want to end that practice?

3. Initially, President Reagan declined to apply any of the provisions of E.O. 12291 and its successors (the Orders) to independent agencies. President Bill Clinton subsequently began the practice of applying the regulatory agenda provisions of the Orders to independent agencies, but to date no President has applied the regulatory analysis or review provisions of the Orders to independent agencies. The Department of Justice and most legal scholars have concluded that there is no legal impediment to applying the Orders to independent agencies. Based on your reading of the cases discussed in this Chapter and in Chapter 2, do you agree with this conclusion? Why do you suppose that Presidents have not been willing to take that step? How would you expect members of Congress to react to such a formal assertion of presidential power over independent agencies? If the President declines to apply the Orders to independent agencies, does it necessarily follow that the President has no influence over decision making by independent agencies?

4. E.O. 12291 repeatedly says that its requirements apply "to the extent permitted by law." Why do you suppose the President included that phrase in every provision that purports to require an agency to take some action? That phrase has enormous implications. Consider the following hypotheticals:

- Assume that you are the EPA Administrator and you are issuing a major rule to implement § 109(b) of the Clean Air Act, 42 U.S.C. § 7409(b). That provision requires the EPA Administrator to promulgate national ambient air quality standards (NAAQS) for air pollutants based on air quality criteria that she concludes are "requisite to protect the public health." In *Whitman v. American Trucking Associations, Inc.*, 531 U.S. 457 (2001), discussed at length in Chapter 2, the Supreme Court construed § 109(b) to preclude cost considerations in the setting of NAAQS. To what extent, if at all, are you "permitted by law" to take the actions required by section 2 of E.O. 12291? To what extent, if at all, are you "permitted by law" to take the actions required by section 3 of E.O. 12291?

- Assume that you are the head of an agency that has just completed a rulemaking that is subject to a statutory or judicial action deadline that has already past. (Statutory and judicial actions deadlines are discussed in Chapter 7.) Are you permitted by law to defer publication of your final rule until OMB has reviewed it?

- Assume that you are the head of an agency that has been ordered by OMB pursuant to section 6(a)(3) of E.O. 12291 to consider a newly available study relevant to a rule that OMB is reviewing. Are you "permitted by law" to consider the study? If so, what else must you do? (You might want to consider this question in conjunction with the requirements of the notice and comment process discussed in Chapter 5.)

5. Agencies and OMB often disagree about the wisdom and/or legality of a rule and/or potential alternatives during the process of OMB review of a rule. When such disagreements occur, the agency often finds itself making arguments to OMB that are, in a sense, the opposite of the arguments they usually make in court. Assume you are the head of an agency that wants to issue a particular rule that OMB finds objectionable. OMB urges you to issue an alternative rule that you and your agency do not want to issue. What arguments can you make? (You might want to consider this question in conjunction with the materials concerning hard look review in Chapter 5 and *Chevron* deference in Chapter 6.)

Major Changes to Executive Order 12291

The most important elements of E.O. 12291 remain in effect. Four years after he issued E.O. 12291, in E.O. 12498, President Reagan expanded significantly the "Regulatory Agenda" requirements from section 5 of E.O. 12291. *See* E.O. 12498, 50 Fed. Reg. 1036 (1985). Every agency must publish regularly, and continuously update, an elaborate regulatory agenda. This requirement is based on the belief that the regulatory review process mandated in section 3 of E.O. 12291 comes too late in the decision making process to have much effect. By the time an agency submits a final rule to OMB, the agency may have devoted a decade or more to the decision making process; it is difficult for OMB to persuade an agency to make major changes in a rule at that late stage. The regulatory agenda requirement is intended to allow political appointees in the White House and in the agencies to learn of a major agency initiative at a point in the decision making process when they can be more effective in influencing the process. It is not clear how effective the regulatory agenda process has been in furthering that goal. In any event, regulated parties, public interest groups aligned with beneficiaries, and lawyers who participate in the agency decision making process find the regulatory agendas extremely useful.

Each President since President Reagan has repromulgated E.O. 12291 and E.O. 12498, often with additions and amendments. President

George H.W. Bush made no significant changes to either. This is not surprising, since he had significant responsibilities in implementing both as Vice President during the Reagan Administration.

President Clinton replaced both E.O. 12291 and E.O. 12498 with E.O. 12866. *See* E.O. 12866, 58 Fed. Reg. 51735 (1993). That Order included all of the basic elements of E.O. 12291 and 12498. The close resemblance between the Reagan/Bush approach and the Clinton approach to control of agencies was somewhat surprising at the time. Candidate Clinton had been highly critical of the E.O.12291 review process, but President Clinton made only three significant changes to that process in E.O. 12866. Persistent critics of the E.O. 12291 review process maintained that OMB often unduly delayed issuance of important rules and that members of the public could not determine the status of a rule once the agency sent it to OMB. Accordingly, E.O. 12866 imposed on OMB review time limits and transparency requirements. Also, E.O. 12866 expanded the definition of a major rule to include any rule that could "significantly hurt the environment, public health, or safety, or diminish the rights of individuals receiving government entitlements, grants, or loans." Lastly, E.O. 12866 created "regulatory policy officers" appointed by agency heads to facilitate compliance with the requirements of E.O. 12866.

President George W. Bush retained E.O. 12866, but later in his tenure issued a potentially important amendment in E.O. 13422. *See* E.O. 13422, 72 Fed. Reg. 2763 (2007). That order expanded the scope of the OMB process to include significant agency "guidance documents" in addition to major rules. As defined in E.O. 13422, guidance documents include policy statements or interpretative rules. We describe the major differences between legislative rules, interpretative rules, and policy statements in detail in Chapter 5. For present purposes, it is enough to note that the process of issuing a major legislative rule is extremely expensive, labor-intensive, and time-consuming; issuing a legislative rule typically requires years. By contrast, an agency often can accomplish roughly similar results by issuing a policy statement or an interpretative rule. Both of those agency actions are exempt from the procedures that make issuing a legislative rule so difficult, so agencies can often issue them quickly and with little commitment of scarce resources. Many agencies have relied increasingly on policy statements and interpretative rules to guide regulated party behavior but avoid the high cost and delay attendant to adopting legislative rules. Until the issuance of E.O. 13422, agencies also could avoid the OMB review process by choosing instead to issue a policy statement or interpretative rule. Presumably, President Bush issued E.O. 13422 to eliminate what he perceived to be an inappropriate loophole in the requirement of OMB review of major rules. E.O. 13422 also required the regulatory policy officers created by President Clinton's E.O. 12866 to be appointed directly by the President, rather than by agency heads. Both of these changes were controversial. Can you think of why that might be the case?

Shortly after taking office, President Obama issued E.O. 13497, revoking President Bush's E.O. 13422 and returning to the Clinton-era E.O. 12866. E.O. 13497, 74 Fed. Reg. 6113 (Jan. 30, 2009). Consequently, President Obama's executive order both removed agency guidance documents from OMB and OIRA oversight and also returned responsibility for appointing regulatory policy officers to agency heads. Also during the Obama Administration, however, OIRA has expanded its role to include coordinator of executive branch review of regulations. When an agency sends OIRA a rule for its review, OIRA sends the rule to every White House office and every agency in government that might have an interest in the rule. If another White House office or agency objects to the rule, OIRA delays its approval of the rule until the White House resolves the differences of opinion between the agency that sent OIRA the rule and the other parts of the executive branch that objected to the rule. Most major rules elicit objections from some other part of the executive branch. Sometimes the objections are based on the merits of the rule and sometimes they are based on the political effects of the rule. The latter have often taken the form of a suggestion that the agency defer issuance of the rule until after either the Presidential election or the mid-term congressional elections. The results of OIRA's performance of these additional roles include unprecedented delay in the review process, major changes to rules as a result of the review process, and widespread OIRA violations of both the time limits and the transparency requirements contained in Executive Order 12866. The expanded role of OIRA has produced intense debate among scholars—many of whom have been participants in the controversial Obama Administration's White House review process. *See, e.g.,* Lisa Heinzerling, *Inside EPA: A Former Insider's Perspective on the Relationship Between EPA and the Obama White House*, 31 Pace Envtl. L. Rev. 325 (2014); Cass Sunstein, *The Office of Information and Regulatory Affairs: Myths and Realities*, 126 Harv. L. Rev. 1838 (2013); Jennifer Nou, *Agency Self-Insulation Under Presidential Review*, 126 Harv. L. Rev. 1755 (2013); Curtis Copeland, *Improving the Timeliness of OIRA Review, Report to the Administrative Conference of the United States* (2013). Is President Obama's approach to agency oversight better or worse than President Bush's approach? How much authority should the President have to oversee the agendas and actions of federal agencies?

In answering these questions, consider the following perspective regarding the evolution of presidential oversight of federal agencies. Although it was written during the administration of President George W. Bush, think about the application of its critique to the Obama Administration's use of OIRA as well.

Peter L. Strauss, Overseer, or "The Decider"? The President in Administrative Law
75 Geo. Wash. L. Rev. (2007).

The accretion of dangerous power does not come in a day. It does come, however slowly, from the generative force of unchecked disregard of the restrictions that fence in even the most disinterested assertion of authority.

All will agree that the Constitution creates a unitary chief executive officer, the President, at the head of the government Congress defines to do the work its statutes detail. Disagreement arises over what his function entails. Once Congress has defined some element of government and specified its responsibilities, we know that the constitutional roles of both Congress and the courts are those of oversight of the agency and its assigned work, not the actual performance of that work. But is it the same for the President? When Congress confers authority on the Environmental Protection Agency ("EPA") to regulate various forms of pollution, on the Occupational Safety and Health Administration to regulate workplace safety, or on the Food and Drug Administration to regulate the safety of food, drugs, and medical devices, is it in the law's contemplation giving the President the authority to decide these matters, or only to oversee the agencies' decision processes?

* * *

The difference between oversight and decision can be subtle, particularly when the important transactions occur behind closed doors and among political compatriots who value loyalty and understand that the President who selected them is their democratically chosen leader. Still, there is a difference between ordinary respect and political deference, on the one hand, and law-compelled obedience, on the other. The subordinate's understanding which of these is owed, and what is her personal responsibility, has implications for what it means to have a government under laws. I cannot improve on the characterization of the problem given half a century ago by Professor Corwin:

> Suppose . . . that the law casts a duty upon a subordinate executive agency *eo nomine*, does the President thereupon become entitled, by virtue of his "executive power" or of his duty to "take care that the laws be faithfully executed," to substitute his own judgment for that of the agency regarding the discharge of such duty? An unqualified answer to this question would invite startling results. An affirmative answer would make all questions of law enforcement questions of discretion, the discretion moreover of an independent and legally uncontrollable branch of the government. By the same token, it would render it impossible for Congress, notwithstanding its broad powers under the "necessary and proper" clause, to leave anything to the specially trained judgment of a subordinate executive official with any assurance that his discretion would not be perverted to political ends for the advantage of the administration in power. At the same time, a flatly negative answer would hold out consequences equally unwelcome. It would, as Attorney General Cushing quaintly phrased it, leave it open to Congress so to divide and transfer "the executive power" by statute as to change the government "into a parliamentary despotism like that of Venezuela or Great Britain with a nominal executive chief or president, who, however, would remain without a shred of actual power."

* * *

To raise these questions is to doubt neither that procedural requirements will sometimes permit private presidential consultations that they do not permit in on-the-record proceedings, nor that when those consultations occur, "undisclosed presidential prodding may direct an outcome that is factually based on the record, but different from the outcome that would have obtained in the absence of presidential involvement." Rather, the question is where legal responsibility for the decision lies. In what frame of mind is this presidential prodding received? Does the recipient of such communications receive them as political wishes expressed by the leadership of her administration respecting how she will exercise a responsibility that by law is hers? Does she think, "In this particular case, Congress confers a discretionary power, and requires reasons if I exercise it. Surely this contemplates responsibility on my part"? Or does she take it as a command that she has a legal as well as a political obligation to honor, and for whose justifications she thus has no particular responsibility?

This is precisely the difference between the oversight and the decisional presidency. In that difference, one may find an ineffable but central question about the psychology of office. Administrative law straddles the difficult, indistinct, inevitable line between politics and law. Save in some inconceivable cyber-age, we could never have a government purely of laws; and we surely do not wish a government just of men. At issue is how we can succeed in applying the constraints of law to the world of politics; and in the argument for a decisional presidency one finds a strong move in the "political" direction. The congressionally specified decision maker, where she is not the President, operates at the head of a professionally staffed agency, charged with decision (and explanation of decision) in accordance with stated and generally transparent procedures and a particular statutory framework. But the President to whom decisional presidency theorists accord a right of decision acts outside these procedures and laws, without their transparency, and subject only to limited political check.

* * *

Distinguishing the legal from the political not only reinforces the psychology of office for the administrator, with its arguable contributions to the reasoned decisionmaking and application of expert judgment that remain major rationales of the administrative state. For presidential administration, it also arms the checks and balances instinct in the necessities of publicly firing a recalcitrant officer, enduring the resulting political reaction, and persuading the Senate to confirm her more compliant replacement. So dramatic a step is not likely to follow from a single disagreement between President and administrator (or, the much likelier situation, presidential staff and agency administration); ordinarily, that will require repeated mismanagement or departures from policies of central importance. These checks are missing if both sides of the conversation inside the executive branch understand and accept that, by law, the President is "the decider" of particular matters.

* * *

Executive Order 13,422, issued by the White House without press release or explanation on Thursday, January 18, appeared in the Federal Register of January 23. It significantly increased White House controls over agency rulemaking. As indicated above, the amendments both added to and subtracted from preexisting provisions respecting the

RPOs that President Clinton's Executive Order 12,866 had required each agency to create to assist in regulatory planning and analysis. Now, an RPO must be a "presidential appointee"—that is, a person both appointed and removable by the President—whose identity would be regularly coordinated with the OMB. Also added was a striking new power for the RPO: "[u]nless specifically authorized by the head of the agency, no rulemaking shall commence nor be included on the [agency's regulatory] Plan without the approval of the agency's Regulatory Policy Office[r]." Removed from the executive order was language tying both the RPO and the agency's annual regulatory plan to the head of the agency. No longer is it provided that an agency's RPO "shall report to the agency head" or that the agency's regulatory plan "shall be approved personally by the agency head." Noted almost immediately by an NGO watchdog, OMB Watch, the amendments were not picked up as a story by the newspapers until Tuesday, January 30, almost two weeks later.

An agency's regulatory plan or regulatory agenda reflects its overall commitments to rulemaking activity. Its priorities for regulation and projected rulemakings appear there long before the formal publication of a notice of proposed rulemaking that commences the notice-and-comment rulemaking process under the APA. It has some obvious connections to the idea of a regulatory budget, long sought by some commentators but not yet established by statute. When President Reagan first elaborated the idea in Executive Order 12,498, Christopher DeMuth, who had responsibilities for these issues in his administration, characterized it as essentially an aid to the political heads of administrative agencies—requiring career staff to reveal their priorities and plans for rulemaking to agency leadership, just as the annual dollar budget process does, and consequently injecting the agency's political leadership into the picture before matters got set in bureaucratic concrete. Seen in this way, the measure supported Congress's assignments of responsibility—it is, after all, on the agency's political leadership alone that Congress's statutes confer the power to adopt rules. To judge by its own actions in measures like the Small Business Regulatory Enforcement Fairness Act, Congress, like the private community, was also attracted by the transparency and added opportunities for broad public participation that early notice of an agency's anticipated rulemaking efforts would provide.

President Clinton's Executive Order 12,866 consolidated the Reagan executive orders on regulatory analysis and regulatory planning that had previously been separate, and in some ways strengthened these measures. It for the first time imposed a structural constraint on agencies, requiring executive agencies to designate an RPO to coordinate general issues under the Executive Order—in effect, to be the agency's designated contact person for OIRA. While there were perhaps hints that the agency's regulatory plan might be used to effect presidential control over agency policy choices, in the intervening years there has been no evidence of this happening. On specific issues of importance to him, as Elena Kagan has detailed, President Clinton would issue directives to particular agencies, but he would do so through his domestic policy office, not OIRA. President Bush's first head of OIRA, John Graham, initiated a practice of occasional "prompt letters" publicly directing agency attention to matters that he concluded might warrant regulation. But a general centralization of actual control over regulatory agendas was never effected—until Executive Order 13,422.

The new executive order purports to confer authority on the RPO to control the initiation of agency rulemaking and, it seems to be intended, its continued processing within the agency. This control appears to run contrary to Congress's judgment about the effect of the regulatory agendas it has required, and has been conferred without statutory authorization. Almost certainly a matter for Congress, the conferral of such authority works a diffusion of political authority within the agency—authority which Congress generally entrusts to the agency head. While statutes often permit an agency head to subdelegate some of her authority to persons she trusts and will take responsibility for, the RPO is to be a "presidential appointee," whose identity is coordinated with OIRA, and who is no longer required to "report to the agency head." While the agency head may override the RPO's judgment in particular instances, it is no longer required that she sign off "personally" on the regulatory plan that now the RPO is to approve. It is at least ambiguous to whom the RPO reports. Anyone aware of the change—the agency head, for example, and the RPO himself—will know that their mandatory relationship and her mandatory responsibility for the regulatory plan have been replaced by a relationship with and responsibility to the President.

Wisely, Congress has rarely permitted agency heads to subdelegate ultimate control over rulemaking, and it certainly would be unwise to permit that to persons controlled by others outside the agency. Congress as well as the President has political relationships with the agency head, and in this political balance the agency head may be assured some independence of action. While the President has a formal capacity to discipline agency heads whose work displeases him, that capacity is sharply limited by the political costs of doing so—including the necessity of securing senatorial confirmation of a successor. A well-connected friend of mine recently remarked that he "personally ha[d] watched two agency heads tell the President to pound sand—they wouldn't do what they were told and the President knew they had the political capital to win." Junior officers, given their responsibilities in a process under close White House supervision, knowing as "presidential appointees" that they can be dismissed by the President (but perhaps not by the agency head) at any moment, and lacking both this political capital and the prospect that their dismissal would have, in itself, political costs for the White House, are not ever going to tell the President or OIRA to pound sand.

Furthermore, the amended order now requires that the RPO be a "presidential appointee," but does not specify what kind of presidential appointee: one who must also be confirmed by the Senate? Or, perhaps, one the President can name without need for confirmation? If it is the latter, then the President has found his way around one constraint insisted upon by the Constitution—that those who exercise major authority in government can do so only with the Senate's blessing as well as his. Then it becomes even more apparent that the President has been able to create a divided administration within each agency, with real power vested in a shadow officer who essentially answers only to him. As my friend also remarked, this would be "disastrous":

> First[,] as a practical matter it takes regulatory power away from the head of the agency where Congress has vested it. Second, it continues the political accretion of power in the bureaucracy of the White House, away from public scrutiny. . . . [T]he worst part from my vantage point is that it treats the agency as a conquered province—the career staff is explicitly told it is distrusted and is not to make recommendations to the agency head but to the White House's political officers. That in turn destroys communication between the staff and the political level of the agency. . . . [T]he agency is quite ineffective when that happens.

* * *

Some may argue that the President is, after all, our chief executive, that our Constitution embodies the theory of a strong, unitary executive; in this light, even if the effect of * * * Executive Order 13,422 is to convert agency judgments about rulemaking into presidential judgments, that would only be accomplishing what the Constitution commands. In my judgment, this argument is not only erroneous, but dangerous to our democracy. The Constitution's text makes the President "Commander in Chief" of the armed forces, but it omits that characterization of his role in domestic government. In domestic government, the Constitution is explicit that Congress may create duties for heads of departments—that is, it is in the heads of departments that duties lie. The President's prerogatives are to consult with them about their performance of those duties, explicitly, and to replace them (with required, and thus politically expensive, senatorial confirmation of their replacement) when their performance of their duties persuades him that he must do so implicitly. Unlike army generals, who may be commanded, the heads of departments the President appoints and the Senate confirms have the responsibility to decide the issues Congress has committed to their care—after appropriate consultation, to be sure—and not simply to obey.

Other Presidential Efforts to Influence Rulemaking

President Bill Clinton began a new form of presidential control of agency action. On 107 occasions, he directed agencies to begin a rulemaking to address a particular problem that he considered unusually important. For example, in 1995, President Clinton initiated a rulemaking to be pursued by the Food and Drug Administration that included six different measures for regulating advertising and distribution of tobacco products to children. In 1999, President Clinton announced and issued a written memorandum directing the Secretary of Labor to develop regulations allowing states to use the unemployment insurance system to provide support for new parents. This degree of presidential involvement in directing agency action is controversial. Elena Kagan, *Presidential Administration*, 114 HARVARD LAW REVIEW 2245 (2001), defended President Clinton's involvement in administrative decision making as an appropriate way in which a President can take a proactive role in the regulatory process, promoting democratic accountability and regulatory effectiveness. By contrast, Peter Strauss, *Presidential Rulemaking*, 72 CHICAGO-KENT LAW REVIEW 965 (1997), has criticized President Clinton's directives as inappropriately politicizing the rulemaking process. What do you see as the advantages and disadvantages of Presidents guiding the regulatory process through such directives? Are there particular circumstances in which a President should or should not take personal responsibility for a rulemaking?

President George W. Bush initiated a program through which regulated firms could nominate rules for reform or even for repeal on the basis that they were no longer needed or unduly burdensome. In 2005, regulated firms nominated 176 rules for reform. The White House concluded that 76 of the rules nominated represented priority reforms, and the OMB directed agencies to prioritize reforming those rules. Is this an appropriate exercise of presidential power? Why or why not?

President Barack Obama has attempted to exert greater control over administrative agencies through the appointment of numerous senior policymakers—colloquially known as "czars—to the White House staff for the purpose of facilitating his domestic policy agenda. Other Presidents have relied on a cadre of deputies and advisers to help them pursue their policy goals, but as Aaron Saiger has documented, President Obama's approach has been unique in a few ways. *See* Aaron J. Saiger, *Obama's "Czars" for Domestic Policy and the Law of the White House Staff*, 79 FORDHAM L. REV. 2577 (2011). First, President Obama has expanded the number of czars relative to his predecessors, up to as many as 50 such appointees. Next, President Obama's czars have been assigned to policy agendas that align quite closely with the portfolios of various Cabinet agencies. Also, many of President Obama's czars possess extensive policymaking experience and substantive expertise in their respective areas of responsibility, rather than political operatives. Indeed, in some instances, the czars have been more senior and more experienced than the Cabinet officials whose portfolios they shared. For example, President Obama appointed former Treasury Secretary Lawrence Summers to direct the National Economic Council in the White House while nominating Summers's protégé, Timothy Geithner, to serve as his Secretary of the Treasury. Similarly, President Obama appointed former EPA Administrator Carol Browner to direct the White House Office of Energy and Climate Change Policy while nominating Lisa Jackson, New Jersey's Commissioner of Environmental Protection, to serve as Administrator of the EPA. Although the Obama Administration has justified its czars as necessary to coordinate regulatory efforts across agencies. According to Saiger, the czars are able to pursue and guide the President's policy goals within the executive bureaucracy without many of the external constraints imposed on Cabinet and other agency officials by the Constitution and by Congress. It is perhaps not too surprising, therefore, that Congress has attempted to curtail the President's ability to appoint the czars as well as the czars' budgets and their duties. *See id.* What do you see as the benefits and costs of allowing the President to expand his advisory staff in this way?

Ad Hoc Jawboning

Finally, beyond the more systematic, if informal, presidential efforts to control agency action, it is important to recognize that every President engages in ad hoc jawboning of agency officials to persuade them to act in ways that he (or his colleagues in the White House) prefers. It is impossible to quantify this method of control or to subject it to careful empirical analysis because most of it takes place behind closed doors. Two recent studies, however, provide partial windows into the dark and murky world of ad hoc presidential jawboning.

In theory, at least, most of the systematic methods of White House control are implemented in a relatively transparent manner by a single office in the White House—the Office of Information and Regulatory Analysis (OIRA) within the Office of Management and Budget. Lisa Bressman and Michael Vandenbergh conducted a study of White House influence over EPA rulemakings that paints a much more complicated picture. *See* Lisa Schultz Bressman & Michael P. Vandenbergh, *Inside the Administrative State: A Critical Look at the Practice of Presidential Control*, 105 MICH. L. REV. 47 (2008). They found that eighteen offices within the White House in addition to OIRA attempted to influence the outcome of major EPA rulemakings during the Presidencies of George H.W. Bush and Bill Clinton. Bressman and Vandenbergh also concluded that the behind-the-scenes efforts of the other offices often were more effective than OIRA's relatively public efforts. "Respondents stated that OIRA had more influence on day-to-day issues; other White House offices had more influence on 'big picture' issues. . . . To further crystallize the point, one respondent commented, 'If asking who kind of mucked around in [rule-making] more, who got into the real details, then OIRA. If asking about big ticket items and who won, the other White House offices." They also found that the other White House offices often took inconsistent positions and seemed to be acting at the behest of some important interest group.

The second study of White House jawboning was conducted by two reporters for the Washington Post, Jo Becker and Barton Gellman. They investigated the manner in which Vice President Cheney exercised influence during the administration of President George W. Bush and then published the results of their investigation in a multi-part series of front-page articles in the Washington Post. In a nutshell, Cheney began by persuading President Bush to appoint about twenty people who were loyal to Vice President Cheney to positions in a wide variety of agencies. A few of Cheney's people were in high positions, *e.g.*, U.N. Ambassador John Bolton, but most were appointed to lower level positions that qualify them as "inferior officers" who may be appointed by the President or a department head without Senate confirmation. Cheney then engaged in ad hoc jawboning by telephone and through his senior staff members in frequently successful attempts to influence the outcome of a variety of agency decision making processes.

From a broad public policy perspective, the most significant incidents reported by Becker and Gellman took place in the context of Cheney's highly successful efforts to shape the manner in which the CIA and other agencies portrayed the situation in Iraq prior to the U.S. invasion. For our purposes, however, the most interesting incident reported by Becker and Gellman was a telephone conversation between

Vice President Cheney and Sue Ellen Woolridge, the *nineteenth ranking* Interior Department official. Becker & Gellman, Leaving No Tracks, Washington Post, June 27, 2007, page 1. According to Becker and Gellman, after the Interior Department announced that it had decided to resolve a major controversy involving releases of scarce waters from dams in Oregon in a manner that would preserve salmon at some cost in the form of reduced crops, Vice President Cheney asked Woolridge to reverse that decision. A few days later, the Interior Department announced the decision's reversal.

Presidents, Vice Presidents, and members of the White House staff always have, and always will, exercise influence over agencies in less formal and less visible ways. The D.C. Circuit explicitly approved of presidential jawboning in *Sierra Club v. Costle*, 657 F.2d 298, 405–06 (D.C. Cir. 1981), discussed at length in Chapter 5; the Supreme Court implicitly did the same when it recognized that the President is "directly accountable to the people" for agency actions in *Chevron U.S.A. Inc. v. Natural Resources Defense Council, Inc.*, 467 U.S. 837, 866 (1984), discussed at length in Chapter 6.

CHAPTER 4

ADJUDICATION

When government agencies act, they typically do so in one of two generalizable formats: rulemaking or adjudication. The following Chapter 5 is dedicated to exploring agency rulemaking. In this Chapter, we consider some of the issues and doctrines that arise when agencies adjudicate.

Agencies adjudicate far more cases than do all courts combined. Much if not most agency action falls into the category of adjudication. Yet, one cannot and should not conceptualize agency adjudication monolithically. Agency adjudications vary tremendously in their complexity, formality, and scope.

Some agency actions resemble nothing so much as court proceedings, with legal adversaries presenting evidence and legal arguments before an independent adjudicator who must evaluate the consequences of past behavior. Relatedly, some agencies use adjudication as a tool for establishing legal policy, issuing published opinions with legal and precedential effect, and articulating therein interpretations of law to which regulated parties are expected to conform their primary behavior. The adjudication category, however, encompasses many agency actions that do not fit these descriptions. Agency officials engage in adjudication when they decide that an individual is eligible for particular government benefits, or when they consider whether or not to award a grant to fund one or another research proposal. An agency official who concludes that a product is subject to an import tariff or who grants a patent to an inventor has conducted an adjudication. Agencies routinely issue licenses or permits authorizing certain private party behavior, and the Administrative Procedure Act (Appendix B) expressly characterizes such agency actions as adjudications.

Agencies use a wide variety of procedures to accomplish these various tasks. In theory, these procedures are outcome-neutral. In practice, however, the procedures that an agency utilizes in adjudicating different matters can have a significant impact on the ultimate resolution of individual matters.

A. THE ROLE OF THE DUE PROCESS CLAUSE

We will begin the process of explaining how agencies choose the procedures they use to adjudicate a class of disputes with an exploration of the requirements of the Due Process Clause of the Constitution.

The Due Process Clause, contained in the Fifth Amendment, provides in relevant part that "no person shall . . . be deprived of life, liberty, or property, without due process of law. . . ."* Only a tiny

---

* The Fifth Amendment's scope is limited to federal government action. The Fourteenth Amendment contains its own Due Process Clause with virtually identical language limiting state government action: "nor shall any State deprive any person of life, liberty, or property,

fraction of procedural disputes involve direct application of the Due Process Clause. Most are resolved by reference to the agency's own procedural rules or to the statutes that govern the agency's choice of procedures. Yet, a simple count of the cases in which agencies or courts invoke due process in connection with agency adjudication would be misleading. Due process considerations play a substantial role in determining which procedures agencies use.

Due process greatly influences agency procedures in several indirect ways. First, when Congress chooses the procedures it requires an agency to use to resolve a class of adjudications, it is influenced by its beliefs with respect to the requirements of due process. Second, Congress often leaves an agency considerable discretion to choose the procedures it will use to resolve a class of adjudications. In that common situation, the agency often relies heavily on judicial decisions that are based on due process-partly because the agency wants to minimize the risk that its procedures will be found to be constitutionally deficient and partly because the agency shares the courts' desire to choose procedures that will yield reasonably accurate results at a tolerable cost.

1. WHEN DUE PROCESS APPLIES

The procedural protections afforded by the Due Process Clause do not apply to every government action with individual implications. First, only certain types of governmental acts raise due process concerns. Second, the act in question must deprive an individual of life, liberty, or property. The following materials examine each of these issues in turn.

a. ADJUDICATION VERSUS RULEMAKING

The influence of judicial decisions based on due process begins with a fundamental distinction in administrative law—the distinction between adjudication and rulemaking. As the following cases make clear, due process requirements attach to agency adjudications, but not to agency rulemaking; hence, the distinction between the two types of agency action is an important one.

The Administrative Procedure Act (Appendix B) defines rules and adjudications, but the statutory definitions are not helpful. "Adjudication" is defined as "agency process for formulation of an order." Although the definition of "order" makes clear that "licensing" is adjudication, the term otherwise is defined merely as "disposition, . . . of an agency in a matter other than a rulemaking. . . ." "Rulemaking" is defined as "agency process for formulating . . . a rule." That leaves the rest of the important work of distinguishing between adjudication and rulemaking to be performed by the definition of "rule." The APA defines rule as "an agency statement of general *or particular* applicability and future effect . . . designed to implement, interpret, or prescribe law or policy. . . ." (emphasis added). With the inexplicable inclusion of "or particular," the APA definition of rule is broad enough to include any

---

without due process of law." Thus, many of the cases in these materials involve interpretations of the Fourteenth Amendment's Due Process Clause, even though only the Fifth Amendment binds federal regulatory agencies.

order issued in an adjudication. The definition of a rule makes reference to future effect, but is prospectivity alone sufficient basis for distinguishing rulemaking from adjudication? The poorly worded statutory definitions of rulemaking and adjudication help to explain why the courts have long relied heavily on the distinction between adjudication and rulemaking that the Supreme Court announced for due process purposes in the following pair of opinions issued a century ago.

Londoner v. Denver

210 U.S. 373 (1908).

■ MR. JUSTICE MOODY delivered the opinion of the court:

The plaintiffs in error began this proceeding in a state court of Colorado to relieve lands owned by them from an assessment of a tax for the cost of paving a street upon which the lands abutted. The relief sought was granted by the trial court, but its action was reversed by the Supreme Court of the State, which ordered judgment for the defendants. The case is here on writ of error. The Supreme Court held that the tax was assessed in conformity with the Constitution and laws of the state, and its decision of that question is conclusive.

The assignments of error relied upon are as follows:

* * *

Fifth. The supreme court of Colorado more particularly erred in holding and deciding that the city authorities, in following the procedure in this Eighth Avenue Paving District, No. 1, of the city of Denver, Colorado, in the manner in which the record, evidence, and decree of the trial court affirmatively shows that they did, constituted due process of law as to these several appellees (now plaintiffs in error) as guaranteed by the Fourteenth Amendment of the Constitution of the United States.

* * *

The tax complained of was assessed under the provisions of the charter of the city of Denver, which confers upon the city the power to make local improvements and to assess the cost upon property specially benefited.

* * *

The fifth assignment, though general, vague, and obscure, fairly raises, we think, the question whether the assessment was made without notice and opportunity for hearing to those affected by it, thereby denying to them due process of law. The trial court found as a fact that no opportunity for hearing was afforded, and the Supreme Court did not disturb this finding.

* * *

In the assessment, apportionment, and collection of taxes upon property within their jurisdiction, the Constitution of the United States imposes few restrictions upon the States. In the enforcement of such restrictions as the Constitution does impose, this court has regarded substance, and not form. But where the legislature of a State, instead of fixing the tax itself, commits to some subordinate body the duty of determining whether, in what amount, and upon whom it shall be levied, and of making its assessment and apportionment, due process of law requires that, at some stage of the proceedings, before the tax becomes irrevocably fixed, the taxpayer shall have an opportunity to be heard, of which he must have notice, either personal, by publication, or by a law fixing the time and place of the hearing. It must be remembered that the law of Colorado denies the landowner the right to object in the courts to the assessment, upon the ground that the objections are cognizable only by the board of equalization.

If it is enough that, under such circumstances, an opportunity is given to submit in writing all objections to and complaints of the tax to the board, then there was a hearing afforded in the case at bar. But we think that something more than that, even in proceedings for taxation, is required by due process of law. Many requirements essential in strictly judicial proceedings may be dispensed with in proceedings of this nature. But even here a hearing, in its very essence, demands that he who is entitled to it shall have the right to support his allegations by argument, however brief: and, if need be, by proof, however informal.

It is apparent that such a hearing was denied to the plaintiffs in error. The denial was by the city council, which, while acting as a board of equalization, represents the State. The assessment was therefore void, and the plaintiffs in error were entitled to a decree discharging their lands from a lien on account of it.

Bi-Metallic Investment Co. v. State Board of Equalization

239 U.S. 441 (1915).

■ MR. JUSTICE HOLMES delivered the opinion of the court:

This is a suit to enjoin the State Board of Equalization and the Colorado Tax Commission from putting in force and the defendant Pitcher, as assessor of Denver, from obeying, an order of the boards, increasing the valuation of all taxable property in Denver forty per cent.

* * *

For the purposes of decision we assume that the constitutional question is presented in the baldest way,—that neither the plaintiff nor the assessor of Denver, who presents a brief on the plaintiff's side, nor any representative of the city and county, was given an opportunity to be heard. . . . On this assumption it is obvious that injustice may be suffered if some property in the county already has been valued at its full worth. But if certain property has been valued at a rate different from that generally prevailing in the county, the owner has had his opportunity to protest and appeal as usual in our system of taxation so that it must be assumed that the property owners in the county all stand alike. The question, then, is whether all individuals have a constitutional right to be heard before a matter can be decided in which all are equally concerned,—here, for instance, before a superior board decides that the local taxing officers have adopted a system of undervaluation throughout a county, as notoriously often has been the case. The answer of this court in the *State Railroad Tax Cases*, 92 U.S. 575 (1875), at least as to any further notice, was that it was hard to believe that the proposition was seriously made.

Where a rule of conduct applies to more than a few people, it is impracticable that everyone should have a direct voice in its adoption. The Constitution does not require all public acts to be done in town meeting or an assembly of the whole. General statutes within the state power are passed that affect the person or property of individuals, sometimes to the point of ruin, without giving them a chance to be heard. Their rights are protected in the only way that they can be in a complex society, by their power, immediate or remote, over those who make the rule. If the result in this case had been reached, as it might have been by the State's doubling the rate of taxation, no one would suggest that the Fourteenth Amendment was violated unless every person affected had been allowed an opportunity to raise his voice against it before the body entrusted by the state Constitution with the power. * * * There must be a limit to individual argument in such matters if government is to go on. In *Londoner v. Denver*, 210 U.S. 373, 385 (1908), a local board had to determine 'whether, in what amount, and upon whom' a tax for paving a street should be levied for special benefit. A relatively small number of persons was concerned, who were exceptionally affected, in each case upon individual grounds, and it was held that they had a right to a hearing. But that decision is far from reaching a general determination dealing only with the principle upon which all the assessments in a county had been laid.

NOTES AND QUESTIONS

1. In *Londoner*, the charter of the city of Denver required the city clerk to publish a notice alerting landowners of the apportionment of costs for improvements to the lots of land to be assessed and inviting those landowners to file written complaints or objections within thirty days. The city clerk followed this procedure, the plaintiff-taxpayers submitted their objections to the assessment in writing within the thirty-day period, and the city council purportedly considered those objections in assessing the taxes. Why was this hearing process inadequate? To what kind of hearing was Londoner entitled?

2. The Court distinguished Bi-Metallic's situation from that of Londoner. What explains the difference between them? Was Bi-Metallic entitled to any sort of hearing before the State increased its taxes? What means of redress do you think Court contemplates for taxpayers like Bi-Metallic who object to the State raising their taxes?

3. The distinction that *Londoner* and *Bi-Metallic* draw between legislation and adjudication remains viable today. The Court relied upon that distinction in some of its most important modern administrative law decisions, such as *Vermont Yankee Nuclear Power Corp. v. NRDC*, 435 U.S. 519, 542 (1978), and *United States v. Florida East Coast Railway*, 410 U.S. 224, 246 (1973), both of which are addressed at some length elsewhere in this casebook. In its 1984 opinion in *Minnesota Board for Community Colleges v. Knight*, 465 U.S. 271, 285 (1984), for instance, the Court emphasized:

> Moreover, the pragmatic considerations identified by Justice Holmes in *Bi-Metallic Investment Co. v. State Board of Equalization* are as weighty today as they were in 1915. Government makes so many policy decisions affecting so many people that it would likely ground to a halt were policymaking constrained by constitutional requirements on whose voices must be heard.

Following the Court's lead, the courts of appeals regularly rely upon *Londoner* and *Bi-Metallic* in evaluating the applicability of due process constraints upon government action. For example, in *Decatur Liquors, Inc. v. District of Columbia*, 478 F.3d 360 (D.C. Cir. 2007), the court characterized as "obviously frivolous" and "absolutely devoid of merit" a due process claim presenting "the classic *Bi-Metallic* scenario"—a statute adopted by a city council prohibiting sales of single containers of beer by all 73 liquor licensees in a particular geographic area plagued by public drunkenness.

4.   The relevance of the *Londoner/Bi-Metallic* distinction extends beyond due process concerns. *Londoner* and *Bi-Metallic* form the basis for the modern relationship between agency rules and agency adjudications, and they remain crucial to legislative and judicial determinations of the types of procedural safeguards that should be provided in various decision-making contexts. Later in this Chapter and in Chapter 5, we will explore the different statutorily-required procedures with which agencies must comply when they engage in rulemaking and adjudication. The courts rely on the principles of *Londoner* and *Bi-Metallic* to decide whether agency action represents rulemaking or adjudication, and thus which statutory procedures the related agency must utilize. *See, e.g., Wisconsin Gas Co. v. F.E.R.C.*, 770 F.2d 1144, 1166 (D.C. Cir. 1985).

5.   Typically, the courts' rely on the *Londoner/Bi-Metallic* distinction as the basis for holdings that due process does not require the government to provide a hearing before it takes an action that adversely affects a class of individuals. Consider the following examples:

- In *75 Acres, LLC v. Miami-Dade County, Fla.*, 338 F.3d 1288 (11th Cir. 2003), rooting its analysis squarely within the tradition of *Londoner* and *Bi-Metallic*, the court determined that a county zoning statute that imposed building moratoria on land under specified circumstances did not trigger due process requirements.

- In *Grand River Enterprises Six Nations v. Pryor*, 425 F.3d 158 (2d Cir. 2005), the court declined to impose a hearing requirement in connection with state laws requiring cigarette manufacturers who opt not to participate in a nationwide settlement agreement to establish escrow funds in case of future damage awards.

- In *Rea v. Matteuchi*, 121 F.3d 483 (9th Cir. 1997), citing Bi-Metallic, the court held that a state law re-classifying some state officers' positions from permanent to at-will employment was generally applicable; thus, the state was not required to conduct a hearing before firing a plaintiff whose job had been so re-classified.

- In *37712, Inc. v. Ohio Department of Liquor Control*, 113 F.3d 614 (6th Cir. 1997), the court determined that due process did not require a hearing before the state could prohibit an otherwise-licensed vendor from selling certain alcoholic beverages, where the prohibition resulted from a plebiscite imposing the same limitation on an entire class of licensees.

- In *Dehainaut v. Pena*, 32 F.3d 1066 (7th Cir. 1994), the court concluded that, where an Executive Order prohibited federal agencies from hiring former air traffic controllers fired for engaging in a strike, a federal agency need not grant a hearing before refusing to consider job applications submitted by such persons.

- In *Interport Pilots Agency v. Sammis*, 14 F.3d 133 (2d Cir. 1994), the court determined that no hearing was required in connection with a state agency policy statement discouraging the use of Connecticut-licensed pilots to steer ships into New York ports.

- In *McMurtray v. Holladay*, 11 F.3d 499 (5th Cir. 1993), relying on *Bi-Mitallic*, the court found that a state law that temporarily removed personnel protections to facilitate a reorganization was aimed at a general class of people; thus, 29 state employees who were terminated in the reorganization were not entitled to due process procedures.

Explaining the *Londoner/Bi-Metallic* Distinction

The distinction between *Londoner* and *Bi-Metallic* can be explained in at least three ways. First, it can be explained on the purely pragmatic basis that the kind of procedural safeguards due process requires for individualized government determinations would be prohibitively expensive and time-consuming if they were required for determinations that affect a large number of people. This explanation fits well with the Court's frequent emphasis on pragmatic considerations. The Court referred to this source of concern in *Bi-Metallic*.

> Where a rule of conduct applies to more than a few people it is impractical that everyone should have a direct voice in its adoption . . . there must be a limit to individual argument in such matters if government is to go on.

The Court reemphasized the pragmatic underpinnings of *Bi-Metallic* in its 1984 opinion in *Minnesota Board for Community Colleges v. Knight*, 465 U.S. 271, 285 (1984):

> Government makes so many policy decisions affecting so many people that it would likely grind to a halt were policymaking constrained by constitutional requirements on whose voices must be heard.

Second, the *Londoner/Bi-Metallic* distinction can be explained based on the nature of the disputed facts on which a government action is based. All government actions necessarily are based on a large number of findings or assumptions concerning many facts. The factual underpinnings of government actions frequently are disputed. As Professor Kenneth Culp Davis famously observed, however, the nature of the disputed facts varies widely depending upon whether the government action in question is legislative or adjudicative. *See, e.g.,* Kenneth Culp Davis, *An Approach to Problems of Evidence in the Administrative Process*, 55 HARV. L. REV. 364, 402–410 (1942).

A determination that an individual committed a crime must be based on findings of historical fact unique to an individual. An individual has a constitutional right to be heard only with respect to resolution of a disputed fact of this type—a fact concerning the individual. Courts refer to facts of this type as adjudicative facts, which usually answer the questions of who did what, where, when, how, why, with what motive or intent; adjudicative facts are roughly the kind of facts that go to a jury in a jury case. Facts related to an individual are intrinsically the kinds of facts that should not be resolved to the individual's detriment without giving the individual an opportunity to be heard with respect to those facts. An individual knows more about the facts concerning herself and her activities than anyone else is likely to know. Thus, an individual is uniquely well-positioned to rebut or explain evidence that bears upon an adjudicative fact concerning her past conduct.

By contrast, a legislative decision to subsidize a particular type of housing is based at least implicitly, and usually explicitly, on factual determinations that the type of housing to be subsidized is particularly valuable to society and that it would not be available in sufficient quantity in the absence of a subsidy. Similarly, the Court based its landmark decision in *Brown v. Board of Education*, 347 U.S. 483 (1954), on factual determinations concerning the effects of educational segregation on members of racial minorities. This second type of fact is a legislative fact. Legislative facts do not describe the individual who is uniquely affected by the government action or that individual's past conduct. Rather, legislative facts are the general facts that help a government institution decide questions of law, policy, and discretion. An individual adversely affected by a government action is not uniquely well-positioned to contribute to the resolution of a dispute with respect to a legislative fact. The most useful sources of data for resolution of disputes concerning legislative facts often are contained in the published literature of the social or natural science disciplines relevant to the legislative fact at issue. Thus, the Constitution permits the institutions of government to resolve disputed legislative facts by relying on sources other than the individuals who are affected by resolution of those facts.

Third, the *Londoner/Bi-Metallic* distinction can be explained based on the theory of government that underlies the Constitution. In his important book, DEMOCRACY AND DISTRUST: A THEORY OF JUDICIAL REVIEW (1980), John Hart Ely argued that the Constitution is principally concerned with providing process of two types:

> [T]he document is overwhelmingly concerned, on the one hand, with procedural fairness in the resolution of individual disputes (process writ small), and on the other, with what might capaciously be designated process writ large—with ensuring broad participation in the processes and distributions of government.

These two forms of process-oriented protection are complementary, as the Pennsylvania Supreme Court recognized in *Ervine's Appeal*, 16 Pa. 256, 268 (1851):

> [W]hen, in the exercise of proper legislative powers, general laws are enacted, which bear or may bear on the whole

community, if they are unjust and against the spirit of the constitution, the whole community will be interested to procure their repeal by a voice potential. And that is the great security for just and fair legislation.

But when individuals are selected from the mass, and laws are enacted affecting their property, . . . who is to stand up for them, thus isolated from the mass, in injury and injustice, or where are they to seek relief from such acts of despotic power?

The Court answered its own question by stating that the only refuge for an individual singled out for adverse treatment is in the judicial process.

The distinction drawn by Dean Ely and by the Pennsylvania Supreme Court has an easy analogy in administrative law. The political process can be trusted to protect classes of people from agency actions adverse to their interests, subject only to two crucial caveats: (1) the judiciary must ensure that the political process can work effectively by enforcing such political rights as freedom of speech and the process of representation; and (2) the judiciary must protect insular minorities from the potential for systematic discrimination by the majority by enforcing the Equal Protection Clause of the Fourteenth Amendment. Thus, there is no need to protect classifications of people (other than insular minorities) through application of the Due Process Clause.

When, however, government singles out an individual for adverse action, the political process provides little protection. Individuals singled out for adverse action can be protected only by forcing the government to use a decision-making process that ensures fairness to the individual. That is the purpose of the Due Process Clause.

DISCUSSION PROBLEM

Federal law allows state authorities that administer public housing projects to evict tenants for drug-related or certain other criminal activities without a grievance hearing only if the Department of Housing and Urban Development (HUD) has determined that state court eviction procedures satisfy due process requirements outlined in federal regulations. Government officials from the state of Washington submitted their state court eviction procedures to HUD for its approval. HUD has decided that those procedures satisfy the aforementioned statutory requirements, and HUD has therefore informed the state of Washington that its public housing authorities may dispense with grievance hearings for crime-related evictions. Federal regulations require HUD to follow certain procedures, including public notice and an opportunity to submit written comments, whenever it engages in substantive rulemaking. HUD did not follow these procedures in deciding that Washington state court eviction procedures satisfy federal due process requirements. HUD claims that it was not required to do so because the decision was adjudication and not rulemaking. Several current tenants of public housing projects in the state of Washington have sued HUD in federal court, claiming that HUD should have followed the rulemaking procedures in reaching its decision. Applying the foregoing materials, consider whether HUD's decision in this matter is rulemaking or adjudication, and thus whether or not HUD was required to satisfy the procedural requirements for rulemaking.

b.   LIFE, LIBERTY, OR PROPERTY

If a court decides that a government action falls on the *Londoner* side of the *Londoner/Bi-Metallic* distinction—*i.e.*, that the action is adjudication—the court then must decide whether the action "deprive[s] any person of life, liberty, or property" and, if so, what process is due the person. Accordingly, judicial opinions considering due process claims often begin by identifying the interest at stake and assessing whether that interest falls within the scope of life, liberty, or property. The courts have struggled with this task.

Prior to 1970, many due process cases rested on traditional, common law notions of life, liberty, or property as an itemized list of separately defined and protected rights. Under this conception, one can ignore the reference to "life." Agencies have vast powers, but none has the authority to deprive a person of life. Courts tended to define property narrowly with reference to the common law, *e.g.*, a government action deprived a person of property only if it took real or personal property from the person. The more abstract liberty included not only freedom from incarceration, but also other traditional freedoms, such as "the opportunity to apply one's labor and skill in an ordinary occupation with proper regard for all reasonable regulations," *New State Ice Co. v. Liebmann*, 285 U.S. 262, 280 (1932), or the choice of parents to send their children to private rather than public schools, *Pierce v. Sisters*, 268 U.S. 510, 535 (1925). Yet, when Dorothy Bailey sought a hearing before losing her civil service job with the federal government for her alleged association with the Communist Party, the court rejected her due process claim with the following brief analysis: "It has been held repeatedly and consistently that Government employ is not 'property' and that in this particular it is not a contract. We are unable to perceive how it could be held to be 'liberty'. Certainly it is not 'life'." *Bailey v. Richardson*, 182 F.2d 46, 57 (D.C. Cir. 1950), aff'd per curiam, 341 U.S. 918 (1951).

In other cases, courts declined to explore the precise contours of property or liberty as separate rights, and instead emphasized a distinction between "rights" and "privileges." By this analysis, while common law rights warranted due process protection, other interests, such as those created by statute and drawing from government resources, were mere "privileges" falling outside the range of the Due Process Clause. Hence, for example, when the Mayor of New Bedford, MA, fired a policeman for disagreeing with him publicly on a matter of public importance, Justice Oliver Wendell Holmes, Jr., then serving on the Massachusetts Supreme Judicial Court, dismissed the policeman's due process claim with the observation that he "may have a constitutional right to talk politics, but he has no constitutional right to be a policeman." *McAuliffe v. City of New Bedford*, 29 N.E. 517, 517 (1892).

The courts were unable to apply the rights/privileges distinction consistently, and eventually this approach to defining the scope of the Due Process Clause proved inadequate. Finally, beginning with the following case, the Court in the early 1970s changed the law under the Due Process Clause dramatically.

Goldberg v. Kelly

397 U.S. 254 (1970).

■ MR. JUSTICE BRENNAN delivered the opinion of the Court.

The question for decision is whether a State that terminates public assistance payments to a particular recipient without affording him the opportunity for an evidentiary hearing prior to termination denies the recipient procedural due process in violation of the Due Process Clause of the Fourteenth Amendment.

This action was brought in the District Court for the Southern District of New York by residents of New York City receiving financial aid under the federally assisted program of Aid to Families with Dependent Children (AFDC) or under New York State's general Home Relief program. Their complaint alleged that the New York State and New York City officials administering these programs terminated, or were about to terminate, such aid without prior notice and hearing, thereby denying them due process of law.

* * *

Pursuant to subdivision (b), the New York City Department of Social Services promulgated Procedure No. 68–18. A caseworker who has doubts about the recipient's continued eligibility must first discuss them with the recipient. If the caseworker concludes that the recipient is no longer eligible, he recommends termination of aid to a unit supervisor. If the latter concurs, he sends the recipient a letter stating the reasons for proposing to terminate aid and notifying him that within seven days he may request that a higher official review the record, and may support the request with a written statement prepared personally or with the aid of an attorney or other person. If the reviewing official affirms the determination of ineligibility, aid is stopped immediately and the recipient is informed by letter of the reasons for the action. Appellees' challenge to this procedure emphasizes the absence of any provisions for the personal appearance of the recipient before the reviewing official, for oral presentation of evidence, and for confrontation and cross-examination of adverse witnesses. However, the letter does inform the recipient that he may request a post-termination "fair hearing." This is a proceeding before an independent state hearing officer at which the recipient may appear personally, offer oral evidence, confront and cross-examine the witnesses against him, and have a record made of the hearing. If the recipient prevails at the "fair hearing" he is paid all funds erroneously withheld. A recipient whose aid is not restored by a "fair hearing" decision may have judicial review. The recipient is so notified, * * *.

The constitutional issue to be decided, therefore, is the narrow one whether the Due Process Clause requires that the recipient be afforded an evidentiary hearing *before* the termination of benefits. The District Court held that only a pre-termination evidentiary hearing would satisfy the constitutional command, and rejected the argument of the state and city officials that the combination of the post-termination "fair hearing" with the informal pre-termination review disposed of all due process claims. The court said: "While post-termination review is relevant, there is one overpowering fact which controls here. By hypothesis, a welfare recipient is destitute, without funds or assets. * * * Suffice it to say that to cut off a welfare recipient in the face of * * * 'brutal need' without a prior hearing of some sort is unconscionable, unless overwhelming considerations justify it." The court rejected the argument that the need to protect the public's tax revenues supplied the requisite "overwhelming consideration." "Against the justified desire to protect public funds must be weighed the individual's overpowering need in this unique situation not to be wrongfully deprived of assistance. * * * While the problem of additional expense must be kept in mind, it does not justify denying a hearing meeting the ordinary standards of due process." * * *

Appellant does not contend that procedural due process is not applicable to the termination of welfare benefits. Such benefits are a matter of statutory entitlement for persons qualified to receive them. Their termination involves state action that adjudicates important rights. The constitutional challenge cannot be answered by an argument that public assistance benefits are "a 'privilege' and not a 'right.' "[8] *Shapiro v. Thompson*, 394 U.S. 618, 627 n.6 (1969). Relevant constitutional restraints apply as much to the withdrawal of public assistance benefits as to disqualification for unemployment compensation, or to denial of a tax exemption, or to discharge from public employment. The extent to which procedural due process must be afforded the recipient is influenced by the extent to which he may be "condemned to suffer grievous loss," *Joint Anti-Fascist Committee v. McGrath*, 341 U.S. 123, 168 (1951) (Frankfurter, J., concurring), and depends upon whether the recipient's interest in avoiding that loss outweighs the governmental interest in summary adjudication. Accordingly, as we said in *Cafeteria & Restaurant Workers Union, etc. v. McElroy*, 367 U.S. 886, 895 (1961), "consideration of what procedures due process may require under any given set of circumstances must begin with a determination of the precise nature of the government function involved as well as of the private interest that has been affected by governmental action."

It is true, of course, that some governmental benefits may be administratively terminated without affording the recipient a pre-termination evidentiary hearing. But we agree with the District Court that when welfare is discontinued, only a pre-termination evidentiary hearing provides the recipient with procedural due process. For

---

[8]   It may be realistic today to regard welfare entitlements as more like "property" than a "gratuity." Much of the existing wealth in this country takes the form of rights that do not fall within traditional common-law concepts of property. It has been aptly noted that

> "[s]ociety today is built around entitlement. The automobile dealer has his franchise, the doctor and lawyer their professional licenses, the worker his union membership, contract, and pension rights, the executive his contract and stock options; all are devices to aid security and independence. Many of the most important of these entitlements now flow from government: subsidies to farmers and businessmen, routes for airlines and channels for television stations; long term contracts for defense, space, and education; social security pensions for individuals. Such sources of security, whether private or public, are no longer regarded as luxuries or gratuities; to the recipients they are essentials, fully deserved, and in no sense a form of charity. It is only the poor whose entitlements, although recognized by public policy, have not been effectively enforced."

Reich, *Individual Rights and Social Welfare: The Emerging Legal Issues*, 74 YALE L.J. 1245, 1255 (1965); *see also* Reich, *The New Property*, 73 YALE L.J. 733 (1964).

qualified recipients, welfare provides the means to obtain essential food, clothing, housing, and medical care. Thus the crucial factor in this context—a factor not present in the case of the blacklisted government contractor, the discharged government employee, the taxpayer denied a tax exemption, or virtually anyone else whose governmental entitlements are ended—is that termination of aid pending resolution of a controversy over eligibility may deprive an *eligible* recipient of the very means by which to live while he waits. Since he lacks independent resources, his situation becomes immediately desperate. His need to concentrate upon finding the means for daily subsistence, in turn, adversely affects his ability to seek redress from the welfare bureaucracy.

Moreover, important governmental interests are promoted by affording recipients a pre-termination evidentiary hearing. From its founding the Nation's basic commitment has been to foster the dignity and well-being of all persons within its borders. We have come to recognize that forces not within the control of the poor contribute to their poverty. This perception, against the background of our traditions, has significantly influenced the development of the contemporary public assistance system. Welfare, by meeting the basic demands of subsistence, can help bring within the reach of the poor the same opportunities that are available to others to participate meaningfully in the life of the community. At the same time, welfare guards against the societal malaise that may flow from a widespread sense of unjustified frustration and insecurity. Public assistance, then, is not mere charity, but a means to "promote the general Welfare, and secure the Blessings of Liberty to ourselves and our Posterity." The same governmental interests that counsel the provision of welfare, counsel as well its uninterrupted provision to those eligible to receive it; pre-termination evidentiary hearings are indispensable to that end.

Appellant does not challenge the force of these considerations but argues that they are outweighed by countervailing governmental interests in conserving fiscal and administrative resources. These interests, the argument goes, justify the delay of any evidentiary hearing until after discontinuance of the grants. Summary adjudication protects the public fisc by stopping payments promptly upon discovery of reason to believe that a recipient is no longer eligible. Since most terminations are accepted without challenge, summary adjudication also conserves both the fisc and administrative time and energy by reducing the number of evidentiary hearings actually held.

We agree with the District Court, however, that these governmental interests are not overriding in the welfare context. The requirement of a prior hearing doubtless involves some greater expense, and the benefits paid to ineligible recipients pending decision at the hearing probably cannot be recouped, since these recipients are likely to be judgment-proof. But the State is not without weapons to minimize these increased costs. Much of the drain on fiscal and administrative resources can be reduced by developing procedures for prompt pre-termination hearings and by skillful use of personnel and facilities. Indeed, the very provision for a post-termination evidentiary hearing in New York's Home Relief program is itself cogent evidence that the State recognizes the primacy of the public interest in correct eligibility determinations and therefore in the provision of procedural safeguards. Thus, the interest of the eligible recipient in uninterrupted receipt of public assistance, coupled with the State's interest that his payments not be erroneously terminated, clearly outweighs the State's competing concern to prevent any increase in its fiscal and administrative burdens. As the District Court correctly concluded, "[t]he stakes are simply too high for the welfare recipient, and the possibility for honest error or irritable misjudgment too great, to allow termination of aid without giving the recipient a chance, if he so desires, to be fully informed of the case against him so that he may contest its basis and produce evidence in rebuttal."

We also agree with the District Court, however, that the pre-termination hearing need not take the form of a judicial or quasi-judicial trial. We bear in mind that the statutory "fair hearing" will provide the recipient with a full administrative review. Accordingly, the pre-termination hearing has one function only: to produce an initial determination of the validity of the welfare department's grounds for discontinuance of payments in order to protect a recipient against an erroneous termination of his benefits. Thus, a complete record and a comprehensive opinion, which would serve primarily to facilitate judicial review and to guide future decisions, need not be provided at the pre-termination stage. We recognize, too, that both welfare authorities and recipients have an interest in relatively speedy resolution of questions of eligibility, that they are used to dealing with one another informally, and that some welfare departments have very burdensome caseloads. These considerations justify the limitation of the pre-termination hearing to minimum procedural safeguards, adapted to the particular characteristics of welfare recipients, and to the limited nature of the controversies to be resolved. We wish to add that we, no less than the dissenters, recognize the importance of not imposing upon the States or the Federal Government in this developing field of law any procedural requirements beyond those demanded by rudimentary due process.

"The fundamental requisite of due process of law is the opportunity to be heard." *Grannis v. Ordean*, 234 U.S. 385, 394 (1914). The hearing must be "at a meaningful time and in a meaningful manner." *Armstrong v. Manzo*, 380 U.S. 545, 552 (1965). In the present context these principles require that a recipient have timely and adequate notice detailing the reasons for a proposed termination, and an effective opportunity to defend by confronting any adverse witnesses and by presenting his own arguments and evidence orally. These rights are important in cases such as those before us, where recipients have challenged proposed terminations as resting on incorrect or misleading factual premises or on misapplication of rules or policies to the facts of particular cases.

* * *

The city's procedures presently do not permit recipients to appear personally with or without counsel before the official who finally determines continued eligibility. Thus a recipient is not permitted to present evidence to that official orally, or to confront or cross-examine adverse witnesses. These omissions are fatal to the constitutional adequacy of the procedures.

The opportunity to be heard must be tailored to the capacities and circumstances of those who are to be heard. It is not enough that a welfare recipient may present his position to the decision maker in writing or secondhand through his caseworker. Written submissions are an unrealistic option for most recipients, who lack the educational attainment necessary to write effectively and who cannot obtain professional assistance. Moreover, written submissions do not afford the flexibility of oral presentations; they do not permit the recipient to mold his argument to the issues the decision maker appears to regard as important. Particularly where credibility and veracity are at issue, as they must be in many termination proceedings, written submissions are a wholly unsatisfactory basis for decision. The secondhand presentation to the decisionmaker by the caseworker has its own deficiencies; since the caseworker usually gathers the facts upon which the charge of ineligibility rests, the presentation of the recipient's side of the controversy cannot safely be left to him. Therefore a recipient must be allowed to state his position orally. Informal procedures will suffice; in this context due process does not require a particular order of proof or mode of offering evidence.

In almost every setting where important decisions turn on questions of fact, due process requires an opportunity to confront and cross-examine adverse witnesses. What we said in *Greene v. McElroy*, 360 U.S. 474, 496–97 (1959), is particularly pertinent here:

> "Certain principles have remained relatively immutable in our jurisprudence. One of these is that where governmental action seriously injures an individual, and the reasonableness of the action depends on fact findings, the evidence used to prove the Government's case must be disclosed to the individual so that he has an opportunity to show that it is untrue. While this is important in the case of documentary evidence, it is even more important where the evidence consists of the testimony of individuals whose memory might be faulty or who, in fact, might be perjurers or persons motivated by malice, vindictiveness, intolerance, prejudice, or jealousy. We have formalized these protections in the requirements of confrontation and cross-examination. They have ancient roots. They find expression in the Sixth Amendment. . . . This Court has been zealous to protect these rights from erosion. It has spoken out not only in criminal cases, . . . but also in all types of cases where administrative . . . actions were under scrutiny."

Welfare recipients must therefore be given an opportunity to confront and cross-examine the witnesses relied on by the department.

"The right to be heard would be, in many cases, of little avail if it did not comprehend the right to be heard by counsel." *Powell v. Alabama*, 267 U.S. 45, 68–69 (1932). We do not say that counsel must be provided at the pre-termination hearing, but only that the recipient must be allowed to retain an attorney if he so desires. Counsel can help delineate the issues, present the factual contentions in an orderly manner, conduct cross-examination, and generally safeguard the interests of the recipient. We do not anticipate that this assistance will unduly prolong or otherwise encumber the hearing.

Finally, the decisionmaker's conclusion as to a recipient's eligibility must rest solely on the legal rules and evidence adduced at the hearing. To demonstrate compliance with this elementary requirement, the decision maker should state the reasons for his determination and indicate the evidence he relied on though his statement need not amount to a full opinion or even formal findings of fact and conclusions of law. And, of course, an impartial decision maker is essential. We agree with the District Court that prior involvement in some aspects of a case will not necessarily bar a welfare official from acting as a decision maker. He should not, however, have participated in making the determination under review.

■ MR. JUSTICE BLACK, dissenting.

In the last half century the United States, along with many, perhaps most, other nations of the world, has moved far toward becoming a welfare state, that is, a nation that for one reason or another taxes its most affluent people to help support, feed, clothe, and shelter its less fortunate citizens. The result is that today more than nine million men, women, and children in the United States receive some kind of state or federally financed public assistance in the form of allowances or gratuities, generally paid them periodically, usually by the week, month, or quarter. Since these gratuities are paid on the basis of need, the list of recipients is not static, and some people go off the lists and others are added from time to time. These ever-changing lists put a constant administrative burden on government and it certainly could not have reasonably anticipated that this burden would include the additional procedural expense imposed by the Court today.

* * *

Representatives of the people of the Thirteen Original Colonies spent long, hot months in the summer of 1787 in Philadelphia, Pennsylvania, creating a government of limited powers. They divided it into three departments—Legislative, Judicial, and Executive. The Judicial Department was to have no part whatever in making any laws. In fact proposals looking to vesting some power in the Judiciary to take part in the legislative process and veto laws were offered, considered, and rejected by the Constitutional Convention. In my judgment there is not one word, phrase, or sentence from the beginning to the end of the Constitution from which it can be inferred that judges were granted any such legislative power. True, *Marbury v. Madison*, 5 U.S. (1 Cranch) 137 (1803), held, and properly, I think, that courts must be the final interpreters of the Constitution, and I recognize that the holding can provide an opportunity to slide imperceptibly into constitutional amendment and law making. But when federal judges use this judicial power for legislative purposes, I think they wander out of their field of vested powers and transgress into the area constitutionally assigned to the Congress and the people. That is precisely what I believe the Court is doing in this case. Hence my dissent.

The more than a million names on the relief rolls in New York, and the more than nine million names on the rolls of all the 50 States were not put there at random. The names are there because state welfare officials believed that those people were eligible for assistance. Probably in the officials' haste to make out the lists many names were put there erroneously in order to alleviate immediate suffering, and undoubtedly some people are drawing relief who are not entitled under the law to do so. Doubtless some draw relief checks from time to time who know they are not eligible, either because they are not actually in need or for some other reason. Many of those who thus draw undeserved gratuities are without sufficient property to enable the government to collect back from them any money they wrongfully receive. But the Court today holds that it would violate the Due Process Clause of the Fourteenth Amendment to stop paying those people weekly or monthly allowances unless the government first affords them a full "evidentiary hearing" even though welfare officials are persuaded that the recipients are not rightfully entitled to receive a penny under the law. In other words, although some recipients might be on the lists for payment wholly because of deliberate fraud on their part, the Court holds that the government is helpless and must continue, until after an evidentiary hearing, to pay money that it does not owe, never has owed, and never could owe. I do not believe there is any provision in our Constitution that should thus paralyze the government's efforts to protect itself against making payments to people who are not entitled to them.

* * *

The Court apparently feels that this decision will benefit the poor and needy. In my judgment the eventual result will be just the opposite. While today's decision requires only an administrative, evidentiary hearing, the inevitable logic of the approach taken will lead to constitutionally imposed, time-consuming delays of a full adversary process of administrative and judicial review. In the next case the welfare recipients are bound to argue that cutting off benefits before judicial review of the agency's decision is also a denial of due process. Since, by hypothesis, termination of aid at that point may still "deprive an *eligible* recipient of the very means by which to live while he waits," I would not be surprised if the weighing process did not compel the conclusion that termination without full judicial review would be unconscionable. After all, at each step, as the majority seems to feel, the issue is only one of weighing the government's pocketbook against the actual survival of the recipient, and surely that balance must always tip in favor of the individual. Similarly, today's decision requires only the opportunity to have the benefit of counsel at the administrative hearing, but it is difficult to believe that the same reasoning process would not require the appointment of counsel, for otherwise the right to counsel is a meaningless one since these people are too poor to hire their own advocates. *Cf. Gideon v. Wainwright*, 372 U.S. 335 (1963). Thus the end result of today's decision may well be that the government, once it decides to give welfare benefits, cannot reverse that decision until the recipient has had the benefits of full administrative and judicial review, including, of course, the opportunity to present his case to this Court. Since this process will usually entail a delay of several years, the inevitable result of such a constitutionally imposed burden will be that the government will not put a claimant on the rolls initially until it has made an exhaustive investigation to determine his eligibility. While this Court will perhaps have insured that no needy person will be taken off the rolls without a full "due process" proceeding, it will also have insured that many will never get on the rolls, or at least that they will remain destitute during the lengthy proceedings followed to determine initial eligibility.

■ [Dissenting opinions by CHIEF JUSTICE BURGER AND JUSTICE STEWART are omitted. Ed.]

NOTES AND QUESTIONS

1. In footnote 8 of its opinion in *Goldberg*, the Court suggests that welfare benefits are "like 'property,'" even though they were not traditionally considered so under the common law. Yet, rather than relying upon such a characterization as the basis of its decision, the Court in *Goldberg* instead emphasized that procedural due process depends upon the extent to which the individual "may be 'condemned to suffer grievous loss'" and whether the individual's "interest in avoiding that loss outweighs the governmental interest in summary adjudication." Does the Court's emphasis on the grievous loss suffered by an individual suggest a shift toward viewing life, liberty, or property as a single, unified concept rather than as an itemized list of protected rights? Would it be better to think of due process in these terms, rather than attempting to categorize interests under the headings of life, liberty, or property? Is the Court's "grievous loss" language incompatible with separate definitions of life, liberty, or property?

2. *Goldberg* marked the beginning of what many have called the due process revolution. In *Goldberg*, the Court expanded the scope of due process dramatically. Before *Goldberg*, the Court probably would have rejected the claim that New York violated the due process rights of AFDC beneficiaries in a brief summary opinion in which the Court stated that they had no property rights in welfare benefits because welfare benefits are not rights but mere privileges. After *Goldberg*, anyone who has a contingent statutory entitlement to anything, including but not limited to welfare, arguably has a protected interest that cannot be deprived without due process of law. Remarkably, the Court made this major change in law without considering any arguments in favor of retaining the status quo. As the Court noted, "Appellant [New York] does not contend that procedural due process is not applicable to the termination of welfare benefits."

The Court relied on only one source to support this revolutionary change in law—the writings of Charles Reich cited in footnote 8 of its opinion. Professor Reich argued that capitalism inevitably produces rich people and poor people; that the U.S. legal system discriminates against poor people by recognizing as property only the intangible assets of rich people and not the intangible assets of the poor people; and, that the Supreme Court should right that wrong by recognizing both a procedural right to welfare and a substantive right to welfare. In other words, Reich argued that the Court should hold that the U.S. must provide adequate welfare benefits to poor people independent of any congressional action. The Court accepted half of Reich's argument in Goldberg, but it has not been willing to accept the other half. Thus, for instance, in Goldberg, the Court extended a procedural right to AFDC beneficiaries because: "Such benefits are a matter of statutory entitlement for persons qualified to receive them." Should the Court adopt the other half of Reich's proposal? Should it have adopted the first half of his proposal?

3. Many government statutes confer opportunities or benefits upon members of the public who satisfy certain criteria. Many government statutes impose obligations upon regulated parties, but within parameters intended to protect those parties' interests. What other kinds of statutes would qualify under the Court's formula as creating due process rights? Would a statute that gives electric utilities in a state a right to "just and reasonable" rates as determined by a government agency create a protected interest under the reasoning of *Goldberg*?

4. In *Goldberg*, the Court held that AFDC benefits are interests protected by the Due Process Clause because they "are a matter of entitlement for persons qualified to receive them." That reasoning fit the language of the welfare statute at issue; the Social Security Act of 1935 provided that an individual was entitled to receive AFDC benefits if she met specified eligibility criteria—basically that she had young children, no assets, no income, and no man in the house who was able to provide support for the children. Congress amended the Social Security Act in 1996 by enacting the Personal Responsibility and Work Opportunity Reconciliation Act. That statute abolished the AFDC program, replaced it with a system of block grants to states for "temporary assistance for needy families," contained no language that entitled anyone to receive the benefits the states are authorized to provide, and underlined the point with an unequivocal statutory declaration: "NO INDIVIDUAL ENTITLEMENT—This part shall not be interpreted to entitle any individual . . . to assistance under any state program funded under this part." Does the amended statute create a protected interest under the reasoning of *Goldberg*?

5. The Court in *Goldberg* requires the state to provide a pre-termination oral evidentiary hearing, including the right to cross-examine adverse witnesses, before a neutral decision maker. The Court reasons that: "Written submissions are an unrealistic option for most recipients, who lack the educational attainment necessary to write effectively and who cannot obtain professional assistance." Consider the implications of this reasoning. Is a welfare recipient who lacks the education necessary to make a written submission likely to be able to cross-examine an adverse witness effectively? If a welfare recipient is unable to obtain professional assistance to complete a written submission, is that same person likely to obtain professional assistance to cross-examine opposing witnesses? Is Justice Black correct in asserting that, under the reasoning of *Goldberg*, AFDC beneficiaries also have a right to state-funded assistance in the form of a state-paid lawyer to represent them in benefits termination hearings?

6. Critique the following claim: the pre-termination hearing required by *Goldberg* will not significantly increase the state's costs of administering the AFDC program because it merely substitutes a judicially-mandated pre-termination oral evidentiary hearing for the post-termination oral evidentiary hearing the state provided voluntarily. Would you expect the number of hearings requested to stay about the same after *Goldberg*? Why or why not? Can you estimate the likely increase in the state's costs of implementation as a result of *Goldberg*? Do you believe that a court can make such an estimate with a tolerable level of accuracy? Should it try, or is that not an appropriate concern for a court in evaluating constitutional requirements?

7. The facts of *Goldberg* involved a situation in which it was easy to characterize the government action at issue as one that deprived a person of an interest protected by the Due Process Clause: the individuals who challenged the adequacy of the procedures the state used had previously been added to the welfare rolls based on a determination that they were eligible, and they were receiving benefits until the state terminated the payments on the basis of its determination that they were not eligible. If you accept the proposition that some statutory benefits are protected interests, then is a person whose initial application for a benefit is denied without a constitutionally adequate hearing deprived of life, liberty, or property without due process of law? The Supreme Court has never answered that question, and the circuit courts are divided:

- In *Mallette v. Arlington County*, 91 F.3d 630 (4th Cir. 1996), the court concluded that a county retirement benefits system promised county employees a property right in potential retirement benefits if they fulfilled certain requirements, and thus that the county's consideration of an employee's application for service-related disability retirement benefits was subject to due process requirements.

- By contrast, in *Kyle v. Morton High School*, 144 F.3d 448 (7th Cir. 1998), the court considered the due process claim of a probationary public school teacher whose contract was not renewed; although many courts have recognized that tenured public school teachers possess property rights in their jobs that give rise to due process protections, the *Kyle* court held that a probationary teacher has no such property interest, observing that his complaint essentially alleged a deprivation of a right to acquire a property interest, rather than a deprivation of an existing property right.

Where a statute contemplates benefits that, post-*Goldberg*, courts recognize as protected interests, should an applicant for such benefits be entitled to the same due process protections as an existing recipient of such benefits?

DISCUSSION PROBLEMS

1. The Social Security Act as amended in 1996 confers on states considerable discretion with respect to the way they provide the "temporary assistance" authorized by federal law. State statutes governing distribution of welfare benefits vary greatly. Assume that a state statute authorizes a state agency to offer reimbursement for medical expenses incurred by disabled children under specified circumstances, but confers discretion on a state agency to provide reimbursement "within the limits of the appropriations made therefor" for "such medical service . . . as in the judgment of the commissioner is needed." Under *Goldberg*, would a disabled child have a protected interest in continued receipt of state reimbursements for payments for medical services?

2. Assume that you are the administrator of the New York AFDC program and that you anticipate that the hearing process that the Court mandated in *Goldberg* will, in fact, increase the costs of administering that program. How would you pay for those increased costs? What result would you expect if you go to the state legislature and/or Congress and ask for an increase in appropriations sufficient to offset the increased costs? (Remember that these are the same legislative bodies that apparently believed that the procedures that the Court required were not necessary and were too expensive.) If the state legislature and Congress refuse to increase appropriations to the extent needed to offset the added costs, what other options might you consider?

———————

Although *Goldberg v. Kelly* is the most prominent representation of the Supreme Court's expansion of life, liberty or property, it is by no means the only such instance. In *Boddie v. Connecticut*, 401 U.S. 371 (1971), for example, the Supreme Court held that indigent individuals have a protected due process interest in seeking a divorce without having to pay filing fees and court costs. In *Bell v. Burson*, 402 U.S. 535 (1971), the Supreme Court recognized continued possession of a state-issued driver's license as potentially "essential in the pursuit of a livelihood" and thus as a protected due process interest. In *Wolff v. McDonnell*, 418 U.S. 539 (1974), the Court concluded that prisoners have a protected due process interest in "good-time credits"—offsets against their sentences for good behavior—granted to them by state statute, and thus that prison officials could not punish prisoners for disciplinary infractions by retracting such good-time credits without due process hearings. The following case offers another oft-cited example of the Supreme Court's expansion of the range of interests protected by the Due Process Clause during this time period.

Wisconsin v. Constantineau

400 U.S. 433 (1971).

■ MR. JUSTICE DOUGLAS delivered the opinion of the Court.

Appellee is an adult resident of Hartford, Wis. She brought suit in a federal district court in Wisconsin to have a Wisconsin statute declared unconstitutional.

The Act provides that designated persons may in writing forbid the sale or gift of intoxicating liquors to one who "by excessive drinking" produces described conditions or exhibits specified traits, such as exposing himself or family "to want" or becoming "dangerous to the peace" of the community.

The chief of police of Hartford, without notice or hearing to appellee, caused to be posted a notice in all retail liquor outlets in Hartford that sales or gifts of liquors to appellee were forbidden for one year. Thereupon this suit was brought against the chief of police claiming damages and asking for injunctive relief.

* * *

We have no doubt as to the power of a State to deal with the evils described in the Act. The police power of the States over intoxicating liquors was extremely broad even prior to the Twenty-first Amendment. The only issue present here is whether the label or characterization given a person by "posting," though a mark of serious illness to some, is to others such a stigma or badge of disgrace that procedural due process requires notice and an opportunity to be heard. We agree with the District Court that the private interest is such that those requirements of procedural due process must be met.

* * *

We reviewed in *Cafeteria Workers v. McElroy*, 367 U.S. 886, 895 (1961), the nature of the various "private interest[s]" that have fallen on one side or the other of the line. Generalizations are hazardous as some state and federal administrative procedures are summary by reason of necessity or history. Yet certainly where the State attaches "a badge of infamy" to the citizen, due process comes into play. *Weiman v. Updegraff*, 344 U.S. 183, 191. "[T]he right to be heard before being condemned to suffer grievous loss of any kind, even though it may not involve the stigma and hardships of a criminal conviction, is a principle basic to our society." *Joint Anti-Fascist Comm. v. McGrath*, 341 U.S. 123, 168 (1951) (Frankfurter, J., concurring).

Where a person's good name, reputation, honor, or integrity is at stake because of what the government is doing to him, notice and an opportunity to be heard are essential. "Posting" under the Wisconsin Act may to some be merely the mark of illness, to others it is a stigma, an official branding of a person. The label is a degrading one. Under the Wisconsin Act, a resident of Hartford is given no process at all. This appellee was not afforded a chance to defend herself. She may have been the victim of an official's caprice. Only when the whole proceedings leading to the pinning of an unsavory label on a person are aired can oppressive results be prevented.

■ [The dissenting opinions of four Justices are omitted. Ed.]

NOTES AND QUESTIONS

In *Constantineau*, the Court identifies a person's reputation as an interest entitled to the protections of procedural due process. Compare the Court's analysis with that in *Goldberg*. Does the Court characterize reputation as a liberty interest, or as a property interest? Does the Court even mention property or liberty? What standard of procedural due process motivates the Court's conclusion?

In the following cases, two of which were decided on the same day, the Supreme Court continued its expansion of the scope of life, liberty or property, but found some limits as well. Arguably, however, the Court's approach to life, liberty or property in these cases contains a different emphasis from that of *Goldberg* and *Constantineau*.

Board of Regents of State Colleges v. Roth

408 U.S. 564 (1972).

■ MR. JUSTICE STEWART delivered the opinion of the Court.

In 1968 the respondent, David Roth, was hired for his first teaching job as assistant professor of political science at Wisconsin State University–Oshkosh. He was hired for a fixed term of one academic year. The notice of his faculty appointment specified that his employment would begin on September 1, 1968, and would end on June

30, 1969. The respondent completed that term. But he was informed that he would not be rehired for the next academic year.

The respondent had no tenure rights to continued employment. Under Wisconsin statutory law a state university teacher can acquire tenure as a "permanent" employee only after four years of year-to-year employment. Having acquired tenure, a teacher is entitled to continued employment "during efficiency and good behavior." A relatively new teacher without tenure, however, is under Wisconsin law entitled to nothing beyond his one-year appointment. There are no statutory or administrative standards defining eligibility for re-employment. State law thus clearly leaves the decision whether to rehire a nontenured teacher for another year to the unfettered discretion of university officials.

The procedural protection afforded a Wisconsin State University teacher before he is separated from the University corresponds to his job security. As a matter of statutory law, a tenured teacher cannot be "discharged except for cause upon written charges" and pursuant to certain procedures. A nontenured teacher, similarly, is protected to some extent during his one-year term. Rules promulgated by the Board of Regents provide that a nontenured teacher "dismissed" before the end of the year may have some opportunity for review of the "dismissal." But the Rules provide no real protection for a nontenured teacher who simply is not re-employed for the next year. He must be informed by February 1 "concerning retention or non-retention for the ensuing year." But "no reason for non-retention need be given. No review or appeal is provided in such case."

In conformance with these Rules, the President of Wisconsin State University–Oshkosh informed the respondent before February 1, 1969, that he would not be rehired for the 1969–1970 academic year. He gave the respondent no reason for the decision and no opportunity to challenge it at any sort of hearing.

The respondent then brought this action in Federal District Court alleging that the decision not to rehire him for the next year infringed his Fourteenth Amendment rights. He attacked the decision both in substance and procedure. First, he alleged that the true reason for the decision was to punish him for certain statements critical of the University administration, and that it therefore violated his right to freedom of speech. Second, he alleged that the failure of University officials to give him notice of any reason for nonretention and an opportunity for a hearing violated his right to procedural due process of law.

The requirements of procedural due process apply only to the deprivation of interests encompassed by the Fourteenth Amendment's protection of liberty and property. When protected interests are implicated, the right to some kind of prior hearing is paramount. But the range of interests protected by procedural due process is not infinite.

The District Court decided that procedural due process guarantees apply in this case by assessing and balancing the weights of the particular interests involved. It concluded that the respondent's interest in re-employment at Wisconsin State University–Oshkosh outweighed the University's interest in denying him re-employment summarily. Undeniably, the respondent's re-employment prospects were of major concern to him—concern that we surely cannot say was insignificant. And a weighing process has long been a part of any determination of the *form* of hearing required in particular situations by procedural due process. But, to determine whether due process requirements apply in the first place, we must look not to the "weight" but to the *nature* of the interest at stake. We must look to see if the interest is within the Fourteenth Amendment's protection of liberty and property.

* * *

Yet, while the Court has eschewed rigid or formalistic limitations on the protection of procedural due process, it has at the same time observed certain boundaries. For the words "liberty" and "property" in the Due Process Clause of the Fourteenth Amendment must be given some meaning.

"While this Court has not attempted to define with exactness the liberty . . . guaranteed [by the Fourteenth Amendment], the term has received much consideration and some of the included things have been definitely stated. Without doubt, it denotes not merely freedom from bodily restraint but also the right of the individual to contract, to engage in any of the common occupations of life, to acquire useful knowledge, to marry, establish a home and bring up children, to worship God according to the dictates of his own conscience, and generally to enjoy those privileges long recognized . . . as essential to the orderly pursuit of happiness by free men." *Meyer v. Nebraska*, 262 U.S. 390, 399 (1923). In a Constitution for a free people, there can be no doubt that the meaning of "liberty" must be broad indeed.

There might be cases in which a State refused to re-employ a person under such circumstances that interests in liberty would be implicated. But this is not such a case.

The State, in declining to rehire the respondent, did not make any charge against him that might seriously damage his standing and associations in his community. It did not base the nonrenewal of his contract on a charge, for example, that he had been guilty of dishonesty, or immorality. Had it done so, this would be a different case. For "[w]here a person's good name, reputation, honor, or integrity is at stake because of what the government is doing to him, notice and an opportunity to be heard are essential." *Wisconsin v. Constantineau*, 400 U.S. 433, 437 (1971). In such a case, due process would accord an opportunity to refute the charge before University officials. In the present case, however, there is no suggestion whatever that the respondent's "good name, reputation, honor, or integrity" is at stake.

Similarly, there is no suggestion that the State, in declining to re-employ the respondent, imposed on him a stigma or other disability that foreclosed his freedom to take advantage of other employment opportunities. The State, for example, did not invoke any regulations to bar the respondent from all other public employment in state universities. Had it done so, this, again, would be a different case. For "[t]o be deprived not only of present government employment but of future opportunity for it certainly is no small injury. . . ." *Joint Anti-Fascist Comm. v. McGrath*, 341 U.S. 123, 185 (1951) (Jackson, J., concurring). The Court has held, for example, that a State, in regulating eligibility for a type of professional employment, cannot foreclose a range of opportunities "in a manner . . . that contravene[s] . . . Due Process," *Schware v. Board of Bar Examiners*, 353 U.S. 232, 238 (1957), and, specifically, in a manner that denies the right to a full prior hearing. In the present case, however, this principle does not come into play.

* * *

Hence, on the record before us, all that clearly appears is that the respondent was not rehired for one year at one university. It stretches the concept too far to suggest that a person is deprived of "liberty" when he simply is not rehired in one job but remains as free as before to seek another.

The Fourteenth Amendment's procedural protection of property is a safeguard of the security of interests that a person has already acquired in specific benefits. These interests—property interests—may take many forms.

Thus, the Court has held that a person receiving welfare benefits under statutory and administrative standards defining eligibility for them has an interest in continued receipt of those benefits that is safeguarded by procedural due process. *Goldberg v. Kelly*, 397 U.S. 254 (1970). Similarly, in the area of public employment, the Court has held that a public college professor dismissed from an office held under tenure provisions, and college professors and staff members dismissed during the terms of their contracts, have interests in continued employment that are safeguarded by due process. Only last year, the Court held that this principle "proscribing summary dismissal from public employment without hearing or inquiry required by due process" also applied to a teacher recently hired without tenure or a formal contract, but nonetheless with a clearly implied promise of continued employment. *Connell v. Higginbotham*, 403 U.S. 207, 208 (1971).

Certain attributes of "property" interests protected by procedural due process emerge from these decisions. To have a property interest in a benefit, a person clearly must have more than an abstract need or desire for it. He must have more than a unilateral expectation of it. He must, instead, have a legitimate claim of entitlement to it. It is a purpose of the ancient institution of property to protect those claims upon which people rely in their daily lives, reliance that must not be arbitrarily undermined. It is a purpose of the constitutional right to a hearing to provide an opportunity for a person to vindicate those claims.

Property interests, of course, are not created by the Constitution. Rather they are created and their dimensions are defined by existing rules or understandings that stem from an independent source such as state law—rules or understandings that secure certain benefits and that support claims of entitlement to those benefits. Thus, the welfare recipients in *Goldberg v. Kelly, supra*, had a claim of entitlement to welfare payments that was grounded in the statute defining eligibility for them. The recipients had not yet shown that they were, in fact, within the statutory terms of eligibility. But we held that they had a right to a hearing at which they might attempt to do so.

Just as the welfare recipients' "property" interest in welfare payments was created and defined by statutory terms, so the respondent's "property" interest in employment at Wisconsin State University–Oshkosh was created and defined by the terms of his appointment. Those terms secured his interest in employment up to June 30, 1969. But the important fact in this case is that they specifically provided that the respondent's employment was to terminate on June 30. They did not provide for contract renewal absent "sufficient cause." Indeed, they made no provision for renewal whatsoever.

Thus, the terms of the respondent's appointment secured absolutely no interest in re-employment for the next year. They supported absolutely no possible claim of entitlement to re-employment. Nor, significantly, was there any state statute or University rule or policy that secured his interest in re-employment or that created any legitimate claim to it. In these circumstances, the respondent surely had an abstract concern in being rehired, but he did not have a *property* interest sufficient to require the University authorities to give him a hearing when they declined to renew his contract of employment.

■ MR. JUSTICE DOUGLAS, dissenting.

Respondent Roth, like Sindermann in the companion case, had no tenure under Wisconsin law and, unlike Sindermann, he had had only one year of teaching at Wisconsin State University–Oshkosh—where during 1968–1969 he had been Assistant Professor of Political Science and International Studies. Though Roth was rated by the faculty as an excellent teacher, he had publicly criticized the administration for suspending an entire group of 94 black students without determining individual guilt. He also criticized the university's regime as being authoritarian and autocratic. He used his classroom to discuss what was being done about the black episode; and one day, instead of meeting his class, he went to the meeting of the Board of Regents.

* * *

There may not be a constitutional right to continued employment if private schools and colleges are involved. But . . . when public schools move against faculty members . . . the First Amendment, applicable to the States by reason of the Fourteenth Amendment, protects the individual against state action when it comes to freedom of speech and of press and the related freedoms guaranteed by the First Amendment; and the Fourteenth protects "liberty" and "property" as stated by the Court in *Sindermann*.

No more direct assault on academic freedom can be imagined than for the school authorities to be allowed to discharge a teacher because of his or her philosophical, political, or ideological beliefs. The same may well be true of private schools, if through the device of financing or other umbilical cords they become instrumentalities of the State.

■ MR. JUSTICE MARSHALL, dissenting.

I would go further than the Court does in defining the terms "liberty" and "property."

The prior decisions of this Court, discussed at length in the opinion of the Court, establish a principle that is as obvious as it is compelling—*i.e.*, federal and state governments and governmental agencies are restrained by the Constitution from acting arbitrarily with respect employment opportunities that they either offer or control. Hence, it is now firmly established that whether or not a private employer is free to act capriciously or unreasonably with respect to employment practices, at least absent statutory or contractual controls, a government employer is different. The government may only act fairly and reasonably.

This Court has long maintained that "the right to work for a living in the common occupation of the community is of the very essence of the personal freedom and opportunity that it was the purpose of the [Fourteenth] Amendment to secure." *Truax v. Raich*, 239 U.S. 33, 41 (1915) (Hughes, J.).

* * *

In my view, every citizen who applies for a government job is entitled to it unless the government can establish some reason for denying the employment. This is the "property" right that I believe is protected by the Fourteenth Amendment and that cannot be denied "without due process of law." And it is also liberty—liberty to work—which is the "very essence of the personal freedom and opportunity" secured by the Fourteenth Amendment.

* * *

Employment is one of the greatest, if not the greatest, benefits that governments offer in modern-day life. When something as valuable as the opportunity to work is at stake, the government may not reward some citizens and not others without demonstrating that its actions are fair and equitable. And it is procedural due process that is our fundamental guarantee of fairness, our protection against arbitrary, capricious, and unreasonable government action.

Perry v. Sindermann

408 U.S. 593 (1972).

■ MR. JUSTICE STEWART delivered the opinion of the Court.

From 1959 to 1969 the respondent, Robert Sindermann, was a teacher in the state college system of the State of Texas. After teaching for two years at the University of Texas and for four years at San Antonio Junior College, he became a professor of Government and Social Science at Odessa Junior College in 1965. He was employed at the college for four successive years, under a series of one-year contracts.

During the 1968–1969 academic year, however, controversy arose between the respondent and the college administration. The respondent was elected president of the Texas Junior College Teachers Association. In this capacity, he left his teaching duties on several occasions to testify before committees of the Texas Legislature, and he became involved in public disagreements with the policies of the college's Board of Regents.

Finally, in May 1969, the respondent's one-year employment contract terminated and the Board of Regents voted not to offer him a new contract for the next academic year. The Regents issued a press release setting forth allegations of the respondent's insubordination. But they provided him no official statement of the reasons for the nonrenewal of his contract. And they allowed him no opportunity for a hearing to challenge the basis of the nonrenewal.

The respondent then brought this action in Federal District Court. He alleged primarily that the Regents' decision not to rehire him was based on his public criticism of the policies of the college administration and thus infringed his right to freedom of speech. He also alleged that their failure to provide him an opportunity for a hearing violated the Fourteenth Amendment's guarantee of procedural due process.

* * *

The first question presented is whether the respondent's lack of a contractual or tenure right to re-employment, taken alone, defeats his claim that the nonrenewal of his contract violated the First and Fourteenth Amendments. We hold that it does not.

For at least a quarter-century, this Court has made clear that even though a person has no "right" to a valuable governmental benefit and even though the government may deny him the benefit for any number of reasons, there are some reasons upon which the government may not rely. It may not deny a benefit to a person on a basis that infringes his constitutionally protected interests—especially, his interest in freedom of speech. For if the government could deny a benefit to a person because of his constitutionally protected speech or associations, his exercise of those freedoms would in effect be penalized and inhibited. This would allow the government to "produce a result which [it] could not command directly." *Speiser v. Randall*, 357 U.S. 513, 526 (1958). Such interference with constitutional rights is impermissible.

* * *

Thus, the respondent's lack of a contractual or tenure "right" to re-employment for the 1969–1970 academic year is immaterial to his free speech claim. Indeed, twice before, this Court has specifically held that the nonrenewal of a nontenured public school teacher's one-year contract may not be predicated on his exercise of First and Fourteenth Amendment rights. We reaffirm those holdings here.

In this case, of course, the respondent has yet to show that the decision not to renew his contract was, in fact, made in retaliation for his exercise of the constitutional right of free speech. The District Court foreclosed any opportunity to make this showing when it granted summary judgment. Hence, we cannot now hold that the Board of Regents' action was invalid.

But we agree with the Court of Appeals that there is a genuine dispute as to "whether the college refused to renew the teaching contract on an impermissible basis—as a reprisal for the exercise of constitutionally protected rights." The respondent has alleged that his nonretention was based on his testimony before legislative committees and his other public statements critical of the Regents' policies. And he has alleged that this public criticism was within the First and Fourteenth Amendments' protection of freedom of speech. Plainly, these allegations present a bona fide constitutional claim. For this Court has held that a teacher's public criticism of his superiors on matters of public concern may be constitutionally protected and may, therefore, be an impermissible basis for termination of his employment.

For this reason we hold that the grant of summary judgment against the respondent, without full exploration of this issue, was improper.

The respondent's lack of formal contractual or tenure security in continued employment at Odessa Junior College, though irrelevant to his free speech claim, is highly relevant to his procedural due process claim. But it may not be entirely dispositive.

We have held today in *Board of Regents v. Roth*, that the Constitution does not require opportunity for a hearing before the nonrenewal of a nontenured teacher's contract, unless he can show that the decision not to rehire him somehow deprived him of an interest in "liberty" or that he had a "property" interest in continued employment, despite the lack of tenure or a formal contract. In *Roth* the teacher had not made a showing on either point to justify summary judgment in his favor.

Similarly, the respondent here has yet to show that he has been deprived of an interest that could invoke procedural due process protection. As in *Roth*, the mere showing that he was not rehired in one particular job, without more, did not amount to a showing of a loss of liberty. Nor did it amount to a showing of a loss of property.

But the respondent's allegations—which we must construe most favorably to the respondent at this stage of the litigation—do raise a genuine issue as to his interest in continued employment at Odessa Junior College. He alleged that this interest, though not secured by a formal contractual tenure provision, was secured by a no less binding understanding fostered by the college administration. In particular, the respondent alleged that the college had a de facto tenure program, and that he had tenure under that program. He claimed that he and others legitimately relied upon an unusual provision that had been in the college's official Faculty Guide for many years:

> "Teacher Tenure: Odessa College has no tenure system. The Administration of the College wishes the faculty member to feel that he has permanent tenure as long as his teaching services are satisfactory and as long as he displays a cooperative attitude toward his co-workers and his superiors, and as long as he is happy in his work."

Moreover, the respondent claimed legitimate reliance upon guidelines promulgated by the Coordinating Board of the Texas College and University System that provided that a person, like himself, who had been employed as a teacher in the state college and university system for seven years or more has some form of job tenure. Thus, the respondent offered to prove that a teacher with his long period of service at this particular State College had no less a "property" interest in continued employment than a formally tenured teacher at other colleges, and had no less a procedural due process right to a statement of reasons and a hearing before college officials upon their decision not to retain him.

We have made clear in *Roth* that "property" interests subject to procedural due process protection are not limited by a few, rigid technical forms. *Bd. of Regents v. Roth*, 408 U.S. 564, 571–72 (1972). Rather, "property" denotes a broad range of interests that are secured by "existing rules or understandings." *Id.* at 577. A person's interest in a benefit is a "property" interest for due process purposes if there are such rules or mutually explicit understandings that support his claim of entitlement to the benefit and that he may invoke at a hearing. *Id.*

A written contract with an explicit tenure provision clearly is evidence of a formal understanding that supports a teacher's claim of entitlement to continued employment unless sufficient "cause" is shown. Yet absence of such an explicit contractual provision may not always foreclose the possibility that a teacher has a "property" interest in reemployment. For example, the law of contracts in most, if not all, jurisdictions long has employed a process by which agreements, though not formalized in writing, may be "implied." 3 A. CORBIN ON CONTRACTS §§ 561–572A (1960). Explicit contractual provisions may be supplemented by other agreements implied from "the promisor's words and conduct in the light of the surrounding circumstances." *Id.*, at § 562. And, "[t]he meaning of [the promisor's] words and acts is found by relating them to the usage of the past." *Id.*

A teacher, like the respondent, who has held his position for a number of years, might be able to show from the circumstances of this service—and from other relevant facts—that he has a legitimate claim of entitlement to job tenure. * * * [T]here may be an unwritten 'common law' in a particular university that certain employees shall have the equivalent of tenure. This is particularly likely in a college or university, like Odessa Junior College, that has no explicit tenure system even for senior members of its faculty, but that nonetheless may have created such a system in practice.

In this case, the respondent has alleged the existence of rules and understandings, promulgated and fostered by state officials, that may justify his legitimate claim of entitlement to continued employment absent 'sufficient cause.' * * * Proof of such a property interest would not, of course, entitle him to reinstatement. But such proof would obligate college officials to grant a hearing at his request, where he could be informed of the grounds for his nonretention and challenge their sufficiency.

NOTES AND QUESTIONS

1.   Compare the Court's conceptions of property and liberty in *Roth* and *Sindermann* with its "grievous loss" reasoning in *Goldberg* and *Constantineau*. Would you characterize the Court's analysis in *Roth* and *Sindermann* as treating life, liberty, or property as a single, unified concept or as a list of separate and distinct items? If the latter, then how does the Court's view of property and liberty compare with its pre-*Goldberg*

definitions? Is the Court's vision of life, liberty, or property in *Roth* and *Sindermann* narrower, broader, or the same as that in *Goldberg*?

2. The Court concluded that Sindermann had both a property interest and a liberty interest protected by due process, and that Roth had neither. Compare Sindermann's circumstances with Roth's. How are they similar, and how are they different? Do you find the differences compelling?

3. Consider the dissenting opinions of Justices Douglas and Marshall in *Roth*. How do their conceptions of life, liberty, or property differ from those of the Court's majority? What would be the effects of a Court opinion that adopts the reasoning of Justice Douglas in *Roth*? What would be the effects of a Court opinion that adopts the reasoning of Justice Marshall in *Roth*?

4. The courts extend the procedural safeguards of due process to all tenured public employees, not just to teachers. Even though the procedural safeguards of due process do not apply to private universities, virtually all private universities extend similar safeguards to tenured professors by contract. Why might the existence of tenure protected by due process in public universities create powerful pressure on private universities to accord similar procedural rights to their professors?

5. At common law, contract rights and property rights were distinct. Each was protected by a different set of remedies. The remedies applicable to property rights were, and are, more powerful than the remedies applicable to contract rights. The Framers of the Constitution referred to property in the Due Process Clauses of the Fifth and Fourteenth Amendments; they referred to contracts in section 10 of Article I: "No state shall . . . pass any . . . Law impairing the Obligation of Contracts." Does the Framers' failure to mention contracts in connection with due process suggest that the Framers intended to exclude government contract rights from the scope of property protected by due process? If not, should the definition of property for due process purposes extend to all government contracts, or just to government employment contracts? The Supreme Court has never extended the scope of due process to include other types of government contracts, and lower courts have explicitly refused to extend it beyond employment contracts. *See, e.g., S & D Maint. Co. v. Goldin*, 844 F.2d 962 (2d Cir. 1988). What justifications can you imagine for treating different types of government contracts differently? What would be the effect of extending due process protection to rights under contracts to supply paper clips or ammunition to the government? For discussion of the many issues raised by the Court's decision to extend due process protection to government employment contracts, see Note, *Breach of Contract as a Due Process Violation: Can the Constitution Be a Font of Contract Law?*, 90 COLUM. L. REV. 1098 (1990).

6. The opinions in *Roth* and *Sindermann* discuss liberty interests as well as property interests protected by due process. As the Court's discussion in *Roth* indicates, however, the Court has always defined liberty more broadly to encompass interests beyond freedom from incarceration. Further, by the time it decided both *Roth* and *Sindermann*, the Court had rejected the parsimonious interpretation of liberty illustrated by Justice Holmes's famous statement in *McAuliffe v. Mayor of New Bedford*, 29 N.E. 517 (1892), mentioned earlier in this Chapter, that a policeman fired for speaking his mind "may have a constitutional right to talk politics, but he has no constitutional right to be a policeman." *Id.* at 220. By the time the Supreme Court decided *Roth* and *Sindermann*, it had adopted the unconstitutional conditions doctrine—*i.e.*, government cannot condition the availability of a benefit such as a government job on an individual's willingness to relinquish a constitutional right. Do you understand why Sindermann arguably fell within the scope of the unconstitutional conditions doctrine independent of whether he had a property interest in his job? Do you understand why the Court remanded the case to the district court to resolve that issue?

Paul v. Davis

424 U.S. 693 (1976).

■ MR. JUSTICE REHNQUIST delivered the opinion of the Court.

We granted certiorari in this case to consider whether respondent's charge that petitioners' defamation of him, standing alone and apart from any other governmental action with respect to him, stated a claim for relief under 42 U.S.C. § 1983 and the Fourteenth Amendment. For the reasons hereinafter stated, we conclude that it does not.

Petitioner Paul is the Chief of Police of the Louisville, Ky., Division of Police, while petitioner McDaniel occupies the same position in the Jefferson County, Ky., Division of Police. In late 1972 they agreed to combine their efforts for the purpose of alerting local area merchants to possible shoplifters who might be operating during the Christmas season. In early December petitioners distributed to approximately 800 merchants in the Louisville metropolitan area a "flyer," which began as follows:

"TO: BUSINESS MEN IN THE METROPOLITAN AREA

"The Chiefs of The Jefferson County and City of Louisville Police Departments, in an effort to keep their officers advised on shoplifting activity, have approved the attached alphabetically arranged flyer of subjects known to be active in this criminal field.

"This flyer is being distributed to you, the business man, so that you may inform your security personnel to watch for these subjects. These persons have been arrested during 1971 and 1972 or have been active in various criminal fields in high density shopping areas.

"Only the photograph and name of the subject is shown on this flyer, if additional information is desired, please forward a request in writing. . . ."

The flyer consisted of five pages of "mug shot" photos, arranged alphabetically. Each page was headed:

"NOVEMBER 1972

CITY OF LOUISVILLE

JEFFERSON COUNTY

POLICE DEPARTMENTS

ACTIVE SHOPLIFTERS"

In approximately the center of page 2 there appeared photos and the name of the respondent, Edward Charles Davis III.

Respondent appeared on the flyer because on June 14, 1971, he had been arrested in Louisville on a charge of shoplifting. He had been arraigned on this charge in September 1971, and, upon his plea of not guilty, the charge had been "filed away with leave [to reinstate]," a disposition which left the charge outstanding. Thus, at the time petitioners caused the flyer to be prepared and circulated respondent had been charged with shoplifting but his guilt or innocence of that offense had never been resolved. Shortly after circulation of the flyer the charge against respondent was finally dismissed by a judge of the Louisville Police Court.

* * *

Respondent's due process claim is grounded upon his assertion that the flyer, and in particular the phrase "Active Shoplifters" appearing at the head of the page upon which his name and photograph appear, impermissibly deprived him of some "liberty" protected by the Fourteenth Amendment. His complaint asserted that the "active shoplifter" designation would inhibit him from entering business establishments for fear of being suspected of shoplifting and possibly apprehended, and would seriously impair his future employment opportunities.

* * *

The second premise upon which the result reached by the Court of Appeals could be rested—that the infliction by state officials of a "stigma" to one's reputation is somehow different in kind from infliction by a state official of harm to other interests protected by state law—is equally untenable. The words "liberty" and "property" as used in the Fourteenth Amendment do not in terms single out reputation as a candidate for special protection over and above other interests that may be protected by state law. While we have in a number of our prior cases pointed out the frequently drastic effect of the "stigma" which may result from defamation by the government in a variety of contexts, this line of cases does not establish the proposition that reputation alone, apart from some more tangible interests such as employment, is either "liberty" or "property" by itself sufficient to invoke the procedural protection of the Due Process Clause. As we have said, the Court of Appeals, in reaching a contrary conclusion, relied primarily upon *Wisconsin v. Constantineau*, 400 U.S. 433 (1971). We think the correct import of that decision, however, must be derived from an examination of the precedents upon which it relied, as well as consideration of the other decisions by this Court, before and after *Constantineau*, which bear upon the relationship between governmental defamation and the guarantees of the Constitution. While not uniform in their treatment of the subject, we think that the weight of our decisions establishes no constitutional doctrine converting every defamation by a public official into a deprivation of liberty within the meaning of the Due Process Clause of the Fifth or Fourteenth Amendment.

* * *

There is undoubtedly language in *Constantineau*, which is sufficiently ambiguous to justify the reliance upon it by the Court of Appeals:

> Yet certainly where the State attaches "a badge of infamy" to the citizen, due process comes into play. *Wieman v. Updegraff*, 344 U.S. 183, 191 (1952). "[T]he right to be heard before being condemned to suffer grievous loss of any kind, even though it may not involve the stigma and hardships of a criminal conviction, is a principle basic to our society." *Joint Anti-Fascist Comm. v. McGrath*, 341 U.S. 123, 168 (1951) (Frankfurter, J., concurring).

> Where a person's good name, reputation, honor, or integrity is at stake *because of what the government is doing to him*, notice and an opportunity to be heard are essential.

Constantineau, 400 U.S. at 437 (emphasis supplied). The last paragraph of the quotation could be taken to mean that if a government official defames a person, without more, the procedural requirements of the Due Process Clause of the Fourteenth Amendment are brought into play. If read that way, it would represent a significant broadening of the holdings of *Wieman v. Updegraff*, 344 U.S. 183 (1952), and *Joint Anti-Fascist Committee v. McGrath*, 341 U.S. 123 (1951), relied upon by the *Constantineau* Court in its analysis in the immediately preceding paragraph. We should not read this language as significantly broadening those holdings without in any way adverting to the fact if there is any other possible interpretation of *Constantineau*'s language. We believe there is.

We think that the italicized language in the last sentence quoted, "because of what the government is doing to him," referred to the fact that the governmental action taken in that case deprived the individual of a right previously held under state law—the right to purchase or obtain liquor in common with the rest of the citizenry. "Posting," therefore, significantly altered her status as a matter of state law, and it was that alteration of legal status which, combined with the injury resulting from the defamation, justified the invocation of procedural safeguards. The "stigma" resulting from the defamatory character of the posting was doubtless an important factor in evaluating the extent of harm worked by that act, but we do not think that such defamation, standing alone, deprived Constantineau of any "liberty" protected by the procedural guarantees of the Fourteenth Amendment.

■ [The dissenting opinion of three Justices is omitted. Ed.]

NOTES AND QUESTIONS

1. Compare the Court's analysis of the stigmatizing effects of government action in *Paul* with that in *Constantineau* and in *Roth*. Does Justice Rehnquist persuade you that the Court did not expand the scope of liberty to include official stigmatization in *Constantineau*, or would it be more accurate to say that the Court expanded the scope of liberty in *Constantineau* and then reduced it in *Paul*?

2. As modified by *Paul*, *Constantineau* is now universally interpreted to adopt the "stigma plus" test. Under this test, loss of some tangible government benefit that is not protected by due process, *e.g.*, an untenured government job, plus official stigmatization, which is not protected by due process, adds up to "stigma plus," which is protected by due process. Students who did well in first grade math may have difficulty understanding the stigma plus test. Under the Court's version of addition, 0 plus 0 equals 1.

Whatever you might think about the logic of the stigma plus test, it is the subject of a great deal of litigation to determine its boundaries. Thus, for instance, all courts agree that the stigmatization must be contemporaneous with the deprivation of the tangible benefit, but courts differ with respect to such important details as whether placement of a statement of stigmatizing reasons for firing an untenured employee in an agency's records at the time the employee is fired qualifies as contemporaneous stigmatization even if the stigmatizing reason is not disclosed to any member of the public until sometime after the employee is fired. The stigma plus test has enormous practical implications for government agencies.

3.   The years since *Goldberg* have seen a retreat on another dimension as well—reductions in the scope of the interests that are protected by due process. In some cases, reductions in the scope of due process have been accomplished by legislative action, *i.e.*, the repeal of the AFDC statute that was the subject of *Goldberg* and its replacement by a new federal welfare statute that is worded in such a way that it cannot possibly be the basis for a holding that it creates "property" within the meaning of *Goldberg*. (This point was discussed in note 4 following *Goldberg*, *supra*.) Of course, legislative bodies are unlikely to eliminate all statutory forms of "property" through that mechanism. It is unlikely, for instance, that Congress will amend the Social Security Act to eliminate the contingent entitlement nature of social security benefits. Why was welfare vulnerable to such a congressional change in status, while social security is at least much less vulnerable to such a change?

4.   In some important contexts, the Supreme Court itself has reduced significantly the scope of the interests protected by due process. The Court's revolutionary expansion of the scope of interests protected by due process in the early 1970s included several cases in which the Court defined liberty to include many interests of prisoners. In its early decisions in the prisoner context, the Court defined the scope of the liberty interest by reference to two criteria: (1) the degree of the restraint on liberty, *i.e.*, whether the prisoner had suffered a grievous loss; and (2) whether the interest was recognized by a statute or rule that limited the discretion of prison personnel. In subsequent cases, however, the Court seemed to ignore the first criterion and to focus entirely on the second criterion. This created an unfortunate situation. During the early 1990s, prisoners filed over 25,000 suits per year in which they alleged violations of their due process rights to liberty predicated on alleged violations of prison rules. A high proportion of these cases involved alleged deprivations of trivial "rights." For example, *Burgin v. Nix*, 899 F.2d 733 (8th Cir. 1990), involved a prisoner's allegation that prison authorities deprived him of his right to a tray lunch, rather than a box lunch, without complying with due process.

The Court eliminated that problem by making a major change in the scope of the protected liberty interests of prisoners in *Sandin v. Conner*, 515 U.S. 472 (1995). The Court held that a prisoner has a liberty interest protected by due process only when prison authorities impose "atypical and significant hardship on the inmate in relation to the normal incidents of life." The majority concluded that the action taken by the prison authorities in the case before it—disciplinary action in the form of 30 days in solitary confinement—did not satisfy the threshold for a deprivation of protected liberty in the circumstances presented. Those circumstances included a confinement system in which solitary confinement did not differ materially from the conditions in which many other inmates were confined. The majority emphasized that its holding was predicated in part on its concern that the Court's prior near-exclusive emphasis on the existence or nonexistence of a rule limiting the discretion of prison personnel was having the unintended and highly undesirable effect of discouraging prison authorities from issuing rules that limited the discretion of prison employees.

DISCUSSION PROBLEMS

1. Assume that you are principal of a public junior high school. You have gotten several report from reliable sources that John Jones, a seventh grade teacher, has engaged in sexual relations with several of his thirteen-year old students. In each case, the student reportedly agreed to have sex with Mr. Jones after he mentioned that the student was in danger of failing but that he might be able to help the student avoid that fate in return for "friendship."

Mr. Jones was hired twenty months ago. He is now teaching under a one-year contract that expires at the end of this school year. A state statute provides that a public school teacher can only be fired "for cause" after the teacher has completed two years of service. Assuming that you want to terminate Mr. Jones, you have three options: (1) conduct a thorough six-month investigation of his conduct to decide whether to terminate him; (2) terminate him immediately for engaging in sexual misconduct with his students; or, (3) terminate him immediately without providing any reason or providing a reason unrelated to his conduct, *e.g.*, the school discovered that it could not afford all of its teachers, so it declined to rehire its newest teacher. Which choice would you make?

2. In its efforts to protect national security, the Transportation Security Administration (TSA), a division of the Department of Homeland Security, has established a transportation watch list system, known colloquially as the "no fly list," that prohibits listed persons from boarding and traveling on airplanes. In December 2004, Congress included language in the Intelligence Reform and Terrorism Prevention Act requiring the TSA to "establish a procedure to enable airline passengers who are delayed or prohibited from boarding a flight" due to their placement on the no fly list that would allow those passengers to "appeal such determination and correct information contained in the system." Does placement on the no fly list implicate procedural due process concerns?

2. PROCEDURES REQUIRED BY DUE PROCESS

The period from 1970 to 1975 is generally referred to as the period of the "due process revolution." As we have seen, during that five-year period, the Court issued many opinions in which it expanded dramatically the scope of due process and conferred powerful (and expensive) procedural rights on the many millions of beneficiaries of the newly-enlarged scope of due process protection. The Court has retreated to some extent in its definition of liberty and property since that revolutionary period. Yet, this is only one dimension of the Court's retreat from *Goldberg*.

The Due Process Clause does not preclude the government from depriving persons of their life, liberty, or property. Rather, the Due Process Clause merely requires that such a deprivation be accomplished through "due process of law." Thus, once it is apparent that government action implicates life, liberty, or property, the question becomes exactly what process the Due Process Clause requires to support a deprivation of that interest.

Prior to 1970, due process jurisprudence recognized that the government must provide some sort of hearing before depriving a person of a protected liberty or property interest, but the scope of such a hearing requirement was not always clear. Again, *Goldberg v. Kelly* was instrumental in affecting legal change.

Recall the array of procedures the Court imposed in *Goldberg* upon states seeking to withdraw eligibility for AFDC benefits, including but not limited to the opportunity to present one's position orally, to confront and cross-examine witnesses, to retain counsel, and to have one's case decided by an impartial decisionmaker. In the years immediately following *Goldberg*, courts extended these procedural requirements to many other government benefit and regulatory programs. Most courts interpreted *Goldberg* to require the government to provide an oral evidentiary hearing before it deprived anyone of "property" in the form of a contingent statutory entitlement; since many other regulatory and benefit programs are governed by statutes that include provisions worded as contingent entitlements, *Goldberg* formed the basis for other, similar holdings.

Agencies and legislators across the country complained that they were unable to implement a wide variety of benefit and regulatory programs efficiently and effectively because of the high cost and decisional delay created by the increasingly widespread judicial demand that agencies conduct pre-deprivation oral evidentiary hearings. Moreover, many scholars concluded that pre-deprivation oral evidentiary hearings were expensive and burdensome, and that they often were less effective than a wide variety of far less expensive and less burdensome procedures for making decisions. *See, e. g.*, Jerry Mashaw, *The Management Side of Due Process*, 59 CORNELL L. REV. 772 (1974). Furthermore, it was quickly apparent that the predictions of Justice Black's dissenting opinion in *Goldberg* were accurate. Justice Black predicted that the pre-deprivation oral evidentiary hearings would be expensive; that legislatures would be unwilling to increase the appropriations to agencies to the extent needed to offset those increased costs; and that, as a result, the intended beneficiaries of the Court's decision would bear the high costs of the decision in various ways, *e.g.*, welfare authorities would not add a new applicant to the list of beneficiaries until after they conducted an investigation of the applicant's eligibility.

The following excerpt from an article by Judge Henry Friendly, a highly-respected member of the Second Circuit, offered further criticism of the Court's opinion in *Goldberg*. *See* Henry J. Friendly, *Some Kind of*

Hearing, 123 U. PA. L. REV. 1267 (1975). The entire article is well worth reading, but the following brief excerpts provide the flavor of Judge Friendly's critical analysis of the Court's opinion in *Goldberg*:

> My rather enigmatic title, "Some Kind of Hearing," is drawn from an opinion by Mr. Justice White rendered not quite a year ago. He stated, "The Court has consistently held that some kind of hearing is required at some time before a person is finally deprived of his property interests." *Wolff v. McDonnell*, 418 U.S. 539, 557–58 (1974). The Court went on to hold that the same not altogether pellucid requirement prevailed where the deprivation was of liberty.
>
> Despite the efforts by some of the Justices to find roots for so broad a constitutional principle deep in the past, these had produced only a few Supreme Court constitutional decisions with respect to executive or administrative action until *Goldberg v. Kelly* in 1970. Since then we have witnessed a due process explosion in which the Court has carried the hearing requirement from one new area of government action to another, an explosion which gives rise to many questions of major importance to our society. Should the executive be placed in a position where it can take no action affecting a citizen without a hearing? When a hearing is required, what kind of hearing must it be? Specifically, how closely must it conform to the judicial model?

* * *

> The term "hearing," like "jurisdiction," is "a verbal coat of too many colors." *United States v. Tucker Truck Lines, Inc.*, 344 U.S. 33, 39 (1952) (Frankfurter, J., dissenting). Professor Davis has defined it as "any oral proceeding before a tribunal." 1 K. DAVIS, ADMINISTRATIVE LAW TREATISE § 7.01, at 407 (1958). Broad as that definition is, it may not be broad enough. Although the term "hearing" has an oral connotation, I see no reason why in some circumstances a "hearing" may not be had on written materials only. In addition the term "tribunal" is hardly apt to convey the notion that hearing requirements may be applied to bodies as diverse as an administrative law judge on the one hand or a city council on the other. The purpose of the hearing may range from the determination of a specific past event—did a government employee steal $50?—to an endeavor to ascertain community feeling about a proposed change in zoning or to determine the efficacy of a new drug.

* * *

> Good sense would suggest that there must be some floor below which no hearing of any sort is required. One wonders whether even the most outspoken of the Justices would require one on the complaint of an AFDC recipient, recounted by Professor Bernard Schwartz, that "I didn't receive one housedress, underwears . . . They gave me two underwears for $14.10 . . . it should have been $17.60 instead of $14.10." B. SCHWARTZ & H. WADE, LEGAL CONTROL OF GOVERNMENT 123 (1972). Although

the value of even small benefits should not be deprecated, given the precarious financial condition of the recipients of AFDC, the cost of providing an evidentiary hearing in such a case must so far outweigh the likelihood or the value of more accurate determinations that final reliance should be placed on the informed good faith of program administrators.

* * *

Perhaps there is more profit in the inquiry, if a hearing, what kind of hearing, to which I now turn.

* * *

The most debated issue is the right of confrontation.

Since the only provision in the Bill of Rights conferring the right of confrontation is limited to criminal cases, one might think the constitutional right of cross-examination was similarly confined. However, in *Greene v. McElroy*, Chief Justice Warren said that the Court had applied this principle "in all types of cases where administrative and regulatory actions were under scrutiny." 360 U.S. 474, 497 (1959). Lofty sentiments on this score are usually accompanied by references to a passage in the Acts of the Apostles, ignoring that it referred to a situation where a man was to be delivered to die, and to Wigmore's statement that cross-examination "is beyond any doubt the greatest legal engine ever invented for the discovery of truth," ignoring that most of the world's legal systems, which are equally intent on discovering the truth, have not seen fit to import the engine. 5 J. WIGMORE, EVIDENCE § 1367, at 32 (1974). Other favorites are characters as diverse as the Emperor Trajan and Wild Bill Hickok of Abilene, Kansas, immortalized by President Eisenhower. Eloquent statements have been made, notably by Mr. Justice Douglas.

While agreeing that these references were wholly appropriate to the witch-hunts of the McCarthy era and that cross-examination is often useful, one must query their universal applicability to the thousands of hearings on welfare, social security benefits, housing, prison discipline, education, and the like which are now held every month—not to speak of hearings on recondite scientific or economic subjects. In many such cases the main effect of cross-examination is delay—an argument not really answered, as any trial judge will confirm, by the easy suggestion that the hearing officer can curtail cross-examination. Lawyers, including those who have gone on the bench, have a vivid recall of the few instances where they destroyed a dishonest witness on cross-examination and forget those where their cross-examination confused an honest one or was ineffective or worse—not to speak of the many cases when they had the good judgment to say "No questions."

* * *

We have traveled over wide areas—from termination of welfare payments to the establishment of incentive per diem for freight cars, from student and prison discipline to rates for natural gas. Yet the problem is always the same—to devise procedures that are both fair and feasible.

In this task we still have far to go. In the mass justice area the Supreme Court has yielded too readily to the notions that the adversary system is the only appropriate model and that there is only one acceptable solution to any problem, and consequently has been too prone to indulge in constitutional codification. There is need for experimentation, particularly for the use of the investigative model, for empirical studies, and for avoiding absolutes. While the Court has been too rigid in some ways, it has been too vague in others. Apart from the field of creditors' preliminary remedies, the lower courts have been furnished little in the way of principle that will enable them to decide with fair assurance as new situations develop. One source of the difficulty has stemmed from the Court's pulling practically all the procedural stops in *Goldberg*, * * * While I applaud the Court's basic initiatives with respect to administrative hearings, the time for some new thinking and also for some tidying up has arrived.

Facing all of this criticism, it is perhaps not surprising that the Supreme Court has since backed away from *Goldberg*'s requirements and required fewer procedures to satisfy due process in other contexts. Indeed, some believe that the retreat from *Goldberg* began with the Court's 1976 opinion in the following case.

Mathews v. Eldridge

424 U.S. 319 (1976).

■ MR. JUSTICE POWELL delivered the opinion of the Court.

The issue in this case is whether the Due Process Clause of the Fifth Amendment requires that prior to the termination of Social Security disability benefit payments the recipient be afforded an opportunity for an evidentiary hearing.

I

Cash benefits are provided to workers during periods in which they are completely disabled under the disability insurance benefits program created by the 1956 amendments to Title II of the Social Security Act. Respondent Eldridge was first awarded benefits in June 1968. In March 1972, he received a questionnaire from the state agency charged with monitoring his medical condition. Eldridge completed the questionnaire, indicating that his condition had not improved and identifying the medical sources, including physicians, from whom he had received treatment recently. The state agency then obtained reports from his physician and a psychiatric consultant. After considering these reports and other information in his file the agency informed Eldridge by letter that it had made a tentative determination that his disability had ceased in May 1972. The letter included a statement of reasons for the proposed termination of benefits, and advised Eldridge that he might request reasonable time in which to obtain and submit additional information pertaining to his condition.

In his written response, Eldridge disputed one characterization of his medical condition and indicated that the agency already had enough evidence to establish his disability. The state agency then made its final determination that he had ceased to be disabled in May 1972. This determination was accepted by the Social Security Administration (SSA), which notified Eldridge in July that his benefits would terminate after that month. The notification also advised him of his right to seek reconsideration by the state agency of this initial determination within six months.

Instead of requesting reconsideration Eldridge commenced this action challenging the constitutional validity of the administrative procedures established by the Secretary of Health, Education, and Welfare for assessing whether there exists a continuing disability. He sought an immediate reinstatement of benefits pending a hearing on the issue of his disability. The Secretary moved to dismiss on the grounds that Eldridge's benefits had been terminated in accordance with valid administrative regulations and procedures and that he had failed to exhaust available remedies. In support of his contention that due process requires a pretermination hearing, Eldridge relied exclusively upon this Court's decision in *Goldberg v. Kelly*, 397 U.S. 254 (1970), which established a right to an "evidentiary hearing" prior to termination of welfare benefits.[4] The Secretary contended that *Goldberg* was not controlling since eligibility for disability benefits, unlike eligibility for welfare benefits, is not based on financial need and since issues of credibility and veracity do not play a significant role in the disability entitlement decision, which turns primarily on medical evidence.

The District Court concluded that the administrative procedures pursuant to which the Secretary had terminated Eldridge's benefits abridged his right to procedural due process. The court viewed the interest of the disability recipient in uninterrupted benefits as indistinguishable from that of the welfare recipient in *Goldberg*. It further noted that decisions subsequent to *Goldberg* demonstrated that the due process requirement of pretermination hearings is not limited to situations involving the deprivation of vital necessities. Reasoning that disability determinations may involve subjective judgments based on conflicting medical and nonmedical evidence, the District Court held that prior to termination of benefits Eldridge had to be afforded an evidentiary hearing of the type required for welfare beneficiaries under Title IV of the Social Security Act. Relying entirely upon the District Court's opinion, the Court of Appeals for the Fourth Circuit affirmed the injunction barring termination of Eldridge's benefits prior to an evidentiary hearing. We reverse.

---

[4] In *Goldberg* the Court held that the pretermination hearing must include the following elements: (1) "timely and adequate notice detailing the reasons for a proposed termination"; (2) "an effective opportunity [for the recipient] to defend by confronting any adverse witnesses and by presenting his own arguments and evidence orally"; (3) retained counsel, if desired; (4) an "impartial" decisionmaker; (5) a decision resting "solely on the legal rules and evidence adduced at the hearing"; (6) a statement of reasons for the decision and the evidence relied on. 397 U.S., at 266–71. In this opinion the term "evidentiary hearing" refers to a hearing generally of the type required in *Goldberg*.

* * *

III

A

Procedural due process imposes constraints on governmental decisions which deprive individuals of "liberty" or "property" interests within the meaning of the Due Process Clause of the Fifth or Fourteenth Amendment. The Secretary does not contend that procedural due process is inapplicable to terminations of Social Security disability benefits. He recognizes, as has been implicit in our prior decisions, that the interests of an individual in continued receipt of these benefits is a statutorily created "property" interest protected by the Fifth Amendment. Rather, the Secretary contends that the existing administrative procedures, detailed below, provide all the process that is constitutionally due before a recipient can be deprived of that interest.

This Court consistently has held that some form of hearing is required before an individual is finally deprived of a property interest. The "right to be heard before being condemned to suffer grievous loss of any kind, even though it may not involve the stigma and hardships of a criminal conviction, is a principle basic to our society." *Joint Anti-Fascist Comm. v. McGrath*, 341 U.S. 123, 168 (1951) (Frankfurter, J., concurring). The fundamental requirement of due process is the opportunity to be heard "at a meaningful time and in a meaningful manner." *Armstrong v. Manzo*, 380 U.S. 545, 552 (1965). Eldridge agrees that the review procedures available to a claimant before the initial determination of ineligibility becomes final would be adequate if disability benefits were not terminated until after the evidentiary hearing stage of the administrative process. The dispute centers upon what process is due prior to the initial termination of benefits, pending review.

In recent years this Court increasingly has had occasion to consider the extent to which due process requires an evidentiary hearing prior to the deprivation of some type of property interest even if such a hearing is provided thereafter. In only one case, *Goldberg v. Kelly*, 397 U.S. at 266–71, has the Court held that a hearing closely approximating a judicial trial is necessary. In other cases requiring some type of pretermination hearing as a matter of constitutional right the Court has spoken sparingly about the requisite procedures.

* * *

These decisions underscore the truism that " '[d]ue process,' unlike some legal rules, is not a technical conception with a fixed content unrelated to time, place and circumstances." *Cafeteria Workers v. McElroy*, 367 U.S. 886, 895 (1961). "[D]ue process is flexible and calls for such procedural protections as the particular situation demands." *Morrissey v. Brewer*, 408 U.S. 471, 481 (1972). Accordingly, resolution of the issue whether the administrative procedures provided here are constitutionally sufficient requires analysis of the governmental and private interests that are affected. More precisely, our prior decisions indicate that identification of the specific dictates of due process generally requires consideration of three distinct factors: First, the private interest that will be affected by the official action; second, the risk of an erroneous deprivation of such interest through the procedures used, and the probable value, if any, of additional or substitute procedural safeguards; and finally, the Government's interest, including the function involved and the fiscal and administrative burdens that the additional or substitute procedural requirement would entail.

We turn first to a description of the procedures for the termination of Social Security disability benefits and thereafter consider the factors bearing upon the constitutional adequacy of these procedures.

B

The disability insurance program is administered jointly by state and federal agencies. State agencies make the initial determination whether a disability exists, when it began, and when it ceased. 42 U.S.C. § 421(a). The standards applied and the procedures followed are prescribed by the Secretary, see § 421(b), who has delegated his responsibilities and powers under the Act to the SSA.

In order to establish initial and continued entitlement to disability benefits a worker must demonstrate that he is unable

> "to engage in any substantial gainful activity by reason of any medically determinable physical or mental impairment which can be expected to result in death or which has lasted or can be expected to last for a continuous period of not less than 12 months. . . ." 42 U.S.C. § 423(d)(1)(A).

To satisfy this test the worker bears a continuing burden of showing, by means of "medically acceptable clinical and laboratory diagnostic techniques," § 423(d)(3), that he has a physical or mental impairment of such severity that

> "he is not only unable to do his previous work but cannot, considering his age, education, and work experience, engage in any other kind of substantial gainful work which exists in the national economy, regardless of whether such work exists in the immediate area in which he lives, or whether a specific job vacancy exists for him, or whether he would be hired if he applied for work." § 423(d)(2)(A).

The principal reasons for benefits terminations are that the worker is no longer disabled or has returned to work. As Eldridge's benefits were terminated because he was determined to be no longer disabled, we consider only the sufficiency of the procedures involved in such cases.

The continuing-eligibility investigation is made by a state agency acting through a "team" consisting of a physician and a nonmedical person trained in disability evaluation. The agency periodically communicates with the disabled worker, usually by mail—in which case he is sent a detailed questionnaire—or by telephone, and requests information concerning his present condition, including current medical restrictions and sources of treatment, and any additional information that he considers relevant to his continued entitlement to benefits.

Information regarding the recipient's current condition is also obtained from his sources of medical treatment. If there is a conflict between the information provided by the beneficiary and that obtained from medical sources such as his physician, or between two sources of treatment, the agency may arrange for an examination by an independent consulting physician. Whenever the agency's tentative assessment of the beneficiary's condition differs from his own assessment, the beneficiary is informed that benefits may be terminated, provided a summary of the evidence upon which the proposed determination to terminate is based, and afforded an opportunity to review the medical reports and other evidence in his case file. He also may respond in writing and submit additional evidence.

The state agency then makes its final determination, which is reviewed by an examiner in the SSA Bureau of Disability Insurance. If, as is usually the case, the SSA accepts the agency determination it notifies the recipient in writing, informing him of the reasons for the decision, and of his right to seek *de novo* reconsideration by the state agency. Upon acceptance by the SSA, benefits are terminated effective two months after the month in which medical recovery is found to have occurred.

If the recipient seeks reconsideration by the state agency and the determination is adverse, the SSA reviews the reconsideration determination and notifies the recipient of the decision. He then has a right to an evidentiary hearing before an SSA administrative law judge. The hearing is nonadversary, and the SSA is not represented by counsel. As at all prior and subsequent stages of the administrative process, however, the claimant may be represented by counsel or other spokesmen. If this hearing results in an adverse decision, the claimant is entitled to request discretionary review by the SSA Appeals Council, and finally may obtain judicial review.

Should it be determined at any point after termination of benefits, that the claimant's disability extended beyond the date of cessation initially established, the worker is entitled to retroactive payments. If, on the other hand, a beneficiary receives any payments to which he is later determined not to be entitled, the statute authorizes the Secretary to attempt to recoup these funds in specified circumstances.

C

Despite the elaborate character of the administrative procedures provided by the Secretary, the courts below held them to be constitutionally inadequate, concluding that due process requires an evidentiary hearing prior to termination. In light of the private and governmental interests at stake here and the nature of the existing procedures, we think this was error.

Since a recipient whose benefits are terminated is awarded full retroactive relief if he ultimately prevails, his sole interest is in the uninterrupted receipt of this source of income pending final administrative decision on his claim. His potential injury is thus similar in nature to that of the welfare recipient in *Goldberg*, ...

Only in *Goldberg* has the Court held that due process requires an evidentiary hearing prior to a temporary deprivation. It was emphasized there that welfare assistance is given to persons on the very margin of subsistence:

> "The crucial factor in this context—a factor not present in the case of . . . virtually anyone else whose governmental entitlements are ended—is that termination of aid pending

resolution of a controversy over eligibility may deprive an *eligible* recipient of the very means by which to live while he waits." 397 U.S., at 264 (emphasis in original).

Eligibility for disability benefits, in contrast, is not based upon financial need. Indeed, it is wholly unrelated to the worker's income or support from many other sources, ...

As *Goldberg* illustrates, the degree of potential deprivation that may be created by a particular decision is a factor to be considered in assessing the validity of any administrative decisionmaking process. The potential deprivation here is generally likely to be less than in *Goldberg*, although the degree of difference can be overstated. As the District Court emphasized, to remain eligible for benefits a recipient must be "unable to engage in substantial gainful activity." * * *

As we recognized last Term in *Fusari v. Steinberg*, 419 U.S. 379, 389 (1975), "the possible length of wrongful deprivation of . . . benefits [also] is an important factor in assessing the impact of official action on the private interests." The Secretary concedes that the delay between a request for a hearing before an administrative law judge and a decision on the claim is currently between 10 and 11 months. Since a terminated recipient must first obtain a reconsideration decision as a prerequisite to invoking his right to an evidentiary hearing, the delay between the actual cutoff of benefits and final decision after a hearing exceeds one year.

In view of the torpidity of this administrative review process, and the typically modest resources of the family unit of the physically disabled worker, the hardship imposed upon the erroneously terminated disability recipient may be significant. Still, the disabled worker's need is likely to be less than that of a welfare recipient. In addition to the possibility of access to private resources, other forms of government assistance will become available where the termination of disability benefits places a worker or his family below the subsistence level. In view of these potential sources of temporary income, there is less reason here than in *Goldberg* to depart from the ordinary principle, established by our decisions, that something less than an evidentiary hearing is sufficient prior to adverse administrative action.

D

An additional factor to be considered here is the fairness and reliability of the existing pretermination procedures, and the probable value, if any, of additional procedural safeguards. Central to the evaluation of any administrative process is the nature of the relevant inquiry. *See* Friendly, *Some Kind of Hearing*, 123 U.PA.L.REV. 1267, 1281 (1975). In order to remain eligible for benefits the disabled worker must demonstrate by means of "medically acceptable clinical and laboratory diagnostic techniques," 42 U.S.C. § 423(d)(3), that he is unable "to engage in any substantial gainful activity by reason of any *medically determinable* physical or mental impairment. . . ." § 423 (d)(1)(A) (emphasis supplied). In short, a medical assessment of the worker's physical or mental condition is required. This is a more sharply focused and easily documented decision than the typical determination of welfare entitlement. In the latter case, a wide variety of information may be deemed relevant, and issues of witness credibility and veracity often are critical to the decisionmaking process. *Goldberg* noted that in such circumstances "written submissions are a wholly unsatisfactory basis for decision." 397 U.S., at 269.

By contrast, the decision whether to discontinue disability benefits will turn, in most cases, upon "routine, standard, and unbiased medical reports by physician specialists," *Richardson v. Perales*, 402 U.S. 389, 404 (1971), concerning a subject whom they have personally examined. In *Richardson* the Court recognized the "reliability and probative worth of written medical reports," emphasizing that while there may be "professional disagreement with the medical conclusions" the "specter of questionable credibility and veracity is not present." *Id.* at 405, 407. To be sure, credibility and veracity may be a factor in the ultimate disability assessment in some cases. But procedural due process rules are shaped by the risk of error inherent in the truth-finding process as applied to the generality of cases, not the rare exceptions. The potential value of an evidentiary hearing, or even oral presentation to the decisionmaker, is substantially less in this context than in *Goldberg*.

The decision in *Goldberg* also was based on the Court's conclusion that written submissions were an inadequate substitute for oral presentation because they did not provide an effective means for the recipient to communicate his case to the decisionmaker. Written submissions were viewed as an unrealistic option, for most recipients lacked the "educational attainment necessary to write effectively" and could not afford professional assistance. In addition, such submissions would not provide the "flexibility of oral presentations" or "permit the recipient to mold his argument to the issues the decision maker appears to regard as important." 397 U.S., at 269. In the context of the disability-benefits-entitlement assessment the administrative procedures under review here fully answer these objections.

The detailed questionnaire which the state agency periodically sends the recipient identifies with particularity the information relevant to the entitlement decision, and the recipient is invited to obtain assistance from the local SSA office in completing the questionnaire. More important, the information critical to the entitlement decision usually is derived from medical sources, such as the treating physician. Such sources are likely to be able to communicate more effectively through written documents than are welfare recipients or the lay witnesses supporting their cause. The conclusions of physicians often are supported by X-rays and the results of clinical or laboratory tests, information typically more amenable to written than to oral presentation.

* * *

E

In striking the appropriate due process balance the final factor to be assessed is the public interest. This includes the administrative burden and other societal costs that would be associated with requiring, as a matter of constitutional right, an evidentiary hearing upon demand in all cases prior to the termination of disability benefits. The most visible burden would be the incremental cost resulting from the increased number of hearings and the expense of providing benefits to ineligible recipients pending decision. No one can predict the extent of the increase, but the fact that full benefits would continue until after such hearings would assure the exhaustion in most cases of this attractive option. Nor would the theoretical right of the Secretary to recover undeserved benefits result, as a practical matter, in any substantial offset to the added outlay of public funds. The parties submit widely varying estimates of the probable additional financial cost. We only need say that experience with the constitutionalizing of government procedures suggests that the ultimate additional cost in terms of money and administrative burden would not be insubstantial.

Financial cost alone is not a controlling weight in determining whether due process requires a particular procedural safeguard prior to some administrative decision. But the Government's interest, and hence that of the public, in conserving scarce fiscal and administrative resources is a factor that must be weighed. At some point the benefit of an additional safeguard to the individual affected by the administrative action and to society in terms of increased assurance that the action is just, may be outweighed by the cost. Significantly, the cost of protecting those whom the preliminary administrative process has identified as likely to be found undeserving may in the end come out of the pockets of the deserving since resources available for any particular program of social welfare are not unlimited.

* * *

We conclude that an evidentiary hearing is not required prior to the termination of disability benefits and that the present administrative procedures fully comport with due process.

■ [The dissenting opinion of JUSTICES BRENNAN and MARSHALL is omitted. Ed.]

NOTES AND QUESTIONS

1. It is easy to see why the district court and the circuit court simply applied the holding in *Goldberg* and held that the procedures used by SSA were inadequate. The two cases seem to be identical in several highly-significant ways. In both, the government cut off benefits to a needy individual based on a contested determination that the individual was no longer eligible. In both, the only pre-deprivation hearing was a paper hearing, in which the individual had an opportunity to submit evidence in writing. In both, the individual had an opportunity to obtain a post-deprivation oral evidentiary hearing approximately a year after the flow of benefits ceased, with retroactive payment of past benefits if the post-deprivation hearing resulted in a finding that the individual was eligible for the benefits. Yet, the Supreme Court distinguished *Goldberg* from *Eldridge* and declined to require a pre-deprivation, oral evidentiary hearing in the latter. What explains the diametrically opposed results in the two cases? What explanations did the *Eldridge* Court offer in attempting to distinguish *Goldberg*?

2. We have already noted that at some length that the Court issued its opinion in *Mathews v. Eldridge* in the face of substantial criticism from numerous directions over the costs—financial and otherwise—of the procedural requirements imposed by *Goldberg v. Kelly*. Many commentators have characterized the Court's opinion in *Eldridge* as responding to those concerns. In what ways does the *Eldridge* Court seem to address the reaction to *Goldberg*? Is the Court's opinion in *Eldridge* an appropriate response to those arguments?

3. Since deciding *Mathews v. Eldridge*, the Supreme Court has consistently invoked the three-part balancing test it announced as the standard for determining what kind of hearing the government must provide and when it must provide that hearing:

> [I]dentification of the specific dictates of due process generally requires consideration of three distinct factors: First, the private interest that will be affected by the official action; second, the risk of an erroneous deprivation of such interest through the procedures used, and the probable value, if any, of additional or substitute procedural safeguards; and finally, the Government's interest, including the function involved and the fiscal and administrative burdens that the additional or substitute procedural requirement would entail.

The *Eldridge* balancing test has been criticized on many grounds. One is that the test is hard to apply. Legislatures and agencies probably are better at applying it than are courts; yet, it is a test courts apply to second guess decisions of legislatures and agencies. Reflecting this practical difficulty, the results of its application vary greatly among judges and Justices, depending on the values each applies.

4. *Goldberg* and *Eldridge* both required oral evidentiary hearings, although they differed as to timing. Yet, one way in which judicial application of the *Eldridge* balancing test varies tremendously is in the types of hearings that satisfy due process, which range from the pre-deprivation oral hearing required by *Goldberg* to no hearing at all. The following examples may give you a feel for the test's variability:

- What kind of hearing, if any, is required before school officials may suspend public school students for disciplinary offenses? In *Goss v. Lopez*, 419 U.S. 565 (1975), a five-Justice majority held that due process is satisfied in that context by a brief, informal, contemporaneous "hearing" before a school official, *e.g.*, a meeting with the vice principal of the school immediately after the incident in which the vice principal listens to the student's story and then suspends him

- What kind of hearing, if any, is required before a public school administers a beating to (*i.e.*, paddles) a student for allegedly engaging in misconduct? In *Ingraham v. Wright*, 430 U.S. 651 (1977), a five-Justice majority found that "corporal punishment in public schools implicates a constitutionally protected liberty interest," but held nevertheless that due process does not require any hearing before or after a student is paddled because tort law and criminal law are adequate to deter abuse of the power to implement corporal punishment.

- What kind of hearing, if any, is required before a trucking company can be compelled to rehire an employee the firm claimed to have fired for misconduct when the government claims he was actually fired for whistle blowing? In *Brock v. Roadway Express*, 481 U.S. 252 (1987), a five-Justice majority upheld as adequate the paper hearing provided by the agency.

5.   Where due process requires an oral evidentiary hearing, when such a hearing must occur is another recurring issue. *Goldberg* is the only case in which the Court has held that due process requires an oral evidentiary hearing before the government may deprive a person of a protected interest. In many cases, the Court has held as it did in *Eldridge* that a pre-deprivation paper hearing is adequate if the individual has the right to a post-deprivation oral evidentiary hearing. Still other cases address the time period that may elapse before a hearing—whether oral or otherwise—is held. The following are merely a few examples:

- A racing commission suspended a jockey for allegedly doping a horse; a five-Justice majority upheld as adequate a pre-suspension ex parte investigation followed by an opportunity for a prompt post-suspension oral evidentiary hearing. *See Barry v. Barchi*, 443 U.S. 55 (1979).

- A university security officer was arrested in a drug raid and charged with a drug felony. The university immediately suspended the security officer without pay, but later merely demoted him to groundskeeper, after a post-suspension oral evidentiary hearing and after the felony charge was dismissed. The Supreme Court unanimously upheld the university's procedures as constitutionally adequate under such circumstances. *See Gilbert v. Homar*, 520 U.S. 924 (1997).

- The Federal Deposit Insurance Corporation (FDIC), a federal administrative agency with oversight authority over banks, suspended the president of a bank who had been indicted for conspiracy to commit mail fraud. Federal law by statute grants a suspended bank officer a post-suspension hearing "within thirty days from service of any notice of suspension" and requires the FDIC to notify the suspended officer of its decision within sixty days of the hearing. The Supreme Court upheld the constitutionality of those time frames. *See Federal Deposit Ins. Corp. v. Mallen*, 486 U.S. 230 (1988).

- The City of Los Angeles towed an illegally-parked car; after paying the fee to recover his car, the owner requested a payment-recovery hearing. After the Court of Appeals for the Ninth Circuit concluded that due process required the city to provide payment-recovery hearings within at least five days, the Supreme Court held that the 27-day actual delay between the towing and the hearing, and perhaps even a somewhat longer delay, were constitutionally permissible. *See City of Los Angeles v. David*, 538 U.S. 715 (2003) (per curiam).

6.   Granting the difficulties inherent in the *Eldridge* test, what alternative test might the Court adopt instead for assessing procedural adequacy? Some have suggested a test based on tradition. Some have suggested a test based on principles of "natural justice." Some have suggested a test based on subjective feelings of justice, *i.e.*, asking what procedures would cause individuals to think that they have been treated fairly. How might each of these approaches work differently from the *Eldridge* three-part balancing model? Do these alternative tests reflect different due process values? What would be the advantages and disadvantages of each test?

DISCUSSION PROBLEM

By law, an individual recipient of public assistance benefits has the opportunity to appeal before an administrative law judge the government's decision to decrease or terminate those benefits. In the past, such hearings were conducted at the recipient's County Board of Assistance, requiring the administrative law judges to travel from county to county to meet with public assistance recipients and their witnesses. Seeking to cut hearing costs, new agency rules require public assistance recipients and their witnesses to travel to one of six regional hearing centers for such hearings. Public assistance recipients who cannot or prefer not to travel to the regional hearing site have the option of presenting their cases to a hearing examiner by telephone conference call.

You work for a legal services office which frequently represents recipients of public assistance benefits. You have been asked to evaluate the due process ramifications of these new hearing rules.

The Bitter with the Sweet Model

Beyond the *Mathews v. Eldridge* balancing test, another approach to curtailing the impact of *Goldberg v. Kelly* seemed, for a time, to gain some traction. When Justice (later Chief Justice) William H. Rehnquist joined the Supreme Court in 1972, he was unhappy with decisions like *Goldberg v. Kelly* in which the Court had expanded the scope of the property to which due process applies to include contingent entitlements in statutes. He seemed to recognize, however, that the Court places such a high value on stare decisis that he was unlikely to be successful in convincing a majority of his colleagues to overrule *Goldberg*. He devised a clever strategy that he hoped would allow him to accomplish the same results through a backdoor route. He called his theory "the bitter with the sweet." His reasoning was simple. If an individual relies on a statute as the basis for a right that is protected by due process, he must take the bitter with the sweet, *i.e.*, he must accept the procedural contours of the right along with the substantive contours of the right. Do you understand how acceptance of this theory would have the practical effect of overruling *Goldberg* in a high proportion of cases in which an individual relies on a statute to create a right protected by due process?

In *Arnett v. Kennedy*, 416 U.S. 134 (1974), the Court considered the due process claim of a nonprobationary federal civil service employee who was fired for falsely and publicly accusing his superior of attempted bribery with only a post-termination opportunity for an evidentiary, trial-type hearing. Justice Rehnquist persuaded a three-Justice plurality to accept and apply his theory, holding that the employee's property interest in his government employment was limited to the procedural protections granted by Congress when it strengthened statutory job protections for civil service workers. "[W]here the grant of a substantive right is inextricably intertwined with the limitations on the procedures which are to be employed in determining that right, a litigant . . . must take the bitter with the sweet." (Although two other Justices agreed with the plurality's outcome on the ground that the procedures offered by the relevant statute satisfied due process, they sided with the four dissenting Justices in rejecting Justice Rehnquist's bitter with the sweet model outright.)

Subsequently, however, in *Bishop v. Wood*, 426 U.S. 341 (1976), the Court evaluated the due process claim of a permanent-status policeman fired for cause, and this time Justice Rehnquist seemed to convince a five-Justice majority to embrace his bitter with the sweet approach. Although the opinion was not a model of clarity, the majority opinion written by Justice Stevens arguably rejected Bishop's due process claim because, while the relevant state and local statutes articulated the circumstances justifying termination, they failed to grant him a right to a hearing and instead left evaluation of the grounds for discharge to a City Manager. (At least, this is how the dissenters in *Bishop* characterized the majority's opinion.)

As a consequence of these two cases, many lower courts applied the bitter with the sweet approach until the Supreme Court issued the following opinion.

Cleveland Board of Education v. Loudermill

470 U.S. 532 (1985).

■ JUSTICE WHITE delivered the opinion of the Court.

In these cases we consider what pretermination process must be accorded a public employee who can be discharged only for cause.

I

In 1979 the Cleveland Board of Education . . . hired respondent James Loudermill as a security guard. On his job application, Loudermill stated that he had never been convicted of a felony. Eleven months later, as part of a routine examination of his employment records, the Board discovered that in fact Loudermill had been convicted of grand larceny in 1968. By letter dated November 3, 1980, the Board's Business Manager informed Loudermill that he had been dismissed because of his dishonesty in filling out the employment application. Loudermill was not afforded an opportunity to respond to the charge of dishonesty or to challenge his dismissal. On November 13, the Board adopted a resolution officially approving the discharge.

Under Ohio law, Loudermill was a "classified civil servant." Ohio Rev. Code Ann. § 124.11 (1984). Such employees can be terminated only for cause, and may obtain administrative review if discharged. § 124.34. Pursuant to this provision, Loudermill filed an appeal with the Cleveland Civil Service Commission on November 12. The Commission appointed a referee, who held a hearing on January 29, 1981. Loudermill argued that he had thought that his 1968 larceny conviction was for a misdemeanor rather than a felony. The referee recommended reinstatement. On July 20, 1981, the full Commission heard argument and orally announced that it would uphold the dismissal. Proposed findings of fact and conclusions of law followed on August 10, and Loudermill's attorneys were advised of the result by mail on August 21.

Although the Commission's decision was subject to judicial review in the state courts, Loudermill instead brought the present suit in the Federal District Court for the Northern District of Ohio. The complaint alleged that § 124.34 was unconstitutional on its face because it did not provide the employee an opportunity to respond to the charges against him prior to removal. As a result, discharged employees were deprived of liberty and property without due process. The complaint also alleged that the provision was unconstitutional as applied because discharged employees were not given sufficiently prompt postremoval hearings.

* * *

Respondents' federal constitutional claim depends on their having had a property right in continued employment. *Bd. of Regents v. Roth*, 408 U.S. 564, 576–78 (1972). If they did, the State could not deprive them of this property without due process.

Property interests are not created by the Constitution, "they are created and their dimensions are defined by existing rules or understandings that stem from an independent source such as state law. . . ." *Roth*, 408 U.S. at 577. The Ohio statute plainly creates such an interest. Respondents were "classified civil service employees," entitled to retain their positions "during good behavior and efficient service," who could not be dismissed "except . . . for . . . misfeasance, malfeasance, or nonfeasance in office," § 124.34. The statute plainly supports the conclusion, reached by both lower courts, that respondents possessed property rights in continued employment. * * *

The [Board] argues, however, that the property right is defined by, and conditioned on, the legislature's choice of procedures for its deprivation. The Board stresses that in addition to specifying the grounds for termination, the statute sets out procedures by which termination may take place. The procedures were adhered to in these cases. According to petitioner, "[t]o require additional procedures would in effect expand the scope of the property interest itself."

This argument, which was accepted by the District Court, has its genesis in the plurality opinion in *Arnett v. Kennedy*, 416 U.S. 134 (1974). *Arnett* involved a challenge by a former federal employee to the procedures by which he was dismissed. The plurality reasoned that where the legislation conferring the substantive right also sets out the procedural mechanism for enforcing that right, the two cannot be separated:

> "The employee's statutorily defined right is not a guarantee against removal without cause in the abstract, but such a guarantee as enforced by the procedures which Congress has designated for the determination of cause.

> * * *

> "[W]here the grant of a substantive right is inextricably intertwined with the limitations on the procedures which are to be employed in determining that right, a litigant in the position of appellee must take the bitter with the sweet." *Id.* at 152–54.

This view garnered three votes in *Arnett*, but was specifically rejected by the other six Justices. Since then, this theory has at times seemed to gather some additional support. *See Bishop v. Wood*, 426 U.S. 341, 355–61 (1976) (White, J., dissenting); *Goss v. Lopez*, 419 U.S. 565, 586–87 (1975) (Powell, J., joined by Burger, C.J., and Blackmun and Rehnquist, J.J., dissenting).

* * *

[T]he "bitter with the sweet" approach misconceives the constitutional guarantee. If a clearer holding is needed, we provide it today. The point is straightforward: the Due Process Clause provides that certain substantive rights—life, liberty, and property—cannot be deprived except pursuant to constitutionally adequate procedures. The categories of substance and procedure are distinct. Were the rule otherwise, the Clause would be reduced to a mere tautology. "Property" cannot be defined by the procedures provided for its deprivation any more than can life or liberty. The right to due process "is conferred, not by legislative grace, but by constitutional guarantee. While the legislature may elect not to confer a property interest in [public] employment, it may not constitutionally authorize the deprivation of such an interest, once conferred, without appropriate procedural safeguards." *Arnett v. Kennedy*, 416 U.S. at 167 (Powell, J., concurring in part and concurring in result in part).

* * *

An essential principle of due process is that a deprivation of life, liberty, or property "be preceded by notice and opportunity for hearing appropriate to the nature of the case." *Mullane v. Cent. Hanover Bank & Trust Co.*, 339 U.S. 306, 313 (1950). We have described "the root requirement" of the Due Process Clause as being "that an individual be given an opportunity for a hearing *before* he is deprived of any significant property interest." *Boddie v. Connecticut*, 401 U.S. 371, 379 (1971) (emphasis in original). This principle requires "some kind of a hearing" prior to the discharge of an employee who has a constitutionally protected property interest in his employment. *Bd. of Regents v. Roth*, 408 U.S., at 569–70; *Perry v. Sindermann*, 408 U.S. 593, 599 (1972). * * *

The need for some form of pretermination hearing, recognized in these cases, is evident from a balancing of the competing interests at stake. These are the private interests in retaining employment, the governmental interest in the expeditious removal of unsatisfactory employees and the avoidance of administrative burdens, and the risk of an erroneous termination. *See Mathews v. Eldridge*, 424 U.S. 319, 335 (1976).

First, the significance of the private interest in retaining employment cannot be gainsaid. We have frequently recognized the severity of depriving a person of the means of livelihood. *See Fusari v. Steinberg*, 419 U.S. 379, 389 (1975); *Bell v. Burson*, 402 U.S. 535, 539 (1971); *Goldberg v. Kelly*, 397 U.S. 254, 264 (1970); *Sniadach v. Family Finance Corp.*, 395 U.S. 337, 340 (1969). While a fired worker may find employment elsewhere, doing so will take some time and is likely to be burdened by the questionable circumstances under which he left his previous job. *See Lefkowitz v. Turley*, 414 U.S. 70, 83–84 (1973).

Second, some opportunity for the employee to present his side of the case is recurringly of obvious value in reaching an accurate decision. Dismissals for cause will often involve factual disputes. *Cf. Califano v. Yamasaki*, 442 U.S. 682, 686 (1979). Even where the facts are clear, the appropriateness or necessity of the discharge may not be; in such cases, the only meaningful opportunity to invoke the discretion of the decisionmaker is likely to be before the termination takes effect. *See Goss v. Lopez*, 419 U.S., at 583–84; *Gagnon v. Scarpelli*, 411 U.S. 778, 784–86 (1973).[8]

* * * As for Loudermill, given the Commission's ruling, we cannot say the discharge was mistaken. Nonetheless, in light of the referee's recommendation, neither can we say that a fully informed decisionmaker might not have exercised its discretion and decided not to dismiss him, notwithstanding its authority to do so. In any event, the termination involved arguable issues,[9] and the right to a hearing does not depend on a demonstration of certain success. *Carey v. Piphus*, 435 U.S. 247, 266 (1978).

The governmental interest in immediate termination does not outweigh these interests. As we shall explain, affording the employee an opportunity to respond prior to termination would impose neither a significant administrative burden nor intolerable delays. Furthermore, the employer shares the employee's interest in avoiding disruption and erroneous decisions; and until the matter is settled, the employer would continue to receive the benefit of the employee's labors. It is preferable to keep a qualified employee on than to train a new one. A governmental employer also has an interest in keeping citizens usefully employed rather than taking the possibly erroneous and counterproductive step of forcing its employees onto the welfare rolls. Finally, in those situations where the employer perceives a significant hazard in keeping the employee on the job, it can avoid the problem by suspending with pay.[10]

---

[8]   This is not to say that where state conduct is entirely discretionary, the Due Process Clause is brought into play. *See Meachum v. Fano*, 427 U.S. 215, 228 (1976). Nor is it to say that a person can insist on a hearing in order to argue that the decisionmaker should be lenient and depart from legal requirements. *See Dixon v. Love*, 431 U.S. 105, 114 (1977). The point is that where there is an entitlement, a prior hearing facilitates the consideration of whether a permissible course of action is also an appropriate one. This is one way in which providing 'effective notice and informal hearing permitting the [employee] to give his version of the events will provide a meaningful hedge against erroneous action. At least the [employer] will be alerted to the existence of disputes about facts and arguments about cause and effect. . . . [H]is discretion will be more informed and we think the risk of error substantially reduced." *Goss v. Lopez*, 419 U.S., at 583–84.

[9]   Loudermill's dismissal turned not on the objective fact that he was an ex-felon or the inaccuracy of his statement to the contrary, but on the subjective question whether he had lied on his application form. His explanation for the false statement is plausible in light of the fact that he received only a suspended 6-month sentence and a fine on the grand larceny conviction.

[10]   * * * As for Loudermill, petitioner states that "to find that we have a person who is an ex-felon as our security guard is very distressful to us." But the termination was based on the presumed misrepresentation on the employment form, not on the felony conviction. In fact, Ohio law provides that an employee "shall not be disciplined for acts," including criminal convictions, occurring more than two years previously. See Ohio Admin. Code. § 124–3–04 (1979). Petitioner concedes that Loudermill's job performance was fully satisfactory.

The foregoing considerations indicate that the pretermination "hearing," though necessary, need not be elaborate. We have pointed out that "[t]he formality and procedural requisites for the hearing can vary, depending upon the importance of the interests involved and the nature of the subsequent proceedings." *Boddie v. Connecticut*, 401 U.S. 371, 378 (1971). In general, "something less" than a full evidentiary hearing is sufficient prior to adverse administrative action. *Mathews v. Eldridge*, 424 U.S. at 343. Under state law, respondents were later entitled to a full administrative hearing and judicial review. The only question is what steps were required before the termination took effect.

In only one case, *Goldberg v. Kelly*, 397 U.S. 254 (1970), has the Court required a full adversarial evidentiary hearing prior to adverse governmental action. However, as the *Goldberg* Court itself pointed out, that case presented significantly different considerations than are present in the context of public employment. Here, the pretermination hearing need not definitively resolve the propriety of the discharge. It should be an initial check against mistaken decisions—essentially, a determination of whether there are reasonable grounds to believe that the charges against the employee are true and support the proposed action. See Bell v. Burson, 402 U.S., at 540.

The essential requirements of due process * * * are notice and an opportunity to respond. The opportunity to present reasons, either in person or in writing, why proposed action should not be taken is a fundamental due process requirement. *See* Friendly, "Some Kind of Hearing," 123 U. Pa. L. Rev. 1267, 1281 (1975). The tenured public employee is entitled to oral or written notice of the charges against him, an explanation of the employer's evidence, and an opportunity to present his side of the story. *See Arnett v. Kennedy*, 416 U.S., at 170–71 (opinion of POWELL, J.); *id.*, at 195–96 (opinion of WHITE, J.); *see also Goss v. Lopez*, 419 U.S., at 581. To require more than this prior to termination would intrude to an unwarranted extent on the government's interest in quickly removing an unsatisfactory employee.

* * *

We conclude that all the process that is due is provided by a pretermination opportunity to respond, coupled with post-termination administrative procedures as provided by the Ohio statute. * * *

■ [The opinion of JUSTICE MARSHALL concurring in part and concurring in the judgment, and the opinion of JUSTICE BRENNAN concurring in part and dissenting in part, are omitted. Ed.]

■ JUSTICE REHNQUIST, dissenting.

In *Arnett v. Kennedy*, six Members of this Court agreed that a public employee could be dismissed for misconduct without a full hearing prior to termination. A plurality of Justices agreed that the employee was entitled to exactly what Congress gave him, and no more.

* * *

In these cases, the relevant Ohio statute provides in its first paragraph that

"[t]he tenure of every officer or employee in the classified service of the state and the counties, civil service townships, cities, city health districts, general health districts, and city school districts thereof, holding a position under this chapter of the Revised Code, shall be during good behavior and efficient service and no such officer or employee shall be reduced in pay or position, suspended, or removed, except ... for incompetency, inefficiency, dishonesty, drunkenness, immoral conduct, insubordination, discourteous treatment of the public, neglect of duty, violation of such sections or the rules of the director of administrative services or the commission, or any other failure of good behavior, or any other acts of misfeasance, malfeasance, or nonfeasance in office." Ohio Rev. Code Ann. § 124.34 (1984).

The very next paragraph of this section of the Ohio Revised Code provides that in the event of suspension of more than three days or removal the appointing authority shall furnish the employee with the stated reasons for his removal. The next paragraph provides that within 10 days following the receipt of such a statement, the employee may appeal in writing to the State Personnel Board of Review or the Commission, such appeal shall be heard within 30 days from the time of its filing, and the Board may affirm, disaffirm, or modify the judgment of the appointing authority.

Thus in one legislative breath Ohio has conferred upon civil service employees such as respondents in these cases a limited form of tenure during good behavior, and prescribed the procedures by which that tenure may be terminated. Here, as in *Arnett*, "[t]he employee's statutorily defined right is not a guarantee against removal without cause in the abstract, but such a guarantee as enforced by the procedures which [the Ohio Legislature] has designated for the determination of cause." 416 U.S., at 152. We stated in *Board of Regents v. Roth*, 408 U.S. 564, 577 (1972):

> "Property interests, of course, are not created by the Constitution. Rather, they are created and their dimensions are defined by existing rules or understandings that stem from an independent source such as state law—rules or understandings that secure certain benefits and that support claims of entitlement to those benefits."

We ought to recognize the totality of the State's definition of the property right in question, and not merely seize upon one of several paragraphs in a unitary statute to proclaim that in that paragraph the State has inexorably conferred upon a civil service employee something which it is powerless under the United States Constitution to qualify in the next paragraph of the statute. This practice ignores our duty under *Roth* to rely on state law as the source of property interests for purposes of applying the Due Process Clause of the Fourteenth Amendment. * * *

3. THE LIMITS OF PROCEDURAL BALANCING

The three-part balancing test of *Mathews v. Eldridge* remains the evaluative standard for assessing whether the procedures utilized by the government in affecting a deprivation of liberty or property satisfy the requirements of due process. Indeed, the framework of modern procedural due process analysis has changed only a little over the past few decades, as the Supreme Court merely tinkers around the edges of cases like *Goldberg*, *Roth*, and *Eldridge*.

Since the catastrophic events of September 11, 2001, new federal government policies concerning national security have yielded numerous allegations of unconstitutional deprivations of liberty interests. These cases are complex, implicating a number of difficult issues including the right of habeas corpus, Congress's constitutional authority to suspend the habeas writ, and other statutory questions as well as due process. Nevertheless, the following case in particular has sparked an interesting revisiting of the nature of liberty and the scope of the *Mathews v. Eldridge* balancing standard outlined above.

Hamdi v. Rumsfeld

542 U.S. 507 (2004).

■ JUSTICE O'CONNOR announced the judgment of the Court and delivered an opinion, in which THE CHIEF JUSTICE, JUSTICE KENNEDY, and JUSTICE BREYER join.

At this difficult time in our Nation's history, we are called upon to consider the legality of the Government's detention of a United States citizen on United States soil as an "enemy combatant" and to address the process that is constitutionally owed to one who seeks to challenge his classification as such. * * * We hold that although Congress authorized the detention of combatants in the narrow circumstances alleged here, due process demands that a citizen held in the United States as an enemy combatant be given a meaningful opportunity to contest the factual basis for that detention before a neutral decisionmaker.

I

On September 11, 2001, the al Qaeda terrorist network used hijacked commercial airliners to attack prominent targets in the United States. Approximately 3,000 people were killed in those attacks. One week later, in response to these "acts of treacherous violence," Congress passed a resolution authorizing the President to "use all necessary and appropriate force against those nations, organizations, or persons he determines planned, authorized, committed, or aided the terrorist attacks" or "harbored such organizations or persons, in order to prevent any future acts of international terrorism against the United States by such nations, organizations or persons." Authorization for Use of Military Force (AUMF), 115 Stat. 224. Soon thereafter, the President ordered United States Armed Forces to Afghanistan, with a mission to subdue al Qaeda and quell the Taliban regime that was known to support it.

This case arises out of the detention of a man whom the Government alleges took up arms with the Taliban during this conflict. His name is Yaser Esam Hamdi. Born in Louisiana in 1980, Hamdi moved with his family to Saudi Arabia as a child. By 2001, the parties agree, he resided in Afghanistan. At some point that year, he was seized by members of the Northern Alliance, a coalition of military groups opposed to the Taliban government, and eventually was turned over to the United States military. The Government asserts that it initially detained and interrogated Hamdi in Afghanistan before transferring him to the United States Naval Base in Guantanamo Bay in January 2002. In April 2002, upon learning that Hamdi is an American citizen, authorities transferred him to a naval brig in Norfolk, Virginia, where he remained until a recent transfer to a brig in Charleston, South Carolina. The Government contends that Hamdi is an "enemy combatant," and that this status justifies holding him in the United States indefinitely—without formal charges or proceedings—unless and until it makes the determination that access to counsel or further process is warranted.

* * *

[Part II of the plurality opinion concludes that Congress gave the President statutory authority to detain citizens who qualify as "enemy combatants" when it adopted the Authorization for Use of Military Force, which sanctioned "all necessary and appropriate force" against "nations, organizations, or persons" associated with the September 11, 2001, terrorist attacks. Ed.]

III

Even in cases in which the detention of enemy combatants is legally authorized, there remains the question of what process is constitutionally due to a citizen who disputes his enemy-combatant status. Hamdi argues that he is owed a meaningful and timely hearing and that "extra-judicial detention [that] begins and ends with the submission of an affidavit based on third-hand hearsay" does not comport with the Fifth and Fourteenth Amendments. The Government counters that any more process than was provided below would be both unworkable and "constitutionally intolerable." Our resolution of this dispute requires a careful examination both of the writ of habeas corpus, which Hamdi now seeks to employ as a mechanism of judicial review, and of the Due Process Clause, which informs the procedural contours of that mechanism in this instance.

* * *

The Government's second argument requires closer consideration. This is the argument that further factual exploration is unwarranted and inappropriate in light of the extraordinary constitutional interests at stake. Under the Government's most extreme rendition of this argument, "[r]espect for separation of powers and the limited institutional capabilities of courts in matters of military decision-making in connection with an ongoing conflict" ought to eliminate entirely any individual process, restricting the courts to investigating only whether legal authorization exists for the broader detention scheme.

* * *

In response, Hamdi emphasizes that this Court consistently has recognized that an individual challenging his detention may not be held at the will of the Executive without recourse to some proceeding before a neutral tribunal to determine whether the Executive's asserted justifications for that detention have basis in fact and warrant in law. * * * The District Court, agreeing with Hamdi, apparently believed that the appropriate process would approach the process that accompanies a criminal trial. * * *

Both of these positions highlight legitimate concerns. And both emphasize the tension that often exists between the autonomy that the Government asserts is necessary in order to pursue effectively a particular goal and the process that a citizen contends he is due before he is deprived of a constitutional right. The ordinary mechanism that we use for balancing such serious competing interests, and for determining the procedures that are necessary to ensure that a citizen is not "deprived of life, liberty, or property, without due process of law," U.S. CONST. amend. V, is the test that we articulated in *Mathews v. Eldridge,* 424 U.S. 319 (1976). *Mathews* dictates that the process due in any given instance is determined by weighing "the private interest that will be affected by the official action" against the Government's asserted interest, "including the function involved" and the burdens the Government would face in providing greater process. 424 U.S., at 335. The *Mathews* calculus then contemplates a judicious balancing of these concerns, through an analysis of "the risk of an erroneous deprivation" of the private interest if the process were reduced and the "probable value, if any, of additional or substitute procedural safeguards." *Id.* We take each of these steps in turn.

1

It is beyond question that substantial interests lie on both sides of the scale in this case. Hamdi's "private interest . . . affected by the official action," *id.,* is the most elemental of liberty interests—the interest in being free from physical detention by one's own government. *Foucha v. Louisiana,* 504 U.S. 71, 80, 112 S.Ct. 1780, 118 L.Ed.2d 437 (1992) "In our society liberty is the norm," and detention without trial "is the carefully limited exception." *Salerno,* 481 U.S. 739, 755 (1987). "We have always been careful not to 'minimize the importance and fundamental nature' of the individual's right to liberty," *Foucha,* 504 U.S. at 80, (quoting *Salerno,* 481 U.S. at 750), and we will not do so today.

Nor is the weight on this side of the *Mathews* scale offset by the circumstances of war or the accusation of treasonous behavior, for "[i]t is clear that commitment for *any* purpose constitutes a significant deprivation of liberty that requires due process protection," *Jones v. United States,* 463 U.S. 354, 361 (1983) (emphasis added; internal quotation marks omitted), and at this stage in the *Mathews* calculus, we consider the interest of the *erroneously* detained individual. Indeed, as *amicus* briefs from media and relief organizations emphasize, the risk of erroneous deprivation of a citizen's liberty in the absence of sufficient process here is very real. Moreover, as critical as the Government's interest may be in detaining those who actually pose an immediate threat to the national security of the United States during ongoing international conflict, history and common sense teach us that an unchecked system of detention carries the potential to become a means for oppression and abuse of others who do not present that sort of threat. Because we live in a society in which "[m]ere public intolerance or animosity cannot constitutionally justify the deprivation of a person's physical liberty," *O'Connor v. Donaldson,* 422 U.S. 563, 575 (1975), our starting point for the *Mathews v. Eldridge* analysis is unaltered by the allegations surrounding the particular detainee or the organizations with which he is alleged to have associated. We reaffirm today the fundamental nature of a citizen's right to be free from involuntary confinement by his own government without due process of law, and we weigh the opposing governmental interests against the curtailment of liberty that such confinement entails.

2

On the other side of the scale are the weighty and sensitive governmental interests in ensuring that those who have in fact fought with the enemy during a war do not return to battle against the United States. As discussed above, the law of war and the realities of combat may render such detentions both necessary and appropriate, and our due process analysis need not blink at those realities. Without doubt, our Constitution recognizes that core strategic matters of warmaking belong in the hands of those who are best positioned and most politically accountable for making them.

The Government also argues at some length that its interests in reducing the process available to alleged enemy combatants are heightened by the practical difficulties that would accompany a system of trial-like process. In its view, military officers who are engaged in the serious work of waging battle would be unnecessarily and dangerously distracted by litigation half a world away, and discovery into military operations would both intrude on the sensitive secrets of national defense and result in a futile search for evidence buried under the rubble of war. To the extent that these burdens are triggered by heightened procedures, they are properly taken into account in our due process analysis.

3

Striking the proper constitutional balance here is of great importance to the Nation during this period of ongoing combat. But it is equally vital that our calculus not give short shrift to the values that this country holds dear or to the privilege that is American citizenship. It is during our most challenging and uncertain moments that our Nation's commitment to due process is most severely tested; and it is in those times that we must preserve our commitment at home to the principles for which we fight abroad.

With due recognition of these competing concerns, we believe that neither the process proposed by the Government nor the process apparently envisioned by the District Court below strikes the proper constitutional balance when a United States citizen is detained in the United States as an enemy combatant. That is, "the risk of an erroneous deprivation" of a detainee's liberty interest is unacceptably high under the Government's proposed rule, while some of the "additional or substitute procedural safeguards" suggested by the District Court are unwarranted in light of their limited "probable value" and the burdens they may impose on the military in such cases. *Mathews*, 424 U.S., at 335.

We therefore hold that a citizen-detainee seeking to challenge his classification as an enemy combatant must receive notice of the factual basis for his classification, and a fair opportunity to rebut the Government's factual assertions before a neutral decisionmaker. *See*

Cleveland Bd. of Ed. v. Loudermill, 470 U.S. 532, 542 (1985). "For more than a century the central meaning of procedural due process has been clear: 'Parties whose rights are to be affected are entitled to be heard; and in order that they may enjoy that right they must first be notified.' It is equally fundamental that the right to notice and an opportunity to be heard 'must be granted at a meaningful time and in a meaningful manner.'" *Fuentes v. Shevin,* 407 U.S. 67, 80 (1972) (quoting *Baldwin v. Hale,* 68 U.S. (1 Wall.) 223, 233 (1864)). These essential constitutional promises may not be eroded.

At the same time, the exigencies of the circumstances may demand that, aside from these core elements, enemy-combatant proceedings may be tailored to alleviate their uncommon potential to burden the Executive at a time of ongoing military conflict. Hearsay, for example, may need to be accepted as the most reliable available evidence from the Government in such a proceeding. Likewise, the Constitution would not be offended by a presumption in favor of the Government's evidence, so long as that presumption remained a rebuttable one and fair opportunity for rebuttal were provided. Thus, once the Government puts forth credible evidence that the habeas petitioner meets the enemy-combatant criteria, the onus could shift to the petitioner to rebut that evidence with more persuasive evidence that he falls outside the criteria. A burden-shifting scheme of this sort would meet the goal of ensuring that the errant tourist, embedded journalist, or local aid worker has a chance to prove military error while giving due regard to the Executive once it has put forth meaningful support for its conclusion that the detainee is in fact an enemy combatant. In the words of *Mathews,* process of this sort would sufficiently address the "risk of an erroneous deprivation" of a detainee's liberty interest while eliminating certain procedures that have questionable additional value in light of the burden on the Government. 424 U.S., at 335.

* * *

■ [The opinion of JUSTICE SOUTER, with whom JUSTICE GINSBURG joined, concurring in part, dissenting in part, and concurring in the judgment, is omitted. Ed.]

■ JUSTICE SCALIA, with whom JUSTICE STEVENS joins, dissenting.

* * *

This case brings into conflict the competing demands of national security and our citizens' constitutional right to personal liberty. Although I share the plurality's evident unease as it seeks to reconcile the two, I do not agree with its resolution.

* * *

The very core of liberty secured by our Anglo-Saxon system of separated powers has been freedom from indefinite imprisonment at the will of the Executive.

* * *

The gist of the Due Process Clause, as understood at the founding and since, was to force the Government to follow those common-law procedures traditionally deemed necessary before depriving a person of life, liberty, or property. When a citizen was deprived of liberty because of alleged criminal conduct, those procedures typically required committal by a magistrate followed by indictment and trial.

* * *

To be sure, certain types of permissible *non*criminal detention—that is, those not dependent upon the contention that the citizen had committed a criminal act—did not require the protections of criminal procedure. However, these fell into a limited number of well-recognized exceptions—civil commitment of the mentally ill, for example, and temporary detention in quarantine of the infectious. It is unthinkable that the Executive could render otherwise criminal grounds for detention noncriminal merely by disclaiming an intent to prosecute, or by asserting that it was incapacitating dangerous offenders rather than punishing wrongdoing.

* * *

The allegations here, of course, are no ordinary accusations of criminal activity. Yaser Esam Mandi has been imprisoned because the Government believes he participated in the waging of war against the United States. The relevant question, then, is whether there is a different, special procedure for imprisonment of a citizen accused of wrongdoing *by aiding the enemy in wartime.*

* * *

It follows from what I have said that Hamdi is entitled to a habeas decree requiring his release unless (1) criminal proceedings are promptly brought, or (2) Congress has suspended the writ of habeas corpus. A suspension of the writ could, of course, lay down conditions for continued detention, similar to those that today's opinion prescribes under the Due Process Clause. But there is a world of difference between the people's representatives' determining the need for that suspension (and prescribing the conditions for it), and this Court's doing so.

* * *

Having found a congressional authorization for detention of citizens where none clearly exists; and having discarded the categorical procedural protection of the Suspension Clause; the plurality then proceeds, under the guise of the Due Process Clause, to prescribe what procedural protections *it* thinks appropriate. It "weigh[s] the private interest . . . against the Government's asserted interest," and—just as though writing a new Constitution—comes up with an unheard-of system in which the citizen rather than the Government bears the burden of proof, testimony is by hearsay rather than live witnesses, and the presiding officer may well be a "neutral" military officer rather than judge and jury. It claims authority to engage in this sort of "judicious balancing" from *Mathews v. Eldridge*, 424 U.S. 319 (1976), a case involving . . . *the withdrawal of disability benefits!* Whatever the merits of this technique when newly recognized property rights are at issue (and even there they are questionable), it has no place where the Constitution and the common law already supply an answer.

■ JUSTICE THOMAS, dissenting.

* * *

This detention falls squarely within the Federal Government's war powers, and we lack the expertise and capacity to second-guess that decision. * * * The plurality reaches a contrary conclusion by failing adequately to consider basic principles of the constitutional structure as it relates to national security and foreign affairs and by using the balancing scheme of *Mathews v. Eldridge,* 424 U.S. 319 (1976). I do not think that the Federal Government's war powers can be balanced away by this Court. Arguably, Congress could provide for additional procedural protections, but until it does, we have no right to insist upon them. But even if I were to agree with the general approach the plurality takes, I could not accept the particulars. The plurality utterly fails to account for the Government's compelling interests and for our own institutional inability to weigh competing concerns correctly. I respectfully dissent.

* * *

Although I do not agree with the plurality that the balancing approach of *Mathews v. Eldridge,* 424 U.S. 319 (1976), is the appropriate analytical tool with which to analyze this case,[5] I cannot help but explain that the plurality misapplies its chosen framework, one that if applied correctly would probably lead to the result I have reached. The plurality devotes two paragraphs to its discussion of the Government's interest, though much of those two paragraphs explain why the Government's concerns are misplaced. But: "It is 'obvious and unarguable' that no governmental interest is more compelling than the security of the Nation." *Haig v. Agee,* 453 U.S. 280, 307 (1981) (quoting *Aptheker v. Sec'y of State,* 378 U.S. 500, 509 (1964)). * * * The Government seeks to further that interest by detaining an enemy soldier not only to prevent him from rejoining the ongoing fight. Rather, as the Government explains, detention can serve to gather critical intelligence regarding the intentions and capabilities of our adversaries, a function that the Government avers has become all the more important in the war on terrorism.

Additional process, the Government explains, will destroy the intelligence gathering function. It also does seem quite likely that, under the process envisioned by the plurality, various military officials will have to take time to litigate this matter. And though the plurality does not say so, a meaningful ability to challenge the Government's factual allegations will probably require the Government to divulge highly classified information to the purported enemy combatant, who might then upon release return to the fight armed with our most closely held secrets.

The plurality manages to avoid these problems by discounting or entirely ignoring them. After spending a few sentences putatively describing the Government's interests, the plurality simply assures the

---

[5]   Evidently, neither do the parties, who do not cite *Mathews* even once.

Government that the alleged burdens "are properly taken into account in our due process analysis." The plurality also announces that "the risk of an erroneous deprivation of a detainee's liberty interest is unacceptably high under the Government's proposed rule." But there is no particular reason to believe that the federal courts have the relevant information and expertise to make this judgment. And ... there is every reason to think that courts cannot and should not make these decisions.

The plurality next opines that "[w]e think it unlikely that this basic process will have the dire impact on the central functions of warmaking that the Government forecasts." Apparently by limiting hearings "to the alleged combatant's acts," such hearings "meddl[e] little, if at all, in the strategy or conduct of war." Of course, the meaning of the combatant's acts may become clear only after quite invasive and extensive inquiry. And again, the federal courts are simply not situated to make these judgments.

Ultimately, the plurality's dismissive treatment of the Government's asserted interests arises from its apparent belief that enemy-combatant determinations are not part of "the actual prosecution of a war," or one of the "central functions of warmaking." This seems wrong: Taking *and holding* enemy combatants is a quintessential aspect of the prosecution of war. Moreover, this highlights serious difficulties in applying the plurality's balancing approach here. First, in the war context, we know neither the strength of the Government's interests nor the costs of imposing additional process.

Second, it is at least difficult to explain why the result should be different for other military operations that the plurality would ostensibly recognize as "central functions of warmaking." As the plurality recounts:

> "Parties whose rights are to be affected are entitled to be heard; and in order that they may enjoy that right they must first be notified. It is equally fundamental that the right to notice and an opportunity to be heard must be granted at a meaningful time and in a meaningful manner." (internal quotation marks omitted).

Because a decision to bomb a particular target might extinguish *life* interests, the plurality's analysis seems to require notice to potential targets. To take one more example, in November 2002, a Central Intelligence Agency (CIA) Predator drone fired a Hellfire missile at a vehicle in Yemen carrying an al Qaeda leader, a citizen of the United States, and four others. It is not clear whether the CIA knew that an American was in the vehicle. But the plurality's due process would seem to require notice and opportunity to respond here as well. I offer these examples not because I think the plurality would demand additional process in these situations but because it clearly would not. The result here should be the same.

* * *

Undeniably, Hamdi has been deprived of a serious interest, one actually protected by the Due Process Clause. Against this, however, is the Government's overriding interest in protecting the Nation. If a deprivation of liberty can be justified by the need to protect a town, the protection of the Nation, *a fortiori,* justifies it.

I acknowledge that under the plurality's approach, it might, at times, be appropriate to give detainees access to counsel and notice of the factual basis for the Government's determination. But properly accounting for the Government's interests also requires concluding that access to counsel and to the factual basis would not always be warranted. Though common sense suffices, the Government thoroughly explains that counsel would often destroy the intelligence gathering function. Equally obvious is the Government's interest in not fighting the war in its own courts, *see, e.g., Johnson v. Eisentrager,* 339 U.S. 763, 779 (1950), and protecting classified information, *see, e.g., Department of Navy v. Egan,* 484 U.S. 518, 527 (1988) (President's "authority to classify and control access to information bearing on national security and to determine" who gets access "flows primarily from [the Commander in Chief Clause] and exists quite apart from any explicit congressional grant"); *Agee,* 453 U.S., at 307 (upholding revocation of former CIA employee's passport in large part by reference to the Government's need "to protect the secrecy of [its] foreign intelligence operations").[7]

NOTES AND QUESTIONS

1. While Justice O'Connor's plurality opinion in *Hamdi* applies the *Mathews v. Eldridge* three-part balancing test to evaluate the government's deprivation of Hamdi's liberty, Justice Scalia's dissenting opinion questions the applicability of *Eldridge* to the case at bar. Obviously Hamdi's physical liberty represents a constitutionally protected due process interest. What is Justice Scalia's objection to applying *Eldridge* to the circumstances of Hamdi's confinement?

2. Reacting to Justice O'Connor's application of *Mathews v. Eldridge* balancing in *Hamdi*, Professor Owen Fiss, *The War Against Terrorism and the Rule of Law*, 26 OXFORD J. LEGAL STUD. 235, 244–45 (2006), suggested the following with respect to constitutionally protected liberty interests and due process:

> . . . Her error was to ignore the distinction between two types of liberties—those that are guaranteed by the Constitution itself, as for example by the First Amendment or by what I have called the principle of freedom, and those liberties that people enjoy in society, but which are not constitutionally protected (one type of liberty can be called constitutional liberty, the other a personal or social liberty).

---

[7] These observations cast still more doubt on the appropriateness and usefulness of *Mathews v. Eldridge,* 424 U.S. 319, 96 S.Ct. 893, 47 L.Ed.2d 18 (1976), in this context. It is, for example, difficult to see how the plurality can insist that Hamdi unquestionably has the right to access to counsel in connection with the proceedings on remand, when new information could become available to the Government showing that such access would pose a grave risk to national security. In that event, would the Government need to hold a hearing before depriving Hamdi of his newly acquired right to counsel even if that hearing would itself pose a grave threat?

A liberty of the latter type might be the liberty a parent has with respect to control of his or her children. * * * I would say that if all that were involved in Hamdi's case were a personal liberty, the *Matthews v. Eldridge* [sic] formula would be applicable, and from that perspective a hearing before a military tribunal might suffice, once again assuming that the tribunal possessed the requisite impartiality. The formula only requires fair procedures.

But for liberties of the first type—liberties guaranteed by the Constitution itself—the individual is entitled to a hearing before a federal court on his or her claim. Imagine a tenured professor being fired by a statute university for criticizing some public official. He can challenge that action as a violation of the First Amendment and is entitled to have that action judged by a federal court, not simply some administrative tribunal within the university structure. He is entitled to something more than fair procedure. Likewise, I maintain that Hamdi was entitled to a hearing before a federal court, not a military tribunal, on his claim that he was being denied the liberty provided by the principle of freedom—a liberty that can be traced to the due process clause of the Fifth Amendment read in its substantive guise and the provision of Article I limiting the suspension of the writ of habeas corpus.

How does Professor Fiss's conception of liberty compare with Justice Scalia's dissenting opinion in *Hamdi*?

3.   The courts have recognized other circumstances in which the courts may deprive individual citizens of their physical liberty with less procedure than a full criminal trial, or even less than a hearing before a judge. For example, numerous cases address the procedures that are due before an individual may be indefinitely detained in a mental health facility. In *Addington v. Texas*, 441 U.S. 418 (1979), the Supreme Court held that state officials seeking a citizen's indefinite involuntary commitment for mental illness need only satisfy the lesser clear and convincing standard rather than the more stringent reasonable-doubt standard due to criminal defendants. In *Parham v. J.R.*, 442 U.S. 584 (1979), the Court concluded that indefinite voluntary commitment of a child to a mental hospital by his or her parents could be accomplished with use of a "neutral factfinder" other than a judge, such as a staff physician, and without a formal hearing. How do these circumstances compare and contrast with those of *Hamdi*? Can you reconcile the outcomes of these cases with the views of due process interests expressed by Justice Scalia and Professor Fiss discussed above?

4.   In the months after the Supreme Court decided *Hamdi*, the Department of Defense established Combatant Status Review Tribunals (CSRTs) to evaluate whether non-citizens seized outside the United States and held at a military detention facility at Guantanamo Bay, Cuba, were properly classified as "enemy combatants." In establishing the CSRTs, the Department of Defense claimed its intent to comply with the guidance provided by Justice O'Connor's plurality opinion in *Hamdi*. In *Boumediene v. Bush*, 128 S.Ct. 2229 (2008), the Supreme Court concluded that the Guantanamo detainees were entitled to the right of habeas corpus and that the military commissions violated that right. In reaching this conclusion, the Supreme Court declined to consider separately whether the military commissions satisfied due process requirements.

B. STATUTES AS A SOURCE OF PROCEDURAL REQUIREMENTS

Statutes often require agencies to use decision-making procedures greater than, or at least different from, the procedures required by due process. In order to determine what procedures a federal agency is statutorily required to provide, the agency must read with care both the statute it is implementing (often referred to as the organic act) and the provisions of the Administrative Procedure Act (APA) that discuss the procedures an agency is required to use to make various types of decisions. Sometimes an agency's organic act specifies the procedures the agency is required to use to adjudicate a class of disputes in some detail. More often, however, the organic act refers to the required procedures briefly and in general terms, *e.g.*, the agency must conduct a "hearing." The question that naturally flows from such provisions is, precisely what sort of hearing do such statutes require?

1. FORMAL ADJUDICATION

Sections 554 to 558 of the APA describe the procedures that are potentially required in agency adjudications. Read those sections with care to determine what procedures an agency must use and in what circumstances the agency must use those procedures. Sections 554, 556, and 557 describe a decision-making procedure that seems to be modeled closely on the institution of a court trial, complete with an Administrative Law Judge (ALJ) who presides over an oral evidentiary hearing and who writes an opinion that includes findings of fact and conclusions of law. Those procedures are generally referred to as "formal adjudication."

ALJs are almost as independent of the agencies at which they preside as federal district judges are of the Executive and Legislative branches of government. ALJ salaries are determined by statute; agencies are prohibited from evaluating the performance of ALJs; agencies must use a random assignment method to assign cases to ALJs; and, agencies cannot fire or otherwise discipline an ALJ except for cause, as determined by another agency in a formal adjudication. *See generally* RICHARD J. PIERCE, JR., SIDNEY A. SHAPIRO & PAUL VERKUIL, ADMINISTRATIVE LAW AND PROCESS 322–23 (5th ed. 2009).

It is important to read APA § 554(a) with care, however, to determine when an agency must use the elaborate formal procedures described in §§ 554, 556, and 557. Specifically, APA § 554(a) provides that those formal procedures apply "in every case of adjudication required by statute to be determined on the record after opportunity for an agency hearing," except as otherwise provided. Many organic statutes, however, do not use precisely this language in calling for agency adjudications. For example, § 402 of the Clean Water Act authorizes the Administrator of the Environmental Protection Agency to issue certain permits "after opportunity for public hearing." Other statutes merely call for "a hearing," with no further elaboration. Is such language sufficiently consistent with APA § 554(a) to trigger the APA's formal procedural requirements? Or do such statutes allow for less formal hearings?

In 1973, the Supreme Court decided a pivotal case concerning when the APA requires a hearing in the context of agency rulemaking, *United States v. Florida East Coast Railway Co.*, 410 U.S. 224. Agency rulemaking and adjudication inhabit different procedural spheres; we discuss agency rulemaking at length in Chapter 5. Nevertheless, it is worth noting here that APA § 553(c) calls for agencies to utilize for rulemaking the same formal procedures prescribed in §§ 556 and 557 for adjudication "[w]hen rules are required by statute to be made on the record after opportunity for an agency hearing." Notice the resemblance of this language to that of APA § 554(a). In *Florida East Coast Railway*, the Supreme Court concluded that the correct reading of APA § 553(c) required an organic statute to expressly include the phrase "on the record," or some similar verbal formulation, before the formal procedures of APA §§ 556 and 557 would apply. An organic statute's mere reference to a "hearing" in connection with rulemaking, by contrast, did not require the administering agency to utilize the formal procedures prescribed in §§ 556 and 557 in promulgating regulations.

Florida East Coast Railway significantly complicated the question of statutory hearing requirements in the context of agency adjudication. For a time, many courts distinguished adjudication from rulemaking and presumed that statutory references to a hearing required the formal procedures of APA §§ 556 and 557 absent clear indication that Congress intended otherwise. *See, e.g., Seacoast Anti-Pollution League v. Costle*, 572 F.2d 872 (1st Cir. 1978); *Marathon Oil Co. v. EPA*, 564 F.2d 1253 (9th Cir. 1977). Other courts noted the similarity between the language of APA §§ 553(c) and 554(a) and concluded that the formal procedural requirements of APA §§ 556 and 557 would only apply if the organic statute included the precise language "on the record," absent some other clear indication that Congress intended to require formal procedures. *See, e.g., City of West Chicago, Illinois v. NRC*, 701 F.2d 632 (7th Cir. 1983).

In 1984, the Supreme Court decided the landmark case of *Chevron U.S.A. Inc. v. Natural Resources Defense Council, Inc.*, 467 U.S. 837 (1984). We discuss the *Chevron* case at length in Chapter 6. For purposes of this discussion, it is enough to note that the Court in *Chevron* adopted a two-part test for judicial review of agency interpretations of statutes that they administer: first determining whether the meaning of the statute is clear ("for the court, as well as the agency, must give effect to the unambiguously expressed intent of Congress"); and second, if the statute is ambiguous, asking whether the agency's interpretation of the statute is a reasonable one. *Id.* at 842–43. In other words, the *Chevron* Court held that courts must defer to an agency's reasonable interpretations of ambiguities in a statute that the agency administers. A few years after the Supreme Court decided *Chevron*, in *Chemical Waste Management, Inc. v. EPA*, 873 F.2d 1477 (1989), the D.C. Circuit Court of Appeals extended *Chevron* deference to the EPA's conclusion that Congress's use of the phrase "public hearing" in the Resource Conservation and Recovery Act did not trigger formal adjudication procedures under APA § 554, 556, and 557. In short, rather than presuming one way or the other based on the statute's requirement of a "public hearing" without the phrase "on the record," the D.C. Circuit deferred to the agency's conclusion regarding whether or not Congress intended to require formal procedures.

Since 1984, every circuit court that has addressed the issue has either held outright that the holding of *Florida East Coast Railway* applies to adjudications or deferred to the agency's interpretation of the statute as not requiring the APA's formal procedures. The following opinion furthers this modern trend among the circuit courts, while also offering a preview of *Chevron* analysis in action.

Dominion Energy Brayton Point, LLC v. Johnson

443 F.3d 12 (1st Cir. 2006).

■ SELYA, CIRCUIT JUDGE.

USGen New England, Inc., now Dominion Energy Brayton Point, LLC (Dominion), filed suit against the U.S. Environmental Protection Agency, its administrator, and its regional office (collectively, the EPA), alleging that the EPA failed to perform a non-discretionary duty when it refused to grant Dominion's request for a formal evidentiary hearing after issuing a proposed final National Pollution Discharge Elimination System (NPDES) permit. The district court dismissed the case for want of subject matter jurisdiction. On appeal, the central question presented concerns the effect of this court's decision in *Seacoast Anti-Pollution League v. Costle*, 572 F.2d 872 (1st Cir.1978), in light of the Supreme Court's subsequent decision in *Chevron U.S.A. Inc. v. Natural Resources Defense Council, Inc.*, 467 U.S. 837 (1984). Concluding, as we do, that *Seacoast* does not control, we affirm the judgment below.

Dominion owns an electrical generating facility in Somerset, Massachusetts (the station). The station opened in the 1960s and, like most power plants of its era, utilizes an "open-cycle" cooling system. Specifically, the station withdraws water from the Lees and Taunton Rivers, circulates that water through the plant's generating equipment as a coolant, and then discharges the water (which, by then, has attained an elevated temperature) into Mount Hope Bay.

The withdrawals and discharges of water are regulated by the Clean Water Act (CWA), 33 U.S.C. §§ 1251–1387. For the last three decades, these actions have been authorized by a series of NPDES permits issued by the EPA pursuant to section 402(a) of the CWA. *See id.* § 1342(a). The standards incorporated into those permits are determined under the thermal variance procedures laid out in section 316(a). *See id.* § 1326(a).

In 1998, the station applied for renewal of its NPDES permit and thermal variance authorization. The EPA issued a proposed final permit on October 6, 2003, in which it rejected the requested thermal variance. On November 4, Dominion sought review before the Environmental Appeals Board (the Board), and asked for an evidentiary hearing. The Board accepted the petition for review but declined to convene an evidentiary hearing.

* * *

Before the EPA either issues an NPDES permit or authorizes a thermal variance, it must offer an "opportunity for public hearing." 33 U.S.C. §§ 1326(a), 1342(a). No definition of "public hearing" is contained within the four corners of the CWA.

The Administrative Procedure Act (APA), 5 U.S.C. § 551 *et seq.*, is also part of the relevant legal landscape. Most pertinent here are those sections that combine to describe the procedures for formal administrative adjudications. *See id.* §§ 554, 556, 557. These procedures apply "in every case of adjudication required by statute to be determined on the record after opportunity for an agency hearing." *Id.* § 554(a). The APA does not directly address whether these procedures apply when a statute simply calls for an "opportunity for public hearing" without any specific indication that the hearing should be "on the record."

In *Seacoast*, this court interpreted "public hearing" (as used in sections 402(a) and 316(a) of the CWA) to mean "evidentiary hearing"— in other words, a hearing that comports with the APA's requirements for a formal adjudication. 572 F.2d at 878, Examining the legislative history of the APA, we adopted a presumption that "unless a statute otherwise specifies, an adjudicatory hearing subject to judicial review must be [an evidentiary hearing] on the record." *Id.* at 877. Applying that presumption to the CWA, we concluded that "the statute certainly does not indicate that the determination need *not* be on the record." *Id.* at 878 (emphasis in original).

So viewed, *Seacoast* established a rebuttable presumption that, in the context of an adjudication, an organic statute that calls for a "public hearing" should be read to require an evidentiary hearing in compliance with the formal adjudication provisions of the APA. Two other circuit courts reached the same conclusion, albeit through different reasoning. *See Marathon Oil Co. v. EPA*, 564 F.2d 1253, 1264 (9th Cir. 1977); *U.S. Steel Corp. v. Train*, 556 F.2d 822, 833–34 (7th Cir. 1977). Acquiescing in this construction, the EPA promulgated regulations that memorialized the use of formal evidentiary hearings in the NPDES permit process.

In 1984, a sea change occurred in administrative law and, specifically, in the interpretation of organic statutes such as the CWA. The Supreme Court held that "[w]hen a court reviews an agency's construction of the statute which it administers," the reviewing court first must ask "whether Congress has directly spoken to the precise question at issue." *Chevron*, 467 U.S. at 842. If Congress's intent is clear, that intent governs—both the court and the agency must give it full effect. If, however, Congress has not directly addressed the question and the agency has stepped into the vacuum by promulgating an interpretive regulation, a reviewing court may "not simply impose its own construction on the statute," but, rather, ought to ask "whether the agency's answer is based on a permissible construction of the statute." *Id.* at 843.

This paradigm, sometimes called the *Chevron* two-step, increases the sphere of influence of agency action. If congressional intent is unclear and an agency's interpretation of a statute that it administers is reasonable, an inquiring court must defer to that interpretation. That is so even if the agency's interpretation is not the one that the court considers to be the best available interpretation.

Armed with the *Chevron* decision and a presidential directive to streamline regulatory programs, *see* Remarks on Regulatory Reform, 31 Weekly Comp. Pres. Doc. 278 (Feb. 21, 1995), the EPA advanced a proposal to eliminate formal evidentiary hearings from the NPDES permitting process. In due course, the EPA adopted that proposal as a final rule. *See* Amendments to Streamline the NPDES Program Regulations: Round Two, 65 Fed. Reg. 30,886, 30,900 (May 15, 2000).

This revision depended heavily on a *Chevron* analysis. The agency began by "finding no evidence that Congress intended to require formal evidentiary hearings or that the text [of section 402(a)] precludes informal adjudication of permit review petitions." *Id.* at 30,896. Then, it weighed the risks and benefits of employing informal hearing procedures for NPDES permit review, "determining that these procedures would not violate the Due Process Clause." *Id.* Finally, it "concluded that informal hearing procedures satisfy the hearing requirement of section 402(a)." *Id.*

It was under this new regulatory scheme that the EPA considered Dominion's request to renew its NPDES permit and to authorize a thermal variance. Thus, it was under this scheme that the EPA denied Dominion's request for an evidentiary hearing.

* * *

One thing is crystal clear: on their face, the current EPA regulations do not establish a non-discretionary duty to provide the evidentiary hearing that Dominion seeks. Prior to the date of Dominion's request, the EPA vitiated the preexisting rule introducing evidentiary hearings into the NPDES permitting process. Dominion concedes this fact, but nonetheless relies on *Seacoast* as the source of a non-discretionary duty to convene an evidentiary hearing.

This reliance is misplaced. Even if *Seacoast* established a non-discretionary duty for section 505(a)(2) purposes when it was decided— a matter upon which we need not opine—Dominion's position ignores two important post-*Seacoast* changes in the legal landscape: the Supreme Court's decision in *Chevron* and the agency's subsequent promulgation of the current "no evidentiary hearing" rule.

* * *

For present purposes, the critical precedent is *National Cable & Telecommunications Ass'n v. Brand X Internet Services*, 545 U.S. 967 (2005). There, the Court examined the relationship between the stare decisis effect of an appellate court's statutory interpretation and the *Chevron* deference due to an administrative agency's subsequent, but contrary, interpretation. Echoing *Chevron*, the Court reiterated that "[f]illing [statutory] gaps . . . involves difficult policy choices that agencies are better equipped to make than courts." *Id.* at 980. Then, concluding that *Chevron*'s application should not turn on the order in which judicial and agency interpretations issue, the Justices held squarely that "[a] court's prior judicial construction of a statute trumps an agency construction otherwise entitled to *Chevron* deference only if the prior court decision holds that its construction follows from the unambiguous terms of the statute and thus leaves no room for agency discretion." *Id.* at 982. This approach "hold[s] judicial interpretations contained in precedents to the same demanding *Chevron* . . . standard that applies if the court is reviewing the agency's construction on a blank slate." *Id.*

Brand X demands that we reexamine pre-*Chevron* precedents through a *Chevron* lens. The *Chevron* two-step applies. At the first step, a court "must look primarily to the plain meaning of the statute, drawing its essence from the particular statutory language at issue, as well as the language and design of the statute as a whole." *Strickland v. Comm'r, Me. Dep't of Human Servs.*, 48 F.3d 12, 16 (1st Cir. 1995). At this step, the court may "examine the legislative history, albeit skeptically, in search of an unmistakable expression of congressional intent." *Id.* at 17. If the precedent at issue finds clarity at step one— that is, if the holding of the case rests on a perception of clear and unambiguous congressional intent—that precedent will govern. *See Brand X*, 545 U.S. at 982. If, however, the precedent operates at *Chevron* step two—that is, if the case holds, in effect, that congressional intent is less than pellucid and proceeds to choose a *"best* reading" rather than "the *only permissible* reading," *id.* at 984 (emphasis in original)—its stare decisis effect will, through *Chevron* deference, yield to a contrary but plausible agency interpretation.

Once this mode of analysis is understood and applied, Dominion's argument collapses. *Seacoast* simply does not hold that Congress clearly intended the term "public hearing" in sections 402(a) and 316(a) of the CWA to mean "evidentiary hearing." To the contrary, the *Seacoast* court based its interpretation of the CWA on a presumption derived from the legislative history of the APA—-a presumption that would hold sway only in the absence of a showing of a contrary congressional intent. In other words, the court resorted to the presumption only because it could find no sign of a plainly discernible congressional intent. A statutory interpretation constructed on such a negative finding is antithetic to a conclusion that Congress's intent was clear and unambiguous.

The short of it is that the *Seacoast* court, faced with an opaque statute, settled upon what it sensibly thought was the best construction of the CWA's "public hearing" language. Such a holding is appropriate at step two of the *Chevron* pavane, not at step one. Consequently, under *Brand X*, *Seacoast* must yield to a reasonable agency interpretation of the CWA's "public hearing" requirement.

The only piece left to this puzzle is to confirm that the EPA's new regulations are, in fact, entitled to *Chevron* deference. This inquiry is a straightforward one. As our earlier discussion suggests (and as the *Seacoast* court correctly deduced), Congress has not spoken directly to the precise question at issue here. Accordingly, we must defer to the EPA's interpretation of the CWA as long as that interpretation is reasonable.

In this instance, the administrative interpretation took into account the relevant universe of factors. *See* 65 Fed.Reg. at 30,898–900 (considering "(1) [t]he private interests at stake, (2) the risk of erroneous decision-making, and (3) the nature of the government interest," and concluding that its new regulation was a reasonable interpretation of the CWA). The agency's conclusion that evidentiary hearings are unnecessary and that Congress, in using the phrase "opportunity for public hearing," did not mean to mandate evidentiary hearings seems reasonable—and Dominion, to its credit, has conceded the point.

NOTES AND QUESTIONS

1. As noted, we discuss *Chevron* in detail in Chapter 6. The First Circuit's opinion in *Dominion Energy* gives you some idea of the significance and effects of *Chevron*, however. Under *Chevron*, an agency has discretion to choose what kind of hearing to provide in an adjudication if its organic act is ambiguous—*e.g.*, if the organic statute specifies only that the agency must provide a hearing—as long as the agency's choice of decision-making procedure is "reasonable." How, if at all, does the reasonableness requirement differ from the decision whether the agency's procedures comply with due process? What kind of hearing do you think is appropriate for determining whether proposed thermal pollution of a water body will have unacceptable adverse effects on aquatic biota?

2. Only a few agency organic acts require the agency to adjudicate "on the record after opportunity for an agency hearing," the language in APA § 554(a) that triggers the duty of the agency to comply with the formal adjudication procedures described in APA §§ 554, 556, and 557. Consequently, the vast bulk of agency adjudications are conducted through use of "informal adjudication" with fewer procedures. Nevertheless, an agency must use procedures that comply with due process in any case in which it is depriving an individual of something that qualifies as property or liberty.

3. The procedures described in APA §§ 554, 556, and 557 are sufficiently elaborate that agencies have an incentive to avoid interpreting statutory hearing requirements as requiring formal adjudication. Nevertheless, agencies often adopt by rule procedures that go beyond the requirements of due process because agencies have an independent interest in using procedures that allow them to make accurate findings of fact and that cause the parties that appear before them to feel that they have been treated fairly and to have confidence in the accuracy and integrity of the agency's decision-making process. If an agency adopts procedural rules that exceed those required by statute or by due process, the agency is required to follow its own rules to the extent that they confer important procedural rights on parties. *See, e.g., Ballard v. Commissioner*, 544 U.S. 40 (2005); *Serv. v. Dulles*, 354 U.S. 363 (1957); *United States ex rel. Accardi v. Shaughnessy*, 347 U.S. 260 (1954).

4. The steady erosion of formal adjudication as a result of the above-described line of cases has been controversial. As agencies and courts have reduced the number of agency adjudications subject to the formal procedural requirements of APA §§ 554, 556, and 557, the American Bar Association has proposed amending the APA to subject more agency adjudications to those procedures. Specifically, in its Resolution 114, dated February 2005, the American Bar Association urged Congress to adopt legislation consistent with a draft bill entitled Federal Administrative Adjudication in the 21st Century. The American Bar Association proposal creates an intermediate or "Type B" category of adjudications where statutes do not explicitly require a hearing "on the record" but nevertheless call for some sort of hearing. Type B adjudications would entail only some of the procedures normally associated with formal adjudications, such as notice, the opportunity to present oral evidence and conduct cross-examination of witnesses, and an impartial and independent decisionmaker. Other APA formal adjudication procedures, such as APA evidence and burden of proof requirements, would not apply to Type B adjudications, and Type B adjudications would be conducted by lesser "presiding officers" rather than Administrative Law Judges (with all of their hiring, firing, and other protections). What concerns do you think might have prompted the American Bar Association to propose such legislation? What difficulties do you think might arise from three rather than two tiers of adjudication rules under the APA?

2. INFORMAL ADJUDICATION

In light of the above jurisprudence, if an agency's organic act lacks the words "on the record," or some other verbal formulation that explicitly requires an oral evidentiary hearing, the agency is free to engage in "informal adjudication." As noted, only a few agency organic acts include the language necessary to trigger formal adjudication procedures described in APA §§ 554, 556, and 557. Thus, the vast bulk of agency adjudications are now conducted through use of informal adjudication. Although due process may impose procedural requirements, APA §§ 554, 556, and 557 do not.

If APA §§ 554, 556, and 557 do not apply, then what procedural requirements does the APA impose upon informal adjudications? The answer is, not many, but a few. The following cases explore these requirements.

Citizens to Preserve Overton Park, Inc. v. Volpe
401 U.S. 402 (1971).

■ Opinion of the Court by MR. JUSTICE MARSHALL, announced by MR. JUSTICE STEWART.

The growing public concern about the quality of our natural environment has prompted Congress in recent years to enact legislation designed to curb the accelerating destruction of our country's natural beauty. We are concerned in this case with § 4(f) of the Department of Transportation Act of 1966, as amended, and § 18(a) of the Federal-Aid Highway Act of 1968. These statutes prohibit the Secretary of Transportation from authorizing the use of federal funds to finance the construction of highways through public parks if a "feasible and prudent" alternative route exists. If no such route is available, the statutes allow him to approve construction through parks only if there has been "all possible planning to minimize harm" to the park.

Petitioners, private citizens as well as local and national conservation organizations, contend that the Secretary has violated these statutes by authorizing the expenditure of federal funds for the construction of a six-lane interstate highway through a public park in Memphis, Tennessee. * * *

Overton Park is 342-acre city park located near the center of Memphis. The park contains a zoo, a nine-hole municipal golf course, an outdoor theater, nature trails, a bridle path, an art academy, picnic areas, and 170 acres of forest. The proposed highway, which is to be a six-lane, high-speed, expressway, will sever the zoo from the rest of the park. Although the roadway will be depressed below ground level except where it crosses a small creek, 26 acres of the park will be destroyed. * * *

* * * In April 1968, the Secretary announced that he concurred in the judgment of local officials that I-40 should be built through the park. And in September 1969 the State acquired the right-of-way inside Overton Park from the city. Final approval for the project—the route as well as the design—was not announced until November 1969, after Congress had reiterated in § 138 of the Federal-Aid Highway Act that highway construction through public parks was to be restricted. Neither announcement approving the route and design of I-40 was accompanied by a statement of the Secretary's factual findings. He did not indicate why he believed there were no feasible and prudent alternative routes or why design changes could not be made to reduce the harm to the park.

Petitioners contend that the Secretary's action is invalid without such formal findings and that the Secretary did not make an independent determination but merely relied on the judgment of the Memphis City Council. They also contend that it would be "feasible and prudent" to route I-40 around Overton Park either to the north or to the south. And they argue that if these alternative routes are not "feasible and prudent," the present plan does not include "all possible" methods for reducing harm to the park. Petitioners claim that I-40 could be built under the park by using either of two possible tunneling methods, and they claim that, at a minimum, by using advanced drainage techniques the expressway could be depressed below ground level along the entire route through the park including the section that crosses the small creek.

Respondents argue that it was unnecessary for the Secretary to make formal findings, and that he did, in fact, exercise his own independent judgment which was supported by the facts. In the District Court, respondents introduced affidavits, prepared specifically for this litigation, which indicated that the Secretary had made the decision and that the decision was supportable. These affidavits were contradicted by affidavits introduced by petitioners, who also sought to take the deposition of a former Federal Highway Administrator who had participated in the decision to route I-40 through Overton Park.

* * *

We agree that formal findings were not required. But we do not believe that in this case judicial review based solely on litigation affidavits was adequate.

A threshold question—whether petitioners are entitled to any judicial review—is easily answered. Section 701 of the Administrative Procedure Act, 5 U.S.C. § 701 (1964 ed., Supp. V), provides that the action of "each authority of the Government of the United States," which includes the Department of Transportation, is subject to judicial review except where there is a statutory prohibition on review or where "agency action is committed to agency discretion by law." In this case, there is no indication that Congress sought to prohibit judicial review and there is most certainly no "showing of 'clear and convincing evidence' of a . . . legislative intent" to restrict access to judicial review. *Abbott Laboratories v. Gardner*, 387 U.S. 136, 141 (1967).

Similarly, the Secretary's decision here does not fall within the exception for action "committed to agency discretion." This is a very narrow exception.

* * *

But the existence of judicial review is only the start: the standard for review must also be determined. For that we must look to § 706 of the Administrative Procedure Act, 5 U.S.C. § 706 (1964 ed., Supp. V), which provides that a "reviewing court shall . . . hold unlawful and set aside agency action, findings, and conclusions found" not to meet six separate standards. In all cases, agency action must be set aside if the action was "arbitrary, capricious, an abuse of discretion, or otherwise not in accordance with law" or if the action failed to meet statutory, procedural, or constitutional requirements. 5 U.S.C. §§ 706(2)(A), (B), (C), (D) (1964 ed., Supp. V). In certain narrow, specifically limited situations, the agency action is to be set aside if the action was not supported by "substantial evidence." And in other equally narrow circumstances the reviewing court is to engage in a *de novo* review of the action and set it aside if it was "unwarranted by the facts." 5 U.S.C. §§ 706(2)(E), (F) (1964 ed., Supp. V).

* * *

Even though there is no *de novo* review in this case and the Secretary's approval of the route of I-40 does not have ultimately to meet the substantial-evidence test, the generally applicable standards of § 706 require the reviewing court to engage in a substantial inquiry. Certainly, the Secretary's decision is entitled to a presumption of regularity. *See, e.g., Pacific States Box & Basket Co. v. White*, 296 U.S. 176, 185 (1935); *United States v. Chemical Foundation*, 272 U.S. 1, 14–15 (1926). But that presumption is not to shield his action from a thorough, probing, in-depth review.

The court is first required to decide whether the Secretary acted within the scope of his authority. *Schilling v. Rogers*, 363 U.S. 666, 676–77 (1960). * * * The reviewing court must consider whether the Secretary properly construed his authority to approve the use of parkland as limited to situations where there are no feasible alternative routes or where feasible alternative routes involve uniquely difficult problems. And the reviewing court must be able to find that the Secretary could have reasonably believed that in this case there are no feasible alternatives or that alternatives do involve unique problems.

Scrutiny of the facts does not end, however, with the determination that the Secretary has acted within the scope of his statutory authority. Section 706(2)(A) requires a finding that the actual choice made was not 'arbitrary, capricious, an abuse of discretion, or otherwise not in accordance with law." 5 U.S.C. § 706(2)(A) (1964 ed., Supp. V). To make this finding, the court must consider whether the decision was based on a consideration of the relevant factors and whether there has been a clear error of judgment. * * *

The final inquiry is whether the Secretary's action followed the necessary procedural requirements. Here the only procedural error alleged is the failure of the Secretary to make formal findings and state his reason for allowing the highway to be built through the park.

Undoubtedly, review of the Secretary's action is hampered by his failure to make such findings, but the absence of formal findings does not necessarily require that the case be remanded to the Secretary. Neither the Department of Transportation Act nor the Federal-Aid Highway Act requires such formal findings. Moreover, the Administrative Procedure Act requirements that there be formal findings in certain rulemaking and adjudicatory proceedings do not apply to the Secretary's action here. *See* 5 U.S.C. §§ 553(a)(2), 554(a). And, although formal findings may be required in some cases in the absence of statutory directives when the nature of the agency action is ambiguous, those situations are rare. *See City of Yonkers v. United States*, 320 U.S. 685 (1944); *American Trucking Assns. v. United States*, 344 U.S. 298, 320 (1953). Plainly, there is no ambiguity here; the Secretary has approved the construction of I-40 through Overton Park and has approved a specific design for the project.

* * *

[T]here is an administrative record that allows the full, prompt review of the Secretary's action that is sought without additional delay which would result from having a remand to the Secretary.

That administrative record is not, however, before us. The lower courts based their review on the litigation affidavits that were presented. These affidavits were merely *"post hoc"* rationalizations, which have traditionally been found to be an inadequate basis for review. And they clearly do not constitute the "whole record" compiled by the agency: the basis for review required by § 706 of the Administrative Procedure Act.

Thus it is necessary to remand this case to the District Court for plenary review of the Secretary's decision. That review is to be based on the full administrative record that was before the Secretary at the time he made his decision. But since the bare record may not disclose the factors that were considered or the Secretary's construction of the evidence it may be necessary for the District Court to require some explanation in order to determine if the Secretary acted within the scope of his authority and if the Secretary's action was justifiable under the applicable standard.

The court may require the administrative officials who participated in the decision to give testimony explaining their action. Of course, such inquiry into the mental processes of administrative decisionmakers is usually to be avoided. *United States v. Morgan*, 313 U.S. 409, 422 (1941). And where there are administrative findings that were made at the same time as the decision, as was the case in *Morgan*, there must be a strong showing of bad faith or improper behavior before such inquiry may be made. But here there are no such formal findings and it may be that the only way there can be effective judicial review is by examining the decisionmakers themselves.

The District Court is not, however, required to make such an inquiry. It may be that the Secretary can prepare formal findings including the information required by DOT Order 5610.1 that will provide an adequate explanation for his action. Such an explanation will, to some extent, be a *"post hoc* rationalization" and thus must be viewed critically. If the District Court decides that additional explanation is necessary, that court should consider which method will prove the most expeditious so that full review may be had as soon as possible.

■ MR. JUSTICE DOUGLAS took no part in the consideration or decision of this case.

■ [Separate concurring opinions of JUSTICES BLACK and BLACKMUN are omitted. Ed.]

Pension Benefit Guaranty Corp. v. LTV Corp.

496 U.S. 633 (1990).

■ JUSTICE BLACKMUN delivered the opinion of the Court.

In this case we must determine whether the decision of the Pension Benefit Guaranty Corporation (PBGC) to restore certain pension plans under § 4047 of the Employee Retirement Income Security Act of 1974 (ERISA), was, as the Court of Appeals concluded, arbitrary and capricious or contrary to law, within the meaning of the Administrative Procedure Act (APA), 5 U.S.C. § 706.

I

Petitioner PBGC is a wholly owned United States Government corporation modeled after the Federal Deposit Insurance Corporation. The Board of Directors of the PBGC consists of the Secretaries of the Treasury, Labor, and Commerce. The PBGC administers and enforces Title IV of ERISA. Title IV includes a mandatory Government insurance program that protects the pension benefits of over 30 million private-sector American workers who participate in plans covered by the Title. In enacting Title IV, Congress sought to ensure that employees and their beneficiaries would not be completely "deprived of anticipated retirement benefits by the termination of pension plans before sufficient funds have been accumulated in the plans." *Pension Benefit Guar. Corp. v. R.A. Gray & Co.*, 467 U.S. 717, 720 (1984).

When a plan covered under Title IV terminates with insufficient assets to satisfy its pension obligations to the employees, the PBGC becomes trustee of the plan, taking over the plan's assets and liabilities. The PBGC then uses the plan's assets to cover what it can of the benefit obligations. The PBGC then must add its own funds to ensure payment of most of the remaining "nonforfeitable" benefits, *i.e.*, those benefits to which participants have earned entitlement under the plan terms as of the date of termination. 29 U.S.C. §§ 1301(a)(8), 1322(a), (b). ERISA does place limits on the benefits PBGC may guarantee upon plan termination, however, even if an employee is entitled to greater benefits under the terms of the plan.

* * *

Termination can be undone by PBGC. * * * When a plan is restored, full benefits are reinstated, and the employer, rather than the PBGC, again is responsible for the plan's unfunded liabilities.

II

This case arose after respondent The LTV Corporation (LTV Corp.) and many of its subsidiaries, including LTV Steel Company Inc. (LTV Steel), (collectively LTV), in July 1986 filed petitions for reorganization under Chapter 11 of the Bankruptcy Code. At that time, LTV Steel was the sponsor of three defined benefit pension plans (Plans) covered by Title IV of ERISA. * * * Chronically underfunded, the Plans, by late 1986, had unfunded liabilities for promised benefits of almost $2.3 billion. Approximately $2.1 billion of this amount was covered by PBGC insurance.

It is undisputed that one of LTV Corp.'s principal goals in filing the Chapter 11 petitions was the restructuring of LTV Steel's pension obligations, a goal which could be accomplished if the Plans were terminated and responsibility for the unfunded liabilities was placed on the PBGC. LTV Steel then could negotiate with its employees for new pension arrangements. LTV, however, could not voluntarily terminate the Plans because two of them had been negotiated in collective bargaining. LTV therefore sought to have the PBGC terminate the Plans.

* * * [T]he PBGC, invoking § 4042(a)(4) of ERISA, 29 U.S.C. § 1342(a)(4), determined that the Plans should be terminated in order to protect the insurance program from the unreasonable risk of large losses, and commenced termination proceedings in the District Court. With LTV's consent, the Plans were terminated effective January 13, 1987.

* * *

In early August 1987, the PBGC determined that the financial factors on which it had relied in terminating the Plans had changed significantly. * * *

The Director issued a notice of restoration on September 22, 1987, indicating the PBGC's intent to restore the terminated Plans. * * *

LTV refused to comply with the restoration decision. * * *

The Court of Appeals for the Second Circuit [held] that the PBGC's restoration decision was "arbitrary and capricious" or contrary to law under the APA, 5 U.S.C. § 706(2)(A), in various ways. * * * [T]he court concluded that the agency's restoration decision was arbitrary and capricious because the PBGC's decisionmaking process of informal adjudication lacked adequate procedural safeguards.

* * *

Finally, we consider the Court of Appeals' ruling that the agency procedures were inadequate in this particular case. Relying upon a passage in *Bowman Transportation, Inc. v. Arkansas-Best Freight System, Inc.,* 419 U.S. 281, 288, n. 4 (1974), the court held that the

PBGC's decision was arbitrary and capricious because the "PBGC neither apprised LTV of the material on which it was to base its decision, gave LTV an adequate opportunity to offer contrary evidence, proceeded in accordance with ascertainable standards . . . , nor provided [LTV] a statement showing its reasoning in applying those standards." The court suggested that on remand the agency was required to do each of these things.

The PBGC argues that this holding conflicts with *Vermont Yankee Nuclear Power Corp. v. Natural Resources Defense Council, Inc.,* 435 U.S. 519 (1978), where, the PBGC contends, this Court made clear that when the Due Process Clause is not implicated and an agency's governing statute contains no specific procedural mandates, the APA establishes the maximum procedural requirements a reviewing court may impose on agencies. * * *

Respondents counter by arguing that courts, under some circumstances, do require agencies to undertake additional procedures. As support for this proposition, they rely on *Citizens to Preserve Overton Park, Inc. v. Volpe,* 401 U.S. 402 (1971). In *Overton Park,* the Court concluded that the Secretary of Transportation's *"post hoc rationalizations"* regarding a decision to authorize the construction of a highway did not provide "an [a]dequate basis for [judicial] review" for purposes of the APA, 5 U.S.C. § 706. *Id.,* at 419. Accordingly, the Court directed the District Court on remand to consider evidence that shed light on the Secretary's reasoning at the time he made the decision. Of particular relevance for present purposes, the Court in *Overton Park* intimated that one recourse for the District Court might be a remand to the agency for a fuller explanation of the agency's reasoning at the time of the agency action. * * *

We believe that respondents' argument is wide of the mark. We begin by noting that although one initially might feel that there is some tension between *Vermont Yankee* and *Overton Park,* the two cases are not necessarily inconsistent. *Vermont Yankee* stands for the general proposition that courts are not free to impose upon agencies specific procedural requirements that have no basis in the APA. At most, *Overton Park* suggests that § 706(2)(A), which directs a court to ensure that an agency action is not arbitrary and capricious or otherwise contrary to law, imposes a general "procedural" requirement of sorts by mandating that an agency take whatever steps it needs to provide an explanation that will enable the court to evaluate the agency's rationale at the time of decision.

Here, unlike in *Overton Park,* the Court of Appeals did not suggest that the administrative record was inadequate to enable the court to fulfill its duties under § 706. * * *

Nor is *Arkansas-Best,* the case on which the Court of Appeals relied, to the contrary. The statement relied upon (which was dictum) said: "A party is entitled, of course, to know the issues on which decision will turn and to be apprised of the factual material on which the agency relies for decision so that he may rebut it." 419 U.S., at 288, n. 4. That statement was entirely correct in the context of *Arkansas-Best,* which involved a formal adjudication by the Interstate Commerce Commission pursuant to the trial-type procedures set forth in §§ 5, 7 and 8 of the APA, 5 U.S.C. §§ 554, 556–57, which include requirements

that parties be given notice of "the matters of fact and law asserted,"
§ 554(b)(3), an opportunity for "the submission and consideration of
facts [and] arguments," § 554(c)(1), and an opportunity to submit
"proposed findings and conclusions" or "exceptions," § 557(c)(1), (2). *See*
5 U.S.C. § 554(a). The determination in this case, however, was lawfully
made by informal adjudication, the minimal requirements for which are
set forth in the APA, 5 U.S.C. § 555, and do not include such elements.
A failure to provide them where the Due Process Clause itself does not
require them (which has not been asserted here) is therefore not
unlawful.

■ [Opinions of JUSTICE WHITE, concurring in part and dissenting in
part, and JUSTICE STEVENS, dissenting, are omitted. Ed.]

NOTES AND QUESTIONS

1. APA § 706, available in Appendix B, requires a reviewing court
evaluating federal agency action to "review the whole record or those parts
of it cited by a party." The Court in *Overton Park* interpreted APA § 706 as
imposing procedural requirements upon federal administrative agencies
engaged in informal adjudication. Reading the two cases together, what if
any procedural requirements do you think the Court interprets APA § 706
as imposing? How do those requirements relate to the language of APA
§ 706?

2. In *LTV Corp.*, the Court identified APA § 555 as setting from "the
minimum requirements" for informal adjudication. APA § 555 is set forth in
Appendix B. Read it carefully. What, if any, procedural requirements for
informal adjudication are imposed by APA § 555?

3. Agencies that are free to use informal adjudication use a wide variety
of procedures in adjudicating disputes. An empirical study of agency
decision-making procedures found that most agencies use a process that
includes (1) notice of issues presented; (2) an opportunity to present data
and arguments in either oral or written form; (3) a decision by a neutral
decisionmaker; and, (4) a statement of reasons for the decision. Paul
Verkuil, *A Study of Informal Adjudication Procedures*, 43 U. CHI. L. REV.
739 (1976).

4. The contexts in which agencies adjudicate disputes vary so greatly
that it is difficult to generalize about the procedures agencies use, or should
use, to conduct informal adjudications. For example, consider the situation
in which a hiker wants to take a hike on a particular trail in a national
park. A park ranger informs the hiker that there is a mother bear with two
cubs a few hundred yards further along the trail, and, therefore, the hiker
cannot continue on the trail. If the hiker contests that decision, we have an
agency adjudication. What procedures should the National Park Service
use to adjudicate such disputes?

C. PERMISSIBLE DECISIONMAKING STRUCTURES AND IMPERMISSIBLE BIAS

The Supreme Court has long held with respect to adjudications
that due process requires a neutral decision-maker, *i.e.*, a decision
maker who is free of impermissible bias. Numerous statutes impose a
similar requirement on courts and agencies, but courts have long

struggled to apply the neutral decision-maker requirement in the context of administrative adjudications. In this Part of Chapter 4, we consider different models for achieving neutral decisionmaking in the context of agencies with overlapping powers.

1. JUDICIAL MODELS: SEPARATION OF FUNCTIONS AND SPLIT-ENFORCEMENT

Administrative agencies often possess and exercise both the power to enforce the law through investigation and prosecution of individual cases and the authority to adjudicate outcomes in those same cases. The Administrative Procedure Act codifies and particularizes the neutral decision-maker requirement for formal adjudications by segregating the investigative and prosecutorial function from that of decision-maker. Read with care APA §§ 554(d) and 556(b), located in Appendix B, restricting which agency employees may preside over the taking of evidence and render decisions in agency adjudications. In particular, APA § 554(d) explicitly prohibits employees serving as adjudicators from performing investigative or prosecutorial functions, and vice versa. § 556(b) meanwhile restricts those presiding over the taking of evidence to "(1) the agency, (2) one or more members of the body which comprises the agency or (3) one or more administrative law judges," all of whom must proceed "in an impartial manner" including possible disqualification for bias. With these provisions, the APA goes well beyond the requirements courts have imposed through interpretations of due process or of the general statutes that require agencies to use an unbiased decision-maker. Do you see why this is so?

The APA requirements are subject, however, to two severe limits. First, these requirements apply only to formal adjudications, not informal ones. Recall the discussion of *Florida East Coast Railway* and the First Circuit's opinion in *Dominion Energy* in Part B of this Chapter. As a result of these and other cases, most agency adjudications are informal rather than formal. Hence, the APA's strictures on which employees can serve as decision-makers do not apply to the vast majority of federal agency adjudications.

Second, even when the formal adjudication provisions of the APA apply, they leave an agency free to substitute its opinion for that of an administrative law judge, and the agency itself is not subject to the structural restriction imposed by the APA. Reconsider APA § 554(d)(2)(C) in conjunction with APA § 557(b), which outlines the decisional relationship where the agency employee presiding over the taking of evidence is not the ultimate decision-maker. Even in a formal adjudication, the agency itself—*i.e.*, the Secretary, the Administrator, or the Commissioners—has the power to order an investigation of conduct that allegedly violated the law, the power to order initiation of a proceeding to enforce the law in the context of the conduct investigated, and the power to make a final decision that the conduct at issue violated the law.

Some participants in and observers of the administrative process believe that the structural safeguards that apply to agency adjudications are inadequate to assure fundamental fairness. The Supreme Court had occasion to consider that argument in the context of a state decision-making structure similar to the structure applicable to APA formal adjudications in the following opinion.

Withrow v. Larkin

421 U.S. 35 (1975).

■ MR. JUSTICE WHITE delivered the opinion for a unanimous Court.

The statutes of the State of Wisconsin forbid the practice of medicine without a license from an Examining Board composed of practicing physicians. The statutes also define and forbid various acts of professional misconduct, proscribe fee splitting, and make illegal the practice of medicine under any name other than the name under which a license has issued if the public would be misled, such practice would constitute unfair competition with another physician, or other detriment to the profession would result. To enforce these provisions, the Examining Board is empowered under Wis. Stat. Ann. §§ 448.17–18 (1974) to warn and reprimand, temporarily to suspend the license, and "to institute criminal action or action to revoke license when it finds probable cause therefor under criminal or revocation statute. . . ." When an investigative proceeding before the Examining Board was commenced against him, appellee brought this suit against appellants, the individual members of the Board, seeking an injunction against the enforcement of the statutes. The District Court issued a preliminary injunction, the appellants appealed, and we noted probable jurisdiction.

Appellee, a resident of Michigan and licensed to practice medicine there, obtained a Wisconsin license in August 1971 under a reciprocity agreement between Michigan and Wisconsin governing medical licensing. . . . On June 20, 1973, the Board sent to appellee a notice that it would hold an investigative hearing on July 12, 1973, . . . to determine whether he had engaged in certain proscribed acts. The hearing would be closed to the public, although appellee and his attorney could attend. They would not, however, be permitted to cross-examine witnesses. Based upon the evidence presented at the hearing, the Board would decide "whether to warn or reprimand if it finds such practice and whether to institute criminal action or action to revoke license if probable cause therefor exists under criminal or revocation statutes."

* * *

The District Court framed the constitutional issue, which it addressed as being whether "for the board temporarily to suspend Dr. Larkin's license at its own contested hearing on charges evolving from its own investigation would constitute a denial to him of his rights to procedural due process." The question was initially answered affirmatively, and in its amended judgment the court asserted that there was a high probability that appellee would prevail on the question. Its opinion stated that the "state medical examining board [did] not qualify as [an independent] decisionmaker [and could not] properly rule with regard to the merits of the same charges it investigated and, as in this case, presented to the district attorney." We disagree. On the present record, it is quite unlikely that appellee would ultimately prevail on the merits of the due process issue presented to the District Court, and it was an abuse of discretion to issue the preliminary injunction.

Concededly, a "fair trial in a fair tribunal is a basic requirement of due process." *In re Murchison*, 349 U.S. 133, 136 (1955). This applies to administrative agencies which adjudicate as well as to courts. *Gibson v. Berryhill*, 411 U.S. 564, 579 (1973). Not only is a biased decisionmaker constitutionally unacceptable but "our system of law has always endeavored to prevent even the probability of unfairness." *Murchison*, 349 U.S. at 136. In pursuit of this end, various situations have been identified in which experience teaches that the probability of actual bias on the part of the judge or decisionmaker is too high to be constitutionally tolerable. Among these cases are those in which the adjudicator has a pecuniary interest in the outcome and in which he has been the target of personal abuse or criticism from the party before him.

The contention that the combination of investigative and adjudicative functions necessarily creates an unconstitutional risk of bias in administrative adjudication has a much more difficult burden of persuasion to carry. It must overcome a presumption of honesty and integrity in those serving as adjudicators; and it must convince that, under a realistic appraisal of psychological tendencies and human weakness, conferring investigative and adjudicative powers on the same individuals poses such a risk of actual bias or prejudgment that the practice must be forbidden if the guarantee of due process is to be adequately implemented.

Very similarly claims have been squarely rejected in prior decisions of this Court. In *FTC v. Cement Institute*, 333 U.S. 683 (1948), the Federal Trade Commission had instituted proceedings concerning the respondents' multiple basing-point delivered-price system. It was demanded that the Commission members disqualify themselves because long before the Commission had filed its complaint it had investigated the parties and reported to Congress and to the President, and its members had testified before congressional committees concerning the legality of such a pricing system. At least some of the members had disclosed their opinion that the system was illegal. The issue of bias was brought here and confronted "on the assumption that such an opinion had been formed by the entire membership of the Commission as a result of its prior official investigations." *Id.* at 700.

The Court rejected the claim saying:

"[T]he fact that the Commission had entertained such views as the result of its prior *ex parte* investigations did not necessarily mean that the minds of its members were irrevocably closed on the subject of the respondents' basing point practices. Here, in contrast to the Commission's investigations, members of the cement industry were legally authorized participants in the hearings. They produced evidence—volumes of it. They were free to point out to the Commission by testimony, by cross-examination of witnesses, and by arguments, conditions of the trade practices under attack which they thought kept these practices within the range of legally permissible business activities." *Id.* at 701.

In specific response to a due process argument, the Court asserted:

> "No decision of this Court would require us to hold that it would be a violation of procedural due process for a judge to sit in a case after he had expressed an opinion as to whether certain types of conduct were prohibited by law. In fact, judges frequently try the same case more than once and decide identical issues each time, although these issues involve questions both of law and fact. Certainly, the Federal Trade Commission cannot possibly be under stronger constitutional compulsions in this respect than a court." *Id.* at 702–03 (footnote omitted).

This Court has also ruled that a hearing examiner who has recommended findings of fact after rejecting certain evidence as not being probative was not disqualified to preside at further hearings that were required when reviewing courts held that the evidence had been erroneously excluded. *NLRB v. Donnelly Garment Co.*, 330 U.S. 219, 236–37 (1946). The Court of Appeals had decided that the examiner should not again sit because it would be unfair to require the parties to try "issues of fact to those who may have prejudged them. . . ." But this Court unanimously reversed, saying:

> "Certainly it is not the rule of judicial administration that, statutory requirements apart . . . a judge is disqualified from sitting in a retrial because he was reversed on earlier rulings. We find no warrant for imposing upon administrative agencies a stiffer rule, whereby examiners would be disentitled to sit because they ruled strongly against a party in the first hearing." 330 U.S. at 236–37.

More recently we have sustained against due process objection a system in which a Social Security examiner has responsibility for developing the facts and making a decision as to disability claims, and observed that the challenge to this combination of functions "assumes too much and would bring down too many procedures designed, and working well, for a governmental structure of great and growing complexity." *Richardson v. Perales*, 402 U.S. 389, 410 (1971).

That is not to say that there is nothing to the argument that those who have investigated should not then adjudicate. The issue is substantial, it is not new, and legislators and others concerned with the operations of administrative agencies have given much attention to whether and to what extent distinctive administrative functions should be performed by the same persons. No single answer has been reached. Indeed, the growth, variety, and complexity of the administrative processes have made any one solution highly unlikely. Within the Federal Government itself, Congress has addressed the issue in several different ways, providing for varying degrees of separation from complete separation of functions to virtually none at all. For the generality of agencies, Congress has been content with § 5 of the Administrative Procedure Act, 5 U.S.C. § 554(d), which provides that no employee engaged in investigating or prosecuting may also participate or advise in the adjudicating function, but which also expressly exempts from this prohibition "the agency or a member or members of the body comprising the agency."

It is not surprising, therefore, to find that "[t]he case law, both federal and state, generally rejects the idea that the combination [of] judging [and] investigating functions is a denial of due process. . . ." 2 KENNETH DAVIS, ADMINISTRATIVE LAW TREATISE § 13.02 (1958). Similarly, our cases, although they reflect the substance of the problem, offer no support for the bald proposition applied in this case by the District Court that agency members who participate in an investigation are disqualified from adjudicating. The incredible variety of administrative mechanisms in this country will not yield to any single organizing principle.

* * *

Nor do we think the situation substantially different because the Board, when it was prevented from going forward with the contested hearing, proceeded to make and issue formal findings of fact and conclusions of law asserting that there was probable cause to believe that appellee had engaged in various acts prohibited by the Wisconsin statutes. These findings and conclusions were verified and filed with the district attorney for the purpose of initiating revocation and criminal proceedings. Although the District Court did not emphasize this aspect of the case before it, appellee stresses it in attempting to show prejudice and prejudgment. We are not persuaded.

Judges repeatedly issue arrest warrants on the basis that there is probable cause to believe that a crime has been committed and that the person named in the warrant has committed it. Judges also preside at preliminary hearings where they must decide whether the evidence is sufficient to hold a defendant for trial. Neither of these pretrial involvements has been thought to raise any constitutional barrier against the judge's presiding over the criminal trial and, if the trial is without a jury, against making the necessary determination of guilt or innocence. Nor has it been thought that a judge is disqualified from presiding over injunction proceedings because he has initially assessed the facts in issuing or denying a temporary restraining order or a preliminary injunction. It is also very typical for the members of administrative agencies to receive the results of investigations, to approve the filing of charges or formal complaints instituting enforcement proceedings, and then to participate in the ensuing hearings. This mode of procedure does not violate the Administrative Procedure Act, and it does not violate due process of law. We should also remember that it is not contrary to due process to allow judges and administrators who have had their initial decisions reversed on appeal to confront and decide the same questions a second time around.

Here, the Board stayed within the accepted bounds of due process. Having investigated, it issued findings and conclusions asserting the commission of certain acts and ultimately concluding that there was probable cause to believe that appellee had violated the statutes.

The risk of bias or prejudgment in this sequence of functions has not been considered to be intolerably high or to raise a sufficiently great possibility that the adjudicators would be so psychologically wedded to their complaints that they would consciously or unconsciously avoid the appearance of having erred or changed position. Indeed, just as there is no logical inconsistency between a finding of probable cause and an acquittal in a criminal proceeding, there is no incompatibility between the agency filing a complaint based on probable cause and a subsequent decision, when all the evidence is in, that there has been no violation of the statute. Here, if the Board now proceeded after an adversary hearing to determine that appellee's license to practice should not be temporarily suspended, it would not implicitly be admitting error in its prior finding of probable cause. Its position most probably would merely reflect the benefit of a more complete view of the evidence afforded by an adversary hearing.

The initial charge or determination of probable cause and the ultimate adjudication have different bases and purposes. The fact that the same agency makes them in tandem and that they relate to the same issues does not result in a procedural due process violation. Clearly, if the initial view of the facts based on the evidence derived from nonadversarial processes as a practical or legal matter foreclosed fair and effective consideration at a subsequent adversary hearing leading to ultimate decision, a substantial due process question would be raised. But in our view, that is not this case.

That the combination of investigative and adjudicative functions does not, without more, constitute a due process violation, does not, of course, preclude a court from determining from the special facts and circumstances present in the case before it that the risk of unfairness is intolerably high. Findings of that kind made by judges with special insights into local realities are entitled to respect, but injunctions resting on such factors should be accompanied by at least the minimum findings required by Rules 52(a) and 65(d).

NOTES AND QUESTIONS

1.   Courts have decided many cases involving allegations of impermissible pecuniary bias. Thus, a mayor may not adjudicate cases in circumstances in which a high proportion of his income is derived from fees assessed against losing parties and in which he receives no compensation if he decides that the accused party did not violate the law, *Tumey v. Ohio*, 273 U.S. 510 (1927), or in which fifty per cent of a town's total revenue is derived from fines imposed by the mayor. *Ward v. Village of Monroeville*, 409 U.S. 57 (1972). It is not hard to understand the Court's conclusions in cases of that type.

Many cases are far more difficult to decide. Compare, for example, *Gibson v. Berryhill*, 411 U.S. 564 (1973), in which the Court held unconstitutional a state statute that required that all members of state board of optometry must be independent on the basis that the board could decide that any optometrist who is affiliated with a corporation is acting unethically, thereby putting all corporate-affiliated optometrists out of business and allowing the independent optometrist board members to profit by obtaining the business of the corporate-affiliated optometrists, with *Friedman v. Rogers*, 440 U.S. 1 (1979), in which a majority of the Court upheld a state statute that required that four of six members of state board of optometry be members of an association that admits only independent optometrists.

2.   Claims of impermissible pecuniary bias rarely arise in the context of federal agency adjudications. Decision-makers in federal agencies are

almost invariably full-time government employees who are subject to elaborate conflict of interest rules. Claims of impermissible pecuniary bias are common, however, in the context of state and local agency adjudications. Why do you think this is? Imagine that you are a part-time state legislator in a relatively small state, or a part-time member of a city council, and that you have decided to create a board with the power to set health and safety standards applicable to some form of professional conduct, *e.g.*, repair of home furnaces, and to implement a licensing system to enforce those standards. How would you go about the process of choosing individuals to serve on the Board? Would you bar from membership on the Board any individual who might profit from a decision to set a particular standard or to deny a license to an applicant? What would be the effects of such a bar?

3. Impermissible bias claims based on prior exposure to an issue or prior expression of views on an issue arise with considerable frequency in the context of federal agencies, as well as state and local agencies. The Federal Trade Commission provides a good context in which to consider how agencies and courts should address claims of that type. The FTC's responsibilities include implementation and enforcement of antitrust law. Assume that you are an FTC Commissioner who is the subject of a motion to recuse based on your alleged impermissible prior expression of views on a contested issue that has arisen in a case in which a firm is accused of engaging in a particular pattern of conduct that the FTC staff alleges to be a violation of antitrust law. Should your reaction to the motion to recuse be the same whether you have previously expressed the view that the pattern of conduct at issue is a violation of antitrust law or the view that the firm has engaged in that pattern of conduct? Can you distinguish those arguable bases for disqualification of a decision-maker?

How well would the legal system function if we disqualified from antitrust decisionmaking any individual who has expressed an opinion on whether horizontal price-fixing or base-point pricing is a violation of antitrust law? Consider then-Justice Rehnquist's explanation for his decision not to recuse himself in an analogous situation in *Laird v. Tatum*, 409 U.S. 824 (1972):

> Since most Justices come to this bench no earlier than their middle years, it would be unusual if they had not by that time formulated at least some tentative notions which would influence them in their interpretation of the sweeping clauses of the Constitution and their interaction with one another. It would be not merely unusual, but extraordinary, if they had not at least given opinions as to constitutional issues in their previous legal careers. Proof that a Justice's mind at the time he joined the Court was a complete tabula rasa in the area of constitutional adjudication would be evidence of lack of qualification, not lack of bias.

* * *

The oath prescribed by 28 U.S.C. § 453 which is taken by each person upon becoming a member of the federal judiciary requires that he "administer justice without respect to persons, and do equal right to the poor and to the rich," that he "faithfully and impartially discharge and perform all the duties incumbent upon [him] . . . agreeably to the Constitution and laws of the United States." Every litigant is entitled to have his case heard by a judge mindful of this oath. But neither the oath, the disqualification statute, nor the practice of the former Justices of this Court guarantee a litigant that each judge will start off from dead center in his willingness or ability to reconcile the opposing arguments of counsel with his understanding of the Constitution and the law. That being the case, it is not a ground for disqualification that a judge has prior to his nomination expressed his then understanding of the meaning of some particular provision of the Constitution.

Based on the foregoing considerations, I conclude that respondents' motion that I disqualify myself in this case should be, and it hereby is denied.

Id. at 835–839.

4. If you were the subject of an enforcement proceeding in which you face the prospect of a large civil penalty for allegedly violating a statute or rule, would you be concerned about the fairness of the decision-making process, knowing that the final decision might well be made by the same person (agency head) who originally authorized the investigation of your conduct and then authorized the initiation of the enforcement proceeding against you? If so, you are not alone. Even though Congress has authorized that type of decision-making structure in most circumstances, and the Supreme Court has upheld it against constitutional attack, many participants in the agency decision-making process continue to believe that it is fundamentally unfair. In some contexts, the critics of the APA model have persuaded Congress to require a different model in an effort to enhance fairness.

The Split-Enforcement Model

The alternative to the APA model is often called the split-enforcement model, dividing responsibility for investigation and enforcement from adjudication. At different times, Congress has adopted this model in various contexts.

In the context of occupational health and safety, one agency—the Occupational Safety and Health Administration (OSHA)—makes rules, investigates alleged violations of rules, and initiates enforcement actions. Another agency—the Occupational Safety and Health Review Commission (OSHRC)—then adjudicates the cases initiated by OSHA. OSHA is headed by a single Administrator who is appointed by the President subject to Senate confirmation and who can be removed by the President at any time without any specification of cause for removal. OSHRC is an "independent agency," that is headed by five Commissioners. The President appoints each Commissioner subject to Senate confirmation. Each Commissioner serves a five-year term and can be removed by the President only for cause. No more than three Commissioners can be members of the same political party, and the Commissioners serve staggered terms.

Congress has adopted a similar regime in the area of mine safety. The Mine Safety and Health Administration (MSHA) is responsible for developing mandatory safety and health standards for the mining industry and also investigating and initiating enforcement actions for violations of those standards. The independent Federal Mine Safety and Health Review Commission (MSHRC) adjudicates the cases initiated by the MSHA. In the past, Congress has used the split-enforcement arrangement in the federal income tax and the federal aviation safety contexts.

If you were subject to regulation, would you prefer the APA model or the split-enforcement model? If you were a beneficiary of occupational safety and health or mine safety regulation, which model would you prefer? What arguments would you make on behalf of a client in support of each model?

2. THE JUDICIAL MODEL VERSUS THE BUREAUCRATIC MODEL

Both the APA model of adjudication and the split-enforcement model are versions of the judicial model of adjudication that U.S. courts use to resolve criminal and civil cases. The judicial model is based on one common conception of due process, *i.e.*, the values reflected in the Due Process Clause are furthered by insulating decision-makers from all external sources of pressure. Thus, the Constitution is designed to insulate federal judges from external sources of pressure by giving them life tenure, and the APA accomplishes the same purpose with respect to ALJs by forbidding agencies from evaluating their performance or setting their pay and by making it extremely difficult for agencies to remove them or to discipline them in any way. This conception of due process furthers important values of our legal system. Thus, for instance, we would be displeased if we believed that the outcome of agency adjudications depended on whether parties were popular or unpopular with the President or members of Congress. The provision of an independent judicial mind to decide agency adjudications greatly reduces the risk of such a disconcerting result.

The judicial model of adjudication has the potential to conflict with an equally appealing conception of the purpose of the Due Process Clause, however. We often think of a decision-making system that complies with due process as a system in which like cases are decided in like manner. Since different "independent judicial minds" can decide like cases in quite different ways, the results of the judicial model have the potential to produce results that diverge from this conception of a fair decision-making process.

Empirical studies of agency adjudication systems have produced disturbing findings. Jaya Ramji-Nogales, Andrew Schoenholtz, and Philip Schrag, *Refugee Roulette: Disparities in Asylum Adjudication*, 60 STAN. L. REV. 295 (2007), found enormous unexplained disparities in the outcome of asylum cases adjudicated by immigration officers and immigration judges. Thus, for instance, Chinese applicants for amnesty have a forty-seven per cent probability of success nationally, but their success rate varies by region from seven per cent in Atlanta to seventy-six per cent in Orlando. Adjudicatory decision-makers in a single regional office vary in their grant rates from zero per cent to sixty-eight per cent. Availability of judicial review does not have a positive effect on the pattern of decisions. Indeed, the study found that judicial review often exacerbated the problem by introducing a new level of unexplained differences in outcomes. Some circuit courts uphold virtually all agency denials of asylum, while others reverse a high proportion of such denials.

Empirical studies of Social Security Administration (SSA) disability decisionmaking have produced similar findings. As the Court discussed in *Mathews v. Eldridge*, 424 U.S. 319 (1976), the SSA initially decides whether to grant an application for disability benefits through a bureaucratic process in which an SSA regional office applies relatively objective criteria to the information contained in a written file. If the application is denied at that level, the SSA provides an opportunity for an oral evidentiary hearing before an SSA ALJ.

A comprehensive interdisciplinary study of the pattern of decisions issued by SSA ALJs in disability cases found that the variable that has the greatest effect on the likely outcome of an SSA disability decision is the identity of the ALJ to whom the case is assigned. MASHAW, GOETZ, GOODMAN, SCHWARTZ, VERKUIL & CARROW, SOCIAL SECURITY HEARINGS AND APPEALS (1978). The average SSA ALJ grants benefits in fifty percent of cases, and forty-five percent of ALJs grant benefits in forty to sixty per cent of cases. Yet, four per cent of ALJs grant benefits in less than twenty-four per cent of case, and eight per cent of ALJs grant benefits in over seventy-six per cent of cases. Since there are about one thousand SSA ALJs, and each decides about 300 cases per year, real differences in the characteristics of the applicants cannot possibly explain most of this large variation in ALJ patterns of decisionmaking.

Moreover, the random possibility of persuading an ALJ to grant benefits when an SSA regional office has denied benefits creates an incentive for applicants to appeal adverse decisions to ALJs. The percentage of cases in which applicants appealed denials of benefits to ALJs soared in the 1980s and 1990s, with large attendant increases in both the unexplained variation in the pattern of decisions and in the delay before a disability proceeding is the subject of a final agency decision. By 2007, the SSA required well over a year to make a final decision in a contested disability proceeding.

During the 1980s, the SSA attempted to address the problem of interdecisional inconsistency among its ALJs and delay in its decision-making process by imposing some constraints on its ALJs. The SSA's ALJs were incensed. They challenged the SSA managerial techniques as violations of both the Constitution and the statutes that govern SSA decisionmaking. The ALJs prevailed in several district courts, but some district courts and the one circuit court that addressed the dispute between SSA and its ALJs approved of SSA's efforts.

Nash v. Bowen

869 F.2d 675 (2d Cir.), cert. denied, 493 U.S. 812 (1989).

■ ALTIMARI, CIRCUIT JUDGE:

The principal issue raised by the instant appeal following a nonjury trial in the United States District Court for the Western District of New York is whether efforts by the Secretary of Health and Human Services (the "Secretary") to improve the quality and efficiency of the work of Administrative Law Judges ("ALJs") impaired their asserted right to "decisional independence" under the Administrative Procedure Act. * * * Because the district court's factual findings underlying the conclusion that the Secretary's policies did not exceed the bounds of legitimate agency supervision are fairly supported by the record and therefore are not clearly erroneous, we agree with the district court that the Secretary's practices did not infringe on the decisional independence of ALJs. We . . . therefore affirm the district court's judgment in all respects.

Plaintiff-appellant, *pro se*, Simon Nash is an Administrative Law Judge ("ALJ") with some thirty years experience in the Social Security Administration. In 1967, he became an ALJ in charge ("ALJIC") of the Buffalo, New York field office of hearings and appeals. By 1975, the Social Security Administration (the "agency") was faced with an administrative crisis due to a backlog of over 100,000 cases. In order to eliminate the backlog and the concomitant delays in processing appeals, former director of the Bureau (now "Office") of Hearings and Appeals Robert L. Trachtenberg instituted a series of reforms which appellant contends interfered with the "decisional independence" of ALJs under the APA, the Social Security Act and the due process clause of the fifth amendment. Nash initially protested the new policies within the agency only to be summarily demoted from his position as ALJIC to ALJ. In his original complaint filed May 30, 1978 in the district court, plaintiff alleged, in addition to a claim concerning his demotion which was later dropped, that the Secretary's newly-instituted "Peer Review Program," monthly production goals, and "Quality Assurance System" infringed upon the "quasi-judicial" status of ALJs.

* * *

Turning, then, to plaintiff's "decisional independence" claims, the challenged practices are threefold. . . . [T]he first allegedly unlawful practice is the "Peer Review Program" (a/k/a/ the "Appellate Appraisal System,") which directed the Office of Hearings and Appeals to review decisions of ALJs outside of the usual appeals procedure conducted by the Appeals Council. The second practice concerns the imposition of allegedly arbitrary monthly production quotas requiring ALJs to render a specified number of decisions per month. The third alleged threat to ALJs' decisional independence is the "Quality Assurance System," which attempted to control the number of ALJ decisions reversing previous state-level determinations declining to award benefits.

* * *

The district court explicitly determined that "[a]lthough the defendants may have engaged in some questionable practices which clearly caused great unrest among ALJs, . . . they did not infringe on the decisional independence of ALJs." The factual components of this conclusion, as with all findings of fact, cannot be set aside on appeal unless they are clearly erroneous.

The district court held that the "Peer Review Program" was intended to respond to the "wide disparity in legal and factual determinations among ALJs." Judge Elfvin concluded that various peer review actions constituted "legitimate administrative steps undertaken to enhance the quality and efficiency of the hearing system." Policies designed to insure a reasonable degree of uniformity among ALJ decisions are not only within the bounds of legitimate agency supervision but are to be encouraged. In this case, "extra-appellate" review of "dead" cases aimed at improving the quality of ALJ decisionmaking is entirely consistent with the prerogative of the agency which retains "all the powers which it would have in making the initial decision." 5 U.S.C. § 557(b). It is, after all, the Secretary who ultimately is authorized to make final decisions in benefit cases. An ALJ is a creature of statute and, as such, is subordinate to the Secretary in matters of policy and interpretation of law. Thus, the Secretary's efforts through peer review to ensure that ALJ decisions conformed with his interpretation of relevant law and policy were permissible so long as such efforts did not directly interfere with "live" decisions. . . . The efforts complained of in this case for promoting quality and efficiency do not infringe upon ALJs' decisional independence. Since Judge Elfvin concluded that the "Peer Review Program" was intended to be, and operated as, a quality control measure, we see no reason to disturb his determination.

Regarding the Secretary's policy of setting a minimum number of dispositions an ALJ must decide in a month, we agree with the district court that reasonable efforts to increase the production levels of ALJs are not an infringement of decisional independence. In a memorandum dated July 1, 1975, then Director Trachtenberg indicated that while he was opposed to the fixing of *quotas*, he was recommending a *goal* of 26 dispositions per four-week period. When Louis B. Hays became Associate Commissioner of the Office of Hearings and Appeals in 1981, he specifically concerned himself with ALJs whose productivity fell below twenty case dispositions per month. The record also reflects continuing pressure from the agency on ALJs to increase monthly dispositions.

The setting of reasonable production goals, as opposed to fixed quotas, is not in itself a violation of the APA. The district court explicitly found that the numbers at issue constituted reasonable goals as opposed to unreasonable quotas. Judge Elfvin explained that

> [a] minimum number of dispositions an ALJ must decide in a given period, provided this number is reasonable and not "etched in stone", is not a prescription of how, or how quickly, an ALJ should decide a particular case. It does not dictate the content of the decision.

Moreover, in view of the significant backlog of cases, it was not unreasonable to expect ALJs to perform at minimally acceptable levels of efficiency. Simple fairness to claimants awaiting benefits required no less. Accordingly, we agree with the district court that the decisional independence of ALJs was not in any way usurped by the Secretary's setting of monthly production goals.

The Secretary's "reversal" rate policy embodied in the "Quality Assurance System," however, is cause for concern. To coerce ALJs into lowering reversal rates—that is, into deciding more cases against claimants—would, if shown, constitute in the district court's words "a clear infringement of decisional independence." In his brief on appeal and at oral argument, Nash characterized the alleged pressure from the agency concerning reversal rates as the heart of the controversy. Plaintiff also maintained that the reversal rate policy, in effect from approximately 1975 to 1985, was implemented under the guise of improving the quality and uniformity of ALJ decisions but was in fact a clear attempt by the Secretary to influence ALJs into deciding more cases in favor of the agency.

The Secretary concedes that he was very concerned about reversal rates, but only to the extent that they might indicate errors in the decisionmaking of ALJs. Testimony in the record revealed that reversal rates were used as a benchmark in deciding whether there might be problems in the adjudicatory methods of particularly high (or low) reversal rate ALJs. Statistical record evidence supported the agency's proffered correlation between actual errors of law or policy in ALJs decisions and extremes in their reversal rates. The agency maintained then, and maintains now, that reducing reversal rates was not the intent of the policy. Indeed, a handwritten notation by Associate Commissioner Hays on a 1982 internal agency memorandum placed the policy in perspective:

> [T]here is *no* goal to reduce reversal rates—there is a goal to improve decisional quality [and] consistency, which is assumed to have as one effect a reduction of the reversal rate.

In view of the foregoing record evidence, therefore, we cannot say that the district court's determination was clearly erroneous. Whatever legitimate concerns there may be about the soundness of the Secretary's practices regarding "reversal" rates, those concerns are more appropriately addressed by Congress or by courts through the usual channels of judicial review in Social Security cases.

NOTES AND QUESTIONS

1.   Unacceptably high rates of inter-decisional inconsistency can arise in any adjudicatory context. The U.S. judicial decision-making and administrative decision-making systems attempt to keep this problem within tolerable bounds through use of several standard techniques. First, we have a hierarchal structure in which higher courts (or, in some instances, intra-agency appeals bodies) review decisions of district judges and ALJs in an effort to enhance uniformity and consistency. Second, the higher courts and intra-agency review bodies typically act in multi-member panels, thereby reducing the effects of differences among individual judges and ALJs. Third, we have statutes and agency rules that limit the decision-making discretion of individual judges and ALJs. Fourth, we have a system of precedents which, when coupled with principles of stare decisis and applications of the arbitrary and capricious standard to agency

adjudications, further reduces the potential for inter-decisional inconsistency.

Each of these methods of keeping inter-decisional inconsistency within tolerable bounds has limits, however, and those limits are particularly serious in contexts like asylum cases and disability cases. Consider the ways that the following characteristics of SSA disability adjudications limit the efficacy of each of our standard methods of managing this problem. The SSA decides over two million cases per year. The decisions are not published or indexed. The adjudications are conducted in many regional offices. The issues that are most frequently contested in the cases that are appealed to ALJs are neurosis and chronic pain. In the vast majority of cases, it is easy to determine that the applicant is suffering from either neurosis or chronic pain, but the question the agency and ALJs must answer is whether the applicant's disability is so severe that he or she "cannot engage in any substantial gainful work which exists in the national economy." The medical profession has not yet devised clear, objective means of determining the level of pain or neurosis an individual is suffering or the extent to which that pain or neurosis is disabling.

If you were the Administrator of the Social Security system, how would you address this problem? By the way, Congress repeatedly chastises SSA for its poor performance but also consistently refuses to increase the appropriations of SSA to address the problems it confronts. If you were a judge, would you uphold the methods of managing this problem the court described in *Nash*?

2.   Congress has adopted a mechanism roughly analogous to the SSA ALJ management tools the court addressed in *Nash* in at least one important context. When Congress detected large unexplained variations in the sentences federal judges were giving in similar cases, it responded by creating a Sentencing Commission and instructing that body to set guidelines that federal judges must follow in sentencing individuals convicted of crimes. The Supreme Court upheld that method of reducing inter-decisional in *Mistretta v. United States*, 488 U.S. 361 (1989), which is discussed in Chapter 2.

3.   The SSA's methods of attempting to limit the discretion of its ALJs encountered great hostility from ALJs and from many federal district judges. Generally federal district judges are far more skeptical of the legitimacy of limits of this type than are circuit court judges and Supreme Court Justices. Thus, a high proportion of the district judges who addressed the merits of the disputes between SSA and its ALJs held the SSA programs unlawful, often in opinions that were harshly critical of SSA, before the Second Circuit upheld the SSA methods of managing their ALJs. Similarly, a high proportion of federal district judges who addressed the merits of the statute that created the Sentencing Commission held it to be unconstitutional before the Supreme Court upheld the statute. Why do you think district judges might differ significantly from circuit judges and Supreme Court Justices with respect to the legitimacy and legality of measures of this type?

4.   Even though the only circuit court that addressed the merits of the dispute between the SSA and its ALJs upheld all of SSA's methods of attempting to limit the discretion of its ALJs, the SSA later abandoned those efforts. The SSA discovered that its rate of reversal in district courts

increased significantly after it began to implement its methods of attempting to manage its ALJs, *i.e.*, district courts began to reverse a higher proportion of SSA decisions through application of the substantial evidence test. Can you think of an explanation for this phenomenon?

5. Other efforts to empower agencies to manage their large numbers of ALJs have met similar fates. In 1992, the Administrative Conference of the United States (ACUS), a government think tank whose past leaders include Justice Scalia and whose past members include Justice Breyer, commissioned a comprehensive study of the federal administrative judiciary. *See* Recommendations and Statements of the Administrative Conference Regarding Administrative Practice and Procedure, 57 Fed. Reg. 61759 (Dec. 29, 1992). The study praised the institution of the ALJ and the performance of ALJs in many respects. It found, however, that the inability of agencies to implement any methods of evaluating the performance of ALJs led to unevenness in the quality of ALJs and to unacceptably high rates of inter-decisional inconsistency and inefficiency in some important contexts. It also found that those problems with the ALJ system had induced most agencies that are not required by statute to use ALJs to hire instead other adjudicatory officers who were often not as good as ALJs and who often had little, if any, independence from the agencies that employed them. As a result, the authors of the study recommended that Congress amend the APA to allow agencies to engage in some limited forms of evaluation of ALJs. The ACUS approved that recommendation and forwarded it to Congress.

The ALJs' union was enraged by the ACUS recommendation and report. They were not content merely to block enactment of the proposed amendment to the APA. They persuaded Congress to abolish ACUS as punishment for its recommendation! In light of the fate of the SSA efforts to enhance inter-decisional consistency in its disability decision-making process, what actions would you recommend to improve inter-decisional consistency in the asylum decision-making process? *See* Margaret H. Taylor, *Refugee Roulette in an Administrative Law Context: the Déjà Vu of Decisional Disparities in Agency Adjudications*, 60 STAN. L. REV. 475 (2007).

Ongoing Issues with ALJs in the Social Security Disability System

Despite the SSA's efforts to address inconsistencies among ALJ decisions regarding disability benefits, more recent studies of the Social Security disability system conducted by the Social Security Advisory Board (SSAB), the Congressional Budget Office (CBO), and researchers at MIT and University of Maryland have painted a picture of an unsustainably generous and incoherent program. *See* CBO, SOCIAL SECURITY DISABILITY INSURANCE: PARTICIPATION RATES AND THEIR FISCAL IMPLICATIONS (2010); SSAB, IMPROVING THE SOCIAL SECURITY HEARING PROCESS (2006); SSAB, CHARTING THE FUTURE OF SOCIAL SECURITY'S DISABILITY PROGRAMS: THE NEED FOR FUNDAMENTAL CHANGE (2001); David Autor & Mark Duggan, *The Growth in the Social Security Disability Rolls: A Fiscal Crisis Unfolding*, 20 J. ECON. PERSPECTIVES 71 (2006). The percent of the population that has been determined to be disabled has doubled since 1970 and the cost of the program has more than quadrupled since 1990. The trust fund

Congress established to fund the program is expected to run out of money by 2018, many years before the trust funds for the Social Security retirement program or the Medicare programs are expected to run out of money.

Like the studies conducted during the 1970s, 1980s, and 1990s, the recent studies identify Social Security Administration (SSA) administrative law judges (ALJs) as one of the major sources of the problems with the disability program. The decision making process begins when a team consisting of a disability examiner and a medical advisor reviews the materials submitted by an applicant for benefits. The team can, and often does, request additional materials and/or examinations and reports by consulting physicians. The team then decides whether the applicant is eligible. If the initial team decides that the applicant is not disabled, the applicant can appeal that decision. In such cases, a second examiner/medical advisor team considers the record independently. The second team also can, and often does, obtain additional materials and/or reports from consulting physicians. The members of the decision making teams are state employees, but their decisions are audited by the SSA quality assurance office, and the team members are provided feedback and additional training to the extent that the SSA finds deficiencies in their decision making process.

If an applicant is determined not to be disabled by both of the examiner/medical advisor teams, he can appeal to an ALJ, who conducts a de novo oral hearing. Over time, ALJs have become increasingly generous in deciding that applicants who have been the subject of two independent SSA determinations that they are not disabled are in fact disabled. On average, ALJs make findings that such applicants are disabled in 60 percent of cases. There is tremendous variability in the patterns of ALJ decision making, however. At least 2 ALJs grant benefits in 100 percent of cases; 27 ALJs grant benefits in over 95 percent of cases; and 100 ALJs grant benefits in over 90 percent of cases. Unlike the examiner/medical advisor teams, SSA ALJs do not have medical advisors, are not subject to any quality assurance program, and cannot be supervised or evaluated by the SSA. An ALJ decision that denies an application is subject to potential review by a federal district court, but an ALJ decision that grants benefits is final and is not reviewable by any government institution.

NOTES AND QUESTIONS

1. Are SSA ALJs employees or officers of the United States? In evaluating this question, reconsider *Landry v. FDIC*, 204 F.3d 1125 (D.C. Cir. 2000), which is excerpted in Chapter 3 of the textbook.

2. An SSA ALJ can only be removed or otherwise disciplined through a process in which the SSA files a petition with the Merit Systems Protection Board (MSPB), the MSPB assigns the case to another ALJ for hearing, and the MSPB decides that the ALJ can be removed for "good cause." The SSA is an independent agency that is headed by a Commissioner who can only be removed by the President for "inefficiency, neglect of duty, or malfeasance of office." The MSPB is also an independent agency that is headed by a three-member Board, each member of which can be removed by the President only for "neglect of duty or malfeasance in office."

Is this structure consistent with the Take Care Clause of the Constitution? In evaluating this question, reconsider the opinions in *Free Enterprise Fund v. Public Co. Accounting Oversight Bd.*, 130 S.Ct. 3138 (2010), excerpted at the start of this update. How many levels of protection separate SSA ALJs from presidential control?

3.   What, if anything, should Congress do to address the variability among ALJs in granting Social Security disability benefits to applicants?

The Bureaucratic Model

Professor Jerry Mashaw has written a book in which he is broadly critical of the U.S. reliance on the judicial model to adjudicate large classes of disputes, including SSA disability cases. MASHAW, BUREAUCRATIC JUSTICE (1983). He notes that most countries use a system of bureaucratic justice, rather than a system of judicial justice, to make decisions in cases like disability cases. He then describes those systems and demonstrates that they operate with greater accuracy, consistency, and efficiency than our system of judicial justice. Mashaw describes the dominant characteristics of systems of bureaucratic justice as follows: decisions are not made by independent individuals but by teams of people who are organized hierarchically and who are instructed to apply objective, verifiable criteria; and both the criteria and the methods of application are constantly reevaluated and revised to enhance accuracy, consistency and efficiency. Would you support a switch to such a bureaucratic model for making important adjudicatory decisions like disability decisions and asylum decisions? Why or why not?

Both the Supreme Court in its due process decisionmaking and the Congress in its statutory drafting assume implicitly that the judicial system of justice is superior to the bureaucratic system. Thus, for instance, in cases like *Goldberg* and *Eldridge*, the Court considers oral evidentiary hearings presided over by ALJs an appropriate and essential means of reducing the errors that are made in the prior bureaucratic decision-making process, and Congress provides for ALJ review of the bureaucratic decisions followed by judicial review of the ALJ decisions. Is it possible that both the Supreme Court and the Congress are mistaken in their evaluations of the merits of the two methods of making decisions?

3.   PUBLIC VERSUS PRIVATE ADJUDICATORS

Concerns about bias in agency adjudications take many forms. Adjudicators may feel strongly about questions of law or policy to the point of suggesting a closed mind. Adjudicators may be personally prejudiced for or against particular individual parties. On occasion, adjudicators may themselves stand to gain or lose by a decision, possessing a personal interest in the outcome of a dispute. Personal interest bias is the most obvious basis for concluding that a judge ought to disqualify herself from hearing and resolving a case. Hence, judges are required to recuse themselves in a variety of circumstances that suggest the potential for personal interest bias. *See* 28 U.S.C. §§ 144 and 455.

Government agencies frequently rely on nongovernmental actors, bodies, or organizations to adjudicate individual cases and claims. These nongovernmental adjudicators are not randomly selected. They are typically selected on the basis of their expertise in the area of the cases and claims they adjudicate. As a result, however, nongovernmental adjudicators generally possess some professional or other economic connection to the concerns being adjudicated. Discerning when such indirect economic interests suggest impermissible bias and ought to be disqualifying has proven challenging for the courts. Consider, for example, the following cases.

Gibson v. Berryhill

411 U.S. 564 (1973).

■ JUSTICE WHITE delivered the opinion of the Court.

Prior to 1965, the laws of Alabama relating to the practice of optometry permitted any person, including a business firm or corporation, to maintain a department in which 'eyes are examined or glasses fitted,' provided that such department was in the charge of a duly licensed optometrist. The permission was expressly conferred by § 210 of Title 46 of the Alabama Code of 940, and also inferentially by § 211 of the Code which regulates the advertising practices of optometrists, and which, until 1965, appeared to contemplate the existence of commercial stores with optical departments. In 1965, § 210 was repealed in its entirety by the Alabama Legislature, and § 211 was amended so as to eliminate any direct reference to optical departments maintained by corporations or other business establishments under the direction of employee optometrists.

Soon after these statutory changes, the Alabama Optometric Association, a professional organization whose membership is limited to independent practitioners of optometry not employed by others, filed charges against various named optometrists, all of whom were duly licensed under Alabama law but were the salaried employees of Lee Optical Co. The charges were filed with the Alabama Board of Optometry, the statutory body with authority to issue, suspend, and revoke licenses for the practice of optometry. The gravamen of these charges was that the named optometrists, by accepting employment from Lee Optical, a corporation, had engaged in 'unprofessional conduct' within the meaning of § 206 of the Alabama optometry statute and hence were practicing their profession unlawfully. More particularly, the Association charged the named individuals with, among other things, aiding and abetting a corporation in the illegal practice of optometry; practicing optometry under a false name, that is, Lee Optical Co.; unlawfully soliciting the sale of glasses; lending their licenses to Lee Optical Co.; and splitting or dividing fees with Lee Optical. It was apparently the Association's position that, following the repeal of § 210 and the amendment of § 211, the practice of optometry by individuals as employees of business corporations was no longer permissible in Alabama, and that, by accepting such employment the named optometrists had violated the ethics of their profession. It was prayed that the Board revoke the licenses of the individuals charged following due notice and a proper hearing.

Meanwhile, following its victory in the trial court, the Board reactivated the proceedings pending before it since 1965 against the individual optometrists employed by Lee, noticing them for hearings to be held on May 26 and 27, 1971. Those individuals countered on May 14, 1971, by filing a complaint in the United States District Court naming as defendants the Board of Optometry and its individual members, as well as the Alabama Optometric Association and other individuals. The suit, brought under the Civil Rights Act of 1871, 42 U.S.C. § 1983, sought an injunction against the scheduled hearings on the grounds that the statutory scheme regulating the practice of optometry in Alabama was unconstitutional insofar as it permitted the Board to hear the pending charges against the individual plaintiffs in the federal suit.[7] The thrust of the complaint was that the Board was biased and could not provide the plaintiffs with a fair and impartial hearing in conformity with due process of law.

A three-judge court was convened in August 1971, and shortly thereafter entered judgment for plaintiffs, enjoining members of the State Board and their successors 'from conducting a hearing on the charges heretofore preferred against the Plaintiffs' and from revoking their licenses to practice optometry in the State of Alabama.

* * *

For the District Court, the inquiry was not whether the Board members were 'actually biased but whether, in the natural course of events, there is an indication of a possible temptation to an average man sitting as a judge to try the case with bias for or against any issue presented to him.' Such a possibility of bias was found to arise in the present case from a number of factors. First, was the fact that the Board, which acts as both prosecutor and judge in delicensing proceedings, had previously brought suit against the plaintiffs on virtually identical charges in the state courts. This the District Court took to indicate that members of the Board might have 'preconceived opinions' with regard to the cases pending before them. Second, the court found as a fact that Lee Optical Co. did a large business in Alabama, and that if it were forced to suspend operations the individual members of the Board, along with other private practitioners of optometry, would fall heir to this business. Thus, a serious question of a personal financial stake in the matter in controversy was raised. Finally, the District Court appeared to regard the Board as a suspect adjudicative body in the cases then pending before it, because only members of the Alabama Optometric Association could be members of the Board, and because the Association excluded from membership optometrists such as the plaintiffs who were employed by other persons or entities. The result was that 92 of the 192 practicing optometrists in Alabama were denied participation in the governance of their own profession.

The court's ultimate conclusion was 'that to require the Plaintiffs to resort to the protection offered by state law in these cases would effectively deprive them of their property, that is, their right to practice

---

[7]   More specifically, the plaintiffs attacked §§ 206 and 192 of the statute which provide, respectively, that the Board shall have the power to entertain delicensing proceedings and that its membership shall be limited to members of the Alabama Optometric Association.

their professions, without due process of law and that irreparable injury would follow in the normal course of events.'

It is against this procedural background that we turn to a consideration of the issues presented by this appeal.

* * *

It is appropriate, therefore, that we consider the District Court's conclusions that the State Board of Optometry was so biased by prejudgment and pecuniary interest that it could not constitutionally conduct hearings looking toward the revocation of appellees' licenses to practice optometry. We affirm the District Court in this respect.

The District Court thought the Board to be impermissibly biased for two reasons. First, the Board had filed a complaint in state court alleging that appellees had aided and abetted Lee Optical Co. in the unlawful practice of optometry and also that they had engaged in other forms of 'unprofessional conduct' which, if proved, would justify revocation of their licenses. These charges were substantially similar to those pending against appellees before the Board and concerning which the Board had noticed hearings following its successful prosecution of Lee Optical in the state trial court.

Secondly, the District Court determined that the aim of the Board was to revoke the licenses of all optometrists in the State who were employed by business corporations such as Lee Optical, and that these optometrists accounted for nearly half of all the optometrists practicing in Alabama. Because the Board of Optometry was composed solely of optometrists in private practice for their own account, the District Court concluded that success in the Board's efforts would possibly redound to the personal benefit of members of the Board, sufficiently so that in the opinion of the District Court the Board was constitutionally disqualified from hearing the charges filed against the appellees.

The District Court apparently considered either source of possible bias—prejudgment of the facts or personal interest—sufficient to disqualify the members of the Board. Arguably, the District Court was right on both scores, but we need reach, and we affirm, only the latter ground of possible personal interest.

It is sufficiently clear from our cases that those with substantial pecuniary interest in legal proceedings should not adjudicate these disputes. *Tumey v. Ohio*, 273 U.S. 510 (1927). And *Ward v. Village of Monroeville*, 409 U.S. 57 (1972), indicates that the financial stake need not be as direct or positive as it appeared to be in *Tumey*. It has also come to be the prevailing view that '(m)ost of the law concerning disqualification because of interest applies with equal force to . . . administrative adjudicators.' K. Davis, Administrative Law Text § 12.04, p. 250 (1972), and cases cited. The District Court proceeded on this basis and, applying the standards taken from our cases, concluded that the pecuniary interest of the members of the Board of Optometry had sufficient substance to disqualify them, given the context in which this case arose. As remote as we are from the local realities underlying this case and it being very likely that the District Court has a firmer grasp of the facts and of their significance to the issues presented, we have no good reason on this record to overturn its conclusion and we affirm it.

* * *

■ The opinion of CHIEF JUSTICE BURGER, concurring, and the opinion of JUSTICE MARSHALL, with whom JUSTICE BRENNAN joins, concurring, are omitted. Ed.]

NOTES AND QUESTIONS

Compare the facts of *Gibson v. Berryhill* with those of *Friedman v. Rogers*, 440 U.S. 1 (1979). The statutory scheme in *Friedman* was substantially similar to that in *Gibson*, except that the Texas statute at issue called for four of six (rather than all) members of the Texas Optometry Board (TOB) to be members of the Texas Optometric Association (TOA). The Court recognized that Texas optometrists were divided into two competing groups with different business models, and that the plaintiff-appellant was ineligible to join the TOA because of the business structure of his practice. Unlike Gibson's challenge against the Alabama Board of Optometry, however, the plaintiff-appellants in *Friedman* were not (yet) the subject of disciplinary proceedings by the TOB. Absent actual disciplinary action by the TOB, the Court rejected the argument that the TOB was structurally biased. Can you reconcile the outcome in *Friedman* with the Court's reasoning in *Gibson v. Berryhill*? Though not mentioned by the Court, do you think the presence of two non-TOA members on the TOB might have prompted the Court's "wait and see" attitude toward the TOB? Why or why not?

Schweiker v. McClure

456 U.S. 188 (1982).

■ JUSTICE POWELL delivered the opinion of the Court.

The question is whether Congress, consistently with the requirements of due process, may provide that hearings on disputed claims for certain Medicare payments be held by private insurance carriers, without a further right of appeal.

I

Title XVIII of the Social Security Act, 42 U.S.C. § 1395 *et seq.* (1976 ed. and Supp.IV), commonly known as the Medicare program, is administered by the Secretary of Health and Human Services. It consists of two parts. Part A, which is not at issue in this case, provides insurance against the cost of institutional health services, such as hospital and nursing home fees. §§ 1395c–1395i–2. Part B is entitled "Supplementary Medical Insurance Benefits for the Aged and Disabled." It covers a portion (typically 80%) of the cost of certain physician services, outpatient physical therapy, X-rays, laboratory tests, and other medical and health care. See §§ 1395k, 1395 *l*, and 1395x(s). Only persons 65 or older or disabled may enroll, and eligibility does not depend on financial need. Part B is financed by the Federal Supplementary Medical Insurance Trust Fund. See § 1395t. This Trust Fund in turn is funded by appropriations from the Treasury, together with monthly premiums paid by the individuals who choose voluntarily to enroll in the Part B program. See §§ 1395j, 1395r, and 1395w (1976 ed. and Supp.IV). Part B consequently resembles a private medical insurance program that is subsidized in major part by the Federal Government.

Part B is a social program of substantial dimensions. More than 27 million individuals presently participate, and the Secretary pays out more than $10 billion in benefits annually. In 1980, 158 million Part B claims were processed. In order to make the administration of this sweeping program more efficient, Congress authorized the Secretary to contract with private insurance carriers to administer on his behalf the payment of qualifying Part B claims. See 42 U.S.C. § 1395u. (In this case, for instance, the private carriers that performed these tasks in California for the Secretary were Blue Shield of California and the Occidental Insurance Co.) The congressional design was to take advantage of such insurance carriers' "great experience in reimbursing physicians." H. R. Rep. No. 213, 89th Cong., 1st Sess., 46 (1965). See also 42 U.S.C. § 1395u(a); S. Rep. No. 404, 89th Cong., 1st Sess., 53 (1965).

The Secretary pays the participating carriers' costs of claims administration. See 42 U.S.C. § 1395u(c). In return, the carriers act as the Secretary's agents. See 42 CFR § 421.5(b) (1980). They review and pay Part B claims for the Secretary according to a precisely specified process. See 42 CFR part 405, subpart H (1980). Once the carrier has been billed for a particular service, it decides initially whether the services were medically necessary, whether the charges are reasonable, and whether the claim is otherwise covered by Part B. See 42 U.S.C. § 1395y(a); 42 CFR § 405.803(b) (1980). If it determines that the claim meets all these criteria, the carrier pays the claim out of the Government's Trust Fund—not out of its own pocket. See 42 U.S.C. §§ 1395u(a)(1), 1395u(b)(3), and 1395u(c).

Should the carrier refuse on behalf of the Secretary to pay a portion of the claim, the claimant has one or more opportunities to appeal. First, all claimants are entitled to a "review determination," in which they may submit written evidence and arguments of fact and law. A carrier employee, other than the initial decisionmaker, will review the written record *de novo* and affirm or adjust the original determination. 42 CFR §§ 405.807–405.812 (1980); *McClure v. Harris*, 503 F.Supp. 409, 411 (ND Cal.1980). If the amount in dispute is $100 or more, a still-dissatisfied claimant then has a right to an oral hearing. See 42 U.S.C. § 1395u(b)(3)(C); 42 CFR §§ 405.820–405.860 (1980). An officer chosen by the carrier presides over this hearing. § 405.823. The hearing officers "do not participate personally, prior to the hearing [stage], in any case [that] they adjudicate." 503 F.Supp., at 414. See 42 CFR § 405.824 (1980).

Hearing officers receive evidence and hear arguments pertinent to the matters at issue. § 405.830. As soon as practicable thereafter, they must render written decisions based on the record. § 405.834. Neither the statute nor the regulations make provision for further review of the hearing officer's decision. See *United States v. Erika, Inc.*, 456 U.S. 201.

II

This case arose as a result of decisions by hearing officers against three claimants.[2] The claimants, here appellees, sued to challenge the constitutional adequacy of the hearings afforded them. The District Court for the Northern District of California certified appellees as representatives of a nationwide class of individuals whose claims had been denied by carrier-appointed hearing officers. On cross-motions for summary judgment, the court concluded that the Part B hearing procedures violated appellees' right to due process "insofar as the final, unappealable decision regarding claims disputes is made by carrier appointees. . . ."

The court reached its conclusion of unconstitutionality by alternative lines of argument. The first rested upon the principle that tribunals must be impartial. The court thought that the impartiality of the carrier's hearing officers was compromised by their "prior involvement and pecuniary interest." "Pecuniary interest" was shown, the District Court said, by the fact that "their incomes as hearing officers are entirely dependent upon the carrier's decisions regarding whether, and how often, to call upon their services."[3] Respecting "prior involvement," the court acknowledged that hearing officers *personally* had not been previously involved in the cases they decided. But it noted that hearing officers "are appointed by, and serve at the will of, the carrier [that] has not only participated in the prior stages of each case, but has twice denied the claims [that] are the subject of the hearing," and that five out of seven of Blue Shield's past and present hearing officers "are former *or current* Blue Shield employees."[4] *Id.*, at 414 (emphasis in original). See also 42 CFR § 405.824 (1980). The District Court thought these links between the carriers and their hearing officers sufficient to create a constitutionally intolerable risk of hearing officer bias against claimants.

The District Court's alternative reasoning assessed the costs and benefits of affording claimants a hearing before one of the Secretary's administrative law judges, "either subsequent to or substituting for the hearing conducted by a carrier appointee." The court noted that

---

[2] Appellee William McClure was denied partial reimbursement for the cost of an air ambulance to a specially equipped hospital. The hearing officer determined that the air ambulance was necessary, but that McClure could have been taken to a hospital closer to home. Appellee Charles Shields was allowed reimbursement for a cholecystectomy but was denied reimbursement for an accompanying appendectomy. The hearing officer reasoned that the appendectomy was merely incidental to the cholecystectomy. Appellee "Ann Doe" was denied reimbursement for the entire cost of a sex-change operation. The hearing officer ruled that the operation was not medically necessary.

[3] The District Court recognized that hearing officer salaries are paid from a federal fund and not the carrier's resources.

[4] In this connection, the court referred to the judicial canon requiring a judge to disqualify himself from cases where a " 'lawyer with whom he previously practiced law served during such association as a lawyer concerning the matter.' " 503 F.Supp., at 414–415, quoting Judicial Conference of the United States, Code of Judicial Conduct, Canon 3C(1)(b). The court found that application to hearing officers of standards more lax than those applicable to the judiciary posed "a constitutionally-unacceptable risk of decisions tainted by bias." Additionally, the court thought it significant that "no meaningful, specific selection criteria govern[ed] the appointment of hearing officers" and that hearing officers were trained largely by the carriers whose decisions they were called upon to review.

Mathews v. Eldridge, 424 U.S. 319, 335 (1976), makes three factors relevant to such an inquiry:

> "First, the private interest that will be affected by the official action; second, the risk of an erroneous deprivation of such interest through the procedures used, and the probable value, if any, of additional or substitute procedural safeguards; and finally, the Government's interest, including the function involved and the fiscal and administrative burdens that the additional or substitute procedural requirement would entail."

Considering the first *Mathews* factor, the court listed three considerations tending to show that the private interest at stake was not overwhelming.[5] The court then stated, however, that "it cannot be gainsaid" that denial of a Medicare beneficiary's claim to reimbursement may impose "considerable hardship."

As to the second *Mathews* factor of risk of erroneous deprivation and the probable value of added process, the District Court found the record "inconclusive." The court cited statistics showing that the two available Part B appeal procedures frequently result in reversal of the carriers' original disposition.[6] But it criticized these statistics for failing to distinguish between partial and total reversals. The court stated that hearing officers were required neither to receive training nor to satisfy "threshold criteria such as having a law degree." On this basis it held that "it must be assumed that additional safeguards would reduce the risk of erroneous deprivation of Part B benefits."

On the final *Mathews* factor involving the Government's interest, the District Court noted that carriers processed 124 million Part B claims in 1978. The court stated that "[o]nly a fraction of those claimants pursue their currently-available appeal remedies," and that "there is no indication that anything but an even smaller group of claimants will actually pursue [an] additional remedy" of appeal to the Secretary. Moreover, the court said, the Secretary already maintained an appeal procedure using administrative law judges for appeals by Part A claimants. Increasing the number of claimants who could use this Part A administrative appeal "would not be a cost-free change from the status quo, but neither should it be a costly one."

Weighing the three *Mathews* factors, the court concluded that due process required additional procedural protection over that presently found in the Part B hearing procedure. The court ordered that the appellees were entitled to a *de novo* hearing of record conducted by an administrative law judge of the Social Security Administration. We noted probable jurisdiction and now reverse.

---

[5] "Eligibility for Part B Medicare benefits is not based on financial need. Part B covers supplementary rather than primary services. Denial of a particular claim in a particular case does not deprive the claimant of reimbursement for other, covered, medical expenses."

[6] "[Appellant] establish[es] that between 1975 and 1978, carriers wholly or partially reversed, upon 'review determination,' their initial determinations in 51–57 percent of the cases considered. Of the adverse determination decisions brought before hearing officers, 42–51 percent of the carriers' decisions were reversed in whole or in part."

III

A

The hearing officers involved in this case serve in a quasi-judicial capacity, similar in many respects to that of administrative law judges. As this Court repeatedly has recognized, due process demands impartiality on the part of those who function in judicial or quasi-judicial capacities. *E.g., Marshall v. Jerrico, Inc.*, 446 U.S. 238, 242–243, and n. 2 (1980). We must start, however, from the presumption that the hearing officers who decide Part B claims are unbiased. See *Withrow v. Larkin*, 421 U.S. 35, 47 (1975); *United States v. Morgan*, 313 U.S. 409, 421 (1941). This presumption can be rebutted by a showing of conflict of interest or some other specific reason for disqualification. See *Gibson v. Berryhill*, 411 U.S. 564, 578–579 (1973); *Ward v. Village of Monroeville*, 409 U.S. 57, 60 (1972). But the burden of establishing a disqualifying interest rests on the party making the assertion.

Fairly interpreted, the factual findings made in this case do not reveal any disqualifying interest under the standard of our cases. The District Court relied almost exclusively on generalized assumptions of possible interest, placing special weight on the various connections of the hearing officers with the private insurance carriers.[9] The difficulty with this reasoning is that these connections would be relevant only if the carriers themselves are biased or interested. We find no basis in the record for reaching such a conclusion.[10] As previously noted, the carriers pay all Part B claims from federal, and not their own, funds. Similarly, the salaries of the hearing officers are paid by the Federal Government. *Marshall v. Jerrico, Inc., supra*, at 245, 251. Further, the carriers operate under contracts that require compliance with standards prescribed by the statute and the Secretary. See 42 U.S.C. §§ 1395u(a)(1)(A)–(B), 1395u(b)(3), and 1395u(b)(4); 42 CFR §§ 421.200, 421.202, and 421.205(a). In the absence of proof of financial interest on the part of the carriers, there is no basis for assuming a derivative bias among their hearing officers.[11]

---

[9] Before this Court, appellees urge that the Secretary himself is biased in favor of inadequate Part B awards. They attempt to document this assertion—not mentioned by the District Court—by relying on the fact that the Secretary both has helped carriers identify medical providers who allegedly bill for more services than are medically necessary and has warned carriers to control overutilization of medical services. This action by the Secretary is irrelevant. It simply shows that he takes seriously his statutory duty to ensure that only *qualifying* Part B claims are paid. See 42 U.S.C. § 1395y(a); 42 CFR § 405.803(b) (1980). It does not establish that the Secretary has sought to discourage payment of Part B claims that *do* meet Part B requirements. Such an effort would violate Congress' direction. Absent evidence, it cannot be presumed.

[10] Similarly, appellees adduced no evidence to support their assertion that, for reasons of psychology, institutional loyalty, or carrier coercion, hearing officers would be reluctant to differ with carrier determinations. Such assertions require substantiation before they can provide a foundation for invalidating an Act of Congress.

[11] The District Court's analogy to judicial canons is not apt. The fact that a hearing officer is or was a carrier employee does not create a risk of partiality analogous to that possibly arising from the professional relationship between a judge and a former partner or associate. We simply have no reason to doubt that hearing officers will do their best to obey the Secretary's instruction manual:

"The individual selected to act in the capacity of [hearing officer] must not have been involved in any way with the determination in question and neither have advised nor given consultation on any request for payment which is a basis for the hearing. Since the hearings are of a nonadversary nature, be particularly responsive to the needs of

B

Appellees further argued, and the District Court agreed, that due process requires an additional administrative or judicial review by a Government rather than a carrier-appointed hearing officer. Specifically, the District Court ruled that "[e]xisting Part B procedures might remain intact so long as aggrieved beneficiaries would be entitled to appeal carrier appointees' decisions to Part A administrative law judges." 503 F.Supp., at 417. In reaching this conclusion, the District Court applied the familiar test prescribed in *Mathews v. Eldridge*, 424 U.S., at 335. We may assume that the District Court was correct in viewing the private interest in Part B payments as "considerable," though "not quite as precious as the right to receive welfare or social security benefits." 503 F.Supp., at 416. We likewise may assume, in considering the third *Mathews* factor, that the additional cost and inconvenience of providing administrative law judges would not be unduly burdensome.[13]

We focus narrowly on the second *Mathews* factor that considers the risk of erroneous decision and the probable value, if any, of the additional procedure. The District Court's reasoning on this point consisted only of this sentence:

> "In light of [appellees'] undisputed showing that carrier-appointed hearing officers receive little or no formal training and are not required to satisfy any threshold criteria such as having a law degree, it must be assumed that additional safeguards would reduce the risk of erroneous deprivation of Part B benefits." 503 F.Supp., at 416 (footnote omitted).

Again, the record does not support these conclusions. The Secretary has directed carriers to select as a hearing officer

> " 'an attorney or other *qualified* individual with the ability to conduct formal hearings and with a general understanding of medical matters and terminology. The [hearing officer] must have a *thorough knowledge* of the Medicare program and the

---

unrepresented parties and protect the claimant's rights, even if the claimant is represented by counsel. The parties' interests must be safeguarded to the full extent of their rights; in like manner, the government's interest must be protected.

"The [hearing officer] should conduct the hearing with dignity and exercise necessary control and order. . . . The [hearing officer] must make independent and impartial decisions, write clear and concise statements of facts and law, secure facts from individuals without causing unnecessary friction, and be objective and free of any influence which might affect impartial judgment as to the facts, while being particularly patient with older persons and those with physical or mental impairments.

"The [hearing officer] must be cognizant of the informal nature of a Part B hearing. . . . The hearing is nonadversary in nature in that neither the carrier nor the Medicare Bureau is in opposition to the party but is interested only in seeing that a proper decision is made.' " Dept. of HEW, Medicare Part B Carriers Manual, ch. XII, pp. 12–21, 12–29 (1980). Cf. *Richardson v. Perales*, 402 U.S. 389, 403 (1971) ("congressional plan" is that social security administrative system will operate essentially "as an adjudicator and not as an advocate or adversary").

13 No authoritative factual findings were made, and perhaps this conclusion would have been difficult to prove. It is known that in 1980 about 158 million Part B claims—up from 124 million in 1978—were filed. Even though the additional review would be available only for disputes in excess of $100, a small percentage of the number of claims would be large in terms of number of cases.

statutory authority and regulations upon which it is based, as well as rulings, policy statements, and general instructions pertinent to the Medicare Bureau.'" Dept. of HEW, Medicare Part B Carriers Manual, ch. VII, p. 12–21 (1980) (emphasis added).

The District Court did not identify any specific deficiencies in the Secretary's selection criteria. By definition, a "qualified" individual already possessing "ability" and "thorough knowledge" would not require further training. The court's further general concern that hearing officers "are not required to satisfy any threshold criteria" overlooks the Secretary's quoted regulation.[14] Moreover, the District Court apparently gave no weight to the qualifications of hearing officers about whom there is information in the record. Their qualifications tend to undermine rather than to support the contention that accuracy of Part B decisionmaking may suffer by reason of carrier appointment of unqualified hearing officers.[15]

"[D]ue Process is flexible and calls for such procedural protections as the particular situation demands." *Morrissey v. Brewer*, 408 U.S. 471, 481 (1972). We have considered appellees' claims in light of the strong presumption in favor of the validity of congressional action and consistently with this Court's recognition of "congressional solicitude for fair procedure. . . ." *Califano v. Yamasaki*, 442 U.S. 682, 693 (1979). Appellees simply have not shown that the procedures prescribed by Congress and the Secretary are not fair or that different or additional procedures would reduce the risk of erroneous deprivation of Part B benefits.

NOTES AND QUESTIONS

1.   Consider the number and type of adjudications at issue in *Schweiker v. McClure* with the circumstances of *Gibson v. Berryhill*. In a footnote in *Schweiker*, the Court noted that the Medicare Part B hearing officers processed 158 million claims in 1980, and that most of those claims were for less than $100. By contrast, one would expect that the Alabama Optometry Board at issue in *Gibson* adjudicated a substantially smaller number of disciplinary actions each year, and also that a decision to suspend or revoke an optometrist's license to practice would have dramatic consequences for that individual. Is it easier to draw inferences regarding personal interest bias in smaller contexts as opposed to larger ones? Should we be more concerned about personal interest bias when the stakes are larger for the individual?

---

[14] The District Court's opinion may be read as requiring that hearing officers always be attorneys. Our cases, however, make clear that due process does not make such a uniform requirement. See *Vitek v. Jones*, 445 U.S. 480, 499 (1980) (POWELL, J., concurring in part); *Parham v. J. R.*, 442 U.S. 584, 607 (1979); *Morrissey v. Brewer*, 408 U.S. 471, 486 (1972). Cf. *Goldberg v. Kelly*, 397 U.S. 254, 271 (1970). Neither the District Court in its opinion nor the appellees before us make a particularized showing of the additional value of a law degree in the Part B context.

[15] The record contains information on nine hearing officers. Two were retired administrative law judges with 15 to 18 years of judging experience, five had extensive experience in medicine or medical insurance, one had been a practicing attorney for 20 years, and one was an attorney with 42 years' experience in the insurance industry who was self-employed as an insurance adjuster.

2.   Although both *Gibson v. Berryhill* and *Schweiker v. McClure* involved nongovernmental actors, it is not unprecedented for courts to find personal interest bias on the part of an agency. In *Esso Standard Oil Co. v. Lopez-Freytes*, 522 F.3d 136 (1st Cir. 2008), the First Circuit held that the Puerto Rico Environmental Quality Board (EQB) was impermissibly biased when it fined Esso $76 million for a gasoline spill. First, the EQB was biased by the fact that the fine was to be deposited in an account over which EQB had complete discretion, given that the fine in question was twice the agency's annual budget and 5,000 times as large as the largest fine the agency had previously imposed. The court rejected the argument that, because the EQB members received salaries for their work, they thus had no personal economic interest in the fine imposed on Esso. According to the court, the EQB's complete discretion over the account into which the fine would have been deposited, when combined with the "unprecedented and extraordinarily large" fine, created an "undeniable and evident" temptation for the EQB. Of the two elements emphasized by the First Circuit in *Esso*— the size of the fine and the EQB's discretion over the funds collected— which do you find more problematic? Would the court have been similarly concerned about the EQB's discretion had it assessed fines of $1 million each against 76 parties, rather than $76 million against on party? Why or why not?

D. JUDICIAL REVIEW OF AGENCY ADJUDICATIONS

Thus far in this Chapter we have focused on procedural constraints imposed upon agency adjudications by the Due Process Clause, by the Administrative Procedure Act, and often by agencies themselves as they manage their internal adjudicators. The courts play a prominent role in policing agency adjudications as they enforce these procedural constraints. Procedural requirements are not the only mechanism, however, for constraining agency behavior in the adjudication context. Courts also limit agency action through judicial review of the outcomes reached in the course of agency adjudication.

Section 706 of the Administrative Procedure Act articulates standards governing judicial review of agency action generally. The APA's standards of review are articulated using different phraseology from the traditional standards of review governing civil litigation more generally. Nevertheless, they operate similarly as a guide to the level of skepticism a reviewing court should adopt in evaluating the outcomes of agency action.

Most of the standards articulated in APA § 706 do not distinguish between rulemaking and adjudication, and there is substantial overlap in the standards and doctrines governing judicial review of both. In contemplating the standards applicable to judicial review of agency action, rather than dividing the universe between rulemaking and adjudication, a better way of organizing the doctrine is to contemplate three separate if overlapping aspects of agency decisionmaking: findings of fact, conclusions of law, and reasoning process. In reviewing these aspects of agency decisionmaking, courts apply the same standards to both the rulemaking and adjudication.

Yet, disputes with respect to agency conclusions of law and the adequacy of an agency's reasoning process tend to dominate judicial review of agency rulemaking, while disputes concerning agency fact finding tend to dominate judicial review of agency adjudication. Hence, we find it easier to address judicial review of agency resolution of legal issues and of the agency reasoning process in the context of rulemaking, and will defer detailed discussion of these topics until Chapters 5 and 6. Our focus in this Chapter concerning adjudication will be on judicial review of agency fact finding.

1. JUDICIAL REVIEW OF AGENCY FACT FINDING

Agency adjudications tend to be fact-intensive, so the issue that is raised most frequently on judicial review of agency adjudications is the adequacy of the evidence to support the agency's findings of fact. In particular, APA § 706(2)(E) provides that "[t]he reviewing court shall . . . hold unlawful and set aside agency action, findings, and conclusions found to be . . . unsupported by substantial evidence. . . ." Shortly after the APA was enacted, the Supreme Court addressed the question of what this language means in conjunction with judicial review of agency action under the Taft-Hartley Act, which employs similar language.

Universal Camera Corp. v. NLRB

340 U.S. 474 (1951).

■ MR. JUSTICE FRANKFURTER delivered the opinion of the Court.

[This case involved the Universal Camera Corp., which fired an employee with the rather unusual name of "Chairman" after he gave testimony at a hearing before the National Labor Relations Board (NLRB) concerning union representation of the company's maintenance employees. Chairman alleged that he was fired in retaliation for his testimony. The company maintained that Chairman was fired because he accused the firm's personnel manager of drunkenness during a heated argument about employee discipline. The hearing examiner was not convinced that the company discharged Chairman because of his NLRB testimony, but on review of the record, a majority of the NLRB found otherwise. The NLRB ordered the company to cease and desist from discharging any employee for filing charges or giving testimony to the NLRB, to offer to reinstate Chairman, and to extend backpay to Chairman. Ed.]

The essential issue raised by this case . . . is the effect of the Administrative Procedure Act and the legislation colloquially known as the Taft-Hartley Act on the duty of Courts of Appeals when called upon to review orders of the National Labor Relations Board.

The Court of Appeals for the Second Circuit granted enforcement of an order directing, in the main, that petitioner reinstate with back pay an employee found to have been discharged because he gave testimony under the Wagner Act and cease and desist from discriminating against any employee who files charges or gives testimony under that Act. The court below, Judge Swan dissenting, decreed full enforcement of the order. Because the views of that court regarding the effect of the new legislation on the relation between the Board and the courts of appeals in the enforcement of the Board's orders conflicted with those of the

Court of Appeals for the Sixth Circuit we brought both cases here. The clash of opinion obviously required settlement by this Court.

* * *

The Wagner Act provided: "The findings of the Board as to the facts, if supported by evidence, shall be conclusive." 29 U.S.C. § 160(e). This Court read "evidence" to mean "substantial evidence," *Washington, Virginia & Maryland Coach Co. v. NLRB*, 301 U.S. 142 (1937), and we said that "[s]ubstantial evidence is more than a mere scintilla. It means such relevant evidence as a reasonable mind might accept as adequate to support a conclusion." *Consol. Edison Co. v. NLRB*, 305 U.S. 197 (1938). Accordingly, it "must do more than create a suspicion of the existence of the fact to be established . . . it must be enough to justify, if the trial were to a jury, a refusal to direct a verdict when the conclusion sought to be drawn from it is one of fact for the jury." *NLRB v. Columbian Enameling & Stamping Co.*, 306 U.S. 292 (1939).

The very smoothness of the "substantial evidence" formula as the standard for reviewing the evidentiary validity of the Board's findings established its currency. But the inevitably variant applications of the standard to conflicting evidence soon brought contrariety of views and in due course bred criticism. Even though the whole record may have been canvassed in order to determine whether the evidentiary foundation of a determination by the Board was "substantial," the phrasing of this Court's process of review readily lent itself to the notion that it was enough that the evidence supporting the Board's result was "substantial" when considered by itself. * * *

Criticism of so contracted a reviewing power reinforced dissatisfaction felt in various quarters with the Board's administration of the Wagner Act in the years preceding the war. The scheme of the Act was attacked as an inherently unfair fusion of the functions of prosecutor and judge. Accusations of partisan bias were not wanting. The "irresponsible admission and weighing of hearsay, opinion, and emotional speculation in place of factual evidence" was said to be a "serious menace." H.R. Rep. No. 1902 76th Cong., 3d Sess. 76 (1940). No doubt some, perhaps even much, of the criticism was baseless and some surely was reckless. What is here relevant, however, is the climate of opinion thereby generated and its effect on Congress. Protests against "shocking injustices," *see Wilson & Co. v. NLRB*, 126 F.2d 114, 117 (7th Cir. 1942), and intimations of judicial "abdication" with which some courts granted enforcement of the Board's order, *see NLRB v. Std. Oil Co.*, 138 F.2d 885, 887 (2d Cir. 1943), stimulated pressures for legislative relief from alleged administrative excesses.

* * *

It is fair to say that in all this Congress expressed a mood. And it expressed its mood not merely by oratory but by legislation. As legislation that mood must be respected, even though it can only serve as a standard for judgment and not as a body of rigid rules assuring sameness of applications. Enforcement of such broad standards implies subtlety of mind and solidity of judgment. But it is not for us to question that Congress may assume such qualities in the federal judiciary.

* * *

Whether or not it was ever permissible for courts to determine the substantiality of evidence supporting a Labor Board decision merely on the basis of evidence which in and of itself justified it, without taking into account contradictory evidence or evidence from which conflicting inferences could be drawn, the new legislation [*i.e.*, the APA] definitively precludes such a theory of review and bars its practice. The substantiality of evidence must take into account whatever in the record fairly detracts from its weight. This is clearly the significance of the requirement in both statutes that courts consider the whole record. * * *

To be sure, the requirement for canvassing "the whole record" in order to ascertain substantiality does not furnish a calculus of value by which a reviewing court can assess the evidence. Nor was it intended to negative the function of the Labor Board as one of those agencies presumably equipped or informed by expertise to deal with a specialized field of knowledge, whose findings within that field carry the authority of an expertness which courts do not possess and therefore must respect. Nor does it mean that even as to matters not requiring expertise a court may displace the Board's choice between two fairly conflicting views, even though the court would justifiably have made a different choice had the matter been before it de novo. Congress has merely made it clear that a reviewing court is not barred from setting aside a Board decision when it cannot conscientiously find that the evidence supporting that decision is substantial, when viewed in the light that the record in its entirety furnishes, including the body of evidence opposed to the Board's view.

* * *

We conclude, therefore, that the Administrative Procedure Act and the Taft-Hartley Act direct that courts must now assume more responsibility for the reasonableness and fairness of Labor Board decisions than some courts have shown in the past. Reviewing courts must be influenced by a feeling that they are not to abdicate the conventional judicial function. Congress has imposed on them responsibility for assuring that the Board keeps within reasonable grounds. That responsibility is not less real because it is limited to enforcing the requirement that evidence appear substantial when viewed, on the record as a whole, by courts invested with the authority and enjoying the prestige of the Courts of Appeals. * * *

* * *

The Taft-Hartley Act provides that "The findings of the Board with respect to questions of fact if supported by substantial evidence on the record considered as a whole shall be conclusive." 29 U.S.C. § 160(e). Surely an examiner's report is as much a part of the record as the complaint or the testimony. According to the Administrative Procedure Act, "All decisions (including initial, recommended, or tentative decisions) shall become a part of the record. . . ." 5 U.S.C. § 1007(b). We found that this Act's provision for judicial review has the same meaning as that in the Taft-Hartley Act. The similarity of the two statutes in language and purpose also requires that the definition of "record" found in the Administrative Procedure Act be construed to be applicable as well to the term "record" as used in the Taft-Hartley Act.

It is therefore difficult to escape the conclusion that the plain language of the statutes directs a reviewing court to determine the substantiality of evidence on the record including the examiner's report. The conclusion is confirmed by the indications in the legislative history that enhancement of the status and function of the trial examiner was one of the important purposes of the movement for administrative reform.

* * *

Apparently it was the Committee's opinion that these recommendations should not be obligatory. For the bill which accompanied the Final Report required only that hearing officers make an initial decision which would become final in the absence of further agency action, and that agencies which differed on the facts from their examiners give reasons and record citations supporting their conclusion. This proposal was further moderated by the Administrative Procedure Act. It permits agencies to use examiners to record testimony but not to evaluate it, and contains the rather obscure provision that an agency which reviews an examiner's report has "all the powers which it would have in making the initial decision."

* * *

We do not require that the examiner's findings be given more weight than in reason and in the light of judicial experience they deserve. The "substantial evidence" standard is not modified in any way when the Board and its examiner disagree. We intend only to recognize that evidence supporting a conclusion may be less substantial when an impartial, experienced examiner who has observed the witnesses and lived with the case has drawn conclusions different from the Board's than when he has reached the same conclusion. The findings of the examiner are to be considered along with the consistency and inherent probability of testimony. The significance of his report, of course, depends largely on the importance of credibility in the particular case. To give it this significance does not seem to us materially more difficult than to heed the other factors which in sum determine whether evidence is "substantial."

NOTES AND QUESTIONS

1. *Universal Camera* contains extensive discussion of the relative significance of the Board's conclusions as they relate to those of the hearing examiner whose findings of fact the Board in that case reversed. (Congress renamed hearing examiners Administrative Law Judges in 1972, but that change had no effect on the scope of review of agency findings.) Do you understand the relationship between ALJ findings and agency findings after *Universal Camera*? Do you understand the statutory basis for that relationship? Does the relationship make sense? Could Congress amend the APA to give ALJs the power to make final decisions consistent with the Appointments Clause? See the discussion of the Appointments Clause in Chapter 3.

2. In *Universal Camera*, the Court compared the substantial evidence standard with the standard applied by courts in reviewing jury verdicts. Later in its opinion, however, the Court held that the substantial evidence standard requires review of the administrative record "as a whole," considering evidence that detracts from the administrative finding as well as evidence that supports it. By contrast, in reviewing jury verdicts, courts typically "draw every reasonable inference in favor of the verdict and may not make credibility determinations or weigh the evidence." *Chen v. Mukasey*, 510 F.3d 797 (8th Cir. 2007). Can you reconcile these aspects of the Court's *Universal Camera* decision?

———

As interpreted in *Universal Camera*, the substantial evidence standard is highly deferential. The Court has reversed circuit courts and admonished them for not extending enough deference to agency findings of fact in many other cases since it decided *Universal Camera*. Occasionally, however, the Court itself applies the test in a non-deferential, intrusive manner that seems to be inconsistent with the Court's description of the standard. Consider as an example the following case.

Allentown Mack Sales & Serv., Inc. v. National Labor Relations Board

522 U.S. 359 (1998).

■ JUSTICE SCALIA delivered the opinion of the Court.

Under longstanding precedent of the National Labor Relations Board, an employer who believes that an incumbent union no longer enjoys the support of a majority of its employees has three options: to request a formal, Board-supervised election, to withdraw recognition from the union and refuse to bargain, or to conduct an internal poll of employee support for the union. The Board has held that the latter two are unfair labor practices unless the employer can show that it had a "good-faith reasonable doubt" about the union's majority support. We must decide whether the Board's standard for employer polling is rational and consistent with the National Labor Relations Act, and whether the Board's factual determinations in this case are supported by substantial evidence in the record.

I

Mack Trucks, Inc., had a factory branch in Allentown, Pennsylvania, whose service and parts employees were represented by Local Lodge 724 of the International Association of Machinists and Aerospace Workers, AFL-CIO (Local 724). Mack notified its Allentown managers in May 1990 that it intended to sell the branch, and several of those managers formed Allentown Mack Sales & Service, Inc., the petitioner here, which purchased the assets of the business on December 20, 1990, and began to operate it as an independent dealership. From December 21, 1990, to January 1, 1991, Allentown hired 32 of the original 45 Mack employees.

During the period before and immediately after the sale, a number of Mack employees made statements to the prospective owners of Allentown Mack Sales suggesting that the incumbent union had lost support among employees in the bargaining unit. In job interviews, eight employees made statements indicating, or at least arguably indicating, that they personally no longer supported the union. In addition, Ron Mohr, a member of the union's bargaining committee and shop steward for the Mack Trucks service department, told an Allentown manager that it was his feeling that the employees did not want a union, and that "with a new company, if a vote was taken, the Union would lose." And Kermit Bloch, who worked for Mack Trucks as a mechanic on the night shift, told a manager that the entire night shift (then five or six employees) did not want the union.

On January 2, 1991, Local 724 asked Allentown Mack Sales to recognize it as the employees' collective-bargaining representative, and to begin negotiations for a contract. The new employer rejected that request by letter dated January 25, claiming a "good faith doubt as to support of the Union among the employees." The letter also announced that Allentown had "arranged for an independent poll by secret ballot of its hourly employees to be conducted under guidelines prescribed by the National Labor Relations Board." The poll, supervised by a Roman Catholic priest, was conducted on February 8, 1991; the union lost 19 to 13. Shortly thereafter, the union filed an unfair-labor-practice charge with the Board.

The Administrative Law Judge (ALJ) concluded that Allentown was a "successor" employer to Mack Trucks, Inc., and therefore inherited Mack's bargaining obligation and a presumption of continuing majority support for the union. The ALJ held that Allentown's poll was conducted in compliance with the procedural standards enunciated by the Board in *Struksnes Constr. Co.,* 165 N.L.R.B. 1062 (1967), but that it violated §§ 8(a)(1) and 8(a)(5) of the National Labor Relations Act (Act), 49 Stat. 452, as amended, 29 U.S.C. §§ 158(a)(1) and 158(a)(5), because Allentown did not have an "objective reasonable doubt" about the majority status of the union. The Board adopted the ALJ's findings and agreed with his conclusion that Allentown "had not demonstrated that it harbored a reasonable doubt, based on objective considerations, as to the incumbent Union's continued majority status after the transition." The Board ordered Allentown to recognize and bargain with Local 724.

On review in the Court of Appeals for the District of Columbia Circuit, Allentown challenged both the facial rationality of the Board's test for employer polling and the Board's application of that standard to the facts of this case. The court enforced the Board's bargaining order, over a vigorous dissent. We granted certiorari.

* * *

III

The Board held Allentown guilty of an unfair labor practice in its conduct of the polling because it "ha[d] not demonstrated that it held a reasonable doubt, based on objective considerations, that the Union continued to enjoy the support of a majority of the bargaining unit employees." We must decide whether that conclusion is supported by substantial evidence on the record as a whole. *Universal Camera Corp. v. NLRB,* 340 U.S. 474 (1951). Put differently, we must decide whether on this record it would have been possible for a reasonable jury to reach the Board's conclusion. See, *e.g., NLRB v. Columbian Enameling & Stamping Co.,* 306 U.S. 292, 300 (1939); *Consolidated Edison Co. v. NLRB,* 305 U.S. 197, 229 (1938).

* * *

The question presented for review, therefore, is whether, on the evidence presented to the Board, a reasonable jury could have found that Allentown lacked a genuine, reasonable uncertainty about whether Local 724 enjoyed the continuing support of a majority of unit employees. In our view, the answer is no. The Board's finding to the contrary rests on a refusal to credit probative circumstantial evidence, and on evidentiary demands that go beyond the substantive standard the Board purports to apply.

The Board adopted the ALJ's finding that 6 of Allentown's 32 employees had made "statements which could be used as objective considerations supporting a good-faith reasonable doubt as to continued majority status by the Union." (These included, for example, the statement of Rusty Hoffman that "he did not want to work in a union shop," and "would try to find another job if he had to work with the Union.") The Board seemingly also accepted (though this is not essential to our analysis) the ALJ's willingness to assume that the statement of a seventh employee (to the effect that he "did not feel comfortable with the Union and thought it was a waste of $35 a month") supported good-faith reasonable doubt of his support for the union—as in our view it unquestionably does. And it presumably accepted the ALJ's assessment that "7 of 32, or roughly 20 percent of the involved employees" was not alone sufficient to create "an objective reasonable doubt of union majority support." The Board did not specify how many express disavowals would have been enough to establish reasonable doubt, but the number must presumably be less than 16 (half of the bargaining unit), since that would establish reasonable *certainty*. Still, we would not say that 20% first-hand-confirmed opposition (even with no countering evidence of union support) is alone enough to *require* a conclusion of reasonable doubt. But there was much more.

For one thing, the ALJ and the Board totally disregarded the effect upon Allentown of the statement of an eighth employee, Dennis Marsh, who said that "he was not being represented for the $35 he was paying." The ALJ, whose findings were adopted by the Board, said that this statement "seems more an expression of a desire for better representation than one for no representation at all." It seems to us that it is, more accurately, simply an expression of dissatisfaction with the union's performance—which *could* reflect the speaker's desire that the union represent him more effectively, but *could also* reflect the speaker's desire to save his $35 and get rid of the union. The statement would assuredly engender an *uncertainty* whether the speaker supported the union, and so could not be entirely ignored.

But the most significant evidence excluded from consideration by the Board consisted of statements of two employees regarding not merely their own support of the union, but support among the work force in general. Kermit Bloch, who worked on the night shift, told an Allentown manager "the entire night shift did not want the Union." The ALJ refused to credit this, because "Bloch did not testify and thus could not explain how he formed his opinion about the views of his fellow employees." Unsubstantiated assertions that other employees do not support the union certainly do not establish *the fact of that disfavor* with the degree of reliability ordinarily demanded in legal proceedings. But under the Board's enunciated test for polling, it is not the fact of disfavor that is at issue (the poll itself is meant to establish that), but rather the existence of a reasonable uncertainty on the part of the employer regarding that fact. On that issue, absent some reason for the employer to know that Bloch had no basis for his information, or that Bloch was lying, reason demands that the statement be given considerable weight.

Another employee who gave information concerning overall support for the union was Ron Mohr, who told Allentown managers that "if a vote was taken, the Union would lose" and that "it was his feeling that the employees did not want a union." The ALJ again objected irrelevantly that "there is no evidence with respect to how he gained this knowledge." In addition, the Board held that Allentown "could not legitimately rely on [the statement] as a basis for doubting the Union's majority status," because Mohr was "referring to Mack's existing employee complement, not to the individuals who were later hired by [Allentown]." This basis for disregarding Mohr's statements is wholly irrational. Local 724 had never won an election, or even an informal poll, within the actual unit of 32 Allentown employees. Its claim to represent them rested entirely on the Board's presumption that the work force of a successor company has the same disposition regarding the union as did the work force of the predecessor company, if the majority of the new work force came from the old one. See *Fall River Dyeing,* 482 U.S., at 43, 46–52. The Board cannot rationally adopt that presumption for purposes of imposing the duty to bargain, and adopt precisely the opposite presumption (*i.e.,* contend that there is no relationship between the sentiments of the two work forces) for purposes of determining what evidence tends to establish a reasonable doubt regarding union support. Such irrationality is impermissible even if, as JUSTICE BREYER suggests, it would further the Board's political objectives.

It must be borne in mind that the issue here is not whether Mohr's statement clearly establishes a majority in opposition to the union, but whether it contributes to a reasonable uncertainty whether a majority in favor of the union existed. We think it surely does. Allentown would reasonably have given great credence to Mohr's assertion of lack of union support, since he was not hostile to the union, and was in a good position to assess antiunion sentiment. Mohr was a union shop steward for the service department, and a member of the union's bargaining committee; according to the ALJ, he "did not indicate personal dissatisfaction with the Union." It seems to us that Mohr's statement has undeniable and substantial probative value on the issue of "reasonable doubt."

Accepting the Board's apparent (and in our view inescapable) concession that Allentown received reliable information that 7 of the bargaining-unit employees did not support the union, the remaining 25 would have had to support the union by a margin of 17 to 8—a ratio of more than 2 to 1—if the union commanded majority support. The statements of Bloch and Mohr would cause anyone to doubt that degree of support, and neither the Board nor the ALJ discussed any evidence that Allentown should have weighed on the other side. The most pro-union statement cited in the ALJ's opinion was Ron Mohr's comment that he personally "could work with or without the Union," and "was there to do his job." The Board cannot covertly transform its presumption of continuing majority support into a working assumption that *all* of a successor's employees support the union until proved otherwise. Giving fair weight to Allentown's circumstantial evidence, we think it quite impossible for a rational factfinder to avoid the conclusion that Allentown had reasonable, good-faith grounds to doubt—to be *uncertain about*—the union's retention of majority support.

* * *

■ [The opinion of CHIEF JUSTICE REHNQUIST, with whom JUSTICE O'CONNOR, JUSTICE KENNEDY, and JUSTICE THOMAS join, concurring in part and dissenting in part, is omitted. Ed.]

■ JUSTICE BREYER, with whom JUSTICE STEVENS, JUSTICE SOUTER, and JUSTICE GINSBURG join, concurring in part and dissenting in part.

[T]he Court holds unlawful an agency conclusion on the ground that it is "not supported by substantial evidence." See 29 U.S.C. § 160(e); 5 U.S.C. § 706(2)(E). That question was not presented to us in the petition for certiorari. In deciding it, the Court has departed from the half-century old legal standard governing this type of review. See *Universal Camera Corp. v. NLRB,* 340 U.S. 474, 490–491 (1951). It has rewritten a National Labor Relations Board (Board) rule without adequate justification. It has ignored certain evidentiary presumptions developed by the Board to provide guidance in the application of this rule. And it has failed to give the kind of leeway to the Board's factfinding authority that the Court's precedents mandate. See, *e.g., Beth Israel Hospital v. NLRB,* 437 U.S. 483, 504 (1978).

To decide whether an agency's conclusion is supported by substantial evidence, a reviewing court must identify the conclusion and then examine and weigh the evidence. As this Court said in 1951, "[w]hether on the record as a whole there is substantial evidence to support agency findings is a question which Congress has placed in the keeping of the Courts of Appeals." *Universal Camera,* 340 U.S., at 491. The Court held that it would "intervene only in what ought to be the rare instance when the standard appears to have been *misapprehended or grossly misapplied." Ibid.* (emphasis added); see *Beth Israel Hospital, supra,* at 507 ("'misapprehended or grossly misapplied'"); *Golden State Bottling Co. v. NLRB,* 414 U.S. 168, 173 (1973) ("'misapprehended or grossly misapplied'"). Consequently, if the majority is to overturn a court of appeals' "substantial evidence" decision, it must identify the agency's conclusion, examine the evidence, and then determine whether the evidence is so *obviously* inadequate to support the conclusion that the reviewing court must have seriously misunderstood the nature of its legal duty.

The majority opinion begins by properly stating the Board's conclusion, namely, that the employer, Allentown Mack Sales & Service, Inc., did not demonstrate that it

"held a reasonable doubt, *based on objective considerations,* that the Union continued to enjoy the support of a majority of the bargaining unit employees."

The opinion, however, then omits the words I have italicized and transforms this conclusion, rephrasing it as:

"Allentown lacked a genuine, reasonable uncertainty about whether Local 724 enjoyed the continuing support of a majority of unit employees."

Key words of a technical sort that the Board has used in hundreds of opinions written over several decades to express what the Administrative Law Judge (ALJ) here called *"objective* reasonable doubt" have suddenly disappeared, leaving in their place what looks like an ordinary jury standard that might reflect not an agency's specialized knowledge of the workplace, but a court's common understanding of human psychology. The only authority cited for the transformation, the dictionary, in fact offers no support, for the majority has looked up the wrong word, namely, "doubt," instead of the right word, "objective." * * *

To illustrate the problem with the majority's analysis, I must describe the factual background, the evidence, and the ALJ's findings in some detail. In December 1990, three managers at Mack Trucks (and several other investors) bought Mack. All of the 45 employees in the union's bargaining unit were dismissed. The new owners changed the company's name to Allentown and then interviewed and rehired 32 of the 45 recently dismissed workers, putting them back to work at jobs similar to those they previously held. The union, which had represented those employees for 17 years, sought continued recognition; Allentown refused it; the Board's general counsel brought unfair labor practice charges; and the ALJ found that Allentown was a "successor" corporation to Mack, a finding that was affirmed by the Board and was not challenged in the Court of Appeals. Because Allentown was found to be a "successor" employer, the union was entitled to a rebuttable presumption of majority status. See *Fall River Dyeing & Finishing Corp. v. NLRB,* 482 U.S. 27, 41 (1987). Absent some extraordinary circumstance, when a union enjoys a rebuttable presumption of majority status, the employer is obligated to recognize the union unless 30% of the union's employees petition the Board for a decertification election (and the union loses), *Texas Petrochemicals Corp.,* 296 N.L.R.B. 1057, 1062, 1989 WL 224426 (1989), enf'd as modified, 923 F.2d 398 (C.A.5 1991); see 29 U.S.C. § 159(c)(1)(A)(ii); 29 C.F.R. § 101.18(a) (1997), or the employer shows that "either (1) the union did not *in fact* enjoy majority support, or (2) the employer had a good-faith doubt, founded on a sufficient objective basis, of the union's majority support," see *NLRB v. Curtin Matheson Scientific, Inc.,* 494 U.S. 775, 778 (1990) (emphasis deleted; internal quotation marks and citations omitted).

Allentown took the last mentioned of these options. According to the ALJ, it sought to show that it had an "objective" good-faith doubt primarily by presenting the testimony of Allentown managers, who, in turn, reported statements made to them by 14 employees. The ALJ set aside the statements of 5 of those employees as insignificant for various reasons—for example because the employees were not among the rehired 32, because their statements were equivocal, or because they made the statements at a time too long before the transition. The majority does not take issue with the ALJ's reasoning with respect to these employees. The ALJ then found that statements made by six, and possibly seven, employees (22% of the 32) helped Allentown show an "objective" reasonable doubt. The majority does not quarrel with this conclusion. The majority does, however, take issue with the ALJ's decision not to count in Allentown's favor three further statements, made by employees Marsh, Bloch, and Mohr. The majority says that these statements *required* the ALJ and the Board to find for Allentown. I cannot agree.

Consider Marsh's statement. Marsh said, as the majority opinion notes, that " 'he was not being represented for the $35 he was paying.' " The majority says that the ALJ was wrong not to count this statement in the employer's favor. But the majority fails to mention that Marsh made this statement to an Allentown manager while the manager was interviewing Marsh to determine whether he would, or would not, be one of the 32 employees whom Allentown would reemploy. The ALJ, when evaluating all the employee statements, wrote that statements made to the Allentown managers during the job interviews were "somewhat tainted as it is likely that a job applicant will say whatever he believes the prospective employer wants to hear." In so stating, the ALJ was reiterating the Board's own normative general finding that employers should not "rely in asserting a good-faith doubt" upon "[s]tatements made by employees during the course of an interview with a prospective employer." *Middleboro Fire Apparatus, Inc.*, 234 N.L.R.B. 888, 894, 1978 WL 7283, enf'd, 590 F.2d 4 (C.A.5 1978). The Board also has found that " '[e]mployee statements of dissatisfaction with a union are not deemed the equivalent of withdrawal of support for the union.' " *Torch Operating Co.*, 322 N.L.R.B. 939, 943, 1997 WL 34911 (1997) (quoting *Briggs Plumbingware, Inc. v. NLRB*, 877 F.2d 1282, 1288 (C.A.6 1989)); see also *Destileria Serralles, Inc.*, 289 N.L.R.B. 51, 1988 WL 214114 (1988), 882 F.2d 19 (C.A.1 1989). Either of these general Board findings (presumably known to employers advised by the labor bar), applied by the ALJ in this particular case, provides more than adequate support for the ALJ's conclusion that the employer could not properly rely upon Marsh's statement as help in creating an "objective" employer doubt.

I do not see how, on the record before us, one could plausibly argue that these relevant general findings of the Board fall outside the Board's lawfully delegated authority. The Board in effect has said that an employee statement *made during a job interview with an employer who has expressed an interest in a nonunionized work force* will often tell us precisely *nothing* about that employee's true feelings. That Board conclusion represents an exercise of the kind of discretionary authority that Congress placed squarely within the Board's administrative and fact-finding powers and responsibilities. See *Radio Officers v. NLRB*, 347 U.S. 17, 49–50. Nor is it procedurally improper for an agency, rather like a common-law court, (and drawing upon its accumulated expertise and exercising its administrative responsibilities) to use adjudicatory proceedings to develop rules of thumb about the likely weight assigned to different kinds of evidence. Cf. *Bell Aerospace,* 416 U.S., at 294; *Chenery,* 332 U.S., at 202.

Consider next Bloch's statement, made during his job interview with Worth, that those on the night shift (five or six employees) "did not want the Union." The ALJ thought this statement failed to provide support, both for reasons that the majority mentions (" 'Bloch did not testify and thus could not explain how he formed his opinion about the views of his fellow employees' "), and for reasons that the majority does not mention ("no showing that [the other employees] made independent representations about their union sympathies to [Allentown] and they did not testify in this proceeding").

The majority says that "reason demands" that Bloch's statement "be given considerable weight." But why? The Board, drawing upon both reason and experience, has said it will "view with suspicion and caution" one employee's statements "purporting to represent the views of other employees." *Wallkill Valley General Hospital,* 288 N.L.R.B. 103, 109, 1988 WL 213698 (1988), enf'd as modified, 866 F.2d 632 (C.A.3 1989). Indeed, the Board specifically has stated that this type of evidence does not qualify as ""objective" within the meaning of the "objective reasonable doubt" standard. *Wallkill Valley General Hospital, supra,* at 109–110 (finding that statement by one employee that other employees opposed the union "cannot be found to provide *objective* considerations" because statement was a "bare assertion," was "subjective," and "lacking in demonstrable foundation"; statement by another employee about the views of others was similarly "insufficiently reliable and definite to contribute to a finding of *objective* considerations" (emphases added)).

How is it unreasonable for the Board to provide this kind of guidance, about what kinds of evidence are more likely, and what kinds are less likely, to support an "objective reasonable doubt" (thereby helping an employer understand just when he may refuse to bargain with an established employee representative, in the absence of an employee—generated union decertification petition)? Why is it unreasonable for an ALJ to disregard a highly general conclusory statement such as Bloch's, a statement that names no names, is unsupported by any other concrete testimony, and was made during a job interview by an interviewer who foresees a nonunionized workforce? To put the matter more directly, how can the majority substitute its own judgment for that of the Board and the ALJ in respect to such detailed workplace-related matters, particularly on the basis of this record, where the question whether we should set aside this kind of Board rule has not even been argued?

Finally, consider the Allentown manager's statement that Mohr told him that "if a vote was taken, the Union would lose." Since, at least from the perspective of the ALJ and the Board, the treatment of this statement presented a closer question, I shall set forth the ALJ's discussion of the matter in full.

The ALJ wrote:

"Should Respondent be allowed to rely on Mohr's opinion? As opposed to Bloch who offered the opinion that the night shift employees did not support the Union, Mohr, as union steward, was arguably in a position to know the sentiments of the service employees in the bargaining unit in this regard. However, there is no evidence with respect to how he gained this knowledge, or whether he was speaking about a large majority of the service employees being dissatisfied with the Union or a small majority. Moreover, he was referring to the existing service employee members of the Mack bargaining unit composed of 32 employees, whereas the Respondent hired only 23 of these men. Certainly the composition of the complement of employees hired would bear on whether this group did or did not support the Union. He also was not in a position to speak for the 11 parts employees of Mack or the 7 parts employees hired by Respondent. Mohr himself did not indicate personal dissatisfaction with the Union."

The ALJ concluded:

"Given the almost off-the-cuff nature of [Mohr's] statement and the Board's historical treatment of unverified assertions by an employee about other employees' sentiments, I do not find that Mohr's statements provides *[sic]* sufficient basis, even when considered with the other employee statements relied upon, to meet the Board's objective reasonable doubt standard for withdrawal of recognition or for polling employees."

One can find reflected in the majority opinion some of the reasons the ALJ gave for discounting the significance of Mohr's statement. The majority says of the ALJ's first reason (namely, that " 'there is no evidence with respect to how' " Mohr " 'gained this knowledge' ") that this reason is "irrelevan[t]." But why so? The lack of any specifics provides some support for the possibility that Mohr was overstating a conclusion, say, in a job-preserving effort to curry favor with Mack's new managers. More importantly, since the absence of detail or support brings Mohr's statement well within the Board's pre-existing cautionary evidentiary principle (about employee statements regarding the views of other employees), it diminishes the reasonableness of any employer reliance.

The majority discusses a further reason, namely, that Mohr was referring to a group of 32 employees of whom Allentown hired only 23, and "the composition of the complement of employees hired would bear on whether this group did or did not support the Union." The majority considers this reason "wholly irrational," because, in its view, the Board cannot "rationally" assume that

"the work force of a successor company has the same disposition regarding the union as did the work force of the predecessor company, if the majority of the new work force came from the old one,"

while adopting an opposite assumption

"for purposes of determining what evidence tends to establish a reasonable doubt regarding union support."

The irrationality of these assumptions, however, is not obvious. The primary objective of the National Labor Relations Act is to secure labor peace. *Fall River Dyeing & Finishing Corp. v. NLRB,* 482 U.S., at 38. To preserve the status quo ante may help to preserve labor peace; the first presumption may help to do so by assuming (in the absence of contrary evidence) that workers wish to preserve that status quo, see *id.,* at 38–40; the second, by requiring detailed evidence before dislodging the status quo, may help to do the same. Regardless, no one has argued that these presumptions are contradictory or illogical.

The majority fails to mention the ALJ's third reason for discounting Mohr's statement, namely, that Mohr did not indicate "whether he was speaking about a large majority of the service employees being dissatisfied with the Union or a small majority." It fails to mention the ALJ's belief that the statement was "almost off-the-cuff." It fails to mention the ALJ's reference to the "Board's historical treatment of unverified assertions by an employee about other employees' sentiments" (which, by itself, would justify a considerable discount). And, most importantly, it leaves out the ALJ's conclusion. The ALJ did not conclude that Mohr's statement lacked evidentiary significance. Rather, the ALJ concluded that the statement did not provide "*sufficient* basis, even when considered with other employee statements relied upon, to meet the Board's objective reasonable doubt standard."

Given this evidence, and the ALJ's reasoning, the Court of Appeals found the Board's conclusion adequately supported. That conclusion is well within the Board's authority to make findings and to reach conclusions on the basis of record evidence, which authority Congress has granted, and this Court's many precedents have confirmed. See, *e.g., Beth Israel Hospital v. NLRB,* 437 U.S., at 504.

In sum, the majority has failed to focus upon the ALJ's actual conclusions, it has failed to consider all the evidence before the ALJ, it has transformed the actual legal standard that the Board has long administered without regard to the Board's own interpretive precedents, and it has ignored the guidance that the Board's own administrative interpretations have sought to provide to the bar, to employers, to unions, and to its own administrative staff. The majority's opinion will, I fear, weaken the system for judicial review of administrative action that this Court's precedents have carefully constructed over several decades.

NOTES AND QUESTIONS

Citing *Universal Camera*, the Court in *Allentown Mack* equated the substantial evidence standard with the standard a reviewing court would apply in evaluating factual determinations made by a jury. "[W]e must decide whether on this record it would have been possible for a reasonable jury to reach the Board's conclusion." The jury standard is notoriously deferential. According to the Court in *Universal Camera*, the substantial evidence standard thus does not allow a reviewing court to "displace the [agency's] choice between two fairly conflicting views, even though the court would justifiably have made a different choice had the matter been before it de novo." Are these pronouncements consistent with the sweeping review of the record both Justice Scalia and Justice Breyer conducted in supporting their conclusions regarding defensibility of the NLRB's decision in *Allentown Mack*?

The Supreme Court's descriptive rhetoric is only minimally helpful in understanding how courts actually apply the substantial evidence standard case by case, In 1958, Professor Frank Cooper conducted an extensive empirical study of the judicial application of the substantial evidence test. Frank E. Cooper, *Administrative Law: The Substantial Evidence Rule*, 44 A.B.A. J. 945, 1002–03 (1958). He derived from this study the following seven guidelines that courts used in applying the test:

(1) hearsay is not substantial evidence, at least if it is opposed by competent evidence;

(2) a finding contrary to uncontradicted testimony is not usually supported by substantial evidence;

(3) evidence that is slight or sketchy in an absolute sense is not substantial evidence;

(4) evidence that is slight in relation to much stronger contrary evidence is not substantial evidence;

(5) an Administrative Law judge's finding contrary to an agency finding can be a significant factor leading a court to conclude that the agency finding is not supported by substantial evidence;

(6) dissenting opinions by members of the agency with respect to agency findings of fact have an effect on a reviewing court comparable to a contrary finding by an Administrative Law judge;

(7) a court is more likely to reverse an agency finding if the agency has engaged in a consistent pattern of crediting the agency's witnesses and discrediting opposing witnesses.

Although these seven simple guidelines have largely stood the test of time, the first requires revision to reflect modern applications of the substantial evidence test, as the following case illustrates.

Richardson v. Perales

402 U.S. 389 (1971).

■ MR. JUSTICE BLACKMUN delivered the opinion of the Court.

In 1966 Pedro Perales, a San Antonio truck driver, then aged 34, height 5'11", weight about 220 pounds, filed a claim for disability insurance benefits under the Social Security Act. [The statute provides] that the term "disability" means "inability to engage in any substantial gainful activity by reason of any medically determinable physical or mental impairment which * * *."[1] Section 205(g), 42 U.S.C. § 405(g), relating to judicial review, states, "The findings of the Secretary as to any fact, if supported by substantial evidence, shall be conclusive. . . ."

The issue here is whether physicians' written reports of medical examinations they have made of a disability claimant may constitute "substantial evidence" supportive of a finding of nondisability, within the § 205(g) standard, when the claimant objects to the admissibility of those reports and when the only live testimony is presented by his side and is contrary to the reports.

---

[1] Not pertinent here are the durational aspects of disability specified in the statute's definition.

I

In his claim Perales asserted that on September 29, 1965, he became disabled as a result of an injury to his back sustained in lifting an object at work. He was seen by a neurosurgeon, Dr. Ralph A. Munslow, who first recommended conservative treatment. When this provided no relief, myelography was performed and surgery for a possible protruded intervertebral disc at L-5 was advised. The patient at first hesitated about surgery and appeared to improve. On recurrence of pain, however, he consented to the recommended procedure. Dr. Munslow operated on November 23. * * * No disc protrusion or other definitive pathology was identified at surgery. The post-operative diagnosis was: "Nerve root compression syndrome, left." The patient was discharged from Dr. Munslow's care on January 25, 1966, with a final diagnosis of "Neuritis, lumbar, mild."

Mr. Perales continued to complain, but Dr. Munslow and Dr. Morris H. Lampert, a neurologist called in consultation, were still unable to find any objective neurological explanation for his complaints. Dr. Munslow advised that he return to work.

In April 1966 Perales consulted Dr. Max Morales, Jr., a general practitioner of San Antonio. Dr. Morales hospitalized the patient from April 15 to May 2. His final discharge diagnosis was: "Back sprain, lumbo-sacral spine."

Perales then filed his claim. As required by § 221 of the Act, 42 U.S.C. § 421, the claim was referred to the state agency for determination. The agency obtained the hospital records and a report from Dr. Morales. The report set forth no physical findings or laboratory studies, but the doctor again gave as his diagnosis: "Back sprain—lumbo-sacral spine," this time "moderately severe," with "Ruptured disk not ruled out." The agency arranged for a medical examination, at no cost to the patient, by Dr. John H. Langston, an orthopedic surgeon. This was done May 25.

Dr. Langston's ensuing report to the Division of Disability Determination was devastating from the claimant's standpoint. The doctor referred to Perales' being "on crutches or cane" since his injury. He noted a slightly edematous condition in the legs, attributed to "inactivity and sitting around"; slight tenderness in some of the muscles of the dorsal spine, thought to be due to poor posture; and "a very mild sprain [of those muscles] which would resolve were he actually to get a little exercise and move." Apart from this, and from the residuals of the pantopaque myelography and hemilaminectomy, Dr. Langston found no abnormalities of the lumbar spine. Otherwise, he described Perales as a "big physical healthy specimen . . . obviously holding back and limiting all of his motions, intentionally. . . . His upper extremities, though they are completely uninvolved by his injury, he holds very rigidly as though he were semi-paralyzed. His reach and grasp are very limited but intentionally so. . . . Neurological examination is entirely normal to detailed sensory examination with pinwheel, vibratory sensations, and light touch. Reflexes are very active and there is no atrophy anywhere." * * *

The state agency denied the claim. Perales requested reconsideration. Dr. Morales submitted a further report to the agency and an opinion to the claimant's attorney. This outlined the surgery and hospitalizations and his own conservative and continuing treatment of the patient, the medicines prescribed, the administration of ultrasound therapy, and the patient's constant complaints. The doctor concluded that the patient had not made a complete recovery from his surgery, that he was not malingering, that his injury was permanent, and that he was totally and permanently disabled. He recommended against any further surgery.

The state agency then arranged for an examination by Dr. James M. Bailey, a board-certified psychiatrist with a sub-specialty in neurology. Dr. Bailey's report to the agency on August 30, 1966, concluded with the following diagnosis:

> "Paranoid personality, manifested by hostility, feelings of persecution and long history of strained interpersonal relationships.
>
> "I do not feel that this patient has a separate psychiatric illness at this time. It appears that his personality is conducive to anger, frustrations, etc."

The agency again reviewed the file. The Bureau of Disability Insurance of the Social Security Administration made its independent review. The report and opinion of Dr. Morales, as the claimant's attending physician, were considered, as were those of the other examining physicians. The claim was again denied.

Perales requested a hearing before a hearing examiner. The agency then referred the claimant to Dr. Langston and to Dr. Richard H. Mattson for electromyography studies. Dr. Mattson's notes referred to "some chronic or past disturbance of function in the nerve supply" to the left and right anterior tibialis muscles and right extensor digitorium brevis muscles that was "strongly suggestive of lack of maximal effort" and was "the kind of finding that is typically associated with a functional or psychogenic component to weakness." There was no evidence of "any active process effecting [sic] the nerves at present." Dr. Langston advised the agency that Dr. Mattson's finding of "very poor effort" verified what Dr. Langston had found on the earlier physical examination.

The requested hearing was set for January 12, 1967, in San Antonio. Written notice thereof was given the claimant with a copy to his attorney. The notice contained a definition of disability, advised the claimant that he should bring all medical and other evidence not already presented, afforded him an opportunity to examine all documentary evidence on file prior to the hearing, and told him that he might bring his own physician or other witnesses and be represented at the hearing by a lawyer.

The hearing took place at the time designated. A supplemental hearing was held March 31. The claimant appeared at the first hearing with his attorney and with Dr. Morales. The attorney formally objected to the introduction of the several reports of Drs. Langston, Bailey, Mattson, and Lampert, and of the hospital records. Various grounds of objection were asserted, including hearsay, absence of an opportunity for cross-examination, absence of proof the physicians were licensed to practice in Texas, failure to demonstrate that the hospital records were proved under the Business Records Act, and the conclusory nature of the reports. These objections were overruled and the reports and hospital records were introduced. The reports of Dr. Morales and of Dr. Munslow were then submitted by the claimant's counsel and admitted.

At the two hearings oral testimony was submitted by claimant Perales, by Dr. Morales, by a former fellow employee of the claimant, by a vocational expert, and by Dr. Lewis A. Leavitt, a physician board-certified in physical medicine and rehabilitation, and chief of, and professor in, the Department of Physical Medicine at Baylor University College of Medicine. Dr. Leavitt was called by the hearing examiner as an independent "medical adviser," that is, as an expert who does not examine the claimant but who hears and reviews the medical evidence and who may offer an opinion. The adviser is paid a fee by the Government. The claimant, through his counsel, objected to any testimony by Dr. Leavitt not based upon examination or upon a hypothetical. Dr. Leavitt testified over this objection and was cross-examined by the claimant's attorney. He stated that the consensus of the various medical reports was that Perales had a mild low-back syndrome of musculo-ligamentous origin.

The hearing examiner, in reliance upon the several medical reports and the testimony of Dr. Leavitt, observed in his written decision, "There is objective medical evidence of impairment which the heavy preponderance of the evidence indicates to be of mild severity. . . . Taken altogether, the Hearing Examiner is of the conclusion that the claimant has not met the burden of proof." He specifically found that the claimant "is suffering from a low back syndrome of musculo-ligamentous origin, and of mild severity"; that while he "has an emotional overlay to his medical impairment it does not require psychiatric treatment and is of minimal contribution, if any, to his medical impairment or to his general ability to engage in substantial gainful activity"; that "[n]either his medical impairment nor his emotional overlay, singly or in combination, constitute a disability as defined" in the Act; and that the claimant is capable of engaging as a salesman in work in which he had previously engaged, of working as a watchman or guard where strenuous activity is not required, or as a ticket-taker or janitor. The hearing examiner's decision then, was that the claimant was not entitled to a period of disability or to disability insurance benefits.

It is to be noted at this point that § 205(d) of the Act, 42 U.S.C. § 405(d), provides that the Secretary has power to issue subpoenas requiring the attendance and testimony of witnesses and the production of evidence and that the Secretary's regulations authorized by § 205(a), 42 U.S.C. § 405(a), provide that a claimant may request the issuance of subpoenas. Perales, however, who was represented by counsel, did not request subpoenas for either of the two hearings.

* * *

II

We therefore are presented with the not uncommon situation of conflicting medical evidence. The trier of fact has the duty to resolve that conflict. We have, on the one hand, an absence of objective findings, an expressed suspicion of only functional complaints, of malingering, and of the patient's unwillingness to do anything about remedying an unprovable situation. We have, on the other hand, the claimant's and his personal physician's earnest pleas that significant and disabling residuals from the mishap of September 1965 are indeed present.

The issue revolves, however, around a system which produces a mass of medical evidence in report form. May material of that kind ever be "substantial evidence" when it stands alone and is opposed by live medical evidence and the client's own contrary personal testimony? The courts below have held that it may not.

III

The Social Security Act has been with us since 1935. It affects nearly all of us. The system's administrative structure and procedures, with essential determinations numbering into the millions, are of a size and extent difficult to comprehend. But, as the Government's brief here accurately pronounces, "Such a system must be fair—and it must work."

Congress has provided that the Secretary

"shall have full power and authority to make rules and regulations and to establish procedures ... necessary or appropriate to carry out such provisions, and shall adopt reasonable and proper rules and regulations to regulate and provide for the nature and extent of the proofs and evidence and the method of taking and furnishing the same in order to establish the right to benefits hereunder." § 205(a), 42 U.S.C. § 405(a).

Section 205(b) directs the Secretary to make findings and decisions; on request to give reasonable notice and opportunity for a hearing; and in the course of any hearing to receive evidence. It then provides:

"Evidence may be received at any hearing before the Secretary even though inadmissible under rules of evidence applicable to court procedure."

In carrying out these statutory duties the Secretary has adopted regulations that state, among other things:

"The hearing examiner shall inquire fully into the matters at issue and shall receive in evidence the testimony of witnesses and any documents which are relevant and material to such matters.... The ... procedure at the hearing generally ... shall be in the discretion of the hearing examiner and of such nature as to afford the parties a reasonable opportunity for a fair hearing." 20 C.F.R. § 404.927.

From this it is apparent that (a) the Congress granted the Secretary the power by regulation to establish hearing procedures; (b) strict rules of evidence, applicable in the courtroom, are not to operate at social security hearings so as to bar the admission of evidence otherwise pertinent; and (c) the conduct of the hearing rests generally in the examiner's discretion. There emerges an emphasis upon the informal rather than the formal. This, we think, is as it should be, for this administrative procedure, and these hearings, should be understandable to the layman claimant, should not necessarily be stiff and comfortable only for the trained attorney, and should be liberal and not strict in tone and operation. This is the obvious intent of Congress so long as the procedures are fundamentally fair.

* * *

We conclude that a written report by a licensed physician who has examined the claimant and who sets forth in his report his medical findings in his area of competence may be received as evidence in a disability hearing and, despite its hearsay character and an absence of cross-examination, and despite the presence of opposing direct medical testimony and testimony by the claimant himself, may constitute substantial evidence supportive of a finding by the hearing examiner adverse to the claimant, when the claimant has not exercised his right to subpoena the reporting physician and thereby provide himself with the opportunity for cross-examination of the physician.

We are prompted to this conclusion by a number of factors that, we feel, assure underlying reliability and probative value:

1.   The identity of the five reporting physicians is significant. Each report presented here was prepared by a practicing physician who had examined the claimant. A majority (Drs. Langston, Bailey, and Mattson) were called into the case by the state agency. Although each received a fee, that fee is recompense for his time and talent otherwise devoted to private practice or other professional assignment. We cannot, and do not, ascribe bias to the work of these independent physicians, or any interest on their part in the outcome of the administrative proceeding beyond the professional curiosity a dedicated medical man possesses.

2.   The vast workings of the social security administrative system make for reliability and impartiality in the consultant reports. We bear in mind that the agency operates essentially, and is intended so to do, as an adjudicator and not as an advocate or adversary. This is the congressional plan. We do not presume on this record to say that it works unfairly.

3.   One familiar with medical reports and the routine of the medical examination, general or specific, will recognize their elements of detail and of value. The particular reports of the physicians who examined claimant Perales were based on personal consultation and personal examination and rested on accepted medical procedures and tests. The operating neurosurgeon, Dr. Munslow, provided his pre-operative observations and diagnosis, his findings at surgery, his post-operative diagnosis, and his post-operative observations. Dr. Lampert, the neurologist, provided the history related to him by the patient, Perales' complaints, the physical examination and neurologic tests, and his professional impressions and recommendations. Dr. Langston, the orthopedist, did the same post-operatively, and described the orthopedic tests and neurologic examination he performed, the results and his impressions and prognosis. Dr. Mattson, who did the post-operative electromyography, described the results of that test, and his impressions. And Dr. Bailey, the psychiatrist, related the history, the patient's complaints, and the psychiatric diagnosis that emerged from the typical psychiatric examination.

These are routine, standard, and unbiased medical reports by physician specialists concerning a subject whom they had seen. That the reports were adverse to Perales' claim is not in itself bias or an indication of nonprobative character.

4. The reports present the impressive range of examination to which Perales was subjected. A specialist in neurosurgery, one in neurology, one in psychiatry, one in orthopedics, and one in physical medicine and rehabilitation add up to definitive opinion in five medical specialties, all somewhat related, but different in their emphases. It is fair to say that the claimant received professional examination and opinion on a scale beyond the reach of most persons and that this case reveals a patient and careful endeavor by the state agency and the examiner to ascertain the truth.

5. So far as we can detect, there is no inconsistency whatsoever in the reports of the five specialists. Yet each result was reached by independent examination in the writer's field of specialized training.

6. Although the claimant complains of the lack of opportunity to cross-examine the reporting physicians, he did not take advantage of the opportunity afforded him under 20 C.F.R. § 404.926 to request subpoenas for the physicians. The five-day period specified by the regulation for the issuance of the subpoenas surely afforded no real obstacle to this, for he was notified that the documentary evidence on file was available for examination before the hearing and, further, a supplemental hearing could be requested. In fact, in this very case there was a supplemental hearing more than two and a half months after the initial hearings. This inaction on the claimant's part supports the Court of Appeals' view that the claimant as a consequence is to be precluded from now complaining that he was denied the rights of confrontation and cross-examination.

7. Courts have recognized the reliability and probative worth of written medical reports even in formal trials and, while acknowledging their hearsay character, have admitted them as an exception to the hearsay rule. * * *

8. Past treatment by reviewing courts of written medical reports in social security disability cases is revealing. Until the decision in this case, the courts of appeals, including the Fifth Circuit, with only an occasional criticism of the medical report practice, uniformly recognized reliability and probative value in such reports. The courts have reviewed administrative determinations, and upheld many adverse ones, where the only supporting evidence has been reports of this kind, buttressed sometimes, but often not, by testimony of a medical adviser such as Dr. Leavitt. In these cases admissibility was not contested, but the decisions do demonstrate traditional and ready acceptance of the written medical report in social security disability cases.

9. There is an additional and pragmatic factor which, although not controlling, deserves mention. This is what Chief Judge Brown has described as "[t]he sheer magnitude of that administrative burden," and the resulting necessity for written reports without "elaboration through the traditional facility of oral testimony." *Page v. Celebrezze*, 311 F.2d 757, 760 (5th Cir. 1963). With over 20,000 disability claim hearings annually, the cost of providing live medical testimony at those hearings,

where need has not been demonstrated by a request for a subpoena, over and above the cost of the examinations requested by hearing examiners, would be a substantial drain on the trust fund and on the energy of physicians already in short supply.

▪ [The opinion of JUSTICE DOUGLAS, dissenting, is omitted. Ed.]

NOTES AND QUESTIONS

1. The Supreme Court in *Universal Camera* called for two things: deferential judicial review of agency fact-finding; and judicial review of the whole record, including evidence discounted as well as evidence relied upon by the agency in reaching its findings of fact. How do you square these two commands? Do you think it is possible for a reviewing court to consider all of the evidence while remaining deferential? Can judicial review of the record be more cursory under a deferential rather than de novo review standard? Or should judicial review of the record always be thorough, just with a more forgiving attitude when applying a deferential standard?

2. Circuit courts have often reversed SSA findings on the basis that SSA failed to attach enough significance to the opinion of the applicant's "treating physician" and attached too much significance to the opinions of "consulting physicians" in determining that an applicant is not disabled. Yet, the Supreme Court reversed a circuit court and criticized it for attaching too much significance to the opinion of a treating physician and not enough significance to the opinions of consulting physicians in *Black & Decker Disability Plan v. Nord*, 538 U.S. 822 (2003). Treating physicians typically are general practitioners who have had a doctor-patient relationship with the applicant for many years, while consulting physicians typically are specialists who have examined the patient only once for purposes of diagnoses. Are treating physicians more credible per se than consulting physicians, or vice versa? Can you think of circumstances in which the reports or testimony of treating physicians might be more persuasive? Can you think of circumstances in which the reports or testimony of consulting physicians might be more persuasive?

3. Read carefully APA § 556(d), available in Appendix B, particularly as it relates to the admissibility of evidence. Compare the APA approach with the long and complicated Federal Rules of Evidence (FRE). For example, the FRE articulate numerous situations in which otherwise relevant evidence is inadmissible for various public policy reasons; preclude the admission of hearsay evidence, subject to more than two dozen exceptions; and identify various bases on which witnesses may or may not be impeached. The FRE are explicitly designed for use in jury trials. Virtually all administrative law and evidence scholars argue that the FRE do not make sense for use by agencies. *See e.g.*, Richard J. Pierce, Jr., *Use of the Federal Rules of Evidence in Federal Agency Adjudications*, 39 ADMIN. L. REV. 1 (1987). Yet, some organic statutes require agencies to conduct adjudications in accordance with the FRE "so far as practicable." *See, e.g.*, National Labor Relations Act, 29 U.S.C. § 160(b). Can you think of reasons why the FRE might or might not be appropriate for use in agency adjudications?

4. The Court in *Richardson v. Perales* makes much of Perales's failure to subpoena the various physicians whose reports contradicted his claim. The SSA does have a rule that authorizes its ALJs to subpoena witnesses, but only when the request for subpoena is accompanied by a persuasive explanation of the value of the testimony the proponent of the subpoena expects to be able to elicit on cross-examination of the witness. Why do you think the SSA takes this attitude toward issuance of subpoenas to consulting physicians? Should a court rely on due process reasoning to require SSA to issue all such subpoenas on demand? What would happen to the cost and accuracy of the SSA decision-making process if any applicant could require any consulting physician to appear for cross-examination? If you represented someone in Mr. Perales's situation today, and you believed that the consulting physicians' opinions were wrong, what would you do?

Fact-Finding in Informal Adjudication

Universal Camera and *Richardson* both concern judicial application of the substantial evidence standard of APA § 706(2)(E). Read that provision, located in Appendix B, in its entirety with care. Note that the APA § 706(2)(E) only calls for judges to apply the substantial evidence standard in cases that are (1) "subject to sections 556 and 557 of this title" or (2) "otherwise reviewed on the record of an agency hearing provided by statute." Think back to Part B of this Chapter discussing the jurisprudence governing formal versus informal adjudication and when the formal adjudication procedures of APA §§ 554, 556, and 557 apply. Recall that most organic statutes do not call for hearings "on the record" and that most agency adjudications are informal adjudications to which §§ 556 and 557 do not apply. In what cases does the substantial evidence standard apply?

There are many cases in which agencies provide some kind of oral or written hearing that falls short of the elaborate formalities required by APA §§ 556 and 557 and then make findings of fact based on the evidence in the record the agency creates. In those cases, courts apply the arbitrary and capricious test of APA § 706(2)(A) to the agency findings. APA § 706(2)(A) instructs reviewing courts to "hold unlawful and set aside agency action, findings, and conclusions found to be . . . arbitrary, capricious, an abuse of discretion, or otherwise not in accordance with law." The Supreme Court has often referred to the arbitrary and capricious test as less demanding than the substantial evidence test. *See e.g., Camp v. Pitts*, 411 U.S. 138, 141–42 (1973). The Court has never articulated, however, the difference between the two tests in their application to findings of fact. Meanwhile, adopting the reasoning of the following case, several circuit courts have declined to distinguish arbitrary and capricious review from the substantial evidence standard.

Ass'n of Data Processing Serv. Organizations, Inc. v. Board of Governors of the Federal Reserve System

745 F.2d 677 (D.C. Cir. 1984).

■ SCALIA, CIRCUIT JUDGE:

The Association of Data Processing Service Organizations, Inc. ("ADAPSO"), a national trade association representing the data processing industry, and two of its members petition this court for review of two orders of the Board of Governors of the Federal Reserve System, pursuant to 12 U.S.C. § 1848 (1982). In No. 82–1910, they seek review of the Board's July 9, 1982 order approving Citicorp's application to establish a subsidiary, Citishare, to engage in certain data processing and transmission services. ("Citicorp Order"). In No. 82–2108, they seek review of the Board's August 23, 1982 order, entered after notice and comment rulemaking, amending those portions of Regulation Y which dealt with the performance of data processing activities by bank holding companies. ("Regulation Y Order"). We consolidated the two appeals.

The Bank Holding Company Act of 1956, ch. 240, 70 Stat. 133 (codified as amended at 12 U.S.C. §§ 1841–50 (1982)) (the "Act"), requires all bank holding companies to seek prior regulatory approval before engaging in nonbanking activities. The restrictions do not apply to:

> activities . . . which the Board after due notice and opportunity for hearing has determined (by order or regulation) to be so closely related to banking or managing or controlling banks as to be a proper incident thereto. . . . In determining whether a particular activity is a proper incident to banking or managing or controlling banks the Board shall consider whether its performance by an affiliate of a holding company can reasonably be expected to produce benefits to the public, such as greater convenience, increased competition, or gains in efficiency, that outweigh possible adverse effects, such as undue concentration of resources, decreased or unfair competition, conflicts of interests, or unsound banking practices.

12 U.S.C. § 1843(c)(8). Section 1848, the source of our review authority, provides that "[t]he findings of the Board as to the facts, if supported by substantial evidence, shall be conclusive." *Id.* § 1848.

On February 23, 1979, Citicorp applied for authority to engage, through its subsidiary Citishare, in the processing and transmission of banking, financial, and economic related data through timesharing, electronic funds transfer, home banking and other techniques. It also sought permission to sell its excess computing capacity and some computer hardware. The Board published notice of Citicorp's application, which was protested by ADAPSO, and set it for formal hearing. Before the hearing was held, Citicorp amended its application to add certain activities and to request amendment of Regulation Y to permit the activities it had specified. The Board published an Amended Order for Hearing and invited public comments and participation. A formal hearing was held before an Administrative Law Judge in which the merits of both the application and the proposed rule were considered. In addition, more than sixty companies and individuals submitted written comments on the proposed rule. On March 29, 1982, the ALJ decided that the activities proposed by Citicorp were closely related to banking and would produce benefits to the public which would outweigh their costs. The ALJ also recommended amendments to Regulation Y that would permit those activities contained in the Citicorp application. On July 9, 1982, the Board adopted the ALJ's recommendation to approve the Citicorp application, with certain restrictions. On August 23, 1982, the Board adopted the ALJ's recommended amendments to Regulation Y, again with certain restrictions. ADAPSO, and two of its members, participants in the actions below, filed these petitions for review.

I.   Standard of Review

We are faced at the outset with a dispute regarding the proper standard of review. These consolidated appeals call for us to review both an on-the-record adjudication and an informal notice and comment rulemaking. Petitioners contend that the substantial evidence standard, which presumably authorizes more rigorous judicial review, should govern our review of both orders. The Board agrees, noting that § 1848 applies a substantial evidence standard to factual determinations. Intervenor Citicorp contends that while the substantial evidence standard should govern review of the Citicorp order, Regulation Y should be upset only if arbitrary or capricious. * * * The parties' submissions on this point reflect considerable confusion, which is understandable when one examines decisions defining the standard of review under this statute.

Both of the Supreme Court's opinions reviewing action of the Board in amending Regulation Y noted that the Board's determination "is entitled to the greatest deference," *Bd. of Governors of the Fed. Reserve Sys. v. Inv. Co. Inst. (ICI)*, 450 U.S. 46, 56 (1981); *Secs. Indus. Ass'n v. Bd. of Governors of the Fed. Reserve Sys. (SIA)*, 468 U.S. 207 (1984), but neither of them discussed the applicable standard of review, or even referred to § 1848. The courts of appeals, however, have applied the substantial evidence standard of § 1848 to Board adjudications such as the authorization in the first order here under review, while applying the arbitrary or capricious standard, despite § 1848, to Board rules, including specifically amendments of Regulation Y. In fact one appellate opinion has, like this one, addressed precisely the situation in which *both* an adjudicatory authorization *and* an amendment of Regulation Y were at issue in the same case—and applied the § 1848 substantial evidence standard to the former but the arbitrary or capricious standard to the latter. This would make a lot of sense if, as the Board has argued in some cases, § 1848 in its totality applies only to adjudication rather than rulemaking, since it is limited to "orders" of the Board, a word which the Administrative Procedure Act ("APA") defines to mean the product of an adjudication. *See* 5 U.S.C. § 551(4), (6) (1982). Such a technical interpretation of the provision, however, has been uniformly and quite correctly rejected. That leaves the courts with the difficult task of explaining why the last sentence of § 1848, unlike all the rest of it, should be deemed to apply only to adjudication and not to rulemaking. Difficult, because there is nothing in either the text or the legislative history of the section to suggest such a result. * * *

We think that there is no basis for giving the last sentence of § 1848 anything less than the general application given to the rest of the section. The Supreme Court's pronouncement that the "greatest deference" is to be given to the determinations of the Board, and the court of appeals decisions applying the arbitrary or capricious test to Board rulemaking, seem to us explicable on quite different grounds—namely, that in their application to the requirement of factual support the substantial evidence test and the arbitrary or capricious test are one and the same. The former is only a specific application of the latter, separately recited in the APA not to establish a more rigorous standard of factual support but to emphasize that in the case of formal proceedings the factual support must be found in the closed record as opposed to elsewhere. We shall elaborate upon this point because it is not uncommon for parties to expend great effort in appeals before us to establish which of the two standards is applicable where in fact their operation is precisely the same.

The "scope of review" provisions of the APA, 5 U.S.C. § 706(2), are cumulative. Thus, an agency action which is supported by the required substantial evidence may in another regard be "arbitrary, capricious, an abuse of discretion, or otherwise not in accordance with law"—for example, because it is an abrupt and unexplained departure from agency precedent. Paragraph (A) of subsection 706(2)—the "arbitrary or capricious" provision—is a catchall, picking up administrative misconduct not covered by the other more specific paragraphs. Thus, in those situations where paragraph (E) has no application (informal rulemaking, for example, which is not governed by §§ 556 and 557 to which paragraph (E) refers), paragraph (A) takes up the slack, so to speak, enabling the courts to strike down, as arbitrary, agency action that is devoid of needed factual support. When the arbitrary or capricious standard is performing that function of assuring factual support, there is no *substantive* difference between what it requires and what would be required by the substantial evidence test, since it is impossible to conceive of a "nonarbitrary" factual judgment supported only by evidence that is not substantial in the APA sense—*i.e.,* not "'enough to justify, if the trial were to a jury, a refusal to direct a verdict when the conclusion sought to be drawn . . . is one of fact for the jury,'" *Ill. Cent. R.R. v. Norfolk & W. Ry.,* 385 U.S. 57 (1966) (quoting *NLRB v. Columbian Enameling & Stamping Co.,* 306 U.S. 292, 300 (1939)).

We have noted on several occasions that the distinction between the substantial evidence test and the arbitrary or capricious test is "largely semantic," *Aircraft Owners & Pilots Ass'n v. FAA,* 600 F.2d 965, 971 n.28 (D.C.Cir.1979); *Pac. Legal Found. v. Dep't of Transp.,* 593 F.2d 1338, 1343 n.35 (D.C.Cir.1979); *Am. Pub. Gas Ass'n v. FPC,* 567 F.2d 1016, 1028–29 (D.C.Cir.1977), and have indeed described that view as "the emerging consensus of the Courts of Appeals," *Pac. Legal Found.,* 593 F.2d at 1343 n.35. Leading commentators agree:

> Does the extent of required factual support for rules depend in part on whether the standard for review is "substantial evidence" or "arbitrary and capricious"? Although from 1946 until some time during the 1970s the dominant answer probably was yes, a change to a no answer has probably occurred during the 1970s. . . .

1 K. DAVIS, ADMINISTRATIVE LAW TREATISE § 6:13 at 512 (2d ed. 1978).

> In review of rules of general applicability made after "notice and comment" rule-making, [substantial evidence and arbitrary or capricious] criteria converge into a test of reasonableness.
>
> . . . .
>
> Review without an agency record thus comes down to review of reasonableness. [T]he question of reasonableness is also the

one which the court must now ask itself in reviewing findings of fact under the post-APA substantial evidence rule.

B. SCHWARTZ, ADMINISTRATIVE LAW 604, 606 (1976).

As noted earlier, this does not consign paragraph (E) of the APA's judicial review section to pointlessness. The distinctive function of paragraph (E)—what it achieves that paragraph (A) does not—is to require substantial evidence to be found *within the record of closed-record proceedings* to which it exclusively applies. The importance of that requirement should not be underestimated. It is true that, as the Supreme Court said in *Camp v. Pitts,* 411 U.S. 138, 142 (1973), even informal agency action (not governed by paragraph (E)) must be reviewed only on the basis of "the administrative record already in existence." But that is quite a different and less onerous requirement, meaning only that whether the administrator was arbitrary must be determined on the basis of what he had before him when he acted, and not on the basis of "some new record made initially in the reviewing court." *Id.* That "administrative record" might well include crucial material that was neither shown to nor known by the private parties in the proceeding-as indeed appears to have been the situation in *Camp v. Pitts* itself. It is true that, in informal rulemaking, at least the most critical factual material that is used to support the agency's position on review must have been made public in the proceeding and exposed to refutation. That requirement, however, does not extend to all data; and it only applies in rulemaking and not in other informal agency action, since it derives not from the arbitrary or capricious test but from the command of 5 U.S.C. § 553(c) that "the agency . . . give interested persons an opportunity to participate in the rule making." *See Portland Cement Ass'n v. Ruckelshaus,* 486 F.2d 375, 393 n.67 (D.C.Cir.1973).

Consolidated cases such as those before us here—involving simultaneous review of a rule (whose factual basis is governed only by paragraph (A)'s catch-all control against "arbitrary or capricious" action) and of a formal adjudication dealing with the same subject (whose factual basis is governed by paragraph (E)'s requirement of substantial evidence)—demonstrate why the foregoing interpretation of the two standards is the only interpretation that makes sense. If the standards were substantively different (and leaving aside for the moment consideration of any special effect of § 1848), the Citicorp order, authorizing one bank holding company's data processing services, would be subject to more rigorous judicial review of factual support than the Regulation Y order which, due to its general applicability, would affect the operations of every bank holding company in the nation. Or, to put the point another way: If the Board had never issued any Regulation Y, and simply determined in the context of a particular application that the provision of timesharing services is "closely related" to banking, that determination, which could be reconsidered and revised in the context of the next adjudication, would require more factual support than the same determination in a rulemaking, which would have immediate nationwide application and, until amended by further rulemaking, would have to be applied to all subsequent applications.

* * *

We hold, therefore, that the § 1848 "substantial evidence" requirement applicable to our review here demands a quantum of factual support no different from that demanded by the substantial evidence provision of the APA, which is in turn no different from that demanded by the arbitrary or capricious standard.

NOTES AND QUESTIONS

1. As noted, several circuit courts of appeals have explicitly adopted the conclusion of the *ADAPSO* court that the substantial evidence standard and the arbitrary and capricious standard are functionally equivalent in the context of judicial review of agency fact-finding. *See, e.g., Ace Telephone Ass'n v. Koppendrayer*, 432 F.3d 876, 880 (8th Cir. 2005); *Sevoian v. Ashcroft*, 290 F.3d 166, 174 (3d Cir. 2002); *GTE South, Inc. v. Morrison*, 199 F.3d 733, 745 n.5 (4th Cir. 1999); *Olenhouse v. Commodity Credit Corp.*, 42 F.3d 1560, 1575 n.25 (10th Cir. 1994). While declining to address the question, the Supreme Court has acknowledged the *ADAPSO* court's equation of the two standards. *See Dickinson v. Zurko*, 527 U.S. 150, 158 (1999).

2. *ADAPSO* involved both a formal adjudication and an informal rulemaking. Justice Scalia justifies equating the substantial evidence and arbitrary and capricious standards in part by saying that, otherwise, an adjudicatory order that applies to only one regulated party would be subject to more rigorous judicial review (under the substantial evidence standard) than a rulemaking of general applicability (subject only to arbitrary and capricious review). Think back to our discussion of the differences between adjudication and rulemaking at the beginning of this Chapter. Although rulemaking is covered in depth in Chapter 5, for now consider also that, while agency adjudications typically involve a dispute between two parties (the government and the regulated party whose actions are at issue), rulemakings of the sort at issue in *ADAPSO* are achieved through public notice and comment procedures, often with extensive public participation in the rulemaking process. Can you think of reasons why we might find more deferential review of agency fact findings in the rulemaking context systemically acceptable?

3. Justice Scalia in *ADAPSO* distinguishes the arbitrary and capricious standard of APA § 706(2)(A) and the substantial evidence standard of APA § 706(2)(E) on the ground that Congress intended the latter merely to limit judicial review to evidence contained in the closed record generated through the agency hearing, while the former is not so limited. Are you persuaded by Justice Scalia's analysis of the text of APA § 706? If so, why do you think Congress chose different phraseologies (arbitrary and capricious versus substantial evidence) in articulating the two standards?

2. JUDICIAL REVIEW OF ISSUES OF LAW AND OF THE AGENCY REASONING PROCESS

As noted, we will defer detailed discussion of judicial review of agency resolution of issues of law and of the agency reasoning process until Chapters 5 and 6. Nevertheless, there are a few characteristics of judicial review of the agency reasoning process that are so closely tied to adjudication that they warrant some discussion in this Chapter.

Judicial review of the agency reasoning process takes place through application of the arbitrary and capricious standard. APA § 706(2)(A) instructs courts to apply that standard to all agency actions. As we discuss in detail in Chapter 5, the Supreme Court has held that an agency must explain its reasoning in support of its action adequately to avoid a judicial conclusion that its action is arbitrary and capricious.

This method of applying the arbitrary and capricious test presents a problem, however, in the context of informal adjudication. As we discussed above, an agency is not statutorily required to adhere to any particular decision-making procedures when it engages in informal adjudication. Thus, a court cannot reverse an agency action taken through use of informal adjudication on the ground that the agency failed to explain the basis for its action because the agency has no duty to explain its action. Yet, a reviewing court must have some basis to determine the adequacy of the agency's reasoning process if an agency adjudicates a dispute through use of informal adjudication and declines to provide any contemporaneous explanation for its action. In both *Overton Park* and *LTV Corp.*, excerpted elsewhere in this Chapter, the Supreme Court addressed this practical problem by instructing reviewing courts to remand such decisions to the agency to allow the agency to explain its action if the agency has declined to provide a contemporaneous explanation for its action or has provided an explanation that is insufficient to allow a court to apply the arbitrary and capricious standard.

The arbitrary and capricious standard also relates to the substantial evidence standard in a way that increases to some extent the stringency of judicial review of agency findings of fact. Reviewing courts require agencies to explain why they chose to credit one item of evidence rather than a conflicting item of evidence in the process of making a finding of fact. A court can vacate and remand an agency action if the court concludes that the agency did not adequately explain why it attached greater significance to some evidence than to other evidence. *E.g.*, *Dia v. Ashcroft*, 353 F.3d 228 (3d Cir. 2003).

Reviewing courts also apply the arbitrary and capricious test in a manner that requires agencies to adhere to a modified version of stare decisis. An agency can issue a decision that is inconsistent with its precedents only if it acknowledges that it is changing course and explains adequately why it is changing course. The Supreme Court explained this doctrine in its unanimous opinion in *INS v. Yang*, 519 U.S. 26, 32 (1996):

> Though the agency's discretion is unfettered at the outset, if it announces and follows—by rule or by settled course of adjudication—a general policy by which its exercise of discretion will be governed, an irrational departure from that policy (as opposed to an avowed alteration of it) could constitute action that must be overturned as "arbitrary, capricious, [or] an abuse of discretion" within the meaning of the Administrative Procedure Act.

Subsequently, in *FCC v. Fox Television Stations, Inc.*, 129 S.Ct. 1800, 1811 (2009), the Supreme Court reiterated and elaborated this position:

An agency may not, for example, depart from a prior policy sub silentio or simply disregard rules that are still on the books. And of course the agency must show that there are good reasons for the new policy. But it need not demonstrate to a court's satisfaction that the reasons for the new policy are better than the reasons for the old one; it suffices that the new policy is permissible under the statute, that there are good reasons for it, and that the agency believes it to be better, which the conscious change of course adequately indicates. This means that the agency need not always provide a more detailed justification than would suffice for a new policy created on a blank slate. Sometimes it must—when, for example, its new policy rests upon factual findings that contradict those which underlay its prior policy; or when its prior policy has engendered serious reliance interests that must be taken into account. It would be arbitrary or capricious to ignore such matters. In such cases it is not that further justification is demanded by the mere fact of policy change; but that a reasoned explanation is needed for disregarding facts and circumstances that underlay or were engendered by the prior policy.

CHAPTER 5

RULES AND RULEMAKING

The other major power that agencies possess is the authority to make rules in the course of administering statutes. If, at least in theory, some agency adjudications compare somewhat to court cases, a subset of agency rules more closely resemble statutes. Yet, any discussion of agency rulemaking must begin by recognizing that there are different types of rules. Specifically, rules are either legislative or nonlegislative. Nonlegislative rules in turn break down into several categories, the most important being interpretative rules, procedural rules, and policy statements.

The Administrative Procedure Act (APA) does not actually use the terms legislative rule and nonlegislative rule. Instead, APA § 553(b) and (c) describes a three-step process for adopting a rule—commonly known as notice-and-comment rulemaking—that entails issuing a notice of proposed rulemaking, soliciting comments on the proposal from interested members of the public, and publishing the final rule with an accompanying statement of its basis and purpose. APA § 553(b) then lists "interpretative rules, general statements of policy, or rules of agency organization, procedure, or practice" as categories of rules that are exempt from those procedural requirements. Courts and commentators have long labeled rules that do not fall within the scope of the exemptions from APA public notice and comment requirements as legislative rules to distinguish them clearly from the exempt categories. Some courts alternatively refer to non-exempt rules as substantive rules instead of legislative rules, but courts and commentators generally treat the two terms as synonymous. Except where there is some need to identify which of the exempt categories a rule falls into, courts and commentators often group procedural rules, interpretative rules, and policy statements under the label of nonlegislative rules for ease of reference while distinguishing them from legislative rules.

Whether a rule is legislative or nonlegislative matters for more than whether its promulgation must satisfy the procedural requirements of notice-and-comment rulemaking. As we will discuss in Chapters 6 and 7, a rule's classification may alter the scope and availability of judicial review. Also, legislative rules carry the same legally binding effect as statutes, and congressional authorization is necessary before an agency may promulgate a legislative rule. *See, e.g.,* *Chrysler Corp. v. Brown*, 441 U.S. 281, 301–02 (1979). By contrast, nonlegislative rules may bind agency employees, but they are not legally enforceable against the public. Legal scholars have long claimed that all agencies have the inherent authority to issue nonlegislative rules, derived from the power to execute the laws; the head of an agency must be able to coordinate the efforts of subordinate employees, and in so doing will establish policies and procedures to guide their actions, including issuing official interpretations of statutes. *See, e.g.,* Thomas W. Merrill & Kristin E. Hickman, *Chevron's Domain*, 89 GEO. L.J. 833, 876 (2001); Kenneth Culp Davis, *Administrative Rules—Interpretative,*

Legislative, and Retroactive, 57 YALE L.J. 919, 930 (1948); John Fairlie, *Administrative Regulation*, 18 MICH. L. REV. 181, 183–88 (1920).

We will discuss in greater depth both the APA's notice-and-comment rulemaking procedures for legislative rules and the nature and scope of the exemptions from those procedures in Parts B and C of this Chapter. First, however, some additional exploration of the relationship between agency rulemaking and agency adjudication is necessary to understand why and under what circumstances agencies choose to engage in rulemaking.

A. WHY RULEMAKING?

Many agencies engage in both rulemaking and adjudication, while some agencies act primarily or even exclusively through one or the other. Is utilization of rulemaking or adjudication a matter of agency choice? If agencies have a choice, how do they decide which to pursue? The following materials address these and related questions.

1. AGENCY POWER TO ISSUE RULES

As noted above, the power to issue legislative rules derives from congressional delegations of rulemaking authority. Statutes express such delegations in a variety of ways.

Most statutes that create agencies or that authorize agencies to take actions to implement a statute are relatively clear in either granting or not granting an agency the power to issue legislative rules. Some of these grants of rulemaking authority are specific, stating that an agency "shall" or "may" issue rules to accomplish a particular, statutorily-identified purpose. Thus,

- The Securities Exchange Act of 1934 provides that the Securities Exchange Commission "shall establish . . . by rules and regulations" applicable to securities brokers or dealers "standards of training, experience, competence, and such other qualifications as the Commission finds necessary or appropriate in the public interest or for the protection of investors," including but not limited to tests that "include questions relating to bookkeeping, accounting, internal control over cash and securities, supervision of employees, maintenance of records, and other appropriate matters." 15 U.S.C. § 78o(a)(7).

- The Clean Air Act states that the Administrator of the Environmental Protection Agency "shall by regulation prescribe (and from time to time revise) in accordance with the provisions of this section, standards applicable to the emission of any air pollutant from any class or classes of new motor vehicles or new motor vehicle engines. . . ." 42 U.S.C. § 7521(a).

- The Communications Act of 1934 provides that the Federal Communications Commission "shall, by rule, prescribe a uniform system of accounts for use by telephone companies." 47 U.S.C. § 220(a)(2).

Others statutory delegations are more general, providing only that an agency may promulgate rules as necessary to effectuate the statute's provisions. Thus,

- The Internal Revenue Code grants the Secretary of the Treasury the authority to "prescribe all needful rules and regulations for the enforcement of this title." 26 U.S.C. § 7805(a).

- The Federal Food, Drug, and Cosmetic Act gives the Secretary of Health and Human Services "the authority to promulgate regulations for the efficient enforcement of this chapter." 21 U.S.C. § 361(a).

- The National Labor Relations Act gives the National Labor Relations Board the power "from time to time to make, amend, and rescind . . . such rules and regulations as may be necessary to carry out the provisions of" the Act. 29 U.S.C. § 156.

Particularly with respect to the latter type of authority grant, a court occasionally has had to decide whether an agency has the power to adopt legislative rules in the context of a statute that is not clear on the issue.

National Petroleum Refiners Ass'n v. FTC

482 F.2d 672 (D.C. Cir.), cert. denied, 415 U.S. 951 (1974).

■ J. SKELLY WRIGHT, CIRCUIT JUDGE.

This case presents an important question concerning the powers and procedures of the Federal Trade Commission. We are asked to determine whether the Commission, under its governing statute, the Trade Commission Act, 15 U.S.C. § 41 *et seq.* (1970), and specifically 15 U.S.C. § 46(g), is empowered to promulgate substantive rules of business conduct or, as it terms them, "Trade Regulation Rules." The effect of these rules would be to give greater specificity and clarity to the broad standard of illegality—"unfair methods of competition in commerce, and unfair or deceptive acts or practices in commerce"—which the agency is empowered to prevent. 15 U.S.C. § 45(a). Once promulgated, the rules would be used by the agency in adjudicatory proceedings aimed at producing cease and desist orders against violations of the statutory standard. The central question in such adjudicatory proceedings would be whether the particular defendant's conduct violated the rule in question.

* * * Specifically at issue in the District Court was the Commission's rule declaring that failure to post octane rating numbers on gasoline pumps at service stations was an unfair method of competition and an unfair or deceptive act or practice. The plaintiffs in the District Court, appellees here, are two trade associations and 34 gasoline refining companies.

* * *

As always, we must begin with the words of the statute creating the Commission and delineating its powers. Section 5 directs the Commission to "prevent persons, partnerships, or corporations * * * from using unfair methods of competition in commerce and unfair or deceptive acts or practices in commerce." 15 U.S.C. § 45(a)(6). Section 5(b) of the Trade Commission Act specifies that the Commission is to accomplish this goal by means of issuance of a complaint, a hearing, findings as to the facts, and issuance of a cease and desist order. The Commission's assertion that it is empowered by Section 6(g) to issue substantive rules defining the statutory standard of illegality in advance of specific adjudications does not in any formal sense circumvent this method of enforcement. For after the rules are issued, their mode of enforcement remains what it has always been under Section 5: the sequence of complaint, hearing, findings, and issuance of a cease and desist order. What rule-making does do, functionally, is to narrow the inquiry conducted in proceedings under Section 5(b). It is the legality of this practice which we must judge.

Appellees argue that since Section 5 mentions only adjudication as the means of enforcing the statutory standard, any supplemental means of putting flesh on that standard, such as rule-making, is contrary to the overt legislative design. But Section 5(b) does not use limiting language suggesting that adjudication alone is the only proper means of elaborating the statutory standard. It merely makes clear that a Commission decision, after complaint and hearing, followed by a cease and desist order, is the way to force an offender to halt his illegal activities. Nor are we persuaded by appellees' argument that, despite the absence of limiting language in Section 5 regarding the role of adjudication in defining the meaning of the statutory standard, we should apply the maxim of statutory construction *expressio unius est exclusio alterius* and conclude that adjudication is the *only* means of defining the statutory standard. * * * Here we have particularly good reason on the face of the statute to reject such arguments. For the Trade Commission Act includes a provision which specifically provides for rule-making by the Commission to implement its adjudicatory functions under Section 5 of the Act. Section 6(g) of the Act, 15 U.S.C. § 46(g), states that the Commission may "[f]rom time to time * * * classify corporations and * * * make rules and regulations for the purpose of carrying out the provisions of sections 41 to 46 and 47 to 58 of this title."

According to appellees, however, this rule-making power is limited to specifying the details of the Commission's nonadjudicatory, investigative and informative functions spelled out in the other provisions of Section 6 and should not be read to encompass substantive rule-making in implementation of Section 5 adjudications. We disagree for the simple reason that Section 6(g) clearly states that the Commission "may" make rules and regulations for the purpose of carrying out the provisions of Section 5 and it has been so applied. For example, the Commission has issued rules specifying in greater detail than the statute the mode of Commission procedure under Section 5 in matters involving service of process, requirements as to the filing of answers, and other litigation details necessarily involved in the Commission's work of prosecuting its complaints under Section 5. Such rule-making by the Commission has been upheld.

* * *

Of course, it is at least arguable that these cases go no farther than to justify utilizing Section 6(g) to promulgate procedural, as opposed to substantive, rules for administration of the Section 5 adjudication and enforcement powers. But we see no reason to import such a restriction on the "rules and regulations" permitted by Section 6(g).

* * *

[T]here is little question that the availability of substantive rule-making gives any agency an invaluable resource-saving flexibility in carrying out its task of regulating parties subject to its statutory mandate. More than merely expediting the agency's job, use of substantive rule-making is increasingly felt to yield significant benefits to those the agency regulates. Increasingly, courts are recognizing that use of rule-making to make innovations in agency policy may actually be fairer to regulated parties than total reliance on case-by-case adjudication.

* * *

Although we believe there are thus persuasive considerations for accepting the FTC's view that the plain meaning of the statute supports substantive rule-making, the question is not necessarily closed. For appellees' contention—that the phrase "rules and regulations for the purpose of carrying out" Section 5 refers only to rules of procedure and practice for carrying out the Commission's adjudicatory responsibility— is not implausible. The opinion of the District Court argues forcefully that, in spite of the clear and unlimited language of Section 6(g) granting rule-making authority to the Commission, the Congress that enacted Section 5 and Section 6(g) gave clear indications of its intent to reject substantive rule-making, that the FTC's own behavior in the years since that time supports a narrow interpretation of its mandate to promulgate "rules and regulations," and that where Congress desired to give the FTC substantive rule-making authority in discrete areas it did so in subsequent years in unambiguous terms. Our own conclusion, based on an independent review of this history, is different. We believe that, while the legislative history of Section 5 and Section 6(g) is ambiguous, it certainly does not compel the conclusion that the Commission was not meant to exercise the power to make substantive rules with binding effect in Section 5(a) adjudications. We also believe that the plain language of Section 6(g), read in light of the broad, clearly agreed-upon concerns that motivated passage of the Trade Commission Act, confirms the framers' intent to allow exercise of the power claimed here.

* * *

[W]hile we believe the historical evidence is indecisive of the question before us, we are convinced that the broad, undisputed policies which clearly motivated the framers of the Federal Trade Commission Act of 1914 would indeed be furthered by our view as to the proper scope of the Commission's rule-making authority. * * *

In determining the legislative intent, our duty is to favor an interpretation which would render the statutory design effective in terms of the policies behind its enactment and to avoid an interpretation which would make such policies more difficult of fulfillment, particularly where, as here, that interpretation is consistent with the plain language of the statute. * * *

The problems of delay and inefficiency that proponents of both a strong and a weak commission aimed to eliminate or minimize have plagued the Trade Commission down to the present. While the Commission has broad common law-like authority to delineate the scope of the statute's prohibitions, like the federal courts it was designed to supplement, it has remained hobbled in its task by the delay inherent in repetitious, lengthy litigation of cases involving complex factual questions under a broad legal standard. Close students of the agency agree that the historic case-by-case purely adjudicatory method of elaborating the Section 5 standard and applying it to discrete business practices has not only produced considerable uncertainty but also has helped to spawn litigation the length of which has frequently been noted ruefully by commentators on the Commission's performance. We believe that, to the extent substantive rule-making to implement Section 5 proceedings is likely to deal with these problems given the statutory authority provided in Section 6(g), the Commission's position should be upheld as a reasonable means of attacking ills the Commission was created to cure.

* * *

This relationship between rule-making's probable benefits and the broad concerns evident when the FTC was created, together with the express language of Section 6(g), help persuade us that any purported ambiguity of the statute be resolved in favor of the Commission's claim. "In a case much more clouded with doubts than this one, we held that we would not 'in the absence of compelling evidence that such was Congress' intention . . . prohibit administrative action imperative for the achievement of an agency's ultimate purposes.'" *Weinberger v. Bentex Pharms., Inc.*, 412 U.S. 645, 653 (1973) (quoting *Permian Basin Area Rate Cases*, 390 U.S. 747, 780 (1968)).

* * *

Our conclusion as to the scope of Section 6(g) is not disturbed by the fact that the agency itself did not assert the power to promulgate substantive rules until 1962 and indeed indicated intermittently before that time that it lacked such power.

NOTES AND QUESTIONS

1. As the *National Petroleum Refiners* court acknowledges, the FTC had consistently interpreted the statutory reference to its power to issue rules as empowering it only to issue procedural rules for the first fifty years of the agency's existence. It had also consistently represented to Congress that it lacked the power to issue legally-binding substantive or legislative rules for that same fifty years. Moreover, the context in which the reference to the FTC's power to issue rules suggested that the reference was only to procedural rules. Many lawyers and commentators were shocked by the D.C. Circuit's decision to hold that the FTC has the power to issue legislative rules in that situation.

2. Thomas Merrill and Kathryn Watts have criticized harshly the D.C. Circuit's opinion in *National Petroleum Refiners* and similar cases. Merrill and Watts argue that a court should hold that an agency has the power to issue legislative rules only when its statute authorizes a court to penalize a party for violating the agency's rules; the FTC's statute contains no such provision. *See* Thomas W. Merrill & Kathryn Tongue Watts, *Agency Rules with the Force of Law*, 116 HARV. L. REV. 467 (2002). Do you find the alternative test urged by Merrill and Watts more persuasive than the D.C. Circuit's approach?

3.   Shortly after the D.C. Circuit held that the FTC had the authority to issue legislative rules, the FTC began to use its newfound power by proposing to issue rules that would restrict the practices of numerous groups, including doctors, lawyers, used car dealers, soft drink bottling companies, and funeral directors. Congress responded to the D.C. Circuit's decision in *National Petroleum Refiners* and to the FTC's efforts to use its new regulatory tool by enacting the Magnuson-Moss Warranty—Federal Trade Commission Improvement Act, Pub. L. No. 93–637, 88 Stat. 2183 (1974) (the "FTC Improvement Act"). That statute confirmed the FTC's power to issue legislative rules, but it required the FTC to use procedures that differ significantly from the simple three-step process described in APA § 553. Under the FTC Improvement Act, the FTC is required to allow an opportunity for presentation of oral evidence and for cross-examination of oral evidence on "disputed material facts" when "necessary for fair determination of . . . the rulemaking proceeding." As we will detail further in Part B of this Chapter in connection with *United States v. Florida East Coast Railway*, 410 U.S. 224 (1973), the procedures FTC must use to issue a rule under the FTC Improvement Act are similar to the "formal rulemaking" procedures that the APA requires any agency to use when the statute the agency is implementing specifies that "rules are required . . . to be made on the record after opportunity for an agency hearing."

Since Congress enacted the FTC Improvement Act, the FTC has almost completely abandoned its efforts to issue legislative rules. Why do you think the FTC has made that choice? If you were counsel for National Petroleum Refiners, and the FTC attempted to issue the octane posting rule after Congress enacted the FTC Improvement Act, what actions would you take in connection with the oral hearing? How many companies would be affected by the rule? How many expert witnesses would each present? Which lawyers would insist on an opportunity to cross-examine the FTC expert witnesses? Would lawyers for one company insist on the opportunity to cross-examine the witnesses presented by other companies? How long would you expect the proceeding to last?

———————

The judges who decided *National Petroleum Refiners* obviously were influenced by their beliefs that FTC should have the power to issue legislative rules. The vast majority of judges, Justices, and administrative law scholars share the belief that legislative rules and the APA process through which such rules are issued offer enormous advantages in comparison with the traditional case-by-case approach to regulation. Consider the following excerpt discussing of those advantages.

Richard J. Pierce, Jr., The Many Advantages of Rules and Rulemaking

Administrative Law Treatise § 6.8 (5th ed. 2010).

Commentators have identified at least nine different advantages of rulemaking over adjudication as a source of generally applicable rules. First, rulemaking can be expected to yield higher quality rules than adjudication. When an agency announces a "rule" in the process of adjudicating a specific dispute, it has before it only the parties to the particular dispute and the evidence those parties tender. Traditionally, that evidence focuses primarily or exclusively on the specific, historical facts related to those parties and their relationship. The factual pattern on which the agency predicates its rule may be widely generalizable or entirely idiosyncratic. The agency has no way of knowing whether the fact pattern before it applies to 100 percent, 50 percent, 10 percent, or 1 percent of superficially analogous relationships or incidents. Other common patterns may suggest entirely different rules. Moreover, the process of making a general rule of conduct should not be based primarily on resolution of specific historical facts. The primary purposes of rules are to effect future conduct and to provide reasonably clear and objective criteria for application to adjudicatory proceedings. Thus, rules should be based on evidence relevant to those goals. An agency contemplating announcement of a rule should search for answers to questions like: How can we channel the future conduct of regulatees or beneficiaries in ways that will further our statutory mission? What is the general relationship between exposure to a particular toxic substance and adverse health effects? An adjudication rarely yields significant, high quality evidence relevant to such questions.

By contrast, all potentially affected members of the public are given an opportunity to participate in a rulemaking proceeding. The frame of reference established by the agency's notice of proposed rulemaking, *e.g.*, "We are considering adoption of the following rules as means of furthering specified statutory goals," invites participants to submit comments relevant to the forward-looking, instrumental purpose of a rule. Parties have a natural incentive to address questions concerning the generalizability of alternative patterns of fact, alternative means of shaping conduct, practical problems in implementing alternative rules, etc. Similarly, parties have incentives to include in their comments studies and affidavits of experts addressing such issues as (1) the frequency of occurrence of various factual patterns, (2) the likely efficacy of alternative rules in shaping conduct, (3) the cost of compliance with alternative rules, and (4) the practical problems inherent in implementing or enforcing alternative rules in varying factual contexts. The rule produced by this process almost certainly will be instrumentally superior to any "rule" produced by the process of adjudicating a specific dispute.

The second advantage of rulemaking inheres in the enhanced political accountability of agency policy decisions adopted through the rulemaking process. Before an agency can make a binding policy decision through the rulemaking process, it must issue a public notice of its proposed rule. This notice of proposed rulemaking enables citizens who oppose or support the proposal to alert the President and members of Congress to the existence of the proposal and to express their views of the agency's proposal to those politically accountable officials. This, in turn, allows the President and Congress to express to the agency their views concerning the proposed policy decision and, through the process of Executive and congressional oversight, to affect agency resolutions of policy disputes. *See* Matthew D. McCubbins, Roger G. Noll & Barry R. Weingast, *Administrative Procedures as Instruments of Political Control*, 3 J.L. ECON. & ORG. 243 (1987). By contrast, when an agency announces a policy decision in the context of resolving a particular adjudicatory dispute, the President and Congress usually have no prior notice that the agency is proposing to make such a decision, and those politically accountable officers have much less ability to influence the agency's policy decision.

Three advantages of rulemaking fit under the broad heading of efficiency. Rulemaking eliminates the need to engage in expensive and time-consuming adjudicatory hearings to address issues of legislative fact; rulemaking eliminates the need to relitigate recurring issues; and rules created through rulemaking are easier and less expensive to enforce and to implement than are "rules" announced in the course of adjudicating specific disputes.

* * *

The other four major advantages of rulemaking fit under the general heading of fairness. Legislative rules provide affected parties with clearer advance notice of permissible and impermissible conduct; they avoid the widely disparate temporal impact of "rules" announced and applied through adjudicatory decisionmaking; they reduce the incidence and magnitude of interdecisional inconsistencies in implementing regulatory and benefit programs; and, they allow all potentially affected members of the public an opportunity to participate in the process of determining the rules that affect them.

DISCUSSION PROBLEM

National Petroleum Refiners concerned a rule imposed by the FTC prohibiting the sale of gasoline without posting the octane content of the gasoline. The FTC decided to promulgate that rule because of complaints from consumers, consumer advocates, and members of Congress, coupled with studies that found that many petroleum refiners were duping consumers out of billions of dollars by selling "premium" grades of gasoline at higher than normal prices based on claims of superior performance in circumstances in which the chemical and functional characteristics of the "premium" grades of gasoline did not justify the claims. Without the power to issue the legislative rule that was challenged in *National Petroleum Refiners*, how could the FTC have addressed this problem?

Without the authority to promulgate legislative rules, FTC would have to begin by filing a complaint against a particular gasoline retailer—*e.g.*, Tom's Shell gas station in Annandale, Virginia—alleging that Tom was engaging in an unfair and deceptive trade practice by failing to post the octane content of the gasoline sold his gas pumps. What actions would you expect Tom to take upon receipt of such a complaint? If you were Tom's local counsel, what actions would you recommend? If the petroleum refiners like Shell were making billion dollar profits as a result of their widespread use of the practice FTC challenged, as FTC believed to be the case, who do you think would provide the financial resources to argue against the FTC in the ensuring hearing, and how much money would you expect them to be willing to devote to an effort to defend Tom's practice? How many expert witnesses, in what areas of expertise, would you expect Tom to call to defend his practice? How many pages of studies and consulting reports would you expect Tom to present through his expert witnesses? How many expert witnesses and supporting studies would FTC need to present to have a decent chance of prevailing in the hearing against Tom? How vigorously would you expect Tom's lawyers to cross-examine the FTC witnesses? How long would you expect it to take for FTC to issue a final decision in the case against Tom and to defend that decision successfully in court?

Assuming that FTC was successful in its case against Tom, would you expect all other gasoline retailers to cease immediately the practice of selling gasoline without posting the octane content? If you represented another gasoline retailer (or, more realistically, another refining company like Exxon), do you think you could find in the inevitably long and detailed FTC opinion in Tom's case some basis on which you could attempt to distinguish your client's marketing practices from those used by Tom without posting the octane content of the various grades of gasoline your client sells? If you believe that other gasoline retailers gradually would begin to post the octane content of their gasoline if FTC prevailed against several retailers, how long would you expect that to take, and would you expect that all retailers would initially post the octane content in a conspicuous location in bold letters?

Assume that you are General Counsel of FTC. Once you recognize the cost to FTC of effectively eliminating the practice and the number of years required to do so, would you recommend that the agency devote its scarce resources to an attempt to eliminate the practice? How many similar widespread deceptive practices could you realistically expect to address through use of this process?

Now consider the situation FTC confronts once it has the power to issue legislative rules. It can use the three-step process described in APA section 553 to issue a rule that prohibits the retail sale of gasoline without posting the octane content of the gasoline. The rule can specify the method the retailer must use to measure octane content, as well as the detailed manner in which the octane must be posted on each pump. Assume you are Tom's lawyer, and that Tom receives an FTC complaint alleging that he is engaged in an unfair and deceptive practice by violating the rule. What actions would you recommend to Tom? If you called the General Counsels of Shell and/or the National Petroleum Refiners Association, what actions would you expect them to recommend?

2. THE FUNCTIONAL RELATIONSHIP BETWEEN RULES AND ADJUDICATIONS

Assuming that an agency has the authority to promulgate legally binding rules, why might it want to do so, particularly when one considers that APA procedural requirements are so much more burdensome for rulemaking than for adjudication? Many reasons exist, and they no doubt vary depending upon the statutory scheme in question. Nevertheless, one reason for pursuing rulemaking over adjudication is that rules provide a means through which agencies can limit the discretion of administrative law judges (ALJs) and other adjudicatory personnel by, inter alia, resolving once and for all one or more issues that otherwise would have to be decided case by case. Limiting the discretion of adjudicators may, in turn, yield some combination of greater accuracy, consistency, and/or efficiency in administering a particular statutory scheme. The social security disability program offers one illustration of this functional relationship in action.

Heckler v. Campbell

461 U.S. 458 (1983).

■ JUSTICE POWELL delivered the opinion of the Court.

The issue is whether the Secretary of Health and Human Services may rely on published medical-vocational guidelines to determine a claimant's right to Social Security disability benefits.

The Social Security Act defines "disability" in terms of the effect a physical or mental impairment has on a person's ability to function in the workplace. It provides disability benefits only to persons who are unable "to engage in any substantial gainful activity by reason of any medically determinable physical or mental impairment." 42 U.S.C. § 423(d)(1)(A). And it specifies that a person must "not only [be] unable to do his previous work but [must be unable], considering his age, education, and work experience, [to] engage in any other kind of substantial gainful work which exists in the national economy, regardless of whether such work exists in the immediate area in which he lives, or whether a specific job vacancy exists for him, or whether he would be hired if he applied for work." 42 U.S.C. § 423(d)(2)(A).

In 1978, the Secretary of Health and Human Services promulgated regulations implementing this definition. *See* 43 Fed. Reg. 55349 (1978) (codified as amended at 20 C.F.R. pt. 404, subpt. P (1982)). The regulations recognize that certain impairments are so severe that they prevent a person from pursuing any gainful work. A claimant who establishes that he suffers from one of these impairments will be considered disabled without further inquiry. If a claimant suffers from a less severe impairment, the Secretary must determine whether the claimant retains the ability to perform either his former work or some less demanding employment. If a claimant can pursue his former occupation, he is not entitled to disability benefits. If he cannot, the Secretary must determine whether the claimant retains the capacity to pursue less demanding work.

The regulations divide this last inquiry into two stages. First, the Secretary must assess each claimant's present job qualifications. The regulations direct the Secretary to consider the factors Congress has identified as relevant: physical ability, age, education and work experience. Second, she must consider whether jobs exist in the national economy that a person having the claimant's qualifications could perform.

Prior to 1978, the Secretary relied on vocational experts to establish the existence of suitable jobs in the national economy. After a claimant's limitations and abilities had been determined at a hearing, a vocational expert ordinarily would testify whether work existed that the claimant could perform. Although this testimony often was based on standardized guides, vocational experts frequently were criticized for their inconsistent treatment of similarly situated claimants. To improve both the uniformity and efficiency of this determination, the Secretary promulgated medical-vocational guidelines as part of the 1978 regulations.

These guidelines relieve the Secretary of the need to rely on vocational experts by establishing through rulemaking the types and numbers of jobs that exist in the national economy. They consist of a matrix of the four factors identified by Congress—physical ability, age, education, and work experience—and set forth rules that identify whether jobs requiring specific combinations of these factors exist in significant numbers in the national economy. Where a claimant's qualifications correspond to the job requirements identified by a rule, the guidelines direct a conclusion as to whether work exists that the claimant could perform. If such work exists, the claimant is not considered disabled.

In 1979, Carmen Campbell applied for disability benefits because a back condition and hypertension prevented her from continuing her work as a hotel maid. After her application was denied, she requested a hearing *de novo* before an Administrative Law Judge. * * * Relying on the medical-vocational guidelines, the Administrative Law Judge found that a significant number of jobs existed that a person of Campbell's qualifications could perform. Accordingly, he concluded that she was not disabled.

* * * The [Court of Appeals for the Second Circuit] found that the medical-vocational guidelines did not provide the specific evidence that it previously had required. It explained that in the absence of such a showing, "the claimant is deprived of any real chance to present evidence showing that she cannot in fact perform the types of jobs that are administratively noticed by the guidelines." The court concluded that because the Secretary had failed to introduce evidence that specific alternative jobs existed, the determination that Campbell was not disabled was not supported by substantial evidence.

* * *

The Social Security Act directs the Secretary to "adopt reasonable and proper rules and regulations to regulate and provide for the nature and extent of the proofs and evidence and the method of taking and furnishing the same" in disability cases. 42 U.S.C. § 405(a). As we previously have recognized, Congress has "conferred on the Secretary exceptionally broad authority to prescribe standards for applying certain sections of the [Social Security] Act." *Schweiker v. Gray Panthers*, 453 U.S. 34, 43 (1981). Where, as here, the statute expressly entrusts the Secretary with the responsibility for implementing a provision by regulation, our review is limited to determining whether the regulations promulgated exceeded the Secretary's statutory authority and whether they are arbitrary and capricious.

We do not think that the Secretary's reliance on medical-vocational guidelines is inconsistent with the Social Security Act. It is true that the statutory scheme contemplates that disability hearings will be individualized determinations based on evidence adduced at a hearing. But this does not bar the Secretary from relying on rulemaking to resolve certain classes of issues. The Court has recognized that even where an agency's enabling statute expressly requires it to hold a hearing, the agency may rely on its rulemaking authority to determine issues that do not require case-by-case consideration. *See FPC v. Texaco, Inc.*, 377 U.S. 33, 41–44 (1964); *United States v. Storer Broad. Co.*, 351 U.S. 192, 205 (1956). A contrary holding would require the agency continually to relitigate issues that may be established fairly and efficiently in a single rulemaking proceeding.

The Secretary's decision to rely on medical-vocational guidelines is consistent with *Texaco* and *Storer*. As noted above, in determining whether a claimant can perform less strenuous work, the Secretary must make two determinations. She must assess each claimant's individual abilities and then determine whether jobs exist that a person having the claimant's qualifications could perform. The first inquiry involves a determination of historic facts, and the regulations properly require the Secretary to make these findings on the basis of evidence adduced at a hearing. We note that the regulations afford claimants ample opportunity both to present evidence relating to their own abilities and to offer evidence that the guidelines do not apply to them. The second inquiry requires the Secretary to determine an issue that is not unique to each claimant—the types and numbers of jobs that exist in the national economy. This type of general factual issue may be resolved as fairly through rulemaking as by introducing the testimony of vocational experts at each disability hearing.

As the Secretary has argued, the use of published guidelines brings with it a uniformity that previously had been perceived as lacking. To require the Secretary to relitigate the existence of jobs in the national economy at each hearing would hinder needlessly an already overburdened agency. We conclude that the Secretary's use of medical-vocational guidelines does not conflict with the statute, nor can we say on the record before us that they are arbitrary and capricious.

■ [The opinion of JUSTICE BRENNAN, concurring, and the opinion of Justice Marshall, concurring in part and dissenting in part, are omitted. Ed.]

NOTES AND QUESTIONS

1.   As the Court notes in *Heckler v. Campbell*, before the Social Security Administration (SSA) issued regulation at issue in that case, known as the "grid rule," the SSA utilized a vocational expert in each individual case to introduce evidence with respect to the existence or non-existence of jobs that could be performed by an individual like the applicant. In some cases, the counsel for the applicant cross-examined the SSA expert, and in some cases the applicant presented his or her own vocational expert. After the SSA issued the grid rule, it did not allow that process in any case in which the grid answered the question of whether one or more jobs existed in the U.S. economy that someone with the applicant's characteristics could perform. This difference in decision-making procedures had enormous

implications for the manner in which the SSA organized its vocational experts and conducted hearings in contested cases.

For example, before it issued the grid rule, most of SSA's vocational experts were assigned to the regional offices that conduct hearings. When an administrative law judge (ALJ) conducted hearings outside his regional office, a vocational expert typically went to the same location and testified in each of the cases in which the ALJ presided. This method of decisionmaking required most SSA vocational experts to be generalists because they would need to discuss the availability of, and the requirements to perform, jobs in the manufacturing sector in one hearing, and then to discuss the availability of, and requirements to perform, jobs in the service sector in the next hearing. After it issued the grid rule, the SSA no longer needed to present testimony from a vocational expert in any case for which the grid answered the vocational questions raised. Consequently, the SSA was able to reorganize most of its vocational experts by subject matter and assign them each to a single location where the SSA could use a hierarchical structure to update the grid.

Which of these two decision-making structures would you expect to yield better results measured with reference to accuracy, consistency, and efficiency?

2.   When the grid does not answer the question, SSA has no choice but to use its traditional method of attempting to determine whether a job exists that the applicant can perform. Would you expect the SSA to be able to construct a grid that answers the critical question of availability of a job for every combination of relevant characteristics of an applicant? How often would you expect the SSA to have to go "off grid?"

———————————

The Court in *Heckler v. Campbell* described the grid rule as identifying "the types and numbers of jobs that exist in the national economy," information that the Court characterized as "not unique to each claimant." The Court contrasted this information with the more individualistic determination of a claimant's job qualifications or abilities. As the Court noted, the SSA must also determine whether a claimant's impairment renders him or her unable to work at all, or whether the impairment is less severe and does not preclude all employment. Would you expect the SSA to be successful in developing rules to assist it in resolving the health state of the applicant and his or her ability to perform various functions? In the following case, the Court addressed just such an attempt at rulemaking.

Bowen v. Yuckert

482 U.S. 137 (1987).

■ JUSTICE POWELL delivered the opinion of the Court.

The question in this case is whether the Secretary of Health and Human Services may deny a claim for Social Security disability benefits on the basis of a determination that the claimant does not suffer from a medically severe impairment that significantly limits the claimant's ability to perform basic work activities.

Title II of the Social Security Act (Act) provides for the payment of insurance benefits to persons who have contributed to the program and who suffer from a physical or mental disability. 42 U.S.C. § 423(a)(1)(D) (1982 ed., Supp. III). Title XVI of the Act provides for the payment of disability benefits to indigent persons under the Supplemental Security Income (SSI) program. § 1382(a). Both titles of the Act define "disability" as the "inability to engage in any substantial gainful activity by reason of any medically determinable physical or mental impairment which can be expected to result in death or which has lasted or can be expected to last for a continuous period of not less than 12 months. . . ." § 423(d)(1)(A); *see* § 1382c(a)(3)(A). The Act further provides that an individual

> "shall be determined to be under a disability only if his physical or mental impairment or impairments are of such severity that he is not only unable to do his previous work but cannot, considering his age, education, and work experience, engage in any other kind of substantial gainful work which exists in the national economy, regardless of whether such work exists in the immediate area in which he lives, or whether a specific job vacancy exists for him, or whether he would be hired if he applied for work." §§ 423(d)(2)(A), 1382c(a)(3)(B).

The Secretary has established a five-step sequential evaluation process for determining whether a person is disabled. 20 C.F.R. §§ 404.1520, 416.920 (1986). Step one determines whether the claimant is engaged in "substantial gainful activity." If he is, disability benefits are denied. If he is not, the decisionmaker proceeds to step two, which determines whether the claimant has a medically severe impairment or combination of impairments. That determination is governed by the "severity regulation" at issue in this case. The severity regulation provides:

> "If you do not have any impairment or combination of impairments which significantly limits your physical or mental ability to do basic work activities, we will find that you do not have a severe impairment and are, therefore, not disabled. We will not consider your age, education, and work experience." §§ 404.1520(c), 416.920(c).

* * *

If the claimant does not have a severe impairment or combination of impairments, the disability claim is denied. If the impairment is severe, the evaluation proceeds to the third step, which determines whether the impairment is equivalent to one of a number of listed impairments that the Secretary acknowledges are so severe as to preclude substantial gainful activity. If the impairment meets or equals one of the listed impairments, the claimant is conclusively presumed to be disabled. If the impairment is not one that is conclusively presumed to be disabling, the evaluation proceeds to the fourth step, which determines whether the impairment prevents the claimant from performing work he has performed in the past. If the claimant is able to perform his previous work, he is not disabled. If the claimant cannot perform this work, the fifth and final step of the process determines whether he is able to perform other work in the national economy in view of his age, education, and work experience. The claimant is entitled to disability benefits only if he is not able to perform other work.

* * *

Respondent Janet Yuckert applied for both Social Security disability insurance benefits and SSI benefits in October 1980. She alleged that she was disabled by an inner ear dysfunction, dizzy spells, headaches, an inability to focus her eyes, and flatfeet. Yuckert had been employed as a travel agent from 1963 to 1977. In 1978 and 1979, she had worked intermittently as a real estate salesperson. Yuckert was 45 years old at the time of her application. She has a high school education, two years of business college, and real estate training.

The Washington Department of Social and Health Services determined that Yuckert was not disabled. The agency reconsidered Yuckert's application at her request, and again determined that she was not disabled. At the next stage of the administrative review process, the ALJ found that, although Yuckert suffered from "episodes of dizziness, or vision problems," "[m]ultiple tests . . . failed to divulge objective clinical findings of abnormalities that support the claimant's severity of the stated impairments." The ALJ also found that Yuckert was pursuing a "relatively difficult" 2-year course in computer programming at a community college and was able to drive her car 80 to 90 miles each week. In light of the medical evidence and the evidence of her activities, the ALJ concluded that her medically determinable impairments were not severe under 20 C.F.R. §§ 404.1520(c) and 416.920(c). The Appeals Council denied Yuckert's request for review on the ground that the results of additional psychological tests supported the ALJ's finding that she had not suffered a significant impairment of any work-related abilities. Yuckert then sought review in the United States District Court for the Western District of Washington. The case was referred to a Magistrate, who concluded that the Secretary's determination was supported by substantial evidence. The District Court adopted the Magistrate's report and affirmed the denial of Yuckert's claim.

The United States Court of Appeals for the Ninth Circuit reversed and remanded without considering the substantiality of the evidence. The court held that the Act does not authorize the Secretary to deny benefits on the basis of a determination that the claimant is not severely impaired. The court focused on the statutory provision that a person is disabled "only if his physical or mental impairment or impairments are of such severity that he is not only unable to do his previous work but cannot, considering his age, education, and work experience, engage in any other kind of substantial gainful work. . . ." In the court's view, this provision requires that "both medical and vocational factors [*i.e.*, age, education, and work experience] be considered in determining disability." * * * Accordingly, the court invalidated the severity regulation. * * *

Our prior decisions recognize that "Congress has 'conferred on the Secretary exceptionally broad authority to prescribe standards for applying certain sections of the Act.'" *Heckler v. Campbell*, 461 U.S.

458, 466 (1983) (quoting *Schweiker v. Gray Panthers*, 453 U.S. 34 (1981)). The Act authorizes the Secretary to "adopt reasonable and proper rules and regulations to regulate and provide for the nature and extent of the proofs and evidence and the method of taking and furnishing the same" in disability cases. 42 U.S.C. § 405(a). We have held that "[w]here, as here, the statute expressly entrusts the Secretary with the responsibility for implementing a provision by regulation, our review is limited to determining whether the regulations promulgated exceeded the Secretary's statutory authority and whether they are arbitrary and capricious." *Heckler v. Campbell*, 461 U.S. at 466. In our view, both the language of the Act and its legislative history support the Secretary's decision to require disability claimants to make a threshold showing that their "medically determinable" impairments are severe enough to satisfy the regulatory standards.

* * *

We have recognized that other aspects of the Secretary's sequential evaluation process contribute to the uniformity and efficiency of disability determinations. *Heckler v. Campbell*, 461 U.S. at 461. The need for such an evaluation process is particularly acute because the Secretary decides more than 2 million claims for disability benefits each year, of which more than 200,000 are reviewed by administrative law judges. The severity regulation increases the efficiency and reliability of the evaluation process by identifying at an early stage those claimants whose medical impairments are so slight that it is unlikely they would be found to be disabled even if their age, education, and experience were taken into account. Similarly, step three streamlines the decision process by identifying those claimants whose medical impairments are so severe that it is likely they would be found disabled regardless of their vocational background.

■ JUSTICE O'CONNOR, with whom JUSTICE STEVENS joins, concurring.

The Court is, I believe, entirely correct to find that the "step two" regulation is not facially inconsistent with the Social Security Act's definition of disability. * * * Step two on its face requires only that the claimant show that he or she suffers from "an impairment or combination of impairments . . . [that] significantly limit[s] . . . physical or mental ability to do basic work activities." 20 C.F.R. § 404.1521(a) (1986). "Basic work activities," the regulation says, include "walking, standing, sitting, lifting, pulling, reaching, carrying, or handling[,] . . . seeing, hearing, and speaking, . . . [u]nderstanding, carrying out, and remembering simple instructions[,] . . . [u]se of judgment . . . [r]esponding appropriately to supervision, co-workers and usual work situations[,] . . . [d]ealing with changes in a routine work setting." § 404.1521(b)(1)–(6). I do not see how a claimant unable to show a significant limitation in any of these areas can possibly meet the statutory definition of disability. * * *

I write separately, however, to discuss the contention of respondent and various *amici* (including 29 States and 5 major cities) that this facially valid regulation has been applied systematically to deny benefits to claimants who *do* meet the statutory definition of disability. Respondent directs our attention to the chorus of judicial criticism concerning the step two regulation, as well as to substantially unrefuted statistical evidence. Despite the heavy deference ordinarily paid to the Secretary's promulgation and application of his regulations, all 11 regional Federal Courts of Appeals have either enjoined the Secretary's use of the step two regulation or imposed a narrowing construction upon it. The frustration expressed by these courts in dealing with the Secretary's application of step two in particular cases is substantial, and no doubt in part accounts for the Court of Appeals' decision in this case to simply enjoin the regulation's further use.

Empirical evidence cited by respondent and the *amici* further supports the inference that the regulation has been used in a manner inconsistent with the statutory definition of disability. Before the step two regulations were promulgated approximately 8% of all claimants were denied benefits at the "not severe" stage of the administrative process; afterwards approximately 40% of all claims were denied at this stage. As the lower federal courts have enjoined use of step two and imposed narrowing constructions, the step two denial rate has fallen to about 25%. Allowance rates in Social Security disability cases have increased substantially when federal courts have demanded that the step two regulation not be used to disqualify those who are statutorily eligible. * * *

To be sure the Secretary faces an administrative task of staggering proportions in applying the disability benefits provisions of the Social Security Act. Perfection in processing millions of such claims annually is impossible. But respondent's evidence suggests that step two has been applied systematically in a manner inconsistent with the statute. Indeed, the Secretary himself has recently acknowledged a need to "clarify" step two in light of this criticism and has attempted to do so by issuing new interpretative guidelines.

In my view, step two may not be used to disqualify those who meet the statutory definition of disability. The statute does not permit the Secretary to deny benefits to a claimant who may fit within the statutory definition without determining whether the impairment prevents the claimant from engaging in either his prior work or substantial gainful employment that, in light of the claimant's age, education, and experience, is available to him in the national economy. Only those claimants with slight abnormalities that do not significantly limit any "basic work activity" can be denied benefits without undertaking this vocational analysis.

■ JUSTICE BLACKMUN, with whom JUSTICE BRENNAN and JUSTICE MARSHALL join, dissenting.

The definition of "disability" for purposes of the disability-insurance benefits program is set forth in § 223(d) of the Social Security Act. Paragraph (2)(A) of that section states: "An individual . . . shall be determined to be under a disability only if his physical or mental *impairment or impairments are of such severity* that he is not only unable to do his previous work but cannot, *considering his age, education, and work experience*, engage in any other kind of substantial gainful work" 42 U.S.C. § 432(d) (1982 ed. Supp. III) (emphasis added). The "severity regulation" promulgated by the Secretary of Health and Human Services for purposes of the program, however, explains to a claimant: "If you do not have any impairment or combination of impairments which significantly limits your physical or mental ability to do basic work activities, we will find that you do not have a *severe impairment* and are, therefore, not disabled. *We will not consider your age, education, and work experience.*" 20 C.F.R. § 404.1520(c) (1986). This regulation, on its very face, directly contradicts the statutory language requiring that a claimant's age, education, and work experience be considered in a case where the claimant cannot perform his past work. It is thus invalid.

NOTES AND QUESTIONS

1. Long before it issued the severity rule that is the subject of the Court's opinions, the SSA issued the rule that requires ALJs to decide disability cases by using the five-step sequential decision-making process that the Court outlines in *Bowen v. Yuckert*. Would you expect the sequencing rule to improve accuracy, consistency, and/or efficiency?

2. Justice O'Connor's concurring opinion in *Bowen v. Yuckert* makes much of the fact that the percentage of benefits claims denied because the claimant's impairments were deemed "not severe" increased substantially after the SSA adopted the severity rule. Justice O'Connor clearly believed that the SSA was applying the severity rule inaccurately to deny valid benefits claims. Assuming that the goals of any decision-making process are accuracy, consistency, and efficiency, would you expect the severity rule to improve the SSA's disability decision-making process in any or all of these respects? Would you vote to uphold the rule if you believed that it would enhance consistency and efficiency but would not improve accuracy? How can a court or anyone else determine what effects a rule will have? Can you think of an alternative explanation for the significant reduction in the rate of grant of benefit applications with the rule?

3. Is the severity rule defensible if SSA intended it not only to improve accuracy, consistency, and efficiency, but also to reduce the rate at which administrative law judges were granting benefits? Is the severity rule defensible if its effect on grant rates is an unintended consequence of a rule that was issued solely to improve accuracy, consistency, and efficiency? How can we tell what SSA intended?

As the last two cases illustrate, agency rules can both limit the issues to be considered in adjudications and limit the discretion of adjudicatory decisionmakers. Sometimes a rule can eliminate completely an entire class of adjudications, as the next case demonstrates.

Yetman v. Garvey

261 F.3d 664 (7th Cir. 2001).

■ FLAUM, CHIEF JUDGE.

Sixty-nine pilots, all either approaching or having reached the age of sixty, petitioned the Federal Aviation Administration ("FAA") for exemptions from the agency's "Age Sixty Rule." The FAA, which has never granted such an exemption, continued that trend by denying the pilots' requests. Petitioners now seek review of the FAA's decision in this court. For the reasons stated herein, we affirm the order of the FAA.

* * *

Under the Federal Aviation Act of 1958, the FAA is charged with promoting safety in the skies by prescribing minimum standards in such areas as aircraft design, aircraft inspection, and pilot qualifications. The Act also requires the FAA to promulgate regulations "in the interest of safety for the maximum . . . periods of service of airmen and other employees of air carriers." 49 U.S.C. § 44701(a)(4). Each responsibility delegated to the FAA by the Act must be carried out in a way which tends to reduce or eliminate the possibility or recurrence of accidents in air transportation. *Id.* § 44701(c).

Responding to its mandate, in 1959, the FAA promulgated what has become known as the Age Sixty Rule, limiting the age past which individuals can pilot certain aircrafts. More specifically, the regulation prohibits any air carrier from using the services of any person as a pilot, and prohibits any person from serving as a pilot, on an airplane engaged in operations under Part 121 if that person has reached his or her 60th birthday. 14 C.F.R. § 121.383(c). As an initial justification for its rule, the agency argued that the regulation promotes air safety, as "available medical studies show that sudden incapacitation due to heart attacks or strokes becomes more frequent as men approach age sixty and present medical knowledge is such that it is impossible to predict with accuracy those individuals most likely to suffer attacks." *Air Line Pilots Ass'n, Int'l v. Quesada*, 276 F.2d 892, 898 (2d Cir. 1960). Notwithstanding advances in the medical field, and the fact that the dictate has been challenged continually over the past forty years, today the Age Sixty Rule remains in force.

Relevant to this review, the Federal Aviation Act also provides for the granting of exemptions to any regulations promulgated by the agency pursuant to the Act. According to 49 U.S.C. § 44701(f), the FAA may grant an exemption from its requirements if it finds that such an exemption is in the public interest. However, the FAA has established a rigorous benchmark for proving that an exemption is in the public interest, as a petition requesting one must contain any information, views, or arguments available to the petitioner to support the action sought, the reasons why the petition would be in the public interest and the reason why the exemption would not adversely affect safety or how the action to be taken by the petitioner would provide a level of safety equal to that provided by the rule from which the exemption is sought. And while that standard had proved insurmountable to pilots for thirty-five years, in 1995, the FAA further hardened its stance, announcing that future petitions for exemptions would be summarily denied unless the petitions contain a proposed technique, not previously discussed, to assess an individual pilot's abilities and risks of subtle and sudden incapacitation.

* * *

[T]he petitioners also present a more specific challenge to the FAA's decision in this case. Their contention is that the agency has disregarded the fact that these pilots have met the promulgated standard for granting exemptions—presenting (and passing) a protocol which can accurately gauge an individual pilot's abilities and risks of sudden incapacitation. The petitioners assert that they have been examined by the Age Sixty Exemption Panel, which was formed in 1999 specifically to evaluate the medical/neuropsychological status of airline pilots seeking to continue their employment after age sixty. According to the pilots, the panel has developed and approved medical and neuropsychological protocols for their use in evaluating the fitness of applicants for exemptions from 14 C.F.R. § 121.383(c). The testing which makes up the Age Sixty Exemption Protocol includes a complete medical history, physical examination, chemscreen profile, hemocult, urinalysis, chest x-ray, audiometry, vision tests, tonometry, electrocardiogram, and exercise stress testing. The protocol also contains neuropsychological testing comprised of CogScreen Aeromedical Edition ("CogScreen-AE"), Wechsler Adult Intelligence Scale-Revised, Rey Auditory Verbal Learning Test, Trail Making Test, Controlled Oral Word Association Test, and the Paced Auditory Serial Addition Test. The Age Sixty Exemption Panel has determined that these tests, performed competently, together with other and further testing which may be medically and psychologically indicated, are sufficient to evaluate the fitness of pilots over sixty. Further, with regard to these sixty-nine pilots, the panel has utilized the protocol and concluded that subject to the satisfactory completion of the customary operational requirements of the FAA, the petitioners should be granted exemptions.

While the Age Sixty Exemption Protocol is certainly comprehensive, the vast majority of the protocol has been previously submitted to the FAA and rejected in the petitions for exemptions in *Aman* and *Baker. See Aman v. FAA*, 856 F.2d 946 (7th Cir. 1988); *Baker v. FAA*, 917 F.2d 318 (7th Cir. 1990). With regard to the medical protocol suggested by the exemption panel, the FAA has concluded that the protocol is essentially identical to the one presented in *Aman*. That protocol was found insufficient to evaluate pilots, and petitioners have not put forth anything to suggest that the protocol, at this point, has any greater predictive value. As for the neuropsychological protocol, we recognize that there are several differences between the present protocol and the one submitted in *Aman*. The Rey Auditory Verbal Learning Test, Controlled Word Association, and Paced Auditory Serial Addition Test in this petition substitute the Welcher Memory Scale, Stroup Color Word Test, and Perceptual Speed Calculation Test relied upon in *Aman*. However, the FAA maintains, and the petitioners do not truly dispute, that these substitutions have been made without improving the test battery's diagnostic or predictive value. Thus, we must focus on what is truly new and relevant in the Age Sixty Exemption Protocol—the CogScreen-AE—and determine whether, when combined with the previously rejected protocol, it provides an adequate means of evaluating petitioners as they reach and pass the age of sixty.

* * *

The FAA does not dispute that CogScreen-AE shows promise as a tool for detecting brain dysfunctions, and for predicting flight performance. The CogScreen-AE was developed and is employed by the

FAA in assessing cognitive function for the grant of special medical exemptions. In fact, the FAA has noted that CogScreen-AE has the potential to serve the agency as a relatively inexpensive and efficient adjunct to traditional neuropsychological assessment in the medical certification of airmen. Studies have clearly demonstrated CogScreen-AE's sensitivity and specificity as a tool for assessing brain dysfunction and for detecting early stages of cognitive pathology. Additionally, there are some research findings which demonstrate that performance of selected CogScreen-AE measures are related to cockpit performance, both in a general aviation simulator and in commercial aviation.

Nonetheless, the agency maintains that the addition of CogScreen-AE to the protocol does not make it sufficient to evaluate pilots as they reach sixty. This conclusion is based upon two serious contentions. First, the FAA notes that CogScreen-AE has not been sufficiently validated for the use proposed in the pilots' protocol. The research to this point does not provide a sufficient basis for determining which CogScreen-AE measures and what level of performance indicate that a person has brain dysfunction that renders the individual unfit to serve as a captain. The FAA points out that with the exception of the initial set of validation studies, there is little additional empirical evidence concerning the degree to which CogScreen-AE is sensitive to alterations in brain functioning associated with substance abuse, trauma, or other illness.

Yet even more troubling to the FAA, the petitioners offer essentially no discussion or analysis of how CogScreen-AE was used to evaluate these petitioners, and the agency suggests that there are serious questions as to how it was in fact used. According to the FAA, it is not clear, for example, what scores on what portions of CogScreen-AE would have proved unsatisfactory to the panel. The agency notes that, in one instance, the panel recommended a certain fifty-four year-old pilot be granted an exemption even though that person had three scores on CogScreen-AE which placed him below the fifth percentile, and four scores which placed him below the fifteenth percentile for speed. While the psychologist administering the test considered the pilot normal, the pilot's results denoted that he had scored lower than eighty percent of the pilots in the fifty-five to seventy normative age group. Furthermore, the FAA notes that the panel considered the Logistic Regression Probability Value ("LRPV"). While the Professional Manual of CogScreen-AE cautions against the use of LRPV, the panel disregarded that warning, as using logistic regression to estimate the probability of brain dysfunction is one of several ways to interpret CogScreen-AE scores. Nevertheless, the panel recommended certain pilots for exemptions whose LRPV's suggested a high probability of brain dysfunction. Finally, the FAA also suggests that it was error for the Age Sixty Exemption Panel to examine pilots' scores in relation to pilots ages fifty-five through seventy, as the purpose of testing is to assess a respondent's absolute level of ability in relation to the total population of pilots. As one report which cautions against the use of such age-adjusted scores correctly points out, older pilots do not have the benefit of landing on age-corrected runway.

We do not doubt that in the future, CogScreen-AE, and similar testing batteries may be sufficient gauges for assessing the abilities of pilots past the age of sixty. However, at this early stage, there is quite simply no evidence in the research literature that allows the FAA to establish a CogScreen-AE score or set of scores to identify when a pilot is incapable of safely operating an aircraft, nor is there evidence that CogScreen-AE provides an appropriate set of cognitive/psychomotor measures for making this prediction. Furthermore, there is limited empirical information available to allow for the use of CogScreen-AE as a clinical tool for adequately determining whether a pilot may have brain damage, especially an older pilot.

As for the application of CogScreen-AE in this case, we believe that the individual problems in testing noted above call into question the validity of the entire CogScreen-AE examination here. That certain pilots could obtain scores that suggest a high probability of brain dysfunction, and still be qualified for exemptions, is highly suspect. Further, if a pilot, age fifty-four, scores below the twentieth percentile of a normative group of pilots age fifty-five through seventy, and is still certified as normal, we must question what pilot would not be considered by the panel as worthy of an exemption. Even a test which has been established as an accurate predictor of future performance in a given field loses all predictive value when the benchmark becomes taking the examination, rather than attaining some minimum score. Here, while there is no doubt that the FAA views CogScreen-AE in high regard, absent established and explained cutoffs, the agency is correct to dismiss the Age Sixty Exemption Panel's reliance on the test.

* * *

We recognize that the FAA's requirements for granting exemptions to the Age Sixty Rule are so demanding that if the agency had initially chosen an age fifty cutoff, pilots above that age would have difficulty meeting those standards. Yet, the rigorous nature of the FAA's exemption requirements is not pertinent at this juncture. Our inquiry is limited to examining whether the FAA has appropriately considered the evidence, and provided sufficient justifications for its decisions. We cannot say that the FAA has failed to take into account new advances in medical technology. The fact that the agency (1) commissioned the Hilton System Study, and (2) developed and utilizes the CogScreen-AE in certifying pilots for flight shows that the agency has not shirked its obligation to keep current with medical progress. Yet given the fact the FAA has nevertheless denied every petition for exemption, an argument could be made that the FAA has examined these studies and protocols only to satisfy the burden which we have placed on the agency. However, that would require that we delve into the motivations of the agency, an inappropriate inquiry under our deferential standard of review. While our review of the evidence submitted by the petitioners might lead us to conclude that a strict age sixty cutoff, without exceptions, is a rule better suited to 1959 than to 2001, this court is not an expert in aerospace medicine, and Congress did not endow this court with the duty to make such a policy judgment. The FAA has the discretionary power to establish a rigid policy, whereby no exemptions are granted, until it is satisfied that medical standards can demonstrate an absence of risk factors in an individual sufficient to warrant a more liberal exemption policy from the Age Sixty Rule. Until the FAA determines that such standards exist, it may adhere inflexibly to a rule whose validity has been upheld by the courts and reevaluated by Congress, so long as it continues to consider, as we are satisfied it has done here, new advances in medical technology.

NOTES AND QUESTIONS

1. Arguably, the FAA's Age Sixty Rule is both overinclusive and underinclusive, in that some commercial pilots who are over sixty present acceptably low risks of sudden incapacitation from heart attack or stroke, while other commercial pilots who have not yet reached sixty present unacceptably high risks of sudden incapacitation. Can you think of a rule that is not similarly both overinclusive and underinclusive? What about rules that set minimum ages for driving, voting, serving in the armed services, or purchasing alcohol or cigarettes? Are rules that are both overinclusive and underinclusive in this manner justifiable? Why or why not?

2. The alternative to a rule like the Age Sixty Rule is an adjudicative system in which the FAA individually evaluates annually each pilot who has reached the age of sixty to determine whether the risk that the individual will suffer a sudden incapacitating heart attack or stroke has reached an unacceptably high level. There are hundreds of pilots over sixty who would like to be able to continue flying commercial passenger planes. How well would you expect that adjudicative system to function? How long would it take to reach a final decision in each case? What should be the status of pilots who are over sixty during the period in which their cases are pending a final decision? What rate of accuracy would you expect from such an adjudicative system?

3. The Supreme Court has often suggested that an agency must provide a means through which an individual can obtain an exemption from a rule. Yet, statements of that type have appeared only as dicta in opinions in which the Court upheld rules; the Court has never actually held that an agency must provide a means to obtain an exemption. Agencies often act as the *Yetman* court alleges that the FAA has with respect to its Age Sixty Rule exception mechanism—*i.e.*, the agency formally provides a means through which an individual can obtain an exemption, but the agency applies its exemption mechanism in a manner that makes it impossible for anyone actually to obtain an exemption. Why might agencies often choose that course of action? Is it defensible? What would happen if an agency created a rule and also created an exemption procedure that provided any individual to whom the rule applies with a colorable claim for an exemption?

4. Most countries have a mandatory age beyond which an individual cannot fly a commercial passenger plane, but most set the age limit at sixty-five. If a judge believes strongly that the cutoff age should be sixty-five, should the judge hold that the Age Sixty Rule is unlawful? If so, on what basis? Should a court be able to compel the FAA to change its age limit to sixty-five? The Supreme Court has repeatedly held that a reviewing court cannot compel an agency to take a particular action except in the rare case in which the court concludes that Congress has specifically required the agency to take that action. In all other cases, a reviewing court only has the power to vacate the action the agency has taken and to remand the case to the agency for further proceedings. *E.g.*, *INS v. Ventura*, 537 U.S. 12 (2002). Such a judicial action leaves the agency with the discretion to take the same action on remand after correcting any procedural error the court identified or after replacing the reasoning the court found to be inadequate or unacceptable with new reasoning.

5. *Yetman* was the fifth unsuccessful attempt to persuade a court to overturn the Age Sixty Rule in the half century that it has been in effect. Pilots whose requests for exemption were denied by the FAA subsequently raised another challenge against the Age Sixty Rule; but while their appeal was pending, Congress enacted and the President signed into law the Fair Treatment for Experienced Pilots Act repealing the Age Sixty Rule.

DISCUSSION PROBLEM

Section 5 of the Federal Trade Commission Act prohibits "unfair or deceptive acts or practices in or affecting commerce." 15 U.S.C. § 45(a)(1). The Federal Trade Commission has received and investigated several complaints regarding instances in which Internet search engines have accepted payment from websites in exchange for being listed at the top of a list of results obtained when consumers search for particular terms. One consumer advocacy group in particular has highlighted this practice as deceptive and misleading to consumers who, absent disclosure, might believe that the listings are objective search results listed by relevance rather than paid advertising. The FTC has sent letters to several Internet search engine companies suggesting that they format their websites to clearly signal which listings are the result of payments received. Some Internet search engines have responded by adjusting their websites, for example by using different fonts for paid and unpaid listings, or segregating paid and unpaid listings. Other Internet search engines have not altered their websites or practices at all. If you were advising the FTC as to how it should proceed, would you recommend the FTC adopt regulations requiring Internet search engines to design their webpages to clearly distinguish paid from unpaid listings, or would you suggest that the FTC pursue case-by-case enforcement against those Internet search engines it deems to be the worst offenders?

3. MAKING "RULES" THROUGH ADJUDICATION

As we noted above and discuss further in Part B of this Chapter, APA § 553(b) and (c) impose upon agencies seeking to issue legislative rules a three-step process involving public notice and opportunity for comment. Is that the only means through which an agency can announce a rule that binds regulated party behavior?

The answer to that question is easy where Congress explicitly instructs an agency to act by legislative rule. Thus, for example, when Congress in the Clean Air Act required the EPA Administrator to adopt regulations prescribing emission standards for motor vehicles, the Administrator has no choice but to use the APA's notice-and-comment rulemaking process to establish those rules. Agencies in such circumstances also remain free to use other means, such as interpretative rules and policy statements, to supplement, clarify, particularize, or announce the manner in which they intend to apply their legislative rules. *See, e.g., Shalala v. Guernsey Mem'l Hosp.*, 514 U.S. 87 (1995).

A more difficult question is whether an agency with the authority to promulgate legislative rules may choose instead to legally binding pronouncements in the same way courts have announced legal rules—by issuing opinions in adjudications that the agency then treats as a binding precedent in later cases. The Supreme Court has addressed this question in the following jurisprudence.

SEC v. Chenery Corp. ("Chenery II")
332 U.S. 194 (1947).

■ MR. JUSTICE MURPHY delivered the opinion of the Court.

This case is here for the second time. In *S.E.C. v. Chenery Corp.*, 318 U.S. 80 (1943), we held that an order of the Securities and Exchange Commission could not be sustained on the grounds upon which that agency acted. We therefore directed that the case be remanded to the Commission for such further proceedings as might be appropriate. On remand, the Commission reexamined the problem, recast its rationale and reached the same result. The issue now is whether the Commission's action is proper in light of the principles established in our prior decision.

When the case was first here, we emphasized a simple but fundamental rule of administrative law. That rule is to the effect that a reviewing court, in dealing with a determination or judgment which an administrative agency alone is authorized to make, must judge the propriety of such action solely by the grounds invoked by the agency. If those grounds are inadequate or improper, the court is powerless to affirm the administrative action by substituting what it considers to be a more adequate or proper basis. To do so would propel the court into the domain which Congress has set aside exclusively for the administrative agency.

We also emphasized in our prior decision an important corollary of the foregoing rule. If the administrative action is to be tested by the basis upon which it purports to rest, that basis must be set forth with such clarity as to be understandable. It will not do for a court to be compelled to guess at the theory underlying the agency's action; nor can a court be expected to chisel that which must be precise from what the agency has left vague and indecisive. In other words, "We must know what a decision means before the duty becomes ours to say whether it is right or wrong." *United States v. Chicago, M., St. P. & P.R. Co.*, 294 U.S. 499, 511 (1935).

Applying this rule and its corollary, the Court was unable to sustain the Commission's original action. The Commission had been dealing with the reorganization of the Federal Water Service Corporation (Federal), a holding company registered under the Public Utility Holding Company Act of 1935. During the period when successive reorganization plans proposed by the management were before the Commission, the officers, directors and controlling stockholders of Federal purchased a substantial amount of Federal's preferred stock on the over-the-counter market. Under the fourth reorganization plan, this preferred stock was to be converted into common stock of a new corporation; on the basis of the purchases of preferred stock, the management would have received more than 10% of this new common stock. It was frankly admitted that the management's purpose in buying the preferred stock was to protect its interest in the new company. It was also plain that there was no fraud or lack of disclosure in making these purchases.

But the Commission would not approve the fourth plan so long as the preferred stock purchased by the management was to be treated on a parity with the other preferred stock. It felt that the officers and directors of a holding company in process of reorganization under the Act were fiduciaries and were under a duty not to trade in the securities of that company during the reorganization period. And so the plan was amended to provide that the preferred stock acquired by the management, unlike that held by others, was not to be converted into the new common stock; instead, it was to be surrendered at cost plus dividends accumulated since the purchase dates. As amended, the plan was approved by the Commission over the management's objections.

The Court interpreted the Commission's order approving this amended plan as grounded solely upon judicial authority. The Commission appeared to have treated the preferred stock acquired by the management in accordance with what it thought were standards theretofore recognized by courts. If it intended to create new standards growing out of its experience in effectuating the legislative policy, it failed to express itself with sufficient clarity and precision to be so understood. Hence the order was judged by the only standards clearly invoked by the Commission. On that basis, the order could not stand. The opinion pointed out that courts do not impose upon officers and directors of a corporation any fiduciary duty to its stockholders which precludes them merely because they are officers and directors, from buying and selling the corporation's stock. Nor was it felt that the cases upon which the Commission relied established any principles of law or equity which in themselves would be sufficient to justify this order.

The opinion further noted that neither Congress nor the Commission had promulgated any general rule proscribing such action as the purchase of preferred stock by Federal's management. And the only judge-made rule of equity which might have justified the Commission's order related to fraud or mismanagement of the reorganization by the officers and directors, matters which were admittedly absent in this situation.

After the case was remanded to the Commission, Federal Water and Gas Corp. (Federal Water), the surviving corporation under the reorganization plan, made an application for approval of an amendment to the plan to provide for the issuance of now common stock of the reorganized company. This stock was to be distributed to the members of Federal's management on the basis of the shares of the old preferred stock which they had acquired during the period of reorganization, thereby placing them in the same position as the public holders of the old preferred stock. The intervening members of Federal's management joined in this request. The Commission denied the application in an order issued on February 7, 1945. That order was reversed by the Court of Appeals, which felt that our prior decision precluded such action by the Commission.

The latest order of the Commission definitely avoids the fatal error of relying on judicial precedents which do not sustain it. This time, after a thorough reexamination of the problem in light of the purposes and standards of the Holding Company Act, the Commission has concluded that the proposed transaction is inconsistent with the standards of §§ 7 and 11 of the Act. It has drawn heavily upon its accumulated experience in dealing with utility reorganizations. And it has expressed its reasons with a clarity and thoroughness that admit of no doubt as to the underlying basis of its order.

The argument is pressed upon us, however, that the Commission was foreclosed from taking such a step following our prior decision. It is said that, in the absence of findings of conscious wrongdoing on the part of Federal's management, the Commission could not determine by an order in this particular case that it was inconsistent with the statutory standards to permit Federal's management to realize a profit through the reorganization purchases. All that it could do was to enter an order allowing an amendment to the plan so that the proposed transaction could be consummated. Under this view, the Commission would be free only to promulgate a general rule outlawing such profits in future utility reorganizations; but such a rule would have to be prospective in nature and have no retroactive effect upon the instant situation.

We reject this contention, for it grows out of a misapprehension of our prior decision and of the Commission's statutory duties. We held no more and no less than that the Commission's first order was unsupportable for the reasons supplied by that agency. But when the case left this Court, the problem whether Federal's management should be treated equally with other preferred stockholders still lacked a final and complete answer. It was clear that the Commission could not give a negative answer by resort to prior judicial declarations. And it was also clear that the Commission was not bound by settled judicial precedents in a situation of this nature. Still unsettled, however, was the answer the Commission might give were it to bring to bear on the facts the proper administrative and statutory considerations, a function which belongs exclusively to the Commission in the first instance. The administrative process had taken an erroneous rather than a final turn. Hence we carefully refrained from expressing any views as to the propriety of an order rooted in the proper and relevant considerations.

When the case was directed to be remanded to the Commission for such further proceedings as might be appropriate, it was with the thought that the Commission would give full effect to its duties in harmony with the views we had expressed. This obviously meant something more than the entry of a perfunctory order giving parity treatment to the management holdings of preferred stock. The fact that the Commission had committed a legal error in its first disposition of the case certainly gave Federal's management no vested right to receive the benefits of such an order. After the remand was made, therefore, the Commission was bound to deal with the problem afresh, performing the function delegated to it by Congress. It was again charged with the duty of measuring the proposed treatment of the management's preferred stock holdings by relevant and proper standards. Only in that way could the legislative policies embodied in the Act be effectuated.

The absence of a general rule or regulation governing management trading during reorganization did not affect the Commission's duties in relation to the particular proposal before it. The Commission was asked to grant or deny effectiveness to a proposed amendment to Federal's reorganization plan whereby the management would be accorded parity treatment on its holdings. It could do that only in the form of an order, entered after a due consideration of the particular facts in light of the relevant and proper standards. That was true regardless of whether those standards previously had been spelled out in a general rule or regulation. Indeed, if the Commission rightly felt that the proposed amendment was inconsistent with those standards, an order giving effect to the amendment merely because there was no general rule or regulation covering the matter would be unjustified.

It is true that our prior decision explicitly recognized the possibility that the Commission might have promulgated a general rule dealing with this problem under its statutory rule-making powers, in which case the issue for our consideration would have been entirely different from that which did confront us. But we did not mean to imply thereby that the failure of the Commission to anticipate this problem and to promulgate a general rule withdrew all power from that agency to perform its statutory duty in this case. To hold that the Commission had no alternative in this proceeding but to approve the proposed transaction, while formulating any general rules it might desire for use in future cases of this nature, would be to stultify the administrative process. That we refuse to do.

Since the Commission, unlike a court, does have the ability to make new law prospectively through the exercise of its rule-making powers, it has less reason to rely upon *ad hoc* adjudication to formulate new standards of conduct within the framework of the Holding Company Act. The function of filling in the interstices of the Act should be performed, as much as possible, through this quasi-legislative promulgation of rules to be applied in the future. But any rigid requirement to that effect would make the administrative process inflexible and incapable of dealing with many of the specialized problems which arise. Not every principle essential to the effective administration of a statute can or should be cast immediately into the mold of a general rule. Some principles must await their own development, while others must be adjusted to meet particular, unforeseeable situations. In performing its important functions in these respects, therefore, an administrative agency must be equipped to act either by general rule or by individual order. To insist upon one form of action to the exclusion of the other is to exalt form over necessity.

In other words, problems may arise in a case which the administrative agency could not reasonably foresee, problems which must be solved despite the absence of a relevant general rule. Or the agency may not have had sufficient experience with a particular problem to warrant rigidifying its tentative judgment into a hard and fast rule. Or the problem may be so specialized and varying in nature as to be impossible of capture within the boundaries of a general rule. In those situations, the agency must retain power to deal with the problems on a case-to-case basis if the administrative process is to be effective. There is thus a very definite place for the case-by-case evolution of statutory standards. And the choice made between proceeding by general rule or by individual, *ad hoc* litigation is one that lies primarily in the informed discretion of the administrative agency.

Hence we refuse to say that the Commission, which had not previously been confronted with the problem of management trading during reorganization, was forbidden from utilizing this particular proceeding for announcing and applying a new standard of conduct. That such action might have a retroactive effect was not necessarily fatal to its validity. Every case of first impression has a retroactive effect, whether the new principle is announced by a court or by an administrative agency. But such retroactivity must be balanced against the mischief of producing a result which is contrary to a statutory design or to legal and equitable principles. If that mischief is greater than the ill effect of the retroactive application of a new standard, it is not the type of retroactivity which is condemned by law.

And so in this case, the fact that the Commission's order might retroactively prevent Federal's management from securing the profits and control which were the objects of the preferred stock purchases may well be outweighed by the dangers inherent in such purchases from the statutory standpoint. If that is true, the argument of retroactivity becomes nothing more than a claim that the Commission lacks power to enforce the standards of the Act in this proceeding. Such a claim deserves rejection.

■ JUSTICE JACKSON, dissenting, joined by JUSTICE FRANKFURTER.

Whether, as matter of policy, corporate managers during reorganization should be prohibited from buying or selling its stock, is not a question for us to decide. But it is for us to decide whether, so long as no law or regulation prohibits them from buying, their purchases may be forfeited, or not, in the discretion of the Commission. If such a power exists in words of the statute or in their implication, it would be possible to point it out and thus end the case. Instead, the Court admits that there was no law prohibiting these purchases when they were made, or at any time thereafter. And, except for this decision, there is none now.

The truth is that in this decision the Court approves the Commission's assertion of power to govern the matter without law, power to force surrender of stock so purchased whenever it will, and power also to overlook such acquisitions if it so chooses. The reasons which will lead it to take one course as against the other remain locked in its own breast, and it has not and apparently does not intend to commit them to any rule or regulation. This administrative authoritarianism, this power to decide without law, is what the Court seems to approve in so many words: 'The absence of a general rule or regulation governing management trading during reorganization did not affect the Commission's duties. . . .' This seems to me to undervalue and to belittle the place of law, even in the system of administrative justice. It calls to mind Mr. Justice Cardozo's statement that 'Law as a guide to conduct is reduced to the level of mere futility if it is unknown and unknowable.'

The Court's averment concerning this order that 'It is the type of judgment which administrative agencies are best equipped to make and which justifies the use of the administrative process,' is the first instance in which the administrative process is sustained by reliance on that disregard of law which enemies of the process have always alleged to be its principal evil. It is the first encouragement this Court has given to conscious lawlessness as a permissible rule of administrative action. This decision is an ominous one to those who believe that men should be governed by laws that they may ascertain and abide by, and which will guide the action of those in authority as well as of those who are subject to authority.

I have long urged, and still believe, that the administrative process deserves fostering in our system as an expeditious and nontechnical method of applying law in specialized fields. I can not agree that it be used, and I think its continued effectiveness is endangered when it is used, as a method of dispensing with law in those fields.

NOTES AND QUESTIONS

1. We have included the Court's opinion in *Chenery II* at this point in the book primarily because of its holding that an agency that has the power to issue rules through the rulemaking process has the discretion to use the traditional common law method of rulemaking instead, *i.e.*, to announce broad rules of conduct in the course of resolving a particular adjudication and then to apply the rules as binding precedent in subsequent cases. The opinion in *Chenery II* is frequently cited to support several other important principles of administrative law, however. What other administrative law principles does the Court announce and apply in *Chenery II*?

2. Many Supreme Court Justices have criticized agencies for evading APA rulemaking procedures by announcing rules of general applicability through adjudication instead. Nevertheless, no more than two Supreme Court Justices at any one time have been willing to hold that practice unlawful. Why do you think so many Justices disapprove of the practice and yet acquiesce in its widespread use?

3. In some important respects, the rules an agency can announce through adjudication differ from legislative rules adopted with public notice and opportunity to comment. Can you imagine how the two types of rules might be different? Can you think of ways in which adjudication and notice-and-comment rulemaking might yield those differences?

The Ongoing Vitality of *Chenery II*

The principal doctrine for which courts routinely cite *Chenery II*—recognizing that agencies have the discretion to announce rules through the process of adjudication—remains valid today. At one time, however, the Court seemed poised to move in a different direction. In particular, in 1969 and 1974, the Supreme Court decided a pair of cases that seemed arguably to repudiate *Chenery II*. Although the Court has since reaffirmed the holding in *Chenery II*, the Court's opinions in these two cases are so difficult to interpret that they remain a source of confusion among students, practitioners, and judges.

The first of these two cases was *NLRB v. Wyman-Gordon Co.*, 394 U.S. 759 (1969). *Wyman-Gordon* involved a rule announced by an NLRB order in a prior case, *Excelsior Underwear Inc.*, 156 N.L.R.B. 1236 (1966). The policy question at issue in *Excelsior* was whether the National Labor Relations Act required the company to furnish a list of its employees' names and addresses to two labor unions. In the course of adjudicating the unions' claim against Excelsior, the NLRB invited certain parties who were unrelated to the case but interested in the broader policy question to file briefs and participate in the hearing. Afterward, the NLRB issued an order requiring employers to give unions the aforementioned employee lists. The NLRB declined, however, to apply that rule to Excelsior, concluding that doing so would be unfair because Excelsior had no reason to believe it was obligated to provide such a list before the NLRB announced its new "rule." Instead, the NLRB made the rule effective prospectively only. When the NLRB subsequently sought to apply the *Excelsior* rule against Wyman-Gordon, the company challenged the validity of the rule on the ground that the NLRB had not satisfied the procedural requirements for rulemaking under the APA. The NLRB maintained the *Excelsior* proceedings satisfied the procedural requirements for adjudication, and thus that APA rulemaking procedures were inapplicable and the *Excelsior* rule was validly issued.

The Court resolved the case in favor of the NLRB, but with a confusing collection of opinions. An opinion written by Justice Fortas on behalf of a plurality of four Justices concluded that the *Excelsior* proceedings were not in fact adjudication at all but instead represented a procedurally flawed rulemaking because the NLRB declined to apply the rule to the party before it at that time, Excelsior.

> There is no question that, in an adjudicatory hearing, the Board could validly decide the issue whether the employer must furnish a list of employees to the union. But that is not what the Board did in Excelsior. The Board did not even apply the rule it made to the parties in the adjudicatory proceeding, the only entities that could properly be subject to the order in that case. Instead, the Board purported to make a rule: *i.e.*, to exercise its quasi-legislative power.
>
> Adjudicated cases may and do, of course, serve as vehicles for the formulation of agency policies, which are applied and announced therein. They generally provide a guide to action that the agency may be expected to take in future cases. Subject to the qualified role of *stare decisis* in the administrative process, they may serve as precedents. But this is far from saying, as the Solicitor General suggests, that commands, decisions, or policies announced in adjudication are "rules" in the sense that they must, without more, be obeyed by the affected public.

Wyman-Gordon, 394 U.S. at 765–66. The plurality upheld the NLRB's order against Wyman-Gordon, however, on the ground that the NLRB issued that order in the course of Wyman-Gordon's adjudicatory hearing. Justices Douglas and Harlan wrote dissenting opinions rejecting the plurality's affirmation of the NLRB's order but agreeing with the plurality that the *Excelsior* rule was invalid as the product of procedurally-flawed rulemaking. For Justices Douglas and Harlan, the NLRB's approach in *Excelsior* was objectionable principally because the agency announced a general rule of broad applicability in the process of adjudicating a dispute, but chose to apply the rule only in subsequent cases and not in the case in which it was announced, and thereby undermined the broader policy behind APA rulemaking procedures. As Justice Douglas observed,

A rule like the one in *Excelsior* is designed to fit all cases at all times. It is not particularized to special facts. It is a statement of far-reaching policy covering all future representation elections.

It should therefore have been put down for the public hearing prescribed by the [Administrative Procedure] Act.

The rule-making procedure performs important functions. It gives notice to an entire segment of society of those controls or regimentation that is forthcoming. It gives an opportunity for persons affected to be heard. * * *

* * * Agencies discover that they are not always repositories of ultimate wisdom; they learn from the suggestions of outsiders and often benefit from that advice.

This is a healthy process that helps make a society viable. * * * Public airing of problems through rule making makes the bureaucracy more responsive to public needs and is an important brake on the growth of absolutism in the regime that now governs all of us.

Id. at 777–78 (Douglas, J., dissenting). By contrast, a concurring opinion written by Justice Black for himself and two others sided with the plurality in supporting the NLRB's order against Wyman-Gordon but also expressed the view that the NLRB properly adopted the *Excelsior* rule through a legitimate adjudicatory process.

[A]lthough it is true that the adjudicatory approach frees an administrative agency from the procedural requirements specified for rule making, the [Administrative Procedure] Act permits this to be done whenever the action involved can satisfy the definition of "adjudication" and then imposes separate procedural requirements that must be met in adjudication. Under these circumstances, so long as the matter involved can be dealt with in a way satisfying the definition of either "rule making" or "adjudication" under the Administrative Procedure Act, that Act, along with the Labor Relations Act, should be read as conferring upon the Board the authority to decide, within its informed discretion, whether to proceed by rule making or adjudication.

Id. at 772 (BLACK, J., concurring).

In short, the holding of *Wyman-Gordon* is opaque because a majority of the Justices expressed the view that the NLRB failed to satisfy the procedural requirements for rulemaking under APA § 553, but a different majority of the Justices voted to uphold the NLRB's order requiring Wyman-Gordon to provide a list of its employees' names and addresses to two labor unions. Hence, one could read the opinions in *Wyman-Gordon* to conclude that a majority of the Court believed that agencies should be free to choose between rulemaking and adjudication procedures in adopting binding rules of general applicability. Yet, one could read those same opinions to conclude that agencies must follow APA rulemaking procedures to promulgate rules intended to govern the actions of regulated parties prospectively.

The outcome in *Wyman-Gordon* was particularly significant because, while Congress has given the NLRB the power to promulgate legislative regulations, the NLRB has rarely chosen to exercise that authority, and instead prefers to announce its rules in lengthy, difficult to interpret decisions issued in adjudicating specific cases. In the aftermath of *Wyman-Gordon*, circuit court judges struggled to understand and apply the four opinions in *Wyman-Gordon*. The Second Circuit in particular interpreted *Wyman-Gordon* as a repudiation of the holding in *Chenery II* and as an invitation to judges to tell agencies that have the power to issue rules through the APA § 533 that they cannot choose instead to announce a rules of general applicability in an adjudication and then apply those rules in subsequent adjudications. *Bell Aerospace Co. Div. of Textron Inc. v. NLRB*, 475 F.2d 485 (2d Cir. 1973).

The second instance in which the Supreme Court arguably seemed to repudiate *Chenery II* came a few years later in *Morton v. Ruiz*, 415 U.S. 199 (1974). The substantive issue in the case was whether the Snyder Act, 25 U.S.C. § 13, and the Department of Interior and Related Agencies Appropriation Act, 1968, Pub. L. 90–28, 81 Stat. 59, 60 (1967), operated to deny general assistance benefits to Native Americans living off but near to reservations. The Bureau of Indian Affairs (BIA), which administered the benefits, in the course of adjudicating individual claims, had established a rule that Native Americans were not eligible for such general assistance benefits unless they lived on a reservation. Applying this rule, the BIA had denied benefits to Ruiz and his family because, while they maintained very close ties to the Papago Indian Reservation in Arizona and were otherwise eligible, they lived roughly fifteen miles outside rather than on the reservation. After documenting numerous examples of inconsistencies in the BIA's explanation and application of the rule, the Court unanimously rejected the BIA's rule.

> No matter how rational or consistent with congressional intent a particular decision might be, the determination of eligibility cannot be made on an *ad hoc* basis by the dispenser of the funds.

> * * *

> This conscious choice of the [BIA] not to treat this extremely significant eligibility requirement affecting rights of needy Indians, as a legislative-type rule, renders it ineffective so far as extinguishing rights of those otherwise within the class of beneficiaries contemplated by Congress is concerned.

> * * * Particularly here, where the BIA has continually represented to Congress, when seeking funds, that Indians living near reservations are within the service area, it is essential that the legitimate expectation of these needy Indians not be extinguished by what amounts to an unpublished *ad hoc* determination of the agency that was not promulgated in accordance with its own procedures, to say nothing of those of the Administrative Procedure Act. * * * Before benefits may be denied to these otherwise entitled Indians, the BIA must first promulgate eligibility requirements according to established procedures.

Ruiz, 415 U.S. at 232, 236.

The Court's broad expressions in *Ruiz* about rules being "ineffective" unless properly promulgated through legislative rulemaking rather than "ad hoc determination" suggests that reviewing courts can deny agencies a choice between rulemaking and adjudication. In fact, in a handful of cases decided since *Ruiz*, circuit courts have required agencies to adopt rules through rulemaking, and have cited *Ruiz* as supporting such a limitation on agency discretion. *See, e.g., Curry v. Block*, 738 F.2d 1556, 1563–64 (11th Cir. 1984).

Nevertheless, in *NLRB v. Bell Aerospace Co.*, 416 U.S. 267 (1974), the Supreme Court reaffirmed *Chenery II* and rejected any notion of repudiating its holding. Here again, as in *Wyman-Gordon*, the NLRB utilized an adjudicatory hearing to announce a broader rule of general applicability, this time concluding that even workers properly classified as "managerial employees" are nevertheless covered by the National Labor Relations Act (NLRA). Relying particularly on the plurality and dissenting opinions in *Wyman-Gordon*, the Court of Appeals below had held that, while the NLRB possessed the authority to interpret the NLRA to include managerial employees, the agency could only adopt such a rule through rulemaking rather than adjudication. The Supreme Court unanimously rejected that conclusion.

> The question is not whether the Board should have resorted to rulemaking, or in fact improperly promulgated a "rule," when in the context of the prior representation proceeding it held that the Act covers all "managerial employees" except those meeting the new "conflict of interest in labor relations" touchstone. * * * Rather, the present question is whether on remand the Board must invoke its rulemaking procedures if it determines, in light of our opinion, that these buyers are not "managerial employees" under the Act. The Court of Appeals thought that rulemaking was required because *any* Board finding that the company's buyers are not "managerial" would be contrary to its prior decisions and would presumably be in the nature of a general rule designed "to fit all cases at all times."

* * *

> The views expressed in *Chenery II* and *Wyman-Gordon* make plain that the Board is not precluded from announcing new principles in an adjudicative proceeding and that the choice between rulemaking and adjudication lies in the first instance within the Board's discretion. Although there may be situations where the Board's reliance on adjudication would amount to an abuse of discretion or a violation of the Act, nothing in the present case would justify such a conclusion.

* * *

> It is true, of course, that rulemaking would provide the Board with a forum for soliciting the informed views of those affected in industry and labor before embarking on a new course. But surely the Board has discretion to decide that the adjudicative procedures in this case may also produce the relevant

information necessary to mature and fair consideration of the
issues. Those most immediately affected, the buyers and the
company in the particular case, are accorded a full opportunity
to be heard before the Board makes its determination.

Bell Aerospace, 416 U.S. at 292, 294–95.

The Court in *Bell Aerospace* declared an agency's choice of
adjudication over rulemaking subject to judicial review for abuse of
discretion. Nevertheless, the Court's unanimous opinion in *Bell
Aerospace*, along with its interpretation of *Wyman-Gordon* in that case
and its continued reliance on *Chenery II*, represent a clear rejection of
judicial attempts to prevent agencies from adopting even rules of
general applicability through adjudication.

The continued vitality of *Chenery II*, and the resulting agency
discretion in choosing whether to bind regulated parties prospectively
through adjudication as well as through rulemaking, raises an
interesting converse question: can agencies employ rulemaking to adopt
rules that they then apply retroactively? The Court addressed just this
issue in the following case.

Bowen v. Georgetown University Hospital

488 U.S. 204 (1988).

■ JUSTICE KENNEDY delivered the opinion of the Court.

Under the Medicare program, health care providers are reimbursed
by the Government for expenses incurred in providing medical services
to Medicare beneficiaries. *See* Social Security Act, Title XVIII, 79 Stat.
291, (codified as amended at 42 U.S.C. § 1395 *et seq.*) (the Medicare
Act). Congress has authorized the Secretary of Health and Human
Services to promulgate regulations setting limits on the levels of
Medicare costs that will be reimbursed. The question presented here is
whether the Secretary may exercise this rulemaking authority to
promulgate cost limits that are retroactive.

I

The Secretary's authority to adopt cost-limit rules is established by
§ 223(b) of the Social Security Amendments of 1972, 86 Stat. 1393,
amending 42 U.S.C. § 1395x(v)(1)(A). * * *

On June 30, 1981, the Secretary issued a cost-limit schedule that
included technical changes in the methods for calculating cost limits.
One of these changes affected the method for calculating the "wage
index," a factor used to reflect the salary levels for hospital employees
in different parts of the country. Under the prior rule, the wage index
for a given geographic area was calculated by using the average salary
levels for all hospitals in the area; the 1981 rule provided that wages
paid by Federal Government hospitals would be excluded from that
computation.

Various hospitals in the District of Columbia area brought suit in
United States District Court seeking to have the 1981 schedule
invalidated. On April 29, 1983, the District Court struck down the 1981
wage-index rule, concluding that the Secretary had violated the

Administrative Procedure Act (APA) by failing to provide notice and an opportunity for public comment before issuing the rule.

* * *

In February 1984, the Secretary published a notice seeking public comment on a proposal to reissue the 1981 wage-index rule, retroactive to July 1, 1981. Because Congress had subsequently amended the Medicare Act to require significantly different cost reimbursement procedures, the readoption of the modified wage-index method was to apply exclusively to a 15-month period commencing July 1, 1981. After considering the comments received, the Secretary reissued the 1981 schedule in final form on November 26, 1984, and proceeded to recoup sums previously paid as a result of the District Court's ruling * * *. In effect, the Secretary had promulgated a rule retroactively, and the net result was as if the original rule had never been set aside.

Respondents, a group of seven hospitals who had benefited from the invalidation of the 1981 schedule, were required to return over $2 million in reimbursement payments. After exhausting administrative remedies, they sought judicial review under the applicable provisions of the APA, claiming that the retroactive schedule was invalid under both the APA and the Medicare Act.

* * *

II

It is axiomatic that an administrative agency's power to promulgate legislative regulations is limited to the authority delegated by Congress. In determining the validity of the Secretary's retroactive cost-limit rule, the threshold question is whether the Medicare Act authorizes retroactive rulemaking.

Retroactivity is not favored in the law. Thus, congressional enactments and administrative rules will not be construed to have retroactive effect unless their language requires this result. By the same principle, a statutory grant of legislative rulemaking authority will not, as a general matter, be understood to encompass the power to promulgate retroactive rules unless that power is conveyed by Congress in express terms. Even where some substantial justification for retroactive rulemaking is presented, courts should be reluctant to find such authority absent an express statutory grant.

The Secretary contends that the Medicare Act provides the necessary authority to promulgate retroactive cost-limit rules in the unusual circumstances of this case. He rests on alternative grounds: first, the specific grant of authority to promulgate regulations to "provide for the making of suitable retroactive corrective adjustments," 42 U.S.C. § 1395x(v)(1)(A)(ii); and second, the general grant of authority to promulgate cost limit rules, 1395hh, 1395ii. We consider these alternatives in turn.

A

The authority to promulgate cost-reimbursement regulations is set forth in § 1395x(v)(1)(A). That subparagraph also provides that:

"Such regulations shall . . . (ii) provide for the making of suitable retroactive corrective adjustments where, for a provider of services for any fiscal period, the aggregate reimbursement produced by the methods of determining costs proves to be either inadequate or excessive." *Id.*

This provision on its face permits some form of retroactive action. We cannot accept the Secretary's argument, however, that it provides authority for the retroactive promulgation of cost-limit rules. To the contrary, we agree with the Court of Appeals that clause (ii) directs the Secretary to establish a procedure for making case-by-case adjustments to reimbursement payments where the regulations prescribing computation methods do not reach the correct result in individual cases. The structure and language of the statute require the conclusion that the retroactivity provision applies only to case-by-case adjudication, not to rulemaking.

* * *

B

The statutory provisions establishing the Secretary's general rulemaking power contain no express authorization of retroactive rulemaking. Any light that might be shed on this matter by suggestions of legislative intent also indicates that no such authority was contemplated. In the first place, where Congress intended to grant the Secretary the authority to act retroactively, it made that intent explicit. As discussed above, § 1395x(v)(1)(A)(ii) directs the Secretary to establish procedures for making retroactive corrective adjustments; in view of this indication that Congress considered the need for retroactive agency action, the absence of any express authorization for retroactive cost-limit rules weighs heavily against the Secretary's position.

The legislative history of the cost-limit provision directly addresses the issue of retroactivity. In discussing the authority granted by § 223(b) of the 1972 amendments, the House and Senate Committee Reports expressed a desire to forbid retroactive cost-limit rules: "The proposed new authority to set limits on costs . . . would be exercised on a prospective, rather than retrospective, basis so that the provider would know in advance the limits to Government recognition of incurred costs and have the opportunity to act to avoid having costs that are not reimbursable." H.R. REP. NO. 92–231, at 83 (1971); *see* S. REP. NO. 92–1230, at 188 (1972), *reprinted in* 1972 U.S.C.C.A.N., 4989, 5070.

The Secretary's past administrative practice is consistent with this interpretation of the statute.

* * *

The Secretary nonetheless suggests that, whatever the limits on his power to promulgate retroactive regulations in the normal course of events, judicial invalidation of a prospective rule is a unique occurrence that creates a heightened need, and thus a justification, for retroactive curative rulemaking. The Secretary warns that congressional intent and important administrative goals may be frustrated unless an invalidated rule can be cured of its defect and made applicable to past time periods. The argument is further advanced that the countervailing reliance interests are less compelling than in the usual case of retroactive rulemaking, because the original, invalidated rule provided at least some notice to the individuals and entities subject to its provisions.

Whatever weight the Secretary's contentions might have in other contexts, they need not be addressed here. The case before us is resolved by the particular statutory scheme in question. Our interpretation of the Medicare Act compels the conclusion that the Secretary has no authority to promulgate retroactive cost-limit rules.

■ JUSTICE SCALIA, concurring.

I agree with the Court that general principles of administrative law suggest that § 223(b) of the Medicare Act, 42 U.S.C. § 1395x(v)(1)(A), does not permit retroactive application of the Secretary of Health and Human Service's 1984 cost-limit rule. I write separately because I find it incomplete to discuss general principles of administrative law without reference to the basic structural legislation which is the embodiment of those principles, the Administrative Procedure Act (APA). * * *

> The first part of the APA's definition of "rule" states that a rule "means the whole or a part of an agency statement of general or particular applicability *and future effect* designed to implement, interpret, or prescribe law or policy or describing the organization, procedure, or practice requirements of an agency. . . ." 5 U.S.C. § 551(4) (emphasis added).

The only plausible reading of the italicized phrase is that rules have legal consequences only for the future. It could not possibly mean that merely *some* of their legal consequences must be for the future, though they may also have legal consequences for the past, since that description would not enable rules to be distinguished from "orders," *see* 5 U.S.C. § 551(6), and would thus destroy the entire dichotomy upon which the most significant portions of the APA are based. (Adjudication—the process for formulating orders, *see* § 551(7)—has future as well as past legal consequences, since the principles announced in an adjudication cannot be departed from in future adjudications without reason.)

Nor could "future effect" in this definition mean merely *"taking effect* in the future," that is, having a future effective date even though, once effective, altering the law applied in the past. That reading, urged by the Secretary of Health and Human Services (Secretary), produces a definition of "rule" that is meaningless, since obviously *all* agency statements have "future effect" in the sense that they do not take effect until after they are made. (One might argue, I suppose, that "future effect" excludes agency statements that take effect immediately, as opposed to one second after promulgation. Apart from the facial silliness of making the central distinction between rulemaking and adjudication hang upon such a thread, it is incompatible with § 553(d), which makes clear that, if certain requirements are complied with, a rule can be effective immediately.) Thus this reading, like the other one, causes § 551(4) to fail in its central objective, which is to distinguish rules from orders. All orders have "future effect" in the sense that they are not effective until promulgated.

In short, there is really no alternative except the obvious meaning, that a rule is a statement that has legal consequences only for the future. If the first part of the definition left any doubt of this, however, it is surely eliminated by the second part (which the Secretary's brief regrettably submerges in ellipsis). After the portion set forth above, the definition continues that a rule

> "includes the approval or prescription *for the future* of rates, wages, corporate or financial structures or reorganizations thereof, prices, facilities, appliances, services or allowances therefor or of valuations, costs, or accounting, or practices bearing on any of the foregoing." 5 U.S.C. § 551(4) (emphasis added).

It seems to me clear that the phrase "for the future"—which even more obviously refers to future operation rather than a future effective date—is not meant to add a requirement to those contained in the earlier part of the definition, but rather to repeat, in a more particularized context, the prior requirement "of future effect." And even if one thought otherwise it would not matter for purposes of the present case, since the HHS "cost-limit" rules governing reimbursement are a "prescription" of "practices bearing on" "allowances" for "services."

* * *

A rule that has unreasonable secondary retroactivity—for example, altering future regulation in a manner that makes worthless substantial past investment incurred in reliance upon the prior rule—may for that reason be "arbitrary" or "capricious," *see* 5 U.S.C. § 706, and thus invalid. In reference to such situations, there are to be found in many cases statements to the effect that "[w]here a rule has retroactive effects, it may nonetheless be sustained in spite of such retroactivity if it is reasonable." *Gen. Tel. Co. of Sw. v. United States,* 449 F.2d 846, 863 (5th Cir. 1971). It is erroneous, however, to extend this "reasonableness" inquiry to purported rules that not merely affect past transactions but change what was the law in the past. Quite simply, a rule is an agency statement "of future effect," not "of future effect and/or reasonable past effect."

The profound confusion characterizing the Secretary's approach to this case is exemplified by its reliance upon our opinion in *SEC v. Chenery Corp.* ("*Chenery II*"), 332 U.S. 194 (1947). Even apart from the fact that that case was not decided under the APA, it has nothing to do with the issue before us here, since it involved adjudication rather than rulemaking. Thus, though it is true that our opinion permitted the Secretary, after his correction of the procedural error that caused an initial reversal, to reach the same substantive result with retroactive effect, the utterly crucial distinction is that *Chenery II* involved that form of administrative action where retroactivity is not only permissible but standard. Adjudication *deals* with what the law was; rulemaking deals with what the law will be. That is why we said in *Chenery II:*

> "Since the Commission, unlike a court, *does have the ability to make new law prospectively through the exercise of its rule-*

making powers, it has less reason to rely upon *ad hoc* adjudication to formulate new standards of conduct. . . . The function of filling in the interstices of the Act should be performed, as much as possible, *through this quasi-legislative promulgation of rules to be applied in the future.*" 332 U.S. at 202 (emphasis added).

And just as *Chenery II* suggested that rulemaking was prospective, the opinions in *NLRB v. Wyman-Gordon Co.*, 394 U.S. 759 (1969), suggested the obverse: that adjudication could *not* be purely prospective, since otherwise it would constitute rulemaking. Both the plurality opinion, joined by four of the Justices, and the dissenting opinions of Justices Douglas and Harlan expressed the view that a rule of law announced in an adjudication, but with exclusively prospective effect, could not be accepted as binding (without new analysis) in subsequent adjudications, since it would constitute rulemaking and as such could only be achieved by following the prescribed rulemaking procedures. Side by side these two cases, *Chenery II* and *Wyman-Gordon*, set forth quite nicely the "dichotomy between rulemaking and adjudication" upon which "the entire [APA] is based."

* * *

It is important to note that the retroactivity limitation applies *only* to rulemaking. Thus, where legal consequences hinge upon the interpretation of statutory requirements, and where no pre-existing interpretive rule construing those requirements is in effect, nothing prevents the agency from acting retroactively through adjudication. *See NLRB v. Bell Aerospace Co.*, 416 U.S. 267, 293–94 (1974); *Chenery II*, 332 U.S. at 202–03.

NOTES AND QUESTIONS

1. In *Georgetown University Hospital*, the Court held that an agency cannot use the APA § 553 process to issue a rule that has any retroactive effect except in the rare case in which Congress has explicitly authorized an agency to issue retroactive rules. Consistent with its reasoning in *Chenery II*, the Court nevertheless recognized that an agency can use the adjudicative process to issue a rule that has retroactive effects? Does *Georgetown University Hospital* add to the growing list of reasons why an agency that has the power to issue rules through the APA § 553 process might choose instead to issue at least some rules through the process of adjudication? Why might an agency consider retroactive application of its rules to be desirable?

2. The foregoing materials seem to present a strong case in favor of agencies choosing adjudication rather than rulemaking to establish rules governing the behavior of regulated parties. Why, then, do you think that so many agencies continue to utilize rulemaking for this purpose?

3. An agency's ability to act retroactively through adjudication is not unlimited. Recall that the Supreme Court in *Chenery II* indicated that retroactive application of rules adopted through adjudication might be impermissible if "the ill effect of the retroactive application of a new standard" outweighed statutory interests. In *Retail, Wholesale, & Department Store Union v. NLRB*, 466 F.2d 380 (D.C. Cir. 1972), the D.C.

Circuit attempted to clarify *Chenery II* and articulate some parameters limiting an agency's discretion to impose rules retroactively through adjudication. In particular, the D.C. Circuit identified several factors that courts should consider in balancing the inequities of retroactive application against the statutory interests advanced thereby:

> Among the considerations that enter into a resolution of the problem are (1) whether the particular case is one of first impression, (2) whether the new rule represents an abrupt departure from well established practice or merely attempts to fill a void in an unsettled area of law, (3) the extent to which the party against whom the new rule is applied relied on the former rule, (4) the degree of the burden which a retroactive order imposes on a party, and (5) the statutory interest in applying a new rule despite the reliance of a party on the old standard.

Id. at 390. Other circuits have adopted these factors as well. *See, e.g., Miguel-Miguel v. Gonzales*, 500 F.3d 941, 951 (9th Cir. 2007). The Fifth Circuit, by contrast, has rejected these factors as "of little practical use" in what it considers a case-by-case evaluation of the costs versus the benefits of retroactive application. *See Microcomputer Tech. Inst. v. Riley*, 139 F.3d 1044, 1050 (5th Cir. 1998). Why do you think the D.C. Circuit considered these factors particularly relevant in reviewing agency rules adopted through adjudication? Do you find one or more of these factors particularly significant? Or do you agree with the Fifth Circuit's assessment that these factors are not particularly helpful?

B. APA RULEMAKING PROCEDURES

Many agencies routinely choose rulemaking as their preferred method for adopting rules of general applicability. When they do, they typically must comply with Administrative Procedure Act procedural requirements. As already discussed in Part A above, the APA explicitly or implicitly recognizes several categories of rules, and imposes different procedural requirements for each.

In a manner of speaking, the APA establishes three separate sets of procedural requirements. The APA imposes very few procedural requirements upon agencies seeking to issue procedural rules, interpretative rules, and policy statements. APA § 552 tells agencies to publish at least some such rules in the Federal Register, and APA § 553(d) requires agencies to publish procedural rules at least thirty days before they become effective. By contrast, APA § 553 prescribes substantially more onerous procedural requirements for legislative rules.

As we have already observed, agencies may only issue legislative rules by following three steps imposed by APA § 553(b) and (c): (1) publishing notice of the proposed rulemaking in the Federal Register; (2) offering all interested persons the opportunity to comment on the proposed rule; and (3) publishing the final rule in the Federal Register, accompanied by a concise statement of the rule's basis and purpose. Typically legislative rules are also subject to thirty day advance publication requirement of APA § 553(d). Agencies, courts, and commentators generally refer to these procedures as informal or notice-and-comment rulemaking.

The third set of procedural requirements, commonly known as formal rulemaking, also applies to legislative rules and tracks the requirements of informal rulemaking except in one very significant way. Agencies engaged in formal rulemaking must conduct an oral evidentiary hearing, described in APA §§ 556 and 557, that is closely analogous to the oral evidentiary hearing that takes place when an agency engages in formal adjudication.

1.   THE DECLINE OF FORMAL RULEMAKING

Most contemporary rulemaking is informal; agencies rarely engage in formal rulemaking, with its oral hearing requirement. In fact, agencies that may only issue legislative rules through formal rulemaking almost invariably abandon all efforts to issue legislative rules. This consequence is not particularly surprising, as the oral, trial-type hearings required by APA §§ 556 and 557 are notoriously time-consuming and expensive. As President Jimmy Carter famously (or perhaps infamously) observed in one speech, the Food and Drug Administration once spent twelve years in an unsuccessful attempt to use formal rulemaking to issue a rule that would determine whether a product must contain 87.5% peanut products or 90% peanut products to call itself peanut butter. 15 WEEKLY COMP. PRES. DOC. 482 (March 15, 1979). Yet, agencies did not always reject formal rulemaking.

When Congress initially adopted the APA, adjudication rather than rulemaking was the norm for agency policymaking. Beginning in the 1960s, however, facing rising caseloads and pressure to develop more definite standards to guide regulated party behavior, federal agencies began to embrace rulemaking, first gradually and then with enthusiasm. Also, in the 1960s and 1970s, Congress adopted legislation creating several new agencies like the National Highway Traffic Safety Administration and the Environmental Protection Agency and expanding the powers of others like the Food and Drug Administration, and in many instances required these agencies to utilize rulemaking. Thus, in 1960, agencies published 498 notices of proposed rulemaking (NOPRs) in the Federal Register, roughly 41 per month. By 1966, the number of NOPRs published in the Federal Register had more than doubled to 86 per month. Agencies published on average 136 NOPRs per month in 1970 and 142 per month in 1972. *See* Reuel E. Schiller, *Rulemaking's Promise: Administrative Law and Legal Culture in the 1960s and 1970s*, 53 ADMIN. L. REV. 1139, 1147 (2001) (documenting the rising popularity of rulemaking among agencies). The trend was facilitated in part by some agencies' assertions of the authority to make legislative rules through informal rulemaking without oral hearings. For example, Thomas Merrill and Kathryn Watts have documented the Food and Drug Administration's changing perceptions of its rulemaking authority along these lines. *See* Thomas W. Merrill & Kathryn Tongue Watts, *Agency Rules with the Force of Law: The Original Convention*, 116 HARV. L. REV. 467, 557–65 (2002). Nevertheless, most agencies believed that they were required to use formal rulemaking where statutes authorized them to act only after a "hearing." The following case radically altered that assumption.

United States v. Florida East Coast Ry. Co.

410 U.S. 224 (1973).

■ MR. JUSTICE REHNQUIST delivered the opinion of the Court.

Appellees, two railroad companies, brought this action in the District Court for the Middle District of Florida to set aside the incentive per diem rates established by appellant Interstate Commerce Commission in a rulemaking proceeding. They challenged the order of the Commission on both substantive and procedural grounds. The District Court sustained appellees' position that the Commission had failed to comply with the applicable provisions of the Administrative Procedure Act, and therefore set aside the order without dealing with the railroads' other contentions. The District Court held that the language of § 1(14)(a) of the Interstate Commerce Act required the Commission in a proceeding such as this to act in accordance with the Administrative Procedure Act, 5 U.S.C. § 556(d), and that the Commission's determination to receive submissions from the appellees only in written form was a violation of that section because the respondents were "prejudiced" by that determination within the meaning of that section.

* * *

This case arises from the factual background of a chronic freight-car shortage on the Nation's railroads, which we described in *United States v. Allegheny-Ludlum Steel Corp.*, 406 U.S. 742 (1972). Judge Simpson, writing for the District Court in this case, noted that "[f]or a number of years portions of the nation have been plagued with seasonal shortages of freight cars in which to ship goods." Judge Friendly, writing for a three-judge District Court in the Eastern District of New York in the related case of *Long Island R. Co. v. United States*, 318 F.Supp. 490, 491 (E.D.N.Y. 1970), described the Commission's order as "the latest chapter in a long history of freight-car shortages in certain regions and seasons and of attempts to ease them." Congressional concern for the problem was manifested in the enactment in 1966 of an amendment to § 1(14)(a) of the Interstate Commerce Act, enlarging the Commission's authority to prescribe per diem charges for the use by one railroad of freight cars owned by another. * * *

The Commission in 1966 commenced an investigation "to determine whether information presently available warranted the establishment of an incentive element increase, on an interim basis, to apply pending further study and investigation." 332 I.C.C. 11, 12 (1967). Statements of position were received from the Commission staff and a number of railroads. Hearings were conducted at which witnesses were examined. In October 1967, the Commission rendered a decision discontinuing the earlier proceeding, but announcing a program of further investigation into the general subject.

In December 1967, the Commission initiated the rulemaking procedure giving rise to the order that appellees here challenge. It directed Class I and Class II line-haul railroads to compile and report detailed information with respect to freight-car demand and supply at numerous sample stations for selected days of the week during 12 four-week periods, beginning January 29, 1968.

Some of the affected railroads voiced questions about the proposed study or requested modification in the study procedures outlined by the Commission in its notice of proposed rulemaking. In response to petitions setting forth these carriers' views, the Commission staff held an informal conference in April 1968, at which the objections and proposed modifications were discussed. Twenty railroads, including appellee Seaboard, were represented at this conference, at which the Commission's staff sought to answer questions about reporting methods to accommodate individual circumstances of particular railroads. The conference adjourned on a note that undoubtedly left the impression that hearings would be held at some future date. * * *

The results of the information thus collected were analyzed and presented to Congress by the Commission during a hearing before the Subcommittee on Surface Transportation of the Senate Committee on Commerce in May 1969. Members of the Subcommittee expressed dissatisfaction with the Commission's slow pace in exercising the authority that had been conferred upon it by the 1966 Amendments to the Interstate Commerce Act. Judge Simpson in his opinion for the District Court said:

> "Members of the Senate Subcommittee on Surface Transportation expressed considerable dissatisfaction with the Commission's apparent inability to take effective steps toward eliminating the national shortage of freight cars. Comments were general that the Commission was conducting too many hearings and taking too little action. Senators pressed for more action and less talk, but Commission counsel expressed doubt respecting the Commission's statutory power to act without additional hearings."

Judge Friendly, describing the same event in *Long Island R. Co. v. United States*, said:

> "To say that the presentation was not received with enthusiasm would be a considerable understatement. Senators voiced displeasure at the Commission's long delay at taking action under the 1966 amendment, engaged in some merriment over what was regarded as an unintelligible discussion of methodology . . . and expressed doubt about the need for a hearing. . . . But the Commission's general counsel insisted that a hearing was needed . . . and the Chairman of the Commission agreed. . . ." 318 F.Supp. at 494.

The Commission, now apparently imbued with a new sense of mission, issued in December 1969 an interim report announcing its tentative decision to adopt incentive per diem charges on standard boxcars based on the information compiled by the railroads. The substantive decision reached by the Commission was that so-called "incentive" per diem charges should be paid by any railroad using on its lines a standard boxcar owned by another railroad. Before the enactment of the 1966 amendment to the Interstate Commerce Act, it was generally thought that the Commission's authority to fix per diem payments for freight car use was limited to setting an amount that reflected fair return on investment for the owning railroad, without any regard being had for the desirability of prompt return to the owning line or for the encouragement of additional purchases of freight cars by the railroads as a method of investing capital. The Commission concluded, however, that in view of the 1966 amendment it could impose additional "incentive" per diem charges to spur prompt return of existing cars and to make acquisition of new cars financially attractive to the railroads. It did so by means of a proposed schedule that established such charges on an across-the-board basis for all common carriers by railroads subject to the Interstate Commerce Act. Embodied in the report was a proposed rule adopting the Commission's tentative conclusions and a notice to the railroads to file statements of position within 60 days, couched in the following language:

> "That verified statements of facts, briefs, and statements of position respecting the tentative conclusions reached in the said interim report, the rules and regulations proposed in the appendix to this order, and any other pertinent matter, are hereby invited to be submitted pursuant to the filing schedule set forth below by an interested person whether or not such person is already a party to this proceeding.

> * * *

> "That any party requesting oral hearing shall set forth with specificity the need therefor and the evidence to be adduced." 337 I.C.C. 183, 213.

Both appellee railroads filed statements objecting to the Commission's proposal and requesting an oral hearing, as did numerous other railroads. In April 1970, the Commission, without having held further "hearings," issued a supplemental report making some modifications in the tentative conclusions earlier reached, but overruling *in toto* the requests of appellees.

The District Court held that in so doing the Commission violated § 556(d) of the Administrative Procedure Act, and it was on this basis that it set aside the order of the Commission.

In *United States v. Allegheny-Ludlum Steel Corp.* we held that the language of § 1(14)(a) of the Interstate Commerce Act authorizing the Commission to act "after hearing" was not the equivalent of a requirement that a rule be made "on the record after opportunity for an agency hearing" as the latter term is used in § 553(c) of the Administrative Procedure Act. Since the 1966 amendment to § 1(14)(a), under which the Commission was here proceeding, does not by its terms add to the hearing requirement contained in the earlier language, the same result should obtain here unless that amendment contains language that is tantamount to such a requirement. Appellees contend that such language is found in the provisions of that Act requiring that:

> "[T]he Commission shall give consideration to the national level of ownership of such type of freight car and to other factors affecting the adequacy of the national freight car supply, and shall, on the basis of such consideration, determine whether compensation should be computed. . . ."

While this language is undoubtedly a mandate to the Commission to consider the factors there set forth in reaching any conclusion as to imposition of per diem incentive charges, it adds to the hearing requirements of the section neither expressly nor by implication. We know of no reason to think that an administrative agency in reaching a decision cannot accord consideration to factors such as those set forth in the 1966 amendment by means other than a trial-type hearing or the presentation of oral argument by the affected parties. Congress by that amendment specified necessary components of the ultimate decision, but it did not specify the method by which the Commission should acquire information about those components.

* * *

Inextricably intertwined with the hearing requirement of the Administrative Procedure Act in this case is the meaning to be given to the language 'after hearing' in § 1(14)(a) of the Interstate Commerce Act. Appellees, both here and in the court below, contend that the Commission procedure here fell short of that mandated by the 'hearing' requirement of § 1(14)(a), even though it may have satisfied § 553 of the Administrative Procedure Act. The Administrative Procedure Act states that none of its provisions 'limit or repeal additional requirements imposed by statute or otherwise recognized by law.' 5 U.S.C. § 559. Thus, even though the Commission was not required to comply with §§ 556 and 557 of that Act, it was required to accord the 'hearing' specified in § 1(14)(a) of the Interstate Commerce Act.

* * *

The term "hearing" in its legal context undoubtedly has a host of meanings. Its meaning undoubtedly will vary, depending on whether it is used in the context of a rulemaking-type proceeding or in the context of a proceeding devoted to the adjudication of particular disputed facts. It is by no means apparent what the drafters of the Esch Car Service Act of 1917, which became the first part of § 1(14)(a) of the Interstate Commerce Act, meant by the term. Such an intent would surely be an ephemeral one if, indeed, Congress in 1917 had in mind anything more specific than the language it actually used, for none of the parties refer to any legislative history that would shed light on the intended meaning of the words 'after hearings.' What is apparent, though, is that the term was used in granting authority to the Commission to make rules and regulations of a prospective nature.

* * *

Under these circumstances, confronted with a grant of substantive authority made after the Administrative Procedure Act was enacted, we think that reference to that Act, in which Congress devoted itself exclusively to questions such as the nature and scope of hearings, is a satisfactory basis for determining what is meant by the term 'hearing' used in another statute. Turning to that Act, we are convinced that the term 'hearing' as used therein does not necessarily embrace either the right to present evidence orally and to cross-examine opposing witnesses, or the right to present oral argument to the agency's decisionmaker.

Section 553 excepts from its requirements rulemaking devoted to 'interpretative rules, general statements of policy, or rules of agency organization, procedure, or practice,' and rulemaking 'when the agency for good cause finds . . . that notice and public procedure thereon are impracticable, unnecessary, or contrary to the public interest.' This exception does not apply, however, 'when notice or hearing is required by statute'; in those cases, even though interpretative rulemaking be involved, the requirements of § 553 apply. But since these requirements themselves do not mandate any oral presentation, see Allegheny-Ludlum, supra, it cannot be doubted that a statute that requires a 'hearing' prior to rulemaking may in some circumstances be satisfied by procedures that meet only the standards of § 553. * * *

Similarly, even where the statute requires that the rulemaking procedure take place 'on the record after opportunity for an agency hearing,' thus triggering the applicability of § 556, subsection (d) provides that the agency may proceed by the submission of all or part of the evidence in written form if a party will not 'be prejudiced thereby.' Again, the Act makes it plain that a specific statutory mandate that the proceedings take place on the record after hearing may be satisfied in some circumstances by evidentiary submission in written form only.

We think this treatment of the term "hearing" in the Administrative Procedure Act affords sufficient basis for concluding that the requirement of a "hearing" contained in § 1(14)(a); in a situation where the Commission was acting under the 1966 statutory rulemaking authority that Congress had conferred upon it, did not by its own force require the Commission either to hear oral testimony, to permit cross-examination of Commission witnesses, or to hear oral argument.

■ [A dissenting opinion by JUSTICE DOUGLAS is omitted. Ed.]

NOTES AND QUESTIONS

1. The Court in *Florida East Coast Railway* based its decision in part on its purported holding the year before in *United States v. Allegheny-Ludlum Steel Corp.*, 406 U.S. 742 (1972). *Allegheny-Ludlum* also involved a challenge to rules issued by the Interstate Commerce Commission (ICC) under § 1(14)(a) of the Interstate Commerce Act, also known as the Esch Car Service Act, which empowered the ICC to establish reasonable rules and practices for railroad cars. The question for decision in *Allegheny-Ludlum* was whether particular regulations adopted by the ICC represented a reasonable interpretation of the statute substantively. The parties had not briefed whether the ICC satisfied APA procedural requirements in promulgating the regulations, and concluding that the Esch Act did not require the ICC to conduct an oral, on the record hearing was irrelevant to the outcome of the case. Nevertheless, the Court included in its opinion a paragraph with a "holding" that the Esch Act's failure to include the language "on the record" excused the ICC from complying with APA §§ 556 and 557. The Court in *Florida East Coast Railway* could have characterized its statement in *Allegheny-Ludlum* as nonbinding dicta, but instead elevated the dicta to a holding.

2. Many regulatory statutes predate the *Florida East Coast Railway* decision by years or even decades, and most do not include the magic words "on the record" in connection with statutory hearing requirements. Hence, as a result of the Court's holding in *Florida East Coast Railway*, agencies have largely ceased to engage in formal rulemaking. This does not necessarily mean that agencies forego oral hearings altogether. For example, the Treasury Department and Internal Revenue Service frequently hold oral hearings in the course of promulgating regulations interpreting the Internal Revenue Code. Nevertheless, these hearings are not the full-blown affairs of the past, with presentation and cross-examination of witnesses.

3. The Court's decision in *Florida East Coast Railway* surprised many practicing attorneys. One of the authors of this casebook was practicing law in Washington D.C. when the Court handed down its decision. Washington lawyers were accustomed to billing many thousands of hours for participating in hearings of the type the ICC avoided in this case. Commonly, an oral hearing under APA §§ 556 and 557 involved dozens of lawyers presenting evidence from hundreds of witnesses and cross examining opposing witnesses over a period of several years. After the Court's decision in *Florida East Coast Railway* excused the ICC and presumably other agencies as well from such hearings, Washington lawyers immediately went into a panic in their efforts to make up for the many thousands of hours that lawyers had previously billed for such work, Do you think that factor played a role in the Supreme Court's decision? Does that practical element influence how you perceive the outcome in *Florida East Coast Railway*?

4. All experienced lobbyists and some legislators know the effect of adding an "on the record" requirement to an agency's power to issue rules or requiring similar procedures: an agency faced with such requirements typically foregoes rulemaking altogether to avoid the procedural burdens associated with oral hearings in rulemaking. In other words, by adding such language to a regulatory statute, Congress as a practical matter substantially reduces or eliminates the agency's ability to utilize rulemaking to effectuate legal policy, and thus erodes the agency's regulatory power. If a party disagrees with a proposal to create a new agency or to assign an existing agency a new task, and the party believes that it lacks the votes needed to block enactment of the statute, the standard second best measure is to burden the agency with many expensive procedural obligations and then to starve the agency of resources in the annual appropriations process. In what political circumstances, therefore, would you expect Congress to require an agency to make rules "on the record?"

2. THE EVOLUTION OF INFORMAL RULEMAKING

The trend in favor of agency rulemaking in the 1960s and 1970s was furthered by agencies claiming the power to promulgate legislative rules through informal rulemaking rather than the oral hearing procedures of APA §§ 556 and 557. With the virtual disappearance of formal rulemaking after *Florida East Coast Railway*, agencies seeking to promulgate legislative rules typically employ the informal notice-and-comment procedures outlined in APA § 553(b) and (c).

Recall that APA § 553(b) and (c) impose three procedural requirements for informal rulemaking: (1) publishing notice of the proposed rulemaking (NOPR) in the Federal Register; (2) offering all interested persons the opportunity to comment on the proposed rule; and (3) publishing the final rule in the Federal Register, accompanied by a concise statement of the rule's basis and purpose. Until 1967, courts rarely reviewed agency rules that were issued through use of informal rulemaking, and courts were not at all demanding of agencies on the rare occasions on which they reviewed these rules. Consequently, agencies had no difficulty complying with the procedural requirements of APA § 553 in a manner that allowed them to use informal rulemaking to issue rules quickly and inexpensively. Both the NOPR that preceded issuance of the rule and the statement of basis and purpose that the agency issued contemporaneously with the final rule usually were brief, as were the public comments the agency received in response to the NOPR. This situation changed greatly during the period from 1967 to 1983, during which time judges interpreted APA § 553(b) and (c) to expand dramatically the procedural burdens of informal rulemaking.

Some students of the administrative process identify the Supreme Court's opinion in *Abbott Laboratories v. Gardner*, 387 U.S. 136 (1967), as the beginning of the judicial transformation of the informal rulemaking process. We discuss *Abbott Labs* in detail in Chapter 7. For now, it is important only to contrast the context in which rules were reviewable prior to *Abbott Labs* with the context in which rules were reviewable after *Abbott Labs*. Prior to *Abbott Labs*, a rule typically was not considered "ripe" for review until an agency applied the rule in an enforcement proceeding. A regulated party seeking to challenge a rule could obtain review of the rule only by violating it and then attempting to defend itself in an enforcement action by arguing that the rule was invalid. If the court upheld the rule, however, the regulated party was subjected to civil or even criminal penalties for violating the rule. Moreover, the party suffered collateral damage to its reputation attributable to the press accounts of the agency decision to charge the firm with a violation and the judicial decision holding that the party had violated the rule. In the pre-*Abbott Labs* environment, the court that considered whether the rule was valid used the record of the enforcement proceeding as the basis for its decision with respect to the validity of the rule. Since agencies typically brought actions to enforce rules only in cases in which the facts were favorable to the agency, the agency usually prevailed when the validity of one of its rules was challenged in an enforcement proceeding. Thus, the pre-*Abbott Labs* environment produced only a few challenges to the validity of agency rules, a high probability that the agency would prevail in each such case, and no judicial demand that an agency defend the validity of a rule based on the record created in a rulemaking proceeding.

Abbott Labs changed all of those characteristics of the context in which most rules are reviewed. In *Abbott Labs*, the Court announced a new test to determine whether a rule is ripe for review, asking whether (1) the issues raised by the petition for review are susceptible to judicial resolution prior to the application of the rule in an enforcement proceeding, and (2) the petitioner would be subject to hardship as a result of deferral of review. The *Abbott Labs* test rendered a high proportion of agency rules ripe for pre-enforcement review. It also encouraged parties to file petitions for pre-enforcement review of virtually all rules they dislike by eliminating the risks attendant to the pre-*Abbott Labs* process of challenging a rule's validity in an enforcement proceeding; there is no downside risk in initiating a pre-enforcement review proceeding to challenge the validity of a rule. As a result, a high proportion of rules were subjected to pre-enforcement review.

Abbott Labs also had substantial second order effects. *Abbott Labs* denied reviewing courts the record of an enforcement proceeding as the basis for evaluating the procedural validity of a regulation. Instead, judges had before them only the record of the rulemaking proceeding, consisting of the NOPR, the comments on the NOPR from the public, and the final rule incorporating a statement of its basis and purpose. Prior to *Abbott Labs*, those records were typically quite short. In the years immediately following *Abbott Labs*, reviewing courts often concluded that rulemaking records were inadequate in one or more respects and vacated rules on the ground that the agency had not created a record sufficient to allow the court to engage in meaningful review.

The judicial demands that agencies create more extensive records in rulemaking proceedings began immediately after the Supreme Court decided *Abbott Labs* and proceeded along three parallel paths: demands that agencies conduct oral evidentiary hearings in many rulemakings, demands that agencies issue elaborate and lengthy NOPRs at the beginning of a major rulemaking, and demands that agencies incorporate long and detailed statements of basis and purpose in some final rules. Each of these paths led to a different destination.

a. ORAL HEARINGS IN INFORMAL RULEMAKING

Prior to the Supreme Court's decision in *Florida East Coast Railway*, most circuit courts held that an agency must conduct an oral evidentiary hearing when it issues a rule if the statute the rule is implementing requires the agency to conduct a "hearing" before it takes an action. Since most agency-administered statutes require the agency to conduct a hearing before it takes a legally-binding action, that judicial practice had the effect of requiring agencies to conduct oral evidentiary hearings in a high proportion of rulemakings. The Supreme Court's decision in *Florida East Coast Railway* eliminated that judicial practice. After *Florida East Coast Railway*, except in the rare case of a statute that requires an agency to issue a rule "on the record after opportunity for an agency hearing" or similarly unambiguous language, a reviewing court could not rely on the language of the APA or any other statute to justify requiring the agency to conduct an oral evidentiary hearing in a rulemaking.

Nevertheless, some reviewing courts continued to require courts to provide limited scope oral evidentiary hearings in some rulemakings even after *Florida East Coast Railway*. If a court concluded that an issue was particularly controversial and important to the outcome of the rulemaking proceeding, the court would vacate the rule and hold that the agency must conduct an oral evidentiary hearing on that issue in order to create record that would be adequate to allow the court to review the agency's resolution of that issue. The Supreme Court ended that practice by issuing the following landmark opinion.

Vermont Yankee Nuclear Power Corp. v. NRDC

435 U.S. 519 (1978).

■ MR. JUSTICE REHNQUIST delivered the opinion of the Court.

In 1946, Congress enacted the Administrative Procedure Act, which was not only "a new, basic and comprehensive regulation of procedures in many agencies," *Wong Yang Sung v. McGrath*, 339 U.S. 33 (1950), but was also a legislative enactment which settled "long-continued and hard-fought contentions, and enacts a formula upon which opposing social and political forces have come to rest." *Id.* at 40. Section 4 of the Act, 5 U.S.C. § 553, dealing with rulemaking, requires in subsection (b) that "notice of proposed rule making shall be published in the Federal Register . . . ," describes the contents of that notice, and goes on to require in subsection (c) that after the notice the agency "shall give interested persons an opportunity to participate in the rule making through submission of written data, views, or arguments with or without opportunity for oral presentation. After consideration of the relevant matter presented, the agency shall incorporate in the rules adopted a concise general statement of their basis and purpose." Interpreting this provision of the Act in *United States v. Allegheny-Ludlum Steel Corp.*, 406 U.S. 742 (1972), and *United States v. Florida East Coast Railway Co.*, 410 U.S. 224 (1973), we held that generally speaking this section of the Act established the maximum procedural requirements which Congress was willing to have the courts impose upon agencies in conducting rulemaking procedures. Agencies are free to grant additional procedural rights in the exercise of their discretion, but reviewing courts are generally not free to impose them if the agencies have not chosen to grant them. This is not to say necessarily that there are no circumstances which would ever justify a court in overturning agency action because of a failure to employ procedures beyond those required by the statute. But such circumstances, if they exist, are extremely rare.

Even apart from the Administrative Procedure Act this Court has for more than four decades emphasized that the formulation of procedures was basically to be left within the discretion of the agencies to which Congress had confided the responsibility for substantive judgments. In *FCC v. Schreiber*, 381 U.S. 279, 290 (1965), the Court explicated this principle, describing it as "an outgrowth of the congressional determination that administrative agencies and administrators will be familiar with the industries which they regulate and will be in a better position than federal courts or Congress itself to design procedural rules adapted to the peculiarities of the industry and the tasks of the agency involved." The Court there relied on its earlier case of *FCC v. Pottsville Broadcasting Co.*, 309 U.S. 134 (1940), where it had stated that a provision dealing with the conduct of business by the Federal Communications Commission delegated to the Commission the power to resolve "subordinate questions of procedure . . . [such as] the scope of the inquiry, whether applications should be heard contemporaneously or successively, whether parties should be allowed to intervene in one another's proceedings, and similar questions."

It is in the light of this background of statutory and decisional law that we granted certiorari to review two judgments of the Court of

Appeals for the District of Columbia Circuit because of our concern that they had seriously misread or misapplied this statutory and decisional law cautioning reviewing courts against engrafting their own notions of proper procedures upon agencies entrusted with substantive functions by Congress. We conclude that the Court of Appeals has done just that in these cases, and we therefore remand them to it for further proceedings. We also find it necessary to examine the Court of Appeals' decision with respect to agency action taken after full adjudicatory hearings. We again conclude that the court improperly intruded into the agency's decisionmaking process, making it necessary for us to reverse and remand with respect to this part of the cases also.

Under the Atomic Energy Act of 1954, the Atomic Energy Commission [later renamed the Nuclear Regulatory Commission (NRC). Ed.] was given broad regulatory authority over the development of nuclear energy. Under the terms of the Act, a utility seeking to construct and operate a nuclear power plant must obtain a separate permit or license at both the construction and the operation stage of the project.

* * *

In December 1967, after the mandatory adjudicatory hearing and necessary review, the Commission granted petitioner Vermont Yankee a permit to build a nuclear power plant in Vernon, Vt. Thereafter, Vermont Yankee applied for an operating license. Respondent Natural Resources Defense Council (NRDC) objected to the granting of a license, however, and therefore a hearing on the application commenced on August 10, 1971. Excluded from consideration at the hearings, over NRDC's objection, was the issue of the environmental effects of operations to reprocess fuel or dispose of wastes resulting from the reprocessing operations. This ruling was affirmed by the Appeal Board in June 1972.

In November 1972, however, the Commission, making specific reference to the Appeal Board's decision with respect to the Vermont Yankee license, instituted rulemaking proceedings "that would specifically deal with the question of consideration of environmental effects associated with the uranium fuel cycle in the individual cost-benefit analyses for light water cooled nuclear power reactors." The notice of proposed rulemaking offered two alternatives, both predicated on a report prepared by the Commission's staff entitled Environmental Survey of the Nuclear Fuel Cycle. The first would have required no quantitative evaluation of the environmental hazards of fuel reprocessing or disposal because the Environmental Survey had found them to be slight. The second would have specified numerical values for the environmental impact of this part of the fuel cycle, which values would then be incorporated into a table, along with the other relevant factors, to determine the overall cost-benefit balance for each operating license.

Much of the controversy in this case revolves around the procedures used in the rulemaking hearing which commenced in February 1973. In a supplemental notice of hearing the Commission indicated that while discovery or cross-examination would not be utilized, the Environmental Survey would be available to the public before the hearing along with the extensive background documents cited therein. All participants would be given a reasonable opportunity to present their position and could be represented by counsel if they so desired. Written and, time permitting, oral statements would be received and incorporated into the record.

* * *

In April 1974, the Commission issued a rule which adopted the second of the two proposed alternatives described above. The Commission also approved the procedures used at the hearing, and indicated that the record, including the Environmental Survey, provided an "adequate data base for the regulation adopted."

* * *

With respect to the challenge of Vermont Yankee's license, the court first ruled that in the absence of effective rulemaking proceedings, the Commission must deal with the environmental impact of fuel reprocessing and disposal in individual licensing proceedings. The court then examined the rulemaking proceedings and, despite the fact that it appeared that the agency employed all the procedures required by 5 U.S.C. § 553 and more, the court determined the proceedings to be inadequate and overturned the rule. Accordingly, the Commission's determination with respect to Vermont Yankee's license was also remanded for further proceedings.

* * *

We next turn to the invalidation of the fuel cycle rule. But before determining whether the Court of Appeals reached a permissible result, we must determine exactly what result it did reach, and in this case that is no mean feat. * * *.

After a thorough examination of the opinion itself, we conclude that while the matter is not entirely free from doubt, the majority of the Court of Appeals struck down the rule because of the perceived inadequacies of the procedures employed in the rulemaking proceedings. The court first determined the intervenors' primary argument to be "that the decision to preclude 'discovery or cross-examination' denied them a meaningful opportunity to participate in the proceedings as guaranteed by due process." The court then went on to frame the issue for decision thus:

"Thus, we are called upon to decide whether the procedures provided by the agency were sufficient to ventilate the issues."

* * *

In prior opinions we have intimated that even in a rulemaking proceeding when an agency is making a "quasi-judicial" determination by which a very small number of persons are "exceptionally affected, in each case upon individual grounds," in some circumstances additional procedures may be required in order to afford the aggrieved individuals due process. *United States v. Fla. E. Coast Ry. Co.*, 410 U.S. at 242–45 (quoting *Bi-Metallic Inv. Co. v. State Bd. of Equalization*, 239 U.S. 441, 446 (1915)). It might also be true, although we do not think the issue is presented in this case and accordingly do not decide it, that a totally unjustified departure from well-settled agency procedures of long standing might require judicial correction.

But this much is absolutely clear. Absent constitutional constraints or extremely compelling circumstances the "administrative agencies 'should be free to fashion their own rules of procedure and to pursue methods of inquiry capable of permitting them to discharge their multitudinous duties.'" *FCC v. Schreiber*, 381 U.S. at 290 (quoting *FCC v. Pottsville Broad. Co.*, 309 U.S. at 143). Indeed, our cases could hardly be more explicit in this regard. The Court has * * * upheld this principle in a variety of applications * * * And the basic reason for this decision was the Court of Appeals' serious departure from the very basic tenet of administrative law that agencies should be free to fashion their own rules of procedure.

* * *

There are compelling reasons for construing § 4 in this manner. In the first place, if courts continually review agency proceedings to determine whether the agency employed procedures which were, in the court's opinion, perfectly tailored to reach what the court perceives to be the "best" or "correct" result, judicial review would be totally unpredictable. And the agencies, operating under this vague injunction to employ the "best" procedures and facing the threat of reversal if they did not, would undoubtedly adopt full adjudicatory procedures in every instance. Not only would this totally disrupt the statutory scheme, through which Congress enacted "a formula upon which opposing social and political forces have come to rest," *Wong Yang Sung v. McGrath*, 339 U.S. at 40, but all the inherent advantages of informal rulemaking would be totally lost.

Secondly, it is obvious that the court in these cases reviewed the agency's choice of procedures on the basis of the record actually produced at the hearing and not on the basis of the information available to the agency when it made the decision to structure the proceedings in a certain way. This sort of Monday morning quarterbacking not only encourages but almost compels the agency to conduct all rulemaking proceedings with the full panoply of procedural devices normally associated only with adjudicatory hearings.

Finally, and perhaps most importantly, this sort of review fundamentally misconceives the nature of the standard for judicial review of an agency rule. The court below uncritically assumed that additional procedures will automatically result in a more adequate record because it will give interested parties more of an opportunity to participate in and contribute to the proceedings. But informal rulemaking need not be based solely on the transcript of a hearing held before an agency. Indeed, the agency need not even hold a formal hearing. *See* 5 U.S.C. § 553(c). Thus, the adequacy of the "record" in this type of proceeding is not correlated directly to the type of procedural devices employed, but rather turns on whether the agency has followed the statutory mandate of the Administrative Procedure Act or other relevant statutes. If the agency is compelled to support the rule which it ultimately adopts with the type of record produced only after a full adjudicatory hearing, it simply will have no choice but to conduct a full adjudicatory hearing prior to promulgating every rule. In sum, this sort of unwarranted judicial examination of perceived procedural shortcomings of a rulemaking proceeding can do nothing but seriously interfere with that process prescribed by Congress.

* * *

There remains, of course, the question of whether the challenged rule finds sufficient justification in the administrative proceedings that it should be upheld by the reviewing court. Judge Tamm, concurring in the result reached by the majority of the Court of Appeals, thought that it did not. There are also intimations in the majority opinion which suggest that the judges who joined it likewise may have thought the administrative proceedings an insufficient basis upon which to predicate the rule in question. We accordingly remand so that the Court of Appeals may review the rule as the Administrative Procedure Act provides. We have made it abundantly clear before that when there is a contemporaneous explanation of the agency decision, the validity of that action must "stand or fall on the propriety of that finding, judged, of course, by the appropriate standard of review. If that finding is not sustainable on the administrative record made, then the Comptroller's decision must be vacated and the matter remanded to him for further consideration." *Camp v. Pitts*, 411 U.S. 138, 143 (1973). The court should engage in this kind of review and not stray beyond the judicial province to explore the procedural format or to impose upon the agency its own notion of which procedures are "best" or most likely to further some vague, undefined public good.

NOTES AND QUESTIONS

1. The D.C. Circuit opinion that the Supreme Court reversed identified only one issue that it concluded should have been the subject of a limited scope oral evidentiary hearing. That was typical of the manner in which circuit courts applied the approach the Supreme Court barred. In the abstract, it sounds like a practical approach that does not impose an undue burden on an agency. The agency could set the one issue for an evidentiary hearing that it might be able to complete in a month or so, thereby adding little to the cost and time required to issue a rule. Yet, a typical major agency rulemaking raises ten to thirty disputed issues, each of which could be characterized as so important that it should be the subject of an evidentiary hearing. Do you think the judicial approach that the Court held unlawful in *Vermont Yankee* caused practical problems for agencies? How well could an agency anticipate the manner in which a reviewing court would apply the D.C. Circuit's approach?

2. The judges who rejected the NRC rule with respect to storage of radioactive waste from nuclear power plants obviously thought the rule was a bad idea. Imagine that you were a law clerk for one of those judges. Suppose the judge for whom you work asks you whether the court has any other way of attempting to block implementation of the rule after *Vermont Yankee*. How might you answer that question? If a reviewing court does not like the policy choices embedded in an agency rule, should it impose additional procedural burdens on the agency as a means of invalidating the rule?

3. On remand of the *Vermont Yankee* case, the D.C. Circuit relied on the last paragraph in the Supreme Court's opinion to vacate the waste storage rule a second time, this time on the basis that the agency rule was arbitrary and capricious because the agency did not provide adequate support for the rule. The Supreme Court unanimously reversed the circuit court in *Baltimore Gas & Electric Co. v. NRDC*, 462 U.S. 87 (1983). The Court characterized the NRC rule as an action the agency had taken based on predictions that are "on the frontiers of knowledge." The Supreme Court admonished reviewing courts that they must be "at their most deferential" in reviewing agency actions of that type.

4. The Supreme Court's opinion in *Vermont Yankee* and its aftermath did nothing to resolve the controversy generally over the safety of nuclear power and more specifically over the safe storage of radioactive waste from nuclear power plants. These controversies continue all over the world today. Do you believe that the additional "ventilation" of the radioactive waste controversy that the circuit court would have required through an oral evidentiary hearing would have been sufficient to resolve that dispute? Do you think that additional "ventilation" would have been of any value to a reviewing court? Why or why not?

DISCUSSION PROBLEM

Imagine that a major agency promulgates a rule. Suppose that the agency conducts an oral evidentiary hearing on one issue that it considers to be of great importance but does not conduct an oral evidentiary hearing on another disputed issue. You represent a party that dislikes the resulting rule. What argument might you make to challenge the rule? Would your answer change if the agency conducted oral evidentiary hearings on two disputed issues but not a third?

Now imagine that you are General Counsel to an agency. Your boss, the head of the agency, asks you how many of the two dozen contested issues the agency must subject to oral hearings to be confident that a reviewing court will not hold the rule invalid because of the agency's failure to conduct a limited-scope oral hearing on a different important contested issue. How would you answer her question?

b. THE NOTICE REQUIREMENT

Regarding the first requirement of informal rulemaking, publishing a notice of proposed rulemaking, APA § 553(b) provides as follows:

> General notice of proposed rulemaking shall be published in the Federal Register, unless persons subject thereto are named and either personally served or otherwise have actual notice thereof in accordance with law. The notice shall include—
>
> (1) A statement of the time, place, and nature of public rule making proceedings;
>
> (2) Reference to the legal authority under which the rule is proposed; and
>
> (3) Either the terms or substance of the proposed rule or a description of the subjects and issues involved.

Congress's intent in adopting the notice requirement was to require agencies to provide sufficient notice of the issues to be addressed in the rulemaking, so that interested parties would be able to present responsive information and arguments.

Before *Abbott Labs*, when reviewing courts paid little attention to agencies' informal rulemaking efforts, and before *Florida East Coast Railway*, when most agencies assumed that rulemaking would necessitate oral, on-the-record hearings, notices of proposed rulemaking (NOPRs) tended to be brief. Since the Supreme Court decided those cases, reviewing courts have adopted more demanding interpretations of APA § 553(b). The Supreme Court's decision in *Vermont Yankee*, precluding reviewing courts from ordering even limited-scope oral hearings in the absence of an unambiguous statutory requirement, merely exacerbated the judicial trend toward more extensive NOPRs. Can you imagine why the courts expanded the demands of the notice requirement?

Most challenges to the adequacy of agency NOPRs fall into two categories: (1) the final rule diverged sufficiently from the proposed rule that the parties affected by the final rule had no way of knowing that the agency was considering one or more critical elements of the final rule; or (2) the agency based a rule on data that was not known or made available to interested parties until the agency published the final rule. In either case, the parties contend that the inadequacy of the agency's NOPR deprived them of the opportunity to submit meaningful comments. The following cases demonstrate the courts' responses to these complaints.

Shell Oil Co. v. EPA

950 F.2d 741 (D.C. Cir. 1991).

■ PER CURIAM:

In these consolidated cases, petitioners challenge both the substance of several rules promulgated by the Environmental Protection Agency pursuant to the Resource Conservation and Recovery Act of 1976 and its compliance with the Administrative Procedure Act's rulemaking requirements.

Consolidated petitioners challenge two rules that categorize substances as hazardous wastes until a contrary showing has been made: the "mixture" rule, which classifies as a hazardous waste any mixture of a "listed" hazardous waste with any other solid waste, and the "derived-from" rule, which so classifies any residue derived from the treatment of hazardous waste. They argue that the EPA failed to provide adequate notice and opportunity for comment when it promulgated the mixture and derived-from rules, and that the rules exceed the EPA's statutory authority.

* * *

Although the EPA acknowledges that neither of the two rules was to be found among the proposed regulations, it nevertheless argues that they were foreseeable—and, therefore, the notice adequate—because certain of the comments received in response to the rulemaking appeared to anticipate both the mixture and the derived-from rules. We are unimpressed by the scanty evidence marshaled in support of this position.

The only comment actually cited by the EPA was made by the Manufacturing Chemists Association, which stated that under the proposed regulations, "a listed waste is a hazardous waste regardless of quantity or concentration," and that "[i]t is not reasonable to classify *all* waste streams which contain *any* concentration of one of the specific wastes as hazardous." This comment, we note, addresses the initial classification of a waste as hazardous rather than the problem of how to deal with residues resulting from the treatment of wastes, or with their subsequent mixture with other, nonhazardous materials.

The EPA also draws attention to a response it made before the close of the comment period to a question posed by the American Mining Congress in which the Agency indicated that the delisting procedure would permit generators to remove wastes from the RCRA system. This, apparently, is supposed to have alerted interested parties that delisting would be the only means of exit from regulation. But examination of the precise words that the EPA used reveals a different message. The EPA stated that "[de]listing provides a means on a case by case basis for [the generator of a given waste] to demonstrate that that waste does not belong in the system at all." This response concerned the exclusion from regulation of wastes included by initial regulatory error, not the deregulation of wastes that have ceased to be hazardous.

The EPA's remaining evidence of implied notice is equally unimpressive. It consists of generalized references to comments urging that wastes be evaluated only according to the four easily testable characteristics and requests that the regulations specifically address the disposition of incinerator ash.

An agency, of course, may promulgate final rules that differ from the proposed regulations. To avoid "the absurdity that . . . the agency can learn from the comments on its proposals only at the peril of starting a new procedural round of commentary," *International Harvester Co. v. Ruckelshaus*, 478 F.2d 615, 632 n.51 (D.C. Cir. 1973), we have held that final rules need only be a "logical outgrowth" of the proposed regulations. *Small Refiner Lead Phase-Down Task Force v. EPA*, 705 F.2d 506, 546–47 (D.C.Cir.1983) (canvassing precedent). But an unexpressed intention cannot convert a final rule into a "logical outgrowth" that the public should have anticipated. Interested parties cannot be expected to divine the EPA's unspoken thoughts. The reasons given by the EPA in support of its contention that interested parties should have anticipated the new rules are simply too insubstantial to justify a finding of implicit notice.

While it is true that such parties might have anticipated the potential for avoiding regulation by simply mixing hazardous and nonhazardous wastes, it was the business of the EPA, and not the public, to foresee that possibility and to address it in its proposed regulations. Moreover, while a comment may evidence a recognition of a problem, it can tell us nothing of how, or even whether, the agency will choose to address it. The comments the EPA cites strike us as sparse and ambiguous at best. Some address similar concerns, but none squarely anticipates the rules.

Even if the mixture and derived-from rules had been widely anticipated, comments by members of the public would not in themselves constitute adequate notice. Under the standards of the APA, "notice necessarily must come—if at all—from the Agency." *Small Refiner*, 705 F.2d at 549. Although we have held that comments raising a foreseeable possibility of agency action can be a factor in providing notice, *NRDC v. Thomas*, 838 F.2d 1224, 1243 (D.C. Cir. 1988), this is not such a case. While, in *Thomas*, the New York State Attorney General's Office suggested a regulatory approach similar to that finally adopted by the EPA, the Agency itself gave warning of its approach two weeks before final promulgation, and the industry petitioners had "at least a limited opportunity to focus a direct attack." *Id*. In fact, they "managed to file objections 7–10 days before the final regulations were signed." *Id*. We nevertheless acknowledged that the case "stretche[d] the concept of 'logical outgrowth' to its limits." *Id*. In contrast, here, the ambiguous comments and weak signals from the agency gave petitioners no such opportunity to anticipate and criticize the rules or to offer alternatives. Under these circumstances, the mixture and derived-from rules exceed the limits of a "logical outgrowth."

The EPA's argument also fails to take into account a marked shift in emphasis between the proposed regulations and the final rules. Under the EPA's initial regulatory strategy, the

> EPA planned to identify and quantitatively define all of the characteristics of hazardous waste. . . . Generators would be required to assess their wastes in accordance with these characteristics and EPA would list hazardous wastes where it had data indicating the wastes exhibited one of the identified characteristics.

45 Fed. Reg. 33,106. As a consequence, listing was to "play [the] largely supplementary function" of increasing the "certainty" of the process. *Id*. Listing was also to have relieved generators of listed wastes of the burden of testing for characteristics "unless they wish to demonstrate that they are not subject" to Subtitle C regulation. 43 Fed. Reg. 58,951. Thus, the proposed regulations imposed, as a generator's principal responsibility, the duty to test wastes for hazardous characteristics and suggested that if the required tests failed to reveal a hazard, the waste would not need to be managed as hazardous.

The final rules, however, place a heavy emphasis on listing. As a consequence, the final criteria for listing are "considerably expanded and more specific" than those proposed. 45 Fed. Reg. 33,106. The EPA justified this "change in emphasis in [its] regulatory strategy," *id*. 33,107, on the basis that it was "not fully confident that it can suitably define and construct testing protocols for [several] characteristics." *Id*.

Whatever the basis for this shift in strategy, it erodes the foundation of the EPA's argument that the mixture rule was implicit in the proposed regulations. A system that would rely primarily on lists of wastes and waste-producing processes might imply inclusion of a waste until it is formally removed from the list. The proposed regulations, however, did not suggest such a system. Rather, their emphasis on characteristics suggested that if a waste did not exhibit the nine characteristics originally proposed, it need not be regulated as hazardous. We conclude, therefore, that the mixture rule was neither implicit in nor a "logical outgrowth" of the proposed regulations.

Similarly, while the derived-from rule may well have been the best regulatory approach the EPA could devise, it was not a logical outgrowth of the proposed regulations. The derived-from rule is not implicit in a system based upon testing wastes for specified hazardous characteristics-the system presented in the proposed regulations. To the contrary, the derived-from rule becomes counterintuitive as applied to processes designed to render wastes nonhazardous. Rather than presuming that these processes will achieve their goals, the derived-from rule assumes their failure.

* * *

The EPA maintains, finally, that it had considered and rejected the points raised by petitioners, and argues that they cannot show prejudice from its failure to provide notice and opportunity to comment. While petitioners must show that they would have submitted new arguments to invalidate rules in the case of certain procedural defaults, such as an agency's failure to provide access to supplemental studies, petitioners need not do so here, where the agency has entirely failed to comply with notice-and-comment requirements, and the agency has offered no persuasive evidence that possible objections to its final rules have been given sufficient consideration.

Because the EPA has not provided adequate notice and opportunity for comment, we conclude that the mixture and derived-from rules must be set aside and remanded to the EPA. In light of the dangers that may be posed by a discontinuity in the regulation of hazardous wastes, however, the agency may wish to consider reenacting the rules, in whole or part, on an interim basis under the "good cause" exemption of 5 U.S.C. § 553(b)(3)(B) pending full notice and opportunity for comment.

As we vacate them on procedural grounds, we do not reach petitioners' argument that the mixture and derived-from rules unlawfully expand the EPA's jurisdiction under Subtitle C of RCRA.

NOTES AND QUESTIONS

1.   The D.C. Circuit in *Shell Oil* spoke in terms of whether the final rule was a "logical outgrowth" of the NOPR or the proposed rule. Courts considering the adequacy of agency NOPRs have applied the logical outgrowth standard since at least 1974, when the First Circuit used that phrase in *South Terminal Corp. v. EPA*, 504 F.2d 646 (1st Cir. 1974). Courts occasionally have used slightly different phraseologies, for example asking whether the NOPR or the proposed rule "sufficiently foreshadowed" the final rule. *See, e.g., American Mining Cong. v. Thomas*, 772 F.2d 617, 633 (10th Cir. 1985). These different rhetorical formulations do not appear to reflect different tests; instead, they seem to be functionally equivalent ways of asking the same question. *See, e.g., Horsehead Res. Dev. Co. v. Browner*, 16 F.3d 1246, 1267–68 (D.C. Cir. 1994) (quoting *Shell Oil* and using both "logical outgrowth" and "sufficiently foreshadowed" phraseology interchangeably).

2.   One criticism of the logical outgrowth test is its susceptibility to judicial manipulation to achieve desired outcomes. It is difficult to

generalize from one opinion how the courts have applied the logical outgrowth test in different cases, because application of that test is so dependent upon the specific details of each individual case and the degree and significance of the divergence between the proposed and final rules. One of the authors of this casebook has been particularly critical of the D.C. Circuit for its aggressive application of the logical outgrowth test to invalidate regulations on several occasions, describing *Shell Oil* in particular as "unusually demanding" and asserting that "many courts would have upheld the rule on the basis that regulation of mixtures and residues was a 'logical outgrowth' of a proposal to regulate toxic wastes." RICHARD J. PIERCE, JR., ADMINISTRATIVE LAW TREATISE § 7.3 (4th Ed. 2004).

3.   While courts on occasion have no doubt applied the logical outgrowth test aggressively, those same courts have also embraced a counterbalancing proposition, that agencies cannot be expected to amend their NOPRs for every unanticipated comment or suggestion to which they respond by altering their proposed rule. *See, e.g., International Harvester Co. v. Ruckelshaus*, 478 F.2d 615, 632 (D.C. Cir. 1973). The point of the notice-and-comment rulemaking process is to enable agencies to improve their proposed regulations based on suggestions from the interested public. As the D.C. Circuit observed in *Shell Oil*, it would be absurd, therefore, to require agencies to begin the notice-and-comment process afresh upon every such change.

Arguments about the application of the logical outgrowth test thus tend to follow a standard pattern. The petitioner alludes to some difference between the proposed rule and the final rule and argues that it had no way of anticipating that the agency would make the change that is implicit in the final rule and, thus, that it was unfairly deprived of an opportunity to argue against the characteristic of the final rule that was not reflected in the proposed rule. The agency responds that: (1) the change it made was a response to the comments it received and, thus, it was acting as Congress intended by taking the comments seriously and making changes in light of the comments; and, (2) it would not make sense to tell an agency that has made changes in response to comments that it must now start the notice and comment process again, this time without making any changes. Because that argument is intractable in the abstract, courts emphasize that applying the "logical outgrowth" test necessarily is a matter of degree that can only be accomplished on an ad hoc, case-by-case basis. Given these arguments and the courts' handling of them, do you find the logical outgrowth test helpful in evaluating the adequacy of notice? Do you find the logical outgrowth test a reasonable interpretation of the language of APA § 553(b)?

4.   Particularly in larger, more complicated rulemaking efforts, agencies often spend years studying a problem before they issue a NOPR to begin the official rulemaking process. In fact, it is not unusual for an agency to issue an advanced notice soliciting initial public input regarding the best way to resolve particular regulatory issues before the agency drafts proposed regulations and publishes the NOPR. Largely in response to the courts' application of the logical outgrowth test in evaluating NOPRs, agencies also often issue supplemental NOPRs as they change their plans in response to public comments. As a result, the actual duration of a rulemaking that yields a major rule usually is several years longer than the time between the issuance of the NOPR and the issuance of the final rule. Each such action creates additional delays, since the agency typically provides an opportunity for parties to submit supplemental comments in response to the supplemental NOPR.

DISCUSSION PROBLEMS

1. A few years ago, the Federal Communications Commission (FCC) issued a NOPR seeking to modify the methodology it employs in calculating the fees that a particular group of users would have to pay to certain service providers. The bulk of the NOPR was dedicated to justifying the change with regard to that particular group of users and explaining the new proposed methodology. In a footnote to the NOPR, however, the FCC suggested that it was contemplating future action to make the same change with respect to the fees paid to the service providers by a second, different group of users. The FCC recently issued the final rule, in which it expanded the scope of its rule change to include both the user group most prominently covered by the NOPR and also the second user group mentioned in the footnote. You are an attorney representing a company that falls in that second user group. Based on the published NOPR, your client had not anticipated that the FCC would change its fee structure in this rulemaking and consequently did not offer its comments regarding the application of the new methodology to the second user group. One of your client's competitors did submit comments based on the footnote, but those were the only comments that the FCC received with respect to the second group of users. Your client wants to challenge the validity of the FCC's new rule. What arguments might you make that the FCC's notice was inadequate with respect to the second user group? What arguments do you expect the FCC might make in response?

2. Imagine that you are a junior attorney at an agency. You have been assigned to draft a NOPR for a major rulemaking. The agency head and the leader of the team that is responsible for the rulemaking provide you with the text of the rule they propose to issue. What else do you need to know to draft a NOPR that is likely to survive the "logical outgrowth" test? Assume that you believe that the agency probably will take about five years to issue a final rule. Do you need to consider the possibility that an intervening Presidential election may yield a President and an agency head whose regulatory philosophies differ from those of the current President and agency head? Do you need to talk to the agency's technical experts to try to anticipate the range of changes that the agency might adopt in response to comments or in response to new ways of thinking about the problems that the proposed rule would address? How long is your NOPR likely to be? How long will it take you to draft the NOPR? When you have completed the draft, how confident are you that the NOPR will survive application of the logical outgrowth test five years later?

Portland Cement Ass'n v. Ruckelshaus

486 F.2d 375 (D.C. Cir. 1973).

■ LEVENTHAL, CIRCUIT JUDGE:

Portland Cement Association seeks review of the action of the Administrator of the Environmental Protection Agency (EPA) in promulgating stationary source standards for new or modified portland cement plants, pursuant to the provisions of Section 111 of the Clean Air Act. * * *

Section 111 of the Clean Air Act directs the Administrator to promulgate "standards of performance" governing emissions of air pollutants by new stationary sources constructed or modified after the effective date of pertinent regulations. The focus of dispute in this case concerns EPA compliance with the statutory language of Section 111(a) which defines "standard of performance" as follows:

> (1) The term "standard of performance" means a standard for emissions of air pollutants which reflects the degree of emission limitation achievable through the application of the best system of emission reduction which (taking into account the cost of achieving such reduction) the Administrator determines has been adequately demonstrated.

After designating portland cement plants as a stationary source of air pollution which may "contribute significantly to air pollution which causes or contributes to the endangerment of public health or welfare", under Section 111(b)(1)(A) of the Act, the Administrator published a proposed regulation establishing standards of performance for portland cement plants. The proposed regulation was accompanied by a document entitled "Background Information For Proposed New-Source Performance Standards," which set forth the justification. Interested parties were afforded an opportunity to participate in the rule making by submitting comments, and more than 200 interested parties did so. The "standards of performance" were adopted by a regulation, issued December 16, 1971, which requires, inter alia, that particulate matter emitted from portland cement plants shall not be:

> (1) In excess of 0.30 lb. per ton of feed to the kiln (0.15 Kg. per metric ton), maximum 2-hour average.

> (2) Greater than 10% opacity, except that where the presence of uncombined water is the only reason for failure to meet the requirements for this subparagraph, such failure shall not be a violation of this section.

The standards were justified by the EPA as follows:

> The standards of performance are based on stationary source testing conducted by the Environmental Protection Agency and/or contractors and on data derived from various other sources, including the available technical literature. In the comments of the proposed standards, many questions were raised as to costs and demonstrated capability of control systems to meet the standards. These comments have been evaluated and investigated, and it is the Administrator's judgment that emission control systems capable of meeting the standards have been adequately demonstrated and that the standards promulgated herein are achievable at reasonable costs.

* * *

We find a critical defect in the decision-making process in arriving at the standard under review in the initial inability of petitioners to obtain—in timely fashion—the test results and procedures used on existing plants which formed a partial basis for the emission control level adopted, and in the subsequent seeming refusal of the agency to respond to what seem to be legitimate problems with the methodology of these tests.

1. *Unavailability of Test Methodology*

The regulations under review were first proposed on August 3, 1971 and then adopted on December 16, 1971. Both the proposed and adopted rule cited certain portland cement testing as forming a basis for the standards. In the statements accompanying the proposed rule, the Administrator stated:

> The standards of performance set forth herein are based on stationary source testing conducted by the Environmental Protection Agency and/or contractors. . . .

On December 16, this test reliance was reiterated:

> The standards of performance are based on stationary source testing conducted by the Environmental Protection Agency and/or contractors. . . .

As indicated in the earlier statement of the case, the proposed standard was accompanied by a Background Document which disclosed some information about the tests, but did not identify the location or methodology used in the one successful test conducted on a dry-process kiln. Further indication was given to petitioners that the Administrator was relying on the tests referred to in the Background Document, when the statement of reasons accompanying the adopted standard were expanded in mid-March of 1972, in the supplemental statement filed while this case was pending on appeal to our court. The Administrator there stated:

> The proposed standard was based principally on particulate levels achieved at a kiln controlled by a fabric filter.

For the first time, however, another set of tests was referred to, as follows:

> After proposal [of the regulation], but prior to promulgation a second kiln controlled by a fabric filter was tested and found to have particulate emissions in excess of the proposed standard. However, based on the revised particulate test method, the second installation showed particulate emissions to be less than 0.3 pound per ton of kiln feed.

These two testing programs were referred to in the March 1972 supplemental statement, but the details, aside from a summary of test results, were not made available to petitioners until mid-April 1972. At that time, it was revealed that the first set of tests was conducted April 29–30, 1971, by a contractor for EPA, at the Dragon Cement Plant, a dry process plant in Northampton, Pennsylvania, and that the second set was performed at the Oregon Portland Cement plant, at Lake Oswego, Oregon, a wet process plant, on October 7 and 8, 1971. The full disclosure of the methodology followed in these tests raised certain problems, in the view of petitioners, on which they had not yet had the opportunity to comment. Their original comments in the period between the proposal and promulgation of the regulation could only respond to the brief summary of the results of the tests that had been disclosed at that time.

After intervenor Northwestern States Portland Cement Company received the detailed test information in mid-April 1972, it submitted the test data, for analysis of reliability and accuracy, to Ralph H. Striker, an engineer experienced in the design of emission control systems for portland cement plants. He concluded that the first series of tests run at the Dragon Cement Company were "grossly erroneous" due to inaccurate sampling techniques to measure particulate matter. Northwestern States then moved this Court to remand the record to EPA so that the agency might consider the additional comments on the tests. This motion was granted on October 31, 1972. This action by the Court was based on "the flexibility and capacity of reexamination that is rooted in the administrative process". *Int'l Harvester v. Ruckelshaus*, 478 F.2d 615, 632 (D.C. Cir. 1973). We considered this opportunity to make further comments necessary to sound execution of our judicial review function.

We are aware that EPA was required to issue its standards within 90 days of the issuance of the proposed regulation, and that this time might not have sufficed to make an adequate compilation of the data from the initial tests, or to fully describe the methodology employed. This was more likely as to the second tests, which were begun during the pendency of the proposed regulation. In contrast, more than three months intervened between the conduct of the first tests and the issuance of the proposed regulation. Even as to the second tests however, as we indicated in *International Harvester*, * * * the fact that the agency chose to perform additional tests and release the results indicates that it did not believe possible agency consideration was frozen. It is not consonant with the purpose of a rule-making proceeding to promulgate rules on the basis of inadequate data, or on data that, [to a] critical degree, is known only to the agency.

NOTES AND QUESTIONS

1.   The last sentence of the excerpt has become a doctrine that all circuit courts apply to rulemakings. Nevertheless, the full scope of an agency's obligation to disclose data sources remains unclear. For example,

- A court may not require an agency to disclose information received after the comment period is closed if the data was publicly available and the challenging party actually responded to it, *see, e.g., Air Pollution Control Dist. v. EPA*, 739 F.2d 1071 (6th Cir. 1984); or where the technical background of a rule has been the subject of extensive debate for a substantial period of time, *see, e.g., Connecticut Light & Power Co. v. NRC*, 673 F.2d 525, 531 (D.C. Cir. 1982); but a court may hold differently if the information is not so exposed to public scrutiny. *See, e.g., Aqua Slide 'N' Dive Corp. v. Consumer Prod. Safety Comm'n*, 569 F.2d 831, 842 (5th Cir. 1978).

- The D.C. Circuit in *Portland Cement* makes much of the agency's decision to perform additional tests and release the results; yet, a court may allow an agency to rely on undisclosed studies or other data that the court does not deem "critical" to the agency's decision-making process for one reason or another, perhaps because such information merely supplements that which the agency disclosed in the NOPR, *see, e.g., Time Warner Entm't Co., L.P. v. FCC*, 240 F.3d 1126, 1140 (D.C. Cir. 2001); *Community Nutrition Inst. v. Block*, 749 F.2d 50, 58 (D.C. Cir. 1984); or because the studies or other data only support secondary justifications for the agency action and information that was disclosed supports the agency's primary rationale for acting. *See, e.g., Personal Watercraft Indus. Ass'n v. Department of Commerce*, 48 F.3d 540, 543–44 (D.C. Cir. 1995).

2. Courts applying the *Portland Cement* doctrine routinely require regulated parties to demonstrate that they were prejudiced by the agency's failure to make particular data available. For example, in *Community Nutrition Institute v. Block*, 749 F.2d 50, 58 (D.C. Cir. 1984), the D.C. Circuit refused to find prejudice where new studies merely expanded on, confirmed, and corrected a methodological flaw in information that the agency had included in the NOPR, and where the challenging party did not suggest that the new data was in any way defective. Similarly, in *Personal Watercraft Industry Ass'n v. Department of Commerce*, 48 F.3d 540, 543–44 (D.C. Cir. 1995), the D.C. Circuit declined to invalidate a rule for the agency's failure to publish a study on which it relied where the petitioner did not question the study's methodology or findings or identify comments that it would have submitted regarding the study if it had been given the opportunity to do so.

3. Consider the implications of the *Portland Cement* doctrine. On the one hand, agencies spend months or even years considering relevant issues and drafting proposed regulations in advance of issuing a NOPR; it seems reasonable to expect agencies to disclose the data on which they have relied in that process, so that regulated parties can comment on that data and participate meaningfully in the rulemaking process. On the other hand, how well can an agency at the time it issues its NOPR anticipate all of the sources on which it will rely in promulgating the final rule? What should an agency do if it discovers a new source of data that it wants to rely on during the between the time it issues its NOPR and the time it issues its final rule? How would you expect an agency to react to new data, in light of the D.C. Circuit's holding in *Portland Cement*?

The doctrine advanced by the D.C. Circuit in *Portland Cement* requires agencies to disclose the data on which they rely in promulgating legislative rules. Yet, the Supreme Court in *Vermont Yankee* held that reviewing courts cannot command agencies to comply with rulemaking procedures beyond those required by statute or by the Constitution. In the following case, members of a panel of the D.C. Circuit debated the relationship between the D.C. Circuit's continued application of the *Portland Cement* doctrine and the Supreme Court's decision in *Vermont Yankee*.

American Radio Relay League, Inc. v. FCC

524 F.3d 227 (D.C. Cir. 2008).

■ ROGERS, CIRCUIT JUDGE:

The American Radio Relay League, Inc., petitions on behalf of licensed amateur radio operators for review of two orders of the Federal Communications Commission promulgating a rule to regulate the use of the radio spectrum by Access Broadband over Power Line ("Access BPL") operators. The Commission concluded that existing safeguards combined with new protective measures required by the rule will prevent harmful interference to licensees from Access BPL radio emissions. The League challenges this conclusion, contending that the Commission has abandoned decades of precedent requiring shut-down and other protections for licensees and that the rule is substantively and procedurally flawed. We grant the petition in part and remand the rule to the Commission. The Commission failed to satisfy the notice and comment requirements of the Administrative Procedure Act ("APA") by redacting studies on which it relied in promulgating the rule and failed to provide a reasoned explanation for its choice of the extrapolation factor for measuring Access BPL emissions.

* * *

The APA requires an agency to publish "notice" of "either the terms or substance of the proposed rule or a description of the subjects and issues involved," in order to "give interested persons an opportunity to participate in the rule making through submission of written data, views, or arguments," and then, "[a]fter consideration of the relevant matter presented, the agency shall incorporate in the rules adopted a concise general statement of their basis and purpose." 5 U.S.C. § 553(b)–(c). Longstanding precedent instructs that "[n]otice is sufficient 'if it affords interested parties a reasonable opportunity to participate in the rulemaking process,' and if the parties have not been 'deprived of the opportunity to present relevant information by lack of notice that the issue was there.' " *WJG Tel. Co., Inc. v. FCC*, 675 F.2d 386, 389 (D.C. Cir. 1982) (citations omitted).

Under APA notice and comment requirements, "[a]mong the information that must be revealed for public evaluation are the 'technical studies and data' upon which the agency relies [in its rulemaking]." *Chamber of Commerce v. SEC (Chamber of Commerce II)*, 443 F.3d 890, 899 (D.C. Cir. 2006) (citation omitted). Construing section 553 of the APA, the court explained long ago that "[i]n order to allow for useful criticism, it is especially important for the agency to identify and make available *technical studies and data* that it has employed in reaching the decisions to propose particular rules." *Conn. Light & Power Co. v. Nuclear Regulatory Comm'n*, 673 F.2d 525, 530 (D.C. Cir. 1982) (emphasis added). More particularly, "[d]isclosure of *staff reports* allows the parties to focus on the information relied on by the agency and to point out where that information is erroneous or where the agency may be drawing improper conclusions from it." *Nat'l Ass'n of Regulatory Util. Comm'rs ("NARUC") v. FCC*, 737 F.2d 1095, 1121 (D.C. Cir. 1984) (emphasis added); *see Portland Cement Ass'n v. Ruckelshaus*, 486 F.2d 375, 393 (D.C. Cir. 1973).

Public notice and comment regarding relied-upon technical analysis, then, are "[t]he safety valves in the use of . . . sophisticated methodology." *Sierra Club v. Costle*, 657 F.2d 298, 334, 397–98 & n.484 (D.C. Cir. 1981).

> By requiring the "most critical factual material" used by the agency be subjected to informed comment, the APA provides a procedural device to ensure that agency regulations are tested through exposure to public comment, to afford affected parties an opportunity to present comment and evidence to support their positions, and thereby to enhance the quality of judicial review.

Chamber of Commerce II, 443 F.3d at 900. Enforcing the APA's notice and comment requirements ensures that an agency does not "fail[ ] to reveal portions of the technical basis for a proposed rule in time to allow for meaningful commentary" so that "a genuine interchange" occurs rather than "allow[ing] an agency to play hunt the peanut with technical information, hiding or disguising the information that it employs." *Conn. Light & Power Co.*, 673 F.2d at 530–31. The failure to disclose for public comment is subject, however, to "the rule of prejudicial error," 5 U.S.C. § 706, and the court will not set aside a rule absent a showing by the petitioners "that they suffered prejudice from the agency's failure to provide an opportunity for public comment," *Gerber v. Norton*, 294 F.3d 173, 182 (D.C. Cir. 2002), in sufficient time so that the agency's "decisions . . . [may be] framed with . . . comment in full view." *NARUC*, 737 F.2d at 1121.

At issue are five scientific studies consisting of empirical data gathered from field tests performed by the Office of Engineering and Technology. Two studies measured specific Access BPL companies' emissions, and three others measured location-specific emissions in pilot Access BPL areas in New York, North Carolina, and Pennsylvania. In placing the studies in the rulemaking record, the Commission has redacted parts of individual pages, otherwise relying on those pages. In responding to the League's FOIA request, the Commission stated that "certain portions of [these] presentations have been redacted, as they represent preliminary or partial results or staff opinions that were part of the deliberative process, exempt from disclosure under Section 0.457(e) of the Commission's rules and Section 552(b)(5) of the FOIA." Letter from Edmond Thomas, Chief, FCC Office of Eng'g & Tech., to Christopher Imlay, Gen. Counsel, Am. Radio Relay League (Jan. 4, 2005). Upon reconsideration, the Commission reaffirmed that "the redacted portions . . . referred to internal communications that were not relied upon in the decision making process," while reiterating that Commission statements in the *Order* "point" to the partially redacted studies—including the Commission's "own field investigations of [Access] BPL experimental sites"—and "clarify[ing] that in this proceeding, the Commission relied . . . on its own internally conducted studies." *Reconsideration Order*, 21 F.C.C.R. at 9324–25. The court, pursuant to the Commission's offer, has reviewed in camera the partially redacted pages in unredacted form; they show staff summaries of test data, scientific recommendations, and test analysis and conclusions regarding the methodology used in the studies. All pages in the studies are stamped "for internal use only."

It would appear to be a fairly obvious proposition that studies upon which an agency relies in promulgating a rule must be made available during the rulemaking in order to afford interested persons meaningful notice and an opportunity for comment. "It is not consonant with the purpose of a rule-making proceeding to promulgate rules on the basis of inadequate data, or on data that, [to a] critical degree, is known only to the agency." *Portland Cement Ass'n*, 486 F.2d at 393. Where, as here, an agency's determination "is based upon 'a complex mix of controversial and uncommented upon data and calculations,'" there is no APA precedent allowing an agency to cherry-pick a study on which it has chosen to rely in part. *See Solite Corp. v. EPA*, 952 F.2d 473, 500 (D.C. Cir. 1991).

The League has met its burden to demonstrate prejudice by showing that it "ha[s] something useful to say" regarding the unredacted studies, *Chamber of Commerce II*, 443 F.3d at 905, that may allow it to "mount a credible challenge" if given the opportunity to comment. *Gerber*, 294 F.3d at 184. As suggested by the League, the partially redacted pages indicate that a study's core scientific recommendations may reveal the limitations of its own data and that its conclusions may reveal methodology or illuminate strengths and weaknesses of certain data or the study as a whole. For example, the League points to the unredacted headings of otherwise redacted pages referring to "New Information Arguing for Caution on HF BPL" and "BPL Spectrum Tradeoffs," subjects on which it seeks the opportunity to comment. The unredacted pages thus appear to "contain information in tension with the [Commission's] conclusion" that "[Access] BPL's acknowledged interference risks are 'manageable.'" Allowing such "omissions in data and methodology" may "ma[ke] it impossible to reproduce" an agency's results or assess its reliance upon them. *City of Brookings Mun. Tel. Co. v. FCC*, 822 F.2d 1153, 1168 (D.C. Cir. 1987).

* * *

The narrowness of our holding under section 553 of the APA is manifest. The redacted studies consist of staff-prepared scientific data that the Commission's partial reliance made "critical factual material." *Owner-Operator Indep. Drivers Ass'n*, 494 F.3d 188, 201 (D.C. Cir. 2007). The Commission has chosen to rely on the data in those studies and to place the redacted studies in the rulemaking record. Individual pages relied upon by the Commission reveal that the unredacted portions are likely to contain evidence that could call into question the Commission's decision to promulgate the rule. Under the circumstances, the Commission can point to no authority allowing it to rely on the studies in a rulemaking but hide from the public parts of the studies that may contain contrary evidence, inconvenient qualifications, or relevant explanations of the methodology employed. The Commission has not suggested that any other confidentiality considerations would be implicated were the unredacted studies made public for notice and comment. The Commission also has not suggested that the redacted portions of the studies contain only "supplementary information" merely "clarify[ing], expand[ing], or amend[ing] other data that has been offered for comment." *Chamber of Commerce II*, 443 F.3d at 903. Of course, it is within the Commission's prerogative to credit only certain parts of the studies. But what it did here was redact parts of those studies that are inextricably bound to the studies as a whole and thus to the data upon which the Commission has stated it relied, parts that explain the otherwise unidentified methodology underlying data cited by the Commission for its conclusions, and parts that signal caution about that data. This is a critical distinction and no precedent sanctions such a "hide and seek" application of the APA's notice and comment requirements.

As our colleague notes, *see* Concurring & Dissenting Op. by JUDGE KAVANAUGH, in *Vermont Yankee Nuclear Power Corp. v. Natural Resources Defense Council*, 435 U.S. 519 (1978), the Supreme Court has limited the extent that a court may order additional agency procedures, but the procedures invalidated in *Vermont Yankee* were not anchored to any statutory provision. *See id.* at 548; Richard J. Pierce, Jr., *Waiting for* Vermont Yankee *III, IV, and V? A Response to Beermann and Lawson*, 75 GEO. WASH. L.REV. 902, 917 (2007). By contrast, the court does not impose any new procedures for the regulatory process, but merely applies settled law to the facts. The Commission made the choice to engage in notice-and-comment rulemaking and to rely on parts of its redacted studies as a basis for the rule. The court, consequently, is not imposing new procedures but enforcing the agency's procedural choice by ensuring that it conforms to APA requirements. It is one thing for the Commission to give notice and make available for comment the studies on which it relied in formulating the rule while explaining its non-reliance on certain parts. It is quite another thing to provide notice and an opportunity for comment on only those parts of the studies that the Commission likes best. Moreover, the court's precedent construing section 553 to require agencies to release for comment the "technical studies and data" or "staff reports" on which they rely during a rulemaking is not inconsistent with the view that "the *Portland Cement* doctrine should be limited to *studies on which the agency actually relies* to support its final rule." 1 RICHARD J. PIERCE, JR., ADMINISTRATIVE LAW TREATISE 437 (4th ed.2002) (emphasis added).

On remand, the Commission shall make available for notice and comment the unredacted "technical studies and data that it has employed in reaching [its] decisions," *Conn. Light & Power Co.*, 673 F.2d at 530, and shall make them part of the rulemaking record. In view of the remand, the court does not reach the League's contention that the late disclosure of redacted portions of the studies also violated the APA.

■ TATEL, CIRCUIT JUDGE, concurring:

> I write separately to emphasize that in my view, the disclosure ordered by the court * * * is particularly important because the Commission's failure to turn over the unredacted studies undermines this court's ability to perform the review function APA section 706 demands. That provision requires us to set aside arbitrary and capricious agency action after reviewing "the whole record," 5 U.S.C. § 706, and the "whole record" in this case includes the complete content of the staff reports the Commission relied upon in promulgating the challenged rule.

* * *

[T]here is little doubt that the Commission deliberately attempted to "exclude[ ] from the record evidence adverse to its position," a circumstance in which "this court [has] recognized that supplementing the administrative record might be proper." *Kent County, Del. Levy Court v. EPA*, 963 F.2d 391, 396 (D.C. Cir. 1992).

■ KAVANAUGH, CIRCUIT JUDGE, concurring in part, concurring in the judgment in part, and dissenting in part.

In issuing its rule, the FCC relied on various technical studies, including an NTIA report; the various interference studies filed in the record, including petitioner's studies; and the unredacted portions of certain internal FCC staff studies. The FCC publicly disclosed all those materials. But the Commission did not release certain redacted portions of the internal staff studies on which it relied. Citing § 553 of the APA, petitioner says the FCC must release the redacted portions of the staff studies so that interested parties can comment on them and so the FCC, in turn, can consider those comments.

Petitioner's argument would be unavailing if analyzed solely under the text of APA § 553. The APA requires only that an agency provide public notice and a comment period before the agency issues a rule. The notice must include "the terms or substance of the proposed rule *or a description of the subjects and issues involved.*" 5 U.S.C. § 553(b)(3) (emphasis added). After issuing a notice and allowing time for interested persons to comment, the agency must issue a "concise general statement" of the rule's "basis and purpose" along with the final rule. § 553(c). One searches the text of APA § 553 in vain for a requirement that an agency disclose other agency information as part of the notice or later in the rulemaking process.

But beginning with the *Portland Cement* case in 1973—which was decided in an era when this Court created several procedural requirements not rooted in the text of the APA—our precedents have required agencies to disclose, in time to allow for meaningful comment, technical data or studies on which they relied in formulating proposed rules.

The majority opinion concludes that the *Portland Cement* requirement does not allow the FCC to redact portions of studies when the studies otherwise must be disclosed under *Portland Cement*. I accept the majority opinion's conclusion as the best interpretation of our *Portland Cement* line of decisions.

I write separately to underscore that *Portland Cement* stands on a shaky legal foundation (even though it may make sense as a policy matter in some cases). Put bluntly, the *Portland Cement* doctrine cannot be squared with the text of § 553 of the APA. And *Portland Cement*'s lack of roots in the statutory text creates a serious jurisprudential problem because the Supreme Court later rejected this kind of freeform interpretation of the APA. In its landmark *Vermont Yankee* decision, which came a few years after *Portland Cement*, the Supreme Court forcefully stated that the text of the APA binds courts: Section 553 of the APA "established the *maximum procedural requirements* which Congress was willing to have the courts impose upon agencies in conducting rulemaking procedures." *Vt. Yankee*

Nuclear Power Corp. v. NRDC, 435 U.S. 519, 524 (1978) (emphasis added).

Because there is "nothing in the bare text of § 553 that could remotely give rise" to the *Portland Cement* requirement, some commentators argue that *Portland Cement* is "a violation of the basic principle of *Vermont Yankee* that Congress and the agencies, but not the courts, have the power to decide on proper agency procedures." Jack M. Beermann & Gary Lawson, *Reprocessing* Vermont Yankee, 75 GEO. WASH. L. REV. 856, 894 (2007). At the very least, others say, the Supreme Court's decision in *Vermont Yankee* raises "a question concerning the continuing vitality of the *Portland Cement* requirement that an agency provide public notice of the data on which it proposes to rely in a rulemaking." 1 RICHARD J. PIERCE, ADMINISTRATIVE LAW TREATISE § 7.3, at 435 (4th ed.2002).

I do not believe *Portland Cement* is consistent with the text of the APA or *Vermont Yankee*. In the wake of *Vermont Yankee*, however, this Court has repeatedly continued to apply *Portland Cement* (albeit without analyzing the tension between *Vermont Yankee* and *Portland Cement*). In these circumstances, this three-judge panel must accept *Portland Cement* as binding precedent and must require the FCC to disclose the redacted portions of its staff studies. I therefore concur in the judgment as to Part IIB of the majority opinion.

NOTES AND QUESTIONS

1. In *American Radio Relay League*, Judge Kavanaugh contends that the notice requirement of APA § 553(b) does not require disclosure of studies on which an agency relies in promulgating a rule. Consider the language of APA § 553(b), both alone and in the context of the rest of APA § 553. How does the text of APA § 553(b) compare with the *Portland Cement* doctrine?

2. Courts and scholars generally accept that the purpose of the notice and comment requirements of APA § 553(b) and (c) is to give the opportunity to participate in the rulemaking process. Whether the rationale for public participation is to benefit agencies or limit their power, or perhaps both at the same time, may be more debatable. Judge Kavanaugh meanwhile contends in *American Radio Relay League* that *Portland Cement* is not consistent with the Supreme Court's holding in *Vermont Yankee* and that APA § 553(b) and *Vermont Yankee* together do not allow a reviewing court to require an agency to disclose in full the studies on which it relies in promulgating a final rule. Is Judge Kavanaugh's argument consistent with the accepted purpose of the notice-and-comment process? The majority opinion asserts that full disclosure is essential for meaningful participation. Can you envision meaningful participation in the notice-and-comment process without full disclosure of the technical information on which the agency relied? Why or why not?

c. THE "CONCISE" STATEMENT OF BASIS AND PURPOSE

APA § 553(c) provides that, "[a]fter notice required by this section, the agency shall give interested persons an opportunity to participate in the rule making through submission of written data, views, or arguments with or without opportunity for oral presentation. After consideration of the relevant matter presented, the agency shall incorporate in the rules adopted a concise general statement of their basis and purpose."

To satisfy the first part of this requirement, agencies typically accept comments from interested parties for some fixed period of time after publishing the NOPR—*e.g.*, sixty or ninety days. Anyone may submit comments irrespective of their expertise or lack thereof concerning the topic of the rulemaking. The real question is whether and to what extent an agency must actually consider the comments submitted. In theory, a regulated party who is unhappy with a final rule might challenge an agency for not accepting comments for a long enough period of time. Such arguments tend not to be successful, however. In *Connecticut Light & Power Co. v. Nuclear Regulatory Commission*, 673 F.2d 525, 534 (D.C. Cir. 1982), for example, the D.C. Circuit allowed that a comment period longer than the thirty days the agency allotted "might have been helpful" given the proposed regulations' technical complexity, but nevertheless declined to find the agency's choice of comment period unreasonable.

By contrast, the requirement that agencies incorporate a concise statement of basis and purpose into their final rules has been the subject of much litigation. This requirement has been the focal point for hard look review under the arbitrary and capricious standard of APA § 706(2)(A), which we discuss at length in Part D of this Chapter 5. For now, it is enough to understand that courts have applied the arbitrary and capricious standard and hard look review to demand that agencies explain in their statements of basis and purpose the full factual and legal bases justifying their actions and choices in the rulemaking process. The result, of course, is that the statements of basis and purpose that accompany final rules are no longer concise.

Relatedly, the statutory requirement that the agency provide interested parties with an opportunity to submit comments raises the questions of just how much consideration the agency must give to the comments it receives and how a court can satisfy itself that the agency duly considered those comments.

United States v. Nova Scotia Food Products Corp.

568 F.2d 240 (2d Cir. 1977).

■ GURFEIN, CIRCUIT JUDGE:

This appeal involving a regulation of the Food and Drug Administration is not here upon a direct review of agency action. It is an appeal from a judgment of the District Court for the Eastern District of New York (Hon. John J. Dooling, Judge) enjoining the appellants, after a hearing, from processing hot smoked whitefish except in accordance with time-temperature-salinity (T-T-S) regulations contained in 21 C.F.R. Part 122 (1977). * * *

The injunction was sought and granted on the ground that smoked whitefish which has been processed in violation of the T-T-S regulation is "adulterated." Food, Drug and Cosmetics Act ("the Act") §§ 302(a), 301(k), 21 U.S.C. §§ 332(a), 331(k).

Appellant Nova Scotia receives frozen or iced whitefish in interstate commerce which it processes by brining, smoking and cooking. The fish are then sold as smoked whitefish.

The regulations cited above require that hot-process smoked fish be heated by a controlled heat process that provides a monitoring system positioned in as many strategic locations in the oven as necessary to assure a continuous temperature through each fish of not less than 180° F. for a minimum of 30 minutes for fish which have been brined to contain 3.5% water phase salt or at 150° F. for a minimum of 30 minutes if the salinity was at 5% water phase. Since *each* fish must meet these requirements, it is necessary to heat an entire batch of fish to even higher temperatures so that the lowest temperature for *any* fish will meet the minimum requirements.

Government inspection of appellants' plant established without question that the minimum T-T-S requirements were not being met. There is no substantial claim that the plant was processing whitefish under "insanitary conditions" in any other material respect. Appellants, on their part, do not defend on the ground that they were in compliance, but rather that the requirements could not be met if a marketable whitefish was to be produced. They defend upon the grounds that the regulation is invalid * * * because there was no adequate statement setting forth the basis of the regulation. * * *

The hazard which the FDA sought to minimize was the outgrowth and toxin formation of Clostridium botulinum Type E spores of the bacteria which sometimes inhabit fish. There had been an occurrence of several cases of botulism traced to consumption of fish from inland waters in 1960 and 1963 which stimulated considerable bacteriological research. These bacteria can be present in the soil and water of various regions. They can invade fish in their natural habitat and can be further disseminated in the course of evisceration and preparation of the fish for cooking. A failure to destroy such spores through an adequate brining, thermal, and refrigeration process was found to be dangerous to public health.

The Commissioner of Food and Drugs ("Commissioner"), employing informal "notice-and-comment" procedures under 21 U.S.C. § 371(a), issued a proposal for the control of C. botulinum bacteria Type E in fish.

* * *

Responding to the Commissioner's invitation in the notice of proposed rulemaking, members of the industry, including appellants and the intervenor-appellant, submitted comments on the proposed regulation.

The Commissioner thereafter issued the final regulations in which he adopted certain suggestions made in the comments, including a suggestion by the National Fisheries Institute, Inc. ("the Institute"), the intervenor herein. The original proposal provided that the fish would have to be cooked to a temperature of 180° F. for at least 30 minutes, if the fish have been brined to contain 3.5% water phase salt, with no alternative. In the final regulation, an alternative suggested by the intervenor "that the parameter of 150° F. for 30 minutes and 5% salt in the water phase be established as an alternate procedure to that stated in the proposed regulation for an interim period until specific parameters can be established" was accepted, but as a permanent part of the regulation rather than for an interim period.

The intervenor suggested that "specific parameters" be established. This referred to particular processing parameters for different species of fish on a "species by species" basis. Such "species by species" determination was proposed not only by the intervenor but also by the Bureau of Commercial Fisheries of the Department of the Interior. That Bureau objected to the general application of the T-T-S requirement proposed by the FDA on the ground that application of the regulation to all species of fish being smoked was not commercially feasible, and that the regulation should therefore specify time-temperature-salinity requirements, as developed by research and study, on a species-by-species basis. The Bureau suggested that "wholesomeness considerations could be more practically and adequately realized by reducing processing temperature and using suitable concentrations of nitrite and salt." The Commissioner took cognizance of the suggestion, but decided, nevertheless, to impose the T-T-S requirement on all species of fish (except chub, which were regulated by 21 C.F.R. 172.177 (1977) [dealing with food additives]).

He did acknowledge, however, in his "basis and purpose" statement required by the Administrative Procedure Act ("APA"), 5 U.S.C. § 553(c), that "adequate times, temperatures and salt concentrations have not been demonstrated for each individual species of fish presently smoked." 35 Fed. Reg. 17,401 (Nov. 13, 1970). The Commissioner concluded, nevertheless, that "the processing requirements of the proposed regulations are the safest now known to prevent the outgrowth and toxin formation of C. botulinum Type E." He determined that "the conditions of current good manufacturing practice for this industry should be established without further delay." *Id.*

The Commissioner did not answer the suggestion by the Bureau of Fisheries that nitrite and salt as additives could safely lower the high temperature otherwise required, a solution which the FDA had accepted in the case of chub. Nor did the Commissioner respond to the claim of Nova Scotia through its trade association, the Association of Smoked Fish Processors, Inc., Technical Center that "[t]he proposed process requirements suggested by the FDA for hot processed smoked fish are neither commercially feasible nor based on sound scientific evidence obtained with the variety of smoked fish products to be included under this regulation."

Nova Scotia, in its own comment, wrote to the Commissioner that "the heating of certain types of fish to high temperatures will completely destroy the product." It suggested, as an alternative, that "specific processing procedures could be established for each species after adequate work and experimentation [sic] has been done but not before." We have noted above that the response given by the Commissioner was in general terms. He did not specifically aver that the T-T-S requirements as applied to whitefish were, in fact, commercially feasible.

When, after several inspections and warnings, Nova Scotia failed to comply with the regulation, an action by the United States Attorney for injunctive relief was filed on April 7, 1976, six years later, and resulted in the judgment here on appeal. The District Court denied a stay pending appeal, and no application for a stay was made to this court.

* * *

Appellants [ ] attack the "concise general statement" required by APA, 5 U.S.C. § 553, as inadequate. We think that, in the circumstances, it was less than adequate. It is not in keeping with the rational process to leave vital questions, raised by comments which are of cogent materiality, completely unanswered. The agencies certainly have a good deal of discretion in expressing the basis of a rule, but the agencies do not have quite the prerogative of obscurantism reserved to legislatures. "Congress did not purport to transfer its legislative power to the unbounded discretion of the regulatory body." *FCC v. RCA Commc'ns, Inc.*, 346 U.S. 86, 90 (1953). As was said in *Envtl. Def. Fund, Inc. v. EPA*, 465 F.2d 528, 540–51 (1972): "We cannot discharge our role adequately unless we hold EPA to a high standard of articulation."

The test of adequacy of the "concise general statement" was expressed by Judge McGowan in the following terms:

> "We do not expect the agency to discuss every item of fact or opinion included in the submissions made to it in informal rulemaking. We do expect that, if the judicial review which Congress has thought it important to provide is to be meaningful, the 'concise general statement of . . . basis and purpose' mandated by Section 4 will enable us to see what major issues of policy were ventilated by the informal proceedings and why the agency reacted to them as it did." *Auto. Parts & Accessories Ass'n v. Boyd*, 407 F.2d 330, 338 (1968).

* * *

The Secretary was squarely faced with the question whether it was necessary to formulate a rule with specific parameters that applied to all species of fish, and particularly whether lower temperatures with the addition of nitrite and salt would not be sufficient. Though this alternative was suggested by an agency of the federal government, its suggestion, though acknowledged, was never answered.

Moreover, the comment that to apply the proposed T-T-S requirements to whitefish would destroy the commercial product was neither discussed nor answered. We think that to sanction silence in the face of such vital questions would be to make the statutory requirement of a "concise general statement" less than an adequate safeguard against arbitrary decision-making.

We cannot improve on the statement of the District of Columbia Circuit in *Industrial Union Dep't, AFL-CIO v. Hodgson*, 499 F.2d 467, 475 (1974).

> "What we are entitled to at all events is a careful identification by the Secretary, when his proposed standards are challenged, of the reasons why he chooses to follow one course rather than another. Where that choice purports to be based on the existence of certain determinable facts, the Secretary must, in form as well as in substance, find those facts from evidence in

the record. By the same token, when the Secretary is obliged to make policy judgments where no factual certainties exist or where facts alone do not provide the answer, he should so state and go on to identify the considerations he found to be persuasive."

One may recognize that even commercial infeasibility cannot stand in the way of an overwhelming public interest. Yet the administrative process should disclose, at least, whether the proposed regulation is considered to be commercially feasible, or whether other considerations prevail even if commercial infeasibility is acknowledged. This kind of forthright disclosure and basic statement was lacking in the formulation of the T-T-S standard made applicable to whitefish. It is easy enough for an administrator to ban everything. In the regulation of food processing, the worldwide need for food also must be taken into account in formulating measures taken for the protection of health. In the light of the history of smoked whitefish to which we have referred, we find no articulate balancing here sufficient to make the procedure followed less than arbitrary.

NOTES AND QUESTIONS

1. The Second Circuit in *Nova Scotia Food Products* required the agency to respond to comments of "cogent materiality." Other courts have used slightly different phraseology, emphasizing that "an agency need not respond to every comment," but that it must "respond[ ] in a reasoned manner to significant comments received," *U.S. Satellite Broad. Co., Inc. v. FCC*, 740 F.2d 1177, 1188 (D.C. Cir. 1984), or "explain how the agency resolved any significant problems raised by the comments." *Action on Smoking & Health v. C.A.B.*, 699 F.2d 1209, 1216 (D.C. Cir. 1983).

2. The courts have often observed that "[t]he basis and purpose statement is inextricably intertwined with the receipt of comments." *See, e.g., Action on Smoking & Health v. C.A.B.*, 699 F.2d 1209, 1216 (D.C. Cir. 1983) (quoting *Rodway v. USDA*, 514 F.2d 809, 817 (D.C. Cir. 1975)). As with hard look review generally, agencies have responded to cases such as *Nova Scotia Food Products* by expanding their treatment of comments received in the statements of basis and purpose that they publish with final regulations.

3. As with the heightened notice requirement discussed in the last part of this Chapter 5, the requirement that agencies address all significant arguments reflects a tradeoff between thoroughness and efficiency in the rulemaking process. Courts may have succeeded in forcing agencies to demonstrate full contemplation of material or significant comments, but processing all of the comments received in this manner consumes both time and limited agency resources. Final rules are delayed, and agencies cannot promulgate as many regulations to address arguably vital issues of statutory administration.

DISCUSSION PROBLEM

Imagine that you are an attorney for an agency engaged in a rulemaking. The agency has received hundreds or perhaps thousands of comments in response to a particularly controversial proposed regulation. How would you assess whether particular comments are material or significant? How do you think you would handle a comment of questionable significance? Would you counsel the agency to respond anyway?

d. EX PARTE COMMUNICATIONS IN RULEMAKINGS

Courts reviewing challenges to the validity of agency rules almost invariably find themselves addressing arguments concerning the adequacy of an agency's NOPR as well as arguments under hard look review, including claims that the agency failed adequately to address material or significant comments. (We discuss hard look review at greater length in Part C of this Chapter Five.) Along with claims that agencies adopted impermissible interpretations of statutory provisions, these arguments account for the vast majority of judicial decisions invalidating agency rules. (We discuss judicial review of agency interpretations of statutes in Chapter 6.) At times, however, circuit courts have entertained other potential bases for invalidating rules, including the existence of ex parte communications in rulemakings and the existence of bias on the part of a decision maker in a rulemaking, as the following cases illustrate. There is much of value to be learned from studying those two judicial false starts.

APA § 557(d)(1) prohibits ex parte communications, but it applies only to formal adjudication and formal rulemaking. The following trilogy of opinions issued by the D.C. Circuit during the period 1977 to 1981 dealt with the legality and propriety of ex parte communications in informal rulemakings.

Home Box Office, Inc. v. FCC

567 F.2d 9 (D.C. Cir. 1977).

■ PER CURIAM:

In these 15 cases, consolidated for purposes of argument and decision, petitioners challenge various facets of four orders of the Federal Communications Commission which, taken together, regulate and limit the program fare "cablecasters" and "subscription broadcast television stations" may offer to the public for a fee set on a per-program or per-channel basis. * * *

At the heart of these cases are the Commission's "pay cable" rules * * *. The effect of these rules is to restrict sharply the ability of cablecasters to present feature film and sports programs if a separate program or channel charge is made for this material. In addition, the rules prohibit cablecasters from devoting more than 90 percent of their cablecast hours to movie and sports programs and further bar cablecasters from showing commercial advertising on cable channels on which programs are presented for a direct charge to the viewer. Virtually identical restrictions apply to subscription broadcast television.

* * *

During the pendency of this proceeding Mr. Henry Geller, a participant before the Commission and an *amicus* here, filed with the Commission a "Petition for Revision of Procedures or for Issuance of Notice of Inquiry or Proposed Rulemaking." In this petition *amicus*

Geller sought to call the Commission's attention to what were alleged to be violations in these proceedings of the *ex parte* communications doctrine set out by this court in *Sangamon Valley Television Corp. v. United States*, 269 F.2d 221 (1959). The Commission took no action in response to the petition, and *amicus* now presses us to set aside the orders under review here because of procedural infirmity in their promulgation.

It is apparently uncontested that a number of participants before the Commission sought out individual commissioners or Commission employees for the purpose of discussing *ex parte* and in confidence the merits of the rules under review here. In fact, the Commission itself solicited such communications in its notices of proposed rulemaking and, without discussing the nature, substance, or importance of what was said, argues before us that we should simply ignore these communications because *amicus'* petition was untimely, because *amicus* is estopped from complaining about a course of conduct in which he also participated, or, alternatively, because *Sangamon* does not apply. In an attempt to clarify the facts this court *sua sponte* ordered the Commission to provide "a list of all of the *ex parte* presentations, together with the details of each, made to it, or to any of its members or representatives, during the rulemaking proceedings." In response to this order the Commission filed a document over 60 pages long which revealed, albeit imprecisely, widespread *ex parte* communications involving virtually every party before this court, including *amicus* Geller.

Unfortunately, the document filed with this court does not allow an assessment of what was said to the Commission by the various persons who engaged in *ex parte* contacts. To give a flavor of the effect of these contacts, however, we think it useful to quote at length from the brief of *amicus* Geller:

> [*Ex parte*] presentations have in fact been made at crucial stages of the proceeding. Thus, in early 1974, then-Chairman Burch sought to complete action in this proceeding. Because the Commission was "leaning" in its deliberations towards relaxing the existing rules "with 'wildcard' rights for 'blockbuster' movies," American Broadcasting Company's representatives contacted "key members of Congress," who in turn successfully pressured the Commission not to take such action. Further, in the final crucial decisional period, the tentative course to be taken by the Commission would leak after each non-public meeting, and industry representatives would rush to make *ex parte* presentations to the Commissioners and staff. On March 10, 1975, the trade journals state that "word of last week's changes . . . got out during the week, and both broadcast and cable lobbyists rushed to the Commission, unhappy with some facets" that broadcast representatives ". . . were calling on commissioners on Friday . . ." to oppose the changes. The following week, the trade press again reported that "various [industry] groups lobbied the Commission, pressing for changes in the tentative decision" that National Association of Broadcasters ". . . staff members met with [FCC] Broadcast Bureau staffers to present

data backing up [an] asserted need for [a more restrictive] standard."

It is important to note that many contacts occurred in the crucial period between the close of oral argument on October 25, 1974 and the adoption of the First Report and Order on March 20, 1975, when the rulemaking record should have been closed while the Commission was deciding what rules to promulgate. The information submitted to this court by the Commission indicates that during this period broadcast interests met some 18 times with Commission personnel, cable interests some nine times, motion picture and sports interests five times each, and "public interest" intervenors not at all.

Although it is impossible to draw any firm conclusions about the effect of *ex parte* presentations upon the ultimate shape of the pay cable rules, the evidence is certainly consistent with often-voiced claims of undue industry influence over Commission proceedings, and we are particularly concerned that the final shaping of the rules we are reviewing here may have been by compromise among the contending industry forces, rather than by exercise of the independent discretion in the public interest the Communications Act vests in individual commissioners. Our concern is heightened by the submission of the Commission's Broadcast Bureau to this court which states that in December 1974 broadcast representatives "described the kind of pay cable regulation that, in their view, broadcasters 'could live with.' " If actual positions were not revealed in public comments, as this statement would suggest, and, further, if the Commission relied on these apparently more candid private discussions in framing the final pay cable rules, then the elaborate public discussion in these dockets has been reduced to a sham.

Even the possibility that there is here one administrative record for the public and this court and another for the Commission and those "in the know" is intolerable. Whatever the law may have been in the past, there can now be no doubt that implicit in the decision to treat the promulgation of rules as a "final" event in an ongoing process of administration is an assumption that an act of reasoned judgment has occurred, an assumption which further contemplates the existence of a body of material—documents, comments, transcripts, and statements in various forms declaring agency expertise or policy—with reference to which such judgment was exercised. Against this material, "the full administrative record that was before [an agency official] at the time he made his decision," it is the obligation of this court to test the actions of the Commission for arbitrariness or inconsistency with delegated authority. *Citizens to Preserve Overton Park, Inc. v. Volpe*, 401 U.S. 402, 420 (1971). Yet here agency secrecy stands between us and fulfillment of our obligation. As a practical matter, *Overton Park*'s mandate means that the public record must reflect what representations were made to an agency so that relevant information supporting or refuting those representations may be brought to the attention of the reviewing courts by persons participating in agency proceedings. This course is obviously foreclosed if communications are made to the agency in secret and the agency itself does not disclose the information presented. Moreover, where, as here, an agency justifies its actions by reference only to information in the public file while failing to disclose the substance of other relevant information that has been presented to it, a reviewing court cannot presume that the agency has acted properly, but must treat the agency's justifications as a fictional account of the actual decisionmaking process and must perforce find its actions arbitrary.

* * *

From what has been said above, it should be clear that information gathered *ex parte* from the public which becomes relevant to a rulemaking will have to be disclosed at some time. On the other hand, we recognize that informal contacts between agencies and the public are the "bread and butter" of the process of administration and are completely appropriate so long as they do not frustrate judicial review or raise serious questions of fairness. Reconciliation of these considerations in a manner which will reduce procedural uncertainty leads us to conclude that communications which are received prior to issuance of a formal notice of rulemaking do not, in general, have to be put in a public file. Of course, if the information contained in such a communication forms the basis for agency action, then, under well established principles, that information must be disclosed to the public in some form. Once a notice of proposed rulemaking has been issued, however, any agency official or employee who is or may reasonably be expected to be involved in the decisional process of the rulemaking proceeding, should "refus[e] to discuss matters relating to the disposition of a [rulemaking proceeding] with any interested private party, or an attorney or agent for any such party, prior to the [agency's] decision * * *," Executive Order 11920, 12 WEEKLY COMP. PRES. DOC. 1040, 1041 (1976). If *ex parte* contacts nonetheless occur, we think that any written document or a summary of any oral communication must be placed in the public file established for each rulemaking docket immediately after the communication is received so that interested parties may comment thereon.[130]

■ [The opinion of DISTRICT JUDGE WEIGEL, concurring, is omitted. Ed.]

■ MACKINNON, CIRCUIT JUDGE, concurring specially:

I agree that this is the proper rule to apply in this case because the rulemaking undeniably involved competitive interests of great monetary value and conferred preferential advantages on vast segments of the broadcast industry to the detriment of other competing business interests. The rule as issued was in effect an adjudication of the respective rights of the parties vis-a-vis each other. And since that is the nature of the case and controversy that we are deciding and to which our opinion is limited, I would make it clear that that is all we are deciding. I would not make an excessively broad statement to include *dictum* that could be interpreted to cover the entire universe of informal rulemaking. There are so many situations where the

---

[130] We do not think these reporting requirements will be unduly burdensome. The overall effect of our opinion will be to require procedures similar to those already in effect in the Consumer Product Safety Commission which the head of that Commission has already stated are not burdensome. Nor do we think disclosure will have the effect of cutting off information vital to the rulemaking process. The scheme we require here is also no more burdensome than that required by the Sunshine Act for formal rulemaking or by Executive Order 11920. * * *

application of such a broad rule would be inappropriate that we should not paint with such a broad brush.

NOTES AND QUESTIONS

1. Imagine that you are an FCC Commissioner. Your assignment in this case is to resolve by rule a series of complicated disputes between traditional over the air broadcasters and newly arrived cablecasters. What sources would you use to educate yourself about the dispute? Would you read the record of the rulemaking, consisting of multiple NOPRs and comments that total tens of thousands of pages? When did you last read something ten thousand pages long? If the answer is never, you are in the same position as every government official who has had a decision-making role in a major rulemaking. Would you read the FCC staff's several hundred page summary of the record? If so, would you be willing to rely solely on that document and on conversations with staff members to educate yourself? Would you like to learn the views of the broadcasters, cablecasters, content providers, and public interest groups? If so, how would you obtain access to those views?

2. Would you expect the requirements imposed by *HBO* to improve or undermine the rulemaking process? Notwithstanding the *HBO* court's assertion in its footnote 130 that its reporting requirements would not be burdensome, it is no exaggeration to say that no agency decisionmaker would actually be willing to live with the restrictions on ex parte communications announced in that case. If those restrictions had remained in effect, how would you expect decisionmakers to avoid them? Hint: a rulemaking only begins when the agency issues its NOPR.

3. What is the basis for the restrictions imposed in *HBO*? The decision was issued a year before *Vermont Yankee*, discussed at length in Part B of this Chapter 5. Can you reconcile the restrictions imposed in *HBO* with the Supreme Court's holding in *Vermont Yankee*?

4. The issue of whether a decisionmaker must actually hear evidence that is presented orally, read transcripts of oral hearings and/or read written evidence came to the Supreme Court four times in the same case. In the case's first visit, the Court held that: "The one who decides must hear." *Morgan v. United States*, 298 U.S. 468 (1936) (*Morgan I*). By the time the Court considered the issue for the fourth time, however, the Justices seemed to have engaged in some reflection on the realities of the agency decision-making process. The Court held that no one was permitted to ask a decisionmaker whether he had heard oral evidence or read written evidence, thus rendering its first holding meaningless. *United States v. Morgan*, 313 U.S. 409 (1941) (*Morgan IV*).

5. Does the universal practice of engaging in ex parte communications in rulemakings render the notice and comment process a "sham" and render judicial review meaningless, as the *HBO* court asserts? Statements of basis and purpose in major rulemakings are 200 to 2000 pages long. Who would you expect to draft those statements? What role, if any, would you expect agency decisionmakers to have in that drafting process? To what extent can we rely on those statements to be an accurate and complete reflection of the actual decision-making process? Are there valuable functions served by the sequence of notice, comments, final rule incorporating a statement of basis and purpose, and judicial review of the final rule based on that record even if the agency's actual decision-making process differed greatly from the process implied by that sequence?

6.   One of the authors participated in a conference of administrative law professors in which a member of the D.C. Circuit made a speech in which she stated that reviewing courts would be more charitable to agencies if agencies were more honest and candid with courts. One of the professors in attendance who had been a decisionmaker at EPA then asked the judge a wonderful question: What if the EPA Administrator were to provide a court the following honest description of the way he decided a rulemaking case? "The industry argued for an emission limit of 10 parts per million, while the public interest groups argued for an emission limit of 1 part per million. The agency lawyers tell me that they can defend reasonably well any limit between 1 and 10, given the conflicting studies and the ambiguous language in the statute. The agency staff is divided between those who favor a limit of 1 and those who favor a limit of 10. The President will be angry if I set the limit below 5, but key members of the House and Senate will be angry if I set the limit above 5. Thus, I hereby set the limit at 5 parts per million." The judge smiled and responded that agencies must be careful not to be too honest and candid with courts.

Action for Children's Television v. FCC

564 F.2d 458 (D.C. Cir. 1977).

■ TAMM, CIRCUIT JUDGE:

This appeal comes to us upon a petition for review of a decision by the Federal Communications Commission (Commission or FCC) not to adopt certain rules proposed by a public-interest organization to improve children's television. We affirm the Commission because we find that it substantially complied with the applicable procedures, provided a reasoned analysis for its action, did not depart from established policies, and did not otherwise abuse its discretion.

* * *

ACT claims at the outset that the manner in which the Commission concluded these rulemaking proceedings "epitomizes abuse of the administrative process" by its failure to solicit public comment on the industry proposals for self-regulation negotiated "behind the closed doors of Chairman Wiley's office in a private meeting with NAB officials . . . [in which] the industry was clearly coerced into action under the threat of FCC regulation." ACT contends that such action undermines the administrative process since it denies public participation at every stage of the regulatory process when issues of critical public importance are considered, frustrates effective judicial review, and renders the extensive comment-gathering stage "little more than a sop. . . ."

* * *

ACT's characterization of the Commission's action as an abuse of the administrative process misconceives the agency's role in, and the flexibility of, the informal rulemaking proceeding through which the Commission explored the issues raised by ACT's petition. In informal rulemaking, an agency must publish notice in the Federal Register of the proposed proceeding, including "either the terms or substance of the proposed rule or a description of the subjects and issues involved." 5 U.S.C. § 553(b)(3). Since the public is generally entitled to submit their views and relevant data on any proposals, the notice "must be sufficient to fairly apprise interested parties of the issues involved . . ." S. Doc. No. 248, 79th Cong., 2d Sess. 258 (1946), but it need not specify "every precise proposal which [the agency] may ultimately adopt as a rule." *Cal. Citizens Band Ass'n v. United States*, 375 F.2d 43, 48 (9th Cir. 1967). The notice publicizing the proceedings on the issues raised by ACT was sufficiently specific, in light of the result, to meet these requirements. The possibility of Commission reliance on industry self-regulation could not have first suggested itself to ACT only when the Commission finally issued its Report. The Commission has traditionally relied upon self-regulation when it comes to programming matters. Moreover, the Notice of Inquiry and Proposed Rulemaking in Docket 19142 specifically requested comments on the "provisions of the NAB Television Code and its guidelines" concerning restrictions on commercials, and the industry urged from the outset of these proceedings, in public comments available to ACT, that self-regulation was the only appropriate avenue for corrective action.

In addition to notice, an agency must permit meaningful public participation by giving "interested parties an opportunity to participate in the rule making through a submission of written data, views, arguments with or without opportunity for oral presentation." The procedures available to satisfy this requirement are correspondingly diverse, though less so than formerly. No hearing is usually required, and generally no procedural uniformity is imposed. The more limited procedural safeguards in informal rulemaking are justified by its more wide-ranging functional emphasis on questions of law, policy and legislatively-conferred discretion rather than on the contested facts of an individual case. The issues facing the Commission in the proceeding *sub judice* were clearly of a legislative nature, policy considerations predominated, and any rules ultimately adopted would have affected the television and advertising industries, and a significant proportion of television programming.

Under section 553, then, ACT and other interested members of the public, including industry representatives, were entitled to a reasonable opportunity to comment and submit data in support of, or in opposition to, the rules proposed. The Commission substantially met this requirement by permitting a lengthy period for the submission of written comments and by holding six days of informal panel discussions and formal oral arguments. The information gathered by the Commission during this informal rulemaking process, along with any information put forth by the agency itself, represent the factual basis on which the agency must necessarily proceed in making its final determination. This factual predicate must be limited in this way in order to give interested parties proper notice of the reasoning behind the agency's actions and to give meaning to the right to submit comments on the proposed rule. While the agency must consider, analyze and rely on these factual materials which are in the public domain, the agency may draw upon its own expertise in interpreting the facts or upon broader policy considerations not present in the record. We believe that the Commission operated within this framework in this case.

We do not consider that ACT's lack of opportunity to respond directly to NAB's specific self-regulatory proposals vitiated the Commission's decision to accept tentatively those proposals, as indicia that self-regulation could prove effective, in lieu of adopting specific rules. On balance, the procedures used by the Commission constitute substantial compliance with the APA's mandate of limited, yet meaningful, public participation.

The Commission's treatment of the various issues and its extended explanation for the action taken detailed in the Report show that ACT's participation in these proceedings was not just *pro forma*, and that its submissions were not simply ignored. We have long recognized that any judicial review of administrative action cannot be meaningfully conducted unless the court is fully informed of the basis for that action. Such review is facilitated by section 553's requirement that an agency incorporate in any rules adopted a statement of their basis and purpose, "[a]fter consideration of the relevant matter presented. . . ." 5 U.S.C. § 553(c). In *Rodway v. USDA*, 514 F.2d 809, 817 (1975), we once again explained the full import of this particular statutory requirement in cautioning that

> [t]he basis and purpose statement is not intended to be an abstract explanation addressed to imaginary complaints. Rather, its purpose is, at least in part, to respond in a reasoned manner to the comments received, to explain how the agency resolved any significant problems raised by the comments, and to show how that resolution led the agency to the ultimate rule.

Here, notwithstanding that no rule was adopted into which the Commission might "incorporate" its basis and purpose, the Commission did explain the reason for its decision to rely for the time being on self-regulation rather than specific rules. This explanation is contained in the record now before us, and it furnishes a basis for effective judicial review.

In holding that ACT's position was not prejudiced by the manner in which the Commission pursued the temporary resolution of these proceedings, we wish to emphasize that we are not insensitive to ACT's disenchantment with what it considered to be the agency's undue deference to the interests of those it was created to regulate. Meaningful public participation is always to be encouraged, since, at the very least, it "[p]ermits administrative agencies to inform themselves and to afford adequate safeguards to private interests." Final Report of the Attorney General's Comm. on Admin. Practice 103 (1941). We previously have warned that "when Congress creates a procedure that gives the public a role in deciding important questions of public policy, that procedure may not lightly be sidestepped by administrators." *Envtl. Def. Fund, Inc. v. Ruckelshaus*, 439 F.2d 584, 594 (1971). Nevertheless, while it may have been impolitic for the Commission not to invite further comment on the NAB's proposals, especially in view of the fact that there was no necessity for deciding these difficult issues quickly, we still cannot say that the Commission abused its discretion in deciding not to, nor are we persuaded that

ACT's interests in these proceedings were inadequately protected, much less subverted, by the Commission's action.

In so concluding, we necessarily are confronted with the recent decision of this court in *Home Box Office, Inc. v. FCC*, which painted a new perspective on ex parte contacts with a rather broad jurisprudential brush. The gist of the *Home Box Office* ex parte ruling was set forth as follows:

> Once a notice of proposed rulemaking has been issued . . . any agency official or employee who is or may reasonably be expected to be involved in the decisional process of the rulemaking proceeding, should "refus[e] to discuss matters relating to the disposition of a [rulemaking proceeding] with any interested private party, or an attorney or agent for any such party, prior to the [agency's] decision." * * *

Home Box Office, 567 F.2d at 57. Executive Order 11920, which the opinion quotes and essentially adopts as an overarching principle of administrative law, is an executive branch prohibition of ex parte contacts with White House staffers regarding international air route allocations when such route certifications are before the President for approval.

For the reasons set forth below, we agree with Judge MacKinnon that the above-quoted rule should not apply—as the opinion clearly would have it—to every case of informal rulemaking. However, notwithstanding our views to the contrary, we hold only that *Home Box Office*'s broad proscription is not to be applied retroactively in the case *sub judice* inasmuch as it constitutes a clear departure from established law when applied to informal rulemaking proceedings such as undertaken in Docket 19142.

In the absence of support for its position in the Administrative Procedure Act, the panel in *Home Box Office* justified its extension of an ex parte prohibition/disclosure rule throughout all manner of informal rulemaking by reasoning from our decision in *Sangamon Valley Television Corp. v. United States*, 269 F.2d 221 (1959), where we held that ex parte contacts by interested parties with FCC members regarding the allocation of specific TV channels vitiated the ultimate allocation decision. That particular case was neither discussed nor cited by the parties now before the court at any point in their briefs, presumably because even petitioner, ACT, considered the case distinguishable. Although *Sangamon* did involve informal rulemaking, as opposed to licensing-by-adjudication, the court there agreed that "whatever the proceeding may be called it involved not only allocation of TV channels among communities *but also resolution of conflicting private claims to a valuable privilege* (i. e., a TV channel), and that basic fairness requires such a proceeding to be carried on in the open." *Id.* at 224 (emphasis added). Surely this is good law, especially in view of the fact that channel allocation via informal rulemaking is rather similar functionally to licensing via adjudication. The proceedings in Docket 19142, however, present a different situation entirely, where the informal rulemaking undertaken did not involve such "conflicting private claims to a valuable privilege" but rather the possible formulation of programming policy revisions of general applicability. Nonetheless, *Home Box Office* would prohibit or require publication and opportunity for comment on all ex parte contacts, no matter how minor, during the notice and comment stage regardless of the nature of the inquiry. The novelty of this requirement should have been apparent to all.

* * *

If we go as far as *Home Box Office* does in its ex parte ruling in ensuring a "whole record" for our review, why not go further to require the decisionmaker to summarize and make available for public comment every status inquiry from a Congressman or any germane material—say a newspaper editorial that he or she reads or their evening-hour ruminations? In the end, why not administer a lie-detector test to ascertain whether the required summary is an accurate and complete one? The problem is obviously a matter of degree, and the appropriate line must be drawn somewhere. In light of what must be presumed to be Congress' intent not to prohibit or require disclosure of all ex parte contacts during or after the public comment stage, we would draw that line at the point where the rulemaking proceedings involve "competing claims to a valuable privilege." *Home Box Office*, 567 F.2d at 61 (McKinnon, J., concurring specially). It is at that point where the potential for unfair advantage outweighs the practical burdens, which we imagine would not be insubstantial, that such a judicially conceived rule would place upon administrators.

NOTES AND QUESTIONS

1. The D.C. Circuit in *Action for Children's Television* articulated its particular conception of the functions of and relationships among the various components of informal rulemaking: notice, comment, and statement of basis and purpose. Are you satisfied with that explanation in the overall context of a procedure in which many of the communications that actually influence the agency take place off the record and behind closed doors?

2. The court in *Action for Children's Television* devoted considerable effort to distinguishing *HBO*. In your view, did the court distinguish *HBO* or did it overrule *HBO* de facto? Like other circuits, the D.C. Circuit has a rule that prohibits one panel of the court from overruling a precedent issued by another panel. The circuit can overrule a precedent created by a panel decision only by convening the entire court *en banc*. Did the *Action for Children's Television* panel comply with that rule?

3. As narrowed by the *Action for Children's Television* panel to accord with the scope of the D.C. Circuit's opinion in *Sangamon Valley*, is the prohibition on ex parte communications in rulemakings defensible consistent with *Vermont Yankee*? On what basis could you defend it? As so narrowed, how many rulemakings would you expect to be subject to the prohibition?

———————

The final opinion in this trilogy involved a routine form of ex parte communication that particularly angers many participants in rulemakings: efforts by the President and members of Congress to influence agency decisions in rulemakings through closed door meetings with agency decision makers. This type of *ex parte* communications particularly upsets some members of the public in part because it is almost invariably effective. Some decry this practice as "politicizing" the agency decision making process. Do you think it is wrong—legally, morally, or politically—for the President or members of Congress to express their views to agency officials or otherwise attempt to influence the process of making policy through rulemaking? What if any role should government officials outside the agency play in the rulemaking process?

Sierra Club v. Costle

657 F.2d 298 (D.C. Cir. 1981).

■ WALD, CIRCUIT JUDGE:

This case concerns the extent to which new coal-fired steam generators that produce electricity must control their emissions of sulfur dioxide and particulate matter into the air. In June of 1979 EPA revised the regulations called "new source performance standards" ("NSPS" or "standards") governing emission control by coal burning power plants. On this appeal we consider challenges to the revised NSPS brought by environmental groups which contend that the standards are too lax and by electric utilities which contend that the standards are too rigorous. Together these petitioners present an array of statutory, substantive, and procedural grounds for overturning the challenged standards. For the reasons stated below, we hold that EPA did not exceed its statutory authority under the Clean Air Act in promulgating the NSPS, and we decline to set aside the standards.

* * *

[We have omitted approximately eighty pages in which the court addressed a wide variety of disputes over the meaning of the relevant statutory language and the adequacy of the agency's explanation (running hundreds of pages in length) of why it chose the emission ceiling it did rather than alternative ceilings proposed in comments. and why it chose to rely on the findings of some studies rather than those of conflicting studies. Ed.]

* * *

EDF objects to nine different meetings. A chronological list and synopsis of the challenged meetings follows:

1. *March 14, 1979*—This was a one and a half hour briefing at the White House for high-level officials from the Department of Energy (DOE), the Council of Economic Advisers (CEA), the White House staff, the Department of Interior, the Council on Environmental Quality (CEQ), the Office of Management and Budget (OMB), and the National Park Service. The meeting was reported in a May 9, 1979 memorandum from EPA to Senator Muskie's staff, responding to the Senator's request for a monthly report of contacts between EPA staff and other federal officials concerning the NSPS. A summary of the meeting and the materials distributed were docketed on May 30, 1979. EDF also obtained, after promulgation of the final rule, a copy of the

memorandum to Senator Muskie in response to its Freedom of Information Act ("FOIA") request.

2.   *April 5, 1979*—The meeting was attended by representatives of EPA, DOE, NCA, EDF, Congressman Paul Simon's office, ICF, Inc. (who performed the microanalysis), and Hunton & Williams (who represented the Electric Utilities). The participants were notified in advance of the agenda for the meeting. Materials relating to EPA's and NCA's presentations during the meeting were distributed and copies were later put into the docket along with detailed minutes of the meeting. Followup calls and letters between NCA and EPA came on April 20, 23, and 29, commenting or elaborating upon the April 5 data. All of these followup contacts were recorded in the docket.

3.   *April 23, 1979*—This was a 30–45 minute meeting held at then Senate Majority Leader Robert Byrd's request, in his office, attended by EPA Administrator Douglas Costle, Chief Presidential Assistant Stuart Eizenstat, and NCA officials. A summary of this meeting was put in the docket on May 1, 1979, and copies of the summary were sent to EDF and to other parties. In its denial of the petition for reconsideration, EPA was adamant that no new information was transmitted to EPA at this meeting.

[The other six meetings were similar to the first three. Ed.]

* * *

This court's scope of review is delimited by the special procedural provisions of the Clean Air Act, which declare that we may reverse the Administrator's decision for procedural error only if (i) his failure to observe procedural requirements was arbitrary and capricious, (ii) an objection was raised during the comment period, or the grounds for such objection arose only after the comment period and the objection is "of central relevance to the outcome of the rule," and (iii) "the errors were so serious and related to matters of such central relevance to the rule that there is a substantial likelihood that the rule would have been significantly changed if such errors had not been made." 42 U.S.C. § 7607(d)(8). The essential message of so rigorous a standard is that Congress was concerned that EPA's rulemaking not be casually overturned for procedural reasons, and we of course must respect that judgment.

Our authority to reverse informal administrative rulemaking for procedural reasons is also informed by *Vermont Yankee Nuclear Power Corp. v. Natural Resources Defense Council, Inc.*, 435 U.S. 519 (1978). In its unanimous opinion, the Supreme Court unambiguously cautioned this court against imposing its own notions of proper procedures upon an administrative agency entrusted with substantive functions by Congress. The Court declared that so long as an agency abided by the minimum procedural requirements laid down by statute, this court was not free to impose additional procedural rights if the agency did not choose to grant them. Except in "extremely rare" circumstances, the Court stated, there is no justification for a reviewing court to overturn agency action because of the failure to employ procedures beyond those required by Congress.

* * *

In contrast to other recent statutes, there is no mention of any restrictions upon "ex parte" contacts. However, the statute apparently did envision that participants would normally submit comments, documentary material, and oral presentations during a prescribed comment period. Only two provisions in the statute touch upon the post-comment period, one of which * * * states that "[a]ll documents which become available after the proposed rule has been published and which the Administrator determines are of central relevance to the rulemaking shall be placed in the docket as soon as possible after their availability." 42 U.S.C. § 7607(d)(4)(B)(i). But since all the post-comment period written submissions which EDF complains of were in fact entered upon the docket, EDF cannot complain that this provision has been violated.

* * *

The statute does not explicitly treat the issue of post-comment period meetings with individuals outside EPA. Oral face-to-face discussions are not prohibited anywhere, anytime, in the Act. The absence of such prohibition may have arisen from the nature of the informal rulemaking procedures Congress had in mind. Where agency action resembles judicial action, where it involves formal rulemaking, adjudication, or quasi-adjudication among "conflicting private claims to a valuable privilege," the insulation of the decisionmaker from ex parte contacts is justified by basic notions of due process to the parties involved. *Sangamon Valley Television Corp. v. United States*, 269 F.2d 221, 224 (D.C. Cir. 1959). But where agency action involves informal rulemaking of a policymaking sort, the concept of ex parte contacts is of more questionable utility.

Under our system of government, the very legitimacy of general policymaking performed by unelected administrators depends in no small part upon the openness, accessibility, and amenability of these officials to the needs and ideas of the public from whom their ultimate authority derives, and upon whom their commands must fall. As judges we are insulated from these pressures because of the nature of the judicial process in which we participate; but we must refrain from the easy temptation to look askance at all face-to-face lobbying efforts, regardless of the forum in which they occur, merely because we see them as inappropriate in the judicial context. Furthermore, the importance to effective regulation of continuing contact with a regulated industry, other affected groups, and the public cannot be underestimated. Informal contacts may enable the agency to win needed support for its program, reduce future enforcement requirements by helping those regulated to anticipate and shape their plans for the future, and spur the provision of information which the agency needs. The possibility of course exists that in permitting ex parte communications with rulemakers we create the danger of "one administrative record for the public and this court and another for the Commission." Under the Clean Air Act procedures, however, "[t]he promulgated rule may not be based (in part or whole) on any information or data which has not been placed in the docket. . . ." Thus EPA must justify its rulemaking solely on the basis of the record it compiles and makes public.

* * *

Lacking a statutory basis for its position, EDF would have us extend our decision in *Home Box Office, Inc. v. FCC*, 567 F.2d 9 (D.C. Cir. 1977), to cover all meetings with individuals outside EPA during the post-comment period. Later decisions of this court, however, have declined to apply *Home Box Office* to informal rulemaking of the general policymaking sort involved here, and there is no precedent for applying it to the procedures found in the Clean Air Act Amendments of 1977.

It still can be argued, however, that if oral communications are to be freely permitted after the close of the comment period, then at least some adequate summary of them must be made in order to preserve the integrity of the rulemaking docket, which under the statute must be the sole repository of material upon which EPA intends to rely. The statute does not require the docketing of all post-comment period conversations and meetings, but we believe that a fair inference can be drawn that in some instances such docketing may be needed in order to give practical effect to section 307(d)(4)(B)(i), which provides that all *documents* "of central relevance to the rulemaking" shall be placed in the docket as soon as possible after their availability. This is so because unless *oral* communications of central relevance to the rulemaking are also docketed in some fashion or other, information central to the justification of the rule could be obtained without ever appearing on the docket, simply by communicating it by voice rather than by pen, thereby frustrating the command of section 307 that the final rule not be "based in part or whole" on any information or data which has not been placed in the docket. . . ." 42 U.S.C. § 7607(d)(6)(C).

EDF is understandably wary of a rule which permits the agency to decide for itself when oral communications are of such central relevance that a docket entry for them is required. Yet the statute itself vests EPA with discretion to decide whether "documents" are of central relevance and therefore must be placed in the docket; surely EPA can be given no less discretion in docketing oral communications, concerning which the statute has no explicit requirements whatsoever. Furthermore, this court has already recognized that the relative significance of various communications to the outcome of the rule is a factor in determining whether their disclosure is required. A judicially imposed blanket requirement that all post-comment period oral communications be docketed would, on the other hand, contravene our limited powers of review, would stifle desirable experimentation in the area by Congress and the agencies, and is unnecessary for achieving the goal of an established, procedure-defined docket, *viz.*, to enable reviewing courts to fully evaluate the stated justification given by the agency for its final rule.

* * *

We have already held that a blanket prohibition against meetings during the post-comment period with individuals outside EPA is unwarranted, and this perforce applies to meetings with White House officials. We have not yet addressed, however, the issue whether such oral communications with White House staff, or the President himself, must be docketed on the rulemaking record, and we now turn to that issue.

* * *

The court recognizes the basic need of the President and his White House staff to monitor the consistency of executive agency regulations with Administration policy. He and his White House advisers surely must be briefed fully and frequently about rules in the making, and their contributions to policymaking considered. The executive power under our Constitution, after all, is not shared—it rests exclusively with the President. The idea of a "plural executive," or a President with a council of state, was considered and rejected by the Constitutional Convention. Instead the Founders chose to risk the potential for tyranny inherent in placing power in one person, in order to gain the advantages of accountability fixed on a single source. To ensure the President's control and supervision over the Executive Branch, the Constitution—and its judicial gloss—vests him with the powers of appointment and removal, the power to demand written opinions from executive officers, and the right to invoke executive privilege to protect consultative privacy. In the particular case of EPA, Presidential authority is clear since it has never been considered an "independent agency," but always part of the Executive Branch.

The authority of the President to control and supervise executive policymaking is derived from the Constitution; the desirability of such control is demonstrable from the practical realities of administrative rulemaking. Regulations such as those involved here demand a careful weighing of cost, environmental, and energy considerations. They also have broad implications for national economic policy. Our form of government simply could not function effectively or rationally if key executive policymakers were isolated from each other and from the Chief Executive. Single mission agencies do not always have the answers to complex regulatory problems. An overworked administrator exposed on a 24-hour basis to a dedicated but zealous staff needs to know the arguments and ideas of policymakers in other agencies as well as in the White House.

We recognize, however, that there may be instances where the docketing of conversations between the President or his staff and other Executive Branch officers or rulemakers may be necessary to ensure due process. This may be true, for example, where such conversations directly concern the outcome of adjudications or quasi-adjudicatory proceedings; there is no inherent executive power to control the rights of individuals in such settings. Docketing may also be necessary in some circumstances where a statute like this one specifically requires that essential "information or data" upon which a rule is based be docketed. 42 U.S.C. § 7607(d)(6)(C). But in the absence of any further Congressional requirements, we hold that it was not unlawful in this case for EPA not to docket a face-to-face policy session involving the President and EPA officials during the post-comment period, since EPA makes no effort to base the rule on any "information or data" arising from that meeting. Where the President himself is directly involved in oral communications with Executive Branch officials, Article II considerations—combined with the strictures of *Vermont Yankee*—

require that courts tread with extraordinary caution in mandating disclosure beyond that already required by statute.

The purposes of full-record review which underlie the need for disclosing ex parte conversations in some settings do not require that courts know the details of every White House contact, including a Presidential one, in this informal rulemaking setting. After all, any rule issued here with or without White House assistance must have the requisite *factual support* in the rulemaking record, and under this particular statute the Administrator may not base the rule in whole or in part on any *"information or data"* which is not in the record, no matter what the source. The courts will monitor all this, but they need not be omniscient to perform their role effectively. Of course, it is always possible that undisclosed Presidential prodding may direct an outcome that is factually based on the record, but different from the outcome that would have obtained in the absence of Presidential involvement. In such a case, it would be true that the political process did affect the outcome in a way the courts could not police. But we do not believe that Congress intended that the courts convert informal rulemaking into a rarified technocratic process, unaffected by political considerations or the presence of Presidential power. In sum, we find that the existence of intra-Executive Branch meetings during the post-comment period, and the failure to docket one such meeting involving the President, violated neither the procedures mandated by the Clean Air Act nor due process.

Finally, EDF challenges the rulemaking on the basis of alleged Congressional pressure, citing principally two meetings with Senator Byrd. EDF asserts that under the controlling case law the political interference demonstrated in this case represents a separate and independent ground for invalidating this rulemaking. But among the cases EDF cites in support of its position, only *D.C. Federation of Civil Associations v. Volpe*, 459 F.2d 1231 (D.C. Cir. 1971), seems relevant to the facts here.

* * *

D.C. Federation * * * requires that two conditions be met before an administrative rulemaking may be overturned simply on the grounds of Congressional pressure. First, the content of the pressure upon the Secretary is designed to force him to decide upon factors not made relevant by Congress in the applicable statute. * * * Second, the Secretary's determination must be affected by those extraneous considerations.

In the case before us, there is no persuasive evidence that either criterion is satisfied. Senator Byrd requested a meeting in order to express "strongly" his already well-known views that the SO_2 standards' impact on coal reserves was a matter of concern to him. EPA initiated a second responsive meeting to report its reaction to the reserve data submitted by the NCA. In neither meeting is there any allegation that EPA made any commitments to Senator Byrd. The meetings did underscore Senator Byrd's deep concerns for EPA, but there is no evidence he attempted actively to use "extraneous" pressures to further his position. Americans rightly expect their elected representatives to voice their grievances and preferences concerning the administration of our laws. We believe it entirely proper for Congressional representatives vigorously to represent the interests of their constituents before administrative agencies engaged in informal, general policy rulemaking, so long as individual Congressmen do not frustrate the intent of Congress as a whole as expressed in statute, nor undermine applicable rules of procedure. Where Congressmen keep their comments focused on the substance of the proposed rule—and we have no substantial evidence to cause us to believe Senator Byrd did not do so here—administrative agencies are expected to balance Congressional pressure with the pressures emanating from all other sources. To hold otherwise would deprive the agencies of legitimate sources of information and call into question the validity of nearly every controversial rulemaking.

* * *

In sum, we conclude that EPA's adoption of the 1.2 lbs./MBtu emissions ceiling was free from procedural error. The post-comment period contacts here violated neither the statute nor the integrity of the proceeding.

NOTES AND QUESTIONS

1. *Sierra Club v. Costle* remains the leading case on the issue of ex parte communications.

- In *New Mexico v. EPA*, 114 F.3d 290 (D.C. Cir. 1997), the D.C. Circuit reaffirmed its holding in a case challenging ex parte communications between the EPA, the Department of Energy, and the Office of Management and Budget; the court found the communications permissible notwithstanding other parties' lack of corresponding opportunity to respond to their contents because the issues addressed had already been "fully aired" through public comments and "added no new data," and the final rule was "plainly sustainable" based on the public record. *Id.* at 295–96.

- In *Strickland v. Comm'r, Me. Dep't of Human Svcs.*, 48 F.3d 12 (1st Cir. 1995), the First Circuit did not find problematic a nonbinding statement in a congressional committee conference report regarding a pending agency rule, given that the agency's change in position was supported by a "reasoned explanation." Indeed, the First Circuit acknowledged that "inter-branch communication and cooperation are not terrible diseases, but rather, are a tested means of improving the health of the body politic." *Id.* at 15.

- In *Radio Ass'n v. Department of Transp.*, 47 F.3d 794 (6th Cir. 1995), the Sixth Circuit held that the agency's rule was not improperly influenced by an appropriations bill rider instructing an agency to commence rulemaking; the agency had clearly stated a basis for its rulemaking, and court did not consider the congressional pressure to be egregious. *See id.* at 807–08.

2. Notwithstanding the D.C. Circuit's general endorsement of ex parte communications in *Sierra Club*, that court in 1999 asserted that its opinion in *HBO* retained some limited validity in the informal rulemaking context, observing that ex parte communications may be unacceptable if they lead to "an unanticipatable change in the final rule." *Air Transp. Ass'n of Am. v.*

FAA, 169 F.3d 1, 7 n.5 (D.C. Cir. 1999). In other words, so long as the agency can explain its rulemaking decision based on the public record, ex parte communications are acceptable. If, however, an agency changes a final rule based on something that interested parties would not anticipate from the public record, and if ex parte communications caused that change, "that would be, of course, objectionable." *Id.*

3. The Sierra Club and other environmental organizations argued that EPA should adopt an SO_2 emission ceiling much lower than the 1.2 lb/MMBTU ceiling EPA adopted in its final rule, *i.e.*, a ceiling of 0.4 lb/MMBTU. A lower standard would have been much better for the environment, but it would have forced many electric utilities to substitute oil or low sulfur coal from Montana and Wyoming for high sulfur Appalachian basin coal. Sierra Club believed that EPA Administrator Costle would have adopted that lower limit if it were not for the meetings Costle had with various government officials outside the EPA. Do you find that plausible? If that is what happened, do you find it inappropriate that other government officials might have influenced Costle, given that the EPA was able to defend the legality of its decision to adopt the 1.2 lb/MMBTU limit?

4. In order to attempt to recreate the conversations that took place at those meetings you must try to turn back the clock to 1979 and recall the circumstances in which the EPA was acting. In 1973, the Organization of Arab Petroleum Exporting Countries (*i.e.*, the Arab members of OPEC plus Egypt and Syria) initiated an embargo in which they substantially curtailed oil shipments to the United States and other countries that supported Israel in the Yom Kippur war. The result was a four-fold increase in the price of oil in 1973 and 1974. Following that incident, in 1979, Islamic militants overthrew the government of the Shah of Iran and replaced it with an Islamic republic. In support of the Iranian Revolution, a group of Islamist students and militants took over the American embassy in Iran and held 53 Americans hostage for more than a year, As a result of these events, the price of oil doubled again. Within the context of these events, President Jimmy Carter sought to obtain American energy independence. Simultaneously, the United States was facing high and rising inflation and unemployment. President Carter was facing an imminent congressional elections and his own presidential re-election campaign. Economic conditions in Appalachia were particularly depressed, Appalachian states rely on coal as a major part of their economy, and President Carter wanted their votes.

Given this environment, what might the Secretary of Energy have said to Costle in an effort to persuade him to adopt a higher SO_2 emission limit? What might the Chair of the President's Council of Economic Advisors have said to Costle in an effort to persuade him to adopt the higher limit? How would the EPA's decision affect the US energy situation? How would the EPA's action affect the performance of the economy? How would the EPA's action affect U.S. relations with other countries? What effect would the EPA's action have on West Virginia? What might Senator Robert Byrd, in his capacity as Senator from West Virginia and as majority leader of the Senate, have said to Costle to influence his decision? How would the EPA's decision affect the political situation in 1979? What might President Carter have said to Costle?

5.   Sierra Club asserted that EPA Administrator Costle should have made his decision the way a judge would—with no communications from outsiders beyond the record from the official notice and comment process. Do you share Sierra Club's belief that Costle was wrong to consult other government officials? If so, how far would you extend the ban on external influences in agency decisionmaking? Should Costle also be prohibited from reading books or newspapers to learn on his own all of the things that were communicated to him at the contested meetings? Suppose that one of the outside participants in one of the meetings had handed Costle a new study that included findings that favored the 1.2 lb/MMBTU limit. What could, or should, Costle do with that study?

6.   Congress probably could amend the APA to prohibit all ex parte communications in rulemakings, though such a prohibition would raise serious constitutional law questions if it precluded the President from communicating with agency officials. If you were told that such a statute would be constitutional, would you support its enactment? Of course, any such prohibition would have to apply to all interested persons, which would include not only the President but also members of Congress. Would you expect Congress to enact a complete prohibition on ex parte communications in rulemakings?

e.   IMPERMISSIBLE BIAS IN RULEMAKINGS

As we discussed in Chapter Four, both due process and the APA require a neutral—*i.e.*, unbiased—decisionmaker in an adjudication. Thus, for instance, a defendant in an adjudicatory proceeding before either a court or an agency would have grounds to force a decisionmaker to recuse herself if the decisionmaker had indicated before the hearing to determine the facts her belief that the defendant engaged in the unlawful conduct of which he was accused. How, if at all, should this important neutrality principle apply to a decisionmaker in a rulemaking? Should a court analogize a rulemaking to a judicial trial or to a legislative action? If you were appearing before a Senate Committee to urge it to enact legislation that would, for example, make it difficult or expensive for electric utilities to use coal, should you be able to force the Senator from West Virginia, home of much coal production, to recuse himself?

Association of National Advertisers v. FTC

627 F.2d 1151 (D.C. Cir. 1979).

■ TAMM, CIRCUIT JUDGE:

Plaintiffs, appellees here, brought an action in the United States District Court for the District of Columbia to prohibit Michael Pertschuk, Chairman of the Federal Trade Commission (Commission), from participating in a pending rulemaking proceeding concerning children's advertising. The district court, citing this court's decision in *Cinderella Career & Finishing Schools, Inc. v. FTC*, 425 F.2d 583 (D.C.Cir.1970), found that Chairman Pertschuk had prejudged issues involved in the rulemaking and ordered him disqualified. We hold that the *Cinderella* standard is not applicable to the Commission's rulemaking proceeding. An agency member may be disqualified from such a proceeding only when there is a clear and convincing showing that he has an unalterably closed mind on matters critical to the disposition of the rulemaking. Because we find that the appellees have failed to demonstrate the requisite prejudgment, the order of the district court is reversed.

On April 27, 1978, the Commission issued a Notice of Proposed Rulemaking that suggested restrictions regarding television advertising directed toward children. The decision to commence rulemaking under section 18 of the Federal Trade Commission (FTC) Act was accompanied by a statement setting forth "with particularity the reason for the proposed rule." The Commission explained that it had decided to propose a rule limiting children's advertising after consideration of a staff report that discussed

> facts which suggest that the televised advertising of any product directed to young children who are too young to understand the selling purpose of, or otherwise comprehend or evaluate, commercials may be unfair and deceptive within the meaning of Section 5 of the Federal Trade Commission Act, requiring appropriate remedy.

43 Fed. Reg. 17,967, 17,969 (1978). The Commission invited interested persons to comment upon any issue raised by the staff proposal.

On May 8, 1978, the Association of National Advertisers, Inc. (ANA), the American Association of Advertising Agencies (AAAA), the American Advertising Federation (AAF), and the Toy Manufacturers of America, Inc. (TMA) petitioned Chairman Pertschuk to recuse himself from participation in the children's advertising inquiry. The petition charged that Pertschuk had made public statements concerning regulation of children's advertising that demonstrated prejudgment of specific factual issues sufficient to preclude his ability to serve as an impartial arbiter. The charges were based on a speech Pertschuk delivered to the Action for Children's Television (ACT) Research Conference in November 1977, on several newspaper and magazine articles quoting Chairman Pertschuk's views on children's television, on the transcript of a televised interview, and on a press release issued by the Commission during the summer of 1977.

On July 13, 1978, Chairman Pertschuk declined to recuse himself from the proceeding. Pertschuk stated his belief that the disqualification standard appropriate for administrative adjudications did not apply to administrative rulemaking, and that, even if adjudicative criteria were relevant, his remarks did not warrant disqualification because they did not concern the petitioners in particular; rather, they addressed the "*issue* of advertising to children and the *policy* questions raised by it." Five days later, the Commission, without Pertschuk participating, also determined that Pertschuk need not be disqualified.

* * *

Before we examine * * * the content of Pertschuk's statements, we review our decision in *Cinderella Career & Finishing Schools, Inc. v. FTC*. In *Cinderella*, we held that the standard for disqualifying an administrator in an adjudicatory proceeding because of prejudgment is whether " 'a disinterested observer may conclude that [the decisionmaker] has in some measure adjudged the facts as well as the law of a particular case in advance of hearing it.'" 425 F.2d at 591. This standard guarantees that the adjudicative hearing of a person facing administrative prosecution for past behavior is before a decisionmaker who has not prejudged facts concerning the events under review.

The facts of the *Cinderella* case illustrate application of the standard. The Commission charged that Cinderella Career College and Finishing Schools, Inc. (Cinderella) made false representations in its advertising and engaged in deceptive practices in contravention of section 5 of the FTC Act. 15 U.S.C. § 45 (1976). For example, the Commission alleged that Cinderella advertised "courses of instruction which qualify students to become airline stewardesses" and that its graduates were "qualified to assume executive positions." 425 F.2d at 584 n.1. An administrative law judge ruled that the Commission had failed to prove that the acts and practices violated the FTC Act, and he dismissed the complaint. Complaint counsel appealed the administrative law judge's decision to the full Commission.

While the appeal was pending before the Commission, Chairman Paul Rand Dixon spoke at the Government Relations Workshop of the National Newspaper Association and stated:

> What kind of vigor can a reputable newspaper exhibit? . . . What standards are maintained on advertising acceptance? . . . What about carrying ads that offer college educations in five weeks, . . . or becoming an airline's hostess by attending a charm school? . . . Granted that newspapers are not in the advertising policing business, their advertising managers are savvy enough to smell deception when the odor is strong enough.

Cinderella, 425 F.2d at 589–90. Six months later, the Commission, with Chairman Dixon participating, found that Cinderella neither awarded nor was capable of awarding academic degrees, and that it offered no course of instruction that would qualify students as airline stewardesses. The Commission concluded that these and other representations were false and misleading in violation of section 5 of the FTC Act and ordered Cinderella to cease and desist from such practices.

On review, we found that Chairman Dixon's remarks gave "the appearance that he ha[d] already prejudged the case and that the ultimate determination of the merits [would] move in predestined grooves." *Cinderella*, 425 F.2d at 590. Accordingly, we held that Chairman Dixon's participation in the proceeding required reversal and remand of the Commission's order.

The district court in the case now before us held that "the standard of conduct delineated in *Cinderella*" governs agency decisionmakers participating in a section 18 proceeding. Section 18 authorizes the Commission to promulgate rules designed to "define with specificity acts or practices which are unfair or deceptive." 15 U.S.C. § 57a(a)(1)(1976). Basically, it allows the Commission to enforce the broad command of section 5 of the FTC Act, which declares "unfair or deceptive acts or practices in or affecting commerce . . . unlawful." 15 U.S.C. § 45(a)(1). The district court ruled that a section 18 proceeding, notwithstanding the appellation rulemaking, "is neither wholly legislative nor wholly adjudicative." According to the district court, the "adjudicative aspects" of the proceeding render *Cinderella* applicable.

* * *

The district court's characterization of section 18 rulemaking as a "hybrid" or quasi-adjudicative proceeding ignores the clear scheme of the APA. Administrative action pursuant to the APA is either adjudication or rulemaking. The two processes differ fundamentally in purpose and focus:

> The object of the rule making proceeding is the implementation or prescription of law or policy for the future, rather than the evaluation of a respondent's past conduct. Typically, the issues relate not to the evidentiary facts, as to which the veracity and demeanor of witnesses would often be important, but rather to the policy-making conclusions to be drawn from the facts. . . . Conversely, adjudication is concerned with the determination of past and present rights and liabilities. Normally, there is involved a decision as to whether past conduct was unlawful, so that the proceeding is characterized by an accusatory flavor and may result in disciplinary action.

Attorney General's Manual on the Administrative Procedure Act 14 (1947).

* * *

[T]he Commission's children's advertising inquiry is designed to determine whether certain acts or practices will, in the future, be considered to contravene the FTC Act. The proceeding is not adjudication or quasi-adjudication. It is a clear exercise of the Commission's rulemaking authority.

The appellees also argue that we must apply *Cinderella* because it involves a factual prejudgment similar to the one now before us. In *Cinderella*, Chairman Dixon made statements that reflected prejudgment that Cinderella Career & Finishing Schools, Inc. had engaged in certain acts. In this case, the appellees accuse Chairman Pertschuk of prejudging issues of material fact in the children's television proceeding. We find that the appellees' argument belies a misunderstanding of the factual basis of rules.

The factual predicate of a rulemaking decision substantially differs in nature and in use from the factual predicate of an adjudicatory decision. The factual predicate of adjudication depends on ascertainment of "facts concerning the immediate parties—who did what, where, when, how, and with what motive or intent." 2 K. DAVIS, ADMINISTRATIVE LAW TREATISE, § 15.03, at 353 (1958). By contrast, the nature of legislative fact is ordinarily general, without reference to specific parties. Adjudicative and legislative facts are also used differently:

> [A]djudicative facts are those to which the law is applied in the process of adjudication. They are the facts that normally go to the jury in a jury case. . . . Legislative facts are the facts which

> help the tribunal determine the content of law and of policy
> and help the tribunal to exercise its judgment or discretion in
> determining what course of action to take.

Id. Thus, legislative facts are crucial to the prediction of future events
and to the evaluation of certain risks, both of which are inherent in
administrative policymaking. The case law demonstrates that the
factual component of generalized rulemaking cannot be severed from
the pure policy aspects of the rule.

* * *

Because legislative facts combine empirical observation with
application of administrative expertise to reach generalized conclusions,
they need not be developed through evidentiary hearings. To the
contrary, however, "[w]here adjudicative, rather than legislative, facts
are involved, the parties must be afforded a hearing to allow them an
opportunity to meet and to present evidence." *Alaska Airlines, Inc. v.
CAB*, 545 F.2d 194, 2000 (D.C. Cir. 1976). This distinction has been
established in judicial, as well as administrative, processes.

* * *

Had Congress amended section 5 of the FTC Act to declare certain
types of children's advertising unfair or deceptive, we would barely
pause to consider a due process challenge. No court to our knowledge
has imposed procedural requirements upon a legislature before it may
act. Indeed, any suggestion that congressmen may not prejudge factual
and policy issues is fanciful. A legislator must have the ability to
exchange views with constituents and to suggest public policy that is
dependent upon factual assumptions. Individual interests impinged
upon by the legislative process are protected, as Justice Holmes wrote,
"in the only way that they can be in a complex society, by [the
individual's] power, immediate or remote, over those who make the
rule." *Bi-Metallic Inv. Co. v. State Bd. of Equalization*, 239 U.S. 441,
445 (1915).

Congress chose, however, to delegate its power to proscribe unfair
or deceptive acts or practices to the Commission because "there were too
many unfair practices for it to define." S. REP. NO. 597, 63d Cong., 2d
Sess. 13 (1914). In determining the due process standards applicable in
a section 18 proceeding, we are guided by its nature as rulemaking.
When a proceeding is classified as rulemaking, due process ordinarily
does not demand procedures more rigorous than those provided by
Congress. *See Vermont Yankee Nuclear Power Corp. v. NRDC*, 435 U.S.
519, 524 n.1, 542 n.16 (1978).

* * *

We never intended the *Cinderella* rule to apply to a rulemaking
procedure such as the one under review. The *Cinderella* rule
disqualifies a decisionmaker if " 'a disinterested observer may conclude
that [he] has in some measure adjudged the facts as well as the law of a
particular case in advance of hearing it.' " *Cinderella*, 425 F.2d at 591
(quoting *Gilligan, Will & Co. v. SEC*, 267 F.2d 461, 469 (2d Cir. 1959)).
As we already have noted, legislative facts adduced in rulemaking
partake of agency expertise, prediction, and risk assessment. In

Cinderella, the court was able to cleave fact from law in deciding whether Chairman Dixon had prejudged particular factual issues. In the rulemaking context, however, the factual component of the policy decision is not easily assessed in terms of an empirically verifiable condition. Rulemaking involves the kind of issues "where a month of experience will be worth a year of hearings." *Am. Airlines, Inc. v. CAB*, 359 F.2d 624, 633 (D.C. Cir. 1966). Application of *Cinderella's* strict law-fact dichotomy would necessarily limit the ability of administrators to discuss policy questions.

The legitimate functions of a policymaker, unlike an adjudicator, demand interchange and discussion about important issues. We must not impose judicial roles upon administrators when they perform functions very different from those of judges. * * *

The *Cinderella* view of a neutral and detached adjudicator is simply an inapposite role model for an administrator who must translate broad statutory commands into concrete social policies. If an agency official is to be effective he must engage in debate and discussion about the policy matters before him.

* * *

Chairman Pertschuk's remarks, considered as a whole, represent discussion, and perhaps advocacy, of the legal theory that might support exercise of the Commission's jurisdiction over children's advertising. The mere discussion of policy or advocacy on a legal question, however, is not sufficient to disqualify an administrator. To present legal and policy arguments, Pertschuk not unnaturally employed the factual assumptions that underlie the rationale for Commission action. The simple fact that the Chairman explored issues based on legal and factual assumptions, however, did not necessarily bind him to them forever. Rather, he remained free, both in theory and in reality, to change his mind upon consideration of the presentations made by those who would be affected.

* * *

In sum, we hold that the materials adduced by the appellees are insufficient to rebut the strong presumption of administrative regularity. The materials, as a whole, merely demonstrate that Pertschuk discussed a legal theory by which the Commission could adopt a rule, if circumstances warranted. The statements do not demonstrate that Chairman Pertschuk is unwilling or unable to consider rationally argument that a final rule is unnecessary because children are either unharmed by sugared products or are able to understand advertising. The appellees have failed to make a clear and convincing showing that Chairman Pertschuk has an unalterably closed mind on matters critical to the children's television proceeding.

■ LEVANTHAL, CIRCUIT JUDGE, concurring:

The ultimate test announced by Judge Tamm as to the merits is that disqualification from a rulemaking proceeding results "only when there has been a clear and convincing showing that [the agency member] has an unalterably closed mind on matters critical to the disposition of the [proceeding]."

* * *

The application of this test to agencies must take into account important differences in function and functioning between the agencies and court systems. In fulfilling the functions of applying or considering the validity of a statute, or a government program, the judge endeavors to put aside personal views as to the desirability of the law or program, and he is not disqualified because he personally deems the program laudable or objectionable. In the case of agency rulemaking, however, the decision-making officials are appointed precisely to implement statutory programs, and with the expectation that they have a personal disposition to enforce them vigilantly and effectively. They work with a combination rather than a separation of functions, in legislative modes, and take action on the basis of information coming from many sources, even though that provides a mindset before a proceeding is begun, subject to reconsideration in the light of the proceeding.

* * *

One can hypothesize beginning an adjudicatory proceeding with an open mind, indeed a blank mind, a tabula rasa devoid of any previous knowledge of the matter. In sharp contrast, one cannot even conceive of an agency conducting a rulemaking proceeding unless it had delved into the subject sufficiently to become concerned that there was an evil or abuse that required regulatory response. It would be the height of absurdity, even a kind of abuse of administrative process, for an agency to embroil interested parties in a rulemaking proceeding, without some initial concern that there was an abuse that needed remedying, a concern that would be set forth in the accompanying statement of the purpose of the proposed rule.

■ MacKINNON, CIRCUIT JUDGE, dissenting in part and concurring in part.

I cannot agree with the holding of the majority that a member of the Commission engaged in the rulemaking proceeding can be disqualified only upon a showing by clear and convincing evidence that he has an *unalterably closed mind* on matters critical to the disposition of the rulemaking. * * * I would hold that the Chairman has disqualified himself in this rulemaking proceeding even if the majority's "unalterably closed mind" standard is applied.

In my opinion the "unalterably closed mind", where it exists, in many cases is practically impossible to prove, imposes too high a barrier to the public's obtaining fair decisionmakers and is a higher standard than the Supreme Court has applied in its recent decisions. I would require any Federal Trade Commissioner to recuse himself, or failing that to be disqualified, upon a showing by the preponderance of evidence that he could not participate fairly in the formulation of the rule because of substantial bias or prejudgment with respect to any critical fact that must be resolved in such formulation.

* * *

The Court's opinion is couched too much in a rulemaking/adjudication dichotomy and tries to pigeonhole Commission action into one or the other. For instance, it states that the "presence of procedures not mandated by Section 553 … does not … convert rulemaking into quasi-adjudication. . . .." That statement however blinks at the reality that exists in this instance of rulemaking. It should also be noted that Professor Davis * * * defines "*adjudicative facts* [as] facts relating to the parties to the case … when a rule is formulated in an on-the-record proceeding." The Commission's action in promulgating the instant rules is required to be supported by substantial evidence in the rulemaking record as a whole. * * *

Professor Davis has pointed out that some rulemakings may involve the determination of adjudicative facts:

> The first step is probably to recognize that the reality [of rulemaking procedures] is a spectrum rather than a dichotomy; some facts are clearly adjudicative, some are clearly legislative, some are probably one or probably the other but not clearly, and some seem impossible to classify. So the adjudicative or legislative character of facts is a variable, and other variables must also be taken into account—the degree of doubt or certainty about the facts, and the degree of their bearing upon the controversy. When facts are clearly adjudicative, disputed, and critical, a party should be entitled to all the procedural protections of a trial. When facts are legislative, reasonably clear, and peripheral to the controversy, the tribunal may assume them without even mentioning them. *The problem cases are those in which the three variables pull against each other.*

DAVIS, ADMINISTRATIVE LAW OF THE SEVENTIES, § 15.00–8, at 375 (1976) (Emphasis added). These observations clearly describe many of the aspects of the [Section 18] Rulemaking and in the last sentences reach the facts of this case.

* * *

[T]he majority considers that one qualifies as an "impartial decisionmaker" unless he is shown by clear and convincing evidence to have an *unalterably closed mind* on matters critical to the children's television proceeding. This rule would establish a legal principle that evidence of bias and prejudice would not be disqualifying unless it could surmount a fence that is horse high, pig tight and bull strong. In my view that is too much protection for a biased decisionmaker. In a great many instances it would deprive the public of decisionmakers that are actually "impartial".

* * *

In addition to understating the Chairman's remarks, the majority does not attempt to actually portray them, or to apply them in all their verbiage, against the standard for disqualification that the majority establishes. This needs to be done.

I begin such analysis with the definite opinions expressed by the Chairman.

* * *

[T]he Chairman stated that the Commission has "not as a body yet approached the question of a remedy for the *evils* we see in children's advertising." So the Commission (we) had already determined that the advertising was "evil". Apparently the only issue was what remedy to apply.

Next, in his speech to the Action for Children's Television Research Conference at Boston on November 8, 1977, he referred to the "*moral myopia* of children's television advertising." (Emphasis added). He also stated that "advertisers *seize* on the child's trust and *exploit* it as a weakness for their gain." (Emphasis added). These remarks evidence definite conclusions, definite opinions and a biased slant. Later he stated: "using sophistication techniques like fantasy and animation, they [TV advertisers] *manipulate* children's attitudes". (Emphasis added). This also indicates a prejudgment of the purpose and intent of TV advertisers.

* * * Can any reasonable person contend that such remarks do not indicate that he has prejudged TV Advertising and decided that it *exploits* children?

* * *

[I]f the Notice of Rulemaking were truthful, so far as Chairman Pertschuk's views were concerned, it would have stated in substance:

> The Commission has decided to make a fundamental assault upon Children's Advertising on TV because we are convinced that it is *evil*, unfair and allowed solely because of the moral myopia of the public and the industry. We solicit comments as to whether it should be prohibited entirely or to some lesser degree.

* * *

It is true that legislators are not required to make findings of fact to support their legislation and that they cannot be disqualified by any court for bias, but there are other safeguards in the legislative process that compensate for the absence of such safeguards as are expressly imposed or implicit in the administrative process. First of all, legislators are *elected* by the voters of their district, and those in the House are elected for a relatively short term—only two years. They can be turned out very quickly if any bias they disclose offends their constituents. Secondly, there is a protection in the sheer size of Congress—535 members of the House and Senate—that implicitly diffuses bias and guarantees that impermissible bias of the individual members will not control. There is safety in numbers and a biased Congressman soon loses influence among the other members, if he ever acquired any. Also, the two house system and the Presidential veto are tremendous guarantees that legislation will not be the result of individual bias or even the impermissible bias of one house.

* * *

We cannot make Congressmen out of Commissioners any more than we could by our decision make errand boys for the court out of the members of the Nuclear Regulatory Commission.

NOTES AND QUESTIONS

1.   The opinions in *Association of National Advertisers* present different conceptions of the role of agency decisionmakers in the rulemaking process. Which vision do you consider to be more accurate? Which do you consider more desirable? Should agency rulemaking be a function of politics and policy making, or should agency rulemaking be more neutral? In thinking about your answers to these questions, consider the following observation from Jack M. Beerman, *Presidential Power in Transitions*, 83 BOSTON U. L. REV. 947, 1002 (2003):

> Agency heads are often chosen, at least in part, based on their previously expressed policy commitments. They make speeches, publish articles, and engage in other forms of communication in which they advocate for government action to deal with particular problems in particular ways. Courts have resisted efforts to disqualify politicians such as these from participating in rulemaking proceedings because disqualification would require a significant transformation in the administrative process. If such a rule were adopted, Presidents would be, at a minimum, seriously hampered in their ability to appoint activists to important agency positions.

2.   The majority opinion in *Association of National Advertisers* alludes to Congress's delegation of policy-making authority to the FTC and analogizes the FTC's rulemaking proceeding to the legislative process. Judge MacKinnon, by contrast, contends that FTC rulemaking is more of a hybrid, in part because the FTC's organic statute requires agency rules to be supported "by substantial evidence in the rulemaking record . . . taken as a whole," 15 U.S.C. § 57(e)(3)(A), and thus agency decisionmakers must include in the record any findings of fact upon which their actions are based.

3.   Courts consistently say that a decisionmaker in a rulemaking is disqualified due to bias if he has "an unalterably closed mind on a matter critical to the outcome of the proceeding," but no court has held that a decisionmaker in a rulemaking is disqualified. If you represented an advertiser of high sugar content cereals on Saturday morning cartoon shows, do you believe that you could "alter" Chairman Pertschuk's mind with respect to whether your client's advertising is good or bad? Do you believe that anyone could alter his mind on that matter? Suppose that Chairman Pertschuk had made a televised speech in which he said: "I have an unalterably closed mind on the morality and legality of advertising high sugar products on children's television programs." Would, or should, a court disqualify him from a rulemaking proceeding concerning that topic?

4.   The FTC also has jurisdiction over many antitrust disputes. Suppose that Chairman Pertschuk made a speech in which he stated: "I have an unalterable view that horizontal minimum price fixing is a violation of antitrust law that should be punished severely." Should he be disqualified from participating in a rulemaking to determine what practices violate antitrust law? Should he be disqualified from participating in an adjudication involving a firm that has allegedly violated antitrust law by allegedly engaging in horizontal minimum price-fixing? Should he be disqualified from participating in such an adjudication if he had said instead: "I have a tentative view that the defendant firm has engaged in

price-fixing, but my view on that issue is not unalterable"? How would you feel about an FTC Commissioner who made a speech in which he said: "I know nothing about the effects of horizontal minimum price-fixing, and I have no views on whether the practice is, or should be, a violation of antitrust law?"

DISCUSSION PROBLEM

The Occupational Safety and Health Administration (OSHA) exercised its statutory authority to issue regulations designed to protect workers from exposure to airborne lead in the workplace. Industry interests have challenged the new regulations on numerous grounds, including the claim that the Assistant Secretary of Labor responsible for overseeing OSHA's rulemaking efforts had prejudged the issues and possessed an unalterably closed mind regarding the matters addressed by the rulemaking proceeding. As evidence for its assertions, industry representatives have noted the following statements made by the Assistant Secretary in a speech to the United Steelworkers of America conference on occupational exposure to lead:

- "I can tell you about a plant within 300 miles of the city where workers are told to go to the hospital from work and receive therapy that would drag out poison and precious metals. And then they're sent back to be poisoned again. I bet I could go down to the hospitals of this city and find a worker that is undergoing kidney dialysis, and I'll bet you a dinner that some of those workers have been in lead plants."

- Regarding the economic feasibility of more stringent lead exposure standards, "I have told some people that I have never aspired to be an economist, but I tell you I can smell a phony issue when I see one. And to say that safety and health regulations are inflationary is phony. . . . I don't understand a society such as ours who is not willing to pay a dollar more for a battery to insure that workers do not have to pay for that battery with their lives."

- The speech went on to urge workers "to control their own destiny" by educating themselves about the lead problem, and called upon workers to support in imminent congressional elections candidates sympathetic to OSHA's goals.

Would you conclude that these statements reflect bias sufficient to invalidate OSHA's new regulations? Would it make a difference to your analysis whether the Assistant Secretary delivered the speech after she approved the regulation's final language, though before her boss, the Secretary of Labor, signed and released the final regulation?

3. EXEMPTIONS FROM APA RULEMAKING PROCEDURES

APA § 553 contains six exemptions from the informal rulemaking process. The significant procedural burdens that the courts have placed on agencies when they undertake notice-and-comment rulemaking increased the significance of those exemptions. As the time and resources required to issue a rule through informal rulemaking has increased, agencies have adopted a strategy of minimizing their use of rules subject to notice and comment requirements and maximizing their issuance of exempt rules. That ubiquitous agency strategy has produced a predictable backlash from regulated parties, who challenge in court many of the most important rules that agencies issue by relying on an exemption from informal rulemaking procedure.

A party who dislikes a rule that an agency claims to be exempt typically argues that the agency's rule is invalid for its failure to satisfy notice and comment requirements and that the rule does not fall within the scope of the exemption the agency claims applies. If the petitioner is able to persuade the court that the rule is not exempt, the rule is then a legal nullity; if the agency did not use informal rulemaking procedures to issue a rule, and no exemption applies, then the rule is procedurally invalid. The exemptions in APA § 553(b)(A) applicable to "interpretative rules" and to "general statements of policy" account for the vast majority of disputes regarding the scope of the exemptions from informal rulemaking procedures, but the other exemptions merit some discussion.

a.   SUBJECT MATTER EXEMPTIONS

Section 553(a) offers two exemptions based on subject matter. Those exemptions apply to rules that involve "(1) a military or foreign affairs function of the United States; or (2) a matter relating to agency management or personnel or to public property, loans, grants, benefits or contracts."

The military or foreign affairs exemption is not particularly controversial, and courts tend to interpret it broadly. Thus, for instance, one court held that this exemption applied to a rule that established a security zone around a naval installation, even though the rule regulated the conduct of civilians, because the rule was intended "to render safe and feasible the performance of a military function." *United States v. Ventura-Melendez*, 321 F.3d 230 (1st Cir. 2003).

By contrast, the agency management exemption has always been controversial. Many scholars consider it overbroad in some of its potential applications. Many of the rules that fall within the scope of this exemption as "relating to . . . public property, loans, grants, benefits, or contracts" are nevertheless subject to mandatory agency use of informal rulemaking procedure for one of two reasons. In some cases, when Congress enacted the statute that authorized the agency to issue such rules, Congress also included language explicitly requiring use of informal rulemaking procedures. In other cases, the agency itself issued a rule binding itself to use informal rulemaking when it issues these types of rules.

b.   THE GOOD CAUSE EXEMPTION

APA § 553(b)(B) exempts rules "when the agency finds (and incorporates the finding and a brief statement of reasons therefor in the rule issued) that notice and public procedure thereon are impracticable, unnecessary, or contrary to the public interest." This language raises both a procedural question and a substantive one, neither of which has been answered consistently by the courts.

Procedurally, the APA text quoted above on its face requires the agency to assert and justify its claim of good cause both explicitly and contemporaneously when it publishes the associated rule. Yet, the courts have not always been consistent in enforcing this requirement. For example, in *Bohner v. Daniels*, 243 F. Supp. 2d 1171, 1176 (D. Or. 2003), the Bureau of Prisons claimed that its statement that it was publishing a regulatory change with only post-promulgation notice and comment "in order to solicit public comment while continuing to provide consideration for early release to qualified inmates" constituted a good cause claim; the court found the language insufficient to invoke the exception. By contrast, other courts have deemed similarly nonexplicit language adequate as an assertion of good cause. *See, e.g., National Customs Brokers & Forwarders Ass'n of Am. v. United States*, 59 F.3d 1219, 1224 (Fed. Cir. 1995).

Even if a court finds a short and nonexplicit statement to be a valid declaration of good cause, however, the court may not deem a brief and nonexplicit good cause claim as providing adequate explanation to satisfy the APA. *See, e.g., Utility Solid Waste Activities Group v. EPA*, 236 F.3d 749, 754–55 (D.C. Cir. 2001). In other words, it may not be enough for an agency merely to claim good cause; rather, the language of APA § 553(b)(B) also requires an agency to justify its finding of good cause with both specificity and particularity. *See, e.g., NRDC v. Evans*, 316 F.3d 904, 912 (9th Cir. 2003). Courts thus generally consider brief and generic declarations of the need for immediate agency action or guidance as inadequate to sustain a finding of good cause. *See, e.g., Xin-Chang Zhang v. Slattery*, 55 F.3d 732, 746 (2d Cir. 1995). Although the length of an agency's explanation in support of its good cause finding is not necessarily determinative, the likelihood of an agency's success in claiming the good cause exception is often directly related to the amount of detail the agency offers.

Substantively, APA § 553(b)(B) allows for good cause where an agency finds the procedural requirements of informal rulemaking to be "impracticable, unnecessary, or contrary to the public interest." Because this language uses the disjunctive "or," the contemporaneously-written Attorney General's Manual on the Administrative Procedure Act and a number of judicial opinions assume that an agency might establish good cause pursuant to three separate and distinct justifications. According to the Attorney General's Manual, notice and comment are impracticable when "due and timely execution of [an agency's] functions would be impeded by" those procedures; unnecessary if the rule is "a minor rule or amendment in which the public is not particularly interested"; and contrary to the public interest if "the interest of the public would be defeated by any requirement of advance notice." U.S. Dep't of Justice, Attorney General's Manual on the Administrative Procedure Act 30–31 (1947).

In sum, the good cause exception exists primarily to give agencies flexibility to deal with emergencies and fix typographical errors, and to allow agencies to impose rules in advance of public notice on those rare occasions in which advance notice would undermine the rule itself. Courts thus sometimes uphold agency invocations of the good cause exemption and sustain temporary legislative rules in emergency situations or when a statutory deadline makes it impossible for the agency to use the notice and comment process before it issues a legislative rule. For example, the D.C. Circuit sustained an agency assertion of good cause for airline pilot certification regulations in the months after terrorists hijacked several commercial airplanes and used them to attack the World Trade Center and the Pentagon on September 11, 2001. *See Jifry v. FAA*, 370 F.3d 1174, 1179–80 (D.C. Cir. 2004). Similarly, the Ninth Circuit upheld an agency's good cause claim for air safety regulations in response to a wave of fatal air tour accidents. *See Hawaii Helicopter Operators Ass'n v. FAA*, 51 F.3d 212, 214 (9th Cir. 1995).

Nevertheless, as the following case exemplifies, courts are often stingy and demanding in their interpretations of the good cause exemption.

Mack Trucks, Inc. v. Environmental Protection Agency

682 F.3d 87 (D.C. Cir. 2012).

■ Brown, Circuit Judge:

In January 2012, EPA promulgated an interim final rule (IFR) to permit manufacturers of heavy-duty diesel engines to pay nonconformance penalties (NCPs) in exchange for the right to sell noncompliant engines. EPA took this action without providing formal notice or an opportunity for comment, invoking the "good cause" exception provided in the Administrative Procedure Act (APA). Because we find that none of the statutory criteria for "good cause" are satisfied, we vacate the IFR.

I

In 2001, pursuant to Section 202 of the Clean Air Act ("the Act"), EPA enacted a rule requiring a 95 percent reduction in the emissions of nitrogen oxide from heavy-duty diesel engines. 66 Fed. Reg. 5,002 (Jan. 18, 2001). By delaying the effective date until 2010, EPA gave industry nine years to innovate the necessary new technologies. (EPA and manufacturers refer to the rule as the "2010 NOx standard." 77 Fed. Reg. 4,678, 4,681 (Jan. 31, 2012).) During those nine years, most manufacturers of heavy-duty diesel engines, including Petitioners, invested hundreds of millions of dollars to develop a technology called "selective catalytic reduction." This technology converts nitrogen oxide into nitrogen and water by using a special aftertreatment system and a diesel-based chemical agent. With selective catalytic reduction, manufacturers have managed to meet the 2010 NOx standard.

One manufacturer, Navistar, took a different approach. For its domestic sales, Navistar opted for a form of "exhaust gas recirculation," but this technology proved less successful; Navistar's engines do not meet the 2010 NOx standard. All else being equal, Navistar would therefore be unable to sell these engines in the United States—unless, of course, it adopted a different, compliant technology. But for the last few years, Navistar has been able to lawfully forestall that result and continue selling its noncompliant engines by using banked emission credits. Simply put, it bet on finding a way to make exhaust gas recirculation a feasible and compliant technology before its finite supply of credits ran out.

Navistar's day of reckoning is fast approaching: its supply of credits is dwindling and its engines remain noncompliant. In October 2011, Navistar informed EPA that it would run out of credits sometime in 2012. EPA, estimating that Navistar "might have as little as three to four months" of available credits before it "would be forced to stop introducing its engines into commerce," leapt into action. Without formal notice and comment, EPA hurriedly promulgated the IFR on January 31, 2012, pursuant to its authority under 42 U.S.C. § 7525(g), to make NCPs available to Navistar.[3]

To issue NCPs under its regulations, EPA must first find that a new emissions standard is "more stringent" or "more difficult to achieve" than a prior standard, that "substantial work will be required to meet the standard for which the NCP is offered," and that "there is likely to be a technological laggard." 40 C.F.R. § 86.1103–87. EPA found these criteria were met. The 2010 NOx standard permits a significantly smaller amount of emissions than the prior standard, so the first criterion is easily satisfied. As for the second, EPA simply said that, because compliant engines (like Petitioners') use new technologies to be compliant, "[i]t is therefore logical to conclude . . . that substantial work was required to meet the emission standard." 77 Fed. Reg. at 4,681. Finally, EPA determined that there was likely to be a technological laggard because "an engine manufacturer [Navistar] . . . has not yet met the requirements for technological reasons" and because "it is a reasonable possibility that this manufacturer may not be able to comply for technological reasons." *Id.*

Having determined that NCPs are appropriate, EPA proceeded to set the amount of the penalty and establish the "upper limit" of emissions permitted even by a penalty-paying manufacturer. The IFR provides that manufacturers may sell heavy-duty diesel engines in model years 2012 and 2013 as long as they pay a penalty of $1,919 per engine and as long as the engines emit fewer than 0.50 grams of nitrogen oxide per horsepower-hour. This "upper limit" thus permits emissions of up to two-and-a-half times the 0.20 grams permitted under the 2010 NOx standard with which Navistar is meant to comply and with which Petitioners do comply.

EPA explained its decision to forego notice and comment procedures by invoking the "good cause" exception of the APA, which provides that an agency may dispense with formal notice and comment procedures if the agency "for good cause finds . . . that notice and public procedure thereon are impracticable, unnecessary, or contrary to the public interest," 5 U.S.C. § 553(b)(B). EPA cited four factors to show the existence of good cause: (1) notice and comment would mean "the possibility of an engine manufacturer [Navistar] . . . being unable to certify a complete product line of engines for model year 2012 and/or 2013," (2) EPA was only "amending limited provisions in existing NCP regulations," (3) the IFR's "duration is limited," and (4) "there is no risk to the public interest in allowing manufacturers to certify using NCPs

---

[3] The NCP is theoretically available to any heavy-duty diesel engine manufacturer, but by discussing only Navistar's predicament in its brief and in the IFR, EPA all but concedes that it issued the IFR for solely Navistar's benefit. Navistar similarly averred in its motion to intervene that "there is no doubt that the engine manufacturer described in EPA's Interim Final Rule is Navistar."

before the point at which EPA could make them available through a full notice-and-comment rulemaking."

* * *

III

* * *

B

Because the Act does not contain any notice-and-comment requirement applicable to the IFR, EPA may invoke the APA's good cause exception. We must therefore determine whether notice and comment were "impracticable, unnecessary, or contrary to the public interest." 5 U.S.C. § 553(b)(B). * * *

We have repeatedly made clear that the good cause exception "is to be narrowly construed and only reluctantly countenanced." *Util. Solid Waste Activities Grp. v. EPA,* 236 F.3d 749, 754 (D.C. Cir. 2001); *Tenn. Gas Pipeline Co. v. FERC,* 969 F.2d 1141, 1144 (D.C.Cir.1992); *New Jersey v. EPA,* 626 F.2d 1038, 1045 (D.C.Cir.1980); *see also Jifry v. FAA,* 370 F.3d 1174, 1179 (D.C. Cir. 2004) ("The exception excuses notice and comment in emergency situations, or where delay could result in serious harm."); *Am. Fed. of Gov't Emps. v. Block,* 655 F.2d 1153, 1156 (D.C.Cir.1981) ("As the legislative history of the APA makes clear, moreover, the exceptions at issue here are not 'escape clauses' that may be arbitrarily utilized at the agency's whim. Rather, use of these exceptions by administrative agencies should be limited to emergency situations. . . .").

First, an agency may invoke the impracticability of notice and comment. 5 U.S.C. § 553(b)(B). Our inquiry into impracticability "is inevitably fact- or context-dependent," *Mid-Tex Electric Coop. v. FERC,* 822 F.2d 1123, 1132 (D.C.Cir.1987). For the sake of comparison, we have suggested agency action could be sustained on this basis if, for example, air travel security agencies would be unable to address threats posing "a possible imminent hazard" to aircraft, persons, and property within the United States," *Jifry,* 370 F.3d at 1179, or if "a safety investigation shows that a new safety rule must be put in place immediately," *Util. Solid Waste Activities Grp.,* 236 F.3d at 755 (ultimately finding that not to be the case and rejecting the agency's argument), or if a rule was of "life-saving importance" to mine workers in the event of a mine explosion, *Council of the S. Mountains, Inc. v. Donovan,* 653 F.2d 573, 581 (D.C.Cir.1981) (describing that circumstance as "a special, possibly unique, case").

By contrast, the context of this case reveals that the only purpose of the IFR is, as Petitioners put it, "to rescue a lone manufacturer from the folly of its own choices." The IFR does not stave off any imminent threat to the environment or safety or national security. It does not remedy any real emergency at all, save the "emergency" facing Navistar's bottom line. Indeed, all EPA points to is "the serious harm to Navistar and its employees" and "the ripple effect on its customers and suppliers," but the same could be said for any manufacturer facing a standard with which its product does not comply.

EPA claims the harm to Navistar and the resulting up- and down-stream impacts should still be enough under our precedents. The only case on which it relies, however, is one in which an entire industry and its customers were imperiled. *See Am. Fed. of Gov't Emps.*, 655 F.2d at 1157. Navistar's plight is not even remotely close to such a weighty, systemic interest, especially since it is a consequence brought about by Navistar's own choice to continue to pursue a technology which, so far, is noncompliant. At bottom, EPA's approach would give agencies "good cause" under the APA every time a manufacturer in a regulated field felt a new regulation imposed some degree of economic hardship, even if the company could have avoided that hardship had it made different business choices. This is both nonsensical and in direct tension with our longstanding position that the exception should be "narrowly construed and only reluctantly countenanced." *Util. Solid Waste Activities Grp.*, 236 F.3d at 754.

Second, an agency may claim notice and comment were "unnecessary." 5 U.S.C. § 553(b)(B). This prong of the good cause inquiry is "confined to those situations in which the administrative rule is a routine determination, insignificant in nature and impact, and inconsequential to the industry and to the public." *Util. Solid Waste Activities Grp.*, 236 F.3d at 755. This case does not present such a situation. Just as in *Utility Solid Waste,* the IFR is a rule "about which these members of the public [the petitioners] were greatly interested," so notice and comment were not "unnecessary." *Id.* EPA argues that since the IFR is just an interim rule, good cause is satisfied because "the interim status of the challenged rule is a significant factor" in determining whether notice and comment are unnecessary. 77 Fed. Reg. at 4,680 (finding good cause because the IFR's "duration is limited"). But we held, in the very case on which EPA relies, that "the limited nature of the rule cannot in itself justify a failure to follow notice and comment procedures." *Mid-Tex Electric Coop.*, 822 F.2d at 1132. And for good reason: if a rule's interim nature were enough to satisfy the element of good cause, then "agencies could issue interim rules of limited effect for any plausible reason, irrespective of the degree of urgency" and "the good cause exception would soon swallow the notice and comment rule." *Tenn. Gas Pipeline*, 969 F.2d at 1145.

EPA's remaining argument that notice and comment were "unnecessary" is that the IFR was essentially ministerial: EPA simply input numbers into an NCP-setting formula without substantially amending the NCP regime. But even if it were true that EPA arrived at the level of the penalty and the upper limit in this way (and Petitioners strenuously argue that EPA actually *amended* the NCP regime in order to arrive at the upper limit level in the IFR[5]), that argument does not account for how EPA determined NCPs were warranted in this case in the first place—another finding to which Petitioners object. EPA's decision to implement an NCP, perhaps even more than the level of the penalty itself, is far from inconsequential or routine, and EPA does not even attempt to defend it as such.

Finally, an agency may invoke the good cause exception if providing notice and comment would be contrary to the public interest.

---

[5] EPA admits in its brief that "Petitioners are correct that in past rules, EPA based the penalty rates [on certain factors]" and that "that was not the case for the Interim Rule."

5 U.S.C. § 553(b)(B). In the IFR, EPA says it has good cause since "there is no risk to the public interest in allowing manufacturers to [use] NCPs before the point at which EPA could make them available through a full notice-and-comment rulemaking," but this misstates the statutory criterion. The question is not whether *dispensing* with notice and comment would be contrary to the public interest, but whether *providing* notice and comment would be contrary to the public interest. By improperly framing the question in this way, the IFR inverts the presumption, apparently suggesting that notice and comment is usually unnecessary. We cannot permit this subtle malformation of the APA. The public interest prong of the good cause exception is met only in the rare circumstance when ordinary procedures—generally presumed to serve the public interest—would in fact harm that interest. It is appropriately invoked when the timing and disclosure requirements of the usual procedures would defeat the purpose of the proposal—if, for example, "announcement of a proposed rule would enable the sort of financial manipulation the rule sought to prevent." *Util. Solid Waste Activities Grp.*, 236 F.3d at 755. In such a circumstance, notice and comment could be dispensed with "in order to prevent the amended rule from being evaded." *Id.* In its brief, EPA belatedly frames the inquiry correctly, but goes on to offer nothing more than a recapitulation of the harm to Navistar and the associated "ripple effects." To the extent this is an argument not preserved by EPA in the IFR, we cannot consider it, *see SEC v. Chenery Corp.*, 332 U.S. 194, 196 (1947), but regardless, it is nothing more than a reincarnation of the impracticability argument we have already rejected.

IV

Because EPA lacked good cause to dispense with required notice and comment procedures, we conclude the IFR must be vacated without reaching Petitioners' alternative arguments. We are aware EPA is currently in the process of promulgating a final rule—with the benefit of notice and comment—on this precise issue. However, we strongly reject EPA's claim that the challenged errors are harmless simply because of the pendency of a properly-noticed final rule. Were that true, agencies would have no use for the APA when promulgating any interim rules. So long as the agency eventually opened a final rule for comment, every error in every interim rule—no matter how egregious—could be excused as a harmless error.

* * *

For now, therefore, we simply hold that EPA lacked good cause for not providing formal notice-and-comment rulemaking, and accordingly vacate the IFR and remand for further proceedings.

DISCUSSION PROBLEM

Section 504 of the Rehabilitation Act of 1973 provides that "[no] otherwise qualified handicapped individual in the United States . . . shall, solely by reason of his handicap, be excluded from the participation in, be denied the benefits of, or be subjected to discrimination under any program or activity receiving Federal financial assistance. . . ." 29 U.S.C. § 794.

In 1982, a child was born in Bloomington, Indiana, with Down's syndrome as well as a surgically-correctible blockage in his digestive tract. His parents refused to consent to the surgery to correct the blockage, and the child, who came to be known as "Baby Doe," died a few days later. The incident gave rise to nationwide controversy about the ethics of withholding life-sustaining medical treatment from newborn infants with severe physical or mental defects.

Approximately one year later, the Secretary of Health and Human Services ("HHS") promulgated an "interim-final" rule to address the issues in the Baby Doe incident. Hospitals were directed to post conspicuous notices declaring that discriminatory denial of food or care to handicapped infants violated federal law. The notices invited anyone with knowledge of such discrimination to call a toll-free "hotline" at HHS to report the violation. Hospitals were also directed to provide access to their records and facilities to officials investigating alleged discrimination of the "Baby Doe" variety. Access would have to be provided outside of normal business hours if HHS officials deemed such access necessary to protect the life or health of a handicapped infant.

The Secretary issued the interim-final rule without notice and comment. Explaining her failure to allow prior notice and comment on the rule, the Secretary noted that HHS investigators already had authority to obtain access to hospital records and facilities. The extension of this authority to compulsory access outside of normal business hours was a "minor technical change and necessary to meet emergency situations." More generally, she said, "[a]ll modifications made in the interim final rule are necessary to protect life from imminent harm. Any delay would leave lives at risk." The regulation was set to go into effect in fifteen days, which the Secretary estimated was the minimum time needed to set up the hotline apparatus.

After the interim-final rule went into effect, the Secretary pursued the notice-and-comment process of APA § 553. After the comment period, the Secretary issued a final rule that was essentially the same as the interim-final rule. Did the Secretary validly assert good cause in promulgating her interim-final rule?

———————

Although the courts regularly claim their intent to construe the good cause exception narrowly, agencies regularly claim good cause to issue rules—sometimes labeled as "interim-final" or "temporary"—without notice and comment. According to a 2012 report issued by the General Accounting Office, about 35 percent of the 568 major rules and 44 percent of the roughly 30,000 nonmajor rules adopted between 2003 and 2010 lacked notice and comment. Agencies asserted the good cause exception for 77 percent of major rules and 61 percent of nonmajor rules published without those procedures. *See* UNITED STATES GENERAL ACCOUNTING OFFICE, REPORT TO CONGRESSIONAL REQUESTERS, FEDERAL RULEMAKING: AGENCIES COULD TAKE ADDITIONAL STEPS TO RESPOND TO PUBLIC COMMENTS, GAO-13-21 (Dec. 2012). Agencies often request comments on these rules after they are issued, and on many occasions issued follow-up rules or otherwise responded to post-promulgation comments received. But they do not always do so. As the GAO further observed,

When agencies do not respond to comments requested, the public does not know whether the agency considered their comments, or if it intends to change the rule. As the courts have recognized, the opportunity to comment is meaningless unless the agency responds to significant points raised by the public. The courts have not consistently resolved the appropriate remedy for cases in which they reject an agency's claim of good cause on behalf of an interim-final or temporary rule, but the agency during the course of litigation has acted to "finalize" the rule through consideration of postpromulgation comments. In some cases, courts have held that the procedural invalidity of an interim-final or temporary rule likewise renders a succeeding final regulation invalid. *See, e.g., Air Transp. Ass'n of Am. v. Department of Transp.*, 900 F.2d 369, 379–80 (D.C. Cir. 1990). Allowing an agency to cure the inadequacy of a good cause claim through postpromulgation notice and comment arguably eviscerates the APA's rulemaking requirements. *See, e.g., NRDC v. EPA*, 683 F.2d 752, 768 (3d Cir. 1982). In other cases, however, courts have refused to invalidate final regulations on such grounds upon finding that the agency's handling of postpromulgation comments in the process of finalizing the regulations demonstrated an "open mind." *See, e.g., Advocates for Highway & Auto Safety v. Federal Highway Admin.*, 28 F.3d 1288, 1292 (D.C. Cir. 1994). Courts are often reluctant to invalidate agency regulations if they do not believe that additional procedures would have altered the outcome. The following case reflects one court's recent effort to resolve this tension.

United States v. Johnson

632 F.3d 912 (5th Cir. 2011).

■ HIGGINBOTHAM, CIRCUIT JUDGE:

Defendant-Appellant Undra Demetrius Johnson appeals his conviction under 18 U.S.C. § 2250(a) for failure to register as a sex offender under the Sex Offender Registration and Notification Act ("SORNA"). He challenges the validity of the Act and the decision of the Attorney General to apply it to persons whose convictions for sex crimes predate its enactment.

I.

As part of a plea agreement, Johnson stipulated to the relevant facts. In 1995, Johnson was convicted in a Mississippi court for gratification of lust, a sex offense. Johnson was sentenced to eight years in prison, four years suspended. Prior to his release in May 1999, Johnson signed an Acknowledgment of Convicted Sex Offender's Duty to Register under Mississippi law. In 2002 and 2004, Johnson signed two additional Mississippi state forms acknowledging his duty to register. In 2005, Johnson moved from Mississippi to Iowa and signed Iowa's Sex Offender Registry Notification of Registration Requirement form. In January 2008, Johnson returned to Mississippi and failed to register as a sex offender with the State of Mississippi.

On January 22, 2009, Johnson was indicted on one count of violating 18 U.S.C. § 2250(a) by traveling in interstate commerce and knowingly failing to register and update a registration in accordance with SORNA. * * * Johnson then entered a guilty plea pursuant to a plea agreement * * *. * * *

II.

On July 27, 2006, President George W. Bush signed into law the Adam Walsh Child Protection and Safety Act of 2006. Title I of the Act includes SORNA, which "establishes a comprehensive national system for the registration of [sex] offenders," requiring all sex offenders to register their residence and place of employment using state-based registries.

* * *

A separate provision of SORNA created a federal criminal offense for traveling interstate and failing to register as a sex offender.

* * *

* * * [T]he Attorney General began enforcing SORNA as though it provided immediate penalties for sex offenders who failed to register. Many defendants challenged SORNA's application to pre-enactment offenders. In response, on February 28, 2007, seven months after SORNA's enactment, the Attorney General issued an interim regulation stating that SORNA's requirements "apply to all sex offenders, including sex offenders convicted of the offense for which registration is required prior to the enactment of that Act."[9] The Attorney General noted that he was issuing the rule to foreclose the argument that SORNA did not apply to defendants with convictions before the Act's enactment, regardless of whether the statute on its face included them or not. The regulation was issued without a notice-and-comment period and without a thirty-day waiting period, both of which are mandated by the Administrative Procedure Act ("APA"). The Attorney General relied upon the good cause exception in the APA to excuse the lack of notice-and-comment and waiting period. He published a justification for good cause at the time the rule was issued:

> The immediate effectiveness of this rule is necessary to eliminate any possible uncertainty about the applicability of the Act's requirements—and related means of enforcement, including criminal liability under 18 U.S.C. 2250 for sex offenders who knowingly fail to register as required—to sex offenders whose predicate convictions predate the enactment of SORNA. Delay in the implementation of this rule would impede the effective registration of such sex offenders and would impair immediate efforts to protect the public from sex offenders who fail to register through prosecution and the imposition of criminal sanctions. The resulting practical dangers include the commission of additional sexual assaults and child sexual abuse or exploitation offenses by sex offenders that could have been prevented had local authorities and the

---

[9] Applicability of the Sex Offender Registration and Notification Act, 72 Fed. Reg. 8894, 8897 (Feb. 28, 2007); *see* 28 C.F.R. pt. 72 (2008).

community been aware of their presence, in addition to greater difficulty in apprehending perpetrators who have not been registered and tracked as provided by SORNA. This would thwart the legislative objective of "protect[ing] the public from sex offenders and offenders against children" by establishing "a comprehensive national system for the registration of those offenders," SORNA § 102, because a substantial class of sex offenders could evade the Act's registration requirements and enforcement mechanisms during the pendency of a proposed rule and delay in the effectiveness of a final rule.

It would accordingly be contrary to the public interest to adopt this rule with the prior notice and comment period normally required under 5 U.S.C. 553(b) or with the delayed effective date normally required under 5 U.S.C. 553(d).

The rule took immediate effect. The Attorney General accepted post-promulgation comments through April 30, 2007, but did not respond to comments in the *Federal Register*.[13] The regulation published in the *Code of Federal Regulations* was identical to the interim rule. On May 30, 2007, the Attorney General issued a notice of rulemaking for the full regulatory implementation of SORNA. This proposal included a subsection on the applicability of SORNA to pre-enactment offenders, noting that the Attorney General had addressed this issue in its earlier rulemaking. Nevertheless, the Attorney General received public comments on SORNA's retroactivity and responded to those comments in the publication of the final SORNA regulations, which were issued and made effective on July 2, 2008.

* * *

VI.

Under the APA, agencies issuing rules must publish notice of proposed rulemaking in the *Federal Register* and "shall give interested persons an opportunity to participate in the rule making" by allowing submission of comments. In addition, the APA requires that publication of a substantive rule "shall be made not less than 30 days before its effective date." The APA provides that both of these requirements may be bypassed if "good cause" exists. The exception states that notice is not required "when the agency for good cause finds . . . that notice and public procedure thereon are impracticable, unnecessary, or contrary to the public interest." In executing his authority under § 16913, the Attorney General failed to comply with either the notice-and-comment procedures or the thirty-day notice provision, relying on the "good cause" exception.

* * *

Here, we do not find the Attorney General's reasons for bypassing the APA's notice-and-comment and thirty day provisions persuasive.

---

[13] In December 2010, the Attorney General took steps to convert the "interim" rule from February 2007 to a "final" rule, which included responding to comments presumably submitted between February and April 2007. The Attorney General noted that these comments "were similar to comments received on the portions of the proposed SORNA Guidelines" from May 2007. *See* 75 Fed. Reg. 81,849, 81,850 (Dec. 29, 2010).

The Attorney General asserted that "[d]elay in the implementation of this rule would impede the effective registration of . . . sex offenders and would impair immediate efforts to protect the public." He argued that delayed implementation would result in more sex offenses by "sex offenders that could have been prevented had local authorities and the community been aware of their presence." Yet the interim rule did not distribute new information to local authorities. Rather, it authorized the federal government to use SORNA to prosecute sex offenders already in violation of state registration laws. Local authorities could have prosecuted most of these offenders before the rule. Moreover, Congress could have expressly waived the APA procedural requirements in SORNA if it feared those requirements would produce significant harm or excessive delay. Congress balanced the costs and benefits of an immediately effective rule against a more deliberate rulemaking process, and it favored the latter. Without good cause, we must enforce Congress's choice in favor of the traditional, deliberative rulemaking process.

The Attorney General argued that foregoing notice and comment was "necessary to eliminate any possible uncertainty about the applicability of the Act's requirements" to pre-SORNA offenders.[98] However, "desire to provide immediate guidance, without more, does not suffice for good cause."[99] Moreover, the goal of reducing uncertainty is undercut by the request for post-promulgation comments, which could have resulted in a rule change. "[T]he possibility of an alteration to the interim rule after its promulgation *increases* rather than eliminates uncertainty."[100] Traditional notice-and-comment process with promptly promulgated final rules was the clearest path to clarify the Act.

Nor does accepting post-promulgation comments excuse compliance with APA procedures. We have previously found that parties will have a greater opportunity for influencing agency decision making if they participate at an early stage, "when the agency is more likely to give real consideration to alternative ideas."[101] If we allowed post-promulgation comments to suffice in this case, "we would make the provisions of § 553 virtually unenforceable."[102]

Lastly, the Attorney General's rule applied federal criminal liabilities to pre-enactment sex offenders. This is not a rule of minimal import. "Certainly, a criminal prosecution founded on an agency rule should be held to the strict letter of the APA."[103] The strict letter requires notice and comment unless there is good cause. Here, the Attorney General has not sufficiently stated that following APA procedures would have been "impracticable, unnecessary, or contrary to the public interest." He did not have good cause for failing to publish

---

[98] 72 Fed. Reg. at 8896.

[99] [*United States v. Cain*, 583 F.3d 408, 421 (6th Cir. 2009)] (quoting *Mobil Oil Corp. v. Dep't of Energy*, 610 F.2d 796, 803 (Temp. Emer. Ct. App. 1979)) (internal quotation marks omitted).

[100] *Gould,* 568 F.3d at 479 (Michael, J., dissenting).

[101] [*U.S. Steel Corp. v. EPA*, 595 F.2d 207, 214 (5th Cir. 1979).]

[102] *U.S. Steel,* 595 F.2d at 214.

[103] *United States v. Picciotto,* 875 F.2d 345, 346 (D.C. Cir.1989).

the rule thirty days before its effective date nor did good cause exist to bypass the notice-and-comment requirements.

VII.

"In administrative law, as in federal civil and criminal litigation, there is a harmless error rule."[104] The APA demands that courts reviewing agency decisions under the Act "[take] due account . . . of the rule of prejudicial error."[105] In this circuit, an administrative body's APA deficiency is not prejudicial "only 'when [it] is one that clearly had no bearing on the procedure used or the substance of decision reached.' "[106] Determining whether an APA deficiency is harmless demands a case-specific inquiry involving "an estimation of the likelihood that the result would have been different, . . . and a hesitancy to generalize too broadly about particular kinds of errors when the specific factual circumstances in which the error arises may well make all the difference."[107] Here, the Attorney General's regulations failed to comply with two separate APA procedures—publishing the rule at least thirty days before the effective date and following notice-and-comment procedures prior to promulgation. We find both errors to be harmless in the particular circumstances of this case.

If the effective date of the interim rule had been in compliance with the APA's thirty-day notice provision, the rule would have been effective on March 30, 2007. If Johnson engaged in interstate travel and failed to register after that date, his actions would properly violate the rule regardless of whether the Attorney General had good cause to bypass the thirty-day notice. Here, Johnson traveled across state lines in January 2008. He was not indicted until January 22, 2009. Even if the Attorney General lacked good cause to waive § 553(d), Johnson was not prejudiced.

Whether Johnson was prejudiced by the lack of notice-and-comment period does not yield so quick an answer. In *United States Steel Corp. v. EPA*, we held that to apply harmless error it must be clear that the petitioner was not prejudiced by APA deficiencies.[108] There, the EPA failed to provide notice-and-comment for air-quality regulations limiting Alabama steel plants' expansion opportunities. The EPA only provided for post-promulgation comments. We held that post-promulgation comments were an inadequate substitute for APA procedures. Moreover, the agency did not have good cause to bypass notice-and-comment nor could it rely on harmless error, as we could not assume the petitioners were not prejudiced.

U.S. Steel did not, however, preclude inquiry into whether petitioners were prejudiced by an agency's procedure, nor did it assert that an error affecting procedure could never be harmless. Rather, a court must determine whether it is clear that the lack of notice and comment did not prejudice the petitioner.

---

[104]   *Nat'l Ass'n of Home Builders v. Defenders of Wildlife,* 551 U.S. 644, 659–60 (2007) (quoting *PDK Labs., Inc. v. Drug Enforcement Admin.,* 362 F.3d 786, 799 (D.C.Cir. 2004)).

[105]   5 U.S.C. § 706.

[106]   *U.S. Steel Corp. v. EPA,* 595 F.2d 207, 215 (5th Cir. 1979) (quoting *Braniff Airways, Inc. v. C.A.B.,* 379 F.2d 453, 466 (D.C.Cir. 1967)).

[107]   *Shinseki v. Sanders,* 129 S.Ct. 1696, 1707 (2009).

[108]   595 F.2d at 215.

The purpose of notice-and-comment rulemaking is to "assure[] fairness and mature consideration of rules having a substantial impact on those regulated."[109] The process allows the agency to "educate itself before adopting a final order."[110] In addition, public notice requires the agency to disclose its thinking on matters that will affect regulated parties.[111] These goals, however, may be achieved in cases where the agency's decision-making process "centered on the identical substantive claims"[112] as those proposed by the party asserting error, even if there were APA deficiencies. It follows that when a party's claims were considered, even if notice was inadequate, the challenging party may not have been prejudiced.[113]

An overreaching harmless error doctrine would allow the agency to inappropriately "avoid the necessity of publishing a notice of a proposed rule and perhaps, most important, [the agency] would not be obliged to set forth a statement of the basis and purpose of the rule, which needs to take account of the major comments—and often is a major focus of judicial review."[114] These concerns support the limited role of the harmless error doctrine in administrative law.[115] With respect to SORNA, we can be confident that Johnson was not prejudiced by the Attorney General's failure to provide notice, in part because the interim rule publication addressed counter-arguments and set forth the basis and purpose of the rule.

While the Attorney General's preamble to the interim rule did not articulate good cause for avoiding APA rulemaking procedures, it did thoroughly engage the issues and challenges inherent in the regulation. Public comment is preferred and ordinarily is required to draw out counter-arguments. Here, the Attorney General was able to address objections in the interim rulemaking itself. After the statute was enacted but before the rule was issued, the Attorney General believed he had authority to prosecute pre-enactment offenders for failing to register. While we have disagreed with the Attorney General's interpretation of SORNA, in the course of those prosecutions, defense counsel for various defendants argued that SORNA should not apply retroactively[116]—the same argument Johnson makes here. The Attorney General considered those arguments and responded to them in his preamble to the interim rule, stating that the rule was being issued because sex offenders with pre-enactment convictions had "devise[d] arguments that SORNA [was] inapplicable to them."[117] He rejected those arguments, concluding that principles of ex post facto were not apt because the registration requirements were non-punitive regulatory

---

[109] *Pennzoil Co. v. Fed. Energy Regulatory Comm'n,* 645 F.2d 360, 371 (5th Cir.1981).

[110] *Id.*

[111] *See United States v. Dean,* 604 F.3d 1275, 1278 (11th Cir. 2010).

[112] *Friends of Iwo Jima v. Nat'l Capital Planning Comm'n,* 176 F.3d 768, 774 (4th Cir. 1999).

[113] *Id.*

[114] *Sugar Cane Growers Co–Op of Fl. v. Veneman,* 289 F.3d 89, 96–97 (D.C.Cir. 2002).

[115] *See U.S. Steel,* 595 F.2d at 215.

[116] *See, e.g., United States v. Madera,* 528 F.3d 852, 854 (11th Cir. 2008) (describing the facts of the case and noting that the defendant moved from New York to Florida in June 2006—prior to the enactment of SORNA, and was arrested for violating SORNA in October 2006—prior to the issuance of the Attorney General's interim rule). * * *

[117] 72 Fed. Reg. 8894, 8896 (Feb. 28, 2007).

measures. Further, the preamble noted that failing to include pre-enactment offenders under SORNA "would thwart the legislative objective."[118] Thus, the error in failing to solicit public comment before issuing the rule was not prejudicial because the Attorney General nevertheless considered the arguments Johnson has asserted and responded to those arguments during the interim rulemaking. There is no suggestion that, if given the opportunity to comment, Johnson would have presented an argument the Attorney General did not consider in issuing the interim rule.

Other circumstances present also point to harmless error. For example, unlike the complex regulatory decision of air-quality designations addressed in *U.S. Steel,* the Attorney General's interim rulemaking here involved a yes or no decision—whether or not to apply SORNA's registration requirements to pre-enactment offenders. This rulemaking starkly contrasts with the vast majority of agency rulemaking, which produces nuanced and detailed regulations that greatly benefit from expert and regulated entity participation.[119] Under those conditions, a finding of harmless error for inadequate notice-and-comment procedures may be rare, but as the Supreme Court has instructed, we should be hesitant to generalize results based on the kind of error. Instead we must focus on the factual circumstances that point to the proper outcome.[120] Given the binary decision made by the Attorney General, harmless error is more fitting under these circumstances than in other agency rulemaking.

Moreover, that the final rulemaking process with full APA comment did not change the Attorney General's decision cannot be ignored.[121] Although it is not completely clear that the later invitation for comment extended to retroactivity as a free-standing issue, that rulemaking process did include retroactivity as part of its regulatory package. The comments received on retroactivity did not sway the Attorney General. Rather, the position of the earlier interim final rule was incorporated into the final publication of the full guidelines promulgated in July 2008.

Finally, Johnson neither proposes comments he would have made during a comment period nor did he choose to involve himself in the post-promulgation comment period. Johnson does not allege that he participated in the Attorney General's subsequent rulemaking process that crafted regulations regarding the more detailed provisions of SORNA, in which the Attorney General also considered the retroactivity of SORNA, free of APA error.[122] While Johnson's

---

[118]   *Id.* at 8897.

[119]   *See United States v. Dean,* 604 F.3d 1275, 1288–89 (11th Cir.2010) (Wilson, J., concurring). The initial rulemaking also contrasts with the Attorney General's later SORNA rulemaking that delved into more detailed provisions and applications.

[120]   *Shinseki,* 129 S.Ct. at 1707.

[121]   This court continues to recognize the limitations of post-promulgation comments, as such comments do not ensure affected parties have an opportunity to influence agency decision-making at an early stage. *See U.S. Steel,* 595 F.2d at 214. Johnson's case is unique because his views were represented in the prosecutions that took place well before the interim rule was published. Those views were reiterated during the comment period offered for the final regulations and remained unpersuasive.

[122]   *See* 73 Fed.Reg. 38,030, 38,036 (July 2, 2008). In response to comments about retroactivity, the Attorney General stated that "no changes have been made in the final

participation in these alternate comment forums is not required to find prejudice, his lack of involvement in all stages of administrative decision-making points to the conclusion that Johnson was not practically harmed by the Attorney General's APA failings.[123] Moreover, Johnson had constructive notice that the Attorney General would apply SORNA to pre-enactment offenders when the Attorney General issued a *Federal Register* notice for the later rulemaking in May 2007,[124] before Johnson crossed interstate lines and failed to register.

In *U.S. Steel,* we held that absence of prejudice "must be clear" before applying harmless error.[125] Because the Attorney General's rulemaking process addressed the same issues raised by Johnson and because Johnson "makes no showing that the outcome of the process would have differed . . . had notice been at its meticulous best,"[126] we find it is clear that the Attorney General's APA violations were harmless error.

NOTES AND QUESTIONS

1. The *Johnson* court concluded that the Attorney General lacked good cause for failing to subject his regulations to pre-promulgation notice and comment, yet held also that the error was harmless. Given the highly case-specific nature of the good cause exception, why do you think the court opted to make this distinction?

2. In evaluating whether the Attorney General's failure to use notice-and-comment rulemaking in initially promulgating the SORNA regulations, the *Johnson* court relied on relied on *Shinseki v. Sanders*, 556 U.S. 396 (2009), in requiring Johnson to demonstrate that the outcome of the rulemaking might have been different had the Attorney General complied with the Administrative Procedure Act. *Shinseki v. Sanders*, however, concerned an agency adjudication rather than an agency rulemaking. Should harmless error be assessed in the same way for rulemakings as for adjudications? Why or why not?

c. THE PROCEDURAL RULE EXEMPTION

APA § 553(b)(3)(A) exempts "rules of agency organization, procedure, or practice." There are frequent disputes in which an agency claims that a rule is exempt as a rule of procedure and a party who dislikes the rule argues that it is actually a substantive rule that is invalid because the agency did not pursue notice and comment. Many rules are easy to categorize. For example, a rule that specifies a time limit for appealing an agency ruling is procedural, while a rule that imposes a new, binding obligation upon regulated parties is

---

guidelines relating to retroactivity based on comments alleging an adverse effect on sex offenders."

[123] *See Air Transp. Ass'n of Amer. v. Civil Aeronautics Bd.,* 732 F.2d 219, 224 n. 11 (D.C.Cir.1984).

[124] *See* 72 Fed.Reg. 30,210, 30,212 (May 30, 2007) ("SORNA's requirements apply to all sex offenders, including those whose convictions predate the enactment of the Act." (citing 28 C.F.R. pt. 72)); *cf. Fed. Crop Ins. Corp. v. Merrill,* 332 U.S. 380, 384–85 (1947) ("Congress has provided that the appearance of rules and regulations in the Federal Register gives legal notice of their contents.").

[125] 595 F.2d at 215.

[126] *Friends of Iwo Jima,* 176 F.3d at 774.

substantive. Many rules, however, may be described so that they just as easily resemble one of these characterizations as the other.

Any student of the federal courts can tell you that, since the Supreme Court decided *Erie R.R. v. Tompkins*, 304 U.S. 64 (1938), the courts have similarly struggled to develop a coherent standard for differentiating substantive and procedural rules in determining whether state or federal law governs the resolution of various issues in cases that reach the federal courts through diversity jurisdiction. In *Hanna v. Plumer*, 380 U.S. 460, 472 (1965), the Court acknowledged the existence of "matters which, though falling within the uncertain area between substance and procedure, are rationally capable of classification as either."

It should come as no surprise, then, that the courts have not settled upon a particular standard for distinguishing procedural rules from substantive ones for purposes of the APA § 553(b) procedural rule exception from notice-and-comment rulemaking requirements. The Supreme Court has never issued an opinion that applies the procedural rule exception of APA § 553(b). Meanwhile, circuit court opinions addressing the applicability of the procedural rule exception have utilized a variety of standards, none of which has proved especially robust.

The D.C. Circuit's approach to assessing the distinction between procedural rules and substantive ones is perhaps best described as an amalgam of rhetorical flourishes that it expresses as it evaluates rules in a relatively ad hoc manner. In *Batterton v. Marshall*, 648 F.2d 694 (D.C. Cir. 1980), for example, the D.C. Circuit identified the "critical feature" of the procedural rule exemption as "that it covers agency actions that do not themselves alter the rights or interests of parties, although it may alter the manner in which the parties present themselves or their viewpoints to the agency." Subsequently, in *American Hospital Ass'n v. Bowen*, 834 F.2d 1037, 1047 (D.C. Cir. 1987), the court described the inquiry as including "whether the agency action also encodes a substantive value judgment or puts a stamp of approval or disapproval on a given type of behavior." The D.C. Circuit has also emphasized the purpose of the exemption as granting agencies "latitude in organizing their internal operations." *Batterton*, 648 F.2d at 707. The D.C. Circuit has applied some or all of these principles simultaneously as follows:

- In *Chamber of Commerce v. Department of Labor*, 174 F.3d 206 (D.C. Cir. 1999), the court characterized as substantive an OSHA "Directive" that gave employers a choice between participation in a compliance program described within the Directive (which included requirements beyond those imposed by preexisting law) or submitting to a comprehensive inspection.

- In *James V. Hurson Associates v. Glickman*, 229 F.3d 277 (D.C. Cir. 2000), the court held as procedural an agency rule that eliminated an expedited face-to-face meeting as a method of obtaining approval of proposed food labels, even though regulated parties claimed that removing that option would impose heavy burdens on them.

- In *National Whistleblower Center v. NRC*, 208 F.3d 256 (D.C. Cir. 2000), the court described as procedural an agency's decision to replace its "good cause" standard for waiving a filing deadline with an "unavoidable and extreme circumstances" test.

In past cases, the Ninth Circuit has focused its analysis on whether a rule regulates "the form of agency action and proceedings," rather than the actions of regulated parties. *Southern Cal. Edison Co. v. FERC*, 770 F.2d 779, 783 (9th Cir. 1985). Thus, for example, in *South California Edison*, the court characterized as procedural regulations that established the process by which the Federal Energy Regulatory Commission would approve rate schedules submitted by regulated parties—*e.g.*, allowing interested parties to intervene in rate hearings, establishing standards for internal review of agency rate determinations, and permitting refunds of excess collections based on interim rates—because they "pertain[ed] to the procedural aspects of FERC's approval" of rate applications without making judgments about the substantive merits of the applications themselves. *Id.* By contrast, in *Sequoia Orange Co. v. Yeutter*, 973 F.2d 752 (9th Cir. 1992), the Ninth Circuit characterized as substantive, and thus subject to notice and comment, rules governing the process by which orange growers, as opposed to agency officials, would vote on a series of amendments to a marketing order that regulated the sale and delivery of their agricultural products. *Id.* at 759.

Finally, some circuits have applied a "substantial impact" standard for determining whether a rule is substantive or procedural. The focus of this test is less on the nature of the rule as substantive or procedural but rather on the magnitude of the burden that a rule imposes on regulated parties. Thus, for example, in *Phillips Petroleum Co. v. Johnson*, 22 F.3d 616 (5th Cir. 1994), the Fifth Circuit concluded that the procedural rule exception was not available to an agency rule adopting a particular methodology for valuing federal offshore natural gas production because the rule restricted the discretion of agency officials and would thereby "dramatically affect[ ] the royalty values of all oil and gas leases." *Id.* at 621. Other circuits have explicitly rejected the substantial impact standard's alternative emphasis on a rule's outcome rather than its essential nature. *See, e.g., Kaspar Wire Works, Inc. v. Secretary of Labor*, 268 F.3d 1123, 1132 (D.C. Cir. 2001); *S. Cal. Edison v. FERC*, 770 F.2d 779, 783 (9th Cir. 1985).

DISCUSSION PROBLEM

The Federal Communications Commission (FCC) is responsible for reviewing license applications and granting operating licenses for radio and television stations. Longstanding FCC rules specify the components of a substantially complete license application. Previously, the FCC gave license applicants notice and an opportunity to correct errors in their applications, with the result that the FCC received a significant percentage of carelessly prepared applications, which caused significant delays in application processing. Anticipating thousands of applications in response to a recent allotment of new radio stations, the FCC adopted a new "hard look" rule without notice and comment. This hard look rule established a fixed filing period for all applications requesting use of a particular channel.

Applications filed within the designated filing period were then reviewed for "substantial compliance." Those meeting this standard were accepted; those that did not were returned to the applicants without opportunity for filing an amended application.

Applicant X filed an application that listed the coordinates for its proposed radio transmitter site as 36° 13' 10" while the accompanying map marked the site at 36° 15' 10". Unable to resolve the inconsistency based on the materials filed, the FCC's staff grew concerned that the wrong coordinates might have been used to generate various engineering reports that accompanied the application. Accordingly, the FCC's staff concluded that Applicant X's application was not in substantial compliance with the application requirements and, under the hard look rule, dismissed and returned the application without giving Applicant X the opportunity to file an amended application correcting the error.

You represent the FCC. Applicant X has challenged the FCC's rejection of its application in federal court. Applicant X contends that the FCC's hard look rule, under which its application was rejected, is invalid because the FCC did not comply with notice-and-comment rulemaking requirements in promulgating the rule. Given these facts, evaluate whether you could argue successfully that the FCC's hard look rule is a procedural rule exempt from notice and comment.

d.   THE INTERPRETATIVE RULE EXEMPTION

APA section 553(b)(3)(A) exempts interpretative rules from informal rulemaking procedural requirements. Non-exempt rules, often called legislative rules, have the same force and effect as a statute. They bind courts, members of the public, and the agency itself. By contrast, interpretative rules do not have any binding effect; they merely interpret the statutes and/or the legislative rules that are binding. Typically, an agency has many, many more interpretative rules than legislative rules. An agency usually uses the informal rulemaking process to make its most important rules, and then issues large numbers of exempt interpretative rules to clarify and to particularize the requirements set forth in its legislative rules.

When an agency relies on the interpretative rule exemption to issue a rule that a regulated party dislikes, that party often files a petition for review in which it argues that the rule is instead a procedurally invalid legislative rule. In most instances in which a regulated party dislikes a rule for which the issuing agency claims the interpretative rule exception, challenging the rule as legislative is the best course of action for three reasons. First, as we discuss in Chapter 7, regulated parties often cannot get substantive review of interpretative rules because their legal challenges cannot survive judicial applications of the tests for ripeness, finality, and/or exhaustion of administrative remedies. Second, even if a party's substantive challenge is justiciable, as we discuss in Chapter 6, courts tend to defer to interpretative rules that announce an agency's interpretation either of a statute that it administers or of the agency's own legislative rules. Third, even when a party is able to convince a court to review an agency's interpretative rule, the court is unlikely to conclude that the rule is arbitrary and capricious under hard look review, which we discuss in Part D of this Chapter 5 below. To understand why that is the case, consider that hard look review demands that agencies explain in the factual and legal bases of their actions and choices in the statement of basis and purpose that accompanies a final rule. If an interpretative rule has not gone through notice and comment, the agency has not issued a statement of basis and purpose, and the rule is nonbinding to boot, on what basis could a court possibly conclude that an exempt rule is arbitrary and capricious?

Courts must distinguish between exempt interpretative rules and procedurally invalid legislative rules in scores of cases every year. The distinction is easy to state. A legislative rule can create or expand the scope of a legal duty, while an interpretative rule can only clarify or particularize the scope of a duty that was previously created by a statute or a legislative rule. In many cases, however, the distinction is difficult to apply.

Although the Supreme Court has often referred to particular regulations as legislative or interpretative, the Court has never articulated a clear standard for distinguishing between the two categories. In *Chrysler Corp. v. Brown*, 441 U.S. 281, 302 (1979), the Court characterized legislative rules as "affecting individual rights and obligations." More recently, in *Long Island Care at Home, Ltd. v. Coke*, 551 U.S. 158 (2007), the Court considered a claim that a particular Department of Labor regulation was "an 'interpretive' regulation not warranting judicial deference." *Id.* at 165. In addressing this question, the Court concluded that the regulation was entitled to deference for several reasons: the Labor Department used notice-and-comment rulemaking procedures to both promulgate and amend the regulation, and otherwise treated the regulation "as a legally binding exercise of its rulemaking authority" for thirty years; the regulation "set[ ] forth important individual rights and duties"; the agency "focuse[d] fully and directly upon" the issue at hand in promulgating the regulation; the regulation "[fell] within the statutory grant of authority"; and the regulation was "reasonable." *Id.* at 173. Ultimately, however, the Court resolved the deference question without actually characterizing the regulation as either legislative or interpretative. We will discuss the relationship between rule characterization and judicial deference in more depth in Chapter 6.

Whether or not these statements might be useful in distinguishing legislative from interpretive rules, the lower courts do not rely upon them for purposes of assessing the applicability of the procedural requirements of APA § 553. Instead, courts and scholars alike generally regard the following opinion to represent the best a court can do in drawing the distinction between legislative and interpretative rules.

American Mining Congress v. Mine Safety & Health Administration

995 F.2d 1106 (D.C. Cir. 1993).

■ STEPHEN WILLIAMS, CIRCUIT JUDGE:

This case presents a single issue: whether Program Policy Letters of the Mine Safety and Health Administration, stating the agency's position that certain x-ray readings qualify as "diagnose[s]" of lung disease within the meaning of agency reporting regulations, are interpretive rules under the Administrative Procedure Act. We hold that they are.

The Federal Mine Safety and Health Act extensively regulates health and safety conditions in the nation's mines and empowers the Secretary of Labor to enforce the statute and relevant regulations. In addition, the Act requires "every operator of a . . . mine . . . [to] establish and maintain such records, make such reports, and provide such information, as the Secretary . . . may reasonably require from time to time to enable him to perform his functions." 30 U.S.C. § 813(h). The Act makes a general grant of authority to the Secretary to issue "such regulations as . . . [he] deems appropriate to carry out" any of its provisions. *Id.* § 957.

Pursuant to its statutory authority, the Mine Safety and Health Administration (acting on behalf of the Secretary of Labor) maintains regulations known as "Part 50" regulations, which cover the "Notification, Investigation, Reports and Records of Accidents, Injuries, Illnesses, Employment, and Coal Production in Mines." 30 C.F.R. Pt. 50. These were adopted via notice-and-comment rulemaking. Subpart C deals with the "Reporting of Accidents, Injuries, and Illnesses" and requires mine operators to report to the MSHA within ten days "each accident, occupational injury, or occupational illness" that occurs at a mine. 30 C.F.R. § 50.20(a). Of central importance here, the regulation also says that whenever any of certain occupational illnesses are "*diagnosed*," the operator must similarly report the diagnosis within ten days. *Id.* (emphasis added). Among the occupational illnesses covered are "[s]ilicosis, asbestosis, coal worker's pneumoconiosis, and other pneumoconioses." *Id.* at § 50.20–6(b)(7)(ii). An operator's failure to report may lead to citation and penalty.

As the statute and formal regulations contain ambiguities, the MSHA from time to time issues Program Policy Letters ("PPLs") intended to coordinate and convey agency policies, guidelines, and interpretations to agency employees and interested members of the public. One subject on which it has done so—apparently in response to inquiries from mine operators about whether certain x-ray results needed to be reported as "diagnos[es]"—has been the meaning of the term diagnosis for purposes of Part 50.

The first of the PPLs at issue here stated that any chest x-ray of a miner who had a history of exposure to pneumonoconiosis-causing dust that rated 1/0 or higher on the International Labor Office (ILO) classification system would be considered a "diagnosis that the x-rayed miner has silicosis or one of the other pneumonoconioses" for the purposes of the Part 50 reporting requirements. (The ILO classification system uses a 12-step scale to measure the concentration of opacities (i.e., areas of darkness or shading) on chest x-rays. A 1/0 rating is the fourth most severe of the ratings.) The 1991 PPL also set up a procedure whereby, if a mine operator had a chest x-ray initially evaluated by a relatively unskilled reader, the operator could seek a reading by a more skilled one; if the latter rated the x-ray below 1/0, the MSHA would delete the "diagnosis" from its files. We explain the multiple-reader rules further in the context of the third PPL, where they took their final form (so far).

The second letter superseded the 1991 PPL but largely repeated its view about a Part 50 diagnosis. In addition, the May 1992 PPL stated the MSHA's position that mere diagnosis of an occupational disease or illness within the meaning of Part 50 did not automatically entitle a miner to benefits for disability or impairment under a workers' compensation scheme. The PPL also said that the MSHA did not intend for an operator's mandatory reporting of an x-ray reading to be equated with an admission of liability for the reported disease.

The final PPL under dispute replaced the May 1992 PPL and again restated the MSHA's basic view that a chest x-ray rating above 1/0 on the ILO scale constituted a "diagnosis" of silicosis or some other pneumoconiosis. The August 1992 PPL also modified the MSHA's position on additional readings. Specifically, when the first reader is not a "B" reader (i.e., one certified by the National Institute of Occupational Safety and Health to perform ILO ratings), and the operator seeks a reading from a "B" reader, the MSHA will stay enforcement for failure to report the first reading. If the "B" reader concurs with the initial determination that the x-ray should be scored a 1/0 or higher, the mine operator must report the "diagnosis". If the "B" reader scores the x-ray below 1/0, the MSHA will continue to stay enforcement if the operator gets a third reading, again from a "B" reader; the MSHA then will accept the majority opinion of the three readers.

The MSHA did not follow the notice and comment requirements of 5 U.S.C. § 553 in issuing any of the three PPLs. In defending its omission of notice and comment, the agency relies solely on the interpretive rule exemption of § 553(b)(3)(A).

* * *

The distinction between those agency pronouncements subject to APA notice-and-comment requirements and those that are exempt has been aptly described as "enshrouded in considerable smog." *Gen. Motors Corp. v. Ruckelshaus*, 742 F.2d 1561, 1565 (D.C. Cir. 1984); *see also Am. Hosp. Ass'n v. Bowen*, 834 F.2d 1037, 1046 (D.C. Cir. 1987) (calling the line between interpretive and legislative rules "fuzzy"); *Community Nutrition Inst. v. Young*, 818 F.2d 943, 946 (D.C. Cir. 1987) (quoting authorities describing the present distinction between legislative rules and policy statements as "tenuous," "blurred" and "baffling").

Given the confusion, it makes some sense to go back to the origins of the distinction in the legislative history of the Administrative Procedure Act. Here the key document is the *Attorney General's Manual on the Administrative Procedure Act* (1947), which offers "the following working definitions":

> *Substantive rules*—rules, other than organizational or procedural under section 3(a)(1) and (2), issued by an agency pursuant to statutory authority and which implement the statute, as, for example, the proxy rules issued by the Securities and Exchange Commission pursuant to section 14 of the Securities Exchange Act of 1934. Such rules have the force and effect of law.

Interpretative rules—rules or statements issued by an agency to advise the public of the agency's construction of the statutes and rules which it administers. . . .

General statements of policy—statements issued by an agency to advise the public prospectively of the manner in which the agency proposes to exercise a discretionary power.

Id. at 30 n.3.

Our own decisions have often used similar language, inquiring whether the disputed rule has "the force of law". We have said that a rule has such force only if Congress has delegated legislative power to the agency and if the agency intended to exercise that power in promulgating the rule.

On its face, the "intent to exercise" language may seem to lead only to more smog, but in fact there are a substantial number of instances where such "intent" can be found with some confidence. The first and clearest case is where, in the absence of a legislative rule by the agency, the legislative basis for agency enforcement would be inadequate. * * * The statute itself forbids *nothing* except acts or omissions to be spelled out by the Commission in "rules or regulations". * * * [S]ection 813(h) merely requires an operator to maintain "such records . . . as the Secretary . . . may reasonably require from time to time". 30 U.S.C. § 813(h). Although the Secretary might conceivably create some "require[ments]" ad hoc, clearly some agency creation of a duty is a necessary predicate to any enforcement against an operator for failure to keep records. Analogous cases may exist in which an agency may offer a government benefit only after it formalizes the prerequisites.

Second, an agency seems likely to have intended a rule to be legislative if it has the rule published in the Code of Federal Regulations; 44 U.S.C. § 1510 limits publication in that code to rules "having general applicability and legal effect".

Third, " '[i]f a second rule repudiates or is irreconcilable with [a prior legislative rule], the second rule must be an amendment of the first; and, of course, an amendment to a legislative rule must itself be legislative.' " *Nat'l Family Planning & Reprod. Health Ass'n v. Sullivan*, 979 F.2d 227, 235 (D.C. Cir. 1992) (quoting Michael Asimow, *Nonlegislative Rulemaking and Regulatory Reform*, 1985 DUKE L.J. 381, 396)).

* * *

The focus on whether the agency *needs* to exercise legislative power (to provide a basis for enforcement actions or agency decisions conferring benefits) helps explain some distinctions that may, out of context, appear rather metaphysical. For example, in *Fertilizer Institute v. EPA*, 935 F.2d 1303 (D.C. Cir. 1991), we drew a distinction between instances where an agency merely "declare[s] its understanding of what a statute requires" (interpretive), and ones where an agency "go[es] beyond the text of a statute" (legislative). *Id.* at 1308. The difficulty with the distinction is that almost every rule may seem to do both.

* * *

A non-legislative rule's capacity to have a binding effect is limited in practice by the fact that agency personnel at every level act under the shadow of judicial review. If they believe that courts may fault them for brushing aside the arguments of persons who contest the rule or statement, they are obviously far more likely to entertain those arguments. And, as failure to provide notice-and-comment rulemaking will usually mean that affected parties have had no prior formal opportunity to present their contentions, judicial review for want of reasoned decisionmaking is likely, in effect, to take place in review of specific agency actions implementing the rule. * * * Because the threat of judicial review provides a spur to the agency to pay attention to facts and arguments submitted in derogation f any rule not supported by notice and comment, even as late as the enforcement stage, *any* agency statement not subjected to notice-and-comment rulemaking will be more vulnerable to attack not only in court but also within the agency itself.

Not only does an agency have an incentive to entertain objections to an interpretive rule, but the ability to promulgate such rules, without notice and comment, does not appear more hazardous to affected parties than the likely alternative. Where a statute or legislative rule has created a legal basis for enforcement, an agency can simply let its interpretation evolve ad hoc in the process of enforcement or other applications (e.g., grants). The protection that Congress sought to secure by requiring notice and comment for legislative rules is not advanced by reading the exemption for "interpretive rule" so narrowly as to drive agencies into pure ad hocery—an ad hocery, moreover, that affords less notice, or less convenient notice, to affected parties.

Accordingly, insofar as our cases can be reconciled at all, we think ~Standard.~ it almost exclusively on the basis of whether the purported interpretive rule has "legal effect", which in turn is best ascertained by asking (1) whether in the absence of the rule there would not be an adequate legislative basis for enforcement action or other agency action to confer benefits or ensure the performance of duties, (2) whether the agency has published the rule in the Code of Federal Regulations, (3) whether the agency has explicitly invoked its general legislative authority, or (4) whether the rule effectively amends a prior legislative rule. If the answer to any of these questions is affirmative, we have a legislative, not an interpretive rule.

Here we conclude that the August 1992 PPL is an interpretive rule. The Part 50 regulations themselves require the reporting of diagnoses of the specified diseases, so there is no legislative gap that required the PPL as a predicate to enforcement action. Nor did the agency purport to act legislatively, either by including the letter in the Code of Federal Regulations, or by invoking its general legislative authority under 30 U.S.C. § 811(a). The remaining possibility therefore is that the August 1992 PPL is a de facto amendment of prior legislative rules, namely the Part 50 regulations.

A rule does not, in this inquiry, become an amendment merely because it supplies crisper and more detailed lines than the authority being interpreted. If that were so, no rule could pass as an interpretation of a legislative rule unless it were confined to parroting the rule or replacing the original vagueness with another.

* * *

A finding of a disease is surely equivalent, in normal terminology, to a diagnosis, and thus the PPLs certainly offer no interpretation that repudiates or is irreconcilable with an existing legislative rule.

NOTES AND QUESTIONS

1.   The MSHA calls its interpretative rules Program Policy Letters, or PPLs. Other agencies use a wide variety of names to refer to their interpretative rules—*e.g.*, guidances, rulings, notices, compliance manuals, and staff instructions. The variety of names agencies use to refer to various types of pronouncements can be a source of confusion. From a legal standpoint, the names the agencies use are irrelevant. A rule is either legislative (or substantive) or it is an exempt interpretative rule or policy statement.

2.   A year after he wrote the opinion in *American Mining Congress*, Judge Williams changed one part of the test by stating that publication of a rule in the Code of Federal Regulations (CFR) is only a "snippet of evidence" that a rule is legislative. *Health Ins. Ass'n of Am., Inc. v. Shalala*, 23 F.3d 412, 423 (D.C. Cir. 1994). He made that change after it was brought to his attention that (1) all interpretative rules are eligible for publication in the CFR because all have at least the "legal effect" of providing notice of the agency's interpretation of its rules or statutes; (2) many agencies follow the practice of publishing their most important interpretative rules in the CFR to maximize their accessibility to affected members of the public; and, (3) retention of publication in CFR as a basis for deciding that a rule is legislative would have the effect of deterring agencies from that socially beneficial practice.

3.   The ideal strategy for any agency would be to use informal rulemaking to issue a legislative rule that says little, if anything, beyond what the statute says and then to rely entirely on issuance of exempt interpretative rules to make all important decisions by "clarifying" and "particularizing" the extraordinarily broad requirements stated in the legislative rules. Do you understand why such a strategy would be attractive to an agency? Although the *American Mining Congress* court did not explicitly list these circumstances among the criteria for characterization as a legislative rule, it suggested and many other courts have held that an agency cannot use this strategy, and that any rule that is a "new rule" rather than merely "an interpretation of an existing rule" is a legislative rule. *Mission Group Kansas, Inc. v. Riley*, 146 F.3d 775, 782 (10th Cir. 1998); *see also Pearson v. Shalala*, 164 F.3d 650, 660–61 (D.C. Cir. 1999). Why do you think the courts have added this criterion as indicative of a legislative rule?

4.   In *American Mining Congress*, the court held that a rule that is inconsistent with a pre-existing legislative rule must itself be a legislative rule, rather than an exempt interpretative rule. Why do you think the court reached that conclusion? In some later opinions, the D.C. Circuit held that a rule that is inconsistent with a pre-existing interpretative rule must be a legislative rule. *See, e.g., Paralyzed Veterans of Am. v. D.C. Arena L.P.*, 117 F.3d 579 (D.C. Cir. 1997). Several scholars have criticized this decision, and one of the authors of this casebook has declared it "a mistake," for several reasons. Richard J. Pierce, Jr., *Distinguishing Legislative Rules from Interpretative Rules*, 52 ADMIN. L. REV. 547, 566 (2000). Can you think why the D.C. Circuit's holding in *Paralyzed Veterans* might be problematic? What result would this holding have produced if the court had applied it to the Program Policy Letter at issue in *American Mining Congress*?

5. As the *American Mining Congress* court noted, the MSHA issued the three Program Policy Letters in response to requests from mine owners and operators to clarify and particularize the meaning of "diagnosis" as that term was used in the part 50 rule. This aspect of the *American Mining Congress* case illustrates an irony that often applies to disputes over rules that agencies claim to be interpretative. Regulated parties as a group crave interpretative guidance from agencies. Without such guidance they have great difficulty knowing what they can do without risking being the subject of an enforcement action. Yet, the same regulated parties that ask agencies to issue interpretative rules also regularly challenge agency claims that the rules are interpretative and urge courts to adopt tests that would make it difficult for an agency to issue the rules the regulated parties seek. Why do you think this is the case?

6. The basic strategy the MSHA pursued in this case is typical of the strategy most agencies use. The MSHA used informal rulemaking to issue the rule that required mine owners and operators to report each occupational illness "diagnosed" and then used exempt interpretative rules to define and to redefine "diagnosis." Why do you think agencies utilize this strategy? What do you consider the disadvantages of pursuing an alternative strategy—*e.g.*, using informal rulemaking to issue each Program Policy Letter? Imagine that you are head of the MSHA. Would you expect to get the definition of diagnosis right the first time you tried to define the term? What would you have to do if you used informal rulemaking to define diagnosis with particularity by reference to the characteristics of x-rays and x-ray readers that qualify as a diagnosis of pneumoconiosis, and then decided that your definition was too narrow or too broad?

7. Most circuit courts have followed the D.C. Circuit's lead and adopted some combination of factors from *American Mining Congress* and its progeny to distinguish between legislative and interpretative rules. At least one circuit, however, applies a different standard. In *Professionals & Patients for Customized Care v. Shalala*, 56 F.3d 592 (5th Cir. 1995), the Fifth Circuit applied a version of the "substantial impact" test, asking two questions: (1) whether the rule at issue is binding in that it imposes "rights and obligations" on regulated parties, and (2) whether the rule leaves the agency and its decisionmakers free to exercise discretion or, conversely, binds the agency as well as regulated parties. Even as other circuits shifted to the *American Mining Congress* test, the Fifth Circuit thus far has declined to follow suit.

e.   THE POLICY STATEMENT EXEMPTION

APA § 553(b)(3)(A) also exempts "general statements of policy." This exemption is second only to the interpretative rule exemption in terms of the number of disputes that it creates. In fact, policy statements resemble interpretative rules in a number of important respects beyond their exemption from the procedural requirements of notice-and-comment rulemaking. Like interpretative rules, policy statements are not legally binding on members of the public or on the courts. Like interpretative rules, many policy statements are not subject to judicial review until they are applied in a particular case due to the ripeness, finality, and exhaustion requirements that we discuss at length in Chapter 7. Finally, as we discuss in Chapter 6, as with interpretative rules, courts tend to be less deferential toward agency legal interpretations advanced in policy statements.

Distinguishing between legislative rules and exempt policy statements can be difficult, for the simple reason that many legislative rules in fact make statements regarding policy. Because legislative rules are legally binding and exempt policy statements are not, courts trying to distinguish the two often ask whether the agency action in question has "binding effect." Courts attempting to apply this binding effect standard have struggled, however, to articulate coherently exactly what constitutes binding effect. The following opinion describes and applies one such attempt. (One of the authors of this casebook knows the case well. He was on the losing side when he was in practice.)

Pacific Gas & Electric Co. v. Federal Power Commission

506 F.2d 33 (D.C. Cir. 1974).

■ MacKINNON, CIRCUIT JUDGE:

Petitioners assert that we have jurisdiction under section 19(b) of the Natural Gas Act to review Order No. 467 which the Federal Power Commission issued on January 8, 1973. Order No. 467 is a "Statement of Policy" on "priorities-of-deliveries by jurisdictional pipelines during periods of curtailment" which the Commission indicated it proposes to implement in all matters arising under the Act. The petitioning customers of pipeline companies, whose deliveries are subject to curtailment during natural gas shortages, contend that Order No. 467 is procedurally defective for failure to comply with the Administrative Procedure Act, * * *.

We hold that as a general statement of policy, Order No. 467 is exempt from the rulemaking requirements of the Administrative Procedure Act. * * *

This country appears to be experiencing a natural gas shortage which necessitates the curtailment of supplies to certain customers during peak demand periods. The problem confronting many pipeline companies is whether to curtail on the basis of existing contractual commitments or on the basis of the most efficient end use of the gas. In some instances the pipeline companies are concerned that withholding gas due under existing contracts may subject them to civil liability.

Recognizing these uncertainties and mindful of the desirability of providing uniform curtailment regulation, the FPC in 1971 issued a Statement of General Policy in the form of Order No. 431 directing jurisdictional pipeline companies which expected periods of shortages to file tariff sheets containing a curtailment plan. Order No. 431 hinted that curtailment priorities should be based on the end use of the gas and stated that curtailment plans approved by the Commission "will control in all respects notwithstanding inconsistent provisions in [prior] sales contracts. . . ." In response to Order No. 431, numerous pipeline companies which had not already done so submitted a variety of curtailment plans for the Commission's approval. As could be expected, the curtailment plans reflected a wide range of views as to the proper priorities for delivery. Some plans were based on end use; others, on contract entitlements. The industry was forced to speculate as to which priorities would later be found to be just and reasonable by the Commission, and the absence of any stated Commission policy hindered effective long range planning by pipelines, distributors and consumers.

Sensing a need for guidance and uniformity in the curtailment area, on January 8, 1973 the Commission promulgated Order No. 467, the order presently under review * * *. Entitled "Statement of Policy," Order No. 467 was issued without prior notice or opportunity for comment. The statement sets forth the Commission's view of a proper priority schedule and expresses the Commission's policy that the national interest would be best served by assigning curtailment priorities on the basis of end use rather than on the basis of prior contractual commitments. Order No. 467 further states the Commission's intent to follow this priority schedule unless a particular pipeline company demonstrates that a different curtailment plan is more in the public interest.

* * *

Petitioners seek review of Order No. 467 in this court under section 19(b) of the Natural Gas Act and advance the following [ ] argument[ ]: that Order No. 467 is in effect a substantive rule which the Commission should have promulgated after a rulemaking proceeding under the Administrative Procedure Act (APA) * * *.

* * *

The APA never defines "general statements of policy" but it does define "rule" to

> [mean] the whole or a part of an agency statement of general or particular applicability and future effect designed to implement, interpret, or prescribe law or policy or describing the organization, procedure, or practice requirements of an agency. . . .

5 U.S.C. § 551(4). This broad definition obviously could be read literally to encompass virtually any utterance by an agency, including statements of general policy. But the statutory provision of an exception to the rulemaking requirements for "general statements of policy" indicates that Congress did not intend the definition of "rule" to be construed so broadly. Congress recognized that certain administrative pronouncements did not require public participation in their formulation. These types of pronouncements are listed in section 553(b)(A) and include "general statements of policy."

* * *

An administrative agency has available two methods for formulating policy that will have the force of law. An agency may establish binding policy through rulemaking procedures by which it promulgates substantive rules, or through adjudications which constitute binding precedents. A general statement of policy is the outcome of neither a rulemaking nor an adjudication; it is neither a rule nor a precedent but is merely an announcement to the public of the policy which the agency hopes to implement in future rulemakings or adjudications. A general statement of policy, like a press release, presages an upcoming rulemaking or announces the course which the agency intends to follow in future adjudications.

As an informational device, the general statement of policy serves several beneficial functions. By providing a formal method by which an agency can express its views, the general statement of policy encourages public dissemination of the agency's policies prior to their actual application in particular situations. Thus the agency's initial views do not remain secret but are disclosed well in advance of their actual application. Additionally, the publication of a general statement of policy facilitates long range planning within the regulated industry and promotes uniformity in areas of national concern.

The critical distinction between a substantive rule and a general statement of policy is the different practical effect that these two types of pronouncements have in subsequent administrative proceedings. A properly adopted substantive rule establishes a standard of conduct which has the force of law. In subsequent administrative proceedings involving a substantive rule, the issues are whether the adjudicated facts conform to the rule and whether the rule should be waived or applied in that particular instance. The underlying policy embodied in the rule is not generally subject to challenge before the agency.

A general statement of policy, on the other hand, does not establish a "binding norm." It is not finally determinative of the issues or rights to which it is addressed. The agency cannot apply or rely upon a general statement of policy as law because a general statement of policy only announces what the agency seeks to establish as policy. A policy statement announces the agency's tentative intentions for the future. When the agency applies the policy in a particular situation, it must be prepared to support the policy just as if the policy statement had never been issued. An agency cannot escape its responsibility to present evidence and reasoning supporting its substantive rules by announcing binding precedent in the form of a general statement of policy.

Often the agency's own characterization of a particular order provides some indication of the nature of the announcement. The agency's express purpose may be to establish a binding rule of law not subject to challenge in particular cases. On the other hand the agency may intend merely to publish a policy guideline that is subject to complete attack before it is finally applied in future cases. When the agency states that in subsequent proceedings it will thoroughly consider not only the policy's applicability to the facts of a given case but also the underlying validity of the policy itself, then the agency intends to treat the order as a general statement of policy.

* * *

The tentative effect of a general statement of policy has ramifications in subsequent judicial review proceedings as well as in administrative proceedings. Because a general statement of policy is adopted without public participation, the scope of review may be broader than the scope of review for a substantive rule. The rulemaking process prescribed by the APA insures a thorough exploration of the relevant issues. The public is notified of the proposed rule and interested parties submit arguments supporting their positions. The rulemaking process culminates in the agency applying its experience and expertise to the issues. A court reviewing a rule that was adopted pursuant to this extensive rulemaking process will defer to the agency's judgment if the rule satisfies the minimal criterion of reasonableness.

But when an agency promulgates a general statement of policy, the agency does not have the benefit of public exploration of the issues. Judicial review may be the first stage at which the policy is subjected to full criticism by interested parties. Consequently a policy judgment expressed as a general statement of policy is entitled to less deference than a decision expressed as a rule or an adjudicative order. Although the agency's expertise and experience cannot be ignored, the reviewing court has some leeway to assess the underlying wisdom of the policy and need not affirm a general statement of policy that merely satisfies the test of reasonableness.

Applying these general principles to the problem at hand, we conclude that Order No. 467 is a general statement of policy. Order No. 467 is entitled and consistently referred to by the Commission as a general statement of policy. Recognizing the "need for Commission guidance in curtailment planning," the Commission announced in Order No. 467 the curtailment policy which it "proposes to implement," the "plan preferred by the Commission" which "will serve as a guide in other proceedings." Thus, the stated purpose of Order No. 467 was not to provide an inflexible, binding rule but to give advance notice of the general policy with respect to curtailment priorities that the Commission prefers.

Order No. 467 does not establish a curtailment plan for any particular pipeline. The effect of the order is to inform the public of the types of plans which will receive initial and tentative FPC approval, but there is no assurance that any such plan will be finally approved. As the Commission stated:

> When applied in specific cases, opportunity will be afforded interested parties to challenge or support this policy through factual or legal presentation as may be appropriate in the circumstances presented.

> Order No. 467, 49 F.P.C. at 85.

> [Order No. 467 is] not finally determinative of the rights and duties of a given pipeline, its customers or ultimate consumers; it expressly envisions further proceedings.

Id. at 585.

* * *

The FPC of course was under no compulsion to issue Order No. 467. The Commission issued the policy statement because the curtailment plans being submitted reflected sharp differences in philosophy which necessitated Commission guidance in the curtailment area. In the absence of such a policy statement, the Commission could have proceeded on an ad hoc basis and tentatively approved curtailment plans filed under section 4 of the Act which the Commission found to be just and reasonable. In following such a course the only difference from the present situation would be that the Commission would be acting under a secret policy rather than under the publicized guidelines of Order No. 467. The argument that an agency must follow rulemaking procedures when it elects to formulate policy by a substantive rule has no application in this case. Order No. 467 does not establish a substantive rule. Although the Commission is free to initiate a rulemaking proceeding to establish a binding substantive rule, the Commission apparently intends to establish its curtailment policies by proceeding through individual adjudications. Order No. 467 merely announces the general policy which the Commission hopes to establish in subsequent proceedings.

NOTES AND QUESTIONS

1.   In the *PG&E* case, the D.C. Circuit stated that, unlike legislative rules, a general statement of policy "does not establish a 'binding norm.'" As a result, the standard articulated by the *PG&E* court for distinguishing between legislative rules and policy statements is often labeled the "binding effects" test or the "legally binding" test to reflect the fact that only legislative rules are legally binding, *i.e.* establish a binding norm. In applying this standard, as in *PG&E*, courts also sometimes speak in terms reminiscent of whether the agency action in question is "finally determinative of the rights and duties" of a particular person or entity.

2.   Like many agency pronouncements that are the subject of characterization disputes, Order 467 contained ambiguous and internally inconsistent language regarding its binding effect. Some passages suggested that the agency intended the order to have no legally binding effect, but other passages suggested the opposite. Do you suppose that the inconsistencies were a function of agency sloppiness, or could they have been intentional instead? Would you expect an agency to specify or hedge its intentions? How would a regulated party or a court know whether or not such inconsistencies were inadvertent? Does a court need to know the answer to that question? How does the court deal with this problem?

3.   In some later adjudicatory proceedings, the agency attempted to give Order 467 a substantive legal effect—*e.g.*, by imposing the burden of proof on a party that proposed curtailment priorities that differed from those set forth in the order. When the agency acted in that manner, reviewing courts vacated the agency action with a reference to the *PG&E* opinion.

4.   If you represented a pipeline that was subject to this agency's jurisdiction, and your client expressed a mild preference to file a curtailment tariff that differed from Order 467, what advice would you give your client? Regulated parties are often "repeat players," engaging a particular agency on numerous matters over time or even simultaneously. Would your advice be influenced by your awareness that the same agency has considerable discretion with respect to the other ways in which it regulates your client—*e.g.*, it decides the rates your client can charge its customers?

5.   After the *PG&E* case, the Federal Power Commission (FPC) spent the next fifteen years trying to implement the policies it announced in Order 467 through case-by-case adjudication. By the time it completed that

SECTION B   APA RULEMAKING PROCEDURES   **555**

process, the natural gas shortage that prompted Order 467 in the first instance had ended because Congress had eliminated the price controls on natural gas that had created the shortage. For an in depth analysis of the costs of this choice, see Richard J. Pierce, Jr., *The Choice Between Rulemaking and Adjudicating for Formulating Energy Policy*, 31 HASTINGS L.J. 1 (1979). In considering this question, notice the proximity of the timing of the *PG&E* case and subsequent FPC adjudications to the judicial climate leading to the Supreme Court's decision in *Vermont Yankee Nuclear Power Corp. v. Natural Resources Defense Council*, 435 U.S. 519 (1978), which we discussed earlier in this Chapter. Can you think how these cases might relate to one another?

———————

The formulation of the binding effect standard articulated in the *PG&E* case, whether the agency action at issue establishes a binding norm, is not the only inquiry that the lower courts have applied to distinguish legislative rules from policy statements. Compare the *PG&E* court's analysis with that of the D.C. Circuit in the next opinion.

Community Nutrition Institute v. Young

818 F.2d 943 (D.C. Cir. 1987).

■ PER CURIAM:

This case makes its second appearance before this court. It presents a challenge by a consortium of organizations and private citizens (collectively referred to as CNI) to the Food and Drug Administration's regulation of certain unavoidable contaminants in food, most particularly, aflatoxins in corn. Pursuant to its statutory mandate to limit the amount of "poisonous or deleterious substances" in food, 21 U.S.C. § 346, FDA establishes "action levels" informing food producers of the allowable levels of unavoidable contaminants such as aflatoxins. Producers who sell products that are contaminated above the action level, which for aflatoxins in corn is currently set at 20 parts per billion, are subject to enforcement proceedings initiated by FDA.

CNI filed suit in federal district court, launching a three-pronged attack on FDA's action level for aflatoxins in corn: (1) in issuing the action level, FDA failed to comply with the rulemaking requirements of the Food, Drug and Cosmetic Act (FDC Act), (2) the action level violated the Administrative Procedure Act because it constitutes a legislative rule issued without the requisite notice-and-comment procedures; and (3) FDA's decision to permit adulterated corn to be blended with unadulterated corn to bring the total contamination within the action level violated the FDC Act. The District Court granted summary judgment in favor of FDA on each issue.

* * *

Under the APA, agency rules may be issued only after the familiar notice-and-comment procedures enumerated in the statute are completed. It is undisputed that the action level at issue here was promulgated *sans* those procedures. FDA, however, argues that notice-and-comment requirements do not apply by virtue of subsection (b)(3)(A) of section 553, which carves out an exception for "interpretative rules [and] general statements of policy." According to the FDA, action levels represent nothing more than nonbinding statements of agency enforcement policy. CNI, on the other hand, argues that the action levels restrict enforcement discretion to such a degree as to constitute legislative rules.

* * *

In this circuit, we are particularly guided by *American Bus Ass'n v. United States*, 627 F.2d 525 (D.C. Cir. 1980). There, in speaking for the court, Judge McGowan identified "two criteria" that courts have used in their efforts to fathom the interpretative/legislative distinction:

> First, courts have said that, unless a pronouncement acts prospectively, it is a binding norm. Thus . . . a statement of policy may not have a present effect: "a 'general statement of policy' is one that does not impose any rights or obligations". . . .
>
> The second criterion is whether a purported policy statement genuinely leaves the agency and its decisionmakers free to exercise discretion.

Id. at 529 (quoting *Texaco v. FPC*, 412 F.2d 740, 744 (3d Cir. 1969)).

* * *

[W]e are persuaded that the FDA action levels are legislative rules and thus subject to the notice-and-comment requirements of section 553. While FDA now characterizes the action levels as policy statements, a variety of factors, when considered in light of the criteria set out in *American Bus*, indicate otherwise.

First. The language employed by FDA in creating and describing action levels suggests that those levels both have a present effect and are binding. Specifically, the agency's regulations on action levels explain an action level in the following way:

> [A]n action level for an added poisonous or deleterious substance . . . may be established to define the level of contamination at which food *will be deemed to be adulterated.* An action level may *prohibit any detectable amount of substance in food.*

21 C.F.R. § 109.4 (1986) (emphasis added). This language, speaking as it does of an action level "defin[ing]" the acceptable level and "prohibit[ing]" substances, clearly reflects an interpretation of action levels as presently binding norms. This type of mandatory, definitive language is a powerful, even potentially dispositive, factor suggesting that action levels are substantive rules. * * *

Second. This view of action levels—as having a present, binding effect—is confirmed by the fact that FDA considers it necessary for food producers to secure *exceptions* to the action levels. A specific regulatory provision allows FDA to "exempt from regulatory action and permit the marketing of any food that is unlawfully contaminated with a poisonous or deleterious substance" if certain conditions exist. *Id.* § 109.8(a). This language implies that in the absence of an exemption, food with aflatoxin contamination over the action level is "unlawful." This putatively unlawful status can derive only from the action level, which, again, indicates that the action level is a presently binding norm.

* * *

We are not unmindful that in a suit to enjoin shipment of allegedly contaminated corn, it appears that FDA would be obliged to prove that the corn is "adulterated," within the meaning of the FDC Act, rather than merely prove non-compliance with the action level. The action level thus does not bind food producers in the sense that producers are automatically subject to enforcement proceedings for violating the action level. This factor, accordingly, points in favor of the agency's characterization. But the fact that action levels do not completely bind food producers as would a more classic legislative rule (where the only issue before the court would be if the agency rule were in fact violated) is not determinative of the issue. For here, we are convinced that FDA has bound itself. As FDA conceded at oral argument, it would be daunting indeed to try to convince a court that the agency could appropriately prosecute a producer for shipping corn with less than 20 ppb aflatoxin. And this type of cabining of an agency's prosecutorial discretion can in fact rise to the level of a substantive, legislative rule. That is exactly what has happened here.

NOTES AND QUESTIONS

1.   Consider how the *Community Nutrition Institute* court seems to alter the binding effect standard as articulated and applied by the D.C. Circuit in *PG&E*, by asking whether the FDA's policy statement purports to bind the agency. Would you expect this added inquiry to narrow or expand the scope of the binding effect standard? Would you expect agencies to alter their behavior based on this modification to the binding effect standard? Why or why not? And how so?

2.   *Community Nutrition Institute* illustrates a common use of policy statements by agencies: to announce the criteria the agency will use in deciding how to exercise its prosecutorial discretion. Should the courts encourage agencies to issue policy statements for this purpose? Are policy statements better than legislative rules for that purpose? Why or why not?

DISCUSSION PROBLEMS

1.   Imagine that you are an agency lawyer. Your agency's chief of enforcement hands you a document entitled "statement of enforcement policies." The document then uses language like "the agency will not bring an enforcement action unless. . . ." You ask the chief of enforcement whether the agency would ever bring an enforcement action in circumstances that are outside the boundaries described in the "policy statement." He says that the agency would never take such an action. How must you edit the document to be able to issue it as an exempt policy statement? Does the *Community Nutrition Institute* test encourage honesty and candor in agency statements of policy? Should courts create doctrines that discourage honest disclosure of enforcement policies and criteria?

2.   Now imagine that you are a lawyer for an entity that is subject to regulation by Agency X. Agency X issues a document that it labels a policy

statement. In that document, Agency X alerts regulated parties that it is concerned that, in the presence of certain specified conditions, a particular pattern of behavior may be inconsistent with the goals of a particular federal statute. Agency X also states that it may exercise its discretionary powers to examine the activities of regulated parties that it suspects are engaged in such behavior to ascertain whether the specified conditions are present, that it plans to use the results of those examinations to develop proposed regulations governing the relevant behavior, and finally, that it may decide to pursue enforcement actions depending upon the results of its examinations. Your client is currently engaged in the pattern of behavior called into question by the policy statement. Your client believes its actions are consistent with both statutory text and statutory goals, and modifying its behavior will be quite costly, but your client is also risk averse and prefers not to become an enforcement target unnecessarily. Assuming you agree with your client's interpretation of its compliance with the relevant statutory text and statutory goals, would you advise your client nevertheless to modify its behavior in accordance with Agency X's preferences? Why or why not? What factors might you consider relevant in advising your client?

The Practically Binding Standard

Even if general statements of policy lack formal binding effect on regulated parties, they may still have coercive effects on regulated party behavior. When an agency with substantial discretionary power uses a nonbinding policy statement to signal its policy preferences, prudent regulated parties are likely to adjust their behavior "voluntarily" to "comply" with those preferences. In other words, even if an agency cannot rely on an exempt policy statement to bind regulated parties to its policy preferences, an agency may be able to use a policy statement to influence regulated parties strongly in that direction.

In 2000, the D.C. Circuit arguably initiated a new test to distinguish between legislative rules and exempt policy statements known as the "practically binding" or "practically binding effect" standard. Under the new test, even if a document that an agency claims to be an exempt policy statement is not "legally binding" in the sense discussed in either *PG & E* or *Community Nutrition Institute*, the document may still be a procedurally invalid legislative rule so long as the reviewing court determines that the document is "practically binding." *See, e.g., Appalachian Power Co. v. EPA*, 208 F.3d 1015 (D.C. Cir. 2000). In suggesting this standard, the D.C. Circuit was clearly reacting to its expressed frustration with what it saw as an abusive pattern of agency behavior:

> The phenomenon we see in this case is familiar. Congress passes a broadly worded statute. The agency follows with regulations containing broad language, open-ended phrases, ambiguous standards and the like. Then as years pass, the agency issues circulars or guidance or memoranda, explaining, interpreting, defining and often expanding the commands in the regulations. One guidance document may yield another and then another and so on. Several words in a regulation may spawn hundreds of pages of text as the agency offers more and more detail regarding what its regulations demand of

regulated entities. Law is made, without notice and comment, without public participation, and without publication in the Federal Register or the Code of Federal Regulations. With the advent of the Internet, the agency does not need these official publications to ensure widespread circulation; it can inform those affected simply by posting its new guidance or memoranda or policy statement on its web site. An agency operating in this way gains a large advantage. "It can issue or amend its real rules, i.e., its interpretative rules or policy statements, quickly and inexpensively without following any statutorily prescribed procedures." Richard J. Pierce, Jr., *Seven Ways to Deossify Agency Rulemaking*, 47 ADMIN. L. REV. 59, 85 (1995).

Appalachian Power Co., 208 F.3d at 1020. Although the court in *Appalachian Power* did not explicitly summarize what makes a rule practically binding for purposes of the procedural requirements of APA § 553, the court did state the following in the context of assessing whether the agency action at issue was final agency action (a requirement for judicial review we discuss at some length in Chapter 7):

> If an agency acts as if a document issued at headquarters is controlling in the field, if it treats the document in the same manner as it treats a legislative rule, if it bases enforcement actions on the policies or interpretations formulated in the document, if it leads private parties or State permitting authorities to believe that it will declare permits invalid unless they comply with the terms of the document, then the agency's document is for all practical purposes "binding."

Id. at 1021. In other words, the court suggests that it will apply the new practically binding test by determining that an agency statement is practically binding if the agency usually acts in a manner consistent with its stated policy when it has discretion with respect to the manner in which it acts. Can you understand why a court might conclude that requiring an agency document to be legally binding might be inadequate to capture the full range of agency actions that should be subject to public notice and comment as legislative rules? Yet, how easy or difficult do you think the practically binding test might be to apply? What effect would you expect it to have on agency incentives to issue policy statements? Without access to policy statements, how can regulated parties determine the boundaries on their conduct and the manner in which agencies will exercise their discretion? What purpose does a policy statement serve unless it indicates the manner in which the agency intends to exercise its discretion in most cases?

Whether or not the D.C. Circuit actually intended to announce a new standard in *Appalachian Power Co.*, that court has a mixed track record in applying the practically binding standard. In *Cement Kiln Recycling Coalition v. EPA*, 493 F.3d 207, 227 (D.C. Cir. 2007), for example, the court indicated that "whether the agency action binds private parties or the agency itself with the 'force of law,'"—that is, whether the agency action is a legislative rule rather than a policy statement—turns on whether "as a practical matter" the agency action "either appears on its face to be binding, or is applied by the agency in a way that indicates it is binding." The court in *Cement Kiln* declined, however, to find the agency action to be a legislative rule. In another recent case, *National Ass'n of Home Builders v. Norton*, 415 F.3d 8 (D.C. Cir. 2005), the court seemed to back away from the practically binding standard, emphasizing the lack of legal consequences rather than the practical implications of the agency action at issue. The court has not repudiated the practical binding standard, but may be attempting to limit its applicability to particularly egregious circumstances.

C. ARBITRARY AND CAPRICIOUS ("HARD LOOK") REVIEW

APA § 706(2)(A) instructs reviewing courts to "set aside agency action . . . found to be . . . arbitrary and capricious. Regulated party challenges against agency regulations as arbitrary and capricious predate the APA, and historically, such claims were easy to rebut. For example, in *Pacific States Box & Basket Co. v. White*, 296 U.S. 176, 186 (1935), the Supreme Court defined arbitrary and capricious to permit an agency to support a legislative rule without any particular findings of fact, statement of reasons, or record support. The agency's lawyer needed only to provide a theoretically plausible justification for the rule to satisfy the arbitrary and capricious standard. Nevertheless, "arbitrary" and "capricious" are malleable terms. Over time, the courts have interpreted the arbitrary and capricious standard as it is used in APA § 706(2)(A) to require substantially more than pre-APA history might suggest.

About the same time that reviewing courts began to interpret the notice and comment requirements of APA § 553(b) and (c) more broadly, they also started to apply a demanding version of the arbitrary and capricious test to rulemakings. Courts began to vacate agency rules if they concluded that the statement of basis and purpose that the agency incorporated in the final rule did not demonstrate that the agency had taken a "hard look" at the issues and that the agency had not explained to the court's satisfaction why it resolved each contested issue as it did. We discussed in Part B of this Chapter 5 above that the courts applied this approach to require agencies to address all material or significant comments submitted in response to a NOPR. The courts have by no means limited the scope of hard look review to that bare procedural requirement, but instead have employed the doctrine to delve much more deeply into the quality and thoroughness of agency reasoning. A trilogy of opinions courts issued in the process of reviewing rules issued by the National Highway Traffic Safety Administration (NHTSA) illustrates the evolution of hard look review, culminating in the Supreme Court's recognition of the doctrine.

The first of the three cases was one of the first cases in which a court considered a petition for pre-enforcement review of a rule, *Automotive Parts & Accessories Ass'n v. Boyd*, 407 F.2d 330 (D.C. Cir. 1968). The rule in that case required all new passenger cars manufactured for sale in the United States to be factory-equipped with front seat head restraints. The court upheld the rule on the basis that NHTSA's relatively brief statement of the rule's basis and purpose was adequate, given the weak evidence and arguments the petitioner had submitted in its comments in opposition to the rule. The court included reasoning in its opinion, however, that has had great significance in future cases.

> We think * * * that the statement in the text of the promulgation of the Standard, when considered in the light of the reasons stated by the Administrator's denial of rehearing, is "a concise general statement" which passes muster under Section 4 of the APA. However, on the occasion of this first challenge to the implementation of the new statute it is appropriate for us to remind the Administrator of the ever present possibility of judicial review, and to caution against an overly literal reading of the statutory terms "concise" and "general." These adjectives must be accommodated to the realities of judicial scrutiny, which do not contemplate that the court itself will, by a laborious examination of the record, formulate in the first instance the significant issues faced by the agency and articulate the rationale of their resolution. We do not expect the agency to discuss every item of fact or opinion included in the submissions made to it in informal rule making. We do expect that, if the judicial review which Congress has thought it important to provide is to be meaningful, the "concise general statement of * * * basis and purpose" mandated by Section 4 will enable us to see what major issues of policy were ventilated by the informal proceedings and why the agency reacted to them as it did.

> Because the "concise general statement" envisaged by Congress is something different from the detailed "findings and conclusions" on all "material issues of fact, law, or discretion" referred to in Section 8, there will inevitably be differences of emphasis and approach in the application of the judicial review standards prescribed in APA § 10. An adversary lawsuit, which most closely resembles the formal hearing of Sections 7 and 8, throws up issues of law and fact in a form quite unlike those which take shape in informal rule making, which has many analogies to a legislative committee hearing. When the issue on appeal is whether a rule made in informal proceedings meets the criteria of Section 10, the court must necessarily go about the application of that standard in a manner unlike its review of findings of fact and conclusions of law compiled in a formal proceeding.

> This exercise need be no less searching and strict in its weighing of whether the agency has performed in accordance with the Congressional purposes, but, because it is addressed to different materials, it inevitably varies from the adjudicatory model. The paramount objective is to see whether the agency, given an essentially legislative task to perform, has carried it out in a manner calculated to negate the dangers of arbitrariness and irrationality in the formulation of rules for general application in the future.

Boyd, 407 F.2d at 338.

> Is it appropriate for a court to tell an agency not take "an overly literal reading" of the language of a statute? What is an overly literal reading, as opposed to a merely literal reading? Is the court's

admonition to the agency consistent with the Supreme Court's subsequently issued opinion in *Vermont Yankee*? Should a court be able to vacate an agency rule on the basis that the agency's several hundred page "concise general statement of basis and purpose" is inadequate?

If you represent a party that strongly opposes a rule proposed by an agency, does the court's opinion in *Automotive Parts & Accessories Ass'n v. Boyd* provide you a hint regarding the strategy you might pursue to increase your client's likelihood of persuading a court to vacate the rule if the agency decides to issue it? Consider the strategy the lawyers for the petitioner implemented in the following case.

National Tire Dealers & Retreaders Ass'n, Inc. v. Brinegar
491 F.2d 31 (D.C. Cir. 1974).

■ WILKEY, CIRCUIT JUDGE:

Petitioner National Tire Dealers and Retreaders Association, Inc. (NTDRA) seeks review of Federal Motor Vehicle Safety Standard No. 117, issued on 23 March 1972 by the National Highway Traffic Safety Administration, * * *

Petitioner focuses its challenge on paragraph S6.3.2 of Standard No. 117, which requires that all pneumatic passenger tires retreaded on or after 1 February 1974 have the following information permanently molded into or on one sidewall of the tire: size; maximum inflation pressure and load; actual number of plies or ply rating; the words "tubeless" or "tube-type," as applicable; and the words "bias/belted" or "radial," as applicable. The administrative record does not adequately demonstrate that these requirements are practicable, nor does it establish any more than a remote relation between the requirements and motor vehicle safety. The [National Traffic and Motor Vehicle Safety Act of 1966] mandates that motor vehicle safety standards promulgated thereunder be "practicable" and "meet the need for motor vehicle safety." 15 U.S.C. § 1392(a) (1970). Therefore, we vacate that portion of the Order establishing Motor Vehicle Safety Standard No. 117 which relates to permanent labeling of tire size, maximum inflation pressure, ply rating, tubeless or tube-type, and bias/belted or radial construction. However, since section 201 of the Act commands that the Secretary promulgate permanent labeling standards with respect to actual number of plies and maximum permissible load, the portion of Standard No. 117 relating to those characteristics must remain in effect.

* * *

In *Boyd* we defined the scope of review of standards promulgated through informal rule-making procedures, such as those employed in the instant case:

> When the issue on appeal is whether a rule made in informal proceedings meets the criteria of Section 10, the court must necessarily go about the application of that standard in a manner unlike its review of findings of fact and conclusions of law compiled in a formal proceeding.

This exercise need be no less searching and strict in its weighing of whether the agency has performed in accordance with the Congressional purposes, but, because it is addressed to different materials, it inevitably varies from the adjudicatory model. The paramount objective is to see whether the agency, given an essentially legislative task to perform, has carried it out in a manner calculated to negate the dangers of arbitrariness and irrationality in the formulation of rules for general application in the future.

Automotive Parts & Accessories Ass'n v. Boyd, 407 F.2d 330, 338 (D.C. Cir. 1968).

* * *

The general requirement that retreaded tires be labeled with the items of information specified in paragraph S6.3.2 of Standard No. 117 clearly bears a substantial relation to the Act's purpose of achieving motor vehicle safety. As the preamble to the publication of Standard No. 117 states:

> Size, maximum load, and maximum permissible inflation pressure are required because each is necessary for proper selection and use of passenger car tires.

* * *

> The words "bias/belted" and "radial" are required, where appropriate, in order to identify tires of different types of construction. There is presently a large body of opinion . . . that mixing tires of differing construction types on the same vehicle or same axle of a vehicle is not in the best interests of safety.

* * *

> The words "tubeless" or "tube type" are also required to be labeled onto completed retreaded tires. Almost all of the comments considered this information to be safety related.

It is indisputable that labeling of tires is necessary to prevent mismatching, overloading, or overinflation, all significant safety hazards.

But the issue here is what relation *permanent* labeling has to avoidance of those hazards. Petitioner recognizes the importance of labeling retreaded tires with the information required by Standard No. 117, and states:

> The retreading industry can and will record such information as is available on a label affixed to the retreaded tire so that the information will be known to the consumer at the time of purchase.

However, petitioner asserts that *the Secretary "has not found* that the information required by S6.3.2 can meet the need for motor vehicle safety *only if it is permanently labeled into the retreaded tire."*

A permanent labeling requirement is clearly unnecessary to protect original purchasers of retreaded tires. A nonpermanent, affixed label can supply such purchasers with all the information specified in

Standard No. 117 and thus permit them to select tires of proper size and construction. Therefore, lack of permanent labeling could become a factor affecting safety only in the event that a retreaded tire is resold or put to some different use after the affixed label has worn off. The Secretary raised this possibility in the preamble to Standard No. 117:

> Tires . . . may be subject to many applications during their useful life. They are transferred from wheel to wheel and from vehicle to vehicle, and each time this takes place the information on the tire sidewall becomes important. Permanent labeling is therefore required if the information is to perform its function, as it can be readily assumed that affixed labels will last little longer than the first time the tire is mounted.

The Secretary has supplied no illustrations or references to the record to amplify these observations. We can hypothesize two situations in which lack of permanent labeling could conceivably affect safety:

1.   An original purchaser of retreaded tires wishes to replace one or more of those tires, and he needs to match up his new tire or tires with the remaining retreads.

2.   Someone wishes to purchase retreaded tires from the original purchaser or from some other second-hand source.

There is no suggestion in the record or briefs of how frequently these hypothetical situations arise. They might occur so rarely that a costly and burdensome permanent labeling requirement geared to ensure safety in such situations is unreasonable. Furthermore, it is not clear that a second-hand purchaser of retreads or an original owner who seeks replacements is dependent on the tires' labeling for information necessary to proper match-ups, inflation, and loading.

* * *

The apparently remote relationship between the permanent labeling requirements of Standard No. 117 and the goal of motor vehicle safety might be tolerable if those standards imposed no significant burden on the tire retreading industry. However, there are numerous indications in the record that permanent labeling of retreaded tires with the information required by Standard No. 117 would be economically unfeasible. In the face of these indications, the Secretary offers mere assertions, unsupported by any citations to the record, that the requirements are practicable. Therefore, the Secretary's Order establishing the permanent labeling requirements of Standard No. 117 is an "arbitrary" agency action that must be set aside under section 10(e) of the APA.

* * *

The record in the case at bar contains considerable comment to the effect that the permanent labeling required by Standard No. 117 would be unreasonably costly and economically unfeasible. The basic problem is that most tire casings received by retreaders either do not bear permanent labeling of the information required by Standard No. 117 or are labeled in a location where the markings are subject to obliteration during the retreading process. * * *

The amended requirements for new tire labeling have little impact on the current inventories of new tire casings maintained by the retreading industry. It has been estimated that only about one third of the casings presently in supply bear the requisite labeling in a location where it is not subject to buffing off during the retreading process. Therefore, Standard No. 117 would force the retreading industry to choose between two equally undesirable alternatives. First, retreaders might use only those new tire casings that bear the requisite information in a permanent location. This course of action would necessarily result in a two-thirds reduction in the volume of retreaded tire production and inevitably cause severe economic dislocation in the industry. Second, retreaders could mold the required information into the tire sidewalls during the retreading process. However, the comments of retreaders in the administrative record indicate that this, too, is far from an economically feasible alternative.

Apparently the retreading process cannot be economically adapted to labeling each tire permanently with the seven items of information required by Standard No. 117. Petitioner describes the retreading process as follows:

1. Careful selection and inspection of the casing as required by S5.2.1 and S5.2.2 of Safety Standard 117.

2. Removing the old tread by a process known as buffing which eliminates the shoulder of the tread and provides a smooth surface to apply the new rubber. During this process, any information appearing above the maximum section width of the tire is subject to being removed.

3. Affixing a new rubber surface to the tire by adhesion of the tread rubber to the casing, and

4. Vulcanizing the new tread to the casing in a mold or matrix under elevated temperatures and pressures. While new tires are produced in substantial factory runs where large quantities of tires should be identical, each retreaded tire is a separate and distinct product.

In order to label tires permanently with the requisite information during this process "it would be necessary for an employee to work with hand-tools on a mold that would have a temperature somewhere between 250 and 300 degrees F. exposing him to the danger of burns in an effort to change the varied plates with this information on it as each tire is changed in the mold." Altering the mold plates in this fashion would be necessary for almost every tire run through the production lines, since the size, number of plies, construction, maximum pressure, and other characteristics vary from tire to tire. As indicated by the table appended to Standard No. 117, there are 57 different tire sizes, three basic ply number-ply rating combinations, three maximum inflation pressures, and nearly 100 different maximum loads. When the tube or tubeless, bias/belted, and radial factors are added to the mix, the possible combinations of characteristics become virtually limitless. Thus, permanent labeling of retreads with the various items specified in Standard No. 117 might be loosely analogized to personalizing a set of wedding invitations by engraving each one with the name of the individual invitee: the engraving plate would have to be changed for each invitation printed. Retreaded tires are usually an economic necessity for the purchaser, not a luxury item.

One retreader has summarized the economic unfeasibility of the permanent labeling requirements specified in Standard No. 117:

> As an experiment, we ran a series of casings that had labeling in the shoulder area that would be removed in the retreading process. Our experience has indicated that the best we can do with a relabeling program is to be 80% Effective, and our additional cost is more than $2.50 per retread. This is an increase of 30%.

Letter from Noyes Tire Co. in support of NTDRA Petition, April 21, 1972.

Of course, the court need not accept at face value the self-serving comments of interested members of the retreading industry. However, such comments raise serious doubts about the practicability of Standard No. 117. In the face of these doubts, the Secretary offers only unsupported and unconvincing assertions that the permanent labeling requirements are practicable and economically feasible, and, in so doing, attempts to equate the data required for safety with that already required for recordkeeping. However, the information required by the Identification and Record Keeping Regulations is significantly different. It consists of such items as the name of the manufacturer and week in which the tire was retreaded. With the exception of the latter, these items do not vary from tire to tire as do the items specified in Standard No. 117; the week of retreading can easily be changed at the start of each week while the retreading molds are cool. The Administration's further suggestion that casings could be sorted into uniform groups before retreading to minimize the frequency of alterations in the retreading mold appears reasonable, but there is nothing in the record to indicate whether such a sorting process would be practicable and not unreasonably costly.

Ultimately the Secretary's position rests on the following statement that appears in the Administration's Denial of Petitions for Reconsideration:

> Many of the petitions request the NHTSA to furnish data supporting specific decisions and determinations reflected in the standard. The decisions and determinations embodied in this standard are based on all the information at the agency's disposal, together with the informed judgment and expertise of agency personnel. Documentary materials relating to NHTSA decisions regarding the standard are part of the public docket. The agency is not obliged by law, nor does it consider it appropriate, to categorize or interpret those records as supporting particular statements or decisions made on rule-making issuances.

37 Fed. Reg. 13992 (1972). While it is true that an agency may act after informal rule-making procedures "upon the basis of information available in its own files, and upon the knowledge and expertise of the agency," *Cal. Citizens' Band Ass'n v. United States*, 375 F.2d 43, 54 (9th Cir. 1967), in the case at bar the Secretary's allusions to information and knowledge outside the record are unpersuasive in light of the

powerful doubts raised by the on-the-record comments of petitioner and others about the practicability of the permanent labeling requirements. The Secretary's statement of the reasons for his conclusion that the requirements are practicable is not so inherently plausible that the court can accept it on the agency's mere *ipse dixit*. We are compelled to conclude that the Secretary's practicability determination was arbitrary and thus requires us to set aside Standard No. 117 under section 10(e) of the APA.

■ [An opinion by CIRCUIT JUDGE ROBINSON, concurring, is omitted. Ed.]

NOTES AND QUESTIONS

1. What was the key to the petitioners' success in this case? Where did the court obtain the factual information it relied on as the basis for its decision? Do you suppose that the most important parts of the comments were written by lawyers? If the comments consisted solely of lawyer-written objections to the proposed rule, do you think the court would have given them as much credence? If you were a lawyer for parties that often seek to challenge the validity of rules, what functional inferences would you draw from the D.C. Circuit's opinions in *Automotive Parts & Accessories Ass'n v. Boyd* and *National Tire Dealers*?

2. On remand from *National Tire Dealers*, NHTSA decided to abandon its attempt to issue a rule of the type the court rejected. It is not unusual for an agency to react to judicial opinions of this type by abandoning the rulemaking. In the other cases, the agency reacts either by reissuing the same rule, or by issuing a similar rule, after taking some additional actions on remand. Imagine that you were General Counsel of NHTSA when the court decided *National Tire Dealers*, and that your boss told you that she considered the rule the court vacated to be crucial to the agency's ability to fulfill its responsibilities. She asks you to describe the actions NHTSA might take on remand in an effort to reissue the same rule or a similar rule with a better chance of persuading a court to uphold the rule. How would you respond to her question? Would you anticipate that it would take NHTSA a long time to take those actions? Would you expect the cost of taking those actions to be high?

———————

The D.C. Circuit decided *National Tire Dealers* four years before the Supreme Court decided *Vermont Yankee Nuclear Power Corp. v. NRDC*, 435 U.S. 519 (1978) (discussed elsewhere in this Chapter) Recall that the Supreme Court in *Vermont Yankee* chastised the circuit courts for imposing procedures on agency rulemaking that exceeded APA requirements. *National Tire Dealers* was one of many examples of circuit courts vacating agency rules through application of the hard look version of the arbitrary and capricious standard of APA § 706(2)(A). The *Vermont Yankee* opinion had two quite different effects on efforts to convince courts to vacate rules through application of hard look review. First, after the Court decided *Vermont Yankee*, prospective petitioners almost invariably followed a strategy similar to the strategy the petitioners used in *National Tire Dealers* and enjoyed considerable success in convincing reviewing courts to vacate rules through application of the hard look doctrine. Second, however, many scholars argued that the Supreme Court should apply the reasoning of *Vermont Yankee* as the basis for an opinion that rejects the hard look doctrine. *See, e.g.*, Paul Verkuil, *Waiting for Vermont Yankee II*, 55 TUL. L. REV. 418 (1981). Why do you think *Vermont Yankee* produced these disparate reactions?

To the surprise of many scholars, the Court did not apply the reasoning of *Vermont Yankee* to ban application of the hard look doctrine. Instead, it issued the following opinion that most scholars interpret as the Supreme Court's endorsement of the hard look doctrine.

Motor Vehicle Manufacturers Ass'n of U.S., Inc. v. State Farm Mutual Auto. Insurance Co.

463 U.S. 29 (1983).

■ JUSTICE WHITE delivered the opinion of the Court.

The development of the automobile gave Americans unprecedented freedom to travel, but exacted a high price for enhanced mobility. Since 1929, motor vehicles have been the leading cause of accidental deaths and injuries in the United States. In 1982, 46,300 Americans died in motor vehicle accidents and hundreds of thousands more were maimed and injured. While a consensus exists that the current loss of life on our highways is unacceptably high, improving safety does not admit to easy solution. In 1966, Congress decided that at least part of the answer lies in improving the design and safety features of the vehicle itself. But much of the technology for building safer cars was undeveloped or untested. Before changes in automobile design could be mandated, the effectiveness of these changes had to be studied, their costs examined, and public acceptance considered. This task called for considerable expertise and Congress responded by enacting the National Traffic and Motor Vehicle Safety Act of 1966. The Act, created for the purpose of "reduc[ing] traffic accidents and deaths and injuries to persons resulting from traffic accidents," 15 U.S.C. § 1381, directs the Secretary of Transportation or his delegate to issue motor vehicle safety standards that "shall be practicable, shall meet the need for motor vehicle safety, and shall be stated in objective terms." 15 U.S.C. § 1392(a). In issuing these standards, the Secretary is directed to consider "relevant available motor vehicle safety data," whether the proposed standard "is reasonable, practicable and appropriate" for the particular type of motor vehicle, and the "extent to which such standards will contribute to carrying out the purposes" of the Act. 15 U.S.C. § 1392(f)(1), (3), (4).

The Act also authorizes judicial review under the provisions of the Administrative Procedure Act (APA), of all "orders establishing, amending, or revoking a Federal motor vehicle safety standard," 15 U.S.C. § 1392(b). Under this authority, we review today whether NHTSA acted arbitrarily and capriciously in revoking the requirement in Motor Vehicle Safety Standard 208 that new motor vehicles produced after September 1982 be equipped with passive restraints to protect the safety of the occupants of the vehicle in the event of a collision. Briefly summarized, we hold that the agency failed to present an adequate basis and explanation for rescinding the passive restraint requirement and that the agency must either consider the matter further or adhere to or amend Standard 208 along lines which its analysis supports.

I

The regulation whose rescission is at issue bears a complex and convoluted history. Over the course of approximately 60 rulemaking notices, the requirement has been imposed, amended, rescinded, reimposed, and now rescinded again.

As originally issued by the Department of Transportation in 1967, Standard 208 simply required the installation of seatbelts in all automobiles. It soon became apparent that the level of seatbelt use was too low to reduce traffic injuries to an acceptable level. The Department therefore began consideration of "passive occupant restraint systems"—devices that do not depend for their effectiveness upon any action taken by the occupant except that necessary to operate the vehicle. Two types of automatic crash protection emerged: automatic seatbelts and airbags. The automatic seatbelt is a traditional safety belt, which when fastened to the interior of the door remains attached without impeding entry or exit from the vehicle, and deploys automatically without any action on the part of the passenger. The airbag is an inflatable device concealed in the dashboard and steering column. It automatically inflates when a sensor indicates that deceleration forces from an accident have exceeded a preset minimum, then rapidly deflates to dissipate those forces. The life-saving potential of these devices was immediately recognized, and in 1977, after substantial on-the-road experience with both devices, it was estimated by NHTSA that passive restraints could prevent approximately 12,000 deaths and over 100,000 serious injuries annually.

In 1969, the Department formally proposed a standard requiring the installation of passive restraints, thereby commencing a lengthy series of proceedings. In 1970, the agency revised Standard 208 to include passive protection requirements, and in 1972, the agency amended the standard to require full passive protection for all front seat occupants of vehicles manufactured after August 15, 1975. In the interim, vehicles built between August 1973 and August 1975 were to carry either passive restraints or lap and shoulder belts coupled with an "ignition interlock" that would prevent starting the vehicle if the belts were not connected. On review, the agency's decision to require passive restraints was found to be supported by "substantial evidence" and upheld. *Chrysler Corp. v. Dep't of Transp.*, 472 F.2d 659 (6th Cir. 1972).

In preparing for the upcoming model year, most car makers chose the "ignition interlock" option, a decision which was highly unpopular, and led Congress to amend the Act to prohibit a motor vehicle safety standard from requiring or permitting compliance by means of an ignition interlock or a continuous buzzer designed to indicate that safety belts were not in use. * * *

The effective date for mandatory passive restraint systems was extended for a year until August 31, 1976. But in June 1976, Secretary of Transportation William Coleman initiated a new rulemaking on the issue. After hearing testimony and reviewing written comments, Coleman extended the optional alternatives indefinitely and suspended the passive restraint requirement. Although he found passive restraints technologically and economically feasible, the Secretary based his decision on the expectation that there would be widespread public resistance to the new systems. He instead proposed a demonstration project involving up to 500,000 cars installed with passive restraints, in order to smooth the way for public acceptance of mandatory passive restraints at a later date.

Coleman's successor as Secretary of Transportation disagreed. Within months of assuming office, Secretary Brock Adams decided that the demonstration project was unnecessary. He issued a new mandatory passive restraint regulation, known as Modified Standard 208. The Modified Standard mandated the phasing in of passive restraints beginning with large cars in model year 1982 and extending to all cars by model year 1984. The two principal systems that would satisfy the Standard were airbags and passive belts; the choice of which system to install was left to the manufacturers. * * * [T]he Court of Appeals upheld Modified Standard 208 as a rational, nonarbitrary regulation consistent with the agency's mandate under the Act. * * *

Over the next several years, the automobile industry geared up to comply with Modified Standard 208. As late as July, 1980, NHTSA reported:

> "On the road experience in thousands of vehicles equipped with airbags and automatic safety belts has confirmed agency estimates of the life-saving and injury-preventing benefits of such systems. When all cars are equipped with automatic crash protection systems, each year an estimated 9,000 more lives will be saved and tens of thousands of serious injuries will be prevented." NHTSA, Automobile Occupant Crash Protection, Progress Report No. 3, at 4.

In February 1981, however, Secretary of Transportation Andrew Lewis reopened the rulemaking due to changed economic circumstances and, in particular, the difficulties of the automobile industry. Two months later, the agency ordered a one-year delay in the application of the standard to large cars, extending the deadline to September 1982, and at the same time, proposed the possible rescission of the entire standard. After receiving written comments and holding public hearings, NHTSA issued a final rule that rescinded the passive restraint requirement contained in Modified Standard 208.

II

In a statement explaining the rescission, NHTSA maintained that it was no longer able to find, as it had in 1977, that the automatic restraint requirement would produce significant safety benefits. This judgment reflected not a change of opinion on the effectiveness of the technology, but a change in plans by the automobile industry. In 1977, the agency had assumed that airbags would be installed in 60% of all new cars and automatic seatbelts in 40%. By 1981 it became apparent that automobile manufacturers planned to install the automatic seatbelts in approximately 99% of the new cars. For this reason, the life-saving potential of airbags would not be realized. Moreover, it now appeared that the overwhelming majority of passive belts planned to be installed by manufacturers could be detached easily and left that way permanently. Passive belts, once detached, then required "the same type of affirmative action that is the stumbling block to obtaining high usage levels of manual belts." Notice 25, 46 Fed. Reg. 53421. For this reason, the agency concluded that there was no longer a basis for reliably predicting that the standard would lead to any significant increased usage of restraints at all.

In view of the possibly minimal safety benefits, the automatic restraint requirement no longer was reasonable or practicable in the agency's view. The requirement would require approximately $1 billion to implement and the agency did not believe it would be reasonable to impose such substantial costs on manufacturers and consumers without more adequate assurance that sufficient safety benefits would accrue. In addition, NHTSA concluded that automatic restraints might have an adverse effect on the public's attitude toward safety. Given the high expense and limited benefits of detachable belts, NHTSA feared that many consumers would regard the standard as an instance of ineffective regulation, adversely affecting the public's view of safety regulation and, in particular, "poisoning popular sentiment toward efforts to improve occupant restraint systems in the future." *Id.* at 53424.

* * *

III

* * * Both the [Motor Vehicle Safety] Act and the 1974 Amendments concerning occupant crash protection standards indicate that motor vehicle safety standards are to be promulgated under the informal rulemaking procedures of the Administrative Procedure Act. 5 U.S.C. § 553. The agency's action in promulgating such standards therefore may be set aside if found to be "arbitrary, capricious, an abuse of discretion, or otherwise not in accordance with law." 5 U.S.C. § 706(2)(A). We believe that the rescission or modification of an occupant-protection standard is subject to the same test. Section 103(b) of the [Motor Vehicle Safety] Act, 15 U.S.C. § 1392(b), states that the procedural and judicial review provisions of the Administrative Procedure Act "shall apply to all orders establishing, amending, or revoking a Federal motor vehicle safety standard," and suggests no difference in the scope of judicial review depending upon the nature of the agency's action.

Petitioner Motor Vehicle Manufacturers Association (MVMA) disagrees, contending that the rescission of an agency rule should be judged by the same standard a court would use to judge an agency's refusal to promulgate a rule in the first place—a standard Petitioner believes considerably narrower than the traditional arbitrary and capricious test. We reject this view. The [Motor Vehicle Safety] Act expressly equates orders "revoking" and "establishing" safety standards; neither that Act nor the APA suggests that revocations are to be treated as refusals to promulgate standards. Petitioner's view would render meaningless Congress' authorization for judicial review of orders revoking safety rules. Moreover, the revocation of an extant regulation is substantially different than a failure to act. Revocation constitutes a reversal of the agency's former views as to the proper course. A "settled course of behavior embodies the agency's informed judgment that, by pursuing that course, it will carry out the policies committed to it by Congress. There is, then, at least a presumption that those policies will be carried out best if the settled rule is adhered to." *Atchison, Topeka & Santa Fe Ry. Co. v. Wichita Bd. of Trade*, 412 U.S. 800, 807–08 (1973). Accordingly, an agency changing its course by rescinding a rule is obligated to supply a reasoned analysis for the change beyond that which may be required when an agency does not act in the first instance.

In so holding, we fully recognize that "[r]egulatory agencies do not establish rules of conduct to last forever," *Am. Trucking Ass'n, Inc. v. Atchison, Topeka & Santa Fe Ry. Co.*, 387 U.S. 397, 416 (1967), and that an agency must be given ample latitude to "adapt their rules and policies to the demands of changing circumstances." *Permian Basin Area Rate Cases*, 390 U.S. 747, 784 (1968). But the forces of change do not always or necessarily point in the direction of deregulation. In the abstract, there is no more reason to presume that changing circumstances require the rescission of prior action, instead of a revision in or even the extension of current regulation. If Congress established a presumption from which judicial review should start, that presumption—contrary to petitioners' views—is not against safety regulation, but against changes in current policy that are not justified by the rulemaking record. While the removal of a regulation may not entail the monetary expenditures and other costs of enacting a new standard, and accordingly, it may be easier for an agency to justify a deregulatory action, the direction in which an agency chooses to move does not alter the standard of judicial review established by law.

* * * The scope of review under the "arbitrary and capricious" standard is narrow and a court is not to substitute its judgment for that of the agency. Nevertheless, the agency must examine the relevant data and articulate a satisfactory explanation for its action including a "rational connection between the facts found and the choice made." *Burlington Truck Lines v. United States*, 371 U.S. 156, 168 (1962). In reviewing that explanation, we must "consider whether the decision was based on a consideration of the relevant factors and whether there has been a clear error of judgment." *Bowman Transp., Inc. v. Arkansas-Best Freight Sys.*, 419 U.S. 281, 285 (1974). Normally, an agency rule would be arbitrary and capricious if the agency has relied on factors which Congress has not intended it to consider, entirely failed to consider an important aspect of the problem, offered an explanation for its decision that runs counter to the evidence before the agency, or is so implausible that it could not be ascribed to a difference in view or the product of agency expertise. The reviewing court should not attempt itself to make up for such deficiencies: "We may not supply a reasoned basis for the agency's action that the agency itself has not given." *SEC v. Chenery Corp.*, 332 U.S. 194, 196 (1947). We will, however, "uphold a decision of less than ideal clarity if the agency's path may reasonably be discerned." *Bowman Transp.*, 419 U.S., at 286.

* * *

V

The ultimate question before us is whether NHTSA's rescission of the passive restraint requirement of Standard 208 was arbitrary and capricious. We conclude, as did the Court of Appeals, that it was. We also conclude, but for somewhat different reasons, that further consideration of the issue by the agency is therefore required. We deal separately with the rescission as it applies to airbags and as it applies to seatbelts.

A

The first and most obvious reason for finding the rescission arbitrary and capricious is that NHTSA apparently gave no consideration whatever to modifying the Standard to require that airbag technology be utilized. Standard 208 sought to achieve automatic crash protection by requiring automobile manufacturers to install either of two passive restraint devices: airbags or automatic seatbelts. There was no suggestion in the long rulemaking process that led to Standard 208 that if only one of these options were feasible, no passive restraint standard should be promulgated. Indeed, the agency's original proposed standard contemplated the installation of inflatable restraints in all cars. Automatic belts were added as a means of complying with the standard because they were believed to be as effective as airbags in achieving the goal of occupant crash protection. At that time, the passive belt approved by the agency could not be detached. Only later, at a manufacturer's behest, did the agency approve of the detachability feature—and only after assurances that the feature would not compromise the safety benefits of the restraint. Although it was then foreseen that 60% of the new cars would contain airbags and 40% would have automatic seatbelts, the ratio between the two was not significant as long as the passive belt would also assure greater passenger safety.

The agency has now determined that the detachable automatic belts will not attain anticipated safety benefits because so many individuals will detach the mechanism. Even if this conclusion were acceptable in its entirety, standing alone it would not justify any more than an amendment of Standard 208 to disallow compliance by means of the one technology which will not provide effective passenger protection. It does not cast doubt on the need for a passive restraint standard or upon the efficacy of airbag technology. In its most recent rule-making, the agency again acknowledged the life-saving potential of the airbag:

> "The agency has no basis at this time for changing its earlier conclusions in 1976 and 1977 that basic airbag technology is sound and has been sufficiently demonstrated to be effective in those vehicles in current use...." NHTSA Final Regulatory Impact Analysis XI–4 (Oct. 1981).

Given the effectiveness ascribed to airbag technology by the agency, the mandate of the [Safety] Act to achieve traffic safety would suggest that the logical response to the faults of detachable seatbelts would be to require the installation of airbags. At the very least this alternative way of achieving the objectives of the Act should have been addressed and adequate reasons given for its abandonment. But the agency not only did not require compliance through airbags, it did not even consider the possibility in its 1981 rulemaking. Not one sentence of its rulemaking statement discusses the airbags-only option. * * * We have frequently reiterated that an agency must cogently explain why it has exercised its discretion in a given manner, and we reaffirm this principle again today.

* * *

Petitioners also invoke our decision in *Vermont Yankee Nuclear Power Corp. v. NRDC*, 435 U.S. 519 (1978), as though it were a talisman under which any agency decision is by definition unimpeachable. Specifically, it is submitted that to require an agency to consider an airbags-only alternative is, in essence, to dictate to the agency the procedures it is to follow. Petitioners both misread *Vermont Yankee* and misconstrue the nature of the remand that is in order. In *Vermont Yankee*, we held that a court may not impose additional procedural requirements upon an agency. We do not require today any specific procedures which NHTSA must follow. Nor do we broadly require an agency to consider all policy alternatives in reaching decision. It is true that a rulemaking "cannot be found wanting simply because the agency failed to include every alternative device and thought conceivable by the mind of man ... regardless of how uncommon or unknown that alternative may have been...." *Vermont Yankee*, 435 U.S. at 551. But the airbag is more than a policy alternative to the passive restraint Standard; it is a technological alternative within the ambit of the existing Standard. We hold only that given the judgment made in 1977 that airbags are an effective and cost-beneficial life-saving technology, the mandatory passive-restraint rule may not be abandoned without any consideration whatsoever of an airbags-only requirement.

B

Although the issue is closer, we also find that the agency was too quick to dismiss the safety benefits of automatic seatbelts. NHTSA's critical finding was that, in light of the industry's plans to install readily detachable passive belts, it could not reliably predict "even a 5 percentage point increase as the minimum level of expected usage increase." Notice 25, 46 Fed. Reg. 53423 (1981). The Court of Appeals rejected this finding because there is "not one iota" of evidence that Modified Standard 208 will fail to increase nationwide seatbelt use by at least 13 percentage points, the level of increased usage necessary for the Standard to justify its cost. Given the lack of probative evidence, the court held that "only a well-justified refusal to seek more evidence could render rescission non-arbitrary."

Petitioners object to this conclusion. In their view, "substantial uncertainty" that a regulation will accomplish its intended purpose is sufficient reason, without more, to rescind a regulation. We agree with petitioners that just as an agency reasonably may decline to issue a safety standard if it is uncertain about its efficacy, an agency may also revoke a standard on the basis of serious uncertainties if supported by the record and reasonably explained. Rescission of the passive restraint requirement would not be arbitrary and capricious simply because there was no evidence in direct support of the agency's conclusion. It is not infrequent that the available data does not settle a regulatory issue and the agency must then exercise its judgment in moving from the facts and probabilities on the record to a policy conclusion. Recognizing that policymaking in a complex society must account for uncertainty, however, does not imply that it is sufficient for an agency to merely recite the terms "substantial uncertainty" as a justification for its actions. The agency must explain the evidence which is available, and must offer a "rational connection between the facts found and the choice made." *Burlington Truck Lines*, 371 U.S. at 168. Generally, one aspect of that explanation would be a justification for rescinding the regulation before engaging in a search for further evidence.

In this case, the agency's explanation for rescission of the passive restraint requirement is not sufficient to enable us to conclude that the rescission was the product of reasoned decisionmaking. To reach this conclusion, we do not upset the agency's view of the facts, but we do appreciate the limitations of this record in supporting the agency's decision. We start with the accepted ground that if used, seatbelts unquestionably would save many thousands of lives and would prevent tens of thousands of crippling injuries. Unlike recent regulatory decisions we have reviewed, the safety benefits of wearing seatbelts are not in doubt and it is not challenged that were those benefits to accrue, the monetary costs of implementing the standard would be easily justified. We move next to the fact that there is no direct evidence in support of the agency's finding that detachable automatic belts cannot be predicted to yield a substantial increase in usage. The empirical evidence on the record, consisting of surveys of drivers of automobiles equipped with passive belts, reveals more than a doubling of the usage rate experienced with manual belts. Much of the agency's rulemaking statement—and much of the controversy in this case—centers on the conclusions that should be drawn from these studies. The agency maintained that the doubling of seatbelt usage in these studies could not be extrapolated to an across-the-board mandatory standard because the passive seatbelts were guarded by ignition interlocks and purchasers of the tested cars are somewhat atypical. Respondents insist these studies demonstrate that Modified Standard 208 will substantially increase seatbelt usage. We believe that it is within the agency's discretion to pass upon the generalizability of these field studies. This is precisely the type of issue which rests within the expertise of NHTSA, and upon which a reviewing court must be most hesitant to intrude.

But accepting the agency's view of the field tests on passive restraints indicates only that there is no reliable real-world experience that usage rates will substantially increase. To be sure, NHTSA opines that "it cannot reliably predict even a 5 percentage point increase as the minimum level of increased usage." Notice 25, 46 Fed. Reg. 53423 (1981). But this and other statements that passive belts will not yield substantial increases in seatbelt usage apparently take no account of the critical difference between detachable automatic belts and current manual belts. A detached passive belt does require an affirmative act to reconnect it, but-unlike a manual seat belt-the passive belt, once reattached, will continue to function automatically unless again disconnected. Thus, inertia—a factor which the agency's own studies have found significant in explaining the current low usage rates for seatbelts—works in *favor* of, not *against*, use of the protective device. Since 20% to 50% of motorists currently wear seatbelts on some occasions, there would seem to be grounds to believe that seatbelt use by occasional users will be substantially increased by the detachable passive belts. Whether this is in fact the case is a matter for the agency to decide, but it must bring its expertise to bear on the question.

* * *

"An agency's view of what is in the public interest may change, either with or without a change in circumstances. But an agency changing its course must supply a reasoned analysis. . . ." *Greater Boston Television Corp. v. FCC*, 444 F.2d 841, 852 (D.C. Cir. 1971). We do not accept all of the reasoning of the Court of Appeals but we do conclude that the agency has failed to supply the requisite "reasoned analysis" in this case. Accordingly, we vacate the judgment of the Court of Appeals and remand the case to that court with directions to remand the matter to the NHTSA for further consideration consistent with this opinion.

■ JUSTICE REHNQUIST, with whom THE CHIEF JUSTICE, JUSTICE POWELL, and JUSTICE O'CONNOR join, concurring in part and dissenting in part.

I join parts I, II, III, IV, and V–A of the Court's opinion. In particular, I agree that, since the airbag and continuous spool automatic seatbelt were explicitly approved in the Standard the agency was rescinding, the agency should explain why it declined to leave those requirements intact. In this case, the agency gave no explanation at all. Of course, if the agency can provide a rational explanation, it may adhere to its decision to rescind the entire Standard.

I do not believe, however, that NHTSA's view of detachable automatic seatbelts was arbitrary and capricious. The agency adequately explained its decision to rescind the Standard insofar as it was satisfied by detachable belts.

The statute that requires the Secretary of Transportation to issue motor vehicle safety standards also requires that "[e]ach such . . . standard shall be practicable [and] shall meet the need for motor vehicle safety." 15 U.S.C. § 1392(a). The Court rejects the agency's explanation for its conclusion that there is substantial uncertainty whether requiring installation of detachable automatic belts would substantially increase seatbelt usage. The agency chose not to rely on a study showing a substantial increase in seatbelt usage in cars equipped with automatic seatbelts *and* an ignition interlock to prevent the car from being operated when the belts were not in place *and* which were voluntarily purchased with this equipment by consumers. It is reasonable for the agency to decide that this study does not support any conclusion concerning the effect of automatic seatbelts that are installed in all cars whether the consumer wants them or not and are not linked to an ignition interlock system.

The Court rejects this explanation because "there would seem to be grounds to believe that seatbelt use by occasional users will be substantially increased by the detachable passive belts," and the agency did not adequately explain its rejection of these grounds. It seems to me that the agency's explanation, while by no means a model, is adequate. The agency acknowledged that there would probably be some increase in belt usage, but concluded that the increase would be small and not worth the cost of mandatory detachable automatic belts. The agency's obligation is to articulate a "rational connection between the facts found and the choice made." *Burlington Truck Lines, Inc. v. United States*, 371 U.S. 156, 168 (1962). I believe it has met this standard.

* * *

The agency's changed view of the standard seems to be related to the election of a new President of a different political party. It is readily apparent that the responsible members of one administration may consider public resistance and uncertainties to be more important than do their counterparts in a previous administration. A change in administration brought about by the people casting their votes is a perfectly reasonable basis for an executive agency's reappraisal of the costs and benefits of its programs and regulations. As long as the agency remains within the bounds established by Congress, it is entitled to assess administrative records and evaluate priorities in light of the philosophy of the administration.

NOTES AND QUESTIONS

1. The Court in *State Farm* held first that the arbitrary and capricious standard of APA § 706(2)(A) applies in the same manner to decisions to issue, amend, or rescind a rule. Assuming that the Court's interpretation of § 706(2)(A) is consistent with Congress's intent in enacting that provision, can you think of reasons why Congress chose to establish a presumption in favor of the status quo ante that an agency can only overcome with a statement of reasons sufficient to justify a change? Would you consider this principle consistent with the U.S. legal system in general?

2. The flip flops on mandatory passive restraints at NHTSA correlated with changes in the political party that controlled the White House: the administration of President Jimmy Carter favored mandatory passive restraints while the administration of President Ronald Reagan opposed them. Should an agency be able to justify a change in its course of action on a controversial matter based solely on changes in the regulatory philosophy of the occupant of the White House caused by a national vote for President? Is this sort of political responsiveness what we should expect from administrative agencies? The four Justices who concurred and dissented in part from the majority's opinion clearly found this justification acceptable. How should the courts respond to the reality that Presidents with differing regulatory philosophies will instruct agency heads to make changes that reflect their philosophies?

3. As the Court notes, second collisions—collisions between car occupants and parts of the interior of cars—were the largest cause of accidental deaths in the country for years. Yet, it took NHTSA about twenty years to issue a passive restraint rule that was effective, was upheld by a court, and remained in effect indefinitely. By contrast, the Steamship Safety Commission of 1852 issued rules within one year that reduced by eighty percent the number of deaths caused by the source of the largest number of accidental deaths in the mid-nineteenth century. *See* Jerry Mashaw, *Administration and "The Democracy": Administrative Law from Jackson to Lincoln, 1829–1861*, 117 YALE L. J. 1568 (2008). The Steamship Safety Commission was not required to use public notice and comment procedures; it was required only to provide a brief explanation for its rules. Moreover, its actions were not subject to judicial review. What inferences do you draw from these contrasting experiences? If you assume that procedural requirements and judicial review delayed NHTSA's passive restraint rule, can you articulate both positive and negative consequences of that delay?

4. The *State Farm* Court unanimously reversed NHTSA's passive restraint rule partly for its failure to discuss the airbag-only alternative at all. The Court stated, however, that an agency is not required to discuss all alternatives to a rule and that NHTSA is free to reject the airbag-only alternative and to re-rescind the passive restraint rule as long as it discusses the airbag-only alternative in some manner. If you were a lawyer for NHTSA, would you advise the agency to take the Court's statement at face value? How would you advise NHTSA to proceed with its efforts to promulgate a passive restraint rule?

5. A five-Justice majority in *State Farm* also reversed NHTSA because the agency did not adequately explain its prediction that automatic seatbelts would not increase use of seatbelts by more than five percent. Four Justices dissented on this issue. Considering their respective arguments, how generalizable do you find this holding? In other words, in what proportion of major rulemakings must an agency make a prediction with respect to uncertain future events based on imperfect, incomplete, or contradictory studies? If you were a lawyer for a firm that wants to be able to challenge a proposed rule, what actions might you take to ensure that a reviewing court will require the agency to explain why it has rejected the findings of a study or refused to adopt a logical alternative to the rule it has proposed?

————————

For many years after deciding *State Farm*, the Supreme Court had little to say about hard look review. With the Supreme Court's acceptance of hard look review in *State Farm*, however, the circuit courts have continued to apply it, raising numerous questions regarding the doctrine's requirements and scope. A few years ago, the Supreme Court had occasion to address two such questions: (1) whether agencies face a heightened burden in justifying agency rules that reflect changes in agency policy, as compared to rules that merely adopt new policies, and (2) whether agencies face a heightened burden in justifying agency rules that raise constitutional concerns.

FCC v. Fox Television Stations, Inc.
129 S.Ct. 1800 (2009).

■ JUSTICE SCALIA delivered the opinion of the Court, except as to Part III–E.

Federal law prohibits the broadcasting of "any . . . indecent . . . language," 18 U.S.C. § 1464, which includes expletives referring to sexual or excretory activity or organs, *see FCC v. Pacifica Foundation*, 438 U.S. 726 (1978). This case concerns the adequacy of the Federal Communications Commission's explanation of its decision that this sometimes forbids the broadcasting of indecent expletives even when the offensive words are not repeated.

* * *

In 2004, the Commission * * * declar[ed] for the first time that a nonliteral (expletive) use of the F- and S-Words could be actionably indecent, even when the word is used only once. The first order to this effect dealt with an NBC broadcast of the Golden Globe Awards, in which the performer Bono commented, "This is really, really, f* * *ing brilliant." *In re Complaints Against Various Broadcast Licensees Regarding Their Airing of the "Golden Globe Awards" Program,* 19 FCC Rcd. 4975, 4976, n.4, 2004 WL 540339 (2004) *(Golden Globes Order).* Although the Commission had received numerous complaints directed at the broadcast, its enforcement bureau had concluded that the material was not indecent because "Bono did not describe, in context, sexual or excretory organs or activities and . . . the utterance was fleeting and isolated." *Id.* at 4975–76. The full Commission reviewed and reversed the staff ruling.

The Commission first declared that Bono's use of the F-Word fell within its indecency definition, even though the word was used as an intensifier rather than a literal descriptor. "[G]iven the core meaning of the 'F-Word,' " it said, "any use of that word . . . inherently has a sexual connotation." *Id.* at 4978. The Commission determined, moreover, that the broadcast was "patently offensive" because the F-Word "is one of the most vulgar, graphic and explicit descriptions of sexual activity in the English language," because "[i]ts use invariably invokes a coarse sexual image," and because Bono's use of the word was entirely "shocking and gratuitous." *Id.* at 4979.

The Commission observed that categorically exempting such language from enforcement actions would "likely lead to more widespread use." *Id.* Commission action was necessary to "safeguard the well-being of the nation's children from the most objectionable, most offensive language." *Id.* The order noted that technological advances have made it far easier to delete ("bleep out") a "single and gratuitous use of a vulgar expletive," without adulterating the content of a broadcast. *Id.* at 4980.

The order acknowledged that "prior Commission and staff action have indicated that isolated or fleeting broadcasts of the 'F-Word' . . . are not indecent or would not be acted upon." It explicitly ruled that "any such interpretation is no longer good law." *Id.* * * *

This case concerns utterances in two live broadcasts aired by Fox Television Stations, Inc., and its affiliates prior to the Commission's *Golden Globes Order*. The first occurred during the 2002 Billboard Music Awards, when the singer Cher exclaimed, "I've also had critics for the last 40 years saying that I was on my way out every year. Right. So f* * * 'em." The second involved a segment of the 2003 Billboard Music Awards, during the presentation of an award by Nicole Richie and Paris Hilton, principals in a Fox television series called "The Simple Life." Ms. Hilton began their interchange by reminding Ms. Richie to "watch the bad language," but Ms. Richie proceeded to ask the audience, "Why do they even call it 'The Simple Life?' Have you ever tried to get cow s* * * out of a Prada purse? It's not so f* * *ing simple." Following each of these broadcasts, the Commission received numerous complaints from parents whose children were exposed to the language.

On March 15, 2006, the Commission released Notices of Apparent Liability for a number of broadcasts that the Commission deemed actionably indecent, including the two described above. * * * The Commission's order on remand upheld the indecency findings for the broadcasts described above. *See In re Complaints Regarding Various*

Television Broadcasts Between February 2, 2002, and March 8, 2005, 21 FCC Rcd. 13299 (2006) (*Remand Order*).

* * *

The order asserted that both broadcasts under review would have been actionably indecent under the staff rulings and Commission dicta in effect prior to the *Golden Globes Order*—the 2003 broadcast because it involved a literal description of excrement, rather than a mere expletive, because it used more than one offensive word, and because it was planned, and the 2002 broadcast because Cher used the F-Word not as a mere intensifier, but as a description of the sexual act to express hostility to her critics. The order stated, however, that the pre-*Golden Globes* regime of immunity for isolated indecent expletives rested only upon staff rulings and Commission dicta, and that the Commission itself had never held "that the isolated use of an expletive . . . was not indecent or could not be indecent." 21 FCC Rcd. at 13307. In any event, the order made clear, the *Golden Globes Order* eliminated any doubt that fleeting expletives could be actionably indecent, and the Commission disavowed the bureau-level decisions and its own dicta that had said otherwise. Under the new policy, a lack of repetition "weigh[s] against a finding of indecency," *id.* at 13325, but is not a safe harbor.

* * *

III. Analysis

A. Governing Principles

The Administrative Procedure Act, which sets forth the full extent of judicial authority to review executive agency action for procedural correctness permits (insofar as relevant here) the setting aside of agency action that is "arbitrary" or "capricious." 5 U.S.C. § 706(2)(A). Under what we have called this "narrow" standard of review, we insist that an agency "examine the relevant data and articulate a satisfactory explanation for its action." *Motor Vehicle Mfrs. Ass'n of United States, Inc. v. State Farm Mut. Auto. Ins. Co.*, 463 U.S. 29, 43 (1983). We have made clear, however, that "a court is not to substitute its judgment for that of the agency," *id.*, and should "uphold a decision of less than ideal clarity if the agency's path may reasonably be discerned," *Bowman Transp., Inc. v. Arkansas-Best Freight System, Inc.*, 419 U.S. 281, 286 (1974).

* * * The Second Circuit has interpreted the Administrative Procedure Act and our opinion in *State Farm* as requiring agencies to make clear " 'why the original reasons for adopting the [displaced] rule or policy are no longer dispositive' " as well as " 'why the new rule effectuates the statute as well as or better than the old rule.' " 489 F.3d, at 456–57. The Court of Appeals for the District of Columbia Circuit has similarly indicated that a court's standard of review is "heightened somewhat" when an agency reverses course. *NAACP v. FCC*, 682 F.2d 993, 998 (1982).

We find no basis in the Administrative Procedure Act or in our opinions for a requirement that all agency change be subjected to more searching review. The Act mentions no such heightened standard. And our opinion in *State Farm* neither held nor implied that every agency action representing a policy change must be justified by reasons more substantial than those required to adopt a policy in the first instance. That case, which involved the rescission of a prior regulation, said only that such action requires "a reasoned analysis for the change beyond that which may be required when an agency *does not act* in the first instance." 463 U.S. at 42 (emphasis added). Treating failures to act and rescissions of prior action differently for purposes of the standard of review makes good sense, and has basis in the text of the statute, which likewise treats the two separately. It instructs a reviewing court to "compel agency action unlawfully withheld or unreasonably delayed," 5 U.S.C. § 706(1), and to "hold unlawful and set aside agency action, findings, and conclusions found to be [among other things] . . . arbitrary [or] capricious," § 706(2)(A). The statute makes no distinction, however, between initial agency action and subsequent agency action undoing or revising that action.

To be sure, the requirement that an agency provide reasoned explanation for its action would ordinarily demand that it display awareness that it *is* changing position. An agency may not, for example, depart from a prior policy *sub silentio* or simply disregard rules that are still on the books. But it need not demonstrate to a court's satisfaction that the reasons for the new policy are *better* than the reasons for the old one; it suffices that the new policy is permissible under the statute, that there are good reasons for it, and that the agency *believes* it to be better, which the conscious change of course adequately indicates. This means that the agency need not always provide a more detailed justification than what would suffice for a new policy created on a blank slate. Sometimes it must—when, for example, its new policy rests upon factual findings that contradict those which underlay its prior policy; or when its prior policy has engendered serious reliance interests that must be taken into account. It would be arbitrary or capricious to ignore such matters. In such cases it is not that further justification is demanded by the mere fact of policy change; but that a reasoned explanation is needed for disregarding facts and circumstances that underlay or were engendered by the prior policy.

In this appeal from the Second Circuit's setting aside of Commission action for failure to comply with a procedural requirement of the Administrative Procedure Act, the broadcasters' arguments have repeatedly referred to the First Amendment. If they mean to invite us to apply a more stringent arbitrary-and-capricious review to agency actions that implicate constitutional liberties, we reject the invitation. The so-called canon of constitutional avoidance is an interpretive tool, counseling that ambiguous statutory language be construed to avoid serious constitutional doubts. We know of no precedent for applying it to limit the scope of authorized executive action. In the same section authorizing courts to set aside "arbitrary [or] capricious" agency action, the Administrative Procedure Act separately provides for setting aside agency action that is "unlawful," 5 U.S.C. § 706(2)(A), which of course includes unconstitutional action. We think that is the only context in which constitutionality bears upon judicial review of authorized agency action. If the Commission's action here was not arbitrary or capricious in the ordinary sense, it satisfies the Administrative Procedure Act's "arbitrary [or] capricious" standard; its lawfulness under the

Constitution is a separate question to be addressed in a constitutional challenge.

B.   Application to This Case

Judged under the above described standards, the Commission's new enforcement policy and its order finding the broadcasts actionably indecent were neither arbitrary nor capricious. First, the Commission forthrightly acknowledged that its recent actions have broken new ground, taking account of inconsistent "prior Commission and staff action" and explicitly disavowing them as "no longer good law." *Golden Globes Order*, 19 FCC Rcd. at 4980. To be sure, the (superfluous) explanation in its *Remand Order* of why the Cher broadcast would even have violated its earlier policy may not be entirely convincing. But that unnecessary detour is irrelevant. There is no doubt that the Commission knew it was making a change. That is why it declined to assess penalties; and it relied on the *Golden Globes Order* as removing any lingering doubt.

Moreover, the agency's reasons for expanding the scope of its enforcement activity were entirely rational. It was certainly reasonable to determine that it made no sense to distinguish between literal and nonliteral uses of offensive words, requiring repetitive use to render only the latter indecent. As the Commission said with regard to expletive use of the F-Word, "the word's power to insult and offend derives from its sexual meaning." *Remand Order*, 21 FCC Rcd. at 13323. And the Commission's decision to look at the patent offensiveness of even isolated uses of sexual and excretory words fits with the context-based approach we sanctioned in *Pacifica,* 438 U.S. at 750. Even isolated utterances can be made in "pander[ing,] . . . vulgar and shocking" manners, *Remand Order*, 21 FCC Rcd. at 13305, and can constitute harmful " 'first blow[s]' " to children. *Id.* at 13309. It is surely rational (if not inescapable) to believe that a safe harbor for single words would "likely lead to more widespread use of the offensive language."

When confronting other requests for *per se* rules governing its enforcement of the indecency prohibition, the Commission has declined to create safe harbors for particular types of broadcasts. The Commission could rationally decide it needed to step away from its old regime where nonrepetitive use of an expletive was *per se* nonactionable because that was "at odds with the Commission's overall enforcement policy." *Golden Globes Order*, 19 FCC Rcd. at 4979.

* * *

The fact that technological advances have made it easier for broadcasters to bleep out offending words further supports the Commission's stepped-up enforcement policy. And the agency's decision not to impose any forfeiture or other sanction precludes any argument that it is arbitrarily punishing parties without notice of the potential consequences of their action.

* * *

E. The Dissents' Arguments

Justice BREYER purports to "begin with applicable law," but in fact begins by stacking the deck. He claims that the FCC's status as an "independent" agency sheltered from political oversight requires courts to be "all the more" vigilant in ensuring "that major policy decisions be based upon articulable reasons." Not so. The independent agencies are sheltered not from politics but from the President, and it has often been observed that their freedom from presidential oversight (and protection) has simply been replaced by increased subservience to congressional direction. Indeed, the precise policy change at issue here was spurred by significant political pressure from Congress.

* * *

Regardless, it is assuredly not "applicable law" that rulemaking by independent regulatory agencies is subject to heightened scrutiny. The Administrative Procedure Act, which provides judicial review, makes no distinction between independent and other agencies, neither in its definition of agency, 5 U.S.C. § 701(b)(1), nor in the standards for reviewing agency action, § 706. Nor does any case of ours express or reflect the "heightened scrutiny" Justice BREYER and Justice STEVENS would impose. Indeed, it is hard to imagine any closer scrutiny than that we have given to the Environmental Protection Agency, which is not an independent agency. *See Massachusetts v. EPA*, 549 U.S. 497, 533–35 (2007). There is no reason to magnify the separation-of-powers dilemma posed by the Headless Fourth Branch by letting Article III judges—like jackals stealing the lion's kill—expropriate some of the power that Congress has wrested from the unitary Executive.

Justice BREYER and Justice STEVENS rely upon two supposed omissions in the FCC's analysis that they believe preclude a finding that the agency did not act arbitrarily. Neither of these omissions could undermine the coherence of the rationale the agency gave, but the dissenters' evaluation of each is flawed in its own right.

First, both claim that the Commission failed adequately to explain its consideration of the constitutional issues inherent in its regulation. We are unaware that we have ever before reversed an executive agency, not for violating our cases, but for failure to discuss them adequately. But leave that aside. According to Justice BREYER, the agency said "next to nothing about the relation between the change it made in its prior 'fleeting expletive' policy and the First-Amendment-related need to avoid 'censorship.'" The *Remand Order* does, however, devote four full pages of small-type, single-spaced text (over 1,300 words not counting the footnotes) to explaining why the Commission believes that its indecency-enforcement regime (which includes its change in policy) is consistent with the First Amendment—and therefore not censorship as the term is understood. * * *

Second, Justice BREYER looks over the vast field of particular factual scenarios unaddressed by the FCC's 35-page *Remand Order* and finds one that is fatal: the plight of the small local broadcaster who cannot afford the new technology that enables the screening of live broadcasts for indecent utterances. The Commission has failed to address the fate of this unfortunate, who will, he believes, be subject to sanction.

We doubt, to begin with, that small-town broadcasters run a heightened risk of liability for indecent utterances. In programming that they originate, their down-home local guests probably employ vulgarity less than big-city folks; and small-town stations generally cannot afford or cannot attract foul-mouthed glitteratae from Hollywood. Their main exposure with regard to self-originated programming is live coverage of news and public affairs. But the *Remand Order* went out of its way to note that the case at hand did not involve "breaking news coverage," and that "it may be inequitable to hold a licensee responsible for airing offensive speech during live coverage of a public event." *Remand Order*, 21 FCC Rcd. at 13311. As for the programming that small stations receive on a network "feed": This *will* be cleansed by the expensive technology small stations (by Justice BREYER's hypothesis) cannot afford.

But never mind the detail of whether small broadcasters are uniquely subject to a great risk of punishment for fleeting expletives. The fundamental fallacy of Justice BREYER's small-broadcaster gloomy scenario is its demonstrably false assumption that the *Remand Order* makes no provision for the avoidance of unfairness—that the single-utterance prohibition will be invoked uniformly, in all situations. The *Remand Order* made very clear that this is not the case. It said that in determining "what, if any, remedy is appropriate" the Commission would consider the facts of each individual case, such as the "possibility of human error in using delay equipment." *Id.* at 13313. * * *

There was, in sum, no need for the Commission to compose a special treatise on local broadcasters. And Justice BREYER can safely defer his concern for those yeomen of the airwaves until we have before us a case that involves one.

■ [The opinion of JUSTICE THOMAS, concurring; the opinion of JUSTICE KENNEDY, concurring in part and concurring in the judgment; the opinion of JUSTICE STEVENS, dissenting; and the opinion of JUSTICE GINSBURG, dissenting, have been omitted. Ed.]

■ JUSTICE BREYER, with whom JUSTICE STEVENS, JUSTICE SOUTER, and JUSTICE GINSBURG join, dissenting.

In my view, the Federal Communications Commission failed adequately to explain *why* it *changed* its indecency policy from a policy permitting a single "fleeting use" of an expletive, to a policy that made no such exception. Its explanation fails to discuss two critical factors, at least one of which directly underlay its original policy decision. Its explanation instead discussed several factors well known to it the first time around, which by themselves provide no significant justification for a *change* of policy. Consequently, the FCC decision is "arbitrary, capricious, an abuse of discretion." 5 U.S.C. § 706(2)(A). * * *

I begin with applicable law. That law grants those in charge of independent administrative agencies broad authority to determine relevant policy. But it does not permit them to make policy choices for purely political reasons nor to rest them primarily upon unexplained policy preferences. Federal Communications Commissioners have fixed terms of office; they are not directly responsible to the voters; and they enjoy an independence expressly designed to insulate them, to a degree, from " 'the exercise of political oversight.' " *Freytag v. Comm'r*, 501 U.S. 868, 916 (1991) (SCALIA, J., concurring in part and concurring in judgment). That insulation helps to secure important governmental objectives, such as the constitutionally related objective of maintaining broadcast regulation that does not bend too readily before the political winds. But that agency's comparative freedom from ballot-box control makes it all the more important that courts review its decisionmaking to assure compliance with applicable provisions of the law—including law requiring that major policy decisions be based upon articulable reasons.

The statutory provision applicable here is the Administrative Procedure Act's (APA) prohibition of agency action that is "arbitrary, capricious, [or] an abuse of discretion," 5 U.S.C. § 706(2)(A). This legal requirement helps assure agency decisionmaking based upon more than the personal preferences of the decisionmakers. Courts have applied the provision sparingly, granting agencies broad policymaking leeway. But they have also made clear that agency discretion is not " 'unbounded.' " *Burlington Truck Lines, Inc. v. United States,* 371 U.S. 156, 167–168 (1962).

* * *

The law has also recognized that it is not so much a particular set of substantive commands but rather it is a *process*, a process of learning through reasoned argument, that is the antithesis of the "arbitrary." This means agencies must follow a "logical and rational" decisionmaking "process." *Allentown Mack Sales & Serv., Inc. v. NLRB*, 522 U.S. 359, 374 (1998). An agency's policy decisions must reflect the reasoned exercise of expert judgment. And, as this Court has specified, in determining whether an agency's policy choice was "arbitrary," a reviewing court "must consider whether the decision was based on a consideration of the relevant factors and whether there has been a clear error of judgment." *Citizens to Preserve Overton Park, Inc. v. Volpe*, 401 U.S. 402, 416 (1971).

Moreover, an agency must act consistently. The agency must follow its own rules. And when an agency seeks to change those rules, it must focus on the fact of change and explain the basis for that change.

To explain a change requires more than setting forth reasons why the new policy is a good one. It also requires the agency to answer the question, "Why did you change?" And a rational answer to this question typically requires a more complete explanation than would prove satisfactory were change itself not at issue. An (imaginary) administrator explaining why he chose a policy that requires driving on the right-side, rather than the left-side, of the road might say, "Well, one side seemed as good as the other, so I flipped a coin." But even assuming the rationality of that explanation for an *initial* choice, that explanation is not at all rational if offered to explain why the administrator *changed* driving practice, from right-side to left-side, 25 years later.

* * *

Contrary to the majority's characterization of this dissent, it would not (and *State Farm* does not) require a "*heightened standard*" of review. Rather, the law requires application of the *same standard* of review to different circumstances, namely circumstances characterized by the fact that *change* is at issue. It requires the agency to focus upon the fact of change where change is relevant, just as it must focus upon any other relevant circumstance. It requires the agency here to focus upon the reasons that led the agency to adopt the initial policy, and to explain why it now comes to a new judgment.

I recognize that *sometimes* the ultimate explanation for a change may have to be, "We now weigh the relevant considerations differently." But at other times, an agency can and should say more. Where, for example, the agency rested its previous policy on particular factual findings. or where an agency rested its prior policy on its view of the governing law, or where an agency rested its previous policy on, say, a special need to coordinate with another agency, one would normally expect the agency to focus upon those earlier views of fact, of law, or of policy and explain why they are no longer controlling. Regardless, to say that the agency here must answer the question "why change" is not to require the agency to provide a justification that is "*better* than the reasons for the old [policy]." It is only to recognize the obvious fact that *change* is sometimes (not always) a relevant background feature that sometimes (not always) requires focus (upon prior justifications) and explanation lest the adoption of the new policy (in that circumstance) be "arbitrary, capricious, an abuse of discretion."

That is certainly how courts of appeals, the courts that review agency decisions, have always treated the matter in practice. The majority's holding could in this respect significantly change judicial review in practice, and not in a healthy direction. After all, if it is *always* legally sufficient for the agency to reply to the question "why change?" with the answer "we prefer the new policy" (even when the agency *has not considered* the major factors that led it to adopt its old policy), then why bother asking the agency to focus on the fact of change? More to the point, *why* would the law exempt this and no other aspect of an agency decision from "arbitrary, capricious" review? Where does, and why would, the APA grant agencies the freedom to change major policies on the basis of nothing more than political considerations or even personal whim?

* * *

We here must apply the general standards set forth in *State Farm* and *Overton Park* to an agency decision that changes a 25-year-old "fleeting expletive" policy from (1) the old policy that would normally permit broadcasters to transmit a single, fleeting use of an expletive to (2) a new policy that would threaten broadcasters with large fines for transmitting even a single use (including its use by a member of the public) of such an expletive, alone with nothing more. The question is whether that decision satisfies the minimal standards necessary to assure a reviewing court that such a change of policy is not "arbitrary, capricious, [or] an abuse of discretion," 5 U.S.C. § 706(2)(A), particularly as set forth in, *e.g., State Farm* and *Overton Park*. The decision, in my view, does not satisfy those standards.

Consider the requirement that an agency at least minimally "consider . . . important aspect[s] of the problem." *State Farm*, 463 U.S. at 43. The FCC failed to satisfy this requirement, for it failed to consider two critically important aspects of the problem that underlay its initial policy judgment (one of which directly, the other of which indirectly). First, the FCC said next to nothing about the relation between the change it made in its prior "fleeting expletive" policy and the First-Amendment-related need to avoid "censorship," a matter as closely related to broadcasting regulation as is health to that of the environment. The reason that discussion of the matter is particularly important here is that the FCC had *explicitly* rested its prior policy in large part upon the need to avoid treading too close to the constitutional line.

* * *

The FCC * * * repeatedly made clear that it based its "fleeting expletive" policy upon the need to avoid treading too close to the constitutional line as set forth in Justice Powell's *Pacifica* concurrence. What then did it say, when it changed its policy, about *why* it abandoned this Constitution-based reasoning? The FCC devoted "four full pages of small-type, single-spaced text," responding to industry arguments that, *e.g.,* changes in the nature of the broadcast industry made *all* indecency regulation, *i.e.,* 18 U.S.C. § 1464, unconstitutional. In doing so it repeatedly *reaffirmed* its view that *Pacifica* remains good law. All the more surprising then that, in respect to *why* it abandoned its prior view about the critical relation between its prior fleeting expletive policy and Justice Powell's *Pacifica* concurrence, it says no more than the following:

> "[O]ur decision is not inconsistent with the Supreme Court ruling in *Pacifica*. The Court explicitly left open the issue of whether an occasional expletive could be considered indecent." *Golden Globes Order*, 19 FCC Rcd. at 4982. And, (repeating what it already had said), "*[Pacifica]* specifically reserved the question of 'an occasional expletive' and noted that it addressed only the 'particular broadcast' at issue in that case." *Remand Order*, 21 FCC Rcd. at 13308–09.

These two sentences are not a summary of the FCC's discussion about why it abandoned its prior understanding of *Pacifica*. They *are* the discussion. These 28 words (repeated in two opinions) do not acknowledge that an entirely different understanding of *Pacifica* underlay the FCC's earlier policy; they do not explain why the agency changed its mind about the line that *Pacifica* draws or its policy's relation to that line; and they tell us nothing at all about what happened to the FCC's earlier determination to search for "compelling interests" and "less restrictive alternatives." They do not explain the transformation of what the FCC had long thought an insurmountable obstacle into an open door. The result is not simply *Hamlet* without the prince, but *Hamlet* with a prince who, in mid-play and without explanation, just disappears.

* * *

Second, the FCC failed to consider the potential impact of its new policy upon local broadcasting coverage. This "aspect of the problem" is particularly important because the FCC explicitly took account of potential broadcasting impact. Indeed, in setting forth "bleeping" technology changes (presumably lowering bleeping costs) as justifying the policy change, it implicitly reasoned that lower costs, making it easier for broadcasters to install bleeping equipment, made it less likely that the new policy would lead broadcasters to reduce coverage, say by canceling coverage of public events.

What then did the FCC say about the likelihood that smaller independent broadcasters, including many public service broadcasters, still would not be able to afford "bleeping" technology and, as a consequence, would reduce local coverage, indeed cancel coverage, of many public events? It said nothing at all.

The FCC cannot claim that local coverage lacks special importance. To the contrary, "the concept of localism has been a cornerstone of broadcast regulation for decades." *In re Broadcast Localism,* 23 FCC Rcd. 1324, 1326, 1327, ¶¶ 3, 5, 2008 WL 216994 (2008). * * *

Neither can the FCC now claim that the impact of its new policy on local broadcasting is insignificant and obviously so. Broadcasters tell us, as they told the FCC, the contrary. They told the FCC, for example, that the costs of bleeping/delay systems, up to $100,000 for installation and annual operation, place that technology beyond the financial reach of many smaller independent local stations. And they ask what the FCC thinks will happen when a small local station without bleeping equipment wants to cover, say a local city council meeting, a high school football game, a dance contest at community center, or a Fourth of July parade.

Relevant literature supports the broadcasters' financial claims.

* * *

What did the FCC say in response to this claim? What did it say about the likely impact of the new policy on the coverage that its new policy is most likely to affect, coverage of *local* live events—city council meetings, local sports events, community arts productions, and the like? It said nothing at all.

The plurality acknowledges that the Commission entirely failed to discuss this aspect of the regulatory problem. But it sees "no need" for discussion in light of its, *i.e.,* the plurality's, own "doubt[s]" that "small-town broadcasters run a heightened risk of liability for indecent utterances" as a result of the change of policy. The plurality's "doubt[s]" rest upon its views (1) that vulgar expression is less prevalent (at least among broadcast guests) in smaller towns, (2) that the greatest risk the new policy poses for "small-town broadcasters" arises when they broadcast local "news and public affairs," and (3) that the *Remand Order* says "little about how the Commission would treat smaller broadcasters who cannot afford screening equipment," while also pointing out that the new policy " 'does not . . . impose undue burdens on broadcasters' " and emphasizing that the case before it did not involve " 'breaking news.' "

As to the first point, about the prevalence of vulgarity in small towns, I confess ignorance. But I do know that there are independent stations in many large and medium sized cities. As to the second point, I too believe that coverage of local public events, if not news, lies at the heart of the problem.

I cannot agree with the plurality, however, about the critical third point, namely that the new policy obviously provides smaller independent broadcasters with adequate assurance that they will not be fined. The new policy removes the "fleeting expletive" exception, an exception that assured smaller independent stations that they would not be fined should someone swear at a public event. In its place, it puts a policy that places all broadcasters at risk when they broadcast fleeting expletives, including expletives uttered at public events. The *Remand Order* says that there "is *no outright news exemption from our indecency rules.*" 21 FCC Rcd. at 13327 (emphasis added). The best it can provide by way of assurance is to say that "it *may* be inequitable to hold a licensee responsible for airing offensive speech during live coverage of a public event *under some circumstances.*" *Id.* at 13311. It does list those circumstances as including the "possibility of human error in using delay equipment." *Id.* at 13313. But it says *nothing* about a station's *inability to afford* delay equipment (a matter that in individual cases could itself prove debatable). All the FCC had to do was to *consider* this matter and either grant an exemption or explain why it did not grant an exemption. But it did not. And the result is a rule that may well chill coverage—the kind of consequence that the law has considered important for decades, to which the broadcasters pointed in their arguments before the FCC, and which the FCC nowhere discusses.

NOTES AND QUESTIONS

1. After the Supreme Court decided the *Fox Television* case, circuit courts almost immediately translated its holding regarding hard look review and changes in agency policy into a three-part test: (1) that the agency's new policy be "permissible under the statute"; (2) that the agency have "good reasons" for the new policy; and (3) that the agency "believe that the new policy is better, 'which the conscious change of course adequately indicates.' " *Handley v. Chapman*, 587 F.3d 273 (5th Cir. 2009); *see also Huvis Corp. v. United States*, 570 F.3d 1347, 1353 (Fed. Cir. 2009).

2. The Court in *Fox Television* declined to impose a heightened explanatory burden on an agency merely because the agency's action might give rise to constitutional concerns. In so doing, the Court distinguished the case at bar from the canon of constitutional avoidance, which the Court has applied in other cases to reject agency rules adopting legal interpretations that might raise doubts as to a statute's constitutionality. Why do you think the Court is so willing to reject agency actions that raise constitutional questions concerning congressional acts (statutes) but to allow agency actions that independently give rise to constitutional concerns?

3. Long before it decided the *Fox Television* case, the Supreme Court arguably, though perhaps more modestly, restricted the scope of hard look review in *Pension Benefit Guaranty Corp. v. LTV Corp.*, 496 U.S. 633 (1990). In that case, the court of appeals rejected as arbitrary and capricious an order of the PBGC reinstating LTV's pension plan after LTV terminated the plan in federal bankruptcy proceedings, on the ground that the PBGC had not considered the relationship between its action and the goals and policies stated in the various federal statutes governing bankruptcy and labor law, In reversing the circuit court, the Supreme Court stated,

> The PBGC points out problems that would arise if federal courts routinely were to require each agency to take explicit account of public policies that derive from federal statutes other than the agency's enabling Act. To begin with, there are numerous federal statutes that could be said to embody countless policies. If agency action may be disturbed whenever a reviewing court is able to point to an arguably relevant statutory policy that was not explicitly considered, then a very large number of agency decisions might be open to judicial invalidation.

Id. at 646. Although the *LTV* case involved the agency's duty of reasoned decisionmaking in informal adjudication, rather than rulemaking, the Court's reasoning seems equally applicable to the rulemaking context, and could foreshadow additional limitations on the scope of hard look review.

4. In *Judulang v. Holder*, 132 S. Ct. 476 (2011), the Supreme Court applied hard look review to conclude that the method used by the Board of Immigration Appeals to determine whether an alien was eligible for discretionary relief from deportation was arbitrary and capricious. In a footnote, the Court said:

> The Government urges us instead to analyze this case under the second step of the test we announced in *Chevron U.S.A. Inc. v. Natural Resources Defense Council, Inc.*, 467 U.S. 837 (1984), to govern judicial review of an agency's statutory interpretations. Were we to do so, our analysis would be the same, because under *Chevron* step two, we ask whether an agency interpretation is arbitrary or capricious in substance.

Id. at 483 n.7 (internal quotation marks and citations omitted). Some scholars have interpreted this footnote as signaling the Court's conclusion that the second step of the *Chevron* review standard, which we discuss in Chapter 6, is the same as hard look review. Afterward, one of us (Professor Pierce) asked the author of the opinion, Justice Kagan, in a public forum whether she intended to communicate that belief. Justice Kagan, who taught administrative law at Harvard Law School before joining the Court, disavowed any intent to make such a fundamental statement of administrative law doctrine with the above language. Nevertheless, as we discuss further in Chapter 6, some lower courts continue to equate the two standards. *See, e.g., National Organization of Veterans' Advocates, Inc. v. Secretary of Veterans' Affairs*, 669 F.3d 1340 (Fed. Cir. 2012).

D. OSSIFICATION AND RESPONSES

Beginning in 1967, petitioners attempted to persuade courts to add major new procedural requirements to the simple three-step informal rulemaking process, with mixed results. Attempts to apply strict neutrality requirements on decisionmakers in rulemakings, the attempts to restrict ex parte access to decisionmakers in rulemakings, and the attempts to require oral evidentiary hearings in informal rulemakings failed. Efforts to require agencies to issue long and elaborate NOPRs and encyclopedic statements of basis and purpose, however, succeeded. Decisions in cases like *Portland Cement*, *Shell Oil*, *Nova Scotia Food Products*, and *State Farm* have greatly increased the time and the agency resources required to issue a major rule.

Arbitrary and capricious or "hard look" review under APA § 706(2)(A) has had a similar effect. A typical major rulemaking involves numerous, even dozens of, contested issues on which a party can commission and submit studies that purport to undermine or conflict with the predicates for the agency's proposed rule. Consider the following highly critical description of the resulting rulemaking process:

> The D.C. Circuit's admonition to agencies to ignore the APA and instead to use the procedures dictated by the D.C. Circuit had dramatic effects on agencies. Before the D.C. Circuit issued its opinion in *Boyd*, the typical agency statement of basis and purpose was one to three pages long; it was "concise" and "general." After the D.C. Circuit announced that the judicially created hard-look doctrine required agencies to ignore the procedures required by the APA, the typical statement of basis and purpose grew to its present gargantuan size of 200 to 1000 pages. Agencies recognized that the D.C. Circuit was correct; to have any chance of successfully running the gauntlet of hard-look review, an agency must ignore the procedures required by statute and must instead issue a statement of basis and purpose that is comprehensive and encyclopedic.

* * *

> The *Vermont Yankee* Court criticized the D.C. Circuit's practice of requiring limited-scope hearings in some rulemakings as one that imposed so much of a procedural burden on the rulemaking process that "all the inherent advantages of informal rulemaking would be totally lost." Like the D.C. Circuit's practice of requiring agencies to conduct limited-scope oral hearings in rulemakings, hard-look review adds years to each major rulemaking, adds many millions of dollars in procedural costs to each rulemaking, and produces rulemaking "records" that usually exceed 10,000 pages. As a result, agencies are extremely reluctant to use informal rulemaking. This is precisely the effect that the Court identified as one of its reasons for forbidding courts from engaging in the practice the Court outlawed in *Vermont Yankee*.

Richard J. Pierce, Jr., *Waiting for Vermont Yankee II, III, and IV*, 75 GEO. WASH. L. REV. 902 (2007). Although the Supreme Court in *Fox Television* arguably narrowed the scope of hard look review somewhat, judges generally have refrained from criticizing the doctrine outright. One notable exception came in the dissenting opinion by Judge Kavanaugh in *American Radio Relay League v. FCC*, 524 F.3d 227 (D.C. Cir. 2008), aspects of which are discussed elsewhere in this Chapter:

> The two issues on which I write separately prompt a broader observation. In appropriate cases or controversies, courts of course must be vigilant in ensuring that agencies adhere to the

plain text of statutes imposing substantive and procedural obligations. But it bears repeating that § 553 of the APA requires only a notice providing a "description of the subjects and issues involved"; time for interested persons to comment; and a "concise general statement" of the rule's "basis and purpose." Courts have incrementally expanded those APA procedural requirements well beyond what the text provides. And courts simultaneously have grown *State Farm*'s "narrow" § 706 arbitrary-and-capricious review into a far more demanding test. Application of the beefed-up arbitrary-and-capricious test is inevitably if not inherently unpredictable—so much so that, on occasion, the courts' arbitrary-and-capricious review itself appears arbitrary and capricious.

Over time, those twin lines of decisions have gradually transformed rulemaking-whether regulatory or deregulatory rulemaking—from the simple and speedy practice contemplated by the APA into a laborious, seemingly never-ending process. The judicially created obstacle course can hinder Executive Branch agencies from rapidly and effectively responding to changing or emerging issues within their authority, such as consumer access to broadband, or effectuating policy or philosophical changes in the Executive's approach to the subject matter at hand. The trend has not been good as a jurisprudential matter, and it continues to have significant practical consequences for the operation of the Federal Government and those affected by federal regulation and deregulation.

Id. at 248 (Kavanaugh, J., concurring in part and dissenting in part).

Accepted wisdom among administrative law scholars holds that the added requirements that judges have imposed on the informal rulemaking process have, in turn, has produced a phenomenon that many scholars call rulemaking ossification—a tendency for agencies to refrain from using the informal rulemaking process at all. Scholars disagree about the merits and extent of such delays. Agencies continue to issue thousands of pages of new rules each year. At least one empirical study of rulemaking across all active federal rule-writing agencies suggests that the ossifying effects of judicially-imposed procedural requirements are limited to a comparatively small number of outliers and situations in which procedural requirements may further slow promulgation of rules that are already taking a long time to finalize. *See* Jason Webb Yackee & Susan Webb Yackee, *Administrative Procedures and Bureaucratic Performance: Is Federal Rulemaking "Ossified"?*, J. PUB. ADMIN. RES. & THEORY (forthcoming 2009).

Regardless, many scholars have urged Congress to amend the APA to make the informal rulemaking process more attractive to agencies by reducing the procedural demands the courts have imposed since 1967. Congress has shown no inclination to make any statutory changes of that type. In some ways, Congress has actually added to agencies' rulemaking burdens, For example, in 1996, Congress amended the Regulatory Flexibility Act to add procedures that an agency must satisfy when it issues a rule that affects "small entities," which essentially requires agencies to further explain the reasons and consequences behind their rules. To a lesser extent, however, Congress, the courts, and agencies themselves have taken some steps and considered others in response to rulemaking ossification.

Negotiated Rulemaking

In 1990, Congress enacted the Negotiated Rulemaking Act. That statute creates an alternative process for issuing a rule known as negotiated rulemaking, also sometimes referred to more colloquially as reg-neg. In the negotiated rulemaking process, the agency assembles representatives of various parties who are interested in the outcome of a rulemaking for the purpose of negotiating the proposed rule. The process begins when an agency issues a public notice announcing its intent to utilize negotiated rulemaking, thereby allowing interested parties who do not believe that their concerns are adequately represented by the proposed negotiating committee to seek better representation. Once the negotiating committee is fully established, a neutral mediator or facilitator chairs the negotiating sessions. The goal of negotiated rulemaking is for the members of the committee to reach a consensus regarding the rule to be proposed. The agency then publishes the negotiated proposed rule in a NOPR and invites public comments, consistent with the standard APA rulemaking process.

Agencies have attempted the negotiated rulemaking process in connection with a number of rulemaking efforts. Negotiated rulemaking has succeeded in creating a rule in about twenty per cent of the cases in which it has been used. Agencies have never used negotiated rulemaking as the exclusive method of crafting a rule in a major rulemaking. Negotiated rulemaking can serve that purpose only if the agency and the interested members of the public can agree on how to resolve the various policy disputes that the rulemaking raises. Congress typically delegates the policy decisions inherent in major rulemakings to agencies because a majority of members of the House and Senate are unable to agree with respect to the resolution of those policy disputes. If members of Congress cannot reach agreement on such matters of policy, what is the likelihood that the agency and the interested parties will be able to do so through the negotiated rulemaking process?

Negotiated rulemaking is controversial. Courts have upheld the use of the alternative process for issuing rules Congress authorized, albeit with expressions of serious misgivings. Judge Posner characterized negotiated rulemaking as "an abdication of regulatory authority to the regulated, the full burgeoning of the interest-group state, and the final confirmation of the 'capture' theory of the administrative state." *USA Group Loan Servs., Inc. v. Riley*, 82 F.3d 708 714 (7th Cir. 1996). In 1997, Duke Law Journal devoted an entire issue to a symposium evaluating negotiated rulemaking.

Proponents of negotiated rulemaking, represented most prominently by Philip Harter, suggest that it reduces the amount of time that an agency needs to promulgate regulations and that it decreases litigation challenging those regulations once the agency finalizes them. *See* Philip J. Harter, *Negotiating Regulations: A Cure for Malaise*, 71 GEO. L.J. 1, 31–42 (1982). Critics argue that, in actual practice, negotiated rulemaking accomplishes neither of these goals.

Rather, they argue, (1) the process heightens conflict by excluding some interested parties from the negotiation committee and calling attention to pressure points in the final rule; (2) any consensus developed in negotiation is likely to unravel as the agency considers other voices through the subsequent notice and comment process; and (3) agencies and interest groups work together in the traditional rulemaking process, too, suggesting that conventional rulemaking offers as much opportunity as negotiated rulemaking for meaningful negotiation and cooperation. *See* Cary Coglianese, *Assessing Consensus: The Promise and Performance of Negotiated Rulemaking*, 46 Duke L.J. 1255 (1997).

Regardless, Jeffrey Lubbers reports that agency utilization of negotiated rulemaking is declining. Lubbers reports that agencies created sixty-three separate negotiation committees from 1991 through 1999 but only twenty-two negotiation committees from 2000 through 2007. Lubbers attributes the decline partly to the demise of the Administrative Conference of the United States, which held certain official responsibilities for the facilitation of negotiated rulemaking but lost its funding in 1995. Lubbers also suggests that agency budgetary issues are a factor: the up-front costs of negotiated rulemaking are quite high, it is not clear whether cost savings at the end from reduced court challenges actually materialized, and most of any savings from reduced litigation would have been pocketed by the Department of Justice (which is responsible for litigating claims against agencies) rather than the agencies themselves. Additionally, Lubbers observes that key staff within the Office of Management and Budget responsible for monitoring agency rulemaking efforts on behalf of the President dislike negotiated rulemaking. *See* Jeffrey S. Lubbers, *Achieving Policymaking Consensus: The (Unfortunate) Waning of Negotiated Rulemaking*, 49 S. Tex. L. Rev. 987 (2008).

Direct Final Rulemaking

Before its demise in 1995, the Administrative Conference of the United States also supported another variation on the notice-and-comment rulemaking process known as direct final rulemaking as a means of reducing ossification and speeding up agency rulemaking. Direct final rulemaking involves issuing regulations in the Federal Register with a notice that they will become final on a given future date unless, within the designated comment period, some interested party files comments requesting changes or criticizing the regulations. Under one version of direct final rulemaking, if the agency receives any negative comments, then the agency withdraws the direct final rules and republishes them as proposed regulations in a more traditional NOPR. Another conception of direct final rulemaking requires the agency withdraw and republish rules only if it receives material or substantial negative comments. Under either approach, however, if the agency receives only favorable comments or no comments at all, the agency may allow the regulations to become final as originally published and without further action. This abbreviated process enables agencies to shift resources from noncontroversial rules to more major rulemaking efforts.

Not all agency rulemakings are major or controversial. Many NOPRs result in few comments or even none at all. As documented by

Ronald Levin, several agencies have used direct final rulemaking successfully to promulgate noncontroversial regulations. *See* Ronald M. Levin, *Direct Final Rulemaking*, 64 GEO. WASH. L. REV. 1 (1995).

Nevertheless, direct final rulemaking is not universally embraced. Lars Noah in particular has criticized direct final rulemaking as contrary to the APA. In particular, Noah contends that allowing direct final rulemaking to proceed in the face of numerous immaterial or insubstantial comments is problematic. The significance of a comment is inherently a subjective inquiry, and an agency's assessment that a particular comment is insignificant could late provide a basis for a legal challenge to the final rule. Further, in the event of a legal challenge, direct final rulemaking could lead to an abbreviated record that might cause frustrated judges to invalidate an otherwise good rule, particularly in light of the hard look doctrine. *See* Lars Noah, *Doubts About Direct Final Rulemaking*, 51 ADMIN. L. REV. 401 (1999).

Remand Without Vacatur

The traditional remedy for agency procedural or process failings in informal rulemaking has been for the reviewing court to reverse or set aside the regulation and remand it back to the agency for further action. As a result, agencies may have devoted substantial time and resources to developing the rule, only to face reversal and remand of its final product. It is hardly surprising that agencies experiencing such outcomes might hesitate before dedicating further time and resources to major rulemaking efforts.

Perhaps perceiving value in rulemaking as a method for agency decisionmaking, reviewing courts have on occasion imposed a less drastic remedy for inadequacies in the agency's NOPR or statement of basis and purpose. In *Allied-Signal, Inc. v. NRC*, 988 F.2d 146 (D.C. Cir. 1993), the D.C. Circuit found that an agency rule was inadequately supported by the record. Rather than reversing the regulation, however, the court decided that "[a]n inadequately supported rule . . . need not necessarily be vacated." Instead, the court remanded the regulation for further agency action while allowing the rule to remain in effect— remand without vacatur (also sometimes labeled remand without vacation). According to the *Allied Signal* court, whether this remedy is appropriate depends upon "the seriousness of the order's deficiencies" as well as "the disruptive consequences" of invalidating the rule.

The remedy of remand without vacatur is controversial. Supporters note that judicial vacation of an agency rule may seriously disrupt agency efforts to implement statutory requirements and accomplish statutory goals. Furthermore, regulated parties may have already arranged their affairs to comply with the rule's requirements or in anticipation of receiving government benefits, implicating reliance interests. But in *Checkosky v. SEC*, 23 F.3d 452, 466 (D.C. Cir. 1994), Judge Raymond Randolph argued in dissent that courts do not possess the discretion to remand an agency action without also vacating that action.

> Once a reviewing court determines that the agency has not adequately explained its decision, the Administrative Procedure Act requires the court—in the absence of any

contrary statute—to vacate the agency's action. * * * Section 706(2)(A) provides that a "reviewing court" faced with an arbitrary and capricious agency decision "shall"—not may— "hold unlawful and set aside" the agency action. Setting aside means vacating; no other meaning is apparent.

* * *

To order only a remand despite the APA's mandate is to act in stubborn defiance of the law. Agencies must conform their actions to the APA. So must the courts.

Id. at 491–93. Daniel Rodriguez has argued further that

The fundamental flaw in the remand without vacatur device is that it creates a remedy that presupposes an activist level of judicial review. . . . Even more problematically, it reinforces this [presupposition] by encouraging the courts to review agency decisions and offer a remedial middle-ground where the agency may be better off with a ground not in the middle, but closer to their preferred place, a place where the agency decision is discretionary and, therefore, not reviewable at all.

Daniel B. Rodriguez, *Of Gift Horses and Great Expectations: Remands Without Vacatur in Administrative Law*, 36 ARIZ. ST. L.J. 599, 635 (1995). Ronald Levin, by contrast, contends that remand without vacatur is a reflection of judicial humility and restraint, allowing courts to grant narrower relief to parties aggrieved by agency action, and thus to avoid intruding too heavily in the administrative sphere. *See* Ronald M. Levin, *"Vacation" at Sea: Judicial Remedies and Equitable Discretion in Administrative Law*, 53 DUKE L.J. 291 (2003).

CHAPTER 6

STATUTORY INTERPRETATION IN ADMINISTRATIVE LAW

Statutory interpretation is a difficult and complicated task for courts. We leave comprehensive treatment of that subject to courses on statutory interpretation. The task is no more or less difficult and complicated when an agency must interpret a statute. Agency statutory interpretation occurs in two contexts. The first involves statutes of general applicability, i.e., statutes the agency is not charged with implementing. Reviewing courts do not confer any special deference on agency interpretations of statutes of general applicability. The other context in which agencies engage in statutory interpretation involves statutes that they administer, i.e., statutes over which Congress has delegated some amount of administrative authority to one or more particular administrative agencies. The question on which we focus in this Chapter is whether the task of statutory interpretation differs when an agency adopts an interpretation of a statute it is responsible for administering.

APA § 706 instructs reviewing courts to "decide all relevant questions of law." That direction contrasts starkly with the instructions APA § 706 gives courts for reviewing agency findings of fact and resolutions of policy disputes. Particularly when it is compared with the deferential substantial evidence standard and the arbitrary and capricious standard as applied in the context of adjudicative facts, the instruction to "decide all relevant questions of law" seems to suggest that courts should ignore agency interpretations of the statutes they administer. Yet, statutes are often susceptible of more than one reasonable interpretation, and choosing between the alternatives may be as much a matter of policy choice as of discerning statutory meaning.

In the realm of statutory interpretation, therefore, what is the most sensible allocation of power between agencies and courts? Do all questions of statutory interpretation represent issues of law? How easy is it to distinguish between "questions of law" and questions of policy? Courts have long struggled to answer these questions in contemplating their own role in reviewing third-party challenges to agency actions in general and to agency legal interpretations in particular.

Contemporary doctrine governing judicial review of agencies' interpretations of the statutes that they administer can largely be summed up in a single word: *Chevron*. Indeed, the Court seemed to make a dramatic change in its approach to judicial review of agency interpretations of agency-administered statutes in 1984 with its opinion in *Chevron U.S.A. Inc. v. Natural Resources Defense Council, Inc.*, 467 U.S. 837 (1984). Many years later, *Chevron* still dominates the field, as other key cases are notable primarily either for how they elaborate or modify *Chevron*'s meaning or scope in some way or for how they prescribe exceptions from *Chevron*. (Of course this overstates the case, but only a little.)

Nevertheless, it is impossible to appreciate the nature and magnitude of the change wrought by *Chevron* without first understanding the pre-*Chevron* approach. It is important to understand the pre-*Chevron* approach for another reason as well: more recent jurisprudence suggests that the Court may be in the process of returning, to some unknown extent, to its pre-*Chevron* approach to judicial review of agency legal interpretations.

In this Chapter, we will particularly consider the judicial approaches to agency interpretations of agency-administered statutes chronologically, using as our breakpoints *Chevron* and another, more recent landmark case, *United States v. Mead Corp.*, 533 U.S. 218 (2001). We will then discuss the special case of agency interpretations of their own regulations.

A. THE PRE-*CHEVRON* APPROACH

As we discussed at length in Chapters 1 and 2, Congress has granted both the Executive Branch and independent agencies extensive authority to adopt legally binding regulations. Some of these authorizations are narrow and specific, for example instructing a specific agency to promulgate regulations to resolve the details necessary to accomplish a particular statutory goal. The Federal Power Act of 1935, for example, gave the Federal Power Commission the power to develop and impose uniform accounting rules upon electric utility companies whose rates were to be regulated and who the statute thus required to file annual reports of their assets, income, and expenses. Other grants of authority are broader and more general, for example instructing agencies to adopt whatever rules and regulations they deem necessary to effectuate and enforce the statutes that they administer. While this distinction between specific and general authority does not carry great significance for contemporary deference doctrine, it was an important element of the pre-*Chevron* deference jurisprudence.

In numerous cases, the Supreme Court conveyed a strongly deferential attitude toward regulations promulgated pursuant to narrow and specific authority grants. In *AT&T v. United States*, 299 U.S. 232, 236–37 (1936), the Court said that it was "not at liberty to substitute its own discretion for that of administrative officers who have kept within the bounds of their administrative powers." In *Atchison, Topeka & Santa Fe Railway v. Scarlett*, 300 U.S. 471 (1937), the Court concluded that the specific authority regulation at issue, "having been made by the [Interstate Commerce Commission] in pursuance of constitutional statutory authority . . . the judgment of the trial court and jury cannot be substituted for that of the commission." In *Commissioner v. South Texas Lumber Co.*, 333 U.S. 496 (1948), the Court opined that such regulations "should not be overruled by the courts unless clearly contrary to the will of Congress." The specific authority regulations at issue in these particular cases were not necessarily adopted using the notice-and-comment procedures that we discussed in Chapter 5; Congress had not yet adopted the Administrative Procedure Act when agencies issued the regulations at issue in these cases. Nevertheless, both before and after the APA's enactment the Court considered specific authority regulations to be legislative rules, as legally binding on regulated parties as the statutes they interpreted. For a more thorough examination of this doctrinal history, see Kristin E. Hickman, *The Need for Mead: Rejecting Tax Exceptionalism in Judicial Deference*, 90 Minn. L. Rev. 1537, 1564–71 (2006).

Most agency legal interpretations, however, do not take the form of specific authority regulations. Rather, most agency legal interpretations rely on more general interpretive authority, fill gaps in statutory meaning that Congress may or may not have anticipated, and may or may not carry the force of law. The Court's pre-*Chevron* attitude toward these regulations was more equivocal and varied, as the following opinions illustrate.

NLRB v. Hearst Publications
322 U.S. 111 (1944).

■ MR. JUSTICE RUTLEDGE delivered the opinion of the Court.

These cases arise from the refusal of respondents, publishers of four Los Angeles daily newspapers, to bargain collectively with a union representing newsboys who distribute their papers on the streets of that city. Respondents[ ] conten[d] that they were not required to bargain because the newsboys are not their "employees" within the meaning of that term in the National Labor Relations Act, 29 U.S.C. § 152 * * *.

The proceedings before the National Labor Relations Board were begun with the filing of four petitions for investigation and certification by Los Angeles Newsboys Local Industrial Union No. 75. Hearings were held in a consolidated proceeding after which the Board made findings of fact and concluded that the regular full-time newsboys selling each paper were employees within the Act and that questions affecting commerce concerning the representation of employees had arisen. It designated appropriate units and ordered elections. At these the union was selected as their representative by majorities of the eligible newsboys. After the union was appropriately certified, the respondents refused to bargain with it. Thereupon proceedings under § 10, 29 U.S.C. § 160, were instituted, a hearing was held and respondents were found to have violated §§ 8(1) and (5) of the Act, 29 U.S.C. § 158(1), (5). They were ordered to cease and desist from such violations and to bargain collectively with the union upon request.

* * *

The newsboys work under varying terms and conditions. They may be "bootjackers," selling to the general public at places other than established corners, or they may sell at fixed "spots." They may sell only casually or part-time, or full-time; and they may be employed regularly and continuously or only temporarily. The units which the Board determined to be appropriate are composed of those who sell full-time at established spots. Those vendors, misnamed boys, are generally mature men, dependent upon the proceeds of their sales for their sustenance, and frequently supporters of families. Working thus as news vendors on a regular basis, often for a number of years, they form a stable group with relatively little turnover, in contrast to schoolboys and others who sell as bootjackers, temporary and casual distributors.

Overall circulation and distribution of the papers are under the general supervision of circulation managers. But for purposes of street distribution each paper has divided metropolitan Los Angeles into geographic districts. Each district is under the direct and close supervision of a district manager. His function in the mechanics of distribution is to supply the newsboys in his district with papers which he obtains from the publisher and to turn over to the publisher the receipts which he collects from their sales, either directly or with the assistance of "checkmen" or "main spot" boys. The latter, stationed at the important corners or "spots" in the district, are newsboys who, among other things, receive delivery of the papers, redistribute them to other newsboys stationed at less important corners, and collect receipts from their sales. For that service, which occupies a minor portion of their working day, the checkmen receive a small salary from the publisher. The bulk of their day, however, they spend in hawking papers at their "spots" like other full-time newsboys. A large part of the appropriate units selected by the Board for the News and the Herald are checkmen who, in that capacity, clearly are employees of those papers.

The newsboys' compensation consists in the difference between the prices at which they sell the papers and the prices they pay for them. The former are fixed by the publishers and the latter are fixed either by the publishers or, in the case of the News, by the district manager. In practice the newsboys receive their papers on credit. They pay for those sold either sometime during or after the close of their selling day, returning for credit all unsold papers. Lost or otherwise unreturned papers, however, must be paid for as though sold. Not only is the 'profit' per paper thus effectively fixed by the publisher, but substantial control of the newsboys' total "take home" can be effected through the ability to designate their sales areas and the power to determine the number of papers allocated to each. While as a practical matter this power is not exercised fully, the newsboys' "right" to decide how many papers they will take is also not absolute. In practice, the Board found, they cannot determine the size of their established order without the cooperation of the district manager. And often the number of papers they must take is determined unilaterally by the district managers.

In addition to effectively fixing the compensation, respondents in a variety of ways prescribe, if not the minutiae of daily activities, at least the broad terms and conditions of work. This is accomplished largely through the supervisory efforts of the district managers, who serve as the nexus between the publishers and the newsboys. The district managers assign "spots" or corners to which the newsboys are expected to confine their selling activities. Transfers from one "spot" to another may be ordered by the district manager for reasons of discipline or efficiency or other cause. Transportation to the spots from the newspaper building is offered by each of respondents. Hours of work on the spots are determined not simply by the impersonal pressures of the market, but to a real extent by explicit instructions from the district managers. Adherence to the prescribed hours is observed closely by the district managers or other supervisory agents of the publishers.

Sanctions, varying in severity from reprimand to dismissal, are visited on the tardy and the delinquent. By similar supervisory controls minimum standards of diligence and good conduct while at work are sought to be enforced. However wide may be the latitude for individual initiative beyond those standards, district managers' instructions in what the publishers apparently regard as helpful sales technique are expected to be followed. Such varied items as the manner of displaying the paper, of emphasizing current features and headlines, and of placing advertising placards, or the advantages of soliciting customers at specific stores or in the traffic lanes are among the subjects of this instruction. Moreover, newsboys are furnished with sales equipment, such as racks, boxes and change aprons, and advertising placards by the publishers. In this pattern of employment the Board found that the newsboys are an integral part of the publishers' distribution system and circulation organization. And the record discloses that the newsboys and checkmen feel they are employees of the papers; and respondents' supervisory employees, if not respondents themselves, regard them as such.

In addition to questioning the sufficiency of the evidence to sustain these findings, respondents point to a number of other attributes characterizing their relationship with the newsboys and urge that on the entire record the latter cannot be considered their employees. They base this conclusion on the argument that by common-law standards the extent of their control and direction of the newsboys' working activities creates no more than an "independent contractor" relationship and that common-law standards determine the "employee" relationship under the Act. They further urge that the Board's selection of a collective bargaining unit is neither appropriate nor supported by substantial evidence.

The principal question is whether the newsboys are "employees." Because Congress did not explicitly define the term, respondents say its meaning must be determined by reference to common-law standards. In their view "common-law standards" are those the courts have applied in distinguishing between "employees" and "independent contractors" when working out various problems unrelated to the Wagner Act's purposes and provisions.

The argument assumes that there is some simple, uniform and easily applicable test which the courts have used, in dealing with such problems, to determine whether persons doing work for others fall in one class or the other. Unfortunately this is not true. Only by a long and tortuous history was the simple formulation worked out which has been stated most frequently as "the test" for deciding whether one who hires another is responsible in tort for his wrongdoing. But this formula has been by no means exclusively controlling in the solution of other problems. And its simplicity has been illusory because it is more largely simplicity of formulation than of application. Few problems in the law have given greater variety of application and conflict in results than the cases arising in the borderland between what is clearly an employer-employee relationship and what is clearly one of independent, entrepreneurial dealing. This is true within the limited field of determining vicarious liability in tort. It becomes more so when the field is expanded to include all of the possible applications of the distinction.

It is hardly necessary to stress particular instances of these variations or to emphasize that they have arisen principally, first, in the struggle of the courts to work out common-law liabilities where the legislature has given no guides for judgment, more recently also under statutes which have posed the same problem for solution in the light of the enactment's particular terms and purposes. It is enough to point out that, with reference to an identical problem, results may be contrary over a very considerable region of doubt in applying the distinction, depending upon the state or jurisdiction where the determination is made; and that within a single jurisdiction a person who, for instance, is held to be an "independent contractor" for the purpose of imposing vicarious liability in tort may be an "employee" for the purposes of particular legislation, such as unemployment compensation. In short, the assumed simplicity and uniformity, resulting from application of "common-law standards," does not exist.

* * *

Both the terms and the purposes of the statute, as well as the legislative history, show that Congress had in mind no such patchwork plan for securing freedom of employees' organization and of collective bargaining. The Wagner Act is federal legislation, administered by a national agency, intended to solve a national problem on a national scale. It is an Act, therefore, in reference to which it is not only proper, but necessary for us to assume, "in the absence of a plain indication to the contrary, that Congress . . . is not making the application of the federal act dependent on state law." *Jerome v. United States*, 318 U.S. 101, 104 (1943). Nothing in the statute's background, history, terms or purposes indicates its scope is to be limited by such varying local conceptions, either statutory or judicial, or that it is to be administered in accordance with whatever different standards the respective states may see fit to adopt for the disposition of unrelated, local problems. Consequently, so far as the meaning of "employee" in this statute is concerned, "the federal law must prevail no matter what name is given to the interest or right by state law." *Morgan v. Comm'r*, 309 U.S. 87, 81 (1940).

* * *

To eliminate the causes of labor disputes and industrial strife, Congress thought it necessary to create a balance of forces in certain types of economic relationships. These do not embrace simply employment associations in which controversies could be limited to disputes over proper "physical conduct in the performance of the service." On the contrary, Congress recognized those economic relationships cannot be fitted neatly into the containers designated "employee" and "employer" which an earlier law had shaped for different purposes. Its Reports on the bill disclose clearly the understanding that "employers and employees not in proximate relationship may be drawn into common controversies by economic forces," and that the very disputes sought to be avoided might involve "employees [who] are at times brought into an economic relationship with employers who are not their employers." S. Rep. No. 573, at 6–7 (74th Cong.). In this light, the broad language of the Act's definitions, which in terms reject conventional limitations on such conceptions as "employee," "employer," and "labor dispute," leaves no doubt that its applicability is to be determined broadly, in doubtful situations, by underlying economic facts rather than technically and exclusively by previously established legal classifications.

Hence "technical concepts pertinent to an employer's legal responsibility to third persons for the acts of his servants" have been rejected in various applications of this Act both here and in other federal courts. There is no good reason for invoking them to restrict the scope of the term "employee" sought to be done in this case. That term, like other provisions, must be understood with reference to the purpose of the Act and the facts involved in the economic relationship. "Where all the conditions of the relation require protection, protection ought to be given." *Lehigh Valley Coal Co. v. Yensavage*, 218 F. 547, 552 (2d Cir. 1914).

It is not necessary in this case to make a completely definitive limitation around the term "employee." That task has been assigned primarily to the agency created by Congress to administer the Act. Determination of "where all the conditions of the relation require protection" involves inquiries for the Board charged with this duty. Everyday experience in the administration of the statute gives it familiarity with the circumstances and backgrounds of employment relationships in various industries, with the abilities and needs of the workers for self-organization and collective action, and with the adaptability of collective bargaining for the peaceful settlement of their disputes with their employers. The experience thus acquired must be brought frequently to bear on the question who is an employee under the Act. Resolving that question, like determining whether unfair labor practices have been committed, "belongs to the usual administrative routine" of the Board. *Gray v. Powell*, 314 U.S. 402, 411 (1941).

In making that body's determinations as to the facts in these matters conclusive, if supported by evidence, Congress entrusted to it primarily the decision whether the evidence establishes the material facts. Hence in reviewing the Board's ultimate conclusions, it is not the court's function to substitute its own inferences of fact for the Board's, when the latter have support in the record. Undoubtedly questions of statutory interpretation, especially when arising in the first instance in judicial proceedings, are for the courts to resolve, giving appropriate weight to the judgment of those whose special duty is to administer the questioned statute. But where the question is one of specific application of a broad statutory term in a proceeding in which the agency administering the statute must determine it initially, the reviewing court's function is limited. Like the commissioner's determination under the Longshoremen's & Harbor Workers' Act, that a man is not a "member of a crew" or that he was injured "in the course of his employment" and the Federal Communications Commission's determination that one company is under the "control" of another, the Board's determination that specified persons are "employees" under this Act is to be accepted if it has "warrant in the record" and a reasonable basis in law.

■ MR. JUSTICE ROBERTS, dissenting.

I think the judgment of the Circuit Court of Appeals should be affirmed. The opinion of that court * * * seems to me adequately to state the controlling facts and correctly to deal with the question of law presented for decision. I should not add anything were it not for certain arguments presented here and apparently accepted by the court.

I think it plain that newsboys are not "employees" of the respondents within the meaning and intent of the National Labor Relations Act. When Congress, in § 2(3) said: "The term 'employee' shall include any employee, . . ." it stated as clearly as language could do it that the provisions of the Act were to extend to those who, as a result of decades of tradition which had become part of the common understanding of our people, bear the named relationship. Clearly also Congress did not delegate to the National Labor Relations Board the function of defining the relationship of employment so as to promote what the Board understood to be the underlying purpose of the statute. The question who is an employee, so as to make the statute applicable to him, is a question of the meaning of the Act and, therefore, is a judicial and not an administrative question.

NOTES AND QUESTIONS

1. The Court in *Hearst Publications* calls for giving the Board's application of the statute "appropriate weight" and for accepting it so long as "it has 'warrant in the record' and a reasonable basis in law." What do you think might be the foundation for this standard of review? In this case, was the Court reviewing a finding of fact, a conclusion of law, or something else? If Congress uses a term in a statute and Congress does not define the term in the statute, does the process of giving the term meaning through adjudication constitute resolving an issue of law?

2. Many regulatory statutes apply to employers and employees, yet Congress has never provided a particularly useful definition of which persons are employees as opposed to managers or independent contractors. If Congress uses an undefined term in a statute, and that term has been interpreted in other contexts, is it safe to assume that Congress intended the term to have the same meaning as it has been given in other contexts? Is it more likely that Congress intended that the term be given a meaning consistent with the context in which it appears in the statute and the purpose of the statute? Should it matter whether the term has been given the same interpretation in each of the other contexts in which it has been used and in each of the jurisdictions in which it has been given meaning? If you believe that undefined terms included in agency-administered statutes should be interpreted in a manner that is consistent with the purpose of the statute, which institution do you think is likely to be able to give the term a meaning that is consistent with the purpose of the statute—a court or the agency responsible for administering the statute?

3. When a term is used in a statute administered by a federal agency, is it desirable that the term be interpreted in the same manner throughout the country? If so, what approach is more likely to yield that result—de novo review by each of the regional circuit courts or deferential review by each?

In addition to the "warrant in the record and a reasonable basis in law" standard applied in *Hearst*, the Court announced another deferential standard of review in the following opinion.

Skidmore v. Swift & Co.

323 U.S. 134 (1944).

■ JUSTICE JACKSON delivered the opinion of the Court.

Seven employees of the Swift and Company packing plant at Fort Worth, Texas, brought an action under the Fair Labor Standards Act, 29 U.S.C. § 201 *et seq.*, to recover overtime, liquidated damages, and attorneys' fees, totalling approximately $77,000. The District Court rendered judgment denying this claim wholly, and the Circuit Court of Appeals for the Fifth Circuit affirmed.

It is not denied that the daytime employment of these persons was working time within the Act. Two were engaged in general fire hall duties and maintenance of fire-fighting equipment of the Swift plant. The others operated elevators or acted as relief men in fire duties. They worked from 7:00 a.m. to 3:30 p.m., with a half-hour lunch period, five days a week. They were paid weekly salaries.

Under their oral agreement of employment, however, petitioners undertook to stay in the fire hall on the Company premises, or within hailing distance, three and a half to four nights a week. This involved no task except to answer alarms, either because of fire or because the sprinkler was set off for some other reason. No fires occurred during the period in issue, the alarms were rare, and the time required for their answer rarely exceeded an hour. For each alarm answered the employees were paid in addition to their fixed compensation an agreed amount, fifty cents at first, and later sixty-four cents. The Company provided a brick fire hall equipped with steam heat and air-conditioned rooms. It provided sleeping quarters, a pool table, a domino table, and a radio. The men used their time in sleep or amusement as they saw fit, except that they were required to stay in or close by the fire hall and be ready to respond to alarms. It is stipulated that "they agreed to remain in the fire hall and stay in it or within hailing distance, subject to call, in event of fire or other casualty, but were not required to perform any specific tasks during these periods of time, except in answering alarms." The trial court found the evidentiary facts as stipulated; it made no findings of fact as such as to whether under the arrangement of the parties and the circumstances of this case, which in some respects differ from those of the *Armour* case, *Armour & Co. v. Wantock et al.*, 323 U.S. 126 (1944), the fire hall duty or any part thereof constituted working time. It said, however, as a "conclusion of law" that "the time plaintiffs spent in the fire hall subject to call to answer fire alarms does not constitute hours worked, for which overtime compensation is due them under the Fair Labor Standards Act, as interpreted by the Administrator and the Courts," and in its opinion observed, "of course we know pursuing such pleasurable occupations or performing such personal chores does not constitute work." The Circuit Court of Appeals affirmed.

For reasons set forth in the *Armour* case, 323 U.S. 126, decided herewith we hold that no principle of law found either in the statute or in Court decisions precludes waiting time from also being working time.

* * *

Congress did not utilize the services of an administrative agency to find facts and to determine in the first instance whether particular cases fall within or without the Act. Instead, it put this responsibility on the courts. *Kirschbaum v. Walling*, 316 U.S. 517, 523 (1942). But it did create the office of Administrator, impose upon him a variety of duties, endow him with powers to inform himself of conditions in industries and employments subject to the Act, and put on him the duties of bringing injunction actions to restrain violations. Pursuit of his duties has accumulated a considerable experience in the problems of ascertaining working time in employments involving periods of inactivity and a knowledge of the customs prevailing in reference to their solution. From these he is obliged to reach conclusions as to conduct without the law, so that he should seek injunctions to stop it, and that within the law, so that he has no call to interfere. He has set forth his views of the application of the Act under different circumstances in an interpretative bulletin and in informal rulings. They provide a practical guide to employers and employees as to how the office representing the public interest in its enforcement will seek to apply it.

The Administrator thinks the problems presented by inactive duty require a flexible solution, rather than the all-in or all-out rules respectively urged by the parties in this case, and his Bulletin endeavors to suggest standards and examples to guide in particular situations. In some occupations, it says, periods of inactivity are not properly counted as working time even though the employee is subject to call. Examples are an operator of a small telephone exchange where the switchboard is in her home and she ordinarily gets several hours of uninterrupted sleep each night; or a pumper of a stripper well or watchman of a lumber camp during the off season, who may be on duty twenty-four hours a day but ordinarily "has a normal night's sleep, has ample time in which to eat his meals, and has a certain amount of time for relaxation and entirely private pursuits." Exclusion of all such hours the Administrator thinks may be justified. In general, the answer depends "upon the degree to which the employee is free to engage in personal activities during periods of idleness when he is subject to call and the number of consecutive hours that the employee is subject to call without being required to perform active work." "Hours worked are not limited to the time spent in active labor but include time given by the employee to the employer. . . ."

The facts of this case do not fall within any of the specific examples given, but the conclusion of the Administrator, as expressed in the brief amicus curiae, is that the general tests which he has suggested point to the exclusion of sleeping and eating time of these employees from the work-week and the inclusion of all other on-call time: although the employees were required to remain on the premises during the entire time, the evidence shows that they were very rarely interrupted in their normal sleeping and eating time, and these are pursuits of a purely private nature which would presumably occupy the employees' time whether they were on duty or not and which apparently could be pursued adequately and comfortably in the required circumstances; the rest of the time is different because there is nothing in the record to suggest that, even though pleasurably spent, it was spent in the ways the men would have chosen had they been free to do so.

There is no statutory provision as to what, if any, deference courts should pay to the Administrator's conclusions. And, while we have given them notice, we have had no occasion to try to prescribe their influence. The rulings of this Administrator are not reached as a result of hearing adversary proceedings in which he finds facts from evidence and reaches conclusions of law from findings of fact. They are not, of course, conclusive, even in the cases with which they directly deal, much less in those to which they apply only by analogy. They do not constitute an interpretation of the Act or a standard for judging factual situations which binds a district court's processes, as an authoritative pronouncement of a higher court might do. But the Administrator's policies are made in pursuance of official duty, based upon more specialized experience and broader investigations and information than is likely to come to a judge in a particular case. They do determine the policy which will guide applications for enforcement by injunction on behalf of the Government. Good administration of the Act and good judicial administration alike require that the standards of public enforcement and those for determining private rights shall be at variance only where justified by very good reasons. The fact that the Administrator's policies and standards are not reached by trial in adversary form does not mean that they are not entitled to respect. This Court has long given considerable and in some cases decisive weight to Treasury Decisions and to interpretative regulations of the Treasury and of other bodies that were not of adversary origin.

We consider that the rulings, interpretations and opinions of the Administrator under this Act, while not controlling upon the courts by reason of their authority, do constitute a body of experience and informed judgment to which courts and litigants may properly resort for guidance. The weight of such a judgment in a particular case will depend upon the thoroughness evident in its consideration, the validity of its reasoning, its consistency with earlier and later pronouncements, and all those factors which give it power to persuade, if lacking power to control.

The courts in the *Armour* case weighed the evidence in the particular case in the light of the Administrator's rulings and reached a result consistent therewith. The evidence in this case in some respects, such as the understanding as to separate compensation for answering alarms, is different. Each case must stand on its own facts. But in this case, although the District Court referred to the Administrator's Bulletin, its evaluation and inquiry were apparently restricted by its notion that waiting time may not be work, an understanding of the law which we hold to be erroneous. Accordingly, the judgment is reversed and the cause remanded for further proceedings consistent herewith.

NOTES AND QUESTIONS

1. The *Hearst* Court applied the standard of whether the agency's interpretation "has 'warrant in the record' and a reasonable basis in law." The *Skidmore* Court counseled considering the agency's experience, thoroughness, valid reasoning, consistency, and other factors that might persuade the court to adopt the agency's interpretation. Do you find these two standards the same or different? If the latter, which standard do you find more deferential?

The Court in *Hearst* offered several circumstances in which it suggested its standard would be appropriate: NLRB interpretations of the National Labor Relations Act, like the one at bar, or the Longshoremen's & Harbor Workers' Act, or the Federal Communications Commission's interpretations of the Communications Act of 1934. The Court noted that all of these contexts involved the agency charged with administering the statute. The Court further observed that Congress had "entrusted to [the NLRB] primarily the decision whether the evidence establishes the material facts" necessary to sustain the Board's legal conclusions regarding the applicability of the statute. By contrast, the Court in *Skidmore* made clear that the Wage and Hour Division did not possess such authority over the Fair Labor Standards Act: "Congress did not utilize the services of an administrative agency to find facts and to determine in the first instance whether particular cases fall within or without the Act. Instead, it put this responsibility on the courts." To the extent you find the *Hearst* and *Skidmore* standards of review distinguishable from one another, do you think this distinction in the scope and nature in the authority of the relevant agencies supports applying different standards of review to their interpretations of the law?

2. The Court applied some variation of the deferential *Hearst* or *Skidmore* standards to allocate primary responsibility to agencies in scores of cases decided in every term through 1983.

- In *Bonanno Linen Service v. NLRB*, 454 U.S. 404, 413 (1982), the Court counseled that the agency's construction of the statute must be affirmed unless it is "arbitrary or contrary to law."

- In *INS v. Wang*, 450 U.S. 139, 145 (1981), the Court said that agencies have authority to adopt a narrow construction of a statutory term "should they deem it wise to do so."

- In *Ford Motor Co. v. NLRB*, 441 U.S. 488, 495 (1979), the Court found that the agency's construction must be affirmed because it "was not an unreasonable or unprincipled construction of the statute."

- In *SEC v. Chenery*, 332 U.S. 194, 207–08 (1947), the Court opined, "The wisdom of the principle adopted is none of our concern. * * * The very breadth of the statutory language precludes reversal of the Commission's judgment save where it has plainly abused its discretion in these matters."

3. In *Batterton v. Francis*, 432 U.S. 416 (1977), many years after deciding *Hearst* and *Skidmore*, and only a few years before issuing its opinion in *Chevron U.S.A. Inc. v. Natural Resources Defense Council, Inc.*, 467 U.S. 837 (1984), the Court evaluated a challenge to a legislative regulation promulgated by the Secretary of Health, Education, and Welfare pursuant to a specific authority grant in the Social Security Act. In evaluating the regulation, the Court offered a particularly thorough summary of its standards for reviewing agency legal interpretations.

> [C]ongress in § 407(a) expressly delegated to the Secretary the power to prescribe standards for determining what constitutes "unemployment" for purposes of AFDC-UF eligibility. In a situation of this kind, Congress entrusts to the Secretary, rather than to the courts, the primary responsibility for interpreting the statutory term. In exercising that responsibility, the Secretary adopts regulations with legislative effect. A reviewing court is not free to set aside those regulations simply because it would have interpreted the statute in a different manner.

> The regulation at issue in this case is therefore entitled to more than mere deference or weight. It can be set aside only if the Secretary exceeded his statutory authority or if the regulation is "arbitrary, capricious, an abuse of discretion, or otherwise not in accordance with law." 5 U.S.C. §§ 706(2)(A), (C).

Batterton, 432 U.S. at 425 (citations omitted). In a footnote accompanying this text, also citing both pre- and post-APA precedents, the Court opined further,

> Legislative, or substantive, regulations are "issued by an agency pursuant to statutory authority and . . . implement the statute, as, for example, the proxy rules issued by the Securities and Exchange Commission. . . . Such rules have the force and effect of law." U.S. Dept. of Justice, Attorney General's Manual on the Administrative Procedure Act 30 n.3 (1947). By way of contrast, a court is not required to give effect to an interpretative regulation. Varying degrees of deference are accorded to administrative interpretations, based on such factors as the timing and consistency of the agency's position, and the nature of its expertise. *See Skidmore v. Swift & Co.*, 323 U.S. 134, 140 (1944).

Batterton, 432 U.S. at 425, n.9.

4.   A common complaint regarding the Court's deference jurisprudence has been the Court's inconsistency in following its own standards. For example, in *NLRB v. Bell Aerospace Co. Division of Textron, Inc.*, 416 U.S. 267 (1974), the Court did precisely what it had so frequently told circuit courts not to do: in the process of determining that buyers are not "employees" for federal labor relations purposes, the Court ignored the agency's construction of its statute and substituted its own independent construction for that of the agency. The Court used this de novo review approach in scores of cases decided in every term through 1983. *See, e.g., Dirks v. SEC*, 463 U.S. 646 (1983); *SEC v. Sloan*, 436 U.S. 103 (1978); *Northeast Marine Terminal v. Caputo*, 432 U.S. 249 (1977); *Office Employees v. NLRB*, 353 U.S. 313 (1957); *Davies Warehouse Co. v. Bowles*, 321 U.S. 144 (1944).

DISCUSSION PROBLEM: *BENZENE* REVISITED

During the pre-*Chevron* period the Justices often divided with respect to the meaning they gave to provisions of agency-administered statutes, as illustrated by the division of the Justices in *Industrial Union Dept., AFL-CIO v. American Petroleum Institute* (the *Benzene* case), 448 U.S. 607

(1980), which we discussed at length in Chapter 2. Reread the opinions in the *Benzene* case. Recall that the Occupational Safety and Health Act (the Act) delegates to the Secretary of Labor the authority to promulgate workplace safety and health standards with little guidance as to their content, and recall that the Justices divided three ways in reviewing one such standard limiting workplace exposure to airborne concentrations of benzene to 1 ppm and imposing complex monitoring and medical testing requirements on employers whose workplaces contained 0.5 ppm of benzene. A four-Justice plurality interpreted the Act to require an agency finding that a pre-existing ceiling applicable to a toxic substance created a "significant risk" to workers before the agency could adopt such stringent standards. In his concurring opinion, Justice Rehnquist took the position that the statute was unconstitutional because Congress did not include in the statute any "intelligible principle" that the agency or a court could use to decide whether to regulate a toxic substance in the workplace. The four dissenting Justices argued that the plurality had made up the "significant risk" standard; they would have upheld the agency's interpretation of the statute as authorizing it to set the strictest limit on a toxic substance that is technologically and economically feasible.

Consider particularly the statutory language quoted by the Court in *Benzene*, which can be found in Chapter 2 of this casebook. Where in the language of the statute did the four-Justice plurality find the "significant risk" prerequisite? If it was not in the statute, how did they support their holding? Where in the language of the statute did the agency and the four dissenting Justices find the "technologically and economically feasible" standard? If it was not in the statute, how did they support their argument? Does the exercise of trying to determine the meaning of this statute allow you to obtain a better appreciation for Justice Rehnquist's opinion?

Many agency decisions are similar to the decision the Court reviewed in *Benzene* in two respects. First, many agency decisions involve difficult scientific questions. Second, a significant subset of those decisions involve exactly the same problem that confronted both the agency and the Justices in *Benzene*: how to extrapolate the shape of a dose-response curve based on a few uncertain data points. In thinking about the latter issue, consider the following hypothetical graph of a typical dose-response curve for a substance that is known to be harmful, e.g., carcinogenic, when people are exposed to high concentrations of the substance for long periods of time.

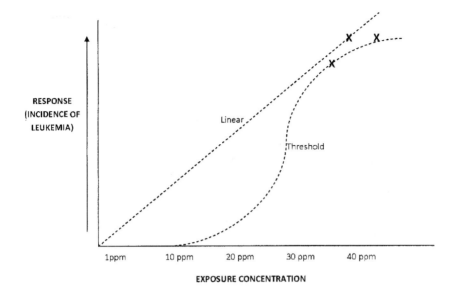

The graph depicts a common situation. The four Xs in the upper right corner represent the findings of four epidemiological studies. Each found that long-term exposure—*e.g.*, exposure for twenty years—to concentrations of the substance in excess of 30 parts per million (ppm) increased significantly the incidence of cancer. The circles around each X indicate the margin of error for each study. Thus, we know with high confidence that the substance is a human carcinogen at concentrations over 30 ppm. Agencies rarely have occasion, however, to take actions with respect to concentrations of substances at levels so high that they have been the subject of epidemiological studies. Typically, the agency's task is to decide whether to retain the pre-existing maximum concentration at a level that is already well below the level for which it has direct evidence— *e.g.*, 10 ppm—or instead to replace that ceiling with a lower ceiling—*e.g.*, 1 ppm. In other words, the question before the agency is whether long term exposure to the substance at concentrations between 1 and 10 ppm will cause an increase in the incidence of cancer.

Ideally, the agency would like to rely on epidemiological studies to make that determination. Epidemiological studies rarely are capable of determining the relationship between long-term exposure to low levels of a substance and the risk of contracting cancer, however, because of the "noisy laboratory effect"—*i.e.*, any population of people who have been subjected to long-term exposure to low levels of a substance have also been exposed to so many other potential sources of cancer that epidemiological studies are not capable of isolating and measuring the effects of exposure the substance of concern. The only reason we often have access to studies that find a causal relationship with long-term exposure to high levels of a substance is because the effect of the exposure to the high concentration is so large that we can safely rule out other potential causes. Even those studies tend to be old and/or from countries other than the U.S. because the U.S. has long prohibited long-term exposure to high levels of substances that are known to be carcinogenic at high concentrations.

In theory, an agency could answer the relevant question and determine the shape of the dose-response curve in the lower left hand corner of the graph by conducting a controlled experiment. It could place ten random samples of one hundred people each in ten enclosed and isolated living spaces and expose each to a different concentration of the substance for twenty years: one population would be exposed to 1 ppm, one would be exposed to 2 ppm, etc. After twenty years, the agency could kill and autopsy all of the people and have pathologists count the number of malignant tumors in each population. We are pleased to report that no agency has given serious consideration to that theoretically perfect way of constructing the part of the dose-response curve that lies in the lower left hand corner of the graph.

In the absence of directly relevant epidemiological evidence, the agency could attempt to extrapolate the relevant portion of the dose-response curve based on the available evidence. It could perform that task by using a standard statistical technique, least squares, to draw a line that represents the best approximation of the shape of the dose-response curve in the upper right hand corner of the graph. It could than extend that line to the extreme lower left hand corner of the graph, and use that extension of the line to determine the magnitude of the increased incidence of cancer at exposure levels of 1 ppm, 2 ppm, etc. That method of extrapolation would be based on the assumption that the substance is a "no-threshold" carcinogen with a linear dose-response curve at all levels of concentration. That is possible, but it is also possible that the substance is not carcinogenic at all until concentrations exceed some unknown level, such as 8 ppm or 12 ppm, or that the dose-response curve is not linear but instead has a steep slope in the lower left hand corner of the graph.

In most cases, including in the *Benzene* case, scientists have no reliable method of extrapolating the dose-response curve to the lower left hand corner of the graph. As a result, there is no scientifically defensible way of estimating whether reducing the exposure ceiling from 10 ppm to something lower, like 5 ppm or 1 ppm, will save a large number of lives or no lives. That is why the inter-agency carcinogen task force decided to try to persuade courts to permit agencies to apply the lowest "technologically and economically feasible standard" criterion that OSHA adopted and a majority of Justices rejected in *Benzene*.

What should an agency do in this common situation? How should courts review agency decisions in this situation? Judges and scholars have long debated the question of how courts should review agency actions that involve difficult scientific disputes. Three schools of thought have merged in this debate. Proponents of one approach argue that judges know too little about the substance of such disputes to engage in meaningful review of the substance of the agency actions, but that judges should apply their expertise with respect to decision-making procedures and process to require agencies to "ventilate" fully all of the issues. Proponents of another approach argue that judges should "immerse" themselves in the substance of such disputes so that they can engage in meaningful review. Proponents of a third approach argue that judges know too little about the substance of such disputes to engage in meaningful review and that mandatory agency "ventilation" is a futile waste of resources. They urge judges to uphold all such agency actions except perhaps in the extreme case where an agency makes an obvious error. What are the advantages and disadvantages of each of the three approaches?

In thinking out your position on this difficult question, you might want to consider an interesting passage from the plurality opinion in *Benzene*. After the plurality held that OSHA could order into effect a lower maximum concentration of a toxic substance only if it first found that the pre-existing ceiling gave rise to a "significant risk," the plurality decided to try to help OSHA understand the Court's holding by using example to illustrate the difference between significant and insignificant risks:

> Some risks are plainly acceptable and others are plainly unacceptable. If, for example, the odds are one in a billion that a person will die from cancer by taking a drink of chlorinated water, the risk clearly could not be considered significant. On the other hand, if the odds are one in a thousand that regular inhalation of gasoline vapors that are 2% benzene will be fatal, a reasonable person might well consider the risk significant and take appropriate steps to decrease or eliminate it.

Which risk is larger—the risk the Court characterizes as significant or the risk the agency characterizes as insignificant? Assume that the does-response curve applicable to the hypothetical chlorinated water risk is linear. How many glasses of water does a person drink in a lifetime? How many people live in the United States? How many residents of the United States would die as a result of the risk the Court calls insignificant? Would you call that number of deaths "insignificant?" How many people would die as a result of the risk the Court considers "significant?" How many people regularly inhale gasoline fumes? What grade would you give the Justices in a Toxicology 101 course? How much of a role do you want them to play in the process of regulating exposure to toxic substances?

B. THE *CHEVRON* "REVOLUTION"

Many lower court judges and administrative law scholars were dissatisfied with the general approach the Court took with respect to judicial review of agency interpretations of agency-administered statutes prior to 1984. They criticized the Court's approach as unprincipled, unpredictable, and highly susceptible to result-oriented application by judges and Justices who tended to uphold agency decisions with which they agreed and to reject agency decisions with which they disagreed. To what extent does the following opinion respond to those criticisms?

Chevron U.S.A. Inc. v. Natural Resources Defense Council, Inc.

467 U.S. 837 (1984).

■ JUSTICE STEVENS delivered the opinion of the Court.

In the Clean Air Act Amendments of 1977, Congress enacted certain requirements applicable to States that had not achieved the national air quality standards established by the Environmental Protection Agency (EPA) pursuant to earlier legislation. The amended Clean Air Act required these "nonattainment" States to establish a permit program regulating "new or modified major stationary sources" of air pollution. Generally, a permit may not be issued for a new or modified major stationary source unless several stringent conditions are met.[1] The EPA regulation promulgated to implement this permit requirement allows a State to adopt a plantwide definition of the term "stationary source."[2] Under this definition, an existing plant that contains several pollution-emitting devices may install or modify one piece of equipment without meeting the permit conditions if the alteration will not increase the total emissions from the plant. The question presented by these cases is whether EPA's decision to allow States to treat all of the pollution-emitting devices within the same industrial grouping as though they were encased within a single "bubble" is based on a reasonable construction of the statutory term "stationary source."

The EPA regulations containing the plantwide definition of the term stationary source were promulgated on October 14, 1981. * * * The Court of Appeals set aside the regulations.

The court observed that the relevant part of the amended Clean Air Act "does not explicitly define what Congress envisioned as a 'stationary source', to which the permit program . . . should apply," and further stated that the precise issue was not "squarely addressed in the legislative history." In light of its conclusion that the legislative history bearing on the question was "at best contradictory," it reasoned that "the purposes of the nonattainment program should guide our decision here." Based on two of its precedents concerning the applicability of the bubble concept to certain Clean Air Act programs, the court stated that the bubble concept was "mandatory" in programs designed merely to maintain existing air quality, but held that it was "inappropriate" in programs enacted to improve air quality. Since the purpose of the permit program—its *"raison d'être*," in the court's view—was to improve air quality, the court held that the bubble concept was inapplicable in these cases under its prior precedents. It therefore set aside the regulations embodying the bubble concept as contrary to law. We granted certiorari to review that judgment, and we now reverse.

The basic legal error of the Court of Appeals was to adopt a static judicial definition of the term "stationary source" when it had decided that Congress itself had not commanded that definition. * * *

When a court reviews an agency's construction of the statute which it administers, it is confronted with two questions. First, always, is the question whether Congress has directly spoken to the precise question

---

[1]   Section 172(b)(6), 42 U.S.C. § 7502(b)(6), provides:

"The plan provisions required by subsection (a) shall—

* * *

"(6) require permits for the construction and operation of new or modified major stationary sources in accordance with section 173 (relating to permit requirements)." 91 Stat. 747.

[2]   "(i) 'Stationary source' means any building, structure, facility, or installation which emits or may emit any air pollutant subject to regulation under the Act.

"(ii) 'Building, structure, facility, or installation' means all of the pollutant-emitting activities which belong to the same industrial grouping, are located on one or more contiguous or adjacent properties, and are under the control of the same person (or persons under common control) except the activities of any vessel." 40 CFR §§ 51.18(j)(1)(i) and (ii) (1983).

at issue. If the intent of Congress is clear, that is the end of the matter; for the court, as well as the agency, must give effect to the unambiguously expressed intent of Congress.[9] If, however, the court determines Congress has not directly addressed the precise question at issue, the court does not simply impose its own construction on the statute, as would be necessary in the absence of an administrative interpretation. Rather, if the statute is silent or ambiguous with respect to the specific issue, the question for the court is whether the agency's answer is based on a permissible construction of the statute.[11]

"The power of an administrative agency to administer a congressionally created ... program necessarily requires the formulation of policy and the making of rules to fill any gap left, implicitly or explicitly, by Congress." *Morton v. Ruiz*, 415 U.S. 199, 231 (1974). If Congress has explicitly left a gap for the agency to fill, there is an express delegation of authority to the agency to elucidate a specific provision of the statute by regulation. Such legislative regulations are given controlling weight unless they are arbitrary, capricious, or manifestly contrary to the statute. Sometimes the legislative delegation to an agency on a particular question is implicit rather than explicit. In such a case, a court may not substitute its own construction of a statutory provision for a reasonable interpretation made by the administrator of an agency.

We have long recognized that considerable weight should be accorded to an executive department's construction of a statutory scheme it is entrusted to administer, and the principle of deference to administrative interpretations

> "has been consistently followed by this Court whenever decision as to the meaning or reach of a statute has involved reconciling conflicting policies, and a full understanding of the force of the statutory policy in the given situation has depended upon more than ordinary knowledge respecting the matters subjected to agency regulations.

> "... If this choice represents a reasonable accommodation of conflicting policies that were committed to the agency's care by the statute, we should not disturb it unless it appears from the statute or its legislative history that the accommodation is not one that Congress would have sanctioned." *United States v. Shimer*, 367 U.S. 374, 382, 383 (1961).

In light of these well-settled principles it is clear that the Court of Appeals misconceived the nature of its role in reviewing the regulations at issue. Once it determined, after its own examination of the legislation, that Congress did not actually have an intent regarding the applicability of the bubble concept to the permit program, the question before it was not whether in its view the concept is "inappropriate" in the general context of a program designed to improve air quality, but

---

[9] The judiciary is the final authority on issues of statutory construction and must reject administrative constructions which are contrary to clear congressional intent. If a court, employing traditional tools of statutory construction, ascertains that Congress had an intention on the precise question at issue, that intention is the law and must be given effect.

[11] The court need not conclude that the agency construction was the only one it permissibly could have adopted to uphold the construction, or even the reading the court would have reached if the question initially had arisen in a judicial proceeding.

whether the Administrator's view that it is appropriate in the context of this particular program is a reasonable one. Based on the examination of the legislation and its history which follows, we agree with the Court of Appeals that Congress did not have a specific intention on the applicability of the bubble concept in these cases, and conclude that the EPA's use of that concept here is a reasonable policy choice for the agency to make.

* * *

The Clean Air Act Amendments of 1977 are a lengthy, detailed, technical, complex, and comprehensive response to a major social issue. A small portion of the statute expressly deals with nonattainment areas. The focal point of this controversy is one phrase in that portion of the Amendments.

* * *

Most significantly for our purposes, the statute provided that each [state implementation] plan (SIP) shall

"(6) require permits for the construction and operation of new or modified major stationary sources in accordance with section 173. . . ." 91 Stat. 747.

Before issuing a permit, § 173 requires (1) the state agency to determine that there will be sufficient emissions reductions in the region to offset the emissions from the new source and also to allow for reasonable further progress toward attainment, or that the increased emissions will not exceed an allowance for growth established pursuant to § 172(b)(5); (2) the applicant to certify that his other sources in the State are in compliance with the SIP, (3) the agency to determine that the applicable SIP is otherwise being implemented, and (4) the proposed source to comply with the lowest achievable emission rate (LAER).

The 1977 Amendments contain no specific reference to the "bubble concept." Nor do they contain a specific definition of the term "stationary source," though they did not disturb the definition of "stationary source" contained in § 111(a)(3), applicable by the terms of the Act to the NSPS program. Section 302(j), however, defines the term "major stationary source" as follows:

"(j) Except as otherwise expressly provided, the terms 'major stationary source' and 'major emitting facility' mean any stationary facility or source of air pollutants which directly emits, or has the potential to emit, one hundred tons per year or more of any air pollutant (including any major emitting facility or source of fugitive emissions of any such pollutant, as determined by rule by the Administrator)." 91 Stat. 770.

The legislative history of the portion of the 1977 Amendments dealing with nonattainment areas does not contain any specific comment on the "bubble concept" or the question whether a plantwide definition of a stationary source is permissible under the permit program. It does, however, plainly disclose that in the permit program Congress sought to accommodate the conflict between the economic interest in permitting capital improvements to continue and the environmental interest in improving air quality. Indeed, the House Committee Report identified the economic interest as one of the "two main purposes" of this section of the bill. * * *

[We have deleted a lengthy description of the EPA's vacillating positions with respect to the "bubble concept," i.e., defining "source" to refer to an entire plant site consisting of many pieces of combustion equipment, prior to 1981. Ed.]

In 1981 a new administration took office and initiated a "Government-wide reexamination of regulatory burdens and complexities." 46 Fed. Reg. 16281. In the context of that review, the EPA reevaluated the various arguments that had been advanced in connection with the proper definition of the term "source" and concluded that the term should be given the same definition in both nonattainment areas and PSD areas.

In explaining its conclusion, the EPA first noted that the definitional issue was not squarely addressed in either the statute or its legislative history and therefore that the issue involved an agency "judgment as how to best carry out the Act." *Id.* It then set forth several reasons for concluding that the plantwide definition was more appropriate. It pointed out that the dual definition "can act as a disincentive to new investment and modernization by discouraging modifications to existing facilities" and "can actually retard progress in air pollution control by discouraging replacement of older, dirtier processes or pieces of equipment with new, cleaner ones." *Id.* Moreover, the new definition "would simplify EPA's rules by using the same definition of 'source' for PSD, nonattainment new source review and the construction moratorium. This reduces confusion and inconsistency." *Id.* Finally, the agency explained that additional requirements that remained in place would accomplish the fundamental purposes of achieving attainment with NAAQS's as expeditiously as possible. These conclusions were expressed in a proposed rulemaking in August 1981 that was formally promulgated in October.

In this Court respondents * * * contend that the text of the Act requires the EPA to use a dual definition—if either a component of a plant, or the plant as a whole, emits over 100 tons of pollutant, it is a major stationary source. They thus contend that the EPA rules adopted in 1980, insofar as they apply to the maintenance of the quality of clean air, as well as the 1981 rules which apply to nonattainment areas, violate the statute.

* * *

The definition in § 302(j) tells us what the word "major" means—a source must emit at least 100 tons of pollution to qualify—but it sheds virtually no light on the meaning of the term "stationary source." It does equate a source with a facility—a "major emitting facility" and a "major stationary source" are synonymous under § 302(j). The ordinary meaning of the term "facility" is some collection of integrated elements which has been designed and constructed to achieve some purpose. Moreover, it is certainly no affront to common English usage to take a reference to a major facility or a major source to connote an entire plant as opposed to its constituent parts. Basically, however, the language of

§ 302(j) simply does not compel any given interpretation of the term "source."

* * *

We are not persuaded that parsing of general terms in the text of the statute will reveal an actual intent of Congress. We know full well that this language is not dispositive; the terms are overlapping and the language is not precisely directed to the question of the applicability of a given term in the context of a larger operation. To the extent any congressional "intent" can be discerned from this language, it would appear that the listing of overlapping, illustrative terms was intended to enlarge, rather than to confine, the scope of the agency's power to regulate particular sources in order to effectuate the policies of the Act.

* * *

Based on our examination of the legislative history, we agree with the Court of Appeals that it is unilluminating. The general remarks pointed to by respondents "were obviously not made with this narrow issue in mind and they cannot be said to demonstrate a Congressional desire. . . ." *Jewell Ridge Coal Corp. v. Mine Workers*, 325 U.S. 161, 168–69 (1945). * * * We find that the legislative history as a whole is silent on the precise issue before us. It is, however, consistent with the view that the EPA should have broad discretion in implementing the policies of the 1977 Amendments.

More importantly, that history plainly identifies the policy concerns that motivated the enactment; the plantwide definition is fully consistent with one of those concerns—the allowance of reasonable economic growth—and, whether or not we believe it most effectively implements the other, we must recognize that the EPA has advanced a reasonable explanation for its conclusion that the regulations serve the environmental objectives as well. Indeed, its reasoning is supported by the public record developed in the rulemaking process, as well as by certain private studies.

Our review of the EPA's varying interpretations of the word "source"—both before and after the 1977 Amendments—convinces us that the agency primarily responsible for administering this important legislation has consistently interpreted it flexibly—not in a sterile textual vacuum, but in the context of implementing policy decisions in a technical and complex arena. The fact that the agency has from time to time changed its interpretation of the term "source" does not, as respondents argue, lead us to conclude that no deference should be accorded the agency's interpretation of the statute. An initial agency interpretation is not instantly carved in stone. On the contrary, the agency, to engage in informed rulemaking, must consider varying interpretations and the wisdom of its policy on a continuing basis. Moreover, the fact that the agency has adopted different definitions in different contexts adds force to the argument that the definition itself is flexible, particularly since Congress has never indicated any disapproval of a flexible reading of the statute.

Significantly, it was not the agency in 1980, but rather the Court of Appeals that read the statute inflexibly to command a plantwide definition for programs designed to maintain clean air and to forbid such a definition for programs designed to improve air quality. The distinction the court drew may well be a sensible one, but our labored review of the problem has surely disclosed that it is not a distinction that Congress ever articulated itself, or one that the EPA found in the statute before the courts began to review the legislative work product. We conclude that it was the Court of Appeals, rather than Congress or any of the decisionmakers who are authorized by Congress to administer this legislation, that was primarily responsible for the 1980 position taken by the agency.

The arguments over policy that are advanced in the parties' briefs create the impression that respondents are now waging in a judicial forum a specific policy battle which they ultimately lost in the agency and in the 32 jurisdictions opting for the "bubble concept," but one which was never waged in the Congress. Such policy arguments are more properly addressed to legislators or administrators, not to judges.

In these cases, the Administrator's interpretation represents a reasonable accommodation of manifestly competing interests and is entitled to deference: the regulatory scheme is technical and complex, the agency considered the matter in a detailed and reasoned fashion, and the decision involves reconciling conflicting policies. Congress intended to accommodate both interests, but did not do so itself on the level of specificity presented by these cases. Perhaps that body consciously desired the Administrator to strike the balance at this level, thinking that those with great expertise and charged with responsibility for administering the provision would be in a better position to do so; perhaps it simply did not consider the question at this level; and perhaps Congress was unable to forge a coalition on either side of the question, and those on each side decided to take their chances with the scheme devised by the agency. For judicial purposes, it matters not which of these things occurred.

Judges are not experts in the field, and are not part of either political branch of the Government. Courts must, in some cases, reconcile competing political interests, but not on the basis of the judges' personal policy preferences. In contrast, an agency to which Congress has delegated policy-making responsibilities may, within the limits of that delegation, properly rely upon the incumbent administration's views of wise policy to inform its judgments. While agencies are not directly accountable to the people, the Chief Executive is, and it is entirely appropriate for this political branch of the Government to make such policy choices—resolving the competing interests which Congress itself either inadvertently did not resolve, or intentionally left to be resolved by the agency charged with the administration of the statute in light of everyday realities.

When a challenge to an agency construction of a statutory provision, fairly conceptualized, really centers on the wisdom of the agency's policy, rather than whether it is a reasonable choice within a gap left open by Congress, the challenge must fail. In such a case, federal judges—who have no constituency—have a duty to respect legitimate policy choices made by those who do. The responsibilities for assessing the wisdom of such policy choices and resolving the struggle between competing views of the public interest are not judicial ones:

"Our Constitution vests such responsibilities in the political branches." *TVA v. Hill*, 437 U.S. 153, 195 (1978).

We hold that the EPA's definition of the term "source" is a permissible construction of the statute which seeks to accommodate progress in reducing air pollution with economic growth. "The Regulations which the Administrator has adopted provide what the agency could allowably view as . . . [an] effective reconciliation of these twofold ends. . . ." *United States v. Shimer*, 367 U.S. 374, 383 (1961).

NOTES AND QUESTIONS

1. Legal scholars often describe the Supreme Court's opinion in *Chevron* as revolutionary. Yet, the scholarly literature also generally concludes that the Supreme Court did not intend its *Chevron* opinion to announce a major shift in deference doctrine. Justice Thurgood Marshall's papers, for example, reflect little discussion among the Justices of either the draft opinion's language or its broader implications. See Robert V. Percival, *Environmental Law in the Supreme Court: Highlights from the Marshall Papers*, 23 ENVTL. L. REP. 10606, 10613 (1993).

2. Irrespective of the Supreme Court's intent, courts and scholars routinely attribute to *Chevron* a new standard for reviewing courts to use when they evaluate agency interpretations of language contained in agency-administered statutes. This standard is now so foundational to modern administrative law that it is worth repeating.

> When a court reviews an agency's construction of the statute which it administers, it is confronted with two questions. First, always, is the question whether Congress has directly spoken to the precise question at issue. If the intent of Congress is clear, that is the end of the matter; for the court, as well as the agency, must give effect to the unambiguously expressed intent of Congress. If, however, the court determines Congress has not directly addressed the precise question at issue, the court does not simply impose its own construction on the statute, as would be necessary in the absence of an administrative interpretation. Rather, if the statute is silent or ambiguous with respect to the specific issue, the question for the court is whether the agency's answer is based on a permissible construction of the statute.

To what extent and in what ways does this test differ from the standards the Court announced and applied in *Hearst* or in *Skidmore*? How does it differ from the Court's articulation of its deference doctrine in *Batterton v. Francis*? Do you think applying the *Chevron* standard would have produced a different outcome in *Benzene*? What effect would the EPA's vacillation with respect to the meaning of "source" have had if the Court had applied the *Skidmore* standard in deciding *Chevron*? What was the effect of that vacillation in *Chevron*? Consider the following passage from the Court's opinion in *Smiley v. Citibank*, 517 U.S. 735, 742 (1996):

> Of course the mere fact that an agency interpretation contradicts a prior agency position is not fatal. Sudden and unexplained change or change that does not take account of legitimate reliance on prior interpretation may be "arbitrary, capricious [or] an abuse of discretion." But if these pitfalls are avoided, change is not invalidating, since the whole point of *Chevron* is to leave the

discretion provided by the ambiguities of a statute with the implementing agency.

3.   *Chevron* is most often cited for its two-step standard, reiterated in the previous note. Arguably, however, this test is remarkable more as a tool for organizing judicial analysis than as a doctrinal statement. Even before *Chevron*, courts did not allow agencies to deviate from the plain meaning of statutes. Although scholars criticized the inconsistency of the Court's pre-*Chevron* deference jurisprudence, the Court had previously advocated strong judicial deference toward legislative regulations promulgated pursuant to express congressional delegations of administrative responsibility. Some legal scholars have found more significance in the Court's observation that legislative delegations may be implicit as well as explicit, and thus its extension of strong deference to agency interpretations adopted under such power. Indeed, the regulation at issue in *Chevron* was adopted by the EPA using its general rulemaking authority to define an unclear statutory term, rather than pursuant to a more specific delegation of rulemaking power. In other words, notwithstanding the EPA's use of notice-and-comment rulemaking, the regulation was an interpretative rule by traditional standards. Legal scholars have identified this aspect of *Chevron* as a transfer of power from the courts to the executive branch. Why do you think this might be the case?

4.   In the prior cases in which the Court had deferred to agency interpretations of agency-administered statutes—e.g., *Hearst* and *Skidmore*—it reasoned that courts should defer to agencies because agencies have superior subject matter expertise. What reason or reasons does the Court in *Chevron* give for instructing courts to defer to agencies? If *Chevron* deference is based at least to some extent on factors other than, or in addition to, subject matter expertise, does that affect the nature and extent of the deference a court should accord an agency?

5.   In his concurring opinion in *Benzene*, Justice Rehnquist argued that the Occupational Safety and Health Act is unconstitutional because Congress cannot "delegate important choices of social policy to politically unresponsive administrators." Does the Court's opinion in *Chevron* reflect a different point of view?

Debating the Theory of *Chevron*

The Supreme Court's *Chevron* decision has prompted an amazing amount of scholarly and judicial analysis, criticism, and debate. The following excerpts offer just the barest glimpse of some of the differing views regarding the *Chevron* standard and its merits.

Antonin Scalia, Judicial Deference to Administrative Interpretations of Law

1989 Duke L.J. 511, 513–17, 521 (1989).

It is not immediately apparent why a court should ever accept the judgment of an executive agency on a question of law. Indeed, on its face the suggestion seems quite incompatible with Marshall's aphorism that "[i]t is emphatically the province and duty of the judicial department to say what the law is." *Marbury v. Madison*, 5 U.S. (1 Cranch) 137, 177 (1803). Surely the law, that immutable product of

Congress, is what it is, and its content—ultimately to be decided by the courts—cannot be altered or affected by what the Executive thinks about it. I suppose it is harmless enough to speak about "giving deference to the views of the Executive" concerning the meaning of a statute, just as we speak of "giving deference to the views of the Congress" concerning the constitutionality of particular legislation—the mealy-mouthed word "deference" not necessarily meaning anything more than considering those views with attentiveness and profound respect, before we reject them. But to say that those views, if at least reasonable, will ever be *binding*—that is, seemingly, a striking abdication of judicial responsibility.

* * *

What, then, is the theoretical justification for allowing reasonable administrative interpretations to govern? The cases, old and new, that accept administrative interpretations, often refer to the "expertise" of the agencies in question, their intense familiarity with the history and purposes of the legislation at issue, their practical knowledge of what will best effectuate those purposes. In other words, they are more likely than the courts to reach the correct result. That is, if true, a good practical reason for accepting the agency's views, but hardly a valid theoretical justification for doing so. * * * If it is, as we have always believed, the constitutional duty of the courts to say what the law is, we must search for something beyond relative competence as a basis for ignoring that principle when agency action is at issue.

One possible validating rationale that has been suggested in some recent articles—and that can perhaps even be derived from some of the language of *Chevron* itself—is that the constitutional principle of separation of powers requires *Chevron*. The argument goes something like this: When, in a statute to be implemented by an executive agency, Congress leaves an ambiguity that cannot be resolved by text or legislative history, the "traditional tools of statutory construction," the resolution of that ambiguity necessarily involves policy judgment. Under our democratic system, policy judgments are not for the courts but for the political branches; Congress having left the policy question open, it must be answered by the Executive.

Now there is no one more fond of our system of separation of powers than I am, but even I cannot agree with this approach. To begin with, it seems to me that the "traditional tools of statutory construction" include not merely text and legislative history but also, quite specifically, the consideration of policy consequences. Indeed, that tool is so traditional that it has been enshrined in Latin: "*Ratio est legis anima; mutata legis ratione mutatur et lex.*" ("The reason for the law is its soul; when the reason for the law changes, the law changes as well.") Surely one of the most frequent justifications courts give for choosing a particular construction is that the alternative interpretation would produce "absurd" results, or results less compatible with the reason or purpose of the statute. This, it seems to me, unquestionably involves judicial consideration and evaluation of competing policies, and for precisely the same purpose for which (in the context we are discussing here) *agencies* consider and evaluate them—to determine which one will best effectuate the statutory purpose. Policy evaluation is, in other words, part of the traditional judicial tool-kit that is used in applying the first step of *Chevron*—the step that determines, *before* deferring to agency judgment, whether the law is indeed ambiguous. Only when the court concludes that the policy furthered by *neither* textually possible interpretation will be clearly "better" (in the sense of achieving what Congress apparently wished to achieve) will it, pursuant to *Chevron*, yield to the agency's choice. But the reason it yields is assuredly *not* that it has no constitutional competence to consider and evaluate policy.

The separation-of-powers justification can be rejected even more painlessly by asking one simple question: If, in the statute at issue in *Chevron*, Congress had specified that in all suits involving interpretation or application of the Clean Air Act the courts were to give no deference to the agency's views, but were to determine the issue de novo, would the Supreme Court nonetheless have acquiesced in the agency's views? I think the answer is clearly no, which means that it is not any constitutional impediment to "policy-making" that explains *Chevron*.

In my view, the theoretical justification for *Chevron* is no different from the theoretical justification for those pre-*Chevron* cases that sometimes deferred to agency legal determinations. As the D.C. Circuit, quoting the First Circuit, expressed it: "The extent to which courts should defer to agency interpretations of law is ultimately 'a function of Congress' intent on the subject as revealed in the particular statutory scheme at issue.'" *Process Gas Consumers Group v. United States Dep't of Agric.*, 694 F.2d 778, 791 (D.C. Cir. 1982) (quoting *Constance v. Sec'y of Health & Human Servs.*, 672 F.2d 990, 995 (1st Cir. 1982)). An ambiguity in a statute committed to agency implementation can be attributed to either of two congressional desires: (1) Congress intended a particular result, but was not clear about it; or (2) Congress had no particular intent on the subject, but meant to leave its resolution to the agency. When the former is the case, what we have is genuinely a question of law, properly to be resolved by the courts. When the latter is the case, what we have is the conferral of discretion upon the agency, and the only question of law presented to the courts is whether the agency has acted within the scope of its discretion—i.e., whether its resolution of the ambiguity is reasonable. As I read the history of developments in this field, the pre-*Chevron* decisions sought to choose between (1) and (2) on a statute-by-statute basis. Hence the relevance of such frequently mentioned factors as the degree of the agency's expertise, the complexity of the question at issue, and the existence of rulemaking authority within the agency. All these factors make an intent to confer discretion upon the agency more likely. *Chevron*, however, if it is to be believed, replaced this statute-by-statute evaluation (which was assuredly a font of uncertainty and litigation) with an across-the-board presumption that, in the case of ambiguity, agency discretion is meant.

It is beyond the scope of these remarks to defend that presumption (I was not on the Court, after all, when *Chevron* was decided). Surely, however, it is a more rational presumption today than it would have been thirty years ago—which explains the change in the law. Broad delegation to the Executive is the hallmark of the modern administrative state; agency rulemaking powers are the rule rather than, as they once were, the exception; and as the sheer number of modern departments and agencies suggests, we are awash in agency "expertise." If the *Chevron* rule is not a 100% accurate estimation of modern congressional intent, the prior case-by-case evaluation was not so either—and was becoming less and less so, as the sheer volume of modern dockets made it less and less possible for the Supreme Court to police diverse application of an ineffable rule. And to tell the truth, the quest for the "genuine" legislative intent is probably a wild-goose chase anyway. In the vast majority of cases I expect that Congress *neither* (1) intended a single result, *nor* (2) meant to confer discretion upon the agency, but rather (3) didn't think about the matter at all. If I am correct in that, then any rule adopted in this field represents merely a fictional, presumed intent, and operates principally as a background rule of law against which Congress can legislate.

If that is the principal function to be served, *Chevron* is unquestionably better than what preceded it. Congress now knows that the ambiguities it creates, whether intentionally or unintentionally, will be resolved, within the bounds of permissible interpretation, not by the courts but by a particular agency, whose policy biases will ordinarily be known. The legislative process becomes less of a sporting event when those supporting and opposing a particular disposition do not have to gamble upon whether, if they say nothing about it in the statute, the ultimate answer will be provided by the courts or rather by the Department of Labor.

* * *

In my experience, there is a fairly close correlation between the degree to which a person is (for want of a better word) a "strict constructionist" of statutes, and the degree to which that person favors *Chevron* and is willing to give it broad scope. The reason is obvious. One who finds *more* often (as I do) that the meaning of a statute is apparent from its text and from its relationship with other laws, thereby finds less often that the triggering requirement for *Chevron* deference exists. It is thus relatively rare that *Chevron* will require me to accept an interpretation which, though reasonable, I would not personally adopt. Contrariwise, one who abhors a "plain meaning" rule, and is willing to permit the apparent meaning of a statute to be impeached by the legislative history, will more frequently find agency-liberating ambiguity, and will discern a much broader range of "reasonable" interpretation that the agency may adopt and to which the courts must pay deference. The frequency with which *Chevron* will require *that* judge to accept an interpretation he thinks wrong is infinitely greater.

Richard J. Pierce, Jr., *Chevron* and Its Aftermath
41 Vand. L. Rev. 301, 304–08 (1988).

Many instances of statutory interpretation require an agency to resolve policy issues, rather than legal issues. Viewed in this light, the first step in the *Chevron* test requires a court to determine whether the issue of statutory interpretation in question is an issue of law or an issue of policy. If the court determines that it is reviewing an agency's resolution of a policy issue, the court then moves to the second part of the test and affirms the agency's interpretation of the statutory provision—and its resolution of the policy issue—if the agency's interpretation is "reasonable."

In determining whether an agency's interpretation of a statute involves an issue of law or policy, it is useful to analyze and characterize the issue prior to Congress' enactment of the statute in question. For example, in *Chevron* most would agree that, prior to the enactment of the Clean Air Act, the question of whether to limit emissions at the plant level or the level of each piece of combustion equipment is a pure question of policy. This question is but one of hundreds of policy issues that some institution of government must resolve in order to implement any regulatory program to reduce air pollution. In the process of enacting the Clean Air Act, or any other regulatory statute, Congress invariably resolves some policy issues but leaves to some other institution of government the task of resolving many other policy issues.

As the Court recognized in *Chevron*, Congress declines to resolve policy issues for many different reasons: Congress simply may have neglected to consider the issue; Congress may have believed that the agency was in a better position to resolve the issue; or finally, Congress may not have been able to forge a coalition or simply may have lacked the political courage necessary to resolve the issue, given that a resolution either way might damage the political future of many members of Congress. The general proposition that Congress cannot and does not resolve all the policy issues raised by its creation of a regulatory scheme probably is not at all controversial.

A more controversial point, however, may be that Congress resolves very few issues when it enacts a statute empowering an agency to regulate. Rather, Congress typically leaves the vast majority of policy issues, including many of the most important issues, for resolution by some other institution of government. Congress accomplishes this through several different statutory drafting techniques, including the use of empty standards, lists of unranked decisional goals, and contradictory standards. Thus, Congress declines to resolve many policy issues by using statutory language that is incapable of meaningful definition and application.

When a court "interprets" imprecise, ambiguous, or conflicting statutory language in a particular manner, the court is resolving a policy issue. Courts frequently resolve policy issues through a process that purports to be statutory interpretation but which, in fact, is not. For lack of a better term, this process will be referred to as "creative" interpretation. Judicial decisions under the Sherman Act provide a good example of judicial policy making through creative statutory interpretation. Whether through congressional inadvertence or by design, courts have interpreted the substantive standard stated in the Sherman Act—whether a restrictive practice should be prohibited as imposing an unreasonable "restraint of trade or commerce"—in many different and inconsistent ways.

As long as courts follow a process of reasoned decision making, judicial policy making through creative interpretation and application of ambiguous statutory provisions is generally appropriate. The function of a court is to resolve cases or controversies. By enacting a statute that raises but does not resolve myriad policy issues, and by permitting parties to bring judicial actions pursuant to that statute, Congress has created a large number of cases or controversies that courts have no choice but to resolve through a process that can only be characterized as judicial policy making. In the context of the Sherman Act, for example, courts and commentators seem increasingly to recognize that judges make antitrust policy. Because Congress has declined to resolve many of the policy decisions raised by the Sherman Act, and because no other institution of government is available to fill that policy making void, the courts regularly must make policy decisions in the guise of interpreting the Sherman Act.

Some judicial policy making in the guise of statutory interpretation seems superficially different from the typical judicial opinion interpreting the Sherman Act. Occasionally courts interpret statutory provisions through lengthy discussions of congressional goals and legislative history. In some cases, this analysis undoubtedly is an exercise in what may be termed "real" statutory interpretation; the judge is honestly convinced from reading the language of the statute and its legislative history that Congress resolved a policy issue in a particular manner. When Congress has resolved a policy issue, the court is dealing with an issue of law, in which case the court's role is limited to implementing congressional intent.

In a high proportion of cases, however, an honest analysis of the language, the congressional goals, and the legislative history of the statute will not support a holding that Congress actually resolved the policy issue presented to the court. This situation often arises because Congress frequently uses ambiguous or conflicting statutory language and invariably promulgates inconsistent congressional goals. While sometimes helpful, the legislative history of a statute is often unclear, inconsistent, or untrustworthy.

* * *

Once a court realizes that it is reviewing an agency's resolution of a policy issue, rather than an issue of law, comparative institutional analysis demonstrates that the agency is a more appropriate institution than a court to resolve the controversy. Because agencies are more accountable to the electorate than courts, agencies should have the dominant role in policy making when the choice is between agencies and courts. A court's function in reviewing a policy decision made by an agency should be the same whether the agency policy decision is made by interpreting an ambiguous statutory provision or by any other means of agency policy making. The court should affirm the agency's policy decision, and hence its statutory interpretation, if the policy is "reasonable." The court should reverse the agency's policy decision if the policy is arbitrary and capricious. Of course, in deciding whether the agency's policy decision is "reasonable," the court should review the agency's decision making process by which the agency determined that its choice of policy was consistent with statutory goals and the contextual facts of the controversy in question.

This characterization of the nature of statutory interpretation by an agency is entirely consistent with the Court's two-step approach to judicial review of agency interpretations of statutory provisions established in *Chevron*. The first step under *Chevron* is for the court to determine if Congress has resolved the policy issue that corresponds to the interpretive issue resolved by the agency. The court should engage in "real" statutory interpretation to determine whether Congress resolved the specific issue that the agency purported to resolve through statutory interpretation. If Congress resolved the specific issue presented, the court is dealing with an issue of law, and the case is at an end because the court is limited to implementing congressional intent.

In the process of applying *Chevron*'s first step, the court should refrain from teasing meaning from the statute's ambiguous or conflicting language and legislative history; it should eschew the process of "creative" statutory interpretation that is otherwise essential and appropriate in judicial decision making. Creative statutory interpretation is not appropriate in the administrative law context because creative statutory interpretation permits judges to make policy decisions that should be made instead by agencies. If the process of "real" statutory interpretation does not produce a determination that Congress resolved the specific issue, the court is dealing with a policy decision made by an agency. Although the court still must insure that the agency made its policy decision through a process of reasoned decision making, the court's role should be influenced greatly by the recognition that it is reviewing a policy decision made by another branch of government.

Lisa Schultz Bressman, *Chevron*'s Mistake
58 Duke L.J. 549, 559–66 (2009).

The conventional theories of statutory interpretation take varying approaches to awkward or imprecise text in part because they hold different pictures about legislative behavior. Intentionalists and purposivists see legislative inadvertence or, more specifically, the inevitable difficulty of capturing all the aspects or applications of a policy in a relatively few words. According to these theorists, Congress has a meaning or a purpose in mind but sometimes chooses words that poorly or incompletely express it. Intentionalists seek to recover the meaning when interpreting words, using legislative history when relevant, and purposivists look for indications of broader statutory purposes. Modern proponents of these theories look for more objective evidence on the assumption that actual legislative intent may be hard to reconstruct given the complexities of the legislative process; but they assume that every enacted law has a reasonable purpose or an "intentionalist stance."

By contrast, modern textualists trace awkward or imprecise text to legislative compromise. They view the legislative process as chaotic and messy. In this environment, legislators cut deals to obtain consensus, and awkward words reflect those deals. Modern textualists adhere to the ordinary meaning of those words to give effect to whatever deal they may manifest. Textualists also maintain a rule-of-law or constitutional defense against the use of legislative history because only the text is enacted.

On the basis of their respective visions, proponents of each theory ask courts to announce the statutory meaning that best reflects what Congress was after—for example, a broad statutory purpose or a specific legislative deal. By construing language in this fashion, those proponents all can claim to position courts as faithful agents of Congress. Undoubtedly, the different camps believe that *their* theory will produce a statutory meaning that most often reflects the legislative design.

The basic law governing interpretation of regulatory statutes reflects a different picture of legislative behavior. *Chevron* establishes a two-step test for courts to apply when reviewing agency interpretations of regulatory statutes. The *Chevron* test tells courts first to determine whether "Congress has directly spoken to the precise question at issue," applying the "traditional tools of statutory construction." But when courts find no meaning for the statutory text, *Chevron* instructs them to defer to the agency interpretation as long as that interpretation is reasonable. *Chevron* recognizes that Congress may intend for agencies rather than courts to fill gaps in regulatory statutes. It notes that Congress may have a variety of reasons for delegating interpretive authority to agencies—for example, to capitalize on agency expertise or to obtain legislative consensus. Regardless of the particular reason, *Chevron* directs courts to accept the legislative assignment of interpretive authority and defer to reasonable agency interpretations. Doing so is consistent not only with congressional delegation but also with administrative expertise and political accountability. Agencies possess more expertise than courts for handling regulatory schemes that are "technical and complex" and for reconciling the "competing interests" that regulatory decisions often involve. Agencies are also accountable to the people, not directly but through the president, and "it is entirely appropriate for this political branch of Government to make such policy choices."

* * *

Chevron mentions the reasons for interpretive delegation as a justification for judicial deference. But it actually directs courts to approach awkward or imprecise statutory language by asking the same question as the standard theories of statutory interpretation: whether "Congress has directly spoken to the precise question at issue." And it tells courts to answer that question applying the "traditional tools of statutory construction." Thus, courts effectively approach interpretive questions mindful of giving effect to broad statutory purposes or finely tuned legislative deals. Only when that effort reveals no clear meaning do courts infer a delegation of interpretive authority. In other words, courts treat a lack of clarity as the exclusive proxy for interpretive delegation. Perhaps, then, it is no wonder that a wide range of legal scholars have characterized the congressional delegation rationale for *Chevron* as a fiction. Because Congress probably does not draft statutes with *Chevron* in mind, courts can justify judicial deference, if at all, using the other values that *Chevron* cites—agency expertise and political accountability.

* * *

The result is that * * * courts approach regulatory statutes with much the same mindset as they approach other statutes. It follows that they are just as likely to find a specific meaning in a case involving an agency as in a case that does not. This is not an empirical claim, although it well might be true. Rather, it is an analytical claim about the framework that courts apply. Because courts approach awkward or imprecise text in regulatory statutes mindful of respecting broad statutory purposes or particular legislative deals, they are unlikely to grant agencies their delegated interpretive authority as often as Congress intends.

Chevron cannot overcome the problem by simply instructing courts to set aside their meaning in favor of an agency's "reasonable" meaning. The thought is a good one, but it is easier said than done. Once courts work actively to construct a meaning for statutory text, as they do under all the dominant theories of statutory interpretation, they will have considerable difficulty recognizing the reasonableness of other interpretations.

* * *

1. HOW CLEAR IS CLEAR?

Irrespective of the extent to which it arguably reflected existing law, the *Chevron* Court's two-step standard of review has only prompted newer and more questions among judges and legal scholars. Many, many lengthy law review articles and even some books have been devoted to exploring the requirements of and relationship between *Chevron*'s two steps. One key question, as yet largely unanswered in any definitive way, concerns just how much statutory clarity *Chevron*'s first step requires. The Court in *Chevron* spoke in terms of "whether Congress has directly spoken to the precise question at issue" and whether "the intent of Congress is clear" after a reviewing court had employed "traditional tools of statutory construction." Given these instructions, how clearly must a statute address the issue at bar? Should a reviewing court look only for an explicit answer in the statute's text (which rarely if ever exists in a case that has made its way to the Supreme Court) or dig deeper before moving on to the reasonableness inquiry of *Chevron* step two? Assuming that principal litigants in a case offer competing constructions of the relevant statute, should the reviewing court resolve the question at step one if it merely believes one of the alternatives offers a somewhat better fit with the statute's text and history? Or must the statute expressly contradict one or another of the competing interpretations? In other words, how clear must a statute be to satisfy *Chevron* step one?

In another passage from his Duke Law Journal article, excerpted above, Justice Scalia offered his interpretation of *Chevron*'s step one most clearly.

> What does it take to satisfy the first step of *Chevron*—that is, when is a statute ambiguous? *Chevron* becomes virtually meaningless, it seems to me, if ambiguity exists only when the arguments for and against the various possible interpretations are in absolute equipoise. If nature knows of such equipoise in legal arguments, the courts at least do not. The judicial task,

every day, consists of finding the right answer, no matter how closely balanced the question may seem to be. In appellate opinions, there is no such thing as a tie. * * * If *Chevron* is to have any meaning, then, congressional intent must be regarded as "ambiguous" not just when no interpretation is even marginally better than any other, but rather when two or more reasonable, though not necessarily equally valid, interpretations exist. This is indeed intimated by the opinion in *Chevron*—which suggests that the opposite of "ambiguity" is not "resolvability" but rather "clarity." Here, of course, is the chink in *Chevron*'s armor—the ambiguity that prevents it from being an absolutely clear guide to future judicial decisions * * *. How clear is clear? It is here, if *Chevron* is not abandoned, that the future battles over acceptance of agency interpretations of law will be fought.

Antonin Scalia, *Judicial Deference to Administrative Interpretations of Law*, 1989 DUKE L.J. 511, 520–21 (1989).

Another, related question is raised by the *Chevron* Court's seeming equation of statutory silence with statutory ambiguity, counseling deference to permissible interpretations in the face of either: Are silence and ambiguity, in fact, synonymous terms? Or are there instances in which a statute's failure to address a particular question in fact reflects clear congressional intent that the issue should fall outside the scope of the agency's power? With these thoughts in mind, compare the Court's approach to *Chevron* step one in the following two cases.

Yellow Transportation, Inc. v. Michigan

537 U.S. 36 (2002).

■ JUSTICE O'CONNOR delivered the opinion of the Court.

We granted certiorari in this case to determine whether the Michigan Supreme Court erred in holding that, under 49 U.S.C. § 14504(c)(2)(B)(iv)(III), only a State's "generic" fee is relevant to determining the fee that was "collected or charged as of November 15, 1991."

Beginning in 1965, Congress authorized States to require interstate motor carriers operating within their borders to register with the State proof of their Interstate Commerce Commission (ICC) interstate operating permits. Congress provided that state registration requirements would not constitute an undue burden on interstate commerce so long as they were consistent with regulations promulgated by the ICC.

Prior to 1994, the ICC allowed States to charge interstate motor carriers annual registration fees of up to $10 per vehicle. As proof of registration, participating States would issue a stamp for each of the carrier's vehicles. The stamp was affixed on a "uniform identification cab car[d]" carried in each vehicle, within the square bearing the name of the issuing State. This system came to be known as the "bingo card" system.

The "bingo card" regime proved unsatisfactory to many who felt that the administrative burdens it placed on carriers and participating

States outweighed the benefits to those States and to the public. In the Intermodal Surface Transportation Efficiency Act of 1991 (ISTEA), Congress therefore directed the ICC to implement a new system to replace the "bingo card" regime.* Under the new system, called the Single State Registration System, "a motor carrier [would be] required to register annually with only one State," and "such single State registration [would] be deemed to satisfy the registration requirements of all other States." 49 U.S.C. §§ 11506(c)(1)(A), (C). Thus, one State would—on behalf of all other participating States—register a carrier's vehicles, file and maintain paperwork, and collect and distribute registration fees. Participation in the Single State Registration System was limited to those States that had elected to participate in the "bingo card" system.

ISTEA also capped the per-vehicle registration fee that participating States could charge interstate motor carriers. Congress directed the ICC to

> "establish a fee system . . . that (I) will be based on the number of commercial motor vehicles the carrier operates in a State and on the number of States in which the carrier operates, (II) will minimize the costs of complying with the registration system, and (III) will result in a fee for each participating State that is equal to the fee, not to exceed $10 per vehicle, that such State collected or charged as of November 15, 1991." § 11506(c)(2)(B)(iv).

Congress provided that the charging or collection of any fee not in accordance with the ICC's fee system would "be deemed to be a burden on interstate commerce." § 11506(c)(2)(C).

The ICC issued its final implementing regulations in May 1993 after notice-and-comment proceedings. The rulemaking gave rise to the central question in this case: whether, under the Single State Registration System, States were free to terminate "reciprocity agreements" that were in place under the "bingo card" regime. Under these agreements, in exchange for reciprocal treatment, some States discounted or waived registration fees for carriers from other States.

In issuing a set of proposed rules and soliciting further comments, the ICC questioned whether it had the power to require States to preserve pre-existing reciprocity agreements. It noted that these agreements were voluntary and mutually beneficial and commented that "as long as no carrier is charged more than [a State's] standard November 15, 1991, fee for all carriers (subject to the $10 limit), the requirements of [ISTEA] are satisfied." *Single State Insurance Registration*, No. MC–100, 1993 WL 17833, at *12 (Jan. 22, 1993).

In its final implementing regulations, however, the ICC concluded, in light of further comments, that its preliminary view on reciprocity agreements was inconsistent with ISTEA's fee-cap provision and with "the intent of the law that the flow of revenue for the States be

---

* Congress abolished the ICC in 1995 and assigned responsibility for administering the new Single State Registration System to the Secretary of Transportation. The Federal Highway Administration, under the Secretary of Transportation, adopted the ICC regulations that implemented the Single State Registration System, and the Federal Motor Carrier Safety Administration now has authority to administer the system. [Ed.]

maintained while the burden of the registration system for carriers be reduced." *Single State Insurance Registration*, 9 I.C.C. 2d 610, 618 (1993). The agency therefore determined that States participating in the Single State Registration System "must consider fees charged or collected under reciprocity agreements when determining the fees charged or collected as of November 15, 1991, as required by § 11506(c)(2)(B)(iv)." *Id.* at 618–19. The National Association of Regulatory Utility Commissioners (NARUC) and 18 state regulatory commissions sought review of the ICC's determination and certain provisions of the Single State Registration System regulations. The United States Court of Appeals for the District of Columbia concluded that the plain language of the statute supported the ICC's determination that States participating in the new system must consider reciprocity agreements under 49 U.S.C. § 11506(c)(2)(B)(iv).

Prior to the implementation of the Single State Registration System, Michigan had participated in the "bingo card" regime. * * *

Petitioner in this case is an interstate trucking company headquartered in Kansas. For calendar years 1990 and 1991, the Michigan Public Service Commission did not levy a fee for petitioner's trucks that were licensed in Illinois pursuant to its policy "not to charge a fee to carriers with vehicles registered in states . . . which did not charge Michigan-based carriers a fee." In 1991, however, the Michigan Public Service Commission announced a change in its reciprocity policy to take effect on February 1, 1992. Under the new policy, the commission granted reciprocity treatment based on the policies of the State in which a carrier maintained its principal place of business rather than the State in which individual vehicles were licensed. Because Michigan had no reciprocal arrangement with Kansas, the Michigan Public Service Commission sent petitioner a bill in September 1991, levying a fee of $10 per vehicle for the 1992 registration year on petitioner's entire fleet, with payment due on January 1, 1992.

Petitioner paid the fees in October 1991 under protest and later brought suit in the Michigan Court of Claims seeking a refund of the fees it paid for its Illinois-licensed vehicles after the Single State Registration System came into effect. Petitioner alleged that, because Michigan had not "collected or charged" a fee for the 1991 registration year for trucks licensed in Illinois, ISTEA's fee-cap provision prohibits Michigan from levying a fee on Illinois-licensed trucks.

* * *

The only issue before this Court * * * is whether States may charge motor carrier registration fees in excess of those charged or collected under reciprocity agreements as of November 15, 1991.

Neither party disputes that *Chevron U.S.A. Inc. v. Natural Resources Defense Council, Inc.*, 467 U.S. 837 (1984), governs the interpretive task at hand. In ISTEA, Congress made an express delegation of authority to the ICC to promulgate standards for implementing the new Single State Registration System. The ICC did so, interpreting ISTEA's fee-cap provision subsequent to a notice-and-comment rulemaking. *See United States v. Mead Corp.*, 533 U.S. 218, 229 (2001) ("[A] very good indicator of delegation meriting *Chevron* treatment [is an] express congressional authorizatio[n] to engage in the process of rulemaking or adjudication that produces regulations or rulings for which deference is claimed"). The Federal Highway Administration adopted the ICC's regulations, and the Single State Registration System is now administered by the Federal Motor Carrier Safety Administration.

Accordingly, the question before us is whether the text of the statute resolves the issue, or, if not, whether the ICC's interpretation is permissible in light of the deference to be accorded the agency under the statutory scheme. If the statute speaks clearly "to the precise question at issue," we "must give effect to the unambiguously expressed intent of Congress." *Chevron*, 467 U.S. at 842–43. If the statute is instead "silent or ambiguous with respect to the specific issue," we must sustain the agency's interpretation if it is "based on a permissible construction of the statute." *Id.* at 843.

ISTEA's fee-cap provision does not foreclose the ICC's determination that fees charged under States' pre-existing reciprocity agreements were, in effect, frozen by the new Single State Registration System. The provision requires that the new system "result in a fee for each participating State that is equal to the fee, not to exceed $10 per vehicle, that such State collected or charged as of November 15, 1991." 49 U.S.C. § 14504(c)(2)(B)(iv)(III). The language "collected or charged" can quite naturally be read to mean fees that a State *actually* collected or charged. The statute thus can easily be read as the ICC chose, making it unlawful "for a State to renounce or modify a reciprocity agreement so as to alter any fee charged or collected as of November 15, 1991, under the predecessor registration system." *American Trucking Associations—Petition for Declaratory Order—Single State Insurance Registration*, 9 I.C.C.2d 1184, 1194 (1993).

The Michigan Supreme Court held that the language of ISTEA's fee-cap provision compels a different result. Although it acknowledged that ISTEA is silent with respect to reciprocity agreements, the court nonetheless concluded that the fee-cap provision mandates that those agreements have no bearing in the determination of what fee a State "collected or charged" as of November 15, 1991. The court reasoned that the Single State Registration System was "based not on the fees collected from one individual company, but on the *fee system* that the state had in place." While such a reading might be reasonable, nothing in the statute compels that particular result.

The fee-cap provision refers not to a "fee system," but to the "fee . . . collected or charged." 49 U.S.C. § 14504(c)(2)(B)(iv)(III). Under the ICC's rule, where a State waives its registration fee, its "fee . . . collected or charged" is zero and must remain zero. The ICC's interpretation is a permissible reading of the language of the statute. And, because there is statutory ambiguity and the agency's interpretation is reasonable, its interpretation must receive deference.

As commenters to the ICC during the rulemaking pointed out, to allow States to disavow their reciprocity agreements so as to alter any fee charged or collected as of November 15, 1991, would potentially permit States to increase their revenues substantially under the new system, a result that the ICC quite reasonably believed Congress did not intend. The ICC concluded that its rule best served the "intent of the law that the flow of revenue for the States be maintained while the burden of the registration system for carriers be reduced." *Single State Insurance Registration*, 9 I.C.C.2d at 618. The agency considered that allowing States to disavow reciprocity agreements and charge a single, uniform fee might reduce administrative burdens, but expressed concern that carriers' registration costs, and state revenues, would balloon.

Respondents argue that Congress intended for each State to set a single, uniform fee. While such a mandate would, indeed, have simplified the new system, it is not compelled by the language of the statute, which instructs the ICC to implement a system under which States charge a fee, not to exceed $10 per vehicle, that is equal to the fee such States "collected or charged as of November 15, 1991."

Respondents also contend that, by freezing the fees charged under reciprocity agreements as part of the fee cap, the ICC added a constraint not within the express language of the statute. The Michigan Supreme Court expressed a similar concern, stating that "[i]t is not for the ICC . . . to insert words into the statute." It was precisely Congress' command, however, that the ICC promulgate standards to govern the Single State Registration System, and it was thus for that agency to resolve any ambiguities and fill in any holes in the statutory scheme. *See Mead Corp.*, 533 U.S. at 229; *Chevron*, 467 U.S. at 843–44. To hold States to the fees they actually collected or charged seems to us a reasonable interpretation of the statute's command that state fees be "equal to the fee, not to exceed $10 per vehicle, that such State collected or charged as of November 15, 1991." 49 U.S.C. § 14504(c)(2)(B)(iv)(III).

Respondents argue that the ICC's rule contravenes ISTEA's fee-cap provision by limiting what a State can charge based on what was collected from or charged to a particular carrier. Respondents point out that the focus of the provision is on the actions of the State, not the actions of any particular carrier. While we agree that the statute focuses on what States "collected or charged" rather than what particular carriers paid, we do not agree that the ICC's rule focuses the inquiry on the latter. Under the "bingo card" regime, States entered into reciprocity agreements that waived or reduced fees charged to particular categories of vehicles. The ICC's rule does not necessarily cap the aggregate fee paid by any particular carrier; rather, it simply requires States to preserve fees at the levels they actually collected or charged pursuant to reciprocity agreements in place as of November 15, 1991.

Because the ICC's interpretation of ISTEA's fee-cap provision is consistent with the language of the statute and reasonably resolves any ambiguity therein, the Michigan Supreme Court erred in declining to enforce it.

■ [The opinion of JUSTICE STEVENS, concurring in the judgment, is omitted. Ed.]

American Bar Association v. Federal Trade Commission

430 F.3d 457 (D.C. Cir. 2005).

■ SENTELLE, CIRCUIT JUDGE.

The Federal Trade Commission ("FTC" or "the Commission") appeals from an order of the District Court granting summary judgment in consolidated cases brought by the appellees American Bar Association and the New York State Bar Association (collectively, "ABA" or "the Bar Associations"). The Bar Associations sought a declaratory judgment that the FTC's decision that attorneys engaged in the practice of law are covered by the Gramm-Leach-Bliley Act ("GLBA" or "the Act") exceeded the statutory authority of the Commission and was therefore invalid as a matter of law. Because we agree with the District Court that the Commission's attempt to regulate the practice of law under the Act fell outside its statutory authority, we affirm the judgment under review.

I. Background

A. *Statutory Framework*

Effective November 12, 1999, Congress enacted the Gramm-Leach-Bliley Financial Modernization Act. The Act declared it to be "the policy of the Congress that each financial institution has an affirmative and continuing obligation to respect the privacy of its customers and to protect the security and confidentiality of those customers' nonpublic personal information." 15 U.S.C. § 6801(a). To further that goal, Congress enacted broad privacy protective provisions, described by one Member of the House of Representatives as "represent[ing] the most comprehensive federal privacy protections ever enacted by Congress." 145 CONG. REC. H11,544 (daily ed. Nov. 4, 1999) (statement of Rep. Sandlin).

The privacy provisions empowered the Federal Trade Commission, along with other federal regulatory agencies, to "prescribe ... such regulations as may be necessary to carry out the purposes of this subchapter with respect to the financial institutions subject to their jurisdiction under section 6805 of this title." 15 U.S.C. § 6804(a)(1). The cited section, 6805, outlines the institutions and persons subject to the jurisdiction of "Federal functional regulators," and in section 6805(a)(7) assigns enforcement "[u]nder the Federal Trade Commission Act . . . [to] the Federal Trade Commission for any other financial institution or other person that is not subject to the jurisdiction of any agency or authority under" the preceding paragraphs of the subsection. The definitional section of the statute, section 6809, defines "financial institution" as "any institution the business of which is engaging in financial activities as described in section 1843(k) of Title 12." *Id.* § 6809(3)(A). Other subsections of section 6809 create exceptions and modifications to the general definition of "financial institution."

Title 12 U.S.C. § 1843(k), referenced in section 6809(a), is a part of the Bank Holding Company Act of 1956 ("BHCA"). The BHCA, in section 1843, limits the ability of the bank holding companies regulated under that statutory scheme to hold interests in nonbanking organizations. Specifically, section 1843(a) provides that

> [e]xcept as otherwise provided in this chapter, no bank holding company shall . . . retain direct or indirect ownership or control of any voting shares of any company which is not a bank or bank holding company or engage in any activities other than (A) those of banking or of managing or controlling banks and other subsidiaries authorized under this chapter or of furnishing services to or performing services for its subsidiaries, and (B) those permitted under [other subsections of the statute].

12 U.S.C. § 1843(a). However, section 1843(k) limits the effect of the general prohibition created by section 1843(a) by providing that

> [n]otwithstanding subsection (a) of this section, a financial holding company may engage in any activity, and may acquire and retain the shares of any company engaged in any activity, that the [Federal Reserve] Board . . . determines (by regulation or order)—(A) to be financial in nature or incidental to such financial activity; or (B) is complementary to a financial activity and does not pose a substantial risk to the safety or soundness of depository institutions or the financial system generally.

Id. § 1843(k)(1). The BHCA declares to be financial in nature activities listed in section 1843(k)(4), to wit:

> (A) Lending, exchanging, transferring, investing for others, or safeguarding money or securities.
>
> (B) Insuring, guaranteeing, or indemnifying against loss, harm, damage, illness, disability, or death, or providing and issuing annuities, and acting as principal, agent, or broker for purposes of the foregoing, in any State.
>
> (C) Providing financial, investment, or economic advisory services, including advising an investment company (as defined in [section 80a–3 of Title 15]).
>
> (D) Issuing or selling instruments representing interests in pools of assets permissible for a bank to hold directly.
>
> (E) Underwriting, dealing in, or making a market in securities.

Id. § 1843(k)(4).

Following the list of activities that "shall be considered" financial in nature, the BHCA enacted the following category of activity, which is most pertinent to the current case:

> (F) Engaging in any activity that the Board has determined, by order or regulation that is in effect on November 12, 1999, to be so closely related to banking or managing or controlling banks as to be a proper incident thereto (subject to the same terms and conditions contained in such order or regulation, unless modified by the [Federal Reserve] Board).

The phrase "order or regulation that is in effect on November 12, 1999" adopts a Federal Reserve Board ("Board") regulation published at 12 C.F.R. § 225.28 (2000), commonly known as Regulation Y. Regulation Y, as is to be expected, deals with the subject matter of section 1843(k), that is, "nonbanking activities and acquisitions by bank holding companies": It lists "permissible nonbanking activities." That list is described in the regulation as activities that are

> (a) Closely related nonbanking activities. The activities listed in paragraph (b) of this section are so closely related to banking or managing or controlling banks as to be a proper incident thereto, and may be engaged in by a bank holding company or its subsidiary in accordance with the requirements of this regulation.

12 C.F.R. § 225.28(a).

* * *

To recapitulate: The GLBA contains extensive privacy protection provisions that apply to "financial institutions." In section 6809, the Act defines "financial institution" as "any institution the business of which is engaging in financial activities as described in section 1843(k) of Title 12." The referenced section of Title 12 is contained in the BHCA. Specifically, that section identifies institutions engaged in nonbanking activities that are financial in nature, such that bank holding companies may retain ownership interests in institutions engaged in their pursuit. The section of the BHCA defining those activities incorporates by reference Regulation Y, which offers an extensive list of examples of such "financial activities" so closely related to banking as to be permissible.

B. *The Commission's Interpretation*

Upon the passage of the Act, the FTC, pursuant to the authority granted it in 15 U.S.C. § 6805(a)(7), undertook a rulemaking. In May 2000, the FTC concluded the rulemaking and issued regulations published at 65 Fed. Reg. 33,646 (codified at 16 C.F.R. pt. 313). Although the FTC relied in the first instance on Congress's definition of "financial institution" as "an institution the business of which is engaging in financial activities," the Commission restated the definition: "An institution that is significantly engaged in financial activities is a financial institution." 16 C.F.R. § 313.3(k)(1).

Like the statute, the regulations at no point describe the statutory or regulatory scheme as governing the practice of law as such. Indeed, the phrase "practice of law" never appears in part 313, and the word "attorneys," while present in two places, appears in the context of describing persons to whom financial institutions can make release of customer information, if authorized, not in the context of defining "financial institutions" as including attorneys. Nonetheless, the breadth of the FTC's regulation, apparently taken in conjunction with statements to or by news media, caused concern among representatives of the bar. Therefore, various bar associations, including the American Bar Association, made inquiry of the Commission as to whether the Commission was taking a position that privacy provisions of the GLBA and the regulations made pursuant thereto governed attorneys engaged in the practice of law.

On April 8, 2002, the Director of the Bureau of Consumer Protection at the Commission sent a letter to the President and the Director of Governmental Affairs of the ABA "in response to your correspondence regarding the application of Title V, Subtitle A, of the

Gramm-Leach-Bliley Act, 15 U.S.C. 6801 *et seq* . . . and the Federal Trade Commission's Rule, Privacy of Consumer Financial Information . . . to attorneys at law." (Citations omitted.) As part of the inquiry, the ABA had also requested exemption from the Act if the Commission purported to regulate the practice of law under the Act. That position has been abandoned by the bar associations during the course of this litigation, but was still a live question between the parties at the time of the FTC's communication to the ABA. Although recognizing that the bar associations' letters had "question[ed] the appropriateness and utility of applying the GLB Act's privacy provisions to attorneys engaged in the practice of law," the Director only directly addressed the ABA's request for exemption. However, in rejecting that request, the Director made it plain that the Commission was purporting to regulate attorneys engaged in the practice of their profession and asserted that "the GLB Act itself states that *entities* engaged in 'financial activities' are subject to the Act." (emphasis supplied).

After some further negotiation, the bar associations brought the present litigation.

II.   The Litigation

The New York State Bar Association and the American Bar Association separately filed actions for declaratory judgment. While the prayers for relief in the two complaints are differently worded, the gist is the same, in that each seeks, *inter alia*, a declaratory order that, in the words of the ABA complaint:

> (a) Congress did not in the GLBA confer authority on the FTC to regulate the confidentiality, privacy and security of information disclosed by clients to their attorneys;

> (b) The FTC's decision that attorneys engaged in the practice of law are covered by the GLBA is unlawful and hereby set aside; . . . .

* * *

III. Analysis

As we analyze the FTC's arguments for the proposition that Congress in the privacy provisions of the GLBA enabled the Commission to regulate the practice of law, we are reminded repeatedly of a recent admonition from the Supreme Court: "[Congress] does not . . . hide elephants in mouseholes." *Whitman v. Am. Trucking Ass'ns*, 531 U.S. 457, 468 (2001). The FTC begins its defense of its attempted turf expansion in the correct place, that is, by recognizing that "the starting point in any case involving the meaning of a statute[ ] is the language of the statute itself." *Group Life & Health Ins. Co. v. Royal Drug Co.*, 440 U.S. 205, 210 (1979). The Commission argues, as it did before the District Court, that the language of the statute evidences a congressional intent to empower the Commission to regulate attorneys engaged in certain types of law practice as "financial institutions" under the privacy regulations promulgated pursuant to the GLBA privacy provisions. More specifically, the Commission notes that the legislation defines "financial institution" quite broadly as "any institution the business of which is engaging in financial activities as described in section 1843(k) of Title 12." The statute in turn deems as "financial in nature" various listed activities, together with those not expressly listed but theretofore listed by the Federal Reserve Board in Regulation Y. Regulation Y, set forth at its staggering full-length above, includes the activities "[p]roviding real estate settlement services," and "[p]roviding tax-planning and tax-preparation services to any person." 12 C.F.R. § 225.28(b)(2)(viii), (b)(6)(vi) (2001). The Commission then asserts, "[t]hus, under the terms of the statute, any institution that is in the business of engaging in a financial activity listed in section 4(k) of the BHCA, including those set forth in Regulation Y, qualifies as a 'financial institution.'" That statement by the Commission is unassailable: Indeed, it does no more than restate the provisions of that statute. That is precisely the problem. The Commission's reasoning, doing no more than restating the statute, leaves as open as ever the question of whether an attorney practicing law is an "institution engaging in the business of financial activities."

The statute certainly does not so plainly grant the Commission the *not plain* authority to regulate attorneys engaged in the practice of law as to entitle the Commission to what is called a *"Chevron* One" disposition. That is, rather simply we cannot hold that Congress has directly and plainly granted the Commission the authority to regulate practicing attorneys as the Commission attempts. *See Chevron U.S.A. Inc. v. Natural Res. Def. Council, Inc.*, 467 U.S. 837, 842–43 (1984). Indeed, such professionals are subject to regulation under the words of the statute only if they are "institutions" and if they are "engaged in the business of financial activity." It is not plain at all to us that Congress has entered such a direct regulatory command by plain language of a statute, a lengthy statute incorporated by reference, and an even more lengthy and detailed regulation incorporated by reference in the second statute, none of which ever mentioned attorneys engaged in the practice of law. Therefore, if the Commission is to prevail, it must do so under a deferential standard of review. That is, to uphold the Commission's regulatory decision, we must conclude first that the words of the statute are ambiguous in such a way as to make the Commission's decision worthy of deference under the second step of *Chevron. Id.* at 843. If we so hold, we will then uphold the agency's interpretation of the ambiguous statute if that interpretation is "permissible," that is, if it is "reasonable." *Id.* at 845.

A. *Chevron* Step One

The first question, whether there is such an ambiguity, is for the court, and we owe the agency no deference on the existence of ambiguity. Deference to the agency's interpretation under *Chevron* is warranted only where "Congress has left a gap for the agency to fill pursuant to an express or implied 'delegation of authority to the agency.'" *Ry. Labor Exec. Ass'n v. Nat'l Mediation Bd.*, 29 F.3d 655, 671 (D.C.Cir.1994) (en banc) (internal citation omitted). The Commission argues along the line suggested by the scant reasoning in the letter announcing its decision. The opinion letter had directed its language principally toward the question of whether the Commission should "exempt attorneys at law from the application of the Privacy Rule." True, the Bar Association had requested such an exemption, but only as a conditional request if the Commission held in the first instance that the privacy provisions of the GLBA covered attorneys engaged in the practice of law, a proposition that the association resisted. The Commission's letter, while claiming that "[w]e have carefully considered your concerns, and recognize the issues you have raised regarding the application of the GLB Act to attorneys at law," addressed only the "significant questions as to the legal authority of the Commission to grant the exemption you request."

The Commission apparently assumed—without reasoning—that it could extend its regulatory authority over attorneys engaged in the practice of law with no other basis than the observation that the Act did not provide for an exemption. * * * While there is limited *post hoc* rationalization in the Commission's brief addressing the inclusion of attorneys in the definition of "financial institution," which we will discuss *infra*, the Commission repeatedly repairs to the position that no language in the statute exempts attorneys from regulation. That is not the question. As we have often cautioned, "[t]o suggest, as the [Commission] effectively does, that *Chevron* step two is implicated any time a statute does not expressly *negate* the existence of a claimed administrative power . . . is both flatly unfaithful to the principles of administrative law . . . and refuted by precedent." Ry. Labor Exec. Ass'n, 29 F.3d at 671 (emphasis in original). Plainly, if we were "to *presume* a delegation of power" from the absence of "an express *withholding* of such power, agencies would enjoy virtually limitless hegemony. . . ." Id. (emphasis in original). Therefore, if there is the sort of ambiguity that supports an implicit congressional delegation of authority to the agency to make a deference-worthy interpretation of the statute, we must look elsewhere than the failure to negate regulation of attorneys. That failure does not advance the Commission's cause at all. Otherwise put, the question is not whether the statute permits exemption from regulation for attorneys, but whether it supports such regulation at all. We will defer to the agency's interpretation on that subject only if the statute "is silent or ambiguous with respect to the specific issue." *Barnhart v. Walton*, 535 U.S. 212, 218 (2002) (internal quotation marks and citation omitted).

We further recognize that the existence of ambiguity is not enough per se to warrant deference to the agency's interpretation. The ambiguity must be such as to make it appear that Congress either explicitly or implicitly delegated authority to cure that ambiguity. "Mere ambiguity in a statute is not evidence of congressional delegation of authority." *Michigan v. EPA*, 268 F.3d 1075, 1082 (D.C. Cir. 2001) (citations omitted). The deference mandated in *Chevron* "comes into play, of course, only as a consequence of statutory ambiguity, and then only if the reviewing court finds an implicit delegation of authority to the agency." *Sea-Land Serv., Inc. v. Dep't of Transp.*, 137 F.3d 640, 645 (D.C. Cir. 1998) (emphasis added). When we examine a scheme of the length, detail, and intricacy of the one before us, we find it difficult to believe that Congress, by any remaining ambiguity, intended to undertake the regulation of the profession of law—a profession never before regulated by "federal functional regulators"—and never mentioned in the statute. To find this interpretation deference-worthy, we would have to conclude that Congress not only had hidden a rather large elephant in a rather obscure mousehole, but had buried the ambiguity in which the pachyderm lurks beneath an incredibly deep mound of specificity, none of which bears the footprints of the beast or any indication that Congress even suspected its presence. We therefore seriously doubt that Congress intended to empower the Commission to undertake that regulation, and we are reluctant to even afford the regulation the deference due agency action that survives the analysis at the first step of *Chevron*.

* * *

Lest it be forgotten, the basic language in which the Commission finds the ambiguity permitting it to regulate the practice of law is that of § 6805 empowering the Federal Trade Commission and other "federal functional regulators" to enforce the statute and regulations prescribed under it with respect to "financial institutions and other persons subject to [the Commission's] jurisdiction. . . ." 15 U.S.C. § 6805(a). That language, even with—perhaps especially with—the layers of incorporated statutory and regulatory language describing financial institutions makes an exceptionally poor fit with the FTC's apparent decision that Congress, after centuries of not doing so, has suddenly decided to regulate the practice of law. This fit is helped but little, if at all, by the congressional definition of "financial institution" as "an institution the business of which is engaging in financial activity." 15 U.S.C. § 6809(3)(A). An attorney, or even a law firm, does not fit very neatly into the niche of a "financial institution." Even if one concedes— and it is quite a concession—that Congress would have intended the word "institution" to include an attorney, or even a law firm, it still requires quite a stretch to conclude that such an institution is a "financial institution." It trims the stretch little, if at all, to read the entire statutory definition of "financial institution" as "any institution the business of which is engaging in financial activities as described in section 1843(k) of Title 12" (set forth above). Without reiterating the language of the incorporated statute, attorneys and law firms, even if viewed as "institutions," are not institutions "the business of which is engaging in financial activities," as defined in the statute. The Commission itself seems to recognize the improbability of Congress's having intended to include law firms within the designation "institutions" in the letter under review, in which it conspicuously substituted the word "entities" for "institutions." Such a dramatic rewriting of the statute is not mere interpretation. Even if we accept the inclusion of "entities" such as law firms within the meaning of "institutions," the "business" of a law firm (if the practice of a profession is properly viewed as business) is the practice of the profession of law.

The Commission distorts the definition slightly but improves the fit but little by its regulatory definition that a financial institution is "an institution that is significantly engaged in financial activities," as opposed to requiring that the institution must be one the business of which is engaging in financial activities. Building on this stretch, the Commission, in its brief, supplies reasoning conspicuously lacking from the letter of determination that we review. Although we cannot affirm an agency's actions based on the *post hoc* rationale of its litigating position, *see, e.g., Motor Vehicle Mfrs. Ass'n v. State Farm Mut. Auto. Ins. Co.*, 463 U.S. 29, 50 (1983), even if we charitably construe the letter to imply the reasoning, it is still inadequate.

The reasoning in the brief relies on the language of Regulation Y, the second tier incorporation. As noted above, Regulation Y, in its original application, described the "closely related nonbanking activities" in which a bank holding company or its subsidiaries might engage. Within that voluminous listing, the regulation included two activities, "[p]roviding real estate settlement services," and "[p]roviding tax-planning and tax-preparation services," in which attorneys sometimes, and apparently in the view of the Commission, *significantly* engage. *See* 16 C.F.R. § 313.3(k)(1). Again, if Congress intended to empower a federal financial regulator to undertake regulation of the practice of law, this seems a strangely unclear method of doing so. The statute after all defined a "financial institution" as "an institution the business of which is engaging in financial activities." Congress did not adopt the approach of the Commission by covering "an institution that is significantly engaged in financial activities." Certainly it did not extend that definition to cover all "entities." In sum, Congress did not leave an ambiguity on the question before us—that is, the power of the Commission to regulate the practice of law—sufficient to compel deference to the Commission's determination to do so.

We further determine that even if we err in our conclusion that the regulation fails at *Chevron* Step One, we are satisfied that the interpretation afforded by the Commission is not sufficiently reasonable to survive that deference at Step Two.

B.   *Chevron* Step Two

All the reasons set forth above for our determination that Congress did not intend to leave sufficient ambiguity to support deferential review return to convince us that the interpretation is not reasonable even if we afford it deference. But our analysis under *Chevron* Step Two need not end there. It is undisputed that the regulation of the practice of law is traditionally the province of the states. Federal law "may not be interpreted to reach into areas of State sovereignty unless the language of the federal law compels the intrusion." *City of Abilene v. FCC*, 164 F.3d 49, 52 (D.C. Cir. 1999). Otherwise put, "if Congress intends to alter the 'usual constitutional balance between the States and the Federal Government,' it must make its intention to do so 'unmistakably clear in the language of the statute.'" *Will v. Mich. Dep't of State Police*, 491 U.S. 58, 65 (1989) (quoting *Atascadero State Hosp. v. Scanlon*, 473 U.S. 234, 242 (1985)). By now it should be abundantly plain that Congress has not made an intention to regulate the practice of law "unmistakably clear" in the language of the GLBA. In *Gregory v. Ashcroft*, 501 U.S. 452 (1991), citing, *inter alia*, *Will* and *Atascadero State Hospital*, the Supreme Court held that

> [t]his plain statement rule is nothing more than an acknowledgment that the States retain substantial sovereign powers under our constitutional scheme, powers with which Congress does not readily interfere.

501 U.S. at 461.

* * * The states have regulated the practice of law throughout the history of the country; the federal government has not. This is not to conclude that the federal government could not do so. We simply conclude that it is not reasonable for an agency to decide that Congress

has chosen such a course of action in language that is, even charitably viewed, at most ambiguous.

NOTES AND QUESTIONS

1. The Supreme Court in *Yellow Transportation* and the D.C. Circuit in *American Bar Association* approached the *Chevron* step one inquiry very differently. In *Yellow Transportation*, the Supreme Court's conclusion, with little textual or other legal analysis, that the statute neither expressly rejected the agency's reading nor particularly compelled that adopted by the Michigan Supreme Court was sufficient to advance the case to *Chevron*'s deferential step two. In *American Bar Association*, by contrast, the court was adamant that the statute's failure to preclude the agency's interpretation explicitly was beside the point; rather, that court saw the step one inquiry as whether the statute actually supported the agency's interpretation, and proceeded to examine the statute in some depth in answering that question. Neither of these approaches has a particular claim at being the "correct" one; variations among *Chevron* step one analysis abound both at the Supreme Court and among circuit court opinions. Do you find one approach to *Chevron* step one preferable to the other? Why or why not?

2. In *Yellow Transportation*, the Supreme Court quickly construed the statute's silence regarding the question at bar as ambiguity and proceeded to examine the permissibility of the agency's interpretation at *Chevron* step two. In other cases, however, the Court's approach to statutory silence has been mixed. In *Entergy Corp. v. Riverkeeper, Inc.*, 129 S.Ct. 1498 (2009), for example, as in Yellow Transportation, the Court interpreted the failure of § 316(b) of the Clean Water Act, 33 U.S.C. § 1326(b), to mention cost-benefit analysis as conferring discretion upon the Environmental Protection Agency. By contrast, in *Whitman v. American Trucking Ass'ns, Inc.*, 531 U.S. 457 (2001), discussed at length in Chapter 2, the Court interpreted the failure of § 109 of the Clean Air Act, 42 U.S.C. § 7409, to reference cost considerations as "unambiguously" precluding cost-benefit analysis given the "statutory and historical context." Interestingly, Justice Scalia wrote the majority opinions in both *Entergy Corp.* and *American Trucking*.

3. The courts have always played a significant role in keeping agencies within the scope of their congressionally delegated authority. Yet, it is often difficult if not impossible to distinguish statutory ambiguities that speak to the scope of an agency's power from those that merely concern the agency's application of clearly delegated authority. This may be particularly true when an agency interprets a statute's failure to preclude regulatory action as permission to act, as the FTC did in *American Bar Association*. For an interesting analysis of this issue, see Nathan Alexander Sales and Jonathan H. Adler, *The Rest is Silence: Chevron Deference, Agency Jurisdiction, and Statutory Silences*, 2009 U. ILL. L. REV. 1497 (2009).

2. THE "TOOLS" OF STEP ONE ANALYSIS

The degree of clarity required at *Chevron* step one is at least partly a function of the evidence the Court is willing to consider in evaluating statutory meaning at that stage of its analysis. To offer just one example, how should the Court react at *Chevron* step one if a statute's text is ambiguous but its legislative history plainly illustrates congressional intent? Is step one analysis limited to a textualist inquiry, or may a reviewing court consider legislative history?

In footnote nine of its opinion in *Chevron*, the Court said:

> The judiciary is the final authority on issues of statutory construction and must reject administrative constructions which are contrary to clear congressional intent. If a court, employing traditional tools of statutory construction, ascertains that Congress had an intention on the precise question at issue, that intention is the law and must be given effect.

[handwritten margin note: traditional tools of Statutory Construction is acceptable]

Footnote nine raises difficult questions. What "traditional tools of statutory construction" should a court use in applying *Chevron* step one, *i.e.*, in deciding what Congress intended when it included particular language in an agency-administered statute? Courts always find some combination of "tools" that are sufficient to allow a court to interpret a judicially-administered statute no matter how ambiguous the statute might be. A court that truly took *Chevron*'s footnote nine at face value would find no room left to accord any deference to an agency interpretation. Thus, the Court could not have intended to authorize reviewing courts to use all of the traditional tools that courts regularly use to interpret judicially-administered statutes. That leads us to the difficult questions: which "tools" should courts use to determine congressional intent for purposes of applying *Chevron* step one and how should they use those tools?

There are five traditional tools of construction that courts use to give meaning to judicially-administered statutes: the plain meaning rule, legislative history, legislative purpose, canons of construction, and stare decisis. Each has advantages and disadvantages for purposes of applying *Chevron* step one.

The Plain Meaning Rule

The plain meaning rule refers to the use of dictionary definitions of words to determine their meaning in a statute. As Fred Schauer has explained, the plain meaning rule facilitates clear communication because legislators, agency administrators, judges, regulatees, and beneficiaries of statutes have access to the same means of determining the meaning of words in statutes. See Frederick Schauer, *Statutory Construction and the Coordinating Function of the Plain Meaning Rule*, 1990 SUP. CT. REV. 231. The plain meaning rule has limited utility, however. Most dictionaries offer multiple definitions for most words, and dictionaries often differ in their definitions of the same word. In some cases, the Supreme Court has used the dictionary definition preferred by a majority of the Justices as the basis for a decision rejecting the agency's interpretation even though the agency's interpretation was consistent with some other dictionary definition. Does that practice seem defensible to you? Why or why not? *See* Richard J. Pierce, Jr., *The Supreme Court's New Hypertextualism: An Invitation to Cacophony and Incoherence in the Administrative State*, 95 COLUM. L. REV. 749 (1995).

Legislative History

Courts have long relied on legislative history as a tool to interpret statutes, but that practice has been subjected to harsh criticism on several bases. Legislative history is often indeterminate because the voluminous history of a major statute frequently offers support for inconsistent interpretations. Further, legislative history is arguably unreliable because lobbyists and congressional staff members often can insert statements into the legislative history of a statute with little, if any, participation or awareness by members of Congress. Finally, legislative history is arguably illegitimate because it was not enacted by Congress. For a particularly harsh criticism of the practice of relying on legislative history, see Adrian Vermeule, *Legislative History and the Limits of Judicial Competence: The Untold Story of Holy Trinity Church*, 50 STAN. L. REV. 1833 (1998). Justices Scalia and Thomas oppose the use of legislative history for any purpose, at least in theory, but the other seven Justices sometimes rely on legislative history to resolve ambiguities in statutory language. If the language of a statute is ambiguous, and the legislative history supports an interpretation of that is inconsistent with the agency's construction, should a court rely on legislative history to support a decision to reject the agency interpretation through application of *Chevron* step one?

Legislative Purpose

Courts have long interpreted statutes in ways that courts expect to further the purpose of the statute. This interpretative tool also has serious limits, however. Few, if any, statutes are enacted to further a single purpose. The *Chevron* Court recognized that Congress had two purposes when it enacted the Clean Air Act amendments of 1977—reducing air pollution and allowing reasonable economic growth. It concluded that Congress had assigned the EPA the task of balancing those two sometimes conflicting purposes. Most statutes are enacted to further multiple, often conflicting, purposes. Should courts police agencies' attempts to reconcile the often competing purposes of statutes? If so, should they do so by applying step one or step two of *Chevron*? Which institution is better at determining whether an action will further a statutory purpose—a court or the agency charged with responsibility to administer the statute? If Congress has said nothing about a national goal or value that is logically-relevant to an agency's decision, should the agency or a reviewing court draw the inference that Congress intended to forbid the agency from considering that goal in its decision-making process. See Richard J. Pierce, Jr., *What Factors Can an Agency Consider in Making a Decision?*, 2009 MICH. ST. L. REV. 67.

Canons of Construction

Canons of construction—customary rules that courts have long utilized to assist them in interpreting statutory language—are another "traditional tool." In his famous essay, *Remarks on the Theory of Appellate Decision and the Rules or Canons About How Statutes Are to Be Construed*, 3 VAND. L. REV. 395 (1950), Karl Llewellyn identified one of the major limitations on the use of the canons: there are scores of canons, and they often support conflicting interpretations. For example, the canon that courts should give effect to every word and clause in a statute is contradicted by the canon that courts should reject as surplusage words that are inadvertently inserted or repugnant to the rest of the statute. *See id.* at 406. Cass Sunstein has suggested that courts abandon the old canons as obsolete and substitute for them a new set of canons that reflects modern values. See Cass Sunstein, *Interpreting Statutes in the Regulatory State*, 103 HARV. L. REV. 405 (1989). Other scholars believe, however, that Sunstein's canonical approach merely creates a new, more complicated version of the problem of internal inconsistency and indeterminacy that Llewellyn attributed to the old canons. See Eben Moglen & Richard J. Pierce, Jr., *Sunstein's New Canons: Choosing the Fictions of Statutory Interpretation*, 57 U. CHI. L. REV. 1203 (1990). Which if any canon should a court use to determine that an otherwise ambiguous provision of a statute reflects a congressional intent that justifies a court in rejecting an agency construction through application of *Chevron* step one?

Furthermore, some canons of construction dictate particular outcomes in the face of statutory ambiguity. For example, the canon of constitutional avoidance instructs reviewing courts to choose interpretations that avoid constitutional questions over constructions that implicate constitutional concerns. Similarly, the rule of lenity counsels interpreting criminal statutes in the light most favorable to the defendant. Although the Court has indicated that *Chevron* review is inapplicable to criminal statutes, the Court has nevertheless on occasion employed the *Chevron* standard in evaluating agency interpretations of regulatory statutes that carry both civil and criminal penalties. In other words, canons such as these only apply when statutes are ambiguous, and they operate specifically to resolve statutory meaning under such circumstances. At times, the Supreme Court has seemed to suggest that such canons ought to displace *Chevron* deference. Yet, if Congress has delegated primary interpretive authority to an agency, should the agency not be able to advance an interpretation that skirts but stays within the boundaries of constitutionality?

Stare Decisis

Ordinarily, of course, the Supreme Court operates under the policy and practice of stare decisis, adhering generally to prior decisions irrespective of whether the current Justices might have decided some cases differently in the first instance. In the context of statutory interpretation, the doctrine of stare decisis would seem to suggest that, once the Supreme Court has reached a conclusion regarding statutory meaning, agencies as well as lower courts would be bound. As should be readily apparent, stare decisis directly contradicts *Chevron*'s presumption that Congress delegated primary interpretive authority over certain statutes to agencies rather than the courts. If Congress has indeed delegated primary responsibility for interpreting a statute to an agency rather than the courts, then it cannot be the case that judicial interpretations necessarily take precedence over contrary agency interpretations. For that matter, the Court in *Chevron* emphasized that "[a]n initial agency interpretation is not instantly carved in stone" and that reviewing courts should allow agencies the flexibility to reconsider and adjust their interpretations—a position that is hardly consistent with the requirements of stare decisis. In fact, in the years following *Chevron*, the circuit courts divided particularly over the question whether or not their own statutory interpretation precedents "trumped" *Chevron* deference.

With these thoughts in mind, consider the Supreme Court's application of *Chevron*'s first step the following cases.

Department of Housing & Urban Development v. Rucker

535 U.S. 125 (2002).

■ CHIEF JUSTICE REHNQUIST delivered the opinion of the Court.

With drug dealers "increasingly imposing a reign of terror on public and other federally assisted low-income housing tenants," Congress passed the Anti-Drug Abuse Act of 1988. The Act, as later amended, provides that each "public housing agency shall utilize leases which . . . provide that any criminal activity that threatens the health, safety, or right to peaceful enjoyment of the premises by other tenants or any drug-related criminal activity on or off such premises, engaged in by a public housing tenant, any member of the tenant's household, or any guest or other person under the tenant's control, shall be cause for termination of tenancy." 42 U.S.C. § 1437d(*l*)(6). Petitioners say that this statute requires lease terms that allow a local public housing authority to evict a tenant when a member of the tenant's household or a guest engages in drug-related criminal activity, regardless of whether the tenant knew, or had reason to know, of that activity. Respondents say it does not. We agree with petitioners.

Respondents are four public housing tenants of the Oakland Housing Authority (OHA). Paragraph 9(m) of respondents' leases, tracking the language of § 1437d(*l*)(6), obligates the tenants to "assure that the tenant, any member of the household, a guest, or another person under the tenant's control, shall not engage in . . . [a]ny drug-related criminal activity on or near the premise[s]." Respondents also signed an agreement stating that the tenant "understand[s] that if I or any member of my household or guests should violate this lease provision, my tenancy may be terminated and I may be evicted."

In late 1997 and early 1998, OHA instituted eviction proceedings in state court against respondents, alleging violations of this lease provision. The complaint alleged: (1) that the respective grandsons of respondents William Lee and Barbara Hill, both of whom were listed as residents on the leases, were caught in the apartment complex parking lot smoking marijuana; (2) that the daughter of respondent Pearlie Rucker, who resides with her and is listed on the lease as a resident, was found with cocaine and a crack cocaine pipe three blocks from Rucker's apartment; and (3) that on three instances within a 2-month period, respondent Herman Walker's caregiver and two others were found with cocaine in Walker's apartment. OHA had issued Walker notices of a lease violation on the first two occasions, before initiating the eviction action after the third violation.

United States Department of Housing and Urban Development (HUD) regulations administering § 1437d(*l*)(6) require lease terms authorizing evictions in these circumstances. The HUD regulations closely track the statutory language, and provide that "[i]n deciding to evict for criminal activity, the [public housing authority] shall have discretion to consider all of the circumstances of the case. . . ." 24 C.F.R. § 966.4(*l*)(5)(i) (2001). The agency made clear that local public housing authorities' discretion to evict for drug-related activity includes those situations in which "[the] tenant did not know, could not foresee, or could not control behavior by other occupants of the unit." 56 Fed. Reg. 51560, 51567 (1991).

After OHA initiated the eviction proceedings in state court, respondents commenced actions against HUD, OHA, and OHA's director in United States District Court. They challenged HUD's interpretation of the statute under the Administrative Procedure Act, 5 U.S.C. § 706(2)(A), arguing that 42 U.S.C. § 1437d(*l*)(6) does not require lease terms authorizing the eviction of so-called "innocent" tenants, and, in the alternative, that if it does, then the statute is unconstitutional. The District Court issued a preliminary injunction, enjoining OHA from "terminating the leases of tenants pursuant to paragraph 9(m) of the 'Tenant Lease' for drug-related criminal activity that does not occur within the tenant's apartment unit when the tenant did not know of and had no reason to know of, the drug-related criminal activity."

A panel of the Court of Appeals reversed, holding that § 1437d(*l*)(6) unambiguously permits the eviction of tenants who violate the lease provision, regardless of whether the tenant was personally aware of the drug activity, and that the statute is constitutional. An en banc panel of the Court of Appeals reversed and affirmed the District Court's grant of the preliminary injunction. That court held that HUD's interpretation permitting the eviction of so-called "innocent" tenants "is inconsistent with Congressional intent and must be rejected" under the first step of *Chevron U.S.A. Inc. v. Natural Resources Defense Council, Inc.*, 467 U.S. 837, 842–43 (1984).

We [hold] that 42 U.S.C. § 1437d(*l*)(6) unambiguously requires lease terms that vest local public housing authorities with the discretion to evict tenants for the drug-related activity of household members and guests whether or not the tenant knew, or should have known, about the activity.

* * *

That this is so seems evident from the plain language of the statute. It provides that "[e]ach public housing agency shall utilize leases which . . . provide that . . . any drug-related criminal activity on or off such premises, engaged in by a public housing tenant, any member of the tenant's household, or any guest or other person under the tenant's control, shall be cause for termination of tenancy." 42 U.S.C. § 1437d(*l*)(6). The en banc Court of Appeals thought the statute did not address "the level of personal knowledge or fault that is required for eviction." Yet Congress' decision not to impose any qualification in the statute, combined with its use of the term "any" to modify "drug-related criminal activity," precludes any knowledge requirement. As we have explained, "the word 'any' has an expansive meaning, that is, 'one or some indiscriminately of whatever kind.'"

#1
Plain language

United States v. Gonzales, 520 U.S. 1, 5 (1997). Thus, *any* drug-related activity engaged in by the specified persons is grounds for termination, not just drug-related activity that the tenant knew, or should have known, about.

The en banc Court of Appeals also thought it possible that "under the tenant's control" modifies not just "other person," but also "member of the tenant's household" and "guest." The court ultimately adopted this reading, concluding that the statute prohibits eviction where the tenant, "for a lack of knowledge or other reason, could not realistically exercise control over the conduct of a household member or guest." But this interpretation runs counter to basic rules of grammar. The disjunctive "or" means that the qualification applies only to "other person." Indeed, the view that "under the tenant's control" modifies everything coming before it in the sentence would result in the nonsensical reading that the statute applies to "a public housing tenant . . . under the tenant's control." HUD offers a convincing explanation for the grammatical imperative that "under the tenant's control" modifies only "other person": "by 'control,' the statute means control in the sense that the tenant has permitted access to the premises." 66 Fed. Reg. 28781 (2001). Implicit in the terms "household member" or "guest" is that access to the premises has been granted by the tenant. Thus, the plain language of § 1437d(*l*)(6) requires leases that grant public housing authorities the discretion to terminate tenancy without regard to the tenant's knowledge of the drug-related criminal activity.

Comparing § 1437d(*l*)(6) to a related statutory provision reinforces the unambiguous text. The civil forfeiture statute that makes all leasehold interests subject to forfeiture when used to commit drug-related criminal activities expressly exempts tenants who had no knowledge of the activity: "[N]o property shall be forfeited under this paragraph . . . by reason of any act or omission established by that owner to have been committed or omitted without the knowledge or consent of that owner." 21 U.S.C. § 881(a)(7). Because this forfeiture provision was amended in the same Anti-Drug Abuse Act of 1988 that created 42 U.S.C. § 1437d(*l*)(6), the en banc Court of Appeals thought Congress "meant them to be read consistently" so that the knowledge requirement should be read into the eviction provision. But the two sections deal with distinctly different matters. The "innocent owner" defense for drug forfeiture cases was already in existence prior to 1988 as part of 21 U.S.C. § 881(a)(7). All that Congress did in the 1988 Act was to add leasehold interests to the property interests that might be forfeited under the drug statute. And if such a forfeiture action were to be brought against a leasehold interest, it would be subject to the pre-existing "innocent owner" defense. But 42 U.S.C. § 1437(d)(*l*)(6), with which we deal here, is a quite different measure. It is entirely reasonable to think that the Government, when seeking to transfer private property to itself in a forfeiture proceeding, should be subject to an "innocent owner defense," while it should not be when acting as a landlord in a public housing project. The forfeiture provision shows that Congress knew exactly how to provide an "innocent owner" defense. It did not provide one in § 1437d(*l*)(6).

#2 related other statutes

The en banc Court of Appeals next resorted to legislative history. The Court of Appeals correctly recognized that reference to legislative

#3 legislative history

history is inappropriate when the text of the statute is unambiguous. Given that the en banc Court of Appeals' finding of textual ambiguity is wrong, there is no need to consult legislative history.

#4
No absurd outcomes

Nor was the en banc Court of Appeals correct in concluding that this plain reading of the statute leads to absurd results. The statute does not require the eviction of any tenant who violated the lease provision. Instead, it entrusts that decision to the local public housing authorities, who are in the best position to take account of, among other things, the degree to which the housing project suffers from "rampant drug-related or violent crime," 42 U.S.C. § 11901(2), "the seriousness of the offending action," 66 Fed. Reg. 22803, and "the extent to which the leaseholder has . . . taken all reasonable steps to prevent or mitigate the offending action." *Id.* It is not "absurd" that a local housing authority may sometimes evict a tenant who had no knowledge of the drug-related activity. Such "no-fault" eviction is a common "incident of tenant responsibility under normal landlord-tenant law and practice." 56 Fed. Reg. 51567. Strict liability maximizes deterrence and eases enforcement difficulties.

And, of course, there is an obvious reason why Congress would have permitted local public housing authorities to conduct no-fault evictions: Regardless of knowledge, a tenant who "cannot control drug crime, or other criminal activities by a household member which threaten health or safety of other residents, is a threat to other residents and the project." 56 Fed.Reg. 51567. With drugs leading to "murders, muggings, and other forms of violence against tenants," and to the "deterioration of the physical environment that requires substantial government expenditures," 42 U.S.C. § 11901(4), it was reasonable for Congress to permit no-fault evictions in order to "provide public and other federally assisted low-income housing that is decent, safe, and free from illegal drugs," § 11901(1).

#5
public issue

In another effort to avoid the plain meaning of the statute, the en banc Court of Appeals invoked the canon of constitutional avoidance. But that canon "has no application in the absence of statutory ambiguity." *United States v. Oakland Cannabis Buyers' Cooperative*, 532 U.S. 483, 494 (2001). "Any other conclusion, while purporting to be an exercise in judicial restraint, would trench upon the legislative powers vested in Congress by Art. I, § 1, of the Constitution." *United States v. Albertini*, 472 U.S. 675, 680 (1985). There are, moreover, no "serious constitutional doubts" about Congress' affording local public housing authorities the discretion to conduct no-fault evictions for drug-related crime. *Reno v. Flores*, 507 U.S. 292, 314 n.9 (1993).

* * *

in all · ·

We hold that "Congress has directly spoken to the precise question at issue." *Chevron*, 467 U.S. at 842. Section 1437d(*l*)(6) requires lease terms that give local public housing authorities the discretion to terminate the lease of a tenant when a member of the household or a guest engages in drug-related activity, regardless of whether the tenant knew, or should have known, of the drug-related activity.

■ JUSTICE BREYER took no part in the consideration or decision of these cases.

General Dynamics Land Systems, Inc. v. Cline

540 U.S. 581 (2004).

■ JUSTICE SOUTER delivered the opinion of the Court.

The Age Discrimination in Employment Act of 1967 (ADEA or Act) forbids discriminatory preference for the young over the old. The question in this case is whether it also prohibits favoring the old over the young. We hold it does not.

I

In 1997, a collective-bargaining agreement between petitioner General Dynamics and the United Auto Workers eliminated the company's obligation to provide health benefits to subsequently retired employees, except as to then-current workers at least 50 years old. Respondents (collectively, Cline) were then at least 40 and thus protected by the Act, but under 50 and so without promise of the benefits. All of them objected to the new terms, although some had retired before the change in order to get the prior advantage, some retired afterwards with no benefit, and some worked on, knowing the new contract would give them no health coverage when they were through.

Before the Equal Employment Opportunity Commission (EEOC or Commission) they claimed that the agreement violated the ADEA, because it "discriminate[d against them] . . . with respect to . . . compensation, terms, conditions, or privileges of employment, because of [their] age," 29 U.S.C. § 623(a)(1). The EEOC agreed, and invited General Dynamics and the union to settle informally with Cline.

When they failed, Cline brought this action against General Dynamics, combining claims under the ADEA and state law. The District Court called the federal claim one of "reverse age discrimination," upon which, it observed, no court had ever granted relief under the ADEA. It dismissed in reliance on the Seventh Circuit's opinion in *Hamilton v. Caterpillar Inc.*, 966 F.2d 1226 (1992), that "the ADEA 'does not protect . . . the younger *against* the older,' " *id.* at 1227 (quoting *Karlen v. City Colls. of Chi.*, 837 F.2d 314, 318 (7th Cir. 1988)).

A divided panel of the Sixth Circuit reversed, with the majority reasoning that the prohibition of § 623(a)(1), covering discrimination against "any individual . . . because of such individual's age," is so clear on its face that if Congress had meant to limit its coverage to protect only the older worker against the younger, it would have said so. * * *

Judge Cole, concurring, saw the issue as one of plain meaning that produced no absurd result, although he acknowledged a degree of tension with *O'Connor v. Consol. Coin Caterers Corp.*, 517 U.S. 308 (1996), in which this Court spoke of age discrimination as giving better treatment to a " 'substantially younger' " worker. Judge Williams dissented in preference for *Hamilton* and the consensus of the federal courts, thinking it "obvious that the older a person is, the greater his or her needs become."

We granted certiorari to resolve the conflict among the Circuits, and now reverse.

II

The common ground in this case is the generalization that the ADEA's prohibition covers "discriminat[ion] ... because of [an] individual's age," 29 U.S.C. § 623(a)(1), that helps the younger by hurting the older. In the abstract, the phrase is open to an argument for a broader construction, since reference to "age" carries no express modifier and the word could be read to look two ways. This more expansive possible understanding does not, however, square with the natural reading of the whole provision prohibiting discrimination, and in fact Congress's interpretive clues speak almost unanimously to an understanding of discrimination as directed against workers who are older than the ones getting treated better.

[handwritten margin note: Cong's interpretive]

Congress chose not to include age within discrimination forbidden by Title VII of the Civil Rights Act of 1964, being aware that there were legitimate reasons as well as invidious ones for making employment decisions on age. Instead it called for a study of the issue by the Secretary of Labor, who concluded that age discrimination was a serious problem, but one different in kind from discrimination on account of race. The Secretary spoke of disadvantage to older individuals from arbitrary and stereotypical employment distinctions (including then-common policies of age ceilings on hiring), but he examined the problem in light of rational considerations of increased pension cost and, in some cases, legitimate concerns about an older person's ability to do the job. When the Secretary ultimately took the position that arbitrary discrimination against older workers was widespread and persistent enough to call for a federal legislative remedy, he placed his recommendation against the background of common experience that the potential cost of employing someone rises with age, so that the older an employee is, the greater the inducement to prefer a younger substitute. The report contains no suggestion that reactions to age level off at some point, and it was devoid of any indication that the Secretary had noticed unfair advantages accruing to older employees at the expense of their juniors.

Congress then asked for a specific proposal, which the Secretary provided in January 1967. Extensive House and Senate hearings ensued.

[handwritten margin note: House Hearings]

The testimony at both hearings dwelled on unjustified assumptions about the effect of age on ability to work. The hearings specifically addressed higher pension and benefit costs as heavier drags on hiring workers the older they got. The record thus reflects the common facts that an individual's chances to find and keep a job get worse over time; as between any two people, the younger is in the stronger position, the older more apt to be tagged with demeaning stereotype. Not surprisingly, from the voluminous records of the hearings, we have found (and Cline has cited) nothing suggesting that any workers were registering complaints about discrimination in favor of their seniors.

Nor is there any such suggestion in the introductory provisions of the ADEA, which begins with statements of purpose and findings that mirror the Wirtz Report and the committee transcripts. The findings stress the impediments suffered by "older workers ... in their efforts to retain ... and especially to regain employment" 81 Stat. 601, § 2(a)(1); "the [burdens] of arbitrary age limits regardless of potential for job performance" *id*. § 2(a)(2); the costs of "otherwise desirable practices [that] may work to the disadvantage of older persons" *id*.; and "the incidence of unemployment, especially long-term unemployment[, which] is, relative to the younger ages, high among older workers," *id*. § 2(a)(3). The statutory objects were "to promote employment of older persons based on their ability rather than age; to prohibit arbitrary age discrimination in employment; [and] to help employers and workers find ways of meeting problems arising from the impact of age on employment." *Id*. § 2(b).

In sum, except on one point, all the findings and statements of objectives are either cast in terms of the effects of age as intensifying over time, or are couched in terms that refer to "older" workers, explicitly or implicitly relative to "younger" ones. The single subject on which the statute speaks less specifically is that of "arbitrary limits" or "arbitrary age discrimination." But these are unmistakable references to the Wirtz Report's finding that "[a]lmost three out of every five employers covered by [a] 1965 survey have in effect age limitations (most frequently between 45 and 55) on new hires which they apply without consideration of an applicant's other qualifications." The ADEA's ban on "arbitrary limits" thus applies to age caps that exclude older applicants, necessarily to the advantage of younger ones.

Such is the setting of the ADEA's core substantive provision, § 4 (as amended, 29 U.S.C. § 623), prohibiting employers and certain others from "discriminat[ion] . . . because of [an] individual's age," whenever (as originally enacted) the individual is "at least forty years of age but less than sixty-five years of age," § 12, 81 Stat. 607. The prefatory provisions and their legislative history make a case that we think is beyond reasonable doubt, that the ADEA was concerned to protect a relatively old worker from discrimination that works to the advantage of the relatively young.

Nor is it remarkable that the record is devoid of any evidence that younger workers were suffering at the expense of their elders, let alone that a social problem required a federal statute to place a younger worker in parity with an older one. Common experience is to the contrary, and the testimony, reports, and congressional findings simply confirm that Congress used the phrase "discriminat[ion] . . . because of [an] individual's age" the same way that ordinary people in common usage might speak of age discrimination any day of the week. One commonplace conception of American society in recent decades is its character as a "youth culture," and in a world where younger is better, talk about discrimination because of age is naturally understood to refer to discrimination against the older.

This same, idiomatic sense of the statutory phrase is confirmed by the statute's restriction of the protected class to those 40 and above. If Congress had been worrying about protecting the younger against the older, it would not likely have ignored everyone under 40. The youthful deficiencies of inexperience and unsteadiness invite stereotypical and discriminatory thinking about those a lot younger than 40, and prejudice suffered by a 40-year-old is not typically owing to youth, as 40-year-olds sadly tend to find out. The enemy of 40 is 30, not 50. Even so, the 40-year threshold was adopted over the objection that some discrimination against older people begins at an even younger age;

female flight attendants were not fired at 32 because they were too young. Thus, the 40-year threshold makes sense as identifying a class requiring protection against preference for their juniors, not as defining a class that might be threatened by favoritism toward seniors.

The federal reports are as replete with cases taking this position as they are nearly devoid of decisions like the one reviewed here. To start closest to home, the best example is *Hazen Paper Co. v. Biggins*, 507 U.S. 604 (1993), in which we held there is no violation of the ADEA in firing an employee because his pension is about to vest, a basis for action that we took to be analytically distinct from age, even though it would never occur without advanced years. We said that "the very essence of age discrimination [is] for an older employee to be fired because the employer believes that productivity and competence decline with old age," *id*. at 610, whereas discrimination on the basis of pension status "would not constitute discriminatory treatment on the basis of age [because t]he prohibited stereotype [of the faltering worker] would not have figured in this decision, and the attendant stigma would not ensue," *id*. at 612. And we have relied on this same reading of the statute in other cases. While none of these cases directly addresses the question presented here, all of them show our consistent understanding that the text, structure, and history point to the ADEA as a remedy for unfair preference based on relative youth, leaving complaints of the relatively young outside the statutory concern.

The Courts of Appeals and the District Courts have read the law the same way, and prior to this case have enjoyed virtually unanimous accord in understanding the ADEA to forbid only discrimination preferring young to old. So the Seventh Circuit held in *Hamilton*, and the First Circuit said in *Schuler*, and so the District Courts have ruled in cases too numerous for citation here in the text. The very strength of this consensus is enough to rule out any serious claim of ambiguity, and congressional silence after years of judicial interpretation supports adherence to the traditional view.

III

Cline and *amicus* EEOC proffer three rejoinders in favor of their competing view that the prohibition works both ways. First, they say (as does Justice THOMAS) that the statute's meaning is plain when the word "age" receives its natural and ordinary meaning and the statute is read as a whole giving "age" the same meaning throughout. And even if the text does not plainly mean what they say it means, they argue that the soundness of their version is shown by a colloquy on the floor of the Senate involving Senator Yarborough, a sponsor of the bill that became the ADEA. Finally, they fall back to the position (fortified by Justice SCALIA's dissent) that we should defer to the EEOC's reading of the statute. On each point, however, we think the argument falls short of unsettling our view of the natural meaning of the phrase speaking of discrimination, read in light of the statute's manifest purpose.

A

The first response to our reading is the dictionary argument that "age" means the length of a person's life, with the phrase "because of such individual's age" stating a simple test of causation: "discriminat[ion] . . . because of [an] individual's age" is treatment that would not have occurred if the individual's span of years had been longer or shorter. The case for this reading calls attention to the other instances of "age" in the ADEA that are not limited to old age, such as 29 U.S.C. § 623(f), which gives an employer a defense to charges of age discrimination when "age is a bona fide occupational qualification." Cline and the EEOC argue that if "age" meant old age, § 623(f) would then provide a defense (old age is a bona fide qualification) only for an employer's action that on our reading would never clash with the statute (because preferring the older is not forbidden).

The argument rests on two mistakes. First, it assumes that the word "age" has the same meaning wherever the ADEA uses it. But this is not so, and Cline simply misemploys the "presumption that identical words used in different parts of the same act are intended to have the same meaning." *Atl. Cleaners & Dyers, Inc. v. United States*, 286 U.S. 427, 433 (1932). Cline forgets that "the presumption is not rigid and readily yields whenever there is such variation in the connection in which the words are used as reasonably to warrant the conclusion that they were employed in different parts of the act with different intent." *Id*. The presumption of uniform usage thus relents when a word used has several commonly understood meanings among which a speaker can alternate in the course of an ordinary conversation, without being confused or getting confusing.

"Age" is that kind of word. As Justice THOMAS agrees, the word "age" standing alone can be readily understood either as pointing to any number of years lived, or as common shorthand for the longer span and concurrent aches that make youth look good. Which alternative was probably intended is a matter of context; we understand the different choices of meaning that lie behind a sentence like "Age can be shown by a driver's license," and the statement, "Age has left him a shut-in." So it is easy to understand that Congress chose different meanings at different places in the ADEA, as the different settings readily show. Hence the second flaw in Cline's argument for uniform usage: it ignores the cardinal rule that "[s]tatutory language must be read in context [since] a phrase 'gathers meaning from the words around it.'" *Jones v. United States*, 527 U.S. 373, 389 (1999). The point here is that we are not asking an abstract question about the meaning of "age"; we are seeking the meaning of the whole phrase "discriminate . . . because of such individual's age," where it occurs in the ADEA. 29 U.S.C. § 623(a)(1). As we have said, social history emphatically reveals an understanding of age discrimination as aimed against the old, and the statutory reference to age discrimination in this idiomatic sense is confirmed by legislative history. For the very reason that reference to context shows that "age" means "old age" when teamed with "discrimination," the provision of an affirmative defense when age is a bona fide occupational qualification readily shows that "age" as a qualification means comparative youth. As context tells us that "age" means one thing in § 623(a)(1) and another in § 623(f), so it also tells us that the presumption of uniformity cannot sensibly operate here.

* * *

B

The second objection has more substance than the first, but still not enough. The record of congressional action reports a colloquy on the Senate floor between two of the legislators most active in pushing for the ADEA, Senators Javits and Yarborough. Senator Javits began the exchange by raising a concern mentioned by Senator Dominick, that "the bill might not forbid discrimination between two persons each of whom would be between the ages of 40 and 65." 113 Cong. Rec. 31255 (1967). Senator Javits then gave his own view that, "if two individuals ages 52 and 42 apply for the same job, and the employer selected the man aged 42 solely . . . because he is younger than the man 52, then he will have violated the act," and asked Senator Yarborough for his opinion. *Id*. Senator Yarborough answered that "[t]he law prohibits age being a factor in the decision to hire, as to one age over the other, whichever way [the] decision went." *Id*.

Although in the past we have given weight to Senator Yarborough's views on the construction of the ADEA because he was a sponsor, his side of this exchange is not enough to unsettle our reading of the statute. * * * What matters is that the Senator's remark, "whichever way [the] decision went," is the only item in all the 1967 hearings, reports, and debates going against the grain of the common understanding of age discrimination. Even from a sponsor, a single outlying statement cannot stand against a tide of context and history, not to mention 30 years of judicial interpretation producing no apparent legislative qualms.

C

The third objection relies on a reading consistent with the Yarborough comment, adopted by the agency now charged with enforcing the statute, as set out at 29 CFR § 1625.2(a) (2003) * * *. When the EEOC adopted § 1625.2(a) in 1981, shortly after assuming administrative responsibility for the ADEA, it gave no reasons for the view expressed, beyond noting that the provision was carried forward from an earlier Department of Labor regulation; that earlier regulation itself gave no reasons.

The parties contest the degree of weight owed to the EEOC's reading, with General Dynamics urging us that *Skidmore v. Swift & Co.*, 323 U.S. 134 (1944), sets the limit, while Cline and the EEOC say that § 1625.2(a) deserves greater deference under *Chevron*. Although we have devoted a fair amount of attention lately to the varying degrees of deference deserved by agency pronouncements of different sorts, *see United States v. Mead Corp.*, 533 U.S. 218 (2001); *Christensen v. Harris County*, 529 U.S. 576 (2000), the recent cases are not on point here. In *Edelman v. Lynchburg College*, 535 U.S. 106, 114 (2002), we found no need to choose between *Skidmore* and *Chevron*, or even to defer, because the EEOC was clearly right; today, we neither defer nor settle on any degree of deference because the Commission is clearly wrong.

Even for an agency able to claim all the authority possible under *Chevron*, deference to its statutory interpretation is called for only when the devices of judicial construction have been tried and found to yield no clear sense of congressional intent. Here, regular interpretive method leaves no serious question, not even about purely textual ambiguity in the ADEA. The word "age" takes on a definite meaning from being in the phrase "discriminat[ion] ... because of such individual's age," occurring as that phrase does in a statute structured and manifestly intended to protect the older from arbitrary favor for the younger.

■ JUSTICE SCALIA, dissenting.

The Age Discrimination in Employment Act of 1967 (ADEA or Act), makes it unlawful for an employer to "discriminate against any individual with respect to his compensation, terms, conditions, or privileges of employment, because of such individual's age." 29 U.S.C. §§ 621–634. The question in this case is whether, in the absence of an affirmative defense, the ADEA prohibits an employer from favoring older over younger workers when both are protected by the Act, *i.e.*, are 40 years of age or older.

The Equal Employment Opportunity Commission (EEOC) has answered this question in the affirmative. In 1981, the agency adopted a regulation which states, in pertinent part:

> "It is unlawful in situations where this Act applies, for an employer to discriminate in hiring or in any other way by giving preference because of age between individuals 40 and over. Thus, if two people apply for the same position, and one is 42 and the other 52, the employer may not lawfully turn down either one on the basis of age, but must make such decision on the basis of some other factor." 29 C.F.R. § 1625.2(a) (2003).

This regulation represents the interpretation of the agency tasked by Congress with enforcing the ADEA.

The Court brushes aside the EEOC's interpretation as "clearly wrong." I cannot agree with the contention upon which that rejection rests: that "regular interpretive method leaves no serious question, not even about purely textual ambiguity in the ADEA." It is evident, for the reasons given in Part II of Justice THOMAS's dissenting opinion, that the Court's interpretive method is anything but "regular." And for the reasons given in Part I of that opinion, the EEOC's interpretation is neither foreclosed by the statute nor unreasonable.

Because § 623(a) "does not unambiguously require a different interpretation, and ... the [EEOC's] regulation is an entirely reasonable interpretation of the text," *Barnhart v. Thomas*, 540 U.S. 20, 29–30 (2003), I would defer to the agency's authoritative conclusion. I respectfully dissent.

■ JUSTICE THOMAS, with whom JUSTICE KENNEDY joins, dissenting.

This should have been an easy case. The plain language of 29 U.S.C. § 623(a)(1) mandates a particular outcome: that the respondents are able to sue for discrimination against them in favor of older workers. The agency charged with enforcing the statute has adopted a regulation and issued an opinion as an adjudicator, both of which adopt this natural interpretation of the provision. And the only portion of legislative history relevant to the question before us is consistent with this outcome. Despite the fact that these traditional tools of statutory interpretation lead inexorably to the conclusion that respondents can state a claim for discrimination against the relatively young, the Court, apparently disappointed by this result, today adopts a different interpretation. In doing so, the Court, of necessity, creates a new tool of statutory interpretation, and then proceeds to give this newly created "social history" analysis dispositive weight. Because I cannot agree with the Court's new approach to interpreting antidiscrimination statutes, I respectfully dissent.

I

"The starting point for [the] interpretation of a statute is always its language," *Cmty. for Creative Non-Violence v. Reid*, 490 U.S. 730, 739 (1989), and "courts must presume that a legislature says in a statute what it means and means in a statute what it says there," *Conn. Nat'l Bank v. Germain*, 503 U.S. 249, 253–54 (1992). Thus, rather than looking through the historical background of the Age Discrimination in Employment Act of 1967 (ADEA), I would instead start with the text of § 623(a)(1) itself, and if "the words of [the] statute are unambiguous," my "judicial inquiry [would be] complete." *Id.* at 254 (internal quotation marks omitted).

The plain language of the ADEA clearly allows for suits brought by the relatively young when discriminated against in favor of the relatively old. The phrase "discriminate . . . because of such individual's age," 29 U.S.C. § 623(a)(1), is not restricted to discrimination because of relatively *older* age. If an employer fired a worker for the sole reason that the worker was under 45, it would be entirely natural to say that the worker had been discriminated against because of his age. I struggle to think of what other phrase I would use to describe such behavior. I wonder how the Court would describe such incidents, because the Court apparently considers such usage to be unusual, atypical, or aberrant.

The parties do identify a possible ambiguity, centering on the multiple meanings of the word "age." As the parties note, "age" does have an alternative meaning, namely, "[t]he state of being old; old age." AMERICAN HERITAGE DICTIONARY 33 (3d ed. 1992). First, this secondary meaning is, of course, less commonly used than the primary meaning, and appears restricted to those few instances where it is clear in the immediate context of the phrase that it could have no other meaning. The phrases "hair white with age," *id.* at 33, or "eyes . . . *dim with age*," RANDOM HOUSE DICTIONARY OF THE ENGLISH LANGUAGE 37 (2d ed. 1987), cannot possibly be using "age" to include "young age," unlike a phrase such as "he fired her because of her age." Second, the use of the word "age" in other portions of the statute effectively destroys any doubt. The ADEA's advertising prohibition, 29 U.S.C. § 623(e), and the bona fide occupational qualification defense, § 623(f)(1), would both be rendered incoherent if the term "age" in those provisions were read to mean only "older age." Although it is true that the " 'presumption that identical words used in different parts of the same act are intended to have the same meaning' " is not "rigid" and can be overcome when the context is clear, the presumption is not rebutted here. As noted, the plain and common reading of the phrase "such individual's age" refers to the individual's chronological age. At the very least, it is manifestly unclear that it bars *only* discrimination against the relatively older. Only by incorrectly concluding that § 623(a)(1) clearly and unequivocally bars only discrimination as "against the older" can the Court then conclude that the "context" of §§ 623(f)(1) and 623(e) allows for an alternative meaning of the term "age."

The one structural argument raised by the Court in defense of its interpretation of "discriminates . . . because of such individual's age" is the provision limiting the ADEA's protections to those over 40 years of age. At first glance, this might look odd when paired with the conclusion that § 623(a)(1) bars discrimination against the relatively young as well as the relatively old, but there is a perfectly rational explanation. Congress could easily conclude that age discrimination directed against those under 40 is not as damaging, since a young worker unjustly fired is likely to find a new job or otherwise recover from the discrimination. A person over 40 fired due to irrational age discrimination (whether because the worker is too young or too old) might have a more difficult time recovering from the discharge and finding new employment. Such an interpretation also comports with the many findings of the Wirtz report and the parallel findings in the ADEA itself.

This plain reading of the ADEA is bolstered by the interpretation of the agency charged with administering the statute. A regulation issued by the Equal Employment Opportunity Commission (EEOC) adopts the view contrary to the Court's, 29 CFR § 1625.2(a) (2003), and the only binding EEOC decision that addresses the question before us also adopted the view contrary to the Court's. I agree with the Court that we need not address whether deference under *Chevron* would apply to the EEOC's regulation in this case. Of course, I so conclude because the EEOC's interpretation is consistent with the best reading of the statute. The Court's position, on the other hand, is untenable. Even if the Court disagrees with my interpretation of the language of the statute, it strains credulity to argue that such a reading is so unreasonable that an agency could not adopt it. To suggest that, in the instant case, the "regular interpretive method leaves no serious question, not even about purely textual ambiguity in the ADEA," is to ignore the entirely reasonable (and, incidentally, correct) contrary interpretation of the ADEA that the EEOC and I advocate.

Finally, the only relevant piece of legislative history addressing the question before the Court—whether it would be possible for a younger individual to sue based on discrimination against him in favor of an older individual—comports with the plain reading of the text. Senator Yarborough, in the only exchange that the parties identified from the legislative history discussing this particular question, confirmed that the text really meant what it said. Although the statute is clear, and hence there is no need to delve into the legislative history, this history merely confirms that the plain reading of the text is correct.

II

Strangely, the Court does not explain why it departs from accepted methods of interpreting statutes. It does, however, clearly set forth its principal reason for adopting its particular reading of the phrase "discriminate . . . based on [an] individual's age" in Part III–A of its opinion. "The point here," the Court states, "is that we are not asking an abstract question about the meaning of 'age'; we are seeking the meaning of the whole phrase 'discriminate . . . because of such individual's age.' . . . As we have said, *social history* emphatically reveals an understanding of age discrimination as aimed against the old, and the statutory reference to age discrimination in this idiomatic sense is confirmed by legislative history." (emphasis added). The Court does not define "social history," although it is apparently something different from legislative history, because the Court refers to legislative history as a separate interpretive tool in the very same sentence. Indeed, the Court has never defined "social history" in any previous opinion, probably because it has never sanctioned looking to "social history" as a method of statutory interpretation. Today, the Court takes this unprecedented step, and then places dispositive weight on the new concept.

It appears that the Court considers the "social history" of the phrase "discriminate . . . because of [an] individual's age" to be the principal evil that Congress targeted when it passed the ADEA. In each section of its analysis, the Court pointedly notes that there was no evidence of widespread problems of antiyouth discrimination, and that the primary concerns of Executive Branch officials and Members of Congress pertained to problems that workers generally faced as they increased in age. The Court reaches its final, legal conclusion as to the meaning of the phrase (that "ordinary" people employing the common usage of language would "talk about discrimination because of age [as] naturally [referring to] discrimination against the older") only after concluding both that "the ADEA was concerned to protect a relatively old worker from discrimination that works to the advantage of the relatively young" and that "the record is devoid of any evidence that younger workers were suffering at the expense of their elders, let alone that a social problem required a federal statute to place a younger worker in parity with an older one." Hence, the Court apparently concludes that if Congress has in mind a particular, principal, or primary form of discrimination when it passes an antidiscrimination provision prohibiting persons from "discriminating because of [some personal quality]," then the phrase "discriminate because of [some personal quality]" only covers the principal or most common form of discrimination relating to this personal quality.

The Court, however, has not typically interpreted nondiscrimination statutes in this odd manner. "[S]tatutory prohibitions often go beyond the principal evil to cover reasonably comparable evils, and it is ultimately the provisions of our laws rather than the principal concerns of our legislators by which we are governed." *Oncale v. Sundowner Offshore Servs., Inc.*, 523 U.S. 75, 79 (1998).

* * *

As the ADEA clearly prohibits discrimination because of an individual's age, whether the individual is too old or too young, I would affirm the Court of Appeals. Because the Court resorts to interpretive sleight of hand to avoid addressing the plain language of the ADEA, I respectfully dissent.

NOTES AND QUESTIONS

1. *Rucker* and *General Dynamics* reflect two very different approaches to *Chevron* step one analysis. The Court in *Rucker* employed a purely textual analysis, employing basic rules of grammar, rejecting outright legislative history and the more substantive canon of constitutional avoidance on the ground that the text was unambiguous. The Court in *General Dynamics* rejected the textual analysis of Justice Thomas's dissent and instead relied principally on legislative history and policy, "idiomatic" meaning, and "social history" to discern statutory meaning. Do you find either of these approaches more consistent with the rationale behind the *Chevron* doctrine? Which if either of these models do you think would be more likely to result in a larger number of cases proceeding to *Chevron* step two?

2. Although a number of Supreme Court cases consider legislative history in the course of *Chevron* step one analysis, some circuit courts have adopted or at least considered a rule of deferring any consideration of legislative history until *Chevron* step two. These cases essentially confine that court's search for clear meaning to textual analysis alone, and consider outside evidence of congressional intent such as legislative history only in evaluating the permissibility of the agency's interpretation at *Chevron* step two. *See, e.g., United States v. Dierckman*, 201 F.3d 915 (7th Cir. 2000) ("The first step of *Chevron* focuses on the text of the statute, leaving legislative history to the second step.") The First Circuit has traced this policy to a footnote by Justice Kennedy in *K Mart Corp. v. Cartier, Inc.*, 486 U.S. 281, 293 n.4 (1988), in a part of the otherwise majority opinion that did not command the support of a majority of the Justices, in which he declared legislative history "irrelevant" in assessing statutory clarity. *See Succar v. Ashcroft*, 394 F.3d 8, 30–31 (1st Cir. 2005). What is your assessment of this model of *Chevron* step one as a faithful interpretation of the Court's opinion in *Chevron*? Should reviewing courts decline to consider legislative history at *Chevron* step one?

3. *CHEVRON* AND SUBSTANTIVE CANONS

The Supreme Court's decision in *Chevron* counsels judicial deference to reasonable agency interpretations of ambiguous statutes. Before reaching *Chevron*'s second step, however, courts first have to ascertain that the statute in question is, in fact, ambiguous. Courts and scholars struggle to discern precisely what it means for a statute to be ambiguous for purposes of *Chevron* deference.

Also in *Chevron*, the Court called upon courts to employ "traditional tools of statutory construction" to evaluate statutory ambiguity, but did not elaborate which tools in the toolbox ought to be used. Substantive canons like constitutional avoidance doctrine and the rule of lenity have traditionally served as ambiguity tie-breakers. Specifically, constitutional avoidance doctrine holds that, in the face of two competing, reasonable interpretations, one of which might make the statute unconstitutional, a reviewing court should instead adopt the alternative interpretation that avoids the constitutional difficulty. Similarly, the rule of lenity generally requires courts to construe ambiguous criminal statutes in the light most favorable to the defendant. While the Supreme Court has declined to extend *Chevron* deference to the Justice Department's interpretations of the criminal code—*see, e.g., Crandon v. United States*, 494 U.S. 152 (1990) (Scalia, J., concurring)—the Court's jurisprudence is more mixed in civil cases involving agency interpretations of statutes with both civil and criminal enforcement potential.

Where the *Chevron* standard applies to counsel deference in the face of ambiguity, but a substantive canon like constitutional avoidance or lenity would resolve ambiguity differently, which should take precedence? In other words, should courts employ substantive canons to resolve ambiguity at *Chevron* step one? In addition to employing various other tools of statutory construction in conjunction with *Chevron* analysis, the following cases address the interaction of the *Chevron* standard with constitutional avoidance doctrine and the rule of lenity, respectively—with arguably different results.

Solid Waste Agency of Northern Cook County v. United States Army Corps of Engineers

531 U.S. 159 (2001).

■ CHIEF JUSTICE REHNQUIST delivered the opinion of the Court.

Section 404(a) of the Clean Water Act (CWA or Act), 33 U.S.C. § 1344(a), regulates the discharge of dredged or fill material into "navigable waters." The United States Army Corps of Engineers (Corps) has interpreted § 404(a) to confer federal authority over an abandoned sand and gravel pit in northern Illinois which provides habitat for migratory birds. We are asked to decide whether the provisions of § 404(a) may be fairly extended to these waters, and, if so, whether Congress could exercise such authority consistent with the Commerce Clause, U.S. Const., Art. I, § 8, cl. 3. We answer the first question in the negative and therefore do not reach the second.

Petitioner, the Solid Waste Agency of Northern Cook County (SWANCC), is a consortium of 23 suburban Chicago cities and villages that united in an effort to locate and develop a disposal site for baled nonhazardous solid waste. The Chicago Gravel Company informed the municipalities of the availability of a 533-acre parcel, bestriding the Illinois counties Cook and Kane, which had been the site of a sand and gravel pit mining operation for three decades up until about 1960. Long since abandoned, the old mining site eventually gave way to a successional stage forest, with its remnant excavation trenches evolving into a scattering of permanent and seasonal ponds of varying size (from under one-tenth of an acre to several acres) and depth (from several inches to several feet).

The municipalities decided to purchase the site for disposal of their baled nonhazardous solid waste. By law, SWANCC was required to file for various permits from Cook County and the State of Illinois before it could begin operation of its balefill project. In addition, because the operation called for the filling of some of the permanent and seasonal ponds, SWANCC contacted federal respondents (hereinafter respondents), including the Corps, to determine if a federal landfill permit was required under § 404(a) of the CWA, 33 U.S.C. § 1344(a).

Section 404(a) grants the Corps authority to issue permits "for the discharge of dredged or fill material into the navigable waters at specified disposal sites." The term "navigable waters" is defined under the Act as "the waters of the United States, including the territorial seas." § 1362(7). The Corps has issued regulations defining the term "waters of the United States" to include

> "waters such as intrastate lakes, rivers, streams (including intermittent streams), mud-flats, sandflats, wetlands, sloughs, prairie potholes, wet meadows, playa lakes, or natural ponds, the use, degradation or destruction of which could affect interstate or foreign commerce. . . ." 33 CFR § 328.3(a)(3) (1999).

In 1986, in an attempt to "clarify" the reach of its jurisdiction, the Corps stated that § 404(a) extends to intrastate waters:

> "a. Which are or would be used as habitat by birds protected by Migratory Bird Treaties; or

> "b. Which are or would be used as habitat by other migratory birds which cross state lines; or

> "c. Which are or would be used as habitat for endangered species; or

> "d. Used to irrigate crops sold in interstate commerce." 51 Fed.Reg. 41217.

This last promulgation has been dubbed the "Migratory Bird Rule."

The Corps initially concluded that it had no jurisdiction over the site because it contained no "wetlands," or areas which support "vegetation typically adapted for life in saturated soil conditions," 33 CFR § 328.3(b) (1999). However, after the Illinois Nature Preserves Commission informed the Corps that a number of migratory bird species had been observed at the site, the Corps reconsidered and ultimately asserted jurisdiction over the balefill site pursuant to subpart (b) of the "Migratory Bird Rule." The Corps found that approximately 121 bird species had been observed at the site, including several known to depend upon aquatic environments for a significant portion of their life requirements. Thus, on November 16, 1987, the Corps formally "determined that the seasonally ponded, abandoned gravel mining depressions located on the project site, while not wetlands, did qualify as 'waters of the United States' . . . based upon the following criteria: (1) the proposed site had been abandoned as a gravel mining operation; (2) the water areas and spoil piles had developed a natural character; and (3) the water areas are used as habitat by migratory bird [sic] which cross state lines." U.S. Army Corps of Engineers, Chicago District, Dept. of Army Permit Evaluation and Decision Document, Lodging of Petitioner, Tab No. 1, p. 6.

* * *

Despite SWANCC's securing the required water quality certification from the Illinois Environmental Protection Agency, the Corps refused to issue a § 404(a) permit.

* * *

Congress passed the CWA for the stated purpose of "restor[ing] and maintain[ing] the chemical, physical, and biological integrity of the Nation's waters." 33 U.S.C. § 1251(a). In so doing, Congress chose to "recognize, preserve, and protect the primary responsibilities and rights of States to prevent, reduce, and eliminate pollution, to plan the development and use (including restoration, preservation, and enhancement) of land and water resources, and to consult with the Administrator in the exercise of his authority under this chapter." § 1251(b). Relevant here, § 404(a) authorizes respondents to regulate the discharge of fill material into "navigable waters," 33 U.S.C. § 1344(a), which the statute defines as "the waters of the United States, including the territorial seas," § 1362(7). Respondents have interpreted these words to cover the abandoned gravel pit at issue here because it is used as habitat for migratory birds. We conclude that the "Migratory Bird Rule" is not fairly supported by the CWA.

* * *

Respondents . . . contend that, at the very least, it must be said that Congress did not address the precise question of § 404(a)'s scope with regard to nonnavigable, isolated, intrastate waters, and that, therefore, we should give deference to the "Migratory Bird Rule." See, e.g., *Chevron U.S.A. Inc. v. Natural Resources Defense Council, Inc.*, 467 U.S. 837 (1984). We find § 404(a) to be clear, but even were we to agree with respondents, we would not extend *Chevron* deference here.

Where an administrative interpretation of a statute invokes the outer limits of Congress' power, we expect a clear indication that Congress intended that result. See *Edward J. DeBartolo Corp. v. Florida Gulf Coast Building & Constr. Trades Council*, 485 U.S. 568, 575 (1988). This requirement stems from our prudential desire not to needlessly reach constitutional issues and our assumption that Congress does not casually authorize administrative agencies to interpret a statute to push the limit of congressional authority. This concern is heightened where the administrative interpretation alters the federal-state framework by permitting federal encroachment upon a traditional state power. See *United States v. Bass*, 404 U.S. 336, 349 (1971) ("[U]nless Congress conveys its purpose clearly, it will not be deemed to have significantly changed the federal-state balance"). Thus, "where an otherwise acceptable construction of a statute would raise serious constitutional problems, the Court will construe the statute to avoid such problems unless such construction is plainly contrary to the intent of Congress." *DeBartolo, supra*, at 575.

Twice in the past six years we have reaffirmed the proposition that the grant of authority to Congress under the Commerce Clause, though broad, is not unlimited. See *United States v. Morrison*, 529 U.S. 598 (2000); *United States v. Lopez*, 514 U.S. 549 (1995). Respondents argue that the "Migratory Bird Rule" falls within Congress' power to regulate intrastate activities that "substantially affect" interstate commerce. They note that the protection of migratory birds is a "national interest of very nearly the first magnitude," *Missouri v. Holland*, 252 U.S. 416, 435 (1920), and that, as the Court of Appeals found, millions of people spend over a billion dollars annually on recreational pursuits relating to migratory birds. These arguments raise significant constitutional questions. For example, we would have to evaluate the precise object or activity that, in the aggregate, substantially affects interstate commerce. This is not clear, for although the Corps has claimed jurisdiction over petitioner's land because it contains water areas used as habitat by migratory birds, respondents now, *post litem motam*, focus upon the fact that the regulated activity is petitioner's municipal landfill, which is "plainly of a commercial nature." But this is a far cry, indeed, from the "navigable waters" and "waters of the United States" to which the statute by its terms extends.

These are significant constitutional questions raised by respondents' application of their regulations, and yet we find nothing approaching a clear statement from Congress that it intended § 404(a) to reach an abandoned sand and gravel pit such as we have here. Permitting respondents to claim federal jurisdiction over ponds and mudflats falling within the "Migratory Bird Rule" would result in a significant impingement of the States' traditional and primary power over land and water use. See, *e.g., Hess v. Port Authority Trans-Hudson Corporation*, 513 U.S. 30, 44 (1994) ("[R]egulation of land use [is] a function traditionally performed by local governments"). Rather than expressing a desire to readjust the federal-state balance in this manner, Congress chose to "recognize, preserve, and protect the primary responsibilities and rights of States . . . to plan the development and use . . . of land and water resources. . . ." 33 U.S.C. § 1251(b). We thus read the statute as written to avoid the significant constitutional and federalism questions raised by respondents' interpretation, and therefore reject the request for administrative deference.

We hold that 33 CFR § 328.3(a)(3) (1999), as clarified and applied to petitioner's balefill site pursuant to the "Migratory Bird Rule," 51 Fed. Reg. 41217 (1986), exceeds the authority granted to respondents under § 404(a) of the CWA.

■ JUSTICE STEVENS, with whom JUSTICE SOUTER, JUSTICE GINSBURG, and JUSTICE BREYER join, dissenting.

Although it might have appeared problematic on a "linguistic" level for the Corps to classify "lands" as "waters" in [*United States v. Riverside Bayview Homes, Inc.*, 474 U.S. 121, 131–132 (1985)], we squarely held that the agency's construction of the statute that it was charged with enforcing was entitled to deference under *Chevron U.S.A. Inc. v. Natural Resources Defense Council, Inc.*, 467 U.S. 837 (1984). Today, however, the majority refuses to extend such deference to the same agency's construction of the same statute. This refusal is unfaithful to both *Riverside Bayview* and *Chevron*. For it is the majority's reading, not the agency's, that does violence to the scheme Congress chose to put into place.

Contrary to the Court's suggestion, the Corps' interpretation of the statute does not "encroac[h]" upon "traditional state power" over land use. "Land use planning in essence chooses particular uses for the land; environmental regulation, at its core, does not mandate particular uses of the land but requires only that, however the land is used, damage to the environment is kept within prescribed limits." *California Coastal Comm'n v. Granite Rock Co.*, 480 U.S. 572, 587 (1987). The CWA is not a land-use code; it is a paradigm of environmental regulation. Such regulation is an accepted exercise of federal power. *Hodel v. Virginia Surface Mining & Reclamation Assn., Inc.*, 452 U.S. 264, 282 (1981).

It is particularly ironic for the Court to raise the specter of federalism while construing a statute that makes explicit efforts to foster local control over water regulation. Faced with calls to cut back on federal jurisdiction over water pollution, Congress rejected attempts to narrow the scope of that jurisdiction and, by incorporating § 404(g), opted instead for a scheme that encouraged States to supplant federal control with their own regulatory programs. S.Rep. No. 95–370, at p. 75 ("The committee amendment does not redefine navigable waters. Instead, the committee amendment intends to assure continued protection of *all the Nation's waters*, but allows States to assume the primary responsibility for protecting those lakes, rivers, streams, swamps, marshes, and other portions of the navigable waters outside the [C]orps program in the so-called phase I waters" (emphasis added)). Because Illinois could have taken advantage of the opportunities offered to it through § 404(g), the federalism concerns to which the majority adverts are misplaced. The Corps' interpretation of the statute as extending beyond navigable waters, tributaries of navigable waters, and wetlands adjacent to each is manifestly reasonable and therefore entitled to deference.

* * *

Whether it is necessary or appropriate to refuse to allow petitioner to fill those ponds is a question on which we have no voice. Whether the Federal Government has the power to require such permission, however, is a question that is easily answered. If, as it does, the Commerce Clause empowers Congress to regulate particular "activities causing air or water pollution, or other environmental hazards that may have effects in more than one State," *Hodel*, 452 U.S., at 282, it also empowers Congress to control individual actions that, in the aggregate, would have the same effect. *Perez*, 402 U.S., at 154; *Wickard*, 317 U.S., at 127–128. There is no merit in petitioner's constitutional argument.

NOTES AND QUESTIONS

1.   Notwithstanding existing precedent labeling § 404(a) of the Clean Water Act as ambiguous for purposes of *Chevron* step one, the Solid Waste Agency majority applied the constitutional avoidance canon to conclude that the statute clearly did not permit the agency interpretation at issue. Courts and scholars often cite *Solid Waste Agency* for the proposition that the constitutional avoidance canon "trumps" or takes precedence over *Chevron* deference. Should it?

2.   *Chevron* deference is premised on the understanding that Congress intended for agencies rather than courts to resolve statutory ambiguity, and thus (at least in theory) reflects judicial respect for legislative supremacy. Similarly, courts and scholars have justified the constitutional avoidance canon as a means by which courts can respect legislative supremacy and maintain the proper separation of powers between Congress and the judicial branch. Others, however, have criticized constitutional avoidance doctrine as displacing legislative supremacy, by permitting courts to substitute their own interpretations for those more likely intended by Congress and by limiting Congress's ability to legislate near the edge of constitutionality. If the goal is respecting Congress and its role in our system of government, then in the context of agency interpretations of ambiguous statutory language, which of *Chevron* deference or the constitutional avoidance canon best achieves that desired end?

3.   *Solid Waste Agency* is not the only case in which the Supreme Court has arguably applied the constitutional avoidance canon rather than *Chevron* deference to resolve statutory ambiguity. In *Rapanos v. United States*, 547 U.S. 715 (2006), the Court again considered an agency interpretation of § 404(a) of the Clean Water Act that arguably pushed the boundaries of Congress's commerce power. Writing for a plurality of the Court, and citing *Solid Waste Agency*, Justice Scalia indicated that the constitutional avoidance canon would render the agency's interpretation of the statute impermissible even if the statute were ambiguous. *Id.* at 737–38. Nor is the Commerce Clause the only constitutional provision invoked by the Court in this sense. For example, in *Edward J. DeBartolo Corp. v. Florida Gulf Coast Building and Construction Trades Council*, 485 U.S. 568 (1988), the Court chose constitutional avoidance over Chevron deference in rejecting a National Labor Relations Board statutory interpretation that raised First Amendment concerns. Should the relationship between constitutional avoidance and *Chevron* deference depend upon the constitutional provision at issue?

4.   Recent empirical research by Professors Abbe Gluck and Lisa Schultz Bressman suggests that the drafters of legislation are more aware of the *Chevron* standard than they are of constitutional avoidance doctrine. *See* Abbe R. Gluck & Lisa Schultz Bressman, *Statutory Interpretation from the Inside—An Empirical Study of Congressional Drafting, Delegation, and the Canons: Part I*, 65 Stan. L. Rev. 901 (2013). Drawing from a survey of 137 congressional counsels with legislation drafting responsibilities, Gluck and Bressman reported that only 25% had heard of the constitutional avoidance canon, although 69% said that how courts might view the constitutionality of statutes was a relevant consideration in the drafting process. By contrast, 82% of survey respondents were aware of and relied upon the Courts' adherence to the *Chevron* standard in drafting legislation. In light of these findings, should the Supreme Court rethink its preference for the constitutional avoidance canon over *Chevron* deference?

Babbitt v. Sweet Home Chapter of Communities for a Greater Oregon

515 U.S. 687 (1995).

■ JUSTICE STEVENS delivered the opinion of the Court.

The Endangered Species Act of 1973 (ESA or Act), 16 U.S.C. § 1531 (1988 ed. and Supp. V), contains a variety of protections designed to save from extinction species that the Secretary of the Interior designates as endangered or threatened. Section 9 of the Act makes it unlawful for any person to "take" any endangered or threatened species. The Secretary has promulgated a regulation that defines the statute's prohibition on takings to include "significant habitat modification or degradation where it actually kills or injures wildlife." This case presents the question whether the Secretary exceeded his authority under the Act by promulgating that regulation.

I

Section 9(a)(1) of the Act provides the following protection for endangered species:

"Except as provided in sections 1535(g)(2) and 1539 of this title, with respect to any endangered species of fish or wildlife listed pursuant to section 1533 of this title it is unlawful for any person subject to the jurisdiction of the United States to—

. . . .

"(B) take any such species within the United States or the territorial sea of the United States." 16 U.S.C. § 1538(a)(1).

Section 3(19) of the Act defines the statutory term "take":

"The term 'take' means to harass, harm, pursue, hunt, shoot, wound, kill, trap, capture, or collect, or to attempt to engage in any such conduct." 16 U.S.C. § 1532(19).

The Act does not further define the terms it uses to define "take." The Interior Department regulations that implement the statute, however, define the statutory term "harm":

"*Harm* in the definition of 'take' in the Act means an act which actually kills or injures wildlife. Such act may include significant habitat modification or degradation where it actually kills or injures wildlife by significantly impairing essential behavioral patterns, including breeding, feeding, or sheltering." 50 CFR § 17.3 (1994).

This regulation has been in place since 1975.

A limitation on the § 9 "take" prohibition appears in § 10(a)(1)(B) of the Act, which Congress added by amendment in 1982. That section authorizes the Secretary to grant a permit for any taking otherwise prohibited by § 9(a)(1)(B) "if such taking is incidental to, and not the purpose of, the carrying out of an otherwise lawful activity." 16 U.S.C. § 1539(a)(1)(B).

* * *

Respondents in this action are small landowners, logging companies, and families dependent on the forest products industries in the Pacific Northwest and in the Southeast, and organizations that represent their interests. They brought this declaratory judgment action against petitioners, the Secretary of the Interior and the Director of the Fish and Wildlife Service, in the United States District Court for the District of Columbia to challenge the statutory validity of the Secretary's regulation defining "harm," particularly the inclusion of habitat modification and degradation in the definition. Respondents challenged the regulation on its face. Their complaint alleged that application of the "harm" regulation to the red-cockaded woodpecker, an endangered species, and the northern spotted owl, a threatened species, had injured them economically.

II

Because this case was decided on motions for summary judgment, we may appropriately make certain factual assumptions in order to frame the legal issue. First, we assume respondents have no desire to harm either the red-cockaded woodpecker or the spotted owl; they merely wish to continue logging activities that would be entirely proper if not prohibited by the ESA. On the other hand, we must assume, *arguendo*, that those activities will have the effect, even though unintended, of detrimentally changing the natural habitat of both listed species and that, as a consequence, members of those species will be killed or injured. Under respondents' view of the law, the Secretary's only means of forestalling that grave result—even when the actor knows it is certain to occur[9]—is to use his § 5 authority to purchase the lands on which the survival of the species depends. The Secretary, on the other hand, submits that the § 9 prohibition on takings, which Congress defined to include "harm," places on respondents a duty to avoid harm that habitat alteration will cause the birds unless respondents first obtain a permit pursuant to § 10.

The text of the Act provides three reasons for concluding that the Secretary's interpretation is reasonable. First, an ordinary understanding of the word "harm" supports it. The dictionary definition of the verb form of "harm" is "to cause hurt or damage to: injure." Webster's Third New International Dictionary 1034 (1966). In the context of the ESA, that definition naturally encompasses habitat modification that results in actual injury or death to members of an endangered or threatened species.

Respondents argue that the Secretary should have limited the purview of "harm" to direct applications of force against protected species, but the dictionary definition does not include the word "directly" or suggest in any way that only direct or willful action that leads to injury constitutes "harm." Moreover, unless the statutory term "harm" encompasses indirect as well as direct injuries, the word has no meaning that does not duplicate the meaning of other words that § 3 uses to define "take." A reluctance to treat statutory terms as surplusage supports the reasonableness of the Secretary's interpretation. See, *e.g., Mackey v. Lanier Collection Agency & Service, Inc.*, 486 U.S. 825, 837, and n. 11 (1988).

Second, the broad purpose of the ESA supports the Secretary's decision to extend protection against activities that cause the precise harms Congress enacted the statute to avoid. In *TVA v. Hill*, 437 U.S. 153 (1978), we described the Act as "the most comprehensive legislation for the preservation of endangered species ever enacted by any nation." Whereas predecessor statutes enacted in 1966 and 1969 had not contained any sweeping prohibition against the taking of endangered species except on federal lands, the 1973 Act applied to all land in the United States and to the Nation's territorial seas. As stated in § 2 of the Act, among its central purposes is "to provide a means whereby the ecosystems upon which endangered species and threatened species depend may be conserved. . . ." 16 U.S.C. § 1531(b).

---

[9]   As discussed above, the Secretary's definition of "harm" is limited to "act[s] which actually kil[l] or injur[e] wildlife." 50 CFR § 17.3 (1994). In addition, in order to be subject to the Act's criminal penalties or the more severe of its civil penalties, one must "knowingly violat[e]" the Act or its implementing regulations. 16 U.S.C. §§ 1540(a)(1), (b)(1). Congress added "knowingly" in place of "willfully" in 1978 to make "criminal violations of the act a general rather than a specific intent crime." H.R.Conf.Rep. No. 95–1804, p. 26 (1978). The Act does authorize up to a $500 civil fine for "[a]ny person who otherwise violates" the Act or its implementing regulations. 16 U.S.C. § 1540(a)(1). * * *

* * *

Respondents advance strong arguments that activities that cause minimal or unforeseeable harm will not violate the Act as construed in the "harm" regulation. Respondents, however, present a facial challenge to the regulation. Thus, they ask us to invalidate the Secretary's understanding of "harm" in every circumstance, even when an actor knows that an activity, such as draining a pond, would actually result in the extinction of a listed species by destroying its habitat. Given Congress' clear expression of the ESA's broad purpose to protect endangered and threatened wildlife, the Secretary's definition of "harm" is reasonable.

Third, the fact that Congress in 1982 authorized the Secretary to issue permits for takings that § 9(a)(1)(B) would otherwise prohibit, "if such taking is incidental to, and not the purpose of, the carrying out of an otherwise lawful activity," 16 U.S.C. § 1539(a)(1)(B), strongly suggests that Congress understood § 9(a)(1)(B) to prohibit indirect as well as deliberate takings. The permit process requires the applicant to prepare a "conservation plan" that specifies how he intends to "minimize and mitigate" the "impact" of his activity on endangered and threatened species, 16 U.S.C. § 1539(a)(2)(A), making clear that Congress had in mind foreseeable rather than merely accidental effects on listed species. No one could seriously request an "incidental" take permit to avert § 9 liability for direct, deliberate action against a member of an endangered or threatened species, but respondents would read "harm" so narrowly that the permit procedure would have little more than that absurd purpose. "When Congress acts to amend a statute, we presume it intends its amendment to have real and substantial effect." *Stone v. INS*, 514 U.S. 386, 397 (1995).

* * *

We need not decide whether the statutory definition of "take" compels the Secretary's interpretation of "harm," because our conclusions that Congress did not unambiguously manifest its intent to adopt respondents' view and that the Secretary's interpretation is reasonable suffice to decide this case. See generally *Chevron U.S.A. Inc. v. Natural Resources Defense Council, Inc.*, 467 U.S. 837 (1984). The latitude the ESA gives the Secretary in enforcing the statute, together with the degree of regulatory expertise necessary to its enforcement, establishes that we owe some degree of deference to the Secretary's reasonable interpretation.[18]

---

[18] Respondents also argue that the rule of lenity should foreclose any deference to the Secretary's interpretation of the ESA because the statute includes criminal penalties. The rule of lenity is premised on two ideas: First, " 'a fair warning should be given to the world in language that the common world will understand, of what the law intends to do if a certain line is passed' "; second, "legislatures and not courts should define criminal activity." *United States v. Bass,* 404 U.S. 336, 347–350 (1971) (quoting *McBoyle v. United States,* 283 U.S. 25, 27 (1931)). We have applied the rule of lenity in a case raising a narrow question concerning the application of a statute that contains criminal sanctions to a specific factual dispute—whether pistols with short barrels and attachable shoulder stocks are short-barreled rifles—where no regulation was present. See *United States v. Thompson/Center Arms Co.,* 504 U.S. 505, 517–518, and n. 9 (1992). We have never suggested that the rule of lenity should provide the standard for reviewing facial challenges to administrative regulations whenever the governing statute authorizes criminal enforcement. Even if there exist regulations whose interpretations of statutory criminal penalties provide such inadequate notice of potential

[The opinion of the Court goes on to analyze the relevant legislative history as further supporting the reasonableness of the Secretary's interpretation of the ESA and to reiterate the Court's conclusion that it owes the agency *Chevron* deference. Ed.]

■ [The opinion of JUSTICE O'CONNOR, concurring, is omitted. Ed.]

■ JUSTICE SCALIA, with whom THE CHIEF JUSTICE and JUSTICE THOMAS join, dissenting.

I think it unmistakably clear that the legislation at issue here (1) forbade the hunting and killing of endangered animals, and (2) provided federal lands and federal funds *for the acquisition of private lands*, to preserve the habitat of endangered animals. The Court's holding that the hunting and killing prohibition incidentally preserves habitat on private lands imposes unfairness to the point of financial ruin—not just upon the rich, but upon the simplest farmer who finds his land conscripted to national zoological use. I respectfully dissent.

* * *

In my view petitioners must lose—the regulation must fall—even under the test of *Chevron U.S.A. Inc. v. Natural Resources Defense Council, Inc.*, 467 U.S. 837, 843 (1984), so I shall assume that the Court is correct to apply *Chevron*.

The regulation has three features which, for reasons I shall discuss at length below, do not comport with the statute. First, it interprets the statute to prohibit habitat modification that is no more than the cause-in-fact of death or injury to wildlife. *Any* "significant habitat modification" that in fact produces that result by "impairing essential behavioral patterns" is made unlawful, regardless of whether that result is intended or even foreseeable, and no matter how long the chain of causality between modification and injury. * * *

Second, the regulation does not require an "act": The Secretary's officially stated position is that an *omission* will do. The previous version of the regulation made this explicit. See 40 Fed. Reg. 44412, 44416 (1975) (" 'Harm' in the definition of 'take' in the Act means an act or omission which actually kills or injures wildlife . . ."). When the regulation was modified in 1981 the phrase "or omission" was taken out, but only because (as the final publication of the rule advised) "the [Fish and Wildlife] Service feels that 'act' is inclusive of either commissions or omissions which would be prohibited by section [1538(a)(1)(B)]." 46 Fed.Reg. 54748, 54750 (1981). * * *

The third and most important unlawful feature of the regulation is that it encompasses injury inflicted, not only upon individual animals, but upon populations of the protected species. "Injury" in the regulation includes "significantly impairing essential behavioral patterns, including *breeding*," 50 CFR § 17.3 (1994) (emphasis added). Impairment of breeding does not "injure" living creatures; it prevents them from propagating, thus "injuring" *a population* of animals which would otherwise have maintained or increased its numbers. * * *

liability as to offend the rule of lenity, the "harm" regulation, which has existed for two decades and gives a fair warning of its consequences, cannot be one of them.

None of these three features of the regulation can be found in the statutory provisions supposed to authorize it. The term "harm" in § 1532(19) has no legal force of its own. An indictment or civil complaint that charged the defendant with "harming" an animal protected under the Act would be dismissed as defective, for the only *operative* term in the statute is to "take." If "take" were not elsewhere defined in the Act, none could dispute what it means, for the term is as old as the law itself. To "take," when applied to wild animals, means to reduce those animals, by killing or capturing, to human control. See, *e.g.*, 11 Oxford English Dictionary (1933) ("Take . . . To catch, capture (a wild beast, bird, fish, etc.)"); Webster's New International Dictionary of the English Language (2d ed. 1949) (take defined as "to catch or capture by trapping, snaring, etc., or as prey"); *Geer v. Connecticut*, 161 U.S. 519, 523 (1896) (" '[A]ll the animals which can be taken upon the earth, in the sea, or in the air, that is to say, wild animals, belong to those who take them' ") (quoting the Digest of Justinian); 2 W. Blackstone, Commentaries 411 (1766) ("Every man . . . has an equal right of pursuing and taking to his own use all such creatures as are *ferae naturae*"). This is just the sense in which "take" is used elsewhere in federal legislation and treaty. See, *e.g.*, Migratory Bird Treaty Act, 16 U.S.C. § 703 (1988 ed., Supp. V) (no person may "pursue, hunt, take, capture, kill, [or] attempt to take, capture, or kill" any migratory bird); Agreement on the Conservation of Polar Bears, Nov. 15, 1973, Art. I, 27 U.S.T. 3918, 3921 (defining "taking" as "hunting, killing and capturing"). And that meaning fits neatly with the rest of § 1538(a)(1), which makes it unlawful not only to take protected species, but also to import or export them, § 1538(a)(1)(A); to possess, sell, deliver, carry, transport, or ship any taken species, § 1538(a)(1)(D); and to transport, sell, or offer to sell them in interstate or foreign commerce, §§ 1538(a)(1)(E), (F). The taking prohibition, in other words, is only part of the regulatory plan of § 1538(a)(1), which covers all the stages of the process by which protected wildlife is reduced to man's dominion and made the object of profit. It is obvious that "take" in this sense—a term of art deeply embedded in the statutory and common law concerning wildlife—describes a class of acts (not omissions) done directly and intentionally (not indirectly and by accident) to particular animals (not populations of animals).

The Act's definition of "take" does expand the word slightly (and not unusually), so as to make clear that it includes not just a completed taking, but the process of taking, and all of the acts that are customarily identified with or accompany that process ("to harass, harm, pursue, hunt, shoot, wound, kill, trap, capture, or collect"); and so as to include attempts. § 1532(19). The tempting fallacy—which the Court commits with abandon—is to assume that *once defined*, "take" loses any significance, and it is only the definition that matters. The Court treats the statute as though Congress had directly enacted the § 1532(19) definition as a self-executing prohibition, and had not enacted § 1538(a)(1)(B) at all. But § 1538(a)(1)(B) is there, and if the terms contained in the definitional section are susceptible of two readings, one of which comports with the standard meaning of "take" as used in application to wildlife, and one of which does not, an agency regulation that adopts the latter reading is necessarily unreasonable, for it reads the defined term "take"—the only operative term—out of the statute altogether.

That is what has occurred here. The verb "harm" has a range of meaning: "to cause injury" at its broadest, "to do hurt or damage" in a narrower and more direct sense. See, e.g., 1 N. Webster, An American Dictionary of the English Language (1828) ("Harm, *v.t.* To hurt; to injure; to damage; *to impair soundness of body, either animal* or vegetable") (emphasis added); American College Dictionary 551 (1970) ("harm . . . n. injury; damage; hurt: *to do him bodily harm*"). In fact the more directed sense of "harm" is a somewhat more common and preferred usage; "*harm* has in it a little of the idea of specially focused hurt or injury, as if a personal injury has been anticipated and intended." J. Opdycke, Mark My Words: A Guide to Modern Usage and Expression 330 (1949). See also American Heritage Dictionary 662 (1985) ("*Injure* has the widest range. . . . *Harm* and *hurt* refer principally to what causes physical or mental distress to living things"). To define "harm" as an act or omission that, however remotely, "actually kills or injures" a population of wildlife through habitat modification is to choose a meaning that makes nonsense of the word that "harm" defines—requiring us to accept that a farmer who tills his field and causes erosion that makes silt run into a nearby river which depletes oxygen and thereby "impairs [the] breeding" of protected fish has "taken" or "attempted to take" the fish. It should take the strongest evidence to make us believe that Congress has defined a term in a manner repugnant to its ordinary and traditional sense.

Here the evidence shows the opposite. "Harm" is merely one of 10 prohibitory words in § 1532(19), and the other 9 fit the ordinary meaning of "take" perfectly. To "harass, pursue, hunt, shoot, wound, kill, trap, capture, or collect" are all affirmative acts (the provision itself describes them as "conduct," see § 1532(19)) which are directed immediately and intentionally against a particular animal—not acts or omissions that indirectly and accidentally cause injury to a population of animals. The Court points out that several of the words ("harass," "pursue," "wound," and "kill") "refer to actions or effects that do not require direct *applications of force*." That is true enough, but force is not the point. Even "taking" activities in the narrowest sense, activities traditionally engaged in by hunters and trappers, do not all consist of direct applications of force; pursuit and harassment are part of the business of "taking" the prey even before it has been touched. What the nine other words in § 1532(19) have in common—and share with the narrower meaning of "harm" described above, but not with the Secretary's ruthless dilation of the word—is the sense of affirmative conduct intentionally directed against a particular animal or animals.

I am not the first to notice this fact, or to draw the conclusion that it compels. In 1981 the Solicitor of the Fish and Wildlife Service delivered a legal opinion on § 1532(19) that is in complete agreement with my reading:

"The Act's definition of 'take' contains a list of actions that illustrate the intended scope of the term. . . . With the possible exception of 'harm,' these terms all represent forms of conduct that are directed against and likely to injure or kill *individual* wildlife. Under the principle of statutory construction, *ejusdem generis*, . . . the term 'harm' should be interpreted to include only those actions that are directed against, and likely to injure or kill, individual wildlife." Memorandum of Apr. 17, reprinted in 46 Fed. Reg. 29490, 29491 (1981) (emphasis in original).

I would call it *noscitur a sociis*, but the principle is much the same: The fact that "several items in a list share an attribute counsels in favor of interpreting the other items as possessing that attribute as well," *Beecham v. United States*, 511 U.S. 368, 371 (1994). The Court contends that the canon cannot be applied to deprive a word of all its "independent meaning." That proposition is questionable to begin with, especially as applied to long lawyers' listings such as this. If it were true, we ought to give the word "trap" in the definition its rare meaning of "to clothe" (whence "trappings")—since otherwise it adds nothing to the word "capture." See *Moskal v. United States*, 498 U.S. 103, 120 (1990) (SCALIA, J., dissenting). In any event, the Court's contention that "harm" in the narrow sense adds nothing to the other words underestimates the ingenuity of our own species in a way that Congress did not. To feed an animal poison, to spray it with mace, to chop down the very tree in which it is nesting, or even to destroy its entire habitat in order to take it (as by draining a pond to get at a turtle), might neither wound nor kill, but would directly and intentionally harm.

The penalty provisions of the Act counsel this interpretation as well. Any person who "knowingly" violates § 1538(a)(1)(B) is subject to criminal penalties under § 1540(b)(1) and civil penalties under § 1540(a)(1); moreover, under the latter section, any person "who otherwise violates" the taking prohibition (*i.e.*, violates it *un*knowingly) may be assessed a civil penalty of $500 for each violation, with the stricture that "[e]ach such violation shall be a separate offense." This last provision should be clear warning that the regulation is in error, for when combined with the regulation it produces a result that no legislature could reasonably be thought to have intended: A large number of routine private activities—for example, farming, ranching, roadbuilding, construction and logging—are subjected to strict-liability penalties when they fortuitously injure protected wildlife, no matter how remote the chain of causation and no matter how difficult to foresee (or to disprove) the "injury" may be (*e.g.*, an "impairment" of breeding). * * *

The Court says that "[to] read a requirement of intent or purpose into the words used to define 'take' . . . ignore[s] [§ 1540's] express provision that a 'knowin[g]' action is enough to violate the Act." This presumably means that because the reading of § 1532(19) advanced here ascribes an element of purposeful injury to the prohibited acts, it makes superfluous (or inexplicable) the more severe penalties provided for a "knowing" violation. That conclusion does not follow, for it is quite possible to take protected wildlife purposefully without doing so knowingly. A requirement that a violation be "knowing" means that the defendant must "know the facts that make his conduct illegal," *Staples v. United States*, 511 U.S. 600, 606 (1994). The hunter who shoots an elk in the mistaken belief that it is a mule deer has not knowingly violated § 1538(a)(1)(B)—not because he does not know that elk are legally protected (that would be knowledge of the law, which is not a requirement), but because he does not know what sort of animal he is shooting. The hunter has nonetheless committed a purposeful taking of protected wildlife, and would therefore be subject to the (lower) strict-liability penalties for the violation.

* * *

The broader structure of the Act confirms the unreasonableness of the regulation. Section 1536 provides:

> "Each Federal agency shall ... insure that any action authorized, funded, or carried out by such agency ... is not likely to jeopardize the continued existence of any endangered species or threatened species or *result in the destruction or adverse modification of habitat* of such species which is determined by the Secretary ... to be critical." 16 U.S.C. § 1536(a)(2) (emphasis added).

The Act defines "critical habitat" as habitat that is "essential to the conservation of the species," §§ 1532(5)(A)(i), (A)(ii), with "conservation" in turn defined as the use of methods necessary to bring listed species "to the point at which the measures provided pursuant to this chapter are no longer necessary," § 1532(3).

These provisions have a double significance. Even if §§ 1536(a)(2) and 1538(a)(1)(B) were totally independent prohibitions—the former applying only to federal agencies and their licensees, the latter only to private parties—Congress's explicit prohibition of habitat modification in the one section would bar the inference of an implicit prohibition of habitat modification in the other section. "[W]here Congress includes particular language in one section of a statute but omits it in another ... , it is generally presumed that Congress acts intentionally and purposely in the disparate inclusion or exclusion." *Keene Corp. v. United States*, 508 U.S. 200, 208 (1993) (internal quotation marks omitted). And that presumption against implicit prohibition would be even stronger where the one section which uses the language carefully defines and limits its application. That is to say, it would be passing strange for Congress carefully to define "critical habitat" as used in § 1536(a)(2), but leave it to the Secretary to evaluate, willy-nilly, impermissible "habitat modification" (under the guise of "harm") in § 1538(a)(1)(B).

In fact, however, §§ 1536(a)(2) and 1538(a)(1)(B) do *not* operate in separate realms; federal agencies are subject to *both*, because the "person[s]" forbidden to take protected species under § 1538 include agencies and departments of the Federal Government. See § 1532(13). This means that the "harm" regulation also contradicts another principle of interpretation: that statutes should be read so far as possible to give independent effect to all their provisions. See *Ratzlaf v. United States*, 510 U.S. 135, 140–141 (1994). By defining "harm" in the definition of "take" in § 1538(a)(1)(B) to include significant habitat modification that injures populations of wildlife, the regulation makes the habitat-modification restriction in § 1536(a)(2) almost wholly superfluous. As "critical habitat" is habitat "essential to the conservation of the species," adverse modification of "critical" habitat by a federal agency would also constitute habitat modification that injures a population of wildlife.

* * *

The Endangered Species Act is a carefully considered piece of legislation that forbids all persons to hunt or harm endangered animals, but places upon the public at large, rather than upon fortuitously accountable individual landowners, the cost of preserving the habitat of endangered species. There is neither textual support for, nor even evidence of congressional consideration of, the radically different disposition contained in the regulation that the Court sustains. For these reasons, I respectfully dissent.

NOTES AND QUESTIONS

1.   Courts and commentators typically offer two rationales as supporting the rule of lenity. The first is rooted in separation of powers principles, holding that legislatures, rather than courts, should be responsible for defining precisely which actions are crimes. The second reflects due process concerns, recognizing that people deserve fair warning that particular activities will subject them to criminal penalties. The Supreme Court in *Sweet Home* addressed only the latter of these, reasoning that the Interior Department regulation at issue had existed for two decades and provided fair warning of the consequences of noncompliance. Do you think the separation of powers concern is satisfied by Congress's delegation of the power to fill interpretive gaps in the Endangered Species Act and the Interior Secretary's exercise of that power?

2.   The brief discussion in *Sweet Home*'s footnote 18 is the Court's most prominent statement to date regarding the relationship between *Chevron* and the rule of lenity, but it arguably is not the only statement. In the *Solid Waste Agency* case excerpted above, the Court noted but declined to address the argument that, because the Clean Water Act carries criminal penalties, the agency's interpretation should fall on lenity grounds. 531 U.S. 159, 174 n.8 (2001). Subsequently, in *National Cable and Telecommunications Association v. Brand X Internet Services*, 545 U.S. 967 (2005), excerpted elsewhere in this Chapter, the Court seemed to suggest that there might be some instances in which a court could rely on the rule of lenity to deny an agency *Chevron* deference. In particular, interpreting a relevant circuit court precedent as consistent with a finding of statutory ambiguity in the case at bar, the Court noted that the circuit court "invoked no other rule of construction (such as the rule of lenity) requiring it to conclude that the statute was unambiguous to reach its judgment." *Id.* at 985.

3.   In discussing the relationship between *Chevron* and the rule of lenity in *Sweet Home*, the Court distinguished the context of that case from that of *United States v. Thomson/Center Arms Co.*, 504 U.S. 505 (1992). Like *Sweet Home*, *Thomson/Center Arms* was a civil case—this time concerning the applicability of an excise tax imposed by the National Firearms Act (NFA). Without mentioning *Chevron* at all, the Court applied the rule of lenity to resolve the case in favor of the challenger, noting that, "although it is a tax statute that we construe now in a civil setting, the NFA has criminal applications that carry no additional requirement of willfulness." The Court in *Sweet Home* recognized the potential for criminal sanctions against persons who violate the Endangered Species Act, and thus the regulation interpreting it. But the Court distinguished *Sweet Home*'s facial challenge to an agency regulation adopted using notice and comment rulemaking from the narrower as-applied challenge to an agency's informal adjudication in *Thomson/Center Arms*. What elements of rulemaking versus adjudication do you think the Court found particularly relevant in deciding to apply *Chevron* rather than lenity in *Sweet Home*?

———————

Seeming inconsistencies in the Supreme Court's jurisprudence regarding the relationship between Chevron deference and the rule of lenity prompted one jurist to draft a concurring opinion attempting to reconcile the two.

Carter v. Welles-Bowen Realty, Inc.

736 F.3d 722 (6th Cir. 2013).

[In this case, customers of a real estate agency appealed a lower court decision that the real estate agency did not violate the Real Estate Settlement Procedures Act, 12 U.S.C. § 2607(a), when it referred them to an affiliated title services company. While the parties agreed that the real estate agency satisfied three prerequisites for a statutory safe harbor for "affiliated business arrangements," they disagreed over whether the real estate agency was required to meet a fourth condition—which employed a multi-factor standard—announced by the Department of Housing and Urban Development (HUD) in a policy statement. HUD intervened and claimed *Chevron* deference for its policy statement as an interpretation of the statute. The court rejected that argument and concluded instead that HUD could not rely on a policy statement to impose additional safe harbor conditions. Since the real estate agency had satisfied the three statutory prerequisites, the safe harbor exempted the real estate agency from liability under the statute. Although the case at bar was a civil one, the opinion for the court observed that the statute carried potential criminal penalties as well, and that the same question regarding the proper interpretation of the affiliated business arrangements safe harbor could arise in a criminal case. Ed.]

■ SUTTON, J., concurring.

Anyone who violates the Real Estate Settlement Procedures Act's ban on referral fees commits a crime. See 12 U.S.C. § 2607(d)(1). The rule of lenity tells all interpreters to resolve uncertainties in laws with criminal applications in favor of the defendant. But the Department of Housing and Urban Development has resolved an ambiguity in the law *against* the defendant, and the government insists that we must defer to this understanding. The doctrine of *Chevron* deference, the government explains, leaves us no choice. This theory would allow one administration to criminalize conduct within the scope of the ambiguity, the next administration to decriminalize it, and the third to recriminalize it, all without any direction from Congress. I am skeptical.

The court does not go into detail in exploring how the rule of lenity interacts with *Chevron* because the issue does not drive the outcome of this case. But because this question will return sooner or later, I write to offer some thoughts on how to address it when it does.

The rule of lenity tells courts to interpret ambiguous criminal laws in favor of criminal defendants. *United States v. Wiltberger*, 5 Wheat. 76, 95 (1820). This principle rests on concerns about notice (the state ought to provide fair warning of what violates the criminal laws) and separation of powers (Congress, not agencies or courts, defines crimes). *United States v. Bass*, 404 U.S. 336, 348 (1971). The *Chevron* doctrine tells courts to defer to an administrative agency's reasonable interpretation of an ambiguous statute. *Chevron U.S.A., Inc. v. Natural Resources Defense Council*, 467 U.S. 837 (1984). This principle rests on the presumption that, when Congress leaves a statutory gap, it means for the agency rather than the court to fill it. *Id.* at 843–44.

The two rules normally operate comfortably in their own spheres. The rule of lenity has no role to play in interpreting humdrum regulatory statutes, which contemplate civil rather than criminal enforcement. And *Chevron* has no role to play in interpreting ordinary criminal statutes, which are "not administered by any agency but by the courts." *Crandon v. United States*, 494 U.S. 152, 177 (1990) (Scalia, J., concurring in the judgment); see *Gonzales v. Oregon*, 546 U.S. 243, 264 (2006).

What happens with a hybrid statute? Today's Act imposes civil *and* criminal penalties for violating the provision at issue. See 12 U.S.C. § 2607(d). And it empowers an executive agency to administer the provision by making rules and holding hearings. *See id.* § 2617. As between the rule of lenity and the agency's interpretation, which one resolves statutory doubt?

One possibility is to apply the rule of lenity in criminal prosecutions and to defer to the agency's position in civil actions. But a statute is not a chameleon. Its meaning does not change from case to case. A single law should have one meaning, and the "lowest common denominator, as it were, must govern" all of its applications. *Clark v. Martinez*, 543 U.S. 371 (2005).

United States v. Thompson/Center Arms Co. illustrates the point. The Court had to interpret a law that included a civil tax penalty and a criminal penalty. Even though *Thompson/Center Arms* was a tax case, the Court applied the rule of lenity. 504 U.S. 505, 518 n. 10 (1992) (plurality opinion); *id.* at 519 (Scalia, J., concurring in the judgment). "The rule of lenity," the lead opinion explained, "is a rule of statutory construction[,] . . . not a rule of administration calling for courts to refrain in criminal cases from applying statutory language that would have been held to apply if challenged in civil litigation." *Id.* at 518 n. 10 (plurality opinion). Recent cases reaffirm the point. *See, e.g., Maracich v. Spears*, 133 S.Ct. 2191, 2209 (2013); *Kasten v. Saint-Gobain Performance Plastics Corp.*, 131 S.Ct. 1325, 1336; Leocal v. Ashcroft, 543 U.S. 1, 11 n. 8 (2004); *Scheidler v. Nat'l Org. for Women*, 537 U.S. 393, 408–09 (2003).

Case law thus makes clear that either the rule of lenity prevails across the board or the agency's interpretation does. But which one? The better approach, it seems to me, is that a court should not defer to an agency's anti-defendant interpretation of a law backed by criminal penalties.

First, the rule of lenity forbids deference to the executive branch's interpretation of a crime-creating law. If an ordinary criminal law contains an uncertainty, every court would agree that it must resolve the uncertainty in the defendant's favor. No judge would think of deferring to the Department of Justice. Allowing prosecutors to fill gaps in criminal laws would "turn the normal construction of criminal statutes upside down, replacing the doctrine of lenity with a doctrine of severity." *Crandon,* 494 U.S. at 178, 110 S.Ct. 997 (Scalia, J., concurring in the judgment).

If the rule of lenity forecloses deference to the Justice Department's interpretation of a crime-creating law in Title 18, does it not follow that it forecloses deference to the Housing Department's interpretation of a crime-creating law in Title 12? Or the immigration authorities' interpretation of a crime-creating law in Title 8? Or the IRS's interpretation of a crime-creating law in Title 26? No principled distinction separates these settings. Allowing housing inspectors and immigration officers and tax collectors to fill gaps in hybrid criminal laws, no less than allowing prosecutors to fill them in pure criminal laws, offends the rule of lenity.

Second, looking at the question within the framework of *Chevron* leads to the same answer. An agency's interpretation of a statute does not prevail whenever the face of the statute contains an ambiguity. Deference comes into play only if a statutory ambiguity lingers after deployment of all pertinent interpretive principles. If you believe that *Chevron* has two steps, you would say that the relevant interpretive rule—the rule of lenity—operates during step one. Once the rule resolves an uncertainty at this step, "there [remains], for *Chevron* purposes, no ambiguity . . . for an agency to resolve." *INS v. St. Cyr,* 533 U.S. 289, 320 n. 45 (2001). If you believe that *Chevron* has only one step, you would say that *Chevron* requires courts "to accept only those agency interpretations that are reasonable in light of the principles of construction courts normally employ." *EEOC v. Arabian American Oil Co.,* 499 U.S. 244, 260 (1991) (Scalia, J., concurring in part and concurring in the judgment). If an interpretive principle resolves a statutory doubt in one direction, an agency may not reasonably resolve it in the opposite direction. *Id.* But the broader point, the critical one, transcends debates about the mechanics of *Chevron*: Rules of interpretation bind all interpreters, administrative agencies included. That means an agency, no less than a court, must interpret a doubtful criminal statute in favor of the defendant.

* * *

Third, the policies that drive lenity and *Chevron* show how to harmonize the two principles. Start with lenity. Making something a crime is serious business. It visits the moral condemnation of the community upon the citizen who engages in the forbidden conduct, and it allows the government to take away his liberty and property. The rule of lenity carries into effect the principle that only the legislature, the most democratic and accountable branch of government, should decide what conduct triggers these consequences. *Bass,* 404 U.S. at 348.

By giving unelected commissioners and directors and administrators carte blanche to decide when an ambiguous statute justifies sending people to prison, the government's theory diminishes this ideal.

The rule of lenity also compels the state to give the citizen fair warning, ideally on the face of the statute, of what the criminal law forbids. *McBoyle v. United States*, 283 U.S. 25, 27 (1931). There are no crimes by implication just as no one is killed by implication. Yet if agencies are free to ignore the rule of lenity, the state could make an act a crime in a remote statement issued by an administrative agency. The agency's pronouncement need not even come in a notice-and-comment rule. All kinds of administrative documents, ranging from manuals to opinion letters, sometimes receive *Chevron* deference. *See, e.g., Barnhart v. Walton*, 535 U.S. 212, 221–22 (2002). Nor is this a figment. In this case, the government has tried to expand a federal criminal law through a policy statement, a theory that runs headlong into "the instinctive distastes against men languishing in prison unless the lawmaker has clearly said they should." Henry Friendly, "Mr. Justice Frankfurter and the Reading of Statutes," in *Benchmarks* 196, 209 (1967).

So much for the purpose of lenity; what of the purpose of *Chevron*? There may be as many accounts of *Chevron* as there are professors of administrative law. But what matters most, *Chevron*'s account of itself, shows that *Chevron* accommodates rather than trumps the lenity principle. Filling a statutory gap, the Supreme Court explained, requires making a policy choice. 467 U.S. at 864–65. But courts should avoid making policy choices, as they enjoy neither expertise in the relevant area nor a democratically accountable pedigree. *Id.* at 865–66. Forced to a choice between the two, the Court concluded that administrators are better equipped than judges to fill the gaps. *Id.* at 866.

This account of *Chevron* says nothing about the present case. When a court applies the rule of lenity, it does not snatch a policy decision from the political branches. It instead insists that the choice to make the conduct criminal be made by the first political branch rather than the second. Put another way, *Chevron* describes how judges and administrators divide power. But power to define crimes is not theirs to divide. The accommodation then becomes straightforward: Allowing agencies to fill gaps in criminal statutes would impair the rule of lenity's purposes, and interpreting these statutes leniently would respect *Chevron*'s aims.

Fourth, uninvited oddities arise if courts but not agencies must adhere to the rule of lenity. *United States v. Mead Corp.*, 533 U.S. 218 (2001), and its follow-on cases hold that an agency interpretation's eligibility for *Chevron* deference depends on the procedure that preceded the interpretation's adoption as well as on factors like "the interstitial nature of the legal question, the related expertise of the Agency, the importance of the question to the administration of the statute, the complexity of that administration, and the careful consideration the Agency has given the question over a long period of time." *Walton*, 535 U.S. at 222. Where the governing statute creates only civil liability, a multi-factor test may be the best one can hope for. *See Mead*, 533 U.S. at 236–37. But it is a bit strange to say that, if

Welles-Bowen wants to know whether it commits a *crime* by falling afoul of a policy statement, it must first endure the "open-ended rough-and-tumble of factors." *Medellin v. Texas*, 552 U.S. 491, 514 (2008).

* * *

The government, both in this case and in similar cases before other courts, offers several lines of argument in response to this approach. None is convincing.

The government points out that several cases show that Congress's authority to define crimes is not exclusive. Although the Constitution as a general matter vests power to define crimes in Congress alone, the modern nondelegation doctrine, it is true, occasionally allows Congress to transfer some responsibility for defining crimes to the executive branch. Hence *United States v. Grimaud*, 220 U.S. 506 (1911), held that Congress could make it a crime to violate regulations issued by the Secretary of Agriculture. *Touby v. United States*, 500 U.S. 160 (1991), held that Congress could direct the Attorney General on an emergency basis to figure out which drugs to classify as controlled substances. And *United States v. O'Hagan*, 521 U.S. 642 (1997), saw nothing objectionable in a law authorizing the Securities and Exchange Commission to make rules combating securities fraud and to make violations of these rules crimes. If the Court allowed Congress to assign responsibility for defining crimes to the executive in those cases, what makes today's case different?

The argument overlooks the reality that, if Congress wants to assign the executive branch discretion to define criminal conduct, it must speak "distinctly." *Grimaud*, 220 U.S. at 519; *United States v. Eaton*, 144 U.S. 677, 688 (1892). This clear-statement rule reinforces horizontal separation of powers in the same way that *Gregory v. Ashcroft*, 501 U.S. 452 (1991), reinforces vertical separation of powers. It compels Congress to legislate deliberately and explicitly before departing from the Constitution's traditional distribution of authority. Cases like *Grimaud*, *Touby* and *O'Hagan* respected this express-statement requirement, but the government's theory flouts it. Under the government's approach, courts could *presume* a congressional delegation of authority to create crimes whenever a criminal statute contains a gap. A presumption does not a clear statement make.

A related analogy to the Court's federalism precedents fortifies the point. The Constitution sometimes allows Congress to upset federalism norms provided it legislates clearly. *See Gregory*, 501 U.S. at 460. But it does not follow that *Chevron* allows agencies to upset federalism norms when Congress legislates ambiguously. *See SWANCC*, 531 U.S. at 172–73. In the same way, Congress may sometimes depart from separation-of-powers principles so long as it legislates clearly. But it does not follow that agencies may depart from separation-of-powers principles when Congress legislates ambiguously.

Quite apart from the clear-statement rule, the Constitution may well also require Congress to state more than an "intelligible principle" when leaving the definition of crime to the executive. The Supreme Court has suggested that "greater congressional specificity [may be] required in the criminal context." Touby, 500 U.S. at 166; *see Yakus v. United States*, 321 U.S. 414, 423–27 (1944). The laws at issue in

Grimaud, Touby and *O'Hagan* honored this principle. But under the government's approach, an agency could fill a gap in a criminal statute even where Congress provides no specific guidance about how to fill it.

The government separately relies heavily on a footnote in *Babbitt v. Sweet Home Chapter of Communities for a Great Oregon*, 515 U.S. 687, 704 n. 18 (1995). *Sweet Home* arose under the Endangered Species Act, which made it an offense (subject to civil and criminal penalties) to "take" any endangered species. 16 U.S.C. § 1538(a)(1). The Interior Department issued a regulation interpreting this provision to prohibit "significant habitat modification or degradation" that kills or injures protected wildlife. 50 C.F.R. § 17.3 (1994). Before the agency could enforce this regulation, landowners challenged it on its face, claiming that it outstripped the agency's statutory authority.

Citing *Chevron*, the Court gave the interpretation contained in the regulation "some degree of deference." *Sweet Home*, 515 U.S. at 703. The Court then dropped this footnote:

> Respondents also argue that the rule of lenity should foreclose any deference to the Secretary's interpretation . . . because the statute includes criminal penalties. . . . We have applied the rule of lenity in a case raising a narrow question concerning the application of a statute that contains criminal sanctions to a specific factual dispute . . . where no regulation was present. *See United States v. Thompson/Center Arms Co.*, 504 U.S. 505, 517–18 & n. 9 (1992). We have never suggested that the rule of lenity should provide the standard for reviewing facial challenges to administrative regulations whenever the governing statute authorizes criminal enforcement. Even if there exist regulations whose interpretations of statutory criminal penalties provide such inadequate notice of potential liability as to offend the rule of lenity, the [present] regulation, which has existed for two decades and gives a fair warning of its consequences, cannot be one of them.

Id. at 704 n. 18. As the government reads it, this passage definitively holds that *Chevron* deference defeats the rule of lenity.

That is a lot to ask of a footnote, more it seems to me than these four sentences can reasonably demand. Note first of all that the government's reading eclipses the just-mentioned *Grimaud/Eaton* line of cases, which hold that, if Congress wants to assign responsibility for crime definition to the executive, it must speak clearly. No one thinks that *Chevron*-triggering ambiguity satisfies a clear-statement requirement. Did the Court mean to overrule these precedents in a footnote that does not even mention them? Not likely. And a case decided after *Sweet Home* expressly declines—in a footnote, no less—to decide how the rule of lenity and *Chevron* interact. See *SWANCC*, 531 U.S. at 174 n. 8. Why did the Court express reluctance to decide a question if, as the government claims, it had already decided it?

The answer is that *Sweet Home*'s footnote 18 lends itself to a narrower reading, one that preserves the clear-statement rule applicable in this setting and one that preserves the obligation of courts *and* agencies to respect the rule of lenity. The footnote merely acknowledges the possibility of a pre-enforcement facial challenge to an agency's regulation—because the agency had no interpretive authority in the first place, because the agency failed to follow the procedures for promulgating the regulation or because the statute plainly forecloses the agency's interpretation. Yet not one of these challenges depends on, or demands consideration of, the rule of lenity. Why else would the Court distinguish cases involving "specific factual dispute[s]" from cases "reviewing facial challenges"? What purpose could this distinction serve unless the Court meant to create a rule for facial challenges? Although the footnote mentions that the Interior Department's two-decade-old regulation comports with one of the rule of lenity's objectives (promoting fair notice), it says nothing about other regulations or the rule of lenity's separation-of-powers objective (reinforcing that Congress, not courts or agencies, define crimes). Before accepting the government's broad reading of the footnote, one would have expected the Court to say more before allowing agencies to trump a doctrine Chief Justice Marshall described as "perhaps not much less old than construction itself." 5 Wheat. at 95.

Not only does the age of the rule counsel against sweeping it aside *sotto voce* in a footnote, but so does its growing significance in interpretive disputes about the meaning of criminal laws. The Court has all but abandoned the practice of interpreting criminal laws against defendants on the basis of legislative history. *Compare, e.g., United States v. Santos*, 553 U.S. 507, 513 n. 3 (plurality opinion), *with, e.g., Dixson v. United States*, 465 U.S. 482, 491 (1984); *see United States v. R.L.C.*, 503 U.S. 291, 307–11 (1992) (Scalia, J., concurring in the judgment). And it has found lenity-triggering ambiguity in criminal laws more readily of late than it did in the past. Compare, e.g., Santos, 553 U.S. at 513–14, *with, e.g., Moskal v. United States*, 498 U.S. 103, 108 (1990). Meanwhile, deference has shrunk in reach. The Court has cabined the range of materials entitled to *Chevron* deference. *See, e.g., Mead*, 533 U.S. at 231. And it has confirmed that Chevron does not permit an agency to trump other rules of interpretation. *See, e.g., St. Cyr*, 533 U.S. at 320 n. 45. Lenity and *Chevron* thus look different now than they did when *Sweet Home* inscrutably footnoted their interaction.

* * *

In the final analysis, the government's theory gives the executive branch an *implied* share of the legislature's power to define crimes. That is no small matter given "the growing power of the administrative state," *City of Arlington v. FCC*, 133 S.Ct. 1863, 1879 (2013) (Roberts, C.J., dissenting), and it is no small matter given the reality that Congress continues to "put[ ] forth an ever-increasing volume . . . of criminal laws," *Sykes v. United States*, 131 S.Ct. 2267, 2288 (2011) (Scalia, J., dissenting). None of the Supreme Court's decisions requires us to accept this theory; many stand in its way. Agencies, no less than courts, must honor the rule of lenity.

NOTES AND QUESTIONS

1. Judge Sutton suggests that, in the face of statutory ambiguity, either lenity or *Chevron* deference must prevail across the board. Is this necessarily the case? Might a statute be sufficiently ambiguous for a reviewing court to conclude that *Chevron* step two applies, but not ambiguous enough to invoke the rule of lenity—e.g., if the court in question only considers legislative history at *Chevron* step two?

2.   Many regulatory statutes follow the hybrid model described by Judge Sutton, relying primarily on civil enforcement but nevertheless imposing criminal penalties under certain circumstances. Not all are as obscure as the Real Estate Settlement Procedures Act at issue in *Carter v. Welles-Bowen Realty, Inc.* Significantly more prominent and sweeping statutes— like the Clean Air Act, the Clean Water Act, the Endangered Species Act, the Federal Food, Drug, and Cosmetics Act, the Securities Exchange Act of 1934, and the Internal Revenue Code, just to name a few—allow for the possibility of criminal prosecution and penalties. If courts extend the rule of lenity to resolve statutory ambiguity in cases interpreting these hybrid statutes, they could curtail substantially judicial deference to agency legal interpretations across the federal government.

3.   Judge Sutton suggests that Congress has the power to give the executive branch some discretion to define the scope of criminal statutes, and thus command *Chevron* deference, so long as Congress clearly states its intent to do so. If courts were to adopt this approach, how explicit do you think they should expect Congress to be? Should courts require Congress to articulate its intent provision by provision? Or should courts be satisfied if Congress merely includes in a statute a general grant of authority to an agency to adopt regulations as necessary to effectuate statutory purposes?

4.   *CHEVRON* STEP TWO: WHAT'S LEFT?

Step two of the *Chevron* test instructs a court to uphold an agency interpretation of an ambiguous provision of an agency-administered statute if, but only if, the interpretation is permissible or reasonable. The Supreme Court rarely rejects agency legal interpretations at *Chevron* step two, nor has it been very explicit in articulating what the step two inquiry entails. So what precisely does *Chevron* step two require a reviewing court to do? How should courts apply step two?

To a great extent, one's perception of the scope *Chevron*'s second step turns on one's view of step one analysis. For example, if a reviewing court pursues a relatively limited inquiry at *Chevron*'s first step and moves on to step two simply because the statutory text on its face does not provide a ready answer to the question at bar, then assessing the reasonableness of the agency's interpretation at step two might entail a evaluation of legislative history and statutory purpose. By contrast, if a court engages in a robust step one inquiry, concluding that the statute is truly ambiguous only after considering all of statutory text and purpose, legislative history, and the applicability of various canons of construction, then one has to ask what could be left for the court to do at *Chevron* step two?

The following two opinions are among the very, very few instances in which the Supreme Court has invalidated an agency legal interpretation by applying *Chevron* step two. Observe the majority's opinion in the first and the plurality opinion in the second were both written by Justice Scalia, who has been quite clear in his support of a robust inquiry at *Chevron* step one. How does that perspective influence Justice Scalia's approach to *Chevron* step two?

AT&T Corp. v. Iowa Utilities Board

525 U.S. 366 (1999).

■ JUSTICE SCALIA delivered the opinion of the Court.

In these cases, we address whether the Federal Communications Commission has authority to implement certain pricing and nonpricing provisions of the Telecommunications Act of 1996, as well as whether the Commission's rules governing unbundled access and "pick and choose" negotiation are consistent with the statute.

Until the 1990's, local phone service was thought to be a natural monopoly. States typically granted an exclusive franchise in each local service area to a local exchange carrier (LEC), which owned, among other things, the local loops (wires connecting telephones to switches), the switches (equipment directing calls to their destinations), and the transport trunks (wires carrying calls between switches) that constitute a local exchange network. Technological advances, however, have made competition among multiple providers of local service seem possible, and Congress recently ended the longstanding regime of state-sanctioned monopolies.

The Telecommunications Act of 1996 (1996 Act or Act) fundamentally restructures local telephone markets. States may no longer enforce laws that impede competition, and incumbent LECs are subject to a host of duties intended to facilitate market entry. Foremost among these duties is the LEC's obligation under 47 U.S.C. § 251(c) to share its network with competitors. Under this provision, a requesting carrier can obtain access to an incumbent's network in three ways: It can purchase local telephone services at wholesale rates for resale to end users; it can lease elements of the incumbent's network "on an unbundled basis"; and it can interconnect its own facilities with the incumbent's network. When an entrant seeks access through any of these routes, the incumbent can negotiate an agreement without regard to the duties it would otherwise have under § 251(b) or § 251(c). But if private negotiation fails, either party can petition the state commission that regulates local phone service to arbitrate open issues, which arbitration is subject to § 251 and the FCC regulations promulgated thereunder.

Six months after the 1996 Act was passed, the FCC issued its First Report and Order implementing the local-competition provisions. The numerous challenges to this rule-making, filed across the country by incumbent LECs and state utility commissions, were consolidated in the United States Court of Appeals for the Eighth Circuit.

* * *

Incumbent LECs also made several challenges, only some of which are relevant here, to the rules implementing the 1996 Act's requirement of unbundled access. Rule 319, the primary unbundling rule, sets forth a minimum number of network elements that incumbents must make available to requesting carriers. *See* 47 CFR § 51.319 (1997). The LECs complained that, in compiling this list, the FCC had virtually ignored the 1996 Act's requirement that it consider whether access to proprietary elements was "necessary" and whether lack of access to nonproprietary elements would "impair" an entrant's ability to provide local service. *See* 47 U.S.C. § 251(d)(2). In addition, the LECs thought that the list included items (like directory assistance and caller I.D.) that did not meet the statutory definition of "network element." *See* § 153(29). The Eighth Circuit rebuffed both arguments, holding that the Commission's interpretations of the "necessary and impair" standard and the definition of "network element" were reasonable and hence lawful under *Chevron U.S.A. Inc. v. Natural Resources Defense Council, Inc.*, 467 U.S. 837 (1984).

* * *

III

A

We turn next to the unbundling rules, and come first to the incumbent LECs' complaint that the FCC included within the features and services that must be provided to competitors under Rule 319 items that do not (as they must) meet the statutory definition of "network element"—namely, operator services and directory assistance, operational support systems (OSS), and vertical switching functions such as caller I.D., call forwarding, and call waiting. See 47 C.F.R. §§ 51.319(f)–(g) (1997). The statute defines "network element" as

> "a facility or equipment used in the provision of a telecommunications service. Such term also includes features, functions, and capabilities that are provided by means of such facility or equipment, including subscriber numbers, databases, signaling systems, and information sufficient for billing and collection or used in the transmission, routing, or other provision of a telecommunications service." 47 U.S.C. § 153(29).

Given the breadth of this definition, it is impossible to credit the incumbents' argument that a "network element" must be part of the physical facilities and equipment used to provide local phone service. Operator services and directory assistance, whether they involve live operators or automation, are "features, functions, and capabilities . . . provided by means of" the network equipment. OSS, the incumbent's background software system, contains essential network information as well as programs to manage billing, repair ordering, and other functions. Section 153(29)'s reference to "databases . . . and information sufficient for billing and collection or used in the transmission, routing, or other provision of a telecommunications service" provides ample basis for treating this system as a "network element." And vertical switching features, such as caller I. D., are "functions . . . provided by means of" the switch, and thus fall squarely within the statutory definition. We agree with the Eighth Circuit that the Commission's application of the "network element" definition is eminently reasonable. *See Chevron*, 467 U.S. at 866.

B

We are of the view, however, that the FCC did not adequately consider the "necessary and impair" standards when it gave blanket access to these network elements, and others, in Rule 319. That Rule requires an incumbent to provide requesting carriers with access to a minimum of seven network elements: the local loop, the network interface device, switching capability, interoffice transmission facilities, signaling networks and call-related data bases, operations support systems functions, and operator services and directory assistance. If a requesting carrier wants access to additional elements, it may petition the state commission, which can make other elements available on a case-by-case basis.

Section 251(d)(2) of the Act provides:

"In determining what network elements should be made available for purposes of subsection (c)(3) of this section, the Commission shall consider, at a minimum, whether—

"(A) access to such network elements as are proprietary in nature is necessary; and

"(B) the failure to provide access to such network elements would impair the ability of the telecommunications carrier seeking access to provide the services that it seeks to offer."

The incumbents argue that § 251(d)(2) codifies something akin to the "essential facilities" doctrine of antitrust theory, opening up only those "bottleneck" elements unavailable elsewhere in the marketplace. We need not decide whether, as a matter of law, the 1996 Act requires the FCC to apply *that* standard; it may be that some other standard would provide an equivalent or better criterion for the limitation upon network-element availability that the statute has in mind. But we do agree with the incumbents that the Act requires the FCC to apply *some* limiting standard, rationally related to the goals of the Act, which it has simply failed to do. In the general statement of its methodology set forth in the First Report and Order, the Commission announced that it would regard the "necessary" standard as having been met regardless of whether "requesting carriers can obtain the requested proprietary element from a source other than the incumbent," since "[r]equiring new entrants to duplicate unnecessarily even a part of the incumbent's network could generate delay and higher costs for new entrants, and thereby impede entry by competing local providers and delay competition, contrary to the goals of the 1996 Act." *In re Implementation of the Local Competition Provisions in the Telecomm. Act of 1996*, ¶ 283, 11 F.C.C. Rcd. 15499 (First Report & Order). And it announced that it would regard the "impairment" standard as having been met if "the failure of an incumbent to provide access to a network element would decrease the quality, or increase the financial or administrative cost of the service a requesting carrier seeks to offer, compared with providing that service *over other unbundled elements in the incumbent LEC's network*," id. ¶ 285 (emphasis added)—which means that comparison with self-provision, or with purchasing from another provider, is excluded. Since any entrant will request the most efficient network element that the incumbent has to offer, it is hard to imagine when the incumbent's failure to give access to the element would not constitute an "impairment" under this standard. The Commission asserts that it deliberately limited its inquiry to the incumbent's own network because no rational entrant would seek access to network elements from an incumbent if it could get better service or prices elsewhere. That may be. But that judgment allows entrants, rather than the Commission, to determine whether access to proprietary elements is necessary, and whether the failure to obtain access to nonproprietary elements would impair the ability to provide services. The Commission cannot, consistent with the statute, blind itself to the availability of elements outside the incumbent's network. That failing alone would require the Commission's rule to be set aside. In addition, however, the Commission's assumption that any increase in cost (or decrease in quality) imposed by denial of a network element renders access to that element "necessary," and causes the failure to provide that element to "impair" the entrant's ability to furnish its desired services, is simply not in accord with the ordinary and fair meaning of those terms. An entrant whose anticipated annual profits from the proposed service are reduced from 100% of investment to 99% of investment has perhaps been "impaired" in its ability to amass earnings, but has not *ipso facto* been "impair[ed] . . . in its ability to provide the services it seeks to offer"; and it cannot realistically be said that the network element enabling it to raise its profits to 100% is "necessary." In a world of perfect competition, in which all carriers are providing their service at marginal cost, the Commission's total equating of increased cost (or decreased quality) with "necessity" and "impairment" might be reasonable; but it has not established the existence of such an ideal world. We cannot avoid the conclusion that, if Congress had wanted to give blanket access to incumbents' networks on a basis as unrestricted as the scheme the Commission has come up with, it would not have included § 251(d)(2) in the statute at all. It would simply have said (as the Commission in effect has) that whatever requested element can be provided must be provided.

When the full record of these proceedings is examined, it appears that that is precisely what the Commission *thought* Congress had said. The FCC was content with its expansive methodology because of its misunderstanding of § 251(c)(3), which directs an incumbent to allow a requesting carrier access to its network elements "at any technically feasible point." The Commission interpreted this to "impos[e] on an incumbent LEC *the duty to provide all network elements for which it is technically feasible to provide access*," and went on to "conclude that we have authority to establish regulations that are coextensive" with this duty. First Report & Order ¶ 278 (emphasis added). As the Eighth Circuit held, that was undoubtedly wrong: Section 251(c)(3) indicates "where unbundled access must occur, not *which* [network] elements must be unbundled." The Commission does not seek review of the Eighth Circuit's holding on this point, and we bring it into our discussion only because the Commission's application of § 251(d)(2) was colored by this error. The Commission began with the premise that an incumbent was obliged to turn over as much of its network as was "technically feasible," and viewed subsection (d)(2) as merely permitting it to soften that obligation by regulatory grace:

> "To give effect to both sections 251(c)(3) and 251(d)(2), we conclude that the proprietary and impairment standards in section 251(d)(2) grant us the authority to refrain from requiring incumbent LECs to provide all network elements for which it is technically feasible to provide access on an unbundled basis."

The Commission's premise was wrong. Section 251(d)(2) does not authorize the Commission to create isolated exemptions from some underlying duty to make all network elements available. It requires the Commission to determine on a rational basis *which* network elements must be made available, taking into account the objectives of the Act and giving some substance to the "necessary" and "impair" requirements. The latter is not achieved by disregarding entirely the availability of elements outside the network, and by regarding *any* "increased cost or decreased service quality" as establishing a "necessity" and an "impair[ment]" of the ability to "provide . . . services."

The Commission generally applied the above described methodology as it considered the various network elements *seriatim*. Though some of these sections contain statements suggesting that the Commission's action might be supported by a higher standard, no other standard is consistently applied and we must assume that the Commission's expansive methodology governed throughout. Because the Commission has not interpreted the terms of the statute in a reasonable fashion, we must vacate 47 CFR § 51.319 (1997).

* * *

It would be gross understatement to say that the 1996 Act is not a model of clarity. It is in many important respects a model of ambiguity or indeed even self-contradiction. That is most unfortunate for a piece of legislation that profoundly affects a crucial segment of the economy worth tens of billions of dollars. The 1996 Act can be read to grant (borrowing a phrase from incumbent GTE) "most promiscuous rights" to the FCC vis-à-vis the state commissions and to competing carriers vis-à-vis the incumbents—and the Commission has chosen in some instances to read it that way. But Congress is well aware that the ambiguities it chooses to produce in a statute will be resolved by the implementing agency, *see Chevron*, 467 U.S. at 842–43. We can only enforce the clear limits that the 1996 Act contains, which in the present cases invalidate only Rule 319.

■ JUSTICE O'CONNOR took no part in the consideration or decision of these cases.

■ JUSTICE SOUTER, concurring in part and dissenting in part.

I agree with the Court's holding that the Federal Communications Commission has authority to implement and interpret the disputed provisions of the Telecommunications Act of 1996, and that deference is due to the Commission's reasonable interpretation under *Chevron*. I disagree with the Court's holding that the Commission was unreasonable in its interpretation of 47 U.S.C. § 251(d)(2), which requires it to consider whether competitors' access to network elements owned by local exchange carriers (LECs) is "necessary" and whether failure to provide access to such elements would "impair" competitors' ability to provide services. Because I think that, under *Chevron*, the Commission reasonably interpreted its duty to consider necessity and impairment, I respectfully dissent from Part III–B of the Court's opinion.

The statutory provision in question specifies that in determining what network elements should be made available on an unbundled basis to potential competitors of the LECs, the Commission "shall consider" whether "access to such network elements as are proprietary in nature is necessary," § 251(d)(2)(A), and whether "the failure to provide access" to network elements "would impair the ability of the telecommunications carrier seeking access to provide the services that it seeks to offer," § 251(d)(2)(B). The Commission interpreted "necessary" to mean "prerequisite for competition," in the sense that without access to certain proprietary network elements, competitors' "ability to compete would be significantly impaired or thwarted." First Report & Order, ¶ 282. On this basis, it decided to require access to such elements unless the incumbent LEC could prove both that the requested network element was proprietary and that the requesting competitor could offer the same service through the use of another, nonproprietary element offered by the incumbent LEC.

The Commission interpreted "impair" to mean "diminished in value," and explained that a potential competitor's ability to offer services would diminish in value when the quality of those services would decline or their price rise, absent the element in question. *Id.* ¶ 285. The Commission chose to apply this standard "by evaluating whether a carrier could offer a service using other unbundled elements within an incumbent LEC's network," *id.*, and decided that whenever it would be more expensive for a competitor to offer a service using other available network elements, or whenever the service offered using those other elements would be of lower quality, the LEC must offer the desired element to the competitor.

In practice, as the Court observes, the Commission's interpretation will probably allow a competitor to obtain access to any network element that it wants; a competitor is unlikely in fact to want an element that would be economically unjustifiable, and a weak economic justification will do. Under *Chevron*, the only question before us is whether the Commission's interpretation, obviously favorable to potential competitors, falls outside the bounds of reasonableness.

As a matter of textual justification, certainly, the Commission is not to be faulted. The words "necessary" and "impair" are ambiguous in being susceptible to a fairly wide range of meanings, and doubtless can carry the meanings the Commission identified. If I want to replace a light bulb, I would be within an ordinary and fair meaning of the word "necessary" to say that a stepladder is "necessary" to install the bulb, even though I could stand instead on a chair, a milk can, or eight volumes of Gibbon. I could just as easily say that the want of a ladder would "impair" my ability to install the bulb under the same circumstances. These examples use the concepts of necessity and impairment in what might be called their weak senses, but these are unquestionably still ordinary uses of the words.

Accordingly, the Court goes too far when it says that under "the ordinary and fair meaning" of "necessary" and "impair," "[a]n entrant whose anticipated annual profits from the proposed service are reduced from 100% of investment to 99% of investment . . . has not *ipso facto* been 'impair[ed] . . . in its ability to provide the services it seeks to offer'; and it cannot realistically be said that the network element enabling it to raise profits to 100% is 'necessary.'" A service is surely "necessary" to my business in an ordinary, weak sense of necessity when that service would allow me to realize more profits, and a business can be said to be "impaired" in delivery of services in an ordinary, weak sense of impairment when something stops the business from getting the profit it wants for those services.

Not every choice of meaning that falls within the bounds of textual ambiguity is necessarily reasonable, to be sure, but the Court's appeal to broader statutory policy comes up short in my judgment. The Court says, with some intuitive plausibility, that "the Act requires the FCC to apply *some* limiting standard, rationally related to the goals of the Act, which it has simply failed to do." In the Court's eyes, the trouble with the Commission's interpretation is that it "allows entrants, rather than the Commission, to determine" necessity and impairment, and so the Court concludes that "if Congress had wanted to give blanket access to incumbents' networks on a basis as unrestricted as the scheme the Commission has come up with, it would not have included § 251(d)(2) in the statute at all."

The Court thus judges the reasonableness of the Commission's rule for implementing § 251(d)(2) by asking how likely it is that Congress would have legislated at all if its point in adopting the criteria of necessity and impairment was to do no more than require economic rationality, and the Court answers that the Commission's notion of the congressional objective in using the ambiguous language is just too modest to be reasonable. The persuasiveness of the Court's answer to its question, however, rests on overlooking the very different question that the Commission was obviously answering when it adopted Rule 319. As the Court itself notes, the Commission explicitly addressed the consequences that would follow from requiring an entrant to satisfy the necessity and impairment criteria by showing that alternative facilities were unavailable at reasonable cost from anyone except the incumbent LEC. To require that kind of a showing, the Commission said, would encourage duplication of facilities and personnel, with obvious systemic costs. The Commission, in other words, was approaching the task of giving reasonable interpretations to "necessary" and "impair" by asking whether Congress would have mandated economic inefficiency as a limit on the objective of encouraging competition through ease of market entry. The Commission concluded, without any apparent implausibility, that the answer was no, and proceeded to implement the necessity and impairment provisions in accordance with that answer.

Before we conclude that the Commission's reading of the statute was unreasonable, therefore, we have to do more than simply ask whether Congress would probably have legislated the necessity and impairment criteria in their weak senses. We have to ask whether the Commission's further question is an irrelevant one, and (if it is not), whether the Commission's answer is reasonably defensible. If the question is sensible and the answer fair, *Chevron* deference surely requires us to respect the Commission's conclusion. This is so regardless of whether the answer to the Commission's question points in a different direction from the answer to the Court's question; there is no apparent reason why deference to the agency should not extend to the agency's choice in responding to mutually ill-fitting clues to congressional meaning. This, indeed, is surely a classic case for such deference, the statute here being infected not only with "ambiguity" but even "self-contradiction." I would accordingly respect the Commission's choice to give primacy to the question it chose.

■ [Opinions of JUSTICE THOMAS, with whom THE CHIEF JUSTICE and JUSTICE BREYER joined, concurring in part and dissenting in part, and of JUSTICE BREYER, concurring in part and dissenting in part, are omitted. Ed.]

NOTES AND QUESTIONS

1. Writing for the majority in *Iowa Utilities Board*, Justice Scalia pointedly did not articulate and require the agency to follow a particular definition of "necessary" and "impair" under § 251(d) of the Telecommunications Act of 1996. Rather, he concluded that those terms served a limiting function in the context of the statute and that the FCC could adopt a variety of rules that accomplished such a purpose, but that the rules at bar failed in that regard. Justice Souter, by contrast, had little difficulty identifying finding that the FCC's existing rules served as an actual, if weak, limitation that was reasonably consistent with statutory purposes. Do you think that, despite his protestations to the contrary, Justice Scalia in fact had a particular definition of "necessary" and "impair" in mind? Do you find the majority's opinion consistent with *Chevron*'s instruction that the courts should defer to reasonable agency legal interpretations? If you represent the FCC—you need rules dictating which features and services local exchange carriers must make available to their competitors, and your rules have been invalidated as insufficiently limiting, but the Court does not tell you exactly what interpretation will pass muster—what do you do now?

2. In *Iowa Utilities Board*, both the majority opinion written by Justice Scalia and Justice Souter writing separately evaluate the FCC's interpretation of the statute using the same sorts of tools that the Court ordinarily employs at *Chevron* step one, particularly statutory text, structure, and purpose. One way of thinking about *Chevron*'s step two in general is to reason that, if a reviewing court has concluded at step one that a statute is ambiguous, i.e., susceptible of more than one reasonable interpretation, then the role of the court at step two is to evaluate whether the construction adopted by the agency falls within or outside the range of permissible alternatives. Under this view, *Chevron*'s second step is as much a statutory inquiry as its first step, involving all the same possible tools for discerning statutory meaning: statutory text and purpose, legislative history, etc. Only the nature of the inquiry has changed, essentially from looking for the "right" answer to assessing plausibility under the statute.

3. Critics of a statutory approach to *Chevron* step two contend that, in reality, rather than merely confining their initial inquiry to discerning whether the statute is ambiguous, reviewing courts already compare the agency's interpretation with the statute at Chevron step one. In other words, these critics argue, the step one inquiry really asks whether or not the statute permits or rejects the agency's interpretation, rendering a statutory inquiry at *Chevron* step two superfluous. *See* M. Elizabeth Magill, *Step Two of* Chevron v. Natural Resources Defense Council, in A GUIDE TO JUDICIAL AND POLITICAL REVIEW OF FEDERAL AGENCIES 85, 90–93 (John F. Duffy & Michael Herz eds., 2005). Of course, those who advance this criticism presumably believe that courts consider legislative history at *Chevron* step one, which some courts have refused to do. Thinking back on what you have learned about the disagreements over the *Chevron* step one inquiry, do you find this criticism of a statutory approach to *Chevron* step two persuasive? Why or why not? If you agree with those who reject a statutory approach to *Chevron* step two as redundant, then what do you think a reviewing court should do at *Chevron* step two?

Rapanos v. United States

547 U.S. 715 (2006).

■ JUSTICE SCALIA announced the judgment of the Court and delivered and opinion, in which THE CHIEF JUSTICE, JUSTICE THOMAS, and JUSTICE ALITO join.

In April 1989, petitioner John A. Rapanos backfilled wetlands on a parcel of land in Michigan that he owned and sought to develop. This parcel included 54 acres of land with sometimes-saturated soil conditions. The nearest body of navigable water was 11 to 20 miles away. Regulators had informed Mr. Rapanos that his saturated fields were "waters of the United States," 33 U.S.C. § 1362(7), that could not be filled without a permit. Twelve years of criminal and civil litigation ensued.

The burden of federal regulation on those who would deposit fill material in locations denominated "waters of the United States" is not trivial. In deciding whether to grant or deny a permit, the U.S. Army Corps of Engineers (Corps) exercises the discretion of an enlightened despot, relying on such factors as "economics," "aesthetics," "recreation," and "in general, the needs and welfare of the people," 33 C.F.R. § 320.4(a) (2004). The average applicant for an individual permit spends 788 days and $271,596 in completing the process, and the average applicant for a nationwide permit spends 313 days and $28,915—not counting costs of mitigation or design changes. Sunding & Zilberman, *The Economics of Environmental Regulation by Licensing: An Assessment of Recent Changes to the Wetland Permitting Process*, 42 NAT. RESOURCES J. 59, 74–76 (2002). "[O]ver $1.7 billion is spent each year by the private and public sectors obtaining wetlands permits." *Id.* at 81. These costs cannot be avoided, because the Clean Water Act "impose[s] criminal liability," as well as steep civil fines, "on a broad range of ordinary industrial and commercial activities." *Hanousek v. United States*, 528 U.S. 1102, 1103 (2000) (Thomas, J., dissenting from denial of certiorari). In this litigation, for example, for backfilling his own wet fields, Mr. Rapanos faced 63 months in prison and hundreds of thousands of dollars in criminal and civil fines.

The enforcement proceedings against Mr. Rapanos are a small part of the immense expansion of federal regulation of land use that has occurred under the Clean Water Act—without any change in the governing statute—during the past five Presidential administrations. In the last three decades, the Corps and the Environmental Protection Agency (EPA) have interpreted their jurisdiction over "the waters of the United States" to cover 270-to-300 million acres of swampy lands in the United States—including half of Alaska and an area the size of California in the lower 48 States. And that was just the beginning. The Corps has also asserted jurisdiction over virtually any parcel of land containing a channel or conduit—whether man-made or natural, broad or narrow, permanent or ephemeral—through which rainwater or drainage may occasionally or intermittently flow. On this view, the federally regulated "waters of the United States" include storm drains, roadside ditches, ripples of sand in the desert that may contain water once a year, and lands that are covered by floodwaters once every 100 years. Because they include the land containing storm sewers and desert washes, the statutory "waters of the United States" engulf entire cities and immense arid wastelands. In fact, the entire land area of the United States lies in some drainage basin, and an endless network of visible channels furrows the entire surface, containing water ephemerally wherever the rain falls. Any plot of land containing such a channel may potentially be regulated as a "water of the United States."

I

Congress passed the Clean Water Act (CWA or Act) in 1972. The Act's stated objective is "to restore and maintain the chemical, physical, and biological integrity of the Nation's waters." 33 U.S.C. § 1251(a). The Act also states that "[i]t is the policy of Congress to recognize, preserve, and protect the primary responsibilities and rights of States to prevent, reduce, and eliminate pollution, to plan the development and use (including restoration, preservation, and enhancement) of land and water resources, and to consult with the Administrator in the exercise of his authority under this chapter." § 1251(b).

One of the statute's principal provisions is 33 U.S.C. § 1311(a), which provides that "the discharge of any pollutant by any person shall be unlawful." "The discharge of a pollutant" is defined broadly to include "any addition of any pollutant to navigable waters from any point source," § 1362(12), and "pollutant" is defined broadly to include not only traditional contaminants but also solids such as "dredged spoil, . . . rock, sand, [and] cellar dirt," § 1362(6). And, most relevant here, the CWA defines "navigable waters" as "the waters of the United States, including the territorial seas." § 1362(7).

The Act also provides certain exceptions to its prohibition of "the discharge of any pollutant by any person." § 1311(a). Section 1342(a) authorizes the Administrator of the EPA to "issue a permit for the discharge of any pollutant, . . . notwithstanding section 1311(a) of this title." Section 1344 authorizes the Secretary of the Army, acting through the Corps, to "issue permits . . . for the discharge of dredged or fill material into the navigable waters at specified disposal sites." § 1344(a), (d). It is the discharge of "dredged or fill material"—which, unlike traditional water pollutants, are solids that do not readily wash downstream—that we consider today.

For a century prior to the CWA, we had interpreted the phrase "navigable waters of the United States" in the Act's predecessor statutes to refer to interstate waters that are "navigable in fact" or readily susceptible of being rendered so. *The Daniel Ball*, 77 U.S. (10 Wall.) 557, 563 (1871); *see also United States v. Appalachian Elec. Power Co.*, 311 U.S. 377, 406 (1940). After passage of the CWA, the Corps initially adopted this traditional judicial definition for the Act's term "navigable waters." After a District Court enjoined these regulations as too narrow, the Corps adopted a far broader definition. The Corps' new regulations deliberately sought to extend the definition of "the waters of the United States" to the outer limits of Congress's commerce power. *See* 42 Fed. Reg. 37144, 37144, n.2 (1977).

The Corps' current regulations interpret "the waters of the United States" to include, in addition to traditional interstate navigable waters, 33 C.F.R. § 328.3(a)(1) (2004), "[a]ll interstate waters including interstate wetlands," § 328.3(a)(2); "[a]ll other waters such as intrastate lakes, rivers, streams (including intermittent streams), mudflats, sandflats, wetlands, sloughs, prairie potholes, wet meadows, playa lakes, or natural ponds, the use, degradation or destruction of which could affect interstate or foreign commerce," § 328.3(a)(3); "[t]ributaries of [such] waters," § 328.3(a)(5); and "[w]etlands adjacent to [such] waters [and tributaries] (other than waters that are themselves wetlands)," § 328.3(a)(7). The regulation defines "adjacent" wetlands as those "bordering, contiguous [to], or neighboring" waters of the United States. § 328.3(c). It specifically provides that "[w]etlands separated from other waters of the United States by man-made dikes or barriers, natural river berms, beach dunes and the like are 'adjacent wetlands.' " *Id.*

We first addressed the proper interpretation of 33 U.S.C. § 1362(7)'s phrase "the waters of the United States" in *United States v. Riverside Bayview Homes, Inc.*, 474 U.S. 121 (1985). That case concerned a wetland that "was adjacent to a body of navigable water," because "the area characterized by saturated soil conditions and wetland vegetation extended beyond the boundary of respondent's property to . . . a navigable waterway." *Id.* at 131. Noting that "the transition from water to solid ground is not necessarily or even typically an abrupt one," and that "the Corps must necessarily choose some point at which water ends and land begins," *id.* at 132, we upheld the Corps' interpretation of "the waters of the United States" to include wetlands that "actually abut[ted] on" traditional navigable waters. *Id.* at 135.

Following our decision in *Riverside Bayview*, the Corps adopted increasingly broad interpretations of its own regulations under the Act. For example, in 1986, to "clarify" the reach of its jurisdiction, the Corps announced the so-called "Migratory Bird Rule," which purported to extend its jurisdiction to any intrastate waters "[w]hich are or would be used as habitat" by migratory birds. 51 Fed. Reg. 41217. In addition, the Corps interpreted its own regulations to include "ephemeral streams" and "drainage ditches" as "tributaries" that are part of the "waters of the United States," *see* 33 C.F.R. § 328.3(a)(5), provided that they have a perceptible "ordinary high water mark" as defined in § 328.3(e). 65 Fed. Reg. 12823 (2000). This interpretation extended "the waters of the United States" to virtually any land feature over which rainwater or drainage passes and leaves a visible mark—even if only "the presence of litter and debris." 33 C.F.R. § 328.3(e). Prior to our decision in *Solid Waste Agency of Northern Cook County v. Army Corps. of Engineers*, 531 U.S. 159 (2001) (SWANCC), lower courts upheld the application of this expansive definition of "tributaries" to such entities as storm sewers that contained flow to covered waters during heavy rainfall, *United States v. Eidson*, 108 F.3d 1336, 1340–42 (11th Cir. 1997), and dry arroyos connected to remote waters through the flow of groundwater over "centuries," *Quivira Mining Co. v. EPA*, 765 F.2d 126, 129 (10th Cir. 1985).

In *SWANCC*, we considered the application of the Corps' "Migratory Bird Rule" to "an abandoned sand and gravel pit in northern Illinois." 531 U.S. at 162. Observing that "[i]t was the *significant nexus* between the wetlands and 'navigable waters' that informed our reading of the CWA in *Riverside Bayview*," *id.* at 167 (emphasis added), we held that *Riverside Bayview* did not establish "that the jurisdiction of the Corps extends to ponds that are not adjacent to open water," *id.* at 168 (emphasis deleted). On the contrary, we held that "nonnavigable, isolated, intrastate waters," *id.* at 171—which, unlike the wetlands at issue in *Riverside Bayview*, did not "actually abu[t] on a navigable waterway," *id.* at 167—were not included as "waters of the United States."

Following our decision in *SWANCC*, the Corps did not significantly revise its theory of federal jurisdiction under § 1344(a). The Corps provided notice of a proposed rulemaking in light of *SWANCC*, but ultimately did not amend its published regulations. Because *SWANCC* did not directly address tributaries, the Corps notified its field staff that they "should continue to assert jurisdiction over traditional navigable waters . . . and, generally speaking, their tributary systems (and adjacent wetlands)." 68 Fed. Reg. 1998. In addition, because *SWANCC* did not overrule *Riverside Bayview*, the Corps continues to assert jurisdiction over waters " 'neighboring' " traditional navigable waters and their tributaries. 68 Fed. Reg. 1997 (quoting 33 C.F.R. § 328.3(c) (2002)).

Even after *SWANCC*, the lower courts have continued to uphold the Corps' sweeping assertions of jurisdiction over ephemeral channels and drains as "tributaries." For example, courts have held that jurisdictional "tributaries" include the "intermittent flow of surface water through approximately 2.4 miles of natural streams and manmade ditches (paralleling and crossing under I-64)," *Treacy v. Newdunn Ass'n*, 344 F.3d 407, 410 (4th Cir. 2003); a "roadside ditch" whose water took "a winding, thirty-two-mile path to the Chesapeake Bay," *United States v. Deaton*, 332 F.3d 698, 702 (4th Cir. 2003); irrigation ditches and drains that intermittently connect to covered waters, *Cmty. Ass'n for Restoration of Env't v. Henry Bosma Dairy*, 305 F.3d 943, 954–55 (9th Cir. 2002); *Headwaters, Inc. v. Talent Irrigation Dist.*, 243 F.3d 526, 534 (9th Cir. 2001); and (most implausibly of all) the "washes and arroyos" of an "arid development site," located in the middle of the desert, through which "water courses . . . during periods of heavy rain," *Save Our Sonoran, Inc. v. Flowers*, 408 F.3d 1113, 1118 (9th Cir. 2005).

These judicial constructions of "tributaries" are not outliers. Rather, they reflect the breadth of the Corps' determinations in the field. The Corps' enforcement practices vary somewhat from district to district because "the definitions used to make jurisdictional determinations" are deliberately left "vague." GAO Report 26. But district offices of the Corps have treated, as "waters of the United States," such typically dry land features as "arroyos, coulees, and washes," as well as other "channels that might have little water flow in a given year." *Id.* at 20–21. They have also applied that definition to such man-made, intermittently flowing features as "drain tiles, storm drains systems, and culverts." *Id.* at 24 (footnote omitted).

In addition to "tributaries," the Corps and the lower courts have also continued to define "adjacent" wetlands broadly after *SWANCC*. For example, some of the Corps' district offices have concluded that wetlands are "adjacent" to covered waters if they are hydrologically connected "through directional sheet flow during storm events," GAO Report 18, or if they lie within the "100-year floodplain" of a body of water—that is, they are connected to the navigable water by flooding, on average, once every 100 years. *Id.* at 17. Others have concluded that presence within 200 feet of a tributary automatically renders a wetland "adjacent" and jurisdictional. *Id.* at 19. And the Corps has successfully defended such theories of "adjacency" in the courts, even after *SWANCC*'s excision of "isolated" waters and wetlands from the Act's coverage. One court has held since *SWANCC* that wetlands separated from flood control channels by 70-foot-wide berms, atop which ran maintenance roads, had a "significant nexus" to covered waters because, *inter alia*, they lay "within the 100 year floodplain of tidal waters." *Baccarat Fremont Developers, LLC v. Army Corps of Engineers*, 425 F.3d 1150, 1152, 1157 (9th Cir. 2005). In one of the cases before us today, the Sixth Circuit held, in agreement with "[t]he majority of courts," that "while a hydrological connection between the non-navigable and navigable waters is required, there is no 'direct abutment' requirement" under *SWANCC* for "'adjacency.'" And even the most insubstantial hydrologic connection may be held to constitute a "significant nexus." One court distinguished *SWANCC* on the ground that "a molecule of water residing in one of these pits or ponds [in *SWANCC*] could not mix with molecules from other bodies of water"— whereas, in the case before it, "water molecules currently present in the wetlands will inevitably flow towards and mix with water from connecting bodies," and "[a] drop of rainwater landing in the Site is certain to intermingle with water from the [nearby river]." *United States v. Rueth Dev. Co.*, 189 F.Supp.2d 874, 877–78 (N.D. Ind. 2002).

II

In these consolidated cases, we consider whether four Michigan wetlands, which lie near ditches or man-made drains that eventually empty into traditional navigable waters, constitute "waters of the United States" within the meaning of the Act. Petitioners deposited fill material without a permit into wetlands on three sites near Midland, Michigan: the "Salzburg site," the "Hines Road site," and the "Pine River site." The wetlands at the Salzburg site are connected to a man-made drain, which drains into Hoppler Creek, which flows into the Kawkawlin River, which empties into Saginaw Bay and Lake Huron. The wetlands at the Hines Road site are connected to something called the "Rose Drain," which has a surface connection to the Tittabawassee River. And the wetlands at the Pine River site have a surface connection to the Pine River, which flows into Lake Huron. It is not clear whether the connections between these wetlands and the nearby drains and ditches are continuous or intermittent, or whether the nearby drains and ditches contain continuous or merely occasional flows of water.

The United States brought civil enforcement proceedings against the Rapanos petitioners. The District Court found that the three described wetlands were "within federal jurisdiction" because they were "'adjacent to other waters of the United States,'" and held petitioners liable for violations of the CWA at those sites. On appeal, the United States Court of Appeals for the Sixth Circuit affirmed, holding that there was federal jurisdiction over the wetlands at all three sites because "there were hydrological connections between all three sites and corresponding adjacent tributaries of navigable waters."

* * *

We granted certiorari and consolidated the cases to decide whether these wetlands constitute "waters of the United States" under the Act, and if so, whether the Act is constitutional.

III

The Rapanos petitioners contend that the terms "navigable waters" and "waters of the United States" in the Act must be limited to the traditional definition of *The Daniel Ball*, which required that the "waters" be navigable in fact, or susceptible of being rendered so. But this definition cannot be applied wholesale to the CWA. The Act uses the phrase "navigable waters" as a *defined* term, and the definition is simply "the waters of the United States." 33 U.S.C. § 1362(7). Moreover, the Act provides, in certain circumstances, for the substitution of state for federal jurisdiction over "navigable waters . . . *other than* those waters which are presently used, or are susceptible to use in their natural condition or by reasonable improvement as a means to transport interstate or foreign commerce . . . including wetlands adjacent thereto." § 1344(g)(1) (emphasis added). This provision shows that the Act's term "navigable waters" includes something more than traditional navigable waters. We have twice stated that the meaning of "navigable waters" in the Act is broader than the traditional understanding of that term, *SWANCC*, 531 U.S. at 167; *Riverside Bayview*, 474 U.S. at 133. We have also emphasized, however, that the qualifier "navigable" is not devoid of significance, *SWANCC*, 531 U.S. at 172.

We need not decide the precise extent to which the qualifiers "navigable" and "of the United States" restrict the coverage of the Act. Whatever the scope of these qualifiers, the CWA authorizes federal jurisdiction only over "waters." 33 U.S.C. § 1362(7). The only natural definition of the term "waters," our prior and subsequent judicial constructions of it, clear evidence from other provisions of the statute, and this Court's canons of construction all confirm that "the waters of the United States" in § 1362(7) cannot bear the expansive meaning that the Corps would give it.

The Corps' expansive approach might be arguable if the CWA defined "navigable waters" as "water of the United States." But "the waters of the United States" is something else. The use of the definite article ("the") and the plural number ("waters") shows plainly that § 1362(7) does not refer to water in general. In this form, "the waters" refers more narrowly to water "[a]s found in streams and bodies forming geographical features such as oceans, rivers, [and] lakes," or "the flowing or moving masses, as of waves or floods, making up such streams or bodies." WEBSTER'S NEW INTERNATIONAL DICTIONARY 2882 (2d ed.1954) (hereinafter WEBSTER'S SECOND). On this definition, "the waters of the United States" include only relatively permanent, standing or flowing bodies of water. The definition refers to water as found in "streams," "oceans," "rivers," "lakes," and "bodies" of water "forming geographical features." All of these terms connote continuously present, fixed bodies of water, as opposed to ordinarily dry channels through which water occasionally or intermittently flows. Even the least substantial of the definition's terms, namely, "streams," connotes a continuous flow of water in a permanent channel—especially when used in company with other terms such as "rivers," "lakes," and "oceans." None of these terms encompasses transitory puddles or ephemeral flows of water.

The restriction of "the waters of the United States" to exclude channels containing merely intermittent or ephemeral flow also accords with the commonsense understanding of the term. In applying the definition to "ephemeral streams," "wet meadows," storm sewers and culverts, "directional sheet flow during storm events," drain tiles, man-made drainage ditches, and dry arroyos in the middle of the desert, the Corps has stretched the term "waters of the United States" beyond parody. The plain language of the statute simply does not authorize this "Land Is Waters" approach to federal jurisdiction.

In addition, the Act's use of the traditional phrase "navigable waters" (the defined term) further confirms that it confers jurisdiction only over relatively *permanent* bodies of water. The Act adopted that traditional term from its predecessor statutes. On the traditional understanding, "navigable waters" included only discrete *bodies* of water. For example, in *The Daniel Ball*, we used the terms "waters" and "rivers" interchangeably. 77 U.S. (10 Wall.) at 563. And in *Appalachian Electric*, we consistently referred to the "navigable waters" as "waterways." 311 U.S. at 407–09. Plainly, because such "waters" had to be navigable in fact or susceptible of being rendered so, the term did not include ephemeral flows. As we noted in *SWANCC*, the traditional term "navigable waters"—even though defined as "the waters of the United States"—carries *some* of its original substance: "[I]t is one thing to give a word limited effect and quite another to give it no effect whatever." 531 U.S. at 172. That limited effect includes, at bare minimum, the ordinary presence of water.

Our subsequent interpretation of the phrase "the waters of the United States" in the CWA likewise confirms this limitation of its scope. In *Riverside Bayview*, we stated that the phrase in the Act referred primarily to "rivers, streams, and other *hydrographic features more conventionally identifiable as 'waters'*" than the wetlands adjacent to such features. 474 U.S. at 131 (emphasis added). We thus echoed the dictionary definition of "waters" as referring to "streams and bodies *forming geographical features* such as oceans, rivers, [and] lakes." WEBSTER'S SECOND 2882. Though we upheld in that case the inclusion of wetlands abutting such a "hydrographic featur[e]"—principally due to the difficulty of drawing any clear boundary between the two—nowhere did we suggest that "the waters of the United States" should be expanded to include, in their own right, entities other than "hydrographic features more conventionally identifiable as 'waters.'" *Riverside Bayview*, 474 U.S. at 131. Likewise, in both *Riverside Bayview* and *SWANCC*, we repeatedly described the "navigable waters" covered by the Act as "open water" and "open waters." Under no rational interpretation are typically dry channels described as "*open* waters."

Most significant of all, the CWA itself categorizes the channels and conduits that typically carry intermittent flows of water separately from "navigable waters," by including them in the definition of " 'point source.' " The Act defines " 'point source' " as "any discernible, confined and discrete conveyance, including but not limited to any pipe, ditch, channel, tunnel, conduit, well, discrete fissure, container, rolling stock, concentrated animal feeding operation, or vessel or other floating craft, from which pollutants are or may be discharged." 33 U.S.C. § 1362(14). It also defines " 'discharge of a pollutant' " as "any addition of any pollutant to navigable waters *from* any point source." § 1362(12)(A). The definitions thus conceive of "point sources" and "navigable waters" as separate and distinct categories. The definition of "discharge" would make little sense if the two categories were significantly overlapping. The separate classification of "ditch[es], channel[s], and conduit[s]"— which are terms ordinarily used to describe the watercourses through which *intermittent* waters typically flow—shows that these are, by and large, *not* "waters of the United States."

Moreover, only the foregoing definition of "waters" is consistent with the CWA's stated "policy of Congress to recognize, preserve, and protect the primary responsibilities and rights of the States to prevent, reduce, and eliminate pollution, [and] to plan the development and use (including restoration, preservation, and enhancement) of land and water resources. . . ." § 1251(b). This statement of policy was included in the Act as enacted in 1972, prior to the addition of the optional state administration program in the 1977 amendments. Thus the policy plainly referred to something beyond the subsequently added state administration program of 33 U.S.C. § 1344(g)–(*l*). But the expansive theory advanced by the Corps, rather than "preserv[ing] the primary rights and responsibilities of the States," would have brought virtually all "plan[ning of] the development and use . . . of land and water resources" by the States under federal control. It is therefore an unlikely reading of the phrase "the waters of the United States."

Even if the phrase "the waters of the United States" were ambiguous as applied to intermittent flows, our own canons of construction would establish that the Corps' interpretation of the statute is impermissible. As we noted in *SWANCC*, the Government's expansive interpretation would "result in a significant impingement of the States' traditional and primary power over land and water use." 531 U.S. at 174. Regulation of land use, as through the issuance of the development permits sought by petitioners in both of these cases, is a quintessential state and local power. The extensive federal jurisdiction urged by the Government would authorize the Corps to function as a *de facto* regulator of immense stretches of intrastate land—an authority the agency has shown its willingness to exercise with the scope of discretion that would befit a local zoning board. *See* 33 C.F.R. § 320.4(a)(1) (2004). We ordinarily expect a "clear and manifest" statement from Congress to authorize an unprecedented intrusion into traditional state authority. *See BFP v. Resolution Trust Corp.*, 511 U.S. 531, 544 (1994). The phrase "the waters of the United States" hardly qualifies.

Likewise, just as we noted in *SWANCC*, the Corps' interpretation stretches the outer limits of Congress's commerce power and raises difficult questions about the ultimate scope of that power. (In developing the current regulations, the Corps consciously sought to extend its authority to the farthest reaches of the commerce power.) Even if the term "the waters of the United States" were ambiguous as applied to channels that sometimes host ephemeral flows of water (which it is not), we would expect a clearer statement from Congress to authorize an agency theory of jurisdiction that presses the envelope of constitutional validity.

In sum, on its only plausible interpretation, the phrase "the waters of the United States" includes only those relatively permanent, standing or continuously flowing bodies of water "forming geographic features" that are described in ordinary parlance as "streams[,] . . . oceans, rivers, [and] lakes." *See* WEBSTER'S SECOND 2882. The phrase does not include channels through which water flows intermittently or ephemerally, or channels that periodically provide drainage for rainfall. The Corps' expansive interpretation of the "the waters of the United States" is thus not "based on a permissible construction of the statute." *Chevron U.S.A. Inc. v. Natural Res. Def. Council, Inc.*, 467 U.S. 837, 843 (1984).

IV

* * *

[O]*nly* those wetlands with a continuous surface connection to bodies that are "waters of the United States" in their own right, so that there is no clear demarcation between "waters" and wetlands, are "adjacent to" such waters and covered by the Act. Wetlands with only an intermittent, physically remote hydrologic connection to "waters of the United States" do not implicate the boundary-drawing problem of *Riverside Bayview*, and thus lack the necessary connection to covered waters that we described as a "significant nexus" in *SWANCC*. 531 U.S. at 167. Thus, establishing that wetlands such as those at the Rapanos [site] are covered by the Act requires two findings: first, that the adjacent channel contains a "wate[r] of the United States," (*i.e.*, a relatively permanent body of water connected to traditional interstate navigable waters); and second, that the wetland has a continuous surface connection with that water, making it difficult to determine where the "water" ends and the "wetland" begins.

V

Respondents and their *amici* urge that such restrictions on the scope of "navigable waters" will frustrate enforcement against traditional water polluters under 33 U.S.C. §§ 1311 and 1342. Because the same definition of "navigable waters" applies to the entire statute, respondents contend that water polluters will be able to evade the permitting requirement of § 1342(a) simply by discharging their pollutants into noncovered intermittent watercourses that lie upstream of covered waters.

That is not so. Though we do not decide this issue, there is no reason to suppose that our construction today significantly affects the enforcement of § 1342, inasmuch as lower courts applying § 1342 have not characterized intermittent channels as "waters of the United States." The Act does not forbid the "addition of any pollutant *directly* to navigable waters from any point source," but rather the "addition of any pollutant to navigable waters." § 1362(12)(A) (emphasis added);

§ 1311(a). Thus, from the time of the CWA's enactment, lower courts have held that the discharge into intermittent channels of any pollutant *that naturally washes downstream* likely violates § 1311(a), even if the pollutants discharged from a point source do not emit "directly into" covered waters, but pass "through conveyances" in between.

In fact, many courts have held that such upstream, intermittently flowing channels themselves constitute "point sources" under the Act. The definition of "point source" includes "any pipe, ditch, channel, tunnel, conduit, well, discrete fissure, container, rolling stock, concentrated animal feeding operation, or vessel or other floating craft, from which pollutants are or may be discharged." 33 U.S.C. § 1362(14). We have held that the Act "makes plain that a point source need not be the original source of the pollutant; it need only convey the pollutant to 'navigable waters.'" *S. Fla. Water Mgmt. Dist. v. Miccosukee Tribe*, 541 U.S. 95, 105 (2004). Cases holding the intervening channel to be a point source include *United States v. Ortiz*, 427 F.3d 1278, 1281 (10th Cir. 2005) (a storm drain that carried flushed chemicals from a toilet to the Colorado River was a "point source"), and *Dague v. Burlington*, 935 F.2d 1343, 1354–55 (2d Cir. 1991) (a culvert connecting two bodies of navigable water was a "point source"). Some courts have even adopted both the "indirect discharge" rationale and the "point source" rationale in the alternative, applied to the same facts. *See, e.g., Concerned Area Residents for Env't v. Southview Farm*, 34 F.3d 114, 118–19 (2d Cir. 1994). On either view, however, the lower courts have seen no need to classify the intervening conduits as "waters of the United States."

In contrast to the pollutants normally covered by the permitting requirement of § 1342(a), "dredged or fill material," which is typically deposited for the sole purpose of staying put, does not normally wash downstream, and thus does not normally constitute an "addition . . . to navigable waters" when deposited in upstream isolated wetlands. §§ 1344(a), 1362(12). The Act recognizes this distinction by providing a separate permitting program for such discharges in § 1344(a). It does not appear, therefore, that the interpretation we adopt today significantly reduces the scope of § 1342.

Respondents also urge that the narrower interpretation of "waters" will impose a more difficult burden of proof in enforcement proceedings under §§ 1311(a) and 1342(a), by requiring the agency to demonstrate the downstream flow of the pollutant along the intermittent channel to traditional "waters." But, as noted above, the lower courts do not generally rely on characterization of intervening channels as "waters of the United States" in applying § 1311 to the traditional pollutants subject to § 1342. Moreover, the proof of downstream flow of pollutants required under § 1342 appears substantially similar, if not identical, to the proof of a hydrologic connection that would be required, on the Sixth Circuit's theory of jurisdiction, to prove that an upstream channel or wetland is a "wate[r] of the United States." In either case, the agency must prove that the contaminant-laden waters ultimately reach covered waters.

Finally, respondents and many *amici* admonish that narrowing the definition of "the waters of the United States" will hamper federal efforts to preserve the Nation's wetlands. It is not clear that the state and local conservation efforts that the CWA explicitly calls for are in any way inadequate for the goal of preservation. In any event, a Comprehensive National Wetlands Protection Act is not before us, and the "wis[dom]" of such a statute is beyond our ken. What is clear, however, is that Congress did not enact one when it granted the Corps jurisdiction over only "the *waters* of the United States."

VI

In an opinion long on praise of environmental protection and notably short on analysis of the statutory text and structure, the dissent would hold that "the waters of the United States" include any wetlands "adjacent" (no matter how broadly defined) to "tributaries" (again, no matter how broadly defined) of traditional navigable waters. For legal support of its policy-laden conclusion, the dissent relies exclusively on two sources: "[o]ur unanimous opinion in *Riverside Bayview*," and "Congress' deliberate acquiescence in the Corps' regulations in 1977." Each of these is demonstrably inadequate to support the apparently limitless scope that the dissent would permit the Corps to give to the Act.

* * *

In a curious appeal to entrenched executive error, the dissent contends that "the appropriateness of the Corps' 30-year implementation of the Clean Water Act should be addressed to Congress or the Corps rather than to the Judiciary." Surely this is a novel principle of administrative law—a sort of 30-year adverse possession that insulates disregard of statutory text from judicial review. It deservedly has no precedent in our jurisprudence. We did not invoke such a principle in *SWANCC*, when we invalidated one aspect of the Corps' implementation.

The dissent contends that "[b]ecause there is ambiguity in the phrase 'waters of the United States' and because interpreting it broadly to cover such ditches and streams advances the purpose of the Act, the Corps' approach should command our deference." Two defects in a single sentence: "[W]aters of the United States" is in *some* respects ambiguous. The *scope* of that ambiguity, however, does not conceivably extend to whether storm drains and dry ditches are "waters," and hence does not support the Corps' interpretation. And as for advancing "the purpose of the Act": We have often criticized that last resort of extravagant interpretation, noting that no law pursues its purpose at all costs, and that the textual limitations upon a law's scope are no less a part of its "purpose" than its substantive authorizations.

Finally, we could not agree more with the dissent's statement that "[w]hether the benefits of particular conservation measures outweigh their costs is a classic question of public policy that should not be answered by appointed judges." Neither, however, should it be answered by appointed officers of the Corps of Engineers in contradiction of congressional direction. It is the dissent's opinion, and not ours, which appeals not to a reasonable interpretation of enacted text, but to the great environmental benefits that a patently unreasonable interpretation can achieve. We have begun our discussion by mentioning, to be sure, the high costs imposed by that interpretation—but they are in no way the basis for our decision, which rests, plainly and simply, upon the limited meaning that can be borne by the phrase "waters of the United States."

■ CHIEF JUSTICE ROBERTS, concurring.

Five years ago, this Court rejected the position of the Army Corps of Engineers on the scope of its authority to regulate wetlands under the Clean Water Act. *SWANCC*, 531 U.S. 159 (2001). The Corps had taken the view that its authority was essentially limitless; this Court explained that such a boundless view was inconsistent with the limiting terms Congress had used in the Act.

In response to the *SWANCC* decision, the Corps and the Environmental Protection Agency (EPA) initiated a rulemaking to consider "issues associated with the scope of waters that are subject to the Clean Water Act (CWA), in light of the U.S. Supreme Court decision in *[SWANCC]*." 68 Fed. Reg. 1991 (2003). The "goal of the agencies" was "to develop proposed regulations that will further the public interest by clarifying what waters are subject to CWA jurisdiction and affording full protection to these waters through an appropriate focus of Federal and State resources consistent with the CWA." *Id.*

Agencies delegated rulemaking authority under a statute such as the Clean Water Act are afforded generous leeway by the courts in interpreting the statute they are entrusted to administer. *See Chevron U.S.A. Inc. v. Natural Res. Def. Council, Inc.*, 467 U.S. 837 (1984). Given the broad, somewhat ambiguous, but nonetheless clearly limiting terms Congress employed in the Clean Water Act, the Corps and the EPA would have enjoyed plenty of room to operate in developing *some* notion of an outer bound to the reach of their authority.

The proposed rulemaking went nowhere. Rather than refining its view of its authority in light of our decision in *SWANCC*, and providing guidance meriting deference under our generous standards, the Corps chose to adhere to its essentially boundless view of the scope of its power. The upshot today is another defeat for the agency.

It is unfortunate that no opinion commands a majority of the Court on precisely how to read Congress' limits on the reach of the Clean Water Act. Lower courts and regulated entities will now have to feel their way on a case-by-case basis. This situation is certainly not unprecedented. What is unusual in this instance, perhaps, is how readily the situation could have been avoided.

■ JUSTICE KENNEDY, concurring in the judgment.

These consolidated cases require the Court to decide whether the term "navigable waters" in the Clean Water Act extends to wetlands that do not contain and are not adjacent to waters that are navigable in fact. In *SWANCC*, the Court held, under the circumstances presented there, that to constitute " 'navigable waters' " under the Act, a water or wetland must possess a "significant nexus" to waters that are or were navigable in fact or that could reasonably be so made. *SWANCC*, 531 U.S. at 167, 172. In the instant cases neither the plurality opinion nor the dissent by Justice STEVENS chooses to apply this test; and though the Court of Appeals recognized the test's applicability, it did not consider all the factors necessary to determine whether the lands in question had, or did not have, the requisite nexus. In my view the cases ought to be remanded to the Court of Appeals for proper consideration of the nexus requirement.

I

Although both the plurality opinion and the dissent by Justice STEVENS (hereinafter the dissent) discuss the background of these cases in some detail, a further discussion of the relevant statutes, regulations, and facts may clarify the analysis suggested here.

[We have deleted Justice KENNEDY's lengthy discussion of the Court's precedents and critique of the plurality and dissenting opinions. Ed.]

* * *

Finally, it should go without saying that because the plurality presents its interpretation of the Act as the only permissible reading of the plain text, the Corps would lack discretion, under the plurality's theory, to adopt contrary regulations. THE CHIEF JUSTICE suggests that if the Corps and EPA had issued new regulations after *SWANCC* they would have "enjoyed plenty of room to operate in developing *some* notion of an outer bound to the reach of their authority" and thus could have avoided litigation of the issues we address today. That would not necessarily be true under the opinion THE CHIEF JUSTICE has joined. New rulemaking could have averted the disagreement here only if the Corps had anticipated the unprecedented reading of the Act that the plurality advances.

* * *

When the Corps seeks to regulate wetlands adjacent to navigable-in-fact waters, it may rely on adjacency to establish its jurisdiction. Absent more specific regulations, however, the Corps must establish a significant nexus on a case-by-case basis when it seeks to regulate wetlands based on adjacency to nonnavigable tributaries. Given the potential overbreadth of the Corps' regulations, this showing is necessary to avoid unreasonable applications of the statute. Where an adequate nexus is established for a particular wetland, it may be permissible, as a matter of administrative convenience or necessity, to presume covered status for other comparable wetlands in the region. That issue, however, is neither raised by these facts nor addressed by any agency regulation that accommodates the nexus requirement outlined here.

* * *

In these consolidated cases I would vacate the judgments of the Court of Appeals and remand for consideration whether the specific wetlands at issue possess a significant nexus with navigable waters.

■ [JUSTICE STEVENS'S lengthy dissenting opinion, critiquing the plurality opinion and defending the agency's interpretation, is omitted. Ed.]

■ JUSTICE BREYER, dissenting.

In my view, the authority of the Army Corps of Engineers under the Clean Water Act extends to the limits of congressional power to regulate interstate commerce. See *SWANCC*, 531 U.S. 159, 181–82 (2001) (Stevens, J., dissenting). I therefore have no difficulty finding that the wetlands at issue in these cases are within the Corps' jurisdiction, and I join Justice STEVENS' dissenting opinion.

My view of the statute rests in part upon the nature of the problem. The statute seeks to "restore and maintain the chemical, physical, and biological integrity of the Nation's waters." 33 U.S.C. § 1251(a). Those waters are so various and so intricately interconnected that Congress might well have decided the only way to achieve this goal is to write a statute that defines "waters" broadly and to leave the enforcing agency with the task of restricting the scope of that definition, either wholesale through regulation or retail through development permissions. That is why I believe that Congress, in using the term "waters of the United States," § 1362(7), intended fully to exercise its relevant Commerce Clause powers.

I mention this because the Court, contrary to my view, has written a "nexus" requirement into the statute. But it has left the administrative powers of the Army Corps of Engineers untouched. That agency may write regulations defining the term—something that it has not yet done. And the courts must give those regulations appropriate deference. *Chevron U.S.A. Inc. v. Natural Res. Def. Council, Inc.*, 467 U.S. 837 (1984).

If one thing is clear, it is that Congress intended the Army Corps of Engineers to make the complex technical judgments that lie at the heart of the present cases (subject to deferential judicial review). In the absence of updated regulations, courts will have to make ad hoc determinations that run the risk of transforming scientific questions into matters of law. That is not the system Congress intended. Hence I believe that today's opinions, taken together, call for the Army Corps of Engineers to write new regulations, and speedily so.

NOTES AND QUESTIONS

1. Depending upon one's view of the relationship between *Chevron*'s two steps, the plurality's opinion in *Rapanos* may be fairly characterized as resolving the case at either step. The plurality never explicitly commits to resolving the case at either step one or step two. On the one hand, in its exhaustive recitation of the history of judicial and agency interpretations of the term "navigable waters" under the Clean Water Act (CWA), the plurality opinion seems to recognize the statute's inherent susceptibility of multiple constructions. Chief Justice Roberts's concurring opinion clearly describes the CWA as ambiguous, according the Army Corps of Engineers "plenty of room" to fashion reasonable regulations. On the other hand, the plurality opinion makes clear its view that the statute unambiguously does not permit the interpretation advanced by the Army Corps of Engineers here. Further, while Justice Kennedy agrees with Chief Justice Roberts's assessment of the statute's ambiguity, he questions whether the plurality opinion finds it so. Reading the opinions carefully, how would you characterize the Court's resolution of the case, and why? Does it matter whether the Court resolves the matter at *Chevron* step one or step two? Why or why not?

2. In a sense, *Rapanos* is all about overreaching. Justice Scalia believes that Congress overreached with a statutory definition of "waters of the United States" so broad that it arguably authorizes the federal government to regulate every intermittent drainage ditch in the country. He further believes that the Corps overreached by stretching that statutory definition to or beyond its limits. By contrast, in his dissenting opinion, which is not included in your excerpt, Justice Stevens clearly signaled his belief that Justice Scalia overreached by using a combination of dictionary definitions and canons of construction to replace the policies of the politically accountable branches of government with a policy that is consistent with the views of politically unaccountable judges. Which form of overreach do you find more troubling? Why?

3. The plurality opinion is typical of Justice Scalia's approach to *Chevron*. As he acknowledged in the article excerpted earlier in this Chapter, he strongly supports *Chevron* deference to reasonable agency interpretations of ambiguous statutes, but he finds statutory ambiguity less frequently than the other Justices. Justice Scalia is the least deferential of the Justices in *Chevron* cases. See Thomas J. Miles & Cass R. Sunstein, *Do Judges Make Regulatory Policy: An Empirical Investigation of Chevron*, 73 U. CHI. L. REV. 823 (2006). Thus, for instance, in *MCI Telecommunications v. AT&T*, 512 U.S. 218 (1994), Justice Scalia wrote an opinion for a five-Justice majority in which he rejected the FCC's definition of "modify" because that definition was not in the dictionary he found most persuasive, even though the FCC's definition appeared in many other dictionaries. See Richard J. Pierce, Jr., *The Supreme Court's New Hypertextualism, An Invitation to Cacophony and Incoherence in the Administrative State*, 95 COLUM. L. REV. 749 (1995).

4. In *Chevron* cases, as in many other cases that the Court decides, Justice Kennedy often provides the deciding vote. Sometimes he writes a separate opinion in which he disagrees with both the plurality and the dissenting positions. His concurring opinion in *Rapanos* has created a lot of confusion in lower courts. Some courts have concluded that Justice Kennedy's "significant nexus" test is now the law, while others have concluded that the plurality's "continuous surface connection" test is the law. For a discussion of this problem, see *United States v. Johnson*, 467 F.3d 56 (1st Cir. 2006).

5. In their separate opinions, both Chief Justice Roberts and Justice Breyer urge the Corps to conduct a rulemaking in which it adopts a new interpretation of "waters of the United States." Given the strong differences of opinion among the Justices apparent in *Rapanos*, is there any reason to expect that the Justices would agree to uphold any interpretation that emerged from such a rulemaking? In their comprehensive study of Supreme Court opinions reviewing agency statutory interpretations, William Eskridge and Lauren Baer found that the Court upheld agency interpretations adopted in notice and comment rulemaking proceedings significantly more often than interpretations adopted through any other means. See William N. Eskridge, Jr. & Lauren E. Baer, *The Continuum of Deference: Supreme Court Treatment of Agency Statutory Interpretations from* Chevron *to* Hamdan, 96 GEO. L.J. 1083 (2008). Is that distinction sensible?

Hard Look Review and *Chevron* Step Two

In both *Iowa Utilities Board* and *Rapanos*, the Justices largely followed a statutory approach to *Chevron* step two analysis, considering statutory text, structure, and purpose, and paying little attention to the process by which the agencies in those cases adopted their respective interpretations, As the notes after both cases indicate, however, it is not always easy to distinguish a statutory-based inquiry at *Chevron* step two from that of *Chevron* step one. Particularly if one subscribes to a robust examination of the statute, its history, and its purpose at *Chevron* step one, then one is left to ask exactly what is left to evaluate at *Chevron* step two.

Some scholars have argued, and many courts have recognized, that step two of *Chevron* overlaps with arbitrary and capricious review under § 706 of the Administrative Procedure Act and *Motor Vehicle Manufacturers Ass'n of United States, Inc. v. State Farm Mutual Automobile Insurance Co.*, 463 U.S. 29 (1983), also known as hard look review. (We discussed hard look review in Part C of Chapter 5.) There is disagreement, however, as to whether the overlap is or should be partial or complete.

In *Arent v. Shalala*, 70 F.3d 610, 619–20 (D.C. Cir. 1995), for example, Judge Wald in a concurring opinion acknowledged the overlap between *Chevron* step two and arbitrary and capricious review under APA § 706 and *State Farm* but claimed them in many if not most cases to be separate inquiries that could lead to different outcomes.

> *Chevron* allocates power to interpret statutes among the branches of government by creating a presumption that agencies, rather than the courts, are the preferred institution for filling in statutory gaps. The first step of *Chevron* is straightforward; if the statutory language is clear, it controls. The second step * * * entrusts agencies with authority to interpret statutory ambiguities, provided they do so in a manner that is reasonable and consistent with the language and purposes of the statute. By contrast, garden-variety APA review under § 706 focuses more heavily on the agency's decisionmaking process; to survive arbitrary and capricious review, "the agency must examine the relevant data and articulate a satisfactory explanation for its action, including a rational connection between the facts found and the choice made." *State Farm*, 463 U.S. at 43.

> Given these differences in the central concerns behind the two analytic frameworks, there are certain situations where a challenge to an agency's regulation will fall squarely within one rubric rather than the other. For example, we might invalidate an agency's decision under *Chevron* as inconsistent with its statutory mandate, even though we do not believe the decision reflects an arbitrary policy choice. Such a result might occur when we believe the agency's course of action to be the most appropriate and effective means of achieving a goal, but determine that Congress had selected a different—albeit, in our eyes, less propitious—path. Conversely, we might determine that although not barred by a statute, an agency's

action is arbitrary and capricious because the agency has not considered certain relevant factors or articulated any rationale for its choice. Or, along similar lines, we might find a regulation arbitrary and capricious, while deciding that *Chevron* is inapplicable because Congress' delegation to the agency is so broad as to be virtually unreviewable.

Ronald Levin has argued, by contrast, that the courts should simply equate *Chevron* step two and hard look review. Levin's argument is premised on the practical realities of judicial review: Litigants and courts already mush together the Chevron and *State Farm* lines of analysis with little if any clear theory for distinguishing their arguments; reviewing courts routinely consider all the relevant sources for discerning statutory meaning and evaluate the validity of the agency's interpretation of the statute in the course of *Chevron* step one analysis, leaving the courts little to do at *Chevron* step two; and wholly merging step two and *State Farm* would both reflect this reality and simplify the process of writing both briefs and court opinions. See Ronald M. Levin, *The Anatomy of* Chevron: *Step Two Reconsidered*, 72 CHI.-KENT L. REV. 1253 (1997).

In *Judulang v. Holder*, 132 S. Ct. 476 (2011), the Supreme Court applied hard look review to conclude that the method used by the Board of Immigration Appeals to determine whether an alien was eligible for discretionary relief from deportation was arbitrary and capricious. In a footnote, the Court said:

> The Government urges us instead to analyze this case under the second step of the test we announced in *Chevron U.S.A. Inc. v. Natural Resources Defense Council, Inc.*, 467 U.S. 837 (1984), to govern judicial review of an agency's statutory interpretations. Were we to do so, our analysis would be the same, because under *Chevron* step two, we ask whether an agency interpretation is arbitrary or capricious in substance.

Id. at 483 n.7 (internal quotation marks and citations omitted). Some scholars have interpreted this footnote as signaling the Court's agreement with Ronald Levin's suggestion to merge *Chevron* step two and hard look review. Afterward, however, one of us (Professor Pierce) asked the author of the opinion, Justice Kagan, in a public forum whether she intended to communicate that belief. Justice Kagan, who taught administrative law at Harvard Law School before joining the Court, disavowed any intent to make such a fundamental statement of administrative law doctrine with the above language. Meanwhile, some lower courts continue to equate the two standards. *See, e.g., National Organization of Veterans' Advocates, Inc. v. Secretary of Veterans' Affairs*, 669 F.3d 1340 (Fed. Cir. 2012).

5. *CHEVRON* APPLIED

Just as many, many legal scholars have debated the theory and wisdom of the *Chevron* standard, numerous scholars have engaged in empirical analysis of the judicial opinions that have applied *Chevron*, with interesting results. Several studies of circuit court applications of *Chevron* in the first fifteen years after the Court issued its opinion in *Chevron* found that circuit courts were applying *Chevron* in ways that furthered the goals that many *Chevron* supporters ascribed to the opinion. Over time, judicial review of agency statutory interpretations in circuit courts became more predictable, more consistent, and more deferential, with a resulting increase in the power of agencies to make policy decisions and a resulting decrease in the power of courts to make policy decisions. Comparing sets of cases from the courts of appeals from immediately before and after *Chevron* as well as from 1988, Peter Schuck and Donald Elliott concluded that affirmances of agency legal interpretations by the courts of appeals in general and the D.C. Circuit in particular increased substantially in response to *Chevron. See* Peter H. Schuck & E. Donald Elliott, *To the Chevron Station: An Empirical Study of Federal Administrative Law*, 1990 DUKE L.J. 984, 1029–43. A few years later, a study of federal appellate cases from 1995 and 1996 found that those courts accepted the agency's interpretation in 89% of Chevron step two applications and 73% of Chevron cases overall. See Orin Kerr, *Shedding Light on Chevron: An Empirical Study of the Chevron Doctrine in the U.S. Courts of Appeals*, 15 YALE J. ON REG. 1 (1998) (finding that federal appellate courts in 1995 and 1996 accepted the agency's view in 89% of *Chevron* step two applications and 73% of *Chevron* cases overall).

Empirical studies of Supreme Court applications of *Chevron* produced quite different findings, however. In two careful studies, Thomas Merrill found that the Supreme Court was massively inconsistent in its applications of *Chevron*. From the outset, the Supreme Court sometimes applied *Chevron* in a highly deferential manner, sometimes ignored it completely, and sometimes characterized and applied the *Chevron* test in strange and inconsistent ways. *See* Thomas W. Merrill, *Textualism and the Future of the Chevron Doctrine*, 72 WASH. U. L.Q. 351 (1994); Thomas W. Merrill, *Judicial Deference to Executive Precedent*, 101 YALE L.J. 969 (1992). More recent studies have found a continuation of the Supreme Court's inconsistent pattern of applications of *Chevron. See* William N. Eskridge, Jr., & Lauren E. Baer, *The Continuum of Deference: Supreme Court Treatments of Agency Statutory Interpretations from* Chevron *to* Hamdan, 96 GEO. L.J. 1083 (2008). They have also observed that the inconsistency of Supreme Court's application of *Chevron* has, not surprisingly, generated confusion and thus inconsistency among the circuit courts, *see* Lisa Schultz Bressman, *How Mead Has Muddled Judicial Review of Agency Action*, 58 VAND. L. REV. 1443 (2005), and that both Justices and judges at least sometimes resolve statutory interpretation disputes in a manner consistent with their individual views of wise policy with little deference to agencies' interpretations of the statutes they administer. *See* Thomas J. Miles & Cass R. Sunstein, *Do Judges Make Regulatory Policy? An Empirical Investigation of* Chevron, 73 U. CHI. L. REV. 823 (2006).

These and other studies of judicial applications of *Chevron* have added to the already lively and complicated debate among legal scholars over the *Chevron* doctrine. Why do you think the courts have been unwilling or unable to maintain consistency in their applications of *Chevron*? What, if anything, should the Supreme Court do to enhance the beneficial effects of *Chevron*?

C. *CHEVRON*'S SCOPE AND THE *MEAD* COUNTER-REVOLUTION

In *Chevron*, the Court applied the *Chevron* test to an agency interpretation of a statute announced in a rule issued under general authority through use of notice-and-comment rulemaking in *Chevron*.[**] Shortly after it decided *Chevron*, the Court applied the *Chevron* standard to agency interpretations of statutes adopted in several formal adjudications, and after that arguably to the occasional informal adjudication, amicus brief, or other informal pronouncement. Until 2000, however, the Court said little that was explicit about whether *Chevron* deference applies to any of the myriad other less formal formats in which agencies often announce interpretations of the statutes they administer. Those contexts include interpretative rules, policy statements, informal adjudications, briefs, letters, and press releases. Thus, between 1984 and 2000, lower courts had no guidance from the Court with respect to the scope of *Chevron* deference. Not surprisingly, lower court opinions differed greatly. Some limited *Chevron* deference to legislative rules and formal adjudications, while some applied *Chevron* deference broadly to almost any of the less formal means through which agencies announce their interpretations of the statutes they administer.

Indeed, the Court's jurisprudence during this period often saw the application of *Chevron* review with very little discussion and seemingly no thought for whether or when *Chevron*'s strongly deferential approach might be inappropriate. The questions within the lower courts were not limited to whether the *Chevron* standard should apply to the different formats in which agencies chose to express their interpretations. The lower courts likewise struggled with whether *Chevron* should apply to informal pronouncements by an agency that lacks the power to issue legislative rules altogether, or to agency interpretations of statutes over which two or more agencies share administrative authority, or to agency interpretations of general principles of common law that might arise in connection with a particular statutory provision, or to agency interpretations of their own regulations. For an exhaustive examination of fourteen separate questions regarding *Chevron*'s scope that had generated circuit splits or otherwise arisen in the lower courts by the late 1990s, see Thomas W. Merrill & Kristin E. Hickman, Chevron*'s Domain*, 89 GEO. L.J. 833 (2001). The Court finally broke its silence on this issue in 2000 with the following opinion.

---

[*]   Although pre-*Chevron* jurisprudence generally would have characterized the regulation at issue in *Chevron* as an interpretative rule because the EPA acted pursuant to its general rulemaking authority, contemporary standards for distinguishing legislative and interpretative rules invariably treat such regulations as legislative rules. We discuss the characterization of agency rules at some length in Chapter 5.

Christensen v. Harris County

529 U.S. 576 (2000).

■ JUSTICE THOMAS delivered the opinion of the Court.

* * *

I

The [Fair Labor Standards Act of 1938] generally provides that hourly employees who work in excess of 40 hours per week must be compensated for the excess hours at a rate not less than 1½ times their regular hourly wage. 29 U.S.C. § 207(a)(1). Although this requirement did not initially apply to public-sector employers, Congress amended the FLSA to subject States and their political subdivisions to its constraints, at first on a limited basis, and then more broadly. States and their political subdivisions, however, did not feel the full force of this latter extension until our decision in *Garcia v. San Antonio Metropolitan Transit Authority*, 469 U.S. 528 (1985), which overruled our holding in *National League of Cities v. Usery*, 426 U.S. 833 (1976), that the FLSA could not constitutionally restrain traditional governmental functions.

In the months following *Garcia*, Congress acted to mitigate the effects of applying the FLSA to States and their political subdivisions, passing the Fair Labor Standards Amendments of 1985. Those amendments permit States and their political subdivisions to compensate employees for overtime by granting them compensatory time at a rate of 1½ hours for every hour worked. To provide this form of compensation, the employer must arrive at an agreement or understanding with employees that compensatory time will be granted instead of cash compensation.

The FLSA expressly regulates some aspects of accrual and preservation of compensatory time. For example, the FLSA provides that an employer must honor an employee's request to use compensatory time within a "reasonable period" of time following the request, so long as the use of the compensatory time would not "unduly disrupt" the employer's operations. § 207(*o*)(5); 29 C.F.R. § 553.25 (1999). The FLSA also caps the number of compensatory time hours that an employee may accrue. After an employee reaches that maximum, the employer must pay cash compensation for additional overtime hours worked. In addition, the FLSA permits the employer at any time to cancel or "cash out" accrued compensatory time hours by paying the employee cash compensation for unused compensatory time. § 207(*o*)(3)(B); 29 C.F.R. § 553.26(a). And the FLSA entitles the employee to cash payment for any accrued compensatory time remaining upon the termination of employment.

Petitioners are 127 deputy sheriffs employed by respondents Harris County, Texas, and its sheriff, Tommy B. Thomas (collectively, Harris County). It is undisputed that each of the petitioners individually agreed to accept compensatory time, in lieu of cash, as compensation for overtime.

As petitioners accumulated compensatory time, Harris County became concerned that it lacked the resources to pay monetary compensation to employees who worked overtime after reaching the statutory cap on compensatory time accrual and to employees who left their jobs with sizable reserves of accrued time. As a result, the county began looking for a way to reduce accumulated compensatory time. It wrote to the United States Department of Labor's Wage and Hour Division, asking "whether the Sheriff may schedule non-exempt employees to use or take compensatory time." The Acting Administrator of the Division replied:

> "[I]t is our position that a public employer may schedule its nonexempt employees to use their accrued FLSA compensatory time as directed if the prior agreement specifically provides such a provision. . . .

> "Absent such an agreement, it is our position that neither the statute nor the regulations permit an employer to require an employee to use accrued compensatory time."

Opinion Letter from Dept. of Labor, Wage, and Hour Div. (Sept. 14, 1992) (hereinafter "Opinion Letter").

After receiving the letter, Harris County implemented a policy under which the employees' supervisor sets a maximum number of compensatory hours that may be accumulated. When an employee's stock of hours approaches that maximum, the employee is advised of the maximum and is asked to take steps to reduce accumulated compensatory time. If the employee does not do so voluntarily, a supervisor may order the employee to use his compensatory time at specified times.

Petitioners sued, claiming that the county's policy violates the FLSA because § 207(o)(5)—which requires that an employer reasonably accommodate employee requests to use compensatory time—provides the exclusive means of utilizing accrued time in the absence of an agreement or understanding permitting some other method. The District Court agreed, granting summary judgment for petitioners and entering a declaratory judgment that the county's policy violated the FLSA. The Court of Appeals for the Fifth Circuit reversed, holding that the FLSA did not speak to the issue and thus did not prohibit the county from implementing its compensatory time policy. Judge Dennis concurred in part and dissented in part, concluding that the employer could not compel the employee to use compensatory time unless the employee agreed to such an arrangement in advance. We granted certiorari because the Courts of Appeals are divided on the issue.

* * *

II

[We have omitted an extended portion of the majority opinion analyzing the statute to reach the following conclusion. Ed.]

At bottom, we think the better reading of § 207(o)(5) is that it imposes a restriction upon an employer's efforts to *prohibit* the use of compensatory time when employees request to do so; that provision says nothing about restricting an employer's efforts to *require* employees to use compensatory time. Because the statute is silent on this issue and because Harris County's policy is entirely compatible with § 207(*o*)(5), petitioners cannot, as they are required to do by 29 U.S.C. § 216(b), prove that Harris County has violated § 207.

* * *

III

In an attempt to avoid the conclusion that the FLSA does not prohibit compelled use of compensatory time, petitioners and the United States contend that we should defer to the Department of Labor's opinion letter, which takes the position that an employer may compel the use of compensatory time only if the employee has agreed in advance to such a practice. Specifically, they argue that the agency opinion letter is entitled to deference under our decision in *Chevron U.S.A. Inc. v. Natural Resources Defense Council, Inc.*, 467 U.S. 837 (1984). In Chevron, we held that a court must give effect to an agency's regulation containing a reasonable interpretation of an ambiguous statute.

Here, however, we confront an interpretation contained in an opinion letter, not one arrived at after, for example, a formal adjudication or notice-and-comment rulemaking. Interpretations such as those in opinion letters—like interpretations contained in policy statements, agency manuals, and enforcement guidelines, all of which lack the force of law—do not warrant *Chevron*-style deference. Instead, interpretations contained in formats such as opinion letters are "entitled to respect" under our decision in *Skidmore v. Swift & Co.*, 323 U.S. 134, 140 (1944), but only to the extent that those interpretations have the "power to persuade." *Id.* As explained above, we find unpersuasive the agency's interpretation of the statute at issue in this case.

Of course, the framework of deference set forth in *Chevron* does apply to an agency interpretation contained in a regulation. But in this case the Department of Labor's regulation does not address the issue of compelled compensatory time. The regulation provides only that "[t]he agreement or understanding [between the employer and employee] *may* include other provisions governing the preservation, use, or cashing out of compensatory time so long as these provisions are consistent with [§ 207(o)]." 29 C.F.R. § 553.23(a)(2) (1999) (emphasis added). Nothing in the regulation even arguably requires that an employer's compelled use policy *must* be included in an agreement. The text of the regulation itself indicates that its command is permissive, not mandatory.

Seeking to overcome the regulation's obvious meaning, the United States asserts that the agency's opinion letter interpreting the regulation should be given deference under our decision in *Auer v. Robbins*, 519 U.S. 452 (1997). In *Auer*, we held that an agency's interpretation of its own regulation is entitled to deference. But *Auer* deference is warranted only when the language of the regulation is ambiguous. The regulation in this case, however, is not ambiguous—it is plainly permissive. To defer to the agency's position would be to permit the agency, under the guise of interpreting a regulation, to create *de facto* a new regulation. Because the regulation is not ambiguous on the issue of compelled compensatory time, *Auer* deference is unwarranted.

* * *

As we have noted, no relevant statutory provision expressly or implicitly prohibits Harris County from pursuing its policy of forcing employees to utilize their compensatory time. In its opinion letter siding with the petitioners, the Department of Labor opined that "it is our position that neither the statute nor the regulations *permit* an employer to require an employee to use accrued compensatory time." Opinion Letter (emphasis added). But this view is exactly backwards. Unless the FLSA *prohibits* respondents from adopting its policy, petitioners cannot show that Harris County has violated the FLSA. And the FLSA contains no such prohibition.

■ JUSTICE SOUTER, concurring.

I join the opinion of the Court on the assumption that it does not foreclose a reading of the Fair Labor Standards Act of 1938 that allows the Secretary of Labor to issue regulations limiting forced use.

■ JUSTICE SCALIA, concurring in part and concurring in the judgment.

I join the judgment of the Court and all of its opinion except Part III, which declines to give effect to the position of the Department of Labor in this case because its opinion letter is entitled only to so-called "*Skidmore* deference," *see Skidmore v. Swift & Co.*, 323 U.S. 134 (1944). *Skidmore* deference to authoritative agency views is an anachronism, dating from an era in which we declined to give agency interpretations (including interpretive regulations, as opposed to "legislative rules") authoritative effect. This former judicial attitude accounts for that provision of the 1946 Administrative Procedure Act which exempted "interpretative rules" (since they would not be authoritative) from the notice-and-comment requirements applicable to rulemaking.

That era came to an end with our watershed decision in *Chevron U.S.A. Inc. v. Natural Resources Defense Council, Inc.*, 467 U.S. 837, 844 (1984), which established the principle that "a court may not substitute its own construction of a statutory provision for a reasonable interpretation made by the administrator of an agency." While *Chevron* in fact involved an interpretive regulation, the rationale of the case was not limited to that context: " 'The power of an administrative agency to administer a congressionally created . . . program necessarily requires the formulation of policy and the making of rules to fill any gap left, implicitly or explicitly, by Congress.' " *Id.* at 843. Quite appropriately, therefore, we have accorded Chevron deference not only to agency regulations, but to authoritative agency positions set forth in a variety of other formats. *See, e.g., INS v. Aguirre-Aguirre*, 526 U.S. 415, 425 (1999) (adjudication); *NationsBank of N.C., N.A. v. Variable Annuity Life Ins. Co.*, 513 U.S. 251, 256–57 (1995) (letter of Comptroller of the Currency); *Pension Benefit Guar. Corp. v. LTV Corp.*, 496 U.S. 633, 647–48 (1990) (decision by Pension Benefit Guaranty Corp. to restore pension benefit plan); *Young v. Cmty. Nutrition Inst.*, 476 U.S. 974, 978–79 (1986) (Food and Drug Administration's "longstanding interpretation of the statute," reflected in no-action notice published in the Federal Register).

In my view, therefore, the position that the county's action in this case was unlawful unless permitted by the terms of an agreement with the sheriff's department employees warrants *Chevron* deference if it represents the authoritative view of the Department of Labor. The fact that it appears in a single opinion letter signed by the Acting Administrator of the Wage and Hour Division might not alone persuade me that it occupies that status. But the Solicitor General of the United States, appearing as an *amicus* in this action, has filed a brief, cosigned by the Solicitor of Labor, which represents the position set forth in the opinion letter to be the position of the Secretary of Labor. That alone, even without existence of the opinion letter, would in my view entitle the position to *Chevron* deference. What we said in a case involving an agency's interpretation of its own regulations applies equally, in my view, to an agency's interpretation of its governing statute:

> "Petitioners complain that the Secretary's interpretation comes to us in the form of a legal brief; but that does not, in the circumstances of this case, make it unworthy of deference. The Secretary's position is in no sense a '*post hoc* rationalizatio[n]' advanced by an agency seeking to defend past agency action against attack, *Bowen v. Georgetown Univ. Hosp.*, 488 U.S. 204, 212 (1988). There is simply no reason to suspect that the interpretation does not reflect the agency's fair and considered judgment on the matter in question." *Auer v. Robbins*, 519 U.S. 452, 462 (1997).

I nonetheless join the judgment of the Court because, for the reasons set forth in Part II of its opinion, the Secretary's position does not seem to me a reasonable interpretation of the statute.

■ [The dissenting opinion of JUSTICE STEVENS, with whom JUSTICE GINSBURG and JUSTICE BREYER join, is omitted. Ed.]

■ JUSTICE BREYER, with whom JUSTICE GINSBURG joins, dissenting.

Justice SCALIA may well be right that the position of the Department of Labor, set forth in both brief and letter, is an "authoritative" agency view that warrants deference under *Chevron U.S.A. Inc. v. Natural Resources Defense Council, Inc.*, 467 U.S. 837 (1984). But I do not object to the majority's citing *Skidmore v. Swift & Co.*, 323 U.S. 134 (1944), instead. And I do disagree with Justice SCALIA's statement that what he calls "*Skidmore* deference" is "an anachronism."

Skidmore made clear that courts may pay particular attention to the views of an expert agency where they represent "specialized experience," 323 U.S. at 139, even if they do not constitute an exercise of delegated lawmaking authority. The Court held that the "rulings, interpretations and opinions of" an agency, "while not controlling upon the courts by reason of their authority, do constitute a body of experience and informed judgment to which courts and litigants may properly resort for guidance." *Id.* at 140. As Justice Jackson wrote for the Court, those views may possess the "power to persuade," even where they lack the "power to control." *Skidmore*, 323 U.S. at 140.

Chevron made no relevant change. It simply focused upon an additional, separate legal reason for deferring to certain agency determinations, namely, that Congress had delegated to the agency the legal authority to make those determinations. And, to the extent there may be circumstances in which *Chevron*-type deference is inapplicable—e.g., where one has doubt that Congress actually intended to delegate interpretive authority to the agency (an "ambiguity" that *Chevron* does not presumptively leave to agency resolution)—I believe that *Skidmore* nonetheless retains legal vitality. If statutes are to serve the human purposes that called them into being, courts will have to continue to pay particular attention in appropriate cases to the experience-based views of expert agencies.

I agree with Justice STEVENS that, when "thoroughly considered and consistently observed," an agency's views, particularly in a rather technical case such as this one, "meri[t] our respect." And, of course, I also agree with Justice STEVENS that, for the reasons he sets forth, the Labor Department's position in this matter is eminently reasonable, hence persuasive, whether one views that decision through *Chevron*'s lens, through *Skidmore*'s, or through both.

NOTES AND QUESTIONS

1. The various opinions in *Christensen* reflect three very different perceptions of the Supreme Court's judicial deference doctrine. Writing for a five-Justice majority, Justice Thomas presents *Chevron* and *Skidmore* as offering separate and competing standards of review for agency legal interpretations, presumably with the third option of no deference at all under some circumstances. Justice Scalia, writing for himself alone in concurrence, rejects *Skidmore* as anachronistic, which leaves a reviewing court with *Chevron* or nothing in evaluating agency legal interpretations. Finally, Justice Breyer, writing in dissent, views all the options of *Chevron*, *Skidmore*, or no deference as merely different points on a single deference continuum, with *Chevron*'s emphasis on delegated authority offering merely an additional factor in deciding just how much deference is appropriate. Given the vagaries and inconsistencies of *Chevron* analysis, do you consider *Skidmore* to be a viable alternative to the *Chevron* standard, or is Justice Breyer more accurate in his recognition that the standards are fundamentally related to one another?

2. A majority of the Justices in *Christensen* agreed with the holding that only agency interpretations advanced in formats that carry "the force of law" are eligible for *Chevron* deference. The majority opinion authored by Justice Thomas offers examples of *Chevron*-ineligible formats but does not otherwise define what it means by the force of law concept. You might recall from Chapter 5 that the D.C. Circuit in *American Mining Congress v. Mine Safety & Health Admin.*, 995 F.2d 1106 (D.C. Cir. 1993), discussed in Chapter 5, recognized "the force of law" as the dividing line between legislative and interpretative rules, and has offered various factors for evaluating in that context whether a particular agency rule carries such force. Do you think the inquiries should be the same for both contexts? Why or why not?

3. Recall that in *Chevron*, the Court emphasized various justifications for its doctrine of strong judicial deference for agency legal interpretations: congressional delegation, superior agency expertise, and the greater democratic accountability of the executive branch. In *Christensen*, a majority of the Justices declined to extend *Chevron*'s strong deference to agency interpretations that do not carry the force of law. What concerns do you think motivated the Court to reduce the scope of *Chevron*'s applicability in this way? By comparison, Justice Scalia in concurrence identified only three circumstances in which he would not apply *Chevron* deference: (1) when the statute is unambiguous; (2) when no interpretation has been made by the responsible agency personnel; and (3) when any such interpretation is not "authoritative, in the sense that it does not represent the official position of the expert agency." On what basis do you think Justice Scalia predicates those exceptions?

4. The Court in *Christensen* addresses the standard of review applicable to various forms of non-legislative agency guidance documents, including but not limited to opinion letters, policy statements, agency manuals, and enforcement guidelines, none of which carry the "force of law." The *Christensen* Court did not address the important question whether the *Chevron* standard applies to agency interpretations of law announced in the course of resolving informal adjudications. Recall our observation from Chapter 4 that informal adjudications represent the largest class of federal agency action. Given the Court's analysis in *Christensen*, do you think the Court would be likely to extend *Chevron* deference to informal adjudications?

Since deciding *Christensen v. Harris County*, the Court has issued a dozen or so opinions in which it has attempted to explain where it draws the line with respect to *Chevron* deference and what, if any, type of deference a court should apply to an agency interpretation that is not entitled to *Chevron* deference. That body of case law is not entirely clear or internally consistent, but lower courts and scholars generally consider the following opinion to be the most definitive statement of the Court's views with respect to the scope of *Chevron* deference, eclipsing even its predecessor, *Christensen*.

United States v. Mead Corp.
533 U.S. 218 (2001).

■ JUSTICE SOUTER delivered the opinion of the Court.

The question is whether a tariff classification ruling by the United States Customs Service deserves judicial deference. The Federal Circuit rejected Customs's invocation of *Chevron*, in support of such a ruling, to which it gave no deference. We agree that a tariff classification has no claim to judicial deference under *Chevron*, there being no indication that Congress intended such a ruling to carry the force of law, but we hold that under *Skidmore*, the ruling is eligible to claim respect according to its persuasiveness.

Imports are taxed under the Harmonized Tariff Schedule of the United States (HTSUS), [The statute] provides that Customs "shall, under rules and regulations prescribed by the Secretary [of the Treasury,] . . . fix the final classification and rate of duty applicable to . . . merchandise" under the HTSUS. 19 U.S.C. § 1500(b). * * *

The Secretary provides for tariff rulings before the entry of goods by regulations authorizing "ruling letters" setting tariff classifications for particular imports. A ruling letter

"represents the official position of the Customs Service with respect to the particular transaction or issue described therein and is binding on all Customs Service personnel in accordance with the provisions of this section until modified or revoked. In the absence of a change of practice or other modification or revocation which affects the principle of the ruling set forth in the ruling letter, that principle may be cited as authority in the disposition of transactions involving the same circumstances." 19 C.F.R. § 177.9(a) (2000).

After the transaction that gives it birth, a ruling letter is to "be applied only with respect to transactions involving articles identical to the sample submitted with the ruling request or to articles whose description is identical to the description set forth in the ruling letter." § 177.9(b)(2). As a general matter, such a letter is "subject to modification or revocation without notice to any person, except the person to whom the letter was addressed," § 177.9(c), and the regulations consequently provide that "no other person should rely on the ruling letter or assume that the principles of that ruling will be applied in connection with any transaction other than the one described in the letter." *Id.* Since ruling letters respond to transactions of the moment, they are not subject to notice and comment before being issued, may be published but need only be made "available for public inspection," 19 U.S.C. § 1625(a), and, at the time this action arose, could be modified without notice and comment under most circumstances. * * *

Any of the 46 port-of-entry Customs offices may issue ruling letters, and so may the Customs Headquarters Office, in providing "[a]dvice or guidance as to the interpretation or proper application of the Customs and related laws with respect to a specific Customs transaction [which] may be requested by Customs Service field offices . . . at any time, whether the transaction is prospective, current, or completed." 19 C.F.R. § 177.11(a). Most ruling letters contain little or no reasoning, but simply describe goods and state the appropriate category and tariff. A few letters, like the Headquarters ruling at issue here, set out a rationale in some detail.

Respondent, the Mead Corporation, imports "day planners," three-ring binders with pages having room for notes of daily schedules and phone numbers and addresses, together with a calendar and suchlike. The tariff schedule on point falls under the HTSUS heading for "[r]egisters, account books, notebooks, order books, receipt books, letter pads, memorandum pads, diaries and similar articles," HTSUS subheading 4820.10, which comprises two subcategories. Items in the first, "[d]iaries, notebooks and address books, bound; memorandum pads, letter pads and similar articles," were subject to a tariff of 4.0% at the time in controversy. Objects in the second, covering "[o]ther" items, were free of duty.

Between 1989 and 1993, Customs repeatedly treated day planners under the "other" HTSUS subheading. In January 1993, however, Customs changed its position, and issued a Headquarters ruling letter classifying Mead's day planners as "Diaries . . . , bound" subject to tariff under subheading 4820.10.20. That letter was short on explanation, but after Mead's protest, Customs Headquarters issued a new letter, carefully reasoned but never published, reaching the same conclusion.

* * *

We granted certiorari in order to consider the limits of *Chevron* deference owed to administrative practice in applying a statute. We hold that administrative implementation of a particular statutory provision qualifies for *Chevron* deference when it appears that Congress delegated authority to the agency generally to make rules carrying the force of law, and that the agency interpretation claiming deference was promulgated in the exercise of that authority. Delegation of such authority may be shown in a variety of ways, as by an agency's power to engage in adjudication or notice-and-comment rulemaking, or by some other indication of a comparable congressional intent. The Customs ruling at issue here fails to qualify, although the possibility that it deserves some deference under *Skidmore* leads us to vacate and remand.

When Congress has "explicitly left a gap for an agency to fill, there is an express delegation of authority to the agency to elucidate a specific provision of the statute by regulation," *Chevron*, 467 U.S. at 843–44, and any ensuing regulation is binding in the courts unless procedurally defective, arbitrary or capricious in substance, or manifestly contrary to the statute. But whether or not they enjoy any express delegation of authority on a particular question, agencies charged with applying a statute necessarily make all sorts of interpretive choices, and while not all of those choices bind judges to follow them, they certainly may influence courts facing questions the agencies have already answered. "[T]he well-reasoned views of the agencies implementing a statute 'constitute a body of experience and informed judgment to which courts and litigants may properly resort for guidance,'" *Bragdon v. Abbott*, 524 U.S. 624, 642 (1998) (quoting *Skidmore*, 323 U.S. at 139–40), and "[w]e have long recognized that considerable weight should be accorded to an executive department's construction of a statutory scheme it is entrusted to administer...." *Chevron*, 467 U.S. at 844. The fair measure of deference to an agency administering its own statute has been understood to vary with circumstances, and courts have looked to the degree of the agency's care, its consistency, formality, and relative expertness, and to the persuasiveness of the agency's position. The approach has produced a spectrum of judicial responses, from great respect at one end to near indifference at the other. Justice Jackson summed things up in *Skidmore v. Swift & Co.*:

> "The weight [accorded to an administrative] judgment in a particular case will depend upon the thoroughness evident in its consideration, the validity of its reasoning, its consistency with earlier and later pronouncements, and all those factors which give it power to persuade, if lacking power to control." 323 U.S. at 140.

Since 1984, we have identified a category of interpretive choices distinguished by an additional reason for judicial deference. This Court in *Chevron* recognized that Congress not only engages in express delegation of specific interpretive authority, but that "[s]ometimes the legislative delegation to an agency on a particular question is implicit." 467 U.S. at 844. Congress, that is, may not have expressly delegated authority or responsibility to implement a particular provision or fill a particular gap. Yet it can still be apparent from the agency's generally conferred authority and other statutory circumstances that Congress would expect the agency to be able to speak with the force of law when it addresses ambiguity in the statute or fills a space in the enacted law, even one about which "Congress did not actually have an intent" as to a particular result. *Chevron*, 467 U.S. at 845. When circumstances implying such an expectation exist, a reviewing court has no business rejecting an agency's exercise of its generally conferred authority to resolve a particular statutory ambiguity simply because the agency's chosen resolution seems unwise, but is obliged to accept the agency's position if Congress has not previously spoken to the point at issue and the agency's interpretation is reasonable.

We have recognized a very good indicator of delegation meriting *Chevron* treatment in express congressional authorizations to engage in the process of rulemaking or adjudication that produces regulations or rulings for which deference is claimed. It is fair to assume generally that Congress contemplates administrative action with the effect of law when it provides for a relatively formal administrative procedure tending to foster the fairness and deliberation that should underlie a pronouncement of such force.[11] Thus, the overwhelming number of our cases applying *Chevron* deference have reviewed the fruits of notice-and-comment rulemaking or formal adjudication. That said, and as significant as notice-and-comment is in pointing to *Chevron* authority, the want of that procedure here does not decide the case, for we have sometimes found reasons for *Chevron* deference even when no such administrative formality was required and none was afforded, see, *e.g.*, *NationsBank of N.C., N. A. v. Variable Annuity Life Ins. Co.*, 513 U.S. 251, 256–257, 263 (1995). The fact that the tariff classification here was not a product of such formal process does not alone, therefore, bar the application of *Chevron*.

There are, nonetheless, ample reasons to deny *Chevron* deference here. The authorization for classification rulings, and Customs's practice in making them, present a case far removed not only from notice-and-comment process, but from any other circumstances reasonably suggesting that Congress ever thought of classification rulings as deserving the deference claimed for them here.

No matter which angle we choose for viewing the Customs ruling letter in this case, it fails to qualify under *Chevron*. On the face of the statute, to begin with, the terms of the congressional delegation give no indication that Congress meant to delegate authority to Customs to issue classification rulings with the force of law. We are not, of course, here making any global statement about Customs's authority, for it is true that the general rulemaking power conferred on Customs authorizes some regulation with the force of law, or "legal norms" * * *. It is true as well that Congress had classification rulings in mind when it explicitly authorized, in a parenthetical, the issuance of "regulations establishing procedures for the issuance of binding rulings prior to the

---

[11] See Merrill & Hickman, Chevron's *Domain*, 89 GEO. L.J. 833, 872 (2001) ("[I]f *Chevron* rests on a presumption about congressional intent, then *Chevron* should apply only where Congress would want *Chevron* to apply. In delineating the types of delegations of agency authority that trigger *Chevron* deference, it is therefore important to determine whether a plausible case can be made that Congress would want such a delegation to mean that agencies enjoy primary interpretational authority").

entry of the merchandise concerned." 19 U.S.C. § 1502(a). The reference to binding classifications does not, however, bespeak the legislative type of activity that would naturally bind more than the parties to the ruling, once the goods classified are admitted into this country. And though the statute's direction to disseminate "information" necessary to "secure" uniformity, id., seems to assume that a ruling may be precedent in later transactions, precedential value alone does not add up to *Chevron* entitlement; interpretive rules may sometimes function as precedents, and they enjoy no *Chevron* status as a class. In any event, any precedential claim of a classification ruling is counterbalanced by the provision for independent review of Customs classifications by the CIT; the scheme for CIT review includes a provision that treats classification rulings on par with the Secretary's rulings on "valuation, rate of duty, marking, restricted merchandise, entry requirements, drawbacks, vessel repairs, or similar matters." § 1581(h). It is hard to imagine a congressional understanding more at odds with the *Chevron* regime.

It is difficult, in fact, to see in the agency practice itself any indication that Customs ever set out with a lawmaking pretense in mind when it undertook to make classifications like these. Customs does not generally engage in notice-and-comment practice when issuing them, and their treatment by the agency makes it clear that a letter's binding character as a ruling stops short of third parties; Customs has regarded a classification as conclusive only as between itself and the importer to whom it was issued, and even then only until Customs has given advance notice of intended change. Other importers are in fact warned against assuming any right of detrimental reliance.

Indeed, to claim that classifications have legal force is to ignore the reality that 46 different Customs offices issue 10,000 to 15,000 of them each year. Any suggestion that rulings intended to have the force of law are being churned out at a rate of 10,000 a year at an agency's 46 scattered offices is simply self-refuting. Although the circumstances are less startling here, with a Headquarters letter in issue, none of the relevant statutes recognizes this category of rulings as separate or different from others; there is thus no indication that a more potent delegation might have been understood as going to Headquarters even when Headquarters provides developed reasoning, as it did in this instance.

Nor do the amendments to the statute made effective after this case arose disturb our conclusion. The new law requires Customs to provide notice-and-comment procedures only when modifying or revoking a prior classification ruling or modifying the treatment accorded to substantially identical transactions; and under its regulations, Customs sees itself obliged to provide notice-and-comment procedures only when "changing a practice" so as to produce a tariff increase, or in the imposition of a restriction or prohibition, or when Customs Headquarters determines that "the matter is of sufficient importance to involve the interests of domestic industry." 19 C.F.R. § 177.10(c)(1), (2) (2000). The statutory changes reveal no new congressional objective of treating classification decisions generally as rulemaking with force of law, nor do they suggest any intent to create a

Chevron patchwork of classification rulings, some with force of law, some without.

In sum, classification rulings are best treated like "interpretations contained in policy statements, agency manuals, and enforcement guidelines." *Christensen*, 529 U.S. at 587. They are beyond the *Chevron* pale.

To agree with the Court of Appeals that Customs ruling letters do not fall within *Chevron* is not, however, to place them outside the pale of any deference whatever. *Chevron* did nothing to eliminate *Skidmore*'s holding that an agency's interpretation may merit some deference whatever its form, given the "specialized experience and broader investigations and information" available to the agency, and given the value of uniformity in its administrative and judicial understandings of what a national law requires. 323 U.S. at 139–40.

There is room at least to raise a *Skidmore* claim here, where the regulatory scheme is highly detailed, and Customs can bring the benefit of specialized experience to bear on the subtle questions in this case: whether the daily planner with room for brief daily entries falls under "diaries," when diaries are grouped with "notebooks and address books, bound; memorandum pads, letter pads and similar articles," and whether a planner with a ring binding should qualify as "bound," when a binding may be typified by a book, but also may have "reinforcements or fittings of metal, plastics, etc." *See* Harmonized Commodity Description and Coding System Explanatory Notes to Heading 4820, at 687. A classification ruling in this situation may therefore at least seek a respect proportional to its "power to persuade," *Skidmore*, 323 U.S. at 140. Such a ruling may surely claim the merit of its writer's thoroughness, logic, and expertness, its fit with prior interpretations, and any other sources of weight.

Underlying the position we take here, like the position expressed by Justice SCALIA in dissent, is a choice about the best way to deal with an inescapable feature of the body of congressional legislation authorizing administrative action. That feature is the great variety of ways in which the laws invest the Government's administrative arms with discretion, and with procedures for exercising it, in giving meaning to Acts of Congress. Implementation of a statute may occur in formal adjudication or the choice to defend against judicial challenge; it may occur in a central board or office or in dozens of enforcement agencies dotted across the country; its institutional lawmaking may be confined to the resolution of minute detail or extend to legislative rulemaking on matters intentionally left by Congress to be worked out at the agency level.

Although we all accept the position that the Judiciary should defer to at least some of this multifarious administrative action, we have to decide how to take account of the great range of its variety. If the primary objective is to simplify the judicial process of giving or withholding deference, then the diversity of statutes authorizing discretionary administrative action must be declared irrelevant or minimized. If, on the other hand, it is simply implausible that Congress intended such a broad range of statutory authority to produce only two varieties of administrative action, demanding either *Chevron* deference or none at all, then the breadth of the spectrum of possible agency action must be taken into account. Justice Scalia's first priority over the years has been to limit and simplify. The Court's choice has been to tailor deference to variety. This acceptance of the range of statutory variation has led the Court to recognize more than one variety of judicial deference, just as the Court has recognized a variety of indicators that Congress would expect *Chevron* deference.

* * *

Since the Skidmore assessment called for here ought to be made in the first instance by the Court of Appeals for the Federal Circuit or the [Court of International Trade], we go no further than to vacate the judgment and remand the case for further proceedings consistent with this opinion.

■ JUSTICE SCALIA, dissenting.

Today's opinion makes an avulsive change in judicial review of federal administrative action. Whereas previously a reasonable agency application of an ambiguous statutory provision had to be sustained so long as it represented the agency's authoritative interpretation, henceforth such an application can be set aside unless "it appears that Congress delegated authority to the agency generally to make rules carrying the force of law," as by giving an agency "power to engage in adjudication or notice-and-comment rulemaking, or . . . some other [procedure] indicati[ng] comparable congressional intent," and "the agency interpretation claiming deference was promulgated in the exercise of that authority." What was previously a general presumption of authority in agencies to resolve ambiguity in the statutes they have been authorized to enforce has been changed to a presumption of no such authority, which must be overcome by affirmative legislative intent to the contrary. And whereas previously, when agency authority to resolve ambiguity did not exist the court was free to give the statute what it considered the best interpretation, henceforth the court must supposedly give the agency view some indeterminate amount of so-called *Skidmore* deference. We will be sorting out the consequences of the *Mead* doctrine, which has today replaced the *Chevron* doctrine, for years to come. I would adhere to our established jurisprudence, defer to the reasonable interpretation the Customs Service has given to the statute it is charged with enforcing, and reverse the judgment of the Court of Appeals.

Only five years ago, the Court described the *Chevron* doctrine as follows: "We accord deference to agencies under *Chevron* . . . because of a presumption that Congress, when it left ambiguity in a statute meant for implementation by an agency, understood that the ambiguity would be resolved, first and foremost, by the agency, and desired the agency (rather than the courts) to possess whatever degree of discretion the ambiguity allows." *Smiley v. Citibank (S.D.), N.A.*, 517 U.S. 735, 740–41 (1996). Today the Court collapses this doctrine, announcing instead a presumption that agency discretion does not exist unless the statute, expressly or impliedly, says so. While the Court disclaims any hard-and-fast rule for determining the existence of discretion-conferring intent, it asserts that "a very good indicator [is] express congressional authorizations to engage in the process of rulemaking or adjudication that produces regulations or rulings for which deference is claimed."

Only when agencies act through "adjudication[,] notice-and-comment rulemaking, or ... some other [procedure] indicati[ng] comparable congressional intent [whatever that means]" is *Chevron* deference applicable—because these "relatively formal administrative procedure[s] [designed] to foster ... fairness and deliberation" bespeak (according to the Court) congressional willingness to have the agency, rather than the courts, resolve statutory ambiguities. Once it is determined that *Chevron* deference is not in order, the uncertainty is not at an end—and indeed is just beginning. Litigants cannot then assume that the statutory question is one for the courts to determine, according to traditional interpretive principles and by their own judicial lights. No, the Court now resurrects, in full force, the pre-*Chevron* doctrine of *Skidmore* deference, whereby "[t]he fair measure of deference to an agency administering its own statute ... var[ies] with circumstances," including "the degree of the agency's care, its consistency, formality, and relative expertness, and ... the persuasiveness of the agency's position." The Court has largely replaced *Chevron*, in other words, with that test most beloved by a court unwilling to be held to rules (and most feared by litigants who want to know what to expect): th'ol' "totality of the circumstances" test.

The Court's new doctrine is neither sound in principle nor sustainable in practice.

As to principle: The doctrine of *Chevron*—that all *authoritative* agency interpretations of statutes they are charged with administering deserve deference—was rooted in a legal presumption of congressional intent, important to the division of powers between the Second and Third Branches. When, *Chevron* said, Congress leaves an ambiguity in a statute that is to be administered by an executive agency, it is presumed that Congress meant to give the agency discretion, within the limits of reasonable interpretation, as to how the ambiguity is to be resolved. By committing enforcement of the statute to an agency rather than the courts, Congress committed its initial and primary interpretation to that branch as well.

* * * Statutory ambiguities, in other words, were left to reasonable resolution by the Executive.

The basis in principle for today's new doctrine can be described as follows: The background rule is that ambiguity in legislative instructions to agencies is to be resolved not by the agencies but by the judges. Specific congressional intent to depart from this rule must be found—and while there is no single touchstone for such intent it can generally be found when Congress has authorized the agency to act through (what the Court says is) relatively formal procedures such as informal rulemaking and formal (and informal?) adjudication, and when the agency in fact employs such procedures. The Court's background rule is contradicted by the origins of judicial review of administrative action. But in addition, the Court's principal criterion of congressional intent to supplant its background rule seems to me quite implausible. There is no necessary connection between the formality of procedure and the power of the entity administering the procedure to resolve authoritatively questions of law. The most formal of the procedures the Court refers to—formal adjudication—is modeled after the process used in trial courts, which of course are not generally accorded deference on questions of law. The purpose of such a procedure is to produce a closed record for determination and review of the facts—which implies nothing about the power of the agency subjected to the procedure to resolve authoritatively questions of law.

As for informal rulemaking: While formal adjudication procedures are *prescribed* (either by statute or by the Constitution), informal rulemaking is more typically authorized but not required. Agencies with such authority are free to give guidance through rulemaking, but they may proceed to administer their statute case-by-case, "making law" as they implement their program (not necessarily through formal adjudication). Is it likely—or indeed even plausible—that Congress meant, when such an agency chooses rulemaking, to accord the administrators of that agency, *and their successors*, the flexibility of interpreting the ambiguous statute now one way, and later another; but, when such an agency chooses case-by-case administration, to eliminate all future agency discretion by having that same ambiguity resolved authoritatively (and forever) by the courts? Surely that makes no sense. It is also the case that certain significant categories of rules—those involving grant and benefit programs, for example, are exempt from the requirements of informal rulemaking. Under the Court's novel theory, when an agency takes advantage of that exemption its rules will be deprived of *Chevron* deference, *i.e.*, authoritative effect. Was this either the plausible intent of the APA rulemaking exemption, or the plausible intent of the Congress that established the grant or benefit program?

Some decisions that are neither informal rulemaking nor formal adjudication are required to be made personally by a Cabinet Secretary, without any prescribed procedures. Is it conceivable that decisions specifically committed to these high-level officers are meant to be accorded no deference, while decisions by an administrative law judge left in place without further discretionary agency review, are authoritative? This seems to me quite absurd, and not at all in accord with any plausible actual intent of Congress.

As for the practical effects of the new rule:

The principal effect will be protracted confusion. As noted above, the one test for *Chevron* deference that the Court enunciates is wonderfully imprecise: whether "Congress delegated authority to the agency generally to make rules carrying the force of law, . . . as by . . . adjudication[,] notice-and-comment rulemaking, or . . . some other [procedure] indicati[ng] comparable congressional intent." But even this description does not do justice to the utter flabbiness of the Court's criterion, since, in order to maintain the fiction that the new test is really just the old one, applied consistently throughout our case law, the Court must make a virtually open-ended exception to its already imprecise guidance: In the present case, it tells us, the absence of notice-and-comment rulemaking (and "[who knows?] [of] some other [procedure] indicati[ng] comparable congressional intent") is not enough to decide the question of *Chevron* deference, "for we have sometimes found reasons for *Chevron* deference even when no such administrative formality was required and none was afforded." The opinion then goes on to consider a grab bag of other factors—including the factor that used to be the sole criterion for *Chevron* deference: whether the interpretation represented the *authoritative* position of the agency. It is hard to know what the lower courts are to make of today's guidance.

* * *

Worst of all, the majority's approach will lead to the ossification of large portions of our statutory law. Where *Chevron* applies, statutory ambiguities remain ambiguities subject to the agency's ongoing clarification. They create a space, so to speak, for the exercise of continuing agency discretion. As *Chevron* itself held, the Environmental Protection Agency can interpret "stationary source" to mean a single smokestack, can later replace that interpretation with the "bubble concept" embracing an entire plant, and if that proves undesirable can return again to the original interpretation. 467 U.S. at 853–59, 865–66. For the indeterminately large number of statutes taken out of *Chevron* by today's decision, however, ambiguity (and hence flexibility) will cease with the first judicial resolution. *Skidmore* deference gives the agency's current position some vague and uncertain amount of respect, but it does not, like *Chevron*, leave the matter within the control of the Executive Branch for the future. Once the court has spoken, it becomes *unlawful* for the agency to take a contradictory position; the statute now *says* what the court has prescribed. It will be bad enough when this ossification occurs as a result of judicial determination (under today's new principles) that there is no affirmative indication of congressional intent to "delegate"; but it will be positively bizarre when it occurs simply because of an agency's failure to act by rulemaking (rather than informal adjudication) before the issue is presented to the courts.

* * *

And finally, the majority's approach compounds the confusion it creates by breathing new life into the anachronism of *Skidmore*, which sets forth a sliding scale of deference owed an agency's interpretation of a statute that is dependent "upon the thoroughness evident in [the agency's] consideration, the validity of its reasoning, its consistency with earlier and later pronouncements, and all those factors which give it power to persuade, if lacking power to control"; in this way, the appropriate measure of deference will be accorded the "body of experience and informed judgment" that such interpretations often embody. 323 U.S. at 140. Justice Jackson's eloquence notwithstanding, the rule of *Skidmore* deference is an empty truism and a trifling statement of the obvious: A judge should take into account the well-considered views of expert observers.

It was possible to live with the indeterminacy of *Skidmore* deference in earlier times. But in an era when federal statutory law administered by federal agencies is pervasive, and when the ambiguities (intended or unintended) that those statutes contain are innumerable, totality-of-the-circumstances *Skidmore* deference is a recipe for uncertainty, unpredictability, and endless litigation. To condemn a vast body of agency action to that regime (all except rulemaking, formal (and informal?) adjudication, and whatever else might now and then be included within today's intentionally vague formulation of affirmative congressional intent to "delegate") is irresponsible.

* * *

To make matters worse, the arguments marshaled by *Christensen* in support of its dictum—its observation that "interpretations contained in policy statements, agency manuals, and enforcement guidelines, all . . . lack the force of law," and its citation of 1 K. Davis & R. Pierce, Administrative Law Treatise § 3.5 (3d ed.1994), 529 U.S. at 587—are not only unpersuasive but bear scant resemblance to the reasoning of today's opinion. Davis and Pierce, and Professor Robert Anthony upon whom they rely, *see* Anthony, *Which Agency Interpretations Should Bind Citizens and the Courts?*, 7 YALE J. ON REG. 1 (1990), do indeed set forth the argument I have criticized above, that congressional authorization of informal rulemaking or formal (and perhaps even informal) adjudication somehow bespeaks a congressional intent to "delegate" power to resolve statutory ambiguities. But their analysis does not permit the broad add-ons that the Court's opinion contains— "some other [procedure] indicati[ng] comparable congressional intent," and "we have sometimes found reasons for *Chevron* deference even when no such administrative formality was required and none was afforded."

To decide the present case, I would adhere to the original formulation of *Chevron*. " 'The power of an administrative agency to administer a congressionally created . . . program necessarily requires the formulation of policy and the making of rules to fill any gap left, implicitly or explicitly by Congress.' " *Chevron*, 467 U.S. at 843. We accordingly presume—and our precedents have made clear to Congress that we presume—that, absent some clear textual indication to the contrary, "Congress, when it left ambiguity in a statute meant for implementation by an agency, understood that the ambiguity would be resolved, first and foremost, by the agency, and desired the agency (rather than the courts) to possess whatever degree of discretion the ambiguity allows." *Smiley*, 517 U.S. at 740–41. *Chevron* sets forth an across-the-board presumption, which operates as a background rule of law against which Congress legislates: Ambiguity means Congress intended agency discretion. Any resolution of the ambiguity by the administering agency that is authoritative—that represents the official position of the agency—must be accepted by the courts if it is reasonable.

* * *

There is no doubt that the Customs Service's interpretation represents the authoritative view of the agency. Although the actual ruling letter was signed by only the Director of the Commercial Rulings Branch of Customs Headquarters' Office of Regulations and Rulings, the Solicitor General of the United States has filed a brief, cosigned by the General Counsel of the Department of the Treasury, that represents the position set forth in the ruling letter to be the official position of the Customs Service.

NOTES AND QUESTIONS

1. Professors Merrill and Hickman suggested, and the *Mead* majority agreed, that the Court needed to limit the scope of *Chevron* deference to contexts in which Congress intended to confer primary interpretative responsibility on agencies. Do you agree with this assessment? If this is to be the case, then the courts must then identify some method of determining congressional intent, since Congress never explicitly addresses this issue. What evidence should a court consider in deciding whether to draw an inference that Congress intended to confer this power on a court? There is no shortage of potential factors a court could plausibly consider. In *Mead* and in other opinions the Court has referred to: (1) whether Congress gave the agency power to issue legislative rules, even if the agency did not adopt the interpretation at issue in a legislative rule; (2) the extent of the public participation in the decision making process the agency allowed; (3) the degree of formality of the decision making procedures the agency used; (4) the extent to which the interpretation has precedential effect; (5) whether the interpretation binds third parties, the agency and/or its employees, (6) whether the agency provided an explanation for the interpretation, and (7) the status of the individual who adopted the interpretation. Which of these factors would you consider in deciding whether Congress intended to give the agency the power to interpret the statute subject only to judicial review in which courts apply *Chevron* deference? Which of these factors does the *Mead* majority consider sufficient? Which of the factors does Justice Scalia consider sufficient?

2. The *Mead* majority described major differences between the classification decisions issued by the 46 port-of-entry customs offices and the classification decisions that are issued by the agency's headquarters. The differences lie in several areas—the level within the agency at which the decision is made, the precedential effect of the interpretation, the binding effect of the interpretation on third parties and on agency employees, provision of an opportunity to contest the classification before it becomes final, and presence or absence of an explanation for the interpretation. Would it make sense to distinguish between those two classes of interpretations for *Chevron* purposes? Would a port-of-entry classification decision satisfy Justice Scalia's test for application of *Chevron*? Was the *Mead* majority wise to reject the agency's argument that the Court should adopt such a distinction?

3. In *Christensen v. Harris County*, 529 U.S. 576 (2000), discussed above, a majority of the Court seemed to hold that only interpretations adopted in legislative rules and adjudications are entitled to *Chevron* deference. As Justice Scalia pointed out in his dissenting opinion in *Mead*, the majority in that case seems to have abandoned the bright-line test it announced in *Christensen* in favor of a more nuanced standard. As you may discern from the citations in the *Mead* opinions, one of us (Professor Hickman) is generally supportive of the approach the Court took in *Mead*, though with some caveats. The other (Professor Pierce) originally urged the Court to maintain the bright-line test it seemed to adopt the year before in *Christensen v. Harris County*, 529 U.S. 576 (2000). More recently, however, Professor Pierce has supported the broader test that Justice Scalia urged in his dissenting opinion in *Mead*. Professor Pierce has concluded that the *Christensen* test created a situation that is hard to defend in a democracy. In Professor Pierce's view, it takes so long for an agency to issue a legislative rule or to conclude a formal adjudication that adoption of the *Christensen* test would create a situation in which each President has no choice but to implement many of the policies of his predecessor even when he disagrees strongly with those policies. *See* Richard J. Pierce, Jr.,

Democratizing the Administrative State, 48 WM. & MARY L. REV. 559 (2006). By contrast, Professor Hickman finds Justice Scalia's willingness to defer to agency interpretations adopted with few or no procedural protections comparatively anti-democratic, given the practical reality of limited congressional and presidential oversight of most agency regulatory activity. Which of the *Mead* majority's approach or Justice Scalia's vision do you find more consistent with democratic accountability? Why?

The *Mead* majority held that an agency interpretation is entitled to *Chevron* deference if it was adopted through use of the relatively formal procedures of informal rulemaking or formal adjudication, but the majority also recognized that the Court has conferred *Chevron* deference on agency interpretations that were not adopted through use of those procedures. To cover that class of cases, the majority referred to "some other procedure [for interpreting a statute] indicat[ing] comparable congressional intent." Only one year after *Mead*, the Court decided the following case, causing some commentators to question the Court's commitment *Mead*'s seeming limitation on the scope of *Chevron*'s applicability.

Barnhart v. Walton

535 U.S. 212 (2002).

■ JUSTICE BREYER delivered the opinion of the Court.

The Social Security Act authorizes payment of disability insurance benefits and Supplemental Security Income to individuals with disabilities. See 49 Stat. 622, as amended, 42 U.S.C. § 401 *et seq.* (1994 ed. and Supp. V) (Title II disability insurance benefits); § 1381 *et seq.* (Title XVI supplemental security income). For both types of benefits the Act defines the key term "disability" as an

> "*inability* to engage in any substantial gainful activity *by reason of* any medically determinable physical or mental *impairment* which can be expected to result in death or *which has lasted or can be expected to last for a continuous period of not less than 12 months.*" § 423(d)(1)(A) (1994 ed.) (Title II) (emphasis added); accord, § 1382c(a)(3)(A) (1994 ed., Supp. V) (Title XVI).

This case presents two questions about the Social Security Administration's interpretation of this definition.

First, the Social Security Administration (which we shall call the Agency) reads the term "inability" as including a "12 month" requirement. In its view, the "inability" (to engage in any substantial gainful activity) must last, or must be expected to last, for *at least 12 months*. Second, the Agency reads the term "expected to last" as applicable only when the "inability" has *not yet* lasted 12 months. In the case of a later Agency determination—where the "inability" *did not* last 12 months—the Agency will automatically assume that the claimant failed to meet the duration requirement. It will not look back to decide hypothetically whether, despite the claimant's actual return to work before 12 months expired, the "inability" nonetheless *might have been* expected to last that long.

The Court of Appeals for the Fourth Circuit held both these interpretations of the statute unlawful. We hold, to the contrary, that both fall within the Agency's lawful interpretive authority. See *Chevron U.S.A. Inc. v. Natural Resources Defense Council, Inc.*, 467 U.S. 837 (1984). Consequently, we reverse.

I

In 1996 Cleveland Walton, the respondent, applied for both Title II disability insurance benefits and Title XVI Supplemental Security Income. The Agency found that (1) by October 31, 1994, Walton had developed a serious mental illness involving both schizophrenia and associated depression; (2) the illness caused him then to lose his job as a full-time teacher; (3) by mid-1995 he began to work again part time as a cashier; and (4) by December 1995 he was working as a cashier full time.

The Agency concluded that Walton's mental illness had prevented him from engaging in any significant work, *i.e.*, from "engag[ing] in any substantial gainful activity," for 11 months—from October 31, 1994 (when he lost his teaching job) until the end of September 1995 (when he earned income sufficient to rise to the level of "substantial gainful activity"). See 20 C.F.R. §§ 404.1574, 416.974 (2001). And because the statute demanded an "inability to engage in any substantial gainful activity" lasting 12, not 11, months, Walton was not entitled to benefits.

* * *

II

The statutory definition of "disability" has two parts. First, it requires a certain kind of "inability," namely, an "inability to engage in any substantial gainful activity." Second it requires an "impairment," namely, a "physical or mental impairment," which provides "reason" for the "inability." The statute adds that the "impairment" must be one that "has lasted or can be expected to last . . . not less than 12 months." But what about the "inability"? Must it also last (or be expected to last) for the same amount of time?

The Agency has answered this question in the affirmative. Acting pursuant to statutory rulemaking authority, 42 U.S.C. §§ 405(a) (Title II), 1383(d)(1) (Title XVI), it has promulgated formal regulations that state that a claimant is not disabled "regardless of [his] medical condition," if he is doing "substantial gainful activity." 20 CFR § 404.1520(b) (2001). And the Agency has interpreted this regulation to mean that the claimant is not disabled if "within 12 months after the onset of an impairment . . . the impairment no longer prevents substantial gainful activity." 65 Fed.Reg. 42774 (2000). Courts grant an agency's interpretation of its own regulations considerable legal leeway. *Auer v. Robbins*, 519 U.S. 452, 461 (1997); *Udall v. Tallman*, 380 U.S. 1, 16–17 (1965). And no one here denies that the Agency has properly interpreted its own regulation.

Consequently, the legal question before us is whether the Agency's interpretation of the statute is lawful. This Court has previously said that, if the statute speaks clearly "to the precise question at issue," we "must give effect to the unambiguously expressed intent of Congress." *Chevron*, 467 U.S., at 842–843. If, however, the statute "is silent or ambiguous with respect to the specific issue," we must sustain the Agency's interpretation if it is "based on a permissible construction" of the Act. *Id.*, at 843. Hence we must decide (1) whether the statute unambiguously forbids the Agency's interpretation, and, if not, (2) whether the interpretation, for other reasons, exceeds the bounds of the permissible. *Ibid.*; see also *United States v. Mead Corp.*, 533 U.S. 218, 227 (2001).

First, the statute does not unambiguously forbid the regulation. The Fourth Circuit believed the contrary primarily for a linguistic reason. It pointed out that, linguistically speaking, the statute's "12-month" phrase modifies only the word "impairment," not the word "inability." And to that extent we agree. After all, the statute, in parallel phrasing, uses the words "which can be expected to result in death." And that structurally parallel phrase makes sense in reference to an "impairment," but makes no sense in reference to the "inability."

Nonetheless, this linguistic point is insufficient. It shows that the particular statutory provision says nothing explicitly about the "inability's" duration. But such silence, after all, normally creates ambiguity. It does not resolve it.

Moreover, a nearby provision of the statute says that an

"individual shall be determined to be under a disability only if his . . . impairment . . . [is] of such severity that he is not only unable to do his previous work but cannot . . . engage in any other kind of substantial gainful work which exists in the national economy." 42 U.S.C. § 423(d)(2)(A) (Title II); accord § 1382c(a)(3)(B) (Title XVI).

In other words, the statute, in the two provisions, specifies that the "impairment" must last 12 months and also be severe enough to prevent the claimant from engaging in virtually any "substantial gainful work." The statute, we concede, nowhere explicitly says that the "impairment" must be *that severe* (*i.e.*, severe enough to prevent "substantial gainful work") for 12 months. But that is a fair inference from the language. At the very least the statute is ambiguous in that respect. And, if so, then it is an equally fair inference that the "inability" must last 12 months. That is because the latter statement (*i.e.*, that the claimant must be unable to "engage in any substantial gainful activity" for a year) is the virtual equivalent of the former statement (*i.e.*, that the "impairment" must remain severe enough to prevent the claimant from engaging in "substantial gainful work" for a year). It simply rephrases the same point in a slightly different way.

Second, the Agency's construction is "permissible." The interpretation makes considerable sense in terms of the statute's basic objectives. The statute demands some duration requirement. No one claims that the statute would permit an individual with a chronic illness—say, high blood pressure—to qualify for benefits if that illness, while itself lasting for a year, were to permit a claimant to return to work after only a week, or perhaps even a day, away from the job. The Agency's interpretation supplies a duration requirement, which the statute demands, while doing so in a way that consistently reconciles the statutory "impairment" and "inability" language.

In addition, the Agency's regulations reflect the Agency's own longstanding interpretation. See Social Security Ruling 82–52, p. 106 (cum. ed. 1982) ("In considering 'duration,' it is the inability to engage in [substantial gainful activity] that must last the required 12-month period"); Disability Insurance State Manual § 316 (Sept. 9, 1965), Government Lodging, Tab C, § 316 ("Duration of impairment refers to that period of time during which an individual is continuously unable to engage in substantial gainful activity because of" an impairment); OASI Disability Insurance Letter No. 39 (Jan. 22, 1957), *id.*, Tab A, p. 1 (duration requirement refers to the "expected duration of the *medical impairment*" at a "level of severity sufficient to preclude substantial gainful activity"). And this Court will normally accord particular deference to an agency interpretation of "longstanding" duration. *North Haven Bd. of Ed. v. Bell*, 456 U.S. 512, 522, n. 12 (1982).

Finally, Congress has frequently amended or reenacted the relevant provisions without change. *E.g.*, Social Security Amendments of 1965, § 303(a)(1), 79 Stat. 366; see also S.Rep. No. 404, 89th Cong., 1st Sess., pt. I, pp. 98–99 (1965), U.S.Code Cong. & Admin.News 1965, pp. 1943, 2039 ("[T]he committee's bill . . . provide[s] for the payment of disability benefits for an insured worker who has been or can be expected to be *totally disabled* throughout a continuous period of 12 calendar months" (emphasis added)); *id.*, at 98, U.S.Code Cong. & Admin.News 1965, pp. 1943, 2038 (rejecting effort to provide benefits to those with "short-term, temporary disabilit[ies]," defined as inability to work for six months); H.R.Rep. No. 92–231, p. 56 (1971) ("No benefit is payable, however, unless the *disability* is expected to last (or has lasted) at least 12 consecutive months" (emphasis added)); S.Rep. No. 744, 90th Cong., 1st Sess., 49 (1967), U.S.Code Cong. & Admin.News 1967, pp. 2834, 2883 ("The committee also believes . . . that an individual who does substantial gainful work despite an impairment or impairments that otherwise might be considered disabling is not disabled for purposes of establishing a period of disability"). These circumstances provide further evidence—if more is needed—that Congress intended the Agency's interpretation, or at least understood the interpretation as statutorily permissible. *Commodity Futures Trading Comm'n v. Schor*, 478 U.S. 833, 845–846 (1986).

Walton points in reply to Title II language stating that a claimant who is "under a disability . . . shall be entitled to a . . . benefit . . . beginning with the first month after" a "waiting period" of "five consecutive calendar months . . . throughout which" he "has been under a disability."*221 42 U.S.C. §§ 423(a)(1)(D)(i), 423(c)(2)(A). He adds that this 5-month "waiting period" assures a lengthy period of time during which the applicant (who must be "under a disability" throughout) has been unable to work. And it thereby provides ironclad protection against the claimant who suffers a chronic, but only briefly disabling, disease, such as the claimant who suffers high blood pressure in our earlier example. This claim does not help Walton, however, for it shows, at most, that the Agency might have chosen other reasonable time periods—a matter not disputed. Regardless, Walton's "waiting period" argument could work only in respect to Title II, not Title XVI. Title XVI has no waiting period, though it uses identical definitional language. And Walton does not explain why we should interpret the same statutory words differently in closely related contexts. See *Department of Revenue of Ore. v. ACF Industries, Inc.*, 510 U.S. 332, 342 (1994) (" '[I]dentical words used in different parts of the same act are intended to have the same meaning' ") (quoting *Sorenson v. Secretary of Treasury*, 475 U.S. 851, 860 (1986) (some internal quotation marks omitted)).

Walton also asks us to disregard the Agency's interpretation of its formal regulations on the ground that the Agency only recently enacted those regulations, perhaps in response to this litigation. We have previously rejected similar arguments. *Smiley v. Citibank (South Dakota), N. A.*, 517 U.S. 735, 741 (1996); *United States v. Morton*, 467 U.S. 822, 835–836, n. 21 (1984).

Regardless, the Agency's interpretation is one of long standing. And the fact that the Agency previously reached its interpretation through means less formal than "notice and comment" rulemaking, see 5 U.S.C. § 553, does not automatically deprive that interpretation of the judicial deference otherwise its due. Cf. *Chevron*, 467 U.S., at 843 (stating, without delineation of means, that the " 'power of an administrative agency to administer a congressionally created . . . program necessarily requires the formulation of policy' " (quoting *Morton v. Ruiz*, 415 U.S. 199, 231 (1974))). If this Court's opinion in *Christensen v. Harris County*, 529 U.S. 576 (2000), suggested an absolute rule to the contrary, our later opinion in *United States v. Mead Corp.*, 533 U.S. 218 (2001), denied the suggestion. *Id.*, at 230–231 ("[T]he want of" notice and comment "does not decide the case"). Indeed, *Mead* pointed to instances in which the Court has applied *Chevron* deference to agency interpretations that did not emerge out of notice-and-comment rulemaking. 533 U.S., at 230–231 (citing *NationsBank of N. C., N.A. v. Variable Annuity Life Ins. Co.*, 513 U.S. 251, 256–257 (1995)). It indicated that whether a court should give such deference depends in significant part upon the interpretive method used and the nature of the question at issue. 533 U.S., at 229–231. And it discussed at length why *Chevron* did not require deference in the circumstances there present—a discussion that would have been superfluous had the presence or absence of notice-and-comment rulemaking been dispositive. 533 U.S., at 231–234.

In this case, the interstitial nature of the legal question, the related expertise of the Agency, the importance of the question to administration of the statute, the complexity of that administration, and the careful consideration the Agency has given the question over a long period of time all indicate that *Chevron* provides the appropriate legal lens through which to view the legality of the Agency interpretation here at issue. See *United States v. Mead Corp., supra*; cf. also 1 K. Davis & R. Pierce, Administrative Law Treatise §§ 1.7, 3.3 (3d ed.1994).

For these reasons, we find the Agency's interpretation lawful.

■ JUSTICE SCALIA, concurring in part and concurring in the judgment.

* * *

I agree that deference is owed to regulations of the Social Security Administration (SSA) interpreting the definition of "disability," 42 U.S.C. §§ 423(d)(1)(A), 1382c(a)(3)(A) (1994 ed. and Supp. V). See 65 Fed. Reg. 42774 (2000). As the Court acknowledges, the recency of these regulations is irrelevant. I would therefore not go on, as the Court does, to address the SSA's prior interpretation of the definition of "disability" in a 1982 Social Security Ruling, a 1965 Disability Insurance State Manual, and a 1957 OASI Disability Insurance Letter.

I do not believe, to begin with, that "particular deference" is owed "to an agency interpretation of 'longstanding' duration." That notion is an anachronism—a relic of the pre-*Chevron* days, when there was thought to be only one "correct" interpretation of a statutory text. A "longstanding" agency interpretation, particularly one that dated back to the very origins of the statute, was more likely to reflect the single correct meaning. See, *e.g., Watt v. Alaska*, 451 U.S. 259, 272–273 (1981). But once it is accepted, as it was in *Chevron*, that there is a range of permissible interpretations, and that the agency is free to move from one to another, so long as the most recent interpretation is reasonable its antiquity should make no difference. Cf. *Rust v. Sullivan*, 500 U.S. 173, 186–187 (1991); *Chevron U.S.A. Inc. v. Natural Resources Defense Council, Inc.*, 467 U.S. 837, 863–864 (1984).

If, however, the Court does wish to credit the SSA's earlier interpretations—both for the purpose of giving the agency's position "particular deference" and for the purpose of relying upon congressional reenactment with presumed knowledge of the agency position—then I think the Court should state why those interpretations were authoritative enough (or whatever-else-enough *Mead* requires) to qualify for deference. See *United States v. Mead Corp.*, 533 U.S. 218 (2001). I of course agree that more than notice-and-comment rulemaking qualifies, but that concession alone does not validate the Social Security Ruling, the Disability Insurance State Manual, and the OASI Disability Insurance Letter. (Only the latter two, I might point out, antedate the congressional reenactments upon which the Court relies.)

The SSA's recently enacted regulations emerged from notice-and-comment rulemaking and merit deference. No more need be said.

NOTES AND QUESTIONS

1. Legal scholars have sharply criticized the Supreme Court for what they see as inconsistency in the Court's explanations of when *Chevron* review is or is not appropriate. Consider the Court's statements in *Barnhart* regarding the scope of *Chevron*'s applicability. How do those statements compare with the Court's opinion in *Mead*? How do they compare with the Justice Breyer's dissenting opinion in *Christensen v. Harris County*? Are *Mead* and *Barnhart* reconcilable?

2. A subsequent Third Circuit case offers an interesting attempt to blend the Supreme Court's analysis from both *Mead* and *Barnhart*. In *Hagans v. Commissioner of Social Security*, 694 F.3d 287 (3d Cir. 2012), the court concluded that *Skidmore* review rather than *Chevron* deference applied to a

Social Security Acquiescence Ruling interpreting statutory standards for terminating disability benefits. Recognizing *Mead*'s two-part test emphasizing the agency's exercise of congressionally delegated power as its "overarching concern," the court went on to draw from *Barnhart* five additional factors for consideration: "(1) the interstitial nature of the legal question; (2) the related expertise of the agency; (3) the importance of the question to administration of the statute; (4) the complexity of that administration; and (5) the careful consideration the agency has given the question over a long period of time." Despite contending that some of these factors, such as Congress's reliance on the Social Security Administration to resolve the program's day-to-day administrative details and the importance of the issue to the administration of the program, weighed in favor of *Chevron* deference, the court decided that the Acquiescence Ruling merited only *Skidmore* review because it did not go through notice and comment procedures, lacked the force of law, and was not well explained.

The Modern *Skidmore* Doctrine

With the Court's apparent resurrection of *Skidmore* review in *Christensen*, *Mead*, and *Barnhart v. Walton*, we must return to a question we asked earlier in this Chapter: what is the difference between *Chevron* deference and *Skidmore* deference? In order to answer that question, you need to know something about the manner in which courts have applied the two deference doctrines and the results of those applications. Many pages of this Chapter Six are devoted to considering various cases in which the Supreme Court has applied *Chevron*'s two steps. But what of *Skidmore*?

Careful review of pre-*Mead* jurisprudence and legal scholarship uncovers two competing visions of *Skidmore* analysis. Colin Diver has suggested that *Skidmore*'s emphasis on deferring to agency legal interpretations based on their power to persuade represents no deference at all, as "the 'weight' assigned to any advocate's position is presumably dependent upon the 'thoroughness evident in its consideration' and the 'validity of its reasoning.'" Colin Diver, *Statutory Interpretation in the Administrative States*, 133 U. PA. L. REV. 549, 565 (1985). Diver comprehends deference under *Skidmore* to depend upon the merits of the agency's interpretation as evaluated by a reviewing court using its independent judgment. Several opinions of the Supreme Court since *Mead* are consistent with this view, with the Court declaring itself persuaded by the agency's interpretation for *Skidmore* purposes based primarily on its own analysis of the best interpretation of the statute and the agency's conformity therewith. *See, e.g., Raymond B. Yates, M.D., P.C. Profit Sharing Plan v. Hendon*, 541 U.S. 1 (2004); *Clackamas Gastroenterology Associates v. Wells*, 538 U.S. 440 (2003).

A competing conception characterizes *Skidmore* as prescribing deference along a continuum or sliding scale, with the degree of deference varying according to the reviewing court's evaluation of various contextual factors. Those factors include those mentioned by Justice Jackson in *Skidmore* itself—thoroughness of consideration, validity of reasoning, and consistency with earlier and later pronouncements—as well as factors relied upon by the courts in subsequent cases, such as whether the interpretation is longstanding or was adopted by the agency shortly after Congress enacted the relevant statutory language, whether the interpretation falls clearly within the realm of the agency's expertise, or whether the agency utilized extensive procedures in vetting the interpretation. At least in theory, the sliding scale model is deferential because courts must evaluate the agency's interpretation by reference to the various factors and may not reject the agency's interpretation solely because it differs from their own preference. The *Mead* opinion, excerpted earlier in this Chapter, and a few of the Supreme Court's post-*Mead* applications of the *Skidmore* standard are consistent with this approach. *See, e.g., Alaska Department of Environmental Conservation v. EPA*, 540 U.S. 461 (2004).

In the only empirical study of judicial applications of *Skidmore* published since the Supreme Court decided *Mead*, Professor Hickman and Matthew Krueger found that, while the Court's application of the *Skidmore* standard tends more often to reflect its independent judgment regarding a statute's best interpretation, the federal courts of appeals overwhelmingly rely on the contextual factors in evaluating agency legal interpretations under *Skidmore*, consistent with the sliding scale model. *See* Kristin E. Hickman & Matthew D. Krueger, *In Search of the Modern* Skidmore *Standard*, 107 COLUM. L. REV. 1235 (2007). Nevertheless, there is great confusion among the circuit courts as to what each factor represents, how the factors relate to one another, and how much weight they should accord to each. For example, does the thoroughness factor test the depth of an agency's explanation in support of its interpretation or the extensiveness of an agency's vetting process in adopting the interpretation? Also, Justice Jackson's opinion in *Skidmore* listed consistency as a factor influencing an interpretation's persuasiveness, yet given the Court's de-emphasis on consistency as a factor influencing judicial deference under the *Chevron* standard, how important is consistency in modern *Skidmore* analysis? Courts often cite expertise as a factor in *Skidmore* analysis, but should the courts simply assume that an agency tasked with administering a statute actually employed its unique expertise in adopting a particular interpretation, or should reviewing courts require some more particular demonstration for *Skidmore* purposes?

D. *CHEVRON* AND STARE DECISIS

For all of its flaws and ambiguities, *Mead* at least acknowledges a need and offers a framework for thinking about *Chevron* deference for certain types of agency actions. *Mead* did not, however, resolve all of the questions concerning the scope of *Chevron*'s applicability. Justice Scalia's dissenting opinion in *Mead* particularly raised the question of the relationship between stare decisis and the *Chevron* standard: if a reviewing court, including but not limited to the Supreme Court, has issued an opinion that reaches a conclusion regarding statutory meaning, does an agency have the authority to adopt an alternative reading of the statute through notice-and-comment rulemaking or formal adjudication; and if so, then is that alternative interpretation entitled to *Chevron* deference? Prior to the Court's decisions in *Christensen* and *Mead*, this issue had divided the circuit courts with respect to their own interpretations of agency-administered statutes. In the following case, the Supreme Court squarely addressed precisely that question.

National Cable & Telecomm. Ass'n v. Brand X Internet Services

545 U.S. 967 (2005).

■ JUSTICE THOMAS delivered the opinion of the Court.

Title II of the Communications Act of 1934 subjects all providers of "telecommunications servic[e]" to mandatory common-carrier regulation. 47 U.S.C. § 153(44). In the order under review, the Federal Communications Commission concluded that cable companies that sell broadband Internet service do not provide "telecommunications servic[e]" as the Communications Act defines that term, and hence are exempt from mandatory common-carrier regulation under Title II. We must decide whether that conclusion is a lawful construction of the Communications Act under *Chevron U.S.A. Inc. v. Natural Resources Defense Council, Inc.*, 467 U.S. 837 (1984), and the Administrative Procedure Act. We hold that it is.

I

The traditional means by which consumers in the United States access the network of interconnected computers that make up the Internet is through "dial-up" connections provided over local telephone facilities. *See In re Inquiry Concerning High-Speed Access to the Internet Over Cable & Other Facilities*, 17 F.C.C. Rcd. 4798, 4802, 4803, ¶ 9 (2002) (hereinafter *Declaratory Ruling*). Using these connections, consumers access the Internet by making calls with computer modems through the telephone wires owned by local phone companies. Internet service providers (ISPs), in turn, link those calls to the Internet network, not only by providing a physical connection, but also by offering consumers the ability to translate raw Internet data into information they may both view on their personal computers and transmit to other computers connected to the Internet. Technological limitations of local telephone wires, however, retard the speed at which data from the Internet may be transmitted through end users' dial-up connections. Dial-up connections are therefore known as "narrowband," or slower speed, connections.

"Broadband" Internet service, by contrast, transmits data at much higher speeds. There are two principal kinds of broadband Internet service: cable modem service and Digital Subscriber Line (DSL) service. Cable modem service transmits data between the Internet and users' computers via the network of television cable lines owned by cable companies. DSL service provides high-speed access using the local telephone wires owned by local telephone companies. Cable companies and telephone companies can either provide Internet access directly to consumers, thus acting as ISPs themselves, or can lease their transmission facilities to independent ISPs that then use the facilities to provide consumers with Internet access. Other ways of transmitting high-speed Internet data into homes, including terrestrial-and satellite-based wireless networks, are also emerging.

II

At issue in these cases is the proper regulatory classification under the Communications Act of broadband cable Internet service. The Act, as amended by the Telecommunications Act of 1996, defines two categories of regulated entities relevant to these cases: telecommunications carriers and information-service providers. The Act regulates telecommunications carriers, but not information-service providers, as common carriers. Telecommunications carriers, for example, must charge just and reasonable, nondiscriminatory rates to their customers, design their systems so that other carriers can interconnect with their communications networks, and contribute to the federal "universal service" fund. These provisions are mandatory, but the Commission must forbear from applying them if it determines that the public interest requires it. Information-service providers, by contrast, are not subject to mandatory common-carrier regulation under Title II, though the Commission has jurisdiction to impose additional regulatory obligations under its Title I ancillary jurisdiction to regulate interstate and foreign communications.

* * *

"Telecommunications service" * * * is "the offering of telecommunications for a fee directly to the public . . . regardless of the facilities used." 47 U.S.C. § 153(46). "Telecommunications" is "the transmission, between or among points specified by the user, of information of the user's choosing, without change in the form or content of the information as sent and received." § 153(43). "Telecommunications carrier[s]"—those subjected to mandatory Title II common-carrier regulation—are defined as "provider[s] of telecommunications services." § 153(44). And "information service"—the analog to enhanced service—is "the offering of a capability for generating, acquiring, storing, transforming, processing, retrieving, utilizing, or making available information via telecommunications. . . ." § 153(20).

In September 2000, the Commission initiated a rulemaking proceeding to, among other things, apply these classifications to cable companies that offer broadband Internet service directly to consumers. In March 2002, that rulemaking culminated in the *Declaratory Ruling* under review in these cases. In the *Declaratory Ruling*, the Commission concluded that broadband Internet service provided by cable companies is an "information service" but not a "telecommunications service" under the Act, and therefore not subject to mandatory Title II common-carrier regulation. * * * Because Internet access provides a capability for manipulating and storing information, the Commission concluded that it was an information service.

The integrated nature of Internet access and the high-speed wire used to provide Internet access led the Commission to conclude that cable companies providing Internet access are not telecommunications providers. * * * [T]he Commission reasoned that consumers use their cable modems not to transmit information "transparently," such as by using a telephone, but instead to obtain Internet access.

The Commission applied this same reasoning to cable companies offering broadband Internet access. Its logic was that, like non-facilities-based ISPs, cable companies do not "offe[r] telecommunications service to the end user, but rather . . . merely us[e] telecommunications to provide end users with cable modem service." *Declaratory Ruling* 4824, ¶ 41. * * * Numerous parties petitioned for judicial review, challenging the Commission's conclusion that cable modem service was not telecommunications service. By judicial lottery, the Court of Appeals for the Ninth Circuit was selected as the venue for the challenge.

* * * [T]he Court of Appeals vacated the ruling to the extent it concluded that cable modem service was not "telecommunications service" under the Communications Act. It held that the Commission could not permissibly construe the Communications Act to exempt cable companies providing Internet service from Title II regulation. Rather than analyzing the permissibility of that construction under the deferential framework of *Chevron*, however, the Court of Appeals grounded its holding in the *stare decisis* effect of *AT&T Corp. v. Portland*, 216 F.3d 871 (9th Cir. 2000). *Portland* held that cable modem service was a "telecommunications service," though the court in that case was not reviewing an administrative proceeding and the Commission was not a party to the case. Nevertheless, *Portland*'s holding, the Court of Appeals reasoned, overrode the contrary interpretation reached by the Commission in the *Declaratory Ruling*.

We granted certiorari to settle the important questions of federal law that these cases present.

III

We first consider whether we should apply *Chevron*'s framework to the Commission's interpretation of the term "telecommunications service." We conclude that we should. We also conclude that the Court of Appeals should have done the same, instead of following the contrary construction it adopted in *Portland*.

A

In *Chevron*, this Court held that ambiguities in statutes within an agency's jurisdiction to administer are delegations of authority to the agency to fill the statutory gap in reasonable fashion. Filling these gaps, the Court explained, involves difficult policy choices that agencies are better equipped to make than courts. If a statute is ambiguous, and if the implementing agency's construction is reasonable, *Chevron* requires a federal court to accept the agency's construction of the statute, even if the agency's reading differs from what the court believes is the best statutory interpretation.

The *Chevron* framework governs our review of the Commission's construction. Congress has delegated to the Commission the authority to "execute and enforce" the Communications Act, § 151, and to "prescribe such rules and regulations as may be necessary in the public interest to carry out the provisions" of the Act, § 201(b); *AT&T Corp. v. Ia. Utilities Bd.*, 525 U.S. 366, 377–78 (1999). These provisions give the Commission the authority to promulgate binding legal rules; the Commission issued the order under review in the exercise of that authority; and no one questions that the order is within the Commission's jurisdiction. *See United States v. Mead Corp.*, 533 U.S. 218, 231–34 (2001). Hence, as we have in the past, we apply the

Chevron framework to the Commission's interpretation of the Communications Act.

Some of the respondents dispute this conclusion, on the ground that the Commission's interpretation is inconsistent with its past practice. We reject this argument. Agency inconsistency is not a basis for declining to analyze the agency's interpretation under the *Chevron* framework. Unexplained inconsistency is, at most, a reason for holding an interpretation to be an arbitrary and capricious change from agency practice under the Administrative Procedure Act. *See Motor Vehicle Mfrs. Ass'n of United States, Inc. v. State Farm Mut. Auto. Ins. Co.*, 463 U.S. 29, 46–57 (1983). For if the agency adequately explains the reasons for a reversal of policy, "change is not invalidating, since the whole point of *Chevron* is to leave the discretion provided by the ambiguities of a statute with the implementing agency." *Smiley v. Citibank (S.D.), N. A.*, 517 U.S. 735, 742 (1996). "An initial agency interpretation is not instantly carved in stone. On the contrary, the agency . . . must consider varying interpretations and the wisdom of its policy on a continuing basis," *Chevron*, 467 U.S. at 863–64, for example, in response to changed factual circumstances, or a change in administrations. That is no doubt why in *Chevron* itself, this Court deferred to an agency interpretation that was a recent reversal of agency policy. We therefore have no difficulty concluding that *Chevron* applies.

B

The Court of Appeals declined to apply *Chevron* because it thought the Commission's interpretation of the Communications Act foreclosed by the conflicting construction of the Act it had adopted in *Portland*. It based that holding on the assumption that *Portland*'s construction overrode the Commission's, regardless of whether *Portland* had held the statute to be unambiguous. That reasoning was incorrect.

A court's prior judicial construction of a statute trumps an agency construction otherwise entitled to *Chevron* deference only if the prior court decision holds that its construction follows from the unambiguous terms of the statute and thus leaves no room for agency discretion. This principle follows from *Chevron* itself. *Chevron* established a "presumption that Congress, when it left ambiguity in a statute meant for implementation by an agency, understood that the ambiguity would be resolved, first and foremost, by the agency, and desired the agency (rather than the courts) to possess whatever degree of discretion the ambiguity allows." *Smiley*, 517 U.S. at 740–41. Yet allowing a judicial precedent to foreclose an agency from interpreting an ambiguous statute, as the Court of Appeals assumed it could, would allow a court's interpretation to override an agency's. *Chevron*'s premise is that it is for agencies, not courts, to fill statutory gaps. The better rule is to hold judicial interpretations contained in precedents to the same demanding *Chevron* step one standard that applies if the court is reviewing the agency's construction on a blank slate: Only a judicial precedent holding that the statute unambiguously forecloses the agency's interpretation, and therefore contains no gap for the agency to fill, displaces a conflicting agency construction.

A contrary rule would produce anomalous results. It would mean that whether an agency's interpretation of an ambiguous statute is entitled to *Chevron* deference would turn on the order in which the interpretations issue: If the court's construction came first, its construction would prevail, whereas if the agency's came first, the agency's construction would command *Chevron* deference. Yet whether Congress has delegated to an agency the authority to interpret a statute does not depend on the order in which the judicial and administrative constructions occur. The Court of Appeals' rule, moreover, would "lead to the ossification of large portions of our statutory law," *Mead*, 533 U.S. at 247 (Scalia, J., dissenting), by precluding agencies from revising unwise judicial constructions of ambiguous statutes. Neither *Chevron* nor the doctrine of *stare decisis* requires these haphazard results.

The dissent answers that allowing an agency to override what a court believes to be the best interpretation of a statute makes "judicial decisions subject to reversal by executive officers." It does not. Since *Chevron* teaches that a court's opinion as to the best reading of an ambiguous statute an agency is charged with administering is not authoritative, the agency's decision to construe that statute differently from a court does not say that the court's holding was legally wrong. Instead, the agency may, consistent with the court's holding, choose a different construction, since the agency remains the authoritative interpreter (within the limits of reason) of such statutes. In all other respects, the court's prior ruling remains binding law (for example, as to agency interpretations to which *Chevron* is inapplicable). The precedent has not been "reversed" by the agency, any more than a federal court's interpretation of a State's law can be said to have been "reversed" by a state court that adopts a conflicting (yet authoritative) interpretation of state law.

The Court of Appeals derived a contrary rule from a mistaken reading of this Court's decisions. It read *Neal v. United States*, 516 U.S. 284 (1996), to establish that a prior judicial construction of a statute categorically controls an agency's contrary construction. *Neal* established no such proposition. *Neal* declined to defer to a construction adopted by the United States Sentencing Commission that conflicted with one the Court previously had adopted in *Chapman v. United States*, 500 U.S. 453 (1991). *Chapman*, however, had held the relevant statute to be unambiguous. Thus, *Neal* established only that a precedent holding a statute to be unambiguous forecloses a contrary agency construction. That limited holding accorded with this Court's prior decisions, which had held that a court's interpretation of a statute trumps an agency's under the doctrine of *stare decisis* only if the prior court holding "determined a statute's *clear* meaning." *Maislin Indus., U.S., Inc. v. Primary Steel, Inc.*, 497 U.S. 116 (1990). Those decisions allow a court's prior interpretation of a statute to override an agency's interpretation only if the relevant court decision held the statute unambiguous.

Against this background, the Court of Appeals erred in refusing to apply *Chevron* to the Commission's interpretation of the definition of "telecommunications service," 47 U.S.C. § 153(46). Its prior decision in *Portland* held only that the *best* reading of § 153(46) was that cable modem service was a "telecommunications service," not that it was the *only permissible* reading of the statute. Nothing in *Portland* held that the Communications Act unambiguously required treating cable Internet providers as telecommunications carriers. Instead, the court noted that it was "not presented with a case involving potential deference to an administrative agency's statutory construction pursuant to the *Chevron* doctrine," *Portland*, 216 F.3d at 876; and the court invoked no other rule of construction (such as the rule of lenity) requiring it to conclude that the statute was unambiguous to reach its judgment. Before a judicial construction of a statute, whether contained in a precedent or not, may trump an agency's, the court must hold that the statute unambiguously requires the court's construction. *Portland* did not do so.

* * *

[The majority's opinion went on to analyze the FCC's action under *Chevron* and to conclude that the statute did not unambiguously resolve the matter, that the FCC's interpretation was reasonable, and that the FCC provided a reasoned explanation in support of its policy. Ed.]

The questions the Commission resolved in the order under review involve a "subject matter [that] is technical, complex, and dynamic." *Nat'l Cable & Telecomms. Ass'n, Inc. v. Gulf Power Co.*, 534 U.S. 327, 339 (2002). The Commission is in a far better position to address these questions than we are. Nothing in the Communications Act or the Administrative Procedure Act makes unlawful the Commission's use of its expert policy judgment to resolve these difficult questions. The judgment of the Court of Appeals is reversed, and the cases are remanded for further proceedings consistent with this opinion.

■ JUSTICE STEVENS, concurring.

While I join the Court's opinion in full, I add this caveat concerning Part III–B, which correctly explains why a court of appeals' interpretation of an ambiguous provision in a regulatory statute does not foreclose a contrary reading by the agency. That explanation would not necessarily be applicable to a decision by this Court that would presumably remove any pre-existing ambiguity.

■ JUSTICE BREYER, concurring.

I join the Court's opinion because I believe that the Federal Communications Commission's decision falls within the scope of its statutorily delegated authority—though perhaps just barely. I write separately because I believe it important to point out that Justice SCALIA, in my view, has wrongly characterized the Court's opinion in *United States v. Mead Corp.*, 533 U.S. 218 (2001). He states that the Court held in *Mead* that "some unspecified degree of formal process" before the agency "was required" for courts to accord the agency's decision deference under *Chevron U.S.A. Inc. v. Natural Res. Def. Council, Inc.*, 467 U.S. 837 (1984).

Justice SCALIA has correctly characterized the way in which he, *in dissent*, characterized the Court's *Mead* opinion. But the Court said the opposite. An agency action qualifies for *Chevron* deference when Congress has explicitly or implicitly delegated to the agency the authority to "fill" a statutory "gap," including an interpretive gap created through an ambiguity in the language of a statute's provisions. The Court said in *Mead* that such delegation "may be shown *in a variety of ways, as by* an agency's power to engage in adjudication or notice-and-comment rulemaking, *or by some other indication of a comparable congressional intent.*" *Mead*, 533 U.S. at 227 (emphasis added). The Court explicitly stated that the absence of notice-and-comment rulemaking did "not decide the case," for the Court has "sometimes found reasons for *Chevron* deference even when no such administrative formality was required and none was afforded." *Id.* at 231. And the Court repeated that it "has recognized *a variety of indicators* that Congress would expect *Chevron* deference." *Id.* at 237.

It is not surprising that the Court would hold that the existence of a formal rulemaking proceeding is neither a necessary nor a sufficient condition for according *Chevron* deference to an agency's interpretation of a statute. It is not a necessary condition because an agency might arrive at an authoritative interpretation of a congressional enactment in other ways, including ways that Justice SCALIA mentions. It is not a sufficient condition because Congress may have intended *not* to leave the matter of a particular interpretation up to the agency, irrespective of the procedure the agency uses to arrive at that interpretation, say, where an unusually basic legal question is at issue.

Thus, while I believe Justice SCALIA is right in emphasizing that *Chevron* deference may be appropriate in the absence of formal agency proceedings, *Mead* should not give him cause for concern.

■ JUSTICE SCALIA, with whom JUSTICE SOUTER and JUSTICE GINSBURG join as to Part I, dissenting.

[Part I of Justice Scalia's dissenting opinion was dedicated to explaining why he thought the FCC and the Court's majority misinterpreted the Communications Act. Ed.]

II

In Part III–B of its opinion, the Court continues the administrative-law improvisation project it began four years ago in *United States v. Mead Corp.*, 533 U.S. 218 (2001). To the extent it set forth a comprehensible rule, Mead drastically limited the categories of agency action that would qualify for deference under *Chevron U.S.A. Inc. v. Natural Resources Defense Council, Inc.*, 467 U.S. 837 (1984). For example, the position taken by an agency before the Supreme Court, with full approval of the agency head, would not qualify. Rather, some unspecified degree of formal process was required—or was at least the only safe harbor.

This meant that many more issues appropriate for agency determination would reach the courts without benefit of an agency position entitled to *Chevron* deference, requiring the courts to rule on these issues *de novo*.[10] As I pointed out in dissent, this in turn meant (under the law as it was understood until today)[11] that many statutory

---

[10] It is true that, even under the broad basis for deference that I propose (viz., any agency position that plainly has the approval of the agency head) some interpretive matters will be decided *de novo*, without deference to agency views. This would be a rare occurrence, however, at the Supreme Court level—at least with respect to matters of any significance to the agency. Seeking to achieve 100% agency control of ambiguous provisions through the complicated method the Court proposes is not worth the incremental benefit.

[11] The Court's unanimous holding in *Neal v. United States*, 516 U.S. 284 (1996), plainly rejected the notion that any form of deference could cause the Court to revisit a prior statutory-construction holding: "Once we have determined a statute's meaning, we adhere to our ruling under the doctrine of *stare decisis*, and we assess an agency's later interpretation of the statute against that settled law." *Id.* at 295. The Court attempts to reinterpret this plain

ambiguities that might be resolved in varying fashions by successive agency administrations would be resolved finally, conclusively, and forever, by federal judges—producing an "ossification of large portions of our statutory law," *Mead*, 533 U.S. at 247. The Court today moves to solve this problem of its own creation by inventing yet another breathtaking novelty: judicial decisions subject to reversal by executive officers.

* * *

This is not only bizarre. It is probably unconstitutional. As we held in *Chicago & Southern Air Lines, Inc. v. Waterman S.S. Corp.*, 333 U.S. 103 (1948), Article III courts do not sit to render decisions that can be reversed or ignored by executive officers. * * * That is what today's decision effectively allows. Even when the agency itself is party to the case in which the Court construes a statute, the agency will be able to disregard that construction and seek *Chevron* deference for its contrary construction the next time around.[12]

Of course, like *Mead* itself, today's novelty in belated remediation of *Mead* creates many uncertainties to bedevil the lower courts. A court's interpretation is conclusive, the Court says, only if it holds that interpretation to be "the *only permissible* reading of the statute," and not if it merely holds it to be "the *best* reading." Does this mean that in future statutory-construction cases involving agency-administered statutes courts must specify (presumably in dictum) which of the two they are holding? And what of the many cases decided in the past, before this dictum's requirement was established? Apparently, silence on the point means that the court's decision is subject to agency reversal: "Before a judicial construction of a statute, whether contained in a precedent or not, may trump an agency's, the court must hold that the statute unambiguously requires the court's construction." (I have not made, and as far as I know the Court has not made, any calculation of how many hundreds of past statutory decisions are now agency-reversible because of failure to include an "unambiguous" finding. I suspect the number is very large.) How much extra work will it entail for each court confronted with an agency-administered statute to determine whether it has reached, not only the right ("best") result, but "the only permissible" result? Is the standard for "unambiguous" under the Court's new agency-reversal rule the same as the standard for

---

language by dissecting the cases *Neal* cited, noting that they referred to previous determinations of " 'a statute's clear meaning.' " *Lechmere, Inc. v. NLRB*, 502 U.S. 527 (1992) (quoting *Maislin Indus., U.S., Inc. v. Primary Steel, Inc.*, 497 U.S. 116 (1990)). But those cases reveal that today's focus on the term "clear" is revisionist. The oldest case in the chain using that word, *Maislin Industries*, did not rely on a prior decision that held the statute to be clear, but on a run-of-the-mill statutory interpretation contained in a 1908 decision. *Id.* at 130–31. When *Maislin Industries* referred to the Court's prior determination of "a statute's clear meaning," it was referring to the fact that the prior decision had made the statute clear, and was not conducting a retrospective inquiry into whether the prior decision had declared the statute itself to be clear on its own terms.

[12] The Court contends that no reversal of judicial holdings is involved, because "a court's opinion as to the best reading of an ambiguous statute . . . is not authoritative." That fails to appreciate the difference between a *de novo* construction of a statute and a decision whether to defer to an agency's position, which does not even *"purport* to give the statute a judicial interpretation." *Mead*, 533 U.S. at 248 (Scalia, J., dissenting). Once a court has decided upon its *de novo* construction of the statute, there no longer is a "different construction" that is "consistent with the court's holding," and available for adoption by the agency.

"unambiguous" under step one of *Chevron*? (If so, of course, every case that reaches step two of *Chevron* will be agency-reversible.) Does the "unambiguous" dictum produce *stare decisis* effect even when a court is *affirming*, rather than *reversing*, agency action—so that in the future the agency *must adhere* to that affirmed interpretation? If so, does the victorious agency have the right to appeal a Court of Appeals judgment in its favor, on the ground that the text in question is in fact not (as the Court of Appeals held) unambiguous, so the agency should be able to change its view in the future?

It is indeed a wonderful new world that the Court creates, one full of promise for administrative-law professors in need of tenure articles and, of course, for litigators. I would adhere to what has been the rule in the past: When a court interprets a statute without *Chevron* deference to agency views, its interpretation (whether or not asserted to rest upon an unambiguous text) is the law. I might add that it is a great mystery why any of this is relevant here. *Whatever* the *stare decisis* effect of *AT&T Corp. v. Portland*, 216 F.3d 871 (9th Cir. 2000), in the Ninth Circuit, it surely does not govern this Court's decision. And— despite the Court's peculiar, self-abnegating suggestion to the contrary—the Ninth Circuit would already be obliged to abandon *Portland*'s holding in the face of *this Court*'s decision that the Commission's construction of "telecommunications service" is entitled to deference and is reasonable. It is a sadness that the Court should go so far out of its way to make bad law.

NOTES AND QUESTIONS

1. Regarding the binding effect of stare decisis on agencies, the Supreme Court in *Brand X* distinguishes between court decisions that find statutes to be unambiguous from those interpreting ambiguous statutes, with only the former limiting agencies' interpretive discretion. Whether or not this outcome is consistent with *Chevron* analysis, as the majority suggests, as a practical matter, how easy would you expect it to be to draw the distinction the Court identifies in each of the thousands of judicial opinions in which courts have upheld agency interpretations of agency-administered statutes?

2. In *Brand X*, the Supreme Court resolved the question of *Chevron* versus stare decisis in favor of *Chevron* after citing *Mead* for the proposition that *Chevron* generally provided the appropriate evaluative standard for the FCC's order. Although the court neither discussed nor even cited *Skidmore*, that standard shares the same tension with stare decisis as *Chevron* previously did. If Congress has not vested an agency with primary interpretive authority, should *Skidmore* factors such as expertise, consistency, and longevity lead courts to reject their own interpretations in favor of those advanced by agencies? Even if an agency does possess the authority to bind regulated parties with the force of law, should a court feel compelled to ignore its own precedent in favor of agency interpretations expressed through thoroughly- and expertly-reasoned opinion letters or amicus briefs? Does the reasoning of *Brand X* offer any hints for resolving this question?

3. Recall our earlier observation regarding the difficulty of discerning whether a traditional canon of construction that dictates a particular outcome in the face of statutory ambiguity should be one of the tools that reviewing courts should use in applying *Chevron* step one. In discussing

AT&T Corp. v. Portland, 216 F.3d 871 (9th Cir. 2000), the *Brand X* Court explicitly referred to the rule of lenity as a "rule of construction . . . requiring [a court] to conclude that the statute was unambiguous." The rule of lenity requires courts to construe statutes in the light most favorable to criminal defendants. In a few civil cases such as *Crandon v. United States*, 494 U.S. 152 (1990), and *United States v. Thompson/Center Arms Co.*, 504 U.S. 505 (1992), the Supreme Court applied the rule of lenity to evaluate agency interpretations of agency-administered statutes that could alternatively support criminal prosecutions. For a more in-depth analysis of this issue, *see* Kristin E. Hickman, *Of Lenity,* Chevron, *and KPMG*, 26 VA. TAX REV. 905 (2007). How seriously should we take the *Brand X* Court's passing reference regarding lenity and statutory ambiguity? Recognizing that many regulatory statutes allow for criminal penalties for more egregious violations, what do you think the implications would be for judicial deference toward agency legal interpretations if the courts routinely applied canons like the rule of lenity at *Chevron* step one?

Brand X concerned whether *Chevron* or stare decisis governed judicial review of an agency regulation in conflict with a federal circuit court precedent. Left unanswered by *Brand X* was whether *Chevron* or stare decisis would govern judicial review of agency action in conflict with a Supreme Court decision. That question has divided the federal circuit courts. With that disagreement in mind, consider the competing opinions in the following case.

United States v. Home Concrete & Supply, LLC

132 S. Ct. 1836 (2012).

■ Justice Breyer delivered the opinion of the Court, except as to Part IV–C.

Ordinarily, the Government must assess a deficiency against a taxpayer within "3 years after the return was filed." 26 U.S.C. § 6501(a) (2000 ed.). The 3-year period is extended to 6 years, however, when a taxpayer *"omits from gross income an amount properly includible therein* which is in excess of 25 percent of the amount of gross income stated in the return." § 6501(e)(1)(A) (emphasis added). The question before us is whether this latter provision applies (and extends the ordinary 3-year limitations period) when the taxpayer *overstates his basis* in property that he has sold, thereby *understating the gain* that he received from its sale. Following *Colony, Inc. v. Commissioner*, 357 U.S. 28 (1958), we hold that the provision does not apply to an overstatement of basis. Hence the 6-year period does not apply.

I

For present purposes the relevant underlying circumstances are not in dispute. We consequently assume that (1) the respondent taxpayers filed their relevant tax returns in April 2000; (2) the returns overstated the basis of certain property that the taxpayers had sold; (3) as a result the returns understated the gross income that the taxpayers received from the sale of the property; and (4) the understatement exceeded the statute's 25% threshold. We also take as undisputed that the Commissioner asserted the relevant deficiency within the extended 6-year limitations period, but outside the default 3-year period. Thus, unless the 6-year statute of limitations applies, the Government's efforts to assert a tax deficiency came too late. Our conclusion—that the extended limitations period does not apply—follows directly from this Court's earlier decision in *Colony*.

II

In *Colony* this Court interpreted a provision of the Internal Revenue Code of 1939, the operative language of which is identical to the language now before us. The Commissioner there had determined

> "that the taxpayer had understated the gross profits on the sales of certain lots of land for residential purposes as a result of having overstated the 'basis' of such lots by erroneously including in their cost certain unallowable items of development expense." *Id.*, at 30.

The Commissioner's assessment came after the ordinary 3-year limitations period had run. And, it was consequently timely only if the taxpayer, in the words of the 1939 Code, had "omit[ted] from gross income an amount properly includible therein which is in excess of 25 per centum of the amount of gross income stated in the return. . . ." 26 U.S.C. § 275(c) (1940 ed.). The Code provision applicable to this case, adopted in 1954, contains materially indistinguishable language. See § 6501(e)(1)(A) (2000 ed.) (same, but replacing "per centum" with "percent").

In *Colony* this Court held that taxpayer misstatements, overstating the basis in property, do not fall within the scope of the statute. But the Court recognized the Commissioner's contrary argument for inclusion. 357 U.S., at 32. Then as now, the Code itself defined "gross income" in this context as the difference between gross revenue (often the amount the taxpayer received upon selling the property) and basis (often the amount the taxpayer paid for the property). Compare 26 U.S.C. §§ 22, 111 (1940 ed.) with §§ 61(a)(3), 1001(a) (2000 ed.). And, the Commissioner pointed out, an overstatement of basis can diminish the "amount" of the gain just as leaving the item entirely off the return might do. 357 U.S., at 32. Either way, the error wrongly understates the taxpayer's income.

But, the Court added, the Commissioner's argument did not fully account for the provision's language, in particular the word "omit." The key phrase says "*omits* . . . an amount." The word "omits" (unlike, say, "reduces" or "understates") means " '[t]o leave out or unmentioned; not to insert, include, or name.' " Thus, taken literally, "omit" limits the statute's scope to situations in which specific receipts or accruals of income are *left out* of the computation of gross income; to inflate the basis, however, is not to "omit" a specific item, not even of profit.

While finding this latter interpretation of the language the "more plausibl[e]," the Court also noted that the language was not "unambiguous." *Colony*, 357 U.S., at 33. It then examined various congressional Reports discussing the relevant statutory language. It found in those Reports

> "persuasive indications that Congress merely had in mind failures to report particular income receipts and accruals, and

did not intend the [extended] limitation to apply whenever gross income was understated. . . ." *Id.*, at 35.

This "history," the Court said, "shows . . . that the Congress intended an exception to the usual three-year statute of limitations only in the restricted type of situation already described," a situation that did not include overstatements of basis. *Id.*, at 36.

The Court wrote that Congress, in enacting the provision,

> "manifested no broader purpose than to give the Commissioner an additional two [now three] years to investigate tax returns in cases where, because of a taxpayer's omission to report some taxable item, the Commissioner is at a special disadvantage . . . [because] the return on its face provides no clue to the existence of the omitted item. . . . [W]hen, *as here* [*i.e.*, where the overstatement of basis is at issue], the understatement of a tax arises from an error in reporting an item disclosed on the face of the return the Commissioner is at no such disadvantage . . . whether the error be one affecting 'gross income' or one, such as overstated deductions, affecting other parts of the return." *Ibid.* (emphasis added).

Finally, the Court noted that Congress had recently enacted the Internal Revenue Code of 1954. And the Court observed that "the conclusion we reach is in harmony with the unambiguous language of § 6501(e)(1)(A)," *id.*, at 37, *i.e.*, the provision relevant in this present case.

III

In our view, *Colony* determines the outcome in this case. The provision before us is a 1954 reenactment of the 1939 provision that Colony interpreted. The operative language is identical. It would be difficult, perhaps impossible, to give the same language here a different interpretation without effectively overruling *Colony*, a course of action that basic principles of *stare decisis* wisely counsel us not to take. *John R. Sand & Gravel Co. v. United States*, 552 U.S. 130, 139 (2008) ("[S]tare decisis in respect to statutory interpretation has special force, for Congress remains free to alter what we have done" (internal quotation marks omitted)); *Patterson v. McLean Credit Union*, 491 U.S. 164, 172–173 (1989).

The Government, in an effort to convince us to interpret the operative language before us differently, points to differences in other nearby parts of the 1954 Code. It suggests that these differences counsel in favor of a different interpretation than the one adopted in *Colony*.

* * *

In our view, these points are too fragile to bear the significant argumentative weight the Government seeks to place upon them.

* * *

IV

A

* * * [T]he Government points to Treasury Regulation § 301.6501(e)–1, which was promulgated in final form in December 2010. See 26 CFR § 301.6501(e)–1 (2011). The regulation, as relevant here, departs from *Colony* and interprets the operative language of the statute in the Government's favor. The regulation says that "an understated amount of gross income resulting from an overstatement of unrecovered cost or other basis constitutes an omission from gross income." § 301.6501(e)–1(a)(1)(iii). In the Government's view this new regulation in effect overturns *Colony*'s interpretation of this statute.

The Government points out that the Treasury Regulation constitutes "an agency's construction of a statute which it administers." *Chevron, U.S.A. Inc. v. Natural Resources Defense Council, Inc.*, 467 U.S. 837, 842 (1984). See also *Mayo Foundation for Medical Ed. and Research v. United States*, 131 S.Ct. 704 (2011) (applying *Chevron* in the tax context). The Court has written that a "court's prior judicial construction of a statute trumps an agency construction otherwise entitled to *Chevron* deference only if the prior court decision holds that its construction follows from the *unambiguous* terms of the statute. . . ." *National Cable & Telecommunications Assn. v. Brand X Internet Services*, 545 U.S. 967, 982 (2005) (emphasis added). And, as the Government notes, in *Colony* itself the Court wrote that "it cannot be said that the language is unambiguous." 357 U.S., at 33. Hence, the Government concludes, *Colony* cannot govern the outcome in this case. The question, rather, is whether the agency's construction is a "permissible construction of the statute." *Chevron, supra*, at 843. And, since the Government argues that the regulation embodies a reasonable, hence permissible, construction of the statute, the Government believes it must win.

B

We do not accept this argument. In our view, *Colony* has already interpreted the statute, and there is no longer any different construction that is consistent with *Colony* and available for adoption by the agency.

C

The fatal flaw in the Government's contrary argument is that it overlooks the *reason why Brand X* held that a "prior judicial construction," unless reflecting an "unambiguous" statute, does not trump a different agency construction of that statute. 545 U.S., at 982. The Court reveals that reason when it points out that "it is for agencies, not courts, to fill statutory gaps." *Ibid.* The fact that a statute is unambiguous means that there is "no gap for the agency to fill" and thus "no room for agency discretion." *Id.*, at 982–983.

In so stating, the Court sought to encapsulate what earlier opinions, including *Chevron*, made clear. Those opinions identify the underlying interpretive problem as that of deciding whether, or when, a particular statute in effect delegates to an agency the power to fill a gap, thereby implicitly taking from a court the power to void a reasonable gap-filling interpretation. Thus, in *Chevron* the Court said that, when

"Congress has explicitly left a gap for the agency to fill, there is
an express delegation of authority to the agency to elucidate a
specific provision of the statute by regulation.... Sometimes
the legislative delegation to an agency on a particular question
is implicit rather than explicit. [But in either instance], a court
may not substitute its own construction of a statutory
provision for a reasonable interpretation made by the
administrator of an agency." 467 U.S., at 843–844.

See also *United States v. Mead Corp.*, 533 U.S. 218, 229 (2001); *Smiley
v. Citibank (South Dakota), N. A.*, 517 U.S. 735, 741 (1996); *INS v.
Cardoza-Fonseca*, 480 U.S. 421, 448 (1987); *Morton v. Ruiz*, 415 U.S.
199, 231 (1974).

Chevron and later cases find in unambiguous language a clear sign
that Congress did *not* delegate gap-filling authority to an agency; and
they find in ambiguous language at least a presumptive indication that
Congress did delegate that gap-filling authority. Thus, in *Chevron* the
Court wrote that a statute's silence or ambiguity as to a particular issue
means that Congress has not "directly addressed the precise question at
issue" (thus likely delegating gap-filling power to the agency). 467 U.S.,
at 843. In *Mead* the Court, describing *Chevron*, explained:

"Congress ... may not have expressly delegated authority or
responsibility to implement a particular provision or fill a
particular gap. Yet it can still be apparent from the agency's
generally   conferred   authority   and   other   statutory
circumstances that Congress would expect the agency to be
able to speak with the force of law when it addresses
ambiguity in the statute or fills a space in the enacted law,
even one about which Congress did not actually have an intent
as to a particular result." 533 U.S., at 229 (internal quotation
marks omitted).

Chevron added that "[i]f a court, *employing traditional tools of
statutory construction*, ascertains that Congress had an intention on the
precise question at issue, that intention is the law and must be given
effect." 467 U.S., at 843, n. 9, 104 S.Ct. 2778 (emphasis added).

As the Government points out, the Court in *Colony* stated that the
statutory language at issue is not "unambiguous." 357 U.S., at 33. But
the Court decided that case nearly 30 years before it decided *Chevron*.
There is no reason to believe that the linguistic ambiguity noted by
Colony reflects a post-*Chevron* conclusion that Congress had delegated
gap-filling power to the agency. At the same time, there is every reason
to believe that the Court thought that Congress had "directly spoken to
the question at hand," and thus left "[no] gap for the agency to fill."
Chevron, supra, at 842–843.

For one thing, the Court said that the taxpayer had the better side
of the textual argument. *Colony*, 357 U.S., at 33. For another, its
examination of legislative history led it to believe that Congress had
decided the question definitively, leaving no room for the agency to
reach a contrary result. It found in that history "persuasive indications"
that Congress intended overstatements of basis to fall outside the
statute's scope, and it said that it was satisfied that Congress "intended
an exception ... only in the restricted type of situation" it had already

described. *Id.*, at 35–36. Further, it thought that the Commissioner's interpretation (the interpretation once again advanced here) would "create a patent incongruity in the tax law." *Id.*, at 36–37. And it reached this conclusion despite the fact that, in the years leading up to *Colony*, the Commissioner had consistently advocated the opposite in the circuit courts. See, *e.g., Uptegrove*, 204 F.2d 570; *Reis*, 142 F.2d 900; Goodenow v. Commisioner, 238 F.2d 20 (C.A.8 1956); *American Liberty Oil Co. v. Commisioner*, 1 T.C. 386 (1942). Cf. *Slaff v. Commisioner*, 220 F.2d 65 (C.A.9 1955); *Davis v. Hightower*, 230 F.2d 549 (C.A.5 1956). Thus, the Court was aware it was rejecting the expert opinion of the Commissioner of Internal Revenue. And finally, after completing its analysis, *Colony* found its interpretation of the 1939 Code "in harmony with the [now] unambiguous language" of the 1954 Code, which at a minimum suggests that the Court saw nothing in the 1954 Code as inconsistent with its conclusion. 357 U.S., at 37.

It may be that judges today would use other methods to determine whether Congress left a gap to fill. But that is beside the point. The question is whether the Court in *Colony* concluded that the statute left such a gap. And, in our view, the opinion (written by Justice Harlan for the Court) makes clear that it did not.

Given principles of *stare decisis*, we must follow that interpretation. And there being no gap to fill, the Government's gap-filling regulation cannot change *Colony*'s interpretation of the statute. We agree with the taxpayer that overstatements of basis, and the resulting understatement of gross income, do not trigger the extended limitations period of § 6501(e)(1)(A). * * *

■ JUSTICE SCALIA, concurring in part and concurring in the judgment.

It would be reasonable, I think, to deny all precedential effect to *Colony, Inc. v. Commissioner*, 357 U.S. 28 (1958)—to overrule its holding as obviously contrary to our later law that agency resolutions of ambiguities are to be accorded deference. Because of justifiable taxpayer reliance I would not take that course—and neither does the Court's opinion, which says that "*Colony* determines the outcome in this case." That should be the end of the matter.

The plurality, however, goes on to address the Government's argument that Treasury Regulation § 301.6501(e)–1 effectively overturned *Colony*. See 26 CFR § 301.6501(e)–1 (2011). In my view, that cannot be: "Once a court has decided upon its *de novo* construction of the statute, there no longer is a different construction that is consistent with the court's holding and available for adoption by the agency." *National Cable & Telecommunications Assn. v. Brand X Internet Services*, 545 U.S. 967, 1018, n. 12 (2005) (SCALIA, J., dissenting) (citation and internal quotation marks omitted). That view, of course, did not carry the day in *Brand X*, and the Government quite reasonably relies on the *Brand X* majority's innovative pronouncement that a "court's prior judicial construction of a statute trumps an agency construction otherwise entitled to *Chevron* deference only if the prior court decision holds that its construction follows from the unambiguous terms of the statute." *Id.*, at 982.

In cases decided pre-*Brand X*, the Court had no inkling that it *must* utter the magic words "ambiguous" or "unambiguous" in order to (poof!)

expand or abridge executive power, and (poof!) enable or disable administrative contradiction of the Supreme Court. Indeed, the Court was unaware of even the utility (much less the necessity) of making the ambiguous/nonambiguous determination in cases decided pre-*Chevron*, before that opinion made the so-called "Step 1" determination of ambiguity *vel non* a customary (though hardly mandatory[1] part of judicial-review analysis. For many of those earlier cases, therefore, it will be incredibly difficult to determine whether the decision purported to be giving meaning to an ambiguous, or rather an unambiguous, statute.

Thus, one would have thought that the *Brand X* majority would breathe a sigh of relief in the present case, involving a pre-*Chevron* opinion that (*mirabile dictu*) makes it *inescapably clear* that the Court thought the statute ambiguous: "It *cannot* be said that the language is *unambiguous*." *Colony, supra*, at 33 (emphasis added). As today's plurality opinion explains, *Colony* "said that the taxpayer had the *better* side of the textual argument"—not what *Brand X* requires to foreclose administrative revision of our decisions: "the *only permissible* reading of the statute." 545 U.S., at 984. Thus, having decided to stand by *Colony* and to stand by *Brand X* as well, the plurality should have found—in order to reach the decision it did—that the Treasury Department's current interpretation was unreasonable.

Instead of doing what *Brand X* would require, however, the plurality manages to sustain the justifiable reliance of taxpayers by revising *yet again* the meaning of *Chevron*—and revising it *yet again* in a direction that will create confusion and uncertainty. See *United States v. Mead Corp.*, 533 U.S. 218, 245–246 (2001) (SCALIA, J., dissenting); Bressman, How *Mead* Has Muddled Judicial Review of Agency Action, 58 Vand. L.Rev. 1443, 1457–1475 (2005). Of course there is no doubt that, with regard to the Internal Revenue Code, the Treasury Department satisfies the *Mead* requirement of some indication "that Congress delegated authority to the agency generally to make rules carrying the force of law." 533 U.S., at 226–227. We have given *Chevron* deference to a Treasury Regulation before. See *Mayo Foundation for Medical Ed. and Research v. United States*, 131 S.Ct. 704, 713–714 (2011). But in order to evade *Brand X* and yet reaffirm *Colony*, the plurality would add yet another lopsided story to the ugly and improbable structure that our law of administrative review has become: To trigger the *Brand X* power of an authorized "gap-filling" agency to give content to an ambiguous text, a pre-*Chevron* determination that language is ambiguous does not alone suffice; the pre-*Chevron* Court must in addition have found that Congress wanted *the particular ambiguity in question* to be resolved by the agency. And here, today's plurality opinion finds, "[t]here is no reason to believe that the linguistic ambiguity noted by *Colony* reflects a post-*Chevron* conclusion that Congress had delegated gap-filling power to the agency." The

---

[1] "Step 1" has never been an essential part of *Chevron* analysis. Whether a particular statute is ambiguous makes no difference if the interpretation adopted by the agency is clearly reasonable—and it would be a waste of time to conduct that inquiry. See *Entergy Corp. v. Riverkeeper, Inc.*, 556 U.S. 208, 218, and n. 4 (2009). The same would be true if the agency interpretation is clearly beyond the scope of any conceivable ambiguity. It does not matter whether the word "yellow" is ambiguous when the agency has interpreted it to mean "purple." See Stephenson & Vermeule, *Chevron* Has Only One Step, 95 Va. L.Rev. 597, 599 (2009).

notion, seemingly, is that post-*Chevron* a finding of ambiguity is accompanied by a finding of agency authority to resolve the ambiguity, but pre-*Chevron* that was not so. The premise is false. Post-*Chevron* cases do not "conclude" that Congress wanted the particular ambiguity resolved by the agency; that is simply the *legal effect* of ambiguity—a legal effect that should obtain whenever the language is in fact (as Colony found) ambiguous.

Does the plurality feel that it ought not give effect to *Colony*'s determination of ambiguity because the Court did not know, in that era, the importance of that determination—that it would empower the agency to (in effect) revise the Court's determination of statutory meaning? But as I suggested earlier, that was an ignorance which all of our cases shared not just pre-*Chevron*, but pre-*Brand X*. Before then it did not really matter whether the Court was resolving an ambiguity or setting forth the statute's clear meaning. The opinion might (or might not) advert to that point in the course of its analysis, but either way the Court's interpretation of the statute would be the law. So it is no small number of still-authoritative cases that today's plurality opinion would exile to the Land of Uncertainty.

Perhaps sensing the fragility of its new approach, the plurality opinion then pivots (as the *à la mode* vernacular has it)—from focusing on whether *Colony* concluded that there was gap-filling authority to focusing on whether *Colony* concluded that there was any gap to be filled: "The question is whether the Court in *Colony* concluded that the statute left such a gap. And, in our view, the opinion . . . makes clear that it did not." How does the plurality know this? Because Justice Harlan's opinion "said that the taxpayer had the better side of the textual argument"; because it found that legislative history indicated "that Congress intended overstatements of basis to fall outside the statute's scope"; because it concluded that the Commissioner's interpretation would "create a patent incongruity in the tax law"; and because it found its interpretation "in harmony with the [now] unambiguous language" of the 1954 Code. But these are the sorts of arguments that courts *always* use in *resolving* ambiguities. They do not prove that no ambiguity existed, unless one believes that an ambiguity resolved is an ambiguity that never existed in the first place. *Colony* said unambiguously that the text was ambiguous, and that should be an end of the matter—unless one wants simply to deny *stare decisis* effect to *Colony* as a pre-*Chevron* decision.

Rather than making our judicial-review jurisprudence curiouser and curiouser, the Court should abandon the opinion that produces these contortions, *Brand X*. I join the judgment announced by the Court because it is indisputable that *Colony* resolved the construction of the statutory language at issue here, and that construction must therefore control. And I join the Court's opinion except for Part IV–C.

* * *

I must add a word about the peroration of the dissent, which asserts that "[o]ur legal system presumes there will be continuing dialogue among the three branches of Government on questions of statutory interpretation and application," and that the "constructive discourse," " 'convers[ations],' " and "instructive exchanges" would be "foreclosed by an insistence on adhering to earlier interpretations of a statute even in light of new, relevant statutory amendments." This passage is reminiscent of Professor K.C. Davis's vision that administrative procedure is developed by "a partnership between legislators and judges," who "working [as] partners produce better law than legislators alone could possibly produce."[2] That romantic, judge-empowering image was obliterated by this Court in *Vermont Yankee Nuclear Power Corp. v. Natural Resources Defense Council, Inc.*, 435 U.S. 519 (1978), which held that Congress prescribes and we obey, with no discretion to add to the administrative procedures that Congress has created. It seems to me that the dissent's vision of a troika partnership (legislative-executive-judicial) is a similar mirage. The discourse, conversation, and exchange that the dissent perceives is peculiarly one-sided. Congress prescribes; and where Congress's prescription is ambiguous the Executive can (within the scope of the ambiguity) clarify that prescription; and if the product is constitutional the courts obey. I hardly think it amounts to a "discourse" that Congress or (as this Court would allow in its *Brand X* decision) the Executive can change its prescription so as to render our prior holding irrelevant. What is needed for the system to work is that Congress, the Executive, and the private parties subject to their dispositions, be able to predict the meaning that the courts will give to their instructions. That goal would be obstructed if the judicially established meaning of a technical legal term used in a very specific context could be overturned on the basis of statutory indications as feeble as those asserted here.

■ JUSTICE KENNEDY, with whom JUSTICE GINSBURG, JUSTICE SOTOMAYOR, and JUSTICE KAGAN join, dissenting.

This case involves a provision of the Internal Revenue Code establishing an extended statute of limitations for tax assessment in cases where substantial income has been omitted from a tax return. See 26 U.S.C. § 6501(e)(1)(A) (2006 ed., Supp. IV). The Treasury Department has determined that taxpayers omit income under this section not only when they fail to report a sale of property but also when they overstate their basis in the property sold. See Treas. Reg. § 301.6501(e)–1, 26 CFR § 301.6501(e)–1 (2011). The question is whether this otherwise reasonable interpretation is foreclosed by the Court's contrary reading of an earlier version of the statute in *Colony, Inc. v. Commissioner*, 357 U.S. 28 (1958).

In *Colony* there was no need to decide whether the meaning of the provision changed when Congress reenacted it as part of the 1954 revision of the Tax Code. Although the main text of the statute remained the same, Congress added new provisions leading to the permissible conclusion that it would have a different meaning going forward. The *Colony* decision reserved judgment on this issue. In my view, the amended statute leaves room for the Department's reading. A summary of the reasons for concluding the Department's interpretation is permissible, and for this respectful dissent, now follows.

---

[2]   1 K. Davis, Administrative Law Treatise § 2.17, p. 138 (1978).

I

* * *

If the Government is to prevail in the instant case the regulation in question must be a proper implementation of the same language the Court considered in *Colony*; but the statutory interpretation issue here cannot be resolved, and the *Colony* decision cannot be deemed controlling, without first considering the inferences that should be drawn from added statutory text. The additional language was not part of the statute that governed the taxpayer's liability in *Colony*, and the Court did not consider it in that case. Congress revised the Internal Revenue Code in 1954, several years before *Colony* was decided but after the tax years in question in that case. Although the interpretation adopted by the Court in *Colony* can be a proper beginning point for the interpretation of the revised statute, it ought not to be the end.

The central language of the new provision remained the same as the old, with the longer period of limitations still applicable where a taxpayer had "omit [ted] from gross income an amount . . . in excess of 25 per[cent] of the amount of gross income stated in the return." In *Colony*, however, the Court left open whether Congress had nonetheless "manifested an intention to clarify or to change the 1939 Code." *Id.*, at 37. The 1954 revisions, of course, could not provide a direct response to *Colony*, which had not yet been decided. But there were indications that, whatever the earlier version of the statute had meant, Congress expected that the overstatement of basis would be considered an omission from gross income as a general rule going forward.

* * *

II

In the instant case the Court concludes these statutory changes are "too fragile to bear the significant argumentative weight the Government seeks to place upon them." But in this context, the changes are meaningful. *Colony* made clear that the text of the earlier version of the statute could not be described as unambiguous, although it ultimately concluded that an overstatement of basis was not an omission from gross income. See 357 U.S., at 33. The statutory revisions, which were not considered in *Colony*, may not compel the opposite conclusion under the new statute; but they strongly favor it. As a result, there was room for the Treasury Department to interpret the new provision in that manner. See *Chevron U.S.A. Inc. v. Natural Resources Defense Council, Inc.*, 467 U.S. 837, 843–845 (1984).

In an earlier case, and in an unrelated controversy not implicating the Internal Revenue Code, the Court held that a judicial construction of an ambiguous statute did not foreclose an agency's later, inconsistent interpretation of the same provision. *National Cable & Telecommunications Assn. v. Brand X Internet Services*, 545 U.S. 967, 982–983 (2005) ("Only a judicial precedent holding that the statute unambiguously forecloses the agency's interpretation, and therefore contains no gap for the agency to fill, displaces a conflicting agency construction"). This general rule recognizes that filling gaps left by ambiguities in a statute "involves difficult policy choices that agencies are better equipped to make than courts." *Id.*, at 980. There has been no opportunity to decide whether the analysis would be any different if an agency sought to interpret an ambiguous statute in a way that was inconsistent with this Court's own, earlier reading of the law. See *id.*, at 1003, (STEVENS, J., concurring).

These issues are not implicated here. In *Colony* the Court did interpret the same phrase that must be interpreted in this case. The language was in a predecessor statute, however, and Congress has added new language that, in my view, controls the analysis and should instruct the Court to reach a different outcome today. The Treasury Department's regulations were promulgated in light of these statutory revisions, which were not at issue in *Colony*. There is a serious difficulty to insisting, as the Court does today, that an ambiguous provision must continue to be read the same way even after it has been reenacted with additional language suggesting Congress would permit a different interpretation. Agencies with the responsibility and expertise necessary to administer ongoing regulatory schemes should have the latitude and discretion to implement their interpretation of provisions reenacted in a new statutory framework. And this is especially so when the new language enacted by Congress seems to favor the very interpretation at issue. The approach taken by the Court instead forecloses later interpretations of a law that has changed in relevant ways. Cf. *United States v. Mead Corp.*, 533 U.S. 218, 247 (2001) (SCALIA, J., dissenting) ("Worst of all, the majority's approach will lead to the ossification of large portions of our statutory law. Where *Chevron* applies, statutory ambiguities remain ambiguities subject to the agency's ongoing clarification"). The Court goes too far, in my respectful view, in constricting Congress's ability to leave agencies in charge of filling statutory gaps.

Our legal system presumes there will be continuing dialogue among the three branches of Government on questions of statutory interpretation and application. See *Blakely v. Washington*, 542 U.S. 296, 326 (2004) (KENNEDY, J., dissenting) ("Constant, constructive discourse between our courts and our legislatures is an integral and admirable part of the constitutional design"); *Mistretta v. United States*, 488 U.S. 361, 408 (1989) ("Our principle of separation of powers anticipates that the coordinate Branches will converse with each other on matters of vital common interest"). In some cases Congress will set out a general principle, to be administered in more detail by an agency in the exercise of its discretion. The agency may be in a proper position to evaluate the best means of implementing the statute in its practical application. Where the agency exceeds its authority, of course, courts must invalidate the regulation. And agency interpretations that lead to unjust or unfair consequences can be corrected, much like disfavored judicial interpretations, by congressional action. These instructive exchanges would be foreclosed by an insistence on adhering to earlier interpretations of a statute even in light of new, relevant statutory amendments. Courts instead should be open to an agency's adoption of a different interpretation where, as here, Congress has given new instruction by an amended statute.

Under the circumstances, the Treasury Department had authority to adopt its reasonable interpretation of the new tax provision at issue. See *Mayo Foundation for Medical Ed. and Research v. United States*,

131 S.Ct. 704, 713 (2011). This was also the conclusion reached in well-reasoned opinions issued in several cases before the Courts of Appeals. *E.g., Intermountain*, 650 F.3d, at 705–706 (reaching this conclusion "because the Court in Colony never purported to interpret [the new provision]; because [the new provision]'s 'omits from gross income' text is at least ambiguous, if not best read to include overstatements of basis; and because neither the section's structure nor its [history and context] removes this ambiguity").

The Department's clarification of an ambiguous statute, applicable to these taxpayers, did not upset legitimate settled expectations. Given the statutory changes described above, taxpayers had reason to question whether Colony's holding extended to the revised § 6501(e)(1). See, *e.g., CC&F Western Operations L.P. v. Commissioner*, 273 F.3d 402, 406, n. 2 (C.A.1 2001) ("Whether Colony's main holding carries over to section 6501(e)(1) is at least doubtful"). Having worked no change in the law, and instead having interpreted a statutory provision without an established meaning, the Department's regulation does not have an impermissible retroactive effect. Cf. *Smiley v. Citibank (South Dakota), N. A.*, 517 U.S. 735, 741, 744, n. 3 (1996) (rejecting retroactivity argument); *Manhattan Gen. Equipment Co. v. Commissioner*, 297 U.S. 129, 135 (1936) (same). It controls in this case.

NOTES AND QUESTIONS

1. Writing for a plurality of the Court, Justice Breyer contends that a pre-*Chevron* reference to statutory ambiguity in a judicial opinion ought not to be interpreted as a conclusion that a statute is ambiguous for purposes of *Chevron* analysis. What are the consequences of this position for judicial review of agency interpretations of other statutory provisions construed by the courts prior to the *Chevron* decision?

2. Some commentators read the *Home Concrete* decision as indicating at least implicitly that the Supreme Court will never allow an agency's interpretation of a statute to overcome a previous interpretation by the Court. Do you concur with this assessment? Do you think such a position is defensible in light of the Court's decision in *Brand X*? Why or why not?

3. Assume you are the head of an agency charged with administering a statute. You believe the statute is ambiguous, and you would like to promulgate a regulation interpreting the statute to resolve a particular issue, but a pre-*Chevron* decision of the Supreme Court interprets the statute differently. In light of the Court's decision in *Home Concrete*, would you be deterred from proceeding with your proposed regulation?

E. *CHEVRON* AND JURISDICTIONAL QUESTIONS

Another challenging issue concerning *Chevron*'s scope is the doctrine's applicability to agency interpretations of statutory questions that speak to the agency's jurisdiction. Agencies sometimes have attempted to leverage ambiguities in statutory text or statutory silence to expand their jurisdiction to include parties or matters previously thought to be beyond their reach. Courts and scholars have often been wary of agency overreach in this way, and courts at times have expressed reluctance to extend *Chevron* deference to such interpretations. For example, in *FDA v. Brown & Williamson Tobacco*

Corp., 529 U.S. 120 (2000), the Supreme Court applied *Chevron*'s first step quite aggressively to conclude that the FDA lacked authority to regulate tobacco advertising. Writing for the majority, Justice O'Connor followed her *Chevron* step one analysis with the following comment.

> Deference under *Chevron* to an agency's construction of a statute that it administers is premised on a theory that a statute's ambiguity constitutes an implicit delegation from Congress to the agency to fill in the statutory gaps. In extraordinary cases, however, there may be reason to hesitate before concluding that Congress has intended such an implicit delegation.

> This is hardly an ordinary case. Contrary to its representations to Congress since 1914, the FDA has now asserted jurisdiction to regulate an industry constituting a significant portion of the American economy. * * * Owing to its unique place in American history and society, tobacco has its own unique political history. Congress, for better or for worse, has created a distinct regulatory scheme for tobacco products, squarely rejected proposals to give the FDA jurisdiction over tobacco, and repeatedly acted to preclude any agency from exercising significant policymaking authority in the area. Given this history and the breadth of the authority that the FDA has asserted, we are obliged to defer not to the agency's expansive construction of the statute, but to Congress' consistent judgment to deny the FDA this power.

Id. at 159 (internal citation omitted). At the same time, many of the most mundane agency statutory interpretations tell regulated parties that they or their actions do or do not fall within statutory mandates, and in this manner define the scope of an agency's jurisdiction. In the following case, the squarely addressed the relationship between *Chevron* review and jurisdictional questions.

City of Arlington, Tex. v. FCC

133 S. Ct. 1863 (2013).

■ JUSTICE SCALIA delivered the opinion of the Court.

We consider whether an agency's interpretation of a statutory ambiguity that concerns the scope of its regulatory authority (that is, its jurisdiction) is entitled to deference under *Chevron U.S.A. Inc. v. Natural Resources Defense Council, Inc.*, 467 U.S. 837 (1984).

I

Wireless telecommunications networks require towers and antennas; proposed sites for those towers and antennas must be approved by local zoning authorities. In the Telecommunications Act of 1996, Congress "impose[d] specific limitations on the traditional authority of state and local governments to regulate the location, construction, and modification of such facilities," *Rancho Palos Verdes v. Abrams*, 544 U.S. 113, 115 (2005), and incorporated those limitations into the Communications Act of 1934. Section 201(b) of that Act empowers the Federal Communications Commission to "prescribe such rules and regulations as may be necessary in the public interest to carry out [its] provisions." 47 U.S.C. § 201(b). Of course, that rulemaking authority extends to the subsequently added portions of the Act.

The Act imposes five substantive limitations, which are codified in 47 U.S.C. § 332(c)(7)(B); only one of them, § 332(c)(7)(B)(ii), is at issue here. That provision requires state or local governments to act on wireless siting applications "within a reasonable period of time after the request is duly filed." Two other features of § 332(c)(7) are relevant. First, subparagraph (A), known as the "saving clause," provides that nothing in the Act, *except* those limitations provided in § 332(c)(7)(B), "shall limit or affect the authority of a State or local government" over siting decisions. Second, § 332(c)(7)(B)(v) authorizes a person who believes a state or local government's wireless-siting decision to be inconsistent with any of the limitations in § 332(c)(7)(B) to "commence an action in any court of competent jurisdiction."

In theory, § 332(c)(7)(B)(ii) requires state and local zoning authorities to take prompt action on siting applications for wireless facilities. But in practice, wireless providers often faced long delays. In July 2008, CTIA—The Wireless Association, which represents wireless service providers, petitioned the FCC to clarify the meaning of § 332(c)(7)(B)(ii)'s requirement that zoning authorities act on siting requests "within a reasonable period of time." In November 2009, the Commission, relying on its broad statutory authority to implement the provisions of the Communications Act, issued a declaratory ruling responding to CTIA's petition. The Commission found that the "record evidence demonstrates that unreasonable delays in the personal wireless service facility siting process have obstructed the provision of wireless services" and that such delays "impede the promotion of advanced services and competition that Congress deemed critical in the Telecommunications Act of 1996." A "reasonable period of time" under § 332(c)(7)(B)(ii), the Commission determined, is presumptively (but rebuttably) 90 days to process a collocation application (that is, an application to place a new antenna on an existing tower) and 150 days to process all other applications.

Some state and local governments opposed adoption of the *Declaratory Ruling* on the ground that the Commission lacked "authority to interpret ambiguous provisions of Section 332(c)(7)." Specifically, they argued that the saving clause, § 332(c)(7)(A), and the judicial review provision, § 337(c)(7)(B)(v), together display a congressional intent to withhold from the Commission authority to interpret the limitations in § 332(c)(7)(B).

* * *

II

A

As this case turns on the scope of the doctrine enshrined in *Chevron*, we begin with a description of that case's now-canonical formulation. "When a court reviews an agency's construction of the statute which it administers, it is confronted with two questions." 467 U.S., at 842. First, applying the ordinary tools of statutory construction, the court must determine "whether Congress has directly spoken to the precise question at issue. If the intent of Congress is clear, that is the end of the matter; for the court, as well as the agency, must give effect to the unambiguously expressed intent of Congress." *Id.*, at 842–843. But "if the statute is silent or ambiguous with respect to the specific issue, the question for the court is whether the agency's answer is based on a permissible construction of the statute." *Id.*, at 843.

Chevron is rooted in a background presumption of congressional intent: namely, "that Congress, when it left ambiguity in a statute" administered by an agency, "understood that the ambiguity would be resolved, first and foremost, by the agency, and desired the agency (rather than the courts) to possess whatever degree of discretion the ambiguity allows." *Smiley v. Citibank (South Dakota), N. A.*, 517 U.S. 735, 740–741 (1996). *Chevron* thus provides a stable background rule against which Congress can legislate: Statutory ambiguities will be resolved, within the bounds of reasonable interpretation, not by the courts but by the administering agency. Congress knows to speak in plain terms when it wishes to circumscribe, and in capacious terms when it wishes to enlarge, agency discretion.

B

The question here is whether a court must defer under *Chevron* to an agency's interpretation of a statutory ambiguity that concerns the scope of the agency's statutory authority (that is, its jurisdiction). The argument against deference rests on the premise that there exist two distinct classes of agency interpretations: Some interpretations—the big, important ones, presumably—define the agency's "jurisdiction." Others—humdrum, run-of-the-mill stuff—are simply applications of jurisdiction the agency plainly has. That premise is false, because the distinction between "jurisdictional" and "nonjurisdictional" interpretations is a mirage. No matter how it is framed, the question a court faces when confronted with an agency's interpretation of a statute it administers is always, simply, *whether the agency has stayed within the bounds of its statutory authority.*

The misconception that there are, for *Chevron* purposes, separate "jurisdictional" questions on which no deference is due derives, perhaps, from a reflexive extension to agencies of the very real division between the jurisdictional and nonjurisdictional that is applicable to courts. In the judicial context, there *is* a meaningful line: Whether the court decided *correctly* is a question that has different consequences from the question whether it had the power to decide *at all*. Congress has the power (within limits) to tell the courts what classes of cases they may decide, but not to prescribe or superintend how they decide those cases. A court's power to decide a case is independent of whether its decision is correct, which is why even an erroneous judgment is entitled to res judicata effect. Put differently, a jurisdictionally proper but substantively incorrect judicial decision is not ultra vires.

That is not so for agencies charged with administering congressional statutes. Both their power to act and how they are to act is authoritatively prescribed by Congress, so that when they act improperly, no less than when they act beyond their jurisdiction, what they do is ultra vires. Because the question—whether framed as an incorrect application of agency authority or an assertion of authority not conferred—is always whether the agency has gone beyond what

Congress has permitted it to do, there is no principled basis for carving out some arbitrary subset of such claims as "jurisdictional."

An example will illustrate just how illusory the proposed line between "jurisdictional" and "nonjurisdictional" agency interpretations is. Imagine the following validly-enacted statute:

COMMON CARRIER ACT

SECTION 1. The Agency shall have jurisdiction to prohibit any common carrier from imposing an unreasonable condition upon access to its facilities.

There is no question that this provision—including the terms "common carrier" and "unreasonable condition"—defines the Agency's jurisdiction. Surely, the argument goes, a court must determine de novo the scope of that jurisdiction.

Consider, however, this alternative formulation of the statute:

COMMON Carrier Act

SECTION 1. No common carrier shall impose an unreasonable condition upon access to its facilities.

SECTION 2. The Agency may prescribe rules and regulations necessary in the public interest to effectuate Section 1 of this Act.

Now imagine that the Agency, invoking its Section 2 authority, promulgates this Rule: "(1) The term 'common carrier' in Section 1 includes Internet Service Providers. (2) The term 'unreasonable condition' in Section 1 includes unreasonably high prices. (3) A monthly fee greater than $25 is an unreasonable condition on access to Internet service." By this Rule, the Agency has claimed for itself jurisdiction that is doubly questionable: Does its authority extend to Internet Service Providers? And does it extend to setting prices? Yet Section 2 makes clear that Congress, in petitioners' words, "conferred interpretive power on the agency" with respect to Section 1. Even under petitioners' theory, then, a court should defer to the Agency's interpretation of the terms "common carrier" and "unreasonable condition"—that is to say, its assertion that its "jurisdiction" extends to regulating Internet Service Providers and setting prices.

In the first case, by contrast, petitioners' theory would accord the agency no deference. The trouble with this is that in both cases, the underlying question is *exactly the same*: Does the statute give the agency authority to regulate Internet Service Providers and cap prices, or not? The reality, laid bare, is that there is *no difference*, insofar as the validity of agency action is concerned, between an agency's exceeding the scope of its authority (its "jurisdiction") and its exceeding authorized application of authority that it unquestionably has. "To exceed authorized application is to exceed authority. Virtually any administrative action can be characterized as either the one or the other, depending on how generally one wishes to describe the 'authority.'" *Mississippi Power & Light Co. v. Mississippi ex rel. Moore*, 487 U.S. 354, 381 (1988) (SCALIA, J., concurring in judgment); see also Monaghan, Marbury *and the Administrative State*, 83 Colum. L. Rev. 1, 29 (1983) ("Administrative application of law is administrative formulation of law whenever it involves elaboration of the statutory norm.").

This point is nicely illustrated by our decision in *National Cable & Telecommunications Assn., Inc. v. Gulf Power Co.*, 534 U.S. 327 (2002). That case considered whether the FCC's "jurisdiction" to regulate the rents utility-pole owners charge for "pole attachments" (defined as attachments by a cable television system or provider of telecommunications service) extended to attachments that provided both cable television and high-speed Internet access (attachments for so-called "commingled services"). *Id.*, at 331–336. We held, sensibly, that *Chevron* applied. 534 U.S., at 333. Whether framed as going to the *scope* of the FCC's delegated authority or the FCC's *application* of its delegated authority, the underlying question was the same: Did the FCC exceed the bounds of its statutory authority to regulate rents for "pole attachments" when it sought to regulate rents for pole attachments providing commingled services?

The label is an empty distraction because every new application of a broad statutory term can be reframed as a questionable extension of the agency's jurisdiction. One of the briefs in support of petitioners explains, helpfully, that "[j]urisdictional questions concern the *who*, *what*, *where*, and *when* of regulatory power: which subject matters may an agency regulate and under what conditions." But an agency's *application* of its authority pursuant to statutory text answers the same questions. *Who* is an "outside salesman"? *What* is a "pole attachment"? *Where* do the "waters of the United States" end? *When* must a Medicare provider challenge a reimbursement determination in order to be entitled to an administrative appeal? These can all be reframed as questions about the scope of agencies' regulatory jurisdiction—and they are all questions to which the *Chevron* framework applies. See *Christopher v. SmithKline Beecham Corp.*, 132 S.Ct. 2156, 2162, 2165 (2012); *National Cable & Telecommunications Assn., supra*, at 331, 333; *United States v. Riverside Bayview Homes, Inc.*, 474 U.S. 121, 123, 131; *Sebelius v. Auburn Regional Medical Center*, 133 S.Ct. 817, 821, 826–827 (2013).

In sum, judges should not waste their time in the mental acrobatics needed to decide whether an agency's interpretation of a statutory provision is "jurisdictional" or "nonjurisdictional." Once those labels are sheared away, it becomes clear that the question in every case is, simply, whether the statutory text forecloses the agency's assertion of authority, or not. The federal judge as haruspex, sifting the entrails of vast statutory schemes to divine whether a particular agency interpretation qualifies as "jurisdictional," is not engaged in reasoned decisionmaking.

C

Fortunately, then, we have consistently held "that *Chevron* applies to cases in which an agency adopts a construction of a jurisdictional provision of a statute it administers." 1 R. Pierce, Administrative Law Treatise § 3.5, p. 187 (2010).

[Justice Scalia then offered several examples of cases in which he said the Supreme Court had previously afforded *Chevron* deference to agencies' interpretations of "jurisdictional provisions." Ed.]

The U.S. Reports are shot through with applications of *Chevron* to agencies' constructions of the scope of their own jurisdiction. * * *

The false dichotomy between "jurisdictional" and "nonjurisdictional" agency interpretations may be no more than a bogeyman, but it is dangerous all the same. Like the Hound of the Baskervilles, it is conjured by those with greater quarry in sight: Make no mistake—the ultimate target here is *Chevron* itself. Savvy challengers of agency action would play the "jurisdictional" card in every case. Some judges would be deceived by the specious, but scary-sounding, "jurisdictional"-"nonjurisdictional" line; others tempted by the prospect of making public policy by prescribing the meaning of ambiguous statutory commands. The effect would be to transfer any number of interpretive decisions—archetypal *Chevron* questions, about how best to construe an ambiguous term in light of competing policy interests—from the agencies that administer the statutes to federal courts. We have cautioned that "judges ought to refrain from substituting their own interstitial lawmaking" for that of an agency. *Ford Motor Credit Co. v. Milhollin*, 444 U.S. 555, 568 (1980). That is precisely what *Chevron* prevents.

III

* * *

B

A few words in response to the dissent. The question on which we granted certiorari was whether "a court should apply *Chevron* to review an agency's determination of its own jurisdiction." Perhaps sensing the incoherence of the "jurisdictional-nonjurisdictional" line, the dissent does not even attempt to defend it, but proposes a much broader scope for *de novo* judicial review: Jurisdictional or not, and even where a rule is at issue and the statute contains a broad grant of rulemaking authority, the dissent would have a court search provision-by-provision to determine "whether [that] delegation covers the 'specific provision' and 'particular question' before the court."

The dissent is correct that *United States v. Mead Corp.*, 533 U.S. 218 (2001), requires that, for *Chevron* deference to apply, the agency must have received congressional authority to determine the particular matter at issue in the particular manner adopted. No one disputes that. But *Mead* denied *Chevron* deference to action, by an agency with rulemaking authority, that was not rulemaking. What the dissent needs, and fails to produce, is a single case in which a general conferral of rulemaking or adjudicative authority has been held insufficient to support *Chevron* deference for an exercise of that authority within the agency's substantive field. There is no such case, and what the dissent proposes is a massive revision of our *Chevron* jurisprudence.

Where we differ from the dissent is in its apparent rejection of the theorem that the whole includes all of its parts—its view that a general conferral of rulemaking authority does not validate rules for *all* the matters the agency is charged with administering. Rather, the dissent proposes that even when general rulemaking authority is clear, *every* agency rule must be subjected to a *de novo* judicial determination of whether *the particular issue* was committed to agency discretion. It offers no standards at all to guide this open-ended hunt for congressional intent (that is to say, for evidence of congressional intent more specific than the conferral of general rulemaking authority). It would simply punt that question back to the Court of Appeals, presumably for application of some sort of totality-of-the-circumstances test—which is really, of course, not a test at all but an invitation to make an ad hoc judgment regarding congressional intent. Thirteen Courts of Appeals applying a totality-of-the-circumstances test would render the binding effect of agency rules unpredictable and destroy the whole stabilizing purpose of *Chevron*. The excessive agency power that the dissent fears would be replaced by chaos. There is no need to wade into these murky waters. It suffices to decide this case that the preconditions to deference under *Chevron* are satisfied because Congress has unambiguously vested the FCC with general authority to administer the Communications Act through rulemaking and adjudication, and the agency interpretation at issue was promulgated in the exercise of that authority.

* * *

Those who assert that applying *Chevron* to "jurisdictional" interpretations "leaves the fox in charge of the henhouse" overlook the reality that a separate category of "jurisdictional" interpretations does not exist. The fox-in-the-henhouse syndrome is to be avoided not by establishing an arbitrary and undefinable category of agency decisionmaking that is accorded no deference, but by taking seriously, and applying rigorously, in all cases, statutory limits on agencies' authority. Where Congress has established a clear line, the agency cannot go beyond it; and where Congress has established an ambiguous line, the agency can go no further than the ambiguity will fairly allow. But in rigorously applying the latter rule, a court need not pause to puzzle over whether the interpretive question presented is "jurisdictional." If "the agency's answer is based on a permissible construction of the statute," that is the end of the matter. *Chevron*, 467 U.S., at 842.

■ JUSTICE BREYER, concurring in part and concurring in the judgment.

I agree with the Court that normally "the question a court faces when confronted with an agency's interpretation of a statute it administers" is, "simply, *whether the agency has stayed within the bounds of its statutory authority*." In this context, "the distinction between 'jurisdictional' and 'non-jurisdictional' interpretations is a mirage."

Deciding just what those statutory bounds are, however, is not always an easy matter, and the Court's case law abounds with discussion of the subject. A reviewing judge, for example, will have to decide independently whether Congress delegated authority to the agency to provide interpretations of, or to enact rules pursuant to, the statute at issue—interpretations or rules that carry with them "the force of law." *United States v. Mead Corp.*, 533 U.S. 218, 229 (2001). If so, the reviewing court must give special leeway or "deference" to the agency's interpretation. See *id.*, at 227–228.

We have added that, if "[e]mploying traditional tools of statutory construction," *INS v. Cardoza-Fonseca*, 480 U.S. 421, 446 (1987), the court determines that Congress has spoken clearly on the disputed question, then "that is the end of the matter," *Chevron U.S.A. Inc. v. Natural Resources Defense Council, Inc.*, 467 U.S. 837, 842 (1984). The agency is due no deference, for Congress has left no gap for the agency to fill. If, on the other hand, Congress has not spoken clearly, if, for example it has written ambiguously, then that ambiguity is a sign—but not always a conclusive sign—that Congress intends a reviewing court to pay particular attention to (*i.e.*, to give a degree of deference to) the agency's interpretation.

I say that the existence of statutory ambiguity is sometimes not enough to warrant the conclusion that Congress has left a deference-warranting gap for the agency to fill because our cases make clear that other, sometimes context-specific, factors will on occasion prove relevant. (And, given the vast number of government statutes, regulatory programs, and underlying circumstances, that variety is hardly surprising.) In *Mead*, for example, we looked to several factors other than simple ambiguity to help determine whether Congress left a statutory gap, thus delegating to the agency the authority to fill that gap with an interpretation that would carry "the force of law." 533 U.S., at 229–231. Elsewhere, we have assessed

> "the interstitial nature of the legal question, the related expertise of the Agency, the importance of the question to administration of the statute, the complexity of that administration, and the careful consideration the Agency has given the question over a long period of time." *Barnhart v. Walton*, 535 U.S. 212, 222 (2002).

The subject matter of the relevant provision—for instance, its distance from the agency's ordinary statutory duties or its falling within the scope of another agency's authority—has also proved relevant. See *Gonzales* [*v. Oregon*, 546 U.S. 243,] 265–266.

Moreover, the statute's text, its context, the structure of the statutory scheme, and canons of textual construction are relevant in determining whether the statute is ambiguous and can be equally helpful in determining whether such ambiguity comes accompanied with agency authority to fill a gap with an interpretation that carries the force of law. Statutory purposes, including those revealed in part by legislative and regulatory history, can be similarly relevant.

Although seemingly complex in abstract description, in practice this framework has proved a workable way to approximate how Congress would likely have meant to allocate interpretive law-determining authority between reviewing court and agency. The question whether Congress has delegated to an agency the authority to provide an interpretation that carries the force of law is for the judge to answer independently. The judge, considering "traditional tools of statutory construction," [*INS v.*] *Cardoza-Fonseca*, [480 U.S. 421,] 446, will ask whether Congress has spoken unambiguously. If so, the text controls. If not, the judge will ask whether Congress would have intended the agency to resolve the resulting ambiguity. If so, deference is warranted. See *Mead, supra*, at 229. Even if not, however, sometimes an agency interpretation, in light of the agency's special expertise, will still have the "power to persuade, if lacking power to control," *Skidmore v. Swift & Co.*, 323 U.S. 134, 140 (1944).

The case before us offers an example. The relevant statutory provision requires state or local governments to act on wireless siting applications "within a reasonable period of time after" a wireless service provider files such a request. 47 U.S.C. § 332(c)(7)(B)(ii). The Federal Communications Commission (FCC) argued that this provision granted it a degree of leeway in determining the amount of time that is reasonable. Many factors favor the agency's view: (1) the language of the Telecommunications Act grants the FCC broad authority (including rulemaking authority) to administer the Act; (2) the words are open-ended—*i.e.* "ambiguous"; (3) the provision concerns an interstitial administrative matter, in respect to which the agency's expertise could have an important role to play; and (4) the matter, in context, is complex, likely making the agency's expertise useful in helping to answer the "reasonableness" question that the statute poses. See § 151 (creating the FCC); § 201(b) (providing rulemaking authority).

In the other side of the coin, petitioners point to two statutory provisions which, they believe, require a different conclusion—namely, that the FCC lacked authority altogether to interpret § 332(c)(7)(B)(ii). First, a nearby saving clause says: "Except as provided in this paragraph, nothing in this chapter shall limit or affect the authority of a State or local government or instrumentality thereof over decisions regarding the placement, construction, and modification of personal wireless service facilities." § 332(c)(7)(A). Second, a judicial review provision, says: "Any person adversely affected by any final action or failure to act by a State or local government or any instrumentality thereof that is inconsistent with this subparagraph may, within 30 days after such action or failure to act, commence an action in any court of competent jurisdiction." § 332(c)(7)(B)(v).

In my view, however, these two provisions cannot provide good reason for reaching the conclusion advocated by petitioners. The first provision begins with an exception, stating that it does *not* apply to (among other things) the "reasonableness" provision here at issue. The second simply sets forth a procedure for judicial review, a review that applies to most government actions. Both are consistent with a statutory scheme that gives States, localities, the FCC, and reviewing courts each some role to play in the location of wireless service facilities. And neither "expressly describ[es] an exception" to the FCC's plenary authority to interpret the Act. *American Hospital Assn. v. NLRB*, 499 U.S. 606, 613 (1991).

For these reasons, I would reject petitioners' argument and conclude that § 332(c)(7)(B)(ii)—the "reasonableness" statute—leaves a gap for the FCC to fill. I would hold that the FCC's lawful efforts to do so carry "the force of law." *Mead*, 533 U.S., at 229. * * * I consequently join the majority's judgment and such portions of its opinion as are consistent with what I have written here.

■ Chief JUSTICE ROBERTS, with whom JUSTICE KENNEDY and JUSTICE ALITO join, dissenting.

My disagreement with the Court is fundamental. It is also easily expressed: A court should not defer to an agency until the court decides, on its own, that the agency is entitled to deference. Courts defer to an agency's interpretation of law when and because Congress has conferred on the agency interpretive authority over the question at issue. An agency cannot exercise interpretive authority until it has it; the question whether an agency enjoys that authority must be decided by a court, without deference to the agency.

I

One of the principal authors of the Constitution famously wrote that the "accumulation of all powers, legislative, executive, and judiciary, in the same hands, . . . may justly be pronounced the very definition of tyranny." The Federalist No. 47, p. 324 (J. Cooke ed. 1961) (J. Madison). Although modern administrative agencies fit most comfortably within the Executive Branch, as a practical matter they exercise legislative power, by promulgating regulations with the force of law; executive power, by policing compliance with those regulations; and judicial power, by adjudicating enforcement actions and imposing sanctions on those found to have violated their rules. The accumulation of these powers in the same hands is not an occasional or isolated exception to the constitutional plan; it is a central feature of modern American government.

The administrative state "wields vast power and touches almost every aspect of daily life." *Free Enterprise Fund v. Public Company Accounting Oversight Bd.*, 130 S.Ct. 3138, 3156 (2010). The Framers could hardly have envisioned today's "vast and varied federal bureaucracy" and the authority administrative agencies now hold over our economic, social, and political activities. *Ibid.* "[T]he administrative state with its reams of regulations would leave them rubbing their eyes." *Alden v. Maine*, 527 U.S. 706, 807 (1999) (Souter, J., dissenting), quoted in *Federal Maritime Comm'n v. South Carolina Ports Authority*, 535 U.S. 743, 755 (2002). And the federal bureaucracy continues to grow; in the last 15 years, Congress has launched more than 50 new agencies. Compare Office of the Federal Register, United States Government Manual 1997/1998, with Office of the Federal Register, United States Government Manual 2012. And more are on the way. See, *e.g.*, Congressional Research Service, C. Copeland, New Entities Created Pursuant to the Patient Protection and Affordable Care Act 1 (2010) (The PPACA "creates, requires others to create, or authorizes dozens of new entities to implement the legislation").

Although the Constitution empowers the President to keep federal officers accountable, administrative agencies enjoy in practice a significant degree of independence. As scholars have noted, "no President (or his executive office staff) could, and presumably none would wish to, supervise so broad a swath of regulatory activity." Kagan, Presidential Administration, 114 Harv. L.Rev. 2245, 2250 (2001). President Truman colorfully described his power over the administrative state by complaining, "I thought I was the president, but when it comes to these bureaucrats, I can't do a damn thing." President Kennedy once told a constituent, "I agree with you, but I don't know if the government will." The collection of agencies housed outside the traditional executive departments, including the Federal Communications Commission, is routinely described as the "headless fourth branch of government," reflecting not only the scope of their authority but their practical independence.

As for judicial oversight, agencies enjoy broad power to construe statutory provisions over which they have been given interpretive authority. In *Chevron U.S.A. Inc. v. Natural Resources Defense Council, Inc.*, we established a test for reviewing "an agency's construction of the statute which it administers." 467 U.S. 837, 842 (1984). If Congress has "directly spoken to the precise question at issue," we said, "that is the end of the matter." A contrary agency interpretation must give way. But if Congress has not expressed a specific intent, a court is bound to defer to any "permissible construction of the statute," even if that is not "the reading the court would have reached if the question initially had arisen in a judicial proceeding." *Id.*, at 843, and n. 11.

When it applies, *Chevron* is a powerful weapon in an agency's regulatory arsenal. Congressional delegations to agencies are often ambiguous—expressing "a mood rather than a message." Friendly, *The Federal Administrative Agencies: The Need for Better Definition of Standards*, 75 Harv. L.Rev. 1263, 1311 (1962). By design or default, Congress often fails to speak to "the precise question" before an agency. In the absence of such an answer, an agency's interpretation has the full force and effect of law, unless it "exceeds the bounds of the permissible." *Barnhart v. Walton*, 535 U.S. 212, 218 (2002).

It would be a bit much to describe the result as "the very definition of tyranny," but the danger posed by the growing power of the administrative state cannot be dismissed. See, *e.g., Talk America, Inc. v. Michigan Bell Telephone Co.*, 131 S.Ct. 2254, 2266 (2011) (Scalia, J., concurring) (noting that the FCC "has repeatedly been rebuked in its attempts to expand the statute beyond its text, and has repeatedly sought new means to the same ends"); *Sackett v. EPA*, 132 S.Ct. 1367, 1374 (2012) (rejecting agency argument that would "enable the strong-arming of regulated parties into 'voluntary compliance' without the opportunity for judicial review").

* * *

It is against this background that we consider whether the authority of administrative agencies should be augmented even further, to include not only broad power to give definitive answers to questions left to them by Congress, but also the same power to decide when Congress has given them that power.

Before proceeding to answer that question, however, it is necessary to sort through some confusion over what this litigation is about. The source of the confusion is a familiar culprit: the concept of "jurisdiction," which we have repeatedly described as a word with " 'many, too many, meanings.' " *Union Pacific R. Co. v. Locomotive Engineers*, 558 U.S. 67, 81 (2009).

The Court states that the question "is whether a court must defer under *Chevron* to an agency's interpretation of a statutory ambiguity that concerns the scope of the agency's statutory authority (that is, its jurisdiction)." That is fine—until the parenthetical. The parties, amici, and court below too often use the term "jurisdiction" imprecisely, which leads the Court to misunderstand the argument it must confront. That argument is not that "there exist two distinct classes of agency interpretations," some "big, important ones" that "define the agency's 'jurisdiction,' " and other "humdrum, run-of-the-mill" ones that "are simply applications of jurisdiction the agency plainly has." The argument is instead that a court should not defer to an agency on whether Congress has granted the agency interpretive authority over the statutory ambiguity at issue.

You can call that "jurisdiction" if you'd like, as petitioners do in the question presented. But given that the term is ambiguous, more is required to understand its use in that question than simply "having read it." It is important to keep in mind that the term, in the present context, has the more precise meaning noted above, encompassing congressionally delegated authority to issue interpretations with the force and effect of law. And that has nothing do with whether the statutory provisions at issue are "big" or "small."

II

"It is emphatically the province and duty of the judicial department to say what the law is." *Marbury v. Madison*, 1 Cranch 137, 177 (1803). The rise of the modern administrative state has not changed that duty. Indeed, the Administrative Procedure Act, governing judicial review of most agency action, instructs reviewing courts to decide "all relevant questions of law." 5 U.S.C. § 706.

We do not ignore that command when we afford an agency's statutory interpretation *Chevron* deference; we respect it. We give binding deference to permissible agency interpretations of statutory ambiguities because Congress has delegated to the agency the authority to interpret those ambiguities "with the force of law." *United States v. Mead Corp.*, 533 U.S. 218, 229 (2001).

But before a court may grant such deference, it must on its own decide whether Congress—the branch vested with lawmaking authority under the Constitution—has in fact delegated to the agency lawmaking power over the ambiguity at issue. Agencies are creatures of Congress; "an agency literally has no power to act . . . unless and until Congress confers power upon it." *Louisiana Pub. Serv. Comm'n v. FCC*, 476 U.S. 355, 374 (1986). Whether Congress has conferred such power is the "relevant question[ ] of law" that must be answered before affording *Chevron* deference. 5 U.S.C. § 706.

III

[Like Justice Scalia, Chief Justice Roberts proceeded to summarize various Supreme Court precedents that he claimed supported the above conclusion. Ed.]

In other words, we do not defer to an agency's interpretation of an ambiguous provision unless Congress wants us to, and whether Congress wants us to is a question that courts, not agencies, must decide. Simply put, that question is "beyond the *Chevron* pale." *Mead, supra,* at 234.

IV

Despite these precedents, the FCC argues that a court need only locate an agency and a grant of general rulemaking authority over a statute. *Chevron* deference then applies, it contends, to the agency's interpretation of any ambiguity in the Act, including ambiguity in a provision said to carve out specific provisions from the agency's general rulemaking authority. If Congress intends to exempt part of the statute from the agency's interpretive authority, the FCC says, Congress "can ordinarily be expected to state that intent explicitly."

If a congressional delegation of interpretive authority is to support *Chevron* deference, however, that delegation must extend to the specific statutory ambiguity at issue. The appropriate question is whether the delegation covers the "specific provision" and "particular question" before the court. *Chevron*, 467 U.S., at 844. A congressional grant of authority over some portion of a statute does not necessarily mean that Congress granted the agency interpretive authority over all its provisions.

An example that might highlight the point concerns statutes that parcel out authority to multiple agencies, which "may be the norm, rather than an exception." Gersen, *Overlapping and Underlapping Jurisdiction in Administrative Law*, 2006 S.Ct. Rev. 201, 208. The Dodd-Frank Wall Street Reform and Consumer Protection Act, for example, authorizes rulemaking by at least eight different agencies. When presented with an agency's interpretation of such a statute, a court cannot simply ask whether the statute is one that the agency administers; the question is whether authority over the particular ambiguity at issue has been delegated to the particular agency.

By the same logic, even when Congress provides interpretive authority to a single agency, a court must decide if the ambiguity the agency has purported to interpret with the force of law is one to which the congressional delegation extends. A general delegation to the agency to administer the statute will often suffice to satisfy the court that Congress has delegated interpretive authority over the ambiguity at issue. But if Congress has exempted particular provisions from that authority, that exemption must be respected, and the determination whether Congress has done so is for the courts alone.

* * *

V

As the preceding analysis makes clear, I do not understand petitioners to ask the Court—nor do I think it necessary—to draw a "specious, but scary-sounding" line between "big, important" interpretations on the one hand and "humdrum, run-of-the-mill" ones on the other. Drawing such a line may well be difficult. Distinguishing between whether an agency's interpretation of an ambiguous term is reasonable and whether that term is for the agency to interpret is not nearly so difficult. It certainly did not confuse the FCC in this proceeding. Nor did it confound the Fifth Circuit. More importantly, if the legitimacy of *Chevron* deference is based on a congressional delegation of interpretive authority, then the line is one the Court must draw.

The majority's hypothetical Common Carrier Acts do not demonstrate anything different. The majority states that in its second Common Carrier Act, Section 2 makes clear that Congress " 'conferred interpretative power on the agency' " to interpret the ambiguous terms "common carrier" and "unreasonable condition." Thus, it says, under anyone's theory a court must defer to the agency's reasonable interpretations of those terms. Correct.

The majority claims, however, that "petitioners' theory would accord the agency no deference" in its interpretation of the same ambiguous terms in the first Common Carrier Act. But as I understand petitioners' argument—and certainly in my own view—a court, in both cases, need only decide for itself whether Congress has delegated to the agency authority to interpret the ambiguous terms, before affording the agency's interpretation *Chevron* deference.

For the second Common Carrier Act, the answer is easy. The majority's hypothetical Congress has spoken clearly and specifically in Section 2 of the Act about its delegation of authority to interpret Section 1. As for the first Act, it is harder to analyze the question, given only one section of a presumably much larger statute. But if the first Common Carrier Act is like most agencies' organic statutes, I have no reason to doubt that the agency would likewise have interpretive authority over the same ambiguous terms, and therefore be entitled to deference in construing them, just as with the second Common Carrier Act. There is no new "test" to worry about; courts would simply apply the normal rules of statutory construction.

That the question might be harder with respect to the first Common Carrier Act should come as no surprise. The second hypothetical Congress has more carefully defined the agency's authority than the first. *Whatever* standard of review applies, it is more difficult to interpret an unclear statute than a clear one. My point is simply that before a court can defer to the agency's interpretation of the ambiguous terms in either Act, it must determine for itself that Congress has delegated authority to the agency to issue those interpretations with the force of law.

The majority also expresses concern that adopting petitioners' position would undermine *Chevron*'s stable background rule against which Congress legislates. That, of course, begs the question of what that stable background rule is. See Merrill & Hickman, Chevron's *Domain*, 89 Geo. L.Rev. 833, 910 (2001) ("Courts have never deferred to agencies with respect to questions such as whether Congress has delegated to an agency the power to act with the force of law through either legislative rules or binding adjudications. Similarly, it has never been maintained that Congress would want courts to give *Chevron* deference to an agency's determination that it is entitled to *Chevron* deference, or should give *Chevron* deference to an agency's determination of what types of interpretations are entitled to *Chevron* deference").

VI

The Court sees something nefarious behind the view that courts must decide on their own whether Congress has delegated interpretative authority to an agency, before deferring to that agency's interpretation of law. What is afoot, according to the Court, is a judicial power-grab, with nothing less than "*Chevron* itself" as "the ultimate target."

The Court touches on a legitimate concern: *Chevron* importantly guards against the Judiciary arrogating to itself policymaking properly left, under the separation of powers, to the Executive. But there is another concern at play, no less firmly rooted in our constitutional structure. That is the obligation of the Judiciary not only to confine itself to its proper role, but to ensure that the other branches do so as well.

An agency's interpretive authority, entitling the agency to judicial deference, acquires its legitimacy from a delegation of lawmaking power from Congress to the Executive. Our duty to police the boundary between the Legislature and the Executive is as critical as our duty to respect that between the Judiciary and the Executive. See *Zivotofsky v. Clinton*, 132 S.Ct. 1421, 1428 (2012). In the present context, that means ensuring that the Legislative Branch has in fact delegated lawmaking power to an agency within the Executive Branch, before the Judiciary defers to the Executive on what the law is. That concern is heightened, not diminished, by the fact that the administrative agencies, as a practical matter, draw upon a potent brew of executive, legislative, and judicial power. And it is heightened, not diminished, by the dramatic shift in power over the last 50 years from Congress to the Executive—a shift effected through the administrative agencies.

We reconcile our competing responsibilities in this area by ensuring judicial deference to agency interpretations under *Chevron*— but only after we have determined on our own that Congress has given interpretive authority to the agency. Our "task is to fix the boundaries of delegated authority," Monaghan, 83 Colum. L.Rev., at 27; that is not a task we can delegate to the agency. We do not leave it to the agency to decide when it is in charge.

* * *

NOTES AND QUESTIONS

1. Justice Scalia is well known for preferring bright-line rules to mushy, open-ended standards. Distinguishing agency interpretations that raise jurisdictional questions from those that do not is often difficult. In defending *Chevron* deference for agency interpretations of jurisdictional provisions, Justice Scalia's majority opinion relies heavily on the argument that courts cannot meaningfully distinguish jurisdictional questions from nonjurisdictional ones. Nevertheless, Justice Scalia further supported his conclusion by identifying several cases in which the Court had previously extended *Chevron* deference to agency interpretations of statutory provisions that raised jurisdictional questions. Note also that Justice O'Connor in *Brown & Williamson Tobacco*, quoted *supra*, had no difficulty concluding that the FDA's attempt to regulate tobacco advertising was an "extraordinary" case concerning a jurisdictional question. Does the difficulty in identifying which cases raise jurisdictional questions justify concluding that

2. The opinions in the *City of Arlington* case all approach the question before the Court as an application of *United States v. Mead Corp.*, 533 U.S. 218 (2001), discussed previously at length in this Chapter 6. Recall that *Mead* holds that *Chevron* provides the appropriate standard of review for agency statutory interpretations when Congress has delegated to an agency the power to act with the force of law and the agency has exercised that authority in advancing the interpretation at issue. Does *Mead*'s first step require a reviewing court to consider merely whether Congress broadly granted an agency the power to act with the force of law in administering all of the statute's provisions? Or does *Mead* instead ask a reviewing court to evaluate congressional intent with respect to each of a statute's provisions independently? The dissenting opinion authored by Chief Justice Roberts advocated the latter. But if a reviewing court were to follow that approach and ask at *Mead*'s first step whether Congress intended to delegate gap-filling power to an agency, then what inquiry remains for the court to conduct at *Chevron* step one?

F. AGENCY INTERPRETATIONS OF AGENCY REGULATIONS

Just as congressionally-enacted statutes are often ambiguous, so too agency regulations that attempt to resolve those statutory ambiguities may themselves prove to be unclear. And, just as agencies promulgate regulations to resolve ambiguous statutory language and fill statutory gaps, agencies often issue rulings, orders, or other guidance that interpret those regulations. Given the deference that reviewing courts give to agency interpretations of the statutes that they administer, should judges also defer to an agency's interpretations of its own regulations?

The Supreme Court in 1945 articulated the standard by which reviewing courts should evaluate those interpretations. In *Bowles v. Seminole Rock & Sand Co.*, 325 U.S. 410 (1945), the Court considered the substantive validity of an Office of Price Administration bulletin that interpreted an earlier Office regulation promulgated in the course of administering the Emergency Price Control Act of 1942. In evaluating the bulletin, the Court offered the following:

> Since this involves an interpretation of an administrative regulation a court must necessarily look to the administrative construction of the regulation if the meaning of the words used is in doubt. The intention of Congress or the principles of the Constitution in some situations may be relevant in the first instance in choosing between various constructions. But the ultimate criterion is the administrative interpretation, which becomes of controlling weight unless it is plainly erroneous or inconsistent with the regulation. * * * In this case the only problem is to discover the meaning of certain portions of Maximum Price Regulation No. 188. Our only tools, therefore, are the plain words of the regulation and any relevant interpretations of the Administrator.

Id. at 413–14.

While the *Chevron* review standard and *Mead*'s refinement of its scope have both been subjected to extensive judicial and scholarly debate, the *Seminole Rock* standard of judicial deference has never been particularly controversial. Nevertheless, much like the *Chevron* standard, *Seminole Rock* review is highly deferential—speaking in terms of "controlling weight" absent plain error or inconsistency with regulatory language. In light of the Court's emphasis in *Chevron* and subsequently in *Mead* on congressional delegation as a requirement for strong judicial deference to agency interpretations of statutory language, some scholars have questioned the comparative logic of strong deference to agency interpretations of regulatory language. As John Manning has observed, for example,

In a *Chevron* case, the reviewing court asks whether agency action—usually the promulgation of a rule, an agency enforcement action, or an adjudication—is consistent with an authorizing statute. If the reviewing court is effectively bound by the agency's interpretation of the statute, separation remains between the relevant lawmaker (Congress) and at least one entity (the agency) with independent authority to interpret the applicable legal text. In contrast, under *Seminole Rock*, the reviewing court asks whether the agency action—typically an enforcement action or adjudication—is consistent with an agency regulation. In those circumstances, if the court is bound by the agency's interpretation of the meaning of its own regulation, there is no independent interpreter; the agency lawmaker has effective control of the exposition of the legal text that is has created. In short, whereas *Chevron* retains one independent interpretive check on lawmaking by Congress, *Seminole Rock* leaves in place no independent interpretive check on lawmaking by an administrative agency."

John Manning, *Constitutional Structure and Judicial Deference to Agency Interpretations of Agency Rules*, 96 Colum. L. Rev. 612, 639 (1996). Manning thus concludes that, unlike *Chevron*, *Seminole Rock* is inconsistent with separation of powers principles, among other flaws. Further, in *Martin v. Occupational Safety & Health Review Commission*, the Court suggested in dicta that *Skidmore* rather than *Seminole Rock* provided the appropriate review standard for "less formal means of interpreting regulations" embodied in such forms as "interpretive rules" and "enforcement guidelines" because they did not derive from the exercise of the Secretary's delegated lawmaking powers." 499 U.S. 144, 157 (1991).

Without addressing the concerns raised by Manning and other scholars, the post-*Chevron* Supreme Court continued to apply *Seminole Rock* review in case after case. In one of the most prominent examples, *Auer v. Robbins*, 519 U.S. 452 (1997), the Court considered an interpretation of regulations under the Fair Labor Standards Act advanced by the Secretary of Labor in an amicus brief filed at the court's request. Without discussion regarding the theory or scope of the Seminole Rock standard, the Court in Auer simply observed that the Secretary's interpretation of his regulation was "under our jurisprudence, controlling unless 'plainly erroneous or inconsistent with the regulation,'" and declared that 'deferential standard . . . easily met" by the amicus brief. *Id*. at 461 (citations omitted).

Post-*Mead*, the Supreme Court likewise continued uncritically to apply the *Seminole Rock* standard, now often alternatively labeled as *Auer* deference. For example,

- In *Federal Express Corp. v. Holowecki*, 552 U.S. 389 (2008), after describing EEOC regulations interpreting the Age Discrimination in Employment Act as "less than clear," the Court deferred to a position taken in the government's amicus brief and various internal EEOC directives as "a reasonable extrapolation of the agency's regulations and . . . as a result . . . dispositive under *Auer*."

- In *Coeur Alaska, Inc. v. Southeast Alaska Conservation Council*, 557 U.S. 261 (2009), the Court concluded that EPA regulations interpreting the Clean Water Act were ambiguous and, applying *Auer* deference, found an interpretation of those regulations contained in an internal EPA memorandum to be "not 'plainly erroneous or inconsistent with the regulation[s],' " and thus "correct."

- In *National Ass'n of Home Builders v. Defenders of Wildlife*, 551 U.S. 644 (2007), the Court observed that an interpretation of agency regulations asserted by regulated parties had been "disclaimed" by "a formal letter" issued by each of three agencies with administrative responsibility over the Endangered Species Act and deferred to the agencies' views as "plainly" satisfying the "deferential standard" of *Auer v. Robbins*.

- In *Christensen v. Harris County*, 529 U.S. 576 (2000), discussed at length elsewhere in this Chapter, the Court acknowledged that "an agency's interpretation of its own regulation is entitled to deference" under *Auer* and *Seminole Rock* but declined to defer to the agency's opinion letter on the ground that, contrary to the agency's argument, the regulation was unambiguous.

The Court's continued commitment to *Seminole Rock* and *Auer* is particularly interesting when one considers that *Mead* denies *Chevron* deference to agency interpretations of statutes expressed in the very guidance formats that agencies typically utilize to articulate their interpretations of their own regulations. Nevertheless, another characteristic of the Court's most recent applications of *Seminole Rock* and *Auer* is its emphasis on the circumstances in which it will not evaluate an agency's interpretations of its regulations under that standard. For example, in *Gonzales v. Oregon*, 546 U.S. 243 (2006), a majority of the Court declined to apply the *Auer* standard in evaluating an Attorney General interpretation of the Controlled Substances Act on the ground that the regulation in question did

> little more than restate the terms of the statute itself. . . . Simply put, the existence of a parroting regulation does not change the fact that the question here is not the meaning of the regulation but the meaning of the statute. An agency does not acquire special authority to interpret its own words when, instead of using its expertise and experience to formulate a regulation, it has elected merely to paraphrase the statutory language.

Id. at 258. Writing in dissent, Justice Scalia objected to the Court's "antiparroting canon."

> [I]t is doubtful that any such exception to the *Auer* rule exists. The Court cites no authority for it, because there is none. To the contrary, our unanimous decision in *Auer* makes clear that broadly drawn regulations are entitled to no less respect than narrow ones.

Id. at 277 (Scalia, J. dissenting).

Subsequently, in *Chase Bank USA, N.A. v. McCoy*, 131 S.Ct. 871 (2011), a unanimous Court applied *Auer* to defer to the Federal Reserve

Board's interpretation of its Regulation Z, promulgated under the Truth-In-Lending Act (TILA). Nevertheless, writing on behalf of the Court, Justice Sotomayor summarized the Court's post-*Mead* approach to the *Auer* standard thusly:

> Under *Auer*, therefore, it is clear that deference to the interpretation in the Board's *amicus* brief is warranted. The cases McCoy cites in which we declined to apply *Auer* do not suggest that deference is unwarranted here. In *Gonzales v. Oregon*, 546 U.S. 243 (2006), we declined to defer because—in sharp contrast to the present case—the regulation in question did "little more than restate the terms of the statute" pursuant to which the regulation was promulgated. *Id.*, at 257. Accordingly, no deference was warranted to an agency interpretation of what were, in fact, Congress' words. In contrast, at the time of the transactions in this case, TILA itself included no requirements with respect to the disclosure of a change in credit terms. In *Christensen v. Harris County*, 529 U.S. 576 (2000), we declined to apply *Auer* deference because the regulation in question was unambiguous, and adopting the agency's contrary interpretation would "permit the agency, under the guise of interpreting a regulation, to create *de facto* a new regulation." 529 U.S., at 588. In light of Regulation Z's ambiguity, there is no such danger here. And our statement in *Christensen* that "deference is warranted only when the language of the regulation is ambiguous," *ibid.*, is perfectly consonant with *Auer* itself; if the text of a regulation is unambiguous, a conflicting agency interpretation advanced in an *amicus* brief will necessarily be "plainly erroneous or inconsistent with the regulation" in question. *Auer*, 519 U.S., at 461 (internal quotation marks omitted). Accordingly, under our precedent deference to the Board's interpretation of its own regulation, as presented in the agency's *amicus* brief, is wholly appropriate.

Just a few months after deciding *Chase Bank*, the Court again unanimously applied *Seminole Rock* and *Auer* in deferring to an agency's interpretation of its own regulations, this time with Justice Scalia expressing a change of heart regarding that standard.

Talk America, Inc. v. Michigan Bell Telephone Co.
131 S.Ct. 2254 (2010).

[In this case between two private parties, the issue was whether the Telecommunications Act of 1996 and Federal Communications Commission (FCC) regulations promulgated thereunder required the respondent to lease certain of its facilities to its competitors at cost-based rates. Although not a party to the case, the FCC filed an amicus briefs before both the Sixth Circuit and the Supreme Court interpreting existing regulations in a manner favorable to the petitioner. Justice Thomas wrote an opinion on behalf of all eight participating Justices deferring to the FCC's interpretation of its own regulations under *Auer v. Robbins*, 519 U.S. 452 (1997), and *Chase Bank USA, N.A. v. McCoy*, 131 S.Ct. 871 (2011). Justice Kagan did not participate in the case. Ed.]

■ JUSTICE SCALIA, concurring.

I join the opinion of the Court. I would reach the same result even without benefit of the rule that we will defer to an agency's interpretation of its own regulations, a rule in recent years attributed to our opinion in *Auer v. Robbins*, 519 U.S. 452, 461 (1997), though it first appeared in our jurisprudence more than half a century earlier, see *Bowles v. Seminole Rock & Sand Co.*, 325 U.S. 410 (1945). In this suit I have no need to rely on *Auer* deference, because I believe the FCC's interpretation is the fairest reading of the orders in question. * * *

It is comforting to know that I would reach the Court's result even without *Auer*. For while I have in the past uncritically accepted that rule, I have become increasingly doubtful of its validity. On the surface, it seems to be a natural corollary—indeed, an *a fortiori* application—of the rule that we will defer to an agency's interpretation of the statute it is charged with implementing, see *Chevron U.S.A. v. Natural Resources Defense Council, Inc.*, 467 U.S. 837 (1984). But it is not. When Congress enacts an imprecise statute that it commits to the implementation of an executive agency, it has no control over that implementation (except, of course, through further, more precise, legislation). The legislative and executive functions are not combined. But when an agency promulgates an imprecise rule, it leaves *to itself* the implementation of that rule, and thus the initial determination of the rule's meaning. And though the adoption of a rule is an exercise of the executive rather than the legislative power, a properly adopted rule has fully the effect of law. It seems contrary to fundamental principles of separation of powers to permit the person who promulgates a law to interpret it as well. "When the legislative and executive powers are united in the same person, or in the same body of magistrates, there can be no liberty; because apprehensions may arise, lest the same monarch or senate should enact tyrannical laws, to execute them in a tyrannical manner." Montesquieu, Spirit of the Laws bk. XI, ch. 6, pp. 151–152 (O. Piest ed., T. Nugent transl.1949).

Deferring to an agency's interpretation of a statute does not encourage Congress, out of a desire to expand its power, to enact vague statutes; the vagueness effectively cedes power to the Executive. By contrast, deferring to an agency's interpretation of its own rule encourages the agency to enact vague rules which give it the power, in future adjudications, to do what it pleases. This frustrates the notice and predictability purposes of rulemaking, and promotes arbitrary government. The seeming inappropriateness of *Auer* deference is especially evident in cases such as these, involving an agency that has repeatedly been rebuked in its attempts to expand the statute beyond its text, and has repeatedly sought new means to the same ends.

There are undoubted advantages to *Auer* deference. It makes the job of a reviewing court much easier, and since it usually produces affirmance of the agency's view without conflict in the Circuits, it imparts (once the agency has spoken to clarify the regulation) certainty and predictability to the administrative process. The defects of *Auer* deference, and the alternatives to it, are fully explored in Manning, Constitutional Structure and Judicial Deference to Agency Interpretations of Agency Rules, 96 Colum. L.Rev. 612 (1996). We have not been asked to reconsider *Auer* in the present case. When we are, I will be receptive to doing so.

———————

With this background, consider the Court's most recent two applications of the standard of review for agency interpretations articulated in *Seminole Rock* and in *Auer*, decided less than a year apart.

Christopher v. SmithKline Beecham Corp.
132 S.Ct. 2156 (2012).

■ JUSTICE ALITO delivered the opinion of the Court.

The Fair Labor Standards Act (FLSA) imposes minimum wage and maximum hours requirements on employers, see 29 U.S.C. §§ 206–207 (2006 ed. and Supp. IV), but those requirements do not apply to workers employed "in the capacity of outside salesman," § 213(a)(1). This case requires us to decide whether the term "outside salesman," as defined by Department of Labor (DOL or Department) regulations, encompasses pharmaceutical sales representatives whose primary duty is to obtain nonbinding commitments from physicians to prescribe their employer's prescription drugs in appropriate cases. We conclude that these employees qualify as "outside salesm[e]n."

I

A

Congress enacted the FLSA in 1938 with the goal of "protect[ing] all covered workers from substandard wages and oppressive working hours." *Barrentine v. Arkansas-Best Freight System, Inc.*, 450 U.S. 728, 739 (1981); see also 29 U.S.C. § 202(a). Among other requirements, the FLSA obligates employers to compensate employees for hours in excess of 40 per week at a rate of 1 1/2 times the employees' regular wages. See § 207(a). The overtime compensation requirement, however, does not apply with respect to all employees. See § 213. As relevant here, the statute exempts workers "employed . . . in the capacity of outside salesman." § 213(a)(1).

Congress did not define the term "outside salesman," but it delegated authority to the DOL to issue regulations "from time to time" to "defin[e] and delimi[t]" the term. *Ibid.* The DOL promulgated such regulations in 1938, 1940, and 1949. In 2004, following notice-and-comment procedures, the DOL reissued the regulations with minor amendments. See 69 Fed. Reg. 22122 (2004). The current regulations are nearly identical in substance to the regulations issued in the years immediately following the FLSA's enactment. See 29 C.F.R. §§ 541.500–541.504 (2011).

Three of the DOL's regulations are directly relevant to this case * * *. * * *

The general regulation sets out the definition of the statutory term "employee employed in the capacity of outside salesman." * * * [U]nder the general regulation, an outside salesman is any employee whose primary duty is making any sale, exchange, contract to sell, consignment for sale, shipment for sale, or other disposition.

The sales regulation restates the statutory definition of sale discussed above and clarifies that "[s]ales within the meaning of [29 U.S.C. § 203(k)] include the transfer of title to tangible property, and in certain cases, of tangible and valuable evidences of intangible property." 29 C.F.R. § 541.501(b).

Finally, the promotion-work regulation identifies "[p]romotion work" as "one type of activity often performed by persons who make sales, which may or may not be exempt outside sales work, depending upon the circumstances under which it is performed." § 541.503(a). Promotion work that is "performed incidental to and in conjunction with an employee's own outside sales or solicitations is exempt work," whereas promotion work that is "incidental to sales made, or to be made, by someone else is not exempt outside sales work." *Ibid.*

Additional guidance concerning the scope of the outside salesman exemption can be gleaned from reports issued in connection with the DOL's promulgation of regulations in 1940 and 1949, and from the preamble to the 2004 regulations. See Dept. of Labor, Wage and Hour Division, Report and Recommendations of the Presiding Officer at Hearings Preliminary to Redefinition (1940) (hereinafter 1940 Report); Dept. of Labor, Wage and Hour Division, Report and Recommendations on Proposed Revisions of Regulations, Part 541 (1949) (hereinafter 1949 Report); 69 Fed. Reg. 22160–22163 (hereinafter Preamble). Although the DOL has rejected proposals to eliminate or dilute the requirement that outside salesmen make their own sales, the Department has stressed that this requirement is met whenever an employee "in some sense make[s] a sale." 1940 Report 46; see also Preamble 22162 (reiterating that the exemption applies only to an employee who "in some sense, has made sales"). And the DOL has made it clear that "[e]xempt status should not depend" on technicalities, such as "whether it is the sales employee or the customer who types the order into a computer system and hits the return button," Preamble 22163, or whether "the order is filled by [a] jobber rather than directly by [the employee's] own employer," 1949 Report 83.

B

Respondent SmithKline Beecham Corporation is in the business of developing, manufacturing, and selling prescription drugs. The prescription drug industry is subject to extensive federal regulation, including the now-familiar requirement that prescription drugs be dispensed only upon a physician's prescription. In light of this requirement, pharmaceutical companies have long focused their direct marketing efforts, not on the retail pharmacies that dispense prescription drugs, but rather on the medical practitioners who possess the authority to prescribe the drugs in the first place. Pharmaceutical companies promote their prescription drugs to physicians through a process called "detailing," whereby employees known as "detailers" or "pharmaceutical sales representatives" provide information to physicians about the company's products in hopes of persuading them to write prescriptions for the products in appropriate cases. See *Sorrell v. IMS Health Inc.*, 131 S.Ct. 2653, 2659–2660 (2011) (describing the process of "detailing"). The position of "detailer" has existed in the pharmaceutical industry in substantially its current form since at least the 1950's, and in recent years the industry has employed more than 90,000 detailers nationwide.

* * *

II

We must determine whether pharmaceutical detailers are outside salesmen as the DOL has defined that term in its regulations. The parties agree that the regulations themselves were validly promulgated and are therefore entitled to deference under *Chevron U.S.A. Inc. v. Natural Resources Defense Council, Inc.*, 467 U.S. 837 (1984). But the parties disagree sharply about whether the DOL's interpretation of the regulations is owed deference under *Auer v. Robbins*, 519 U.S. 452 (1997). It is to that question that we now turn.

A

The DOL first announced its view that pharmaceutical detailers are not exempt outside salesmen in an *amicus* brief filed in the Second Circuit in 2009, and the Department has subsequently filed similar amicus briefs in other cases, including the case now before us. While the DOL's ultimate conclusion that detailers are not exempt has remained unchanged since 2009, the same cannot be said of its reasoning. In both the Second Circuit and the Ninth Circuit, the DOL took the view that "a 'sale' for the purposes of the outside sales exemption requires a consummated transaction directly involving the employee for whom the exemption is sought." Secretary's Novartis Brief 11; see also Brief for Secretary of Labor as *Amicus Curiae* in No. 10–15257 (CA9), p. 12. Perhaps because of the nebulous nature of this "consummated transaction" test, the Department changed course after we granted certiorari in this case. The Department now takes the position that "[a]n employee does not make a 'sale' for purposes of the 'outside salesman' exemption unless he actually transfers title to the property at issue." Brief for United States as *Amicus Curiae* 12–13 (hereinafter U.S. Brief). Petitioners and the DOL assert that this new interpretation of the regulations is entitled to controlling deference.[14]

Although *Auer* ordinarily calls for deference to an agency's interpretation of its own ambiguous regulation, even when that interpretation is advanced in a legal brief, see *Chase Bank USA, N.A. v. McCoy*, 131 S.Ct. 871, 880 (2011); *Auer*, 519 U.S., at 461–462, this general rule does not apply in all cases. Deference is undoubtedly inappropriate, for example, when the agency's interpretation is "plainly erroneous or inconsistent with the regulation." *Id.*, at 461. And deference is likewise unwarranted when there is reason to suspect that the agency's interpretation "does not reflect the agency's fair and considered judgment on the matter in question." *Auer, supra*, at 462; see also, *e.g.*, *Chase Bank, supra*, at 881. This might occur when the agency's interpretation conflicts with a prior interpretation, see, *e.g.*,

---

[14] Neither petitioners nor the DOL asks us to accord controlling deference to the "consummated transaction" interpretation the Department advanced in its briefs in the Second Circuit and Ninth Circuit, nor could we given that the Department has now abandoned that interpretation. See *Estate of Cowart v. Nicklos Drilling Co.*, 505 U.S. 469, 480 (1992) (noting that "it would be quite inappropriate to defer to an interpretation which has been abandoned by the policymaking agency itself").

Thomas Jefferson Univ. v. Shalala, 512 U.S. 504 (1994), or when it appears that the interpretation is nothing more than a "convenient litigating position," *Bowen v. Georgetown Univ. Hospital*, 488 U.S. 204, 213 (1988), or a "'*post hoc* rationalizatio[n]' advanced by an agency seeking to defend past agency action against attack," *Auer*, *supra*, at 462 (quoting *Bowen*, *supra*, at 212).

In this case, there are strong reasons for withholding the deference that *Auer* generally requires. Petitioners invoke the DOL's interpretation of ambiguous regulations to impose potentially massive liability on respondent for conduct that occurred well before that interpretation was announced. To defer to the agency's interpretation in this circumstance would seriously undermine the principle that agencies should provide regulated parties "fair warning of the conduct [a regulation] prohibits or requires." *Gates & Fox Co. v. Occupational Safety and Health Review Comm'n*, 790 F.2d 154, 156 (C.A.D.C.1986) (SCALIA, J.). Indeed, it would result in precisely the kind of "unfair surprise" against which our cases have long warned. See *Long Island Care at Home, Ltd. v. Coke*, 551 U.S. 158, 170–171 (2007) (deferring to new interpretation that "create[d] no unfair surprise" because agency had proceeded through notice-and-comment rulemaking); *Martin v. Occupational Safety and Health Review Comm'n*, 499 U.S. 144, 158 (1991) (identifying "adequacy of notice to regulated parties" as one factor relevant to the reasonableness of the agency's interpretation); *NLRB v. Bell Aerospace Co.*, 416 U.S. 267, 295 (1974) (suggesting that an agency should not change an interpretation in an adjudicative proceeding where doing so would impose "new liability . . . on individuals for past actions which were taken in good-faith reliance on [agency] pronouncements" or in a case involving "fines or damages").

This case well illustrates the point. Until 2009, the pharmaceutical industry had little reason to suspect that its longstanding practice of treating detailers as exempt outside salesmen transgressed the FLSA. The statute and regulations certainly do not provide clear notice of this.
* * *

Even more important, despite the industry's decades-long practice of classifying pharmaceutical detailers as exempt employees, the DOL never initiated any enforcement actions with respect to detailers or otherwise suggested that it thought the industry was acting unlawfully.[16] We acknowledge that an agency's enforcement decisions are informed by a host of factors, some bearing no relation to the agency's views regarding whether a violation has occurred. See, *e.g.*, *Heckler v. Chaney*, 470 U.S. 821, 831 (1985) (noting that "an agency decision not to enforce often involves a complicated balancing of a number of factors which are peculiarly within its expertise"). But where, as here, an agency's announcement of its interpretation is preceded by a very lengthy period of conspicuous inaction, the potential for unfair surprise is acute. As the Seventh Circuit has noted, while it

---

[16] Neither petitioners nor the DOL asks us to accord controlling deference to the "consummated transaction" interpretation the Department advanced in its briefs in the Second Circuit and Ninth Circuit, nor could we given that the Department has now abandoned that interpretation. See *Estate of Cowart v. Nicklos Drilling Co.*, 505 U.S. 469, 480 (1992) (noting that "it would be quite inappropriate to defer to an interpretation which has been abandoned by the policymaking agency itself").

may be "possible for an entire industry to be in violation of the [FLSA] for a long time without the Labor Department noticing," the "more plausible hypothesis" is that the Department did not think the industry's practice was unlawful. *Yi v. Sterling Collision Centers, Inc.*, 480 F.3d 505, 510–511 (2007). There are now approximately 90,000 pharmaceutical sales representatives; the nature of their work has not materially changed for decades and is well known; these employees are well paid; and like quintessential outside salesmen, they do not punch a clock and often work more than 40 hours per week. Other than acquiescence, no explanation for the DOL's inaction is plausible.

Our practice of deferring to an agency's interpretation of its own ambiguous regulations undoubtedly has important advantages, but this practice also creates a risk that agencies will promulgate vague and open-ended regulations that they can later interpret as they see fit, thereby "frustrate[ing] the notice and predictability purposes of rulemaking." *Talk America, Inc. v. Michigan Bell Telephone Co.*, 131 S.Ct. 2254, 2266 (2011) (SCALIA, J., concurring). It is one thing to expect regulated parties to conform their conduct to an agency's interpretations once the agency announces them; it is quite another to require regulated parties to divine the agency's interpretations in advance or else be held liable when the agency announces its interpretations for the first time in an enforcement proceeding and demands deference.

Accordingly, whatever the general merits of *Auer* deference, it is unwarranted here. We instead accord the Department's interpretation a measure of deference proportional to the " 'thoroughness evident in its consideration, the validity of its reasoning, its consistency with earlier and later pronouncements, and all those factors which give it power to persuade.' " *United States v. Mead Corp.*, 533 U.S. 218, 228 (2001) (quoting *Skidmore v. Swift & Co.*, 323 U.S. 134, 140 (1944)).

B

We find the DOL's interpretation of its regulations quite unpersuasive. The interpretation to which we are now asked to defer— that a sale demands a transfer of title—plainly lacks the hallmarks of thorough consideration. Because the DOL first announced its view that pharmaceutical sales representatives do not qualify as outside salesmen in a series of amicus briefs, there was no opportunity for public comment, and the interpretation that initially emerged from the Department's internal decisionmaking process proved to be untenable. After arguing successfully in the Second Circuit and then unsuccessfully in the Ninth Circuit that a sale for present purposes simply requires a "consummated transaction," the DOL advanced a different interpretation in this Court. Here, the DOL's brief states unequivocally that "[a]n employee does not make a 'sale' for purposes of the 'outside salesman' exemption unless he actually transfers title to the property at issue."

* * *

In support of its new interpretation, the DOL relies heavily on its sales regulation, which states in part that "[s]ales [for present purposes] *include* the transfer of title to tangible property," 29 C.F.R. § 541.501(b) (emphasis added). This regulation, however, provides little support for the DOL's position.

* * *

In light of our conclusion that the DOL's interpretation is neither entitled to *Auer* deference nor persuasive in its own right, we must employ traditional tools of interpretation to determine whether petitioners are exempt outside salesmen.

[The Court's opinion finally analyzes statutory and regulatory text and purpose to conclude that "petitioners qualify as outside salesmen under the most reasonable interpretation of the DOL's regulations." Ed.]

■ JUSTICE BREYER, with whom JUSTICE GINSBURG, JUSTICE SOTOMAYOR, and JUSTICE KAGAN join, dissenting.

The Fair Labor Standards Act (FLSA) exempts from federal maximum hour and minimum wage requirements "any employee employed . . . in the capacity of outside salesman." 29 U.S.C. § 213(a)(1). The question is whether drug company detailers fall within the scope of the term "outside salesman." In my view, they do not.

* * *

As summarized, I agree with the Court's description of the job. In light of important, near contemporaneous differences in the Justice Department's views as to the meaning of relevant Labor Department regulations, I also agree that we should not give the Solicitor General's current interpretive view any especially favorable weight. Thus, I am willing to assume, with the Court, that we should determine whether the statutory term covers the detailer's job as here described through our independent examination of the statute's language and the related Labor Department regulations. But, I conclude on that basis that a detailer is not an "outside salesman."

Decker v. Northwest Environmental Defense Center

133 S. Ct. 1326 (2013).

■ JUSTICE KENNEDY delivered the opinion of the Court.

These cases present the question whether the Clean Water Act (Act) and its implementing regulations require permits before channeled stormwater runoff from logging roads can be discharged into the navigable waters of the United States. Under the statute and its implementing regulations, a permit is required if the discharges are deemed to be "associated with industrial activity." 33 U.S.C. § 1342(p)(2)(B). The Environmental Protection Agency (EPA), with the responsibility to enforce the Act, has issued a regulation defining the term "associated with industrial activity" to cover only discharges "from any conveyance that is used for collecting and conveying storm water and that is directly related to manufacturing, processing or raw materials storage areas at an industrial plant." The EPA interprets its regulation to exclude the type of stormwater discharges from logging roads at issue here. For reasons now to be explained, the Court concludes the EPA's determination is a reasonable interpretation of its own regulation; and, in consequence, deference is accorded to the interpretation under *Auer v. Robbins*, 519 U.S. 452 (1997).

I

A

Congress passed the Clean Water Act in 1972 to "restore and maintain the chemical, physical, and biological integrity of the Nation's waters." 33 U.S.C. § 1251(a). A central provision of the Act is its requirement that individuals, corporations, and governments secure National Pollutant Discharge Elimination System (NPDES) permits before discharging pollution from any point source into the navigable waters of the United States. The Act defines "point source" as

> "any discernible, confined and discrete conveyance, including but not limited to any pipe, ditch, channel, tunnel, conduit, well, discrete fissure, container, rolling stock, concentrated animal feeding operation, or vessel or other floating craft, from which pollutants are or may be discharged. This term does not include agricultural stormwater discharges and return flows from irrigated agriculture." § 1362(14).

When the Act took effect, the EPA found it difficult to process permit applications from countless owners and operators of point sources throughout the country. * * * [T]he EPA issued new regulations to define with more precision which categories of discharges qualified as point sources in the first place. Among these regulations was the so-called Silvicultural Rule. This rule is at issue here. It provides:

> "*Silvicultural point source* means any discernible, confined and discrete conveyance related to rock crushing, gravel washing, log sorting, or log storage facilities which are operated in connection with silvicultural activities and from which pollutants are discharged into waters of the United States. The term does not include non-point source silvicultural activities such as nursery operations, site preparation, reforestation and subsequent cultural treatment, thinning, prescribed burning, pest and fire control, harvesting operations, surface drainage, or road construction and maintenance from which there is natural runoff." 40 C.F.R. § 122.27(b)(1).

Under the quoted rule, any discharge from a logging-related source that qualifies as a point source requires an NPDES permit unless some other federal statutory provision exempts it from that coverage. In one such provision, 33 U.S.C. § 1342(p), Congress has exempted certain discharges of stormwater runoff.

* * *

As relevant here, Congress directed the EPA to continue to require permits for stormwater discharges "associated with industrial activity." § 1342(p)(2)(B). The statute does not define that term, but the EPA adopted a regulation (hereinafter Industrial Stormwater Rule) in which it defined it as "the discharge from any conveyance that is used for collecting and conveying storm water and that is directly related to manufacturing, processing or raw materials storage areas at an industrial plant. The term does not include discharges from facilities or activities excluded from the NPDES program under this part 122. For the categories of industries identified in this section, the term includes, but is not limited to, storm water discharges from . . . immediate access roads and rail lines used or traveled by carriers of raw materials, manufactured products, waste material, or by-products used or created by the facility. . . ." 40 C.F.R. § 122.26(b)(14) (2006).

The Industrial Stormwater Rule also specified that, with one exception not relevant here, "[f]acilities classified as Standard Industrial Classificatio[n] 24" are "considered to be engaging in 'industrial activity' for purposes of paragraph (b)(14)." *Ibid.* The Standard Industrial Classifications are a system used by federal agencies to categorize firms engaged in different types of business activity. Standard Industrial Classification 24 identifies industries involved in the field of "Lumber and Wood Products." This includes the "Logging" industry, defined as "[e]stablishments primarily engaged in cutting timber and in producing . . . primary forest or wood raw materials."

On November 30, 2012—three days before the instant cases were argued in this Court—the EPA issued its final version of an amendment to the Industrial Stormwater Rule. The amendment was the agency's response to the Court of Appeals' ruling now under review.

* * *

It is fair to say the purpose of the amended regulation is to bring within the NPDES permit process only those logging operations that involve the four types of activity (rock crushing, gravel washing, log sorting, and log storage facilities) that are defined as point sources by the explicit terms of the Silvicultural Rule.

* * *

B

At issue are discharges of channeled stormwater runoff from two logging roads in Oregon's Tillamook State Forest, lying in the Pacific Coast Range about 40 miles west of Portland. Petitioner Georgia-Pacific West, along with other logging and paper-products companies, has a contract with the State of Oregon to harvest timber from the forest. It uses the roads for that purpose. When it rains (which it does often in the mountains of northwest Oregon, averaging in some areas more than 100 inches per year), water runs off the graded roads into a system of ditches, culverts, and channels that discharge the water into nearby rivers and streams. The discharges often contain large amounts of sediment, in the form of dirt and crushed gravel from the roads. There is evidence that this runoff can harm fish and other aquatic organisms.

In September 2006, respondent Northwest Environmental Defense Center (NEDC) filed suit in the United States District Court for the District of Oregon. It invoked the Clean Water Act's citizen-suit provision, 33 U.S.C. § 1365, and named as defendants certain firms involved in logging and paper-products operations (including petitioner Georgia-Pacific West), as well as state and local governments and officials (including the State Forester of Oregon, who is now petitioner Doug Decker). The suit alleged that the defendants caused discharges of channeled stormwater runoff into two waterways—the South Fork Trask River and the Little South Fork Kilchis River. The defendants had not obtained NPDES permits, and so, the suit alleged, they had violated the Act.

* * *

III

Under the Act, petitioners were required to secure NPDES permits for the discharges of channeled stormwater runoff only if the discharges were "associated with industrial activity," 33 U.S.C. § 1342(p)(2)(B), as that statutory term is defined in the preamendment version of the Industrial Stormwater Rule, 40 C.F.R. § 122.26(b)(14) (2006). Otherwise, the discharges fall within the Act's general exemption of "discharges composed entirely of stormwater" from the NPDES permitting scheme. 33 U.S.C. § 1342(p)(1).

NEDC first contends that the statutory term "associated with industrial activity" unambiguously covers discharges of channeled stormwater runoff from logging roads. See *Chevron U.S.A. Inc. v. Natural Resources Defense Council, Inc.*, 467 U.S. 837, 842–843 (1984). That view, however, overlooks the multiple definitions of the terms "industrial" and "industry." These words can refer to business activity in general, yet so too can they be limited to "economic activity concerned with the processing of raw materials and manufacture of goods in factories." Oxford Dict. 887. The latter definition does not necessarily encompass outdoor timber harvesting. The statute does not foreclose more specific definition by the agency, since it provides no further detail as to its intended scope.

Somewhat more plausible is NEDC's claim that the preamendment version of the Industrial Stormwater Rule unambiguously required a permit for the discharges at issue. NEDC reasons that under the rule, "[f]or the categories of industries identified in this section," NPDES permits are required for, among other things, "storm water discharges from . . . immediate access roads . . . used or traveled by carriers of raw materials." 40 C.F.R. § 122.26(b)(14) (2006). Yet this raises the question whether logging is a "categor[y] of industr[y]" identified by the section. The regulation goes on to identify a list of "categories of facilities" that "are considered to be engaging in 'industrial activity' for purposes" of the Industrial Stormwater Rule. *Ibid.* In the earlier version of the regulation, this list included "[f]acilities classified as Standard Industrial Classificatio[n] 24," which encompasses "Logging." Hence, NEDC asserts, logging is among the categories of industries for which "storm water discharges from . . . immediate access roads . . . used or traveled by carriers of raw materials" required NPDES permits under the earlier version of the Industrial Stormwater Rule. § 122.26(b)(14). NEDC further notes, in support of its reading of the regulation, that modern logging is a large-scale, highly mechanized enterprise, using sophisticated harvesting machines weighing up to 20 tons.

The EPA takes a different view. It concludes that the earlier regulation invoked Standard Industrial Classification 24 " 'to regulate traditional *industrial* sources such as sawmills.' " It points to the regulation's reference to "facilities" and the classification's reference to "establishments," which suggest industrial sites more fixed and permanent than outdoor timber-harvesting operations. This reading is reinforced by the Industrial Stormwater Rule's definition of discharges associated with industrial activity as discharges "from any conveyance that is used for collecting and conveying storm water and that is directly related to manufacturing, processing or raw materials storage areas at an industrial plant." 40 C.F.R. § 122.26(b)(14) (2006). This language lends support to the EPA's claim that the regulation does not cover temporary, outdoor logging installations. It was reasonable for the agency to conclude that the conveyances at issue are "directly related" only to the harvesting of raw materials, rather than to "manufacturing," "processing," or "raw materials storage areas." See Oxford Dict. 1066 (manufacturing is "mak[ing] (something) on a large scale using machinery"); *id.*, at 1392 (processing is "perform [ing] a series of mechanical or chemical operations on (something) in order to change or preserve it"). In addition, even if logging as a general matter is a type of economic activity within the regulation's scope, a reasonable interpretation of the regulation could still require the discharges to be related in a direct way to operations "at an industrial plant" in order to be subject to NPDES permitting.

NEDC resists this conclusion, noting that elsewhere in the Industrial Stormwater Rule the EPA has required NPDES permits for stormwater discharges associated with other types of outdoor economic activity. See § 122.26(b)(14)(iii) (mining); § 122.26(b)(14)(v) (landfills receiving industrial waste); § 122.26(b)(14)(x) (large construction sites). The EPA reasonably could conclude, however, that these types of activities tend to be more fixed and permanent than timber-harvesting operations are and have a closer connection to traditional industrial sites. In light of the language of the regulation just discussed, moreover, the inclusion of these types of economic activity in the Industrial Stormwater Rule need not be read to mandate that all stormwater discharges related to these activities fall within the rule, just as the inclusion of logging need not be read to extend to all discharges from logging sites. The regulation's reach may be limited by the requirement that the discharges be "directly related to manufacturing, processing or raw materials storage areas at an industrial plant." § 122.26(b)(14).

It is well established that an agency's interpretation need not be the only possible reading of a regulation—or even the best one—to prevail. When an agency interprets its own regulation, the Court, as a general rule, defers to it "unless that interpretation is 'plainly erroneous or inconsistent with the regulation.' " *Chase Bank USA, N.A. v. McCoy*, 131 S.Ct. 871, 880 (2011) (quoting Auer, 519 U.S., at 461). The EPA's interpretation is a permissible one. Taken together, the regulation's references to "facilities," "establishments," "manufacturing," "processing," and an "industrial plant" leave open the rational interpretation that the regulation extends only to traditional industrial buildings such as factories and associated sites, as well as other relatively fixed facilities.

There is another reason to accord *Auer* deference to the EPA's interpretation: there is no indication that its current view is a change from prior practice or a post hoc justification adopted in response to litigation. See *Christopher v. SmithKline Beecham Corp.*, 132 S.Ct. 2156, 2166–2167 (2012). The opposite is the case. The agency has been consistent in its view that the types of discharges at issue here do not require NPDES permits.

The EPA's decision exists against a background of state regulation with respect to stormwater runoff from logging roads. The State of Oregon has made an extensive effort to develop a comprehensive set of best practices to manage stormwater runoff from logging roads. These practices include rules mandating filtration of stormwater runoff before it enters rivers and streams, requiring logging companies to construct roads using surfacing that minimizes the sediment in runoff, and obligating firms to cease operations where such efforts fail to prevent visible increases in water turbidity. Oregon has invested substantial time and money in establishing these practices. In addition, the development, siting, maintenance, and regulation of roads—and in particular of state forest roads—are areas in which Oregon has considerable expertise. In exercising the broad discretion the Clean Water Act gives the EPA in the realm of stormwater runoff, the agency could reasonably have concluded that further federal regulation in this area would be duplicative or counterproductive. Indeed, Congress has given express instructions to the EPA to work "in consultation with State and local officials" to alleviate stormwater pollution by developing the precise kind of best management practices Oregon has established here. 33 U.S.C. § 1342(p)(6).

* * *

The preamendment version of the Industrial Stormwater Rule, as permissibly construed by the agency, exempts discharges of channeled stormwater runoff from logging roads from the NPDES permitting scheme. * * *

■ JUSTICE BREYER took no part in the consideration or decision of these cases.

■ CHIEF JUSTICE ROBERTS, with whom JUSTICE ALITO joins, concurring.

The opinion concurring in part and dissenting in part raises serious questions about the principle set forth in *Bowles v. Seminole Rock & Sand Co.*, 325 U.S. 410 (1945), and *Auer v. Robbins*, 519 U.S. 452 (1997). It may be appropriate to reconsider that principle in an appropriate case. But this is not that case.

Respondent suggested reconsidering *Auer*, in one sentence in a footnote, with no argument. Petitioners said don't do it, again in a footnote. Out of 22 *amicus* briefs, only two—filed by dueling groups of law professors—addressed the issue on the merits.

The issue is a basic one going to the heart of administrative law. Questions of *Seminole Rock* and *Auer* deference arise as a matter of course on a regular basis. The bar is now aware that there is some interest in reconsidering those cases, and has available to it a concise statement of the arguments on one side of the issue.

I would await a case in which the issue is properly raised and argued. The present cases should be decided as they have been briefed and argued, under existing precedent.

■ JUSTICE SCALIA, concurring in part and dissenting in part.

I join Parts I and II of the Court's opinion * * *. I do not join Part III. The Court there gives effect to a reading of EPA's regulations that is not the most natural one, simply because EPA says that it believes the unnatural reading is right. It does this, moreover, even though the agency has vividly illustrated that it can write a rule saying precisely what it means—by doing *just that* while these cases were being briefed.

Enough is enough.

I

For decades, and for no good reason, we have been giving agencies the authority to say what their rules mean, under the harmless-sounding banner of "defer[ring] to an agency's interpretation of its own regulations." *Talk America, Inc. v. Michigan Bell Telephone Co.*, 131 S.Ct. 2254, 2265 (2011) (SCALIA, J., concurring). This is generally called *Seminole* Rock or Auer deference. See *Bowles v. Seminole Rock & Sand Co.*, 325 U.S. 410 (1945); *Auer v. Robbins*, 519 U.S. 452 (1997).

Two Terms ago, in my separate concurrence in *Talk America*, I expressed doubts about the validity of this practice. In that case, however, the agency's interpretation of the rule was also the fairest one, and no party had asked us to reconsider *Auer*. Today, however, the Court's deference to the agency makes the difference (note the Court's defensive insistence that the agency's interpretation need not be "the best one." And respondent has asked us, if necessary, to " 'reconsider *Auer.*' " I believe that it is time to do so. This is especially true because the circumstances of these cases illustrate *Auer*'s flaws in a particularly vivid way.

The canonical formulation of *Auer* deference is that we will enforce an agency's interpretation of its own rules unless that interpretation is "plainly erroneous or inconsistent with the regulation." *Seminole Rock* at 414. But of course whenever the agency's interpretation of the regulation is different from the fairest reading, it is in that sense "inconsistent" with the regulation. Obviously, that is not enough, or there would be nothing for *Auer* to do. In practice, *Auer* deference is *Chevron* deference applied to regulations rather than statutes. See *Chevron U.S.A. Inc. v. Natural Resources Defense Council, Inc.*, 467 U.S. 837 (1984). The agency's interpretation will be accepted if, though not the fairest reading of the regulation, it is a plausible reading—within the scope of the ambiguity that the regulation contains.

Our cases have not put forward a persuasive justification for Auer deference. The first case to apply it, *Seminole Rock*, offered no justification whatever—just the *ipse dixit* that "the administrative interpretation . . . becomes of controlling weight unless it is plainly erroneous or inconsistent with the regulation." 325 U.S., at 414. Our later cases provide two principal explanations, neither of which has much to be said for it. See generally Stephenson & Pogoriler, *Seminole Rock*'s Domain, 79 Geo. Wash. L.Rev. 1449, 1454–1458 (2011). First, some cases say that the agency, as the drafter of the rule, will have some special insight into its intent when enacting it. *E.g., Martin v.*

Occupational Safety and Health Review Comm'n, 499 U.S. 144, 150–153, 111 S.Ct. 1171, 113 L.Ed.2d 117 (1991). The implied premise of this argument—that what we are looking for is the agency's *intent* in adopting the rule—is false. There is true of regulations what is true of statutes. As Justice Holmes put it: "[w]e do not inquire what the legislature meant; we ask only what the statute means." *The Theory of Legal Interpretation*, 12 Harv. L.Rev. 417, 419 (1899). Whether governing rules are made by the national legislature or an administrative agency, we are bound *by what they say*, not by the unexpressed intention of those who made them.

The other rationale our cases provide is that the agency possesses special expertise in administering its " 'complex and highly technical regulatory program.' " See, *e.g., Thomas Jefferson Univ. v. Shalala*, 512 U.S. 504, 512 (1994). That is true enough, and it leads to the conclusion that agencies and not courts should make regulations. But it has nothing to do with who should interpret regulations—unless one believes that the purpose of interpretation is to make the regulatory program work in a fashion that the current leadership of the agency deems effective. Making regulatory programs effective is the purpose of *rulemaking*, in which the agency uses its "special expertise" to formulate the best rule. But the purpose of interpretation is to determine the fair meaning of the rule—to "say what the law is," *Marbury v. Madison*, 1 Cranch 137 (1803). Not to make policy, but to determine what policy has been made and promulgated by the agency, to which the public owes obedience. Indeed, since the leadership of agencies (and hence the policy preferences of agencies) changes with Presidential administrations, an agency head can only be sure that the application of his "special expertise" to the issue addressed by a regulation *will be given effect* if we adhere to predictable principles of textual interpretation rather than defer to the "special expertise" of his successors. If we take agency enactments as written, the Executive has a stable background against which to write its rules and achieve the policy ends it thinks best.

Another conceivable justification for *Auer* deference, though not one that is to be found in our cases, is this: If it is reasonable to defer to agencies regarding the meaning of statutes that *Congress* enacted, as we do per *Chevron*, it is *a fortiori* reasonable to defer to them regarding the meaning of regulations *that they themselves crafted*. To give an agency less control over the meaning of its own regulations than it has over the meaning of a congressionally enacted statute seems quite odd.

But it is not odd at all. The theory of *Chevron* (take it or leave it) is that when Congress gives an agency authority to administer a statute, including authority to issue interpretive regulations, it implicitly accords the agency a degree of discretion, which the courts must respect, regarding the meaning of the statute. See *Smiley v. Citibank (South Dakota), N. A.*, 517 U.S. 735, 740–741 (1996). While the implication of an agency power to clarify the statute is reasonable enough, there is surely no congressional implication that the agency can resolve ambiguities in its own regulations. For that would violate a fundamental principle of separation of powers—that the power to write a law and the power to interpret it cannot rest in the same hands. "When the legislative and executive powers are united in the same person . . . there can be no liberty; because apprehensions may arise, lest the same monarch or senate should enact tyrannical laws, to execute them in a tyrannical manner." Montesquieu, Spirit of the Laws bk. XI, ch. 6, pp. 151–152 (O. Piest ed., T. Nugent transl. 1949). Congress cannot enlarge its *own* power through *Chevron*—whatever it leaves vague in the statute will be worked out *by someone else*. *Chevron* represents a presumption about who, as between the Executive and the Judiciary, that someone else will be. (The Executive, by the way—the competing political branch—is the less congenial repository of the power as far as Congress is concerned.) So Congress's incentive is to speak as clearly as possible on the matters it regards as important.

But when an agency interprets its *own* rules—that is something else. Then the power to prescribe is augmented by the power to interpret; and the incentive is to speak vaguely and broadly, so as to retain a "flexibility" that will enable "clarification" with retroactive effect. "It is perfectly understandable" for an agency to "issue vague regulations" if doing so will "maximiz[e] agency power." *Thomas Jefferson Univ., supra*, at 525 (THOMAS, J., dissenting). Combining the power to prescribe with the power to interpret is not a new evil: Blackstone condemned the practice of resolving doubts about "the construction of the Roman laws" by "stat[ing] the case to the emperor in writing, and tak[ing] his opinion upon it." 1 W. Blackstone, Commentaries on the Laws of England 58 (1765). And our Constitution did not mirror the British practice of using the House of Lords as a court of last resort, due in part to the fear that he who has "agency in passing bad laws" might operate in the "same spirit" in their interpretation. The Federalist No. 81, pp. 543–544 (J. Cooke ed. 1961). *Auer* deference encourages agencies to be "vague in framing regulations, with the plan of issuing 'interpretations' to create the intended new law without observance of notice and comment procedures." Anthony, *The Supreme Court and the APA: Sometimes They Just Don't Get It*, 10 Admin. L.J. Am. U. 1, 11–12 (1996). *Auer* is not a logical corollary to *Chevron* but a dangerous permission slip for the arrogation of power. See *Talk America*, 131 S.Ct., at 2266 (SCALIA, J., concurring); Manning, *Constitutional Structure and Judicial Deference to Agency Interpretations of Agency Rules*, 96 Colum. L.Rev. 612 (1996).

It is true enough that *Auer* deference has the same beneficial pragmatic effect as *Chevron* deference: The country need not endure the uncertainty produced by divergent views of numerous district courts and courts of appeals as to what is the fairest reading of the regulation, until a definitive answer is finally provided, years later, by this Court. The agency's view can be relied upon, unless it is, so to speak, beyond the pale. But the duration of the uncertainty produced by a vague regulation need not be as long as the uncertainty produced by a vague statute. For as soon as an interpretation uncongenial to the agency is pronounced by a district court, the agency can begin the process of amending the regulation to make its meaning entirely clear. The circumstances of this case demonstrate the point. While these cases were being briefed before us, EPA issued a rule designed to respond to the Court of Appeals judgment we are reviewing. It did so (by the standards of such things) relatively quickly: The decision below was handed down in May 2011, and in December 2012 the EPA published an amended rule setting forth in unmistakable terms the position it argues here. And there is another respect in which a lack of *Chevron*-type deference has less severe pragmatic consequences for rules than for statutes. In many cases, when an agency believes that its rule permits conduct that the text arguably forbids, it can simply exercise its discretion not to prosecute. That is not possible, of course, when, as here, a party harmed by the violation has standing to compel enforcement.

In any case, however great may be the efficiency gains derived from *Auer* deference, beneficial effect cannot justify a rule that not only has no principled basis but contravenes one of the great rules of separation of powers: He who writes a law must not adjudge its violation.

II

I would therefore resolve these cases by using the familiar tools of textual interpretation to decide: Is what the petitioners did here proscribed by the fairest reading of the regulations? * * * The fairest reading of the statute and regulations is that these discharges were from point sources, and were associated with industrial activity.

[Justice Scalia's opinion goes on to utilize traditional tools of statutory interpretation to support his view of the statute's meaning. Ed.]

* * *

Because the fairest reading of the agency's rules proscribes the conduct at issue in these cases, I would affirm the judgment below. It is time for us to presume (to coin a phrase) that an agency says in a rule what it means, and means in a rule what it says there.

NOTES AND QUESTIONS

1. The *Christopher* majority supported its decision not to apply *Seminole Rock* and *Auer* by citing several cases in which courts have refused to apply *Auer* to support the imposition of penalties for violating an agency rule first announced after the conduct that the agency sought to punish took place, where the regulated party had no contemporaneous reason to believe that its conduct was unlawful. The Court also cited Pierce's Administrative Law Treatise for the proposition that, "in penalty cases, courts will not accord substantial deference to an agency's interpretation of an ambiguous rule in circumstances where the rule did not place the individual or firm on notice that the conduct at issue constituted a violation of the rule." While past courts have declined to apply *Seminole Rock/Auer* deference when the agency relies on the new interpretation as the basis to impose a penalty, however, there was no penalty at issue in *Christopher*. Rather, Christopher sought backpay and liquidated damages. The Department of Labor, which is the only entity with the power to impose a penalty for the conduct at issue, was not even a party to the case. If the Court conceives the concept of a penalty broadly, as it appears to do in *Christopher*, then does the penalty exception from *Seminole Rock* and *Auer* effectively eliminate their controlling weight standard?

2. If the *Christopher* approach to the penalty exception from *Seminole Rock* and *Auer* does substantially curtail the scope of the controlling weight standard, the shift could be significant. A study by William Eskridge and

Lauren Baer of judicial deference standards in the Supreme Court found a 91% deference rate when the Court applied the *Seminole Rock/Auer* standard. *See* William N. Eskridge, Jr. & Lauren E. Baer, *The Continuum of Deference: Supreme Court Treatment of Agency Statutory Interpretations from* Chevron *to* Hamdan, 96 Geo. L.J. 1083 (2008). The high deference rate in *Seminole Rock/Auer* in the Supreme Court stands in sharp contrast to other administrative law standards of review, as two recent articles summarizing empirical studies in the area demonstrate. *See* Richard J. Pierce, Jr., *What Do the Studies of Judicial Review of Agency Actions Mean?*, 63 Admin. L. Rev. 77 (2011); David Zaring, *Reasonable Agencies*, 96 Va. L. Rev. 135 (2010). To quote Pierce,

> With one notable exception, the studies suggest that a court's choice of which doctrine to apply in reviewing an agency action is not an important determinant of outcomes in the Supreme Court or the circuit courts. The ranges of affirmance rates by doctrine are as follows: *Chevron*, 60% to 81.3%; *Skidmore*, 55.1 to 73.5%; *State Farm*, 64%; substantial evidence, 64% to 71.2%; and de novo, 66%. All of the ranges of findings overlap, and doctrinally-based differences in outcome are barely detectable. The one notable exception is the *Auer* doctrine. The Supreme Court affirms agency interpretations of agency rules at a much higher rate—90%—than the roughly 70% rate at which it upholds other agency decisions.

Pierce, *supra*, at 85. The Eskridge and Baer study, and Pierce's acknowledgment of *Seminole Rock/Auer* deference as highly and uniquely deferential, are countered somewhat by findings offered in a forthcoming article by Pierce and Joshua Weiss. They document a 76% affirmance rate for agency interpretations of agency rules in lower federal courts applying *Seminole Rock* and *Auer* prior to the Supreme Court's decision in *Christopher*. *See* Richard J. Pierce, Jr. & Joshua A. Weiss, *An Empirical Study of Judicial Review of Agency Interpretations of Agency Rules*, 63 ADMIN. L. REV. 515 (2011).

3. While the majority of the Court in *Christopher* concluded that the employer in lacked adequate notice of the Labor Department's interpretation of its regulations when it engaged in the conduct at issue, the dissent maintained that "[t]aken together, the statute, regulations, ethical codes, and Labor Department Reports" all indicated that the detailers were not exempt as outside salesmen. Thus, four Justices obviously believed that the existing rules provided fair warning to firms that they were required to pay overtime to the detailers. If fair warning justifies the controlling weight extended by *Seminole Rock* and *Auer*, in what ways might an agency provide adequate notice regarding its interpretations of its regulations?

4. Notwithstanding the skepticism he expressed in *Talk America* regarding the continued vitality of *Seminole Rock* and *Auer*, Justice Scalia joined a majority opinion in *Christopher* that arguably carved back but did not challenge the continued vitality of *Seminole Rock/Auer*. Only one term later, in *Decker*, Justice Scalia offered a full-throated denunciation of *Seminole Rock* and *Auer*. Can you reconcile the positions taken by Justice Scalia in these two decisions?

CHAPTER 7

PREREQUISITES TO JUDICIAL REVIEW

In addition to imposing procedural requirements upon agencies pursuing rulemaking and formal adjudication and articulating standards for judicial review of agencies' factual findings and legal interpretations, the Administrative Procedure Act contains a number of provisions that limit when and under what conditions the courts may consider legal challenges to agency action. Particularly as regards the question of who may challenge a particular agency action, Article III of the United States Constitution also serves a limiting function. Consequently, in a high proportion of cases, agencies argue that a court cannot review an action because it is not reviewable at all, it is not reviewable at this time, and/or it is not reviewable at the behest of the petitioner raising the legal challenge. As a result, lawyers and judges who are involved in litigation of administrative law disputes devote significant time to disputes with respect to these prerequisites to judicial review.

In this chapter we will discuss three categories of limitations on judicial review of agency action. First, we will consider the question of reviewability generally—that is, which agency actions are subject to judicial review. Second, we will examine four separate but overlapping doctrines that limit the time at which an agency action is subject to judicial review—finality, ripeness, exhaustion, and primary jurisdiction—along with the judicial response to the problem of agency delay stemming particularly from the exhaustion requirement. Finally, we will address the question of standing—that is, who can obtain judicial review of an action.

A. REVIEWABILITY

Principles of sovereign immunity hold that no person may sue the United States without its consent. Consistent with this doctrine, until the 1960s, the law with respect to the availability of judicial review of agency actions was relatively simple. An agency action was not reviewable unless a statute authorized judicial review or a statute commanded or prohibited an agency action in such a clear and unambiguous manner that a court was willing to characterize the action as ministerial and nondiscretionary. During the nineteenth century, the vast majority of federal agency decisions were not subject to judicial review. The only recourse available to a party who objected to a federal agency action was a common law action for trespass or conversion against the federal employee in a state court. Judicial review of federal agency actions became more common gradually during the first half of the twentieth century as a result of an increasing number of statutes that authorized judicial review. During the late 1960s and early 1970s, however, the Supreme Court issued a series of opinions that interpreted the APA in ways that greatly expanded the availability of judicial review of agency actions.

In one of these cases in particular, *Abbott Laboratories v. Gardner*, 387 U.S. 136 (1967), and in many other cases since, the Supreme Court has emphasized that the APA "embodies the basic presumption of judicial review" and its own conclusion that the APA's "generous review provisions must be given a hospitable interpretation." *Id.* at 140–41 (internal quotations omitted). Of course, such a presumption is neither a promise nor a guarantee of reviewability. Irrespective of the Court's broad reading of the APA's stance on reviewability, Congress can and sometimes does enact statutory provisions limiting reviewability in particular circumstances. Notwithstanding its general support for judicial review of agency action, even the APA recognizes the potential for congressionally-imposed limitations. APA § 701(a) provides that the APA's other judicial review provisions apply "except to the extent that (1) statutes preclude judicial review; or (2) agency action is committed to agency discretion by law."

The following materials consider the limitations on reviewability imposed by APA § 701(a). As we will see, at one time the Supreme Court characterized both APA § 701(a)(1) and (a)(2) in ways that rendered them ineffective in insulating the vast majority of agency actions from review. As will become apparent when you read some of the Court's later opinions, however, both exceptions to reviewability have greater scope and significance today.

1. PRECLUSION

Many regulatory statutes administered by government agencies contain judicial review provisions with language that either clearly or arguably limits reviewability. A question that repeatedly arises is how broadly or narrowly the courts should read these provisions, given the APA's presumption of reviewability. In other words, when these provisions seem possibly to limit judicial review but are unclear, or perhaps where they provide for judicial review in some contexts but are silent as to others, how should courts approach the task of deciding whether they preclude judicial review for purposes of APA § 701(a)(1)?

a. EXPRESS PRECLUSION

If a statute clearly and unequivocally precludes all judicial review of an agency action, then the courts will generally give the statute effect. Yet, even when Congress has adopted explicit language precluding judicial review of at least some agency actions, the presumption of reviewability often induces courts to interpret Congress's words narrowly. The courts have been particularly protective of the ability of petitioners to obtain judicial review of credible claims that agency actions violate their constitutional rights.

Johnson v. Robison

415 U.S. 361 (1974).

■ MR. JUSTICE BRENNAN delivered the opinion of the Court.

A draftee accorded Class I-O conscientious objector status and completing performance of required alternative civilian service does not qualify under 38 U.S.C. § 1652(a)(1) as a "veteran who . . . served on active duty" and is therefore not an "eligible veteran" entitled under 38 U.S.C. § 1661(a) to veterans' educational benefits provided by the Veterans' Readjustment Benefits Act of 1966. Appellants, the Veterans' Administration and the Administrator of Veterans' Affairs, for that reason, denied the application for educational assistance of appellee Robison, a conscientious objector who filed his application after he satisfactorily completed two years of alternative civilian service at the Peter Bent Brigham Hospital, Boston. Robison thereafter commenced this class action in the United States District Court for the District of Massachusetts, seeking a declaratory judgment that 38 U.S.C. §§ 101(21), 1652(a)(1), and 1661(a), read together, violated the First Amendment's guarantee of religious freedom and the Fifth Amendment's guarantee of equal protection of the laws. Appellants moved to dismiss the action on the ground, among others, that the District Court lacked jurisdiction because of 38 U.S.C. § 211(a) which prohibits judicial review of decisions of the Administrator.[5] * * *

We consider first appellants' contention that § 211(a) bars federal courts from deciding the constitutionality of veterans' benefits legislation. Such a construction would, of course, raise serious questions concerning the constitutionality of § 211(a), and in such case "it is a cardinal principle that this Court will first ascertain whether a construction of the statute is fairly possible by which the [constitutional] question[s] may be avoided." *United States v. Thirty-Seven Photographs*, 402 U.S. 363, 369 (1971).

Plainly, no explicit provision of § 211(a) bars judicial consideration of appellee's constitutional claims. That section provides that "the *decisions* of the Administrator on any question of law or fact under any law administered by the Veterans' Administration providing benefits for veterans . . . shall be final and conclusive and no . . . court of the United States shall have power or jurisdiction to review any such decision. . . ." (Emphasis added). The prohibitions would appear to be aimed at review only of those decisions of law or fact that arise in the *administration* by the Veterans' Administration of a *statute* providing benefits for veterans. A decision of law or fact "under" a statute is made by the Administrator in the interpretation or application of a particular provision of the statute to a particular set of facts, Appellee's constitutional challenge is not to any such decision of the Administrator, but rather to a decision of *Congress* to create a statutory

---

[5]   Title 38 U.S.C. § 211(a) provides: "(a) On and after October 17, 1940, except as provided in sections 775, 784, and as to matters arising under chapter 37 of this title, the decisions of the Administrator on any question of law or fact under any law administered by the Veterans' Administration providing benefits for veterans and their dependents or survivors shall be final and conclusive and no other official or any court of the United States shall have power or jurisdiction to review any such decision by an action in the nature of mandamus or otherwise."

class entitled to benefits that does not include I-O conscientious objectors who performed alternative civilian service. Thus, as the District Court stated: "The questions of law presented in these proceedings arise under the Constitution, not under the statute whose validity is challenged."

NOTES AND QUESTIONS

1. *Robison* was not the first case in which the courts considered the reviewability of decisions regarding veterans' benefits. Congress had previously attempted to insulate those decisions from the scrutiny of judicial review. A version of the same statutory provision adopted in 1958 had barred judicial review of "decisions of the Administrator on any question of law or fact concerning a claim for benefits or payments under any law administered by the Veterans' Administration," but decisions by the D.C. Circuit had interpreted that language narrowly as only precluding judicial review of an initial decision to grant or deny benefits, as opposed to other types of VA determinations concerning benefits. *See, e.g., Tracy v. Gleason*, 379 F.2d 469, 473 (D.C. Cir. 1967) (concerning a forfeiture of previously awarded benefits); *Thompson v. Gleason*, 317 F.2d 901, 907 (D.C. Cir. 1962) (same). Congress in effect overruled these decisions when it amended the statute in 1970 to remove the phrase "concerning a claim for benefits" from 38 U.S.C. § 211(a). It was this amended statute that the Court considered in *Robison*.

For some time, whether Congress intended the amended § 211(a) to do more than overrule the D.C. Circuit's prior decisions was a matter of debate. Some courts interpreted *Robison* narrowly to allow judicial review under the amended § 211(a) only in cases challenging the constitutionality of veterans' benefits legislation. *See, e.g., Cabiya San Miguel v. United States Veterans Admin.*, 592 F.Supp. 21 (D.P.R. 1984). Other courts construed *Robison* and the amended § 211(a) as permitting review of constitutional or statutory challenges to V.A. regulations, policies, and procedures. *See, e.g., American Fed'n of Gov't Employees, AFL-CIO*, 711 F.2d 28, 31 (4th Cir. 1983). In *Traynor v. Turnage*, 485 U.S. 535, 545 (1988), the Supreme Court interpreted the amended § 211(a) as allowing judicial review of constitutional challenges against VA regulations interpreting the Rehabilitation Act, which no one government agency is responsible for administering.

In 1988, Congress adopted the Veterans' Judicial Review Act, which among other things granted the Federal Circuit jurisdiction to consider challenges to VA regulations, established the Board of Veterans' Appeals (BVA) expressly to review benefits claims determinations, and created an Article I court, now known as the Court of Appeals for Veterans Claims, with exclusive jurisdiction to consider appeals from BVA decisions. Decisions of the Court of Appeals for Veterans Claims are also appealable to the Federal Circuit and, after that, the Supreme Court.

2. Given that 38 U.S.C. § 211(a) at least seems unambiguously to instruct courts that they are not to review Veterans Administration decisions regarding veterans' benefits, perhaps the Court's conclusion fares better as an application of the canon of constitutional avoidance. The constitutional questions the Court avoided deciding is both difficult and potentially explosive: can Congress preclude courts from deciding whether a statute is unconstitutional? By issuing opinions like its opinion in *Robison*, the Court has avoided a potential constitutional crisis by refraining from answering this question. Presumably, the Court would be forced to answer the question if Congress enacted a no-review provision that explicitly prohibited courts from considering the constitutionality of a statute, but Congress has never enacted a no-review provision of that type. Do you applaud or condemn the apparent decisions of the judicial and legislative branches to avoid answering this important question?

3. In *Califano v. Sanders*, 430 U.S. 99, 109 (1977), the Supreme Court explicitly stated that "[c]onstitutional questions obviously are unsuited to resolution in administrative hearing procedures and, therefore, access to the courts is essential to the decision of such questions." In the same opinion, however, the Court suggested that it might read a statute as precluding judicial review of constitutional claims if Congress's intent to foreclose review "is manifested by clear and convincing evidence." *Id.* (internal quotations omitted). Why might Congress want to preclude judicial review of agency decisions concerning benefits claims? Should Congress be able to preclude judicial review of constitutional challenges to determinations regarding benefits claims?

DISCUSSION PROBLEM

The Farm Service Agency is responsible for administering a program that offers deficiency payments when the actual market price for certain agricultural products falls below the target price set by the Secretary of Agriculture. The FSA may reduce such deficiency payments if a farm experiences a decrease in its expected production, unless that decrease occurs because of a natural disaster or other condition beyond the farmer's control. A group of Kansas farmers objected to a decision by the FSA to reduce its deficiency payments without considering that fall rains that delayed fall plantings and reduced their yields were a condition beyond the farmers' control. In particular, the farmers claim that the imposed reductions in their deficiency payments violated their due process rights under the Fifth Amendment of the United States Constitution.

The relevant statute, 7 U.S.C. § 1385, provides as follows:

> The facts constituting the basis for . . . any payment under the wheat, feed grain, upland cotton, extra long staple cotton, and rice programs authorized by [the Agriculture Act of 1949] . . . or the amount thereof . . . shall be final and conclusive and shall not be reviewable by any other office or agency of the Government.

Should a reviewing court read this statutory provision as precluding judicial review of the farmers' due process claim against the FSA? Why or why not?

b.   IMPLIED PRECLUSION

One might think that, if the courts generally interpret express limitations on reviewability narrowly, then they must be reluctant to entertain arguments that statutory language is implicitly preclusive of judicial review. This has, in fact, not always been so. Consider and compare the following two cases.

Block v. Community Nutrition Institute

467 U.S. 340 (1984).

■ JUSTICE O'CONNOR delivered the opinion of the Court.

This case presents the question whether ultimate consumers of dairy products may obtain judicial review of milk market orders issued by the Secretary of Agriculture (Secretary) under the authority of the Agricultural Marketing Agreement Act of 1937 (Act). We conclude that consumers may not obtain judicial review of such orders.

I

A

In the early 1900's, dairy farmers engaged in intense competition in the production of fluid milk products. To bring this destabilizing competition under control, the 1937 Act authorizes the Secretary to issue milk market orders setting the minimum prices that handlers (those who process dairy products) must pay to producers (dairy farmers) for their milk products. 7 U.S.C. § 608c. The "essential purpose [of this milk market order scheme is] to raise producer prices," S. REP. No. 1011, at 3 (1935), and thereby to ensure that the benefits and burdens of the milk market are fairly and proportionately shared by all dairy farmers.

Under the scheme established by Congress, the Secretary must conduct an appropriate rulemaking proceeding before issuing a milk market order. The public must be notified of these proceedings and provided an opportunity for public hearing and comment. An order may be issued only if the evidence adduced at the hearing shows "that [it] will tend to effectuate the declared policy of this chapter with respect to such commodity." 7 U.S.C. § 608c(4). Moreover, before any market order may become effective, it must be approved by the handlers of at least 50% of the volume of milk covered by the proposed order and at least two-thirds of the affected dairy producers in the region. If the handlers withhold their consent, the Secretary may nevertheless impose the order. But the Secretary's power to do so is conditioned upon at least two-thirds of the producers consenting to its promulgation and upon his making an administrative determination that the order is "the only practical means of advancing the interests of the producers." 7 U.S.C. § 608c(9)(B).

The Secretary currently has some 45 milk market orders in effect.

* * *

In particular, the Secretary has regulated the price of "reconstituted milk"—that is, milk manufactured by mixing milk powder with water—since 1964. The Secretary's orders assume that handlers will use reconstituted milk to manufacture surplus milk products. Handlers are therefore required to pay only the lower Class II minimum price. However, handlers are required to make a "compensatory payment" on any portion of the reconstituted milk that their records show has not been used to manufacture surplus milk products. 7 C.F.R. §§ 1012.44(a)(5)(i), 1012.60(e) (1984). The compensatory payment is equal to the difference between the Class I and Class II milk product prices. Handlers make these payments to the regional pool, from which moneys are then distributed to producers of fresh fluid milk in the region where the reconstituted milk was manufactured and sold.

B

In December 1980, respondents brought suit in District Court, contending that the compensatory payment requirement makes reconstituted milk uneconomical for handlers to process. Respondents, as plaintiffs in the District Court, included three individual consumers of fluid dairy products, a handler regulated by the market orders, and a nonprofit organization. The District Court concluded that the consumers and the nonprofit organization did not have standing to challenge the market orders. In addition, it found that Congress had intended by the Act to preclude such persons from obtaining judicial review. The District Court dismissed the milk handler's complaint because he had failed to exhaust his administrative remedies.

The Court of Appeals affirmed in part and reversed in part, and remanded the case for a decision on the merits. The Court of Appeals agreed that the milk handler and the nonprofit organization had been properly dismissed by the District Court. But the court concluded that the individual consumers had standing: they had suffered an injury-in-fact, their injuries were redressable, and they were within the zone of interests arguably protected by the Act. The Court also concluded that the statutory structure and purposes of the Act did not reveal "the type of clear and convincing evidence of congressional intent needed to overcome the presumption in favor of judicial review." * * *

We granted certiorari to resolve the conflict in the Circuits. We now reverse the judgment of the Court of Appeals in this case.

II

Respondents filed this suit under the Administrative Procedure Act (APA), 5 U.S.C. § 701 *et seq.* The APA confers a general cause of action upon persons "adversely affected or aggrieved by agency action within the meaning of a relevant statute," 5 U.S.C. § 702, but withdraws that cause of action to the extent the relevant statute "preclude[s] judicial review," 5 U.S.C. § 701(a)(1). Whether and to what extent a particular statute precludes judicial review is determined not only from its express language, but also from the structure of the statutory scheme, its objectives, its legislative history, and the nature of the administrative action involved. Therefore, we must examine this statutory scheme "to determine whether Congress precluded all judicial review, and, if not, whether Congress nevertheless foreclosed review to the class to which the [respondents] belon[g]." *Barlow v. Collins,* 397 U.S. 159, 173 (1970) (Brennan, J., concurring and dissenting).

It is clear that Congress did not intend to strip the judiciary of all authority to review the Secretary's milk market orders. The Act's predecessor, the Agricultural Adjustment Act of 1933, contained no provision relating to administrative or judicial review. In 1935, however, Congress added a mechanism by which dairy handlers could obtain review of the Secretary's market orders. That mechanism was retained in the 1937 legislation and remains in the Act as § 608c(15) today. Section 608c(15) requires handlers first to exhaust the administrative remedies made available by the Secretary. After these formal administrative remedies have been exhausted, handlers may obtain judicial review of the Secretary's ruling in the federal district court in any district "in which [they are] inhabitant[s], or ha[ve their] principal place[s] of business." 7 U.S.C. § 608c(15)(B). These provisions for handler-initiated review make evident Congress' desire that some persons be able to obtain judicial review of the Secretary's market orders.

The remainder of the statutory scheme, however, makes equally clear Congress' intention to limit the classes entitled to participate in the development of market orders. The Act contemplates a cooperative venture among the Secretary, handlers, and producers the principal purposes of which are to raise the price of agricultural products and to establish an orderly system for marketing them. Handlers and producers—but not consumers—are entitled to participate in the adoption and retention of market orders. 7 U.S.C. §§ 608c(8), (9), (16)(B). The Act provides for agreements among the Secretary, producers, and handlers, 7 U.S.C. § 608(2), for hearings among them, §§ 608(5), 608c(3), and for votes by producers and handlers, §§ 608c(8)(A), (9)(B), (12), 608c(19). Nowhere in the Act, however, is there an express provision for participation by consumers in any proceeding. In a complex scheme of this type, the omission of such a provision is sufficient reason to believe that Congress intended to foreclose consumer participation in the regulatory process.

To be sure, the general purpose sections of the Act allude to general consumer interests. But the preclusion issue does not only turn on whether the interests of a particular class like consumers are implicated. Rather, the preclusion issue turns ultimately on whether Congress intended for that class to be relied upon to challenge agency disregard of the law. The structure of this Act indicates that Congress intended only producers and handlers, and not consumers, to ensure that the statutory objectives would be realized.

Respondents would have us believe that, while Congress unequivocally directed handlers first to complain to the Secretary that the prices set by milk market orders are too high, it was nevertheless the legislative judgment that the same challenge, if advanced by consumers, does not require initial administrative scrutiny. There is no basis for attributing to Congress the intent to draw such a distinction. The regulation of agricultural products is a complex, technical undertaking. Congress channelled disputes concerning marketing orders to the Secretary in the first instance because it believed that only he has the expertise necessary to illuminate and resolve questions about them. Had Congress intended to allow consumers to attack provisions of marketing orders, it surely would have required them to pursue the administrative remedies provided in § 608c(15)(A) as well. The restriction of the administrative remedy to handlers strongly suggests that Congress intended a similar restriction of judicial review of market orders.

Allowing consumers to sue the Secretary would severely disrupt this complex and delicate administrative scheme. It would provide handlers with a convenient device for evading the statutory requirement that they first exhaust their administrative remedies. A handler may also be a consumer and, as such, could sue in that capacity. Alternatively, a handler would need only to find a consumer who is willing to join in or initiate an action in the district court. The consumer or consumer-handler could then raise precisely the same exceptions that the handler must raise administratively. Consumers or consumer-handlers could seek injunctions against the operation of market orders that "impede, hinder, or delay" enforcement actions, even though such injunctions are expressly prohibited in proceedings properly instituted under 7 U.S.C. § 608c(15). Suits of this type would effectively nullify Congress' intent to establish an "equitable and expeditious procedure for testing the validity of orders, without hampering the Government's power to enforce compliance with their terms." S. REP. NO. 1011, at 14 (1935). For these reasons, we think it clear that Congress intended that judicial review of market orders issued under the Act ordinarily be confined to suits brought by handlers in accordance with 7 U.S.C. § 608c(15).

III

* * *

The presumption favoring judicial review of administrative action is just that—a presumption. This presumption, like all presumptions used in interpreting statutes, may be overcome by specific language or specific legislative history that is a reliable indicator of congressional intent. The congressional intent necessary to overcome the presumption may also be inferred from contemporaneous judicial construction barring review and the congressional acquiescence in it or from the collective import of legislative and judicial history behind a particular statute. More important for purposes of this case, the presumption favoring judicial review of administrative action may be overcome by inferences of intent drawn from the statutory scheme as a whole. In particular, at least when a statute provides a detailed mechanism for judicial consideration of particular issues at the behest of particular persons, judicial review of those issues at the behest of other persons may be found to be impliedly precluded.

* * *

In this case, the Court of Appeals * * * recited this Court's oft-quoted statement that "only upon a showing of 'clear and convincing evidence' of a contrary legislative intent should the courts restrict access to judicial review." *Abbott Labs. v. Gardner*, 387 U.S. 136, 141 (1967). According to the Court of Appeals, the "clear and convincing evidence" standard required it to find unambiguous proof, in the traditional evidentiary sense, of a congressional intent to preclude judicial review at the consumers' behest. Since direct statutory language or legislative history on this issue could not be found, the Court of Appeals found the presumption favoring judicial review to be controlling.

This Court has, however, never applied the "clear and convincing evidence" standard in the strict evidentiary sense the Court of Appeals thought necessary in this case. Rather, the Court has found the standard met, and the presumption favoring judicial review overcome, whenever the congressional intent to preclude judicial review is "fairly discernible in the statutory scheme." *Data Processing Serv. v. Camp*,

397 U.S. 150, 157 (1970). In the context of preclusion analysis, the "clear and convincing evidence" standard is not a rigid evidentiary test but a useful reminder to courts that, where substantial doubt about the congressional intent exists, the general presumption favoring judicial review of administrative action is controlling. That presumption does not control in cases such as this one, however, since the congressional intent to preclude judicial review is "fairly discernible" in the detail of the legislative scheme. Congress simply did not intend for consumers to be relied upon to challenge agency disregard of the law.

* * *

[P]reclusion of consumer suits will not threaten realization of the fundamental objectives of the statute. Handlers have interests similar to those of consumers. Handlers, like consumers, are interested in obtaining reliable supplies of milk at the cheapest possible prices. Handlers can therefore be expected to challenge unlawful agency action and to ensure that the statute's objectives will not be frustrated. Indeed, as noted above, consumer suits might themselves frustrate achievement of the statutory purposes. The Act contemplates a cooperative venture among the Secretary, producers, and handlers; consumer participation is not provided for or desired under the complex scheme enacted by Congress. Consumer suits would undermine the congressional preference for administrative remedies and provide a mechanism for disrupting administration of the congressional scheme.

Bowen v. Michigan Academy of Family Physicians

476 U.S. 667 (1986).

■ JUSTICE STEVENS delivered the opinion of the Court.

The question presented in this case is whether Congress, in either § 1395ff or § 1395ii of Title 42 of the United States Code, barred judicial review of regulations promulgated under Part B of the Medicare program.

Respondents, who include an association of family physicians and several individual doctors, filed suit to challenge the validity of 42 C.F.R. § 405.504(b) (1985), which authorizes the payment of benefits in different amounts for similar physicians' services. The District Court held that the regulation contravened several provisions of the statute governing the Medicare program:

> "There is no basis to justify the segregation of allopathic family physicians from all other types of physicians. Such segregation is not rationally related to any legitimate purpose of the Medicare statute. To lump MDs who are family physicians, but who have chosen not to become board certified family physicians for whatever motive, with chiropractors, dentists, and podiatrists for the purpose of determining Medicare reimbursement defies all reason."

Because it ruled in favor of respondents on statutory grounds, the District Court did not reach their constitutional claims. The Court of

Appeals agreed with the District Court that the Secretary's regulation was "obvious[ly] inconsisten[t] with the plain language of the Medicare statute" and held that "this regulation is irrational and is invalid." Like the District Court, it too declined to reach respondents' constitutional claims.

The Secretary of Health and Human Services has not sought review of the decision on the merits invalidating the regulation. Instead, he renews the contention, rejected by both the District Court and the Court of Appeals, that Congress has forbidden judicial review of all questions affecting the amount of benefits payable under Part B of the Medicare program. Because the question is important and has divided the Courts of Appeals, we granted the petition for a writ of certiorari. We now affirm.

I

We begin with the strong presumption that Congress intends judicial review of administrative action. From the beginning "our cases [have established] that judicial review of a final agency action by an aggrieved person will not be cut off unless there is persuasive reason to believe that such was the purpose of Congress." *Abbott Labs. v. Gardner*, 387 U.S. 136, 140 (1967). In *Marbury v. Madison*, 5 U.S. (1 Cranch) 137, 163,(1803), a case itself involving review of executive action, Chief Justice Marshall insisted that "[t]he very essence of civil liberty certainly consists in the right of every individual to claim the protection of the laws." Later, in the lesser known but nonetheless important case of *United States v. Nourse*, 34 U.S. (9 Pet.) 8, 28–29 (1835), the Chief Justice noted the traditional observance of this right and laid the foundation for the modern of judicial review:

> "It would excite some surprise if, in a government of laws and of principle, furnished with a department whose appropriate duty it is to decide questions of right, not only between individuals, but between the government and individuals; a ministerial officer might, at his discretion, issue this powerful process . . . leaving to the debtor no remedy, no appeal to the laws of his country, if he should believe the claim to be unjust. But this anomaly does not exist; this imputation cannot be cast on the legislature of the United States."

Committees of both Houses of Congress have endorsed this view. In undertaking the comprehensive rethinking of the place of administrative agencies in a regime of separate and divided powers that culminated in the passage of the Administrative Procedure Act (APA), 5 U.S.C. §§ 551–559, 701–706, the Senate Committee on the Judiciary remarked:

> "Very rarely do statutes withhold judicial review. It has never been the policy of Congress to prevent the administration of its own statutes from being judicially confined to the scope of authority granted or to the objectives specified. Its policy could not be otherwise, for in such a case statutes would in effect be blank checks drawn to the credit of some administrative officer or board." S. REP. NO. 752, at 26 (1945).

The Committee on the Judiciary of the House of Representatives agreed that Congress ordinarily intends that there be judicial review, and emphasized the clarity with which a contrary intent must be expressed:

> "The statutes of Congress are not merely advisory when they relate to administrative agencies, any more than in other cases. To preclude judicial review under this bill a statute, if not specific in withholding such review, must upon its face give clear and convincing evidence of an intent to withhold it. The mere failure to provide specially by statute for judicial review is certainly no evidence of intent to withhold review." H.R. REP. NO. 1980, at 41 (1946).

Taking up the language in the House Committee Report, Justice Harlan reaffirmed the Court's holding in *Rusk v. Cort*, 369 U.S. 367, 379–80 (1962), that "only upon a showing of 'clear and convincing evidence' of a contrary legislative intent should the courts restrict access to judicial review." *Abbott Labs.*, 387 U.S. at 141. This standard has been invoked time and again when considering whether the Secretary has discharged "the heavy burden of overcoming the strong presumption that Congress did not mean to prohibit all judicial review of his decision," *Dunlop v. Bachowski*, 421 U.S. 560, 567 (1975).

Subject to constitutional constraints, Congress can, of course, make exceptions to the historic practice whereby courts review agency action. The presumption of judicial review is, after all, a presumption, and "like all presumptions used in interpreting statutes, may be overcome by," *inter alia*, "specific language or specific legislative history that is a reliable indicator of congressional intent," or a specific congressional intent to preclude judicial review that is "'fairly discernible' in the detail of the legislative scheme." *Block v. Cmty. Nutrition Inst.*, 467 U.S. 340, 349, 351 (1984).

In this case, the Government asserts that two statutory provisions remove the Secretary's regulation from review under the grant of general federal-question jurisdiction found in 28 U.S.C. § 1331. First, the Government contends that 42 U.S.C. § 1395ff(b), which authorizes "Appeal by individuals," impliedly forecloses administrative or judicial review of any action taken under Part B of the Medicare program by failing to authorize such review while simultaneously authorizing administrative and judicial review of "any determination . . . as to . . . the amount of benefits under part A," § 1395ff(b)(1)(C). Second, the Government asserts that 42 U.S.C. § 1395ii, which makes applicable 42 U.S.C. § 405(h), of the Social Security Act to the Medicare program, expressly precludes all administrative or judicial review not otherwise provided in that statute. We find neither argument persuasive.

II

Section 1395ff on its face is an explicit authorization of judicial review, not a bar.[5] As a general matter, " '[t]he mere fact that some acts

---

[5]   The pertinent text of § 1395ff reads as follows:

"(a) Entitlements to and amount of benefits

"The determination of whether an individual is entitled to benefits under part A or part B, and the determination of the amount of benefits under part A, shall be made by the Secretary in accordance with regulations prescribed by him.

"(b) Appeal by individuals

are made reviewable should not suffice to support an implication of exclusion as to others. The right to review is too important to be excluded on such slender and indeterminate evidence of legislative intent.'" *Abbott Labs.*, 387 U.S. at 141 (quoting L. JAFFE, JUDICIAL CONTROL OF ADMINISTRATIVE ACTION 357 (1965)).

In the Medicare program, however, the situation is somewhat more complex. Under Part B of that program, which is at issue here, the Secretary contracts with private health insurance carriers to provide benefits for which individuals voluntarily remit premiums. This optional coverage, which is federally subsidized, supplements the mandatory institutional health benefits (such as coverage for hospital expenses) provided by Part A. Subject to an amount-in-controversy requirement, individuals aggrieved by delayed or insufficient payment with respect to benefits payable under Part B are afforded an "opportunity for a fair hearing by the *carrier*," 42 U.S.C. § 1395u(b)(3)(C) (emphasis added); in comparison, and subject to a like amount-in-controversy requirement, a similarly aggrieved individual under Part A is entitled "to a hearing thereon by the *Secretary* . . . and to judicial review," 42 U.S.C. § 1395ff(b)(1)(C), (b)(2). "In the context of the statute's precisely drawn provisions," we held in *United States v. Erika, Inc.*, 456 U.S. 201, 208 (1982), that the failure "to authorize further review for determinations of the amount of Part B awards . . . provides persuasive evidence that Congress deliberately intended to foreclose further review of such claims." Not limiting our consideration to the statutory text, we investigated the legislative history which "confirm[ed] this view," *id.*, and disclosed a purpose to "'avoid overloading the courts'" with "'trivial matters,'" a consequence which would "'unduly ta[x]'" the federal court system with "'little real value'" to be derived by participants in the program. *Id.* at 210 n.13 (quoting 118 CONG. REC. 33882 (1972) (remarks of Sen. Bennett)).

Respondents' federal-court challenge to the validity of the Secretary's regulation is not foreclosed by § 1395ff as we construed that provision in *Erika*. The reticulated statutory scheme, which carefully details the forum and limits of review of "any determination . . . of . . . the amount of benefits under part A," 42 U.S.C. § 1395ff(b)(1)(C), and of the "amount of . . . payment" of benefits under Part B, 42 U.S.C. § 1395u(b)(3)(C), simply does not speak to challenges mounted against the *method* by which such amounts are to be determined rather than the *determinations* themselves. As the Secretary has made clear, "the legality, constitutional or otherwise, of any provision of the Act or regulations relevant to the Medicare Program" is not considered in a

---

"(1) Any individual dissatisfied with any determination under subsection (a) of this section as to—

"(A) whether he meets the conditions of section 426 or section 426a of this title [which set forth eligibility requirements to be satisfied before an individual is permitted to participate in Part A of the Medicare program], or

"(B) whether he is eligible to enroll and has enrolled pursuant to the provisions of part B of [the Medicare program] . . . , or,

"(C) the amount of the benefits under part A (including a determination where such amount is determined to be zero)

shall be entitled to a hearing thereon by the Secretary to the same extent as is provided in section 405(b) of this title and to judicial review of the Secretary's final decision after such hearing as is provided in section 405(g) of this title."

"fair hearing" held by a carrier to resolve a grievance related to a determination of the amount of a Part B award. As a result, an attack on the validity of a regulation is not the kind of administrative action that we described in *Erika* as an "amount determination" which decides "the amount of the Medicare payment to be made on a particular claim" and with respect to which the Act impliedly denies judicial review. 456 U.S. at 208.

That Congress did not preclude review of the method by which Part B awards are computed (as opposed to the computation) is borne out by the very legislative history we found persuasive in *Erika*. The Senate Committee Report on the original 1965 legislation reveals an intention to preclude "judicial review of a determination concerning the *amount of benefits* under part B where claims will probably be for substantially smaller amounts than under part A." S. REP. NO. 404, at 54–55 (1965) (emphasis added). The Report makes plain that "carriers, not the Secretary, would review beneficiary complaints regarding the *amount of benefits*." *Id.* (emphasis added). The legislative history of the pertinent 1972 amendment likewise reveals that judicial review was precluded only as to controversies regarding determinations of amounts of benefits. The Conference Report on the 1972 amendment explains that "there is no authorization for an appeal to the Secretary or for judicial review on matters *solely involving amounts of benefits under Part B*." H. REP. NO. 92–1605, at 61 (1972) (Conf. Rep.) (emphasis added). Senator Bennett's introductory explanation to the amendment confirms that preclusion of judicial review of Part B awards—designed "to avoid overloading the courts with quite minor matters"—embraced only "decisions on a claim for payment for a given service." 118 CONG. REC. 33992 (1972). The Senator feared that "[i]f judicial review is made available where any claim is denied, as some court decisions have held, the resources of the Federal court system would be unduly taxed and little real value would be derived by the enrollees. The proposed amendment would merely clarify the original intent of the law and prevent the overloading of the courts with trivial matters because the intent is considered unclear." *Id.* As we found in *Erika*, 456 U.S. at 206, Congress has precluded judicial review only "of adverse hearing officer determinations of the amount of Part B payments."

Careful analysis of the governing statutory provisions and their legislative history thus reveals that Congress intended to bar judicial review only of determinations of the amount of benefits to be awarded under Part B. Congress delegated this task to carriers who would finally determine such matters in conformity with the regulations and instructions of the Secretary. We conclude, therefore, that those matters which Congress did *not* leave to be determined in a "fair hearing" conducted by the carrier—including challenges to the validity of the Secretary's instructions and regulations—are not impliedly insulated from judicial review by 42 U.S.C. § 1395ff.

III

In light of Congress' express provision for carrier review of millions of what it characterized as "trivial" claims, it is implausible to think it intended that there be *no* forum to adjudicate statutory and constitutional challenges to regulations promulgated by the Secretary. The Government nevertheless maintains that this is precisely what

Congress intended to accomplish in 42 U.S.C. § 1395ii. That section states that 42 U.S.C. § 405(h), along with a string citation of 10 other provisions of Title II of the Social Security Act, "shall also apply with respect to this subchapter to the same extent as they are applicable with respect to subchapter II of this chapter." Section 405(h), in turn, reads in full as follows:

> "(h) Finality of Secretary's decision
>
> "The findings and decision of the Secretary after a hearing shall be binding upon all individuals who were parties to such hearing. No findings of fact or decision of the Secretary shall be reviewed by any person, tribunal, or governmental agency except as herein provided. No action against the United States, the Secretary, or any officer or employee thereof shall be brought under section 1331 or 1346 of title 28 to recover on any claim arising under this subchapter."

The Government contends that the third sentence of § 405(h) by its terms prevents any resort to the grant of general federal-question jurisdiction contained in 28 U.S.C. § 1331. * * *

[W]e need not pass on the meaning of § 405(h) in the abstract to resolve this case. Section 405(h) does not apply on its own terms to Part B of the Medicare program, but is instead incorporated *mutatis mutandis* by § 1395ii. The legislative history of both the statute establishing the Medicare program and the 1972 amendments thereto provides specific evidence of Congress' intent to foreclose review only of "amount determinations"—*i.e.*, those "quite minor matters," 118 CONG. REC. 33992 (1972) (remarks of Sen. Bennett), remitted finally and exclusively to adjudication by private insurance carriers in a "fair hearing." By the same token, matters which Congress did *not* delegate to private carriers, such as challenges to the validity of the Secretary's instructions and regulations, are cognizable in courts of law. In the face of this persuasive evidence of legislative intent, we will not indulge the Government's assumption that Congress contemplated review by carriers of "trivial" monetary claims, but intended no review at all of substantial statutory and constitutional challenges to the Secretary's administration of Part B of the Medicare program. This is an extreme position, and one we would be most reluctant to adopt without "a showing of 'clear and convincing evidence,'" *Abbott Labs.*, 387 U.S. at 141, to overcome the "strong presumption that Congress did not mean to prohibit all judicial review" of executive action, *Dunlop v. Bachowski*, 421 U.S. 560, 567 (1975). We ordinarily presume that Congress intends the executive to obey its statutory commands and, accordingly, that it expects the courts to grant relief when an executive agency violates such a command. That presumption has not been surmounted here.

NOTES AND QUESTIONS

1. The Supreme Court in *Block* clearly frames its analysis of the case in terms APA § 701(a)(1) and statutory preclusion of judicial review. Interestingly, however, preclusion was not the issue that animated the lower courts' consideration of the case. When the Community Nutrition Institute first sought to challenge the Secretary of Agriculture's milk market orders both on behalf of individual consumers and as a plaintiff in

its own right, the federal district court dismissed the claim for lack of standing. On appeal, the D.C. Circuit held that individual consumers had standing but that the Community Nutrition Institute as an organization did not. Then-Judge Scalia, concurring in part and dissenting in part from the circuit panel's decision, expressed the view that the individual consumers lacked standing to challenge the milk market orders as well. Perhaps because of this background, many legal scholars and courts characterize the Supreme Court's decision in *Block* as concerning consumer standing rather than statutory preclusion. We discuss the standing issue in Part C of this Chapter.

2. In *Block*, the Supreme Court quoted its opinion in *Abbott Laboratories v. Gardner*, 387 U.S. 136, 141 (1967), for the proposition that the presumption in favor of reviewability of agency action may be rebutted by "a showing of 'clear and convincing evidence' of a contrary legislative intent." The Court then identified five sources of such clear and convincing evidence: (1) specific statutory language, (2) specific legislative history, (3) contemporaneous judicial construction followed by congressional acquiescence, (4) the collective import of the legislative and judicial history of the statute, and (5) inferences of intent drawn from the statutory scheme as a whole. The Court in *Block* then reviewed the entire statutory scheme at bar and, given express language concerning the reviewability of challenges raised by processors of dairy products and dairy farmers but statutory silence regarding the reviewability of consumer claims, inferred legislative intent to preclude judicial review. By contrast, the Court in *Bowen* refused to draw a similar inference from statutory silence concerning the reviewability of physician challenges to regulations under Medicare Part B, notwithstanding express language concerning the reviewability of other claims under the statute. Do you find the Court's opinion in *Bowen* consistent with *Block*'s analytical approach to APA § 701(a)(1) and the presumption of reviewability? If not, can you draw from *Bowen* an alternative view of what constitutes clear and convincing evidence of legislative intent to preclude judicial review?

3. Also in *Block*, the Supreme Court stated that, "Whether and to what extent a particular statute precludes judicial review is determined not only from its express language, but also from the structure of the statutory scheme, its objectives, its legislative history, and the nature of the administrative action involved." Some federal appellate courts have interpreted this statement as dictating the collection of factors that courts should consider in assessing the applicability of APA § 701(a)(1). *See, e.g., High Country Citizens Alliance v. Clarke*, 454 F.3d 1177, 1182–83 (10th Cir. 2006). Would an inquiry that focuses on these elements differ from one that considers the five sources of clear and convincing evidence highlighted in the previous note? How so? Do you find the *Bowen* opinion more consistent with one or the other of these interpretations of *Block*?

2. COMMITTED TO AGENCY DISCRETION

As difficult as it may be to discern whether or under precisely which circumstances statutory language precludes judicial review, the limitation on reviewability imposed by APA § 701(a)(2) when "agency action is committed to agency discretion by law" is positively cryptic. Ronald Levin suggests that those involved in drafting the APA must have known that the language of APA § 701(a)(2) was ambiguous. Levin documents that, rather than pursue clearer statutory language, different parties in the APA's enactment process loaded the APA's legislative history with statements supporting their competing views of the provision's meaning. *See* Ronald M. Levin, *Understanding Unreviewability in Administrative Law*, 74 MINN. L. REV. 689, 695–99 (1990). Of course, conflicting statements within the legislative history only complicate the task of evaluating the scope and meaning of the committed to agency discretion limitation on reviewability.

Given that the Supreme Court has long accepted statutory delegations of tremendous discretion to administrative agencies, one might be forgiven for thinking that APA § 701(a)(2) represents an exception from reviewability that subsumes the general presumption in favor thereof. Such a reading seems implausible, however, when one considers the APA § 706(2)(A) expressly calls upon courts to "set aside agency action, findings, and conclusions found to be . . . an abuse of discretion." In fact, the courts have interpreted the committed to agency discretion exception from the presumption of reviewability more narrowly. Nevertheless, as the following materials demonstrate, the courts have not always been consistent in their assessment of the limitation's scope.

Citizens to Preserve Overton Park, Inc. v. Volpe

401 U.S. 402 (1971).

■ Opinion of the Court by MR. JUSTICE MARSHALL.

The growing public concern about the quality of our natural environment has prompted Congress in recent years to enact legislation designed to curb the accelerating destruction of our country's natural beauty. We are concerned in this case with § 4(f) of the Department of Transportation Act of 1966, as amended, 49 U.S.C. § 1653(f), and § 18(a) of the Federal-Aid Highway Act of 1968, 23 U.S.C. § 138. These statutes prohibit the Secretary of Transportation from authorizing the use of federal funds to finance the construction of highways through public parks if a "feasible and prudent" alternative route exists. 49 U.S.C. § 1653(f). If no such route is available, the statutes allow him to approve construction through parks only if there has been "all possible planning to minimize harm" to the park. *Id.*

* * *

Overton Park is 342-acre city park located near the center of Memphis. The park contains a zoo, a nine-hole municipal golf course, an outdoor theater, nature trails, a bridle path, an art academy, picnic areas, and 170 acres of forest. The proposed highway, which is to be a six-lane, high-speed, expressway, will sever the zoo from the rest of the park. Although the roadway will be depressed below ground level except where it crosses a small creek, 26 acres of the park will be destroyed. The highway is to be a segment of Interstate Highway I-40, part of the National System of Interstate and Defense Highways. I-40 will provide Memphis with a major east-west expressway which will allow easier access to downtown Memphis from the residential areas on the eastern edge of the city.

Although the route through the park was approved by the Bureau of Public Roads in 1956 and by the Federal Highway Administrator in 1966, the enactment of § 4(f) of the Department of Transportation Act prevented distribution of federal funds for the section of the highway designated to go through Overton Park until the Secretary of Transportation determined whether the requirements of § 4(f) had been met. * * * In April 1968, the Secretary announced that he concurred in the judgment of local officials that I-40 should be built through the park. * * * Neither announcement approving the route and design of I-40 was accompanied by a statement of the Secretary's factual findings. He did not indicate why he believed there were no feasible and prudent alternative routes or why design changes could not be made to reduce the harm to the park.

Petitioners contend that the Secretary's action is invalid without such formal findings and that the Secretary did not make an independent determination but merely relied on the judgment of the Memphis City Council. They also contend that it would be "feasible and prudent" to route I-40 around Overton Park * * *

Respondents argue that it was unnecessary for the Secretary to make formal findings, and that he did, in fact, exercise his own independent judgment which was supported by the facts. In the District Court, respondents introduced affidavits, prepared specifically for this litigation which indicated that the Secretary had made the decision and that the decision was supportable. These affidavits were contradicted by affidavits introduced by petitioners, who also sought to take the deposition of a former Federal Highway Administrator who had participated in the decision to route I-40 through Overton Park.

The District Court and the Court of Appeals found that formal findings by the Secretary were not necessary and refused to order the deposition of the former Federal Highway Administrator because those courts believed that probing of the mental processes of an administrative decisionmaker was prohibited. And, believing that the Secretary's authority was wide and reviewing courts' authority narrow in the approval of highway routes, the lower courts held that the affidavits contained no basis for a determination that the Secretary had exceeded his authority.

We agree that formal findings were not required. But we do not believe that in this case judicial review based solely on litigation affidavits was adequate.

A threshold question—whether petitioners are entitled to any judicial review—is easily answered. Section 701 of the Administrative Procedure Act provides that the action of "each authority of the Government of the United States," which includes the Department of Transportation, is subject to judicial review except where there is a statutory prohibition on review or where "agency action is committed to agency discretion by law." 5 U.S.C. § 701. In this case, there is no indication that Congress sought to prohibit judicial review and there is most certainly no "showing of 'clear and convincing evidence' of a . . . legislative intent" to restrict access to judicial review. *Abbott Labs. v. Gardner*, 387 U.S. 136, 141 (1967).

Similarly, the Secretary's decision here does not fall within the exception for action "committed to agency discretion." This is a very narrow exception. The legislative history of the Administrative Procedure Act indicates that it is applicable in those rare instances where "statutes are drawn in such broad terms that in a given case there is no law to apply." S. REP. NO. 752, 79th Cong., 1st Sess., 26 (1945).

Section 4(f) of the Department of Transportation Act and § 138 of the Federal-Aid Highway Act are clear and specific directives. Both the Department of Transportation Act and the Federal-Aid to Highway Act provide that the Secretary "shall not approve any program or project" that requires the use of any public parkland "unless (1) there is no feasible and prudent alternative to the use of such land, and (2) such program includes all possible planning to minimize harm to such park. . . ." 23 U.S.C. § 138; 49 U.S.C. § 1653(f). This language is a plain and explicit bar to the use of federal funds for construction of highways through parks—only the most unusual situations are exempted.

Despite the clarity of the statutory language, respondents argue that the Secretary has wide discretion. They recognize that the requirement that there be no "feasible" alternative route admits of little administrative discretion. For this exemption to apply the Secretary must find that as a matter of sound engineering it would not be feasible to build the highway along any other route. Respondents argue, however, that the requirement that there be no other "prudent" route requires the Secretary to engage in a wide-ranging balancing of competing interests. They contend that the Secretary should weigh the detriment resulting from the destruction of parkland against the cost of other routes, safety considerations, and other factors, and determine on the basis of the importance that he attaches to these other factors whether, on balance, alternative feasible routes would be "prudent."

But no such wide-ranging endeavor was intended. It is obvious that in most cases considerations of cost, directness of route, and community disruption will indicate that parkland should be used for highway construction whenever possible. Although it may be necessary to transfer funds from one jurisdiction to another, there will always be a smaller outlay required from the public purse when parkland is used since the public already owns the land and there will be no need to pay for right-of-way. And since people do not live or work in parks, if a highway is built on parkland no one will have to leave his home or give up his business. Such factors are common to substantially all highway construction. Thus, if Congress intended these factors to be on an equal footing with preservation of parkland there would have been no need for the statutes.

Congress clearly did not intend that cost and disruption of the community were to be ignored by the Secretary. But the very existence of the statutes indicates that protection of parkland was to be given paramount importance. The few green havens that are public parks were not to be lost unless there were truly unusual factors present in a particular case or the cost or community disruption resulting from alternative routes reached extraordinary magnitudes. If the statutes are to have any meaning, the Secretary cannot approve the destruction of parkland unless he finds that alternative routes present unique problems.

Plainly, there is "law to apply" and thus the exemption for action "committed to agency discretion" is inapplicable. But the existence of judicial review is only the start: the standard for review must also be determined. For that we must look to § 706 of the Administrative Procedure Act, which provides that a "reviewing court shall . . . hold unlawful and set aside agency action, findings, and conclusions found" not to meet six separate standards. In all cases agency action must be set aside if the action was "arbitrary, capricious, an abuse of discretion, or otherwise not in accordance with law" or if the action failed to meet statutory, procedural, or constitutional requirements. 5 U.S.C. § 706(2)(A)–(D). In certain narrow, specifically limited situations, the agency action is to be set aside if the action was not supported by "substantial evidence." And in other equally narrow circumstances the reviewing court is to engage in a de novo review of the action and set it aside if it was "unwarranted by the facts." 5 U.S.C. § 706(E), (F).

* * *

Review under the substantial-evidence test is authorized only when the agency action is taken pursuant to a rulemaking provision of the Administrative Procedure Act itself, or when the agency action is based on a public adjudicatory hearing. The Secretary's decision to allow the expenditure of federal funds to build I-40 through Overton Park was plainly not an exercise of a rulemaking function. And the only hearing that is required by either the Administrative Procedure Act or the statutes regulating the distribution of federal funds for highway construction is a public hearing conducted by local officials for the purpose of informing the community about the proposed project and eliciting community views on the design and route. The hearing is nonadjudicatory, quasi-legislative in nature. It is not designed to produce a record that is to be the basis of agency action—the basic requirement for substantial-evidence review.

* * *

Certainly, the Secretary's decision is entitled to a presumption of regularity. But that presumption is not to shield his action from a thorough, probing, in-depth review.

* * *

Section 706(2)(A) requires a finding that the actual choice made was not "arbitrary, capricious, an abuse of discretion, or otherwise not in accordance with law." To make this finding the court must consider whether the decision was based on a consideration of the relevant factors and whether there has been a clear error of judgment. Although this inquiry into the facts is to be searching and careful, the ultimate standard of review is a narrow one. The court is not empowered to substitute its judgment for that of the agency.

The final inquiry is whether the Secretary's action followed the necessary procedural requirements. Here the only procedural error alleged is the failure of the Secretary to make formal findings and state his reason for allowing the highway to be built through the park.

Undoubtedly, review of the Secretary's action is hampered by his failure to make such findings, but the absence of formal findings does not necessarily require that the case be remanded to the Secretary. Neither the Department of Transportation Act nor the Federal-Aid Highway Act requires such formal findings. Moreover, the Administrative Procedure Act requirements that there be formal findings in certain rulemaking and adjudicatory proceedings do not apply to the Secretary's action here.

* * *

Thus it is necessary to remand this case to the District Court for plenary review of the Secretary's decision. That review is to be based on the full administrative record that was before the Secretary at the time he made his decision. But since the bare record may not disclose the factors that were considered or the Secretary's construction of the evidence it may be necessary for the District Court to require some explanation in order to determine if the Secretary acted within the scope of his authority and if the Secretary's action was justifiable under the applicable standard.

The court may require the administrative officials who participated in the decision to give testimony explaining their action. Of course, such inquiry into the mental processes of administrative decisionmakers is usually to be avoided. *United States v. Morgan*, 313 U.S. 409, 422 (1941). And where there are administrative findings that were made at the same time as the decision, as was the case in *Morgan*, there must be a strong showing of bad faith or improper behavior before such inquiry may be made. But here there are no such formal findings and it may be that the only way there can be effective judicial review is by examining the decisionmakers themselves.

The District Court is not, however, required to make such an inquiry. It may be that the Secretary can prepare formal findings * * * that will provide an adequate explanation for his action. Such an explanation will, to some extent, be a "*post hoc* rationalization" and thus must be viewed critically. If the District Court decides that additional explanation is necessary, that court should consider which method will prove the most expeditious so that full review may be had as soon as possible.

NOTES AND QUESTIONS

1. The facts of *Overton Park* are hardly unusual. Many economic historians rank President Eisenhower's project to construct a network of interstate highways as one of the three most important government projects in history in terms of its contribution to the remarkable growth of the U.S. economy. (The other two are the construction of transcontinental railroads, which opened the west to trade and settlement in the late nineteenth century, and the World War II GI Bill, which dramatically expanded access to a college education in the late 1940s and early 1950s.) Choosing the routes of interstate highways was one of the most difficult and contentious political issues to confront government officials from the 1950s through the early 1970s. Route choices were often life or death decisions for the many small towns that had grown up alongside state highways that the new interstates rendered largely obsolete. Routing

decisions within urban areas were extremely controversial for other reasons; any route chosen would disrupt residential and commercial living patterns and separate communities from the stores and churches they had long patronized.

Congress anticipated the complicated politics of the interstate highway routing process by establishing an intergovernmental decisionmaking process in which state and local authorities had the dominant roles while the federal government had a veto power over the final routing decision. Concerning *Overton Park* in particular, Peter Strauss documents a process that engaged all of the citizens of Memphis over a two decade period in which the routing decision was a major issue in mayoral and city council elections, and even in gubernatorial and state legislature races. Throughout the process, all levels of government, including the federal government, focused a great deal of attention on the effects of the routing decision on parks generally and on Overton Park in particular. Citizens to Preserve Overton Park participated in this lengthy and complicated debate, but it eventually lost at the local, state, and federal level. *See* Peter Strauss, *Revisiting* Overton Park, 39 UCLA L. REV. 1251 (1992). Strauss concludes that the political decisionmaking process Congress created worked well in the case of the decision to route Interstate 40 through Memphis, and that judicial review was incompatible with that process. Do you believe that, when Congress created this political decisionmaking process and provided no express role for the courts, it implicitly intended to authorize judicial review of the decisions?

2.   The Court decided *Overton Park* toward the end of the multi-decade period in which the U.S. implemented Eisenhower's plan for a network of interstate highways. If the Court had issued its *Overton Park* decision at the beginning of that period, what effect do you think its opinion would have had on the interstate highway project? How much delay in the implementation process so you think the opinion would have created if the Court had issued it in 1956, for instance, rather than in 1971? How much would that delay have cost the nation?

3.   Again, APA § 701(a) provides "This chapter applies, according to the provisions thereof, except to the extent that (1) statutes preclude review; or (2) agency action is committed to agency discretion by law." Although the *Overton Park* opinion characterized these statutory exceptions to the reviewability of agency actions so narrowly as to sustain the reviewability of the vast majority of agency actions, even at that time many circuit courts interpreted § 701(a)(1) and (2) more broadly than *Overton Park* suggested. A pair of circuit court opinions involving the same statute illustrate both the tendency of many lower courts to apply those two provisions with greater effect than the Supreme Court suggested and also the significant overlap between the two provisions of APA § 701(a).

In *Hahn v. Gottlieb*, 430 F.2d 1243 (1st Cir. 1970), the First Circuit was asked to review a decision of the Department of Housing and Urban Development (HUD) to allow an owner of Title 8 property to increase the rents it charged tenants. Title 8 is a statutory program that is intended to make low cost housing available to poor people by providing subsidies to private parties who build low cost housing that complies with HUD specifications and then to rent that housing to poor people at rents regulated by HUD. That statute anticipates that the owners of Title 8 housing might have to increase the rent that they charge over time due to changed conditions. It empowers HUD to grant requests to increase rents in some circumstances. Like the Federal Aid to Highways Act that was at issue in *Overton Park*, the housing statute is silent with respect to the reviewability of HUD decisions to allow increases in the rent charged poor tenants in Title 8 housing. The First Circuit held that such decisions were unreviewable because they were "committed to agency discretion by law." The court acknowledged that the poor tenants had a powerful interest in obtaining judicial review of HUD decisions that require them to pay higher rent, but it expressed concern that (1) courts lack the expertise needed to evaluate HUD decisions authorizing rent increases; (2) courts may unintentionally cause more harm than good by attempting to perform this task; and (3) availability of judicial review of rent increase decisions may harm poor people by deterring prospective investors from investing in Title 8 properties. Do you find the *Hahn* opinion consistent with the Supreme Court's characterization of APA § 701(a)(2) in *Overton Park*?

A year after the First Circuit issued its opinion in *Hahn*, the Second Circuit addressed the same question in *Langevin v. Chenango Court, Inc.*, 447 F.2d 296 (2d Cir. 1971). The Second Circuit criticized the reasoning and holding of the First Circuit on two bases. First, it noted that courts had long reviewed agency decisions that are analogous to HUD rent increase decisions. For many decades, courts had engaged in review of agency decisions to authorize electricity and natural gas companies to increase the rates they charged. As the Second Circuit noted, that class of agency actions differs from HUD decisions to authorize rent increases in only one arguably important respect—Congress specifically instructed courts to review the rate increases, while it was silent with respect to judicial review of HUD rent increase decisions. Second, the Second Circuit criticized the First Circuit's conclusion that rent increase decisions were committed to HUD's discretion. For these reasons, the Second Circuit rejected the argument that APA § 701(a)(2) operated to deny reviewability in such cases. Yet, the Second Circuit continued by agreeing with the policy concerns expressed by the First Circuit and by holding that HUD decisions authorizing rent increases are not reviewable because Congress implicitly precluded review of such decisions within the meaning of APA § 701(a)(1). Do you find the Second Circuit's application of APA § 701(a)(1) under such circumstances consistent with the Supreme Court's characterization of that provision in *Overton Park*?

One way of thinking about judicial opinions is as a means through which courts communicate with other institutions of government. What message did the First Circuit send Congress in *Hahn*? What message did the Second Circuit send Congress in *Langevin*? Which of those messages is more accurate and more helpful to members of Congress who might want to amend the housing statute in ways that would authorize and enable courts to review HUD rent increase decisions?

4. Courts routinely cite the *Overton Park* opinion to support many propositions in addition to the presumption of reviewability. For example, the Court in *Overton Park* characterized arbitrary and capricious review under APA § 706 as "thorough, in-depth," "searching and careful," and "narrow." Given this characterization, what might you expect arbitrary and capricious review to entail? Of course, the Court has since elaborated on the meaning of arbitrary and capricious under APA § 706 in opinions that we discuss in Chapters 4 and 5.

5.   The Supreme Court in *Overton Park* described the "committed to agency discretion" limitation of APA § 701(a)(2) as denying reviewability when "statutes are drawn in such broad terms that in a given case there is no law to apply." Recall that, in Chapter 2, we considered the Supreme Court's repeated assertions under the nondelegation doctrine that congressional delegations of discretionary authority to agencies are only constitutional if they establish "intelligible principles" that limit agency discretion and guide agency behavior. Of course, the Court has rarely found that a statute's delegation does not set forth intelligible principles. Nevertheless, do you find *Overton Park*'s "no law to apply" standard consistent with the principles espoused by the nondelegation doctrine?

6.   The Court in *Overton Park* also held that the agency was not required to provide any contemporaneous explanation of its decision. The Court reasoned that APA § 553 did not apply to the decision to provide federal funding for the section of interstate 40 that would go through Overton Park because the agency was not engaged in a rulemaking of any type, and that APA §§ 554, 556, and 557 did not apply because the statute lacked the requirement that the agency act "on the record after agency hearing" and, thus, did not require the agency to engage in formal adjudication. By default, that meant that the action the agency took was an informal adjudication, and the APA does not require an agency to explain why its action when it engages in informal adjudication. The vast majority of agency actions fall into that category. The Court reaffirmed that holding in *PBGC v. LTV Corp.*, 496 U.S. 633 (1990). In *LTV*, the Court held that only APA § 555 applies to an informal adjudication.

Nevertheless, in *Overton Park*, the Court suggested that the district court might require the decisionmaker, Transportation Secretary Volpe, to explain the reasons for his actions in testimony in the proceedings on remand so the court would have basis for applying the statutory standard and the arbitrary and capricious test to the agency's decision. In *LTV* and several other later cases, the Court has made it clear that a court cannot require an agency decisionmaker to testify except in the rare case where a petitioner can present powerful extrinsic evidence of wrongdoing by the decisionmaker. The Court has repeatedly said that a reviewing court should instead require an agency to provide the court with a written explanation for its action if the agency provided no contemporaneous explanation for an action it took through use of informal adjudication or if the contemporaneous explanation the agency provided is inadequate to permit the court to apply the applicable statutory standards and the arbitrary and capricious test. If you represented an agency, would you find it easier to contemporaneously document the reasoning behind a decision in an informal adjudication or to recreate that reasoning after the fact in the course of litigation?

Between the 1950s and the early 1970s, judicial attitudes concerning the appropriate role of the judiciary changed. Over that period, many judges and Justices saw serious problems in the United States that they believed the judiciary could, and should, solve. Many scholars view the Court's famous opinion in *Brown v. Board of Education*, 347 U.S. 483 (1954), as the most important illustration of this period of judicial activism and of the optimism about the constructive role courts could play in solving the nation's problems. In the mid-1970s, however, this general attitude began to change. Judges and Justices began to recognize the institutional limitations of the judicial branch as an agent for major change. They also became increasingly concerned about the burdens that both the courts and Congress had imposed on the judiciary by increasing dramatically the number of disputes the courts were required to address and by assigning the courts broad roles in addressing numerous serious social problems.

In retrospect, the *Overton Park* opinion is one of the last opinions to reflect the attitude that prevailed in the federal courts in the period 1950 to 1975. In Chapter 4, we recognized the Supreme Court's opinions interpreting the Due Process as demonstrating this general change in the attitude of the federal judiciary. The Court issued a series of opinions from 1968 through 1972 in which it dramatically increased the role of courts in prescribing the decisionmaking procedures agencies were require to use. In 1976, however, the Court began to issue opinions in which it reduced the role of the courts in that process. The same general change in attitude is apparent in the Court's opinions with respect to reviewability. During the period 1967 to 1975, the Court issued a series of opinions in which it announced and applied a powerful presumption of reviewability that applied to virtually all agency actions. *Overton Park* is one of those opinions. We include several other important opinions that illustrate this attitude later in this Chapter. In the second half of the decade of the 1970s, however, the Court began to reduce both the power and the scope of the presumption of reviewability, as will become apparent in many of the other opinions we include later in this chapter. The presumption still exists, but it is both weaker and narrower than the Court's description of it in *Overton Park* suggested.

Fourteen years after deciding *Overton Park*, the Supreme Court again addressed the question of when an action is committed to agency discretion in *Heckler v. Chaney*, 470 U.S. 821 (1985). The Court's opinion in *Chaney* is perhaps better known for its discussion of enforcement discretion and agency inaction; we discuss this issue and the *Chaney* decision at some length beginning on page 713 of this Chapter. Nevertheless, *Chaney* is also notable for its discussion of the committed to agency discretion limitation on judicial review of agency action. In an opinion authored by then-Justice Rehnquist, the majority offered the following analysis of the Court's *Overton Park* opinion.

> First, it clearly separates the exception provided by § (a)(1) from the § (a)(2) exception. The former applies when Congress has expressed an intent to preclude judicial review. The latter applies in different circumstances; even where Congress has not affirmatively precluded review, review is not to be had if the statute is drawn so that a court would have no meaningful standard against which to judge the agency's exercise of discretion. In such a case, the statute ("law") can be taken to have "committed" the decisionmaking to the agency's judgment absolutely.

Id. at 830. The Court in *Chaney* did not seem to consider its "no meaningful standard" articulation of the committed to agency discretion limitation to be substantially different from the "no law to apply" phraseology used by the Court in *Overton Park*. Do you agree?

A few years later, the Court had yet another opportunity to consider the meaning of APA § 701(a)(2) in the following case.

Webster v. Doe

486 U.S. 592 (1988).

■ CHIEF JUSTICE REHNQUIST delivered the opinion of the Court.

Section 102(c) of the National Security Act of 1947 provides that:

"[T]he Director of Central Intelligence may, in his discretion, terminate the employment of any officer or employee of the Agency whenever he shall deem such termination necessary or advisable in the interests of the United States. . . ." 50 U.S.C. § 403(c).

In this case we decide whether, and to what extent, the termination decisions of the Director under § 102(c) are judicially reviewable.

I

Respondent John Doe was first employed by the Central Intelligence Agency (CIA or Agency) in 1973 as a clerk-typist. He received periodic fitness reports that consistently rated him as an excellent or outstanding employee. By 1977, respondent had been promoted to a position as a covert electronics technician.

In January 1982, respondent voluntarily informed a CIA security officer that he was a homosexual. Almost immediately, the Agency placed respondent on paid administrative leave pending an investigation of his sexual orientation and conduct. On February 12 and again on February 17, respondent was extensively questioned by a polygraph officer concerning his homosexuality and possible security violations. Respondent denied having sexual relations with any foreign nationals and maintained that he had not disclosed classified information to any of his sexual partners. After these interviews, the officer told respondent that the polygraph tests indicated that he had truthfully answered all questions. The polygraph officer then prepared a five-page summary of his interviews with respondent, to which respondent was allowed to attach a two-page addendum.

On April 14, 1982, a CIA security agent informed respondent that the Agency's Office of Security had determined that respondent's homosexuality posed a threat to security, but declined to explain the nature of the danger. Respondent was then asked to resign. When he refused to do so, the Office of Security recommended to the CIA Director that respondent be dismissed. After reviewing respondent's records and the evaluations of his subordinates, the Director "deemed it necessary and advisable in the interests of the United States to terminate [respondent's] employment with this Agency pursuant to section 102(c) of the National Security Act. . . ."

Respondent then filed an action against petitioner in the United States District Court for the District of Columbia. Respondent's amended complaint asserted a variety of statutory and constitutional claims against the Director. Respondent alleged that the Director's decision to terminate his employment violated the Administrative Procedure Act (APA) because it was arbitrary and capricious, represented an abuse of discretion, and was reached without observing the procedures required by law and CIA regulations. He also complained that the Director's termination of his employment deprived him of constitutionally protected rights to property, liberty, and privacy in violation of the First, Fourth, Fifth, and Ninth Amendments. Finally, he asserted that his dismissal transgressed the procedural due process and equal protection of the laws guaranteed by the Fifth Amendment.

* * *

II

The APA's comprehensive provisions allow any person "adversely affected or aggrieved" by agency action to obtain judicial review thereof, so long as the decision challenged represents a "final agency action for which there is no other adequate remedy in a court." 5 U.S.C. §§ 701–706. Typically, a litigant will contest an action (or failure to act) by an agency on the ground that the agency has neglected to follow the statutory directives of Congress. Section 701(a), however, limits application of the entire APA to situations in which judicial review is not precluded by statute, *see* § 701(a)(1), and the agency action is not committed to agency discretion by law, *see* § 701(a)(2).

In *Citizens to Preserve Overton Park, Inc. v. Volpe*, 401 U.S. 402 (1971), this Court explained the distinction between §§ 701(a)(1) and (a)(2). Subsection (a)(1) is concerned with whether Congress expressed an intent to prohibit judicial review; subsection (a)(2) applies "in those rare instances where 'statutes are drawn in such broad terms that in a given case there is no law to apply.'" 401 U.S. at 410 (citing S. REP. No. 752, at 26 (1945)).

We further explained what it means for an action to be "committed to agency discretion by law" in *Heckler v. Chaney*, 470 U.S. 821 (1984). *Heckler* required the Court to determine whether the Food and Drug Administration's decision not to undertake an enforcement proceeding against the use of certain drugs in administering the death penalty was subject to judicial review. We noted that, under § 701(a)(2), even when Congress has not affirmatively precluded judicial oversight, "review is not to be had if the statute is drawn so that a court would have no meaningful standard against which to judge the agency's exercise of discretion." 470 U.S. at 830.

* * *

In the present case, respondent's claims against the CIA arise from the Director's asserted violation of § 102(c) of the NSA. As an initial matter, it should be noted that § 102(c) allows termination of an Agency employee whenever the Director "shall *deem* such termination necessary or advisable in the interests of the United States" (emphasis added), not simply when the dismissal *is* necessary or advisable to those interests. This standard fairly exudes deference to the Director, and appears to us to foreclose the application of any meaningful judicial standard of review. Short of permitting cross-examination of the Director concerning his views of the Nation's security and whether the discharged employee was inimical to those interests, we see no basis on which a reviewing court could properly assess an Agency termination decision. The language of § 102(c) thus strongly suggests that its implementation was "committed to agency discretion by law."

So too does the overall structure of the NSA. Passed shortly after the close of the Second World War, the NSA created the CIA and gave its Director the responsibility "for protecting intelligence sources and methods from unauthorized disclosure." Section 102(c) is an integral part of that statute, because the Agency's efficacy, and the Nation's security, depend in large measure on the reliability and trustworthiness of the Agency's employees. As we recognized in *Snepp v. United States*, 444 U.S. 507 (1980), employment with the CIA entails a high degree of trust that is perhaps unmatched in Government service.

* * *

We thus find that the language and structure of § 102(c) indicate that Congress meant to commit individual employee discharges to the Director's discretion, and that § 701(a)(2) accordingly precludes judicial review of these decisions under the APA. * * *

III

In addition to his claim that the Director failed to abide by the statutory dictates of § 102(c), respondent also alleged a number of constitutional violations in his amended complaint. Respondent charged that petitioner's termination of his employment deprived him of property and liberty interests under the Due Process Clause of the Fifth Amendment, denied him equal protection of the laws, and unjustifiably burdened his right to privacy.

* * *

Petitioner maintains that, no matter what the nature of respondent's constitutional claims, judicial review is precluded by the language and intent of § 102(c). In petitioner's view, all Agency employment termination decisions, even those based on policies normally repugnant to the Constitution, are given over to the absolute discretion of the Director, and are hence unreviewable under the APA. We do not think § 102(c) may be read to exclude review of constitutional claims. We emphasized in *Johnson v. Robison*, 415 U.S. 361, 373–74 (1974), that where Congress intends to preclude judicial review of constitutional claims its intent to do so must be clear. * * * We require this heightened showing in part to avoid the "serious constitutional question" that would arise if a federal statute were construed to deny any judicial forum for a colorable constitutional claim.

Our review of § 102(c) convinces us that it cannot bear the preclusive weight petitioner would have it support. As detailed above, the section does commit employment termination decisions to the Director's discretion, and precludes challenges to these decisions based upon the statutory language of § 102(c). A discharged employee thus cannot complain that his termination was not "necessary or advisable in the interests of the United States," since that assessment is the Director's alone. Subsections (a)(1) and (a)(2) of § 701, however, remove from judicial review only those determinations specifically identified by Congress or "committed to agency discretion by law." Nothing in

§ 102(c) persuades us that Congress meant to preclude consideration of colorable constitutional claims arising out of the actions of the Director pursuant to that section; we believe that a constitutional claim based on an individual discharge may be reviewed by the District Court.

■ JUSTICE O'CONNOR, concurring in part and dissenting in part.

I agree that the Administrative Procedure Act (APA) does not authorize judicial review of the employment decisions referred to in § 102(c) of the National Security Act of 1947. Because § 102(c) does not provide a meaningful standard for judicial review, such decisions are clearly "committed to agency discretion by law" within the meaning of the provision of the APA set forth in 5 U.S.C. § 701(a)(2). I do not understand the Court to say that the exception in § 701(a)(2) is necessarily or fully defined by reference to statutes "drawn in such broad terms that in a given case there is no law to apply." *Citizens to Preserve Overton Park, Inc. v. Volpe*, 401 U.S. 402, 410 (1971).

I disagree, however, with the Court's conclusion that a constitutional claim challenging the validity of an employment decision covered by § 102(c) may nonetheless be brought in a federal district court. Whatever may be the exact scope of Congress' power to close the lower federal courts to constitutional claims in other contexts, I have no doubt about its authority to do so here. The functions performed by the Central Intelligence Agency and the Director of Central Intelligence lie at the core of "the very delicate, plenary and exclusive power of the President as the sole organ of the federal government in the field of international relations." *United States v. Curtiss-Wright Export Corp.*, 299 U.S. 304, 320 (1936). The authority of the Director of Central Intelligence to control access to sensitive national security information by discharging employees deemed to be untrustworthy flows primarily from this constitutional power of the President, and Congress may surely provide that the inferior federal courts are not used to infringe on the President's constitutional authority. Section 102(c) plainly indicates that Congress has done exactly that, and the Court points to nothing in the structure, purpose, or legislative history of the National Security Act that would suggest a different conclusion. Accordingly, I respectfully dissent from the Court's decision to allow this lawsuit to go forward.

■ JUSTICE SCALIA, dissenting.

I agree with the Court's apparent holding in Part II of its opinion that the Director's decision to terminate a CIA employee is "committed to agency discretion by law" within the meaning of 5 U.S.C. § 701(a)(2). But because I do not see how a decision can, either practically or legally, be both unreviewable and yet reviewable for constitutional defect, I regard Part III of the opinion as essentially undoing Part II. I therefore respectfully dissent from the judgment of the Court.

Before proceeding to address Part III of the Court's opinion, which I think to be in error, I must discuss one significant element of the analysis in Part II. Though I subscribe to most of that analysis, I disagree with the Court's description of what is required to come within subsection (a)(2) of § 701, which provides that judicial review is unavailable "to the extent that . . . agency action is committed to agency discretion by law." The Court's discussion suggests that the Court of

Appeals below was correct in holding that this provision is triggered only when there is "no law to apply." Our precedents amply show that "commit[ment] to agency discretion by law" includes, but is not limited to, situations in which there is "no law to apply."

* * *

The "no law to apply" test can account for the nonreviewability of certain issues, but falls far short of explaining the full scope of the areas from which the courts are excluded. For the fact is that there is no governmental decision that is not subject to a fair number of legal constraints precise enough to be susceptible of judicial application—beginning with the fundamental constraint that the decision must be taken in order to further a public purpose rather than a purely private interest; yet there are many governmental decisions that are not at all subject to judicial review. A United States Attorney's decision to prosecute, for example, will not be reviewed on the claim that it was prompted by personal animosity. Thus, "no law to apply" provides much less than the full answer to whether § 701(a)(2) applies.

The key to understanding the "committed to agency discretion *by law*" provision of § 701(a)(2) lies in contrasting it with the "*statutes* preclude judicial review" provision of § 701(a)(1). Why "statutes" for preclusion, but the much more general term "law" for commission to agency discretion? The answer, as we implied in *Heckler v. Chaney*, 470 U.S. 821, 832 (1985), is that the latter was intended to refer to "the 'common law' of judicial review of agency action,"—a body of jurisprudence that had marked out, with more or less precision, certain issues and certain areas that were beyond the range of judicial review. That jurisprudence included principles ranging from the "political question" doctrine, to sovereign immunity (including doctrines determining when a suit against an officer would be deemed to be a suit against the sovereign), to official immunity, to prudential limitations upon the courts' equitable powers, to what can be described no more precisely than a traditional respect for the functions of the other branches reflected in the statement in *Marbury v. Madison*, 5 U.S. (1 Cranch) 137, 170–71, (1803), that "[w]here the head of a department acts in a case, in which executive discretion is to be exercised; in which he is the mere organ of executive will; it is again repeated, that any application to a court to control, in any respect, his conduct, would be rejected without hesitation." Only if all that "common law" were embraced within § 701(a)(2) could it have been true that, as was generally understood, "[t]he intended result of [§ 701(a)] is to restate the existing law as to the area of reviewable agency action." ATTORNEY GENERAL'S MANUAL ON THE ADMINISTRATIVE PROCEDURE ACT 94 (1947). Because that is the meaning of the provision, we have continued to take into account for purposes of determining reviewability, post-APA as before, not only the text and structure of the statute under which the agency acts, but such factors as whether the decision involves "a sensitive and inherently discretionary judgment call," *Dep't of Navy v. Egan*, 484 U.S. 518, 527 (1988), whether it is the sort of decision that has traditionally been nonreviewable, *Chaney*, 470 U.S. at 832, and whether review would have "disruptive practical consequences." *S. R.R. Co. v. Seabord Allied Milling Corp.*, 442 U.S. 444, 457 (1979). This explains the seeming contradiction between § 701(a)(2)'s disallowance of review to the extent that action is "committed to agency discretion," and § 706's injunction that a court shall set aside agency action that constitutes "an abuse of discretion." Since, in the former provision, "committed to agency discretion by law" means "of the sort that is traditionally unreviewable," it operates to keep certain categories of agency action out of the courts; but when agency action is appropriately in the courts, abuse of discretion is of course grounds for reversal.

All this law, shaped over the course of centuries and still developing in its application to new contexts, cannot possibly be contained within the phrase "no law to apply." It is not surprising, then, that although the Court recites the test it does not really apply it. Like other opinions relying upon it, this one essentially announces the test, declares victory and moves on. It is not really true " 'that a court would have no meaningful standard against which to judge the agency's exercise of discretion,' " The standard set forth in § 102(c) of the National Security Act of 1947, "necessary or advisable in the interests of the United States," at least excludes dismissal out of personal vindictiveness, or because the Director wants to give the job to his cousin. Why, on the Court's theory, is respondent not entitled to assert the presence of such excesses, under the "abuse of discretion" standard of § 706?

* * *

Before taking the reader through the terrain of the Court's holding that respondent may assert constitutional claims in this suit, I would like to try to clear some of the underbrush, consisting primarily of the Court's ominous warning that "[a] 'serious constitutional question' . . . would arise if a federal statute were construed to deny any judicial forum for a colorable constitutional claim."

The first response to the Court's grave doubt about the constitutionality of denying all judicial review to a "colorable constitutional claim" is that the denial of all judicial review is not at issue here, but merely the denial of review in United States district courts. As to that, the law is, and has long been, clear. Article III, § 2, of the Constitution extends the judicial power to "all Cases . . . arising under this Constitution." But Article III, § 1, provides that the judicial power shall be vested "in one supreme Court, *and in such inferior Courts as the Congress may from time to time ordain and establish*" (emphasis added). We long ago held that the power not to create any lower federal courts at all includes the power to invest them with less than all of the judicial power.

> "The Constitution has defined the limits of the judicial power of the United States, but has not prescribed how much of it shall be exercised by the Circuit Court; consequently, the statute which does prescribe the limits of their jurisdiction, cannot be in conflict with the Constitution, unless it confers powers not enumerated therein." *Sheldon v. Sill*, 49 U.S. (8 How.) 441, 449 (1850).

Thus, if there is any truth to the proposition that judicial cognizance of constitutional claims cannot be eliminated, it is, at most, that they cannot be eliminated from state courts, and from this Court's appellate jurisdiction over cases from state courts (or cases from federal courts, should there be any) involving such claims. Narrowly viewed, therefore, there is no shadow of a constitutional doubt that we are free to hold that the present suit, whether based on constitutional grounds or not, will not lie.

It can fairly be argued, however, that our interpretation of § 701(a)(2) indirectly implicates the constitutional question whether state courts can be deprived of jurisdiction, because if they cannot, then interpreting § 701(a)(2) to exclude relief here would impute to Congress the peculiar intent to let state courts review Federal Government action that it is unwilling to let federal district courts review—or, alternatively, the peculiar intent to let federal district courts review, upon removal from state courts pursuant to 28 U.S.C. § 1442(a)(1), claims that it is unwilling to let federal district courts review in original actions. I turn, then, to the substance of the Court's warning that judicial review of all "colorable constitutional claims" arising out of the respondent's dismissal may well be constitutionally required. What could possibly be the basis for this fear? Surely not some general principle that *all* constitutional violations must be remediable in the courts. The very text of the Constitution refutes that principle, since it provides that "[e]ach House shall be the Judge of the Elections, Returns and Qualifications of its own Members," art. I, § 5, and that "for any Speech or Debate in either House, [the Senators and Representatives] shall not be questioned in any other Place," art. I, § 6. Claims concerning constitutional violations committed in these contexts—for example, the rather grave constitutional claim that an election has been stolen—cannot be addressed to the courts. Even apart from the strict text of the Constitution, we have found some constitutional claims to be beyond judicial review because they involve "political questions." The doctrine of sovereign immunity—not repealed by the Constitution, but to the contrary at least partly reaffirmed as to the States by the Eleventh Amendment—is a monument to the principle that some constitutional claims can go unheard. No one would suggest that, if Congress had not passed the Tucker Act, the courts would be able to order disbursements from the Treasury to pay for property taken under lawful authority (and subsequently destroyed) without just compensation. And finally, the doctrine of equitable discretion, which permits a court to refuse relief, even where no relief at law is available, when that would unduly impair the public interest, does not stand aside simply because the basis for the relief is a constitutional claim. In sum, it is simply untenable that there must be a judicial remedy for every constitutional violation. Members of Congress and the supervising officers of the Executive Branch take the same oath to uphold the Constitution that we do, and sometimes they are left to perform that oath unreviewed, as we always are.

Perhaps, then, the Court means to appeal to a more limited principle, that although there may be areas where judicial review of a constitutional claim will be denied, the scope of those areas is fixed by the Constitution and judicial tradition, and cannot be affected by *Congress,* through the enactment of a statute such as § 102(c). That would be a rather counter-intuitive principle, especially since Congress has in reality been the principal determiner of the scope of review, for constitutional claims as well as all other claims, through its waiver of the pre-existing doctrine of sovereign immunity. On the merits of the point, however: It seems to me clear that courts would not entertain, for example, an action for backpay by a dismissed Secretary of State claiming that the reason he lost his Government job was that the President did not like his religious views—surely a colorable violation of the First Amendment. I am confident we would hold that the President's choice of his Secretary of State is a "political question." But what about a similar suit by the Deputy Secretary of State? Or one of the Under Secretaries? Or an Assistant Secretary? Or the head of the European Desk? Is there really a constitutional line that falls at some immutable point between one and another of these offices at which the principle of unreviewability cuts in, and which cannot be altered by congressional prescription? I think not. I think Congress can prescribe, at least within broad limits, that for certain jobs the dismissal decision will be unreviewable—that is, will be "committed to agency discretion by law."

Once it is acknowledged, as I think it must be, (1) that not all constitutional claims require a judicial remedy, and (2) that the identification of those that do not can, even if only within narrow limits, be determined by Congress, then it is clear that the "serious constitutional question" feared by the Court is an illusion. Indeed, it seems to me that if one is in a mood to worry about serious constitutional questions the one to worry about is not whether Congress can, by enacting § 102(c), give the President, through his Director of Central Intelligence, unreviewable discretion in firing the agents that he employs to gather military and foreign affairs intelligence, but rather whether Congress could constitutionally *permit* the courts to review all such decisions if it wanted to. We have acknowledged that the courts cannot intervene when there is "a textually demonstratable constitutional commitment of the issue to a coordinate political department." *Baker v. Carr*, 369 U.S. 186, 217 (1962). We have recognized "the insistence (evident from the number of Clauses devoted to the subject) with which the Constitution confers authority over the Army, Navy, and militia upon the political branches." *United States v. Stanley*, 483 U.S. 669, 682 (1987). We have also recognized "the very delicate, plenary and exclusive power of the President as the sole organ of the federal government in the field of international relations—a power which does not require as a basis for its exercise an act of Congress." *United States v. Curtiss-Wright Export Corp.*, 299 U.S. 304, 320 (1936). And finally, we have acknowledged that "[i]t is impossible for a government wisely to make critical decisions about foreign policy and national defense without the benefit of dependable foreign intelligence." *Snepp v. United States*, 444 U.S. 507, 512 n.7 (1980). We have thus recognized that the "authority to classify and control access to information bearing on national security and to determine whether an individual is sufficiently trustworthy to occupy a position in the Executive Branch that will give that person access to such information flows primarily from this constitutional investment of power in the President *and exists quite apart from any explicit congressional grant.*" *Dep't of Navy v. Egan*, 484 U.S. at 527 (emphasis added).

I think it entirely beyond doubt that if Congress intended, by the APA in 5 U.S.C. § 701(a)(2), to exclude judicial review of the President's decision (through the Director of Central Intelligence) to dismiss an officer of the Central Intelligence Agency, that disposition would be constitutionally permissible.

I turn, then, to whether that executive action is, within the meaning of § 701(a)(2), "committed to agency discretion by law." My discussion of this point can be brief, because the answer is compellingly obvious. Section 102(c) of the National Security Act of 1947 states:

> "*Notwithstanding . . . the provisions of any other law*, the Director of Central Intelligence, *may, in his discretion,* terminate the employment of any officer or employee of the Agency *whenever he shall deem* such termination necessary or advisable in the interests of the United States. . . ." 50 U.S.C. § 403(c) (emphasis added).

Further, as the Court declares, § 102(c) is an "integral part" of the National Security Act, which throughout exhibits "extraordinary deference to the Director." Given this statutory text, and given (as discussed above) that the area to which the text pertains is one of predominant executive authority and of traditional judicial abstention, it is difficult to conceive of a statutory scheme that more clearly reflects that "commit[ment] to agency discretion by law" to which § 701(a)(2) refers.

It is baffling to observe that the Court seems to agree with the foregoing assessment, holding that "the language and structure of § 102(c) indicate that Congress meant to commit individual employee discharges to the Director's discretion." Nevertheless, without explanation the Court reaches the conclusion that "a constitutional claim based on an individual discharge may be reviewed by the District Court." It seems to me the Court is attempting the impossible feat of having its cake and eating it too. The opinion states that "[a] discharged employee . . . cannot complain that his termination was not 'necessary or advisable in the interests of the United States,' *since that assessment is the Director's alone.*" But two sentences later it says that "[n]othing in § 102(c) persuades us that Congress meant to preclude consideration of colorable constitutional claims arising out of the actions of the Director pursuant to that section." Which are we to believe? If the former, the case should be at an end. If the § 102(c) assessment is really "the Director's alone," the only conceivable basis for review of respondent's dismissal (which is what this case is about) would be that the dismissal was not *really* the result of a § 102(c) assessment by the Director. But respondent has never contended that, nor could he. Not only was his counsel formally advised, by letter of May 11, 1982, that "the Director has deemed it necessary and advisable in the interests of the United States to terminate your client's employment with this Agency pursuant to section 102(c)," but the petitioner filed with the court an affidavit by the Director, dated September 17, 1982, stating that "[a]fter careful consideration of the matter, I determined that the termination of Mr. Doe's employment was necessary and advisable in the interests of the United States and, exercising my discretion under the authority granted by section 102(c) . . . I terminated Mr. Doe's employment." Even if the basis for the Director's assessment was the respondent's homosexuality, and even if the connection between that and the interests of the United States is an irrational and hence an unconstitutional one, if that assessment is really "the Director's alone" there is nothing more to litigate about. I cannot imagine what the Court expects the "further proceedings in the District Court" which it commands to consist of, unless perhaps an academic seminar on the relationship of homosexuality to security risk. For even were the District Court persuaded that no such relationship exists, "that assessment is the Director's alone."

Since the Court's disposition contradicts its fair assurances, I must assume that the § 102(c) judgment is no longer "the Director's alone," but rather only "the Director's alone except to the extent it is colorably claimed that his judgment is unconstitutional." I turn, then, to the question of where this exception comes from. As discussed at length earlier, the Constitution assuredly does not require it. Nor does the text of the statute. True, it only gives the Director absolute discretion to dismiss "[n]otwithstanding ... the provisions of any other *law*" (emphasis added). But one would hardly have expected it to say "[n]otwithstanding the provisions of any other law *or of the Constitution.*" What the provision directly addresses is the authority to dismiss, not the authority of the courts to review the dismissal. And the Director does *not* have the authority to dismiss in violation of the Constitution, nor could Congress give it to him. The implication of nonreviewability in this text, its manifestation that the action is meant to be "committed to agency discretion," is no weaker with regard to constitutional claims than nonconstitutional claims, unless one accepts the unacceptable proposition that the only basis for such committal is "no law to apply."

Perhaps, then, a constitutional right is by its nature so much more important to the claimant than a statutory right that a statute which plainly excludes the latter should not be read to exclude the former unless it says so. That principle has never been announced—and with good reason, because its premise is not true. An individual's contention that the Government has reneged upon a $100,000 debt owing under a contract is much more important to him—both financially and, I suspect, in the sense of injustice that he feels—than the same individual's claim that a particular federal licensing provision requiring a $100 license denies him equal protection of the laws, or that a particular state tax violates the Commerce Clause. A citizen would much rather have his statutory entitlement correctly acknowledged after a constitutionally inadequate hearing, than have it incorrectly denied after a proceeding that fulfills all the requirements of the Due Process Clause. The *only* respect in which a constitutional claim is necessarily more significant than any other kind of claim is that, regardless of how trivial its real-life importance may be in the case at hand, it can be asserted against the action of the legislature itself, whereas a nonconstitutional claim (no matter how significant) cannot. That is an important distinction, and one relevant to the constitutional analysis that I conducted above. But it has no relevance to the question whether, as between executive violations of statute and executive violations of the Constitution—both of which are equally unlawful, and neither of which can be said, *a priori*, to be more harmful or more unfair to the plaintiff—one or the other category should be favored by a presumption against exclusion of judicial review.

Even if we were to assume, however, contrary to all reason, that every constitutional claim is *ipso facto* more worthy, and every statutory claim less worthy, of judicial review, there would be no basis for writing that preference into a statute that makes no distinction between the two. We have rejected such judicial rewriting of legislation even in the more appealing situation where particular applications of a statute are not merely less desirable but in fact raise "grave constitutional doubts." That, we have said, only permits us to adopt one rather than another permissible reading of the statute, but not, by altering its terms, "to ignore the legislative will in order to avoid constitutional adjudication." *Commodity Futures Trading Comm'n v. Schor*, 478 U.S. 833, 841 (1986). There is no more textual basis for reading this statute as barring only nonconstitutional claims than there is to read it as barring only claims with a monetary worth of less than $1 million. Neither of the two decisions cited by the Court to sustain its power to read in a limitation for constitutional claims remotely supports that proposition. In *Johnson v. Robison*, 415 U.S. 361 (1974), we considered a statute precluding judicial review of " 'the *decisions* of the Administrator on any question of law or fact *under* any law administered by the Veterans' Administration.' " *Id.* at 367 (quoting 38 U.S.C. § 211(a)). We concluded that this statute did not bar judicial review of a challenge to the constitutionality of the statute itself, since that was a challenge not to a decision of the Administrator but to a decision of Congress. Our holding was based upon the text, and not upon some judicial power to read in a "constitutional claims" exception.

* * *

The harm done by today's decision is that, contrary to what Congress knows is preferable, it brings a significant decisionmaking process of our intelligence services into a forum where it does not belong. Neither the Constitution, nor our laws, nor common sense gives an individual a right to come into court to litigate the reasons for his dismissal as an intelligence agent. It is of course not just *valid* constitutional claims that today's decision makes the basis for judicial review of the Director's action, but all *colorable* constitutional claims, whether meritorious or not. And in determining whether what is colorable is in fact meritorious, a court will necessarily have to review the entire decision. If the Director denies, for example, respondent's contention in the present case that he was dismissed because he was a homosexual, how can a court possibly resolve the dispute without knowing what other good, intelligence-related reasons there might have been? * * * Of course the Agency can seek to protect itself, ultimately, by an authorized assertion of executive privilege, but that is a power to be invoked only *in extremis,* and any scheme of judicial review of which it is a central feature is extreme. I would, in any event, not like to be the agent who has to explain to the intelligence services of other nations, with which we sometimes cooperate, that they need have no worry that the secret information they give us will be subjected to the notoriously broad discovery powers of our courts, because, although we have to litigate the dismissal of our spies, we have available a protection of somewhat uncertain scope known as executive privilege, which the President can invoke if he is willing to take the political damage that it often entails.

Today's result, however, will have ramifications far beyond creation of the world's only secret intelligence agency that must litigate the dismissal of its agents. If constitutional claims can be raised in this highly sensitive context, it is hard to imagine where they cannot. The assumption that there are any executive decisions that cannot be hauled into the courts may no longer be valid. Also obsolete may be the assumption that we are capable of preserving a sensible common law of judicial review.

NOTES AND QUESTIONS

1.   Recall that the Court in *Overton Park* characterized the committed to agency discretion limitation of APA § 701(a)(2) in terms of "no law to apply," while the court in *Heckler v. Chaney* described the limitation using the phrase "no meaningful standard against which to judge the agency's exercise of discretion." The Court in *Webster* cites both explanations of APA § 701(a)(2). Do you find one or the other more descriptive of the Court's analysis of the National Security Act, or do you find them indistinguishable? Given the Court's analysis in *Webster*, how would you characterize the committed to agency discretion limitation of APA § 701(a)(2) if asked to describe it?

2.   In *Webster*, the Court clearly held that decisions of the CIA Director to fire an employee are committed to the Director's unreviewable discretion within the meaning of APA § 701(a)(2). Can you reconcile that opinion with the holding and reasoning of *Overton Park*? Can you reconcile it with APA § 706(2)(A), which authorizes a court to set aside agency action if it is an abuse of discretion? Do you think the Court would have held that the Secretary of Housing and Urban Development has unreviewable discretion to terminate an employee if Congress amended the HUD statute to include the same "deems . . . advisable" standard that it included in the CIA statute? What, if anything, does the *Webster* opinion tell you about the Court's interpretation of APA § 701(a)(1)? How different are the two sections that exempt agency actions from judicial review?

3.   Dissenting in *Webster*, Justice Scalia questions the workability of the "no law to apply" approach to APA § 701(a)(2) and supports an approach to the committed to agency discretion limitation that emphasizes traditional areas of nonreviewability. He also expresses doubts that all constitutional claims must necessarily be reviewable. Justice Scalia makes both theoretical and practical arguments in support of both expanding the scope of the committed to agency discretion exemption from judicial review in this manner and also reducing the scope of the avoidance canon to allow Congress to exempt statutes from constitutional review.

Consider particularly Justice Scalia's dissenting opinion in *Webster v. Doe* as you read the following opinion of the Court issued just five years later.

Lincoln v. Vigil

508 U.S. 182 (1993).

■ JUSTICE SOUTER delivered the opinion of the Court.

For several years in the late 1970's and early 1980's, the Indian Health Service provided diagnostic and treatment services, referred to collectively as the Indian Children's Program (Program), to handicapped Indian children in the Southwest. In 1985, the Service decided to reallocate the Program's resources to a nationwide effort to assist such children. We hold that the Service's decision to discontinue the Program was "committed to agency discretion by law" and therefore not subject to judicial review under the Administrative Procedure Act, 5 U.S.C. § 701(a)(2), and that the Service's exercise of that discretion was not subject to the notice-and-comment rulemaking requirements imposed by § 553.

I

The Indian Health Service, an agency within the Public Health Service of the Department of Health and Human Services, provides health care for some 1.5 million American Indian and Alaska Native people. The Service receives yearly lump-sum appropriations from Congress and expends the funds under authority of the Snyder Act and the Indian Health Care Improvement Act. So far as it concerns us here, the Snyder Act authorizes the Service to "expend such moneys as Congress may from time to time appropriate, for the benefit, care, and assistance of the Indians," for the "relief of distress and conservation of health." 25 U.S.C. § 13. The Improvement Act authorizes expenditures for, *inter alia*, Indian mental-health care, and specifically for "therapeutic and residential treatment centers." 25 U.S.C. § 1621(a)(4)(D).

The Service employs roughly 12,000 people and operates more than 500 health-care facilities in the continental United States and Alaska. This case concerns a collection of related services, commonly known as the Indian Children's Program, that the Service provided from 1978 to 1985. In the words of the Court of Appeals, a "clou[d] [of] bureaucratic haze" obscures the history of the Program, *Vigil v. Rhoades*, 953 F.2d 1225, 1226 (10th Cir. 1992), which seems to have grown out of a plan "to establish therapeutic and residential treatment centers for disturbed Indian children." H.R. REP. NO. 94–1026, pt. 1, at 80 (1976). These centers were to be established under a "major cooperative care agreement" between the Service and the Bureau of Indian Affairs, *id.*, at 81, and would have provided such children "with intensive care in a residential setting." *Id.*, at 80.

Congress never expressly appropriated funds for these centers. In 1978, however, the Service allocated approximately $292,000 from its fiscal year 1978 appropriation to its office in Albuquerque, New Mexico, for the planning and development of a pilot project for handicapped Indian children, which became known as the Indian Children's Program. The pilot project apparently convinced the Service that a building was needed, and, in 1979, the Service requested $3.5 million from Congress to construct a diagnostic and treatment center for handicapped Indian children. The appropriation for fiscal year 1980 did not expressly provide the requested funds, however, and legislative reports indicated only that Congress had increased the Service's funding by $300,000 for nationwide expansion and development of the Program in coordination with the Bureau.

Plans for a national program to be managed jointly by the Service and the Bureau were never fulfilled, however, and the Program continued simply as an offering of the Service's Albuquerque office, from which the Program's staff of 11 to 16 employees would make monthly visits to Indian communities in New Mexico and southern Colorado and on the Navajo and Hopi Reservations. * * * Congress never authorized or appropriated moneys expressly for the Program, and the Service continued to pay for its regional activities out of annual lump-sum appropriations from 1980 to 1985, during which period the Service repeatedly apprised Congress of the Program's continuing operation.

Nevertheless, the Service had not abandoned the proposal for a nationwide treatment program, and in June 1985 it notified those who referred patients to the Program that it was "re-evaluating [the Program's] purpose . . . as a national mental health program for Indian children and adolescents." In August 1985, the Service determined that Program staff hitherto assigned to provide direct clinical services should be reassigned as consultants to other nationwide Service programs, and discontinued the direct clinical services to Indian children in the Southwest. The Service announced its decision in a memorandum, dated August 21, 1985, addressed to Service offices and Program referral sources:

"As you are probably aware, the Indian Children's Program has been involved in planning activities focusing on a national program effort. This process has included the termination of all direct clinical services to children in the Albuquerque, Navajo and Hopi reservation service areas. During the months of August and September, . . . staff will [see] children followed by the program in an effort to update programs, identify alternative resources and facilitate obtaining alternative services. In communities where there are no identified resources, meetings with community service providers will be scheduled to facilitate the networking between agencies to secure or advocate for appropriate services."

The Service invited public "input" during this "difficult transition," and explained that the reallocation of resources had been "motivated by our goal of increased mental health services for all Indian [c]hildren."

Respondents, handicapped Indian children eligible to receive services through the Program, subsequently brought this action for declaratory and injunctive relief against petitioners, the Director of the Service and others (collectively, the Service), in the United States District Court for the District of New Mexico. Respondents alleged, *inter alia*, that the Service's decision to discontinue direct clinical services violated the federal trust responsibility to Indians, the Snyder Act, the Improvement Act, the Administrative Procedure Act, various agency regulations, and the Fifth Amendment's Due Process Clause.

II

* * *

First is the question whether it was error for the Court of Appeals to hold the substance of the Service's decision to terminate the Program reviewable under the APA. The APA provides that "[a] person suffering legal wrong because of agency action, or adversely affected or aggrieved by agency action within the meaning of a relevant statute, is entitled to judicial review thereof," 5 U.S.C. § 702, and we have read the APA as embodying a "basic presumption of judicial review," *Abbott Labs. v. Gardner*, 387 U.S. 136, 140 (1967). This is "just" a presumption, however, and under § 701(a)(2) agency action is not subject to judicial review "to the extent that" such action "is committed to agency discretion by law." As we explained in *Heckler v. Chaney*, 470 U.S. 821, 830 (1985), § 701(a)(2) makes it clear that "review is not to be had" in those rare circumstances where the relevant statute "is drawn so that a court would have no meaningful standard against which to judge the agency's exercise of discretion." *See also Webster v. Doe*, 486 U.S. 592, 599–600 (1988); *Citizens to Preserve Overton Park, Inc. v. Volpe*, 401 U.S. 402, 410 (1971). "In such a case, the statute ('law') can be taken to have 'committed' the decisionmaking to the agency's judgment absolutely." *Heckler*, 470 U.S. at 830.

Over the years, we have read § 701(a)(2) to preclude judicial review of certain categories of administrative decisions that courts traditionally have regarded as "committed to agency discretion." In *Heckler* itself, we held an agency's decision not to institute enforcement proceedings to be presumptively unreviewable under § 701(a)(2). *Heckler*, 470 U.S. at 831. An agency's "decision not to enforce often involves a complicated balancing of a number of factors which are peculiarly within its expertise," *id.*, and for this and other good reasons, we concluded, "such a decision has traditionally been 'committed to agency discretion,'" *id.*, at 832. Similarly, in *ICC v. Locomotive Engineers*, 482 U.S. 270, 282 (1987), we held that § 701(a)(2) precludes judicial review of another type of administrative decision traditionally left to agency discretion, an agency's refusal to grant reconsideration of an action because of material error. In so holding, we emphasized "the impossibility of devising an adequate standard of review for such agency action." *Id.* Finally, in *Webster*, 486 U.S. at 599–601, we held that § 701(a)(2) precludes judicial review of a decision by the Director of Central Intelligence to terminate an employee in the interests of national security, an area of executive action "in which courts have long been hesitant to intrude." *Franklin v. Massachusetts*, 505 U.S. 788, 819 (1992) (Stevens, J., concurring in part and concurring in judgment).

The allocation of funds from a lump-sum appropriation is another administrative decision traditionally regarded as committed to agency discretion. After all, the very point of a lump-sum appropriation is to give an agency the capacity to adapt to changing circumstances and meet its statutory responsibilities in what it sees as the most effective or desirable way. For this reason, a fundamental principle of appropriations law is that where "Congress merely appropriates lump-sum amounts without statutorily restricting what can be done with those funds, a clear inference arises that it does not intend to impose legally binding restrictions, and indicia in committee reports and other legislative history as to how the funds should or are expected to be spent do not establish any legal requirements on" the agency. *LTV Aerospace Corp.*, 55 Comp. Gen. 307, 319 (1975). Put another way, a lump-sum appropriation reflects a congressional recognition that an agency must be allowed "flexibility to shift . . . funds within a particular . . . appropriation account so that" the agency "can make necessary adjustments for 'unforeseen developments'" and "'changing requirements'" *Id.* at 318 (citation omitted).

Like the decision against instituting enforcement proceedings, then, an agency's allocation of funds from a lump-sum appropriation requires "a complicated balancing of a number of factors which are peculiarly within its expertise": whether its "resources are best spent" on one program or another; whether it "is likely to succeed" in fulfilling its statutory mandate; whether a particular program "best fits the agency's overall policies"; and, "indeed, whether the agency has enough resources" to fund a program "at all." *Heckler*, 470 U.S. at 831. As in *Heckler*, so here, the "agency is far better equipped than the courts to deal with the many variables involved in the proper ordering of its priorities." *Id.* at 831–32. Of course, an agency is not free simply to disregard statutory responsibilities: Congress may always circumscribe agency discretion to allocate resources by putting restrictions in the operative statutes (though not, as we have seen, just in the legislative history). *See id.* at 833. And, of course, we hardly need to note that an agency's decision to ignore congressional expectations may expose it to grave political consequences. But as long as the agency allocates funds from a lump-sum appropriation to meet permissible statutory objectives, § 701(a)(2) gives the courts no leave to intrude. "[T]o [that] extent," the decision to allocate funds "is committed to agency discretion by law." § 701(a)(2).

The Service's decision to discontinue the Program is accordingly unreviewable under § 701(a)(2). As the Court of Appeals recognized, the appropriations Acts for the relevant period do not so much as mention the Program, and both the Snyder Act and the Improvement Act likewise speak about Indian health only in general terms. It is true that the Service repeatedly apprised Congress of the Program's continued operation, but, as we have explained, these representations do not translate through the medium of legislative history into legally binding obligations. The reallocation of agency resources to assist handicapped Indian children nationwide clearly falls within the Service's statutory mandate to provide health care to Indian people, and respondents, indeed, do not seriously contend otherwise. The decision to terminate the Program was committed to the Service's discretion.

* * *

One final note: although respondents claimed in the District Court that the Service's termination of the Program violated their rights under the Fifth Amendment's Due Process Clause, that court expressly declined to address respondents' constitutional arguments, as did the Court of Appeals. Thus, while the APA contemplates, in the absence of a clear expression of contrary congressional intent, that judicial review will be available for colorable constitutional claims, *see Webster*, 486 U.S. at 603–04, the record at this stage does not allow mature consideration of constitutional issues, which we leave for the Court of Appeals on remand.

* * *

The judgment of the Court of Appeals is reversed, and the case is remanded for further proceedings consistent with this opinion.

NOTES AND QUESTIONS

The Court in *Overton Park* described the limitation on judicial review posed by APA § 701(a)(2) in terms of there being "no law to apply." The Court in *Heckler v. Chaney* explained the limitation as applying where a statute offers "no meaningful standard" by which to judge agency action. Justice Scalia's dissenting opinion in *Webster v. Doe* emphasized traditional areas of unreviewability. Recognizing that Justice Souter in *Vigil* wrote on behalf of a unanimous Court and cited all three of these cases, can you reconcile his analysis of the committed to agency discretion limitation of APA § 701(a)(2) with one or more of them? If you were asked to explain when APA § 701(a)(2) applies, how would you answer?

3. AGENCY INACTION

The Court began to apply the powerful presumption of reviewability to agency actions in the late 1960s, and it has continued to apply at least a somewhat weaker version of that presumption to agency actions through the date of publication of this book. The history of the reviewability of agency decisions not to act differs considerably from the history of the reviewability of agency action. Until 1975, the Supreme Court routinely held that agency decisions not to investigate and agency decisions not to bring an enforcement action when the agency has reason to believe that someone has committed a violation of law within its jurisdiction are committed to the agency's unreviewable discretion. The Court interpreted and applied broadly the centuries-old British common law prohibition on review of exercises of prosecutorial discretion even when Congress enacted a statute that used the language of command in an arguable attempt to require prosecution of all offenses within an agency's jurisdiction. For example, in the *Confiscation Cases*, 74 U.S. (7 Wall) 454 (1868), the Court held that a reviewing court cannot require a U.S. Attorney to bring an action to force a property owner to forfeit an asset under statutorily-specified circumstances, even though the statute giving U.S. Attorneys the power to pursue such actions used the language of command by providing that a U.S. Attorney "shall" bring such an action in the specified circumstances.

Beginning in the late 1960s, public interest groups attempted to obtain judicial review of many agency decisions not to act. They argued that the then newly-announced presumption of reviewability should apply to agency decisions not to act, as well as to decisions to act, because many agencies were refusing to take the kinds of aggressive enforcement actions that Congress expected them to take to enforce the many newly-enacted agency-administered statutes that were designed to protect public health, public safety, and the environment. By the time the Supreme Court issued the following opinion in 1975, public interest groups had been successful in persuading some circuit courts to apply the presumption of reviewability to agency decisions not to act.

Dunlop v. Bachowski

421 U.S. 560 (1975).

■ Mr. Justice Brennan delivered the opinion of the Court.

On February 13, 1973, the United Steelworkers of America (USWA) held district officer elections in its several districts. Respondent Bachowski (hereinafter respondent) was defeated by the incumbent in the election for that office in District 20. After exhausting his remedies within USWA, respondent filed a timely complaint with petitioner, the Secretary of Labor, alleging violations of § 401 of the Labor-Management Reporting and Disclosure Act of 1959 (LMRDA), thus invoking 29 U.S.C. §§ 482(a), (b) which require that the Secretary investigate the complaint and decide whether to bring a civil action to set aside the election.[2] * * * With respect to the election in District 20, [the Secretary] advised respondent by letter dated November 7, 1973, that "[b]ased on the investigative findings, it has been determined . . . that civil action to set aside the challenged election is not warranted."

On November 7, 1973, respondent filed this action against the Secretary and USWA in the District Court for the Western District of Pennsylvania. The complaint asked that, among other relief, "the Court declare the actions of the Defendant Secretary to be arbitrary and capricious and order him to file suit to set aside the aforesaid election." The District Court conducted a hearing on November 8, and after argument on the question of reviewability of the Secretary's decision, concluded that the court lacked "authority" to find that the action was capricious and to order him to file suit. The Court of Appeals for the Third Circuit reversed.

The Court of Appeals held, *first*, that the District Court had jurisdiction of respondent's suit under 28 U.S.C. § 1337 as a case arising under an Act of Congress regulating commerce, the LMRDA, *second*, that the Administrative Procedure Act, 5 U.S.C. §§ 702, 704, subjected the Secretary's decision to judicial review as "final agency action for which there is no other adequate remedy in a court," § 704, and that his decision was not, as the Secretary maintained, agency action pursuant to "(1) statutes [that] preclude judicial review; or (2) agency action [that] is committed to agency discretion by law," excepted by § 701(a) from judicial review, and, *third*, that the scope of judicial review—governed by § 706(2)(A), "to ensure that the Secretary's actions are not arbitrary, capricious, or an abuse of discretion,"—entitled respondent, who sought "to challenge the factual basis for [the Secretary's] conclusion either that no violations occurred or that they

---

[2]   Title 29 U.S.C. § 482 provides:

"(a) Filing of complaint; presumption of validity of challenged election.

* * *

"(b) Investigation of complaint; commencement of civil action by Secretary; jurisdiction; preservation of assets.

"The Secretary shall investigate such complaint and, if he finds probable cause to believe that a violation of this subchapter has occurred and has not been remedied, he shall, within sixty days after the filing of such complaint, bring a civil action against the labor organization as an entity in the district court of the United States in which such labor organization maintains its principal office to set aside the invalid election, if any, and to direct the conduct of an election or hearing and vote upon the removal of officers under the supervision of the Secretary. . . ."

did not affect the outcome of the election," "to a sufficiently specific statement of the factors upon which the Secretary relied in reaching his decision . . . so that [respondent] may have information concerning the allegations contained in his complaint." * * *

We agree that 28 U.S.C. § 1337 confers jurisdiction upon the District Court to entertain respondent's suit, and that the Secretary's decision not to sue is not excepted from judicial review by 5 U.S.C. § 701(a); rather, §§ 702 and 704 subject the Secretary's decision to judicial review under the standard specified in § 706(2)(A). We hold, however, that the Court of Appeals erred insofar as its opinion construes § 706(2)(A) to authorize a trial-type inquiry into the factual bases of the Secretary's conclusion that no violations occurred affecting the outcome of the election. * * *

The LMRDA contains no provision that explicitly prohibits judicial review of the decision of the Secretary not to bring a civil action against the union to set aside an allegedly invalid election. * * *

In the absence of an express prohibition in the LMRDA, the Secretary, therefore, bears the heavy burden of overcoming the strong presumption that Congress did not mean to prohibit all judicial review of his decision. "The question is phrased in terms of 'prohibition' rather than 'authorization' because a survey of our cases shows that judicial review of a final agency action by an aggrieved person will not be cut off unless there is persuasive reason to believe that such was the purpose of Congress." *Abbott Labs. v. Gardner*, 387 U.S. 136, 140 (1967). "[O]nly upon a showing of 'clear and convincing evidence' of a contrary legislative intent should the courts restrict access to judicial review." *Id.* at 141; *see also Citizens to Preserve Overton Park v. Volpe*, 401 U.S. 402, 410 (1971).

* * *

Our examination of the relevant materials persuades us, however, that although no purpose to prohibit all judicial review is shown, a congressional purpose narrowly to limit the scope of judicial review of the Secretary's decision can, and should, be inferred in order to carry out congressional objectives in enacting the LMRDA.

Four prior decisions of the Court construing the LMRDA identify the congressional objectives and thus put the scope of permissible judicial review in perspective. Congress "decided to utilize the special knowledge and discretion of the Secretary of Labor in order best to serve the public interest . . . [and] decided not to permit individuals to block or delay union elections by filing federal-court suits. . . ." *Calhoon v. Harvey*, 379 U.S. 134, 140 (1964). Congress' concern was "to settle as quickly as practicable the cloud on the incumbents' titles to office," and in "deliberately [giving] exclusive enforcement authority to the Secretary . . . emphatically asserted a vital public interest in assuring free and democratic union elections that transcends the narrower interest of the complaining union member. . . ." *Wirtz v. Bottle Blowers Ass'n*, 389 U.S. 463, 468 n.7, 473–75 (1968). "[I]t is most improbable that Congress deliberately settled exclusive enforcement jurisdiction on the Secretary and granted him broad investigative powers to discharge his responsibilities, yet intended the shape of the enforcement action to be immutably fixed by the artfulness of a layman's complaint. . . . The expertise and resources of the Labor Department were surely meant to have a broader play. . . ." *Wirtz v. Laborers' Union*, 389 U.S. 477, 482 (1968). ". . . Congress made suit by the Secretary the exclusive post-election remedy for two principal reasons: (1) to protect unions from frivolous litigation and unnecessary judicial interference with their elections, and (2) to centralize in a single proceeding such litigation as might be warranted. . . ." *Trbovich v. Mine Workers*, 404 U.S. 528, 532 (1972). ". . . Congress intended to prevent members from pressing claims not thought meritorious by the Secretary, and from litigating in forums or at times different from those chosen by the Secretary." *Id.* at 536. "[T]he statute gives the individual union members certain rights against their union, and 'the Secretary of Labor in effect becomes the union member's lawyer' for purposes of enforcing those rights. . . ." *Id.* at 538–39.

* * * Section 482(b) leaves to the Secretary, in terms, only the question whether he has probable cause to believe that a violation has occurred, and not the question whether the outcome of the election was probably affected by the violation. *Bottle Blowers* construed § 482(b), however, as conferring upon the Secretary discretion to determine both the probable violation and the probable effect. "[T]he Secretary may not initiate an action until his own investigation confirms that a violation . . . probably infected the challenged election." 389 U.S. at 472.

* * *

Two conclusions follow from this survey of our decisions: (1) since the statute relies upon the special knowledge and discretion of the Secretary for the determination of both the probable violation and the probable effect, clearly the reviewing court is not authorized to substitute its judgment for the decision of the Secretary not to bring suit; (2) therefore, to enable the reviewing court intelligently to review the Secretary's determination, the Secretary must provide the court and the complaining witness with copies of a statement of reasons supporting his determination. "[W]hen action is taken by [the Secretary] it must be such as to enable a reviewing Court to determine with some measure of confidence whether or not the discretion, which still remains in the Secretary, has been exercised in a manner that is neither arbitrary nor capricious. . . . [I]t is necessary for [him] to delineate and make explicit the basis upon which discretionary action is taken, particularly in a case such as this where the decision taken consists of a failure to act after the finding of union election irregularities." *DeVito v. Schultz (DeVito I)*, 300 F. Supp. 381, 383 (D.D.C. 1969).

* * *

The necessity that the reviewing court refrain from substitution of its judgment for that of the Secretary thus helps define the permissible scope of review. Except in what must be the rare case, the court's review should be confined to examination of the "reasons" statement, and the determination whether the statement, without more, evinces that the Secretary's decision is so irrational as to constitute the decision arbitrary and capricious. Thus, review may not extend to cognizance or trial of a complaining member's challenges to the factual bases for the

Secretary's conclusion either that no violations occurred or that they did
not affect the outcome of the election. The full trappings of adversary
trial-type hearings would be defiant of congressional objectives not to
permit individuals to block or delay resolution of post-election disputes,
but rather "to settle as quickly as practicable the cloud on the
incumbents' titles to office"; and "to protect unions from frivolous
litigation and unnecessary interference with their elections." "If . . . the
Court concludes . . . there is a rational and defensible basis [stated in
the reasons statement] for [the Secretary's] determination, then that
should be an end of this matter, for it is not the function of the Court to
determine whether or not the case should be brought or what its
outcome would be." *DeVito v. Schultz (DeVito II)*, 72 L.R.R.M. 2682,
2683 (D.D.C. 1969).

NOTES AND QUESTIONS

1.   The LMRDA instructs DOL to initiate an enforcement proceeding
when it finds "probable cause." In *Bachowski*, the Supreme Court said that
that the LMRDA provides a standard a court can apply to determine
whether the DOL is required to initiate an enforcement proceeding. Indeed,
courts have applied that standard for centuries in the context of searches
and arrests. In such cases, the court asks whether the agency had probable
cause when the agency claims to have had probable cause. In the LMRDA,
a court must ask instead whether an agency had so much evidence of
wrongdoing that it was required to make a probable cause determination.
Can you think of any other context in which a court is required to apply the
"probable cause" standard to an agency that claims that it did not have
probable cause? Is "probable cause" a standard a court can apply in that
context?

2.   Can you reconcile *Bachowski* with the many prior cases in which the
Court had held that exercises of prosecutorial discretion are committed to
the unreviewable discretion of the prosecutor? The Supreme Court did not
even attempt to distinguish the prior cases, but the circuit court attempted
to do so on two grounds. First, Congress used the language of command,
i.e., it provided that the Secretary "shall" bring an enforcement action if he
finds probable cause to believe that the party who prevailed in a union
election had violated the law by engaging in an unfair election practice and
that the violation was determinative of the outcome of the election. Second,
the exclusive remedy provided in the statute was designed to further the
private rights of unsuccessful candidates for union office rather than the
rights of the general public. What do you think of those bases for
distinguishing the many prior cases? Do those reasons suffice to distinguish
the Court's 1868 holding in the *Confiscation Cases*?

3.   The circuit court in *Bachowski* held that the agency must provide a
statement of its reasons for declining to initiate an enforcement proceeding
in response to a complaint and that the reviewing court must then review
the statement of reasons to determine whether the agency decision was
consistent with the statute and was not arbitrary and capricious. The
circuit court also held that the agency or the reviewing court must conduct
a hearing to determine whether the reasons given by the agency are
consistent with the facts. The Supreme Court upheld the circuit court with
respect to the reviewability of the class of agency actions at issue, the
requirement that the agency provide a statement of reasons, and the duty

of a court to review the statement of reasons. The Supreme Court rejected, however, the mandatory hearing part of the remedy ordered by the circuit court. Do you understand why that remedy was inconsistent with the purposes of the statute? How effective is the mandatory statement of reasons remedy if the agency can state reasons that accord with the statute but that are inconsistent with the underlying facts? How far can courts go in forcing agencies to act? If the agency devotes inadequate resources to an investigation or prosecution, can a court order the agency to increase the quantity and/or quality of the resources it commits?

4. Like all agencies, the LMRDA enforcement section within the Department of Labor does not have anywhere near the resources needed to bring an enforcement action in every case in which it has reason to believe that someone has violated the LMRDA. Assume that you are head of the LMRDA enforcement section and that you have enough resources to bring an enforcement action in ten percent of the cases in which you believe that someone violated the LMRDA. Assume further that you have just completed an informal preliminary investigation of a complaint in which an unsuccessful candidate for office in a local chapter of a union alleged that the leadership of the union allowed large numbers of members to transfer from one local to another immediately prior to the election in a successful attempt to defeat the candidate who filed the complaint. Your informal preliminary investigation persuades you that the practice of permitting transfers on the eve of an election to change the result is an unfair election practice and that use of that practice changed the outcome of the election in the case that is the subject of the investigation. Assume finally that your agency has never previously stated that such eve-of-election transfers are an unfair election practice; your agency has received recent complaints about several other practices that are far worse and that you had previously declared to be unlawful; and your agency has enough resources to bring enforcement actions in only a fraction of those cases. You respond to the complaint with an accurate recitation of those facts and with announcement of a decision not to bring an enforcement action in response to the complaint. You explain your decision by stating that (1) you have concluded that the practice of allowing eve-of-election transfers is an unfair election practice; (2) in the future you will bring enforcement actions in cases in which unions change election results through use of that practice; (3) you are not going to bring an enforcement action in this case partly because you had not previously placed unions on notice that the practice was unlawful and partly because you have decided to commit your scarce resources to other cases in which the conduct that was the subject of the complaint was clearly unlawful and was particularly egregious. Should you be praised or condemned for taking that approach?

In *Shelley v. Brock*, 793 F.2d 1368 (D.C. Cir. 1986), on facts identical to those hypothesized above, the D.C. Circuit applied *Bachowski* and held that the agency has discretion not to bring an enforcement action in response to a complaint of an alleged violation of the LMRDA only if it finds either that there is no probable cause to believe that the conduct complained of is unlawful or that there is no probable cause to believe that the conduct determined the outcome of the election. The D.C. Circuit held that the agency was required to initiate an enforcement action in response to the complaint, since the agency expressed its belief that the conduct at issue was unlawful and that it was determinative of the outcome of the election. After *Bachowski* and *Shelley*, what must the agency say to avoid judicial reversal when it decides not to initiate an enforcement proceeding? Will that statement be accurate in all cases? Do you like the effects of *Bachowski* and *Shelley*?

———————

Many circuit courts interpreted *Bachowski* broadly and ordered agencies to take actions they did not want to take, much to the delight of many public interest groups, until the Supreme Court issued the following opinion. The opinion resolved a dispute that was the subject of great controversy within the public interest law community. The case began as a result of a petition filed by public interest groups that want to stop the use of the death penalty. Other public interest groups that are committed to improving environmental and health regulation tried unsuccessfully to persuade the advocates of abolition of the death penalty not to file the petition. They feared that the Supreme Court, now under the leadership of Justices more conservative then the Justices who decided *Bachowski*, would issue the kind of opinion that the Court issued, thereby depriving the public interest groups of one of their most valued legal weapons.

Heckler v. Chaney

470 U.S. 821 (1985).

■ JUSTICE REHNQUIST delivered the opinion of the Court.

This case presents the question of the extent to which a decision of an administrative agency to exercise its "discretion" not to undertake certain enforcement actions is subject to judicial review under the Administrative Procedure Act. Respondents are several prison inmates convicted of capital offenses and sentenced to death by lethal injection of drugs. They petitioned the Food and Drug Administration (FDA), alleging that under the circumstances the use of these drugs for capital punishment violated the Federal Food, Drug, and Cosmetic Act and requesting that the FDA take various enforcement actions to prevent these violations. The FDA refused their request. We review here a decision of the Court of Appeals for the District of Columbia Circuit, which held the FDA's refusal to take enforcement actions both reviewable and an abuse of discretion, and remanded the case with directions that the agency be required "to fulfill its statutory function."

Respondents have been sentenced to death by lethal injection of drugs under the laws of the States of Oklahoma and Texas. Those States, and several others, have recently adopted this method for carrying out the capital sentence. Respondents first petitioned the FDA, claiming that the drugs used by the States for this purpose, although approved by the FDA for the medical purposes stated on their labels, were not approved for use in human executions. They alleged that the drugs had not been tested for the purpose for which they were to be used, and that, given that the drugs would likely be administered by untrained personnel, it was also likely that the drugs would not induce the quick and painless death intended. They urged that use of these drugs for human execution was the "unapproved use of an approved drug" and constituted a violation of the Act's prohibitions against "misbranding." * * * They therefore requested the FDA to take various investigatory and enforcement actions to prevent these perceived violations. * * *

The FDA Commissioner responded, refusing to take the requested actions. The Commissioner first detailed his disagreement with respondents' understanding of the scope of FDA jurisdiction over the unapproved use of approved drugs for human execution, concluding that FDA jurisdiction in the area was generally unclear but in any event should not be exercised to interfere with this particular aspect of state criminal justice systems. He went on to state:

> "Were FDA clearly to have jurisdiction in the area, moreover, we believe we would be authorized to decline to exercise it under our inherent discretion to decline to pursue certain enforcement matters. The unapproved use of approved drugs is an area in which the case law is far from uniform. Generally, enforcement proceedings in this area are initiated only when there is a serious danger to the public health or a blatant scheme to defraud. We cannot conclude that those dangers are present under State lethal injection laws, which are duly authorized statutory enactments in furtherance of proper State functions. . . ."

Respondents then filed the instant suit in the United States District Court for the District of Columbia, claiming the same violations of the FDCA and asking that the FDA be required to take the same enforcement actions requested in the prior petition. The District Court granted summary judgment for petitioner. It began with the proposition that "decisions of executive departments and agencies to *refrain* from instituting investigative and enforcement proceedings are essentially unreviewable by the courts." * * *

A divided panel of the Court of Appeals for the District of Columbia Circuit [held that the FDA decision was reviewable and set aside that decision.] The majority began by discussing the FDA's jurisdiction over the unapproved use of approved drugs for human execution, and concluded that the FDA did have jurisdiction over such a use. The court then addressed the Government's assertion of unreviewable discretion to refuse enforcement action. It first discussed this Court's opinions which have held that there is a general presumption that all agency decisions are reviewable under the APA, at least to assess whether the actions were "arbitrary, capricious, or an abuse of discretion." It noted that the APA, 5 U.S.C. § 701, only precludes judicial review of final agency action—including refusals to act, *see* 5 U.S.C. § 551(13)—when review is precluded by statute, or "committed to agency discretion by law." Citing this Court's opinions in *Dunlop v. Bachowski*, 421 U.S. 560 (1975), and *Citizens to Preserve Overton Park v. Volpe*, 401 U.S. 402 (1971), for the view that these exceptions should be narrowly construed, the court held that the "committed to agency discretion by law" exception of § 701(a)(2) should be invoked only where the substantive statute left the courts with "no law to apply." The court cited *Dunlop* as holding that this presumption "applies with no less force to review of . . . agency decisions to refrain from enforcement action."

The court found "law to apply" in the form of a FDA policy statement which indicated that the agency was "obligated" to investigate the unapproved use of an approved drug when such use became "widespread" or "endanger[ed] the public health." The court held that this policy statement constituted a "rule" and was considered binding by the FDA. Given the policy statement indicating that the FDA should take enforcement action in this area, and the strong presumption that all agency action is subject to judicial review, the court concluded that review of the agency's refusal was not foreclosed. It then proceeded to assess whether the agency's decision not to act was "arbitrary, capricious, or an abuse of discretion." Citing evidence that the FDA assumed jurisdiction over drugs used to put animals to sleep and the unapproved uses of drugs on prisoners in clinical experiments, the court found that the FDA's refusal, for the reasons given, was irrational, and that respondents' evidence that use of the drugs could lead to a cruel and protracted death was entitled to more searching consideration. The court therefore remanded the case to the District Court, to order the FDA "to fulfill its statutory function."

* * *

The APA's comprehensive provisions for judicial review of "agency actions," are contained in 5 U.S.C. §§ 701–706. Any person "adversely affected or aggrieved" by agency action; *see* § 702, including a "failure to act," is entitled to "judicial review thereof," as long as the action is a "final agency action for which there is no other adequate remedy in a court," *see* § 704. The standards to be applied on review are governed by the provisions of § 706. But before any review at all may be had, a party must first clear the hurdle of § 701(a). That section provides that the chapter on judicial review "applies, according to the provisions thereof, except to the extent that—(1) statutes preclude judicial review; or (2) agency action is committed to agency discretion by law." Petitioner urges that the decision of the FDA to refuse enforcement is an action "committed to agency discretion by law" under § 701(a)(2).

This Court has not had occasion to interpret this second exception in § 701(a) in any great detail. On its face, the section does not obviously lend itself to any particular construction; indeed, one might wonder what difference exists between § (a)(1) and § (a)(2). The former section seems easy in application; it requires construction of the substantive statute involved to determine whether Congress intended to preclude judicial review of certain decisions. * * * But one could read the language "committed to agency discretion *by law*" in § (a)(2) to require a similar inquiry. In addition, commentators have pointed out that construction of § (a)(2) is further complicated by the tension between a literal reading of § (a)(2), which exempts from judicial review those decisions committed to agency "discretion," and the primary scope of review prescribed by § 706(2)(A)—whether the agency's action was "arbitrary, capricious, or an *abuse of discretion*." How is it, they ask, that an action committed to agency discretion can be unreviewable and yet courts still can review agency actions for abuse of that discretion? * * *

This Court first discussed § (a)(2) in *Citizens to Preserve Overton Park v. Volpe*, 401 U.S. 402 (1971). * * * After setting out the language of § 701(a), the Court stated:

* * *

[T]he Secretary's decision here does not fall within the exception for action 'committed to agency discretion.' This is a very narrow exception.... The legislative history of the Administrative Procedure Act indicates that it is applicable in those rare instances where 'statutes are drawn in such broad terms that in a given case there is no law to apply.' *Overton Park*, 401 U.S. at 410 (quoting S. REP. NO. 752, 79th Cong., 1st Sess., at 26 (1945)).

* * *

To this point our analysis does not differ significantly from that of the Court of Appeals. That court purported to apply the "no law to apply" standard of *Overton Park*. We disagree, however, with that court's insistence that the "narrow construction" of § (a)(2) required application of a presumption of reviewability even to an agency's decision not to undertake certain enforcement actions. Here we think the Court of Appeals broke with tradition, case law, and sound reasoning.

Overton Park did not involve an agency's refusal to take requested enforcement action. It involved an affirmative act of approval under a statute that set clear guidelines for determining when such approval should be given. Refusals to take enforcement steps generally involve precisely the opposite situation, and in that situation we think the presumption is that judicial review is not available. This Court has recognized on several occasions over many years that an agency's decision not to prosecute or enforce, whether through civil or criminal process, is a decision generally committed to an agency's absolute discretion. This recognition of the existence of discretion is attributable in no small part to the general unsuitability for judicial review of agency decisions to refuse enforcement.

The reasons for this general unsuitability are many. First, an agency decision not to enforce often involves a complicated balancing of a number of factors which are peculiarly within its expertise. Thus, the agency must not only assess whether a violation has occurred, but whether agency resources are best spent on this violation or another, whether the agency is likely to succeed if it acts, whether the particular enforcement action requested best fits the agency's overall policies, and, indeed, whether the agency has enough resources to undertake the action at all. An agency generally cannot act against each technical violation of the statute it is charged with enforcing. The agency is far better equipped than the courts to deal with the many variables involved in the proper ordering of its priorities. Similar concerns animate the principles of administrative law that courts generally will defer to an agency's construction of the statute it is charged with implementing, and to the procedures it adopts for implementing that statute.

* * *

We of course only list the above concerns to facilitate understanding of our conclusion that an agency's decision not to take enforcement action should be presumed immune from judicial review under § 701(a)(2). For good reasons, such a decision has traditionally been "committed to agency discretion," and we believe that the Congress enacting the APA did not intend to alter that tradition. In so stating, we emphasize that the decision is only presumptively unreviewable; the presumption may be rebutted where the substantive statute has provided guidelines for the agency to follow in exercising its enforcement powers.[4] Thus, in establishing this presumption in the APA, Congress did not set agencies free to disregard legislative direction in the statutory scheme that the agency administers. Congress may limit an agency's exercise of enforcement power if it wishes, either by setting substantive priorities, or by otherwise circumscribing an agency's power to discriminate among issues or cases it will pursue. How to determine when Congress has done so is the question left open by *Overton Park*.

Dunlop v. Bachowski, 421 U.S. 560 (1975), relied upon heavily by respondents and the majority in the Court of Appeals, presents an example of statutory language which supplied sufficient standards to rebut the presumption of unreviewability. * * * This Court held that review was available. It rejected the Secretary's argument that the statute precluded judicial review, and in a footnote it stated its agreement with the conclusion of the Court of Appeals that the decision was not "an unreviewable exercise of prosecutorial discretion." 421 U.S. at 567 n.7. Our textual references to the "strong presumption" of reviewability in *Dunlop* were addressed only to the § (a)(1) exception; we were content to rely on the Court of Appeals' opinion to hold that the § (a)(2) exception did not apply. The Court of Appeals, in turn, had found the "principle of absolute prosecutorial discretion" inapplicable, because the language of the LMRDA indicated that the Secretary was required to file suit if certain "clearly defined" factors were present. The decision therefore was not " 'beyond the judicial capacity to supervise.' " *Bachowski v. Brennan*, 502 F.2d 79, 87–88 (3rd Cir. 1974).

Dunlop is thus consistent with a general presumption of unreviewability of decisions not to enforce. The statute being administered quite clearly withdrew discretion from the agency and provided guidelines for exercise of its enforcement power. Our decision that review was available was not based on "pragmatic considerations," such as those cited by the Court of Appeals that amount to an assessment of whether the interests at stake are important enough to justify intervention in the agencies' decisionmaking. The danger that agencies may not carry out their delegated powers with sufficient vigor does not necessarily lead to the conclusion that courts are the most appropriate body to police this aspect of their performance. That decision is in the first instance for Congress, and we therefore turn to the FDCA to determine whether in this case Congress has provided us with "law to apply." If it has indicated an intent to circumscribe agency enforcement discretion, and has provided meaningful standards for

---

[4] We do not have in this case a refusal by the agency to institute proceedings based solely on the belief that it lacks jurisdiction. Nor do we have a situation where it could justifiably be found that the agency has "consciously and expressly adopted a general policy" that is so extreme as to amount to an abdication of its statutory responsibilities. *See, e.g., Adams v. Richardson*, 480 F.2d 1159 (1973) (en banc). Although we express no opinion on whether such decisions would be unreviewable under § 701(a)(2), we note that in those situations the statute conferring authority on the agency might indicate that such decisions were not "committed to agency discretion."

defining the limits of that discretion, there is "law to apply" under § 701(a)(2), and courts may require that the agency follow that law; if it has not, then an agency refusal to institute proceedings is a decision "committed to agency discretion by law" within the meaning of that section.

To enforce the various substantive prohibitions contained in the FDCA, the Act provides for injunctions, criminal sanctions, and seizure of any offending food, drug, or cosmetic article. The Act's general provision for enforcement provides only that "[t]he Secretary is *authorized* to conduct examinations and investigations . . ." 21 U.S.C. § 332 (emphasis added). Unlike the statute at issue in *Dunlop*, § 332 gives no indication of when an injunction should be sought, and § 334, providing for seizures, is framed in the permissive—the offending food, drug, or cosmetic "shall be liable to be proceeded against." The section on criminal sanctions states baldly that any person who violates the Act's substantive prohibitions "shall be imprisoned . . . or fined." Respondents argue that this statement mandates criminal prosecution of every violator of the Act but they adduce no indication in case law or legislative history that such was Congress' intention in using this language, which is commonly found in the criminal provisions of Title 18 of the United States Code. We are unwilling to attribute such a sweeping meaning to this language, particularly since the Act charges the Secretary only with recommending prosecution; any criminal prosecutions must be instituted by the Attorney General. The Act's enforcement provisions thus commit complete discretion to the Secretary to decide how and when they should be exercised.

* * *

We also find singularly unhelpful the agency "policy statement" on which the Court of Appeals placed great reliance. We would have difficulty with this statement's vague language even if it were a properly adopted agency rule. Although the statement indicates that the agency considered itself "obligated" to take certain investigative actions, that language did not arise in the course of discussing the agency's discretion to exercise its enforcement power, but rather in the context of describing agency policy with respect to unapproved uses of approved drugs by physicians. In addition, if read to circumscribe agency enforcement discretion, the statement conflicts with the agency rule on judicial review, which states that "[t]he Commissioner shall object to judicial review . . . if (i) [t]he matter is committed by law to the discretion of the Commissioner, *e.g.*, a decision to recommend or not to recommend civil or criminal enforcement action. . . ." 21 C.F.R. § 10.45(d)(2) (1984).

Respondents' third argument, based upon § 306 of the FDCA, merits only slightly more consideration. That section provides:

> "Nothing in this chapter shall be construed as requiring the Secretary to report for prosecution, or for the institution of libel or injunction proceedings, minor violations of this chapter whenever he believes that the public interest will be adequately served by a suitable written notice or ruling." 21 U.S.C. § 336.

Respondents seek to draw from this section the negative implication that the Secretary is *required* to report for prosecution all "major" violations of the Act, however those might be defined, and that it therefore supplies the needed indication of an intent to limit agency enforcement discretion. We think that this section simply does not give rise to the negative implication which respondents seek to draw from it. The section is not addressed to agency proceedings designed to discover the existence of violations, but applies only to a situation where a violation has already been established to the satisfaction of the agency. We do not believe the section speaks to the criteria which shall be used by the agency for investigating *possible* violations of the Act.

We therefore conclude that the presumption that agency decisions not to institute proceedings are unreviewable under 5 U.S.C. § 701(a)(2) is not overcome by the enforcement provisions of the FDCA. The FDA's decision not to take the enforcement actions requested by respondents is therefore not subject to judicial review under the APA. The general exception to reviewability provided by § 701(a)(2) for action "committed to agency discretion" remains a narrow one, but within that exception are included agency refusals to institute investigative or enforcement proceedings, unless Congress has indicated otherwise. In so holding, we essentially leave to Congress, and not to the courts, the decision as to whether an agency's refusal to institute proceedings should be judicially reviewable. No colorable claim is made in this case that the agency's refusal to institute proceedings violated any constitutional rights of respondents, and we do not address the issue that would be raised in such a case.

NOTES AND QUESTIONS

1. In both *Bachowski* and *Chaney*, the Supreme Court considered at some length whether Congress spoke in permissive or commanding terms in the statutes at issue. In comparing the Court's analysis of the two statutes, do you find that the Court gives the language of command, *i.e.*, statements that the agency "shall" undertake some action, the same effect in both cases?

2. The Court in *Chaney* seems to acknowledge implicitly that the presumption of unreviewability of agency inaction may in some instances be rebutted by a legislative rule that couples the language of command with a justiciable standard. For example, an agency might adopt a legislative rule providing that the agency "shall initiate an investigation when it receives any complaint that. . . ." Circuit courts have interpreted the Court's opinion in *Chaney* as allowing regulated parties to assert an agency's own regulations in rebutting the presumption of unreviewability. *See, e.g., Greater Los Angeles Council on Deafness v. Baldrige*, 827 F.2d 1353, 1361 (9th Cir. 1987). Of course, judicial decisions that give this effect to legislative rules essentially require agencies to commit themselves to take specific actions in specific circumstances. Given that legislative rules have the same binding legal effect as statutes in governing the actions of agencies as well as regulated parties, does it make sense to give legislative rules the same effect as statutes for purposes of rebutting the presumption of unreviewability of agency inaction?

3. In the *Chaney* case, the D.C. Circuit gave the FDA's policy statement with respect to drugs used for unapproved purposes the effect of a legislative rule that bound the agency to act in the circumstances presented. The Supreme Court reversed the D.C. Circuit on that issue. Looking back upon our discussion of policy statements in Chapters 5 and 6, do you understand why a policy statement can never rebut the presumption of unreviewability? Do you understand why the particular policy statement at issue could not rebut the presumption even if it had been a legislative rule?

4. FDA has long struggled to address the problems presented by unapproved uses of approved drugs. It does not like the practice, but it has been both unable and unwilling to stop the practice. About 25% of all prescriptions are for unapproved uses of drugs that FDA approved for other uses. FDA prohibits pharmaceutical companies from promoting the use of drugs for unapproved uses. FDA cannot stop doctors from prescribing drugs for unapproved uses, however, because it does not have the power to regulate the practice of medicine. Even if the FDA had that power, it would not exercise its power in all cases. It is quite common for doctors and medical researchers to discover a drug that has been approved for one purpose is effective for a different purpose. The firm that markets the drug can go through the process of obtaining FDA approval of the drug for that newly-discovered use. Firms often go through that process in order to be able to promote a drug for a newly-discovered use. The approval process is very long and expensive, however, so firms sometimes choose not apply for approval for a new use even when many doctors are prescribing the drug for that use. Moreover, the approval process often requires many years to complete, so a drug often is prescribed for unapproved uses for years before the firm that makes the drug obtains approval for the new use. In this complicated situation, it is not surprising that FDA does not bind itself to take any specific action in specific circumstances. FDA asserts the discretion to take unspecified actions to stop unapproved uses of an approved drug when it concludes that public health considerations justify some form of action, *e.g.*, when it discovers that a drug is being widely prescribed for uses for which it is unsuited because its risks far outweigh its benefits.

In addition to whether agency regulations can rebut the presumption that agency decisions not to act are unreviewable, the Court left open many other questions about the scope of that presumption. Under what circumstances (if ever) is an agency's refusal to issue a rule or initiate a rulemaking subject to judicial review? What if an agency begins a rulemaking process but then decides to suspend the process, or initially pursues an enforcement action but then withdraws its complaint? Can a court ever claim broad supervisory authority over an agency based on the agency's conscious and systematic refusal to enforce a statute? The D.C. Circuit addressed one of the most important of those questions in the following opinion.

American Horse Protection Ass'n, Inc. v. Lyng

812 F.2d 1 (D.C. Cir. 1987).

■ WILLIAMS, CIRCUIT JUDGE:

The regulations at issue concern the practice of deliberately injuring show horses to improve their performance in the ring. This practice, called soring, may involve fastening heavy chains or similar equipment, called action devices, on a horse's front limbs. As a result of wearing action devices, the horse may suffer intense pain as its forefeet touch the ground. This pain causes it to adopt a high-stepping gait that is highly prized in Tennessee walking horses and certain other breeds. In the Horse Protection Act, Congress sought to end this practice by forbidding the showing or selling of sored horses. 15 U.S.C. §§ 1821–24. Exercising broadly phrased rulemaking power under 15 U.S.C. § 1828, the Secretary issued regulations that prohibited soring devices and other soring methods in both general and specific terms. The general prohibition, 9 C.F.R. § 11.2(a) (1986), states:

> Notwithstanding the provisions of paragraph (b) of this section [containing specific prohibitions], no chain, boot, roller, collar, action device, nor any other device, method, practice, or substance shall be used with respect to any horse at any horse show, horse exhibition, or horse sale or auction if such use causes or can reasonably be expected to cause such horse to be sore.

The regulations' specific prohibitions include the use of chains weighing more than eight or ten ounces (depending on the age of the horse), rollers weighing more than fourteen ounces, and certain padded shoes on young horses. *Id.* § 11.2(b). Lighter chains and rollers are not specifically prohibited.

Use of action devices in violation of either the general or specific prohibitions is unlawful and may subject the violator to both criminal and civil penalties. Under the general prohibition, however, there is no penalty unless the use of the device is shown to have caused soreness or the device can "reasonably be expected to cause" soreness. Use of pain killers may make detection of actual soring difficult. The regulations give no guidance as to when a device not specifically prohibited may reasonably be expected to cause soreness. There are no such definitional difficulties, of course, when a violation involves a device specifically prohibited.

The Association here contends that developments since these regulations were originally promulgated have demonstrated their inadequacy and that, accordingly, the Secretary should revise them in a new rulemaking. In fact, in its original rulemaking the agency made quite clear its recognition that the premises for not enacting broader specific prohibitions might erode. In its notice of proposed rulemaking, it stated that it relied on evidence from three test clinics which appeared to exonerate action devices weighing less than those that it proposed to forbid. When the final rule was issued, the agency stated that it would consider prohibiting all action devices and padded shoes if the practice of soring continued. At the same time it also mentioned that the agency had recently commissioned "a study of soring methods and techniques at a major university" that might eventually result in further changes in the regulations. 44 Fed. Reg. 25,172, at 25,174 (1979).

This study was conducted at the Auburn University School of Veterinary Medicine between September 1978 and December 1982. The Auburn study evaluated use of eight-and ten-ounce chains and fourteen-ounce rollers—devices that the agency had declined to prohibit on the grounds that they did not cause soring when properly used under actual training conditions. The study concluded that ten-ounce chains caused lesions, bleeding, edema, and inflammation. It also considered the effects of eight-and ten-ounce chains and fourteen-ounce rollers on scarred horses, and found that these devices caused raw lesions. The effects of these devices thus fell within the statutory definition of sore. * * * The Association relies on these results in challenging the Agriculture Department's regulations.

* * *

The reviewability of a refusal to institute a rulemaking has been a source of some uncertainty since the Supreme Court held refusals to take ad hoc enforcement steps presumptively unreviewable in *Heckler v. Chaney*, 470 U.S. 821 (1985). Although the Court expressly noted that *Chaney* did not "involve the question of agency discretion not to invoke rulemaking proceedings," *id*. at 825 n.2, its reasoning applies to some extent to a refusal to institute a rulemaking. Our examination of *Chaney* persuades us, however, that it does not bar review of the agency's decision here.

The *Chaney* Court relied on three features of nonenforcement decisions in arriving at its negative presumption. First, such decisions require a high level of agency expertise and coordination in setting priorities. Second, the agency in such situations will not ordinarily be exercising "its *coercive* power over an individual's liberty or property rights." *Id*. at 832 (emphasis in original). Third, such nonenforcement decisions are akin to prosecutorial decisions not to indict, which traditionally involve executive control and judicial restraint. The first and second of these features are likely to be involved in an agency's refusal to institute a rulemaking, but the third is another matter.

Chaney says little about this third feature. To a degree, of course, it recapitulates and underscores the prior points about resource allocation and non-coercion. The analogy between prosecutorial discretion and agency nonenforcement is strengthened, however, by two other shared characteristics. First, both prosecutors and agencies constantly make decisions not to take enforcement steps; such decisions thus are numerous. Second, both types of nonenforcement are typically based mainly on close consideration of the facts of the case at hand, rather than on legal analysis. Refusals to institute rulemakings, by contrast, are likely to be relatively infrequent and more likely to turn upon issues of law. This analysis of the third *Chaney* feature finds support in the Court's distinguishing of cases where an agency "has 'consciously and expressly adopted a general policy' that is so extreme as to amount to an abdication of its statutory responsibilities." *Id*. at 833 n.4. Such abdications are likely both to be infrequent and to turn on matters remote from the specific facts of individual cases.

Furthermore, the Administrative Procedure Act serves to distinguish between *Chaney* nonenforcement decisions and refusals to institute rulemakings. The *Chaney* Court noted that "when an agency *does* act to enforce, that action itself provides a focus for judicial review" since a court can "at least . . . determine whether the agency exceeded its statutory powers." APA provisions governing agency refusals to initiate rulemakings give a similar focal point. The APA requires agencies to allow interested persons to "petition for the issuance, amendment, or repeal of a rule," 5 U.S.C. § 553(e) (1982), and, when such petitions are denied, to give "a brief statement of the grounds for denial," *id.* § 555(e). These two provisions suggest that Congress expected that agencies denying rulemaking petitions must explain their actions.

Thus, refusals to institute rulemaking proceedings are distinguishable from other sorts of nonenforcement decisions insofar as they are less frequent, more apt to involve legal as opposed to factual analysis, and subject to special formalities, including a public explanation. *Chaney* therefore does not appear to overrule our prior decisions allowing review of agency refusals to institute rulemakings.

The District Court was thus correct in finding that this case requires a determination of whether the Secretary's failure to act was "arbitrary, capricious, an abuse of discretion, or otherwise not in accordance with law." Review under the "arbitrary and capricious" tag line, however, encompasses a range of levels of deference to the agency, and *Chaney* surely reinforces our frequent statements that an agency's refusal to institute rulemaking proceedings is at the high end of the range. Such a refusal is to be overturned "only in the rarest and most compelling of circumstances," *WWHT, Inc. v. FCC*, 656 F.2d 807, 817 (D.C. Cir. 1981), which have primarily involved "plain errors of law, suggesting that the agency has been blind to the source of its delegated power." *State Farm Mut. Auto. Ins. Co. v. Dep't of Transp.*, 680 F.2d 206, 221 (D.C. Cir. 1982), *vacated on other grounds*, 463 U.S. 29 (1983).

[The court went on to hold that the agency's refusal to initiate a rulemaking in response to the petition for rulemaking was arbitrary and capricious because the agency had not complied with the duty to engage in reasoned decisionmaking the Supreme Court announced in *State Farm*, which we discuss at length in Part C of Chapter 5. Ed.]

NOTES AND QUESTIONS

1. A five-Justice majority expressed its approval of the reasoning and holding in *AHPA v. Lyng* in the global warming case, *Massachusetts v. EPA*, 549 U.S. 497 (2007). As we discuss in Part C of this Chapter, the majority went on to hold that Massachusetts had standing to obtain review of the EPA's decision not to initiate a rulemaking to determine limits on automobile emissions of global warming gases in response to a petition to conduct such a rulemaking, and also to hold that the EPA was arbitrary and capricious in denying that petition for rulemaking. In so doing, the majority adopted the holding and reasoning of the D.C. Circuit in *AHPA v. Lyng*.

As we have repeated time and again, an agency has broad discretion to choose how best to marshal its limited resources and personnel to carry out its delegated responsibilities. That discretion is at its height when the agency decides not to bring an enforcement action. Therefore, in *Heckler v. Chaney*, 470 U.S. 821 (1985), we held that an agency's refusal to initiate enforcement proceedings is not ordinarily subject to judicial review. Some debate remains, however, as to the rigor with which we review an agency's denial of a petition for rulemaking.

There are key differences between a denial of a petition for rulemaking and an agency's decision not to initiate an enforcement action. *See Am. Horse Protection Ass'n, Inc. v. Lyng*, 812 F.2d 1, 3–4 (D.C. Cir. 1987). In contrast to nonenforcement decisions, agency refusals to initiate rulemaking "are less frequent, more apt to involve legal as opposed to factual analysis, and subject to special formalities, including a public explanation." *Id.* at 4. They moreover arise out of denials of petitions for rulemaking which (at least in the circumstances here) the affected party had an undoubted procedural right to file in the first instance. Refusals to promulgate rules are thus susceptible to judicial review, though such review is "extremely limited" and "highly deferential." *Nat'l Customs Brokers & Forwarders Ass'n of Am., Inc. v. United States*, 883 F.2d 93, 96 (D.C. Cir. 1989).

EPA concluded in its denial of the petition for rulemaking that it lacked authority under 42 U.S.C. § 7521(a)(1) to regulate new vehicle emissions because carbon dioxide is not an "air pollutant" as that term is defined in § 7602. In the alternative, it concluded that even if it possessed authority, it would decline to do so because regulation would conflict with other administration priorities. As discussed earlier, the Clean Air Act expressly permits review of such an action. § 7607(b)(1). We therefore "may reverse any such action found to be . . . arbitrary, capricious, an abuse of discretion, or otherwise not in accordance with law." § 7607(d)(9).

Massachusetts v. EPA, 549 U.S. at 527–28. Writing on behalf of four Justices in dissent, Justice Scalia did not explicitly refer to the majority's adoption of *AHPA v. Lyng*, so it may be that there was no difference of opinion among the Justices on that question. Justice Scalia's opinion was hardly the picture of clarity, however, regarding the reviewability of the EPA's inaction. At one point, Justice Scalia opined,

I am willing to assume, for the sake of argument, that the Administrator's discretion in this regard is not entirely unbounded—that if he has no reasonable basis for deferring judgment he must grasp the nettle at once.

Id. at 550 (Scalia, J., dissenting). These words would seem to suggest the dissenters' support for reviewability, else how could the Court determine whether or not the Administrator had a reasonable basis for deferring judgment? Indeed, Justice Scalia went on to find the reasons offered by the Administrator for not acting presently to be "perfectly valid." In the same part of his opinion, however, Justice Scalia offered the following analysis.

As the Court recognizes, the statute "condition[s] the exercise of EPA's authority on its formation of a 'judgment.'" There is no dispute that the Administrator has made no such judgment in this case.

The question thus arises: Does anything *require* the Administrator to make a "judgment" whenever a petition for rulemaking is filed? Without citation of the statute or any other authority, the Court says yes. Why is that so? When Congress wishes to make private action force an agency's hand, it knows how to do so. Where does the CAA say that the EPA Administrator is required to come to a decision on this question whenever a rulemaking petition is filed? The Court points to no such provision because none exists.

* * *

EPA's interpretation of the discretion conferred by the statutory reference to "its judgment" is not only reasonable, it is the most natural reading of the text. The Court nowhere explains why this interpretation is incorrect, let alone why it is not entitled to deference under *Chevron, U.S.A., Inc. v. Natural Res. Def. Council, Inc.*, 467 U.S. 837 (1984). As the Administrator acted within the law in declining to make a "judgment" for the policy reasons above set forth, I would uphold the decision to deny the rulemaking petition on that ground alone.

Id. at 549–53. Would you read this language from Justice Scalia's dissenting opinion in *Massachusetts v. EPA* unequivocally as an endorsement of judicial review of agency decisions not to pursue a rulemaking? Why or why not?

2.   It is now easy to obtain review of an agency's denial of a petition for rulemaking, but it remains extremely difficult to persuade a reviewing court to overturn such a decision. Imagine that you are an agency lawyer who is given responsibility to explain why your agency has decided to deny a petition for rulemaking addressed to a problem that is clearly exists and that is within your agency's jurisdiction. How would you go about that task? Hint: it is often a good idea to quote Supreme Court opinions when you try to defend your agency's actions. Are there passages in the Court's opinion in *Chenery II* [discussed beginning on page 371 of this casebook] that you can combine with passages from the Court's opinion in *Chaney* to draft an explanation that is likely to be effective in most circumstances?

DISCUSSION PROBLEM

The Occupational Safety and Health Act grants the Secretary of Labor the authority to promulgate workplace health and safety standards. More specifically, it provides that the Secretary "may by rule promulgate, modify, or revoke any occupational safety or health standard" according to a process prescribed by statute. That process includes that he "may request the recommendations of" an advisory committee regarding proposed rules "[w]henever [he] . . . determines that a rule should be promulgated." After the Secretary appoints an advisory committee and determines that a rule should be issued, the statute states that "he shall publish the proposed rule within sixty days after the submission of the advisory committee's recommendations. . . ." Once the Secretary issues a proposed standard, the statute provides that he "shall afford interested persons a period of thirty days after publication to submit written data or comments" and that, "[w]ithin sixty days after" the expiration of that comment period, "the Secretary shall issue a rule promulgating . . . an occupational safety or health standard or make a determination that a rule should not be issued." 29 U.S.C. § 655(b).

X is an organization that represents agricultural workers. X petitioned the Secretary of Labor to adopt a field sanitation standard requiring employers to provide workers in the fields with access to drinking water, handwashing facilities, and portable toilets. The Secretary did not respond, and one year later, X brought suit to compel the Secretary to issue the standard. After the suit was filed, the Secretary referred X's petition to an advisory committee, which timely responded with a proposed standard. The Secretary failed to act upon the committee's recommendation, however, so after yet another year, a federal district court ordered the Secretary to proceed within statutory time limits toward publishing final field sanitation standards. On appeal, the circuit court held that the federal district court exceeded its authority but, citing *Heckler v. Chaney*, concluded that the Secretary's discretion was not limitless, so it remanded the case to the district court for further proceedings. Some months thereafter, the Secretary published a notice of proposed rulemaking that expressly recognized a substantial need for a field sanitation standard to prevent disease and invited public comment for the following ninety-day period. Notwithstanding the notice of proposed rulemaking, another year went by, and the Secretary still had not issued a final rule. The district court requested a status report, and the Secretary reported back that the field sanitation standard was simply a lower priority than other Department initiatives and that, because of limited agency resources, he did not know when the rule might be finalized. Litigation over the matter continued, and after three years, the Secretary promised in a settlement agreement to make a good faith effort to complete a field sanitation standard within another two years. At the end of that two year period (and nine years after X filed its initial petition), the Secretary issued a decision withdrawing the earlier proposed field sanitation standard and publishing a new notice of proposed rulemaking that he said corrected problems with the earlier proposed standard. After allowing another ninety-day comment period, the Secretary issued a "final determination" that he would not issue a federal field sanitation standard "at this time," claiming that the Department lacked the resources to enforce a federal standard and asserting that, consistent with principles of federalism, the states were better suited to regulate the problem.

X is contemplating bringing suit again to challenge the Secretary of Labor's inaction in failing to promulgate a field sanitation standard. Can the courts review such a claim?

B. THE TIMING OF JUDICIAL REVIEW

Reviewability is only one of several obstacles to judicial review a petitioner must overcome. Even if the petitioner can persuade a court that the agency action is reviewable, the petitioner must persuade the court that it is reviewable at this time and in its present posture. To be reviewable at the present time and in the present procedural posture, the action must be "final" and "ripe" for judicial review, and the petitioner must have exhausted available administrative remedies. In the following section, we will focus on Supreme Court opinions that treat each of the timing doctrines as independent of each other. As you will see, the tests courts use to apply each doctrine differ. You also should be aware, however, that the factors courts consider in applying the three doctrines overlap significantly. You also should be aware that the agency has an advantage in all arguments with respect to the timing doctrines because the petitioner must prevail with respect to all three doctrines while the agency can win by prevailing with respect to any one of the doctrines.

The best illustration of the significant overlap among the timing doctrines is the decision of the D.C. Circuit in *Ticor Title Insurance Co. v. FTC*, 814 F.2d 731 (D.C. Cir. 1987). The court dismissed the petition for review as premature, and the three members of the panel all agreed with respect to the court's disposition of the case. Yet, the judges disagreed completely regarding the basis for that disposition. One judge concluded that the agency action was final and ripe but that review was premature because the petitioner had not yet exhausted administrative remedies. One judge concluded that the action was final and that the petitioner had exhausted administrative remedies but that review was premature because the action was not yet ripe for review. The third judge concluded that the action was ripe for review and that the petitioner had exhausted administrative remedies but that review was premature because the action was not yet final.

1.   FINAL AGENCY ACTION

APA section 704 provides:

> Agency action made reviewable by statute and final agency action for which there is no other adequate remedy in a court are subject to judicial review. A preliminary, procedural, or intermediate agency action or ruling not directly reviewable is subject to review on the review of the final agency action. Except as otherwise expressly required by statute, agency action otherwise final is final for the purposes of this section whether or not there has been presented or determined an application for a declaratory order, for any form of reconsiderations, or, unless the agency otherwise requires by rule and provides that the action meanwhile is inoperative, for an appeal to superior agency authority.

Unless some other statute authorizes review of a non-final action, finality is a necessary prerequisite for judicial review of agency action. The APA does not define finality, however, so courts have given the term meaning. Compare the Court's conclusions regarding finality in the following cases.

Franklin v. Massachusetts

505 U.S. 788 (1992).

■ JUSTICE O'CONNOR delivered the opinion of the Court, except as to Part III.

As one season follows another, the decennial census has again generated a number of reapportionment controversies. This decade, as a result of the 1990 census and reapportionment, Massachusetts lost a seat in the House of Representatives. Appellees Massachusetts and two of its registered voters brought this action against the President, the Secretary of Commerce (Secretary), Census Bureau officials, and the Clerk of the House of Representatives, challenging, among other things, the method used for counting federal employees serving overseas. In particular, the appellants' allocation of 922,819 overseas military personnel to the State designated in their personnel files as their "home of record" altered the relative state populations enough to shift a Representative from Massachusetts to Washington.

* * *

Under the automatic reapportionment statute, the Secretary of Commerce takes the census "in such form and content as [s]he may determine." 13 U.S.C. § 141(a). The Secretary is permitted to delegate her authority for establishing census procedures to the Bureau of the Census. "The tabulation of total population by States . . . as required for the apportionment of Representatives in Congress . . . shall be completed within 9 months after the census date and reported by the Secretary to the President of the United States." § 141(b). After receiving the Secretary's report, the President "shall transmit to the Congress a statement showing the whole number of persons in each State . . . as ascertained under the . . . decennial census of the population, and the number of Representatives to which each State would be entitled under an apportionment of the then existing number of Representatives by the method known as the method of equal proportions. . . ." 2 U.S.C. § 2a(a). "Each State shall be entitled . . . to the number of Representatives shown" in the President's statement, and the Clerk of the House of Representatives must "send to the executive of each State a certificate of the number of Representatives to which such State is entitled." § 2a(b).

* * *

In July 1990, six months before the census count was due to be reported to the President, the Census Bureau decided to allocate the Department of Defense's overseas employees to the States based on their "home of record." It chose the home of record designation over other data available, including legal residence and last duty station, because home of record most closely resembled the Census Bureau's standard measure of state affiliation—"usual residence." Legal residence was thought less accurate because the choice of legal residence may have been affected by state taxation. Indeed, the Congressional Research Service found that in 1990 "the nine States with either no income taxes, or those which tax only interest and dividend income, have approximately 9 percent more of the overseas military personnel claiming the States for tax purposes, than those same States receive using *home of record*." For similar reasons, last duty station was rejected because it would provide only a work address, and the employee's last home address might have been in a different State, as with those, for example, who worked in the District of Columbia but lived in Virginia or Maryland. Residence at a "last duty station" may also have been of a very short duration and may not have reflected the more enduring tie of usual residence. Those military personnel for whom home of record information was not available were allocated based on legal residence or last duty station, in that order.

The Census Bureau invited 40 other federal agencies with overseas employees to submit counts of their employees as well. Of those, only 30 actually submitted counts, and only 20 agencies included dependents in their enumeration. Four of the agencies could not provide a home State for all of their overseas employees.

* * *

The APA sets forth the procedures by which federal agencies are accountable to the public and their actions subject to review by the courts. The Secretary's report to the President is an unusual candidate for "agency action" within the meaning of the APA, because it is not promulgated to the public in the Federal Register, no official administrative record is generated, and its effect on reapportionment is felt only after the President makes the necessary calculations and reports the result to the Congress. Only after the President reports to Congress do the States have an entitlement to a particular number of Representatives.

The APA provides for judicial review of "final agency action for which there is no other adequate remedy in a court." 5 U.S.C. § 704. At issue in this case is whether the "final" action that appellees have challenged is that of an "agency" such that the federal courts may exercise their powers of review under the APA. We hold that the final action complained of is that of the President, and the President is not an agency within the meaning of the Act. Accordingly, there is no final agency action that may be reviewed under the APA standards.

To determine when an agency action is final, we have looked to, among other things, whether its impact "is sufficiently direct and immediate" and has a "direct effect on . . . day-to-day business." *Abbott Labs. v. Gardner*, 387 U.S. 136, 152 (1967). An agency action is not final if it is only "the ruling of a subordinate official," or "tentative." *Id.* at 151. The core question is whether the agency has completed its decisionmaking process, and whether the result of that process is one that will directly affect the parties. In this case, the action that creates an entitlement to a particular number of Representatives and has a direct effect on the reapportionment is the President's statement to Congress, not the Secretary's report to the President.

Unlike other statutes that expressly require the President to transmit an agency's report directly to Congress, § 2a does not. After receiving the Secretary's report, the President is to "transmit to the Congress a statement showing the whole number of persons in each State . . . as ascertained under the . . . decennial census of the population." 2 U.S.C. § 2a(a). Section 2a does not expressly require the

President to use the data in the Secretary's report, but, rather, the data from the "decennial census." There is no statute forbidding amendment of the "decennial census" itself after the Secretary submits the report to the President. For potential litigants, therefore, the "decennial census" still presents a moving target, even after the Secretary reports to the President. In this case, the Department of Commerce, in its press release issued the day the Secretary submitted the report to the President, was explicit that the data presented to the President was still subject to correction. Moreover, there is no statute that rules out an instruction by the President to the Secretary to reform the census, even after the data are submitted to him. It is not until the President submits the information to Congress that the target stops moving, because only then are the States entitled by § 2a to a particular number of Representatives. Because the Secretary's report to the President carries no direct consequences for the reapportionment, it serves more like a tentative recommendation than a final and binding determination. It is, like "the ruling of a subordinate official," *Abbott Labs.*, 387 U.S. at 151, not final and therefore not subject to review.

* * *

Appellees claim that because the President exercises no discretion in calculating the numbers of Representatives, his "role in the statutory scheme was intended to have no substantive content," and the final action is the Secretary's, not the President's. They cite the Senate Report for the bill that became 2 U.S.C. § 2a, which states that the President is to report "upon a problem in mathematics which is standard, and for which rigid specifications are provided by Congress itself, and to which there can be but one mathematical answer." S. REP. No. 2, at 4–5 (71st Cong., 1st Sess.).

The admittedly ministerial nature of the apportionment calculation itself does not answer the question whether the apportionment is foreordained by the time the Secretary gives her report to the President. To reiterate, § 2a does not curtail the President's authority to direct the Secretary in making policy judgments that result in "the decennial census"; he is not expressly required to adhere to the policy decisions reflected in the Secretary's report. Because it is the President's personal transmittal of the report to Congress that settles the apportionment, until he acts there is no determinate agency action to challenge. The President, not the Secretary, takes the final action that affects the States.

* * *

As enacted, 2 U.S.C. § 2a provides that the Secretary cannot act alone; she must send her results to the President, who makes the calculations and sends the final apportionment to Congress. That the final act is that of the President is important to the integrity of the process and bolsters our conclusion that his duties are not merely ceremonial or ministerial. Thus, we can only review the APA claims here if the President, not the Secretary of Commerce, is an "agency" within the meaning of the Act.

The APA defines "agency" as "each authority of the Government of the United States, whether or not it is within or subject to review by another agency, but does not include—(A) the Congress; (B) the courts of the United States; (C) the government of the territories or possessions of the United States; (D) the government of the District of Columbia." 5 U.S.C. §§ 701(b)(1), 551(1). The President is not explicitly excluded from the APA's purview, but he is not explicitly included, either. Out of respect for the separation of powers and the unique constitutional position of the President, we find that textual silence is not enough to subject the President to the provisions of the APA. We would require an express statement by Congress before assuming it intended the President's performance of his statutory duties to be reviewed for abuse of discretion. As the APA does not expressly allow review of the President's actions, we must presume that his actions are not subject to its requirements. Although the President's actions may still be reviewed for constitutionality, see *Youngstown Sheet & Tube Co. v. Sawyer*, 343 U.S. 579 (1952); *Panama Refining Co. v. Ryan*, 293 U.S. 388 (1935), we hold that they are not reviewable for abuse of discretion under the APA.

■ [Opinions of JUSTICE STEVENS, with whom JUSTICE BLACKMUN, JUSTICE KENNEDY, and JUSTICE SOUTER join, concurring in part and concurring in the judgment, and of JUSTICE SCALIA, concurring in part and concurring in the judgment, are omitted. Ed.]

———————————

Dalton v. Specter

511 U.S. 462 (1994).

■ CHIEF JUSTICE REHNQUIST delivered the opinion of the Court.

Respondents sought to enjoin the Secretary of Defense (Secretary) from carrying out a decision by the President to close the Philadelphia Naval Shipyard. This decision was made pursuant to the Defense Base Closure and Realignment Act of 1990 (1990 Act or Act). The Court of Appeals held that judicial review of the decision was available to ensure that various participants in the selection process had complied with procedural mandates specified by Congress. We hold that such review is not available.

The decision to close the shipyard was the end result of an elaborate selection process prescribed by the 1990 Act. Designed "to provide a fair process that will result in the timely closure and realignment of military installations inside the United States," § 2901(b),[2] the Act provides for three successive rounds of base closings—in 1991, 1993, and 1995, § 2903(c)(1). For each round, the Secretary must prepare closure and realignment recommendations, based on selection criteria he establishes after notice and an opportunity for public comment. § 2903(b), (c).

The Secretary submits his recommendations to Congress and to the Defense Base Closure and Realignment Commission (Commission), an independent body whose eight members are appointed by the President, with the advice and consent of the Senate. §§ 2903(c)(1); 2902(a),

———————————

[2] For ease of reference, all citations to the 1990 Act are to the relevant sections of the Act as it appears in note following 10 U.S.C. § 2687 (1988 ed., Supp. IV).

(c)(1)(A). The Commission must then hold public hearings and prepare a report, containing both an assessment of the Secretary's recommendations and the Commission's own recommendations for base closures and realignments. § 2903(d)(1)–(2). Within roughly three months of receiving the Secretary's recommendations, the Commission has to submit its report to the President. § 2903(d)(2)(A).

Within two weeks of receiving the Commission's report, the President must decide whether to approve or disapprove, in their entirety, the Commission's recommendations. § 2903(e)(1)–(3). If the President disapproves, the Commission has roughly one month to prepare a new report and submit it to the President. § 2903(e)(3). If the President again disapproves, no bases may be closed that year under the Act. § 2903(e)(5). If the President approves the initial or revised recommendations, the President must submit the recommendations, along with his certification of approval, to Congress. § 2903(e)(2), (e)(4). Congress may, within 45 days of receiving the President's certification (or by the date Congress adjourns for the session, whichever is earlier), enact a joint resolution of disapproval. §§ 2904(b), 2908. If such a resolution is passed, the Secretary may not carry out any closures pursuant to the Act; if such a resolution is not passed, the Secretary must close all military installations recommended for closure by the Commission. § 2904(a), (b)(1).

In April 1991, the Secretary recommended the closure or realignment of a number of military installations, including the Philadelphia Naval Shipyard. After holding public hearings in Washington, D.C., and Philadelphia, the Commission recommended closure or realignment of 82 bases. The Commission did not concur in all of the Secretary's recommendations, but it agreed that the Philadelphia Naval Shipyard should be closed. In July 1991, President Bush approved the Commission's recommendations, and the House of Representatives rejected a proposed joint resolution of disapproval by a vote of 364 to 60.

Two days before the President submitted his certification of approval to Congress, respondents filed this action under the Administrative Procedure Act (APA), 5 U.S.C. § 701 *et seq.*, and the 1990 Act. Their complaint contained three counts, two of which remain at issue. Count I alleged that the Secretaries of Navy and Defense violated substantive and procedural requirements of the 1990 Act in recommending closure of the Philadelphia Naval Shipyard. Count II made similar allegations regarding the Commission's recommendations to the President, asserting specifically that, *inter alia*, the Commission used improper criteria, failed to place certain information in the record until after the close of public hearings, and held closed meetings with the Navy.

The United States District Court for the Eastern District of Pennsylvania dismissed the complaint in its entirety, on the alternative grounds that the 1990 Act itself precluded judicial review and that the political question doctrine foreclosed judicial intervention. A divided panel of the United States Court of Appeals for the Third Circuit affirmed in part and reversed in part. *Specter v. Garrett*, 971 F.2d 936 (1992) (*Specter I*). * * * The Court of Appeals decided that there could be judicial review of the President's decision because the "actions of the

President have never been considered immune from judicial review solely because they were taken by the President." *Id.* at 945. The dissenting judge took the view that the 1990 Act precluded judicial review of all statutory claims, procedural and substantive.

Shortly after the Court of Appeals issued its opinion, we decided *Franklin v. Massachusetts*, 505 U.S. 788 (1992), in which we addressed the existence of "final agency action" in a suit seeking APA review of the decennial reapportionment of the House of Representatives. * * * Because of the similarities between *Franklin* and this case, we granted the petition for certiorari, vacated the judgment of the Court of Appeals, and remanded for further consideration in light of *Franklin.*

On remand, the same divided panel of the Court of Appeals adhered to its earlier decision, and held that *Franklin* did not affect the reviewability of respondents' procedural claims. *Specter v. Garrett*, 995 F.2d 404 (1993) (*Specter II*). Although apparently recognizing that APA review was unavailable, the Court of Appeals felt that adjudging the President's actions for compliance with the 1990 Act was a "form of constitutional review," and that *Franklin* sanctioned such review. * * * We now reverse.

We begin our analysis on common ground with the Court of Appeals. In *Specter II*, that court acknowledged, at least tacitly, that respondents' claims are not reviewable under the APA. A straightforward application of *Franklin* to this case demonstrates why this is so. *Franklin* involved a suit against the President, the Secretary of Commerce, and various public officials, challenging the manner in which seats in the House of Representatives had been apportioned among the States. The plaintiffs challenged the method used by the Secretary of Commerce in preparing her census report, particularly the manner in which she counted federal employees working overseas. The plaintiffs raised claims under both the APA and the Constitution. In reviewing the former, we first sought to determine whether the Secretary's action, in submitting a census report to the President, was "final" for purposes of APA review. (The APA provides for judicial review only of "*final* agency action." 5 U.S.C. § 704 (emphasis added).) Because the President reviewed (and could revise) the Secretary's report, made the apportionment calculations, and submitted the final apportionment report to Congress, we held that the Secretary's report was "not final and therefore not subject to review." 505 U.S. at 798.

* * *

In this case, respondents brought suit under the APA, alleging that the Secretary and the Commission did not follow the procedural mandates of the 1990 Act. But here, as in *Franklin*, the prerequisite to review under the APA—"final agency action"—is lacking. The reports submitted by the Secretary and the Commission, like the report of the Secretary of Commerce in *Franklin*, "carr[y] no direct consequences" for base closings. 505 U.S. at 798. The action that "will directly affect" the military bases is taken by the President, when he submits his certification of approval to Congress. Accordingly, the Secretary's and Commission's reports serve "more like a tentative recommendation than a final and binding determination." *Id.* The reports are, "like the ruling of a subordinate official, not final and therefore not subject to review."

Id. The actions of the President, in turn, are not reviewable under the APA because, as we concluded in *Franklin*, the President is not an "agency."

Respondents contend that the 1990 Act differs significantly from the Census Act at issue in *Franklin*, and that our decision in *Franklin* therefore does not control the question whether the Commission's actions here are final. Respondents appear to argue that the President, under the 1990 Act, has little authority regarding the closure of bases. Consequently, respondents continue, the Commission's report must be regarded as final. This argument ignores the *ratio decidendi* of *Franklin*.

First, respondents underestimate the President's authority under the Act, and the importance of his role in the base closure process. Without the President's approval, no bases are closed under the Act; the Act, in turn, does not by its terms circumscribe the President's discretion to approve or disapprove the Commission's report. Second, and more fundamentally, respondents' argument ignores "[t]he core question" for determining finality: "whether the agency has completed its decisionmaking process, and whether the result of that process is one that will directly affect the parties." *Franklin*, 505 U.S. at 797. That the President cannot pick and choose among bases, and must accept or reject the entire package offered by the Commission, is immaterial. What is crucial is the fact that "[t]he President, not the [Commission], takes the final action that affects" the military installations. *Id.* at 799. Accordingly, we hold that the decisions made pursuant to the 1990 Act are not reviewable under the APA.

* * *

In sum, we hold that the actions of the Secretary and the Commission cannot be reviewed under the APA because they are not "final agency actions." The actions of the President cannot be reviewed under the APA because the President is not an "agency" under that Act. * * *

Respondents tell us that failure to allow judicial review here would virtually repudiate *Marbury v. Madison*, 5 U.S. (1 Cranch) 137 (1803), and nearly two centuries of constitutional adjudication. But our conclusion that judicial review is not available for respondents' claim follows from our interpretation of an Act of Congress, by which we and all federal courts are bound. The judicial power of the United States conferred by Article III of the Constitution is upheld just as surely by withholding judicial relief where Congress has permissibly foreclosed it, as it is by granting such relief where authorized by the Constitution or by statute.

■ [Opinions of JUSTICE BLACKMUN, concurring in part and concurring in the judgment, and JUSTICE SOUTER, with whom JUSTICE BLACKMUN, JUSTICE STEVENS, and JUSTICE GINSBURG join, concurring in part and concurring in the judgment, have been omitted. Ed.]

NOTES AND QUESTIONS

1. The Court in *Franklin* and *Dalton* concluded that the challenged reports of the Census Bureau and the Base Closure Commission,

respectively, were not final agency action for APA review purposes because they had "no direct consequences;" another stage of action was required, in these cases by the President. Many regulatory regimes rely on a two-stage decisionmaking process. Typically, the second stage requires the agency to comply with more elaborate procedural requirements, which is hardly surprising given that the agency's second-stage action leads to more serious or permanent consequences. Nevertheless, the potentially harmful impacts of first-stage actions are not trivial. Accordingly, courts often receive petitions to review the agency's action at the conclusion of the first stage of the decisionmaking process and must then decide whether they can review those actions.

2.   *Franklin* and *Dalton* involved circumstances in which the Court declared that the actions of the Census Bureau and the Base Closure Commission, respectively, were not reviewable under the APA because they were not final, but that the acts of the President that finalized those agency actions rendered them unreviewable because the APA does not apply to the President. As the Court observed in *Franklin*, the constitutionality of the President's actions are still reviewable under the framework articulated in *Youngstown Sheet & Tube Co. v. Sawyer*, 343 U.S. 579 (1952), which we discussed in Chapter 3. Nevertheless, these cases suggest the potentially unfettered ability of Presidents and agencies to utilize statutory arrangements such as these to assert the broadest possible statutory authority. Why do you think Congress might have wanted to remove the reports of the Census Bureau and the Base Closure Commission from judicial oversight?

3.   While *Franklin* and *Dalton* make clear that Congress may structure a decisionmaking process to avoid judicial review, the Court has at least implicitly acknowledged that Congress has the power to declare an agency action final and reviewable. In *Department of Commerce v. U.S. House of Representatives*, 525 U.S. 316 (1999), the Court considered a challenge to another Census Bureau report. In this case, however, Congress had learned in advance that the Census Bureau was considering using a statistical methodology known as sampling in conducting the 2000 census. Given that information, Congress had enacted a statute declaring that the Census 2000 Report and the Census 2000 Operating Plan "shall be deemed to constitute final agency action regarding the use of statistical methods in the 2000 decennial census." In considering the legal challenge, the Court did not address the question of finality, but rather simply noted that "Congress has eliminated any prudential concerns in this case."

Although the Court has not repudiated the outcomes of *Franklin* and *Dalton*, in the following opinion issued just a few years after deciding those cases, the Court articulated a new two-part test for determining whether an agency action is "final agency action" under APA § 704.

Bennett v. Spear

520 U.S. 154 (1997).

■ JUSTICE SCALIA delivered the opinion of the Court.

This is a challenge to a biological opinion issued by the Fish and Wildlife Service in accordance with the Endangered Species Act of 1973 (ESA), concerning the operation of the Klamath Irrigation Project by the Bureau of Reclamation, and the project's impact on two varieties of endangered fish. * * *

The ESA requires the Secretary of the Interior to promulgate regulations listing those species of animals that are "threatened" or "endangered" under specified criteria, and to designate their "critical habitat." 16 U.S.C. § 1533. The ESA further requires each federal agency to "insure that any action authorized, funded, or carried out by such agency . . . is not likely to jeopardize the continued existence of any endangered species or threatened species or result in the destruction or adverse modification of habitat of such species which is determined by the Secretary . . . to be critical." § 1536(a)(2). If an agency determines that action it proposes to take may adversely affect a listed species, it must engage in formal consultation with the Fish and Wildlife Service, as delegate of the Secretary, after which the Service must provide the agency with a written statement (the Biological Opinion) explaining how the proposed action will affect the species or its habitat. If the Service concludes that the proposed action will "jeopardize the continued existence of any [listed] species or threatened species or result in the destruction or adverse modification of [critical habitat]," § 1536(a)(2), the Biological Opinion must outline any "reasonable and prudent alternatives" that the Service believes will avoid that consequence. § 1536(b)(3)(A). * * *

The Klamath Project, one of the oldest federal reclamation schemes, is a series of lakes, rivers, dams, and irrigation canals in northern California and southern Oregon. The project was undertaken by the Secretary of the Interior pursuant to the Reclamation Act of 1902, and is administered by the Bureau of Reclamation, which is under the Secretary's jurisdiction. In 1992, the Bureau notified the Service that operation of the project might affect the Lost River Sucker and Shortnose Sucker species of fish that were listed as endangered in 1988. After formal consultation with the Bureau, the Service issued a Biological Opinion which concluded that the " 'long-term operation of the Klamath Project was likely to jeopardize the continued existence of the Lost River and shortnose suckers.' " The Biological Opinion identified "reasonable and prudent alternatives" the Service believed would avoid jeopardy, which included the maintenance of minimum water levels on Clear Lake and Gerber reservoirs. The Bureau later notified the Service that it intended to operate the project in compliance with the Biological Opinion.

Petitioners, two Oregon irrigation districts that receive Klamath Project water and the operators of two ranches within those districts, filed the present action against the director and regional director of the Service and the Secretary of the Interior. * * *

Petitioners' complaint included three claims for relief that are relevant here. The first and second claims allege that the Service's jeopardy determination with respect to Clear Lake and Gerber reservoirs, and the ensuing imposition of minimum water levels, violated § 7 of the ESA. The third claim is that the imposition of minimum water elevations constituted an implicit determination of critical habitat for the suckers, which violated § 4 of the ESA because it failed to take into consideration the designation's economic impact. Each of the claims also states that the relevant action violated the APA's prohibition of agency action that is "arbitrary, capricious, an abuse of discretion, or otherwise not in accordance with law." 5 U.S.C. § 706(2)(A).

The complaint asserts that petitioners' use of the reservoirs and related waterways for "recreational, aesthetic and commercial purposes, as well as for their primary sources of irrigation water," will be "irreparably damaged" by the actions complained of and that the restrictions on water delivery "recommended" by the Biological Opinion "adversely affect plaintiffs by substantially reducing the quantity of available irrigation water." In essence, petitioners claim a competing interest in the water the Biological Opinion declares necessary for the preservation of the suckers.

[We have omitted lengthy parts of the opinion in which the Court concludes that the action is reviewable and that the petitioners have standing to obtain review. Ed.]

The Government contends that petitioners may not obtain judicial review under the APA on the theory that the Biological Opinion does not constitute "final agency action," 5 U.S.C. § 704, because it does not conclusively determine the manner in which Klamath Project water will be allocated. * * * As a general matter, two conditions must be satisfied for agency action to be "final": First, the action must mark the "consummation" of the agency's decisionmaking process, *Chicago & S. Air Lines, Inc. v. Waterman S. S. Corp.*, 333 U.S. 103, 113 (1948)—it must not be of a merely tentative or interlocutory nature. And second, the action must be one by which "rights or obligations have been determined," or from which "legal consequences will flow." *Port of Boston Marine Terminal Ass'n v. Rederiaktiebolaget Transatl.*, 400 U.S. 62, 71 (1970). It is uncontested that the first requirement is met here; and the second is met because, as we have discussed above, the Biological Opinion and accompanying Incidental Take Statement alter the legal regime to which the action agency is subject, authorizing it to take the endangered species if (but only if) it complies with the prescribed conditions. In this crucial respect the present case is different from the cases upon which the Government relies, *Franklin v. Massachusetts*, 505 U.S. 788 (1992), and *Dalton v. Specter*, 511 U.S. 462 (1994). In the former case, the agency action in question was the Secretary of Commerce's presentation to the President of a report tabulating the results of the decennial census; our holding that this did not constitute "final agency action" was premised on the observation that the report carried "no direct consequences" and served "more like a tentative recommendation than a final and binding determination." 505 U.S. at 798. And in the latter case, the agency action in question was submission to the President of base closure recommendations by the Secretary of Defense and the Defense Base Closure and Realignment Commission; our holding that this was not "final agency action" followed from the fact that the recommendations were in no way binding on the President, who had absolute discretion to accept or reject them. Unlike the reports in *Franklin* and *Dalton*, which were purely advisory and in no way affected the legal rights of the relevant actors, the Biological Opinion at issue here has direct and appreciable legal consequences.

NOTES AND QUESTIONS

1. The final agency action test articulated in *Bennett* is particularly difficult to apply in the context of the many regulatory statutes that authorize a two-step decisionmaking process. The Federal Insecticide, Fungicide, and Rodenticide Act (FIFRA), 7 U.S.C. §§ 136–136y, illustrates this problem. FIFRA provides that no one can sell a pesticide in interstate commerce unless and until it is registered. The process of registration requires the manufacturer to conduct a series of tests and to report those tests to EPA, so that EPA can determine whether the pesticide provides enough benefits to offset its costs in terms of potential adverse effects on health and the environment. FIFRA contains provisions that authorize EPA to remove a pesticide from the market by suspending or canceling its registration. EPA can cancel a registration only if it makes a finding that the costs of using a pesticide exceed its benefits. EPA can cancel a registration only if it makes the required findings after it has completed an elaborate decisionmaking process that can take years to complete. Congress foresaw the possibility that some pesticides might pose such high costs and risks to health and to the environment that EPA would need to remove them from the market before it completed a typically lengthy cancellation proceeding. FIFRA authorizes EPA to suspend the registration of a pesticide if it finds that the pesticide creates an imminent hazard to the public. EPA can issue an emergency suspension order without first engaging in an elaborate decisionmaking procedure like the procedure it must follow in a cancellation proceeding.

It is easy to determine that an EPA decision to initiate a cancellation proceeding is not a final agency action and that an EPA decision to cancel or not to cancel a registration taken after conducting a cancellation proceeding is a final agency action. In many cases, however, EPA initiates a cancellation proceeding and then either suspends the registration pending the outcome of the cancellation proceeding or refuses to suspend the registration until it completes the cancellation proceeding. Either of those decisions is almost invariably the subject of a petition for review. Consumer and environmental groups regularly seek review of EPA decisions not to suspend pesticide registrations, while pesticide manufacturers and pesticide users regularly seek review of EPA decisions to suspend pesticide registrations. Those petitions raise two questions. First, are decisions to suspend pesticide registrations final actions that are reviewable immediately? Second, are decisions not to suspend pesticide registrations final actions that are reviewable immediately? How would you apply the test for finality to those two types of decisions, and with what results? The circuit courts are divided with respect to both questions, and the Supreme Court has never addressed either.

2. In *Sackett v. EPA*, 132 S. Ct. 1367 (2012), the Supreme Court held unanimously that an Administrative Compliance Order (ACO) issued by the EPA is a final agency action that is immediately reviewable. The

Sacketts were owners of residential property in Idaho whose property was located near a lake but separated from the water by several other lots with permanent buildings on them. In preparing to build a house, the Sacketts filled in part of their land with dirt and rock. The EPA sent the Sacketts the ACO declaring their property to be wetlands subject to EPA jurisdiction under the Clean Water Act (CWA) and ordering them to restore the site pursuant to an EPA-approved Restoration Work Plan and subject to EPA oversight. Failure to comply with the ACO exposed the Sacketts to potential financial penalties in future enforcement proceedings. The EPA declined the Sackett's request for a hearing to contest the ACO, but the EPA also maintained that the ACO was not final agency action because it invited the Sacketts to "engage in informal discussion" of the order's terms and requirements and to inform the agency of "any allegations [t]herein which [they] believe[d] to be inaccurate. Applying the two-part *Bennett* test, the Court disagreed, concluding that "[t]he mere possibility that an agency might reconsider in light of 'informal discussion' and invited contentions of inaccuracy does not suffice to make an otherwise final agency action nonfinal." *Id.* at 1372.

DISCUSSION PROBLEM

An association of retail stores writes to the Administrator of the Wage and Hour Division in the Department of Labor, the person in charge of enforcing the federal minimum wage and overtime laws, seeking to clarify the effect on its members of recent amendments to these laws. The Administrator responded in a lengthy letter explaining his interpretation of the effect of the amendments on the association's members and the basis for his interpretation. The Administrator's letter is not legally binding, but employers who comply with such letters may rely upon them in defending against employee suits based on alternative legal interpretations. Is the Administrator's letter "final agency action" for purposes of APA § 704?

Note: Notice that this is the same sort of agency action at issue in *Skidmore v. Swift* and in *Christensen v. Harris County*, both of which cases are discussed at length in Chapter 6.

2.   RIPENESS FOR JUDICIAL REVIEW

Ripeness law serves two basic purposes. First, it conserves judicial resources for problems that are real and present or imminent, by prohibiting their expenditure on problems that are abstract, hypothetical, or remote. Second, it limits the ability of courts to intrude excessively on the policymaking domains of the politically accountable Branches by instructing courts to review government actions only when the government's position has crystallized to the point at which a court can identify a relatively discrete dispute.

The Court transformed the law of ripeness dramatically in 1967. As a result, much of the reasoning in the pre-1967 opinions that held agency actions unreviewable on ripeness grounds has limited value today. Prior to 1967, the Court was reluctant to consider the validity of any statute, rule, or informal statement of an agency's position except in the context of a party's attempt to defend its conduct in an enforcement proceeding. The Court's general reasoning could be summarized as follows: (1) the case or controversy limitation precludes us from issuing advisory opinions; (2) an abstract declaration that a statute or rule is invalid would be an advisory opinion; (3) the case or controversy limitation precludes us from resolving a dispute between the government and an individual unless the government is acting in a way that harms the individual; and (4) "harm" is defined very narrowly to cover only direct and formal actions, such as imposition of a fine or incarceration.

The old approach is illustrated by *United Public Workers v. Mitchell*, 330 U.S. 75 (1947). Twelve federal employees sued members of the Civil Service Commission to enjoin enforcement of the Hatch Act and regulations under the Act; they also sought a declaratory judgment. The Act forbade federal employees to "take any active part in political management or in political campaigns." The Commission had implemented the Act with regulations that employees may express political opinions but "not such as to amount to taking an active part in an organized political campaign," and that employees "may not write for publication . . . any letter or article" or serve as election officers. The complaint alleged that the employees desired to do some of the prohibited acts, specifying the particular acts. The Supreme Court held that the case was unripe for consideration, except with respect to one employee who had violated the Act. The Court said:

> [T]he federal courts established pursuant to Article III of the Constitution do not render advisory opinions. * * * These appellants seem clearly to seek advisory opinions. * * * [T]he facts of their personal interest in their civil rights, of the general threat of possible interference with those rights by the Civil Service Commission under its rules, if specified things are done by appellants, does not make a justiciable case or controversy. * * * It is beyond the competence of courts to render such a decision.

Mitchell, 330 U.S. at 89.

The Court did not mention that each of the appellants was confronted with the dilemma of either refraining from political activity he desired to engage in or risking penalties for violating the Act, including discharge. The Court offered no explanation of why that dilemma did not suffice to prevent a determination from being an advisory opinion. Prior to 1967, the Court applied the same reasoning to most attempts to challenge the validity of agency rules that it applied to attempts to challenge the validity of statutes like the Hatch Act.

The pre-1967 law of ripeness created unfairness to regulated firms and individuals, but it had enormous advantages from the perspective of agencies. A regulated party typically could only obtain judicial review of a rule by violating it and then arguing that the rule was invalid in the ensuing enforcement proceeding. The "record" the court used to review the legality of the rule consisted of the record of the enforcement proceeding and not of the proceedings that generated the rule. Since agencies usually bring enforcement actions only in cases in which the underlying conduct harms the public, the record of the enforcement proceeding typically was favorable to the agency. Agencies prevailed in most cases in which regulated parties challenged the validity of rules in enforcement proceedings. This legal regime provided powerful deterrents to judicial challenges to the validity of agency rules. Even when a regulated party strongly believed that a rule was invalid, it was extremely reluctant to violate the rule and to take the high risk that it would lose in an enforcement proceeding and suffer significant civil, criminal, and/or collateral penalties for violating the rule.

Moreover, even if the regulated party prevailed in the enforcement proceeding, it often suffered significant damage to its reputation as a result of press accounts of the agency's claim that the firm had violated the law. Thus, for instance, to peak ahead at the facts of the case that led the Court to change the law of ripeness, a pharmaceutical firm that FDA claims to have violated an agency rule might be charged with selling "adulterated drugs," and newspapers would run stories with headlines like "Government Accuses Ajax Pharmaceuticals of Selling Adulterated Drugs." In many cases, the public relations harm that would be caused by even an unsuccessful agency enforcement action far exceeded the cost of complying with the rule the firm believed to be invalid.

In this legal environment, most firms "voluntarily" complied with rules even when they believed they were invalid; judicial challenges to rules were rare; and, successful challenges were even rarer. As a result, agencies could issue rules expeditiously and inexpensively with little concern that the rule might be held arbitrary and capricious or otherwise unlawful. The Court changed the legal regime applicable to judicial review of rules dramatically in the following opinion.

Abbott Laboratories v. Gardner

387 U.S. 136 (1967).

■ MR. JUSTICE HARLAN delivered the opinion of the Court.

In 1962 Congress amended the Federal Food, Drug, and Cosmetic Act to require manufacturers of prescription drugs to print the "established name" of the drug "prominently and in type at least half as large as that used thereon for any proprietary name or designation for such drug," on labels and other printed material. 21 U.S.C. § 352(e)(1)(B). The "established name" is one designated by the Secretary of Health, Education, and Welfare; the "proprietary name" is usually a trade name under which a particular drug is marketed. The underlying purpose of the 1962 amendment was to bring to the attention of doctors and patients the fact that many of the drugs sold under familiar trade names are actually identical to drugs sold under their "established" or less familiar trade names at significantly lower prices. The Commissioner of Food and Drugs, exercising authority delegated to him by the Secretary, published proposed regulations designed to implement the statute. After inviting and considering comments submitted by interested parties the Commissioner promulgated the following regulation for the "efficient enforcement" of the Act:

> "If the label or labeling of a prescription drug bears a proprietary name or designation for the drug or any ingredient thereof, the established name, if such there be, corresponding to such proprietary name or designation, shall accompany each appearance of such proprietary name or designation." 21 C.F.R. § 1.104(g)(1).

A similar rule was made applicable to advertisements for prescription drugs.

The present action was brought by a group of 37 individual drug manufacturers and by the Pharmaceutical Manufacturers Association, of which all the petitioner companies are members, and which includes manufacturers of more than 90% of the Nation's supply of prescription drugs. They challenged the regulations on the ground that the Commissioner exceeded his authority under the statute by promulgating an order requiring labels, advertisements, and other printed matter relating to prescription drugs to designate the established name of the particular drug involved every time its trade name is used anywhere in such material.

* * * The Court of Appeals for the Third Circuit * * * held first that under the statutory scheme provided by the Federal Food, Drug, and Cosmetic Act pre-enforcement review of these regulations was unauthorized and therefore beyond the jurisdiction of the District Court. Second, the Court of Appeals held that no "actual case or controversy" existed and, for that reason, that no relief under the Administrative Procedure Act or under the Declaratory Judgment Act was in any event available. * * *

The first question we consider is whether Congress by the Federal Food, Drug, and Cosmetic Act intended to forbid pre-enforcement review of this sort of regulation promulgated by the Commissioner. The question is phrased in terms of "prohibition" rather than "authorization" because a survey of our cases shows that judicial review of a final agency action by an aggrieved person will not be cut off unless there is persuasive reason to believe that such was the purpose of Congress. Early cases in which this type of judicial review was entertained have been reinforced by the enactment of the Administrative Procedure Act, which embodies the basic presumption of judicial review to one "suffering legal wrong because of agency action, or adversely affected or aggrieved by agency action within the meaning of a relevant statute," 5 U.S.C. § 702, so long as no statute precludes such relief or the action is not one committed by law to agency discretion, 5 U.S.C. § 701(a). * * *

Given this standard, we are wholly unpersuaded that the statutory scheme in the food and drug area excludes this type of action. The Government relies on no explicit statutory authority for its argument that pre-enforcement review is unavailable, but insists instead that because the statute includes a specific procedure for such review of certain enumerated kinds of regulations, not encompassing those of the kind involved here, other types were necessarily meant to be excluded from any pre-enforcement review. The issue, however, is not so readily resolved; we must go further and inquire whether in the context of the entire legislative scheme the existence of that circumscribed remedy evinces a congressional purpose to bar agency action not within its purview from judicial review.

* * *

The only other argument of the Government requiring attention on the preclusive effect of the statute is that *Ewing v. Mytinger & Casselberry, Inc.*, 339 U.S. 594 (1950), counsels a restrictive view of judicial review in the food and drug area. In that case the Food and Drug Administrator found that there was probable cause that a drug was "adulterated" because it was misbranded in such a way as to be "fraudulent" or "misleading to the injury or damage of the purchaser or consumer." 21 U.S.C. § 334(a). Multiple seizures were ordered through libel actions. The manufacturer of the drug brought an action to challenge directly the Administrator's finding of probable cause. This Court held that the owner could raise his constitutional, statutory, and factual claims in the libel actions themselves, and that the mere finding of probable cause by the Administrator could not be challenged in a separate action. That decision was quite clearly correct, but nothing in its reasoning or holding has any bearing on this declaratory judgment action challenging a promulgated regulation.

The Court in *Ewing* first noted that the "administrative finding of probable cause required by § 304(a) is merely the statutory prerequisite to the bringing of the lawsuit," at which the issues are aired. 339 U.S. at 598. Such a situation bears no analogy to the promulgation, after formal procedures, of a rule that must be followed by an entire industry. To equate a finding of probable cause for proceeding against a particular drug manufacturer with the promulgation of a self-operative industry-wide regulation, such as we have here, would immunize nearly all agency rulemaking activities from the coverage of the Administrative Procedure Act.

Second, the determination of probable cause in *Ewing* has "no effect in and of itself," 339 U.S. at 598; only some action consequent upon such a finding could give it legal life. As the Court there noted, like a determination by a grand jury that there is probable cause to proceed against an accused, it is a finding which only has vitality once a proceeding is commenced, at which time appropriate challenges can be made. The Court also noted that the unique type of relief sought by the drug manufacturer was inconsistent with the policy of the Act favoring speedy action against goods in circulation that are believed on probable cause to be adulterated.

* * *

A further inquiry must, however, be made. The injunctive and declaratory judgment remedies are discretionary, and courts traditionally have been reluctant to apply them to administrative determinations unless these arise in the context of a controversy "ripe" for judicial resolution. Without undertaking to survey the intricacies of the ripeness doctrine it is fair to say that its basic rationale is to prevent the courts, through avoidance of premature adjudication, from entangling themselves in abstract disagreements over administrative policies, and also to protect the agencies from judicial interference until an administrative decision has been formalized and its effects felt in a concrete way by the challenging parties. The problem is best seen in a twofold aspect, requiring us to evaluate both the fitness of the issues for judicial decision and the hardship to the parties of withholding court consideration.

As to the former factor, we believe the issues presented are appropriate for judicial resolution at this time. First, all parties agree that the issue tendered is a purely legal one: whether the statute was properly construed by the Commissioner to require the established name of the drug to be used *every time* the proprietary name is employed. * * * [B]oth sides have approached this case as one purely of congressional intent, and * * * the Government made no effort to justify the regulation in factual terms.

Second, the regulations in issue we find to be "final agency action" within the meaning of § 10 of the Administrative Procedure Act, 5 U.S.C. § 704, as construed in judicial decisions. * * *

This is also a case in which the impact of the regulations upon the petitioners is sufficiently direct and immediate as to render the issue appropriate for judicial review at this stage. These regulations purport to give an authoritative interpretation of a statutory provision that has a direct effect on the day-to-day business of all prescription drug companies; its promulgation puts petitioners in a dilemma that it was the very purpose of the Declaratory Judgment Act to ameliorate. As the District Court found on the basis of uncontested allegations, "Either they must comply with the every time requirement and incur the costs of changing over their promotional material and labeling or they must follow their present course and risk prosecution." The regulations are clear-cut, and were made effective immediately upon publication; as noted earlier the agency's counsel represented to the District Court that immediate compliance with their terms was expected. If petitioners wish to comply they must change all their labels, advertisements, and promotional materials; they must destroy stocks of printed matter; and they must invest heavily in new printing type and new supplies. The alternative to compliance—continued use of material which they believe in good faith meets the statutory requirements, but which clearly does not meet the regulation of the Commissioner—may be even more costly. That course would risk serious criminal and civil penalties for the unlawful distribution of "misbranded" drugs.

It is relevant at this juncture to recognize that petitioners deal in a sensitive industry, in which public confidence in their drug products is especially important. To require them to challenge these regulations only as a defense to an action brought by the Government might harm them severely and unnecessarily. Where the legal issue presented is fit for judicial resolution, and where a regulation requires an immediate and significant change in the plaintiffs' conduct of their affairs with serious penalties attached to noncompliance, access to the courts under the Administrative Procedure Act and the Declaratory Judgment Act must be permitted, absent a statutory bar or some other unusual circumstance, neither of which appears here.

* * *

Finally, the Government urges that to permit resort to the courts in this type of case may delay or impede effective enforcement of the Act. We fully recognize the important public interest served by assuring prompt and unimpeded administration of the Pure Food, Drug, and Cosmetic Act, but we do not find the Government's argument convincing. First, in this particular case, a pre-enforcement challenge by nearly all prescription drug manufacturers is calculated to speed enforcement. If the Government prevails, a large part of the industry is bound by the decree; if the Government loses, it can more quickly revise its regulation.

The Government contends, however, that if the Court allows this consolidated suit, then nothing will prevent a multiplicity of suits in various jurisdictions challenging other regulations. The short answer to this contention is that the courts are well equipped to deal with such eventualities. The venue transfer provision may be invoked by the Government to consolidate separate actions. Or, actions in all but one jurisdiction might be stayed pending the conclusion of one proceeding. A court may even in its discretion dismiss a declaratory judgment or injunctive suit if the same issue is pending in litigation elsewhere. * * *

Further, the declaratory judgment and injunctive remedies are equitable in nature, and other equitable defenses may be interposed. If a multiplicity of suits are undertaken in order to harass the Government or to delay enforcement, relief can be denied on this ground alone. The defense of laches could be asserted if the Government is prejudiced by a delay. And courts may even refuse declaratory relief for the nonjoinder of interested parties who are not, technically speaking, indispensable.

In addition to all these safeguards against what the Government fears, it is important to note that the institution of this type of action does not by itself stay the effectiveness of the challenged regulation. There is nothing in the record to indicate that petitioners have sought to stay enforcement of the "every time" regulation pending judicial review. *See* 5 U.S.C. § 705. If the agency believes that a suit of this type will significantly impede enforcement or will harm the public interest, it need not postpone enforcement of the regulation and may oppose any motion for a judicial stay on the part of those challenging the regulation. It is scarcely to be doubted that a court would refuse to postpone the effective date of an agency action if the Government could show, as it made no effort to do here, that delay would be detrimental to the public health or safety.

The same day the Supreme Court decided *Abbott Labs*, it also decided the following companion case.

Toilet Goods Ass'n, Inc. v. Gardner

387 U.S. 158 (1967).

■ MR. JUSTICE HARLAN delivered the opinion of the Court.

Petitioners in this case are the Toilet Goods Association, an organization of cosmetics manufacturers accounting for some 90% of annual American sales in this field, and 39 individual cosmetics manufacturers and distributors. They brought this action in the United States District Court for the Southern District of New York seeking declaratory and injunctive relief against the Secretary of Health, Education, and Welfare and the Commissioner of Food and Drugs, on the ground that certain regulations promulgated by the Commissioner exceeded his statutory authority under the Color Additive Amendments to the Federal Food, Drug and Cosmetic Act.

* * *

The Commissioner of Food and Drugs, exercising power delegated by the Secretary, under statutory authority "to promulgate regulations for the efficient enforcement" of the Act, 21 U.S.C. § 371(a), issued the following regulation after due public notice and consideration of comments submitted by interested parties:

"(a) When it appears to the Commissioner that a person has:

* * *

"(4) Refused to permit duly authorized employees of the Food and Drug Administration free access to all manufacturing facilities, processes, and formulae involved in the manufacture of color additives and intermediates from which such color additives are derived;

"he may immediately suspend certification service to such person and may continue such suspension until adequate corrective action has been taken." 28 Fed. Reg. 6445–46; 21 C.F.R. § 8.28.

* * *

In determining whether a challenge to an administrative regulation is ripe for review a twofold inquiry must be made: first to determine whether the issues tendered are appropriate for judicial resolution, and second to assess the hardship to the parties if judicial relief is denied at that stage.

As to the first of these factors, we agree with the Court of Appeals that the legal issue as presently framed is not appropriate for judicial resolution. This is not because the regulation is not the agency's considered and formalized determination, for we are in agreement with petitioners that * * * there can be no question that this regulation—promulgated in a formal manner after notice and evaluation of submitted comments—is a "final agency action" under the Administrative Procedure Act. 5 U.S.C. § 704. Also, we recognize the force of petitioners' contention that the issue as they have framed it presents a purely legal question: whether the regulation is totally beyond the agency's power under the statute, the type of legal issue that courts have occasionally dealt with without requiring a specific attempt at enforcement or exhaustion of administrative remedies.

These points which support the appropriateness of judicial resolution are, however, outweighed by other considerations. The regulation serves notice only that the Commissioner *may* under certain circumstances order inspection of certain facilities and data, and that further certification of additives *may* be refused to those who decline to permit a duly authorized inspection until they have complied in that regard. At this juncture we have no idea whether or when such an inspection will be ordered and what reasons the Commissioner will give to justify his order. The statutory authority asserted for the regulation is the power to promulgate regulations "for the efficient enforcement" of the Act. § 701(a). Whether the regulation is justified thus depends not only, as petitioners appear to suggest, on whether Congress refused to include a specific section of the Act authorizing such inspections, although this factor is to be sure a highly relevant one, but also on whether the statutory scheme as a whole justified promulgation of the regulation. This will depend not merely on an inquiry into statutory purpose, but concurrently on an understanding of what types of enforcement problems are encountered by the FDA, the need for various sorts of supervision in order to effectuate the goals of the Act, and the safeguards devised to protect legitimate trade secrets. We believe that judicial appraisal of these factors is likely to stand on a much surer footing in the context of a specific application of this regulation than could be the case in the framework of the generalized challenge made here.

We are also led to this result by considerations of the effect on the petitioners of the regulation, for the test of ripeness, as we have noted, depends not only on how adequately a court can deal with the legal issue presented, but also on the degree and nature of the regulation's present effect on those seeking relief. The regulation challenged here is not [one] * * * where the impact of the administrative action could be said to be felt immediately by those subject to it in conducting their day-to-day affairs.

This is not a situation in which primary conduct is affected—when contracts must be negotiated, ingredients tested or substituted, or special records compiled. This regulation merely states that the Commissioner may authorize inspectors to examine certain processes or formulae; no advance action is required of cosmetics manufacturers, who since the enactment of the 1938 Act have been under a statutory duty to permit reasonable inspection of a "factory, warehouse, establishment, or vehicle and all pertinent equipment, finished and unfinished materials; containers, and labeling therein." § 704(a). Moreover, no irremediable adverse consequences flow from requiring a later challenge to this regulation by a manufacturer who refuses to allow this type of inspection. Unlike the other regulations challenged in this action, in which seizure of goods, heavy fines, adverse publicity for distributing "adulterated" goods, and possible criminal liability might penalize failure to comply, a refusal to admit an inspector here would at most lead only to a suspension of certification services to the particular party, a determination that can then be promptly challenged through an administrative procedure, which in turn is reviewable by a court. Such review will provide an adequate forum for testing the regulation in a concrete situation.

■ [We have omitted the opinion of three Justices that concurred in *Toilet Goods* and dissented in *Abbott Labs*. The bases for their dissent in *Abbott Labs* were the concerns expressed by FDA and discussed by the *Abbott Labs* majority in the last four paragraphs of the majority opinion. Ed.]

NOTES AND QUESTIONS

1.   The FDA's "every time" rule at issue in *Abbott Labs* and the statutory amendment that FDA issued the rule to implement were motivated by numerous studies that found that doctors often prescribed an aggressively promoted the brand name version of a drug even though it cost two to five times as much as the generic equivalent manufactured by another firm.

FDA believed that doctors would curtail this practice if they were reminded of the generic name every time the manufacturer of the brand name version of the drug advertised its product. On remand, FDA and the petitioners settled the case by agreeing on a new rule that required mention of the generic name less often than every time the brand name appears in labeling or advertising.

2. In many cases, there may be several bases on which a petitioner might challenge the validity of a rule. Some of the issues raised might be "ripe" for pre-enforcement review, while others might be susceptible to meaningful review only in the context of application of the rule in a particular case. Note, however, that challenges to rules based on alleged inadequacies in the procedures an agency used to issue a rule are always ripe for pre-enforcement review (though such challenges may be subject to other limitations on reviewability, such as standing). Thus, for instance, a petitioner typically can persuade a court to engage in pre-enforcement review of a rule to determine whether the agency provided an adequate notice of proposed rulemaking or whether the agency's statement of basis and purpose contains enough explanation of each of the steps in the agency's reasoning process to overcome a claim that the issuance of the rule is arbitrary and capricious. Before *Abbott Labs*, courts rarely considered those types of challenges to the validity of rules. After *Abbott Labs*, many if not most major rules are challenged as arbitrary and capricious, and a high proportion are challenged on the basis that the agency did not provide adequate notice. The massive increase in the proportion of rules that are the subject of review petitions and the increase in the demands of the reviewing courts for voluminous notices of proposed rulemaking and statements of basis and purpose have, in turn, greatly increased the cost of conducting a rulemaking and the length of time required to issue a rule.

3. The Declaratory Judgment Act, 28 U.S.C. § 2201, broadly creates a cause of action for those seeking declaratory relief from agency action. The Declaratory Judgment Act does not, however, apply to controversies "with respect to Federal taxes." As a result, the circuit courts that have considered the question have declined to allow pre-enforcement judicial review of tax regulations issued by the Treasury Department and the Internal Revenue Service. *See* Kristin E. Hickman, *A Problem of Remedy: Responding to Treasury's (Lack of) Compliance with Administrative Procedure Act Rulemaking Requirements*, 76 GEO. WASH. L. REV. 1153 (2008). Applying more recent Supreme Court jurisprudence, however, the D.C. Circuit challenged this conclusion in *Cohen v. United States*, 578 F.3d 1 (D.C. Cir. 2009). Would you predict the denial of pre-enforcement review to have adverse effects? Assuming your answer is affirmative, do you see any offsetting benefits of the legal regime that applies to tax rules? Which legal regime do you prefer?

4. The Court in *Toilet Goods* concluded that the petitioners and regulation at bar did not satisfy the second part of the *Abbott Labs* test—hardship of deferring review. In evaluating the Court's application of that prong of the *Abbott Labs* test, it might help you to know that the suspension of certification services the Court discounts as a consequence of a refusal to provide immediate access to an FDA inspector has the effect of prohibiting a firm from selling anything made at the facility in question in interstate commerce, and that the administrative and judicial remedies for a wrongful suspension that the Court describes as prompt can easily take many years to complete. Currently, the D.C. Circuit applies only the first part of the *Abbott Labs* test, based on its belief that a court should resolve any issue that is appropriate for pre-enforcement review in a pre-enforcement review proceeding no matter what might be the adverse effects of deferral of review. Does that approach make more sense than the Supreme Court's approach?

5. The potential adverse effects of the *Abbott Labs* decision that FDA raised and that were the basis for the dissenting opinion in *Abbott Labs* have not proven to be serious. The courts have kept those effects to a manageable level through use of the tools the *Abbott Labs* majority referred to in the last four paragraphs of the opinion. As we discussed at length in Chapter 5, however, *Abbott Labs* arguably has had the effect of ossifying the rulemaking process and discouraging agencies from engaging in rulemaking. Some scholars have urged the Court to overrule *Abbott Labs* to avoid those adverse effects. *See, e.g.*, Richard J. Pierce, Jr., *Seven Ways to Deossify the Rulemaking Process*, 47 ADMIN. L. REV. 59 (1995). What is your opinion with respect to that proposal?

6. The *Abbott Labs* majority argued that the government might actually find the availability of pre-enforcement review advantageous because it allows an agency to find out quickly whether a rule is valid. In at least some contexts, Congress seems to agree with that belief. Thus, for instance, the Clean Air Act limits the availability of judicial review of a rule establishing an emission standard to thirty days after the EPA issued the rule, thereby precluding challenges to the validity of the rule in an enforcement proceeding and requiring anyone who wants to obtain judicial review of such a rule to file a petition for pre-enforcement review of the rule within thirty days of its issuance. The Court upheld that strict limit on the availability of judicial review of a rule in *Adamo Wrecking Co. v. United States*, 434 U.S. 275 (1978).

7. *Abbott Labs* remains the law, but with some major qualifications. In *Thunder Basin Coal Co. v. Reich*, 510 U.S. 200 (1994), the Court held that mine owners could not obtain pre-enforcement review of rules issued to implement the Mine Safety and Health Act because the statute explicitly provided for an alternative method of obtaining review—a challenge to the validity of the rule in an enforcement proceeding. Unlike its reasoning in *Abbott Labs*, the Court interpreted the existence of an explicit alternative means of challenging a rule in the statute as an implicit decision to preclude pre-enforcement review. Also, in *Shalala v. Illinois Council on Long Term Care*, 529 U.S. 1 (2000), the Justices engaged in a lively debate about the presumption in favor of pre-enforcement review. The majority said that "any such presumption must be far weaker than a presumption against preclusion of all review. . . ." *Id.* at 19–20. One dissenting Justice said, "preenforcement review is better described as the background rule, which can be displaced by any reasonable implication * * * from the statute." *Id.* at 32. Three other dissenting Justices referred to "our longstanding presumption in favor of preenforcement judicial review," but even they acknowledged that "the presumption [of reviewability] may not be quite as strong when the question is now-or-later instead of now-or-never." *Id.* at 33, 45.

Finally, both *Abbott Labs* and *Toilet Goods* considered the justiciability of challenges to agency regulations, adopted through notice-and-comment rulemaking, that imposed compliance burdens on regulated parties. Consequently, much of the Court's analysis considered the likelihood that those regulated parties would suffer legal consequences for noncompliance. As many of the cases in this casebook demonstrate, however, not all agency actions impose burdens. Some provide benefits. How should ripeness doctrine apply to judicial review of agency actions regarding benefit eligibility requirements? Consider the following case.

Reno v. Catholic Social Services, Inc.

509 U.S. 43 (1993).

■ JUSTICE SOUTER delivered the opinion of the Court.

This petition joins two separate suits, each challenging a different regulation issued by the Immigration and Naturalization Service (INS) in administering the alien legalization program created by Title II of the Immigration Reform and Control Act of 1986. In each instance, a District Court struck down the regulation challenged and issued a remedial order directing the INS to accept legalization applications beyond the statutory deadline; the Court of Appeals consolidated the INS's appeals from these orders, and affirmed the District Courts' judgments. We are now asked to consider whether the District Courts had jurisdiction to hear the challenges, and whether their remedial orders were permitted by law. * * *

I

On November 6, 1986, the President signed the Immigration Reform and Control Act of 1986, Title II of which established a scheme under which certain aliens unlawfully present in the United States could apply, first, for the status of a temporary resident and then, after a 1-year wait, for permission to reside permanently. An applicant for temporary resident status must have resided continuously in the United States in an unlawful status since at least January 1, 1982, 8 U.S.C. § 1255a(a)(2)(A); must have been physically present in the United States continuously since November 6, 1986, the date the Reform Act was enacted, § 1255a(a)(3)(A); and must have been otherwise admissible as an immigrant, § 1255a(a)(4). The applicant must also have applied during the 12-month period beginning on May 5, 1987. § 1255a(a)(1).

The two separate suits joined before us challenge regulations addressing, respectively, the first two of these four requirements. The first, *Reno v. Catholic Social Services, Inc. (CSS), et al.,* focuses on an INS interpretation of 8 U.S.C. § 1255a(a)(3), the Reform Act's requirement that applicants for temporary residence prove "continuous physical presence" in the United States since November 6, 1986. To mitigate this requirement, the Reform Act provides that "brief, casual, and innocent absences from the United States" will not break the required continuity. § 1255a(a)(3)(B). In a telex sent to its regional offices on November 14, 1986, however, the INS treated the exception narrowly, stating that it would consider an absence "brief, casual, and innocent" only if the alien had obtained INS permission, known as "advance parole," before leaving the United States; aliens who left without it would be "ineligible for legalization." The INS later softened this limitation somewhat by regulations issued on May 1, 1987, forgiving a failure to get advance parole for absences between November 6, 1986, and May 1, 1987. But the later regulation confirmed that any absences without advance parole on or after May 1, 1987, would not be considered "brief, casual, and innocent" and would therefore be taken to have broken the required continuity. See 8 CFR § 245a.1(g) (1992).

The *CSS* plaintiffs challenged the advance parole regulation as an impermissible construction of the Reform Act. * * *

The second of the two lawsuits, styled *INS v. League of United Latin American Citizens (LULAC) et al.,* goes to the INS's interpretation of 8 U.S.C. § 1255a(a)(2)(A), the Reform Act's "continuous unlawful residence" requirement. The Act provides that certain brief trips abroad will not break an alien's continuous unlawful residence (just as certain brief absences from the United States would not violate the "continuous physical presence" requirement). See § 1255a(g)(2)(A). Under an INS regulation, however, an alien would fail the "continuous unlawful residence" requirement if he had gone abroad and reentered the United States by presenting "facially valid" documentation to immigration authorities. 8 CFR § 245a.2(b)(8) (1992). On the INS's reasoning, an alien's use of such documentation made his subsequent presence "lawful" for purposes of § 1255a(a)(2)(A), thereby breaking the continuity of his unlawful residence. Thus, an alien who had originally entered the United States under a valid nonimmigrant visa, but had become an unlawful resident by violating the terms of that visa in a way known to the Government before January 1, 1982, was eligible for relief under the Reform Act. If, however, the same alien left the United States briefly and then used the same visa to get back in (a facially valid visa that had in fact become invalid after his earlier violation of its terms), he rendered himself ineligible.

In July 1987, the *LULAC* plaintiffs brought suit challenging the reentry regulation as inconsistent both with the Act and the equal protection limitation derived from Fifth Amendment due process.

* * *

II

* * *

[The Court held first that § 1255a(f)(1) of the Reform Act did not preclude judicial review of the plaintiffs' claims. Ed.]

Section 1255a(f)(1), however, is not the only jurisdictional hurdle in the way of the *CSS* and *LULAC* plaintiffs, whose claims still must satisfy the jurisdictional and justiciability requirements that apply in the absence of a specific congressional directive. To be sure, a statutory source of jurisdiction is not lacking, since 28 U.S.C. § 1331, generally granting federal question jurisdiction, "confer[s] jurisdiction on federal courts to review agency action." *Califano v. Sanders,* 430 U.S. 99, 105 (1977). Neither is it fatal that the Reform Act is silent about the type of judicial review those plaintiffs seek. We customarily refuse to treat such silence "as a denial of authority to [an] aggrieved person to seek appropriate relief in the federal courts," *Stark v. Wickard,* 321 U.S. 288, 309 (1944), and this custom has been "reinforced by the enactment of the Administrative Procedure Act, which embodies the basic presumption of judicial review to one 'suffering legal wrong because of agency action, or adversely affected or aggrieved by agency action within the meaning of a relevant statute.'" *Abbott Laboratories v. Gardner,* 387 U.S. 136, 140 (1967) (quoting 5 U.S.C. § 702).

As we said in *Abbott Laboratories,* however, the presumption of available judicial review is subject to an implicit limitation: "injunctive and declaratory judgment remedies," what the respondents seek here, "are discretionary, and courts traditionally have been reluctant to apply them to administrative determinations unless these arise in the context of a controversy 'ripe' for judicial resolution,"[18] 387 U.S., at 148, that is to say, unless the effects of the administrative action challenged have been "felt in a concrete way by the challenging parties," *id.,* at 148–149. In some cases, the promulgation of a regulation will itself affect parties concretely enough to satisfy this requirement, as it did in *Abbott Laboratories* itself. There, for example, as well as in *Gardner v. Toilet Goods Assn., Inc.,* 387 U.S. 167 (1967), the promulgation of the challenged regulations presented plaintiffs with the immediate dilemma to choose between complying with newly imposed, disadvantageous restrictions and risking serious penalties for violation. *Abbott Laboratories, supra,* 387 U.S., at 152–153; *Gardner, supra,* 387 U.S., at 171–172. But that will not be so in every case. In *Toilet Goods Assn., Inc. v. Gardner,* 387 U.S. 158 (1967), for example, we held that a challenge to another regulation, the impact of which could not "be said to be felt immediately by those subject to it in conducting their day-to-day affairs," *id.,* at 164, would not be ripe before the regulation's application to the plaintiffs in some more acute fashion, since "no irremediabl[y] adverse consequences flow[ed] from requiring a later challenge," *ibid.*

The regulations challenged here fall on the latter side of the line. They impose no penalties for violating any newly imposed restriction, but limit access to a benefit created by the Reform Act but not automatically bestowed on eligible aliens. Rather, the Act requires each alien desiring the benefit to take further affirmative steps, and to satisfy criteria beyond those addressed by the disputed regulations.[19] It

---

[18] We have noted that ripeness doctrine is drawn both from Article III limitations on judicial power and from prudential reasons for refusing to exercise jurisdiction. See, *e.g., Buckley v. Valeo,* 424 U.S. 1 (1976) (*per curiam*); *Socialist Labor Party v. Gilligan,* 406 U.S. 583, 588 (1972). Even when a ripeness question in a particular case is prudential, we may raise it on our own motion, and "cannot be bound by the wishes of the parties." *Regional Rail Reorganization Act Cases,* 419 U.S. 102, 138 (1974). Although the issue of ripeness is not explicitly addressed in the questions presented in the INS's petition, it is fairly included and both parties have touched on it in their briefs before this Court.

[19] Justice O'CONNOR contends that "if the court can make a firm prediction that the plaintiff will apply for the benefit, and that the agency will deny the application by virtue of the [challenged] rule[,] then there may well be a justiciable controversy that the court may find prudent to resolve." Even if this is true, however, we do not see how such a "firm prediction" could be made in this case. As for the prediction that the plaintiffs "will apply for the benefit," we are now considering only the cases of those plaintiffs who, in fact, failed to file timely applications. As for the prediction that "the agency will deny the application by virtue of the [challenged] rule," we reemphasize that in this case, access to the benefit in question is

delegates to the INS the task of determining on a case-by-case basis whether each applicant has met all of the Act's conditions, not merely those interpreted by the regulations in question. In these circumstances, the promulgation of the challenged regulations did not itself give each *CSS* and *LULAC* class member a ripe claim; a class member's claim would ripen only once he took the affirmative steps that he could take before the INS blocked his path by applying the regulation to him.[20]

Ordinarily, of course, that barrier would appear when the INS formally denied the alien's application on the ground that the regulation rendered him ineligible for legalization. A plaintiff who sought to rely on the denial of his application to satisfy the ripeness requirement, however, would then still find himself at least temporarily barred by the Reform Act's exclusive review provisions, since he would be seeking "judicial review of a determination respecting an application." 8 U.S.C. § 1255a(f)(1). The ripeness doctrine and the Reform Act's jurisdictional provisions would thus dovetail neatly, and not necessarily by mere coincidence. Congress may well have assumed that, in the ordinary case, the courts would not hear a challenge to regulations specifying limits to eligibility before those regulations were actually applied to an individual, whose challenge to the denial of an individual application would proceed within the Reform Act's limited scheme. The *CSS* and *LULAC* plaintiffs do not argue that this limited scheme would afford them inadequate review of a determination based on the regulations they challenge, presumably because they would be able to obtain such review on appeal from a deportation order, if they become subject to such an order * * *.

This is not the end of the matter, however, because the plaintiffs have called our attention to an INS policy that may well have placed some of them outside the scope of § 1255a(f)(1). The INS has issued a manual detailing procedures for its offices to follow in implementing the Reform Act's legalization programs and instructing INS employees called "Legalization Assistants" to review certain applications in the presence of the applicants before accepting them for filing. See Procedures Manual for the Legalization and Special Agricultural

---

conditioned on several nontrivial rules other than the two challenged. This circumstance makes it much more difficult to predict firmly that the INS would deny a particular application "by virtue of the [challenged] rule," and not by virtue of some other, unchallenged rule that it determined barred an adjustment of status.

[20] Justice O'CONNOR maintains that the plaintiffs' actions are now ripe because they have amended their complaints to seek the additional remedy of extending the application period, and the application period is now over. We do not see how these facts establish ripeness. In both cases before us, the plaintiffs' underlying claim is that an INS regulation implementing the Reform Act is invalid. Because the Act requires each alien desiring legalization to take certain affirmative steps, and because the Act's conditions extend beyond those addressed by the challenged regulations, one cannot know whether the challenged regulation actually makes a concrete difference to a particular alien until one knows that he will take those affirmative steps and will satisfy the other conditions. Neither the fact that the application period is now over, nor the fact that the plaintiffs would now like the period to be extended, tells us anything about the willingness of the class members to take the required affirmative steps, or about their satisfaction of the Reform Act's other conditions. The end of the application period may mean that the plaintiffs no longer have an opportunity to take the steps that could make their claims ripe; but this fact is significant only for those plaintiffs who can claim that the Government prevented them from filing a timely application. See *infra* (discussing the INS's "front-desking" practice).

Worker Programs of the Immigration Reform and Control Act of 1986 (Legalization Manual or Manual).[21] According to the Manual, "[m]inor correctable deficiencies such as incomplete responses or typographical errors may be corrected by the [Legalization Assistant]." *Id.,* at IV–6. "[I]f the applicant is statutorily ineligible," however, the Manual provides that "the application *will be rejected* by the [Legalization Assistant]." *Ibid.* (emphasis added). Because this prefiling rejection of applications occurs at the front desk of an INS office, it has come to be called "front-desking."[22] While the regulations challenged in *CSS* and *LULAC* were in force, Legalization Assistants who applied both the regulations and the Manual's instructions may well have "front-desked" the applications of class members who disclosed the circumstances of their trips outside the United States, and affidavits on file in the *LULAC* case represent that they did exactly that.

As respondents argue, a class member whose application was "front-desked" would have felt the effects of the "advance parole" or "facially valid document" regulation in a particularly concrete manner, for his application for legalization would have been blocked then and there; his challenge to the regulation should not fail for lack of ripeness. Front-desking would also have a further, and untoward, consequence for jurisdictional purposes, for it would effectively exclude an applicant from access even to the limited administrative and judicial review procedures established by the Reform Act. He would have no formal denial to appeal to the Associate Commissioner for Examinations, nor would he have an opportunity to build an administrative record on which judicial review might be based. Hence, to construe § 1255a(f)(1) to bar district court jurisdiction over his challenge, we would have to impute to Congress an intent to preclude judicial review of the legality of INS action entirely under those circumstances. As we stated recently in *McNary,* however, there is a "well-settled presumption favoring interpretations of statutes that allow judicial review of administrative action," *McNary,* 498 U.S., at 496; and we will accordingly find an intent to preclude such review only if presented with " 'clear and convincing evidence,' " *Abbott Laboratories,* 387 U.S., at 141 (quoting *Rusk v. Cort,* 369 U.S. 367, 379–380 (1962)).

There is no such clear and convincing evidence in the statute before us. Although the phrase "a determination respecting an application for

---

[21] Under the Manual's procedures, only those applications that were not prepared with the assistance of a "Qualified Designated Entity" (the Reform Act's designation for private organizations that serve as intermediaries between applicants and the INS, see 8 U.S.C. § 1255a(c)(1)) are subject to review by Legalization Assistants. The applications that were prepared with the help of Qualified Designated Entities skip this step. See Legalization Manual, at IV–5, IV–6. There is no evidence in the record indicating how many *CSS* and *LULAC* class members were assisted by Qualified Designated Entities in preparing their applications.

[22] The INS forwards a different interpretation of the policy set forth in the Legalization Manual. According to the INS, the Manual reflects a policy, motivated by "charitable concern," of "inform[ing] aliens of [the INS's] view that their applications are deficient before it accepts the filing fee, so that they can make an informed choice about whether to pay the fee if they are not going to receive immediate relief." The "rejection" policy, argues the INS, did not really bar applicants from filing applications; another sentence in the Manual proves that the door remains open, for it provides that "[i]f an applicant whose application has been rejected by the [Legalization Assistant] insists on filing, the application will be routed through a fee clerk to an adjudicator with a routing slip from the [Legalization Assistant] stating the noted deficiency(ies)." Legalization Manual, at IV–6.

adjustment of status" could conceivably encompass a Legalization Assistant's refusal to accept the application for filing at the front desk of a Legalization Office, nothing in the statute suggests, let alone demonstrates, that Congress was using "determination" in such an extended and informal sense. Indeed, at least one related statutory provision suggests just the opposite. Section 1255a(f)(3)(B) limits administrative appellate review to "the administrative record established at the time of the determination on the application"; because there obviously can be no administrative record in the case of a front-desked application, the term "determination" is best read to exclude front-desking. Thus, just as we avoided an interpretation of 8 U.S.C. § 1160(e) in *McNary* that would have amounted to "the practical equivalent of a total denial of judicial review of generic constitutional and statutory claims," *McNary, supra,* 498 U.S., at 497, so here we avoid an interpretation of § 1255a(f)(1) that would bar front-desked applicants from ever obtaining judicial review of the regulations that rendered them ineligible for legalization.

Unfortunately, however, neither the *CSS* record nor the *LULAC* record contains evidence that particular class members were actually subjected to front-desking. None of the named individual plaintiffs in either case alleges that he or she was front-desked, and while a number of affidavits in the *LULAC* record contain the testimony of immigration attorneys and employees of interested organizations that the INS has "refused," "rejected," or "den[ied] individuals the right to file" applications, the testimony is limited to such general assertions; none of the affiants refers to any specific incident that we can identify as an instance of front-desking.

This lack of evidence precludes us from resolving the jurisdictional issue here, because, on the facts before us, the front-desking of a particular class member is not only sufficient to make his legal claims ripe, but necessary to do so. As the case has been presented to us, there seems to be no reliable way of determining whether a particular class member, had he applied at all (which, we assume, he did not), would have applied in a manner that would have subjected him to front-desking. As of October 16, 1987, the INS had certified 977 Qualified Designated Entities which could have aided class members in preparing applications that would not have been front-desked, see 52 Fed. Reg. 44812 (1987); n. 21, *supra,* and there is no prior history of application behavior on the basis of which we could predict who would have applied without Qualified Designated Entity assistance and therefore been front-desked. Hence, we cannot say that the mere existence of a front-desking policy involved a "concrete application" of the invalid regulations to those class members who were not actually front-desked.[28] Because only those class members (if any) who were front-desked have ripe claims over which the District Courts should exercise jurisdiction, we must vacate the judgment of the Court of Appeals, and

---

[28] The record reveals relatively little about the application of the front-desking policy and surrounding circumstances. Although we think it unlikely, we cannot rule out the possibility that further facts would allow class members who were not front-desked to demonstrate that the front-desking policy was nevertheless a substantial cause of their failure to apply, so that they can be said to have had the "advanced parole" or "facially valid document" regulation applied to them in a sufficiently concrete manner to satisfy ripeness concerns.

remand with directions to remand to the respective District Courts for proceedings to determine which class members were front-desked.

■ JUSTICE O'CONNOR, concurring in the judgment.

* * *

Our prior cases concerning anticipatory challenges to agency rules do not specify when an anticipatory suit may be brought against a benefit-conferring rule, such as the INS regulations here. An anticipatory suit by a would-be beneficiary, who has not yet applied for the benefit that the rule denies him, poses different ripeness problems than a pre-enforcement suit against a duty-creating rule, see *Abbott Laboratories v. Gardner,* 387 U.S. 136, 148–156 (1967) (permitting pre-enforcement suit). Even if he succeeds in his anticipatory action, the would-be beneficiary will not receive the benefit until he actually applies for it; and the agency might then deny him the benefit on grounds other than his ineligibility under the rule. By contrast, a successful suit against the duty-creating rule will relieve the plaintiff immediately of a burden that he otherwise would bear.

Yet I would not go so far as to state that a suit challenging a benefit-conferring rule is necessarily unripe simply because the plaintiff has not yet applied for the benefit. "Where the inevitability of the operation of a statute against certain individuals is patent, it is irrelevant to the existence of a justiciable controversy that there will be a time delay before the disputed provisions will come into effect." *Regional Rail Reorganization Act Cases,* 419 U.S. 102 (1974). If it is "inevitable" that the challenged rule will "operat[e]" to the plaintiff's disadvantage—if the court can make a firm prediction that the plaintiff will apply for the benefit, and that the agency will deny the application by virtue of the rule—then there may well be a justiciable controversy that the court may find prudent to resolve.

I do not mean to suggest that a simple anticipatory challenge to the INS regulations would be ripe under the approach I propose. That issue need not be decided because, as explained below, these cases are *not* a simple anticipatory challenge. My intent is rather to criticize the Court's reasoning—its reliance on a categorical rule that would-be beneficiaries cannot challenge benefit-conferring regulations until they apply for benefits.

Certainly the line of cases beginning with *Abbott Laboratories* does not support this categorical approach. That decision itself discusses with approval an earlier case that involved an anticipatory challenge to a benefit-conferring rule.

> "[I]n *United States v. Storer Broadcasting Co.,* 351 U.S. 192 (1956), the Court held to be a final agency action . . . an FCC regulation announcing a Commission policy that it would not issue a television license to an applicant already owning five such licenses, *even though no specific application was before the Commission.*" 387 U.S., at 151 (emphasis added).

More recently, in *EPA v. National Crushed Stone Assn.,* 449 U.S. 64 (1980), the Court held that a facial challenge to the variance provision of an EPA pollution-control regulation was ripe even "prior to application of the regulation to a particular [company's] request for a variance." *Id.,* at 72, n. 12. And in *Pacific Gas & Elec. Co. v. State Energy Resources Conservation and Development Comm'n,* 461 U.S. 190 (1983), the Court permitted utilities to challenge a state law imposing a moratorium on the certification of nuclear power plants, even though the utilities had not yet applied for a certificate. See *id.,* at 200–202. To be sure, all of these decisions involved licenses, certificates, or variances, which exempt the bearer from otherwise-applicable duties; but the same is true of the instant cases. The benefit conferred by the Reform Act—an adjustment in status to lawful temporary resident alien, see 8 U.S.C. § 1255a(a)—readily can be conceptualized as a "license" or "certificate" to remain in the United States, or a "variance" from the immigration laws.

As for *Lujan v. National Wildlife Federation,* 497 U.S. 871 (1990), the Court there stated:

> "Absent [explicit statutory authorization for immediate judicial review], a regulation is not ordinarily considered the type of agency action 'ripe' for judicial review under the APA until the scope of the controversy has been reduced to more manageable proportions, and its factual components fleshed out, by some concrete action applying the regulation to the claimant's situation in a fashion that harms or threatens to harm him. (The major exception, of course, is a substantive rule which as a practical matter requires the plaintiff to adjust his conduct immediately. Such agency action is 'ripe' for review at once, whether or not explicit statutory review apart from the APA is provided.)" *Id.,* at 891–892.

This language does not suggest that an anticipatory challenge to a benefit-conferring rule will of necessity be constitutionally unripe, for otherwise an "explicit statutory review" provision would not help cure the ripeness problem. Rather, *Lujan* points to the prudential considerations that weigh in the ripeness calculus: the need to "fles[h] out" the controversy and the burden on the plaintiff who must "adjust his conduct immediately." These are just the kinds of factors identified in the two-part, prudential test for ripeness that *Abbott Laboratories* articulated. "The problem is best seen in a twofold aspect, requiring us to evaluate both the fitness of the issues for judicial decision and the hardship to the parties of withholding court consideration." 387 U.S., at 149. At the very least, where the challenge to the benefit-conferring rule is purely legal, and where the plaintiff will suffer hardship if he cannot raise his challenge until later, a justiciable, anticipatory challenge to the rule may well be ripe in the prudential sense. Thus I cannot agree with the Court that ripeness will never obtain until the plaintiff actually applies for the benefit.

■ JUSTICE STEVENS, with whom JUSTICE WHITE and JUSTICE BLACKMUN join, dissenting.

* * *

Our test for ripeness is two pronged, "requiring us to evaluate both the fitness of the issues for judicial decision and the hardship to the parties of withholding court consideration." *Abbott Laboratories v. Gardner,* 387 U.S. 136, 149 (1967). Whether an issue is fit for judicial review, in turn, often depends on "the degree and nature of [a] regulation's present effect on those seeking relief," *Toilet Goods Assn., Inc. v. Gardner,* 387 U.S. 158, 164 (1967), or, put differently, on whether there has been some "concrete action applying the regulation to the claimant's situation in a fashion that harms or threatens to harm him," *Lujan v. National Wildlife Federation,* 497 U.S. 871, 891 (1990). As Justice O'CONNOR notes, we have returned to this two-part test for ripeness time and again, and there is no question but that the *Abbott Laboratories* formulation should govern this case.

As to the first *Abbott Laboratories* factor, I think it clear that the challenged regulations have an impact on respondents sufficiently "direct and immediate," 387 U.S., at 152, that they are fit for judicial review. My opinion rests, in part, on the unusual character of the amnesty program in question. As we explained in *McNary:*

> "The Immigration Reform and Control Act of 1986 (Reform Act) constituted a major statutory response to the vast tide of illegal immigration that had produced a 'shadow population' of literally millions of undocumented aliens in the United States. . . . [I]n recognition that a large segment of the shadow population played a useful and constructive role in the American economy, but continued to reside in perpetual fear, the Reform Act established two broad amnesty programs to allow existing undocumented aliens to emerge from the shadows." 498 U.S., at 481–483 (footnotes omitted).

A major purpose of this ambitious effort was to eliminate the fear in which these immigrants lived, " 'afraid to seek help when their rights are violated, when they are victimized by criminals, employers or landlords or when they become ill.' " *Ayuda, Inc. v. Thornburgh,* 292 U.S. App. D.C. 150, 168 (1991) (Wald, J., dissenting). Indeed, in recognition of this fear of governmental authority, Congress established a special procedure through which "qualified designated entities," or "QDE's," would serve as a channel of communication between undocumented aliens and the INS, providing reasonable assurance that "emergence from the shadows" would result in amnesty and not deportation. 8 U.S.C. § 1255a(c)(2); see *Ayuda,* 292 U.S. App. D.C., at 168, and n. 1.

Under these circumstances, official advice that specified aliens were ineligible for amnesty was certain to convince those aliens to retain their "shadow" status rather than come forward. At the moment that decision was made—at the moment respondents conformed their behavior to the invalid regulations—those regulations concretely and directly affected respondents, consigning them to the shadow world from which the Reform Act was designed to deliver them, and threatening to deprive them of the statutory entitlement that would otherwise be theirs. Cf. *Lujan,* 497 U.S., at 891 (concrete application threatening harm as basis for ripeness).

The majority concedes, of course, that class members whose applications were "front-desked" felt the effects of the invalid regulations concretely, because their applications were "blocked then and there." Why "then and there," as opposed to earlier and elsewhere, should be dispositive remains unclear to me; whether a potential application is thwarted by a front-desk Legalization Assistant, by advice from a QDE, by consultation with a private attorney, or even by word of mouth regarding INS policies, the effect on the potential applicant is equally concrete, and equally devastating. In my view, there is no relevant difference, for purposes of ripeness, between respondents who were "front-desked" and those who can demonstrate, like the *LULAC* class, that they " 'learned of their ineligibility following promulgation of the policy and who, relying upon information that they were ineligible, did not apply,' " or, like the class granted relief in *CSS,* that they " 'knew of [the INS'] unlawful regulation and thereby concluded that they were ineligible for legalization and by reason of that conclusion did not file an application.' " As Judge Wald explained in *Ayuda:*

> "[T]he majority admits that if low level INS officials had refused outright to accept legalization applications for filing, the district court could hear the suit. Even if the plaintiffs' affidavits are read to allege active discouragement rather than outright refusal to accept, this is a subtle distinction indeed, and one undoubtedly lost on the illegal aliens involved, upon which to grant or deny jurisdiction to challenge the practice." 292 U.S. App. D.C., at 169, n. 3 (Wald, J., dissenting).

The second *Abbott Laboratories* factor, which focuses on the cost to the parties of withholding judicial review, also weighs heavily in favor of ripeness in this case. Every day during which the invalid regulations were effective meant another day spent in the shadows for respondents, with the attendant costs of that way of life. Even more important, with each passing day, the clock on the application period continued to run, increasing the risk that review, when it came, would be meaningless because the application period had already expired. See *Ayuda,* 292 U.S. App. D.C., at 178 (Wald, J., dissenting). Indeed, the dilemma respondents find themselves in today speaks volumes about the costs of deferring review in this situation. Cf. *Toilet Goods Assn.,* 387 U.S., at 164 (challenge not ripe where "no irremediable adverse consequences flow from requiring a later challenge").

Under *Abbott Laboratories,* then, I think it plain that respondents' claims were ripe for adjudication at the time they were filed. The Court's contrary holding, which seems to rest on the premise that respondents cannot challenge a condition of legalization until they have satisfied all other conditions is at odds not only with our ripeness case law, but also with our more general understanding of the way in which government regulation affects the regulated. In *Northeastern Fla. Chapter, Associated Gen. Contractors of America v. Jacksonville,* 508 U.S. 656 (1993), for instance, we held that a class of contractors could challenge an ordinance making it more difficult for them to compete for public business without making any showing that class members were actually in a position to receive such business, absent the challenged regulation. We announced the following rule:

> "When the government erects a barrier that makes it more difficult for members of one group to obtain a benefit than it is for members of another group, a member of the former group seeking to challenge the barrier need not allege that he would have obtained the benefit but for the barrier in order to establish standing. The 'injury in fact' in an equal protection case of this variety is the denial of equal treatment resulting

from the imposition of the barrier, not the ultimate inability to obtain the benefit." *Id.,* at 666.[4]

Our decision in the *Jacksonville* case is well supported by precedent; the Court's ripeness holding today is notable for its originality.

Though my approach to the ripeness issue differs from that of Justice O'CONNOR, we are in agreement in concluding that respondents' claims are ripe for adjudication.

* * *

NOTES AND QUESTIONS

1. In *Catholic Social Services*, the five-Justice majority held that petitioners could not obtain pre-application review of benefit eligibility rules because, unlike the regulated parties in *Abbott Labs* threatened by statutory penalties for noncompliance with agency rules potential applicants for benefits would not suffer hardship from deferring review of the rules until they are applied as the basis to deny an applicant benefits. Justice O'Connor in concurrence contended that

2. The *Catholic Social Services* majority potentially distinguished a potential claimant who had done nothing to apply for benefits from one who had been "front desked"—*i.e.*, who had not formally applied but had been told informally by agency employees that their application would be denied if submitted. Why do you think the Court considered these two scenarios distinguishable? What aspects of front desking are key in altering the ripeness analysis? What evidence should a reviewing court require to substantiate such a ripeness claim? Should it matter for ripeness analysis whether the agency employees engaging in such behavior possess or lack the training or formal decisionmaking authority to make such assessments?

3. DUTY TO EXHAUST ADMINISTRATIVE REMEDIES

Courts have long required prospective petitioners to exhaust administrative remedies as a prerequisite to the availability of judicial review. The common law exhaustion requirement is flexible, pragmatic, and subject to several judge-made exceptions. Ironically, one of the Court's most comprehensive efforts to justify common law exhaustion doctrine is contained in the following opinion in which the Court held that the petitioner was excused from exhausting his administrative remedies.

---

[4]   *Jacksonville* is, of course, an equal protection case, while respondents in this case are seeking a statutory benefit. If this distinction has any relevance to a ripeness analysis, then it should mitigate in favor of finding ripeness here; I assume we should be more reluctant to overcome jurisdictional hurdles to decide constitutional issues than to effectuate statutory programs.

McKart v. United States

395 U.S. 185 (1969).

■ MR. JUSTICE MARSHALL, delivered the opinion of the Court.

Petitioner was indicted for willfully and knowingly failing to report for and submit to induction into the Armed Forces of the United States. At trial, petitioner's only defense was that he should have been exempt from military service because he was the "sole surviving son" of a family whose father had been killed in action while serving in the Armed Forces of the United States. Selective Service Act of 1948, § 6(*o*), 50 U.S.C. § 456(*o*). The District Court held that he could not raise that defense because he had failed to exhaust the administrative remedies provided by the Selective Service System. Accordingly, petitioner was convicted and sentenced to three years' imprisonment. * * *

[We have omitted the Court's lengthy recitation of the complicated facts of the case. McKart was originally classified by his local selective service (draft) board as a sole surviving son, an exempt classification for which he clearly qualified. When his local draft board later erroneously reclassified him as I-A, and hence as immediately eligible to be drafted, McKart did not appeal that decision, apparently because he was one of the many young men who refused to cooperate with the draft board because they objected to the Vietnam War on moral grounds. He was then ordered to report for a pre-induction physical and did not appear. Failure to appear in response to such an order was a crime at the time. McKart was indicted and attempted to defend himself in the criminal proceeding by arguing that he was exempt from the draft as a sole surviving son. Ed.]

The Government maintains, however, that petitioner cannot raise the invalidity of his I-A classification and subsequent induction order as a defense to a criminal prosecution for refusal to report for induction. According to the Government, petitioner's failure to appeal his reclassification * * * constitutes a failure to exhaust available administrative remedies and therefore should bar all judicial review. For the reasons set out below, we cannot agree.

The doctrine of exhaustion of administrative remedies is well established in the jurisprudence of administrative law. The doctrine provides "that no one is entitled to judicial relief for a supposed or threatened injury until the prescribed administrative remedy has been exhausted." *Myers v. Bethlehem Shipbuilding Corp.*, 303 U.S. 41, 50–51 (1938). The doctrine is applied in a number of different situations and is, like most judicial doctrines, subject to numerous exceptions. Application of the doctrine to specific cases requires an understanding of its purposes and of the particular administrative scheme involved.

Perhaps the most common application of the exhaustion doctrine is in cases where the relevant statute provides that certain administrative procedures shall be exclusive. The reasons for making such procedures exclusive, and for the judicial application of the exhaustion doctrine in cases where the statutory requirement of exclusivity is not so explicit, are not difficult to understand. A primary purpose is, of course, the avoidance of premature interruption of the administrative process. The agency, like a trial court, is created for the purpose of applying a statute in the first instance. Accordingly, it is normally desirable to let the agency develop the necessary factual background upon which decisions should be based. And since agency decisions are frequently of a discretionary nature or frequently require expertise, the agency should be given the first chance to exercise that discretion or to apply that expertise. And of course it is generally more efficient for the administrative process to go forward without interruption than it is to permit the parties to seek aid from the courts at various intermediate stages. The very same reasons lie behind judicial rules sharply limiting interlocutory appeals.

Closely related to the above reasons is a notion peculiar to administrative law. The administrative agency is created as a separate entity and invested with certain powers and duties. The courts ordinarily should not interfere with an agency until it has completed its action, or else has clearly exceeded its jurisdiction. As Professor Jaffe puts it, "[t]he exhaustion doctrine is, therefore, an expression of executive and administrative autonomy." L. JAFFE, JUDICIAL CONTROL OF ADMINISTRATIVE ACTION 425 (1965). This reason is particularly pertinent where the function of the agency and the particular decision sought to be reviewed involve exercise of discretionary powers granted the agency by Congress, or require application of special expertise.

Some of these reasons apply equally to cases like the present one, where the administrative process is at an end and a party seeks judicial review of a decision that was not appealed through the administrative process. Particularly, judicial review may be hindered by the failure of the litigant to allow the agency to make a factual record, or to exercise its discretion or apply its expertise. In addition, other justifications for requiring exhaustion in cases of this sort have nothing to do with the dangers of interruption of the administrative process. Certain very practical notions of judicial efficiency come into play as well. A complaining party may be successful in vindicating his rights in the administrative process. If he is required to pursue his administrative remedies, the courts may never have to intervene. And notions of administrative autonomy require that the agency be given a chance to discover and correct its own errors. Finally, it is possible that frequent and deliberate flouting of administrative processes could weaken the effectiveness of an agency by encouraging people to ignore its procedures.

* * *

We are not here faced with a premature resort to the courts—all administrative remedies are now closed to petitioner. We are asked instead to hold that petitioner's failure to utilize a particular administrative process—an appeal—bars him from defending a criminal prosecution on grounds which could have been raised on that appeal. We cannot agree that application of the exhaustion doctrine would be proper in the circumstances of the present case.

First of all, it is well to remember that use of the exhaustion doctrine in criminal cases can be exceedingly harsh. The defendant is often stripped of his only defense; he must go to jail without having any judicial review of an assertedly invalid order. The deprivation of judicial review occurs not when the affected person is affirmatively asking for assistance from the courts but when the Government is attempting to impose criminal sanctions on him. Such a result should not be tolerated unless the interests underlying the exhaustion rule clearly outweigh the severe burden imposed upon the registrant if he is denied judicial review. The statute as it stood when petitioner was reclassified said nothing which would require registrants to raise all their claims before the appeal boards. We must ask, then, whether there is in this case a governmental interest compelling enough to outweigh the severe burden placed on petitioner. Even if there is no such compelling interest when petitioner's case is viewed in isolation, we must also ask whether allowing all similarly situated registrants to bypass administrative appeal procedures would seriously impair the Selective Service System's ability to perform its functions.

The question of whether petitioner is entitled to exemption as a sole surviving son is, as we have seen, solely one of statutory interpretation. The resolution of that issue does not require any particular expertise on the part of the appeal board; the proper interpretation is certainly not a matter of discretion. In this sense, the issue is different from many Selective Service classification questions which do involve expertise or the exercise of discretion, both by the local boards and the appeal boards. Petitioner's failure to take his claim through all available administrative appeals only deprived the Selective Service System of the opportunity of having its appellate boards resolve a question of statutory interpretation. Since judicial review would not be significantly aided by an additional administrative decision of this sort, we cannot see any compelling reason why petitioner's failure to appeal should bar his only defense to a criminal prosecution. There is simply no overwhelming need for the court to have the agency finally resolve this question in the first instance, at least not where the administrative process is at an end and the registrant is faced with criminal prosecution.

We are thus left with the Government's argument that failure to require exhaustion in the present case will induce registrants to bypass available administrative remedies. The Government fears an increase in litigation and a consequent danger of thwarting the primary function of the Selective Service System, the rapid mobilization of manpower. This argument is based upon the proposition that the Selective Service System will, through its own processes, correct most errors and thus avoid much litigation. The exhaustion doctrine is assertedly necessary to compel resort to these processes. The Government also speculates that many more registrants will risk criminal prosecution if their claims need not carry into court the stigma of denial not only by their local boards, but also by at least one appeal board.

We do not, however, take such a dire view of the likely consequences of today's decision. At the outset, we doubt whether many registrants will be foolhardy enough to deny the Selective Service System the opportunity to correct its own errors by taking their chances with a criminal prosecution and a possibility of five years in jail. The very presence of the criminal sanction is sufficient to ensure that the great majority of registrants will exhaust all administrative remedies before deciding whether or not to continue the challenge to their classifications. And, today's holding does not apply to every registrant who fails to take advantage of the administrative remedies provided by the Selective Service System. For, as we have said, many classifications require exercise of discretion or application of expertise; in these cases, it may be proper to require a registrant to carry his case through the administrative process before he comes into court. Moreover, we are not convinced that many in this rather small class of registrants will bypass the Selective Service System with the thought that their ultimate chances of success in the courts are enhanced thereby. In short, we simply do not think that the exhaustion doctrine contributes significantly to the fairly low number of registrants who decide to subject themselves to criminal prosecution for failure to submit to induction. Accordingly, in the present case, where there appears no significant interest to be served in having the System decide the issue before it reaches the courts, we do not believe that petitioner's failure to appeal his classification should foreclose all judicial review.

■ [Opinions by JUSTICE DOUGLAS, concurring, and an opinion by JUSTICE WHITE, concurring in the result, are omitted. Ed.]

Although the Court in *McKart* recognized the need for flexibility in common law exhaustion requirements and excused the petitioner's failure to exhaust administrative remedies, litigants are ill advised to rely on the Court's holding in that case to predict the outcome of many other efforts to avoid the exhaustion requirement. The following opinion demonstrates the narrow scope of the *McKart* exception to the common law exhaustion requirement

McGee v. United States

402 U.S. 479 (1971).

■ MR. JUSTICE MARSHALL delivered the opinion of the Court.

Petitioner was convicted of failing to submit to induction and other violations of the draft laws. His principal defense involves the contention that he had been incorrectly classified by his local Selective Service board. The Court of Appeals ruled that this defense was barred because petitioner had failed to pursue and exhaust his administrative remedies. We granted certiorari to consider the applicability of the "exhaustion of administrative remedies" doctrine in the circumstances of this case.

In February 1966, while attending the University of Rochester, petitioner applied to his local Selective Service board for conscientious objector status. In support of his claim to that exemption he submitted the special form for conscientious objectors (SSS Form 150), setting forth his views concerning participation in war. The board continued petitioner's existing classification—student deferment—and advised him that the conscientious objector claim would be passed upon when student status no longer applied.

In April 1967 petitioner wrote to President Johnson, Johnson, enclosing the charred remnants of his draft cards and declaring his conviction that he must "sever every link with violence and war." The letter included a statement that petitioner had "already been accepted for graduate study in a program where I would probably qualify for the theological deferment." A copy of the letter was forwarded to the local board; the board continued petitioner's student deferment. Petitioner graduated in June 1967, and thereafter the board sent him a current information questionnaire which asked *inter alia* for specific information concerning his future educational plans and generally for any information he thought should be called to the board's attention. Petitioner returned the questionnaire unanswered and announced in a cover letter that henceforth he would adhere to a policy of noncooperation with the Selective Service System.

In September 1967 the board reviewed petitioner's file, rejected the pending conscientious objector claim, and reclassified petitioner I-A. In response to his reclassification petitioner sought neither a personal appearance before the local board nor review by the appeal board. Indeed, pursuant to his policy of noncooperation, he returned to the board, unopened, the communication notifying him of the reclassification and of his right to appear before the local board, to confer with the Government appeal agent, and to appeal. Petitioner did not appear for a physical examination ordered to take place in October 1967. He did respond to an order to appear for induction in January 1968, and he took a physical examination at that time. However, he refused to submit to induction.

Petitioner was prosecuted, under § 12(a) of the Military Selective Service Act of 1967 and applicable Selective Service regulations, for failing to submit to induction (count I), failing to report for a pre-induction physical examination (count II), failing to keep possession of a valid classification notice (count III), and failing to submit requested information relevant to his draft status (count IV). Petitioner was convicted on all four counts and sentenced to two years' imprisonment on each count. Petitioner's principal defense to liability for refusing induction was that the local board had erred in classifying him I-A. The Court of Appeals, with one judge dissenting, held that the defense of incorrect classification was barred because petitioner had failed to exhaust the administrative remedies available for correction of such an error. The conviction was affirmed by the Court of Appeals.

Two Terms ago, in *McKart v. United States*, 395 U.S. 185 (1969), the Court surveyed the place of the exhaustion doctrine in Selective Service cases, and the policies that underpin the doctrine. As it has evolved, the doctrine when properly invoked operates to restrict judicial scrutiny of administrative action having to do with the classification of a registrant, in the case of a registrant who has failed to pursue normal administrative remedies and thus has side-stepped a corrective process which might have cured or rendered moot the very defect later complained of in court. *McKart* stands for the proposition that the doctrine is not to be applied inflexibly in all situations, but that decision also plainly contemplates situations where a litigant's claims will lose vitality because the litigant has failed to contest his rights in an administrative forum. The result in a criminal context is no doubt a substantial detriment to the defendant whose claims are barred. Still this unhappy result may be justified in particular circumstances by considerations relating to the integrity of the Selective Service classification process and the limited role of the courts in deciding the proper classification of draft registrants.

After *McKart* the task for the courts, in deciding the applicability of the exhaustion doctrine to the circumstances of a particular case, is to ask "whether allowing all similarly situated registrants to bypass [the administrative avenue in question] would seriously impair the Selective Service System's ability to perform its functions." 395 U.S. at 197. *McKart* specified the salient interests that may be jeopardized by a registrant's failure to pursue administrative remedies. Certain failures to exhaust may deny the administrative system important opportunities "to make a factual record" for purposes of classification, or "to exercise its discretion or apply its expertise" in the course of decisionmaking. *Id.* at 194. There may be a danger that relaxation of exhaustion requirements, in certain circumstances, would induce "frequent and deliberate flouting of administrative processes," thereby undermining the scheme of decisionmaking that Congress has created. *Id.* at 195. And of course, a strict exhaustion requirement tends to ensure that the agency have additional opportunities "to discover and correct its own errors," and thus may help to obviate all occasion for judicial review. *Id.*

To be weighed against the interests in exhaustion is the harsh impact of the doctrine when it is invoked to bar any judicial review of a registrant's claims. Surely an insubstantial procedural default by a registrant should not shield an invalid order from judicial correction, simply because the interest in time-saving self-correction by the agency is involved. That single interest is conceivably slighted by any failure to exhaust, however innocuous the bypass in other respects, and *McKart* recognizes that the exhaustion requirement is not to be applied "blindly in every case." *Id.* at 201. *McKart* also acknowledges that the fear of "frequent and deliberate flouting" can easily be overblown, since in the normal case a registrant would be "foolhardy" indeed to withhold a valid claim from administrative scrutiny. *Id.* at 200. Thus the contention that the rigors of the exhaustion doctrine should be relaxed is not to be met by mechanical recitation of the broad interests usually served by the doctrine but rather should be assessed in light of a discrete analysis of the particular default in question, to see whether there is "a governmental interest compelling enough" to justify the forfeiting of judicial review. *Id.* at 197.

In the *McKart* case, the focal interest for purposes of analysis was the interest in allowing the agency "to make a factual record, or to exercise its discretion or apply its expertise." There the registrant had failed to take an administrative appeal from the local board's denial of "sole surviving son" status. Later the issue of McKart's entitlement to that exempt status arose in a criminal context, and the Court held that the claim should be heard as a defense to liability despite the failure to exhaust. The validity of the claim was a question "solely . . . of statutory interpretation." *Id.* at 197–98. McKart's failure to exhaust did not inhibit the making of an administrative record—all the relevant facts had been presented. The issue was not one of fact and thus its resolution would not have been aided by the exercise of special administrative expertise; and proper interpretation of the statutory provision in question was not a matter for agency discretion.

In the present case the same interest is pivotal—but here it is apparent that McGee's failure to exhaust did jeopardize the interest in full administrative fact gathering and utilization of agency expertise, rather than the contrary. Unlike the dispute about statutory interpretation involved in *McKart*, McGee's claims to exempt status—as a ministerial student or a conscientious objector—depended on the application of expertise by administrative bodies in resolving underlying issues of fact. Factfinding for purposes of Selective Service classification is committed primarily to the administrative process, with very limited judicial review to ascertain whether there is a "basis in fact" for the administrative determination. *McKart* expressly noted that as to classification claims turning on the resolution of particularistic fact questions, "the Selective Service System and the courts may have a stronger interest in having the question decided in the first instance by the local board and then by the appeal board, which considers the question anew." 395 U.S. at 198 n.16. This "stronger interest," in the circumstances of the present case, has become compelling and fully sufficient to justify invocation of the exhaustion doctrine.

* * *

That petitioner's failure to exhaust should cut off judicial review of his conscientious objector claim may seem too hard a result, assuming, as the Government admits, that the written information available to the board provided no basis in fact for denial of the exemption, and as the Court of Appeals ruled, that neither did petitioner's conduct in relation to the conscription system or other acts that came into view. But even assuming the above, petitioner's dual failure to exhaust—his failure either to secure a personal appearance or to take an administrative appeal—implicates decisively the policies served by the exhaustion requirement, especially the purpose of ensuring that the Selective Service System have full opportunity to "make a factual record" and "apply its expertise" in relation to a registrant's claims. When a claim to exemption depends ultimately on the careful gathering and analysis of relevant facts, the interest in full airing of the facts within the administrative system is prominent, and as the Court of Appeals noted, the exhaustion requirement "cannot properly be limited to those persons whose claims would fail in court anyway."

Conscientious objector claims turn on the resolution of factual questions relating to the nature of a registrant's beliefs concerning war, the basis of the objection in conscience and religion, and the registrant's sincerity. Petitioner declined to contest the denial of his conscientious objector claim before the local board by securing a personal appearance, and the Selective Service System was thereby deprived of one opportunity to supplement the record of relevant facts. The opportunity would have been restored had petitioner sought review by the appeal board. While the local board apparently was satisfied that classification should be made on the basis of the record it confronted, the appeal board, which classifies *de novo*, might have determined that the record should be supplemented by the local board. In the circumstances of this case, petitioner's failure to take an administrative appeal not only deprived the appeal board of the opportunity to "apply its expertise" in factfinding to the record that was available; it also removed an opportunity to supplement a record containing petitioner's own submissions but not containing the results of any specific inquiry into sincerity.

The Government contends that unless the exhaustion requirement is imposed to bar judicial review when the failure to exhaust has the present character, registrants would be encouraged to sidestep the administrative processes once a prima facie claim to conscientious objector status is made out by submission of a carefully drafted Form 150. Should the claim be denied at the local board level, the claimant might be tempted to circumvent further fact-gathering processes, and take a chance on showing in court that the only administrative record available contains no basis in fact for denial of the claim. This somewhat extreme situation is indeed presented by the circumstances of the present case, though, of course, there is no reason to question the bona fides of McGee's own supervening policy of noncooperation with the conscription system. It remains that McGee's failure to pursue his administrative remedies was deliberate and without excuse. And it is not fanciful to think that "frequent and deliberate flouting of administrative processes" might occur if McGee and others similarly situated were allowed to press their claims in court despite a dual failure to exhaust.

We conclude that petitioner's failure to exhaust administrative remedies bars the defense of erroneous classification, and therefore the judgment below is affirmed.

■ [An opinion by JUSTICE DOUGLAS, dissenting, is omitted. Ed.]

NOTES AND QUESTIONS

1.   The opinions in *McGee* and *McKart* differ in tone. After giving a long list of reasons in support of the exhaustion doctrine, the *McKart* Court excused the petitioner's failure to exhaust and said that the exhaustion doctrine is "subject to numerous exceptions." Yet, the *McGee* opinion suggested that the doctrine is strong and that the exceptions are few and narrow. The *McGee* opinion is a more accurate reflection of the manner in which courts apply the exhaustion doctrine. Thus, for instance, the doctrine has always been subject to an exception that applies when an attempt to persuade an agency to take the action desired by the petitioner would be an exercise in futility, but courts typically apply the futility exception only when the petitioner can "provide a clear and positive showing" that exhaustion would be an exercise in futility. *E.g.*, *Wilson v. MVM, Inc.*, 475 F.3d 166, 175–76 (3d Cir. 2007).

2.   Although *McKart* and *McGee* both involved failures to pursue administrative appeals of agency adjudications, the courts have applied exhaustion doctrine to deny judicial review in the rulemaking context as well. In *Association of Flight Attendants-CWA v. Chao*, 493 F.3d 155, 159 (D.C. Cir. 2007), the court declined to hear a union's challenge to the refusal by the Occupational Safety and Health Administration (OSHA) to apply certain working condition standards to airline industry crewmembers until the union first exhausted administrative remedies by petitioning OSHA to undertake a rulemaking to gather facts and adopt new standards reflecting the union's preferences.

While the Supreme Court's decision in *McGee* makes clear that litigants should take care not to construe the Court's opinion in *McKart* too broadly, the courts nevertheless have recognized a number of exceptions from the common law exhaustion requirement. In the following case, the Court articulated additional circumstances in which it may be appropriate to consider a litigant's claim notwithstanding a failure to exhaust administrative remedies.

<h1 style="text-align:center">McCarthy v. Madigan</h1>
503 U.S. 140 (1992).

■ JUSTICE BLACKMUN delivered the opinion of the Court.

The issue in this case is whether a federal prisoner must resort to the internal grievance procedure promulgated by the Federal Bureau of Prisons before he may initiate a suit, pursuant to the authority of *Bivens v. Six Unknown Federal Narcotics Agents*, 403 U.S. 388 (1971), solely for money damages. The Court of Appeals for the Tenth Circuit ruled that exhaustion of the grievance procedure was required. We granted certiorari to resolve a conflict among the Courts of Appeals.

I

While he was a prisoner in the federal penitentiary at Leavenworth, petitioner John J. McCarthy filed a *pro se* complaint in the United States District Court for the District of Kansas against four prison employees: the hospital administrator, the chief psychologist, another psychologist, and a physician. McCarthy alleged that respondents had violated his constitutional rights under the Eighth Amendment by their deliberate indifference to his needs and medical condition resulting from a back operation and a history of psychiatric problems. On the first page of his complaint, he wrote: "This Complaint seeks Money Damages Only."

The District Court dismissed the complaint on the ground that petitioner had failed to exhaust prison administrative remedies. Under 28 C.F.R. 542 (1991), setting forth the general "Administrative Remedy Procedure for Inmates" at federal correctional institutions, a prisoner may "seek formal review of a complaint which relates to any aspect of his imprisonment." § 542.10. When an inmate files a complaint or appeal, the responsible officials are directed to acknowledge the filing with a "signed receipt" which is returned to the inmate, to "[c]onduct an investigation," and to "[r]espond to and sign all complaints or appeals." §§ 542.11(a)(2)–(4). The general grievance regulations do not provide for any kind of hearing or for the granting of any particular type of relief.

To promote efficient dispute resolution, the procedure includes rapid filing and response timetables. An inmate first seeks informal resolution of his claim by consulting prison personnel. § 542.13(a). If this informal effort fails, the prisoner "may file a formal written complaint on the appropriate form, within fifteen (15) calendar days of the date on which the basis of the complaint occurred." § 542.13(b). Should the warden fail to respond to the inmate's satisfaction within 15 days, the inmate has 20 days to appeal to the Bureau's Regional Director, who has 30 days to respond. If the inmate still remains unsatisfied, he has 30 days to make a final appeal to the Bureau's general counsel, who has another 30 days to respond. §§ 542.14, 542.15.

If the inmate can demonstrate a "valid reason for delay," he "shall be allowed" an extension of any of these time periods for filing. § 542.13(b).

Petitioner McCarthy filed with the District Court a motion for reconsideration under Federal Rule of Civil Procedure 60(b), arguing that he was not required to exhaust his administrative remedies, because he sought only money damages which, he claimed, the Bureau could not provide. The court denied the motion.

The Court of Appeals, in affirming, observed that because *Bivens* actions are a creation of the judiciary, the courts may impose reasonable conditions upon their filing. The exhaustion rule, the court reasoned, "is not keyed to the type of relief sought, but to the need for preliminary fact-finding" to determine "whether there is a possible *Bivens* cause of action." Accordingly, " '[a]lthough the administrative apparatus could not award money damages . . . , administrative consideration of the possibility of corrective action and a record would have aided a court in measuring liability and determining the *extent* of the damages.' " Exhaustion of the general grievance procedure was required notwithstanding the fact that McCarthy's request was solely for money damages.

II

The doctrine of exhaustion of administrative remedies is one among related doctrines—including abstention, finality, and ripeness—that govern the timing of federal-court decisionmaking. Of "paramount importance" to any exhaustion inquiry is congressional intent. *Patsy v. Bd. of Regents of Fla.*, 457 U.S. 496, 501 (1982). Where Congress specifically mandates, exhaustion is required. But where Congress has not clearly required exhaustion, sound judicial discretion governs. *McGee v. United States*, 402 U.S. 479, 483, n.6 (1971). Nevertheless, even in this field of judicial discretion, appropriate deference to Congress' power to prescribe the basic procedural scheme under which a claim may be heard in a federal court requires fashioning of exhaustion principles in a manner consistent with congressional intent and any applicable statutory scheme.

A

This Court long has acknowledged the general rule that parties exhaust prescribed administrative remedies before seeking relief from the federal courts. Exhaustion is required because it serves the twin purposes of protecting administrative agency authority and promoting judicial efficiency.

As to the first of these purposes, the exhaustion doctrine recognizes the notion, grounded in deference to Congress' delegation of authority to coordinate branches of Government, that agencies, not the courts, ought to have primary responsibility for the programs that Congress has charged them to administer. Exhaustion concerns apply with particular force when the action under review involves exercise of the agency's discretionary power or when the agency proceedings in question allow the agency to apply its special expertise. The exhaustion doctrine also acknowledges the commonsense notion of dispute resolution that an agency ought to have an opportunity to correct its own mistakes with respect to the programs it administers before it is haled into federal court. Correlatively, exhaustion principles apply with special force when "frequent and deliberate flouting of administrative processes" could weaken an agency's effectiveness by encouraging disregard of its procedures. *McKart v. United States*, 395 U.S. 185, 195 (1969).

As to the second of the purposes, exhaustion promotes judicial efficiency in at least two ways. When an agency has the opportunity to correct its own errors, a judicial controversy may well be mooted, or at least piecemeal appeals may be avoided. And even where a controversy survives administrative review, exhaustion of the administrative procedure may produce a useful record for subsequent judicial consideration, especially in a complex or technical factual context.

B

Notwithstanding these substantial institutional interests, federal courts are vested with a "virtually unflagging obligation" to exercise the jurisdiction given them. *Colo. River Water Conservation Dist. v. United States*, 424 U.S. 800, 817–18 (1976). "We have no more right to decline the exercise of jurisdiction which is given, than to usurp that which is not given." *Cohens v. Virginia*, 19 U.S. (6 Wheat.) 264, 404 (1821). Accordingly, this Court has declined to require exhaustion in some circumstances even where administrative and judicial interests would counsel otherwise. In determining whether exhaustion is required, federal courts must balance the interest of the individual in retaining prompt access to a federal judicial forum against countervailing institutional interests favoring exhaustion. "[A]dministrative remedies need not be pursued if the litigant's interests in immediate judicial review outweigh the government's interests in the efficiency or administrative autonomy that the exhaustion doctrine is designed to further." *West v. Bergland*, 611 F.2d 710, 715 (8th Circ. 1979). Application of this balancing principle is "intensely practical," *Bowen v. City of New York*, 476 U.S. 467, 484 (1986), because attention is directed to both the nature of the claim presented and the characteristics of the particular administrative procedure provided.

C

This Court's precedents have recognized at least three broad sets of circumstances in which the interests of the individual weigh heavily against requiring administrative exhaustion. First, requiring resort to the administrative remedy may occasion undue prejudice to subsequent assertion of a court action. Such prejudice may result, for example, from an unreasonable or indefinite timeframe for administrative action. Even where the administrative decisionmaking schedule is otherwise reasonable and definite, a particular plaintiff may suffer irreparable harm if unable to secure immediate judicial consideration of his claim. By the same token, exhaustion principles apply with less force when an individual's failure to exhaust may preclude a defense to criminal liability.

Second, an administrative remedy may be inadequate "because of some doubt as to whether the agency was empowered to grant effective relief." *Gibson v. Berryhill*, 411 U.S. 564, 575, n.14 (1973). For example, an agency, as a preliminary matter, may be unable to consider whether to grant relief because it lacks institutional competence to resolve the particular type of issue presented, such as the constitutionality of a statute. In a similar vein, exhaustion has not been required where the challenge is to the adequacy of the agency procedure itself, such that " 'the question of the adequacy of the administrative remedy . . . [is] for all practical purposes identical with the merits of [the plaintiff's] lawsuit.' " *Barry v. Barchi*, 443 U.S. 55, 63, n.10 (1979). Alternatively, an agency may be competent to adjudicate the issue presented, but still lack authority to grant the type of relief requested.

Third, an administrative remedy may be inadequate where the administrative body is shown to be biased or has otherwise predetermined the issue before it.

III

In light of these general principles, we conclude that petitioner McCarthy need not have exhausted his constitutional claim for money damages. As a preliminary matter, we find that Congress has not meaningfully addressed the appropriateness of requiring exhaustion in this context. Although respondents' interests are significant, we are left with a firm conviction that, given the type of claim McCarthy raises and the particular characteristics of the Bureau's general grievance procedure, McCarthy's individual interests outweigh countervailing institutional interests favoring exhaustion.

A

Turning first to congressional intent, we note that the general grievance procedure was neither enacted nor mandated by Congress. Respondents, however, urge that Congress, in effect, has acted to require exhaustion by delegating power to the Attorney General and the Bureau of Prisons to control and manage the federal prison system. We think respondents confuse what Congress could be claimed to allow by implication with what Congress affirmatively has requested or required. By delegating authority, in the most general of terms, to the Bureau to administer the federal prison system, Congress cannot be said to have spoken to the particular issue whether prisoners in the custody of the Bureau should have direct access to the federal courts.

* * *

B

Because Congress has not *required* exhaustion of a federal prisoner's *Bivens* claim, we turn to an evaluation of the individual and institutional interests at stake in this case. The general grievance procedure heavily burdens the individual interests of the petitioning inmate in two ways. First, the procedure imposes short, successive filing deadlines that create a high risk of forfeiture of a claim for failure to comply. Second, the administrative "remedy" does not authorize an award of monetary damages—the only relief requested by McCarthy in this action. The combination of these features means that the prisoner seeking only money damages has everything to lose and nothing to gain from being required to exhaust his claim under the internal grievance procedure.

The filing deadlines for the grievance procedure require an inmate, within 15 days of the precipitating incident, not only to attempt to resolve his grievance informally but also to file a formal written complaint with the prison warden. Then, he must successively hurdle 20-day and 30-day deadlines to advance to the end of the grievance process. Other than the Bureau's general and quite proper interest in having early notice of any claim, we have not been apprised of any urgency or exigency justifying this timetable. As a practical matter, the filing deadlines, of course, may pose little difficulty for the knowledgeable inmate accustomed to grievances and court actions. But they are a likely trap for the inexperienced and unwary inmate, ordinarily indigent and unrepresented by counsel, with a substantial claim.

Respondents argue that the deadlines are not jurisdictional and may be extended for any "valid" reason. *See* 28 C.F.R. §§ 542.13(b), 542.15. Yet the regulations do not elaborate upon what a "valid" reason is. Moreover, it appears that prison officials—perhaps the very officials subject to suit—are charged with determining what is a "valid" reason.

All in all, these deadlines require a good deal of an inmate at the peril of forfeiting his claim for money damages. The "first" of "the principles that necessarily frame our analysis of prisoners' constitutional claims" is that "federal courts must take cognizance of the valid constitutional claims of prison inmates." *Turner v. Safley*, 482 U.S. 78, 84 (1987). Because a prisoner ordinarily is divested of the privilege to vote, the right to file a court action might be said to be his remaining most "fundamental political right, because preservative of all rights." *Yick Wo v. Hopkins*, 118 U.S. 356, 370 (1886). The rapid filing deadlines counsel strongly against exhaustion as a prerequisite to the filing of a federal-court action.

As we have noted, the grievance procedure does not include any mention of the award of monetary relief. Respondents argue that this should not matter, because "in most cases there are other things that the inmate wants." This may be true in some instances. But we cannot presume, as a general matter, that when a litigant has deliberately forgone any claim for injunctive relief and has singled out discrete past wrongs, specifically requesting monetary compensation only, that he is likely interested in "other things." The Bureau, in any case, is always free to offer an inmate administrative relief in return for withdrawal of his lawsuit. We conclude that the absence of any monetary remedy in the grievance procedure also weighs heavily against imposing an exhaustion requirement.

In the alternative, respondents argue that, despite the absence of any provision in the general grievance procedure for the award of money damages, such damages in fact are available for most prisoners asserting *Bivens* claims. As to *Bivens* claims that could have been brought under the Federal Tort Claims Act (FTCA), respondents contend that a grievance asking for money damages can be "converted" by prison officials to a FTCA claim for which prison officials are authorized, under 28 C.F.R. § 543.30, to award money damages. This "conversion" authority does not appear in the regulations having to do with the grievance procedure, which raises substantial doubt that an inmate would have sufficient notice as to how his claim would be treated. In any event, respondents have not pointed to anything in the record showing that prison officials have a practice of converting a claim filed under the general grievance procedure to a claim under the FTCA procedure. We agree with petitioner that it is implausible to think that they do. The availability of a money damages remedy is, at best, uncertain, and the uncertainty of the administrative agency's authority to award relief counsels against requiring exhaustion.

We do not find the interests of the Bureau of Prisons to weigh heavily in favor of exhaustion in view of the remedial scheme and particular claim presented here. To be sure, the Bureau has a substantial interest in encouraging internal resolution of grievances and in preventing the undermining of its authority by unnecessary resort by prisoners to the federal courts. But other institutional concerns relevant to exhaustion analysis appear to weigh in hardly at all. The Bureau's alleged failure to render medical care implicates only tangentially its authority to carry out the control and management of the federal prisons. Furthermore, the Bureau does not bring to bear any special expertise on the type of issue presented for resolution here.

The interests of judicial economy do not stand to be advanced substantially by the general grievance procedure. No formal factfindings are made. The paperwork generated by the grievance process might assist a court somewhat in ascertaining the facts underlying a prisoner's claim more quickly than if it has only a prisoner's complaint to review. But the grievance procedure does not create a formal factual record of the type that can be relied on conclusively by a court for disposition of a prisoner's claim on the pleadings or at summary judgment without the aid of affidavits.

C

In conclusion, we are struck by the absence of supporting material in the regulations, the record, or the briefs that the general grievance procedure here was crafted with any thought toward the principles of exhaustion of claims for money damages. The Attorney General's professed concern for internal dispute resolution has not translated itself into a more effective grievance procedure that might encourage the filing of an administrative complaint as opposed to a court action. Congress, of course, is free to design or require an appropriate administrative procedure for a prisoner to exhaust his claim for money damages. Even without further action by Congress, we do not foreclose the possibility that the Bureau itself may adopt an appropriate administrative procedure consistent with congressional intent.

■ CHIEF JUSTICE REHNQUIST, with whom JUSTICE SCALIA and JUSTICE THOMAS join, concurring in the judgment.

I agree with the Court's holding that a federal prisoner need not exhaust the procedures promulgated by the Federal Bureau of Prisons. My view, however, is based entirely on the fact that the grievance procedure at issue does not provide for any award of monetary damages. As a result, in cases such as this one where prisoners seek monetary relief, the Bureau's administrative remedy furnishes no effective remedy at all, and it is therefore improper to impose an exhaustion requirement.

Because I would base the decision on this ground, I do not join the Court's extensive discussion of the general principles of exhaustion, nor do I agree with the implication that those general principles apply without modification in the context of a *Bivens* claim. In particular, I disagree with the Court's reliance on the grievance procedure's filing deadlines as a basis for excusing exhaustion. As the majority observes, we have previously refused to require exhaustion of administrative remedies where the administrative process subjects plaintiffs to unreasonable delay or to an indefinite timeframe for decision. This principle rests on our belief that when a plaintiff might have to wait seemingly forever for an agency decision, agency procedures are "inadequate" and therefore need not be exhausted.

But the Court makes strange use of this principle in holding that filing deadlines imposed by agency procedures may provide a basis for finding that those procedures need not be exhausted. Whereas before we have held that procedures without "reasonable time limit[s]" may be inadequate because they make a plaintiff wait too long, *Coit Independence Joint Venture v. FSLIC*, 489 U.S. 561, 587 (1989), today the majority concludes that strict filing deadlines might also contribute to a finding of inadequacy because they make a plaintiff move too quickly. But surely the second proposition does not follow from the first. In fact, short filing deadlines will almost always promote quick decisionmaking by an agency, the very result that we have advocated repeatedly in the cases cited above. So long as there is an escape clause, as there is here, and the time limit is within a zone of reasonableness, as I believe it is here, the length of the period should not be a factor in deciding the adequacy of the remedy.

NOTES AND QUESTIONS

1.   *McCarthy* involved a claim solely for money damages filed by a federal prisoner against four federal prison employees under *Bivens v. Six Unknown Named Agents of the Federal Bureau of Narcotics*, 403 U.S. 388 (1971), and its progeny. Since the Court decided *McCarthy*, Congress enacted 42 U.S.C. § 1997e(a) as part of the Prison Litigation Reform Act (PLRA), Pub. L. No. 104–134, 110 Stat. 1321 (1996), in an effort to address severe problems that had been created by the flood of thousands of largely frivolous civil rights actions brought by prisoners in federal courts each year. The provision uses absolute language: "No action shall be brought with respect to prison conditions . . . by a prisoner . . . until such administrative remedies as are available are exhausted." Yet, some circuits adopted narrow interpretations of § 1997e(a) by excluding from its scope: (1) cases in which a prisoner seeks relief that is not available from a prison, *e.g.*, money damages; (2) cases involving violations of the rights of individual prisoners, as opposed to cases challenging general prison conditions; and (3) cases involving claims of use of excessive force. In *Booth v. Churner*, 532 U.S. 731 (2001), the Supreme Court unanimously rejected the first of these exclusions; in *Porter v. Nussle*, 534 U.S. 516 (2002), the Court unanimously rejected the second and third. The Court concluded that Congress intended to require exhaustion in all prisoners' rights cases and interpreted § 1997e(a) as a comprehensive ban on judicial consideration of any prisoner's claim that his civil rights were violated unless the prisoner first exhausts prison grievance procedures. The Court also noted that Congress can make exhaustion mandatory in all cases and can eliminate all judicial discretion to excuse a petitioner's failure to exhaust, as the Court concluded that Congress did when it enacted § 1997e(a).

Nevertheless, for a few years after the Court's decisions in *Booth* and *Porter*, the circuit courts were divided over whether a prisoner who failed to satisfy a prison grievance system's procedural requirements and saw his claims dismissed by prison officials as a result could nevertheless claim to have exhausted administrative remedies. *Compare, e.g., Thomas v. Woolum*, 337 F.3d 720, 723 (6th Cir. 2003), *with Ross v. County of Bernalillo*, 365 F.3d 1181, 1185–86 (10th Cir. 2004), *and Pozo v. McCaughtry*, 286 F.3d 1022, 1035 (7th Cir. 2002). In *Woodford v. Ngo*, 548 U.S. 81 (2006), the Supreme Court held that the PLRA's exhaustion provision "requires proper exhaustion," including satisfaction of a prison grievance system's procedural requirements. To hold otherwise, said the Court, would merely incentivize prisoners to circumvent the prison grievance process and turn the PLRA's exhaustion provision "into a largely useless appendage." *Id.* at 93. In sum, while *McCarthy*'s overall description of common law exhaustion doctrine remains valid and is often relied upon by the courts, the PLRA's exhaustion provision and the Supreme Court's subsequent jurisprudence have repudiated *McCarthy*'s application to prisoner suits.

2. In identifying "at least" three potential exceptions from common law exhaustion requirements, the Supreme Court in *McCarthy* did not foreclose that other circumstances might similarly excuse a failure to exhaust administrative remedies. A number of appellate courts have adopted and applied a three-part test for waiving common law exhaustion requirements originally proposed by Kenneth Culp Davis. *See* 3 KENNETH CULP DAVIS, ADMINISTRATIVE LAW TREATISE § 20.03 (1958). Under this three-part test, a reviewing court will excuse a litigant's failure to exhaust administrative remedies if "(1) there is clear evidence that exhaustion of administrative remedies will result in irreparable injury; (2) the agency's jurisdiction is plainly lacking; and (3) the agency's special expertise will be of no help on the question of jurisdiction." *E.g., General Atomics v. U.S. Nuclear Regulatory Comm'n*, 75 F.3d 536, 541 (9th Cir. 1996); *Rogers v. Bennett*, 873 F.2d 1387, 1393 (11th Cir. 1989).

3. As the Court recognized in *McCarthy*, agencies often lack and even disclaim outright the authority to examine constitutional issues, at which point the only avenue of relief for litigants seeking to raise constitutional challenges to agency action would be through judicial review. In some cases, courts have declined to require exhaustion of administrative remedies in cases raising legitimate constitutional challenges to an agency's actions or procedures. *See, e.g., Bangura v. Hansen*, 434 F.3d 487, 494 (6th Cir. 2006); *Wilkins v. United States*, 279 F.3d 782, 789 (9th Cir. 2002). In other cases raising such claims, courts have declined to waive common law exhaustion requirements so that agencies have the opportunity to address the concerns of regulated parties as best they can within their jurisdiction and pursue other remedies at their disposal, and otherwise to allow fuller development of the case record consistent with agency procedural requirements. *See, e.g., Bonhometre v. Gonzales*, 414 F.3d 442, 447–48 (3d Cir. 2005).

4. The *McCarthy* Court offered an exception from common law exhaustion requirements for circumstances in which agency bias or predetermination of the outcome would render pursuit of administrative remedies "inadequate." The courts have long expressed a willingness to excuse a litigant's failure to exhaust administrative remedies when doing so would be an exercise in futility. *See, e.g., Weinberger v. Salfi*, 422 U.S. 749, 765–66 (1975); *Brown v. Secretary of Health & Human Servs.*, 46 F.3d 102, 114–15 (1st Cir. 1995). The courts have often, however, limited the futility exception to those circumstances in which an adverse decision is certain. As the Seventh Circuit explained in *Greene v. Meese*, 875 F.2d 639, 641 (7th Cir. 1989):

> Lightning may strike; and even if it doesn't, in denying relief the Bureau may give a statement of its reasons that is helpful to the district court in considering the merits of the claim.

DISCUSSION PROBLEM

Assume that you represent a national chain of pizza restaurants. The FDA has just concluded that the pizza your client sells is actually a drug, rather than food, because your client made claims in its advertising that its pizza has beneficial effects on human health. A drug cannot be lawfully sold in interstate commerce unless it has first been determined to be safe and effective. The process of testing a drug to determine whether it is safe and effective takes about ten years and costs the manufacturer hundreds of millions of dollars. The FDA takes the position that your client cannot sell any more pizza until it goes through that process. You believe that the FDA is wrong, *i.e.*, you believe that the health claims your client makes for its product do not convert it from the category of food to the category of drug. You want to obtain judicial review of the FDA's decision that your client's pizza is a drug. The FDA moves to dismiss your petition to review on the grounds that it has not taken a final action, its action is not ripe for review, and your client must exhaust its remedies by testing its pizza to determine whether it is safe and effective before your client can obtain review of the FDA's decision that its pizza is a drug. How would you argue this case for your client? How would you expect a court to resolve the dispute?

Statutory Exhaustion

Until the 1990s, the duty to exhaust administrative remedies existed only as a judge-made doctrine that was subject to judge-made exceptions. In the 1990s, the Supreme Court began to recognize that statutes can impose and define the duty, and Congress began to enact some statutes that explicitly imposed statutory duties to exhaust. Thus, while the common law exhaustion doctrine continues to exist and to have powerful effects where it has not been modified by statute, the judge-made version of the doctrine is now subject to statutory exceptions that take precedence in the circumstances in which the statutes apply. A statute can either exempt a class of actions from the duty or impose a stronger version of the doctrine.

The APA addresses exhaustion in § 704:

> Agency action made reviewable by statute and final agency action for which there is no other adequate remedy in a court are subject to judicial review. A preliminary, procedural, or intermediate agency action or ruling not directly reviewable is subject to review on the review of the final agency action. Except as otherwise expressly required by statute, agency action otherwise final is final for the purposes of this section whether or not there has been presented or determined an application for a declaratory order, for any form of reconsideration, or, unless the agency otherwise requires by

rule and provides that the action meanwhile is inoperative, for
an appeal to superior agency authority.

By its terms, this provision requires exhaustion of the remedies of
"reconsideration" or "appeal to superior agency authority" only when a
statute or agency rule requires exhaustion of those remedies. Judicial
opinions on exhaustion rarely referred to § 704 until 1993, when the
Court addressed the relationship in the following case.

Darby v. Cisneros

509 U.S. 137 (1993).

■ JUSTICE BLACKMUN delivered the opinion of the Court.

This case presents the question whether federal courts have the
authority to require that a plaintiff exhaust available administrative
remedies before seeking judicial review under the Administrative
Procedure Act (APA), 5 U.S.C. § 701 *et seq.*, where neither the statute
nor agency rules specifically mandate exhaustion as a prerequisite to
judicial review. At issue is the relationship between the judicially
created doctrine of exhaustion of administrative remedies and the
statutory requirements of § 10(c) of the APA.[3]

I

Petitioner R. Gordon Darby is a self-employed South Carolina real
estate developer who specializes in the development and management
of multifamily rental projects. In the early 1980's, he began working
with Lonnie Garvin, Jr., a mortgage banker, who had developed a plan
to enable multifamily developers to obtain single-family mortgage
insurance from respondent Department of Housing and Urban
Development (HUD). Respondent Secretary of HUD (Secretary) is
authorized to provide single-family mortgage insurance under § 203(b)
of the National Housing Act. Although HUD also provides mortgage
insurance for multifamily projects under § 207 of the National Housing
Act, 12 U.S.C. § 1713, the greater degree of oversight and control over
such projects makes it less attractive for investors than the single-
family mortgage insurance option.

The principal advantage of Garvin's plan was that it promised to
avoid HUD's "Rule of Seven." This rule prevented rental properties
from receiving single-family mortgage insurance if the mortgagor
already had financial interests in seven or more similar rental

---

[3]   Section 10(c), 80 Stat. 392–93, 5 U.S.C. § 704, provides:

"Agency action made reviewable by statute and final agency action for which there is
no other adequate remedy in a court are subject to judicial review. A preliminary,
procedural, or intermediate agency action or ruling not directly reviewable is subject
to review on the review of the final agency action. Except as otherwise expressly
required by statute, agency action otherwise final is final for the purposes of this
section whether or not there has been presented or determined an application for a
declaratory order, for any form of reconsideration, or, unless the agency otherwise
requires by rule and provides that the action meanwhile is inoperative, for an appeal
to superior agency authority."

We note that the statute as codified in the United States Code refers to "any form of
reconsiderations," with the last word being in the plural. The version of § 10(c) as currently
enacted, however, uses the singular "reconsideration." We quote the text as enacted in the
Statutes at Large.

properties in the same project or subdivision. Under Garvin's plan, a person seeking financing would use straw purchasers as mortgage insurance applicants. Once the loans were closed, the straw purchasers would transfer title back to the development company. Because no single purchaser at the time of purchase would own more than seven rental properties within the same project, the Rule of Seven appeared not to be violated. HUD employees in South Carolina apparently assured Garvin that his plan was lawful and that he thereby would avoid the limitation of the Rule of Seven.

Darby obtained financing for three separate multiunit projects, and, through Garvin's plan, Darby obtained single-family mortgage insurance from HUD. Although Darby successfully rented the units, a combination of low rents, falling interest rates, and a generally depressed rental market forced him into default in 1988. HUD became responsible for the payment of over $6.6 million in insurance claims.

HUD had become suspicious of Garvin's financing plan as far back as 1983. In 1986, HUD initiated an audit but concluded that neither Darby nor Garvin had done anything wrong or misled HUD personnel. Nevertheless, in June 1989, HUD issued a limited denial of participation (LDP) that prohibited petitioners for one year from participating in any program in South Carolina administered by respondent Assistant Secretary of Housing. Two months later, the Assistant Secretary notified petitioners that HUD was also proposing to debar them from further participation in all HUD procurement contracts and in any nonprocurement transaction with any federal agency.

Petitioners' appeals of the LDP and of the proposed debarment were consolidated, and an Administrative Law Judge (ALJ) conducted a hearing on the consolidated appeals in December 1989. The judge issued an "Initial Decision and Order" in April 1990, finding that the financing method used by petitioners was "a sham which improperly circumvented the Rule of Seven." The ALJ concluded, however, that most of the relevant facts had been disclosed to local HUD employees, that petitioners lacked criminal intent, and that Darby himself "genuinely cooperated with HUD to try [to] work out his financial dilemma and avoid foreclosure." In light of these mitigating factors, the ALJ concluded that an indefinite debarment would be punitive and that it would serve no legitimate purpose; good cause existed, however, to debar petitioners for a period of 18 months.

Under HUD regulations,

> "The hearing officer's determination shall be final unless, pursuant to 24 CFR part 26, the Secretary or the Secretary's designee, within 30 days of receipt of a request decides as a matter of discretion to review the finding of the hearing officer. The 30 day period for deciding whether to review a determination may be extended upon written notice of such extension by the Secretary or his designee. Any party may request such a review in writing within 15 days of receipt of the hearing officer's determination." 24 C.F.R. § 24.314(c) (1992).

Neither petitioners nor respondents sought further administrative review of the ALJ's "Initial Decision and Order."

On May 31, 1990, petitioners filed suit in the United States District Court for the District of South Carolina. They sought an injunction and a declaration that the administrative sanctions were imposed for purposes of punishment, in violation of HUD's own debarment regulations, and therefore were "not in accordance with law" within the meaning of § 10(e)(B)(1) of the APA, 5 U.S.C. § 706(2)(A).

Respondents moved to dismiss the complaint on the ground that petitioners, by forgoing the option to seek review by the Secretary, had failed to exhaust administrative remedies. The District Court denied respondents' motion to dismiss, reasoning that the administrative remedy was inadequate and that resort to that remedy would have been futile. In a subsequent opinion, the District Court granted petitioners' motion for summary judgment, concluding that the "imposition of debarment in this case encroached too heavily on the punitive side of the line, and for those reasons was an abuse of discretion and not in accordance with the law."

The Court of Appeals for the Fourth Circuit reversed. It recognized that neither the National Housing Act nor HUD regulations expressly mandate exhaustion of administrative remedies prior to filing suit. The court concluded, however, that the District Court had erred in denying respondents' motion to dismiss, because there was no evidence to suggest that further review would have been futile or that the Secretary would have abused his discretion by indefinitely extending the time limitations for review.

The court denied petitioners' petition for rehearing with suggestion for rehearing en banc. In order to resolve the tension between this and the APA, as well as to settle a perceived conflict among the Courts of Appeals, we granted certiorari.

II

Section 10(c) of the APA bears the caption "Actions reviewable." It provides in its first two sentences that judicial review is available for "final agency action for which there is no other adequate remedy in a court," and that "preliminary, procedural, or intermediate agency action . . . is subject to review on the review of the final agency action." The last sentence of § 10(c) reads:

> "Except as otherwise expressly required by statute, agency action otherwise final is final for the purposes of this section whether or not there has been presented or determined an application for a declaratory order, for any form of reconsideration, or, unless the agency otherwise requires by rule and provides that the action meanwhile is inoperative, for an appeal to superior agency authority." 5 U.S.C. § 704.

Petitioners argue that this provision means that a litigant seeking judicial review of a final agency action under the APA need not exhaust available administrative remedies unless such exhaustion is expressly required by statute or agency rule. According to petitioners, since § 10(c) contains an explicit exhaustion provision, federal courts are not free to require further exhaustion as a matter of judicial discretion.

Respondents contend that § 10(c) is concerned solely with timing, that is, when agency actions become "final," and that Congress had no intention to interfere with the courts' ability to impose conditions on the timing of their exercise of jurisdiction to review final agency actions. Respondents concede that petitioners' claim is "final" under § 10(c), for neither the National Housing Act nor applicable HUD regulations require that a litigant pursue further administrative appeals prior to seeking judicial review. However, even though nothing in § 10(c) precludes judicial review of petitioners' claim, respondents argue that federal courts remain free under the APA to impose appropriate exhaustion requirements.

We have recognized that the judicial doctrine of exhaustion of administrative remedies is conceptually distinct from the doctrine of finality:

> "[T]he finality requirement is concerned with whether the initial decisionmaker has arrived at a definitive position on the issue that inflicts an actual, concrete injury; the exhaustion requirement generally refers to administrative and judicial procedures by which an injured party may seek review of an adverse decision and obtain a remedy if the decision is found to be unlawful or otherwise inappropriate." *Williamson County Regional Planning Comm'n v. Hamilton Bank of Johnson City*, 473 U.S. 172, 193 (1985).

Whether courts are free to impose an exhaustion requirement as a matter of judicial discretion depends, at least in part, on whether Congress has provided otherwise, for "[o]f 'paramount importance' to any exhaustion inquiry is congressional intent," *McCarthy v. Madigan*, 503 U.S. 140, 144 (1992). We therefore must consider whether § 10(c), by providing the conditions under which agency action becomes "final for the purposes of" judicial review, limits the authority of courts to impose additional exhaustion requirements as a prerequisite to judicial review.

* * *

[T]he text of the APA leaves little doubt that petitioners are correct. Under § 10(a) of the APA, "[a] person suffering legal wrong because of agency action, or adversely affected or aggrieved by agency action within the meaning of a relevant statute, *is entitled to judicial review thereof*." 5 U.S.C. § 702 (emphasis added). Although § 10(a) provides the general right to judicial review of agency actions under the APA, § 10(c) establishes when such review is available. When an aggrieved party has exhausted all administrative remedies expressly prescribed by statute or agency rule, the agency action is "final for the purposes of this section" and therefore "subject to judicial review" under the first sentence. While federal courts may be free to apply, where appropriate, other prudential doctrines of judicial administration to limit the scope and timing of judicial review, § 10(c), by its very terms, has limited the availability of the doctrine of exhaustion of administrative remedies to that which the statute or rule clearly mandates.

The last sentence of § 10(c) refers explicitly to "any form of reconsideration" and "an appeal to superior agency authority." Congress clearly was concerned with making the exhaustion requirement unambiguous so that aggrieved parties would know precisely what administrative steps were required before judicial review would be available. If courts were able to impose additional exhaustion requirements beyond those provided by Congress or the agency, the last sentence of § 10(c) would make no sense. To adopt respondents' reading would transform § 10(c) from a provision designed to " 'remove obstacles to judicial review of agency action,' " *Bowen v. Massachusetts*, 487 U.S. 879, 904 (1988), into a trap for unwary litigants. Section 10(c) explicitly requires exhaustion of all intra-agency appeals mandated either by statute or by agency rule; it would be inconsistent with the plain language of § 10(c) for courts to require litigants to exhaust optional appeals as well.

III

[We have omitted the Court's lengthy discussion of APA legislative history and pre-APA common law regarding administrative exhaustion, which part of the opinion THE CHIEF JUSTICE, JUSTICE SCALIA, and JUSTICE THOMAS declined to join, and which the opinion itself declared to be "unnecessary in light of the plain meaning of the statutory text." Ed.]

IV

We noted just last Term in a non-APA case that

> "appropriate deference to Congress' power to prescribe the basic procedural scheme under which a claim may be heard in a federal court requires fashioning of exhaustion principles in a manner consistent with congressional intent and any applicable statutory scheme." *McCarthy*, 503 U.S. at 144.

Appropriate deference in this case requires the recognition that, with respect to actions brought under the APA, Congress effectively codified the doctrine of exhaustion of administrative remedies in § 10(c). Of course, the exhaustion doctrine continues to apply as a matter of judicial discretion in cases not governed by the APA. But where the APA applies, an appeal to "superior agency authority" is a prerequisite to judicial review *only* when expressly required by statute or when an agency rule requires appeal before review and the administrative action is made inoperative pending that review. Courts are not free to impose an exhaustion requirement as a rule of judicial administration where the agency action has already become "final" under § 10(c).

The judgment of the Court of Appeals is reversed, and the case is remanded for further proceedings consistent with this opinion.

NOTES AND QUESTIONS

1. The opinion in *Darby* has the salutary effect of forcing federal agencies to describe the nature and effect of available intra-agency appeals clearly and explicitly in their rules. Most agencies have the discretion to make available a wide variety of procedures for intra-agency review of actions that are, or become, final in the absence of such review. Those procedures can be either optional or mandatory. Before *Darby*, some agencies attempted to have it both ways, *i.e.*, to describe an intra-agency review procedure as optional but then to seek dismissal of a petition for judicial

review of an agency action if a party declined to avail itself of the putatively optional administrative appeal. After *Darby*, that option is not available to an agency in a proceeding governed by the APA. An agency can make an intra-agency review procedure a mandatory prerequisite to the availability of judicial review only by describing it as such in its rules and by providing that the action that is subject to the intra-agency review procedure "meanwhile is inoperative." If the agency simply makes such a procedure available, however, a party can obtain judicial review of an otherwise final action without first pursuing the available intra-agency review procedure except in the relatively unusual case in which a statute makes exhaustion of the intra-agency review procedure a prerequisite to the availability of judicial review. In the post-*Darby* world, a party to an agency proceeding should be able to distinguish between optional and mandatory intra-agency review procedures simply by reading the applicable provisions of statutes and agency rules.

2.   In some recent statutes, Congress has described in detail the often elaborate administrative procedures a petitioner must exhaust as a prerequisite to obtaining judicial review of a class of agency actions. When Congress requires exhaustion of specified administrative procedures, courts have no discretion to review an agency action unless and until the petitioner exhausts the statutorily-specified administrative procedures. A court cannot apply any exception to such a statutorily-prescribed exhaustion requirement. The Prison Litigation Reform Act, discussed after *McCarthy v. Madigan* on pages 766–767 of this casebook, represents one example.

Issue Exhaustion

A logical corollary to the common law exhaustion doctrine requires a petitioner to raise an objection to an agency action at each stage in the agency decision making process as a prerequisite to the petitioner's ability to convince a court to consider the objection. Thus, for instance, in *Department of Transp. v. Public Citizen*, 541 U.S. 752, 764–65 (2004), the Court refused to consider an argument that an agency had not adequately considered alternatives to the final rule it adopted because the petitioner had not urged the agency to consider those alternatives.

A number of statutes have adopted issue exhaustion requirements. The National Labor Relations Act, for example, provides that "[n]o objection that has not been urged before the Board . . . shall be considered by the court unless the failure or neglect to urge such objection shall be excused because of extraordinary circumstances." 29 U.S.C. § 160(e). Similarly, the Clean Air Act provides that "[o]nly an objection to a rule or procedure which was raised with reasonable specificity during the period for public comment . . . may be raised during judicial review." 42 U.S.C. § 7607(d)(7)(B).

Issue exhaustion requirements, particularly at common law, are not absolute. For example, in *Sims v. Apfel*, 530 U.S. 103 (2000), the Supreme Court held that a Social Security disability applicant may seek judicial review of an issue that he or she failed to raise initially in asking the Social Security Appeals Council to review of an unfavorable decision by an administrative law judge. Writing on behalf of a four-judge plurality, Justice Thomas recognized that issue exhaustion is mandatory when a statute or agency regulation requires it. He also reasoned that, particularly when a statute or agency regulation anticipates that the parties will develop the issues in adversarial administrative proceedings resembling the trial process, common law will typically require issue exhaustion, just as it does when a litigant wishes to appeal a decision of the district court. Where administrative proceedings are not particularly adversarial, however, as in the case of Social Security disability hearings (where the agency is responsible for developing the factual record and applicants often are not represented by attorneys), the analogy to trial and appellate courts does not hold. Finally, in the particular case at bar, the agency's rules and forms suggested that it did not require issue exhaustion; for example, the form to appeal an administrative law judge's decision to the Social Security Appeals Council provided only three lines for the review request, and an accompanying notice suggested that completing the form should only take ten minutes. In a separate concurring opinion, Justice O'Connor relied principally on the lack of an agency rule requiring issue exhaustion and a suggestion on the agency's forms that it did not require parties to specify the issues they intended to raise on appeal.

Perhaps not surprisingly, the Supreme Court's decision in *Sims* has resulted in extensive litigation over whether or not particular agency proceedings are sufficiently nonadversarial or otherwise dissimilar from judicial trials to justify an exception from common law issue exhaustion requirements. In *Woodford v. Ngo*, 548 U.S. 81 (2006), the Justices in dicta disagreed over the scope of common law exhaustion requirements in light of *Sims*. The majority of the Court in *Woodford* interpreted *Sims* as offering only a narrow exception to the duty to exhaust for cases in which agency proceedings are inquisitorial rather than adversarial, while the three dissenting Justices contended that *Sims* eliminated common law exhaustion requirements in any situation in which judicial review of an agency decision does not resemble appellate review of a trial court decision.

4. AGENCY DELAY

The duty to exhaust administrative remedies and the requirements of ripeness and finality contribute to a serious problem in the administrative state. Agencies often take a long time to take an action. Thus, for instance, the Social Security Administration requires twelve to eighteen months to issue a final decision in a contested disability case, while EPA complies with statutory deadlines to issue rules in only 17 percent of cases. In many if not most cases, agencies issue rules many years after the action deadline Congress imposed on the agency by statute. Regulated parties and beneficiaries are frustrated by the torpor of the agency decision-making process, but no one has yet identified a politically viable solution to the problem.

It may well be that delay in agency decision-making sometimes is caused by an agency's lack of enthusiasm to do that which it is required by statute to do. In the vast majority of cases, however, agency delay is attributable to more prosaic causes: Congress has ordered agencies to take more actions than the agencies can take, given the often demanding procedures Congress requires the agencies to use and the limited resources Congress makes available to the agencies. *See*

Richard J. Pierce, Jr., *Judicial Review of Agency Actions in a Period of Diminishing Agency Resources*, 49 ADMIN. L. REV. 61 (1997).

APA § 706(1) authorizes a court to "compel agency action . . . unreasonably delayed." Someone who is injured by agency delay can file an action pursuant to that section. In *Telecommunications Research & Action Center v. FCC*, 750 F.2d 70 (D.C. Cir. 1984) (*TRAC*), the D.C. Circuit held that all APA § 706(1) actions are within the exclusive jurisdiction of the court that has jurisdiction to review the agency action that is the subject of the § 706(1) proceeding. Thus, in the *TRAC* case, the D.C. Circuit had exclusive jurisdiction over the § 706(1) proceeding because circuit courts have exclusive jurisdiction to review actions taken by the Federal Communications Commission (FCC).

The *TRAC* court relied partly on formal reasoning and partly on policy-based reasoning. Formally, the court relied on the All Writs Act, 28 U.S.C. § 1651(a). That statute authorizes any court to issue "all writs necessary or appropriate in aid of their jurisdiction." The circuit court concluded that the All Writs Act conferred on it exclusive jurisdiction to consider the APA § 706(1) petition to compel the agency to act, since the agency's action, once taken, was subject to exclusive circuit court review jurisdiction. The *TRAC* court reinforced this formal reasoning with policy analysis. The court concluded that a circuit court with exclusive jurisdiction to review an agency's actions has greater familiarity with the agency because of its review role. That preexisting knowledge of the agency's responsibilities would be helpful to the circuit court in assessing the claim that the agency has "unreasonably delayed" its action in a specific case. In particular, the circuit court would have a comparative advantage over a district court, which is likely to have no preexisting knowledge of the agency because of the statutory assignment of exclusive review jurisdiction to circuit courts.

The jurisdictional decision in *TRAC* had the effect of reducing significantly a petitioner's prospects for success in an APA § 706(1) action. It is often easy to paint a picture of apparent irresponsible delay by focusing only on the manner in which an agency has handled a particular matter. It is much more difficult to demonstrate that delay of a particular matter is "unreasonable" when the inquiry focuses instead on the agency's total workload and its scarce resources available to accomplish all of the important tasks it has been assigned.

The second doctrine that makes it difficult for petitioners to prevail in APA § 706(1) proceedings is substantive. After it announced its jurisdictional holding, the *TRAC* court set forth a six-part test for determining whether an agency action has been unreasonably delayed:

> (1) [T]he time agencies take to make decisions must be governed by a "rule of reason"; (2) where Congress has provided a timetable or other indication of the speed with which it expects the agency to proceed in the enabling statute, that statutory scheme may supply context for this rule of reason; (3) delays that might be reasonable in the sphere of economic regulation are less tolerable when human health and welfare are at stake; (4) the court should consider the effect of expediting delayed action on agency activities of a higher or competing priority; (5) the court should also take into account the nature and extent of the interest prejudiced by delay; and,

(6) the court need not "find any impropriety lurking behind agency lassitude in order to hold that agency action is unreasonably delayed."

TRAC, 750 F.2d at 80 (citations omitted).

It is difficult for a petitioner to prevail under this deferential standard, and most do not. Petitioners sometimes obtain relief of a sort, however, even if they are unable to convince the court to impose a deadline on the agency. Sometimes the agency responds to the pressure implicit in the § 706(1) petition by "voluntarily" presenting to the court a proposed timetable for acting in the matter. The court typically accepts the agency's timetable and expresses its approval of the agency's then-announced intention to act more expeditiously in the matter. This, in turn, creates continuing pressure on the agency to conform to its timetable.

It is easier to prevail in a § 706(1) case when Congress establishes a statutory deadline applicable to the action, but even in that situation courts have limited ability to take actions that are effective in responding to the problem of agency delay. If Congress imposed decisional deadlines selectively and based on a realistic assessment of the nature of the assigned tasks and the resources available to accomplish the tasks, statutory deadlines could serve a socially beneficial purpose. They would send a signal from Congress that the agency should attach an unusually high priority to a particular item on its agenda. Unfortunately, statutory deadlines are not imposed in this manner.

Congress establishes so many deadlines for so many actions by the same agency that the agency cannot possibly use the presence of a deadline as an indication that Congress attaches a priority to one or a few actions. The EPA typifies this problem. A 1985 study found that the EPA was then subject to 328 statutory deadlines. Environmental & Energy Study Institute and Environmental Law Institute, Statutory Deadlines in Environmental Legislation (1985). The Clean Air Act Amendments of 1990 added hundreds more. The statutory deadlines are totally unrealistic. The 1985 study found that the EPA had been able to meet only 17 percent of the deadlines Congress had imposed on the agency.

As a formal matter, courts are required to enforce statutory deadlines, just as they are required to enforce any other statutory obligation. To ensure that deadlines are enforced, Congress typically includes a provision authorizing "any person" to obtain a court order enforcing a deadline. *See, e.g.,* 42 U.S.C. § 7609(a)(2). As a practical matter, however, the unrealistic statutory deadlines Congress imposes are about as easy to enforce as would be a statute requiring all citizens to run the 100 meter dash in 8 seconds. When a petitioner complains to a court that an agency has not met a statutory deadline, the judge typically issues an order requiring that the agency act by some subsequent judicially determined deadline. More often than not, the agency fails to meet that deadline, and the court establishes a new deadline. The sequence continues until the agency finally acts in the matter, usually years after the original statutory deadline. *See, e.g., Association of Am. R.R. v. Costle,* 562 F.2d 1310 (D.C. Cir. 1977); *Natural Res. Def. Council, Inc. v. Train,* 510 F.2d 692 (D.C. Cir. 1975).

This sequence does have the effect of placing the agency under constant pressure to expedite any matter that is (1) subject to a statutory deadline and (2) subject to a judicial petition for an order to enforce that deadline. With so many agency actions subject to unrealistic statutory deadlines, however, the main effect of the deadlines is to confer on the private parties who are potential petitioners the discretion to determine the agency's priorities and its allocation of resources among the tasks that are subject to deadlines. *See* R. Shep Melnick, *Administrative Law and Bureaucratic Reality*, 44 ADMIN. L. REV. 245 (1992). In Professor Melnick's words: "It is hard to imagine a worse way to apportion agency resources."

None of the many studies of statutory deadlines has concluded that they provide an effective and efficient remedy for agency delay. Indeed, all researchers have reached conclusions similar to those of Alden Abbott: "[S]tatutory deadlines . . . impose three types of costs on society: (1) wasted resource costs . . . ; (2) agency resource mis-allocation costs . . . ; and (3) regulatory inefficiency costs. . . ." *See* Alden F. Abbott, *Case Studies on the Costs of Federal Statutory and Judicial Deadlines*, 39 ADMIN. L. REV. 467 (1987). In a careful empirical analysis, Jacob Gersen & Anne O'Connell found that decisional deadlines imposed on agencies by statutes and by courts reduce average decisionmaking time by modest amounts at significant cost in the form of reduced quality of decisionmaking. *See* Jacob E. Gersen & Anne Joseph O'Connell, *Deadlines in Administrative Law*, 156 U. PENN. L. REV. 923 (2008); *see also* CARNEGIE COMMISSION ON SCIENCE, TECHNOLOGY, AND GOVERNMENT, RISK AND THE ENVIRONMENT: IMPROVING REGULATORY DECISIONMAKING 58–59 (1993).

The Court limited the scope of § 706(1) in *Norton v. Southern Utah Wilderness Alliance*, 542 U.S. 55 (2004). In that case, the Court held that "a claim under § 706(1) can proceed only where an agency failed to take a *discrete* agency action that it is *required to take.*" *Id.* at 64 (emphasis in original.) The Court in *Southern Utah Wilderness Alliance* concluded that a statute that requires the Bureau of Land Management (BLM) "to continue to manage Wilderness Study Areas . . . in a manner so as not to impair the suitability of such areas for preservation as wilderness," while mandatory, was not specific enough to support a court order requiring BLM to take any discrete action. The Court reasoned that a contrary conclusion would create judicial entanglement in abstract policy debates, permit judicial interference with lawful exercises of agency discretion, and invite pervasive oversight by federal courts over the manner and pace of agency compliance with broad statutory mandates. The Court also concluded that BLM land use plans cannot be the basis for a court order requiring BLM to take a discrete action "absent a binding commitment in the terms of the plan." The Court concluded that such plans are merely projections of the agency's intended future actions. Finally, the Court concluded that a statement in a particular plan that BLM would conduct supervision and monitoring of activities in an area—"like other 'will do' projections of agency action set forth in land use plans—are not a legally binding commitment enforceable under § 706(1)." *Id.* at 72.

DISCUSSION PROBLEM

The Mashpee Wampanoag Tribal Council, Inc. (Mashpee) petitioned the Secretary of the Interior and the Bureau of Indian Affairs (BIA) to be recognized by the United States as an Indian tribe. After initially reviewing the petition, the BIA sent Mashpee a "letter of obvious deficiency" requesting additional information. Five years later, Mashpee filed its response. Upon receiving the response, the BIA notified Mashpee that it was placing the petition on its list of applications "ready, waiting for active consideration." Petitions on the ready list are considered in the order in which they are placed on the list. Petitions under active consideration are evaluated according to a complex set of criteria by a historian, a cultural anthropologist, and a genealogist, a time-consuming and resource-intensive process. No statute or regulation sets a particular deadline for processing petitions once the BIA deems them complete; by contrast, once the BIA moves a petition into active consideration, BIA regulations establish series of deadlines for agency action respecting the petition. *See* 25 C.F.R. § 83.10(h)–(*l*). Six years after Mashpee's petition was placed on the ready list, there are thirteen petitions under active consideration and ten more petitions on the ready list. Six petitions, including Mashpee's, have been waiting on the ready list for at least five years. Throughout that time, roughly a dozen BIA staff have been assigned to the task of evaluating recognition petitions. The BIA estimates that it will take fifteen years to resolve all of the petitions on the ready list. The BIA and Mashpee agree that the delay experienced by Mashpee and other groups seeking recognition is mostly due to a shortage of resources. Interested parties have repeatedly asked Congress to provide additional funding for processing recognition petitions, to no avail. Regardless, unhappy with the time frame for action on its petition, Mashpee has sued the Secretary of the Interior and the BIA claiming unreasonable delay under the APA and seeking an order compelling the BIA to act on its petition. Do you think a reviewing court is likely to hear Mashpee's claim?

5. PRIMARY JURISDICTION

The doctrine of primary jurisdiction typically arises not in a proceeding before an administrative agency but in litigation before a court. Agency and court jurisdiction to resolve disputes and issues frequently overlap, leading to potential conflicts in resolving those disputes and issues. Primary jurisdiction is a doctrine used by courts to allocate initial decisionmaking responsibility between agencies and courts where such overlaps and potential for conflicts exist. Since the boundaries between judicial and agency responsibilities often are not clear and may depend on expert analysis of factual patterns, courts often use primary jurisdiction to allocate to an agency initial responsibility to decide whether an overlap that is likely to lead to conflicts actually exists.

If a court concludes that a dispute brought before the court is within the exclusive jurisdiction of an agency, it will dismiss the action on the basis that it should be brought before the agency instead. However, if a court concludes that an issue raised in an action before the court is within the primary jurisdiction of an agency, the court will defer any decision in the action before it until the agency has addressed the issue that is within its primary jurisdiction. The court retains jurisdiction over the action itself and all other issues raised by the case, but it cannot resolve the case until the agency has resolved the issue that is in its primary jurisdiction.

Primary jurisdiction is conceptually analogous to exhaustion of administrative remedies. Both are prudential doctrines created by the courts to allocate between courts and agencies the initial responsibility for resolving issues and disputes in a manner that recognizes the differing responsibilities and comparative advantages of agencies and courts. There is no fixed formula for determining whether an agency has primary jurisdiction over a dispute or an issue raised in a dispute. In making such determinations, courts consider several factors, including (1) the extent to which the agency's specialized expertise makes it a preferable forum for resolving the issue, (2) the need for uniform resolution of the issue, and (3) the potential that judicial resolution of the issue will have an adverse impact on the agency's performance of its regulatory responsibilities. Increasingly, however, courts balance the considerations that favor allocation of initial decisionmaking responsibility to an agency against the likelihood that application of primary jurisdiction will unduly delay resolution of the dispute before the court.

United States v. Western Pacific R.R. Co., 352 U.S. 59 (1956), illustrates the typical effect of primary jurisdiction. The government refused to pay a freight bill tendered by Western Pacific on the basis that Western Pacific had billed under its tariff provision applicable to "incendiary bombs," while the government maintained that the fuseless napalm bombs shipped were eligible for the lower tariff rate applicable to gasoline. Western Pacific sued in the court of claims, where both parties and the court assumed that the court had the power to interpret the tariff and to determine which rate applied. The Supreme Court raised the question of primary jurisdiction to interpret Western Pacific's tariff *sua sponte* and held that issue to be within Interstate Commerce Commission's primary jurisdiction. (The ICC was the agency responsible for regulating rail rates and for approving rail tariffs at the time.) As a result, while the court of claims retained ultimate power to resolve the overall dispute between Western Pacific and the government, it was required to suspend its decisionmaking process and to refer to ICC the issue of which tariff provision applied to the government's shipment.

The *Western Pacific* Court explained the effects of the primary jurisdiction doctrine:

> "primary jurisdiction" * * * applies where a claim is originally cognizable in the courts, and comes into play whenever enforcement of the claim requires the resolution of issues which, under a regulatory scheme, have been placed within the special competence of an administrative body; in such a case the judicial process is suspended pending referral of such issues to the administrative body for its views.

Id. at 63–64.

Later in the opinion, the Court emphasized the full significance of the doctrine: "The doctrine of primary jurisdiction thus does 'more than prescribe the mere procedural time table of the lawsuit. It is a doctrine allocating the lawmaking power over certain aspects' of commercial relations. 'It transfers from court to agency the power to determine' some of the incidents of such relations." *Id.* at 65.

C. STANDING TO OBTAIN JUDICIAL REVIEW

One might expect the law governing standing to obtain judicial review of an agency action to be simple. When a court is called upon to resolve a standing dispute, it needs to answer only one easy question: can this particular petitioner obtain review of this otherwise final, ripe, and reviewable agency action? Yet, the law of standing is extraordinarily complicated. Courts have blended constitutional reasoning, statutory reasoning, and prudential reasoning in a rich stew of which no one can be sure of the ingredients. Moreover, courts often impose standing limitations for undisclosed purposes that seem logically irrelevant to the question of who can obtain review of an agency action. Further, courts often use standing as a substitute for reviewability, *i.e.*, as a means of insulating completely some class of actions from judicial review at the behest of any potential petitioner. The Supreme Court has issued over five hundred opinions that addressed standing in the past forty years. It is impossible to rationalize fully the resulting maze of often inconsistent statements contained in those opinions. We will attempt to provide a framework in which you can understand the many ways in which courts use standing to further a wide variety of unstated goals on which the Justices often differ.

Modern standing doctrine consists of both constitutional and statutory requirements. Constitutional standing requirements derive from Article III of the United States Constitution, which limits federal court jurisdiction to "cases" or "controversies." Beyond constitutional standing requirements, the courts for many years also recognized certain statutory and prudential limitations on plaintiff standing in federal court. Recent cases have moved away from the "prudential standing" phraseology by recharacterizing concerns previously labeled as prudential instead as either constitutional or statutory. In the following materials, we discuss constitutional standing and statutory standing in turn. First, however, consider the following opinion, in which the Supreme Court summarizes the requirements of modern standing doctrine.

Association of Data Processing Service Organizations, Inc. v. Camp

397 U.S. 150 (1970).

■ MR. JUSTICE DOUGLAS delivered the opinion of the Court.

Petitioners sell data processing services to businesses generally. In this suit they seek to challenge a ruling by respondent Comptroller of the Currency that, as an incident to their banking services, national banks, including respondent American National Bank & Trust Company, may make data processing services available to other banks and to bank customers. * * *

Generalizations about standing to sue are largely worthless as such. One generalization is, however, necessary and that is that the question of standing in the federal courts is to be considered in the framework of Article III which restricts judicial power to "cases" and "controversies." * * *

The first question is whether the plaintiff alleges that the challenged action has caused him injury in fact, economic or otherwise. There can be no doubt but that petitioners have satisfied this test. The petitioners not only allege that competition by national banks in the business of providing data processing services might entail some future loss of profits for the petitioners, they also allege that respondent American National Bank & Trust Company was performing or preparing to perform such services for two customers for whom petitioner Data Systems, Inc., had previously agreed or negotiated to perform such services. The petitioners' suit was brought not only against the American National Bank & Trust Company, but also against the Comptroller of the Currency. The Comptroller was alleged to have caused petitioners injury in fact by his 1966 ruling which stated:

> "Incidental to its banking services, a national bank may make available its data processing equipment or perform data processing services on such equipment for other banks and bank customers." COMPTROLLER'S MANUAL FOR NATIONAL BANKS ¶ 3500 (Oct. 15, 1966).

* * *

The question of standing * * * concerns, apart from the "case" or "controversy" test, the question whether the interest sought to be protected by the complainant is arguably within the zone of interests to be protected or regulated by the statute or constitutional guarantee in question. Thus the Administrative Procedure Act grants standing to a person "aggrieved by agency action within the meaning of a relevant statute." 5 U.S.C. § 702. That interest, at times, may reflect "aesthetic, conservational, and recreational" as well as economic values. *Scenic Hudson Preservation Conference v. FPC*, 354 F.2d 608, 616 (1957). A person or a family may have a spiritual stake in First Amendment values sufficient to give standing to raise issues concerning the Establishment Clause and the Free Exercise Clause. We mention these noneconomic values to emphasize that standing may stem from them as well as from the economic injury in which petitioners rely here. Certainly he who is "likely to be financially" injured, *FCC v. Sanders Bros. Radio Station*, 309 U.S. 470, 477 (1940), may be a reliable private attorney general to litigate the issues of the public interest in the present case.

Apart from Article III jurisdictional questions, problems of standing, as resolved by this Court for its own governance, have involved a "rule of self-restraint." *Barrows v. Jackson*, 346 U.S. 249, 255 (1953). Congress can, of course, resolve the question one way or another, save as the requirements of Article III dictate otherwise.

Where statutes are concerned, the trend is toward enlargement of the class of people who may protest administrative action. The whole drive for enlarging the category of aggrieved "persons" is symptomatic of that trend. In a closely analogous case we held that an existing entrepreneur had standing to challenge the legality of the entrance of a newcomer into the business, because the established business was allegedly protected by a valid city ordinance that protected it from unlawful competition. *Chicago v. Atchison, T. & S.F.R. Co.*, 357 U.S. 77, 83–84 (1958). In that tradition was *Hardin v. Kentucky Utilities Co.*, 390 U.S. 1 (1968), which involved a section of the TVA Act designed primarily to protect, through area limitations, private utilities against TVA competition. We held that no explicit statutory provision was necessary to confer standing, since the private utility bringing suit was within the class of persons that the statutory provision as designed to protect.

It is argued that the *Chicago case* and the *Hardin* case are relevant here because of § 4 of the Bank Service Corporation Act of 1962, which provides:

> "No bank service corporation may engage in any activity other than the performance of bank services for banks."

The Court of Appeals for the First Circuit held in Arnold Tours, Inc. v. Camp, 408 F.2d 1147, 1153, that by reason of § 4 a data processing company has standing to contest the legality of a national bank performing data processing services for other banks and bank customers:

> "Section 4 had a broader purpose than regulating only the service corporations. It was also a response to the fears expressed by a few senators, that without such a prohibition, the bill would have enabled 'banks to engage in a nonbanking activity,' S. Rep. No. 2105 (87th Cong., 2d Sess., 7–12) (Supplemental views of Senators Proxmire, Douglas, and Neuberger), and thus constitute 'a serious exception to the accepted public policy which strictly limits banks to banking.' (Supplemental views of Senators Muskie and Clark). We think Congress has provided the sufficient statutory aid to standing even though the competition may not be the precise kind Congress legislated against."

We do not put the issue in those words, for they implicate the merits. We do think, however, that § 4 arguably brings a competitor within the zone of interests protected by it.

* * *

Both [the Bank Service Corporation Act and the National Bank Act] are clearly 'relevant' statutes within the meaning of § 702. The Acts do not in terms protect a specified group. But their general policy is apparent; and those whose interests are directly affected by a broad or narrow interpretation of the Acts are easily identifiable. It is clear that petitioners, as competitors of national banks which are engaging in data processing services, are within that class of 'aggrieved' persons who, under § 702, are entitled to judicial review of 'agency action.'

* * *

We hold that petitioners have standing to sue and that the case should be remanded for a hearing on the merits.

1. CONSTITUTIONAL STANDING

The Supreme Court has interpreted the case or controversy requirement of Article III as limiting standing to raise a claim in federal court to those plaintiffs who satisfy three elements. First, as the Court indicated in *ADAPSO,* a plaintiff must establish that she has suffered an "injury in fact." Second, a plaintiff must demonstrate a causal connection between her injury and the conduct that gives rise to her complaint. In other words, the injury must be "fairly traceable to the challenged action of the defendant." Finally, a plaintiff must show that a decision by the courts in her favor will likely redress her injury.

Having set forth these three requirements—injury in fact, causation, and redressability, the courts have struggled to apply them consistently. Consider, for example, the Supreme Court's approach to the causation element in the following opinion.

Allen v. Wright

468 U.S. 737 (1984).

■ JUSTICE O'CONNOR delivered the opinion of the Court.

Parents of black public school children allege in this nation-wide class action that the Internal Revenue Service (IRS) has not adopted sufficient standards and procedures to fulfill its obligation to deny tax-exempt status to racially discriminatory private schools. They assert that the IRS thereby harms them directly and interferes with the ability of their children to receive an education in desegregated public schools. The issue before us is whether plaintiffs have standing to bring this suit. We hold that they do not.

* * *

It is in their complaint's second claim of injury that respondents allege harm to a concrete, personal interest that can support standing in some circumstances. The injury they identify—their children's diminished ability to receive an education in a racially integrated school—is, beyond any doubt, not only judicially cognizable but, as shown by cases from *Brown v. Board of Education,* 347 U.S. 483 (1954), to *Bob Jones University v. United States,* 461 U.S. 574 (1983), one of the most serious injuries recognized in our legal system. Despite the constitutional importance of curing the injury alleged by respondents, however, the federal judiciary may not redress it unless standing requirements are met. In this case, respondents' second claim of injury cannot support standing because the injury alleged is not fairly traceable to the Government conduct respondents challenge as unlawful.

The illegal conduct challenged by respondents is the IRS's grant of tax exemptions to some racially discriminatory schools. The line of causation between that conduct and desegregation of respondents' schools is attenuated at best. From the perspective of the IRS, the injury to respondents is highly indirect and "results from the independent action of some third party not before the court," As the Court pointed out in *Warth v. Seldin,* 422 U.S. 490, 505 (1975), "the indirectness of the injury . . . may make it substantially more difficult to meet the minimum requirement of Art. III. . . ."

The diminished ability of respondents' children to receive a desegregated education would be fairly traceable to unlawful IRS grants of tax exemptions only if there were enough racially discriminatory private schools receiving tax exemptions in respondents' communities for withdrawal of those exemptions to make an appreciable difference in public school integration. Respondents have made no such allegation. It is, first, uncertain how many racially discriminatory private schools are in fact receiving tax exemptions. Moreover, it is entirely speculative whether withdrawal of a tax exemption from any particular school would lead the school to change its policies. It is just as speculative whether any given parent of a child attending such a private school would decide to transfer the child to public school as a result of any changes in educational or financial policy made by the private school once it was threatened with loss of tax-exempt status. It is also pure speculation whether, in a particular community, a large enough number of the numerous relevant school officials and parents would reach decisions that collectively would have a significant impact on the racial composition of the public school.

■ JUSTICE STEVENS, with whom JUSTICE BLACKMUN joins, dissenting.

Three propositions are clear to me: (1) respondents have adequately alleged "injury in fact"; (2) their injury is fairly traceable to the conduct that they claim to be unlawful; and (3) the "separation of powers" principle does not create a jurisdictional obstacle to the consideration of the merits of their claim.

* * *

We have held that when a subsidy makes a given activity more or less expensive, injury can be fairly traced to the subsidy for purposes of standing analysis because of the resulting increase or decrease in the ability to engage in the activity. Indeed, we have employed exactly this causation analysis in the same context at issue here—subsidies given private schools that practice racial discrimination. Thus, in *Gilmore v. City of Montgomery*, 417 U.S. 556 (1974), we easily recognized the causal connection between official policies that enhanced the attractiveness of segregated schools and the failure to bring about or maintain a desegregated public school system. Similarly, in *Norwood v. Harrison*, 413 U.S. 455 (1973), we concluded that the provision of textbooks to discriminatory private schools "has a significant tendency to facilitate, reinforce, and support private discrimination." *Id.* at 466.

* * *

This causation analysis is nothing more than a restatement of elementary economics: when something becomes more expensive, less of it will be purchased. * * * If racially discriminatory private schools lose the "cash grants" that flow from the operation of the statutes, the education they provide will become more expensive and hence less of their services will be purchased. Conversely, maintenance of these tax benefits makes an education in segregated private schools relatively more attractive, by decreasing its cost. Accordingly, without tax-exempt status, private schools will either not be competitive in terms of cost, or have to change their admissions policies, hence reducing their competitiveness for parents seeking "a racially segregated alternative" to public schools, which is what respondents have alleged many white parents in desegregating school districts seek. In either event the process of desegregation will be advanced in the same way that it was advanced in *Gilmore* and *Norwood*—the withdrawal of the subsidy for segregated schools means the incentive structure facing white parents who seek such schools for their children will be altered. Thus, the laws of economics, not to mention the [tax] laws of Congress, compel the conclusion that the injury respondents have alleged—the increased segregation of their children's schools because of the ready availability of private schools that admit whites only—will be redressed if these schools' operations are inhibited through the denial of preferential tax treatment.

■ [An opinion by JUSTICE BRENNAN, dissenting, is omitted. Ed.]

NOTES AND QUESTIONS

1.   Supreme Court precedent generally requires the causal chain to be relatively direct to satisfy constitutional standing requirements. In *Allen*, the Court's majority contended that the plaintiffs had failed to establish a sufficient causal relationship between the IRS's decision to grant tax exempt status to racially discriminatory private schools and the insufficient desegregation of public schools, at least in part because it was unclear whether and to what extent the implicit tax subsidy actually influenced the decisions of individual schools and parents. How much do you think the tax laws affect the conduct of taxpayers? How might a taxpayer satisfy the causation standard the majority applied?

2.   In *Allen*, the Court denied standing to petitioners who sought to argue that the IRS was not adequately enforcing two provisions of the tax code. Prior to 1985, the Court used reasoning similar to that of the *Allen* majority to deny standing in several other cases that, in a sense, resembled *Allen*. The Court denied standing to petitioners who sought to challenge a prosecutor's decision not to prosecute a father for failure to provide child support in *Linda R.S. v. Richard D.*, 410 U.S. 614 (1973), and it denied standing to petitioners who argued that the IRS was not adequately enforcing a different provision of the tax code in *Simon v. Eastern Ky. Welfare Rights Org.*, 426 U.S. 26 (1976). The Court has not used reasoning like that it used in *Allen* to decide a case of this type since it issued its opinion in *Heckler v. Chaney*, 470 U.S. 821 (1985), which we discussed at length earlier in this Chapter. Can you draw from these cases a pattern that suggests why the *Allen* Court adopted and applied a test of causation that seems to be impossible to satisfy?

The *ADAPSO* Court interpreted the case or controversy requirement of Article III to limit standing to a petitioner who alleges that the challenged action has caused him to suffer "injury-in-fact, economic or otherwise." As with causation, the Court has had tremendous difficulty applying the injury-in-fact requirement consistently. The Court does not accept all injuries as sufficient to qualify as an injury-in-fact. "Concrete" and "particularized" injuries qualify, while "abstract" or "generalized" injuries do not. Mere anger over an allegedly unlawful government action is insufficient to qualify as an injury for standing purposes. Beyond that, however, the Justices often disagree over the parameters of this distinction. For example, the Justices often disagree about whether an "injury shared by the many" is sufficient to confer standing on a petitioner. The following case illustrates this common source of disagreement regarding the injury in fact element of constitutional standing doctrine.

FEC v. Akins

524 U.S. 11 (1998).

■ JUSTICE BREYERS delivered the opinion of the Court.

The Federal Election Commission (FEC) has determined that the American Israel Public Affairs Committee (AIPAC) is not a "political committee" as defined by the Federal Election Campaign Act of 1971 (FECA), and, for that reason, the FEC has refused to require AIPAC to make disclosures regarding its membership, contributions, and expenditures that FECA would otherwise require. We hold that respondents, a group of voters, have standing to challenge the Commission's determination in court, and we remand this case for further proceedings.

* * * [T]he FECA seeks to remedy any actual or perceived corruption of the political process in several important ways. The Act imposes limits upon the amounts that individuals, corporations, "political committees" (including political action committees), and political parties can contribute to a candidate for federal political office. 2 U.S.C. §§ 441a(a)–(b), 441b.

This case concerns requirements in the Act that extend beyond these better-known contribution and expenditure limitations. In particular, the Act imposes extensive recordkeeping and disclosure requirements upon groups that fall within the Act's definition of a "political committee." Those groups must register with the FEC, appoint a treasurer, keep names and addresses of contributors, track the amount and purpose of disbursements, and file complex FEC reports that include lists of donors giving in excess of $200 per year (often, these donors may be the group's members), contributions, expenditures, and any other disbursements irrespective of their purposes.

* * *

This case arises out of an effort by respondents, a group of voters with views often opposed to those of AIPAC, to persuade the FEC to treat AIPAC as a "political committee." [We have omitted the Court's discussion of FEC's decision refusing to characterize AIPAC as a political committee. Ed.]

The Solicitor General argues that respondents lack standing to challenge the FEC's decision not to proceed against AIPAC. He claims that they have failed to satisfy the "prudential" standing requirements upon which this Court has insisted. He adds that respondents have not shown that they "suffe[r] injury in fact," that their injury is "fairly traceable" to the FEC's decision, or that a judicial decision in their favor would "redres[s]" the injury. *See, e.g., Bennett v. Spear*, 520 U.S. 154, 162 (1997). In his view, respondents' District Court petition consequently failed to meet Article III's demand for a "case" or "controversy."

We do not agree with the FEC's "prudential standing" claim. Congress has specifically provided in FECA that "[a]ny person who believes a violation of this Act . . . has occurred, may file a complaint with the Commission." § 437(g)(a)(1). It has added that "[a]ny party aggrieved by an order of the Commission dismissing a complaint filed by such party . . . may file a petition" in district court seeking review of that dismissal. § 437(g)(8)(A). History associates the word "aggrieved" with a congressional intent to cast the standing net broadly—beyond the common-law interests and substantive statutory rights upon which "prudential" standing traditionally rested. *See, e.g., FCC v. Sanders Bros. Radio Station*, 309 U.S. 470 (1940).

Moreover, prudential standing is satisfied when the injury asserted by a plaintiff "arguably [falls] within the zone of interests to be protected or regulated by the statute . . . in question." *National Credit Union Admin.(NCUA) v. First Nat'l Bank & Trust Co.*, 522 U.S. 479, 488 (1998) (quoting *Ass'n of Data Processing Serv. Orgs., Inc. v. Camp*, 397 U.S. 150, 153 (1970)). The injury of which respondents complain— their failure to obtain relevant information—is injury of a kind that FECA seeks to address; political committees must disclose contributors and disbursements to help voters understand who provides which candidates with financial support. We have found nothing in the Act that suggests Congress intended to exclude voters from the benefits of these provisions, or otherwise to restrict standing, say, to political parties, candidates, or their committees.

Given the language of the statute and the nature of the injury, we conclude that Congress, intending to protect voters such as respondents from suffering the kind of injury here at issue, intended to authorize this kind of suit. Consequently, respondents satisfy "prudential" standing requirements.

Nor do we agree with the FEC or the dissent that Congress lacks the constitutional power to authorize federal courts to adjudicate this lawsuit. Article III, of course, limits Congress' grant of judicial power to "cases" or "controversies." That limitation means that respondents must show, among other things, an "injury in fact"—a requirement that helps assure that courts will not "pass upon . . . abstract, intellectual problems," but adjudicate "concrete, living contest[s] between adversaries." *Coleman v. Miller*, 307 U.S. 433, 460 (1939) (Frankfurter, J., dissenting). In our view, respondents here have suffered a genuine "injury in fact."

The "injury in fact" that respondents have suffered consists of their inability to obtain information—lists of AIPAC donors (who are, according to AIPAC, its members), and campaign-related contributions and expenditures—that, on respondents' view of the law, the statute requires that AIPAC make public. There is no reason to doubt their claim that the information would help them (and others to whom they would communicate it) to evaluate candidates for public office, especially candidates who received assistance from AIPAC, and to evaluate the role that AIPAC's financial assistance might play in a specific election. Respondents' injury consequently seems concrete and particular. Indeed, this Court has previously held that a plaintiff suffers an "injury in fact" when the plaintiff fails to obtain information which must be publicly disclosed pursuant to a statute.

The dissent refers to *United States v. Richardson*, 418 U.S. 166 (1974), a case in which a plaintiff sought information (details of Central Intelligence Agency (CIA) expenditures) to which, he said, the Constitution's Accounts Clause, art. I, § 9, cl. 7, entitled him. The Court held that the plaintiff there lacked Article III standing. The dissent says that *Richardson* and this case are "indistinguishable." But as the parties' briefs suggest—for they do not mention *Richardson*—that case does not control the outcome here.

Richardson's plaintiff claimed that a statute permitting the CIA to keep its expenditures nonpublic violated the Accounts Clause, which requires that "a regular Statement and Account of the Receipts and Expenditures of all public Money shall be published from time to time." art. I, § 9, cl. 7. The Court held that the plaintiff lacked standing because there was "no 'logical nexus' between the [plaintiff's] asserted status of taxpayer and the claimed failure of the Congress to require the Executive to supply a more detailed report of the [CIA's] expenditures." *Richardson*, 418 U.S. at 175.

In this case, however, the "logical nexus" inquiry is not relevant. Here, there is no constitutional provision requiring the demonstration of the "nexus" the Court believed must be shown in *Richardson*. Rather, there is a statute which, as we previously pointed out, does seek to protect individuals such as respondents from the kind of harm they say they have suffered, *i.e.*, failing to receive particular information about campaign-related activities.

* * *

The FEC's strongest argument is its contention that this lawsuit involves only a "generalized grievance." * * * The FEC points out that respondents' asserted harm (their failure to obtain information) is one which is "shared in substantially equal measure by all or a large class of citizens." *Warth v. Seldin*, 422 U.S. 490, 499 (1975). This Court, the FEC adds, has often said that "generalized grievance[s]" are not the kinds of harms that confer standing. Whether styled as a constitutional or prudential limit on standing, the Court has sometimes determined that where large numbers of Americans suffer alike, the political process, rather than the judicial process, may provide the more appropriate remedy for a widely shared grievance.

The kind of judicial language to which the FEC points, however, invariably appears in cases where the harm at issue is not only widely shared, but is also of an abstract and indefinite nature—for example, harm to the "common concern for obedience to law." *L. Singer & Sons v. Union Pac. R.R. Co.*, 311 U.S. 295, 303 (1940). The abstract nature of the harm—for example, injury to the interest in seeing that the law is obeyed—deprives the case of the concrete specificity that characterized those controversies which were "the traditional concern of the courts at Westminster," *Coleman*, 307 U.S. at 460 (Frankfurter, J., dissenting), and which today prevents a plaintiff from obtaining what would, in effect, amount to an advisory opinion.

Often the fact that an interest is abstract and the fact that it is widely shared go hand in hand. But their association is not invariable, and where a harm is concrete, though widely shared, the Court has found "injury in fact." Thus the fact that a political forum may be more readily available where an injury is widely shared (while counseling against, say, interpreting a statute as conferring standing) does not, by itself, automatically disqualify an interest for Article III purposes. Such an interest, where sufficiently concrete, may count as an "injury in fact." This conclusion seems particularly obvious where (to use a hypothetical example) large numbers of individuals suffer the same common-law injury (say, a widespread mass tort), or where large numbers of voters suffer interference with voting rights conferred by law. We conclude that, similarly, the informational injury at issue here, directly related to voting, the most basic of political rights, is sufficiently concrete and specific such that the fact that it is widely shared does not deprive Congress of constitutional power to authorize its vindication in the federal courts.

■ JUSTICE SCALIA, with whom JUSTICE O'CONNOR and JUSTICE THOMAS join, dissenting.

The provision of law at issue in this case is an extraordinary one, conferring upon a private person the ability to bring an Executive agency into court to compel its enforcement of the law against a third party. Despite its liberality, the Administrative Procedure Act does not allow such suits, since enforcement action is traditionally deemed "committed to agency discretion by law." 5 U.S.C. § 701(a)(2); *Heckler v. Chaney*, 470 U.S. 821, 827–35 (1985). If provisions such as the present one were commonplace, the role of the Executive Branch in our system of separated and equilibrated powers would be greatly reduced, and that of the Judiciary greatly expanded.

Because this provision is so extraordinary, we should be particularly careful not to expand it beyond its fair meaning. In my view the Court's opinion does that. Indeed, it expands the meaning beyond what the Constitution permits.

* * *

In *Richardson*, we dismissed for lack of standing a suit whose "aggrievement" was precisely the "aggrievement" respondents assert here: the Government's unlawful refusal to place information within the public domain. The only difference, in fact, is that the aggrievement there was more direct, since the Government already had the information within its possession, whereas here respondents seek enforcement action that will bring information within the Government's possession and *then* require the information to be made public. The plaintiff in *Richardson* challenged the Government's failure to disclose the expenditures of the Central Intelligence Agency (CIA), in alleged violation of the constitutional requirement, art. I, § 9, cl. 7, that "a regular Statement and Account of the Receipts and Expenditures of all public Money shall be published from time to time." We held that such a claim was a nonjusticiable "generalized grievance" because "the impact on [plaintiff] is plainly undifferentiated and common to all members of the public." 418 U.S. at 176–77.

It was alleged in *Richardson* that the Government had denied a right conferred by the Constitution, whereas respondents here assert a right conferred by statute—but of course "there is absolutely no basis for making the Article III inquiry turn on the source of the asserted right." *Lujan v. Defenders of Wildlife*, 504 U.S. 555, 576 (1992). The Court today distinguishes *Richardson* on a different basis—a basis that reduces it from a landmark constitutional holding to a curio. According to the Court, "*Richardson* focused upon taxpayer standing, . . . not voter standing." In addition to being a silly distinction, given the weighty governmental purpose underlying the "generalized grievance" prohibition—viz., to avoid "something in the nature of an Athenian democracy or a New England town meeting to oversee the conduct of the National Government by means of lawsuits in federal courts," *Richardson*, 418 U.S. at 179—this is also a distinction that the Court in *Richardson* went out of its way explicitly to eliminate. It is true enough that the narrow question presented in *Richardson* was " '[w]hether a federal taxpayer has standing.' " *Id.* at 167 n.1. But the *Richardson* Court did not hold only, as the Court today suggests, that the plaintiff failed to qualify for the exception to the rule of no taxpayer standing established by the "logical nexus" test of *Flast v. Cohen*. The plaintiff's complaint in *Richardson* had also alleged that he was " 'a member of the electorate,' " 418 U.S. at 167 n.1, and he asserted injury in that capacity as well. The *Richardson* opinion treated that as fairly included within the taxpayer-standing question, or at least as plainly indistinguishable from it:

> "The respondent's claim is that without detailed information on CIA expenditures—and hence its activities—he cannot intelligently follow the actions of Congress or the Executive, *nor can he properly fulfill his obligations as a member of the electorate in voting for candidates seeking national office. * * *"* *Id.* at 176–77 (citations and internal quotations omitted) (emphasis added).

* * * Fairly read, and applying a fair understanding of its important purposes, *Richardson* is indistinguishable from the present case.

* * *

What is noticeably lacking in the Court's discussion of our generalized-grievance jurisprudence is all reference to two words that have figured in it prominently: "particularized" and "undifferentiated." "Particularized" means that "the injury must affect the plaintiff in a personal and individual way." *Lujan*, 504 U.S. at 560 n.1. If the effect is "undifferentiated and common to all members of the public," *Richardson*, 418 U.S. at 177, the plaintiff has a "generalized grievance" that must be pursued by political, rather than judicial, means. These terms explain why it is a gross oversimplification to reduce the concept of a generalized grievance to nothing more than "the fact that [the grievance] is widely shared," thereby enabling the concept to be dismissed as a standing principle by such examples as "large numbers of individuals suffer[ing] the same common-law injury (say, a widespread mass tort), or . . . large numbers of voters suffer[ing] interference with voting rights conferred by law." The exemplified injuries are widely shared, to be sure, but each individual suffers a particularized and differentiated harm. One tort victim suffers a burnt leg, another a burnt arm—or even if both suffer burnt arms they are *different* arms. One voter suffers the deprivation of *his* franchise, another the deprivation of *hers*. With the generalized grievance, on the other hand, the injury or deprivation is not only widely shared but it is *undifferentiated*. The harm caused to Mr. Richardson by the alleged disregard of the Statement-of-Accounts Clause was precisely the same as the harm caused to everyone else: unavailability of a description of CIA expenditures. Just as the (more indirect) harm caused to Mr. Akins by the allegedly unlawful failure to enforce FECA is precisely the same as the harm caused to everyone else: unavailability of a description of AIPAC's activities.

The Constitution's line of demarcation between the Executive power and the judicial power presupposes a common understanding of the type of interest needed to sustain a "case or controversy" against the Executive in the courts. A system in which the citizenry at large could sue to compel Executive compliance with the law would be a system in which the courts, rather than the President, are given the primary responsibility to "take Care that the Laws be faithfully executed," art. II, § 3. We do not have such a system because the common understanding of the interest necessary to sustain suit has included the requirement, affirmed in *Richardson*, that the complained-of injury be particularized and differentiated, rather than common to all the electorate. When the Executive can be directed by the courts, at the instance of any voter, to remedy a deprivation that affects the entire electorate in precisely the same way—and particularly when that deprivation (here, the unavailability of information) is one inseverable part of a larger enforcement scheme—there has occurred a shift of political responsibility to a branch designed not to protect the public at large but to protect individual rights. "To permit Congress to convert the undifferentiated public interest in executive officers' compliance with the law into an 'individual right' vindicable in the courts is to permit Congress to transfer from the President to the courts the Chief Executive's most important constitutional duty. . . ." *Lujan*, 504 U.S. at 577. If today's decision is correct, it is within the power of Congress to authorize any interested person to manage (through the courts) the Executive's enforcement of any law that includes a requirement for the filing and public availability of a piece of paper. This is not the system we have had, and is not the system we should desire.

NOTES AND QUESTIONS

1. The dissent in *Akins* considered that case indistinguishable from *United States v. Richardson*, 418 U.S. 166 (1974), while the majority distinguished *Richardson*. In *Richardson*, the Court held unanimously that neither taxpayers nor voters (nor presumably anyone else) had standing to challenge the refusal of the government to make public the details of the CIA's budget, arguably in violation of Article I, Section 9, Clause 7 of the Constitution. In *Schlesinger v. Reservists Committee to Stop the War*, 418 U.S. 208 (1974), in an opinion issued the same day as *Richardson*, the Court held unanimously that neither taxpayers nor voters could challenge the then-widespread practice of members of Congress holding reserve commissions in the military, arguably in violation of Article I, Section 6, Clause 2 of the Constitution. Why do you suppose the Justices held unanimously that no one has standing to obtain judicial consideration of those issues?

2. The *Akins* majority distinguished the case at bar from *Richardson* on the basis that Congress had explicitly created a statutory right to the information that was at issue in *Akins* and had explicated instructed courts to enforce that statutory right. As the opinions in *Akins* illustrate, this is another issue on which the Justices differ. Some consider the existence of a statutory right that Congress wants courts to enforce to be relevant, and perhaps even dispositive, in establishing constitutional standing, while other Justices consider it irrelevant.

In *ADAPSO*, the Court emphasized that injuries to "noneconomic values" such as "aesthetic, conservational, and recreational" values can qualify a petitioner for standing. Cases in which petitioners argue that they have standing based on alleged environmental injuries have been a major subject of debate among the Justices since 1990. Between 1970 and 1990, the Court decided several cases in which it seemed to welcome petitioners who relied on alleged environmental injuries to support their claims to standing. In some cases, the Court accepted as adequate claims of injury and/or alleged causal relationships with injuries that were tenuous at best. In *United States v. Students Challenging Regulatory Agency Procedures (SCRAP)*, 412 U.S. 669 (1973), for example, the Court held that a group of law students at George Washington University had standing to obtain review of a decision in which the ICC authorized an across-the-board increase in rail freight rates. The students claimed to have been injured in their capacity as air breathers. They argued that the ICC caused injury to their lungs by (1) refusing to exempt scrap metal from the rate increase (2) thereby decreasing the economic attractiveness of using recycled metal, (3) thereby increasing the amount of new metal that must be made, and (4) thereby increasing the pollutants in the air the students breathed by the amount of the difference between the pollution produced in the process of making new metal and the amount of pollution produced in the process of making an equivalent amount of recycled metal.

The Court's extremely accommodating attitude toward environmental petitioners began to change when Justice Scalia joined the Court. Before he joined the Court, Justice Scalia wrote *The Doctrine of Standing as an Essential Element of the Separation of Powers*, 17 SUFFOLK U. L. REV. 881 (1983). He argued that the Take Care Clause in Article II authorizes only the President to enforce and administer laws that are intended to benefit the general public. Thus, in his view, it is unconstitutional for a court to entertain a lawsuit in which a citizen seeks to enforce an environmental statute. Justice Scalia has devoted much of his time and energy on the Court to persuading a majority of his colleagues to adopt his view of the law of standing, with mixed results to date.

Lujan v. National Wildlife Federation

497 U.S. 871 (1990).

■ JUSTICE SCALIA delivered the opinion of the Court.

In this case we must decide whether respondent, the National Wildlife Federation (hereinafter respondent), is a proper party to challenge actions of the Federal Government relating to certain public lands.

Respondent filed this action in 1985 in the United States District Court for the District of Columbia against petitioners the United States Department of the Interior, the Secretary of the Interior, and the Director of the Bureau of Land Management (BLM), an agency within the Department. In its amended complaint, respondent alleged that petitioners had violated the Federal Land Policy and Management Act of 1976 (FLPMA), the National Environmental Policy Act of 1969 (NEPA) and § 10(e) of the Administrative Procedure Act (APA), 5 U.S.C. § 706, in the course of administering what the complaint called the "land withdrawal review program" of the BLM.

* * *

Pursuant to the directives of the FLPMA, petitioners engage in a number of different types of administrative action with respect to the various tracts of public land within the United States. First, the BLM conducts the review and recommends the determinations required by 43 U.S.C. § 1714(*l*) with respect to withdrawals in 11 Western States. * * *

Second, the Secretary revokes some withdrawals under § 204(a) of the Act, which the Office of the Solicitor has interpreted to give the Secretary the power to process proposals for revocation of withdrawals made during the "ordinary course of business." * * *

Third, the Secretary engages in the ongoing process of classifying public lands, either for multiple use management, for disposal, or for other uses.

* * *

[R]espondent claims a right to judicial review under § 10(a) of the APA, which provides:

> "A person suffering legal wrong because of agency action, or adversely affected or aggrieved by agency action within the meaning of a relevant statute, is entitled to judicial review thereof." 5 U.S.C. § 702.

This provision contains two separate requirements. First, the person claiming a right to sue must identify some "agency action" that affects him in the specified fashion; it is judicial review "thereof" to which he is entitled. The meaning of "agency action" for purposes of § 702 is set forth in 5 U.S.C. § 551(13), which defines the term as "the whole or a part of an agency rule, order, license, sanction, relief, or the equivalent or denial thereof, or failure to act." When, as here, review is sought not pursuant to specific authorization in the substantive statute, but only under the general review provisions of the APA, the "agency action" in question must be "final agency action." *See* 5 U.S.C. § 704.

Second, the party seeking review under § 702 must show that he has "suffer[ed] legal wrong" because of the challenged agency action, or is "adversely affected or aggrieved" by that action "within the meaning of a relevant statute." Respondent does not assert that it has suffered "legal wrong," so we need only discuss the meaning of "adversely affected or aggrieved . . . within the meaning of a relevant statute." * * * [W]e have said that to be "adversely affected or aggrieved . . . within the meaning" of a statute, the plaintiff must establish that the injury he complains of (*his* aggrievement, or the adverse effect *upon him*) falls within the "zone of interests" sought to be protected by the statutory provision whose violation forms the legal basis for his complaint.

* * *

We turn, then, to whether the specific facts alleged in the two affidavits considered by the District Court raised a genuine issue of fact as to whether an "agency action" taken by petitioners caused respondent to be "adversely affected or aggrieved . . . within the meaning of a relevant statute."

As for the "agency action" requirement, we think that each of the affidavits can be read, as the Court of Appeals believed, to complain of a particular "agency action" as that term is defined in § 551. The parties agree that the Peterson affidavit, judging from the geographic area it describes, must refer to that one of the BLM orders listed in the appendix to the complaint that appears at 49 Fed. Reg. 19904–05, an order captioned W–6228 and dated April 30, 1984, terminating the withdrawal classification of some 4,500 acres of land in that area. * * *

We also think that whatever "adverse effect" or "aggrievement" is established by the affidavits was "within the meaning of the relevant statute"—*i.e.*, met the "zone of interests" test. The relevant statute, of course, is the statute whose violation is the gravamen of the complaint—both the FLPMA and NEPA. We have no doubt that "recreational use and aesthetic enjoyment" are among the *sorts* of interests those statutes were specifically designed to protect. The only issue, then, is whether the facts alleged in the affidavits showed that those interests *of Peterson* * * * were actually affected.

* * *

The District Court found the Peterson affidavit inadequate for the following reasons:

> "Peterson . . . claims that she uses federal lands *in the vicinity* of the South Pass-Green Mountain area of Wyoming for recreational purposes and for aesthetic enjoyment and that her recreational and aesthetic enjoyment has been and continues to be adversely affected as the result of the decision of BLM to open it to the staking of mining claims and oil and gas leasing. * * *

* * *

[The requirement that the petitioner allege an injury] is assuredly not satisfied by averments which state only that one of respondent's members uses unspecified portions of an immense tract of territory, on some portions of which mining activity has occurred or probably will occur by virtue of the governmental action.

* * *

It is impossible that the affidavits would suffice, as the Court of Appeals held, to enable respondent to challenge the entirety of petitioners' so-called "land withdrawal review program." That is not an "agency action" within the meaning of § 702, much less a "final agency action" within the meaning of § 704. The term "land withdrawal review program" (which as far as we know is not derived from any authoritative text) does not refer to a single BLM order or regulation, or even to a completed universe of particular BLM orders and regulations. It is simply the name by which petitioners have occasionally referred to the continuing (and thus constantly changing) operations of the BLM in reviewing withdrawal revocation applications and the classifications of public lands and developing land use plans as required by the FLPMA. It is no more an identifiable "agency action"—much less a "final agency action"—than a "weapons procurement program" of the Department of Defense or a "drug interdiction program" of the Drug Enforcement Administration. As the District Court explained, the "land withdrawal review program" extends to, currently at least, "1250 or so individual classification terminations and withdrawal revocations."

Respondent alleges that violation of the law is rampant within this program—failure to revise land use plans in proper fashion, failure to submit certain recommendations to Congress, failure to consider multiple use, inordinate focus upon mineral exploitation, failure to provide required public notice, failure to provide adequate environmental impact statements. Perhaps so. But respondent cannot seek *wholesale* improvement of this program by court decree, rather than in the offices of the Department or the halls of Congress, where programmatic improvements are normally made.

■ JUSTICE BLACKMUN, with whom JUSTICE BRENNAN, JUSTICE MARSHALL, and JUSTICE STEVENS join, dissenting.

In my view, the affidavit[ ] of Peggy Kay Peterson * * *, in conjunction with other record evidence before the District Court on the motions for summary judgment, w[as] sufficient to establish the standing of the National Wildlife Federation (Federation or NWF) to bring this suit.

The Federation's asserted injury in this case rested upon its claim that the Government actions challenged here would lead to increased mining on public lands; that the mining would result in damage to the environment; and that the recreational opportunities of NWF's members would consequently be diminished. Abundant record evidence supported the Federation's assertion that on lands newly opened for mining, mining in fact would occur. Similarly, the record furnishes ample support for NWF's contention that mining activities can be expected to cause severe environmental damage to the affected lands.

NOTES AND QUESTIONS

NWF illustrates perhaps the most common manner in which standing disputes come before courts. Typically, a membership organization—a union, a trade association, or a public interest organization—files a petition for review in which it relies on the doctrine of associational or derivative standing to support its claim of standing. The Court established a test for an association's standing derivative of that of its members in *Hunt v. Washington Apple Advertising Comm'n*, 432 U.S. 333, 343 (1977):

> [A]n association has standing to bring suit on behalf of its members when: (a) its members would otherwise have standing to sue in their own right; (b) the interests it seeks to protect are germane to the organization's purpose; and (c) neither the claim asserted nor the relief requested requires the participation of individual members in the lawsuit.

During the Reagan Administration, the government argued that an association never has standing; only an individual can have standing. A five-Justice majority rejected that argument in *International Union, United Auto., Aerospace & Agricultural Implement Workers of Amer. v. Brock*, 477 U.S. 274 (1986). Political scientists have explained why a small number of individuals or firms, each with a large amount at stake, has a major advantage over a large number of people, each with a small amount at stake, in both political and legal forums. *See* MANCUR OLSON, THE LOGIC OF COLLECTIVE ACTION (1965). What, if any, relationship do you see between that characteristic of the political and legal systems and the associational standing doctrine?

When an association files a petition for review, it must rely on some combination of evidence already in the record made at the agency and affidavits from members to support its claim to standing. Since agencies are not bound by the case or controversy limitation of Article III, a party does not need to establish Article III standing to participate in an agency proceeding. As a result, agencies have no occasion to resolve such standing disputes and the record made at the agency alone usually is inadequate to support the association's claim of standing. Thus, associations almost always must submit member affidavits that recite facts sufficient to support the association's claim of derivative standing to avoid being subject to a successful motion to dismiss or motion for summary judgment based on alleged lack of standing. Some circuits require that the petitioner submit such affidavits at or before the time it submits its initial brief even if the government does not raise the standing issue. *See, e.g., Sierra Club v. EPA*, 292 F.3d 895 (D.C. Cir. 2002).

In *NWF*, Justice Scalia persuaded a majority of his colleagues to make a modest incremental change—addition of a geographic proximity requirement—in the Court's approach to environmental standing disputes. In the next case, he persuaded at least three of his colleagues to make much more dramatic changes in the law of standing.

Lujan v. Defenders of Wildlife

504 U.S. 555 (1992).

■ JUSTICE SCALIA delivered the opinion of the Court with respect to Parts I, II, III–A, and IV, and an opinion with respect to Part III–B, in which THE CHIEF JUSTICE, JUSTICE WHITE, and JUSTICE THOMAS join.

This case involves a challenge to a rule promulgated by the Secretary of the Interior interpreting § 7 of the Endangered Species Act of 1973 (ESA) in such fashion as to render it applicable only to actions within the United States or on the high seas. The preliminary issue, and the only one we reach, is whether respondents here, plaintiffs below, have standing to seek judicial review of the rule.

I

The ESA seeks to protect species of animals against threats to their continuing existence caused by man. The ESA instructs the Secretary of the Interior to promulgate by regulation a list of those species which are either endangered or threatened under enumerated criteria, and to define the critical habitat of these species. Section 7(a)(2) of the Act then provides, in pertinent part:

"Each Federal agency shall, in consultation with and with the assistance of the Secretary [of the Interior], insure that any action authorized, funded, or carried out by such agency . . . is not likely to jeopardize the continued existence of any endangered species or threatened species or result in the destruction or adverse modification of habitat of such species which is determined by the Secretary, after consultation as appropriate with affected States, to be critical." 16 U.S.C. § 1536(a)(2).

In 1978, the Fish and Wildlife Service (FWS) and the National Marine Fisheries Service (NMFS), on behalf of the Secretary of the Interior and the Secretary of Commerce respectively, promulgated a joint regulation stating that the obligations imposed by § 7(a)(2) extend to actions taken in foreign nations. The next year, however, the Interior Department began to reexamine its position. A revised joint regulation, reinterpreting § 7(a)(2) to require consultation only for actions taken in the United States or on the high seas, was proposed in 1983 and promulgated in 1986.

Shortly thereafter, respondents, organizations dedicated to wildlife conservation and other environmental causes, filed this action against the Secretary of the Interior, seeking a declaratory judgment that the new regulation is in error as to the geographic scope of § 7(a)(2) and an injunction requiring the Secretary to promulgate a new regulation restoring the initial interpretation. * * *

II

While the Constitution of the United States divides all power conferred upon the Federal Government into "legislative Powers," art. I, § 1, "[t]he executive Power," art. II, § 1, and "[t]he judicial Power," art. III, § 1, it does not attempt to define those terms. To be sure, it limits the jurisdiction of federal courts to "Cases" and "Controversies," but an executive inquiry can bear the name "case" (the Hoffa case) and a legislative dispute can bear the name "controversy" (the Smoot-Hawley controversy). Obviously, then, the Constitution's central mechanism of separation of powers depends largely upon common understanding of what activities are appropriate to legislatures, to executives, and to courts. * * *

Over the years, our cases have established that the irreducible constitutional minimum of standing contains three elements. First, the plaintiff must have suffered an "injury in fact"—an invasion of a legally protected interest which is (a) concrete and particularized, *Allen v. Wright*, 468 U.S. 737, 756 (1984), and (b) "actual or imminent, not 'conjectural' or 'hypothetical.' " *Whitmore v. Arkansas*, 495 U.S. 149, 155 (quoting *Los Angeles v. Lyons*, 461 U.S. 95, 102 (1983)). Second, there must be a causal connection between the injury and the conduct complained of—the injury has to be "fairly . . . trace[able] to the challenged action of the defendant, and not . . . th[e] result [of] the independent action of some third party not before the court." *Simon v. E. Ky. Welfare Rights Org.*, 426 U.S. 26, 41, 42 (1976). Third, it must be "likely," as opposed to merely "speculative," that the injury will be "redressed by a favorable decision." *Id.* at 38, 43.

* * *

When the suit is one challenging the legality of government action or inaction, the nature and extent of facts that must be averred (at the summary judgment stage) or proved (at the trial stage) in order to establish standing depends considerably upon whether the plaintiff is himself an object of the action (or forgone action) at issue. If he is, there is ordinarily little question that the action or inaction has caused him injury, and that a judgment preventing or requiring the action will redress it. When, however, as in this case, a plaintiff's asserted injury arises from the government's allegedly unlawful regulation (or lack of regulation) of *someone else*, much more is needed. In that circumstance, causation and redressability ordinarily hinge on the response of the regulated (or regulable) third party to the government action or inaction—and perhaps on the response of others as well. The existence of one or more of the essential elements of standing "depends on the unfettered choices made by independent actors not before the courts and whose exercise of broad and legitimate discretion the courts cannot presume either to control or to predict," *ASARCO Inc. v. Kadish*, 490 U.S. 605, 615 (1989), and it becomes the burden of the plaintiff to adduce facts showing that those choices have been or will be made in such manner as to produce causation and permit redressability of injury. Thus, when the plaintiff is not himself the object of the government action or inaction he challenges, standing is not precluded, but it is ordinarily "substantially more difficult" to establish. *Allen*, 468 U.S. at 758.

III

* * *

A

Respondents' claim to injury is that the lack of consultation with respect to certain funded activities abroad "increas[es] the rate of extinction of endangered and threatened species." Of course, the desire to use or observe an animal species, even for purely esthetic purposes, is undeniably a cognizable interest for purpose of standing. "But the 'injury in fact' test requires more than an injury to a cognizable interest. It requires that the party seeking review be himself among the injured." *Sierra Club v. Morton*, 405 U.S. 727, 734–35 (1972). To survive the Secretary's summary judgment motion, respondents had to submit affidavits or other evidence showing, through specific facts, not only that listed species were in fact being threatened by funded activities abroad, but also that one or more of respondents' members would thereby be "directly" affected apart from their " 'special interest' in th[e] subject." *Id.* at 735, 739.

With respect to this aspect of the case, the Court of Appeals focused on the affidavits of two Defenders' members—Joyce Kelly and Amy Skilbred. Ms. Kelly stated that she traveled to Egypt in 1986 and "observed the traditional habitat of the endangered nile crocodile there and intend[s] to do so again, and hope[s] to observe the crocodile directly," and that she "will suffer harm in fact as the result of [the] American ... role ... in overseeing the rehabilitation of the Aswan High Dam on the Nile ... and [in] develop[ing] ... Egypt's ... Master Water Plan." Ms. Skilbred averred that she traveled to Sri Lanka in 1981 and "observed th[e] habitat" of "endangered species such as the Asian elephant and the leopard" at what is now the site of the Mahaweli project funded by the Agency for International Development (AID), although she "was unable to see any of the endangered species"; "this development project," she continued, "will seriously reduce endangered, threatened, and endemic species habitat including areas that I visited ... [, which] may severely shorten the future of these species"; that threat, she concluded, harmed her because she "intend[s] to return to Sri Lanka in the future and hope[s] to be more fortunate in spotting at least the endangered elephant and leopard." When Ms. Skilbred was asked at a subsequent deposition if and when she had any plans to return to Sri Lanka, she reiterated that "I intend to go back to Sri Lanka," but confessed that she had no current plans: "I don't know [when]. There is a civil war going on right now. I don't know. Not next year, I will say. In the future."

We shall assume for the sake of argument that these affidavits contain facts showing that certain agency-funded projects threaten listed species—though that is questionable. They plainly contain no facts, however, showing how damage to the species will produce "imminent" injury to Mses. Kelly and Skilbred. That the women "had visited" the areas of the projects before the projects commenced proves nothing. As we have said in a related context, " 'Past exposure to illegal conduct does not in itself show a present case or controversy regarding injunctive relief ... if unaccompanied by any continuing, present adverse effects.' " *Lyons*, 461 U.S. at 102 (quoting *O'Shea v. Littleton*, 414 U.S. 488, 495–96 (1974)). And the affiants' profession of an "inten[t]" to return to the places they had visited before—where they will presumably, this time, be deprived of the opportunity to observe animals of the endangered species—is simply not enough. Such "some day" intentions—without any description of concrete plans, or indeed even any specification of *when* the some day will be—do not support a finding of the "actual or imminent" injury that our cases require.

Besides relying upon the Kelly and Skilbred affidavits, respondents propose a series of novel standing theories. The first, inelegantly styled "ecosystem nexus," proposes that any person who uses *any part* of a "contiguous ecosystem" adversely affected by a funded activity has standing even if the activity is located a great distance away. This approach, as the Court of Appeals correctly observed, is inconsistent with our opinion in *National Wildlife Federation*, which held that a plaintiff claiming injury from environmental damage must use the area affected by the challenged activity and not an area roughly "in the vicinity" of it. 497 U.S. at 887–89. It makes no difference that the general-purpose section of the ESA states that the Act was intended in part "to provide a means whereby the ecosystems upon which endangered species and threatened species depend may be conserved." 16 U.S.C. § 1531(b). To say that the Act protects ecosystems is not to say that the Act creates (if it were possible) rights of action in persons who have not been injured in fact, that is, persons who use portions of an ecosystem not perceptibly affected by the unlawful action in question.

Respondents' other theories are called, alas, the "animal nexus" approach, whereby anyone who has an interest in studying or seeing the endangered animals anywhere on the globe has standing; and the "vocational nexus" approach, under which anyone with a professional interest in such animals can sue. Under these theories, anyone who goes to see Asian elephants in the Bronx Zoo, and anyone who is a keeper of Asian elephants in the Bronx Zoo, has standing to sue because the Director of the Agency for International Development (AID) did not consult with the Secretary regarding the AID-funded project in Sri Lanka. This is beyond all reason. Standing is not "an ingenious academic exercise in the conceivable," *United States v. Students Challenging Regulatory Agency Procedures (SCRAP)*, 412 U.S. 669, 688 (1973), but as we have said requires, at the summary judgment stage, a factual showing of perceptible harm. It is clear that the person who observes or works with a particular animal threatened by a federal decision is facing perceptible harm, since the very subject of his interest will no longer exist. It is even plausible—though it goes to the outermost limit of plausibility—to think that a person who observes or works with animals of a particular species in the very area of the world where that species is threatened by a federal decision is facing such harm, since some animals that might have been the subject of his interest will no longer exist. It goes beyond the limit, however, and into pure speculation and fantasy, to say that anyone who observes or works with an endangered species, anywhere in the world, is appreciably harmed by a single project affecting some portion of that species with which he has no more specific connection.

B

* * *

The most obvious problem in the present case is redressability. Since the agencies funding the projects were not parties to the case, the District Court could accord relief only against the Secretary: He could be ordered to revise his regulation to require consultation for foreign projects. But this would not remedy respondents' alleged injury unless the funding agencies were bound by the Secretary's regulation, which is very much an open question. * * *

Respondents assert that this legal uncertainty did not affect redressability (and hence standing) because the District Court itself could resolve the issue of the Secretary's authority as a necessary part of its standing inquiry. Assuming that it is appropriate to resolve an issue of law such as this in connection with a threshold standing inquiry, resolution by the District Court would not have remedied respondents' alleged injury anyway, because it would not have been binding upon the agencies. They were not parties to the suit, and there is no reason they should be obliged to honor an incidental legal determination the suit produced. * * *

A further impediment to redressability is the fact that the agencies generally supply only a fraction of the funding for a foreign project. AID, for example, has provided less than 10% of the funding for the Mahaweli project. Respondents have produced nothing to indicate that the projects they have named will either be suspended, or do less harm to listed species, if that fraction is eliminated. * * * [I]t is entirely conjectural whether the nonagency activity that affects respondents will be altered or affected by the agency activity they seek to achieve.

IV

The Court of Appeals found that respondents had standing for an additional reason: because they had suffered a "procedural injury." The so-called "citizen-suit" provision of the ESA provides, in pertinent part, that "any person may commence a civil suit on his own behalf (A) to enjoin any person, including the United States and any other governmental instrumentality or agency . . . who is alleged to be in violation of any provision of this chapter." 16 U.S.C. § 1540(g). The court held that, because § 7(a)(2) requires interagency consultation, the citizen-suit provision creates a "procedural righ[t]" to consultation in all "persons"—so that *anyone* can file suit in federal court to challenge the Secretary's (or presumably any other official's) failure to follow the assertedly correct consultative procedure, notwithstanding his or her inability to allege any discrete injury flowing from that failure. To understand the remarkable nature of this holding one must be clear about what it does *not* rest upon: This is not a case where plaintiffs are seeking to enforce a procedural requirement the disregard of which could impair a separate concrete interest of theirs (*e.g.*, the procedural requirement for a hearing prior to denial of their license application, or the procedural requirement for an environmental impact statement before a federal facility is constructed next door to them).[7] Nor is it

---

[7]   There is this much truth to the assertion that "procedural rights" are special: The person who has been accorded a procedural right to protect his concrete interests can assert that right without meeting all the normal standards for redressability and immediacy. Thus, under our case law, one living adjacent to the site for proposed construction of a federally licensed dam has standing to challenge the licensing agency's failure to prepare an environmental impact statement, even though he cannot establish with any certainty that the statement will cause the license to be withheld or altered, and even though the dam will not be completed for many years. (That is why we do not rely, in the present case, upon the Government's argument that, *even if* the other agencies were obliged to consult with the Secretary, they might not have followed his advice.) What respondents' "procedural rights" argument seeks, however, is quite different from this: standing for persons who have no concrete interests affected—persons who live (and propose to live) at the other end of the country from the dam.

simply a case where concrete injury has been suffered by many persons, as in mass fraud or mass tort situations. Nor, finally, is it the unusual case in which Congress has created a concrete private interest in the outcome of a suit against a private party for the Government's benefit, by providing a cash bounty for the victorious plaintiff. Rather, the court held that the injury-in-fact requirement had been satisfied by congressional conferral upon *all* persons of an abstract, self-contained, noninstrumental "right" to have the Executive observe the procedures required by law. We reject this view.

* * *

[We have omitted the plurality's lengthy description of the many cases in which the Court refused to consider the alleged unconstitutionality of a practice on the basis that the petitioner was asserting only generalized grievance against the government. Ed.]

To be sure, our generalized-grievance cases have typically involved Government violation of procedures assertedly ordained by the Constitution rather than the Congress. But there is absolutely no basis for making the Article III inquiry turn on the source of the asserted right. Whether the courts were to act on their own, or at the invitation of Congress, in ignoring the concrete injury requirement described in our cases, they would be discarding a principle fundamental to the separate and distinct constitutional role of the Third Branch—one of the essential elements that identifies those "Cases" and "Controversies" that are the business of the courts rather than of the political branches. "The province of the court," as Chief Justice Marshall said in *Marbury v. Madison*, 5 U.S. (1 Cranch) 137, 170 (1803), "is, solely, to decide on the rights of individuals." Vindicating the *public* interest (including the public interest in Government observance of the Constitution and laws) is the function of Congress and the Chief Executive. The question presented here is whether the public interest in proper administration of the laws (specifically, in agencies' observance of a particular, statutorily prescribed procedure) can be converted into an individual right by a statute that denominates it as such, and that permits all citizens (or, for that matter, a subclass of citizens who suffer no distinctive concrete harm) to sue. If the concrete injury requirement has the separation-of-powers significance we have always said, the answer must be obvious: To permit Congress to convert the undifferentiated public interest in executive officers' compliance with the law into an "individual right" vindicable in the courts is to permit Congress to transfer from the President to the courts the Chief Executive's most important constitutional duty, to "take Care that the Laws be faithfully executed," art. II, § 3. It would enable the courts, with the permission of Congress, "to assume a position of authority over the governmental acts of another and co-equal department," *Massachusetts v. Mellon*, 262 U.S. 447, 489 (1923), and to become " 'virtually continuing monitors of the wisdom and soundness of Executive action.' " *Allen*, 468 U.S. at 760 (quoting *Laird v. Tatum*, 408 U.S. 1, 15 (1972)). We have always rejected that vision of our role.

■ JUSTICE KENNEDY, with whom JUSTICE SOUTER joins, concurring in part and concurring in the judgment.

Although I agree with the essential parts of the Court's analysis, I write separately to make several observations.

I agree with the Court's conclusion that, on the record before us, respondents have failed to demonstrate that they themselves are "among the injured." *Sierra Club v. Morton*, 405 U.S. 727, 735 (1972). * * *

While it may seem trivial to require that Mses. Kelly and Skilbred acquire airline tickets to the project sites or announce a date certain upon which they will return, this is not a case where it is reasonable to assume that the affiants will be using the sites on a regular basis, nor do the affiants claim to have visited the sites since the projects commenced. With respect to the Court's discussion of respondents' "ecosystem nexus," "animal nexus," and "vocational nexus" theories, I agree that on this record respondents' showing is insufficient to establish standing on any of these bases. I am not willing to foreclose the possibility, however, that in different circumstances a nexus theory similar to those proffered here might support a claim to standing.

In light of the conclusion that respondents have not demonstrated a concrete injury here sufficient to support standing under our precedents, I would not reach the issue of redressability that is discussed by the plurality in Part III–B.

I also join the Court's opinion with the following observations. As Government programs and policies become more complex and farreaching, we must be sensitive to the articulation of new rights of action that do not have clear analogs in our common-law tradition. Modern litigation has progressed far from the paradigm of Marbury suing Madison to get his commission, * * *. In my view, Congress has the power to define injuries and articulate chains of causation that will give rise to a case or controversy where none existed before, and I do not read the Court's opinion to suggest a contrary view. In exercising this power, however, Congress must at the very least identify the injury it seeks to vindicate and relate the injury to the class of persons entitled to bring suit. The citizen-suit provision of the Endangered Species Act does not meet these minimal requirements, because while the statute purports to confer a right on "any person . . . to enjoin . . . the United States and any other governmental instrumentality or agency . . . who is alleged to be in violation of any provision of this chapter," it does not of its own force establish that there is an injury in "any person" by virtue of any "violation." 16 U.S.C. § 1540(g)(1)(A).

The Court's holding that there is an outer limit to the power of Congress to confer rights of action is a direct and necessary consequence of the case and controversy limitations found in Article III. I agree that it would exceed those limitations if, at the behest of Congress and in the absence of any showing of concrete injury, we were to entertain citizen suits to vindicate the public's nonconcrete interest in the proper administration of the laws. While it does not matter how many persons have been injured by the challenged action, the party bringing suit must show that the action injures him in a concrete and personal way. This requirement is not just an empty formality. It preserves the vitality of the adversarial process by assuring both that the parties before the court have an actual, as opposed to professed, stake in the outcome, and that "the legal questions presented . . . will be resolved, not in the rarified atmosphere of a debating society, but in a concrete factual context conducive to a realistic appreciation of the consequences of judicial action." *Valley Forge Christian Coll. v. Ams. United for Separation of Church & State, Inc.*, 454 U.S. 464, 472 (1982). In addition, the requirement of concrete injury confines the Judicial Branch to its proper, limited role in the constitutional framework of Government.

■ JUSTICE STEVENS, concurring in the judgment.

Because I am not persuaded that Congress intended the consultation requirement in § 7(a)(2) of the Endangered Species Act of 1973 (ESA) to apply to activities in foreign countries, I concur in the judgment of reversal. I do not, however, agree with the Court's conclusion that respondents lack standing because the threatened injury to their interest in protecting the environment and studying endangered species is not "imminent." Nor do I agree with the plurality's additional conclusion that respondents' injury is not "redressable" in this litigation.

In my opinion a person who has visited the critical habitat of an endangered species has a professional interest in preserving the species and its habitat, and intends to revisit them in the future has standing to challenge agency action that threatens their destruction. Congress has found that a wide variety of endangered species of fish, wildlife, and plants are of "aesthetic, ecological, educational, historical, recreational, and scientific value to the Nation and its people." 16 U.S.C. 1531(a)(3). Given that finding, we have no license to demean the importance of the interest that particular individuals may have in observing any species or its habitat, whether those individuals are motivated by esthetic enjoyment, an interest in professional research, or an economic interest in preservation of the species. Indeed, this Court has often held that injuries to such interests are sufficient to confer standing, and the Court reiterates that holding today.

The Court nevertheless concludes that respondents have not suffered "injury in fact" because they have not shown that the harm to the endangered species will produce "imminent" injury to them. I disagree. An injury to an individual's interest in studying or enjoying a species and its natural habitat occurs when someone (whether it be the Government or a private party) takes action that harms that species and habitat. In my judgment, therefore, the "imminence" of such an injury should be measured by the timing and likelihood of the threatened environmental harm, rather than—as the Court seems to suggest by the time that might elapse between the present and the time when the individuals would visit the area if no such injury should occur.

■ JUSTICE BLACKMUN, with whom JUSTICE O'CONNOR joins, dissenting.

I part company with the Court in this case * * * I believe that respondents have raised genuine issues of fact—sufficient to survive summary judgment—both as to injury and as to redressability. * * * I fear the Court seeks to impose fresh limitations on the constitutional authority of Congress to allow citizen suits in the federal courts for injuries deemed "procedural" in nature. I dissent.

* * *

I think a reasonable finder of fact could conclude from the information in the affidavits and deposition testimony that either Kelly or Skilbred will soon return to the project sites, thereby satisfying the "actual or imminent" injury standard.

* * *

I have difficulty imagining this Court applying its rigid principles of geographic formalism anywhere outside the context of environmental claims. * * *

[We have omitted the dissenting Justices lengthy point-by-point rebuttal of the reasoning in the plurality opinion. Ed.]

In conclusion, I cannot join the Court on what amounts to a slash-and-burn expedition through the law of environmental standing. In my view, "[t]he very essence of civil liberty certainly consists in the right of every individual to claim the protection of the laws, whenever he receives an injury." *Marbury v. Madison*, 5 U.S. (1 Cranch) 137, 163 (1803).

NOTES AND QUESTIONS

1. One of the tasks of a lawyer for a membership organization is to find, recruit, or create members who can provide affidavits sufficient to support the organization's claim of derivative standing. Six Justices held that *Defenders* lacked standing to challenge the EPA's rule and implicitly held that the citizen's suit provision of the Endangered Species Act is unconstitutional in its potential application to the facts of this case. The four-Justice plurality relied on seven separate bases for its conclusion. Which of those bases do the two concurring Justices accept as valid? Is the lack of temporal proximity and temporal certainty the only basis the concurring Justices embrace? Do you think the concurring Justices would have voted differently if Joyce Kelly had bought a nonrefundable ticket to Egypt and had booked a tour of the habitat of the Nile crocodile in the area that would be affected by the AID funded project in Egypt? Could *Defenders* pay for Kelly's ticket and tour? Can you answer these questions based on the concurring opinion?

2. The plurality opinion in *Defenders* is unprecedented in many respects. As the plurality acknowledged, it is the first case in which the Court held that a petitioner lacked standing even though Congress explicitly granted the petitioner standing. None of the many prior cases in which the Court had referred to the Article III limit on standing involved a situation in which Congress explicitly authorized standing by statute. Thus, all of the prior references to constitutional limits on standing necessarily were dicta. Should it matter for purposes of the Constitution whether Congress has explicitly authorized standing by statute? Should the Court recognize as having suffered an "injury-in-fact" any person that Congress says is injured by a violation of a statutory right? Would Joyce Kelly or Amy Skilbred suffer such a qualifying injury if Congress amended the Endangered Species Act (ESA) to confer on each citizen a right of joint ownership of each endangered species? Would *Defenders* have standing if Congress amended the ESA by providing that any citizen who prevails in a citizen suit is entitled to one dollar from the Treasury, or even merely to one peppercorn? For arguments that either amendment should change the outcome in *Defenders*, see Cass R. Sunstein, *What's Standing After* Lujan? *Of Citizen Suits, "Injuries," and Article III*, 91 MICH. L. REV. 163 (1992).

3. Like many modern standing opinions, the plurality opinion in *Defenders* refers to the Article III limit on standing and to the "injury-in-fact" requirement as if both are ancient doctrines that U.S. courts have long applied. Four scholars have engaged in comprehensive research in an effort to locate the roots of the modern constitutional law of standing. All have reached the same conclusions: no court referred to constitutional limits on standing or to the injury-in-fact requirement until relatively late in the twentieth century, and U.S. courts regularly decided cases that would not satisfy the injury-in-fact requirement prior to that time. *See* Cass R. Sunstein, *What's Standing After* Lujan? *Of Citizen Suits, "Injuries," and Article III*, 91 MICH. L. REV. 163 (1992); Steven L. Winter, *The Metaphor of Standing and the Problem of Self-Governance*, 40 STANFORD L. REV. 1371 (1988); Raoul Berger, *Standing to Sue in Public Actions: Is It a Constitutional Requirement?*, 78 YALE L.J. 816 (1969); Louis L. Jaffe, *Standing to Secure Judicial Review: Public Actions*, 74 HARV. L. REV. 1265 (1961). The Article II Take Care Clause basis for limiting standing, discussed by the plurality opinion, has a pedigree that is even less impressive; it did not appear in any Supreme Court opinion until Justice Scalia joined the Court, and its first appearance in the scholarly literature was in Justice Scalia's own article, *The Doctrine of Standing as an Essential Element of the Separation of Powers*, 17 SUFFOLK U. L. REV. 881 (1983).

4. The plurality opinion in *Defenders* also was the first opinion in which the Court applied the redressability requirement in a manner that was independent of the causation requirement. In all prior cases, the Court had equated the two requirements—*i.e.*, if the challenged agency action caused the injury, then a court decision vacating that agency action would redress the injury. In *Defenders*, the plurality conceded the causal relationship between the challenged agency action and the alleged injury but still concluded that Defenders lacked standing because a court could not redress that injury. In evaluating the plurality's reasoning with respect to redressability, you might want to consider that the Court held that the redressability requirement is satisfied if it is "likely" that a judicial decision would redress the petitioner's injury; consider also that the Court has held that a judicial decision that is directed to one agency of government estops all other agencies of government form acting in a manner inconsistent with the opinion because all agencies of government are in privity with each other. *See Sunshine Anthracite Coal Co. v. Adkins*, 310 U.S. 381 (1940). Do you find Justice Scalia's opinion in *Defenders* consistent with his opinion in *Bennett v. Spear*, 520 U.S. 154 (1997), excerpted earlier in this Chapter.

5. Surprisingly, the plurality opinion in *Defenders* is the first opinion in which the Court discussed the availability of standing in cases in which a petitioner alleges that it has been injured by an agency's failure to provide a procedure to which it is entitled. In footnote seven, the majority recognized that procedural rights are "special" in some respects—*e.g.*, a petitioner who alleges that he has been denied a procedural right need not establish that provision of that right will change the outcome of the case. The Court's recognition of the special nature of procedural rights is critical to an understanding of administrative law. Most of the judicial opinions in this book would never have been issued were it not for the special nature of procedural rights for standing purposes. Do you understand why that is the case?

6.   The composition of the Court has changed significantly since the Court decided *Defenders*. Before he became Chief Justice, John Roberts was an Assistant Solicitor General who played a major role in arguing standing cases before the Supreme Court. He gave his views on the issues the Court addressed in *Defenders* in a debate with one of the authors that took place shortly after the Court decided *Defenders*. Compare John G. Roberts, Jr., *Article III Limits on Statutory Standing*, 42 DUKE L.J. 1219 (1993), with Richard J. Pierce, Jr., Lujan v. Defenders of Wildlife: *Standing As A Judicially-Imposed Limit on Legislative Power*, 42 DUKE L.J. 1170 (1993).

Justice Scalia followed up his major victory in *Defenders* with another major victory in the following case.

Steel Co. v. Citizens for a Better Environment

523 U.S. 83 (1998).

■ JUSTICE SCALIA delivered the opinion of the Court.

This is a private enforcement action under the citizen-suit provision of the Emergency Planning and Community Right-To-Know Act of 1986 (EPCRA). The case presents the merits question, answered in the affirmative by the United States Court of Appeals for the Seventh Circuit, whether EPCRA authorizes suits for purely past violations. It also presents the jurisdictional question whether respondent, plaintiff below, has standing to bring this action.

Respondent, an association of individuals interested in environmental protection, sued petitioner, a small manufacturing company in Chicago, for past violations of EPCRA. EPCRA establishes a framework of state, regional, and local agencies designed to inform the public about the presence of hazardous and toxic chemicals, and to provide for emergency response in the event of health-threatening release. Central to its operation are reporting requirements compelling users of specified toxic and hazardous chemicals to file annual "emergency and hazardous chemical inventory forms" and "toxic chemical release forms," which contain, *inter alia*, the name and location of the facility, the name and quantity of the chemical on hand, and, in the case of toxic chemicals, the waste-disposal method employed and the annual quantity released into each environmental medium. 42 U.S.C. §§ 11022, 11023. * * *

Enforcement of EPCRA can take place on many fronts. The Environmental Protection Agency (EPA) has the most powerful enforcement arsenal: it may seek criminal, civil, or administrative penalties. State and local governments can also seek civil penalties, as well as injunctive relief. For purposes of this case, however, the crucial enforcement mechanism is the citizen-suit provision, which likewise authorizes civil penalties and injunctive relief. This provides that "any person may commence a civil action on his own behalf against . . . [a]n owner or operator of a facility for failure," among other things, to "[c]omplete and submit an inventory form * * *". § 11046(a)(1). As a prerequisite to bringing such a suit, the plaintiff must, 60 days prior to filing his complaint, give notice to the Administrator of the EPA, the State in which the alleged violation occurs, and the alleged violator. The citizen suit may not go forward if the Administrator "has commenced and is diligently pursuing an administrative order or civil action to enforce the requirement concerned or to impose a civil penalty." § 11046(e).

In 1995 respondent sent a notice to petitioner, the Administrator, and the relevant Illinois authorities, alleging—accurately, as it turns out—that petitioner had failed since 1988, the first year of EPCRA's filing deadlines, to complete and to submit the requisite hazardous-chemical inventory and toxic-chemical release forms * * *. Upon receiving the notice, petitioner filed all of the overdue forms with the relevant agencies. The EPA chose not to bring an action against petitioner, and when the 60-day waiting period expired, respondent filed suit in Federal District Court. Petitioner promptly filed a motion to dismiss contending that, because its filings were up to date when the complaint was filed, the court had no jurisdiction to entertain a suit for a present violation; and that, because EPCRA does not allow suit for a purely historical violation, respondent's allegation of untimeliness in filing was not a claim upon which relief could be granted.

* * *

Petitioner, however, both in its petition for certiorari and in its briefs on the merits, has raised the issue of respondent's standing to maintain the suit, and hence this Court's jurisdiction to entertain it. Though there is some dispute on this point, this would normally be considered a threshold question that must be resolved in respondent's favor before proceeding to the merits. Justice STEVENS' opinion concurring in the judgment, however, claims that the question whether [EPCRA] permits this cause of action is *also* "jurisdictional," and so has equivalent claim to being resolved first. Whether that is so has significant implications for this case and for many others, and so the point warrants extended discussion.

* * *

[We have omitted the lengthy section of the opinion in which the majority held that a court cannot address a merits issue without first deciding whether it has jurisdiction to decide the case and that Article III standing is a jurisdictional issue while the existence of a cause of action is not. Ed.]

Having reached the end of what seems like a long front walk, we finally arrive at the threshold jurisdictional question: whether respondent, the plaintiff below, has standing to sue. Article III, § 2, of the Constitution extends the "judicial Power" of the United States only to "Cases" and "Controversies."

* * *

[We have omitted the majority's discussion of the general requirements to establish Article III standing. Ed.]

[R]espondent asserts petitioner's failure to provide EPCRA information in a timely fashion, and the lingering effects of that failure, as the injury in fact to itself and its members. We have not had occasion to decide whether being deprived of information that is supposed to be disclosed under EPCRA—or at least being deprived of it when one has a particular plan for its use—is a concrete injury in fact that satisfies Article III. And we need not reach that question in the present case because, assuming injury in fact, the complaint fails the third test of standing, redressability.

The complaint asks for (1) a declaratory judgment that petitioner violated EPCRA; (2) authorization to inspect periodically petitioner's facility and records (with costs borne by petitioner); (3) an order requiring petitioner to provide respondent copies of all compliance reports submitted to the EPA; (4) an order requiring petitioner to pay civil penalties of $25,000 per day for each violation of [the EPCRA]; (5) an award of all respondent's "costs, in connection with the investigation and prosecution of this matter, including reasonable attorney and expert witness fees, as authorized by Section 326(f) of [EPCRA]"; and (6) any such further relief as the court deems appropriate. None of the specific items of relief sought, and none that we can envision as "appropriate" under the general request, would serve to reimburse respondent for losses caused by the late reporting, or to eliminate any effects of that late reporting upon respondent.

The first item, the request for a declaratory judgment that petitioner violated EPCRA, can be disposed of summarily. There being no controversy over whether petitioner failed to file reports, or over whether such a failure constitutes a violation, the declaratory judgment is not only worthless to respondent, it is seemingly worthless to all the world.

Item (4), the civil penalties authorized by the statute, might be viewed as a sort of compensation or redress to respondent if they were payable to respondent. But they are not. These penalties—the only damages authorized by EPCRA—are payable to the United States Treasury. In requesting them, therefore, respondent seeks not remediation of its own injury—reimbursement for the costs it incurred as a result of the late filing—but vindication of the rule of law—the "undifferentiated public interest" in faithful execution of EPCRA. *Lujan v. Defenders of Wildlife*, 504 U.S. 555, 577 (1992). This does not suffice. Justice STEVENS thinks it is enough that respondent will be gratified by seeing petitioner punished for its infractions and that the punishment will deter the risk of future harm. * * * Obviously, such a principle would make the redressability requirement vanish. By the mere bringing of his suit, *every* plaintiff demonstrates his belief that a favorable judgment will make him happier. But although a suitor may derive great comfort and joy from the fact that the United States Treasury is not cheated, that a wrongdoer gets his just deserts, or that the Nation's laws are faithfully enforced, that psychic satisfaction is not an acceptable Article III remedy because it does not redress a cognizable Article III injury. Relief that does not remedy the injury suffered cannot bootstrap a plaintiff into federal court; that is the very essence of the redressability requirement.

Item (5), the "investigation and prosecution" costs "as authorized by Section 326(f)," would assuredly benefit respondent as opposed to the citizenry at large. Obviously, however, a plaintiff cannot achieve standing to litigate a substantive issue by bringing suit for the cost of bringing suit. The litigation must give the plaintiff some other benefit besides reimbursement of costs that are a byproduct of the litigation itself. An "interest in attorney's fees is . . . insufficient to create an Article III case or controversy where none exists on the merits of the underlying claim." *Lewis v. Continental Bank Corp.*, 494 U.S. 472, 480 (1990) (citing *Diamond v. Charles*, 476 U.S .54, 70–71 (1986)).

■ [We have omitted the concurring opinions of three Justices in which they argued that Citizens for a Better Environment had standing but that EPCRA did not authorize a private right of action for wholly past violations of EPCRA. Ed.]

NOTES AND QUESTIONS

The majority opinion in *Steel Co.* had enormous implications for enforcement of environmental statutes. Understanding the effects of the opinion requires some contextual knowledge of federal environmental law. Most federal environmental statutes include a private right of action provision similar to the provision in EPCRA. In the view of many environmental advocates, private rights of action provisions are critical to the successful implementation of environmental statutes. The limited resources available to federal and state agencies to enforce environmental statutes precludes them from bringing enforcement actions in all but the most extreme cases. By authorizing private suits to enforce such statutes (and by authorizing courts to award the costs of bringing such suits to private parties and their lawyers when they prevail), Congress enlisted the assistance of "private attorney generals" who would supplement the limited enforcement resources of agencies by monitoring compliance with environmental statutes and bringing enforcement actions against firms that violate those statutes.

Lower courts interpreted *Steel Co.* broadly to stand for the principle that civil penalties paid to the United States can never redress an injury to a private individual. That, in turn, created a situation in which a firm could violate an environmental statute with no fear that it would ever have to pay damages as a result of a private right of action proceeding. As long as the firm ceased its pattern of violating the statute before the court issued a final decision in response to the private action, the court would be required to dismiss the case for lack of standing, since a court cannot issue a declaratory judgment with respect to conduct that a defendant concedes to have been unlawful and civil penalties do not qualify as redress of a private party's injury.

The effect and the general tenor of the majority opinion in *Steel Co.* also suggested to many observers of the Court that Justice Scalia had persuaded a majority of his colleagues to embrace his view that private individuals never have standing to enforce an environmental statute either against a firm or against an agency. Lower courts also began to interpret the ambiguous opinions in *Defenders* as if a majority of the Justices had adopted the reasoning of the plurality opinion in *Defenders*. Morale was low among environmental advocates until the Court issued the following opinion.

Friends of the Earth, Inc. v. Laidlaw
Environmental Services

528 U.S. 167 (2000).

■ JUSTICE GINSBURG delivered the opinion of the Court

This case presents an important question concerning the operation of the citizen-suit provisions of the Clean Water Act. Congress authorized the federal district courts to entertain Clean Water Act suits initiated by "a person or persons having an interest which is or may be adversely affected." 33 U.S.C. §§ 1365(a), (g). To impel future compliance with the Act, a district court may prescribe injunctive relief in such a suit; additionally or alternatively, the court may impose civil penalties payable to the United States Treasury. In the Clean Water Act citizen suit now before us, the District Court determined that injunctive relief was inappropriate because the defendant, after the institution of the litigation, achieved substantial compliance with the terms of its discharge permit. The court did, however, assess a civil penalty of $405,800. The "total deterrent effect" of the penalty would be adequate to forestall future violations, the court reasoned, taking into account that the defendant "will be required to reimburse plaintiffs for a significant amount of legal fees and has, itself, incurred significant legal expenses."

The Court of Appeals vacated the District Court's order. The case became moot, the appellate court declared, once the defendant fully complied with the terms of its permit and the plaintiff failed to appeal the denial of equitable relief. "[C]ivil penalties payable to the government," the Court of Appeals stated, "would not redress any injury Plaintiffs have suffered." Nor were attorneys' fees in order, the Court of Appeals noted, because absent relief on the merits, plaintiffs could not qualify as prevailing parties.

We reverse the judgment of the Court of Appeals. The appellate court erred in concluding that a citizen suitor's claim for civil penalties must be dismissed as moot when the defendant, albeit after commencement of the litigation, has come into compliance. In directing dismissal of the suit on grounds of mootness, the Court of Appeals incorrectly conflated our case law on initial standing to bring suit with our case law on postcommencement mootness. A defendant's voluntary cessation of allegedly unlawful conduct ordinarily does not suffice to moot a case. The Court of Appeals also misperceived the remedial potential of civil penalties. Such penalties may serve, as an alternative to an injunction, to deter future violations and thereby redress the injuries that prompted a citizen suitor to commence litigation.

* * *

In 1986, defendant-respondent Laidlaw Environmental Services bought a hazardous waste incinerator facility in Roebuck, South Carolina, that included a wastewater treatment plant. * * * Shortly after Laidlaw acquired the facility, the South Carolina Department of Health and Environmental Control (DHEC), acting under 33 U.S.C. § 1342(a)(1), granted Laidlaw an NPDES permit authorizing the company to discharge treated water into the North Tyger River. The permit, which became effective on January 1, 1987, placed limits on Laidlaw's discharge of several pollutants into the river, including—of particular relevance to this case—mercury, an extremely toxic pollutant. The permit also regulated the flow, temperature, toxicity, and pH of the effluent from the facility, and imposed monitoring and reporting obligations.

Once it received its permit, Laidlaw began to discharge various pollutants into the waterway; repeatedly, Laidlaw's discharges exceeded the limits set by the permit. In particular, despite experimenting with several technological fixes, Laidlaw consistently failed to meet the permit's stringent 1.3 ppb (parts per billion) daily average limit on mercury discharges.

* * *

On June 12, 1992, FOE filed this citizen suit against Laidlaw under § 505(a) of the Act, alleging noncompliance with the NPDES permit and seeking declaratory and injunctive relief and an award of civil penalties. Laidlaw moved for summary judgment on the ground that FOE had failed to present evidence demonstrating injury in fact, and therefore lacked Article III standing to bring the lawsuit. In opposition to this motion, FOE submitted affidavits and deposition testimony from members of the plaintiff organizations. After examining this evidence, the District Court denied Laidlaw's summary judgment motion, finding—albeit "by the very slimmest of margins"—that FOE had standing to bring the suit.

* * *

On January 22, 1997, the District Court issued its judgment. It found that Laidlaw had gained a total economic benefit of $1,092,581 as a result of its extended period of noncompliance with the mercury discharge limit in its permit. The court concluded, however, that a civil penalty of $405,800 was adequate * * *. In particular, the District Court stated that the lesser penalty was appropriate taking into account the judgment's "total deterrent effect." In reaching this determination, the court "considered that Laidlaw will be required to reimburse plaintiffs for a significant amount of legal fees." The court declined to grant FOE's request for injunctive relief, stating that an injunction was inappropriate because "Laidlaw has been in substantial compliance with all parameters in its NPDES permit since at least August 1992."

* * *

On July 16, 1998, the Court of Appeals for the Fourth Circuit issued its judgment. The Court of Appeals assumed without deciding that FOE initially had standing to bring the action, but went on to hold that the case had become moot. The appellate court stated, first, that the elements of Article III standing—injury, causation, and redressability—must persist at every stage of review, or else the action becomes moot. Citing our decision in *Steel Co.*, the Court of Appeals reasoned that the case had become moot because "the only remedy currently available to [FOE]—civil penalties payable to the government—would not redress any injury [FOE has] suffered." The court therefore vacated the District Court's order and remanded with instructions to dismiss the action. In a footnote, the Court of Appeals added that FOE's "failure to obtain relief on the merits of [its] claims precludes any recovery of attorneys' fees or other litigation costs because such an award is available only to a 'prevailing or substantially prevailing party.'" (quoting 33 U.S.C. § 1365(d)).

* * *

Laidlaw contends first that FOE lacked standing from the outset even to seek injunctive relief, because the plaintiff organizations failed to show that any of their members had sustained or faced the threat of any "injury in fact" from Laidlaw's activities. In support of this contention Laidlaw points to the District Court's finding, made in the course of setting the penalty amount, that there had been "no demonstrated proof of harm to the environment" from Laidlaw's mercury discharge violations.

The relevant showing for purposes of Article III standing, however, is not injury to the environment but injury to the plaintiff. To insist upon the former rather than the latter as part of the standing inquiry (as the dissent in essence does) is to raise the standing hurdle higher than the necessary showing for success on the merits in an action alleging noncompliance with an NPDES permit. Focusing properly on injury to the plaintiff, the District Court found that FOE had demonstrated sufficient injury to establish standing. For example, FOE member Kenneth Lee Curtis averred in affidavits that he lived a half-mile from Laidlaw's facility; that he occasionally drove over the North Tyger River, and that it looked and smelled polluted; and that he would like to fish, camp, swim, and picnic in and near the river between 3 and 15 miles downstream from the facility, as he did when he was a teenager, but would not do so because he was concerned that the water was polluted by Laidlaw's discharges.

* * *

These sworn statements, as the District Court determined, adequately documented injury in fact. We have held that environmental plaintiffs adequately allege injury in fact when they aver that they use the affected area and are persons "for whom the aesthetic and recreational values of the area will be lessened" by the challenged activity. *Sierra Club v. Morton*, 405 U.S. 727, 735 (1972).

* * *

[I]t is undisputed that Laidlaw's unlawful conduct—discharging pollutants in excess of permit limits—was occurring at the time the complaint was filed. Under *Lyons*, then, the only "subjective" issue here is "[t]he reasonableness of [the] fear" that led the affiants to respond to that concededly ongoing conduct by refraining from use of the North Tyger River and surrounding areas. Unlike the dissent, we see nothing "improbable" about the proposition that a company's continuous and pervasive illegal discharges of pollutants into a river would cause nearby residents to curtail their recreational use of that waterway and would subject them to other economic and aesthetic harms. The proposition is entirely reasonable, the District Court found it was true in this case, and that is enough for injury in fact.

Laidlaw argues next that even if FOE had standing to seek injunctive relief, it lacked standing to seek civil penalties. Here the asserted defect is not injury but redressability. Civil penalties offer no redress to private plaintiffs, Laidlaw argues, because they are paid to the Government, and therefore a citizen plaintiff can never have standing to seek them.

* * *

We have recognized on numerous occasions that "all civil penalties have some deterrent effect." *Hudson v. United States*, 522 U.S. 93, 102 (1997). More specifically, Congress has found that civil penalties in Clean Water Act cases do more than promote immediate compliance by limiting the defendant's economic incentive to delay its attainment of permit limits; they also deter future violations. This congressional determination warrants judicial attention and respect. "The legislative history of the Act reveals that Congress wanted the district court to consider the need for retribution and deterrence, in addition to restitution, when it imposed civil penalties. . . . [The district court may] seek to deter future violations by basing the penalty on its economic impact." *Tull v. United States*, 481 U.S. 412, 422–23 (1987).

It can scarcely be doubted that, for a plaintiff who is injured or faces the threat of future injury due to illegal conduct ongoing at the time of suit, a sanction that effectively abates that conduct and prevents its recurrence provides a form of redress. Civil penalties can fit that description. To the extent that they encourage defendants to discontinue current violations and deter them from committing future ones, they afford redress to citizen plaintiffs who are injured or threatened with injury as a consequence of ongoing unlawful conduct.

* * *

Justice Frankfurter's observations for the Court, made in a different context nearly 60 years ago, hold true here as well:

> "How to effectuate policy—the adaptation of means to legitimately sought ends—is one of the most intractable of legislative problems. Whether proscribed conduct is to be deterred by *qui tam* action or triple damages or injunction, or by criminal prosecution, or merely by defense to actions in contract, or by some, or all, of these remedies in combination, is a matter within the legislature's range of choice. Judgment on the deterrent effect of the various weapons in the armory of the law can lay little claim to scientific basis." *Tigner v. Texas*, 310 U.S. 141, 148 (1940).

* * *

Laidlaw contends that the reasoning of our decision in *Steel Co.* directs the conclusion that citizen plaintiffs have no standing to seek civil penalties under the Act. We disagree. *Steel Co.* established that citizen suitors lack standing to seek civil penalties for violations that have abated by the time of suit. *See* 523 U.S. at 106–07. We specifically noted in that case that there was no allegation in the complaint of any continuing or imminent violation, and that no basis for such an allegation appeared to exist. In short, *Steel Co.* held that private plaintiffs, unlike the Federal Government, may not sue to assess penalties for wholly past violations, but our decision in that case did not reach the issue of standing to seek penalties for violations that are ongoing at the time of the complaint and that could continue into the future if undeterred.

Satisfied that FOE had standing under Article III to bring this action, we turn to the question of mootness.

The only conceivable basis for a finding of mootness in this case is Laidlaw's voluntary conduct—either its achievement by August 1992 of substantial compliance with its NPDES permit or its more recent shutdown of the Roebuck facility. It is well settled that "a defendant's voluntary cessation of a challenged practice does not deprive a federal court of its power to determine the legality of the practice." *City of Mesquite v. Aladdin's Castle, Inc.*, 455 U.S. 283, 289 (1982). "[I]f it did, the courts would be compelled to leave '[t]he defendant . . . free to return to his old ways.'" *Id.* At 289 n.10 (citing *United States v. W.T. Grant Co.*, 345 U.S. 629, 632 (1953)). In accordance with this principle, the standard we have announced for determining whether a case has been mooted by the defendant's voluntary conduct is stringent: "A case might become moot if subsequent events made it absolutely clear that the allegedly wrongful behavior could not reasonably be expected to recur." *United States v. Concentrated Export Ass'n, Inc.*, 393 U.S. 199, 203 (1968). The "heavy burden of persua[ding]" the court that the challenged conduct cannot reasonably be expected to start up again lies with the party asserting mootness. *Id.*

■ JUSTICE SCALIA, with whom JUSTICE THOMAS joins, dissenting.

The Court begins its analysis by finding injury in fact on the basis of vague affidavits that are undermined by the District Court's express finding that Laidlaw's discharges caused no demonstrable harm to the environment. It then proceeds to marry private wrong with public remedy in a union that violates traditional principles of federal standing—thereby permitting law enforcement to be placed in the hands of private individuals. Finally, the Court suggests that to avoid mootness one needs even less of a stake in the outcome than the Court's watered-down requirements for initial standing. I dissent from all of this.

* * *

Typically, an environmental plaintiff claiming injury due to discharges in violation of the Clean Water Act argues that the discharges harm the environment, and that the harm to the environment injures him. This route to injury is barred in the present case, however, since the District Court concluded after considering all the evidence that there had been "no demonstrated proof of harm to the environment," that the "permit violations at issue in this citizen suit did not result in any health risk or environmental harm," that "[a]ll available data . . . fail to show that Laidlaw's *actual* discharges have resulted in harm to the North Tyger River," [and] that "the overall quality of the river exceeds levels necessary to support * * * recreation in and on the water."

* * *

By accepting plaintiffs' vague, contradictory, and unsubstantiated allegations of "concern" about the environment as adequate to prove injury in fact, and accepting them even in the face of a finding that the environment was not demonstrably harmed, the Court makes the injury-in-fact requirement a sham. If there are permit violations, and a member of a plaintiff environmental organization lives near the offending plant, it would be difficult not to satisfy today's lenient standard.

The Court's treatment of the redressability requirement—which would have been unnecessary if it resolved the injury-in-fact question correctly—is equally cavalier. As discussed above, petitioners allege ongoing injury consisting of diminished enjoyment of the affected waterways and decreased property values. They allege that these injuries are caused by Laidlaw's continuing permit violations. But the remedy petitioners seek is neither recompense for their injuries nor an injunction against future violations. Instead, the remedy is a statutorily specified "penalty" for past violations, payable entirely to the United States Treasury. Only last Term, we held that such penalties do not redress any injury a citizen plaintiff has suffered from past violations. *Steel Co. v. Citizens for Better Env't*, 523 U.S. 83, 106–07 (1998).

■ [Opinions by JUSTICE STEVENS and JUSTICE KENNEDY, concurring, are omitted. Ed.]

NOTES AND QUESTIONS

It is hard to overstate the significance of the *Laidlaw* opinion. The Court changed dramatically the nature of the injury an environmental petitioner must establish. Before *Laidlaw*, many courts required environmental petitioners to prove that a particular illegal emission of a pollutant caused actual harm to the environment downstream of the source. The petitioner had to hire experts to try to track the substance that was emitted as it commingled with a mix of other substances that exceeded the magnitude of the emitted substance by a factor of at least one trillion to one. That process was extremely expensive, and it was often impossible to "prove" that any particular illegal emission produced a measurable injury to the environment. After *Laidlaw*, a petitioner need establish only that he changed his conduct, *e.g.*, by no longer fishing within a mile downstream of the source of the illegal emissions, based on "reasonable fear" that the illegal emissions rendered his prior conduct, *e.g.*, fishing, dangerous to his health. Would you fear that eating fish caught downstream of illegal emissions of a toxic substance would expose you to a health hazard? Would your fear be reasonable? Of course, there are some limits to the new test. Presumably, it would not be reasonable to fear the adverse effects of emissions on activities like fishing upstream of the source or one hundred miles downstream of the source.

Laidlaw also changed dramatically the Court's approach to proof of redressability. The *Laidlaw* Court adopted an extremely narrow interpretation of the redressability holding in *Steel Co.* It also equated redressability with deterrence; recognized that civil penalties paid to the government redress an injury to a private individual by deterring a party from repeating the injurious conduct; and suggested strongly that courts should defer to any congressional determination that any statutory sanction redresses an injury through its deterrent effect.

Laidlaw also suggested that Justice Scalia had failed in his twenty year effort to persuade a majority of the Court to adopt his approach to standing to enforce public laws—*i.e.*, that the Take Care Clause prohibits Congress from authorizing anyone but the President to bring an action to enforce a public law. Justice Scalia appeared to have persuaded at least four Justices to adopt his view when the Court decided *Defenders* in 1992, and he appeared to have persuaded six Justices to adopt his view when the Court decided *Steel Co.* in 1998. Yet, two years later in *Laidlaw*, he could persuade only one other Justice to join his dissenting opinion. Seven Justices joined a majority opinion that rejected every aspect of Justice Scalia's position on environmental standing. Environmental advocates celebrated their apparent victory, but their celebration may have been overly optimistic as the following opinion illustrates.

Massachusetts v. EPA

549 U.S. 497 (2007).

■ JUSTICE STEVENS delivered the opinion of the Court.

A well-documented rise in global temperatures has coincided with a significant increase in the concentration of carbon dioxide in the atmosphere. Respected scientists believe the two trends are related. For when carbon dioxide is released into the atmosphere, it acts like the ceiling of a greenhouse, trapping solar energy and retarding the escape of reflected heat. It is therefore a species—the most important species—of a "greenhouse gas."

Calling global warming "the most pressing environmental challenge of our time," a group of States, local governments, and private organizations, alleged in a petition for certiorari that the Environmental Protection Agency (EPA) has abdicated its responsibility under the Clean Air Act to regulate the emissions of four greenhouse gases, including carbon dioxide. Specifically, petitioners asked us to answer two questions concerning the meaning of § 202(a)(1) of the Act: whether EPA has the statutory authority to regulate greenhouse gas emissions from new motor vehicles; and if so, whether its stated reasons for refusing to do so are consistent with the statute.

* * *

Section 202(a)(1) of the Clean Air Act, as amended, provides:

"The [EPA] Administrator shall by regulation prescribe (and from time to time revise) in accordance with the provisions of this section, standards applicable to the emission of any air pollutant from any class or classes of new motor vehicles or new motor vehicle engines, which in his judgment cause, or contribute to, air pollution which may reasonably be anticipated to endanger public health or welfare. . . ." 42 U.S.C. § 7521(a)(1).

* * *

On October 20, 1999, a group of 19 private organizations filed a rulemaking petition asking EPA to regulate "greenhouse gas emissions from new motor vehicles under § 202 of the Clean Air Act."

* * *

[We have omitted the Court's lengthy description of the process through which EPA decided to deny the petition for rulemaking on the bases that it cannot establish emissions limits on carbon dioxide because carbon dioxide is not a pollutant, and that, even if it has the power to set such limits, it declines to exercise its discretion to do so at this time for a variety of policy reasons. Ed.]

Article III of the Constitution limits federal-court jurisdiction to "Cases" and "Controversies." Those two words confine "the business of federal courts to questions presented in an adversary context and in a form historically viewed as capable of resolution through the judicial process." *Flast v. Cohen*, 392 U.S. 83, 95 (1968). It is therefore familiar learning that no justiciable "controversy" exists when parties seek adjudication of a political question, when they ask for an advisory opinion, or when the question sought to be adjudicated has been mooted by subsequent developments. This case suffers from none of these defects.

The parties' dispute turns on the proper construction of a congressional statute, a question eminently suitable to resolution in federal court. Congress has moreover authorized this type of challenge to EPA action. That authorization is of critical importance to the standing inquiry: "Congress has the power to define injuries and articulate chains of causation that will give rise to a case or controversy where none existed before." *Lujan v. Defenders of Wildlife*, 504 U.S. 555, 580 (1992) (Kennedy, J., concurring in part and concurring in the judgment). "In exercising this power, however, Congress must at the very least identify the injury it seeks to vindicate and relate the injury to the class of persons entitled to bring suit." *Id.* We will not, therefore, "entertain citizen suits to vindicate the public's nonconcrete interest in the proper administration of the laws." *Id.* at 581.

* * *

To ensure the proper adversarial presentation, *Lujan* holds that a litigant must demonstrate that it has suffered a concrete and particularized injury that is either actual or imminent, that the injury is fairly traceable to the defendant, and that it is likely that a favorable decision will redress that injury. However, a litigant to whom Congress has "accorded a procedural right to protect his concrete interests,"—here, the right to challenge agency action unlawfully withheld,—"can assert that right without meeting all the normal standards for redressability and immediacy." *Id.* at 572, n.7; 42 U.S.C. § 7607(b)(1). When a litigant is vested with a procedural right, that litigant has standing if there is some possibility that the requested relief will prompt the injury-causing party to reconsider the decision that allegedly harmed the litigant.

Only one of the petitioners needs to have standing to permit us to consider the petition for review. We stress here, as did Judge Tatel below, the special position and interest of Massachusetts. It is of considerable relevance that the party seeking review here is a sovereign State and not, as it was in *Lujan*, a private individual.

Well before the creation of the modern administrative state, we recognized that States are not normal litigants for the purposes of invoking federal jurisdiction. As Justice Holmes explained in *Georgia v. Tennessee Copper Co.*, 206 U.S. 230 (1907), a case in which Georgia sought to protect its citizens from air pollution originating outside its borders:

> "The case has been argued largely as if it were one between two private parties; but it is not. The very elements that would be relied upon in a suit between fellow-citizens as a ground for equitable relief are wanting here. The State owns very little of the territory alleged to be affected, and the damage to it capable of estimate in money, possibly, at least, is small. This is a suit by a State for an injury to it in its capacity of *quasi-sovereign*. In that capacity the State has an interest independent of and behind the titles of its citizens, in all the earth and air within its domain. It has the last word as to whether its mountains shall be stripped of their forests and its inhabitants shall breathe pure air."

Just as Georgia's "independent interest . . . in all the earth and air within its domain" supported federal jurisdiction a century ago, so too does Massachusetts' well-founded desire to preserve its sovereign territory today. That Massachusetts does in fact own a great deal of the "territory alleged to be affected" only reinforces the conclusion that its stake in the outcome of this case is sufficiently concrete to warrant the exercise of federal judicial power.

When a State enters the Union, it surrenders certain sovereign prerogatives. Massachusetts cannot invade Rhode Island to force reductions in greenhouse gas emissions, it cannot negotiate an emissions treaty with China or India, and in some circumstances the exercise of its police powers to reduce in-state motor-vehicle emissions might well be pre-empted.

These sovereign prerogatives are now lodged in the Federal Government, and Congress has ordered EPA to protect Massachusetts (among others) by prescribing standards applicable to the "emission of any air pollutant from any class or classes of new motor vehicle engines, which in [the Administrator's] judgment cause, or contribute to, air pollution which may reasonably be anticipated to endanger public health or welfare." 42 U.S.C. § 7521(a)(1). Congress has moreover recognized a concomitant procedural right to challenge the rejection of its rulemaking petition as arbitrary and capricious. Given that procedural right and Massachusetts' stake in protecting its quasi-sovereign interests, the Commonwealth is entitled to special solicitude in our standing analysis.

With that in mind, it is clear that petitioners' submissions as they pertain to Massachusetts have satisfied the most demanding standards of the adversarial process. EPA's steadfast refusal to regulate greenhouse gas emissions presents a risk of harm to Massachusetts that is both "actual" and "imminent." *Lujan*, 504 U.S. at 560. There is, moreover, a "substantial likelihood that the judicial relief requested" will prompt EPA to take steps to reduce that risk. *Duke Power Co. v. Carolina Env'tl Study Group, Inc.*, 438 U.S. 59, 79 (1978).

The harms associated with climate change are serious and well recognized. Indeed, the NRC [National Research Council] Report itself—which EPA regards as an "objective and independent assessment of the relevant science," 68 Fed. Reg. 52930—identifies a number of environmental changes that have already inflicted significant harms, including "the global retreat of mountain glaciers, reduction in snow-cover extent, the earlier spring melting of rivers and lakes, [and] the accelerated rate of rise of sea levels during the 20th century relative to the past few thousand years. . . ." NRC REPORT 16.

Petitioners allege that this only hints at the environmental damage yet to come. According to the climate scientist Michael MacCracken, "qualified scientific experts involved in climate change research" have reached a "strong consensus" that global warming threatens (among other things) a precipitate rise in sea levels by the end of the century, "severe and irreversible changes to natural ecosystems," a "significant reduction in water storage in winter snowpack in mountainous regions with direct and important economic consequences," and an increase in the spread of disease. He also observes that rising ocean temperatures may contribute to the ferocity of hurricanes.

That these climate-change risks are "widely shared" does not minimize Massachusetts' interest in the outcome of this litigation. *See FEC v. Akins*, 524 U.S. 11, 24 (1998). According to petitioners' unchallenged affidavits, global sea levels rose somewhere between 10 and 20 centimeters over the 20th century as a result of global warming. These rising seas have already begun to swallow Massachusetts' coastal land. Because the Commonwealth "owns a substantial portion of the state's coastal property," it has alleged a particularized injury in its capacity as a landowner. The severity of that injury will only increase over the course of the next century: If sea levels continue to rise as predicted, one Massachusetts official believes that a significant fraction of coastal property will be "either permanently lost through inundation or temporarily lost through periodic storm surge and flooding events." Remediation costs alone, petitioners allege, could run well into the hundreds of millions of dollars.

EPA does not dispute the existence of a causal connection between man-made greenhouse gas emissions and global warming. At a minimum, therefore, EPA's refusal to regulate such emissions "contributes" to Massachusetts' injuries.

EPA nevertheless maintains that its decision not to regulate greenhouse gas emissions from new motor vehicles contributes so insignificantly to petitioners' injuries that the agency cannot be haled into federal court to answer for them. For the same reason, EPA does not believe that any realistic possibility exists that the relief petitioners seek would mitigate global climate change and remedy their injuries.

That is especially so because predicted increases in greenhouse gas emissions from developing nations, particularly China and India, are likely to offset any marginal domestic decrease.

But EPA overstates its case. Its argument rests on the erroneous assumption that a small incremental step, because it is incremental, can never be attacked in a federal judicial forum. Yet accepting that premise would doom most challenges to regulatory action. Agencies, like legislatures, do not generally resolve massive problems in one fell regulatory swoop. They instead whittle away at them over time, refining their preferred approach as circumstances change and as they develop a more-nuanced understanding of how best to proceed. That a first step might be tentative does not by itself support the notion that federal courts lack jurisdiction to determine whether that step conforms to law.

And reducing domestic automobile emissions is hardly a tentative step. Even leaving aside the other greenhouse gases, the United States transportation sector emits an enormous quantity of carbon dioxide into the atmosphere—according to the MacCracken affidavit, more than 1.7 billion metric tons in 1999 alone. That accounts for more than 6% of worldwide carbon dioxide emissions. To put this in perspective: Considering just emissions from the transportation sector, which represent less than one-third of this country's total carbon dioxide emissions, the United States would still rank as the third-largest emitter of carbon dioxide in the world, outpaced only by the European Union and China. Judged by any standard, U.S. motor-vehicle emissions make a meaningful contribution to greenhouse gas concentrations and hence, according to petitioners, to global warming.

While it may be true that regulating motor-vehicle emissions will not by itself *reverse* global warming, it by no means follows that we lack jurisdiction to decide whether EPA has a duty to take steps to *slow* or *reduce* it. Because of the enormity of the potential consequences associated with man-made climate change, the fact that the effectiveness of a remedy might be delayed during the (relatively short) time it takes for a new motor-vehicle fleet to replace an older one is essentially irrelevant. Nor is it dispositive that developing countries such as China and India are poised to increase greenhouse gas emissions substantially over the next century: A reduction in domestic emissions would slow the pace of global emissions increases, no matter what happens elsewhere.

* * *

In sum—at least according to petitioners' uncontested affidavits— the rise in sea levels associated with global warming has already harmed and will continue to harm Massachusetts. The risk of catastrophic harm, though remote, is nevertheless real. That risk would be reduced to some extent if petitioners received the relief they seek. We therefore hold that petitioners have standing to challenge the EPA's denial of their rulemaking petition.

[The majority then held that a court can review an agency decision to deny a petition for rulemaking, EPA has the power to regulate emissions of carbon dioxide from autos because carbon dioxide is a pollutant, and EPA refusal to initiate a rulemaking to set such emissions limits was arbitrary and capricious. Ed.]

■ CHIEF JUSTICE ROBERTS, with whom JUSTICE SCALIA, JUSTICE THOMAS, and JUSTICE ALITO join, dissenting.

Global warming may be a "crisis," even "the most pressing environmental problem of our time." Indeed, it may ultimately affect nearly everyone on the planet in some potentially adverse way, and it may be that governments have done too little to address it. It is not a problem, however, that has escaped the attention of policymakers in the Executive and Legislative Branches of our Government, who continue to consider regulatory, legislative, and treaty-based means of addressing global climate change.

Apparently dissatisfied with the pace of progress on this issue in the elected branches, petitioners have come to the courts claiming broad-ranging injury, and attempting to tie that injury to the Government's alleged failure to comply with a rather narrow statutory provision. I would reject these challenges as nonjusticiable. Such a conclusion involves no judgment on whether global warming exists, what causes it, or the extent of the problem. Nor does it render petitioners without recourse. This Court's standing jurisprudence simply recognizes that redress of grievances of the sort at issue here "is the function of Congress and the Chief Executive," not the federal courts. *Lujan v. Defenders of Wildlife*, 504 U.S. 555, 576 (1992). I would vacate the judgment below and remand for dismissal of the petitions for review.

* * *

Our modern framework for addressing standing is familiar: "A plaintiff must allege personal injury fairly traceable to the defendant's allegedly unlawful conduct and likely to be redressed by the requested relief." *Allen v. Wright*, 468 U.S. 737, 751 (1984). Applying that standard here, petitioners bear the burden of alleging an injury that is fairly traceable to the Environmental Protection Agency's failure to promulgate new motor vehicle greenhouse gas emission standards, and that is likely to be redressed by the prospective issuance of such standards.

Before determining whether petitioners can meet this familiar test, however, the Court changes the rules. It asserts that "States are not normal litigants for the purposes of invoking federal jurisdiction," and that given "Massachusetts' stake in protecting its quasi-sovereign interests, the Commonwealth is entitled to *special solicitude* in our standing analysis." (emphasis added).

Relaxing Article III standing requirements because asserted injuries are pressed by a State, however, has no basis in our jurisprudence, and support for any such "special solicitude" is conspicuously absent from the Court's opinion. The general judicial review provision cited by the Court affords States no special rights or status. The Court states that "Congress has ordered EPA to protect Massachusetts (among others)" through the statutory provision at issue, and that "Congress has . . . recognized a concomitant procedural right to challenge the rejection of its rulemaking petition as arbitrary and capricious." The reader might think from this unfortunate phrasing that Congress said something about the rights of States in this particular provision of the statute. Congress . . . has done nothing of the sort here. Under the law on which petitioners rely, Congress treated public and private litigants exactly the same.

Nor does the case law cited by the Court provide any support for the notion that Article III somehow implicitly treats public and private litigants differently. The Court has to go back a full century in an attempt to justify its novel standing rule, but even there it comes up short. The Court's analysis hinges on *Georgia v. Tennessee Copper Co.*, 206 U.S. 230 (1907)—a case that did indeed draw a distinction between a State and private litigants, but solely with respect to available remedies. The case had nothing to do with Article III standing.

* * *

All of this presumably explains why petitioners never cited *Tennessee Copper* in their briefs before this Court or the D.C. Circuit. It presumably explains why not one of the legion of *amici* supporting petitioners ever cited the case. And it presumably explains why not one of the three judges writing below ever cited the case either. Given that one purpose of the standing requirement is "to assure that concrete adverseness which sharpens the presentation of issues upon which the court so largely depends for illumination," *Baker v. Carr*, 369 U.S. 186, 204 (1962), it is ironic that the Court today adopts a new theory of Article III standing for States without the benefit of briefing or argument on the point.

It is not at all clear how the Court's "special solicitude" for Massachusetts plays out in the standing analysis, except as an implicit concession that petitioners cannot establish standing on traditional terms. But the status of Massachusetts as a State cannot compensate for petitioners' failure to demonstrate injury in fact, causation, and redressability.

When the Court actually applies the three-part test, it focuses on the State's asserted loss of coastal land as the injury in fact. If petitioners rely on loss of land as the Article III injury, however, they must ground the rest of the standing analysis in that specific injury. That alleged injury must be "concrete and particularized," *Lujan*, 504 U.S. at 560, and "distinct and palpable." *Allen*, 468 U.S. at 751. Central to this concept of "particularized" injury is the requirement that a plaintiff be affected in a "personal and individual way," *Lujan*, 504 U.S. at 560 n.1, and seek relief that "directly and tangibly benefits him" in a manner distinct from its impact on "the public at large." *Id.* at 573–74. Without "particularized injury, there can be no confidence of 'a real need to exercise the power of judicial review' or that relief can be framed 'no broader than required by the precise facts to which the court's ruling would be applied.'" *Warth v. Seldin*, 422 U.S. 490, 508 (1975) (quoting *Schlesinger v. Reservists Comm. to Stop the War*, 418 U.S. 208, 221–22 (1974)).

The very concept of global warming seems inconsistent with this particularization requirement. Global warming is a phenomenon "harmful to humanity at large," and the redress petitioners seek is focused no more on them than on the public generally—it is literally to change the atmosphere around the world.

If petitioners' particularized injury is loss of coastal land, it is also that injury that must be "actual or imminent, not conjectural or hypothetical," *Lujan*, 504 U.S. at 560, "real and immediate," *Los Angeles v. Lyons*, 461 U.S. 95, 102 (1983), and "certainly impending." *Whitmore v. Arkansas*, 495 U.S. 149, 158 (1990).

As to "actual" injury, the Court observes that "global sea levels rose somewhere between 10 and 20 centimeters over the 20th century as a result of global warming" and that "[t]hese rising seas have already begun to swallow Massachusetts' coastal land." But none of petitioners' declarations supports that connection. One declaration states that "a rise in sea level due to climate change is occurring on the coast of Massachusetts, in the metropolitan Boston area," but there is no elaboration. And the declarant goes on to identify a "significan[t]" *non*-global-warming cause of Boston's rising sea level: land subsidence.

The Court's attempts to identify "imminent" or "certainly impending" loss of Massachusetts coastal land fares no better. One of petitioners' declarants predicts global warming will cause sea level to rise by 20 to 70 centimeters *by the year 2100*. * * * [A]ccepting a century-long time horizon and a series of compounded estimates renders requirements of imminence and immediacy utterly toothless. "Allegations of possible future injury do not satisfy the requirements of Art. III. A threatened injury must be *certainly impending* to constitute injury in fact." *Whitmore*, 495 U.S. at 158 (emphasis added).

Petitioners' reliance on Massachusetts's loss of coastal land as their injury in fact for standing purposes creates insurmountable problems for them with respect to causation and redressability. To establish standing, petitioners must show a causal connection between that specific injury and the lack of new motor vehicle greenhouse gas emission standards, and that the promulgation of such standards would likely redress that injury. As is often the case, the questions of causation and redressability overlap. And importantly, when a party is challenging the Government's allegedly unlawful regulation, or lack of regulation, of a third party, satisfying the causation and redressability requirements becomes "substantially more difficult." *Lujan*, 504 U.S. at 562.

Petitioners view the relationship between their injuries and EPA's failure to promulgate new motor vehicle greenhouse gas emission standards as simple and direct: Domestic motor vehicles emit carbon dioxide and other greenhouse gases. Worldwide emissions of greenhouse gases contribute to global warming and therefore also to petitioners' alleged injuries. Without the new vehicle standards, greenhouse gas emissions—and therefore global warming and its attendant harms—have been higher than they otherwise would have been; once EPA changes course, the trend will be reversed.

The Court ignores the complexities of global warming, and does so by now disregarding the "particularized" injury it relied on in step one, and using the dire nature of global warming itself as a bootstrap for finding causation and redressability. First, it is important to recognize the extent of the emissions at issue here. Because local greenhouse gas emissions disperse throughout the atmosphere and remain there for anywhere from 50 to 200 years, it is global emissions data that are relevant. According to one of petitioners' declarations, domestic motor vehicles contribute about 6 percent of global carbon dioxide emissions and 4 percent of global greenhouse gas emissions. The amount of global emissions at issue here is smaller still; § 202(a)(1) of the Clean Air Act covers only *new* motor vehicles and *new* motor vehicle engines, so petitioners' desired emission standards might reduce only a fraction of 4 percent of global emissions.

This gets us only to the relevant greenhouse gas emissions; linking them to global warming and ultimately to petitioners' alleged injuries next requires consideration of further complexities. As EPA explained in its denial of petitioners' request for rulemaking,

> "predicting future climate change necessarily involves a complex web of economic and physical factors including: our ability to predict future global anthropogenic emissions of [greenhouse gases] and aerosols; the fate of these emissions once they enter the atmosphere (e.g., what percentage are absorbed by vegetation or are taken up by the oceans); the impact of those emissions that remain in the atmosphere on the radiative properties of the atmosphere; changes in critically important climate feedbacks (e.g., changes in cloud cover and ocean circulation); changes in temperature characteristics (e.g., average temperatures, shifts in daytime and evening temperatures); changes in other climatic parameters (e.g., shifts in precipitation, storms); and ultimately the impact of such changes on human health and welfare (e.g., increases or decreases in agricultural productivity, human health impacts)."

Petitioners are never able to trace their alleged injuries back through this complex web to the fractional amount of global emissions that might have been limited with EPA standards. In light of the bit-part domestic new motor vehicle greenhouse gas emissions have played in what petitioners describe as a 150-year global phenomenon, and the myriad additional factors bearing on petitioners' alleged injury—the loss of Massachusetts coastal land—the connection is far too speculative to establish causation.

Redressability is even more problematic. To the tenuous link between petitioners' alleged injury and the indeterminate fractional domestic emissions at issue here, add the fact that petitioners cannot meaningfully predict what will come of the 80 percent of global greenhouse gas emissions that originate outside the United States. As the Court acknowledges, "developing countries such as China and India are poised to increase greenhouse gas emissions substantially over the next century," so the domestic emissions at issue here may become an increasingly marginal portion of global emissions, and any decreases produced by petitioners' desired standards are likely to be overwhelmed many times over by emissions increases elsewhere in the world.

Petitioners offer declarations attempting to address this uncertainty, contending that "[i]f the U.S. takes steps to reduce motor vehicle emissions, other countries are very likely to take similar actions regarding their own motor vehicles using technology developed in response to the U.S. program." In other words, do not worry that other countries will contribute far more to global warming than will U.S. automobile emissions; someone is bound to invent something, and places like the People's Republic of China or India will surely require use of the new technology, regardless of cost. The Court previously has explained that when the existence of an element of standing "depends on the unfettered choices made by independent actors not before the courts and whose exercise of broad and legitimate discretion the courts cannot presume either to control or to predict," a party must present facts supporting an assertion that the actor will proceed in such a manner. *Lujan*, 504 U.S. at 562 (quoting *ASARCO Inc. v. Kadish*, 490 U.S. 605, 615 (1989) (Kennedy, J.)). The declarations' conclusory (not to say fanciful) statements do not even come close.

No matter, the Court reasons, because *any* decrease in domestic emissions will "slow the pace of global emissions increases, no matter what happens elsewhere." Every little bit helps, so Massachusetts can sue over any little bit.

The Court's sleight-of-hand is in failing to link up the different elements of the three-part standing test. What must be *likely* to be redressed is the particular injury in fact. The injury the Court looks to is the asserted loss of land. The Court contends that regulating domestic motor vehicle emissions will reduce carbon dioxide in the atmosphere, *and therefore* redress Massachusetts's injury. But even if regulation *does* reduce emissions—to some indeterminate degree, given events elsewhere in the world—the Court never explains why that makes it *likely* that the injury in fact—the loss of land—will be redressed. Schoolchildren know that a kingdom might be lost "all for the want of a horseshoe nail," but "likely" redressability is a different matter. The realities make it pure conjecture to suppose that EPA regulation of new automobile emissions will *likely* prevent the loss of Massachusetts coastal land.

Petitioners' difficulty in demonstrating causation and redressability is not surprising given the evident mismatch between the source of their alleged injury—catastrophic global warming—and the narrow subject matter of the Clean Air Act provision at issue in this suit. The mismatch suggests that petitioners' true goal for this litigation may be more symbolic than anything else. The constitutional role of the courts, however, is to decide concrete cases-—not to serve as a convenient forum for policy debates.

[The dissenting Justices went on to argue that the Court should uphold EPA's determination that carbon dioxide is not a pollutant and that EPA engaged in reasoned decisionmaking when it decided not to exercise any discretion it might have to conduct a rulemaking to set emissions limits applicable to carbon dioxide at the time. Ed.]

NOTES AND QUESTIONS

1. With one change in the text of the opinions in *Massachusetts v. EPA*, the opinions should seem familiar. If you substitute the name of an individual—*e.g.*, landowner John Jones—for Massachusetts in the discussions of injury, causation, and redressability, the opinions are similar to the opinions the Court issued in cases like *Defenders*, *Steel Co.*, and

Laidlaw. One group of Justices applied easy-to-satisfy versions of the tests for injury, causation, and redressability and concluded that the environmental petitioner had standing. Another group of Justices applied an impossible-to-meet version of the tests for injury, causation, and redressability and concluded that the environmental petitioner lacked standing. Viewed in this way, the case is remarkable only as an indication that changes in the composition of the Court since *Laidlaw* have allowed Justice Scalia to add two more converts to his view that private parties never have standing to enforce a public law, thus bringing to four the number of Justices who share that view.

2.   It is impossible to make sense of the majority opinion in *Massachusetts v. EPA*, however, with the deletion of all references to Massachusetts. In *Massachusetts v. EPA*, the Court held that states have a special, preferred status in standing disputes. The majority repeatedly refers to the significance of a state as the petitioner and explicitly distinguishes the (apparently) less legally-significant potential interests of private parties. This position is unprecedented. The Court had never even hinted at the existence of such a special status for states prior to its opinion in *Massachusetts v. EPA*. As the dissenting opinion noted, no petitioner, intervenor, or amicus cited the sole case the majority relied upon to support its states-are-special holding, for a good reason. That case said nothing about standing and was considered totally irrelevant to the dispute by all of the hundreds of lawyers involved in the case. Would the Court have resolved the standing dispute the same way in the absence of a state as a co-petitioner, or would the Court have held, five-to-four, that a private petitioner lacked standing? In order to prevail in future environmental standing disputes, must public interest groups enlist a state as a co-petitioner in every case? Can you justify such a legal regime?

3.   It is impossible for an outsider to the decisionmaking process to know why the Justices voted as they did or reasoned as they did in *Massachusetts v. EPA*. Many scholars believe, however, that both the outcome of the case and important parts of the reasoning in the opinions can be explained only as a function of the critical role that Justice Kennedy played in the Court's decisionmaking process at the time the Court decided *Massachusetts v. EPA*. During that period, the Justices were sharply divided along political and ideological lines. Four Justices were conservatives who shared Justice Scalia's views on many issues, including standing in public law disputes. Four Justices were liberals who disagreed strongly with the Scalia group on many issues and who believed that any private individual who could satisfy the temporal and geographic criteria recognized by the majority in *Laidlaw* had standing in public law disputes. Justice Kennedy did not fit comfortably in either group. As a consequence, his views often prevailed in cases that raised issues that divided the other Justices. Many scholars, including the authors of this book, believe that the Justices were divided four-to-four in *Massachusetts v. EPA* and that Justice Kennedy took the position that he would join the majority opinion if, but only if, the majority agreed to change its opinion to add the states-are-special reasoning and language suggesting strongly that the case would have been decided the other way in the absence of a state as a co-petitioner.

This theory is supported by the patterns of voting of the Justices in many other federalism cases. In many other federalism disputes, the four Justices who dissented in *Massachusetts v. EPA* joined with Justice

Kennedy in deciding the case in favor of states' rights, while the other four Justices who joined the majority opinion in *Massachusetts v. EPA* wrote a dissenting opinion in which they expressed the contrary view. It seems unlikely that the other justices who joined Justice Kennedy in the majority opinion became overnight converts to the strong states' rights position they had rejected in many other contexts. If Justice Kennedy is the only Justice who actually embraces the states-are-special aspect of the *Massachusetts v. EPA* opinion, is that likely to be a durable part of the law of standing?

4. The dissenting Justices in *Massachusetts v. EPA* accused the majority of engaging in "symbolic" decisionmaking. That is plausible, given the miniscule contribution that limits on emissions of carbon dioxide from new cars could conceivably make to mitigation of anthropogenic global warming. There is a broad consensus that global warming can be addressed effectively only by a global decision to adopt strict limits on carbon dioxide emissions that would reduce such emissions by about 80% or by a global tax on emissions so high that it would accomplish the same result. *See* Richard J. Pierce, Jr., *Energy Independence and Global Warming*, 37 ENVTL. L. 595 (2007). No country can do anything unilaterally that is likely to be effective.

5. *Massachusetts v. EPA* is not the Court's last word on constitutional standing doctrine. In *Clapper v. Amnesty International*, 133 S. Ct. 1138 (2013), a five-Justice majority held that no petitioner had standing to obtain review of the constitutionality of a provision of the Foreign Intelligence Surveillance Act (FISA) that authorizes the government to listen to the conversations of individuals who are believed not to be U.S. citizens and who are believed not to be in the U.S. at the time of the conversation. The government can take that action only with judicial authorization, but the FISA court has never denied a government request to do so. The petitioners fell in several categories of individuals who had reasons to believe that their conversations were the subject of FISA surveillance—*e.g.*, foreign correspondents, lawyers representing non-U.S. persons accused of acts of terrorism, and officials of international human rights organizations. The petitioners alleged two types of injuries: (1) future injuries in the form of their expectation that the government would listen to some of their conversations in the future; and (2) present injuries in the form of a variety of actions that they were already taking to make it more difficult for the government to listen to their conversations based on their belief that some of their conversations were already targets of FISA surveillance.

The five-Justice majority held that the alleged future injuries were too speculative because they did not satisfy what might be described as a newly-announced standard for establishing injury in fact—i.e., a future or probable injury must be "certainly impending" to be judicially cognizable for standing purposes. The majority also applied the new "certainly impending" standard to resolve the issue of whether the challenged action caused the alleged injury. Thus, the majority denied standing based in part on its reasoning that, even if the government was listening to the petitioners' conversations, it might be doing so pursuant to some other statutory authority.

In addition, the majority seemed to eliminate the availability of standing based on the theory the Court embraced in *Friends of the Earth, Inc. v. Laidlaw Environmental Services*, 528 U.S. 167 (2000), which is excerpted and discussed above in this Part C of Chapter 7. Recall that in *Laidlaw*, the district court found that the tiny quantity of mercury that the defendant had illegally discharged into a river upstream of the locations where the plaintiffs used the river for fishing and swimming could not possibly cause injury in the form of danger to the health of the petitioners. The Court held that the petitioners had demonstrated a different form of judicially-cognizable injury, however, in the form of changes in their behavior based on their "reasonable concern" that the illegal discharge might have exposed them to hazards to their health. While the majority in *Clapper* attempted to distinguish *Laidlaw*, its explanation makes little sense on its face. In both cases, the petitioners made changes to their behavior based on their reasonable concern that something bad would happen to them if they did not. The only difference was that the risk of occurrence of the bad consequence that caused the change in behavior was non-existent in *Laidlaw*, while it probably existed in *Clapper*. Thus, the case for standing would seem to have been stronger in *Clapper* than in *Laidlaw*.

The dissenting Justices in *Clapper* described many prior cases in which the Court found standing based on a standard that was much easier to satisfy than the new "certainly impending" standard and based on facts that could not possibly satisfy a "certainly impending" requirement. The dissenting Justices expressed the view that the Court should have applied a standard like "high probability" and that the *Clapper* petitioners had easily satisfied such a requirement.

It remains to be seen whether a majority of the Court continues to pursue the limited approach to constitutional standing articulated in *Clapper*. If the Court applies the new "certainly impending" standard on a consistent basis, the Court will have virtually eliminated access to the courts for anyone who relies on either an expected future injury or a probable injury to obtain standing. That is a big "if," however, given the Court's historic unwillingness to adhere to consistent standards in this area of law.

2.   STATUTORY STANDING AND THE "ZONE OF INTERESTS"

Beyond the requirements of constitutional standing, the courts have recognized a number of statutory or prudential limitations on who may raise a claim in federal court. For example, while plaintiffs may assert their own injuries, outside of the associational standing principles discussed earlier in this Chapter, the courts generally deny third parties standing to raise claims based on the injuries of others. *See, e.g., Singleton v. Wulff*, 428 U.S. 106, 113–14 (1976). Although the burden of taxation represents an injury in fact, because that injury is shared by many or even all taxpayers, individual taxpayers typically must demonstrate more direct and individualized injuries than their mere status as taxpayers to establish standing to challenge the legitimacy of government actions. *See, e.g., Frothingham v. Mellon*, 262 U.S. 447 (1923). Yet another limitation, derived from the *ADAPSO* case excerpted earlier in this Chapter, holds that a plaintiff raising a statutory claim must fall within the "zone of interests" that Congress intended the statute to address with the statute. *ADAPSO*, 397 U.S. 150, 153 (1970). As the Supreme Court summarized in *Allen v. Wright*, 468 U.S. 737 (1984),

Standing doctrine embraces several judicially self-imposed limits on the exercise of federal jurisdiction, such as the general prohibition on a litigant's raising another person's legal rights, the rule barring adjudication of generalized grievances more appropriately addressed in the representative branches, and the requirement that a plaintiff's complaint fall within the zone of interests protected by the law invoked.

Id. at 751. Following this rhetorical lead, courts have routinely grouped all of these limitations on plaintiff standing under the label of "prudential standing."

More recently, the Supreme Court has moved away from the prudential standing label, recharacterizing at least some of these limitations as either variants of the Article III standing requirements or as purely statutory in nature. In *Lexmark Int'l, Inc. v. Static Control Components, Inc.*, 134 S. Ct. 1377 (2014), writing for a unanimous Court, Justice Scalia offered the following observations:

In recent decades, however, we have adverted to a "prudential" branch of standing, a doctrine not derived from Article III and "not exhaustively defined" but encompassing (we have said) at least three broad principles: " 'the general prohibition on a litigant's raising another person's legal rights, the rule barring adjudication of generalized grievances more appropriately addressed in the representative branches, and the requirement that a plaintiff's complaint fall within the zone of interests protected by the law invoked.' " *Elk Grove Unified School Dist. v. Newdow*, 542 U.S. 1, 12, (2004) (quoting *Allen v. Wright*, 468 U.S. 737, 751 (1984)).

* * *

Although we admittedly have placed [the zone-of-interests] test under the "prudential" rubric in the past, see, *e.g., Elk Grove, supra,* at 12, it does not belong there * * *. Whether a plaintiff comes within "the 'zone of interests' " is an issue that requires us to determine, using traditional tools of statutory interpretation, whether a legislatively conferred cause of action encompasses a particular plaintiff's claim. See *Steel Co. v. Citizens for Better Environment*, 523 U.S. 83, 97, and n. 2 (1998); *Clarke v. Securities Industry Assn.*, 479 U.S. 388, 394–395 (1987). As Judge Silberman of the D.C. Circuit recently observed, " 'prudential standing' is a misnomer" as applied to the zone-of-interests analysis, which asks whether "this particular class of persons ha[s] a right to sue under this substantive statute." *Association of Battery Recyclers, Inc. v. EPA*, 716 F.3d 667, 675–676 (2013) (concurring opinion).

Id. at 1386–87. In a footnote, Justice Scalia added,

The zone-of-interests test is not the only concept that we have previously classified as an aspect of "prudential standing" but for which, upon closer inspection, we have found that label inapt. Take, for example, our reluctance to entertain generalized grievances— *i.e.*, suits "claiming only harm to [the plaintiff's] and every citizen's interest in proper application of the Constitution and laws, and seeking relief that no more directly and tangibly benefits him than it does the public at large." *Lujan v. Defenders of Wildlife,* 504 U.S. 555, 573–574 (1992). While we have at times grounded our reluctance to entertain such suits in the "counsels of prudence" (albeit counsels "close[ly] relat[ed] to the policies reflected in" Article III), *Valley Forge Christian College v. Americans United for Separation of Church and State, Inc.,* 454 U.S. 464, 475 (1982), we have since held that such suits do not present constitutional "cases" or "controversies." See, *e.g., Lance v. Coffman,* 549 U.S. 437, 439 (2007) (*per curiam*); *DaimlerChrysler Corp. v. Cuno,* 547 U.S. 332, 344–346 (2006); *Defenders of Wildlife, supra,* at 573–574. They are barred for constitutional reasons, not "prudential" ones.

Id. at 1387 n.3. The *Lexmark* Court left the proper characterization of third-party standing for another day, *id.*; but given the Court's unanimity in *Lexmark*, the prudential standing label may well be headed for the dustbin of jurisprudential history.

Nevertheless, the Court has always considered statutes relevant to the resolution of standing disputes. Prior to enactment of the APA, the test the Court applied to determine whether a petitioner had standing to obtain review of an agency action depended critically on the language of the statute that authorized the agency action at issue. If that statute was silent with respect to standing, as many were, the Court applied a test that was extremely difficult to satisfy, the legal right test. However, the Court was open to the possibility of a broader approach to standing if it interpreted the statute as authorizing a more liberal test.

The legal right test is illustrated by *Alexander Sprunt & Son, Inc. v. United States*, 281 U.S. 249 (1930). Based on complaints from shippers, the Interstate Commerce Commission (ICC) initiated an investigation into the rates charged to ship cotton to Houston. The ICC found the preexisting rate relationship unduly discriminatory because the ship-side rate was lower than the city-delivery rate. It ordered the railroads to eliminate the discriminatory relationship by equalizing the two rates. The railroads complied with the ICC order and declined to seek judicial review. Alexander Sprunt & Son owned a shipside warehouse. It sought judicial review of the ICC order, claiming that the order and the resulting change in rate relationships caused it to lose business and that the ICC erred in concluding that the preexisting rate relationship was unduly discriminatory.

The Court recognized that the ICC action caused economic harm to Alexander Sprunt & Son, but it held that Alexander Sprunt & Son lacked standing to obtain judicial review of the ICC order on two grounds. First, the Court found that the statute conferred upon shippers a legal right only to reasonable service at reasonable rates and without undue discrimination. Alexander Sprunt & Son was not asserting a violation of that right. Only carriers had the legal right to maintain the specific rates in effect, and Alexander Sprunt & Son could not assert that right on behalf of the carriers that had chosen not to assert that right in court. Second, the Court concluded that judicial reversal of the ICC order would be an exercise in futility, since the carriers would remain free to keep the newly equalized rates in effect on a voluntary basis even if a court held that the ICC could not force the carriers to maintain such a rate relationship. Thus, the Court concluded that Alexander Sprunt & Son's sole remedy was to file a complaint with the ICC alleging that the new rates were unreasonable or unduly discriminatory.

To understand the effect of the holding in *Alexander Sprunt & Son*, and the pernicious effect of the legal right test, requires a basic understanding of the substantive law of rate regulation. The statute at issue prohibited only unreasonable or unduly discriminatory rates and rate relationships. Thus, it is quite possible that both the preexisting rates the ICC held unlawful and the rates in effect after the ICC order were statutorily permissible. If that was the situation, the ICC order that injured Alexander Sprunt & Son was itself unlawful. We will never know, since the Court refused to allow Alexander Sprunt & Son to obtain judicial review of the order.

The Court's second point in *Alexander Sprunt & Son* is formally accurate but irrelevant. It is true that the railroads could have selected voluntarily the rate structure that injured Alexander Sprunt & Son. Yet, they did not do so. When they believed the preexisting rates were permissible, the railroads voluntarily chose the preexisting rates. The railroads adopted the rates that injured Alexander Sprunt & Son only because the ICC held that the preexisting rates were no longer permissible. Thus, the ICC action definitely caused Alexander Sprunt & Son injury, and there was every reason to expect that a court order holding the ICC order invalid would redress that injury, since there was every reason to expect that the railroads would return to the preexisting rates if they were permitted to do so.

The legal right test was criticized on many grounds. *See, e.g.,* Kenneth Culp Davis, *The Liberalized Law of Standing*, 37 U. CHI. L. REV. 450 (1970). Perhaps the most telling criticism was based on its confusion of the issue of access to the courts with the issue of whether a party should prevail on the merits of a dispute. Under the legal right test, a court was required to determine whether the petitioner's claim had merit in order to decide whether the petitioner was entitled to have the merits of its case considered by the court. This circular reasoning process is unnecessary to the determination of the threshold question of access to judicial review, and it can force a court to determine the merits of a claim at such an early stage that the court does not focus enough attention on the merits. Thus, considering the merits of a party's claim as part of the process of determining whether the party has standing to assert that claim invites poorly reasoned summary judicial disposition of the merits of the claim. *Alexander Sprunt & Son* illustrates that frequent result.

However, in some pre-APA cases the Court applied a much broader "adversely affected" test, as announced in *FCC v. Sanders Bros. Radio Station*, 309 U.S. 470 (1940). Sanders Bros. owned a radio station in East Dubuque, Illinois. Another party applied to the Federal Communications Commission (FCC) for a license to operate a radio station in Dubuque, Iowa. The FCC granted the license over the objection of Sanders Bros. that a second station would erode its market share and revenue base. Sanders Bros. sought and obtained judicial review of the FCC order. The court of appeals granted judicial review on the theory that the FCC was required to consider allegations of potential economic injury to competitors in the process of deciding whether to grant a broadcast license to a new applicant. The applicant asked the Supreme Court to reverse the court of appeals because the statute did not make harm to competitors a basis for denial of a license and, therefore, the FCC grant of the license did not deny Sanders Bros. any legal right.

The Supreme Court affirmed the court of appeals, but on an entirely different basis. The Court agreed with the applicant that potential harm to competitors was not a factor to be considered by the FCC in granting or denying a license. It held, however, that Sanders Bros. had standing to obtain judicial review of the FCC order despite the fact that the order did not violate any legal right of Sanders Bros. Congress provided an explicit statutory right to judicial review to any person aggrieved or adversely affected by an FCC order granting or denying an application for a broadcast license. The Court concluded that Congress established this permissive standard for access to the courts in recognition of the fact that competitors often are the only persons with sufficient incentive "to bring to the attention of the appellate court errors of law in the action of the Commission in granting the license." Thus, while Sanders Bros. could not argue on the merits that grant of the license impermissibly caused it economic harm, it could use that economic harm as the basis for standing, and then argue on the merits that the FCC action was unlawful on some other basis.

Recall that, in the *ADAPSO* case, excerpted earlier in this Chapter, the Court discussed language in the APA as granting standing to persons "aggrieved by agency action within the meaning of a relevant statute." 5 U.S.C. § 702. The Court in *ADAPSO* described the question raised by this language as "whether the interest sought to be protected by the complainant is arguably within the zone of interests to be protected by the statute or constitutional guarantee in question." The Court considered not only the language of APA § 702 but also at language from the statute under which the agency took its action, the Bank Service Corporations Act (BSCA). The language from the BSCA on which the *ADAPSO* Court focused was not a special judicial review provision addressing standing but, rather, substantive provisions of the BSCA central to the agency's action. It was this statutory language that the Court decided brought a competitor within the zone of interests protected by the statute. The *ADAPSO* Court also recognized that this approach to statutory standing was broader than even the sort of economic harm asserted in *Sanders Bros. Radio Station*, encompassing "aesthetic, conservational, and recreational" concerns as well.

Perhaps because of that breadth, in the decades since deciding *ADAPSO*, the Court has struggled to define the scope and even the nature of the zone of interests test. The Court has interpreted standing under APA § 702 to require reference to other statutes and the zone of interests test. Yet, most statutes that delegate authority to an administering agency are silent regarding standing. Which provisions of a statute must a reviewing court consider in evaluating standing to raise a statutory claim against agency action? In the face of statutory silence regarding the standing issue, what if any role should congressional intent play in deciding whether or not to allow a plaintiff's claim against agency action proceed? Is it enough that the statute's provisions arguably implicate the plaintiff's interests, or is it necessary that Congress consciously intended to benefit or protect the plaintiff's interests?

The Supreme Court's answers to these questions have varied tremendously over the past few decades. In speaking of protecting "aesthetic, conservational, and recreational" as well as economic interests and a trend of "enlarge[ing] . . . the class of people who may protest of administrative action," the *ADAPSO* Court clearly anticipated a broad application of APA § 702 and the zone of interests test. Subsequently, the Court suggested that the zone of interests test "is not meant to be especially demanding." *Clarke v. Securities Industry Ass'n*, 479 U.S. 388 (1987). Yet, the Court has at times applied the zone of interests test to deny standing notwithstanding the plaintiff's ability to satisfy the requirements of Article III. For example, in applying the zone of interests test in *Air Courier Conf. of Amer. v. Amer. Postal Workers Union, AFL-CIO*, 498 U.S. 517 (1991), the Court both narrowed its inquiry to the subset of statutory provisions under which the agency had acted, rather than the entire statute, and also required evidence of congressional intent to benefit the plaintiffs with those particular provisions—and thus denied standing to the plaintiffs notwithstanding the obvious economic injury they suffered as a result of the agency's action.

The opinions in the following case neatly demonstrate the arguments over the nature and scope of the zone of interests test that prevailed for so long. Can you identify the points of doctrinal disagreement?

National Credit Union Administration v. First National Bank & Trust Co.

522 U.S. 479 (1991).

■ JUSTICE THOMAS delivered the opinion of the Court.

In 1934, during the Great Depression, Congress enacted the [Federal Credit Union Act (FCUA)], which authorizes the chartering of credit unions at the national level and provides that federal credit unions may, as a general matter, offer banking services only to their members. Section 109 of the FCUA, which has remained virtually unaltered since the FCUA's enactment, expressly restricts membership in federal credit unions. In relevant part, it provides:

> "Federal credit union membership shall consist of the incorporators and such other persons and incorporated and unincorporated organizations, to the extent permitted by rules and regulations prescribed by the Board, as may be elected to membership and as such shall each, subscribe to at least one share of its stock and pay the initial installment thereon and a uniform entrance fee if required by the board of directors; *except that Federal credit union membership shall be limited to groups having a common bond of occupation or association, or*

to groups within a well-defined neighborhood, community, or rural district." 12 U.S.C. § 1759 (emphasis added).

Until 1982, the [National Credit Union Administration (NCUA)] and its predecessors consistently interpreted § 109 to require that the *same* common bond of occupation unite every member of an occupationally defined federal credit union. In 1982, however, the NCUA reversed its longstanding policy in order to permit credit unions to be composed of multiple unrelated employer groups. See IRPS 82–1, 47 Fed. Reg. 16775 (1982). It thus interpreted § 109's common bond requirement to apply only to each employer group in a multiple-group credit union, rather than to every member of that credit union. See IRPS 82–3, 47 Fed. Reg. 26808 (1982). Under the NCUA's new interpretation, all of the employer groups in a multiple-group credit union had to be located "within a well-defined area," *ibid.,* but the NCUA later revised this requirement to provide that each employer group could be located within "an area surrounding the [credit union's] home or a branch office that can be reasonably served by the [credit union] as determined by NCUA." IRPS 89–1, 54 Fed. Reg. 31170 (1989). Since 1982, therefore, the NCUA has permitted federal credit unions to be composed of wholly unrelated employer groups, each having its own distinct common bond.

After the NCUA revised its interpretation of § 109, petitioner AT&T Family Federal Credit Union (ATTF) expanded its operations considerably by adding unrelated employer groups to its membership. As a result, ATTF now has approximately 110,000 members nationwide, only 35% of whom are employees of AT&T and its affiliates. The remaining members are employees of such diverse companies as the Lee Apparel Company, the Coca-Cola Bottling Company, the Ciba-Geigy Corporation, the Duke Power Company, and the American Tobacco Company.

In 1990, after the NCUA approved a series of amendments to ATTF's charter that added several such unrelated employer groups to ATTF's membership, respondents brought this action. Invoking the judicial review provisions of the Administrative Procedure Act (APA), 5 U.S.C. § 702, respondents claimed that the NCUA's approval of the charter amendments was contrary to law because the members of the new groups did not share a common bond of occupation with ATTF's existing members, as respondents alleged § 109 required.

* * *

Respondents claim a right to judicial review of the NCUA's chartering decision under § 10(a) of the APA, which provides:

> "A person suffering legal wrong because of agency action, or adversely affected or aggrieved by agency action within the meaning of a relevant statute, is entitled to judicial review thereof." 5 U.S.C. § 702.

We have interpreted § 10(a) of the APA to impose a prudential standing requirement in addition to the requirement, imposed by Article III of the Constitution, that a plaintiff have suffered a sufficient injury in fact. See, *e.g., Association of Data Processing Service Organizations, Inc.*

v. Camp, 397 U.S. 150, 152 (1970) *(Data Processing).*[4] For a plaintiff to have prudential standing under the APA, "the interest sought to be protected by the complainant [must be] arguably within the zone of interests to be protected or regulated by the statute . . . in question." *Id.,* at 153.

Based on four of our prior cases finding that competitors of financial institutions have standing to challenge agency action relaxing statutory restrictions on the activities of those institutions, we hold that respondents' interest in limiting the markets that federal credit unions can serve is arguably within the zone of interests to be protected by § 109. Therefore, respondents have prudential standing under the APA to challenge the NCUA's interpretation.

Although our prior cases have not stated a clear rule for determining when a plaintiff's interest is "arguably within the zone of interests" to be protected by a statute, they nonetheless establish that we should not inquire whether there has been a congressional intent to benefit the would-be plaintiff. In *Data Processing, supra,* the Office of the Comptroller of the Currency (Comptroller) had interpreted the National Bank Act's incidental powers clause, Rev. Stat. § 5136, 12 U.S.C. § 24 Seventh, to permit national banks to perform data processing services for other banks and bank customers. See *Data Processing, supra,* at 151. The plaintiffs, a data processing corporation and its trade association, alleged that this interpretation was impermissible because providing data processing services was not, as was required by the statute, "[an] incidental powe[r] . . . necessary to carry on the business of banking." See 397 U.S., at 157, n. 2.

In holding that the plaintiffs had standing, we stated that § 10(a) of the APA required only that "the interest sought to be protected by the complainant [be] arguably within the zone of interests to be protected or regulated by the statute . . . in question." *Id.,* at 153. In determining that the plaintiffs' interest met this requirement, we noted that although the relevant federal statutes—the National Bank Act, 12 U.S.C. § 24 Seventh, and the Bank Service Corporation Act, 12 U.S.C. § 1864—did not "in terms protect a specified group[,] . . . their general policy is apparent; and those whose interests are directly affected by a broad or narrow interpretation of the Acts are easily identifiable." *Data Processing,* 397 U.S., at 157. "[A]s competitors of national banks which are engaging in data processing services," the plaintiffs were within that class of "aggrieved persons" entitled to judicial review of the Comptroller's interpretation. *Ibid.*

Less than a year later, we applied the "zone of interests" test in *Arnold Tours, Inc. v. Camp,* 400 U.S. 45 (1970) *(per curiam) (Arnold Tours).* There, certain travel agencies challenged a ruling by the Comptroller, similar to the one contested in *Data Processing,* that permitted national banks to operate travel agencies. See 400 U.S., at 45. In holding that the plaintiffs had prudential standing under the APA, we noted that it was incorrect to view our decision in *Data Processing* as resting on the peculiar legislative history of § 4 of the Bank Service Corporation Act, which had been passed in part at the

---

[4]   In this action, it is not disputed that respondents have suffered an injury in fact because the NCUA's interpretation allows persons who might otherwise be their customers to be members, and therefore customers, of ATTF.

behest of the data processing industry. See 400 U.S., at 46. We stated explicitly that "we did not rely on any legislative history showing that Congress desired to protect data processors alone from competition." *Ibid.* We further explained:

> "In *Data Processing* . . . [w]e held that § 4 arguably brings a competitor within the zone of interests protected by it. Nothing in the opinion limited § 4 to protecting only competitors in the data-processing field. When national banks begin to provide travel services for their customers, they compete with travel agents no less than they compete with data processors when they provide data-processing services to their customers." *Ibid.* (internal citations and quotation marks omitted).

A year later, we decided *Investment Company Institute v. Camp,* 401 U.S. 617 (1971) (*ICI*). In that case, an investment company trade association and several individual investment companies alleged that the Comptroller had violated, *inter alia,* § 21 of the Glass-Steagall Act[5] by permitting national banks to establish and operate what in essence were early versions of mutual funds. We held that the plaintiffs, who alleged that they would be injured by the competition resulting from the Comptroller's action, had standing under the APA and stated that the case was controlled by *Data Processing.* See 401 U.S., at 621. Significantly, we found unpersuasive Justice Harlan's argument in dissent that the suit should be dismissed because "neither the language of the pertinent provisions of the Glass-Steagall Act nor the legislative history evince[d] any congressional concern for the interests of petitioners and others like them in freedom from competition." *Id.,* at 640.

Our fourth case in this vein was *Clarke v. Securities Industry Assn.,* 479 U.S. 388 (1987) (*Clarke*). There, a securities dealers trade association sued the Comptroller, this time for authorizing two national banks to offer discount brokerage services both at their branch offices and at other locations inside and outside their home States. See *id.,* at 391. The plaintiff contended that the Comptroller's action violated the McFadden Act, which permits national banks to carry on the business of banking only at authorized branches, and to open new branches only in their home States and only to the extent that state-chartered banks in that State can do so under state law. See *id.,* at 391–392.

We again held that the plaintiff had standing under the APA. Summarizing our prior holdings, we stated that although the "zone of interests" test "denies a right of review if the plaintiff's interests are . . . marginally related to or inconsistent with the purposes implicit in the statute," *id.,* at 399, "there need be no indication of congressional purpose to benefit the would-be plaintiff," *id.,* at 399–400 (citing *ICI*). We then determined that by limiting the ability of national banks to do business outside their home States, "Congress ha[d] shown a concern to keep national banks from gaining a monopoly control over credit and money." 479 U.S., at 403. The interest of the securities dealers in preventing national banks from expanding into the securities markets

---

[5]   Under § 21 of the Glass–Steagall Act, it is unlawful "[f]or any person, firm, [or] corporation . . . engaged in the business of issuing . . . securities, to engage at the same time to any extent whatever in the business of receiving deposits." § 21 of the Banking Act of 1933, 12 U.S.C. § 378(a).

directly implicated this concern because offering discount brokerage services would allow national banks "access to more money, in the form of credit balances, and enhanced opportunities to lend money, viz., for margin purchases." *Ibid.* The case was thus analogous to *Data Processing* and *ICI:* "In those cases the question was what activities banks could engage in at all; here, the question is what activities banks can engage in without regard to the limitations imposed by state branching law." 479 U.S., at 403.

Our prior cases, therefore, have consistently held that for a plaintiff's interests to be arguably within the "zone of interests" to be protected by a statute, there does not have to be an "indication of congressional purpose to benefit the would-be plaintiff." *Id.,* at 399–400 (citing *ICI*); see also *Arnold Tours,* 400 U.S., at 46 (citing *Data Processing*). The proper inquiry is simply "whether the interest sought to be protected by the complainant is *arguably* within the zone of interests to be protected . . . by the statute." *Data Processing,* 397 U.S., at 153 (emphasis added). Hence in applying the "zone of interests" test, we do not ask whether, in enacting the statutory provision at issue, Congress specifically intended to benefit the plaintiff. Instead, we first discern the interests "arguably . . . to be protected" by the statutory provision at issue; we then inquire whether the plaintiff's interests affected by the agency action in question are among them.

Section 109 provides that "[f]ederal credit union membership shall be limited to groups having a common bond of occupation or association, or to groups within a well-defined neighborhood, community, or rural district." 12 U.S.C. § 1759. By its express terms, § 109 limits membership in every federal credit union to members of definable "groups." Because federal credit unions may, as a general matter, offer banking services only to members, see, *e.g.,* 12 U.S.C. §§ 1757(5)–(6), § 109 also restricts the markets that every federal credit union can serve. Although these markets need not be small, they unquestionably are limited. The link between § 109's regulation of federal credit union membership and its limitation on the markets that federal credit unions can serve is unmistakable. Thus, even if it cannot be said that Congress had the specific purpose of benefiting commercial banks, one of the interests "arguably . . . to be protected" by § 109 is an interest in limiting the markets that federal credit unions can serve. This interest is precisely the interest of respondents affected by the NCUA's interpretation of § 109. As competitors of federal credit unions, respondents certainly have an interest in limiting the markets that federal credit unions can serve, and the NCUA's interpretation has affected that interest by allowing federal credit unions to increase their customer base.

* * *

We therefore cannot accept petitioners' argument that respondents do not have standing because there is no evidence that the Congress that enacted § 109 was concerned with the competitive interests of commercial banks. To accept that argument, we would have to reformulate the "zone of interests" test to require that Congress have specifically intended to benefit a particular class of plaintiffs before a plaintiff from that class could have standing under the APA to sue. We have refused to do this in our prior cases, and we refuse to do so today.

* * *

Respondents' interest in limiting the markets that credit unions can serve is "arguably within the zone of interests to be protected" by § 109. Under our precedents, it is irrelevant that in enacting the FCUA, Congress did not specifically intend to protect commercial banks. Although it is clear that respondents' objectives in this action are not eleemosynary in nature, under our prior cases that, too, is beside the point.

■ JUSTICE O'CONNOR, with whom JUSTICE STEVENS, JUSTICE SOUTER, and JUSTICE BREYER join, dissenting.

In determining that respondents have standing under the zone-of-interests test to challenge the National Credit Union Administration's (NCUA's) interpretation of the "common bond" provision of the Federal Credit Union Act (FCUA), 12 U.S.C. § 1759, the Court applies the test in a manner that is contrary to our decisions and, more importantly, that all but eviscerates the zone-of-interests requirement. In my view, under a proper conception of the inquiry, "the interest sought to be protected by" respondents in this action is not "arguably within the zone of interests to be protected" by the common bond provision. *Association of Data Processing Service Organizations, Inc. v. Camp*, 397 U.S. 150, 153 (1970). Accordingly, I respectfully dissent.

* * *

[R]espondents must establish that the injury they assert is "within the meaning of a relevant statute," *i.e.*, satisfies the zone-of-interests test. *Air Courier Conference v. Postal Workers*, 498 U.S. 517, 52 (1991); *Lujan v. National Wildlife Federation*, 497 U.S. 871, 883, 886 (1990). Specifically, "the plaintiff must establish that the injury he complains of (*his* aggrievement, or the adverse effect *upon him*), falls within the 'zone of interests' sought to be protected by the statutory provision whose violation forms the legal basis for his complaint." *National Wildlife Federation, supra*, at 883; see also *Air Courier, supra*, at 523–524.

The "injury respondents complain of," as the Court explains, is that the NCUA's interpretation of the common bond provision "allows persons who might otherwise be their customers to be . . . customers" of petitioner AT&T Family Federal Credit Union. Put another way, the injury is a loss of respondents' customer base to a competing entity, or more generally, an injury to respondents' commercial interest as a competitor. The relevant question under the zone-of-interests test, then, is whether injury to respondents' commercial interest as a competitor "falls within the zone of interests sought to be protected by the [common bond] provision." *E.g., Air Courier, supra*, at 523–524. For instance, in *Data Processing*, where the plaintiffs—like respondents here—alleged competitive injury to their commercial interest, we found that the plaintiffs had standing because "their commercial interest was sought to be protected by the . . . provision which they alleged had been violated." *Bennett v. Spear*, 520 U.S. 154, 176 (1997) (discussing *Data Processing*).

The Court adopts a quite different approach to the zone-of-interests test today, eschewing any assessment of whether the common bond provision was intended to protect respondents' commercial interest. The Court begins by observing that the terms of the common bond provision—"[f]ederal credit union membership shall be limited to groups having a common bond of occupation or association, or to groups within a well-defined neighborhood, community, or rural district," 12 U.S.C. § 1759—expressly limit membership in federal credit unions to persons belonging to certain "groups." Then, citing other statutory provisions that bar federal credit unions from serving nonmembers, see §§ 1757(5)–(6), the Court reasons that one interest sought to be protected by the common bond provision "is an interest in limiting the markets that federal credit unions can serve." The Court concludes its analysis by observing simply that respondents, "[a]s competitors of federal credit unions, . . . certainly *have* [that] interest . . . , and the NCUA's interpretation has affected that interest."

Under the Court's approach, every litigant who establishes injury in fact under Article III will automatically satisfy the zone-of-interests requirement, rendering the zone-of-interests test ineffectual. See *Air Courier, supra,* at 524 ("mistak[e]" to "conflat[e] the zone-of-interests test with injury in fact"). That result stems from the Court's articulation of the relevant "interest." In stating that the common bond provision protects an "interest in limiting the markets that federal credit unions can serve," the Court presumably uses the term "markets" in the sense of *customer* markets, as opposed to, for instance, product markets: The common bond requirement and the provisions prohibiting credit unions from serving nonmembers combine to limit the customers a credit union can serve, not the services a credit union can offer.

With that understanding, the Court's conclusion that respondents "have" an interest in "limiting the [customer] markets that federal credit unions can serve" means little more than that respondents "have" an interest in enforcing the statute. The common bond requirement limits a credit union's membership, and hence its customer base, to certain groups, 12 U.S.C. § 1759, and in the Court's view, it is enough to establish standing that respondents "have" an interest in limiting the customers a credit union can serve. The Court's additional observation that respondents' interest has been "affected" by the NCUA's interpretation adds little to the analysis; agency interpretation of a statutory restriction will of course affect a party who has an interest in the restriction. Indeed, a party presumably will bring suit to vindicate an interest only if the interest has been affected by the challenged action. The crux of the Court's zone-of-interests inquiry, then, is simply that the plaintiff must "have" an interest in enforcing the pertinent statute.

A party, however, will invariably have an interest in enforcing a statute when he can establish injury in fact caused by an alleged violation of that statute. An example we used in *National Wildlife Federation* illustrates the point. There, we hypothesized a situation involving "the failure of an agency to comply with a statutory provision requiring 'on the record' hearings." 497 U.S., at 883. That circumstance "would assuredly have an adverse effect upon the company that has the contract to record and transcribe the agency's proceedings," and so the company would establish injury in fact. *Ibid.* But the company would not satisfy the zone-of-interests test, because "the provision was obviously enacted to protect the interests of the parties to the proceedings and not those of the reporters." *Ibid.;* see *Air Courier,* 498 U.S., at 524. Under the Court's approach today, however, the reporting company would have standing under the zone-of-interests test: Because the company is injured by the failure to comply with the requirement of on-the-record hearings, the company would certainly "have" an interest in enforcing the statute.

Our decision in *Air Courier,* likewise, cannot be squared with the Court's analysis in this action. *Air Courier* involved a challenge by postal employees to a decision of the Postal Service suspending its statutory monopoly over certain international mailing services. The postal employees alleged a violation of the Private Express Statutes (PES)—the provisions that codify the Service's postal monopoly—citing as their injury in fact that competition from private mailing companies adversely affected their employment opportunities. 498 U.S., at 524. We concluded that the postal employees did not have standing under the zone-of-interests test, because "the PES were not designed to protect postal employment or further postal job opportunities." *Id.,* at 528. As with the example from *National Wildlife Federation,* though, the postal employees would have established standing under the Court's analysis in this action: The employees surely "had" an interest in enforcing the statutory monopoly, given that suspension of the monopoly caused injury to their employment opportunities.

In short, requiring simply that a litigant "have" an interest in enforcing the relevant statute amounts to hardly any test at all. That is why our decisions have required instead that a party "establish that the *injury he complains* of . . . falls within the 'zone of interests' sought to be protected by the statutory provision" in question. *National Wildlife Federation, supra,* at 883 (emphasis added); see *Bennett,* 520 U.S., at 176. In *Air Courier,* for instance, after noting that the asserted injury in fact was "an adverse effect on employment opportunities of postal workers," we characterized "[t]he question before us" as "whether the adverse effect on the employment opportunities of postal workers . . . is within the zone of interests encompassed by the PES." 498 U.S., at 524.

* * *

The same approach should lead the Court to ask in this action whether respondents' injury to their commercial interest as competitors falls within the zone of interests protected by the common bond provision. Respondents recognize that such an inquiry is mandated by our decisions. They argue that "the competitive interests of banks *were* among Congress's concerns when it enacted the Federal Credit Union Act," and that the common bond provision was motivated by "[c]ongressional concerns that chartering credit unions could inflict an unwanted competitive injury on the commercial banking industry." The Court instead asks simply whether respondents have an interest in enforcing the common bond provision, an approach tantamount to abolishing the zone-of-interests requirement altogether.

Contrary to the Court's suggestion, its application of the zone-of-interests test in this action is not in concert with the approach we followed in a series of cases in which the plaintiffs, like respondents here, alleged that agency interpretation of a statute caused competitive injury to their commercial interests. In each of those cases, we focused * * * on whether competitive injury to the plaintiff's commercial interest fell within the zone of interests protected by the relevant statute.

* * *

It is true, as the Court emphasizes repeatedly, that we did not require in this line of decisions that the statute at issue was designed to benefit the particular party bringing suit. See *Clarke, supra,* at 399–400. * * *

In each of the competitor standing cases, though, we found that Congress had enacted an "anti-competition limitation," see *Bennett,* 520 U.S., at 176 (discussing *Data Processing*), or, alternatively, that Congress had "legislated against . . . competition," see *Clarke, supra,* at 403; *ICI, supra,* at 620–621, and accordingly, that the plaintiff-competitor's "commercial interest was sought to be protected by the anti-competition limitation" at issue, *Bennett, supra,* at 176. We determined, in other words, that "the injury [the plaintiff] complain[ed] of . . . [fell] within the zone of interests sought to be protected by the [relevant] statutory provision." *National Wildlife Federation,* 497 U.S., at 883. The Court fails to undertake that analysis here.

Applying the proper zone-of-interests inquiry to this action, I would find that competitive injury to respondents' commercial interests does not arguably fall within the zone of interests sought to be protected by the common bond provision. The terms of the statute do not suggest a concern with protecting the business interests of competitors. The common bond provision limits "[f]ederal credit union membership . . . to groups having a common bond of occupation or association, or to groups within a well-defined neighborhood, community, or rural district." 12 U.S.C. § 1759. And the provision is framed as an exception to the preceding clause, which confers membership on "incorporators and such other persons and incorporated and unincorporated organizations . . . as may be elected . . . and as such shall each, subscribe to at least one share of its stock and pay the initial installment thereon and a uniform entrance fee." *Ibid.* The language suggests that the common bond requirement is an internal organizational principle concerned primarily with defining membership in a way that secures a financially sound organization. There is no indication in the text of the provision or in the surrounding language that the membership limitation was even arguably designed to protect the commercial interests of competitors.

Nor is there any nontextual indication to that effect. Significantly, the operation of the common bond provision is much different from the statutes at issue in *Clarke, ICI,* and *Data Processing.* Those statutes evinced a congressional intent to legislate against competition, *e.g., Clarke, supra,* at 403, because they imposed direct restrictions on banks generally, specifically barring their entry into certain markets. In *Data Processing* and *ICI,* "the question was what activities banks could engage in at all," and in *Clarke,* "the question [was] what activities banks [could] engage in without regard to the limitations imposed by state branching law." 479 U.S., at 403.

The operation of the common bond provision does not likewise denote a congressional desire to legislate against competition. First, the common bond requirement does not purport to restrict credit unions from becoming large, nationwide organizations, as might be expected if the provision embodied a congressional concern with the competitive consequences of credit union growth.

More tellingly, although the common bond provision applies to all credit unions, the restriction operates against credit unions individually: The common bond requirement speaks only to whether a *particular* credit union's membership can include a given group of customers, not to whether credit unions *in general* can serve that group. Even if a group of would-be customers does not share the requisite bond with a particular credit union, nothing in the common bond provision prevents that same group from joining a different credit union that is within the same "neighborhood, community, or rural district" or with whose members the group shares an adequate "occupation[al] or association[al]" connection. 12 U.S.C. § 1759. Also, the group could conceivably form its own credit union. In this sense, the common bond requirement does not limit credit unions collectively from serving any customers, nor does it bar any customers from being served by credit unions.

* * *

The circumstances surrounding the enactment of the FCUA also indicate that Congress did not intend to legislate against competition through the common bond provision. As the Court explains, the FCUA was enacted in the shadow of the Great Depression; Congress thought that the ability of credit unions to "come through the depression without failures, when banks have failed so notably, is a tribute to the worth of cooperative credit and indicates clearly the great potential value of rapid national credit union extension." S. Rep. No. 555, 73d Cong., 2d Sess., 3–4 (1934). Credit unions were believed to enable the general public, which had been largely ignored by banks, to obtain credit at reasonable rates. See *id.*, at 2–3; *First Nat'l Bank & Trust Co. v. National Credit Union Administration*, 988 F.2d 1272, 1274 (C.A.D.C.), cert. denied, 510 U.S. 907 (1993). The common bond requirement "was seen as the cement that united credit union members in a cooperative venture, and was, therefore, thought important to credit unions' continued success." 988 F.2d, at 1276. "Congress assumed implicitly that a common bond amongst members would ensure both that those making lending decisions would know more about applicants and that borrowers would be more reluctant to default." *Ibid.*; A. Burger & T. Dacin, Field of Membership: An Evolving Concept 7–8 (2d ed. 1992).

The requirement of a common bond was thus meant to ensure that each credit union remains a cooperative institution that is economically stable and responsive to its members' needs. See 988 F.2d, at 1276. As a principle of internal governance designed to secure the viability of individual credit unions in the interests of the membership, the common bond provision was in no way designed to impose a restriction on all credit unions in the interests of institutions that might one day become competitors. "Indeed, the very notion seems anomalous, because

Congress' general purpose was to encourage the proliferation of credit unions, which were expected to provide service to those would-be customers that banks disdained." *Id.,* at 1275.

That the common bond requirement would later come to be viewed by competitors as a useful tool for curbing a credit union's membership should not affect the zone-of-interests inquiry. The pertinent question under the zone-of-interests test is whether Congress *intended* to protect certain interests through a particular provision, not whether, irrespective of congressional intent, a provision may have the *effect* of protecting those interests. See *Clarke,* 479 U.S., at 394 (the "matter [is] basically one of interpreting congressional intent"). Otherwise, competitors could bring suits challenging the interpretation of a host of provisions in the FCUA that might have the unintended effect of furthering their competitive interest, such as restrictions on the loans credit unions can make or on the sums credit unions can borrow. See 12 U.S.C. §§ 1757(5), (6).

In this light, I read our decisions as establishing that there must at least be *some* indication in the statute, beyond the mere fact that its enforcement has the effect of incidentally benefiting the plaintiff, from which one can draw an inference that the plaintiff's injury arguably falls within the zone of interests sought to be protected by that statute. The provisions we construed in *Clarke, ICI,* and *Data Processing* allowed such an inference: Where Congress legislates against competition, one can properly infer that the statute is at least arguably intended to protect competitors from injury to their commercial interest, even if that is not the statute's principal objective. See *Bennett,* 520 U.S., at 176–177 (indicating that zone-of-interests test is satisfied if one of several statutory objectives corresponds with the interest sought to be protected by the plaintiff). Accordingly, "[t]here [was] sound reason to infer" in those cases "that Congress intended [the] class [of plaintiffs] to be relied upon to challenge agency disregard of the law." *Clarke, supra,* at 403 (internal quotation marks omitted).

The same cannot be said of respondents in this action, because neither the terms of the common bond provision, nor the way in which the provision operates, nor the circumstances surrounding its enactment, evince a congressional desire to legislate against competition. This, then, is an action "the plaintiff's interests are so marginally related to or inconsistent with the purposes implicit in the statute that it cannot reasonably be assumed that Congress intended to permit the suit." 479 U.S., at 399. The zone-of-interests test "seeks to exclude those plaintiffs whose suits are more likely to frustrate than to further statutory objectives," *id.,* at 397, n. 12, and one can readily envision circumstances in which the interests of competitors, who have the incentive to suppress credit union expansion in all circumstances, would be at odds with the statute's general aim of supporting the growth of credit unions that are cohesive and hence financially stable.

* * *

Prudential standing principles "are 'founded in concern about the proper—and properly limited—role of the courts in a democratic society.'" *Bennett, supra,* at 162 (quoting *Warth v. Seldin,* 422 U.S. 490, 498 (1975)). The zone-of-interests test is an integral part of the prudential standing inquiry, and we ought to apply the test in a way that gives it content. The analysis the Court undertakes today, in my view, leaves the zone-of-interests requirement a hollow one. As with the example in *National Wildlife Federation,* where the reporting company suffered injury from the alleged statutory violation, but the injury to the company's commercial interest was not within the zone of interests protected by the statute, here, too, respondents suffer injury from the NCUA's interpretation of the common bond requirement, but the injury to their commercial interest is not within the zone of interests protected by the provision. Applying the zone-of-interests inquiry as it has been articulated in our decisions, I conclude that respondents have failed to establish standing. I would therefore vacate the judgment of the Court of Appeals and remand the action with instructions that it be dismissed.

NOTES AND QUESTIONS

1. Statutory standing doctrine presumes that Congress can deny standing via statute in cases where the Constitution's Article III otherwise would allow a plaintiff's claim to proceed. Yet, in explaining the statute-focused zone of interests test, the Court in *Nat'l Credit Union* de-emphasized congressional intent to protect a particular class of plaintiffs with a statute in favor of a judicial assessment of "the interests 'arguably . . . to be protected' by the statutory provision at issue." The latter approach arguably allows courts to hear more cases, but is it consistent with a premise of Congress imposing limits on judicial review?

2. Congress is free to impose statutory standing limitations on judicial review of agency action. Yet, most cases in which the courts apply the zone of interests test involve statutes that are facially silent regarding the standing question. In some sense, therefore, the *Nat'l Credit Union* majority's de-emphasis on congressional intent in the zone-of-interests context operates similarly to a clear statement rule. Congress may constrain judicial review beyond the requirements of Article III if it wants to do so. But in the absence of a clear statement to that effect, if the plaintiff's claim bears some reasonable relationship to the subject matter of the statute giving rise to the claim, then the Court is disinclined to infer congressional intent to limit plaintiff standing.

3. Justice O'Connor's dissenting opinion complained that the *Nat'l Credit Union* majority "all but eviscerates the zone of interests requirement." In other words, according to the dissent, any plaintiff able to satisfy the Article III injury in fact requirement will also have standing under the zone of interests test. Is Justice O'Connor's characterization of the majority's approach accurate? Why or why not?

The sharp disagreement among the Justices in *Nat'l Credit Union* is emblematic of past cases regarding the nature and scope of statutory standing and the zone of interests test. With the Court's most recent consideration of statutory standing and the zone of interests test, that disagreement seems to have faded.

Match-E-Be-Nash-She-Wish Band of Pottawatomi Indians v. Patchak

132 S. Ct. 2199 (2012).

■ JUSTICE KAGAN delivered the opinion of the Court.

A provision of the Indian Reorganization Act (IRA), 25 U.S.C. § 465, authorizes the Secretary of the Interior (Secretary) to acquire property "for the purpose of providing land for Indians." Ch. 576, § 5, 48 Stat. 985. The Secretary here acquired land in trust for an Indian tribe seeking to open a casino. Respondent David Patchak lives near that land and challenges the Secretary's decision in a suit brought under the Administrative Procedure Act (APA), 5 U.S.C. § 701 *et seq.* Patchak claims that the Secretary lacked authority under § 465 to take title to the land, and alleges economic, environmental, and aesthetic harms from the casino's operation.

We consider two questions arising from Patchak's action. * * * The second is whether Patchak has prudential standing to challenge the Secretary's acquisition. We think he does. We therefore hold that Patchak's suit may proceed.

I

The Match-E-Be-Nash-She-Wish Band of Pottawatomi Indians (Band) is an Indian tribe residing in rural Michigan. Although the Band has a long history, the Department of the Interior (DOI) formally recognized it only in 1999. See 63 Fed. Reg. 56936 (1998). Two years later, the Band petitioned the Secretary to exercise her authority under § 465 by taking into trust a tract of land in Wayland Township, Michigan, known as the Bradley Property. The Band's application explained that the Band would use the property "for gaming purposes," with the goal of generating the "revenue necessary to promote tribal economic development, self-sufficiency and a strong tribal government capable of providing its members with sorely needed social and educational programs."[1]

In 2005, after a lengthy administrative review, the Secretary announced her decision to acquire the Bradley Property in trust for the Band. See 70 Fed. Reg. 25596. In accordance with applicable regulations, the Secretary committed to wait 30 days before taking action, so that interested parties could seek judicial review. See *ibid.*; 25 C.F.R. § 151.12(b) (2011). * * *

* * * Patchak filed this suit under the APA * * *. He asserted that § 465 did not authorize the Secretary to acquire property for the Band because it was not a federally recognized tribe when the IRA was enacted in 1934. To establish his standing to bring suit, Patchak contended that he lived "in close proximity to" the Bradley Property and that a casino there would "destroy the lifestyle he has enjoyed" by causing "increased traffic," "increased crime," "decreased property values," "an irreversible change in the rural character of the area," and

---

[1] Under the Indian Gaming Regulatory Act, 25 U.S.C. §§ 2701–2721, an Indian tribe may conduct gaming operations on "Indian lands," § 2710, which include lands "held in trust by the United States for the benefit of any Indian tribe," § 2703(4)(B). The application thus requested the Secretary to take the action necessary for the Band to open a casino.

"other aesthetic, socioeconomic, and environmental problems." Notably, Patchak did not assert any claim of his own to the Bradley Property.

* * *

This Court has long held that a person suing under the APA must satisfy not only Article III's standing requirements, but an additional test: The interest he asserts must be "arguably within the zone of interests to be protected or regulated by the statute" that he says was violated. *Association of Data Processing Service Organizations, Inc. v. Camp,* 397 U.S. 150, 153 (1970). Here, Patchak asserts that in taking title to the Bradley Property, the Secretary exceeded her authority under § 465, which authorizes the acquisition of property "for the purpose of providing land for Indians." And he alleges that this statutory violation will cause him economic, environmental, and aesthetic harm as a nearby property owner. The Government and Band argue that the relationship between § 465 and Patchak's asserted interests is insufficient. That is so, they contend, because the statute focuses on land *acquisition,* whereas Patchak's interests relate to the land's *use* as a casino. We find this argument unpersuasive.

The prudential standing test Patchak must meet "is not meant to be especially demanding." *Clarke v. Securities Industry Assn.,* 479 U.S. 388, 399 (1987). We apply the test in keeping with Congress's "evident intent" when enacting the APA "to make agency action presumptively reviewable." *Ibid.* We do not require any "indication of congressional purpose to benefit the would-be plaintiff." *Id.,* at 399–400.[7] And we have always conspicuously included the word "arguably" in the test to indicate that the benefit of any doubt goes to the plaintiff. The test forecloses suit only when a plaintiff's "interests are so marginally related to or inconsistent with the purposes implicit in the statute that it cannot reasonably be assumed that Congress intended to permit the suit." *Id.,* at 399.

Patchak's suit satisfies that standard, because § 465 has far more to do with land use than the Government and Band acknowledge. Start with what we and others have said about § 465's context and purpose. As the leading treatise on federal Indian law notes, § 465 is "the capstone" of the IRA's land provisions. F. Cohen, Handbook of Federal Indian Law § 15.07[1][a], p. 1010 (2005 ed.) (hereinafter Cohen). And those provisions play a key role in the IRA's overall effort "to rehabilitate the Indian's economic life," *Mescalero Apache Tribe v. Jones,* 411 U.S. 145, 152 (1973) (internal quotation marks omitted). "Land forms the basis" of that "economic life," providing the foundation for "tourism, manufacturing, mining, logging, . . . and gaming." Cohen § 15.01, at 965. Section 465 thus functions as a primary mechanism to foster Indian tribes' economic development. * * * So when the Secretary obtains land for Indians under § 465, she does not do so in a vacuum. Rather, she takes title to properties with at least one eye directed

---

[7]   For this reason, the Band's statement that Patchak is "not an Indian or tribal official seeking land" and does not "claim an interest in advancing tribal development" is beside the point. The question is not whether § 465 seeks to benefit Patchak; everyone can agree it does not. The question is instead, as the Band's and the Government's main argument acknowledges, whether issues of land use (arguably) fall within § 465's scope—because if they do, a neighbor complaining about such use may sue to enforce the statute's limits.

toward how tribes will use those lands to support economic development.

The Department's regulations make this statutory concern with land use crystal clear. Those regulations permit the Secretary to acquire land in trust under § 465 if the "land is necessary to facilitate tribal self-determination, economic development, or Indian housing." 25 CFR § 151.3(a)(3). And they require the Secretary to consider, in evaluating any acquisition, both "[t]he purposes for which the land will be used" and the "potential conflicts of land use which may arise." §§ 151.10(c), 151.10(f); see § 151.11(a). For "off-reservation acquisitions" made "for business purposes"—like the Bradley Property—the regulations further provide that the tribe must "provide a plan which specifies the anticipated economic benefits associated with the proposed use." § 151.11(c). DOI's regulations thus show that the statute's implementation centrally depends on the projected use of a given property.

The Secretary's acquisition of the Bradley Property is a case in point. The Band's application to the Secretary highlighted its plan to use the land for gaming purposes. Similarly, DOI's notice of intent to take the land into trust announced that the land would "be used for the purpose of construction and operation of a gaming facility," which the Department had already determined would meet the Indian Gaming Regulatory Act's requirements. 70 Fed. Reg. 25596; 25 U.S.C. §§ 2701–2721. So from start to finish, the decision whether to acquire the Bradley Property under § 465 involved questions of land use.

And because § 465's implementation encompasses these issues, the interests Patchak raises—at least arguably—fall "within the zone . . . protected or regulated by the statute." If the Government had violated a statute specifically addressing how federal land can be used, no one would doubt that a neighboring landowner would have prudential standing to bring suit to enforce the statute's limits. The difference here, as the Government and Band point out, is that § 465 specifically addresses only land acquisition. But for the reasons already given, decisions under the statute are closely enough and often enough entwined with considerations of land use to make that difference immaterial. As in this very case, the Secretary will typically acquire land with its eventual use in mind, after assessing potential conflicts that use might create. See 25 CFR §§ 151.10(c), 151.10(f), 151.11(a). And so neighbors to the use (like Patchak) are reasonable—indeed, predictable—challengers of the Secretary's decisions: Their interests, whether economic, environmental, or aesthetic, come within § 465's regulatory ambit.

■ [The dissenting opinion of JUSTICE SOTOMAYOR addressed a different issue and is omitted. Ed.]

NOTES AND QUESTIONS

In describing the zone of interests test, the Court in *Match-E-Be-Nash-She-Wish Band* continues the de-emphasis on congressional intent observed in the majority opinion in *Nat'l Credit Union Admin. v. First Nat'l Bank & Trust Co.*, 522 U.S. 479 (1991). Here, however, the Court linked a permissive approach toward the zone of interests test with the APA's general presumption in favor of judicial review of agency action. Can you explain how the two policies might be related to one another?

APPENDIX A

THE CONSTITUTION OF THE UNITED STATES

PREAMBLE

We the People of the United States, in Order to form a more perfect Union, establish Justice, insure domestic Tranquility, provide for the common defence, promote the general Welfare, and secure the Blessings of Liberty to ourselves and our Posterity, do ordain and establish this Constitution for the United States of America.

ARTICLE I

Section 1. All legislative Powers herein granted shall be vested in a Congress of the United States, which shall consist of a Senate and House of Representatives.

Section 2. The House of Representatives shall be composed of Members chosen every second Year by the People of the several States, and the Electors in each State shall have the Qualifications requisite for Electors of the most numerous Branch of the State Legislature.

No Person shall be a Representative who shall not have attained to the age of twenty five Years, and been seven Years a Citizen of the United States, and who shall not, when elected, be an Inhabitant of that State in which he shall be chosen.

Representatives and direct Taxes shall be apportioned among the several States which may be included within this Union, according to their respective Numbers, which shall be determined by adding to the whole Number of free Persons, including those bound to Service for a Term of Years, and excluding Indians not taxed, three fifths of all other Persons. The actual Enumeration shall be made within three Years after the first Meeting of the Congress of the United States, and within every subsequent Term of ten Years, in such Manner as they shall by Law direct. The Number of Representatives shall not exceed one for every thirty Thousand, but each State shall have at Least one Representative; and until such enumeration shall be made, the State of New Hampshire shall be entitled to chuse three, Massachusetts eight, Rhode-Island and Providence Plantations one, Connecticut five, New-York six, New Jersey four, Pennsylvania eight, Delaware one, Maryland six, Virginia ten, North Carolina five, South Carolina five, and Georgia three.

When vacancies happen in the Representation from any State, the Executive Authority thereof shall issue Writs of Election to fill such Vacancies.

The House of Representatives shall chuse their Speaker and other Officers; and shall have the sole Power of Impeachment.

Section 3. The Senate of the United States shall be composed of two Senators from each State, chosen by the Legislature thereof, for six Years; and each Senator shall have one Vote.

Immediately after they shall be assembled in Consequence of the first Election, they shall be divided as equally as may be into three Classes. The Seats of the Senators of the first Class shall be vacated at the Expiration of the second Year, of the second Class at the Expiration of the fourth Year, and of the third Class at the Expiration of the sixth Year, so that one third may be chosen every second Year; and if Vacancies happen by Resignation, or otherwise, during the Recess of the Legislature of any State, the Executive thereof may make temporary Appointments until the next Meeting of the Legislature, which shall then fill such Vacancies.

No Person shall be a Senator who shall not have attained to the Age of thirty Years, and been nine Years a Citizen of the United States, and who shall not, when elected, be an Inhabitant of that State for which he shall be chosen.

The Vice President of the United States shall be President of the Senate but shall have no Vote, unless they be equally divided.

The Senate shall chuse their other Officers, and also a President pro tempore, in the Absence of the Vice President, or when he shall exercise the Office of President of the United States.

The Senate shall have the sole Power to try all Impeachments. When sitting for that Purpose, they shall be on Oath or Affirmation. When the President of the United States is tried the Chief Justice shall preside: And no Person shall be convicted without the Concurrence of two thirds of the Members present.

Judgment in Cases of Impeachment shall not extend further than to removal from Office, and disqualification to hold and enjoy any Office of honor, Trust or Profit under the United States: but the Party convicted shall nevertheless be liable and subject to Indictment, Trial, Judgment and Punishment, according to Law.

Section 4. The Times, Places and Manner of holding Elections for Senators and Representatives, shall be prescribed in each State by the Legislature thereof; but the Congress may at any time by Law make or alter such Regulations, except as to the Places of chusing Senators.

The Congress shall assemble at least once in every Year, and such Meeting shall be on the first Monday in December, unless they shall by Law appoint a different Day.

Section 5. Each House shall be the Judge of the Elections, Returns and Qualifications of its own Members, and a Majority of each shall constitute a Quorum to do Business; but a smaller Number may adjourn from day to day, and may be authorized to compel the Attendance of absent Members, in such Manner, and under such Penalties as each House may provide.

Each House may determine the Rules of its Proceedings, punish its Members for disorderly Behaviour, and, with the Concurrence of two thirds, expel a Member.

Each House shall keep a Journal of its Proceedings, and from time to time publish the same, excepting such Parts as may in their Judgment require Secrecy; and the Yeas and Nays of the Members of either House on any question shall, at the Desire of one fifth of those Present, be entered on the Journal.

Neither House, during the Session of Congress, shall, without the Consent of the other, adjourn for more than three days, nor to any other Place than that in which the two Houses shall be sitting.

Section 6. The Senators and Representatives shall receive a Compensation for their Services, to be ascertained by Law, and paid out of the Treasury of the United States. They shall in all Cases, except Treason, Felony and Breach of the Peace, be privileged from Arrest during their Attendance at the Session of their respective Houses, and in going to and returning from the same; and for any Speech or Debate in either House, they shall not be questioned in any other Place.

No Senator or Representative shall, during the Time for which he was elected, be appointed to any civil Office under the Authority of the United States, which shall have been created, or the Emoluments whereof shall have been increased during such time; and no Person holding any Office under the United States, shall be a Member of either House during his Continuance in Office.

Section 7. All Bills for raising Revenue shall originate in the House of Representatives; but the Senate may propose or concur with amendments as on other Bills.

Every Bill which shall have passed the House of Representatives and the Senate, shall, before it become a law, be presented to the President of the United States: If he approve he shall sign it, but if not he shall return it, with his Objections to that House in which it shall have originated, who shall enter the Objections at large on their Journal, and proceed to reconsider it. If after such Reconsideration two thirds of that House shall agree to pass the Bill, it shall be sent, together with the Objections, to the other House, by which it shall likewise be reconsidered, and if approved by two thirds of that House, it shall become a Law. But in all such Cases the Votes of both Houses shall be determined by Yeas and Nays, and the Names of the Persons voting for and against the Bill shall be entered on the Journal of each House respectively. If any Bill shall not be returned by the President within ten Days (Sundays excepted) after it shall have been presented to him, the Same shall be a Law, in like Manner as if he had signed it, unless the Congress by their Adjournment prevent its Return, in which Case it shall not be a Law.

Every Order, Resolution, or Vote to which the Concurrence of the Senate and House of Representatives may be necessary (except on a question of Adjournment) shall be presented to the President of the United States; and before the Same shall take Effect, shall be approved by him, or being disapproved by him, shall be repassed by two thirds of the Senate and House of Representatives, according to the Rules and Limitations prescribed in the Case of a Bill.

Section 8. The Congress shall have Power To lay and collect Taxes, Duties, Imposts and Excises, to pay the Debts and provide for the common Defence and general Welfare of the United States; but all Duties, Imposts and Excises shall be uniform throughout the United States;

To borrow Money on the credit of the United States;

To regulate Commerce with foreign Nations, and among the several States, and with the Indian Tribes;

To establish an uniform Rule of Naturalization, and uniform Laws on the subject of Bankruptcies throughout the United States;

To coin Money, regulate the Value thereof, and of foreign Coin, and fix the Standard of Weights and Measures;

To provide for the Punishment of counterfeiting the Securities and current Coin of the United States;

To establish Post Offices and post Roads;

To promote the Progress of Science and useful Arts, by securing for limited Times to Authors and Inventors the exclusive Right to their respective Writings and Discoveries;

To constitute Tribunals inferior to the supreme Court;

To define and punish Piracies and Felonies committed on the high Seas, and Offences against the Law of Nations;

To declare War, grant Letters of Marque and Reprisal, and make Rules concerning Captures on Land and Water;

To raise and support Armies, but no Appropriation of Money to that Use shall be for a longer Term than two Years;

To provide and maintain a Navy;

To make Rules for the Government and Regulation of the land and naval Forces;

To provide for calling forth the Militia to execute the Laws of the Union, suppress Insurrections and repeal Invasions;

To provide for organizing, arming, and disciplining, the Militia, and for governing such Part of them as may be employed in the Service of the United States, reserving to the States respectively, the Appointment of the Officers, and the Authority of training the Militia according to the discipline prescribed by Congress;

To exercise exclusive Legislation in all Cases whatsoever, over such District (not exceeding ten Miles square) as may, by Cession of Particular States, and the Acceptance of Congress, become the Seat of the Government of the United States, and to exercise like Authority over all Places purchased by the Consent of the Legislature of the State in which the Same shall be, for the Erection of Forts, Magazines, Arsenals, dock-Yards and other needful Buildings;—And

To make all Laws which shall be necessary and proper for carrying into Execution the foregoing Powers and all other Powers vested by this Constitution in the Government of the United States, or in any Department or Officer thereof.

Section 9. The Migration or Importation of such Persons as any of the States now existing shall think proper to admit, shall not be prohibited by the Congress prior to the Year one thousand eight hundred and eight, but a Tax or duty may be imposed on such Importation, not exceeding ten dollars for each Person.

The Privilege of the Writ of Habeas Corpus shall not be suspended, unless when in Cases or Rebellion or Invasion the public Safety may require it.

No Bill of Attainder or ex post facto Law shall be passed.

No Capitation, or other direct, Tax shall be laid, unless in Proportion to the Census of Enumeration herein before directed to be taken.

No Tax or Duty shall be laid on Articles exported from any State.

No Preference shall be given by any Regulation of Commerce or Revenue to the Ports of one State over those of another: nor shall Vessels bound to, or from, one State, be obliged to enter, clear or pay Duties in another.

No Money shall be drawn from the Treasury, but in Consequence of Appropriations made by Law; and a regular Statement and Account of the Receipts and Expenditures of all public Money shall be published from time to time.

No Title of Nobility shall be granted by the United States: And no Person holding any Office of Profit or Trust under them, shall, without the Consent of the Congress, accept of any present, Emolument, Office, or Title, of any kind whatever, from any King, Prince or foreign State.

Section 10. No State shall enter into any Treaty, Alliance, or Confederation; grant Letters of Marque and Reprisal; coin Money; emit Bills of Credit; make any Thing but gold and silver Coin a Tender in Payment of Debts; pass any Bill of Attainder, ex post facto Law, or Law impairing the Obligation of Contracts, or grant any Title of Nobility.

No State shall, without the Consent of the Congress, lay any Imposts or Duties on Imports or Exports, except what may be absolutely necessary for executing it's inspection Laws: and the net Produce of all Duties and Imposts, laid by any State on Imports or Exports, shall be for the Use of the Treasury of the United States; and all such Laws shall be subject to the Revision and Controul of the Congress.

No State shall, without the Consent of Congress, lay any Duty of Tonnage, keep Troops, or Ships of War in time of Peace, enter into any Agreement or Compact with another State, or with a foreign Power, or engage in War, unless actually invaded, or in such imminent Danger as will not admit of delay.

ARTICLE II

Section 1. The executive Power shall be vested in a President of the United States of America. He shall hold his Office during the Term of four Years, and, together with the Vice President, chosen for the same Term, be elected, as follows:

Each State shall appoint, in such Manner as the Legislature thereof may direct, a Number of Electors, equal to the whole Number of Senators and Representatives to which the State may be entitled in the Congress: but no Senator or Representative, or Person holding an Office of Trust or Profit under the United States, shall be appointed an Elector.

The Electors shall meet in their respective States, and vote by Ballot for two Persons, of whom one at least shall not be an Inhabitant of the same State with themselves. And they shall make a List of all the Persons voted for, and of the Number of Votes for each; which List they shall sign and certify, and transmit sealed to the Seat of the Government of the United States, directed to the President of the

Senate. The President of the Senate shall, in the Presence of the Senate and House of Representatives, open all the Certificates, and the Votes shall then be counted. The Person having the greatest Number of Votes shall be the President, if such Number be a Majority of the whole Number of Electors appointed; and if there be more than one who have such Majority, and have an equal Number of Votes, then the House of Representatives shall immediately chuse by Ballot one of them for President; and if no Person have a Majority, then from the five highest on the List the said House shall in like Manner chuse the President. But in chusing the President, the Votes shall be taken by States, the Representatives from each State having one Vote; a quorum for this Purpose shall consist of a Member or Members from two thirds of the States, and a Majority of all the States shall be necessary to a Choice. In every Case, after the Choice of the President, the Person having the greatest Number of Votes of the Electors shall be the Vice President. But if there should remain two or more who have equal Votes, the Senate shall chuse from them by Ballot the Vice President.

The Congress may determine the Time of chusing the Electors, and the Day on which they shall give their Votes; which Day shall be the same throughout the United States.

No Person except a natural born Citizen, or a Citizen of the United States, at the time of the Adoption of this Constitution, shall be eligible to the Office of President; neither shall any person be eligible to that Office who shall not have attained to the Age of thirty five Years, and been fourteen Years a Resident within the United States.

In Case of the Removal of the President from Office, or of his Death, Resignation, or Inability to discharge the Powers and Duties of the said Office, the Same shall devolve on the Vice President, and the Congress may by Law provide for the Case of Removal, Death, Resignation or Inability, both of the President and Vice President, declaring what Officer shall then act as President, and such Officer shall act accordingly, until the Disability be removed, or a President shall be elected.

The President shall, at stated Times, receive for his Services, a Compensation, which shall neither be increased nor diminished during the Period for which he shall have been elected, and he shall not receive within that Period any other Emolument from the United States, or any of them.

Before he enter on the Execution of his Office, he shall take the following Oath or Affirmation:—"I do solemnly swear (or affirm) that I will faithfully execute the Office of President of the United States, and will to the best of my Ability, preserve, protect and defend the Constitution of the United States."

Section 2. The President shall be Commander in Chief of the Army and Navy of the United States, and of the Militia of the several States, when called into the actual Service of the United States; he may require the Opinion, in writing, of the principal Officer in each of the executive Departments, upon any Subject relating to the Duties of their respective Offices, and he shall have Power to Grant Reprieves and Pardons for Offences against the United States, except in Cases of Impeachment.

He shall have Power, by and with the Advice and Consent of the Senate, to make Treaties, provided two thirds of the Senators present concur; and he shall nominate, and by and with the Advice and Consent of the Senate, shall appoint Ambassadors, other public Ministers and Consuls, Judges of the supreme Court, and all other Officers of the United States, whose Appointments are not herein otherwise provided for, and which shall be established by Law: but the Congress may by Law vest the Appointment of such inferior Officers, as they think proper, in the President alone, in the Courts of Law, or in the Heads of Departments.

The President shall have Power to fill up all Vacancies that may happen during the Recess of the Senate, by granting Commissions which shall expire at the End of their next Session.

Section 3. He shall from time to time give to the Congress Information on the State of the Union, and recommend to their Consideration such Measures as he shall judge necessary and expedient; he may, on extraordinary Occasions, convene both Houses, or either of them, and in Case of Disagreement between them, with Respect to the Time of Adjournment, he may adjourn them to such Time as he shall think proper; he shall receive Ambassadors and other public Ministers; he shall take Care that the Laws be faithfully executed, and shall Commission all the Officers of the United States.

Section 4. The President, Vice President and all Civil Officers of the United States, shall be removed from Office on Impeachment for and Conviction of, Treason, Bribery, or other high Crimes and Misdemeanors.

ARTICLE III

Section 1. The judicial Power of the United States, shall be vested in one supreme Court, and in such inferior Courts as the Congress may from time to time ordain and establish. The Judges, both of the supreme and inferior Courts, shall hold their Offices during good Behaviour, and shall, at stated Times, receive for their Services, a Compensation, which shall not be diminished during their Continuance in Office.

Section 2. The judicial Power shall extend to all Cases, in Law and Equity, arising under this Constitution, the Laws of the United States, and Treaties made, or which shall be made, under their Authority;—to all Cases affecting Ambassadors, other public ministers and Consuls;—to all Cases of admiralty and maritime Jurisdiction;—to Controversies to which the United States shall be a Party;—to Controversies between two or more States;—between a State and Citizens of another State;—between Citizens of different States;—between Citizens of the same State claiming Lands under Grants of different States, and between a State, or the Citizens thereof, and foreign States, Citizens or Subjects.

In all Cases affecting Ambassadors, other public Ministers and Consuls, and those in which a State shall be Party, the supreme Court shall have original Jurisdiction. In all the other Cases before mentioned, the supreme Court shall have appellate Jurisdiction, both as to Law and Fact, with such Exceptions, and under such Regulations as the Congress shall make.

The Trial of all Crimes, except in Cases of Impeachment, shall be by Jury; and such Trial shall be held in the State where the said Crimes shall have been committed; but when not committed within any State, the Trial shall be at such Place or Places as the Congress may by Law have directed.

Section 3. Treason against the United States, shall consist only in levying War against them, or in adhering to their Enemies, giving them Aid and Comfort. No Person shall be convicted of Treason unless on the Testimony of two Witnesses to the same overt Act, or on Confession in open Court.

The Congress shall have Power to declare the Punishment of Treason, but no Attainder of Treason shall work Corruption of Blood, or Forfeiture except during the Life of the Person attainted.

ARTICLE IV

Section 1. Full Faith and Credit shall be given in each State to the public Acts, Records, and judicial Proceedings of every other State. And the Congress may by general Laws prescribe the Manner in which such Acts, Records and Proceedings shall be proved, and the Effect thereof.

Section 2. The Citizens of each State shall be entitled to all Privileges and Immunities of Citizens in the several States.

A Person charged in any State with Treason, Felony, or other Crime, who shall flee from Justice, and be found in another State, shall on Demand of the executive Authority of the State from which he fled, be delivered up, to be removed to the State having Jurisdiction of the Crime.

No Person held to Service or Labour in one State, under the Laws thereof, escaping into another, shall, in Consequence of any Law or Regulation therein, be discharged from such Service or Labour, but shall be delivered up on Claim of the Party to whom such Service or Labour may be due.

Section 3. New States may be admitted by the Congress into this Union; but no new State shall be formed or erected within the Jurisdiction of any other State; nor any State be formed by the Junction of two or more States, or Parts of States, without the Consent of the Legislatures of the States concerned as well as of the Congress.

The Congress shall have Power to dispose of and make all needful Rules and Regulations respecting the Territory or other Property belonging to the United States; and nothing in this Constitution shall be so construed as to Prejudice any Claims of the United States, or of any particular State.

Section 4. The United States shall guarantee to every State in this Union a Republican Form of Government, and shall protect each of them against Invasion; and on Application of the Legislature, or of the Executive (when the Legislature cannot be convened) against domestic Violence.

ARTICLE V

The Congress, whenever two thirds of both Houses shall deem it necessary, shall propose Amendments to this Constitution, or, on the Application of the Legislatures of two thirds of the several States, shall call a Convention for proposing Amendments, which, in either Case, shall be valid to all Intents and Purposes, as Part of this Constitution, when ratified by the Legislatures of three fourths of the several States, or by Conventions in three fourths thereof, as the one or the other Mode of Ratification may be proposed by the Congress; Provided that no Amendment which may be made prior to the Year One thousand eight hundred and eight shall in any Manner affect the first and fourth Clauses in the Ninth Section of the first Article; and that no State, without its Consent, shall be deprived of its equal Suffrage in the Senate.

ARTICLE VI

All Debts contracted and Engagements entered into, before the Adoption of this Constitution, shall be as valid against the United States under this Constitution, as under the Confederation.

This Constitution, and the Laws of the United States which shall be made in Pursuance thereof; and all Treaties made, or which shall be made, under the Authority of the United States, shall be the supreme Law of the Land; and the Judges in every State shall be bound thereby, any Thing in the Constitution or Laws of any state to the Contrary notwithstanding.

The Senators and Representatives before mentioned, and the Members of the several State Legislatures, and all executive and judicial Officers, both of the United States and of the several States, shall be bound by Oath or Affirmation, to support this Constitution; but no religious Test shall ever be required as a Qualification to any Office or public Trust under the United States.

ARTICLE VII

The Ratification of the Conventions of nine States, shall be sufficient for the Establishment of this Constitution between the States so ratifying the same.

AMENDMENT I (1791)

Congress shall make no law respecting an establishment of religion, or prohibiting the free exercise thereof; or abridging the freedom of speech, or of the press; or the right of the people peaceably to assemble, and to petition the Government for a redress of grievances.

AMENDMENT II (1791)

A well regulated Militia, being necessary to the security of a free State, the right of the people to keep and bear Arms, shall not be infringed.

AMENDMENT III (1791)

No Soldier shall, in time of peace be quartered in any house, without the consent of the Owner, nor in time of war, but in a manner to be prescribed by law.

AMENDMENT IV (1791)

The right of the people to be secure in their persons, houses, papers, and effects, against unreasonable searches and seizures, shall not be violated, and no Warrants shall issue, but upon probable cause, supported by Oath or affirmation, and particularly describing the place to be searched, and the persons or things to be seized.

AMENDMENT V (1791)

No person shall be held to answer for a capital, or otherwise infamous crime, unless on a presentment or indictment of a Grand Jury, except in cases arising in the land or naval forces, or in the Militia, when in actual service in time of War or public danger; nor shall any person be subject for the same offence to be twice put in jeopardy of life or limb; nor shall be compelled in any criminal case to be a witness against himself, nor be deprived of life, liberty, or property, without due process of law; nor shall private property be taken for public use, without just compensation.

AMENDMENT VI (1791)

In all criminal prosecutions, the accused shall enjoy the right to a speedy and public trial, by an impartial jury of the State and district wherein the crime shall have been committed, which district shall have been previously ascertained by law, and to be informed of the nature and cause of the accusation; to be confronted with the witnesses against him; to have compulsory process for obtaining witnesses in his favor, and to have the Assistance of Counsel for his defence.

AMENDMENT VII (1791)

In Suits at common law, where the value in controversy shall exceed twenty dollars, the right of trial by jury shall be preserved, and no fact tried by a jury, shall be otherwise re-examined in any Court of the United States, than according to the rules of the common law.

AMENDMENT VIII (1791)

Excessive bail shall not be required, nor excessive fines imposed, nor cruel and unusual punishments inflicted.

AMENDMENT IX (1791)

The enumeration in the Constitution, of certain rights, shall not be construed to deny or disparage others retained by the people.

AMENDMENT X (1791)

The powers not delegated to the United States by the Constitution, nor prohibited by it to the States, are reserved to the States respectively, or to the people.

AMENDMENT XI (1795)

The Judicial power of the United States shall not be construed to extend to any suit in law or equity, commenced or prosecuted against one of the United States by Citizens of another State, or by Citizens or Subjects of any Foreign State.

AMENDMENT XII (1804)

The Electors shall meet in their respective states, and vote by ballot for President and Vice-President, one of whom, at least, shall not be an inhabitant of the same state with themselves; they shall name in their ballots the person voted for as President, and in distinct ballots the person voted for as Vice-President, and they shall make distinct lists of all persons voted for as President, and of all persons voted for as Vice-President, and of the number of votes for each, which lists they shall sign and certify, and transmit sealed to the seat of the government of the United States, directed to the President of the Senate;—The President of the Senate shall, in the presence of the Senate and House of Representatives, open all the certificates and the votes shall then be counted;—The person having the greatest number of votes for President, shall be the President, if such number be a majority of the whole number of Electors appointed; and if no person have such majority, then from the persons having the highest numbers not exceeding three on the list of those voted for as President, the House of Representatives shall choose immediately, by ballot, the President. But in choosing the President, the votes shall be taken by states, the representation from each state having one vote; a quorum for this purpose shall consist of a member or members from two-thirds of the states, and a majority of all the states shall be necessary to a choice. And if the House of Representatives shall not choose a President whenever the right of choice shall devolve upon them, before the fourth day of March next following, then the Vice-President shall act as President, as in the case of the death or other constitutional disability of the President.—The person having the greatest number of votes as Vice-President, shall be the Vice-President, if such number be a majority of the whole number of Electors appointed, and if no person have a majority, then from the two highest numbers on the list, the Senate shall choose the Vice-President; a quorum for the purpose shall consist of two-thirds of the whole number of Senators, and a majority of the whole number shall be necessary to a choice. But no person constitutionally ineligible to the office of President shall be eligible to that of Vice-President of the United States.

AMENDMENT XIII (1865)

Section 1. Neither slavery nor involuntary servitude, except as a punishment for crime whereof the party shall have been duly convicted, shall exist within the United States, or any place subject to their jurisdiction.

Section 2. Congress shall have power to enforce this article by appropriate legislation.

AMENDMENT XIV (1868)

Section 1. All persons born or naturalized in the United States, and subject to the jurisdiction thereof, are citizens of the United States and of the State wherein they reside. No State shall make or enforce any law which shall abridge the privileges or immunities of citizens of the United States; nor shall any State deprive any person of life, liberty, or property, without due process of law; nor deny to any person within its jurisdiction the equal protection of the laws.

Section 2. Representatives shall be apportioned among the several States according to their respective numbers, counting the whole number of persons in each State, excluding Indians not taxed. But when the right to vote at any election for the choice of electors for President and Vice President of the United States, Representatives in Congress, the Executive and Judicial officers of a State, or the members of the Legislature thereof, is denied to any of the male inhabitants of such State, being twenty-one years of age, and citizens of the United States, or in any way abridged, except for participation in rebellion, or other crime, the basis of representation therein shall be reduced in the proportion which the number of such male citizens shall bear to the whole number of male citizens twenty-one years of age in such State.

Section 3. No person shall be a Senator or Representative in Congress, or elector of President and Vice President, or hold any office, civil or military, under the United States, or under any State, who, having previously taken an oath, as a member of Congress, or as an officer of the United States, or as a member of any State legislature, or as an executive or judicial officer of any State, to support the Constitution of the United States, shall have engaged in insurrection or rebellion against the same, or given aid or comfort to the enemies thereof. But Congress may by a vote of two-thirds of each House, remove such disability.

Section 4. The validity of the public debt of the United States, authorized by law, including debts incurred for payment of pensions and bounties for services in suppressing insurrection or rebellion, shall not be questioned. But neither the United States nor any State shall assume or pay any debt or obligation incurred in aid of insurrection or rebellion against the United States, or any claim for the loss or emancipation of any slave; but all such debts, obligations and claims shall be held illegal and void.

Section 5. The Congress shall have power to enforce, by appropriate legislation, the provisions of this article.

AMENDMENT XV (1870)

Section 1. The right of citizens of the United States to vote shall not be denied or abridged by the United States or by any State on account of race, color, or previous condition of servitude.

Section 2. The Congress shall have power to enforce this article by appropriate legislation.

AMENDMENT XVI (1913)

The Congress shall have power to lay and collect taxes on incomes, from whatever source derived, without apportionment among the several States, and without regard to any census or enumeration.

AMENDMENT XVII (1913)

The Senate of the United States shall be composed of two Senators from each State, elected by the people thereof, for six years; and each Senator shall have one vote. The electors in each State shall have the qualifications requisite for electors of the most numerous branch of the State legislatures.

When vacancies happen in the representation of any State in the Senate, the executive authority of such State shall issue writs of election to fill such vacancies: Provided, That the legislature of any State may empower the executive thereof to make temporary appointments until the people fill the vacancies by election as the legislature may direct.

This amendment shall not be so construed as to affect the election or term of any Senator chosen before it becomes valid as part of the Constitution.

AMENDMENT XVIII (1919)

Section 1. After one year from the ratification of this article the manufacture, sale, or transportation of intoxicating liquors within, the importation thereof into, or the exportation thereof from the United States and all territory subject to the jurisdiction thereof for beverage purposes is hereby prohibited.

Section 2. The Congress and the several States shall have concurrent power to enforce this article by appropriate legislation.

Section 3. This article shall be inoperative unless it shall have been ratified as an amendment to the Constitution by the legislatures of the several States, as provided in the Constitution, within seven years from the date of the submission hereof to the States by the Congress.

AMENDMENT XIX (1920)

The right of citizens of the United States to vote shall not be denied or abridged by the United States or by any State on account of sex.

Congress shall have power to enforce this article by appropriate legislation.

AMENDMENT XX (1933)

Section 1. The terms of the President and Vice President shall end at noon on the 20th day of January, and the terms of Senators and Representatives at noon on the 3d day of January, of the years in which such terms would have ended if this article had not been ratified; and the terms of their successors shall then begin.

Section 2. The Congress shall assemble at least once in every year, and such meeting shall begin at noon on the 3d day of January, unless they shall by law appoint a different day.

Section 3. If, at the time fixed for the beginning of the term of the President, the President elect shall have died, the Vice President elect shall become President. If a President shall not have been chosen before the time fixed for the beginning of his term, or if the President elect shall have failed to qualify, then the Vice President elect shall act as President until a President shall have qualified; and the Congress may by law provide for the case wherein neither a President elect nor a Vice President elect shall have qualified, declaring who shall then act as President, or the manner in which one who is to act shall be selected, and such person shall act accordingly until a President or Vice President shall have qualified.

Section 4. The Congress may by law provide for the case of the death of any of the persons from whom the House of Representatives may choose a President whenever the right of choice shall have devolved upon them, and for the case of the death of any of the persons from whom the Senate may choose a Vice President whenever the right of choice shall have devolved upon them.

Section 5. Sections 1 and 2 shall take effect on the 15th day of October following the ratification of this article.

Section 6. This article shall be inoperative unless it shall have been ratified as an amendment to the Constitution by the legislatures of three-fourths of the several States within seven years from the date of its submission.

AMENDMENT XXI (1933)

Section 1. The eighteenth article of amendment to the Constitution of the United States is hereby repealed.

Section 2. The transportation or importation into any State, Territory, or possession of the United States for delivery or use therein of intoxicating liquors, in violation of the laws thereof, is hereby prohibited.

Section 3. This article shall be inoperative unless it shall have been ratified as an amendment to the Constitution by conventions in the several States, as provided in the Constitution, within seven years from the date of the submission hereof to the States by the Congress.

AMENDMENT XXII (1951)

Section 1. No person shall be elected to the office of the President more than twice, and no person who has held the office of President, or acted as President, for more than two years of a term to which some other person was elected President shall be elected to the office of the President more than once. But this article shall not apply to any person holding the office of President when this article was proposed by the Congress, and shall not prevent any person who may be holding the office of President, or acting as President, during the term within which this article becomes operative from holding the office of President or acting as President during the remainder of such term.

Section 2. This article shall be inoperative unless it shall have been ratified as an amendment to the Constitution by the legislatures of three-fourths of the several states within seven years from the date of its submission to the states by the Congress.

AMENDMENT XXIII (1961)

Section 1. The District constituting the seat of government of the United States shall appoint in such manner as the Congress may direct:

A number of electors of President and Vice President equal to the whole number of Senators and Representatives in Congress to which the District would be entitled if it were a state, but in no event more than the least populous state; they shall be in addition to those appointed by the states, but they shall be considered, for the purposes of the election of President and Vice President, to be electors appointed by a state; and they shall meet in the District and perform such duties as provided by the twelfth article of amendment.

Section 2. The Congress shall have power to enforce this article by appropriate legislation.

AMENDMENT XXIV (1964)

Section 1. The right of citizens of the United States to vote in any primary or other election for President or Vice President, for electors for President or Vice President, or for Senator or Representative in Congress, shall not be denied or abridged by the United States or any state by reason of failure to pay any poll tax or other tax.

Section 2. The Congress shall have power to enforce this article by appropriate legislation.

AMENDMENT XXV (1967)

Section 1. In case of the removal of the President from office or of his death or resignation, the Vice President shall become President.

Section 2. Whenever there is a vacancy in the office of the Vice President, the President shall nominate a Vice President who shall take office upon confirmation by a majority vote of both Houses of Congress.

Section 3. Whenever the President transmits to the President pro tempore of the Senate and the Speaker of the House of Representatives his written declaration that he is unable to discharge the powers and duties of his office, and until he transmits to them a written declaration to the contrary, such powers and duties shall be discharged by the Vice President as Acting President.

Section 4. Whenever the Vice President and a majority of either the principal officers of the executive departments or of such other body as Congress may by law provide, transmit to the President pro tempore of the Senate and the Speaker of the House of Representatives their written declaration that the President is unable to discharge the powers and duties of his office, the Vice President shall immediately assume the powers and duties of the office as Acting President.

Thereafter, when the President transmits to the President pro tempore of the Senate and the Speaker of the House of Representatives his written declaration that no inability exists, he shall resume the powers and duties of his office unless the Vice President and a majority of either the principal officers of the executive department or of such other body as Congress may by law provide, transmit within four days to the President pro tempore of the Senate and the Speaker of the House of Representatives their written declaration that the President is unable to discharge the powers and duties of his office. Thereupon Congress shall decide the issue, assembling within forty-eight hours for that purpose if not in session. If the Congress, within twenty-one days after receipt of the latter written declaration, or, if Congress is not in session, within twenty-one days after Congress is required to assemble, determines by two-thirds vote of both Houses that the President is unable to discharge the powers and duties of his office, the Vice President shall continue to discharge the same as Acting President; otherwise, the President shall resume the powers and duties of his office.

AMENDMENT XXVI (1971)

Section 1. The right of citizens of the United States, who are 18 years of age or older, to vote, shall not be denied or abridged by the United States or any state on account of age.

Section 2. The Congress shall have the power to enforce this article by appropriate legislation.

AMENDMENT XXVII (1992)

No law varying the compensation for the services of the Senators and Representatives shall take effect until an election of Representatives shall have intervened.

APPENDIX B

ADMINISTRATIVE PROCEDURE ACT

TITLE 5, U.S. CODE

CHAPTER 5—ADMINISTRATIVE PROCEDURE

§ 551. DEFINITIONS

For the purpose of this subchapter—

(1) "agency" means each authority of the Government of the United States, whether or not it is within or subject to review by another agency, but does not include—

(A) the Congress;

(B) the courts of the United States;

(C) the governments of the territories or possessions of the United States;

(D) the government of the District of Columbia; or except as to the requirements of section 552 of this title—

(E) agencies composed of representatives of the parties or of representatives of organizations of the parties to the disputes determined by them;

(F) courts martial and military commissions;

(G) military authority exercised in the field in time of war or in occupied territory; or

(H) functions conferred by sections 1738, 1739, 1743, and 1744 of title 12; chapter 2 of title 41; or sections 1622, 1884, 1891–1902, and former section 1641(b)(2), of title 50, appendix;

(2) "person" includes an individual, partnership, corporation, association, or public or private organization other than an agency;

(3) "party" includes a person or agency named or admitted as a party, or properly seeking and entitled as of right to be admitted as a party, in an agency proceeding, and a person or agency admitted by an agency as a party for limited purposes;

(4) "rule" means the whole or a part of an agency statement of general or particular applicability and future effect designed to implement, interpret, or prescribe law or policy or describing the organization, procedure, or practice requirements of an agency and includes the approval or prescription for the future of rates, wages, corporate or financial structures or reorganizations thereof, prices, facilities, appliances, services or allowances therefor or of valuations, costs, or accounting, or practices bearing on any of the foregoing;

(5) "rule making" means agency process for formulating, amending, or repealing a rule;

(6) "order" means the whole or a part of a final disposition, whether affirmative, negative, injunctive, or declaratory in form, of an agency in a matter other than rule making but including licensing;

(7) "adjudication" means agency process for the formulation of an order;

(8) "license" includes the whole or a part of an agency permit, certificate, approval, registration, charter, membership, statutory exemption or other form of permission;

(9) "licensing" includes agency process respecting the grant, renewal, denial, revocation, suspension, annulment, withdrawal, limitation, amendment, modification, or conditioning of a license;

(10) "sanction" includes the whole or a part of an agency.

(A) prohibition, requirement, limitation, or other condition affecting the freedom of a person;

(B) withholding of relief;

(C) imposition of penalty or fine;

(D) destruction, taking, seizure, or withholding of property;

(E) assessment of damages, reimbursement, restitution, compensation, costs, charges, or fees;

(F) requirement, revocation, or suspension of a license; or

(G) taking other compulsory or restrictive action;

(11) "relief" includes the whole or a part of an agency—

(A) grant of money, assistance, license, authority, exemption, exception, privilege, or remedy;

(B) recognition of a claim, right, immunity, privilege, exemption, or exception; or

(C) taking of other action on the application or petition of, and beneficial to, a person;

(12) "agency proceeding" means an agency process as defined by paragraphs (5), (7), and (9) of this section;

(13) "agency action" includes the whole or a part of an agency rule, order, license, sanction, relief, or the equivalent or denial thereof, or failure to act; and

(14) "ex parte communication" means an oral or written communication not on the public record with respect to which reasonable prior notice to all parties is not given, but it shall not include requests for status reports on any matter or proceeding covered by this subchapter.

(Pub. L. 89–554, Sept. 6, 1966, 80 Stat. 381; Pub. L. 94–409, Sec. 4(b), Sept. 13, 1976, 90 Stat. 1247; Pub. L. 103–272, Sec. 5(a), July 5, 1994, 108 Stat. 1373.)

§ 553. RULEMAKING

(a) This section applies, according to the provisions thereof, except to the extent that there is involved—

(1) a military or foreign affairs function of the United States; or

(2) a matter relating to agency management or personnel or to public property, loans, grants, benefits, or contracts.

(b) General notice of proposed rule making shall be published in the Federal Register, unless persons subject thereto are named and either personally served or otherwise have actual notice thereof in accordance with law. The notice shall include—

(1) a statement of the time, place, and nature of public rule making proceedings;

(2) reference to the legal authority under which the rule is proposed; and

(3) either the terms or substance of the proposed rule or a description of the subjects and issues involved.

Except when notice or hearing is required by statute, this subsection does not apply—

(A) to interpretative rules, general statements of policy, or rules of agency organization, procedure, or practice; or

(B) when the agency for good cause finds (and incorporates the finding and a brief statement of reasons therefor in the rules issued) that notice and public procedure thereon are impracticable, unnecessary, or contrary to the public interest.

(c) After notice required by this section, the agency shall give interested persons an opportunity to participate in the rule making through submission of written data, views, or arguments with or without opportunity for oral presentation. After consideration of the relevant matter presented, the agency shall incorporate in the rules adopted a concise general statement of their basis and purpose. When rules are required by statute to be made on the record after opportunity for an agency hearing, sections 556 and 557 of this title apply instead of this subsection.

(d) The required publication or service of a substantive rule shall be made not less than 30 days before its effective date, except—

(1) a substantive rule which grants or recognizes an exemption or relieves a restriction;

(2) interpretative rules and statements of policy; or

(3) as otherwise provided by the agency for good cause found and published with the rule.

(e) Each agency shall give an interested person the right to petition for the issuance, amendment, or repeal of a rule. (Pub. L. 89–554, Sept. 6,1966, 80 Stat. 383.)

§ 554. ADJUDICATIONS

(a) This section applies, according to the provisions thereof, in every case of adjudication required by statute to be determined on the record after opportunity for an agency hearing, except to the extent that there is involved—

(1) a matter subject to a subsequent trial of the law and the facts de novo in a court;

(2) the selection or tenure of an employee, except a administrative law judge appointed under section 3105 of this title;

(3) proceedings in which decisions rest solely on inspections, tests, or elections;

(4) the conduct of military or foreign affairs functions;

(5) cases in which an agency is acting as an agent for a court; or

(6) the certification of worker representatives.

(b) Persons entitled to notice of an agency hearing shall be timely informed of—

(1) the time, place, and nature of the hearing;

(2) the legal authority and jurisdiction under which the hearing is to be held; and

(3) the matters of fact and law asserted. When private persons are the moving parties, other parties to the proceeding shall give prompt notice of issues controverted in fact or law; and in other instances agencies may by rule require responsive pleading. In fixing the time and place for hearings, due regard shall be had for the convenience and necessity of the parties or their representatives.

(c) The agency shall give all interested parties opportunity for—

(1) the submission and consideration of facts, arguments, offers of settlement, or proposals of adjustment when time, the nature of the proceeding, and the public interest permit; and

(2) to the extent that the parties are unable so to determine a controversy by consent, hearing and decision on notice and in accordance with sections 556 and 557 of this title.

(d) The employee who presides at the reception of evidence pursuant to section 556 of this title shall make the recommended decision or initial decision required by section 557 of this title, unless he becomes unavailable to the agency. Except to the extent required for the disposition of ex parte matters as authorized by law, such an employee may not—

(1) consult a person or party on a fact in issue, unless on notice and opportunity for all parties to participate; or

(2) be responsible to or subject to the supervision or direction of an employee or agent engaged in the performance of investigative or prosecuting functions for an agency. An employee or agent engaged in the performance of investigative or prosecuting functions for an agency in a case may not, in that or a factually related case, participate or advise in the decision, recommended decision, or agency review pursuant to section 557 of this title, except as witness or counsel in public proceedings. This subsection does not apply—

(A) in determining applications for initial licenses;

(B) to proceedings involving the validity or application of rates, facilities, or practices of public utilities or carriers; or

(C) to the agency or a member or members of the body comprising the agency.

(e) The agency, with like effect as in the case of other orders, and in its sound discretion, may issue a declaratory order to terminate a controversy or remove uncertainty.

(Pub. L. 89–554, Sept. 6, 1966, 80 Stat. 384; Pub. L. 95–251, Sec. 2(a)(1), Mar. 27, 1978, 92 Stat. 183.)

§ 555. ANCILLARY MATTERS

(a) This section applies, according to the provisions thereof, except as otherwise provided by this subchapter.

(b) A person compelled to appear in person before an agency or representative thereof is entitled to be accompanied, represented, and advised by counsel or, if permitted by the agency, by other qualified representative. A party is entitled to appear in person or by or with counsel or other duly qualified representative in an agency proceeding. So far as the orderly conduct of public business permits, an interested person may appear before an agency or its responsible employees for the presentation, adjustment, or determination of an issue, request, or controversy in a proceeding, whether interlocutory, summary, or otherwise, or in connection with an agency function. With due regard for the convenience and necessity of the parties or their representatives and within a reasonable time, each agency shall proceed to conclude a matter presented to it. This subsection does not grant or deny a person who is not a lawyer the right to appear for or represent others before an agency or in an agency proceeding.

(c) Process, requirement of a report, inspection, or other investigative act or demand may not be issued, made, or enforced except as authorized by law. A person compelled to submit data or evidence is entitled to retain or, on payment of lawfully prescribed costs, procure a copy or transcript thereof, except that in a nonpublic investigatory proceeding the witness may for good cause be limited to inspection of the official transcript of his testimony.

(d) Agency subpoenas authorized by law shall be issued to a party on request and, when required by rules of procedure, on a statement or showing of general relevance and reasonable scope of the evidence sought. On contest, the court shall sustain the subpoena or similar process or demand to the extent that it is found to be in accordance with law. In a proceeding for enforcement, the court shall issue an order requiring the appearance of the witness or the production of the evidence or data within a reasonable time under penalty of punishment for contempt in case of contumacious failure to comply.

(e) Prompt notice shall be given of the denial in whole or in part of a written application, petition, or other request of an interested person made in connection with any agency proceeding. Except in affirming a prior denial or when the denial is self-explanatory, the notice shall be accompanied by a brief statement of the grounds for denial.

(Pub. L. 89–554, Sept. 6,1966, 80 Stat. 385.)

§ 556. HEARINGS; PRESIDING EMPLOYEES; POWERS AND DUTIES; BURDEN OF PROOF; EVIDENCE; RECORD AS BASIS OF DECISION

(a) This section applies, according to the provisions thereof, to hearings required by section 553 or 554 of this title to be conducted in accordance with this section.

Either rulemaking or adjudication

(b) There shall preside at the taking of evidence—

(1) the agency;

(2) one or more members of the body which comprises the agency; or

(3) one or more administrative law judges appointed under section 3105 of this title. This subchapter does not supersede the conduct of specified classes of proceedings, in whole or in part, by or before boards or other employees specially provided for by or designated under statute. The functions of presiding employees and of employees participating in decisions in accordance with section 557 of this title shall be conducted in an impartial manner. A presiding or participating employee may at any time disqualify himself. On the filing in good faith of a timely and sufficient affidavit of personal bias or other disqualification of a presiding or participating employee, the agency shall determine the matter as a part of the record and decision in the case.

power to decision makers.

(c) Subject to published rules of the agency and within its powers, employees presiding at hearings may—

(1) administer oaths and affirmations;

(2) issue subpoenas authorized by law;

(3) rule on offers of proof and receive relevant evidence;

(4) take depositions or have depositions taken when the ends of justice would be served;

(5) regulate the course of the hearing;

(6) hold conferences for the settlement or simplification of the issues by consent of the parties or by the use of alternative means of dispute resolution as provided in subchapter IV of this chapter;

(7) inform the parties as to the availability of one or more alternative means of dispute resolution, and encourage use of such methods;

(8) require the attendance at any conference held pursuant to paragraph (6) of at least one representative of each party who has authority to negotiate concerning resolution of issues in controversy;

(9) dispose of procedural requests or similar matters;

(10) make or recommend decisions in accordance with section 557 of this title; and

(11) take other action authorized by agency rule consistent with this subchapter.

about the evidence

(d) Except as otherwise provided by statute, the proponent of a rule or order has the burden of proof. Any oral or documentary evidence may be received, but the agency as a matter of policy shall provide for the exclusion of irrelevant, immaterial, or unduly repetitious evidence. A sanction may not be imposed or rule or order issued except on consideration of the whole record or those parts thereof cited by a party and supported by and in accordance with the reliable, probative, and substantial evidence. The agency may, to the extent consistent with the interests of justice and the policy of the underlying statutes administered by the agency, consider a violation of section 557(d) of this title sufficient grounds for a decision adverse to a party who has knowingly committed such violation or knowingly caused such violation to occur. A party is entitled to present his case or defense by oral or documentary evidence, to submit rebuttal evidence, and to conduct such cross-examination as may be required for a full and true disclosure of the facts. In rule making or determining claims for money or benefits or applications for initial licenses an agency may, when a party will not be prejudiced thereby, adopt procedures for the submission of all or part of the evidence in written form.

(e) The transcript of testimony and exhibits, together with all papers and requests filed in the proceeding, constitutes the exclusive record for decision in accordance with section 557 of this title and, on payment of lawfully prescribed costs, shall be made available to the parties. When an agency decision rests on official notice of a material fact not appearing in the evidence in the record, a party is entitled, on timely request, to an opportunity to show the contrary.

(Pub. L. 89–554, Sept. 6, 1966, 80 Stat. 386; Pub. L. 94–409, Sec. 4(c), Sept. 13, 1976, 90 Stat. 1247; Pub. L. 95–251, Sec. 2(a)(1), Mar. 27, 1978, 92 Stat. 183; Pub. L. 101–552, Sec. 4(a), Nov. 15, 1990, 104 Stat. 2737.)

§ 557. INITIAL DECISIONS; CONCLUSIVENESS; REVIEW BY AGENCY; SUBMISSIONS BY PARTIES; CONTENTS OF DECISIONS; RECORD

(a) This section applies, according to the provisions thereof, when a hearing is required to be conducted in accordance with section 556 of this title.

(b) When the agency did not preside at the reception of the evidence, the presiding employee or, in cases not subject to section 554(d) of this title, an employee qualified to preside at hearings pursuant to section 556 of this title, shall initially decide the case unless the agency requires, either in specific cases or by general rule, the entire record to be certified to it for decision. When the presiding employee makes an initial decision, that decision then becomes the decision of the agency without further proceedings unless there is an appeal to, or review on motion of, the agency within time provided by rule. On appeal from or review of the initial decision, the agency has all the powers which it would have in making the initial decision except as it may limit the issues on notice or by rule. When the agency makes the decision without having presided at the reception of the evidence, the presiding employee or an employee qualified to preside at hearings pursuant to section 556 of this title shall first recommend a decision, except that in rule making or determining applications for initial licenses—

(1) instead thereof the agency may issue a tentative decision or one of its responsible employees may recommend a decision; or

(2) this procedure may be omitted in a case in which the agency finds on the record that due and timely execution of its functions imperatively and unavoidably so requires.

(c) Before a recommended, initial, or tentative decision, or a decision on agency review of the decision of subordinate employees, the parties are entitled to a reasonable opportunity to submit for the consideration of the employees participating in the decisions—

(1) proposed findings and conclusions; or

(2) exceptions to the decisions or recommended decisions of subordinate employees or to tentative agency decisions; and

(3) supporting reasons for the exceptions or proposed findings or conclusions. The record shall show the ruling on each finding, conclusion, or exception presented. All decisions, including initial, recommended, and tentative decisions, are a part of the record and shall include a statement of—

> (A) findings and conclusions, and the reasons or basis therefor, on all the material issues of fact, law, or discretion presented on the record; and

> (B) the appropriate rule, order, sanction, relief, or denial thereof.

(d)(1) In any agency proceeding which is subject to subsection (a) of this section, except to the extent required for the disposition of ex parte matters as authorized by law—

> (A) no interested person outside the agency shall make or knowingly cause to be made to any member of the body comprising the agency, administrative law judge, or other employee who is or may reasonably be expected to be involved in the decisional process of the proceeding, an ex parte communication relevant to the merits of the proceeding;

> (B) no member of the body comprising the agency, administrative law judge, or other employee who is or may reasonably be expected to be involved in the decisional process of the proceeding, shall make or knowingly cause to be made to any interested person outside the agency an ex parte communication relevant to the merits of the proceeding;

> (C) a member of the body comprising the agency, administrative law judge, or other employee who is or may reasonably be expected to be involved in the decisional process of such proceeding who receives, or who makes or knowingly causes to be made, a communication prohibited by this subsection shall place on the public record of the proceeding:

>> (i) all such written communications;

>> (ii) memoranda stating the substance of all such oral communications; and

>> (iii) all written responses, and memoranda stating the substance of all oral responses, to the materials described in clauses (i) and (ii) of this subparagraph;

> (D) upon receipt of a communication knowingly made or knowingly caused to be made by a party in violation of this subsection, the agency, administrative law judge, or other employee presiding at the hearing may, to the extent consistent with the interests of justice and the policy of the underlying statutes, require the party to show cause why his claim or interest in the proceeding should not be dismissed, denied, disregarded, or otherwise adversely affected on account of such violation; and

(E) the prohibitions of this subsection shall apply beginning at such time as the agency may designate, but in no case shall they begin to apply later than the time at which a proceeding is noticed for hearing unless the person responsible for the communication has knowledge that it will be noticed, in which case the prohibitions shall apply beginning at the time of his acquisition of such knowledge.

(2) This subsection does not constitute authority to withhold information from Congress.

(Pub. L. 89–554, Sept. 6, 1966, 80 Stat. 387; Pub. L. 94–409, Sec. 4(a), Sept. 13, 1976, 90 Stat. 1246.)

§ 558. IMPOSITION OF SANCTIONS; DETERMINATION OF APPLICATIONS FOR LICENSES; SUSPENSION, REVOCATION, AND EXPIRATION OF LICENSES

(a) This section applies, according to the provisions thereof, to the exercise of a power or authority.

(b) A sanction may not be imposed or a substantive rule or order issued except within jurisdiction delegated to the agency and as authorized by law.

(c) When application is made for a license required by law, the agency, with due regard for the rights and privileges of all the interested parties or adversely affected persons and within a reasonable time, shall set and complete proceedings required to be conducted in accordance with sections 556 and 557 of this title or other proceedings required by law and shall make its decision. Except in cases of willfulness or those in which public health, interest, or safety requires otherwise, the withdrawal, suspension, revocation, or annulment of a license is lawful only if, before the institution of agency proceedings therefor, the licensee has been given—

(1) notice by the agency in writing of the facts or conduct which may warrant the action; and

(2) opportunity to demonstrate or achieve compliance with all lawful requirements. When the licensee has made timely and sufficient application for a renewal or a new license in accordance with agency rules, a license with reference to an activity of a continuing nature does not expire until the application has been finally determined by the agency.

(Pub. L. 89–554, Sept. 6,1966, 80 Stat. 388.)

§ 559. EFFECT ON OTHER LAWS; EFFECT OF SUBSEQUENT STATUTE

This subchapter, chapter 7, and sections 1305, 3105, 3344, 4301(2)(E), 5372, and 7521 of this title, and the provisions of section 5335(a)(B) of this title that relate to administrative law judges, do not limit or repeal additional requirements imposed by statute or otherwise recognized by law. Except as otherwise required by law, requirements or privileges relating to evidence or procedure apply equally to agencies and persons. Each agency is granted the authority necessary to comply with the requirements of this subchapter through the issuance of rules or otherwise. Subsequent statute may not be held to supersede or modify this subchapter, chapter 7, sections 1305, 3105, 3344, 4301(2)(E), 5372, or 7521 of this title, or the provisions of section 5335(a)(B) of this title that relate to administrative law judges, except to the extent that it does so expressly.

(Pub. L. 89–554, Sept. 6, 1966, 80 Stat. 388; Pub. L. 90–623, Sec. 1(1), Oct. 22, 1968, 82 Stat. 1312; Pub. L. 95–251, Sec. 2(a)(1), Mar. 27, 1978, 92 Stat. 183; Pub. L. 95–454, title VIII, Sec. 801(a)(3)(B)(iii), Oct. 13,1978, 92 Stat. 1221.)

CHAPTER 7—JUDICIAL REVIEW

§ 701. APPLICATION; DEFINITIONS

requirement of judicial review

(a) This chapter applies, according to the provisions thereof, except to the extent that—

(1) statutes preclude judicial review; or

(2) agency action is committed to agency discretion by law.

(b) For the purpose of this chapter—

(1) "agency" means each authority of the Government of the United States, whether or not it is within or subject to review by another agency, but does not include—

(A) the Congress;

(B) the courts of the United States;

(C) the governments of the territories or possessions of the United States;

(D) the government of the District of Columbia;

(E) agencies composed of representatives of the parties or of representatives of organizations of the parties to the disputes determined by them;

(F) courts martial and military commissions;

(G) military authority exercised in the field in time of war or in occupied territory; or

(H) functions conferred by sections 1738, 1739, 1743, and 1744 of title 12; chapter 2 of title 41; or sections 1622, 1884, 1891–1902, and former section 1641(b)(2), of title 50, appendix; and

(2) "person", "rule", "order", "license", "sanction", "relief", and "agency action" have the meanings given them by section 551 of this title.

(Pub. L. 89–554, Sept. 6, 1966, 80 Stat. 392; Pub. L. 103–272, Sec. 5(a), July 5, 1994, 108 Stat. 1373.)

§ 702. RIGHT OF REVIEW

A person suffering legal wrong because of agency action, or adversely affected or aggrieved by agency action within the meaning of a relevant statute, is entitled to judicial review thereof. An action in a court of the United States seeking relief other than money damages and stating a claim that an agency or an officer or employee thereof acted or failed to act in an official capacity or under color of legal authority shall not be dismissed nor relief therein be denied on the ground that it is against the United States or that the United States is an indispensable party. The United States may be named as a defendant in any such action, and a judgment or decree may be entered against the United States: Provided, That any mandatory or injunctive decree shall specify the Federal officer or officers (by name or by title), and their successors in office, personally responsible for compliance. Nothing herein (1) affects other limitations on judicial review or the power or duty of the court to dismiss any action or deny relief on any other appropriate legal or equitable ground; or (2) confers authority to grant relief if any other statute that grants consent to suit expressly or impliedly forbids the relief which is sought.

(Pub. L. 89–554, Sept. 6, 1966, 80 Stat. 392; Pub. L. 94–574, Sec. 1, Oct. 21, 1976, 90 Stat. 2721.)

§ 703. FORM AND VENUE OF PROCEEDING

The form of proceeding for judicial review is the special statutory review proceeding relevant to the subject matter in a court specified by statute or, in the absence or inadequacy thereof, any applicable form of legal action, including actions for declaratory judgments or writs of prohibitory or mandatory injunction or habeas corpus, in a court of competent jurisdiction. If no special statutory review proceeding is applicable, the action for judicial review may be brought against the United States, the agency by its official title, or the appropriate officer. Except to the extent that prior, adequate, and exclusive opportunity for judicial review is provided by law, agency action is subject to judicial review in civil or criminal proceedings for judicial enforcement.

(Pub. L. 89–554, Sept. 6, 1966, 80 Stat. 392; Pub. L. 94–574, Sec. 1, Oct. 21, 1976, 90 Stat. 2721.)

§ 704. ACTIONS REVIEWABLE

Agency action made reviewable by statute and final agency action for which there is no other adequate remedy in a court are subject to judicial review. A preliminary, procedural, or intermediate agency action or ruling not directly reviewable is subject to review on the review of the final agency action. Except as otherwise expressly required by statute, agency action otherwise final is final for the purposes of this section whether or not there has been presented or determined an application for a declaratory order, for any form of reconsiderations, or, unless the agency otherwise requires by rule and provides that the action meanwhile is inoperative, for an appeal to superior agency authority.

(Pub. L. 89–554, Sept. 6, 1966, 80 Stat. 392.)

§ 705. RELIEF PENDING REVIEW

When an agency finds that justice so requires, it may postpone the effective date of action taken by it, pending judicial review. On such conditions as may be required and to the extent necessary to prevent irreparable injury, the reviewing court, including the court to which a case may be taken on appeal from or on application for certiorari or other writ to a reviewing court, may issue all necessary and appropriate process to postpone the effective date of an agency action or to preserve status or rights pending conclusion of the review proceedings.

(Pub. L. 89–554, Sept. 6,1966, 80 Stat. 393.)

§ 706. SCOPE OF REVIEW

To the extent necessary to decision and when presented, the reviewing court shall decide all relevant questions of law, interpret constitutional and statutory provisions, and determine the meaning or applicability of the terms of an agency action. The reviewing court shall—

(1) compel agency action unlawfully withheld or unreasonably delayed; and

(2) hold unlawful and set aside agency action, findings, and conclusions found to be—

(A) arbitrary, capricious, an abuse of discretion, or otherwise not in accordance with law;

(B) contrary to constitutional right, power, privilege, or immunity;

(C) in excess of statutory jurisdiction, authority, or limitations, or short of statutory right;

(D) without observance of procedure required by law;

(E) unsupported by substantial evidence in a case subject to sections 556 and 557 of this title or otherwise reviewed on the record of an agency hearing provided by statute; or

(F) unwarranted by the facts to the extent that the facts are subject to trial de novo by the reviewing court.

In making the foregoing determinations, the court shall review the whole record or those parts of it cited by a party, and due account shall be taken of the rule of prejudicial error.

(Pub. L. 89–554, Sept. 6,1966, 80 Stat. 393.)

INDEX

References are to Pages

ACCOUNTABILITY
Policy delegations to agencies,
  accountability evading by Congress,
  37, 43
Rulemaking process, political
  accountability inherent in, 425

ADAPSO TEST
Case opinion, 408
Standing
  Generally, 922
  Noneconomic injuries, 932
  Zone of interest, 972

ADJUDICATION
Generally, 277
Administrative Law Judges, this index;
  Public/Private Rights Distinction,
  this index
Agency assertions vs express
  congressional delegations, 114
Alcohol sales restrictions to named
  persons, due process requirements,
  297
APA judicial review standards, 385
APA model
  Generally, 259
  Split-enforcement model compared,
  366
APA requirements
  Generally, 343
  Formal adjudications, 343
  Informal adjudications, 350
  On the record formal adjudication
  requirements, 344
Article I courts and agency adjudications
  distinguished
  Delegated adjudicatory power, 98,
  105
Article III challenges to delegated
  adjudicatory power, 92
Bias
  Cinderella rule, 517
  Impermissible, 357
Binding precedent and common law
  rulemaking, 447
Bureaucratic vs judicial models, 366
Chevron deference in rulemaking vs
  adjudicatory interpretations, 711
Cinderella rule, 517
Commodity Exchange Act, 106
Common law rulemaking, 447
Congressional interference in decisional
  process, 129
Constitutional fact doctrine
  Generally, 98
  Deferential standard of judicial
  review, 120
Cross-examination of witnesses, 359
Decisional process, congressional
  interference in, 129

Deferential vs de novo judicial review, 407
Definition, 277, 278
Delegated powers
  Generally, 23, 108 et seq.
  Agency assertions vs express
  congressional delegations, 114
  Article I courts and agency
  adjudications distinguished,
  98, 105
  Article III challenges, 92
  Breadth of delegation, 97, 105, 110
  Commodity Exchange Act, 106
  Constitutional fact doctrine
  Generally, 98
  Deferential standard of
  judicial review, 120
  Economic regulatory disputes, 98
  Federal Insecticide, Fungicide &
  Rodenticide Act, 105
  Health care court proposals, 121
  Jurisdictional fact doctrine
  Generally, 98
  Deferential standard of
  judicial review, 120
  Longshoremen's and Harbor
  Workers Act, 93
  Medical malpractice court proposals,
  121
  Public/Private Rights Distinction,
  this index
  Right of judiciary to protect Article
  III jurisdiction, 115
  Seventh Amendment challenges, 92
  Social Security claims, 92
  Waivers of right of recourse to
  Article III courts, 115
Due process requirements
  Generally, 277 et seq.
  Alcohol sales restrictions to named
  persons, 297
  Bitter with the sweet theory, 326
  Cross-examination of witnesses, 359
  Fact finding adjudications, 283
  Fundamental fairness standards,
  358
  Hearings
  Generally, 314
  Three-part balancing test, 324
  Informal adjudications, 349, 350
  Legislative and adjudicative
  factfinding distinguished, 283
  Life, liberty, or property,
  adjudications affecting, 286 et
  seq.
  Limits of procedural balancing, 332
  Pre-deprivation hearings in benefit
  cases, 324
  Pre-termination hearing rights of
  public employees, 327
  Procedural restraints, 277

Procedures required by due process, below
Public employment rights of individuals, below
Rulemaking vs adjudication requirements, 278
Social Security benefits determinations, 316
Stigma claims, 308
Tax assessments, 279
Terrorist detentions, 332
Welfare benefits determinations, 286, 313
Economic regulatory disputes, 98
Erosion of formal adjudication requirements, 350
Fact finding
Due process requirements, 283
Judicial review, 386
Reasoning processes applicable to, 413
Fact-finding
Informal adjudications, 408
Federal Insecticide, Fungicide & Rodenticide Act, 105
Formal adjudications
Generally, 343
Erosion of requirements, 350
Separation of investigation and prosecution functions, 357
Standard of review, 412
Functional relationship between rules and adjudications, 426 et seq.
Fundamental fairness standards, 358
Health care court proposals, 121
Hearings
Due process requirements
Generally, 314
Three-part balancing test, 324
Formal adjudications, 343
On the record formal adjudication requirements, 344
Oral vs written hearings, 324
Pre-deprivation hearings in benefit cases, 324
Pre-termination hearing rights of public employees, 327
Public hearing requirements, 345
Three-part balancing test, 324
Immigration law proceedings criticisms, 366, 371
Informal adjudications
Generally, 350
Chevron deference, 711
Due process requirements, 350
Due process requirements of, 349
Fact-finding, 408
Federal-Aid Highway Act, 350, 818
Judicial review of reasoning processes, 413
Minimum requirements, 357
Separation of investigation and prosecution functions, 357
Standard of review, 412
Inter-decisional inconsistency, 367, 370

Judicial models of decision-making structures
Generally, 357
Bureaucratic models compared, 366
Judicial review
Generally, 385 et seq.
Agency reasoning processes, 413
APA standards, 385
Arbitrary and capricious standard, 408
Deferential vs de novo review, 407
Fact finding review, 386
Hearsay, substantial evidence standard, 400
Law issues, 413
Refusal to institute adjudication, 853
Remands to explain reasoning processes, 413, 442
Rulemaking review standards compared, 386
Substantial evidence standard, 386
Whole record review, 386, 407
Jurisdictional fact doctrine
Generally, 98
Deferential standard of judicial review, 120
Law issues, judicial review, 413
Legislative and adjudicative factfinding distinguished, 283
Legislative vetoes affecting, 142
Licensing as adjudication, 278
Life, liberty, or property, adjudications affecting
Generally, 286 et seq., 332 et seq.
Stigma claims, 308
Longshoremen's and Harbor Workers Act
Delegated adjudicatory power, 93
Medical malpractice court proposals
Delegated adjudicatory power, 120
Mine Safety and Health Administration, split-enforcement model, 366
Neutral decision-maker requirements, 357
Occupational Safety and Health Administration, split-enforcement model, 259
On the record formal adjudication requirements, 344
Oral vs written hearings, 324
Permissible decision-making structures, 357
Policy expressing, 448
Policy setting in adjudications, 277
Policy statements, prosecutorial discretion criteria, 557
Pre-deprivation hearings in benefit cases, 324
Pre-termination hearing rights of public employees, 327
Prior exposure bias claims, 364
Procedure
Procedures required by due process, below
APA requirements, 343

Hearings, due process requirements
　　Generally, 314
　　　Three-part balancing test, 324
　　Limits of procedural balancing, 332
　　Social Security benefits
　　　determinations, due process
　　　requirements, 316
　　Statutory requirements, 343
Procedures required by due process
　　Generally, 277, 312 et seq.
　　Bitter with the sweet theory, 326
　　Due process requirements, above
　　Hearings, 314, 324
　　Limits of procedural balancing, 332
　　Social Security benefits
　　　determinations, 316
　　Terrorist detentions, 332
　　Welfare benefits matters, 313
Prosecutorial discretion criteria as policy
　　statements, 557
Prospectivity
　　Rulemaking compared, 279
　　Rules expressed in adjudications,
　　　447
Public employment, adjudications
　　affecting
　　　Generally, 286
　　　Pre-termination hearing rights, 327
　　　Teachers, 298, 303
Public hearing requirements, 345

Reasoning processes, judicial review, 413
Refusal to institute adjudication, judicial
　　review, 853
Retroactivity of rules adopted in, 442, 457
Right of judiciary to protect Article III
　　jurisdiction, 115
Rule-creating adjudications, 264, 441 et
　　seq.
Rulemaking compared
　　Generally, 277, 418
　　Advantages of rulemaking, 424
　　APA distinctions, 278
　　Bias rules, 517
　　Due process requirements, 278
　　Fact finding standards, 517
　　Functional relationship between
　　　rules and adjudications, 426 et
　　　seq.
　　Order issuances, 410
　　Prospectivity, 279
　　Retroactivity, 442, 457
　　Standard of judicial review, 413
Rules avoiding classes of adjudications,
　　435
Scope of adjudication, 277
Separation of investigation and
　　prosecution functions, 357
Seventh Amendment challenges, 92
Social Security benefits determinations
　　Criticisms of processes, 367, 371
　　Delegated adjudicatory power, 92
　　Due process requirements, 316
Split-enforcement model
　　Generally, 259
　　APA model compared, 366

Stare decisis principle, 414
Statutory procedural requirements, 343
Stigma claims, due process requirements,
　　308
Sub silentio departures from prior policy,
　　414, 581
Subpoenas, 407
Substantial evidence standard of judicial
　　review, 386
Tax assessments, due process
　　requirements, 279
Waivers of right of recourse to Article III
　　courts, 115
Welfare benefits determinations, due
　　process requirements, 286, 313
Whole record judicial review, 386, 407

ADJUDICATIVE FACT
Definition, 283

ADMINISTRATIVE AUTHORITY
　　STATUTES
Generally, 597
See also *Chevron* Deference, this index

ADMINISTRATIVE LAW JUDGES
　　(ALJS)
Alternative adjudicatory officers systems,
　　372
Appointments of, 168
Collective bargaining by, 372
Efficiency standards, 370
Independence standards
　　Generally, 343, 366
　　Judicial protection, 368
　　Management conflicts, 372
Judicial protection of independence
　　standards, 368
Management conflicts with independence
　　standards, 372
Officers of the United States, 169
Peer review program, 368
Powers of
　　Generally, 168
　　Appointment Clause limitations,
　　　389
Production quotas, 368
Quality assurance system, 368
Reversal rate standards, 370
Salary, 343
Social Security disability claims,
　　criticisms of processes, 367
Tenure, 343
Unionization, 372

ADMINISTRATIVE PROCEDURE
　　ACT (APA)
Adjudication requirements
　　Generally, 343
　　Formal adjudications, 343
　　Informal adjudications, 350
　　On the record formal adjudication
　　　requirements, 344
　　Rulemaking distinctions, 278
Agencies defined, 5
Agency management exemptions from
　　rulemaking requirements, 524

Arbitrary and capricious standard, 354, 408, 560
Congressional control of agencies through, 121
Congressional Review Act, 144
Definitions, 279
Emergency exemptions from rulemaking requirements, 525
Enactment, 18
Evidence rules, federal rules compared, 407
Evolution of informal rulemaking, 465 et seq.
Foreign affairs exemptions from rulemaking requirements, 524
Formal adjudications, 343
Good cause exemptions from rulemaking requirements, 524
Informal adjudications
        Generally, 350
        Due process requirements, 350
        Minimum requirements, 357
Informal rulemaking, evolution of, 465 et seq.
Interpretative rules
        Generally, 417
        Exemptions from rulemaking requirements, 542
Judicial review
        Generally, 795
        Exhaustion of administrative remedies, 907
        Presumptive reviewability, 796, 803, 810, 836
Legislative and interpretive rules distinguished, 542
Legislative compromises reflected in, 19
Legislative vetoes, 135
Military exemptions from rulemaking requirements, 524
Negotiated Rulemaking Act, 593
Notice-and-comment rulemaking, 417
Notices of Proposed Rulemaking, this index
On-the-record requirements
        Adjudication, 344
        Rulemaking, 464
Orders defined, 410
Organic acts, 343
Policy statements
        Exemptions from rulemaking requirements, 549
        Rules distinguished, 551
Powers of agencies, policy debates, 19
Practically binding policy statements, exemptions from rulemaking requirements, 558
Procedural rules
        Generally, 417
        Exemptions from rulemaking requirements, 539
Public property exemptions from rulemaking requirements, 524
Retroactive application of rules, 455
Rule defined, 279

Rulemaking
        Generally, 457 et seq.
        See also Rulemaking and Regulations, this index
    Adjudication distinctions, 278
    Policy statements, 417
Scope of regulation, 5
Standing, prudential, 970
Statutory interpretation authority
        Generally, 597
        See also *Chevron* Deference, this index
Subject matter exemptions from rulemaking requirements, 524

AGE DISCRIMINATION IN EMPLOYMENT ACT
Chevron deference, 651, 661

AGENCIES
Generally, 1
Agencies within agencies, 11
Ambiguous legislative power grants, effect on Presidential control, 254
Appointment Power, this index
Appropriations process, congressional influence through, 127
Cabinet level and department level agencies, 10
Confirmations of agency officers, 127
Congressional influences
        Generally, 121 et seq.
        Administrative Procedure Act, this index
        Ambiguous legislative grants of power, 254
        Appropriations process, 127
        Casework communications on behalf of constituents, 128
        Civil Service Act, 125
        Confirmations of agency officers, 127
        Congressional Review Act, 144
        Decisional process, congressional interference, 129
        Due process limitations, 129
        Freedom of Information Act, 122
        Gramm-Rudman-Hollings Act, 145
        Informal influences on agency actions, 135
        Information Quality Act, 126
        Legislative Vetoes, this index
        Limitations on congressional power, 129 et seq.
        National Environmental Policy Act, 124
        Oversight process, 128
        Policy, this index
        Standing, statutory, of agencies, 126
        Supreme Court, statutory authority to litigate before, 127 167
Congressional power delegations
        Adjudication, this index
        Policy, this index
Congressional Review Act as mechanism of congressional control, 145

Constitutional bases of Presidential control, 155
Creation, 14
Deadlines for agency actions
  Generally, 913
  Enforcement, 915
Decisional process in pending adjudication, congressional interference with, 129
Definitions, 5
Delegations of Power, this index
Department of Justice, litigation conducted through, 126
Departments of government as, 23
Due process limitations on congressional influences, 129
Executive branch agencies, 10, 12
Executive departments as agencies, 23
FOIA vs APA definitions of agency, 6
Freedom of Information Act, congressional influences through, 122
Gramm-Rudman-Hollings Act, 145
Independent agencies, 12
Independent Agencies, this index
Informal congressional influences on agency actions, 135
Information Quality Act, congressional influence exercised through, 126
Judicial review of actions
  Generally, 795 et seq.
  See also Judicial Review, this index
  Discretionary acts, 810
  Inaction, review of, 836
National Environmental Policy Act, congressional influence through, 124
Nature and scope of Presidential authority over, 247
Officers, this index
Oversight process, congressional influences exercised through, 128
Policy statements. See Rulemaking and Regulations, this index
Powers of, policy debates, 19
Presidential control of
  Generally, 155 et seq.
  Ad hoc jawboning, 274
  Ambiguous legislative power grants, 254
  Appointment Power, this index
  Constitutional bases, 155
  Executive Orders, 258
  Nature and scope of presidential authority, 247
  OMB oversight control, 265
  Removal Power, this index
  Rulemaking, efforts to influence, 272
  Signing statements, effect of, 257
  Solicitor General control of Supreme Court litigation, 127 167
  Steel Seizure Case, 248, 253
Primary jurisdiction doctrine, 917
Public interest theory of, 20

Public/Private Rights Distinction, this index
Quasi-legislative and quasi-judicial functions, 14, 225
Rulemaking, presidential efforts to influence, 272
Separation of Powers, this index
Solicitor General control of Supreme Court litigation, 127, 167
Standing, statutory, of agencies, 126
Statutory agencies, 5
Statutory Interpretation, 599
Substantial independent authority standard, 9
Supreme Court, statutory authority to litigate before, 127, 167
Traditional Agencies, this index

AGENCY CAPTURE
History of administrative law, 20
Negotiated rulemaking as, 593

AGRICULTURAL MARKETING AGREEMENT ACT OF 1937
Preclusion of judicial review, 799
Standing to seek judicial review, 810

ALCOHOLIC BEVERAGES
Sales restrictions to named persons as adjudication requiring due process requirements, 297

ALL WRITS ACT
Judicial review, 914

AMBIGUITIES
  See also Statutory Interpretation, this index
Chevron deference to agency interpretations, 344
Congressional intent determinations, 604
Delegation ambiguities, *Chevron* deference, 643
How clear is clear, 629
Intentional and unintentional, 642
Legislative grants of power to agencies, 254
Regulations, interpretation, 774
Signing statements for ambiguous statutes, 257
Statutory silence as statutory ambiguity, 629

ANTI-DRUG ABUSE ACT OF 1988
Chevron deference, 647, 661

ANTITRUST LAW
Bias rules and policy-based agency head appointments, inherent tension, 521

APPOINTMENT POWER
  Generally, 157 et seq.
  See also Officers, this index; Removal Power, this index
Administrative Law Judges
  Generally, 168
  Powers of ALJs, Appointment Clause limitations, 389

Citizen suits conflicts, 171
Commissioners of independent agencies, 162
Courts of Law, 183, 187
Department Heads, 183, 187
Federal Election Commission, Commissioners of, 158, 164
Independent agencies, appointment of heads of, 162
Independent counsels, 171
Non-cabinet agency officials, 191
Officers of the United States, 157, 158 et seq.
Political implications of exercises, 255
Principal and inferior officer distinctions, 171
Recess appointments, 193
Removal power distinctions, 219
Scope of power, 158 et seq.
Tax Court judges, 170
Tax Court Special Trial Judges, 183
Traditional vs independent agencies, 191

APPROPRIATIONS
Congressional control of agencies through
    Generally, 127
        Lump sum appropriations, 834
        Riders, prohibitions in, 127
Endangered Species Act listings, appropriations riders limiting, 128
Freedom of Information Act funding deficiencies, 123
Gramm-Rudman-Hollings Act, 145
Lump sum appropriations, discretionary disbursement, 834
Presidential discretion to spend appropriated funds, 145
Riders, prohibitions in, 127
Separation of powers implications of appropriations process, 145

ARBITRARY AND CAPRICIOUS REVIEW STANDARD
Abandonment of rule after review, 567
Adjudications, reviews of, 408
Agency reasoning processes, 413
APA, 354, 408, 560
Automobile restraints, hard look review, 560
Basis and purpose statements, hard look review, 560, 590
Chevron deference and hard look at step two, 708
Constitutional concerns, rules involving, 589
Effect of hard look rule review, 591
Effect on rulemaking procedures, 590
Evolution of standard, 560
Fact findings, 408
Federal-Aid Highway Act, 818
Hard look review
    Automobile restraints, 560
    Chevron deference at step two, 708
    Development of, 560
    Effect of, 591

Effect on rulemaking procedures, 590
Evolution of standard, 560
Purpose statements, 560, 590
Retread tire labeling, 562
Seatbelt standards, 568
Three part test, 589
History of, 21
National Highway Traffic Safety Administration rules, review of, 560 et seq.
Policy changes, rules reflecting, 578
Purpose statements, hard look rule review, 560, 590
Reasonableness analysis, 411
Retread tire labeling, hard look review, 562
Rules, review of
    Generally, 560 et seq.
    Abandonment of rule after review, 567
    Amendments of rules, 577
    Constitutional concerns, rules involving, 589
    Hard look review, above
    National Highway Traffic Safety Administration, 560 et seq.
    Policy changes, rules reflecting, 578
    Pre-enforcement review, 560
    Rescissions of rules, 577
Seatbelt standards, hard look review, 568
Substantial evidence standard compared, 408
Three part hard look test, 589

ARTICLE I COURTS
    See also Congressional Powers, this index
Agency adjudications and Article I courts distinguished, 98, 105
Bankruptcy jurisdiction, 98
Core proceedings in bankruptcy courts, 115, 119
Delegations of power to agencies, 23
Judicial powers of Article III vs Article I Courts, 183, 187
Jury trials in, 118
Public/Private Rights Distinction, this index
Standing, this index
Tax Court, 183

ARTICLE II
See Presidential Powers, this index

ARTICLE III COURTS
Judicial powers of Article III vs Article I Courts, 183, 187

ARTICLE III COURTS
    See also Judicial Powers, this index
Bankruptcy jurisdiction, 98
Case or controversy limitation, 919, 957
Constitutional purpose, 109
Delegations of power to agencies, 23
Economic regulatory disputes, 98

Exhaustion of administrative remedies.
    See Standing, this index
Health care court proposals, 121
Medical malpractice court proposals, 121
Public/Private Rights Distinction, this
    index
Right of judiciary to protect Article III
    jurisdiction, 115
Waivers of right of recourse to, 115

AUER DEFERENCE
Interpretation of regulations, 775–776

BANKRUPTCY COURTS
Article I vs Article III, 98
Core proceedings, 115, 119
Jury trial rights in, 115
Public/private rights distinction, 101, 105

BIAS
Adjudication and rulemaking bias rules
    compared, 517
Informal rulemaking
        Generally, 513
        Challenges to, 494
Legislative and adjudicative fact finding
    distinguished, 517
Policy-based agency head appointments
    and bias rules, inherent tension, 521
Rulemaking and adjudication bias rules
    compared, 517

BUREAU OF INDIAN AFFAIRS
Adjudication, rulemaking through, 450
Rulemaking through adjudication, 450

BUREAU OF LAND MANAGEMENT
Agency delay problem, 917
Standing to challenge actions of, 932

CANONS OF CONSTRUCTION
Chevron deference, 645, 746

CARCINOGENS
See Toxic Substance Standards, this index

CASEWORK
Congressional communications with
    agencies on behalf of constituents,
    128

CENSUS BUREAU
    REAPPORTIONMENTS
Judicial review, final agency action
    requirement, 857

***CHEVRON* DEFERENCE**
        Generally, 613
        See also Statutory Interpretation,
            this index
Adjudicatory vs rulemaking
    interpretations, 711
Administrative authority statutes and
    general applicability statutes
    distinguished, 597
Age Discrimination in Employment Act,
    651, 661
Ambiguity determinations, 629

Ambiguity resolution, agency authority as
    to, 344, 621
Anti-Drug Abuse Act of 1988, 647, 661
Auer deference compared, 775–776
Bright line test of *Chevron* applicability,
    712, 729
Canons of construction, 645, 746
Case opinion, 613
Clean Water Act, step two invalidation of
    agency interpretation, 693, 706
Conflicting policies committed to agency's
    care, 615
Customs Service, 718
Debating *Chevron* theory, 621
Deference defined, 621
Department of Housing and Urban
    Development, 647, 661
Empirical analyses of *Chevron*, 709
Environmental Protection Agency, 613
Environmental Protection Agency, step
    two invalidation of agency
    interpretation, 693, 706
Equal Employment Opportunity
    Commission, 651, 661
Fair Labor Standards Act, 712
Federal Communications Commission
        Generally, 708
        Chevron step two invalidation of
            agency interpretation, 684
        Scope of *Chevron*, 738
Federal Motor Carrier Safety
    Administration, 630
Federal Trade Commission, 635
Force of law assertions, 717
General applicability statutes and
    administrative authority statutes
    distinguished, 597
Gramm-Leach-Bliley Act, 635
Hard look review and *Chevron* step two,
    708
Hearing requirement determinations, 349
How clear is clear, 629
Impact of *Chevron* decision, 597
Informal adjudications, application to, 711
Intentional and unintentional ambiguity,
    642
Interpretative rules, application to, 711
Interstate Commerce Commission, 630
Law question deference, 621
Legislative history as interpretive tool
        Generally, 645, 656, 659
        Step one vs step two, 661
Mead counter-revolution, 711 et seq.
Opinion letters, 712, 746
Plain meaning rule, 643, 651
Policies committed to agency's care, 615
Policy aspects of *Chevron* principle, 621
Policy resolution through statutory
    interpretation, 625
Policy statements, application to, 711
Policy-related questions, application to, 53
Pre-*Chevron* approach to judicial review,
    598
Purpose-based interpretation, 645
Regulations, interpretation of
        Auer deference compared, 775–776

Skidmore deference compared, 775
Revolutionary nature of *Chevron* opinion, 620
Rule of, 620
Rulemaking vs adjudicatory interpretations, 711
Scope of *Chevron*
    Generally, 711 et seq.
    Bright line test, 712, 729
    Fair Labor Standards Act, 712
    Federal Communications Commission, 738
    Force of law assertions, 717
    Opinion letters, 712
    Tariff classifications, 718
Separation of powers as support for *Chevron*, 621
Separation of powers implications of *Chevron*, 621
Skidmore deference compared
    Generally, 714, 717, 724
    Modern *Skidmore* doctrine, 736
    Regulations, interpretation of, 775
Stare decisis, 347, 647, 737, 746
Statutory silence as statutory ambiguity, 629
Strict constructionists and, 624
Subject matter expertise, 621
Tools of step one analysis, 643
Two-step approach
    Generally, 346, 621
    Ambiguity determinations, 629
    First step limitations, 627
    Hard look review and step two, 708
    Legislative history, place of, 661
    Step one inquiries, 643
    Step two, 661
    Tools of step one analysis, 643

CINDERELLA RULE
Generally, 517

CITIZEN SUITS
Appointment powers conflicts, 171
Causation tests, 955
Clean Water Act, 950
Constitutional standing, 940
Emergency Planning and Community Right-To-Know Act, 946
Endangered Species Act, 940
Environmental protection litigation, 949
Generalized grievances, 941
Redressibility, 955
Standing, 940

CIVIL SERVICE ACT
Congressional control of agencies through, 125
Political appointment exemptions, 125
Regulation challenges, ripeness, 868
Unintended adverse effects, 125

CLEAN AIR ACT
Ex parte communications in rulemakings, 504
Judicial review ripeness, statutory requirements, 878

Nondelegation doctrine, applicability to, 55, 60

CLEAN WATER ACT
Chevron deference, 693, 706
Citizens suits, 950
Hearings, permit, 345
Permit hearings, 345

CODE OF FEDERAL REGULATIONS
Rules, publication in, 18, 546, 559

COMBATANT STATUS REVIEW TRIBUNALS
Terrorist detentions, 342

COMMODITY EXCHANGE ACT
Adjudicatory power delegations to agencies, 106

COMMODITY FUTURES TRADING COMMISSION
Traditional agency status, 110

COMPTROLLER GENERAL
Gramm-Rudman-Hollings Act, 145, 153

CONFIRMATIONS
Agency officers, 127

CONGRESSIONAL POWERS
    Generally, 23 et seq.
    See also Separation of Powers, this index
Accountability-evading policy delegations to agencies, 37, 43
Administrative Procedure Act, this index
Agencies, creation by Congress, 14
Agency control
    Generally, 121 et seq.
    Administrative Procedure Act, this index
    Ambiguous legislative grants of power, 254
    Appropriations process, 127
    Casework communications on behalf of constituents, 128
    Civil Service Act, 125
    Confirmations of agency officers, 127
    Congressional Review Act, 145
    Decisional process, congressional interference, 129
    Due process limitations, 129
    Freedom of Information Act, 122
    Gramm-Rudman-Hollings Act, 145
    Informal influences on agency actions, 135
    Information Quality Act, 126
    Legislative Vetoes, this index
    Limitations on congressional power, 129 et seq.
    National Environmental Policy Act, 124
    Oversight process, 128
    Policy, this index
    Standing, statutory, of agencies, 126

Supreme Court, statutory authority
to litigate before, 127, 167
Ambiguous legislative grants of power to
agencies, 254
Appropriations process as mechanism of
agency control, 127
Article I vs Article III Courts
Generally, 183, 187
See also Article I Courts, this index
Casework communications on behalf of
constituents, 128
Civil Service Act as agency control
mechanism, 125
Confirmations of agency officers, 127
Congressional Review Act as agency
control mechanism, 145
Decisional process in pending
adjudication, congressional
interference with, 129
Delegations to agencies
Adjudication, this index
Delegations of Power, this index
Policy, this index
Due process limitations on power over
agencies, 129
Freedom of Information Act, agency
control by, 122
Gramm-Rudman-Hollings Act, 145
Informal influences on agency actions,
135
Information Quality Act as agency control
mechanism, 126
Legislative Vetoes, this index
Limitations on congressional power over
agencies, 129 et seq.
National Environmental Policy Act as
mechanism of agency control, 124
Oversight process as agency control
mechanism, 128
Politically-motivated policy delegations to
agencies, 37, 43
Solicitor General control of Supreme
Court litigation by agencies, 127,
167
Standing of agencies, statutory provisions
for, 126
Supreme Court, agencies' statutory
authority to litigate before, 127, 167

CONGRESSIONAL REVIEW ACT
Congressional control of agencies through,
145

**CONSTITUTIONAL FACT
DOCTRINE**
Adjudicatory power delegations to
agencies
Generally, 98
Deferential standard of judicial
review, 120
Deferential standard of judicial review,
120

CONSTITUTIONAL LAW
Adjudicatory power delegations to
agencies, Seventh Amendment
challenges, 92

Agencies, Constitutional bases of
presidential control, 155
Article I Courts, this index
Article III Courts, this index
Case or controversy limitation, 919, 957
Judicial review limitations, 795
Judicial review of constitutional questions
Generally, 825
Statutory preclusion, 797
Relationships, constitutional, 2
Seventh Amendment, this index
Standing, this index

CONSTRUCTION
Regulations. See Rulemaking and
Regulations, this index.
Statutes. See Statutory Interpretation,
this index.

**CONSUMER PRODUCT SAFETY
COMMISSION**
Ex parte communications in rulemakings,
499

CONSUMER PROTECTION
Bias rules and policy-based agency head
appointments, inherent tension, 521

CONTRACT RIGHTS
Property rights compared, 307

CONTROLLED SUBSTANCES ACT
Prescription regulations, interpretation
of, 776

COPYRIGHT ROYALTY JUDGES
Officer status, 183

CUSTOMS SERVICE
Chevron deference, 718

DATA QUALITY ACT
See Information Quality Act, this index

DE NOVO REVIEW
Constitutional facts, 98
Deferential review compared, 407
Legal determinations of agencies, 110
Social Security claims denials, 320, 428
Statutory interpretations, 605, 609

DECLARATORY JUDGMENT ACT
Judicial review of agency actions, 877

**DEFENSE BASE CLOSURE AND
REALIGNMENT ACT OF 1990**
Judicial review, final agency action
requirement, 860

DEFINITIONS
Adjudication, 277, 278
Adjudicative fact, 283
Administrative authority statute, 597
Agency, 5
ALJ, 107
APA, 5
Casework, 128
CEA, 106
Chevron two-step, 346
Constitutional fact doctrine, 98

CSA, 125
CSRT, 342
Deference, 621
Department, 183, 191
Executive branch agency, 10
FACA, 6
FOIA, 6
General applicability statute, 597
Hearing, 314
Holdover clause, 217
Independent agency, 11
Inferior officer, 169, 171
Interpretation of undefined terms in
        statutes, 604
Interpretative rule, 417
IQA, 126
Jurisdiction, 314
Jurisdictional fact, 98
Legislative fact, 283
Legislative power, 664
Legislative rule, 417
Major rule, 264
NEPA, 124
Nondelegation, 23
Nonlegislative rule, 417
Notice-and-comment rulemaking, 417
Officer, 127
Officer of the United States, 127, 157
OIRA, 259
OMB, 126
Order, 410
Organic act, 343
Ossification, rulemaking, 591
Plenary jurisdiction, 98
Policy statement, 417
Principal officer, 171
Private rights, 97, 101, 117
Procedural rule, 417, 539
Public officer, 127
Public rights, 97, 101, 117
Rule, 279
Rulemaking, 279
Substantive rule, 417, 539
Summary jurisdiction, 98
Traditional agencies, 10

DELANEY CLAUSE
Detailed delegation of powers problems,
        88

DELEGATIONS OF POWER
Adjudicatory powers
        Generally, 23, 108 et seq.
        See also Adjudication, this index
Ambiguous legislative grants of power to
        agencies
        Generally, 254
        Chevron deference, 643
Article I powers, 23
Article III powers, 23
Authorizations to agencies to interpret
        statutes, 598
Bankruptcy jurisdiction, 98
Breadth of delegation, adjudicatory
        powers, 97, 105, 110

Carcinogenics regulations, detailed
        delegation problems, 88
Chevron deference application to
        delegation ambiguities, 643
Congress and agencies, 23 et seq.
Delaney Clause, detailed delegation
        problems, 88
Executive delegations theory of policy
        delegations to agencies, 53
Food Stamp Program, detailed delegation
        problems, 85
History of administrative law, 115
Implicit and explicit, 621
Interpretation to avoid unconstitutional
        delegations, 59
Legislative Vetoes, this index
Policy delegations to agencies
                Generally, 23 et seq.
        See also Policy, this index
Politically-motivated policy delegations to
        agencies, 37, 43
Public interest theory of policy
        delegations to agencies, 43
Public/Private Rights Distinction, this
        index
Pure delegations, 51
Realities of agency delegations, 23
Responsibility vs power delegations, 53
Rulemaking, 23
Rules and regulations authority, 37
Social choice theory of policy delegations,
        45
Social policies affected by policy
        delegations, 42, 53
Statutory interpretation authorizations,
        598

DEPARTMENTS OF GOVERNMENT
Agencies, treatment as, 23
Appointment power determinations, 183,
        191
Traditional vs independent agencies, 191

DISCRETION
Judicial review of discretionary acts
                Generally, 810
        See also Judicial Review, this index
Lump sum appropriations, discretionary
        disbursement, 834
National Security Act, 820
No law to apply rule, discretionary acts
        where, 811, 831
No meaningful standard for discretionary
        acts, 820, 836
Prosecutorial discretion criteria, 557

DUE PROCESS
Adjudicatory due process
                Generally, 129, 277 et seq.
        See also Adjudication, this index
Congressional control of agencies, due
        process limitations, 129
Fundamental fairness standards, 358
Informal adjudications, 350
Informal rulemaking, 513

Life, liberty, or property, adjudications affecting
    Generally, 286 et seq.
    Stigma claims, 308
    Terrorist detentions, 332 et seq.
Limitations, congressional control of agencies, 129
Public employment of individuals, adjudications affecting
    Generally, 286
    Pre-termination hearing rights, 327
    Teachers, 298, 303
Tax assessments as adjudications requiring, 279
Terrorist detentions, 332
Welfare benefits determinations, 286, 313

ECONOMIC REGULATORY DISPUTES
Article III vs administrative adjudication, 98

ECONOMIC STABILIZATION ACT OF 1970
Policy delegations to agencies, 35

EMERGENCY PLANNING AND COMMUNITY RIGHT-TO-KNOW ACT
Citizen suits, 946

ENDANGERED SPECIES ACT
Citizen suits, 940
Constitutional standing to challenge actions of, 936
Judicial review, final agency action requirement, 864
Listings, appropriations riders limiting, 128

ENVIRONMENTAL PROTECTION
Citizen suits, 949
Standing of environmental petitioners, 932

ENVIRONMENTAL PROTECTION AGENCY
Chevron deference
    Generally, 613
    Step two invalidation of agency interpretation, 693, 706
Data sources, disclosure obligations, 479
Deadlines for agency actions, 915
Delay of agency problem, 913
Ex parte communications in rulemakings, 504, 511
Global warming rulemaking inaction, 852, 956
Judicial review
    Final agency action requirement, 866
    Inaction, reviewability, 852, 956
Notices of proposed rulemaking, 473
Rulemaking
    Generally, 418
    Data sources, disclosure obligations, 479

EQUAL EMPLOYMENT OPPORTUNITY COMMISSION
Chevron deference, 651, 661

EVIDENCE RULES
APA and federal rules compared, 407

EX PARTE COMMUNICATIONS
    Generally, 495 et seq.
Clean Air Act rulemaking, 504
Congressional communications, 504
Consumer Product Safety Commission rulemaking, 499
Environmental Protection Agency rulemaking, 504, 511
Federal Communications Commission rulemaking, 495, 500
Post-comment communications, 507
Presidential communications, 504

EXECUTIVE DEPARTMENTS
See Departments of Government, this index

EXECUTIVE ORDERS
    Generally, 258
Independent agencies, application Executive Order 12291 to, 264
Office of Management and Budget, 259
Rulemaking, Executive Order 12291
    Generally, 260
    Changes and modifications, 266
    Independent agencies, application to, 264
Separation of powers implications, 259

EXECUTIVE POWERS
See Presidential Powers, this index

EXHAUSTION OF REMEDIES
See Judicial Review, this index

FACT FINDING
Adjudication and rulemaking compared, 517
Adjudicative and legislative facts distinguished, 517
Arbitrary and capricious standard, 408
Legislative and adjudicative facts distinguished, 517
Reasoning processes applicable to, 413
Rulemaking and adjudication compared, 517
Substantial evidence standard, 408

FAIR LABOR STANDARDS ACT
Chevron deference, 712
Statutory interpretation authority, 605, 608

FEDERAL ADVISORY COMMITTEE ACT (FACA)
Agencies subject to, 6

FEDERAL BUREAU OF PRISONS
Regulations challenges, exhaustion of administrative remedies, 898

FEDERAL COMMUNICATIONS COMMISSION
Chevron deference
Generally, 708
Scope of *Chevron*, 738
Step two invalidation of agency interpretation, 684
Ex parte communications in rulemakings, 495, 500
Informal rulemaking, 483
Policy changes, judicial review of rules reflecting, 578
Rulemaking power, 419
Statutory interpretation authority, 604, 608

FEDERAL ELECTION COMMISSION
Adjudication challenges, standing, 927
Appointment powers, 158, 164
Officers of the United States status of commissioners, 158

FEDERAL INSECTICIDE, FUNGICIDE & RODENTICIDE ACT
Adjudicatory power delegations to agencies, 105
Judicial review, final agency action requirement, 866
Public/private rights distinction, 105

FEDERAL MOTOR CARRIER SAFETY ADMINISTRATION
Chevron deference, 630

FEDERAL POWER COMMISSION
Creation, 17
Policy statement exemptions from APA rulemaking requirements, 549

FEDERAL REGISTER
Rulemaking publications, 122, 460, 559

FEDERAL TRADE COMMISSION
Antitrust positions and prior exposure bias claims, 364
Bias, impermissible in informal rulemaking, 513
Chevron deference, 635
Creation, 17
Informal rulemaking, impermissible bias, 513
Rulemaking power, 419

FEDERAL-AID HIGHWAY ACT
Arbitrary and capricious review standard, 818
Informal adjudications, 350, 818
Judicial review of discretionary acts, 811

FOOD AND DRUG ADMINISTRATION
Judicial review
Discretionary acts, 820
Refusals to act, 842
Notice-and-comment rulemaking, 490
Policy statement exemptions from APA rulemaking requirements, 555

Regulation challenges, ripeness, 869, 874

FOOD STAMP PROGRAM
Detailed delegations of powers, problems with, 85

FOREIGN AFFAIRS MATTERS
Policy delegations to agencies, 35

FORMAL ADJUDICATION
See Adjudication, this index

FORMAL RULEMAKING
See Rulemaking and Regulations, this index

FORMALISM
Separation of powers, formalism vs functionalism approaches, 155

FREEDOM OF INFORMATION ACT (FOIA)
Agencies subject to, 6
Congressional control of agencies through, 122
Congressional intent, 7
Costs to agencies of compliance, 123
Deliberative process exemptions, 485
Exemptions, 122
Funding to cover agency costs, 123
Notices of proposed rulemaking, FOIA requests of underlying data, 485
Presidential staff, applicability to, 7
Procedure, 122
Unintended adverse effects, 122
White House Office of Administration as agency subject to, 7

FUNCTIONALISM
Separation of powers, formalism vs functionalism approaches, 155

GLOBAL WARMING
Judicial review of EPA rulemaking inaction, 852, 956

GOVERNMENT IN THE SUNSHINE ACT
Agencies subject to, 6

GRAMM-LEACH-BLILEY ACT
Chevron deference, 635

GRAMM-RUDMAN-HOLLINGS ACT
Generally, 145
Comptroller General powers under, 145, 153
Policy delegations to agencies, 151

HARD LOOK REVIEW STANDARD
Generally, 560
See also Arbitrary and Capricious Review Standard, this index

HAZARDOUS SUBSTANCES
See Toxic Substance Standards, this index

HEARINGS
Adjudication, this index

Chevron deference to determinations of hearing requirements, 349
Informal rulemaking, oral hearings in, 467
On-the-record hearing requirements, 464
Oral hearings in informal rulemaking, 467
Permit hearings, 345
Rulemaking hearing requirements, 344

HEARSAY
Substantial evidence standards, 400

HISTORY OF ADMINISTRATIVE LAW
Generally, 15
Agency capture theories, 20
Agency powers, policy debates, 19
APA enactment, 18
Arbitrary and capricious standard
Development of, 21
Evolution of standard, 560
Delegations of administrative powers, 15
Federal Power Commission, 17
Federal Trade Commission, 17
Interstate Commerce Commission creation, 17
Judicial review of agency actions, 16
Judicial review standards, development, 21
Modern era, 21
New Deal Era, 17
1960s and 1970s, 20
Policy delegation questions, 21
Policy delegations to agencies, 21
Progressive Era, 17
Rulemaking practices, 459
Securities and Exchange Commission, 17
Social Security Board, 18
Steamship Safety Act, 16
Transmission belt model of administration, 16

HORSE PROTECTION ACT
Judicial review of agency inaction, 850

HOUSING AND URBAN DEVELOPMENT DEPARTMENT
Chevron deference, 647, 661

IMMIGRATION AND NATIONALITY ACT
Adjudication processes, criticisms, 366, 371
Legislative vetoes, 135

IMPARTIALITY
See Bias, this index

INDEPENDENT AGENCIES
Appointment power, 162, 191
Characteristics of, 153
Definition, 11
Department status, traditional vs independent agencies, 191
Legislative veto as control mechanism, 142

Quasi-legislative and quasi-judicial functions, 225
Removal power, 153, 225
Rulemaking, Executive Order 12291, application to, 264

INDEPENDENT COUNSELS
Appointment powers, 171
Inferior vs principal officer status, 230
Officer status of, 174
Removal powers, 228
Saturday Night Massacre, 178

INDIAN HEALTH CARE IMPROVEMENT ACT
Judicial review of discretionary acts, 832

INFERIOR OFFICERS
See also Officers, this index
Appointments, principal and inferior officer distinctions, 171
Definition, 169, 171

INFORMAL ADJUDICATION
See Adjudication, this index

INFORMAL RULEMAKING
See Rulemaking and Regulations, this index

INFORMATION QUALITY ACT (IQA)
Congressional control of agencies through, 126
Office of Management and Budget implementation duties, 126

INHERENT NECESSITIES DOCTRINE
Policy delegations to agencies, 43, 46

INTELLIGIBLE PRINCIPLE STANDARD
Policy delegations to agencies, 25, 34, 45, 60

INTERNAL REVENUE SERVICE
Tax exemption rules, standing to challenge, 922

INTERPRETATION
Regulations. See Rulemaking and Regulations, this index
Statutes. See Statutory Interpretation, this index

INTERSTATE COMMERCE COMMISSION
Chevron deference, 630
Creation and abolition, 17, 630
Hearing requirements for formal rulemaking, 460
Primary jurisdiction doctrine, 918
Standing, prudential, 970

INTERSTITIAL POLICYMAKING
Generally, 25

INVESTIGATIONS
Separation of investigation and prosecution functions, 357

**IRREBUTTABLE PRESUMPTION
  DOCTRINE**
Judicial review, 88
Nondelegation doctrine compared, 88

JOHNSON, ANDREW
Officers, presidential authority to remove,
  14, 222

JUDICIAL POWERS
Adjudication, this index
Appointment powers of Courts of Law,
  183, 187
Article III vs Article I Courts
          Generally, 183, 187
          See also Article III Courts, this
                index
Chevron deference, separation of powers
  implications, 621
Constitutional bases, 99
Constitutional principles, 114
Delegations of Power, this index
Evolution of judicial review exercises of,
  818
Law question deference after *Chevron*,
  621
Primary jurisdiction doctrine, 917
Public/Private Rights Distinction, this
  index
References to magistrates, 101
Right of judiciary to protect Article III
  jurisdiction, 115
Separation of Powers, this index

JUDICIAL REVIEW
          Generally, 795 et seq.
Adjudication inactivity, 853
Adjudications, reviews of
          Generally, 385 et seq.
          Agency reasoning processes, 413
          APA standards, 385
          Arbitrary and capricious standard,
                408
          Deferential vs de novo review, 407
          Fact finding review, 386
          Failure to adjudicate, 853
          Hearsay, substantial evidence
                standard, 400
          Law issues, 413
          Rulemaking review standards
                compared, 386, 413
          Substantial evidence standard, 386
          Whole record review, 386, 407
Agency discretion. Discretionary acts,
  below
Agency findings of fact, 98
Agency reasoning processes, 413
All Writs Act, 914
Amendments of rules, 577
APA
          Generally, 597, 795
          Adjudications, reviews of, 385
          Exhaustion of administrative
                remedies, 907
          Presumptive reviewability, 796, 803,
                810, 836

Arbitrary and Capricious Review
  Standard, this index
Article II, formalism vs functionalism in
  construction of, 155
Auer Deference, this index
Chevron Deference, this index
Citizen Suits, this index
Clean Air Act ripeness requirements, 878
Congressional finality statements, 864
Congressional intent, exhaustion
  requirement, 899, 904
Constitutional concerns, rules involving,
  589
Constitutional fact doctrine
          Generally, 98
          Deferential standard of review, 120
Constitutional issues
          Generally, 799, 825
          Statutory preclusion, 797
Constitutional limitations
          Generally, 795
          Standing, this index
De Novo Review, this index
Deadlines for agency actions
          Generally, 913
          Enforcement, 915
Declaratory Judgment Act, 877
Deference defined, 621
Deferential vs de novo review of
  adjudications, 407
Delay of agency problem, 913
Direct consequences, final agency action
  requirement, 864
Discretionary acts
          Generally, 810 et seq.
          Employment decisions of agencies,
                820, 822
          Federal-Aid Highway Act, 811
          Food and Drug Administration, 820
          Indian Health Care Improvement
                Act, 832
          Lump sum appropriations,
                discretionary applications, 834
          National Security Act, 820
          No law to apply rule, 811, 831
          No meaningful standard, 820, 836
          Public Health Service programs, 832
Employment decisions of agencies, 820,
  822
Environmental Protection Agency
  inaction, reviewability, 852, 956
Evolution of judicial power exercises
  through, 818
Exhaustion of administrative remedies
          Generally, 878 et seq.
          APA, 907
          Congressional intent as to
                requirement, 899, 904
          Delay of agency problem, 913
          Federal Bureau of Prisons
                regulations, 898
          Futility exception, 898
          Inadequacy exception, 898, 905
          Issue exhaustion, 911
          National Housing Act, 907

National Labor Relations Board, issue exhaustion, 912
Optional and mandatory intra-agency remedies, 911
Prison Litigation Reform Act, 904
Rulemaking challenges, 898
Selective Service System, 890, 893
Three-part test for waiver, 905
Express statutory preclusion, 796
Fact finding review of agency adjudications, 386
Final agency action requirement
    Generally, 855 et seq.
    Census Bureau reapportionments, 857
    Congressional finality statements, 864
    Defense Base Closure and Realignment Act of 1990, 860
    Direct consequences, 864
    Endangered Species Act, 865
    Environmental Protection Agency, 866
    Federal Insecticide, Fungicide, and Rodenticide Act, 866
    Two-part test, 864
Finality
    Delay of agency problem, 913
    Standing, this index
Findings of fact, agency, 98
Food and Drug Administration refusals to act, 842
Formal vs informal rulemaking, 471
Formalism vs functionalism in construction of Article II, 155
Global warming rulemaking inaction, 852, 956
Hardship of timeliness deferrals to challenges, 877
Hearsay, substantial evidence standard, 400
History of administrative law, 16
History of standards development, 21
Implied preclusion, 799
Inaction, agency
    Generally, 836 et seq.
    Adjudication inactivity, 853
    Deadlines for agency actions
        Generally, 913
        Enforcement, 915
    Environmental Protection Agency, 852, 956
    Food and Drug Administration, 842
    Global warming rulemaking, 852, 956
    Horse Protection Act, 850
    Labor-Management Reporting and Disclosure Act, 837
    Probable cause to act, 840
    Reasons for inaction, 840
    Refusal to act, above
    Rulemaking inactivity, 851
Inadequacy of administrative remedies and exhaustion, 898, 905
Intelligible Principle Standard, this index

Interpretation of statutory preclusions, 796
Interrelationship of timing doctrines, 855
Irrebuttable presumption doctrine, 88
Issue exhaustion, 911
Jurisdiction, 917
Jurisdictional fact doctrine
    Generally, 98
    Deferential standard of review, 120
Law issues in adjudications, 413
Law questions and policy questions, distinguishing, 597
Limitations on reviewability
    Generally, 795 et seq.
    Preclusion, below
    Standing, this index
Lump sum appropriations, discretionary applications, 834
Multiple issues, ripe and unripe, 876
National Labor Relations Board adjudications, 386
No law to apply rule, discretionary acts, 811, 831
No meaningful standard for discretionary acts, 820, 836
Nondelegation doctrine
    Generally, 23
    See also Policy, this index
Notices of proposed rulemaking, review based on, 466
Overlap of timing doctrines, 855
Policy changes, rules reflecting, 578
Policy statements, 847
Preclusion
    Agricultural Marketing Agreement Act of 1937, 800
    Implied, 799
    Medicare program, 804
    Veterans' Readjustment Benefits Act, 797
Pre-enforcement review of regulations, 869, 877
Pre-enforcement review of rules, 560
Presumptive reviewability
    Generally, 810
    Agency inaction, 836
    APA, 796, 803
Primary jurisdiction doctrine, 917
Probable cause to act, inaction in face of, 840
Reasons for inaction, statements of, 840
Record requirements, rulemaking, 467
Refusals to act
    Adjudication failures, 853
    Food and Drug Administration, 842
    Inaction, agency, 836 et seq.
    Rulemaking failures, 851
Regulations, interpretation of
    Generally, 774 et seq.
    See also Rulemaking and Regulations, this index
Remand without vacatur of challenged rules, 595
Remands to explain reasoning processes, 413, 442
Rescissions of rules, 577

Ripeness
    Generally, 868
    Civil Service Commission regulation
        challenges, 868
    Clean Air Act ripeness
        requirements, 878
    Delay of agency problem, 913
    Food and Drug Administration
        regulation challenges, 869,
        874
    Hardship of deferring review, 877
    Mine Safety and Health Act rule
        challenges, 878
    Multiple issues, ripe and unripe,
        876
    Pre-enforcement review of
        regulations, 869, 877
    Rule, reviews, 466
    Standing, this index
    Tax regulation challenges, 877
Rulemaking
    Generally, 560 et seq.
    Abandonment of rule after review,
        567
    Adjudication compared, 413
    Adjudication review standards
        compared, 386
    Amendments of rules, 577
    Constitutional concerns, rules
        involving, 589
    Inactivity, 851
    Pre-enforcement review, 560
    Record requirements, 467
    Remand without vacatur, 595
    Rescissions of rules, 577
    Ripeness for review, 466
Seminole Rock standard of judicial
    deference, 775, 776
Separation of powers implications, 14
Skidmore Deference, this index
Sovereign immunity limitations, 795
Standards of Review, this index
Standing, this index
Statutory authorizations, 796
Statutory interpretations of agencies
    Generally, 597
    See also *Chevron* Deference, this
        index
Statutory preclusion
    Constitutional challenges, 797
    Express, 796
Subject matter expertise of agency,
    deference based on, 621
Substantial evidence standard of
    adjudications, 386
Termination, congressional finality
    statements, 864
Timing of review
    Generally, 855 et seq.
    Census Bureau reapportionments,
        857
    Civil Service Commission regulation
        challenges, 868
    Clean Air Act ripeness
        requirements, 878

    Defense Base Closure and
        Realignment Act of 1990, 860
    Delay of agency problem, 913
    Direct consequences, 864
    Environmental Protection Agency
        actions, 866
    Exhaustion of administrative
        remedies, above
    Federal Insecticide, Fungicide, and
        Rodenticide Act, 866
    Final agency action requirement,
        855
    Food and Drug Administration
        regulation challenges, 869,
        874
    Hardship of deferring review, 877
    Interrelationship of timing
        doctrines, 855
    Mine Safety and Health Act rule
        challenges, 878
    Multiple issues, ripe and unripe,
        876
    Overlap of timing doctrines, 855
    Pre-enforcement review of
        regulations, 869, 877
    Ripe and unripe issues, 876
    Ripeness, 868
    Tax regulation challenges, 877
    Two-part test of finality of agency
        action, 864
Timing questions
    Standing, this index
Two-part test of finality of agency action,
    864
Whole record review of adjudications, 386,
    407

JURISDICTION
    See also Article I Courts, this index;
        Article III Courts, this index
Bankruptcy, Article I vs Article III courts,
    98
Plenary jurisdiction, 98
Primary jurisdiction doctrine, 917
Right of judiciary to protect Article III
    jurisdiction, 115
Standing, this index
Summary jurisdiction, 98

JURISDICTIONAL FACT DOCTRINE
Adjudicatory power delegations to
    agencies
        Generally, 98
    Deferential standard of judicial
        review, 120
Deferential standard of judicial review,
    120

JURY TRIAL RIGHTS
See Seventh Amendment, this index

JUSTICE DEPARTMENT
Agency litigation conducted by, 126

**LABOR-MANAGEMENT REPORTING
AND DISCLOSURE ACT**
Judicial review of agency inaction, 837

LEGISLATIVE FACT
Definition, 283

LEGISLATIVE HISTORY
Chevron deference
    Generally, 645, 656, 659
    Step one vs step two tool, 661

LEGISLATIVE POWERS
See Congressional Powers, this index

LEGISLATIVE STANDARDS TEST
Policy delegations to agencies, 25

LEGISLATIVE VETOES
    Generally, 135
Adjudications, legislative vetoes affecting, 142
Administrative Procedure Act, 135
Alternative control mechanisms, 144
Congressional removal powers questions, 222
Congressional Review Act, 144
Constitutionality, 135
Immigration and Nationality Act, 135
Independent agencies, control of, 142
Nondelegation doctrine, relation to, 142
One-house vetoes, 137, 144
Policy effects, 142
Presentment Clause challenge, 138
Separation of powers implications, 142

LICENSING
Adjudication, treatment as, 278

LINE ITEM VETOES
Signing statement parallels, 257

LONGSHOREMEN'S & HARBOR WORKERS' ACT
Adjudicatory power delegations to agencies, 93
Statutory interpretation authority, 608

MEDICARE PROGRAM
Judicial review preclusion, 804

MINE SAFETY AND HEALTH ADMINISTRATION
Adjudications, split-enforcement model, 366
Legislative and interpretive rules distinguished, 543
Program Policy Letters, 548
Ripeness of rule challenges, 878

NAMED CONTINGENCY TEST
Policy delegations to agencies, 25

NATIONAL BANK ACT
Standing to challenge regulations, 972

NATIONAL ENVIRONMENTAL POLICY ACT
Congressional control of agencies through, 124
Unintended adverse effects, 124

NATIONAL HIGHWAY TRAFFIC SAFETY ADMINISTRATION
Hard look review of rules of, 560 et seq.

NATIONAL HOUSING ACT
Exhaustion of administrative remedies, 907

NATIONAL INDUSTRIAL RECOVERY ACT
Policy delegations to agencies, 25

NATIONAL LABOR RELATIONS BOARD
Adjudication, rulemaking through, 447
Decisions, standard of review, 388
Exhaustion of administrative remedies, 912
Judicial review of adjudications of, 386
Rulemaking through adjudication, 447
Statutory interpretation authority, 599, 608, 609

NATIONAL POLLUTION DISCHARGE ELIMINATION SYSTEM (NPDES)
Hearings on permits, 345
Permit hearings, 345

NATIONAL SECURITY ACT
Judicial review of discretionary acts, 820

NEGOTIATED RULEMAKING ACT
Generally, 593

NEW DEAL ERA
History of administrative law, 17
Policy delegations to agencies challenges, 25, 47
Removal powers disputes, 225

NONDELEGATION DOCTRINE
    Generally, 23
    See also Policy, this index
Legislative vetoes, relation of doctrine to, 142

NOTICE-AND-COMMENT RULEMAKING
See Rulemaking and Regulations, this index

NOTICES OF PROPOSED RULEMAKING (NOPR)
    Generally, 473
Adequacy challenges, 473
Advanced notices, 478
APA requirements, 473
Data sources, disclosure obligations, 479, 483
Direct final rulemaking proposals, 594
FOIA requests of underlying data, 485
Implied notice of specific proposals, 473
Informal rulemaking notice requirements, 473
Judicial review based on, 466
Logical outgrowth standard, 475, 477
Negotiated Rulemaking Act, 593
Portland Cement requirement, 479, 488

Prejudicial effect of notice errors, 483, 485
Publication requirements, 460
Reasonableness standard, 483
Reform proposals, 590
Responses to comments, notice of, 477
Scope of notice, 473
Time for responses, 490
What proposals must be noticed, 473

NUCLEAR REGULATORY COMMISSION
Oral hearings in informal rulemaking, 467

OCCUPATIONAL SAFETY AND HEALTH ACT
Adjudications, split-enforcement model, 259
Policy delegations to agencies, 38, 43
Statutory interpretation authority, 609

OFFICE OF INFORMATION AND REGULATORY AFFAIRS (OIRA)
Generally, 259
Presidential influence on agencies through, 274

OFFICE OF MANAGEMENT AND BUDGET (OMB)
Agency control functions, 265
Executive orders, 259
Information Quality Act implementation, 126

OFFICERS
Administrative Law Judges as, 169
Appointments
    Generally, 157 et seq.
    See also Appointment Power, this index
    Principal and inferior officer distinctions, 171
Commissioners of independent agencies, 162
Copyright Royalty Judges, 183
Definition, 127, 157
Federal Election Commission, commissioners of, 158
Holdover clauses, 217
Independent counsels
    Inferior vs principal officer status, 230
    Officer status of, 174
Inferior, 171
Inferior status criteria, 174
Military court personnel, 179
Presidential authority to remove, 14, 222
Principal, 171
Principal/inferior status, distinguishing criteria, 171, 183
Removal
    See also Removal Power, this index
    Independent agency officers, 153
    Status and removal conditions, 174–175
Subordinate status, 179

Tax court special judges, 183

OPINION LETTERS
Chevron deference, 712, 746
Rules expressed in, 264

OPPORTUNITY TO RESPOND
See Notices of Proposed Rulemaking, this index

ORDERS
Definition, 410

ORGANIC ACTS
Definition, 343

OSSIFICATION
Rulemaking, 591, 877

PARTIALITY
See Bias, this index

PERMITS
Hearings on, 345

PLAIN MEANING RULE
Chevron deference, 643, 651

POLICY
Generally, 23 et seq.
Accountability-evading delegations to agencies, 37, 43
Adjudications, policy setting in, 277
Air quality standards promulgation, nondelegation doctrine, 55, 60
Bias rules and policy-based agency head appointments, inherent tension, 521
Broad vs detailed delegations, 84
Canons of construction reflecting purpose of nondelegation doctrine, 55
Carcinogenics regulations, detailed delegation problems, 88
Casework on behalf of congressional constituents, implications of, 128
Chevron deference applicability to policy-related questions, 53
Chevron deference as policy delegation, 621
Chevron deference where conflicting policies committed to agency's care, 615
Congressional failures to set policy, reasons for, 624
Delaney Clause, detailed delegation problems, 88
Delegated authority as to
    Generally, 23 et seq.
    Accountability-evading delegations to agencies, 37, 43
    Air quality standards promulgation, 55, 60
    Bias rules and policy-based agency head appointments, inherent tension, 521
    Broad vs detailed delegations, 84
    Canons of construction reflecting purpose of nondelegation doctrine, 55

Carcinogenics regulations, detailed delegation problems, 88

Casework on behalf of congressional constituents, implications of, 128

Chevron deference as a policy delegation, 621

Chevron deference where conflicting policies committed to agency's care, 615

Chevron doctrine applicability to policy-related questions, 53

Congressional failures to set policy, reasons for, 624

Delaney Clause, detailed delegation problems, 88

Detailed vs broad delegations, 84

Economic Stabilization Act of 1970, 35

Executive delegations theory, 53

Failures of Congress to set policy, reasons for, 624

Food Stamp Program, detailed delegation problems, 85

Foreign affairs matters, 35

Gramm-Rudman-Hollings Act, 151

History of administrative law, 21

Inherent necessities justifying broad grants, 43, 46

Intelligible principle standard
 Generally, 25, 34, 45, 60
 Nondelegation doctrine, 818

Interpretation to avoid unconstitutional delegations, 59

Interstitial policymaking, 25

Irrebuttable presumption doctrine, nondelegation doctrine compared, 88

Legislative power, definitional problems, 64

Legislative standards test, 25

Legislative vetoes, policy effects, 142

Named contingency test, 25

National Industrial Recovery Act, 25

New Deal Era, 25, 47

New nondelegation doctrine, 55

Nondelegation doctrine, below

Occupational Safety and Health Act, 38, 43

Origin of nondelegation doctrine, 23

Politically-motivated policy delegations to agencies, 37, 43

Public interest theory, 43

Public interests justifying broad grants, 43

Pure delegations, 51

Realities of agency delegations, 23

Responsibility vs power delegations, 53

Rules and regulations authority, 37

Sentencing Commission, 445

Separation of powers implications, 151

Social choice theory of policy delegations, 45

Social policies affected, 42, 53

Sources of policy guidance, 43

Standard of review, 21

Tariff-setting powers, 23

Toxic substances exposure standards, 38, 43

Detailed vs broad delegations, 84

Economic Stabilization Act of 1970, 35

Executive delegations theory, 53

Failures of Congress to set policy, reasons for, 624

Food Stamp Program, detailed delegation problems, 85

Foreign affairs matters, nondelegation doctrine, 35

Gramm-Rudman-Hollings Act, delegated policy authority, 151

History of delegated policy authority, 21

Inherent necessities justifying broad grants, 43, 46

Intelligible principle standard
 Delegated policy authority, 25, 34, 45, 60
 Nondelegation doctrine, 25, 34, 45, 60, 818

Interpretation to avoid unconstitutional delegations, 59

Interstitial policymaking, 25

Irrebuttable presumption doctrine, nondelegation doctrine compared, 88

Law questions and policy questions, distinguishing, 597

Legislative power, definitional problems, 64

Legislative standards test
 Delegated policy authority, 25
 Nondelegation doctrine, 25

Legislative vetoes
 Policy effects, 142
 Relation to nondelegation doctrine, 143

Named contingency test
 Delegated policy authority, 25
 Nondelegation doctrine, 25

National Industrial Recovery Act
 Delegated policy authority, 25
 Nondelegation doctrine, 25

New Deal Era nondelegation, 25, 47

New nondelegation doctrine
 Delegated policy authority, 55
 Nondelegation doctrine, 53, 55

Nondelegation doctrine, above XREF, New nondelegation doctrine
 Generally, 23 et seq.
 Air quality standards promulgation, 55, 60
 Canons of construction reflecting purpose of, 55
 Decline of the doctrine, 35
 Executive delegations theory, 53
 Foreign affairs matters, 35
 Future of nondelegation problem, 84

Intelligible principle standard, 25, 34, 45, 60, 818
Interpretation to avoid unconstitutionality, 59
Interstitial policymaking, 25
Irrebuttable presumption doctrine compared, 88
Legislative standards test, 25
Legislative vetoes, relation to, 142
Named contingency test, 25
National Industrial Recovery Act, 25
New Deal Era, 25, 47
Occupational Safety and Health Act, 38, 43
Origin, 23
Platitudinous support, 55
Pure delegations, 51
Purpose of doctrine, 442
Realities of agency delegations, 23
Reinvigoration, 37
Rejection of reinvigoration, 45
Renewed interest in doctrine, 37
Responsibility vs power delegations, 53
Rules and regulations authority, 37
Sentencing Commission, 445
Social policies affected, 42, 53
Occupational Safety and Health Act, 38, 43
Origin of nondelegation doctrine, 23
Platitudinous support for nondelegation doctrine, 55
Politically-motivated policy delegations to agencies, 37, 43
Public interests justifying broad grants, 43
Pure delegations, 51
Purpose of nondelegation doctrine, 42
Questions of law and questions of policy, distinguishing, 597
Realities of agency delegations, 23
Reinvigoration of nondelegation doctrine, 37
Rejection of reinvigoration of nondelegation doctrine, 45
Removal power, policy decision powers of removed officer as factor, 231
Renewed interest in nondelegation doctrine, 37
Responsibility vs power delegations, 53
Rules and regulations authority and delegated policy authority, 37
Rules reflecting policy changes, judicial review of, 578
Sentencing Commission, nondelegation doctrine, 445
Separation of powers implications of delegated policy authority, 151
Social choice theory of policy delegations, 45
Social policies affected by delegated policy authority, 42, 53
Sources of policy guidance, 43
Standard of review of delegated policy authority, 21

Statements of agency policy. See Rulemaking and Regulations, this index
Statutory interpretation
Policy influences, 597
Policy resolutions, 625
Sub silentio departures from prior policy, 414, 581
Tariff-setting powers, 23
Toxic substances exposure standards, 38, 43

POLICY STATEMENTS
See Rulemaking and Regulations, this index

POLITICS
Appointment powers, political implications of exercises, 255
Bias rules and policy-based agency head appointments, inherent tension, 521
Policy delegations to agencies, politically-motivated, 37, 43
Removal powers, political implications of exercises, 256
Removals for political reasons, 222, 226
Rulemaking, politics impacting, 522
Rulemaking process, political accountability inherent in, 425
Standing jurisprudence, political differences reflected in Supreme Court opinions, 968

PREJUDICE
See Bias, this index

PRESIDENTIAL POWERS
Agencies, control of
Generally, 155 et seq.
Ad hoc jawboning, 274
Ambiguous legislative power grants, 254
Appointment Power, this index
Constitutional bases, 155
Nature and scope of presidential authority, 247
OMB oversight control, 265
Removal Power, this index
Rulemaking, efforts to influence, 272
Signing statements, effect of, 257
Steel Seizure Case, 248, 253
Agencies, presidential creation, 13
Agency policy delegations as delegations to the executive branch, 53
Ambiguous legislative power grants to agencies, 254
Appointment Power, this index
Appropriations, presidential discretion as to, 145
Chevron deference, separation of powers implications, 621
Commander-in-Chief powers, 255
Constitutional bases of control over agencies, 155
Discretion to spend appropriated funds, 145

Executive Orders, this index
FOIA applicability to presidential staff, 7
Formalism vs functionalism in
    construction of Article II, 155
Johnson impeachment, 14, 222
Nature and scope of presidential
    authority over agencies, 247
Officers, authority to remove, 14, 222
Policy delegations to agencies, executive
    delegations theory of, 53
Prosecution, 178
Removal Power, this index
Rulemaking, efforts to influence, 272
Separation of Powers, this index
Signing statements, effect of, 257
Steel Seizure Case, 248, 253
Unitary executive theory, 253
War powers, 255

PRINCIPAL OFFICERS
See Officers, this index

PRISON LITIGATION REFORM ACT
Exhaustion of administrative remedies,
    904

PRIVACY ACT
Agencies subject to, 6

PROCEDURAL RULES
See Rulemaking and Regulations, this
    index

PROGRESSIVE ERA
History of administrative law, 17

PROPERTY RIGHTS
Contract rights compared, 307

PROSECUTORIAL POWERS
Generally, 178

PUBLIC EMPLOYMENT
Adjudications affecting, due process rights
        Generally, 286
    Pre-termination hearing rights, 327
    Teachers, 298, 303
Pre-termination hearing rights, 327

**PUBLIC HEALTH SERVICE
    PROGRAMS**
Judicial review, discretionary acts, 832

**PUBLIC INTEREST THEORY OF
    AGENCIES**
Generally, 20

PUBLIC OFFICERS
See Officers, this index

**PUBLIC/PRIVATE RIGHTS
    DISTINCTION**
Article I courts, 105
Article III vs administrative adjudications
    of disputes, 97
Bankruptcy disputes, 101, 105
Distinguishing public rights, 106
Evolution of Supreme Court
    jurisprudence, 120
Federal Insecticide, Fungicide &
    Rodenticide Act, 105
Government as party, significance of, 117
Jury trial rights, 115
New statutory public rights, 116
Origin of public rights doctrine, 100
Rejection of doctrine, 106, 110
Separation of powers implications, 100
Workers' compensation regimes, 120

**QUASI-LEGISLATIVE AND QUASI-
    JUDICIAL FUNCTIONS OF
    AGENCIES**
Generally, 14, 225
Executive functions distinguished, 230
Removal of officers, 225, 227

REMOVAL POWER
        Generally, 217 et seq.
    See also Appointment Power, this
        index; Officers, this index
Appointment power distinctions, 219
Cause, removal without, 222, 226
Consent of Senate to removal, 217
Executive powers of removed officer as
    factor, 222, 230
Faithful execution duties, implications of,
    221
For-cause removals, 225
Holdover clauses, 217
Independent agencies, removals from,
    153, 225
Independent counsels
        Generally, 228
    Saturday Night Massacre, 178
Johnson impeachment, 14, 222
Legislative vetoes and congressional
    removal powers questions, 222
Limitations on presidential removals, 222,
    226
New Deal Era removal power disputes,
    225
Policy decision powers of removed officer
    as factor, 231
Political implications of exercises, 256
Political reason removals, 222, 226
Quasi-judicial functions, 227
Quasi-legislative and quasi-judicial
    functions of agencies, 225, 228
Saturday Night Massacre, 178
Separation of powers, 217, 222
Tenure in Office Act, 217, 222

RESPONSIBILITIES
Delegations of distinguished from power
    delegations, 53

RULEMAKING AND REGULATIONS
        Generally, 417 et seq.
Adjudication, rule-creating, 441 et seq.
Adjudication compared
        Generally, 277, 418
    Advantages of rulemaking, 424
    APA distinctions, 278
    Bias rules, 517
    Due process requirements, 278
    Fact finding standards, 517

Functional relationship between rules and adjudications, 426 et seq.
Order issuances, 410
Prospectivity, 279
Retroactivity, 442, 457
Standard of judicial review, 413
Adjudication requirements for validity challenges, 466
Adjudication-avoiding rules, 435
Adjudications, policy expressing, 448
Adjudicatory opinions, rules expressed in, 264
Advanced notices, 478
Advantages of rulemaking over adjudication, 424
Agency management exemptions from APA requirements, 524
Ambiguities in regulations, interpretation, 774
Amendments of rules, judicial review, 577
APA requirements
Generally, 457 et seq.
Decline of formal rulemaking, 459
Evolution of informal rulemaking, 465 et seq.
Exemptions from APA requirements, below
Hearing requirements for formal rulemaking, 460
Informal rulemaking, evolution of, 465 et seq.
Informal rulemaking, oral hearings in, 467
Interpretive rules, 459
Notices of Proposed Rulemaking, this index
On-the-record hearing requirements, 464
Oral hearings in informal rulemaking, 467
Policy statements, 459
Procedural rules, 459
Retroactive application of rules, 455
Three sets of procedural requirements, 459
Arbitrary and Capricious Review Standard, this index
Auer deference, interpretation of regulations, 775–776
Basis and purpose statements
Generally, 494, 502
Hard look review, effect on, 590
Bias challenges, informal rulemaking, 495, 513
Binding norms, policy statements distinguished, 552, 554
Chevron deference in adjudicatory vs rulemaking interpretations, 711
Code of Federal Regulations publication, 18, 546, 559
Cogent materiality, response to comments of, 494
Common law rulemaking, 447
Concise general statement requirement
Informal rulemaking, 465, 488, 493

Concise statement of basis and purpose, 489
Congressional ex parte communications, informal rulemaking, 504
Constitutional concerns, judicial review of rules involving, 589
Data sources, disclosure obligations, 479, 482
Decline of formal rulemaking, 459
Definition, 279
Delegations of authority to establish, 337
Delegations of power, 23
Direct final rulemaking proposals, 594
Due process, informal rulemaking, 513
Emergency exemptions from APA requirements, 525
Environmental Protection Agency, rulemaking power, 418
Evolution of hard look judicial review, 560
Evolution of informal rulemaking, 465 et seq.
Ex parte communications in rulemakings, 495 et seq.
Executive Order 12291
Generally, 260
Changes and modifications, 266
Independent agencies, application to, 264
Exemptions from APA requirements
Generally, 523 et seq.
Agency management, 524
Categories, exempt, 417
Emergencies, 525
Federal Aviation Administration Age Sixty Rule, 435
Foreign affairs, 524
Good cause exemption, 524
Interpretive rules, 542
Military, 524
Notice-and-comment rulemaking, effect of, 523
Policy statements, 549
Practically binding policy statements, 558
Procedural rule exemptions, 539
Public property, 524
Subject matter, 524
When required, 440
Federal Aviation Administration Age Sixty Rule, 435
Federal Communications Commission rulemaking power, 419
Federal Register publication, 122, 460, 559
Federal Trade Commission rulemaking power, 419
Force of law assertions, *Chevron* deference, 717
Foreign affairs exemptions from APA requirements, 524
Formal rulemaking
Decline of, 459
Exemptions from APA requirements, above
Hearing requirements, 460

Judicial review of formal vs informal rulemaking, 471
Functional relationship between rules and adjudications, 426 et seq.
Good cause exemptions from APA requirements, 524
Hearing requirements
    Generally, 344
    Formal rulemaking, 460
    Informal rulemaking, 467
    Oral hearings, 467
History of rulemaking practices, 459
Informal rulemaking
    Generally, 465 et seq., 483
    Bias challenges, 494
    Cogent materiality, response to comments of, 494
    Concise general statement requirement, 465, 488, 493
    Concise statement of basis and purpose, 489
    Congressional ex parte communications, 504
    Data sources, disclosure obligations, 479, 482
    Due process, 513
    Evolution of, 465 et seq.
    Ex parte communications in rulemakings, 495 et seq.
    Judicial review of formal vs informal rulemaking, 471
    Notice requirements, 473
    Notice-and-comment, 490
    Oral hearings in, 467
    Ossification of process, 591, 877
    Portland Cement requirement, 479, 488
    Post-comment ex parte communications, 507
    Presidential ex parte communications, 504
    Reform proposals, 590
Informal rulemaking and impermissible bias, 513
Interpretation of regulations
    Generally, 774
    Ambiguities in regulations, 774
    APA requirements, 459
    Auer deference, 775–776
    Controlled Substances Act prescription regulations, 776
    Interpretive rules, below
    Skidmore deference, 775
Interpretive rules
    Generally, 417, 442
    APA requirements, 459
    Chevron deference, 711
    Exemptions from APA requirements, 542
Judicial review
    Generally, 560 et seq.
    Abandonment of rule after review, 567
    Adjudication review standards compared, 386
    Amendments of rules, 577

Constitutional concerns, rules involving, 589
Evolution of hard look review, 560
Exhaustion of administrative remedies, 898
Formal vs informal rulemaking, 471
Policy changes, rules reflecting, 578
Pre-enforcement review, 560
Record requirements, 467
Refusal to institute rulemaking, 851
Remand without vacatur, 595
Rescissions of rules, 577
Ripeness of rule for, 466
Legislative rules
    Chevron deference, 711
    Nonlegislative rules compared, 417
    Statutory requirements, 442
Major rules, 264
Military exemptions from APA requirements, 524
National Highway Traffic Safety Administration rules, review of, 560 et seq.
Negotiated Rulemaking Act, 593
Non-exempt rules, 417
Notice requirements, informal rulemaking, 473
Notice-and-comment rulemaking
    Generally, 490
    Definition, 417
    Exemptions from APA requirements, 523
Notices of Proposed Rulemaking, this index
On-the-record hearing requirements, 464
Opinion letters, *Chevron* deference, 712
Ossification, 591, 877
Policy changes, judicial review of rules reflecting, 578
Policy expressing adjudications, 448
Policy statements
    Generally, 417, 442
    APA requirements, 459
    Binding norms distinguished, 552, 554
    Chevron deference, 711
    Exemptions from APA requirements, 549
    Judicial review, 847
    Practically binding policy statements, 558
    Prosecutorial discretion criteria, 557
    Rules distinguished, 551
Political accountability and rulemaking process, 425
Politics impacting, 512
Post-comment ex parte communications, informal rulemaking, 507
Powers, rulemaking
    Environmental Protection Agency, 418
    Federal Communications Commission, 419
    Federal Trade Commission, 419
    Procedural vs substantive rules, 419, 422

Securities Exchange Commission, 418

Practically binding policy statements, exemptions from APA requirements, 558

Pre-enforcement judicial review, 560

Prejudicial effect of notice errors, 483, 485

Presidential ex parte communications and informal rulemaking, 504

Procedural rules
  Generally, 417
  APA requirements, 459
  Exemptions from APA requirements, 539

Procedural vs substantive rulemaking powers, 419, 422

Procedure
  Arbitrary and capricious review standard, effect on, 590
  Direct final rulemaking proposals, 594
  Hard look reviews, effect on procedures, 590
  Informal rulemaking, 590
  Negotiated Rulemaking Act, 593
  Ossification of informal rulemaking, 591, 877
  Reform of informal rulemaking, proposals for, 590

Prosecutorial discretion criteria as policy statements, 557

Prospectivity
  Adjudication compared, 279
  Rules expressed in adjudications, 447

Public property exemptions from APA requirements, 524

Purpose statements
  Generally, 494, 502
  Hard look review, effect on, 590

Record required for judicial review, 467

Reform proposals, informal rulemaking, 590

Refusal to institute rulemaking, judicial review, 851

Regulatory agenda requirements, 265

Rescissions of rules, judicial review, 577

Responses to comments, notice of, 477

Retroactive application of rules, 452

Retroactivity, adjudicatory rules compared, 442, 457

Ripeness of rule for judicial review, 466

Securities Exchange Commission rulemaking power, 418

Seminole Rock standard of judicial deference, 775, 776

Skidmore deference, interpretation of regulations, 775

Statutes and rules compared, 417

Statutory interpretation, rulemaking vs adjudicatory situations, 708

Statutory powers, retroactive application of rules, 454

Statutory requirements, 442

Subject matter exemptions from APA requirements, 524

Substantive rules, 417

Substantive vs procedural rule determinations, 539

Validity challenges, adjudication requirements, 466

RULES
Definition, 279

SECURITIES AND EXCHANGE COMMISSION
Adjudication, rulemaking through, 442
Creation, 17
Rulemaking power, 418
Rulemaking through adjudication, 442

SELECTIVE SERVICE SYSTEM
Exhaustion of administrative remedies, 890, 893

SEMINOLE ROCK STANDARD
Agency interpretations, 775, 776

SENTENCING COMMISSION
  Generally, 371
Policy delegations to agencies, 45

SEPARATION OF POWERS
Adjudication, this index
Agencies, creation of, 14
Appropriations process, separation of powers implications, 145
Chevron deference, effect of, 621
Chevron deference as principle of, 621
Constitutional bases, 15
Executive orders, 259
Formalism vs functionalism in construction of vesting clauses, 155
Judicial review of agency actions, 14
Legislative vetoes, 142
Officers, presidential authority to remove, 14, 222
Policy delegations to agencies, 151
Presumption of proper exercise, 149
Prosecutorial powers, 178
Public vs private rights adjudications, 100
Quasi-legislative and quasi-judicial functions of agencies, 14, 225
Removal power, 217
State law character of claim, determination of, 110

SEVENTH AMENDMENT
Adjudicatory power delegations to agencies, 92
Article I forums, jury trials in, 118
Bankruptcy courts, jury trial in, 115
Health care court proposals, 121
Public/private rights distinction and jury trial rights, 115

SIGNING STATEMENTS
Ambiguous statutes, 257
Line item veto parallels, 267
Presidential power implications, 257

SKIDMORE DEFERENCE
  Generally, 605
Case opinion, 605

Chevron deference compared, 714, 717, 724
Interpretation of regulations, 775
Modern *Skidmore* doctrine, 736
Regulations, interpretation of, 775

SOCIAL CHOICE THEORY
Policy delegations to agencies, 45

SOCIAL SECURITY ADMINISTRATION
Adjudications processes
    Criticisms, 367, 371
    Interdecisonal inconsistency, 367
Benefits determinations, due process requirements, 316
Claims
    Denials, de novo review of, 320, 428
    Grid rule, 429
    Impairment determinations, adjudicative vs rulemaking approaches to, 430
    Medical reports hearsay, substantial evidence standard of review, 400
    Treating vs consulting physicians' opinions, 407
Creation of Social Security Board, 18
De novo review of claim denials, 320
Delay of agency problem, 913
Due process requirements, benefits determinations, 316
Functional relationship between rules and adjudications, 426
Grid rule, 429
Impairment determinations, adjudicative vs rulemaking approaches to, 430
Medical reports hearsay, substantial evidence standard of review, 400
Retroactive application of rules, 452
Subpoenas, 407
Treating vs consulting physicians' opinions, 407

SOLICITOR GENERAL
Agency litigation at Supreme Court level, control over, 127, 167

SOVEREIGN IMMUNITY
Judicial review limitations, 795

STANDARDS OF REVIEW
Adjudication reviews
    Fact finding review, 386
    Rulemaking review compared, 413
APA mandates, 597
APA standards for adjudication reviews, 385
Arbitrary and Capricious Review Standard, this index
Auer deference, 775–776
Chevron Deference, this index
Constitutional concerns, rules involving, 589
Constitutional facts, findings of, 120
De Novo Review, this index

Fact finding review of agency adjudications, 386
Formal vs informal adjudications, 412
Hard look review. See Arbitrary and Capricious Standard, this index
Hearsay, substantial evidence standard, 400
Heightened scrutiny of rules involving constitutional concerns, 589
Heightened scrutiny of rules reflecting policy changes, 578
History of standards development, 21
Intelligible Principle Standard, this index
Jurisdictional facts, findings of, 120
Law questions and policy questions, distinguishing, 597
National Labor Relations Board adjudications, 386
National Labor Relations Board decisions, 388
Policy changes, heightened scrutiny of rules reflecting, 578
Policy delegations to agencies, 21
Regulations, interpretation of
    Generally, 774 et seq.
    See also Rulemaking and Regulations, this index
Rulemaking, adjudication review compared, 413
Seminole Rock standard of judicial deference, 775, 776
Skidmore Deference, this index
Statutory interpretation challenges, 411
Substantial evidence standard of adjudications, 386
Tax Court decisions, 187

STANDING
Generally, 919 et seq.
ADAPSO test, 922, 932, 972
Agencies, statutory standing to litigate, 126
Aggrievement showing, constitutional standing, 928
Agricultural Marketing Agreement Act of 1937, 810
APA, prudential standing, 970
Associational standing, 934, 944
Bureau of Land Management action challenges, constitutional standing, 932
Case or controversy limitation, 919, 957
Causation tests
    Citizens' suits, 955
    Constitutional standing, 922, 927
Citizen Suits, this index
Clean Water Act, citizens suits, 950
Constitutional standing
    Generally, 922 et seq., 946
    Aggrievement showing, 928
    Associational standing, 934, 944
    Bureau of Land Management action challenges, 932
    Case or controversy limitation, 919, 957
    Causation tests, 922, 927, 955

Citizen suits, 940
Clean Water Act, citizens suits, 950
Derivative standing, 934, 944
Endangered Species Act, 936
Environmental petitioners
        Generally, 932
        Citizen suits, 949
Evolution of, 944
Federal Election Commission
        adjudication challenges, 927
Generalized grievances, 927
Injury in fact, 922
Internal Revenue Service tax
        exemption rules, 922
Noneconomic injuries, 932
Procedural rights conferrals, 941
Redressibility, 922, 955
States as litigants, 958, 966
Three-part standing test, 965
Traceability, 922
Department of Justice, agency litigation
        conducted through, 126
Derivative standing, 934, 944
Emergency Planning and Community
        Right-To-Know Act, citizen suits,
        946
Endangered Species Act
        Citizen suits, 940
        Constitutional standing to challenge
                actions of, 936
Environmental petitioners
        Citizen suits, 949
        Constitutional standing, 932
Evolution of constitutional standing, 944
Federal Election Commission adjudication
        challenges, 927
Generalized grievances
        Citizen suits, 941
        Constitutional standing, 927
Injury in fact
        Constitutional standing, 922
        Noneconomic injuries, 932
Internal Revenue Service tax exemption
        rules, constitutional standing, 922
Interstate Commerce Commission,
        prudential standing, 970
Legal right test, prudential standing, 970
Modern standing doctrine, 919
National Bank Act regulation challenges,
        972
Noneconomic injuries, constitutional
        standing, 932
Political differences reflected in Supreme
        Court opinions, 968
Procedural rights conferrals,
        constitutional standing, 941
Prudential standing
        Generally, 968 et seq.
        APA, 970
        Interstate Commerce Commission,
                970
        Legal right test, 970
        National Bank Act regulation
                challenges, 972
        Taxpayers, 97
        Zone of interests, 968 et seq.

Redressibility
        Citizens' suits, 955
        Constitutional standing, 922
Solicitor General control of agency
        litigation at Supreme Court level,
        127, 167
States as litigants, constitutional
        standing, 958, 966
Statutory standing of agencies, 126
Supreme Court, agencies' statutory
        authority to litigate before, 127, 167
Taxpayer standing, 970
Three-part standing test, constitutional
        standing, 965
Traceability, constitutional standing, 922
Zone of interests
        Generally, 968 et seq.

STARE DECISIS
Adjudications, application of principle to,
        414
Chevron deference, 347, 647, 737, 746
Sub silentio departures from prior policy,
        414, 581

STATUTORY INTERPRETATION
        Generally, 597 et seq.
Administrative authority statutes, 597
Ambiguities, this index
APA mandates, 597
Auer deference
        Regulations, interpretation of, 775–
                776
Authorizations to agencies to interpret
        statutes, 598
Broad authorizations to agencies to
        interpret statutes, 598
Canons of construction
        Chevron deference, 645, 746
        Nondelegation doctrine, canon
                reflecting purpose of, 55
Creative, 625
De novo review of agency interpretations,
        605, 609
Delegations, unconstitutional,
        interpretation to avoid, 59
Environmental Protection Agency, 613
Fair Labor Standards Act, 605, 608
Federal Communications Commission,
        604, 608
Federal vs local interpretations, 605
Force of law assertions, *Chevron*
        deference, 717
Gap-filling authority of agencies, 599
General applicability statutes, 597
Intentionalists, 627
Judicial review preclusions, 796
Law and policy issue distinctions, 624
Law question deference after *Chevron*,
        621
Legislative history, *Chevron* deference
                Generally, 645, 656, 659
                Step one vs step two tool, 661
Longshoremen's & Harbor Workers' Act,
        608

National Labor Relations Board, 599, 608, 609
National vs local interpretations, 605
Nondelegation doctrine, canons of construction reflecting purpose of, 55
Occupational Safety and Health Act, 609
Plain meaning rule, *Chevron* deference, 643, 651
Policy aspects of interpretation, 623
Policy influences, 597
Policy resolutions masquerading as, 625
Power delegation ambiguities, 643
Purpose-based interpretation, *Chevron* deference, 645
Purposivists, 627
Regulations, interpretation of
    Generally, 774 et seq.
    See also Rulemaking and
    Regulations, this index
Rulemaking vs adjudicatory interpretations, 708
Seminole Rock standard of judicial deference, 775, 776
Signing statements for ambiguous statutes, 257
Silence as ambiguity, 629
Skidmore deference
    Generally, 605
    Chevron deference compared, 714, 717, 724
    Modern *Skidmore* doctrine, 736
    Regulations, interpretation of, 775
Specific and general agency authority, 598
Specific authorizations to agencies to interpret statutes, 598
Stare decisis, *Chevron* deference, 347, 647, 737, 746
Statutory silence as statutory ambiguity, 629
Strict constructionists and *Chevron* deference, 624
Subject matter expertise of agency, deference based on, 621
Textualists, 627
Toxic substance standards, 609
Two-step approach, law and policy issue distinctions, 624
Unconstitutional delegations, interpretation to avoid, 59
Undefined terms, 604

STIGMA
Adjudication creating, due process requirements, 308

SUBJECT MATTER EXPERTISE
Statutory interpretation deference based on, 621

SUBSTANTIAL EVIDENCE STANDARD
Arbitrary and capricious standard compared, 408
Fact findings, 408
Hearsay, 400

Judicial review of agency adjudications, 386
Reasonableness analysis, 412
Seven guidelines, 400

SUBSTANTIAL INDEPENDENT AUTHORITY STANDARD
Agency status determinations, 9

SUPREME COURT
Agencies, statutory authority to litigate before, 127, 167
Congressional control over agencies' statutory authority to litigate before, 127, 167
Standing of agencies to litigate before, 127, 167
Statutory authority to litigate before, 127, 167

TARIFF-SETTING POWERS
Policy delegations to agencies, 23

TAX COURT
    Generally, 183
Judges, appointment powers, 170

TAX REGULATIONS
Ripeness of challenges, 877

TENURE IN OFFICE ACT
Removal power, 222

TERRORIST DETENTIONS
Combatant Status Review Tribunals, 342
Due process requirements, 332

TOXIC SUBSTANCE STANDARDS
Detailed delegation of powers problems, 88
Nondelegation doctrine, applicability to promulgation of, 38, 43
Policy delegations to agencies, 38, 43
Statutory interpretation authority, 609

TRADITIONAL AGENCIES
Appointment power, traditional vs independent agencies, 191
Commodity Futures Trading Commission, 110
Definition, 10
Department status, traditional vs independent agencies, 191

TRANSMISSION BELT MODEL OF ADMINISTRATION
History of administrative law, 16

UNITARY EXECUTIVE THEORY
Presidential power, 254

VETERANS' READJUSTMENT BENEFITS ACT
Judicial review preclusion, 797

VETOES
Legislative Vetoes, this index
Line Item Vetoes, this index
Signing Statements, this index

WELFARE BENEFITS
Adjudication of rights, due process
requirements, 286, 313
Entitlement and nonentitlement statutes,
295

**WORKERS' COMPENSATION
REGIMES**
Public/private rights distinction, 120

WRITS
All Writs Act, judicial review, 914